A Field Guide to
The Life and Times of
ROGER CONANT

by
Roger Conant

Including Photographs by
Isabelle Hunt Conant

Sponsored by the Toledo Zoo

Selva
An imprint of Canyonlands Publishing Group, L.C.
Provo, Utah USA

SELVA, an imprint of
Canyonlands Publishing Group, L.C.
2544 North 530 East
Provo, Utah 84604 USA

ISBN 0-9657446-0-4

Printed in the United States of America
FIRST EDITION

To my Parents

CHARLES FRANCIS CONANT

and especially my mother

CLARA ELIZABETH ROGERS

who was my boyhood pal.

*They gave me the opportunity of visiting
this wonderful world for nearly ninety years,
maybe more. I was born at a time when most
wildlife was abundant and not yet suffering
from the frightening proliferation of mankind.*

CONTENTS

THE LIFE AND TIMES OF ROGER CONANT

ANCILLARY ESSAYS

AN ASSEMBLAGE OF ANECDOTES

VIGNETTES

Sponsor's Preface

Dr. Roger Conant is truly a remarkable individual. For nearly fifty years he managed to combine a distinguished zoo career with that of a meticulous field scientist. It is with no small amount of satisfaction that we, and the rest of the staff at the Toledo Zoological Gardens can boast that it all started for Dr. Conant back in Toledo in March, 1929, as he assumed his new duties as Curator of Reptiles at the Toledo Zoo. Inspired by Ruthven et al.'s, "Herpetology of Michigan," Dr. Conant was soon at work on plans to survey the reptiles of Ohio. His fieldwork and subsequent publication of "The Reptiles of Ohio" soon eclipsed anything that Ruthven or any of his contemporaries had ever accomplished. In fact, for many years the collection on which this work was based was housed in the Zoo's Museum of Science, and many of the stories presented in this volume stem from that frenetic period in his life. I doubt that Dr. Conant knew, as he embarked on this and other ambitious projects, how momentous his efforts would prove to be, not only for North American herpetology, but also for The Toledo Zoo. For some time he had harbored a dream about constructing a state-of-the-art reptile building at The Toledo Zoo. Never a person who failed to couple planning with action, Dr. Conant drew up plans for his facility. The timing was perfect, as it coincided with a search for projects to employ men in the Toledo area under the Civil Works Administration as the Great Depression deepened. Dr. Conant suggested that CWA labor be employed in the construction of this edifice, and by February of 1934 the building was under construction. After its completion it was so imposing and its inauguration was so auspicious that zoo and scientific authorities from across the country attended the grand opening. The construction of the Reptile Building provided the impetus for CWA/ FERA/WPA construction of five additional major buildings at the Zoo and made the facility into one the finest in the nation. Before he left the Zoo in 1935, Dr. Conant had been elevated in position to General Curator and Educational Director. The staff at the Toledo Zoo and the citizens of Toledo will always be grateful for the contributions he made while at the Toledo Zoological Gardens, and in our hearts he will always be one of us. We are extremely proud to sponsor this volume, "A Field Guide to the Life and Times of Roger Conant."

William V.A. Dennler
Executive Director, The Toldeo Zoo

Peter J. Tolson
Conservation Biologist, The Toledo Zoo

Foreword

No doubt my story is no different than that of most who read this, a fact which makes Conant's singular achievements all the more amazing. Like so many others born with an intense interest in herpetology, I spent a frustrated youth, craving answers to my many questions, books to read, and teachers who could tell me about the animals themselves. Armed with my "Golden Nature Guide to Reptiles and Amphibians" by Zim and Smith, I spent evenings thumbing through the tiny pages, staring intently at James Gordon Irving's beautiful illustrations, and dreaming of seeing the fabulous creatures he depicted. Then someone gave me a book entitled "What Snake is That? A Field Guide to the Snakes of the United States East of the Rocky Mountains." It was written by Roger Conant and William Bridges, published in 1939, and illustrated with Ed Malnate's wonderful line drawings. It opened my eyes to a whole new way of looking at reptiles.

In short order I would find influential books by Raymond L. Ditmars, Bessie M. Hecht, and others, and they fueled my fantasies of creatures on other continents, or in captivity. But nothing so galvanized my interest as Conant's "A Field Guide to Reptiles and Amphibians of Eastern North America," published in 1958. It would become the most widely read title in herpetology, and a landmark in the Peterson Field Guide series. Here was a book that dealt with all the topics I could imagine: how to find reptiles and amphibians, identify them, or keep them. The illustrations included the late Isabelle Hunt Conant's outstanding photographs, and the text was vintage Roger: concise, accurate, and a joy to read. The book went with me everywhere, and I began to feel as though Roger accompanied me during my hikes in the woods. At last there were answers to my questions, and more importantly—I had a source of inspiration.

Clearly, Roger Conant never obeyed the dictum about most of us leading lives of quiet desperation. I believe he would agree with the late Archie Carr, who observed that adventure is a state of mind, and a very good one at that. For Roger is an adventurer in the finest sense, having managed to combine a life of scholarship, tedious tasks, and responsibilities, with the thrill of discovery, travel, and constant learning. And he has done it with an unfailing good sense of humour.

I count myself among the lucky thousands who have benefitted from Roger Conant's enthusiasm and teaching. But it also has been my rare privilege to have him as a friend. Knowing Roger has allowed me to peer at an age gone by—a time of civility, self-discipline, and unfailing politeness. His life is a tribute to organization and consistency. I am constantly amazed by Roger's ability to pinpoint facts about events preceding my birth, and by the rigor with which he has documented his every move.

After a lifetime of productivity, this consummate professional has found yet another way to entertain, teach, and inspire us: by revealing the stories behind-the-scenes, the great personalities he has known, and the histories of the two marvelous zoos at Toledo and Philadephia that shaped so much of his career. Through it all he has maintained a lively sense of wonder, and it has kept him young. Just last week he and his wife Catherine travelled to Costa Rica to attend a herpetological symposium. Afterwards they toured the backroads of the country so Roger could see the land that gives rise to such a diverse herpetofauna. So, at 89 years of age, this man continues to exemplify the essence of his memoir: that life is a great adventure, meant to be savored to the last. Roger, you're a class act!

William W. Lamar
Tyler, Texas
August 1, 1997

Acknowledgments

Many persons assisted in a variety of ways in the preparation of these recollections.

The late Frederick A. Ulmer, Jr., who was Curator of Mammals at the Philadelphia Zoological Garden for more than 25 years, made several trips to the zoo on my behalf in recent years to obtain or verify facts or to identify persons portrayed in the zoo's photographic collection. He also critically reviewed several portions of the manuscript. J. Kevin Bowler and John D. Groves, both of whom served as Curator of Reptiles, contributed important information. Stephen R. Wylie, Assistant Curator of Birds, also helped. All four of those men were actively associated with me during parts of my long tenure in Philadelphia.

Jeanne Segal Gaughan and Allie Almario expedited the loan of photographs from the files of the Philadelphia Zoo, many of which were taken by Isabelle Hunt Conant or Franklin Williamson. Photographs from the Toledo Zoological Gardens were very kindly supplied by William V. A. Dennler, Peter J. Tolson, and Don Red-Fox. A few illustrations are from other sources, as indicated by the credit lines accompanying them. Because so many of the photographs were taken by my late wife and others by me, I have avoided frequent repetition in the captions by using just our initials—IHC and RC.

Sherman A. Minton very kindly reviewed medical aspects in my text, particularly in the "Snakebite!" and "On Staying Healthy" chapters.

Many other persons helped in various ways. Some furnished information or photographs or reviewed portions of the text, notably the vignettes about herpetologists and zoo personalities whom I knew. They are Kraig Adler, Richard D. Alexander, John S. Applegarth, Reeve M. Bailey, Dale Belcher, Ellin Beltz, Albert P. Blair, Martha R. Bogert, William S. Brown, Brooks M. Burr, Marjorie Harris Carr, Ellen J. Censky, Gary K. Clarke, Roger K. Conant, William G. Conway, Timothy L. Corley, Clifford S. Crawford, Douglas L. Crowell, Margaret A. Dankworth, William G. Degenhardt, Mark A. Dimmitt, Michael A. Dloogatch, William E. Duellman, Lee A. Fitzgerald, Barney Gardner, J. Whitfield Gibbons, Leonard J. Goss, Arthur M. Greenhall, Christine Conant Gross, Joanne Hammershoy, Margaret W. Hartweg, Robert W. Henderson, René E. Honegger, Ben Huo, Robert S. Ingersoll, Peter B. Ives, Steven P. Johnson, Marvin L. Jones, Ken Kawata, Kay A. Kenyon, Joan D. and John H. Lemmler, Spencer G. Lucas, Edmond V. Malnate, William J. Maloney, William C. Martin, Dennis J. Miller, Robert R. Miller, Joseph C. Mitchell, William B. Montgomery, Daniel H. Moreno, George W. Myers, M. Graham Netting, Murray A. Newman, Steve Platania, Louis W. Porras, Ken Redman, Heather Rex, Ximena Reyes, Michael Richard, Christian R. Schmidt, Laura and Gordon W. Schuett, James F. Scudday, A. Carl Segal, Christine Sheppard, Dorothy D. Smith, Hobart M. Smith, Robert L. Snyder, S. Bret Snyder, Barbara N. Timmermann, Thomas R. Van Devender, Robert O. Wagner, and Er-mi Zhao.

Special thanks are due to several persons who gave me permission to use all or parts of contributions I made some years ago to publications or journals for which they are or were responsible. Their names and pertinent comments follow:

Robert J. Crankshaw, President of the Medford Historical Society, which organization published the book "Medford/Pioneering Township" in 1975. It includes a chapter of mine based on information about the geological history and ecology of the New Jersey Pine Barrens that I assembled during the quarter of a century when my late, beloved wife, Isabelle, and I lived at Taunton Lake.

Robert W. Hansen, Editor of "Herpetological Review," granted me permission to use material from obituaries about several colleagues that I had written over a period of many years.

Martin J. Rosenberg, longtime Editor of "Notes from Noah," the newsletter of The Northern Ohio Association of Herpetologists, printed my "Herpetological Memories of a Day in Spain" in their tenth anniversary number in 1984.

William V. Donaldson, late President of the Zoological Society of Philadelphia, gave me carte blanche to use anything and everything I had written in publications of the Zoological Society.

Alexander L. Hoskins, President of the Zoological Society of Philadelphia, has supplemented my use of such material, and has given me permission to reproduce any illustrations that appeared in Philadelphia Zoo publications during my long association with that institution.

The maps in the text showing regions in which I did considerable fieldwork (Ohio, the Delmarva Peninsula, southern New Jersey, and Mexico) bear legends concerning their origins and the names of the publications or persons to whom I am indebted for their use.

A few of the illustrations in this book first appeared in "Snakes of the *Agkistrodon* Complex," by Howard K. Gloyd and Roger Conant, published by the Society for the Study of Amphibians and Reptiles. Kraig Adler, who served as editor of that lengthy tome, has granted me permission to reproduce the original pictures again. Each is accompanied by the abbreviation SSAR.

The pictures of the Cape water snake and the place where I caught it during 1961 in the then neowilderness of southern Baja California were previously published in the Bulletin of the American Museum of Natural History.

Several chapters, written expressly for these recollections, were printed in advance with the understanding that I could use them in this book without restrictions. For this, I express my thanks to Michael A. Dloogatch, Publications Secretary of the Chicago Herpetological Society. The three chapters entitled "Attempting the Impossible," the two on "Closing the Gap," "The Great Barrancas," and the anecdote on "The Oldest Snake" appeared in the Society's bulletin. My appreciation is also extended to: Arnold Norden, Editor of "Maryland Naturalist," who published my chapter on "The Delmarva Peninsula"; Erica Ramus and Norman Frank of "Reptile and Amphibian Magazine," who printed my vignette on Howard K. Gloyd; and Tim Hoen, human spark plug of the Mid-Atlantic Reptile Show, who used the anecdote on "Los Coronados" in the program for the 1995 show.

Friends, colleagues, and amateur herpetologists have solved an exasperating problem for me. The words "amphibians and reptiles" constitute a mouthful when used in conversation. We had long needed a short collective noun with which to refer to all of them. I used the word "herptiles" in the first edition of our field guide, Isabelle's and mine, but it met with little favor and some criticism, so I dropped it in the second edition. That word is seldom seen anymore, except occasionally in British herpetological literature. For a while "herpetozoa" came into use but it, too, found little favor.

Gradually, a slang expression has taken over that is now so widespread and generally accepted that, predictably, it will soon appear in dictionaries. It is simply "herp," and it is used for the animals of both groups. It also means a person who works in herpetology or herpetoculture, although the derivation "herper" may be employed in that sense. So I have followed the trend in the pages that follow, and I am happy that, at long last, we have a simple word for amphibians and reptiles that is almost universally accepted by the herpetological community.

Mindy Conner, a thoroughly competent copy editor, greatly improved the manuscript, but I fear she may regard me as a stubborn old-timer who refused, in some cases, to abandon certain writing styles I had used for decades.

Margie Crisp, a professional book designer, visited me in Albuquerque, patiently went over the several hundred illustrations I had selected for possible use in this volume, and together we culled out a great many because of space limitations. Then, using her expertise, she greatly improved the appearance of the book and created its clever paper jacket.

Louis W. Porras, whose kind invitation to accompany him and Gordon W. Schuett to his native Costa Rica while I was working on the Gloyd/Conant *Agkistrodon* manuscript, opened up a whole new world of research for me. It prompted me to visit the Orient. Also, as an unexpected spinoff during my first evening in Central America, I received the impetus for writing these lengthy recollections. Louis has been constantly supportive, and I thank him for his splendid help with the illustrations.

The National Science Foundation supported most of my fieldwork in Mexico, and I am indebted to it for grants G-9040, G-22657, and GB-2177.

I am especially grateful to Candice R. Corley, my part-time secretary, who painstakingly copied my roughed-out manuscript into her computer so the type could be set from disks. She is a good editor and speller who corrected many of my mistakes. She magnanimously refused to charge me for most of the work, thus making a truly major contribution to these lengthy musings of an octogenarian.

There are two ladies whose contributions have been invaluable: Isabelle Hunt Conant and Kathryn J. Gloyd, widow of my esteemed friend, Howard K. Gloyd. Isabelle and I worked together for 34 years, and we were inseparable as husband and wife for almost 30. Her detailed diaries have been extremely useful in compiling these memoirs and in recalling details of our travels and adventures, and of our daily lives. She also left me a legacy of thousands of photographs depicting reptiles, amphibians, and other animals, as well as our personal activities at the Philadelphia Zoo and in the field. I surely would like to include a great many more of them in this book. Kathryn and I each lost our beloved spouses at about the same time, and we have been married for more than 17 years. She has been my constant and indispensable companion during our excursions to many distant parts of the world. Without either of those two ladies, my life would have been lonely and incomplete.

There are also two very good friends without whose help this book would not have been finished and published.

After visiting my home in Albuquerque to read a large part of my manuscript and assess my huge reservoir of pictures and maps for illustrations, William W. Lamar agreed to be my publisher. He patiently answered my questions and skillfully guided me through a labyrinth of problems that developed while this personal opus was being completed and then making its way through the press. The electronic technologies that have drastically changed printing methods are so intricate that I fear I will never fully master them. Through it all, Bill Lamar—herpetologist, explorer, entrepreneur, and publisher of books—was developing his ecotourism business "Greentracks." He was personally conducting clients on trips to the great rain forest of the Amazon basin and to Costa Rica with its numerous wildlife reserves. How busy he was. Yet he found time to assist me with innumerable details, and he put together a team of experts who made this book a truly professional publication. We are all very grateful to Houghton Mifflin, and especially Harry Foster, Field Guide Editor, for its willingness to let us use a facsimile of the early

editions of my field guide on our dust jacket. How indebted I am to Bill Lamar for the many ways in which he has befriended me.

One of the staunchest supporters of this book is William V. A. Dennler, a good friend of many years' standing, and now the distinguished Executive Director of the Toledo Zoological Gardens. What superb success he has had in making the Toledo Zoo one of the greatest institutions of its kind in the world today and for a long time to come. And how nostalgic it is for me to recall that Toledo was where I received my professional start in the zoo business. Incredible though it may seem, that was almost "three score years and ten" ago, the traditional life span of the average man. Bill, through the magic of his personality and his trust in my humble writing efforts, was able to find the working capital to make the publication of this book possible. He and his organization have my profound and enduring thanks.

Finally, I acknowledge that any flaws or errors in the text or picture captions are mine. I have tried my best to keep everything accurate, but errors have an uncanny way of creeping in no matter how carefully any long work has been written or printed. Also, I hope I have not repeated myself too many times, but I have had to reset the stage here and there, partly because I realize that the average reader will do a few chapters at a time and may have forgotten some of the details that have gone before. Scientific names of various animals are largely as of the time about which I was writing and not necessarily those currently in vogue. The manuscript was completed as of December 31, 1996.

By Way of Introduction

There was a time, not so long ago, when I thought anyone who wrote an autobiography was either vain or self-centered—excepting, of course, such famous patriots as Benjamin Franklin. Possibly that is why I so long resisted committing to paper some of the interesting, exciting, and humorous adventures that befell me during the many years I worked with animals, both in zoos and in the field. I had often regaled my friends, male ones especially, with my stories, and they finally convinced me that I owed it to them, and especially to younger zoo fans and herpetologists who might like to read about things as they used to be. I yielded, and here are the results.

Social changes have so thoroughly swept away the mores of the recent past that I now feel free to record things as they happened and without deferring to the ladies. My dear mother, a strict and proper product of the Victorian age, would be both shocked and horrified by what her "little boy" has written, but times have changed, and she, poor soul, is no longer with us.

Oddly enough, these memoirs had their final impetus in, of all places, the heart of San José, Costa Rica. Louis W. Porras, Gordon W. Schuett, and I were crowded together in the cell-like room of a *posada* (inn) on a hot, sweaty night in 1982. It was a temporary stopping place and, on the morrow, under Louis's guidance, we were to finish assembling our collecting permits. Sleep did not come easily in that tiny room, and I found myself telling some of the more humorous adventures that befell me during the days when I did fieldwork in Ohio a half century earlier. My audience of two was so interested and so convulsed with laughter that I soon thereafter took the first hesitant step toward setting down the same tales and several others in a booklet of some 65 pages that was published by the Toledo Herpetological Society. That little pamphlet reached other friends and colleagues, who then convinced me that, instead of feeling vain and self-centered, I should consider it my duty to write all I could for posterity.

Putting together an account of a single field trip or two, as I did in the Ohio booklet, was easy. Each was a chapter in itself. But how should I approach a long narrative that spanned decades? To my way of thinking, any attempt to present happenstances in exact chronological order makes very dull reading. There would be high spots, but far too many lows. I finally decided to retain the chapter approach, and to focus on some special event or series of events, but to make each chapter a unit of its own. Some chapters became too long, so I split them into segments, as, for example, "Attempting the Impossible." Other subjects did not lend themselves to partitioning. The record-breaking "Let's Visit the Zoo" program, which was aired weekly on Philadelphia's radio station KYW, lasted for more than a third of a century. Writing about that presented a problem. To get around it I kept everything on that subject in one chapter instead of referring to the program over and over again. With these and a few other comparable exceptions, each chapter appears in roughly chronological order. I switch back and forth, however, between my two major interests, zoos and herpetology. My early, vigorous years come first, and my more sedentary musings as a senior citizen are last.

I suspect that this arrangement was subconsciously suggested by James Herriot's delightful tales of his experiences as a Yorkshire veterinarian. He used such chapters in "All Things Wise and Wonderful" and his other books, and they served as my bedtime stories, to be read a chapter or two at a time and then set aside for the morrow or even later. Without realizing that I was employing his pattern, I followed suit. I have kept each chapter more or less as a unit, even though that has meant repeating a sentence or two here and there to set the stage for a subsequent chapter.

Several of my many friends who very kindly read portions of my manuscript, and who made helpful comments and suggestions, asked me, "How in the world do you remember all these details?"

Fortunately, I have an abundant supply of resources. First, I have done a lot of writing in my time, and I started publishing at an early age. I have copies of all my papers on herpetology, of course, but I also was the zoo editor

My two children, Skip (10) and Susan (8), bagging a garter snake. Dutch Mountain, Pennsylvania (1940). Photo by RC.

of "Parks and Recreation" magazine for 20 years. "Zoo reporter" would be a more appropriate title for that responsibility, because few persons ever submitted manuscripts for editing, and I had to solicit information and prepare it for publication myself. So I chronicled pieces of zoo history for two decades. Even earlier I wrote about events in the Philadelphia Zoo, as well as about my trip to study European zoos way back in 1937, when Hitler was in power in Germany and World War II was imminent. All such source material is available to corroborate or emend my own recollections of what transpired. I recall most of my youthful days with crystal clarity. Very unhappily, however, I cannot remember the full names or even the names at all of some of the persons who helped me on my way that long ago.

Second, I have all my correspondence with herpetologists from the late 1920s onward—many thousands of their letters to me and my replies. My files, therefore, are a gold mine of information. I wish I had made copies of some of my zoo correspondence as well. Because it was concerned chiefly with the Philadelphia Zoological Garden and, in a sense, belonged to it, I left it there when I retired as Director in 1973.

There were also my letters to my mother. As a dutiful son I wrote to her every Saturday for more than 40 years, sometimes only briefly. She saved the more interesting ones about my zoo and field activities, and gave them back to me a few years before she died in 1975.

Finally, I have an extraordinarily useful running account of our daily activities for the almost 30 years that I was married to my late wife, née Isabelle dePeyster Hunt. She kept a daily diary, and, when we were on field trips together, she went into great detail. What a marvelous source of information! Here and there I have quoted verbatim from her thousands of handwritten pages. In a very real sense Isabelle's diaries are indispensable mnemonics, or memory prompters, if you are not familiar with that unusual word.

There is no lack of illustrations. Beginning with our work for our "Field Guide to Reptiles and Amphibians" (see "Attempting the Impossible: Part I") and for a great many years thereafter we amassed a huge reservoir of almost 10,000 black-and-white prints with all their respective negatives. They are willed to the American Museum of Natural History, in New York, which has agreed to accept them as the Isabelle Hunt Conant Memorial Photographic Collection. There are also a great many color slides and some color prints, the bulk of them exposed during our numerous field excursions. Including both color and black-and-white, we took about 2,500 pictures during our seven weeks in Africa in 1968—Uganda, Kenya, Tanzania, South Africa, and Swaziland, in that order.

I confess that I have not told all. There are skeletons in my closet, and it is best to let them hang. I have made enemies. Don't we all? Most of them are now dead, and there is no point in resurrecting them. I have hinted here and there, however, about some of the unhappiness they caused me. My first marriage was a colossal failure, but I stuck it out, far beyond endurance, and fought back as best I could against a tyrannical father-in-law. The only thing good that resulted from that union were my beloved children. First, there was my son, Roger Karl "Skip" Conant. He and his lovely wife, Virginia, and their adorable little girls have brought much happiness into my life. My daughter, Jane Susan Conant Megraw, died suddenly when she was in her mid-50s, much to our dismay. Her memory lives on in my talented grandson, Richard Baldwin Megraw.

My main topic, as mentioned above, is to recount many of the unusual, exciting, and humorous adventures that befell me during 45 years of zoo work and an even greater length of time spent in pursuit of the serpent, the frog, and all the rest—on all the habitable continents. I don't count Antarctica, because there are no herps there, at least not now. The discovery of fossil remains of the weird-looking reptile, *Lystrosaurus*, in the Coalsack Bluff of that frigid part of the world, by Edwin H. Colbert and his party helped prove that the Reptilia were represented there in the past. Those fossils were so similar to others known from Africa and India that their discovery clinched the fact that all three now widely separated land masses were once united as part of Gondwanaland. Plate tectonics! What a fascinating subject; it revolutionized the science of geology during the 1960s. How I wish I knew more about geology. I follow its findings and developments as best I can, but I am a mere layman on that subject.

Occasionally I have digressed to write about some of the ways of life that were so different during my early years. When I was a boy, automobiles were few. Radio came into existence. I had my own set, a cat's whisker and a chunk of galena with which, if I were lucky, I might hear some static-laden music or chatter from New York at my home in Red Bank, New Jersey. Aviation was in its infancy, and I, like all Americans, thrilled over Lindbergh's historic flight. Jets came many years later. Television arrived, and so did the nuclear age, and men walked on the moon. Now we have computers and word processors and a bewildering array of electronic gadgets. What wonders I have seen come into existence and develop! So many of the things that people take for granted today didn't even exist when I was younger. Also, my life span embraced the entire period of existence of the Soviet Union.

On the downside, I cannot remember when there wasn't a war, revolution, insurrection, guerrilla uprising, coup, or the ascendency of a dictator occurring in some part of the world. I lived through two world wars, the first when I was quite young. Every morning I eagerly scanned Philadelphia's daily "North American" newspaper for the map showing where the trenches were. Naval battles, with their accompanying maps, especially intrigued me, and my intense, lifelong interest in geography undoubtedly began at that time. During World War II I realized I would not be drafted for combat because of my crippled hand (see "Snakebite!"), but I helped as much as I could by joining the Volunteer Port Security Force of the U.S. Coast Guard, and I wore its regulation uniform and side arm when I was on duty every five days. Even today, think of the riots, hostages, street warfare, and drive-by shootings, and the general breakdown of respect for law and order, the rights of man, and even for life itself. What a savage century it has been!

My last chapters ("Breed and Greed" and "Some Final Thoughts") are devoted to some of the problems we face today and inevitably will in the future. I also mention the distressful condition of so many kinds of wildlife that are declining in most disheartening ways because of the proliferation and greed of the human species. I am so glad I lived when I did. Many of my experiences, especially in the field, could not be duplicated today. I feel sorry for the younger and still-to-come generations that will be denied seeing what I did and experiencing the thrills I had. Also, they will be subjected to many more stresses than I had to endure.

It has been a joy to write these pages. For me, they have dripped with nostalgia. They have provided a chance for me to visit vicariously with my beloved Isabelle as we struggled to promote the Philadelphia Zoo, to write and illustrate our field guides, and to pursue our fieldwork in Africa, every state of Mexico, and in most of our own 48 contiguous ones. Also, they have taken me, with Kathryn J. Gloyd, twice around the world and to such exotic places as Bangkok, Bombay, Guangzhou (Canton), Hong Kong, Singapore, Sydney, Taipei, and Tokyo, as well as to several cities in Europe and South America. How extremely lucky I have been to see and to do so many things!

Chapter 1

Youthful Trials and Triumphs

Roger Conant was baptized on April 9, 1592, at East Budleigh, Devonshire, England. In March 1623, he sailed for the New World, and three years later founded the colony that became Salem, Massachusetts.

When I came along at Mamaroneck, New York, a few centuries later (on May 6, 1909), it was natural that I, a lineal descendent, should be named for my illustrious ancestor, especially since my mother's maiden name was Rogers (née Clara Elizabeth Rogers). My father, Charles Francis Conant, was in the iron and steel business, and he had the extraordinary gift of being able to look at a long column of multidigit numbers and stating moments later what their sum was. I have seen only one other person who could equal him, and that was the chap who tallied the vote count on television on election nights before the advent of computers.

We lived in Reading, Pennsylvania, for a while, but moved to Philadelphia when I was about five or six. My grammar school days were spent in West Philadelphia. I can remember some of my boyhood friends and how we climbed all over the scaffolds on a church being constructed nearby, and how we walked for blocks underground through a huge new water main that was being laid under our street. Its diameter was so large that we could stand upright in it. Meantime, my poor mother worried herself sick with visions of accidents until I came back late each afternoon to our row house safe and sound.

I had a normal childhood until about my twelfth birthday, when disaster struck. I lost my father. After our trauma had somewhat subsided, Mother and I realized we were virtual paupers. Our house had a large mortgage, and we had very little equity in it. We would soon have to get out, and Mother had no marketable skills. As an only child I suddenly found myself the "man (?) of the house."

We had no automobile. My father never owned one. Long-distance telephone calls were expensive luxuries. I doubt if my mother had ever made one until she called someone in Red Bank, New Jersey, who relayed word to my grandparents about our tragedy. They expressed their sympathies and told us to come to them when we were ready. Somehow Mother managed to keep things going until the school semester was over in June. Friends and neighbors rallied round to help her sell the furniture and do the packing. I was able to get a small, temporary newspaper route after school, but I have no recollection of the dreadful melee that must have whirled around my poor mother. How did she ship such things as clothing and my father's Globe-Wernicke sectional bookcases—which, miraculously, I still have?

I do recall the train trip, however, because I had previously traversed the route to "Grandmother's house." We took the ferryboat to Camden. There were no bridges across the lower Delaware River in those days. We boarded a train for Atlantic City, but changed at Winslow Junction to a northbound train. That one rolled through the New Jersey Pine Barrens, stopping at every tiny settlement, including Elm, Chatsworth, Woodmansie, and Pasadena, and towns like Lakehurst and Lakewood. (The tracks were removed long ago, but the wooden ties were left to rot, and they became hiding places for the eagerly sought rare snakes of the region.) At Red Bank we had to part with some of our precious money for a taxi. Neither my grandfather nor my uncle owned a car. It was much too far to walk, and we had a plethora of baggage. We were hugged and kissed and welcomed when we reached our haven at last.

Unexpectedly we had a lucky break, one that was to have a profound influence on me. It also gave Mother a brief respite, and the opportunity to pick up a little "pin money" working part-time in an office doing some simple things such as filing. Friends in Stamford, Connecticut, invited us to spend the summer with them. There were two boys in the family, one my age and the other a couple of years older. They and I were to spend eight weeks at a Boy Scout camp that straddled the state line. We ate and played ball in Connecticut and swam and slept in New York, or some such combination. I quickly learned the ropes, and I was sworn in as a "tenderfoot" even before camp started.

What a memorable summer that was. I entered into

Our first formal picture. My beautiful mother and her little boy of about three (1912).

the Boy Scout program with great enthusiasm, passed my tests, and quickly became a second- and then a first-class scout. The camp counselors waived the time requirements. I even earned some merit badges. Most important, my interest in herpetology was aroused, something I have retained all my life. Dr. Albert H. Wright, an authority on reptiles and amphibians, was then a professor at Cornell University, and two of his students were camp counselors. We boys, of course, took every frog, salamander, and small snake we caught to them for identification, and two or three of us plied them with questions. One day, on a brief hike with one of the counselors just before camp was due to close for the season, I spotted an adult copperhead lying among leaves at the side of the path we were following. Perhaps as a reward for my sharp eyes, I was permitted to participate in its capture. That did it. I was hooked. I wanted to be a herpetologist.

Mother and I returned to Red Bank and resumed our stay with my grandparents. I joined Troop 17 of the Monmouth County Council, Boy Scouts of America, and continued to earn merit badges. I hoped to become an Eagle Scout, but the lifesaving merit badge was required. I easily passed my swimming badge, but the other necessitated both skill and strength, especially for breaking strangleholds in the water. I was well into my

fourteenth year before I finally passed, and I became the first Eagle Scout in Monmouth County. The Scout Executive saw an opportunity for some good publicity, and he alerted the "Red Bank Register" and papers in other parts of the county, including the large summer resorts of Long Branch and Asbury Park. It worked out well for the Boy Scout office but not for me. Because the last merit badge was lifesaving, that topic was featured in the news stories. My male school mates promptly nicknamed me "Hero," which I detested, but I was stuck with it all through my high school days: "Hi, Hero, how many people did you save today?" Kids, even teenagers, could be cruel.

I continued in scouting, serving as a camp counselor for several summers, a scoutmaster for a while, and a merit badge counselor for decades. I wrote several editions of the reptile study merit badge pamphlet that spanned a period of nearly 50 years.

Mother found a few small jobs, but they did little to help. I ran errands, distributed circulars, and worked on Saturdays in a grocery store and later in a butcher shop. It would be a long time before supermarkets arrived. Shoppers in the 1920s visited several stores, not just one, and they brought containers with them to carry home their purchases.

My grandfather, a Civil War veteran, was on a small pension. He had been the engineer on a ferryboat in New York Harbor. His funds were meager but sufficient to pay the taxes on his house, which he had built himself, and there was enough left over to buy meat occasionally and such staples as salt, flour, and sugar. He had a large truck garden, however, and we all pitched in to help prepare the crop for canning. By late fall each year the shelves in the basement were filled with hundreds of mason jars containing vegetables, jams, jellies, and fruits. The root and other vegetables, such as potatoes, carrots, cabbages, turnips, and parsnips, were kept in a cold room, where they lasted all winter.

During my first spring in Red Bank my grandfather assigned part of the garden to me. I became an amateur farmer and raised an excellent and varied crop under his watchful eye. I felt as though I were doing something to help. In retrospect, I think that over several years' time I must have pulled strings on thousands of beans, shelled a ton of peas, and peeled a zillion tomatoes that had been dipped in boiling water to loosen the skins.

In those days, the people in small country towns were self-sustaining, except for a few rich folks. We had a wood stove in the kitchen with a water jacket at the side, so sometimes we had hot water, but mostly not. Grandfather kept chickens. Periodically he would catch one, cut its throat with a penknife, and hang it by the legs to drain off the blood. Then there was the tedious chore of plucking the feathers. Finally, it had to be eviscerated and all the edible entrails saved. We rarely ever had beef, lamb, or pork. In season, we sometimes went crabbing or fishing to augment the larder.

We were dirt poor, but we didn't know it. No one had yet come up with a definition of a poverty level. Traumatized as I was by the loss of my father, there was a valuable by-product. At a very early age I learned the value of hard work and money.

Grandpa became my surrogate father, and I learned to love him and Grandma dearly. He was calm and patient. He not only taught me to garden, but also how to use all kinds of hand tools. He never referred to the extra burden Mother and I brought to him and Grandma simply by our presence. The strongest expletive I ever heard him utter was "by George." Grandma was a delight. Nothing was too much trouble. She worked from dawn until well after suppertime, and then, in the evening, she would crochet or mend all our sox and stockings by the light of a kerosene lantern. During the school year, I studied my lessons on the other side of the same light. In essence, I had a real taste of what today we would consider as primitive conditions. We walked everywhere, although Grandpa rode his bicycle into downtown Red Bank once a week to buy a few necessities. I walked to school, and it was a long way, especially in winter with the temperature way down and the wind blowing hard. What was a school bus? We never heard of one.

Mother had a way with children, and it soon became clear that teaching was the goal toward which she should work. Eventually, no doubt through a friend, she found a job at a mission on the Bowery in New York City. It was chiefly a sustenance one, but she received a small stipend that enabled her, every three or four months, to pay the railroad fare back and forth to Red Bank. Despite the lurid tales about the tenements and rough neighborhoods of the area, it was still safe for a woman to walk alone there during daylight hours. Our communication with Mother was by mail, I think for two cents a letter.

To lighten the load on my grandparents, my aunt, Mother's sister, suggested that, while Mother was away, I should spend two weeks with them and two weeks with the old folks. So for a couple of years, while Mother was teaching orphans and other unfortunate youngsters at the mission and learning steadily from the other teachers, I made my biweekly pilgrimage, loading my clothes and other necessities into an express wagon someone had given me, and hiking the mile between the two residences. My aunt was kind to me, but my uncle, a tin-

smith by trade, was difficult to get along with. He, too, had a truck garden, and I helped all I could, but I missed Grandpa's patience and kindliness. My aunt and uncle had two children, a boy and a girl, both a little younger than I, and my cousins were good company for me.

Happily, both places had indoor plumbing, but some of our friends just outside of town still used outdoor privies. Heat was meager at both houses, except in the kitchens. At my aunt's there was a coal furnace in the basement that supplied hot air to flow through a large open grille in the dining room floor. There was another much smaller grille in the hall on the second floor through which a small amount of heat trickled upward, at least in the early mornings after my uncle added a shovelful of coal to the furnace. We kids dressed over the grille in wintertime. There were no radiators.

But enough about those early difficult years. I have recounted something about them chiefly to provide a glimpse of what life was like during yesteryear. Almost everyone was self-sufficient, and welfare didn't exist. Handicapped persons were cared for by relatives and friends, and there was always the poorhouse.

I was a good student, so much so that I skipped another semester, my fourth. Mother was very proud of me, but there was a major drawback. I was too young for my class, and I missed out on many of the social activities. I was just a kid to my classmates. I graduated from high school only a little more than a month after I turned 16.

By that time Mother had passed her examinations, and she was qualified, under the New Jersey state rules, to teach kindergarten and first grade, but she was only a substitute, and work and paychecks were intermittent. With the small amount I could give her, we rented a little apartment, but I soon left for my fourth summer as a Boy Scout counselor. Like Mother's stint on the Bowery, my job at camp was chiefly sustenance, but I did get something like $50 for my summer's work of being on duty from first call and reveille to taps, seven days a week. Incidentally, I was the camp bugler, and I had to be the first one up every morning.

In the autumn I went hunting for a real job, and I found one, but it wouldn't be ready for more than a month. So I filled in again with odds and ends, including back to the grocery store where I had long, hard days, especially on Saturdays. Way back then, customers arrived with a list, sometimes written but often verbal, and clerks, such as I was, ran back and forth to the various shelves, assembling cans, bottles, and packages until the list was complete. I was young and quick, but I never did get the hang of cutting off a pound of butter with a single stroke from the store's tub-sized supply.

During that period in the 1920s, I was able to earn a little money by taking a few of my pet snakes to Boy Scout troop meetings all over Monmouth County. A wealthy patron who liked to help boys gave me five dollars a talk and transportation in his chauffeur-driven automobile! I even addressed a few adult audiences and gained valuable experience as a public speaker.

My promised job was with the Monmouth County Social Service organization, where a typist and I had the responsibility of getting the annual Christmas Seals into the mail. Everything was done by hand: stuffing and sealing envelopes, and sticking on stamps. Once the money started coming in we posted it on donors' file cards, sent them a form letter of thanks, and prepared deposit slips for each day's receipts. That was all over by mid-February and I was looking for a job again.

Work was difficult to find. One day, almost in desperation, I took the bus to Middletown, which was only a few miles from Red Bank. I stopped at the Twin Brook Zoo, a small new establishment operated by Oliver W. Holton, a wealthy man who had a deep and abiding interest in animals. He was kind enough to interview me, but he said he had nothing to offer. He had a game-keeper and a small group of other employees, but there were no openings. Fortunately for me, a girl I knew and who had graduated in a class or two ahead of mine, was his secretary. As soon as I departed and had walked out to the highway to wait for the return bus, she put in a good word for me by stating that I was an Eagle Scout and a good student. The result was that Holton himself came out to see me at the curb and told me to return in April when he expected paying visitors would start coming in numbers. He would need a cashier, and Margaret had assured him I was "as honest as they come."

I began my new job in April, as planned, and found it very boring. Scarcely anyone came in the mornings, and, at first, only a few in the afternoons. It was early in the season, but Mr. Holton wanted me to be well broken in before the rush came. I read books, studied Spanish, with which I was getting rather proficient, and I made it my job to sweep out and tidy up the entrance room and the path leading to it from the ample parking lot and the bus stop. The first Sunday I was busy selling tickets from late morning until late afternoon. On Monday, Holton was out of town and Margaret, who could see my cashier's cage from her desk, suggested that I go out and look around the zoo. She would keep an eye open for possible visitors. I had been through the grounds and had seen all the animals, of course, but that Monday I stepped into a new world, as it were, one that changed my entire approach to my future.

The zoo consisted of one large building filled with about eight spacious cages for large cats, such as lions and tigers, although some of them were occupied by other kinds of animals. The grounds, a few acres in extent, held numerous wire cages, ponds, and paddocks of various sizes. Notable were a fine row of pheasant pens and two tall "flight" cages, one for birds and the other for monkeys. The latter was well equipped with branches and swings, and it was a lively place, especially at feeding time when monkeys of several species leaped and swung around after they had grabbed a handful of food and raced away from the dominant male, who tried to hog everything. The Twin Brook Zoo was tastefully designed and well planted and tended. It was a far cry from the dirty, dingy roadside menageries that proliferated as tourist traps along highways as the motorcar age gathered momentum.

As I wandered around that Monday morning I heard a shout and hastened to its source. Several men were struggling with a heavy iron grille, trying to get it into an upright position to bolt to a cage front. I ran over to give them a hand, and my few extra pounds of push, added to theirs, were sufficient. They thanked me. I had made some friends, one of whom was a keeper who had been pressed momentarily into service to help the construction men. I trailed along with him as he worked, and he even let me carry a pail and some of his tools, which I handed to him as they were needed. He responded by answering my flood of questions.

By noontime I had returned to my cashier's cage, but the next morning I was back in the zoo following another keeper and helping him as best I could. It was the same on Wednesday and Thursday. When Holton returned at the end of the week, the men told him about my enthusiasm. He called me into his office, and we had a long talk, the outcome of which was that he let me spend every morning working in the zoo, except on Saturdays, Sundays, and holidays. My days off were erratic, and I usually took them when the weather forecasts predicted rain, which meant few, if any, visitors.

I have never forgotten Oliver W. Holton's great kindness. It was he, in a very real sense, who started me on my zoo career.

I remember with great clarity some of the many things I learned about handling animals. When a pheasant got out of its cage it was never chased. Its normal tendency was to walk back and forth trying to rejoin its mates. So you propped open the gate at an angle to form a partial barrier for it. You walked slowly toward it, in a sense driving it in front of you, and when it came to the open gate it would turn into its own quarters. The same trick could be used for deer and other animals. The secret was to be calm and quiet and not to forget that the escapee was bewildered by being where it didn't belong, and was more than willing to go back "home." It was OK to talk to the animals in a low voice.

When you entered the large monkey cage, you locked the gate behind you. If the lock was left hanging on the wire it was virtually certain to disappear, thanks to simian curiosity and mischievousness.

When feeding lions, tigers, or other great cats you should be sure the chunk of meat you were giving them, including any piece of bone, was cut small enough to pass clean through or under the bars. If it stuck, you never used your hand to push it through. An iron bar was provided for that purpose. The huge claws of such animals were dangerous, and any of the cats could extend a foreleg far through the bars.

Another trick I learned but didn't see put into action was related to me by one of the keepers who had once worked for a carnival. If a monkey or baboon escaped, he said, you should go at once to the snake charmer and have her show the runaway her big snake at as close range as possible. The errant primate would run for the safety of its cage. He said it worked every time.

Speaking of snakes, the Twin Brook Zoo exhibited a few and, as soon as Holton learned that I had some of my own and knew how to handle them, more were acquired for the zoo display, and I was put in charge of them.

Twin Brook served as a receiving and holding station for animals imported by dealers, who did a thriving business in those days before many legal restrictions were imposed. So there was a passing parade of wildlife with which I became familiar. The construction crew erected additional paddocks outside the zoo, but on land belonging to the Holton estate. I recall with sorrow how a herd of about 20 zebras was placed in them, but not for long. An epizootic (animal epidemic), obviously contracted before their arrival, raced through the group and all were soon dead. Their carcasses were moved to some empty ground outside the zoo and left to rot. A couple of years later I returned with a technician from the University of Pennsylvania, and we collected a full skeleton and several skulls.

I learned another lesson when a large Malay tapir arrived. It must have weighed at least 500 pounds. Like all adults of its kind, it was black with a broad pale gray, almost white, saddle on the posterior part of its body. Except for its protruding snout (proboscis), it resembled a giant pig. Technically it was related to the horse and rhinoceros. Because of its odd appearance Holton decided to put the tapir in a large empty paddock right inside the zoo. Its crate was worked through the gate and the door was lifted. The tapir poked out its head, looked around, and one of the men gave it a whack on

its rump. It started to run, picking up speed as it went. It failed to see the wire at the other end of the paddock, which was inconspicuous against the distant background of shrubbery. The animal crashed into it, and the wire acted like a vertical trampoline, bouncing the tapir onto its back. We were appalled, but it seemed to be all right. Later we learned it had sustained a serious injury. In later years when nervous or freshly caught animals were introduced into paddocks, I always made sure there was a visible barrier at the opposite end, even if it was only a line of keepers standing where they easily could be seen.

One day a large shipment of animals, both common and rare, arrived from Singapore, which was then the major shipping center for the Far East. I saw my first birds-of-paradise, cockatoos, Java sparrows, orangutans, and gibbons, among others. The shipment, which, of course, had come by boat and was en route for months, had traveled in the custody of a young Malay in his 20s. Since Singapore was then a British colony, he was fluent in English. We hit it off well, and I listened with rapt attention to his many tales about capturing animals in the East Indies. One evening I told my mother I wanted to go to Singapore, and she was horrified. She hadn't the foggiest notion where it was, but she knew it was far away. I was all she had, and the thought of my going any real distance from her was shattering. I finally visited Singapore twice, but that wasn't until the 1980s, long after Mother had died. It was a wonderful city, flower-bedecked and spotlessly clean.

One morning late in the season, I arrived at the zoo before nine o'clock as usual, but I found the entrance locked and bolted. I went to the fence on each side of the building, but not a soul was in sight. I called, even yelled, but got no response. Sensing that something was very wrong, I climbed over the fence, started to walk through the grounds, and suddenly confronted a fellow employee with a rifle cradled in his arm. "The leopard's loose," he said.

Just the day before we had received a full-grown spotted leopard that had seriously injured someone at a circus or carnival. The owners wanted to get rid of it, and my boss accepted it as a valuable addition to his zoo. It had been put in one of the large cat cages.

"How did it get loose?" I asked. "We don't know," he replied, "but it ain't in the building. We've searched every inch of it."

I went inside. The lock was in place and everything looked normal except there was no leopard in the cage. Just then a very worried looking Oliver W. Holton entered, and, simultaneously, I had an inspiration. I asked him, "Do you mind if I have a look?" When he shook his head no, I climbed up the barred grille of the cage front and discovered how the big cat had made its exit. The sloping roof rafters passed over the grille, leaving a gap between the roof and the steel. It seemed like an incredibly small space for such a big beast, but I found telltale claw marks left by the leopard as it struggled to get through. An open window had given it access to the out-of-doors. There was nothing to indicate when the escape had occurred. Perhaps it was right after the zoo closed for the previous day, or it might have been much later. In any event, the leopard had a good start on us.

We searched every part of the zoo and its immediate vicinity, but, by noon, it was obvious that Holton would have to sound the alarm. He called the police and, almost at once, the event became a sensation. The newspapers played it up and, for a few days, mothers in Middletown and vicinity kept their children and dogs indoors.

Reports of seeing the leopard were frequent, and we followed up on every one of them. Bert Farrow, one of Holton's close friends, had a roadster, and I was young enough to feel very important sitting in the rumble seat with another staff member, each of us clutching a high-powered rifle. Every sighting proved to be a bust. Large dogs, mistakenly identified after dark or in shrubs or shadows, were the source of almost all of them. A few times we were shown pug marks in moist earth, but claw marks were evident in all of them. That meant a dog had made them. Dog claws protrude, but, in all the true cats, the claws are sheathed and make no marks as the animals walk.

Eventually things settled down, and, a week or so later, we were accused of fabricating the whole thing to get publicity for the zoo.

The sequel to all the excitement was truly amazing. It occurred months later when my mind was on other things and I was far away. In the autumn a family living at Island Heights began to miss chickens, and a chap named Willard Irons decided to set a trap for the raccoon or whatever other predator was responsible. Very early the next morning the family was aroused by a commotion in the henhouse, and Willard went to investigate. No sooner had he opened the back door of the residence when the leopard, caught by two or three toes, lunged at him. The trap chain held and the cat took a tumble. Willard slammed the door shut, reloaded his gun with buckshot instead of the birdshot it held, opened the door cautiously, and then shot the leopard dead. Holton gave him a reward, and the runaway's body lay in state at the zoo entrance for a couple of days before it was skinned and mounted.

It wasn't difficult to reconstruct what had happened.

There was a thick woods close to the Twin Brook Zoo, and the cat evidently took refuge there the first day. It moved off at night, kept hidden during daylight hours, and eventually reached the vast New Jersey Pine Barrens, the edge of which was not too far away. In the 1920s the Barrens constituted a virtual wilderness, seldom visited and appreciated only by a few naturalists, hunters, and trappers. Once in that haven the leopard was safe. It no doubt killed and fed on deer and lesser game of the region. Island Heights was also near the edge of the Pine Barrens, but on the opposite side. Why the animal ventured out of the Barrens to prey on the Irons' chickens is anyone's guess. It was roughly 30 miles, as the crow flies, from Middletown to Island Heights.

The Twin Brook Zoo survived that episode and probably even profited through increased attendance. But it succumbed a year or two later following a dreadful accident. As a result of human carelessness, a wolf escaped from its cage and, by an extraordinarily unlucky stroke of fate, it chanced to pass close to the Holton residence, which was nearby. The wolf killed the baby of the family, which was momentarily unattended in its playpen in the yard. The State of New Jersey shut the zoo down.

I felt dreadfully sorry for the Holtons, but I was far away at the time and could express my sorrow only by mail. Many years later, Oliver W. Holton looked me up when I was at the Philadelphia Zoo, and we reminisced for a while, but neither of us mentioned the tragedy. There was another child, George, whom I was destined to meet as a full-grown man in, of all places, Taxco, Mexico.

During my summer at Twin Brook I made up my mind. I wanted to become the director of a zoo. For that, a college career seemed indicated. I suggested Cornell, but Mother wouldn't hear of it. Too far away. So we compromised on the University of Pennsylvania. At least it was close, and either of us could get back or forth in a day. I took a cram course in Spanish, which had been my foreign language in high school, passed my exams, and, with what money we had been able to save plus a frighteningly large amount we had to borrow, I made it for a couple of years.

I sustained a rude shock when I arrived at Penn. I had needed Spanish to matriculate, but I could not take it for credit. It wasn't a scientific language! I had to take either French or German instead. That was a hidebound rule, and my pleas fell on deaf ears. Since I was hoping to complete the course in biology, I took French—hated it, struggled with it, but made good grades, as I did in all my subjects.

College life was a grueling grind, because I had to work every waking minute I wasn't in class or studying. The Great Depression had not yet officially arrived, but things were already tightening up for unskilled persons, such as I was. Part-time jobs off-campus were very difficult to find, and I had to do far more than wait on table in a fraternity house, which assured me of my meals for one semester. So I had to give up. I consoled myself by rationalizing. The biology course was strongly slanted toward medicine, and I was learning little that would help me to run a zoo.

It was quite a while before Mother and I were able to pay off our debt.

Chapter 2

The Toledo Years

It was by sheer chance that I went to Toledo for my first truly professional zoo job. Things had begun to look up for us at last. Mother was fully accredited, and she had a full-time job with the Red Bank school system and a comfortable little apartment. I could quit peddling magazine subscriptions from door to door in Philadelphia and its suburbs, which had been my most successful method of bringing in money.

I knew C. Emerson Brown, Director of the Philadelphia Zoo, from having visited him on several occasions, and, when I asked him for help, he graciously gave me the names and addresses of the directors of a dozen zoos. I laboriously typed an original letter to each, and I had two responses. My first choice was St. Louis, but the employee who had left his post, to go into business with his father, had second thoughts and returned. That left only Toledo for me.

In a sense it was a lucky break. Already I was deeply interested in reptiles, and there were two important factors in my favor at Toledo. First, only a few snakes were on display there, whereas St. Louis had an excellent, well-stocked reptile house. At Toledo I would have free rein to build a good collection, whereas at St. Louis I would have been low man on the totem pole, so to speak, with R. Marlin Perkins and his assistant, Moody J. R. Lentz, as my superiors. Second, Toledo was close to Ann Arbor and the University of Michigan, which was then the systematic herpetological capital of the United States.

I well recall my arrival at the old Pennsylvania Railroad station after a virtually sleepless night on the *Red Arrow Express*. It was Inauguration Day, March 4, 1929. President Herbert Hoover and I started our new assignments at the same time.

After a day of introductions and a complete tour of the Toledo Zoo I was told what my duties would be. I was assigned to curate the few reptiles, which seldom required more than a half hour daily, and, more important, I was put to work in the relatively new giraffe house. Just a few days previously, a male nilgai, largest of the Asian antelopes, had seriously gored two keepers with his short, sharp horns. I have often wondered why they put a complete greenhorn, who readily admitted he had never previously worked with hoofed stock, in charge of such dangerous animals. But I survived, and when the reptile collection eventually was greatly enlarged and moved to temporary quarters in the elephant house, I spent most of my time with it.

My six years at Toledo constituted an extremely valuable training period for things to come. There were times when all the keepers, including me, had to pitch in to do unusual things, such as moving animals when considerable manpower was required. When a keeper was sick, a substitute was needed to clean and feed his stock. We all worked a six-day week. Swingmen, who were knowledgeable about several different parts of the zoo, filled in when each regular man had his day off. Eventually I became a part-time swingman myself. I couldn't have hoped for a better opportunity to learn the zoo business on a broad basis from the ground up.

The Toledo Zoo had evolved from a few animals in Walbridge Park to a good but still small institution by the time I arrived. The Toledo Zoological Society had made the difference. Frank L. Skeldon, a reporter for the "Toledo Blade," lived on Shadow Lawn Drive right across the street from the small park menagerie. He well knew what good stories animals could generate, and he was close at hand to garner scoops for his paper when anything interesting happened. He realized the value of enlarging the collection, and he solicited the help of a few leading citizens of Toledo to form a zoological society. Skeldon eventually approached Percy C. Jones, an able and strong-willed person who was the son of Samuel Milton "Golden Rule" Jones who had been mayor of Toledo for 16 years. Percy Jones's reaction to Skeldon's appeal was blunt: "If I kept the animals on my farm like you keep your animals in Walbridge Park, I'd be in jail." Jones was elected president of the infant Society, and things began to happen.

By the time of my arrival the entire zoo had been fenced, although admission was free. There were public entrances that could be closed at night by large gates.

There were also a few much smaller gates, including one directly across the street from Skeldon's house, through which he could enter quickly, or leave, simply by using a key in a padlock. Numerous pens, pools, and enclosures for birds and small mammals were scattered around the grounds. More impressive installations were the elephant house, modeled after the one at Detroit's Belle Isle Zoo; a new and ornate lion house; and an old "buffalo barn" from which paddocks radiated for bison, deer, kangaroos, and other species that were relatively tractable. An ancient catchall building housed the few snakes along with a variety of zoological odds and ends. The giraffe house, where I received my initiation as a keeper, was populated by zebras, antelopes, and a young African buffalo, as well as a pair of giraffes. Normally they all could be transferred to outdoor paddocks while I cleaned inside, even for short periods in winter weather. I was forbidden to let the giraffes out when there was snow on the ground, however. That meant I had to enter their spacious indoor pen with them while I cleaned up and tossed pitchforks full of hay into high racks so the lofty, lanky animals could eat standing up. Once, when I was looking up to toss the hay, the male giraffe kicked at me with one of his long hind legs. He caught me in a particularly tender spot, and I nearly fainted. Fortunately, it was a spent blow and, despite the pain, I was able to exit from the pen promptly.

When I arrived at the Toledo Zoo I had not yet reached my twentieth birthday, although I tried to conceal that fact as best I could by making myself two years older. Some of the veteran employees resented the presence of a young whippersnapper on the staff. Lou Scherer, the head keeper and former superintendent of the entire zoo, was one of them. Some of his friends among the citizenry at large criticized the zoo board for hiring me. Percy Jones's reply was, "We're trying to get someone on the staff who knows a lot about animals. Do you know anybody in Toledo who does?" Lou and I eventually became friends, but I realized how very little education he had when I saw the report he prepared about the death of an ostrich. He spelled it "austrije."

After I had graduated from the giraffe house to the reptile exhibit in the lobby of the elephant house, an event occurred that eradicated all animosity toward me. At the time, a small mammal house was under construction, and I was walking past it one morning when I heard a scream. I looked for its source and saw Charlie Conners, the keeper who had succeeded me in the giraffe house, lying on the ground in one of the outdoor paddocks. A stallion zebra was furiously kicking and biting at him. Without a second's hesitation I grabbed the nearest tool, a shovel, raced for the chain-link wire

RC at the age of 19, in a photo taken professionally just before he left Philadelphia for Toledo.

fence, and scrambled up and over it like a monkey. I was joined by a young workman with a piece of pipe. Together we beat off the zebra, and Charlie was able to get up and run into the building. He had several smashed ribs, and part of one ear had been bitten off.

My companion dropped his length of pipe and climbed out, but I, like an idiot, tried to throw my shovel over the fence. It didn't quite make the top, bounced back, and the handle struck me under one of my eyes, giving me one of the most terrific "shiners" I ever endured. When Skeldon and a news photographer arrived at the zoo to record the story for his paper, one of the two "heroes" had a beautiful black eye that was portrayed on the front page for everyone to see. My fellow employees congratulated me on going to Charlie's rescue, and, after that episode, I was accepted as one of them.

Percy Jones, the Society's president, took a liking to me despite my youth. He realized that I was several cuts above the hard-working laborers who served as the other keepers. I was invited to his beautiful home for dinner, and more than once. He let me assume the title of Curator of Reptiles and gave me every encouragement to acquire something to curate, besides the few snakes in the zoo's oldest building. He underwrote a train trip to St. Louis for two or three days so I could see and study the splendid reptile house over which Marlin Perkins presided.

Percy C. Jones, President of the Toledo Zoological Society, and RC's benefactor. Toledo Zoo photo, taken about 1935.

Toledo, at the time, was the third-largest railway terminal in the nation, following Chicago and St. Louis. I had two choices, the Wabash and the Nickel Plate Railroads. I chose the Wabash and enjoyed it so much that I used it on several subsequent trips to St. Louis. It was an overnight run, and I had a lower berth and ate in the dining car, a new and pleasant experience for me.

Marlin and his deputy, Moody Lentz, welcomed me, and the three of us soon became fast friends. They, too, were young, although several years my senior. They not only showed me the collection and all the intricacies of the building, but they also pointed out details that should be avoided in planning any similar structure. They taught me many tricks for getting recalcitrant snakes and other reptiles to feed properly.

My enthusiasm was sufficient so that a rather elaborate reptile exhibit was installed in the lobby of Toledo's elephant house. There were quarters for many kinds of reptiles, even a large python. Because we were forced to fit the cages into the existing and rather cramped dimensions below and between the large windows that admitted light, we lacked most of the safety features that had been built into the St. Louis Zoo's reptile house. Once the new battery of cages was installed, I was relieved of my giraffe house duties and I devoted most of my time to the reptiles. The Society bought a number of specimens, mostly of exotic species from animal dealers, but the local kinds I had to go out and catch myself.

One happy spinoff of the latter responsibility, again sponsored by Percy Jones, was a truly memorable trip to the fabulous snake dens near Murphysboro in southern Illinois, for which Marlin and Moody served as guides and companions. Thousands of snakes of many kinds, but largely timber rattlesnakes and cottonmouths, occupied upland, rocky hibernating areas during cold weather, but they migrated in season to a large swampy area in the floodplain of the Mississippi River. In spring and fall they were subjected to frightful persecution by mankind. We went in August, when gravid females were present close to the wintering dens. We collected a few, including a cottonmouth that gave birth to young at Toledo and was the first of three captive generations of her species.

On Sunday mornings the officers of the Zoological Society assembled in a small building, formerly a restroom, where the zoo's secretary had her desk, typewriter, and files. Percy Jones invited me to join them one day, and I soon became a regular guest of the weekly "bull sessions." Some of the conversation was aptly described by that slang expression, but important business was also discussed, including problems with the city. The Toledo Zoo belonged to the city. Our paychecks were drawn on the public treasury, and all foodstuffs and supplies had to be requisitioned through the purchasing department with its annoying red tape and endless delays. There was no provision for emergencies, which are inevitably a part of every zoo. The Society maintained a petty cash fund for the quick acquisition of various commodities, especially medications. Dr. Reuben Hilty was the zoo's veterinarian, and also an officer of the board. He did as well as any "vet" could possibly have done, given the primitive techniques available in those days long before antibiotics. His difficulties remind me of the delightful stories told by James Herriott about caring for farm animals in his native Yorkshire, England, in such books as his "All Things Bright and Beautiful." Dr. Hilty was almost always present on Sunday mornings and so was Frank D. Butler, the Zoological Society's treasurer. Those two, along with Jones and Skeldon, actually ran the zoo. They were all members of the Zoological Board of Management, a device engineered by the Society and approved by city ordinance. There were also four members of the administration in power and the mayor. That made nine in all, but, in actual practice, two or more of the city people were always absent from the meetings. The Board of Management was a useful liaison between the city and the Society.

Raymond L. Ditmars, the best known herpetologist of his day, visited the Toledo Zoo during the early 1930s. The press demanded a picture. He, as a former newspaper reporter, suggested that we pretend a tree cobra had a case of "mouth rot." He held the snake, RC with a swab dipped in antiseptic. Toledo Zoo photo.

As a reptile curator, I had many problems. Our 16-foot regal python wouldn't eat. I tried all the tricks I knew—slowly increasing the heat in its quarters, introducing food slowly and cautiously in the evening so there would be no one around to disturb it, using live or freshly killed rabbits and chickens—but with no success. There seemed nothing to do but to force-feed it. On one of my visits to St. Louis, Marlin and Moody had demonstrated how they did it with a python considerably larger than ours.

I obtained a piece of sturdy rubber hose about four feet long and with an inside diameter of about two inches. The hose was packed with ground rabbit, fur and entrails included. We boiled a few pieces of slippery elm bark and smeared the resultant slime thoroughly over half the hose. A wooden ramrod, small enough to fit inside the hose and carefully marked so I would not insert it too far, was also at hand. Next, the python had to be caught and held. With heavily gloved hands, I reached into its cage and seized it right behind the head. In quick succession a series of men, 8 or 10 in number, grabbed the snake, and we held it as straight as we could. I then relinquished my hold on the snake's head to a trusted keeper. The snake obligingly held its mouth open ready to bite. I slowly and carefully inserted the slippery end of the rubber hose into its esophagus, and then used the ramrod to push the rabbit hash well down the snake's gullet. After I removed the hose, again gently, the snake was returned to its cage, tail end first. Happily, the python never regurgitated. We fed it the same way every few months and kept it alive for several years.

By modern standards of reptile husbandry the procedure just described was little short of brutal, but it was the accepted method in use, those 60 years ago, in all American zoos that maintained reptile collections. A line of men holding a large snake while food was rammed down its throat was always good for publicity pictures. The San Diego Zoo even used a sausage-stuffing machine, and "volunteers" paid for the privilege of helping to hold the snake while it was fed.

The keepers who regularly assisted with the force-feeding of our python were always amused by the ignorance of newcomers, and I suspected them of purposely recruiting helpers who had never held the snake before. WPA maintenance workers, assigned to sweep sidewalks, wash windows, and to do other chores, and who never had close contact with any of the animals, were the usual victims. To be sure of having enough manpower, I always made certain that one or two of them were at hand. On being confronted by the large, formidable-looking python and told what was expected of them, the usual reaction was, "Boy, I'm keeping away from the head of that thing. I'll hold the tail." The keepers would wink at one another. The snake invariably defecated during the feeding process, and that event was immediately followed by loud guffaws from the men in the know. I remember, even yet, seeing one of the innocent helpers standing out of sight of visitors in the work passage of the elephant house, with his pants off and scrubbing them with soap and water.

Even back in my Twin Brook Zoo days I realized the vast potential for educating the public inherent in large collections of animals. At Toledo I had an opportunity to put that thought into action. The zoo officers learned that I had experience as a public speaker, and the next thing I knew I was invited to address the Toledo Rotary Club, whose members consisted largely of leading citizens. I would have preferred to warm up with a less prestigious group, but I need not have worried. The audience was so responsive that I was quickly put at ease, and I probably gave one of my best lectures ever. After it was over they plied me with questions about snakes for a full hour. Next it was the Kiwanis Club, then the Lions Club, and all the rest of the service, civic, and charitable organizations of the city. That was followed by invitations from similar groups in nearby towns. All my talks were free, but I had convinced the zoo's officers that I was able to drum up interest in the zoo just by talking about it. I soon acquired the additional title of Educational Director.

I visited biology classes in all the city's high schools, taking a few live harmless snakes with me, and I returned to talk again the next semester or year when the students had changed. I even had the temerity, at my young age, to present a paper entitled "The Educational Duty of the Zoological Park" at a meeting of the American Association of Zoological Parks and Aquariums.

I met classes by appointment at the zoo gates and gave them tours of the entire zoo. I conducted courses for Boy Scouts who sought to earn the reptile study merit badge, and I soon had a small retinue of young men who often came to the zoo after school just for the fun of it. I put some of them to work doing such things as making charts and helping me with my research on the reptiles of Ohio (see the "Ohio Reptile Survey" chapters). A few of them, especially eager young Barney Gardner, then in his early teens, I invited to go on field trips with me. My daily routine at the zoo soon consisted of looking after the reptiles most mornings and living up to my new title the rest of the day. I was also active during many evenings, giving lectures and attending meetings of such organizations as the Field Naturalists' Association and the Toledo Aquarium Society.

So many things happened at the Toledo Zoo that I could go on recounting them for a great many more pages. There actually is a separate chapter on the origin of the new reptile house and several more concerned with our extensive fieldwork throughout Ohio. A few events, however, should be recorded here.

In 1933 I received an unexpected promotion. Lou Scherer had been demoted to keeper of the lion house, and the supervision of all the employees, except me, had been delegated to the superintendent of maintenance. He had managed quite well despite his lack of knowledge about animals. There were enough experienced keepers to help him over any rough spots. He was well-liked and his orders were obeyed. But then sex reared its ugly head. We were still deeply immersed in the Victorian era, and the very word "sex" was absolutely taboo. Someone tipped Skeldon off about what was going on. A woman, a practitioner of the world's oldest profession, had literally been having rolls in the hay with some of the employees in the lofts of the giraffe house and buffalo barn. Because I was in such close touch with the Society's officers and was regarded as their "fair-haired boy," I was kept under surveillance when the woman was in the zoo, so I knew nothing about it. An investigation was inaugurated, quietly and with no outside leaks, and the superintendent finally admitted he had known what was transpiring. He even was suspected of having been directly involved, and more than once. He was fired along with two or three of the younger employees. The officers met in emergency session, and I was told that, henceforth, it was up to me to run the zoo. So, at the age of 24, and with no experience in handling men, I faced a great challenge.

Instinctively I let them pretty much alone. Almost every animal man, veterans all, knew his individual duties. All I asked of them was to tell me at once when any problems arose. The assistant superintendent of maintenance was promoted and took charge of the other employees, which was good. I still had to look after the reptiles. There was no backup or swingman for me, but my charges, in emergencies, could be neglected for even two or three days, except for a cursory daily inspection. Also, I was soon to be deeply involved with the planning of the new reptile house. The only real advantages to my promotion were an increase in salary and the new title of just plain Curator, although it should have been "General Curator." I had problems, some of them serious, but I managed to settle them—thanks, at least in some cases, because of my close liaison with the officers of the Society.

One amusing event is worthy of comment: the case of the errant kangaroo. One summer day, Barney and I were doing something in the office when the telephone rang and I was told that a kangaroo was loose. The clean-up man, who drove a horse and wagon (and later a truck) to pick up the manure in the various pens where the keepers had piled it, had opened the gate into one of the paddocks, driven in, and failed to notice the kangaroo as it slipped past him onto the public walk before he closed the gate. Some boys began to chase it, not realizing that they had no hope whatsoever of catching up with it. By the time I was alerted, a couple of the keepers had stopped the boys, but the kangaroo had passed through one of the exit gates on the southwest side of the zoo and was calmly eating grass at the curb. My plan was to get past it and quietly urge it back into the zoo. Because it was on the outside, however, I decided to take my car, which was nearby, just in case. Before I arrived a passing vehicle spooked the kangaroo, and it started hopping down a quiet residential street. I stopped at the gate, picked up the two keepers, and, with them and Barney on the running boards, started slowly after the animal. It kept picking up speed, and so did I, but our quarry managed effortlessly to keep ahead of us. We turned into Harvard Drive and were doing 30 miles an hour, as Barney clearly remembers, when the kangaroo suddenly slowed down and hopped between two houses. I had to stop the car, of course, while Barney and the men jumped off and followed the animal. I was not far behind. The backyard was fenced, but vines growing upward made the wire barrier invisible. The kangaroo slowed, but not quite in time to avoid hitting the fence and being bounced back into our waiting arms. I grabbed it by the tail. One of the keepers took my place, held on to the tail, and, in the approved fashion with kangaroos, let it hop slowly all the way back to the zoo and its pen.

In the meantime, I offered our apologies to the ladies who had been sunning themselves in the yard, one of them quite elderly and with her hair done up in paper curlers. They had been startled, to say the least, when a kangaroo, with a posse in hot pursuit, came dashing past them. After I told them the animal was quite harmless, and they had seen how easy it was for us to handle it, they had a good laugh and a wonderful story to tell their friends and relatives.

As the zoo's curator I was on call for all sorts of problems. One night, well after 1:00 A.M., the telephone rang. I answered sleepily, and the night watchman literally shouted, "Fanny's out!" My groggy reply was, "Whose fanny's out?" Once I was fully awake I remembered that Fanny was a black bear and the mother of a small but ambulatory cub.

"Where is she?" I asked. "Up a tree," he replied, "along Amherst Drive just outside our fence." I told him to go to the spot and stand by at a safe distance pending my arrival. I dressed as rapidly as possible and got my car. When I arrived, there were a half dozen automobiles, all with their lights trained on the tree next to the fence that the mother bear had ascended to the first horizontal limb. The cub was pacing back and forth, still inside the fence, and bawling loudly for its mother. I quickly surveyed the situation and then went to each car and asked the drivers to keep their lights on but not to step out under any circumstances. By luck, one of the

perimeter gates was close by. I unlocked it with my key and propped it open at an angle with a stick. My hope was that the bear would eventually go down to her cub, walk along the fence, and then turn into the zoo when she reached the open gate. Meanwhile, with my high-powered flashlight ready to turn on, I kept my distance but talked gently to Fanny. Soon she grasped the bole of the tree with her arms and legs and started down, rear end first. "Good," I whispered to myself, but no.

A siren sounded in the distance and it grew louder and louder until a police car drew up, screeched to a stop, and two officers leaped out, each with a rifle, which they promptly aimed at the bear.

Believe it or not, I had to plead with them not to shoot; I was even forced to push their rifle barrels upward. They knew who I was and tolerated my behavior, but the temptation to shoot was difficult for them to suppress.

They finally agreed to give me a few minutes, but they kept their weapons trained on Fanny, who had climbed back up to the horizontal limb. By gestures I cautioned everyone to be quiet. I resumed talking to her gently, and soon she came down and walked away from me along the fence toward the gate. She passed through it into the zoo and was reunited with her cub. She started off at once, walking leisurely in the direction of her cage, followed, in sequence, by me with my light shining brightly to keep her in sight, the two trigger-happy cops, and the night watchman, who had closed the gate. Fanny went right home, with the cub at her heels, and stepped inside her chain-link cage, which was equipped with a shelter. It and a couple of others like it constituted our bear dens. I closed the gate behind the two animals and reached for the padlock, which the keeper had hooked over the wire and carelessly neglected to put back into place. I snapped it shut. I turned to the officers and shrugged my shoulders. One of them said, "I'll be damned! You were right. I'm glad we didn't shoot." I escorted them to the gate and locked it behind them. All the other cars were gone, except mine and the one from the police department.

In the morning I had the difficult but necessary chore of bawling out the keeper. He hung his head and then apologized. He knew he was wrong, and he also knew I could fire him. I didn't. We were deep in the Great Depression, and jobs were almost impossible to find. I happened to know he had a family to support. He had learned his lesson, and from that time on he was one of our best keepers.

Who had sounded the alarm? A young couple had been necking in a car near where Fanny climbed the fence and tree. They drove to a phone and called the zoo, then promptly returned to watch the excitement, if

Babe, the rogue male Indian elephant, taking a stroll in Walbridge Park. During earlier days, long before RC arrived in Ohio, Babe managed to escape from the zoo many times. He often terrorized the human neighbors, some of whom must have left a car in haste. Toledo Zoo photo from Don RedFox.

any. They turned on their lights, and that attracted other cars from along the "lovers' lane" that our fence and a quiet drive made possible. One car, I learned from the watchman, had driven off before my arrival, and presumably its driver had called the police.

I took my responsibilities very seriously. I was constantly checking pens and cages for weak spots where the animals gnawed or shook the bars or wire, or where they tried to dig their way to freedom. After the incident with Fanny and her cub I also became lock-conscious and looked at all of them, and sometimes even checked them with my hand to make sure they were securely fastened. During the winters I worried about the heat. There were no furnaces at the zoo. All of our heat was from hot water piped from the old pumping station many blocks away on Broadway. The system was archaic. Once, during one of the summers of my tenure at Toledo, the line to the zoo was dug up, and the old rusty pipes were replaced with new ones. Even so, the pumping station was sometimes shut down for hours or even days for repairs. The winter of 1934-35 was an especially severe one, with temperatures dropping to 10 or more degrees below zero night after night. The wind-chill factor reminded us of stories we had heard about Siberia. I worried about a possible breakdown and the devastating

effect it would have on many of the animals. I kept in close touch with the people at the pumping station, and several times I sallied forth from home into the bitter weather to visit the zoo at night to make sure all was well.

In general, my supervisory job was going well, but there was an ominous development that was both unexpected and certainly no fault of mine. One of my bosses had a severe drinking problem, and I suddenly found myself on the receiving end of a steady stream of invective. I'll not go into detail, but the unfair persecution I had to endure was my chief reason for leaving Toledo, and moving back to Philadelphia, which I did during late June of 1935. Inadvertently, my tormentor did me a big favor. Dr. William M. Mann, Director of the National Zoo in Washington, summed it up a few years later by telling me, "You were a big frog in a little pond, but you moved to a big pond where you could become a really big frog." The potential for my career advancement at the Philadelphia Zoo was enormous, although I didn't realize it then.

No account of the Toledo years would be complete without writing a few paragraphs about Babe, the zoo's enormous Indian bull elephant, of which I was mortally afraid. He was the most truculent, the most treacherous, and the most dangerous animal in the entire zoo. He has been dead for decades, but my memories of him remain clear even though more than 60 years have passed since I saw him last.

Babe stood about 10 feet 5 inches tall at the shoulder—not that we ever tried to measure him accurately. He was too rambunctious for that, but we sighted along a huge beam that was part of his cage, and we probably made a close estimate. It had been years since he was on a scale, but we guessed that he weighed six tons or thereabouts. He was a monstrous brute.

At one time Babe had belonged to a circus but, after killing two of his attendants, he was donated to the infant Toledo Zoo where he killed another man. Before the elephant house, with its massive steel construction, became available, virtually nothing could contain Babe. Occasionally he escaped from the chains tying his feet together and made forays around the neighborhood, often taking housewives' clean laundry and clotheslines down with him as he moved along. He would pull up and eat cabbages and other truck garden produce. Sometimes, in the early dawn, he would walk between houses in the nearby residential areas. He would even poke his long trunk through second-story windows and, by pushing on the frames or sashes, make enough noise to scare the daylights out of the sleeping occupants of the room.

When Babe was moved into the elephant house, long before my arrival on the scene, the zoo staff gave a sigh of relief, especially since a small female named Toots had been purchased as a mate for him. Some problems still remained for me, however.

The new reptile exhibit in the lobby of the elephant house looked nice, but it lacked all the amenities necessary for the care of live animals. There was no water and no place to dispose of waste. That meant I had to carry water in one bucket and debris in another, and the shortest route to the keepers' passageway was through Toots's cage. The bars were far enough apart so I could easily pass through them. I stayed as far away as possible from Babe and from the rhino and hippo, which completed the foursome of pachyderms on exhibition. They, too, could be quite dangerous. Toots was friendly toward me, but she bulked large and sometimes playfully pushed me against the wall or tried to sample the contents of my pails. Babe, on the other hand, seemed to hate me. (Because I didn't feed him like the other employees did?) He had a nasty trick of swinging his trunk back and forth and then throwing it out straight in my direction to shower me with mucus (snot, to be vulgar) if I was not on my guard. Also, whenever I was fairly close, he sometimes would make a wild grab for me with his trunk.

Babe had three pens, in the broadest sense of the word. First, there was a rather spacious outdoor yard surrounded by steel beams deeply imbedded in concrete and buttressed with more steel set at an angle. Second, his exhibition cage inside the building was separated from Toots's pen by a sturdy reinforced concrete wall. There was a gate in it so the two elephants could be put together when Toots came into estrus. The third was a large holding pen between the two others, and barred at the side toward the keepers' work passage. Babe could be kept in it while his indoor quarters were being cleaned. He was also confined there when he came into that strictly elephantine phenomenon known as "musth," pronounced "must." At such times he became a rogue elephant and was especially dangerous. Musth was thought then to be a sexual manifestation, and Dr. Hilty prescribed large quantities of saltpeter, to be added to Babe's drinking water, to reduce his ardor.

Musth is accompanied by the oozing of a dark, odoriferous fluid from the male's temporal glands, through slitlike openings, one on each side of his head between the eye and ear, and the thick exudate might even run down to his mouth. The condition can last for weeks or even months. Recent research indicates that musth is associated with a strong increase of the hormone testosterone, but it also is now known that males can mate successfully whether they are in musth or not. The excretion may serve as a mechanism to assert dominance among males, which have been seen marking trees with the sides of their heads, presumably to stake out territory. During musth, male work elephants in India were always chained, we were told, between trees or heavy posts until the phenomenon passed. Musth comes from a Hindi word that translates as "intoxicated."

There was a large, heavy, steel-barred gate between the holding pen and Babe's exhibition cage. It was operated by an electric motor that pulled a cable across a big pulley and wound it onto a drum as the gate was raised. In theory it worked well, but Babe was so incredibly strong that, at times, whether he was in musth or not, he would raise the gate with his big trunk for a foot or two and then let it drop with a terrific bang. Occasionally the blow would jerk the cable off the pulley, rendering the electric mechanism inoperable. The gate was supposed to be chained to a steel ring imbedded in the floor when it was down, but sometimes Babe was so ornery that he wouldn't permit his keeper to put the chain in place. Normally he tolerated the men who took care of him. If the weather was warm, Babe could be put out-of-doors while the cable was restored to its proper place. One day, however, in the midst of a spell of bitterly cold weather, it slipped off, and Babe could not go outside. What to do?

An elaborate plan was worked out. Lou Scherer, who had taken care of Babe during earlier years, could still control him to some extent. Lou was consulted, and he asked for a supply of Babe's favorite delicacy, banana stalks from which all the fruit had been removed. Someone was dispatched to the produce market's garbage pile for the goodies. Lou would keep Babe as far away from the gate as possible, feeding him the stalks from the keepers' passage, one by one, to keep him busy. Meantime, someone with a crowbar would go up a short ladder in Toots's pen, stand on top of the wall between the two elephant cages, and attempt to put the cable back in place. Who would do it?

The man who was then the superintendent of the zoo pointed at me. "It's up to you," he said. "You're the most agile person around here, and you're tall enough to reach the cable. Nobody else can do it." Frankly, I was scared to death. Once I was in position, Babe could easily reach far enough to grab my ankle with his trunk and slam me down onto the concrete floor far below. I felt like refusing, but I was young and vain enough so that I didn't want to be called a coward, so up I went. It was all I could do to reach the cable. I struggled with it for what seemed like an eternity, but I finally pried it into place. I was shaking from head to foot when I was finally down—and safe.

Twice again during the following winter I had to repeat the operation, but the maintenance men rigged a heavy box they could anchor atop the wall on which I could stand, and it gave me sufficient additional elevation to do the job quickly and easily.

The zoo business never lacked for problems. Sometimes it could be downright dangerous.

Chapter 3

Snakebite!

Quite early in my career I sustained a bite from a relatively small rattlesnake. It was rather a severe bite, but, worse yet, the medical treatment I received was so badly botched that I nearly died. When I finally recovered, months later, the attending physician had to leave town.

The locale was the Toledo Zoo; the reptile involved was *Crotalus mitchellii*, the speckled rattlesnake; and the date was September 16, 1929.

Several months after I arrived in Toledo, my enthusiasm prompted the zoo authorities to erect a series of display cages for reptiles, chiefly snakes, in the spacious lobby of the elephant house. The new installation was an instant success, and it was invariably crowded with visitors on busy days.

Even at that early date I was interested in research and in the dissemination of information that might help to dispel the ugly stigma that all snakes suffered at the time. I hoped someday to write a pamphlet on the subject, but I envisioned an even more ambitious project. The Antivenin Institute of America, a division of the Mulford Biological Laboratories, had recently been founded, and the Mulford company had developed an antivenin for use in case of snakebite. How wonderful it would be if I could influence them into establishing a midwestern venom-collecting station at the Toledo Zoo. If that were to happen, I would need to do the extractions myself. So I began practicing with a collecting glass firmly attached to a heavy board. Snakes from dealers often arrived in job lots in those days, and almost invariably they would include emaciated rattlesnakes that were probably already too far gone to survive. They became my subjects. In the fashion of the day, I would pin down the head of each snake with a snake hook, then pick it up with my index finger on the top of the head and my thumb and middle finger pressing against the neck posterior to the venom glands. With the other hand I held and supported the snake. Usually the mouth opened as soon as the snake was grasped, and it was a simple matter to hook the fangs over the glass and press against the glands to force the maximum amount of venom from them.

Despite the fact that I am right-handed, I used my left hand to pick up and hold the snakes' heads. Marlin Perkins, who served then as the St. Louis Zoo's Curator of Reptiles, but who later attained fame as a television narrator about animals in general, had recently sustained a nearly fatal bite from a Gaboon viper, a large, heavy-bodied African snake. Marlin strongly advised me to use my left hand because, in the event of a bite, my right hand would not be at risk. After milking (extracting venom from) at least a dozen rattlers, I became quite skillful with my left hand.

The speckled rattlesnake had arrived from a dealer in Arizona, and it was such a nice-looking and supposedly rare snake that I wanted to photograph it for my proposed pamphlet. So, on a September weekday when there were very few visitors in the zoo, I removed the reptile from its cage with a snake hook, carried it outdoors into the sunshine, and took several pictures with my Graflex, one of the best cameras of the day. When I had finished I picked up the snake as I had done with the milkers. All went well until I was putting it back in its cage, when I gently tossed it onto the bed of soft sand on the cage floor. Somehow I did not synchronize my hands, and the snake turned in midair and buried its fangs in the basal (proximal) phalanx of my left thumb. It hung on, and I had to lift it off my thumb with my other hand.

After shutting the cage door, I instinctively reached for the snakebite first-aid kit that was out of sight behind a nearby cage. It contained a piece of rubber tubing and a scalpel. The prescribed treatment at the time was to apply a tourniquet on the bitten limb to prevent the venom from spreading, and then to make incisions at or near the site of the bite and start sucking out the blood and venom with one's mouth. Although first-aid treatment for snakebite remains controversial to this day, tourniquets, cutting, and sucking are all known to cause serious complications, and they now are almost universally avoided. Unfortunately, my bite happened long ago.

The piece of rubber tubing had to go around my left

The biter, a speckled rattlesnake. Photo by RC.

arm, but how was I to attach it with a single, unpracticed hand? The elephant house was empty of visitors, but, as I looked up, a man came in the door. I called to him for help and he responded promptly, but, believe it or not, he had only one arm! That was enough, however, and the two of us, working together, managed to put the tourniquet in place. I then walked to the zoo office, which was directly adjacent to the elephant house, and asked the secretary to call the doctor. He had an office nearby, and he was related in some way to one of the members of the zoo's board of directors. We had been instructed to call him in case of any emergency. He was in, and he arrived so quickly that I hadn't yet attempted any cutting. He immediately took charge. With the scalpel, he made a great gash along my thumb, slashing through nerves and blood vessels. With that single cut he effectively amputated my thumb.

I started sucking (and expectorating) while he drove his car at high speed, slowing down but not stopping for red lights, until we reached St. Agnes Hospital. I was put into bed, and he injected an ampule of the Mulford antivenin into one of my buttocks. Meanwhile, I kept on sucking, but my whole hand soon began to swell and I was extracting nothing, so I stopped. A wet dressing was applied to my hand. Whether or not I received any additional antivenin, I don't know, but I probably did while I was asleep. I was in considerable pain and I was given something that caused me to drowse off rather quickly. It would be helpful if the hospital records were available, but normally they are kept for only a decade or less, so I must depend on my memory for such details as I can recall.

The next day the swelling reached its maximum, involving my entire left arm and also the adjacent pectoral region of my chest. There was considerable discoloration, and that, in addition to the great swelling, made my fingers resemble a bunch of red bananas. During the next day the swelling subsided, and three or

four days later it had disappeared altogether, even from my hand, which, although still discolored, looked almost normal—except, of course, for my thumb.

About a week after the bite I had a severe serum reaction, and for a full day I itched like fury and large blebs appeared on many parts of my body. Following that episode my general progress was good. Someone gave me a sponge rubber "Easter egg," and I squeezed it for hours daily with my left hand, keeping my fingers supple.

Back in those days, so many decades ago, there was no rush to move patients out of hospitals as soon as possible. Rates were low, my case was compensable because I was an employee of the City of Toledo, and the hospital was not crowded. So I was retained as a patient, even well after I was ambulatory. It was well that they kept me, because on the twenty-first day I came down with a classic case of lockjaw. The doctor had forgotten to give me a tetanus shot!

For weeks I was mercifully sedated with chloral hydrate. I had a few lucid moments when the effects were wearing off, but, for most of what happened during that long period, I am dependent on what I can remember hearing from the several doctors who became involved, the nurses, and a few good friends who visited often and kept tabs on me.

Tetanus (tetanus bacillus exotoxin) overstimulates the muscles, making them contract to their fullest. My jaws were clamped shut. The back of my head and my heels were on the hospital bed, but the large muscles of my back were so tight that my body was arched upward and supported by a pile of pillows. I was on a liquid diet, and all food was strained through my teeth. I can remember sucking Campbell's tomato soup through a straw. My weight dropped by more than 30 pounds—and I was a slender person to begin with.

The best doctors in the city entered the case. I was injected with what must have been massive doses of tetanus antitoxin. After I had begun to recover, one of my special nurses calculated, from my chart, that I had received almost a half liter of it. Much of it was injected into the epidural space of my spinal column. The next step would have been to drive a hypodermic needle into the medulla oblongata at the base of my brain, which surely would have killed me. Fortunately, I began the long, slow period of relaxation before such drastic treatment was thought necessary. One of the specialists did some research, and he told me that, insofar as he could determine, I was only the sixth or seventh person who had ever recovered from tetanus. I was finally discharged after seven weeks, but I had to return a fortnight later to have my necrotic thumb properly amputated. One serious side effect was that adhesions developed in the palm of my left hand, which was severely traumatized from lack of use for so many weeks. I have never since been able to spread my fingers wide apart or to make a clenched fist. How grateful I was to Marlin Perkins! My right hand was intact.

During my long incarceration I think that every doctor in Toledo and many surrounding towns and cities stopped in to have a look at me. My case certainly was widely publicized, with almost daily updates on my condition appearing in the newspapers. Snakebite in Ohio was a rarity and tetanus almost unknown.

The bite was assuredly my own fault, and I probably would have lost my thumb in any event, but the complications that developed were another matter. The antivenin I received may have helped me a little, but it was far less efficacious than the antivenom now available.

Someone kindly had my film developed and I still have the negatives of the speckled rattlesnake in my files. It was not so lucky as I was. It died before I left the hospital.

My compensation from the State of Ohio for the loss of my thumb was somewhat in excess of $1,100. Suits for medical malpractice were virtually unheard of 60 and more years ago, but given today's frequency of such events and the high awards being made by juries, I might be a millionaire if a good lawyer had pressed the loss of my thumb, my stiff hand, and, especially, the tetanus. Back then I was glad to have the $1,100. I spent most of it for a car of my own that I used for my extensive fieldwork in Ohio, which eventually enabled me to write and help illustrate the "Reptiles of Ohio."

It is no wonder that throughout the rest of my life I have stressed the need for great care in handling venomous snakes. I have always discouraged the keeping of such snakes as pets. Too often the possession of one or more dangerous serpents meant that the owner was showing off and bragging about what a great guy he was. Curiously, a number of such persons, to whom I talked, were little impressed by my pain and suffering when I tried to dissuade them from such foolhardy practices. But they obviously were shocked when I told them how large my hospital bill had been. Most assuredly, the cost of such a complicated case as mine would be astronomical today.

Chapter 4

The Ohio Reptile Survey:
Part I. The Plight of Two Water Snakes

A few weeks after being invited to join the officers of the Toledo Zoological Society at their weekly Sunday morning meetings and bull sessions, I summoned up enough courage to mention I would like to attempt a survey of the reptiles of Ohio. Frank Skeldon was interested at once. He smelled a good newspaper story. He was the Zoological Society's secretary and the "dollar-a-year director" of the Toledo Zoo, but he made his living as a reporter for the "Toledo Blade," the city's leading newspaper. He plied me with many questions while the others listened.

Some of my answers were: I hoped to find a vehicle that would permit me to travel to various parts of the state. I would attempt to obtain help from people in various colleges and universities. I would assemble a small cadre of friends to go afield with me.

Later, Skeldon pumped me for details with which to pad his story, which occupied almost a full page in a Friday edition of his paper. It was a good beginning, because it was read by many persons. An automobile dealer donated an ancient vehicle, shaped like a Victorian brougham, for which he undoubtedly took a tax write-off. Local naturalists volunteered to help. A steady stream of reptiles came into the zoo as donations. I recorded the locality where each was collected and other pertinent data.

After my snakebite I used most of the compensation I received for the loss of my thumb to buy a new Chevrolet sedan. I also found many staunch friends, one or more of whom joined me on every regular field trip. In the meantime, I began assembling a preserved collection that included all the specimens with good field data that died at the zoo, and all the dead, but salvageable, ones found run over on the road. The Ohio reptile survey was off and running, surprisingly only a few months after my arrival in Toledo in 1929.

I was permitted to go afield on weekends throughout each spring for several years and occasionally during the autumn. We were then on a six-day week. My day off was Saturday, and I appreciated the privilege of so many free Sundays. For the first month or so, the Toledo

Zoo reimbursed me for gasoline, which then cost less than 20 cents a gallon. Those were the days of the Great Depression and its aftermath, however, so even that meager financial support soon came to an end, and we were on our own. All the participants on any one trip shared the cost of gasoline, but each was responsible for his personal food and lodging. Some of us brought sandwiches and cookies and thermos bottles of milk or coffee from home. Food was cheap in those days. It was usually possible to find a tourist home for a dollar a night, where one had his own bed but shared the bathroom with the residents in a private house. With care we could get by on a dollar or two a day.

Our usual procedure was to leave Toledo on Friday evening after dinner. Often we were off by 7:00 P.M., but to reach the Cincinnati area, the Pymatuning Swamp region in northeastern Ohio, or the hill country of the southeastern counties required long hours of driving. There were no divided throughways in those days. Many of the roads were paved with bricks, virtually all were only two-laned, and even the most direct routes had numerous right-angled turns in them. In any event, we usually drove long enough to reach our general destination, where we slept in the car or on the ground for a few hours. Then we collected all day Saturday, often used a tourist home that night if we had the money, and then continued our fieldwork on Sunday until late afternoon, when we faced the homeward ordeal of fighting the weekend traffic on the narrow roads. Usually it was midnight or later before we arrived back in Toledo. But by the following weekend we were always ready to do it all over again.

One of my first great interests was to confirm or refute the tales I'd heard about huge numbers of water snakes on the Lake Erie islands. There were so many, according to some informants, that it was difficult to walk without stepping on them. I discounted such claims, but I was unprepared for what we discovered later.

During the early days, when I still lacked my own transportation, friends took me to Catawba, and the sight of a dozen or more water snakes during an hour of walking and wading along the rocky peninsula, whetted my appetite to be off to the islands, the southernmost of which was clearly visible from the Catawba ferry dock.

Our first trip was to Put-in-Bay on South Bass Island. It was a formal excursion of sorts with some elderly friends, who were certainly not dressed for snake hunting, and neither was I. Out of respect for them I had donned my only good suit and shoes, but I had stuffed a small snake bag in my coat pocket. While they were inspecting the Commodore Perry Memorial with its tall shaft commemorating his naval victory over the British in 1813, I sneaked down to the water's edge and started overturning slabs of rock. As I recall, I had only about 10 minutes' time, but I uncovered at least 20 water snakes and caught a couple of small ones to take back with me. That was the beginning. After that I visited the islands at every opportunity, using any available over-water transportation.

It was obvious almost at once that the insular snakes were different from the water snakes of the same species on the Ohio mainland. They lacked patterns on both back and belly, or had the markings only vaguely represented. In contrast, the mainland snakes were strongly blotched and their venters sported dark half-moons, sometimes with reddish centers. So I began keeping score on the patterns. Eventually William M. Clay and I described the island populations as a new race, *Natrix (=Nerodia) sipedon insularum*. Bill was then a Ph.D. candidate at the University of Michigan, and his dissertation was on water snakes, so I invited him to participate.

Our experiences on the islands were varied and interesting. One time we learned about a special boat trip to the Canadian Pelee Island, so we went along. Such excursions were popular in those days of Prohibition, and the steamer was crowded, mostly with men who betook themselves to the liquor store as soon as we landed. My companions and I headed for the shoreline, but its rocky shingle, with no places for water snakes to hide, was a poor place to collect. We soon discovered, however, that snakes were present among the rocks in the landing dock itself, and from it we extracted what later became the type series of specimens on which the description of the new subspecies was based.

In some favorable localities the island water snakes were incredibly abundant. On June 1, 1935, three of us, working along the northeastern shore of South Bass Island, caught 234 snakes in exactly four hours, an average of almost one a minute! If we hadn't bagged them, an accurate count would have been impossible. Many times, when a slab of rock was overturned, a dozen or 15 large ones would suddenly be exposed, and several

invariably escaped—either into the water of the lake or under larger rocks that couldn't be moved. We had sampled only a small fraction of the shoreline, and it was futile to continue. We estimated the water snake population on that one island alone as being in the high thousands. We liberated most of those we caught.

On April 30, 1949, a time of year when the snakes may have been coming out of hibernation, Joseph C. Camin and six associates collected about 400 water snakes in five hours on the much smaller Middle Island in Canadian waters. Camin was interested in studying the effects of predation, possibly by gulls, on the water snake populations, and he planned to mark large numbers of young specimens on Middle Island for future identification. He wanted to test the survival value of the pale unmarked patterns in comparison with the more strongly blotched markings that were present on smaller numbers of the island snakes. In essence, would a gull be able to see and catch a patterned snake more readily than a pale one that almost exactly matched the rocks on which it was resting? If so, natural selection would favor the survival of the light-colored specimens. Unfortunately, when Camin returned to Middle Island, he found many summer homes under construction and realized that human persecution would soon have ruined his experiment if he had started it.

Probably all the Lake Erie islands were once a virtual utopia for water snakes. They provided innumerable slabs of limestone rock for shelters, as well as an abundance of food that, at times, consisted of windrows of small fishes that had died or were dying, for one reason or another, and were washed onto the rocky shores by the waves. The snakes apparently were little affected by natural enemies, but that champion slayer and polluter, man, decimated their populations in short order wherever he arrived in numbers.

One experience on the archipelago stands out in my memory above all others. The small Rattlesnake Island, which lies due west of Middle Bass Island, received its name, we were told, because of its somewhat attenuated shape and the two tiny islets at its western end. The ensemble vaguely resembles a snake with two rattles. I learned that the island belonged to Hubert D. Bennett, President of the Toledo Scale Company. We readily obtained his permission for a visit, and he even promised to help. During the first week of September 1930, Reeve M. Bailey and I set off to try our luck. We drove to Catawba and took the boat to Put-in-Bay. The following morning I called Mr. Bennett, who had a telephone on his island. He said he would be right over for us, and in due course he picked us up in his speedboat, set us down at his landing, and told us to help ourselves to any

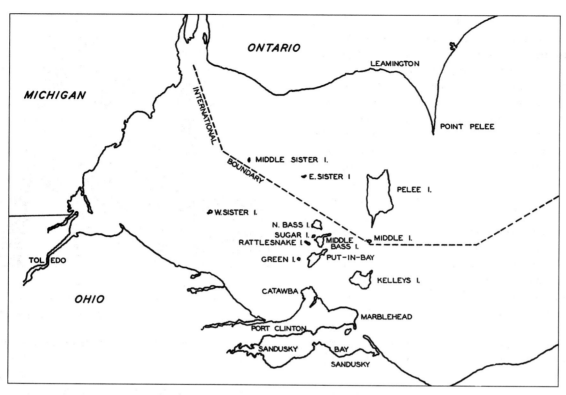

The archipelago in the western end of Lake Erie. From Occasional Papers of the Museum of Zoology, University of Michigan, no. 346, 1937.

snakes we could find. We worked diligently all the rest of the morning, with the net result of having only one small brown snake, *Storeria dekayi*, in our bag. We reported back to his lodge about noon. Whereas we were crestfallen, he was elated.

"If you two experts could only find that little thing," he said, "it proves how efficient we've been in getting rid of the snakes here. But I'm afraid I've played rather a dirty trick on you. To make amends how would you like me to take you over to Green Island where there are lots of snakes?" With that, he waved his arm toward the southwest where we could vaguely see what was to be our next destination. He soon landed us on the dock at Green Island, where there was a small lighthouse and an unoccupied Coast Guard station. "I'll pick you up before dark," he told us, and with that he was off for his own island.

We ate the lunch we had brought with us and then set out to explore the well-wooded speck of land on which we found ourselves. The shores, like those of Rattlesnake Island, were largely sheer cliffs, perhaps 15 to 20 feet high and with only a very few places where one could scramble up from the water's edge. We decided our best bet would be to swim around the island, which we did in leisurely fashion. We found a few small water snakes, and I discovered a hatchling Blanding's turtle, *Emydoidea*

blandingii, crawling toward the water at a spot where several rocks had fallen from the cliff wall. What an extraordinary place to find a turtle that, on the mainland, usually turned up in marshes or was wandering on land, usually near a stream. And a hatchling at that!

By late afternoon we had circumnavigated the island. We dried ourselves, dressed, and then had another look, with no success, through the woods. At sunset we sat on the dock, ate the oranges left over from lunch, and waited for our host. Soon it was dark. Still no boat and, with some hesitancy, we built a signal fire that we hoped could be seen from Rattlesnake Island. That was almost a calamity, but we put out the flames before they did any damage. The realization descended upon us that we were marooned.

Because the statute of limitations has long since passed and I have atoned, many times over, by serving for two years in the Volunteer Port Security Force of the U.S. Coast Guard during World War II, it is now probably safe to admit that we took shelter in the small station building by pushing open a loose window. We were sorely tempted to raid the cans of food with which the place was stocked, presumably for any coastguardsmen who, like ourselves, had to remain overnight on the island. But we resisted and slept fitfully on empty stomachs.

At dawn we were back at the dock. Soon we saw a

boat in the far distance, and by attaching snake bags to our collecting hooks, we made and waved flags trying to attract attention. No luck. An hour or two later, when the boat was returning from the mainland, someone saw our signal, and we were rescued—at a cost of two dollars a head! Miller's Boat Livery, an island institution, had delivered us from our isolation and hunger.

Back in Put-in-Bay, I telephoned Mr. Bennett and told him we had spent the night on Green Island. After a moment of silence, he exploded. "The hell you did. I forgot all about you!"

There is a sequel to this narrative. Years later I transferred my affiliation to the Philadelphia Zoo, which at that time had a large gorilla, named Bamboo, who was the first of his kind to survive in captivity for any length of time. We had no idea how much the big brute weighed. Because I was getting started in my career as the zoo's publicity man, I thought how wonderful it would be to have a scale with a large dial on which zoo visitors could read Bamboo's weight. I wrote to Mr. Bennett, who was still head of the Toledo Scale Company, explained what we needed, and reminded him of how he had deserted us.

We got our scale promptly. Bamboo weighed 435 pounds.

But back to the snakes. What has happened to them? What is their present status?

For several decades I've been dismayed by reports of their great decrease in numbers. Their natural habitat is along the shorelines of the islands, where both food and shelter are abundant. They are rarely, if ever, found in the interior of the larger islands. Unfortunately, the shoreline is precisely the prime site for cottages and docks for use as summertime or vacation second homes. This brings human beings and snakes into close contact, and the reptiles are killed on sight in the belief they are venomous "water moccasins." Actually they are harmless scavengers.

The slaughter has been unremitting, and the water snake, *Nerodia sipedon insularum*, is now a rarity on many of the islands. In fact, so much so that the U.S. Fish and Wildlife Service proposed in the summer of 1993 that it be placed on the list of "Threatened" organisms that might easily become endangered. Such action would give it some protection. The Canadian government had already acted to help the water snakes on the islands within its own territorial waters.

Thus, well within my lifetime, the Lake Erie water snake has dwindled from an extraordinarily abundant serpent to one about which we need to worry. I recall, during the 1930s, how I found so many in so many places that I was reminded of the legendary island of Sindbad the Sailor,

Searching for Lake Erie water snakes on a dock on Pelee Island, Canada, June 9, 1935. From left: David E. Delzell, RC, and Frederick R. Flickinger. Photo by William M. Clay.

who couldn't walk without stepping on snakes. Now seeing even one, on some of the Lake Erie islands, is a rarity.

Concurrently, another Ohio water snake has also suffered greatly. But first let me review how I discovered it, quite unexpectedly. Not too long after the reptile survey was publicly announced, I was visited at the Toledo Zoo by Charles L. Burris who wanted to tell me about redbellied black snakes he had found near Mount Victory in Hardin County. What could they be? I interrogated him thoroughly. They were sometimes more than three feet long and they had plain red bellies, he told me, but with no other markings—no dark half-moons and no pale longitudinal areas down the center. Furthermore, he said, they were often seen far from water, so that eliminated the northern water snake. What in the devil had he found? He seemed like an intelligent, serious-minded person who was not trying to pull my leg, as the saying goes. So I asked him to catch one for me.

When Burris delivered a specimen in August 1929, I was flabbergasted and not a little puzzled. It was big, it was black, and the belly was bright red. From its general appearance it obviously was a water snake, but what scientific name should be applied to it? The status of the species *erythrogaster* was in dispute at the time. Stejneger and Barbour, whose checklist was widely considered to be *the* authority, dismissed it in a footnote by stating, in essence, that the name had been applied to rufescent specimens of both the common (*sipedon*) and banded (*fasciata*) water snakes. In short, they didn't recognize it as a good taxonomic form. On the other hand, Blanchard included *erythrogaster* in his key to the snakes of the United States, but he considered it to be a subspecies of the northern water snake (*sipedon*), and indicated that it occurred no farther north than southern Illinois. Edward H. Taylor, in a work on the herpetology of Kansas, was the first to place it in its true perspective, when he listed the blotched water snake (*transversa*) as a subspecies of *erythrogaster* and pointed out that it was specifically distinct from the northern water snake (*sipedon*). All this I learned in due course, but the discovery of the copperbelly water snake in Ohio set me off on a series of research projects that involved a number of published papers based on specimens of the complex from such widely diverse areas as from Delaware to New Mexico and from Michigan to Zacatecas, in old Mexico.

We found another colony of *erythrogaster* near Blakesley, in Williams County, Ohio, and I soon learned that it also had been reported from Olivet, Michigan, way back in 1903 by Hubert Lyman Clark, although scarcely anyone, including Blanchard and Stejneger and Barbour, had paid any attention to his paper. Later, after I had published on *erythrogaster* in Ohio, Clark sent me a letter, which I still have and treasure, thanking me for proving he had been right all along. Eventually, Bill Clay, Howard Gloyd, and I made a trip to Clark's old Olivet locality, and the species was still there. Ironically, Howard and I each caught a specimen, but Bill, who was deeply involved with water snakes at the time, came away empty-handed, except for the photographs he took during our excursion. Since then, *erythrogaster* has been found in several other Ohio and Michigan localities, as well as in Indiana, initially as a result of fieldwork by Kraig Adler, David M. Dennis, and Otto E. Ehrhart, but later by a number of other people.

In the late 1940s bulldozers moved into the Mount Victory area. They eliminated the remaining swamp forest to provide more land for agriculture, and the red-bellied water snakes lost their habitat. The Blakesley locality suffered a similar fate. Evidently, this snake needs a swamp forest or similar environment in order to thrive. Pools are often present in wet weather, but it can wander well away from them and survive, at least temporarily, without immediate access to water.

Stimulated by the stunning discovery of *erythrogaster* in Ohio, I began my studies on the species as a whole. In 1949, I described the black populations in Ohio and other states as *Natrix (=Nerodia) erythrogaster neglecta*, a new subspecies, and suggested "northern copperbelly" as a common name for it.

It surely achieved its northerly distribution during the warm period of a great many centuries ago, during what is known as the Hypsithermal. After the return of cooler, more humid climates, its range became fragmented. Following the arrival of European settlers, the fragmentation greatly accelerated, as the snakes' swamp forest habitats were altered by the felling of the trees and drainage of the land in preparation for the planting of crops.

Simultaneously with its announcement about the Lake Erie water snake, the U.S. Fish and Wildlife Service also proposed "Threatened" status for *neglecta*.

Perhaps I may be excused for feeling like the godfather of the two water snakes, *insularum* and *neglecta*, but I was the herpetologist who made them both known to science, and thus to naturalists in general. How sad to see them both in trouble. How symptomatic of the mass destruction that is taking place all over the world as the human population increases far beyond all reason. Do we face a future world when the only surviving animals will be domesticated species and such commensal pests as rats and mice? One can but wonder how long it will be until our national parks and wildlife sanctuaries are engulfed to make room for growing food to feed more hordes of humans.

Chapter 5

The Ohio Reptile Survey:
Part II. The Landscape of the Buckeye State

My "Reptiles of Ohio" was published in 1938 by the "American Midland Naturalist" as a separate bound book of 200 pages. It was a formal, scientific report containing information I assembled over a period of six years, and it included the results of intensive fieldwork in virtually all parts of Ohio in the company of several boon companions.

It would have been out of place in such a dignified publication to mention our adventures, foibles, and mishaps during our collecting trips. We had our share of flat tires and miscalculations that plunged us, up to our waists or even further, in mud or water and forced us to swim to save ourselves. We had a lot of fun along with all our hard work. We were young and enthusiastic, and there were no restrictions other than those imposed by the financial problems of the Great Depression and an ironclad regulation that prevented us from using turtle traps. We grew up in an era of deep respect for private property. We always asked permission before we hunted snakes, and, with few exceptions, the response was, "Help yourselves. I'm glad to get rid of the varmints."

That's the way it was. The only good snake was a dead one. Basking turtles were suitable for target practice with shotgun or rifle. Big frogs were edible in part. Small frogs and salamanders were useful only as fish bait. Herps had few friends. No one had ever proposed the drafting of lists of rare and endangered species.

In the previous chapter I described how the survey came about and how we operated in season, and I called special attention to two water snakes that are now the subjects of grave concern.

In 1982 I prepared a lengthy manuscript that was published by the Toledo Herpetological Society. It bore the title of "Herpetology in Ohio—Fifty Years Ago." In it, I recounted many of the interesting adventures and humorous experiences that befell us during our fieldwork in the early 1930s. Much of what is included in the four "Ohio Reptile Survey" chapters here is abstracted from that 65-page booklet.

My most frequent companion was Barney Gardner, an enthusiastic teenager who loved the fun and excitement of our many trips. Even now, some 60 years later, I see him often. We both live in Albuquerque. David E. Delzell was a little older than Barney, he was an excellent driver, and he frequently spelled me at the wheel of my little Chevy when we were headed for faraway places in Ohio. Robert H. Mattlin, who later spent his professional life in the zoo business, as I did, frequently joined us. Older than any of us was Malcolm K. Murphy, a businessman whose hobby, believe it or not, was hunting turtles. Others went along from time to time, including Reeve M. Bailey, who spent the night marooned with me on Green Island. Sometimes his brother, Joseph R. Bailey, also participated. Charles F. Walker, of the Ohio State Museum, was a virtual oracle on wildlife and natural habitats in the Buckeye State, and, whenever possible, we stopped in Columbus to take him along with us, and to learn as much from him as we could.

Ohio had been glaciated in part, and it boasted parts of five distinct physiographic provinces, which offered a wide variety of places for us to hunt—some excellent and others not so good. Toledo, our home base, is in the Lake Plains, a flat, rather monotonous area that once formed the bed of postglacial Lake Maumee. Southward to the Ohio River are the Till Plains, an area covered with glacial till and moraines that offer some relief here and there. Both the Lake and Till Plains had long since been cut over, and agriculture and grazing occupied much of their large extent.

The eastern half of Ohio is on the Allegheny Plateau, which is deeply dissected, especially toward the south, where the glaciers didn't penetrate. For orientation, see the accompanying map, which is taken from the second edition of the "Reptiles of Ohio," a 1951 reprint of the first edition with a lengthy updating entitled "Revisionary Addenda."

Southeastern Ohio escaped glaciation, as mentioned, and the erosion of the Allegheny Plateau resulted in the formation of innumerable ravines, some of which—such as those at Ash Cave, Conkle's Hollow, Old Man's Cave, Rock House, and other formations in the black-hand conglomerate—are of spectacular beauty. In

The 1930 Chevrolet sedan that took us to every part of Ohio and four of its most frequent users. From left: Robert H. Mattlin, Byron L. "Barney" Gardner, Jr., RC, and David E. Delzell. Photo by Otto E. Ehrhart.

numerous places, we found tree-covered, rock-strewn hillsides where, in the springtime, rock turning, log rolling, and breaking apart rotting stumps or logs often produced prizes for a herpetological collector.

So also was another type of habitat that was man-made, but which has long since disappeared. It was the abandoned sawdust pile, often quite large and strewn with bark slabs cut off before the logs were sawed into boards. Overturning slabs on well-stabilized sawdust piles, i.e., ones that had been undisturbed for years, often revealed herpetological goodies. On September 11, 1932, a large, slab-covered pile in Hocking County yielded a fence lizard, three young broad-headed skinks, a northern water snake, 11 hatchling black rat snakes, and two juvenile copperheads. We often found milk snakes and toads in similar places.

The sawdust usually remained moist beneath the outer inch or two of its surface, even in the driest seasons, thus providing a shelter against desiccation and a good medium for the deposition of snake and lizard eggs. The slabs made excellent hiding places, and food, in the form of small mammals and insects, was often abundant. As we wound our way along the narrow, curving roads of the hill country, the driver, his attention devoted to his task, didn't always see such habitats, but all the passengers were prompt in calling out "sawdust pile" whenever they spotted one, up an obscure side road, for example. We always stopped to inspect

even the smallest of them, although it was often difficult to find a place to pull the car off the narrow, sometimes one-lane roads.

Sixty and more years ago, portable, itinerant sawmills were set up in the woods wherever there was enough timber to provide several weeks or months of cutting. The boards were loaded by hand onto trucks, or sometimes horse-drawn wagons, and conveyed to town. The sawdust piles remained for years, and traces of them sometimes survived after second growth had replaced the trees removed earlier. Eventually the procedure was changed. Logs were hauled to a central sawmill site, usually in or close to a small town, where all the sawing was done and the sawdust was often burned. We found slab and sawdust piles in many parts of Ohio during the 1930s, but they were especially abundant in the hill country, where the timber grew on slopes too steep to cultivate. In most other parts of the state, and especially in the Lake Plains and Till Plains, they were seldom found. The original forest had been eliminated from them when the land was prepared for agriculture, and the numerous small woodlots of second growth were not large enough to sustain a lumber industry.

Southeastern Ohio, although much of it had long since been cut over, was in a relatively pristine condition during our fieldwork those many years ago. The forest had regrown, and there were ample opportunities for exploration. We often followed trails or paths

The physiographic areas of Ohio. Reproduced from the second edition of the Reptiles of Ohio, published by the American Midland Naturalist in 1951. Isabelle delineated the various boundaries on a county outline map used with the permission of the George F. Cram Company.

for considerable distances into the woods or up and down the hills. Once, when Barney was in the lead, we stumbled onto a moonshiner's hideout. The operator seized his shotgun, all set to fight the "revenuers" who were invading his domain. I was out of earshot, but Barney reported that the man quickly realized we were not the law. He offered to sell us some of his stock real cheap, at three dollars a jugful, because it was a "mite scorched."

The language in use among the hillbillies who lived in the woods or in the smaller towns was picturesque and to the point. It's regrettable that we didn't include some of it in our field notes. Portable tape recorders were unheard of in those days. Much of the uniqueness and color of the local conversations has now been lost because of such innovations as district schools, to which the children are transported by bus. More recently, America has become homogenized by radio and television. Nowadays we all

hear much the same language, and the charm of the hillbilly patois has largely and lamentably vanished, like so many other fragments of Americana.

Two typical items linger in my memory, however. During one of our excursions to Pike County, someone told us to look up a person called Yancey who knew where all the sawdust piles were situated. When we finally found his humble abode, three or four towheaded youngsters came out of the house to stare at us and listen to our conversation. Evidently they had been eating, because their faces showed strong evidences of strawberry jam. Yancey turned to the most besmeared of the group and commanded, "Go in an' wash yerself. Yer mouth looks like a jaybird's ass in pokeberry time."

Once when we had stopped at McArthur, the tiny county seat of Vinton County, someone asked, "Doesn't this town ever grow? It always looks the same. Aren't any babies ever born here?" To that, the prompt response was, "Ever'time one's born some son-of-a-bitch has to leave town."

One weekend, when Memorial Day, May 30, fell on a Monday, we had remarkable success in Scioto County. We were especially lucky in finding several of the smaller snakes which, at that time, had seldom been encountered in the field in Ohio. The weather had been perfect and we found many herps under rocks in the moist woods, so I decided to extend our field trip by a day and not to drive back on Sunday. Partly because of my elation and partly because, in all good conscience, I needed to let the folks at home know about our delay in returning, I dispatched the following 10-word telegram when we stopped in a small town: "Just took Virginia and eight Carphophis will be home Monday." When I handed over my Western Union form, the local operator could not contain his curiosity, and I had to explain that the message was not in code and that I was the reptile man at the Toledo Zoo. I have often wondered, however, what the reaction was of the chap who took the message off the wire in Toledo, especially if he momentarily mistook "eight" for its homonym "ate."

The charm of the Ohio hill country lay largely in the fact that it was mostly wild in those days. Agriculture was confined to the valleys, and second growth had reclothed the hillsides and many other areas to the point where the forest had more or less returned to its original climax stage. Also, there were many objects to overturn, and there was always the chance of finding something unusual beneath any log or rock. Springs and streams, both clear and muddy, abounded. In short, there was a great variety of habitats to explore. The net result was that we probably spent more man-hours in the hill country than in any other part of the state. Southeastern Ohio was unquestionably our favorite collecting area.

Often my traveling companions didn't know until our time of departure what our weekend destination was to be. Weather conditions and sometimes a last-minute confirmation of where and when we might meet friends in the field could influence our plans. When I announced we were headed for the hill country, I was invariably greeted by cheers, but when our goal was southwestern Ohio, the groans were loud and long.

Collecting in the Till Plains, with a few exceptions, was poor. Early in 1931, when I indicated I wanted to visit Butler County to check on some old records, Charles Walker responded by writing, "Don't expect too much. It is rather uniform and civilized country, with few attractive collecting spots. The woods are almost gone and there is a paucity of swamps."

The same description could easily have been applied to a large block of counties in southwestern Ohio. Almost all of them were under intensive cultivation or in pasturage, and fences were everywhere. There were a few woodlots, but they were mostly small and unproductive. Occasionally we might find a narrow strip of potential habitat along a stream, but whereas reptiles were present in the general area, they were reduced in numbers and difficult to find. Usually our catch was small and chiefly confined to the more common species. For a group of eager young men, fun and excitement were lacking, but I stuck to my goal of sampling the herpetofauna of all of Ohio. I will frankly admit, however, that we made a considerably less sustained effort in the southwestern counties than we did almost anywhere else.

It was Barney who invented the term "moving van country." He maintained that one might just as well nap inside a moving van while traveling through that highly cultivated part of the state. Scarcely anything of interest would be missed in the process. The term stuck with us all through the years of our fieldwork.

We did find a few places of interest in the "moving van country," virtually all associated in one way or another with water. The arbor vitae swamp in Champaign County was one, and so were two lakes, Indian and St. Mary's, but even there we met with only moderate success, possibly because the fishermen and others were persecuting reptiles whenever they saw them. We did, however, obtain a Kirtland's snake near Lake St. Mary's and a massasauga at Indian Lake. In the latter case the snake was sunning itself not too far from a wooded shoreline on a tuft of vegetation that was entirely surrounded by water. We managed to catch it, without getting ourselves wet, while we teetered in a rented canoe.

Once we had a brief bit of excitement as we rounded a curve along a road and saw three men, armed with big sticks, in hot pursuit of a sizable racer. They were so intent on the kill that some of us literally had to fend them off while another member of our party caught the snake. Although we explained our purpose and showed them our official letter of identification from the Toledo Zoo, we drove away feeling that they were mad as hell at us. Our guess was that we had cheated them out of a victim and a chance to regale their friends with a tale, probably to be embroidered with imaginary details, about how they had rid the vicinity of a menace. Snakes engendered mighty little sympathy from the general public in those days.

As an example of how hard up we were to find places to collect, I should mention Ray Lake. I've long ago forgotten just where in the southwestern counties we were at the time. We began seeing signs tacked to phone poles reading "Ray Lake" in large letters, but with the rest of the wording too small to read from a moving car. One of my companions said, "Hey! Where's Ray Lake? Maybe we could find something there." I suggested that he check the road map, which he did with no success. I couldn't recall any such place, and it was my usual practice to review our route carefully either before we started on a trip or while we were rolling along with someone else at the wheel of the car. So the next time we saw one of the signs I stopped and let one of the boys hop out to read it. He came back with a long face and announced, "It says to vote for Ray Lake."

One warm afternoon we were driving through southwestern Ohio in a typical "moving van" area. Traffic was light, there were fields and other signs of civilization on all sides, and we were discouraged, as we usually were in that part of the state. We had found only a few herps despite a weekend of searching, and we were glad to be homeward bound. I was driving along at a moderate speed, keeping my eyes on the road and its shoulders looking for any reptiles, dead or alive. Barney was in front with me, and the other members of the party were asleep behind us. All of a sudden Barney almost shouted, "Turtle."

I hadn't seen it, but I slammed on the brakes, rudely awakening the backseat nappers, and Barney hopped out and ran back along the road. I watched him through the rear-view mirror. Presently he stopped, leaned partway over, promptly stood erect again, and then, in disgust, vigorously kicked aside a well-formed horse dropping that I had noted as we passed over it. But suddenly he knelt down on the road, picked up something, and brought it back to the car. Wonder of wonders! It was a baby painted turtle that had been mashed flat, no doubt by a passing vehicle, and the horse inadvertently had covered it up as it relieved itself.

Poor Barney! We teased him unmercifully about his "X-ray" eyes that enabled him to see a turtle right through a chunk of horse manure.

Chapter 6

The Ohio Reptile Survey:
Part III. In Pursuit of the Turtle

Not everything went smoothly as we pursued our fieldwork. We had our troubles and problems, most of which we overcame with hard work or ingenuity. There was one that wouldn't budge, however, and which severely restricted our work with turtles.

Several colleagues had urged us to use turtle traps. They are effective, and they attract and catch specimens while you are otherwise occupied in the field. So Murphy, with a token amount of help from me, set about making a couple for a try-out. For ease in carrying they were collapsible. Heavy cotton netting was attached to sturdy metal hoops. The resultant trap was drum-shaped with a narrow, horizontal throat fashioned at each end through which a turtle could enter to get at the bait but out of which it was almost impossible to escape. The traps had to be set in shallow water, so any turtles that were caught could get to the surface to breathe. Rods of reinforcing steel were pushed through the netting at each "corner," and then they were driven down into the mud or other substrate to hold the trap in place.

I do not now recall how many times Murphy and I used them, but they worked well. On one occasion, much to our amazement, an even 50 painted turtles managed to squeeze their way into the two traps overnight. They may have been especially hungry to be attracted by the chopped medium-sized fish we used for bait in each trap, but they seemed well nourished when we examined them before turning almost all of them loose. Maybe our brand of fish was especially enticing.

We had visions of great success with the turtle part of the reptile survey, but our hopes were dashed as quickly as they were raised. We learned belatedly that no traps could be set "in Ohio waters" with meshes less than four inches in diameter. That regulation, which we were told was rigidly enforced, was not intended for turtles. Not at all. It was to allow small fishes to escape from similar traps. But it also meant that a majority of the turtles could walk or swim right through the large meshes, especially the small musk turtle or stinkpot.

Murphy and I were disturbed, but I felt sure we could get a collecting permit to use the traps, and I undertook

a special trip to the Conservation Division of the State of Ohio, in Columbus, to make application. The people there were sympathetic and cooperative, especially E. L. Wickliff, as he proved repeatedly over the years, but a permit could not be issued for the use of turtle traps. It would have required an act of the Ohio State Legislature to make that possible, or so I was told. The Division offered to help us if we got into trouble, but the prospective scenario sounded so grim that we decided not to tempt fate, at least not too often. If we were picked up by a game protector during one of our field trips, we could be held until Monday morning for court action. The Conservation Division people said that, if we telephoned them then, they would try to get us out of any difficulty in which we found ourselves. What a nice prospect! Spend maybe most of our precious weekend in the "clink," and then perhaps face a fine or even a jail sentence or both, as well as having our traps confiscated. We did a little trapping after that, but always in obscure bodies of water where there was no evidence of fishermen or game protectors. We reported our take to the Conservation Division, but our hopes for a good, statewide trapping campaign were never realized.

The Ohio law was eventually liberalized to permit scientists to use turtle traps, but in our day we were badly frustrated. It was a bitter pill to swallow, and, as a result, our records for musk turtles were poor. In all probability, we would have done much better with virtually all the other kinds of turtles, at least by catching young ones, if we had been free to use our traps wherever and whenever we wished. We soon would have learned just where, in relation to the turtles' immediate environment, traps should be placed for the greatest success. I eventually developed almost a sixth sense for that, based on my subsequent turtle trapping over a period of many decades in New Jersey, on the Delmarva Peninsula, and especially in Mexico.

We seldom met game protectors in the field, except on a few prearranged occasions. Most were quite cooperative, once they knew our purpose, but such was not the case with a crusty character we encountered at Nettle Lake, in Williams County, one Fourth of July weekend. We planned to investigate a rumor that red-bellied water snakes occurred around the borders of the lake. We had just hired a boat and were shoving off when a loud voice yelled at us to stop. We were asked what we were doing and, when I explained, the "gentleman" wanted to know who had given me the authority to collect snakes. I told him that I represented the Toledo Zoo and that our fieldwork had the full approval of the Bureau of Scientific Research of the Ohio Division of Conservation. Next he ordered me to produce my credentials. Because he was so obnoxious, I retaliated by asking to see his. He was a game protector, according to his card, but I reminded him that there were no laws in Ohio prohibiting or restricting the catching of snakes. After voicing his opinion about the "damned, fish-eating snakes," he calmed down and allowed us to proceed.

We had been on the lake for a good half hour, skirting its shoreline, when the same character arrived in a boat similar to ours but with an outboard motor on it. He had come, of course, to check up on us. He shut off his motor, rowed over, and demanded to know how many assistants I was allowed to have while collecting snakes! I convinced him the number didn't matter. After inspecting the contents of our boat he left, but he was unable to get his motor started again. The last we saw of him, he was struggling to row back to the fishermen's landing against a stiff breeze. We controlled ourselves, but once we had rounded the next small point along the shore and were out of sight and sound, we had a hearty laugh. We found no snakes, but we did see a number of big softshell turtles swimming in the open lake.

With turtle trapping so severely restricted, I was extraordinarily fortunate to have the help of Malcolm Kenneth Murphy. He was an enthusiast of the first order. As a boy, in his native Indiana, he had hunted turtles along the Eel River, and his hobby had continued into manhood. He enjoyed being out in the country, wading in streams, and matching his wits against the escape reflexes of his quarry, some members of which were exceedingly difficult to catch with no other tool than a landing net.

Murphy was very proud of his net. It was about six feet long, with a triangular hoop at one end that supported a bag of cotton mesh, similar to a fisherman's landing net but of sturdier material. At the other end was a snake "hook" that could be used for pinning down a serpent. The handle was of hardwood, but the metal at each extremity was of spring steel that snapped back into place, no matter how great the tension to which it was subjected. Murphy took great care of his net, but even he had to admit that it was a little unwieldy to transport when there were four or five people in such a small car as mine, especially when the mesh bag at the hoop end was wet.

I thought I knew how to catch turtles, but Murphy's techniques were far superior to mine. I promptly and willingly became his pupil.

One day we were exploring a pond that had suffered much from a summer-long drought. Its acre of area had shrunk to a tenth that size, and great wallows of thick brown mud surrounded the remaining water. Turtle tracks, arranged in neat parallel rows, ran in every direction. Murphy waded in without hesitation, first across the mud and then into the water until he was almost thigh-deep. Presently he stopped, stared up at the sky, and then beckoned to me to come. Gingerly I picked my way through the gluey mess, fearful lest a false step should result in disaster. Eventually I reached him and he calmly announced, "I'm standing on a snapper."

And he was—on a big one that had sought refuge in the deepest remnant of the pond. It was completely invisible beneath the muck and turbid water, but, when my companion stepped aside and bade me to take his place, I could feel its shell through the sturdy soles of my boots. Instinctively it had pulled in its head, limbs, and tail.

"Now the trick is to find its tail," Murphy instructed me. "Run your toe around the edge of the shell and when you touch the rough part, that will be its hind end."

Because I was familiar with snapping turtle anatomy, I knew what he meant. Forward and to both port and starboard the perimeter of a snapper's shell is smooth, but aft is a series of deep sawtooth edges that I could easily detect, heavily shod though I was. A quick probe with a hand followed and, shortly, we had our catch firmly gripped by the tail. It struggled valiantly; the huge, webbed feet flailed mud in all directions, and the mouth was held wide open ready to snap shut on any object. Once ashore we examined our prize. It must have weighed 20 pounds.

Such is the art of noodeling, or muddling—feeling for turtles with the hands and feet. Professional hunters had developed it to a high degree of proficiency in their efforts to supply the demand for snapper soup, then a delicacy esteemed by gourmets. Not much turtle soup is made anymore, partly because preparing it requires much skill and many hours of work. It was long popular in Baltimore, Washington, and especially Philadelphia, but few people hunt turtles for the market nowadays.

On another occasion Murphy and I were wading in the shallow riffles of a small river. We purposely worked upstream, so that any sediment stirred up by our feet would flow away behind us. Suddenly Murphy stood stock-still, tense with anticipation. He pointed to a sandbar directly ahead and said, "There. Do you see that swirl?"

I had to look twice before I spotted it, but, sure enough, there was a little eddy settling back on the bar. Cautioning me to play the outfield in case his technique should fail, he approached the spot, poked his fingers downward in exploratory fashion, and a moment later came up with a big softshell turtle. He held it tightly, each hand gripping an opposite side of the flat shell, and far enough back to avoid the scissorlike jaws. The small tail was, of course, useless as a handle.

The turtle had lain buried just beneath the surface of the sand, in water shallow enough for its long, snaky neck to reach upward for an occasional breath of air. As we approached, the snout and eyes had been just above the sand. Sensing danger, the turtle had yanked in its head. Murphy had seen the resulting swirl.

Together we explored innumerable bodies of water, and under the master's tutelage I learned that no suspicious item should remain unexamined, that little bumps of mud, chunks of wood, and many another innocent-looking object actually were turtles. Some kinds had to be stalked, whereas others would come right back up to the water's surface after plunging downward when we disturbed their sunny siestas. Still other kinds had to be rushed, the hunter racing to the water's edge, stepping in boldly, and making a dexterous dip with his long-handled net after the fleeing quarry.

Murphy's enthusiasm and determination to "get that turtle" earned the admiration of all of us. One spring, he and I were invited to participate in a trip to Reelfoot Lake, in western Tennessee, with a party from the University of Michigan led by Norman E. Hartweg, one of the nation's outstanding cheloniologists. Reelfoot had an enormous population of turtles, and for many decades it was one of the chief sources of the literally millions of baby turtles that ended up in dime and pet stores, and few of which survived very long.

It was early April, and as we drove south we were enjoying the sunshine. For the first time in months it was warm enough to ride with the car windows open. We had just endured a frightful winter, replete with below-zero days and an overabundance of snow and ice.

Naturally our enthusiasm was at a high pitch; already we had seen a few turtles basking on distant logs. The Mississippi and all its tributaries were on a seasonal rampage, and every ditch and stream was over its banks. Fields were flooded, here and there, and we noted how vastly larger had become the domain of all aquatic wildlife. Once, as we passed along a high levee, we stopped to stretch our legs. Scarcely had we stepped from the car when someone made a discovery. Not 50 yards ahead of us, at the water's edge, a whole squadron of big turtles was lined up on a floating plank, absorbing the rays of the sun.

Here was a perfect setup for Murphy. Swiftly he removed his net from the trailer we were towing, and then he paused for a moment to reconnoiter. This operation called for a combination of stalking and rushing. A few clumps of willows offered some shelter. With his skill Murphy could get within 20 feet of his quarry without their becoming aware of his presence. But the final gap would have to be closed with all possible speed.

The rest of us watched from a distance. We saw Murphy snake his way forward like an Indian, using the willows as a screen. Ahead of him the turtles dozed lazily. They made quite a sight, set off by a few scraggly plants that grew out of the shallow water before and beyond them.

Suddenly one of them raised its head in alarm and its feet assumed a position of readiness for a quick dive. It was now or never. Murphy rose, his net outstretched in front, and he raced most of the distance before the turtles plopped overboard. Into the water he stepped, and a split second later he disappeared from sight. His hat floated away, and we stood there aghast, not knowing whether to laugh or to rush to the rescue.

Presently he surfaced. Streamers of green vegetation hung from his glasses and, as he floundered ashore, he looked like Father Neptune stepping forth from the sea. His precious net, held like the legendary trident, added to the illusion. What we had all mistaken for shallow water was quite deep, and the scraggly plants were really the topmost twigs of an inundated tree that grew close to the steep-sided levee.

Our guffaws were loud and uncontrolled. But somehow Murphy's misadventure didn't seem quite so amusing when, months later, I plunged into a pond clear up to my armpits.

Murphy was in seventh heaven at Reelfoot Lake. He had never seen so many turtles or so many different kinds in one place, or had so much fun catching them. That trip was probably the highlight of his hobby career.

Murphy was so turtle-oriented that he sometimes declined to accompany the rest of us when we were headed for the hill country, where the only species he could be fairly sure of finding was the box turtle. He did, however, develop an interest in massasaugas, possibly because he had had a long acquaintance with them in Indiana. He made several trips with his brother, Cecil, and a few friends in search of "swamp rattlers" while the rest of us were on field excursions to parts of Ohio where turtles were not often seen. His favorite collecting grounds were near Mount Victory, in Hardin County, and the New Haven Marsh, portions of which were in Crawford, Huron, Richland, and Seneca Counties. The latter area had been drained and was largely devoted to agriculture, but massasaugas were still fairly common in the general region.

One weekend, possibly because I mentioned that there were turtles in small tributaries of the Ohio River, he agreed to accompany me on a trip to the extreme southern part of the state. Ironton, in Lawrence County, was our destination. We left in the evening, as usual, and Barney Gardner accompanied us. It was a long tiresome drive, even though Murphy and I took turns at the wheel. It was some 265 miles, and just about as far away from Toledo as one could get and still be in the Buckeye State. By the time we reached Ironton, sometime after midnight, both Murphy and I were ready for bed and a good night's sleep. We drove around the town looking for a tourist home, but the few signs we saw were not illuminated, which meant there was either no vacancy or the home owners had tired of waiting for guests and had gone to bed. What to do? The prospect of sleeping in the car or on the ground after our long drill down from Toledo was not very inviting. Then we rounded a corner near the edge of town and, miraculously, at a dead end directly ahead of us, was a brightly illuminated sign with the single word "Hotel" on it.

We drove up, parked, and went inside, and were told by the young lady desk clerk that we could have three separate rooms at a dollar each, a surprisingly low price for a hotel. As we ascended the long staircase that looked out over the lobby we saw two or three other girls quietly reading. Barney was shown to a room near the head of the stairs, but Murphy and I were taken down a long corridor and given rooms well apart. Just as soon as we were in our respective quarters, Murphy and I realized that we had blundered into what, in those days, was known as a house of "ill repute," where one

could foregather with "ladies of the evening." I was appalled, especially because of Barney, who was then only 14 years old. I quickly went down to Murphy's room where we consulted. His opinion was that the girls would let Barney strictly alone because of his age, and, since there was no other place to sleep in town, we might as well stay put. I agreed. The beds were clean, and so was the washstand and sink with which each room was equipped, but there were no locks on the doors. Both Murphy and I propped chairs under the doorknobs so we wouldn't be disturbed. Despite our dilemma we both slept soundly.

Barney was not so lucky, as we learned the next morning. He had slept most of the way down in the car and he felt wide awake. He was a resourceful person, however, and with nothing to read, he invented a game that kept him occupied for quite some time. The room, which was equipped with a large ashtray, was also well populated with cockroaches. He would catch one alive and put it under the overturned ashtray. Then he would catch another and another, the object being to see how many he could get and keep under the ashtray. Each time he lifted it a little to slip in another insect, one of the others would try to get out, sometimes successfully. His final score was 12. Eventually he tired of the game, so about 2:00 A.M. he went downstairs, where there were several girls in various stages of undress, and asked them if they had some magazines he could read, because he couldn't get to sleep. The ladies obliged him, but told him he would have to go to bed because they were closing up for the night.

Barney, like the rest of us, had been brought up in the age of innocence, and he was unaware of what had happened. He didn't mention the experience again until many years later when he was in his late 50s, and then he asked me, almost in a whisper, "Was that a whorehouse we got into that night in Ironton?" I answered, "Yes, Barney, it was."

Chapter 7

The Ohio Reptile Survey
Part IV. The Venomous Snakes

Unlike several of my professional colleagues, I have never had an overpowering desire to catch and maintain venomous snakes. Carl F. Kauffeld, of the Staten Island (New York) Zoo, was a fanatic on the subject. He was an avid field collector who spent most of his vacations in the Southwest, where there are many different kinds of rattlesnakes, and he would let nothing interfere, not even stopping to eat, if there was even a remote chance of finding a desired specimen. His collection at the zoo was maintained in splendid condition, and it usually included all, or almost all, the forms of rattlers native to the United States. Howard K. Gloyd, one of the leading experts on pit vipers, once told me that, if he was in the field far from his base, he would find some way, somehow, to pack out 100 pounds of rattlers or copperheads, but a couple of turtles would "break his back." I admired their enterprise and the fine contributions they and others with kindred enthusiasms made to herpetology, but my interests were more catholic. I had equal thrills from finding some of the rarer or smaller species of herps, even among the frogs and salamanders.

If I had been a rattlesnake enthusiast, we doubtless would have spent more time looking for them. Our total catch of timber rattlers, *Crotalus horridus horridus*, was only two, and one of those I found soon after daybreak as it was returning to its daytime retreat under a row of large stones. Its head and neck were already out of sight, but I seized it by the tail and yanked it into the open where it could be pinned down with a snake hook. R. L. Pope, of Hillsboro, in Highland County, helped make up for the deficit by catching several timbers, as well as copperheads, for us in Ross and Scioto Counties. From 1936 through 1939, approximately 60 timber rattlers were killed in the Zaleski Forest by the Civilian Conservation Corps.

In prepioneer days the species probably ranged over a considerable part of Ohio, at least in areas where there were suitable habitats. Kraig Adler, in 1961, after delving into historical accounts by early writers, reported he had found apparently authentic records for the timber rattlesnake from Franklin, Licking, Mahoning, Pickaway, and Trumbull Counties, and possibly Summit County. He also personally found bones and fangs identifiable as that species in caves at the site of the former, but long extirpated, colony among the bluffs along the Scioto River north of Columbus. Later, Charles J. Chantell found similar remains of this rattlesnake, estimated to be not more than 150 years old, in caves in Miami County in the midst of the Till Plains. Habitat destruction and persecution by man probably were the two principal factors in the shrinking of the species' range.

Rattlers managed to survive, however, on the rocky limestone peninsulas in Ottawa County and on at least one of the larger islands nearby in Lake Erie. The Catawba colony remained stable for many years but, according to Gordon W. Schuett, none has been seen there since 1955. Milton B. Trautman, who collected fishes all over Ohio and in the adjacent waters of Lake Erie, advised me that the last sighting on South Bass Island was at about the same time. The timber rattlesnake is now considered an endangered species in Ohio.

The massasauga, *Sistrurus catenatus catenatus*, mentioned in a previous chapter, was still a common snake in several localities during the 1930s. Although it was generally recognized as being potentially dangerous, many persons paid little attention to it. A family of migrant laborers from Georgia, who had arrived in the New Haven Marsh area to work on a celery farm, told us they had seen a rattler crawl under the cement slab that served as a doorstep to their ramshackle abode. When they overturned the slab, they found five massasaugas hiding beneath it. They showed little concern, even though a dozen barefooted children played in the yard daily.

For a time the massasauga survived at Mount Victory, and on one occasion 13 were found in a single day. All were adults, and, as was always the case in that locality, all were jet black, or melanistic. Charles A. Triplehorn, who visited the locality in late 1947, found bulldozers at work ripping up the area. The following spring, Bob Mattlin, who was then the Cleveland Zoo's curator of

Snapshot of four fieldworkers assembled at Neotoma, the rural cottage of naturalist Edward S. Thomas in Hocking County, Ohio, during September 1931. From left: Charles F. Walker, Joseph R. Bailey, Reeve M. Bailey, and RC.

Professional portrait of the four friends sitting in the same order during June 1972. By that time each of us had served as president of the American Society of Ichthyologists and Herpetologists.

reptiles, reported that the Mount Victory habitat had been completely converted to agriculture and the remnants of the swamp forest had been drained. Mattlin also found that massasaugas had become a rarity in the New Haven Marsh area, which had been under heavy cultivation even during our day. The same fate doubtless befell most of the other habitats of the species in Ohio.

Mass destruction of habitats has been a major factor in the reduction in numbers or extirpation of both plant and animal species over large areas. Some few of the persons who read these pages may look askance, no doubt, about our having collected series of specimens of reptiles of a number of kinds. My reply is that it was a good thing we did, and that we preserved them for future study and reference. In comparison with the enormous destruction of wildlife that has resulted from human beings advancing their own, often greedy interests, the specimens we took were an infinitesimal fraction. One should also bear in mind that, during past decades, virtually every reptile was considered fair game and was slaughtered on sight. Not too many years ago the Commonwealth of Pennsylvania was still awarding a medal to boys between the ages of 9 and 16 who killed 10 water snakes. The role of natural predators was not commonly understood until rather recently.

Public attitudes toward wildlife have changed drastically for the better, and there is now a general understanding that a great many species, by losing their habitats or by being exposed to pollution, have become rare and need protection. Milton B. Trautman, in the revised edition (1981) of his "Fishes of Ohio," reviewed the truly stupendous alterations to habitats in Ohio that have occurred since we were actively working in the state. In view of what has happened, I marvel that only three species of reptiles are currently classified as being endangered. Two of them, the copperbelly water snake and the plains garter snake, were rare even in the 1930s in the sense that they occupied only a few relict areas. The third is the timber rattler. A number of other species whose status is of concern are currently listed by the Ohio Department of Natural Resources. The Lake Erie water snake and Kirtland's snake are considered as threatened. Eight other reptiles are designated as of special interest, and all of them are worthy of careful monitoring. Included are the spotted and Blanding's turtles, coal skink, black kingsnake, rough green snake, fox snake, massasauga, and the black (melanistic) phase of the common garter snake.

The copperhead, *Agkistrodon contortrix mokasen*, has fared far better than the other venomous snakes. The rough, rugged portions of its habitat are not coveted for farms or developments, and it also lives in the Wayne National Forest and other heavily wooded areas where it comes into relatively little contact with human persecutors.

I noted that the range of the copperhead almost exactly matched that of the fence lizard when I plotted my distribution maps in the 1930s. Also, the massasauga and the copperhead had complementary but mutually exclusive ranges. Although the copperhead crossed the glacial boundary in a few places, the massa-sauga did not. The former's stronghold was in the hill country, whereas the latter's was throughout most of the rest of the state except in the extreme southwest.

We didn't find copperheads during every field trip into their territory, but they turned up frequently. On warm days in early spring they might be sunning, but most of them were beneath objects we overturned. Probably half were among or under bark slabs associated with sawdust piles. On one very warm, sultry day in late June, on our last trip of the spring season, we were in Monroe County not too far from the Ohio River. We were tired and uncomfortable, and we had decided to start our long trip back to Toledo earlier than usual. At least it was cooler driving than tramping through the wooded hillsides. As we rounded a turn, however, a moderate-sized sawdust pile came into view. For the first time ever the boys groaned when I stopped the car near it. Almost reluctantly they followed me to the pile. It contained nothing of interest except the omnipresent large, shiny black, patent-leather beetles, then designated as *Passalus cornutus*, that made a creaking, hissing noise when we picked them up. My companions headed back to the car, grateful to retreat into its shade, but I elected to walk a bit farther to where I could see a single fairly large bark slab lying on an otherwise bare expanse of sawdust. I flipped it over, and there, each neatly coiled and lined up in a row, were three adult copperheads. What to do? They were warm and poised to take off, probably in several directions, at any instant. Almost without thinking I planted the sole of one of my big shoes on each of two of them, meanwhile shifting my weight to my heels in order to apply a minimum of pressure on the snakes. The third I pinned down with my snake hook, and then I started yelling. That time the boys came on the run, and the snakes were all in the bag in minutes. All three were females, and all three had litters of young at the Toledo Zoo.

When the weather was quite warm, copperheads became nocturnal and we would sometimes see them crossing the paving. What a wonderful car my Chevy was for riding the roads at night. It had running boards! One of the boys could stand on either side ready to hop off and grab anything of interest. With a fourth member of the party alongside me in the front seat, there were four pairs of eyes watching. I doubt that we missed very much. With the car windows open, the boys could hang on to the door posts and be in no danger of falling off when I made sudden stops. We also had the help of an expensive extravagance, for which I saved every cent and dollar I could all one winter. It was a spotlight, mounted on the roof of the car, and it was operable in any direction from inside at the will of the driver. If a snake were moving fast we could follow it and keep it illuminated until the outside persons caught up with it.

The spotlight was also helpful in other ways. On narrow, winding roads we used it almost constantly when traffic was light or nonexistent, and sometimes it was indispensable. In the 1930s almost all railroads, where they intersected rural roads, were at grade crossings that were not always properly protected by lights or gates. Twice at night we suddenly came upon freight trains, the cars of which were completely blocking our way. We were thankful for the bright light that alerted us before we had to slam on the brakes with full force to avoid a crack-up. In Holmes County and some other parts of Ohio, the Dunkers or Dunkards, a religious sect of the Amish group, used one-horse, closed black buggies for transportation. They even drove on the paved roads at night with no lights whatsoever on their vehicles. Several times we passed over the crest of a hill in the road and found ourselves in imminent danger of crashing into the rear of one. Once we had acquired the spotlight, however, we employed it freely in any area where we might encounter hazards. Using unlighted vehicles on public roads at night is now prohibited. Presumably the Dunkards depended on their faith to protect them.

No discussion of venomous snakes would be complete without some reference to the tall tales they've engendered. Count the joints in a rattler's string, and that's its exact age in years. They had to coil and rattle before they could strike. A pair of fangs imbedded in leather boots, but with the points inside, pricked and killed anyone who wore the boots, even years later. Copperheads smelled like fresh cucumbers. We answered "false" to all of them, but I had second thoughts about the copperhead scent after my Coast Guard training during World War II. We were asked to sniff a small bottle containing a liquid that simulated a deadly gas the Germans were alleged to have in their arsenal. Half the class said it smelled like a common substance, but the other half disagreed. Obviously our senses of smell did not all react the same way. The odor of copperheads bore no resemblance to cucumbers, I thought, but perhaps to another person it did. In any event, we knew all the yarns, or thought we did. But we were to hear a brand new snake story.

One evening, Charles Walker, the Bailey brothers, Joe and Reeve, and I were riding through a wooded area, more or less paralleling the Ohio River, when Charles suddenly announced that he would like to stop at the next building we saw. A friend of his, named Watters, ran a gas station and small restaurant and he had been instrumental in helping to obtain several interesting specimens. Charles warned us not to mention snakes, however, or we might be there for hours. That was wishful thinking. The moment Watters laid eyes on him, he said, "Well hello, Mr. Walker. How are all the snakes?"

That did it, and we went inside for a long round of yarns to which several local characters, who were loafing over cups of coffee, did most of the contributing. Finally the conversation died down, and a portly, middle-aged chap, who had talked but little, spoke up and said he'd like to tell us his snake story. Evidently he had something to do with river boats or barges, because he had been introduced as Captain Appleby.

After clearing his throat and looking at each of us in turn, he said, "Ya know we folks down here in the country don't have none a them fancy flush toilets like you do in the city. We have to use back houses." He paused, and then continued with, "Couple a nights ago, I woke up kinda sudden and found I hadda go out there. But soon's I sat down, somethin' stung me. Now I know tweren't no copperhead or I wouldn't be here now. Maybe it was one of them there milk snakes. Here, let me show you what it did."

He beckoned for the four of us to follow him behind the counter, he slipped his suspenders off his shoulders, dropped his pants and underdrawers, and showed us some scratches on a tender part of his anatomy. With that he pulled up his clothes and, as he leisurely hoisted one side of his suspenders back into place, he remarked, "Wall, I guess anybody what lets it pile up that high deserves to get snakebit."

Chapter 8

The Miracle at the Toledo Zoo

Toledo suffered severely from the Great Depression of the 1930s. Factories closed, there were massive layoffs, and unemployment was at a staggering figure well in excess of 50 percent. In desperation, men swarmed aboard freight trains when they slowed to pass through the city, and threw lumps of coal from the open gondolas onto the right of way, to be picked up and taken home later. Some of the more venturesome made forays into the countryside at night and raided farmers' fields to provide food for their families. Things went from bad to worse, and I well remember the mournful cry of newsboys hawking a special edition of the "Toledo Blade" as they announced in loud, monotonous voices, "Extry! Extry! Read all about it. Three Toledo banks close."

Times were grim, as they were all over the nation, but Toledo was hit as hard as, if not harder than, any other American city. Yet, despite all the misery, the Toledo Zoo profited immensely from the Depression.

To explain this paradox I must pause and review what happened, because I, fortuitously and completely unexpectedly, had a small part in it.

I arrived at the Toledo Zoo in March 1929, seven months before the disastrous stock market crash of October 29. My chief interest was in reptiles, but the zoo's collection of those fascinating animals was tiny, and it could be curated in less than an hour. So I was given the added and much more formidable duty of keeper of the antelope and giraffe house. In deference to my ever-present enthusiasm and constant urging, however, a modest, inexpensive, but impressive reptile display was established in the lobby of the old elephant house. It was instantly popular and was invariably crowded on busy days. There things stood while the Depression deepened.

Through a member of the zoo's Board of Directors I learned about a Toledo architect who was trying to keep the key members of his staff together despite the lack of business. Would he be interested in donating his time and talent toward roughing out some plans for a large new reptile house? He would, and with the blessing of my bosses, I was soon spending an afternoon a week with Paul Robinette, a young, keen, and highly imaginative draftsman and first assistant to the architect. Our conferences lasted for only a few months when the inevitable happened. The office closed. But we had acquired a set of basic plans for a new building. Would its construction ever come to pass? Probably not, judging from the desperate times through which we were passing.

Franklin Delano Roosevelt took office as President of the United States on March 4, 1933, and immediately declared a two-week bank holiday as a cooling off period. That decelerated the feeling of panic that affected us all, but it led to some ludicrous incidents. I had a bit of change, a few small bills, and a twenty. After the smaller denominations had been spent, I might as well have been a pauper. No one could or would change the twenty.

Under Roosevelt's leadership Congress created the Works Progress Administration (WPA). Carefully selected military officers, noted for their ability to get things done, were assigned to each state and large city to put men to work on public projects as quickly as possible. Colonel John S. Shetler was dispatched to Toledo, and the day he arrived the "Toledo Blade" delegated one of its top reporters, Frank L. Skeldon, to be the Colonel's shadow and to gather material for news stories.

The Colonel's first visit was to one of Toledo's spacious parks, where a few score men were raking leaves as a recently implemented and simple method of work relief. Once they had raked all the leaves to one end of the park, they turned around and raked them all back again. The Colonel exploded. "My God, this is disgraceful," he said. "Isn't there anything worthwhile these men can do?" Skeldon, who also served as Secretary of the Toledo Zoological Society, replied, "We have some plans at the zoo for a new reptile house."

Colonel Shetler's response was brief and to the point. "Bring them to me at once."

As though some genie had waved a magic wand, things began to happen with bewildering speed. The WPA acquired an empty warehouse and gathered up the city's unemployed architects and draftsmen, which meant all of them. They were provided with desks and

Entrance to the handmade reptile house at the Toledo Zoo. WPA photograph.

The main lobby. WPA photograph.

drawing boards, and, almost before we knew it, we were off and running. I was designated to help part-time, and, best of all, Paul Robinette was put in charge of the entire operation.

As the drawings progressed, a huge effort was initiated to find building materials that could be salvaged by hand and thus put more men to work. Old buildings that qualified as tax liabilities or eyesores were torn down piece by piece, and squads of men chipped mortar from bricks and stacked them in piles. Others removed nails from lumber and carefully cleaned it. Huge blocks of stone from the locks of the long abandoned Miami and Erie Canal were hauled to the zoo. Other stone arrived from the piers of the old Wabash Railroad shops, as well as enormous white pine timbers from the 75-year-old Wabash Building. Wood from packing crates that were used to ship relief supplies to Toledo was saved, and a huge log of perfectly preserved black walnut was found in the old canal. Eventually it would be used for the handrails in front of the reptile cages.

The rule of the day was to do everything possible by hand. If a timber could be worked with an adze, then no plane or saw was used. Amazingly, a few artisans were found who were still skillful with that old-fashioned tool. Stonecutters laboriously split blocks of limestone with special chisels and trimmed and smoothed them, and three elderly stone carvers chipped, rasped, and painstakingly executed motifs of reptiles and amphibians either as free-standing statues or in bas-relief. Mortar was mixed by hand. Machinery was used only when segments of the project absolutely required it, such as hoisting heavy blocks of limestone or transporting material to the zoo. But everything that possibly

could be was loaded on and off the trucks by the men.

Human morale, which had been badly shattered by the setbacks of the Depression, improved immensely when the workers saw the results of their efforts emerging as the building rose foot by foot. Bricklayers, even in bad weather, laid more bricks per day than the commercial average. Carpenters and metal workers executed intricate designs for the graceful chandeliers and the hand-carved trim around and above the cage fronts. Artists painted habitat backgrounds for the four largest snake cages. A skilled mason with a willingness to depart from tradition was assigned to me. Together we built rock ledges, waterfalls, and other naturalistic backgrounds which, along with logs, stumps, and other "cage furniture," gave some suggestion of places in the field where one might find the snakes and other reptiles and amphibians soon to be exhibited. There was a high spirit of camaraderie among the workmen representing so many different skills. I, a member of management, was highly flattered to be invited to attend a Labor Day union picnic in Walbridge Park to sample the delicious snapping-turtle soup, which one of the men was singularly skilled at preparing.

The reptile house fully deserved its proud designation as a handmade structure, and many of its features and embellishments represented examples of dying arts. When the Depression waned with the sudden rush to rearm for World War II, efficient machines with their quicker results replaced the hand-wrought work of the artisans of yesteryear. In a very real sense the reptile house was the swan song of the old-timers. I always think of that building, which still stands, as useful and beautiful as ever, as a cathedral assembled by a multitude of tender, loving hands.

The reptile house, so successfully and exquisitely completed, turned out to be only the beginning. There followed, in rapid succession, a natural history museum, an outdoor amphitheater, a bird house, and what was then the largest freshwater aquarium in the country, plus a number of smaller structures, all inspired as an architectural motif from the original Toledo, in Spain. Under Paul Robinette and his associates, including landscape expert Ellwood Allen, the Toledo Zoological Park was transformed from little more than a menagerie into one of the great zoos of America, all as a result of the worst financial crisis the nation ever sustained. And just to think, it all came about because we had some plans on paper and had the outstanding leadership of Colonel John S. Shetler, who had the vision and determination to get things done. Many members of the zoo board and staff aided and abetted the process, but the result was an astounding miracle that has no parallel.

Chapter 9

Back to Philadelphia

On January 1, 1934, Solon T. Klotz became mayor of Toledo, and his first official act was to fire the heads of all city departments. Because I had the title of Curator of the Zoo (actually I was serving as General Curator), my name was included. The dismissal didn't last long, because Percy C. Jones, President of the Toledo Zoological Society, had political clout. I was back at work the next day, but the experience jolted me into realizing how fragile my job really was.

Almost concurrently there was another unhappy development. My immediate superior, who had a serious drinking problem, decided to make me his whipping boy. Let the least little thing go wrong, and I was in hot water. I suspected he even told some of the employees to ignore my instructions, but I could never prove it. When celebrities visited the zoo, he attempted to embarrass me by implying that I had misidentified some of the animals. Edmund Heller, the great naturalist who accompanied Theodore Roosevelt on his famous expedition to Africa, was asked in my presence if a certain bird was actually what it was labeled. Heller, who was then the Director of the Milwaukee Zoo and a close friend despite the great disparity in our ages, adroitly sidestepped that trap by stating he was a mammalogist and knew little about birds. The same trick was played on reptile expert Raymond L. Ditmars when he visited the zoo, and he detected it just as quickly. Both men sensed my problem, and Ditmars even offered to help me find a new job.

The crowning humiliation came when I was purposely not invited to sit on the platform with the various dignitaries, many from other zoos, when the dedication ceremonies were held for the new reptile house. I was the titular head of the zoo, and it was I who had originally conceived the project, designed the building, and worked hard with the architects. I had personally supervised the installation of all the habitat backgrounds of stone and oil paintings in the various enclosures and, in fact, had worked like a dog getting the building and the livestock ready. Some other person on the zoo board noted the omission, and I was eventually asked to step up to the platform to take a token bow.

It was useless to attempt an open fight. My persecutor was too deeply entrenched. Before I arrived, he had fancied himself as "Mr. Zoo," but I inadvertently had taken that appellation away from him. Almost everyone in town knew me, at least by name.

There had been other problems in Toledo. Politics were always with us, and more than once there was talk of abolishing the Zoological Board of Management and giving the zoo completely back to the city, to be run by a political appointee. Doubtless Mayor Klotz had that in mind. For a while, during the Depression, we were paid not with money, but by city script, virtually worthless paper that could be redeemed only at the State of Ohio's relief warehouse. I have forgotten most of the details, but there were about a dozen different things we could get: a 50-pound bag of sugar, a 100-pound bag of flour, a bushel of potatoes, a case of toilet paper, a large slab of salt pork, and similar dainties. We couldn't have a pound of sugar. No indeed! We had to take the entire 50-pound bag, and it was the same with everything else. What a dreary situation, even when several of us went to the warehouse together and shared things. We could tolerate such hardships because of the difficult times through which we were passing, but I could not endure the constant barrage of abuse aimed at me by a psychotic alcoholic who was motivated by jealousy.

So I decided to leave Toledo, and I passed the word around. I had served as Secretary of the American Association of Zoological Parks and Aquariums. Because of that, I was well known to several sympathetic zoo men who offered to help, but they had nothing available at their respective institutions suitable for my talents. Then, quite unexpectedly, there was an opening at the Philadelphia Zoo. My old friend C. Emerson Brown had retired fairly recently as Director of the zoo, and his place was taken by Roderick Macdonald, who was looking for an eager young herpetologist. I began my new job as Curator of Reptiles on July 1, 1935, and eventually it turned out to be a wise move.

I had roots and contacts in Philadelphia, where I had

The antiquated reptile house that RC inherited when he returned to the East. Philadelphia Zoo archives.

lived and gone to school for a number of years, and it seemed like a good place to start over. I knew the zoo well from visiting it intermittently from the time I was a small boy. When I arrived, however, I was both shocked and discouraged. The zoo had deteriorated badly during my six years in Toledo. Further, very little had been accomplished through the WPA and other federal work programs. They had meant salvation for the Toledo Zoo, but Philadelphia was then a Republican stronghold. Had the zoo and the city been reluctant to take FDR's tainted money because it was Democratic?

The Philadelphia Zoo opened on July 1, 1874, exactly 61 years before I started my new job. Unlike most zoos in other American cities, which originated with a few deer, swans, or raccoons in public parks, the Philadelphia Zoological Garden opened as a full-fledged institution with several buildings, bear pits, barns, and other enclosures all well stocked with animals. There were hundreds of specimens on opening day, and, by the time of its first birthday, the infant zoo's animal inventory was so large and varied that it would have rivaled some of the collections in existence a century later. Those facts, coupled with the charter granted to the Zoological Society of Philadelphia on March 21, 1859, by the Commonwealth of Pennsylvania, made it rank as America's First Zoo in point of time. Difficult financial problems followed by the Great Depression had taken their toll, however, and it was far from first in quality. The zoo was operated by the Zoological Society, which received most of its revenue from its meager admission charge of a quarter for adults and a dime for children. It did not begin to receive financial help from the City of Philadelphia until 1891, and the annual grant from that

source was small. When I arrived in 1935, the old buildings were virtually held together with the proverbial paint and baling wire. It would take many of us, working together for years, to restore the zoo to its proper position as a leading institution. But more of that later.

Dr. Macdonald, the new Managing Director, had earned a reputation as a marine biologist, and it was quickly apparent that he had a lot to learn about running a zoo. I found myself in the unenviable position of occupying a relatively lowly post, even though I knew far more about zoos in general than he ever would. I kept my mouth shut, however, and concentrated on the reptile collection, which assuredly needed my attention. I had "two strikes on me," to use an old expression derived from baseball. Instead of waiting for a month or so until my arrival (I felt obliged to give notice at Toledo before leaving), Macdonald rushed ahead to get things ready for me.

First, he had stonemasons cement piles of rocks together in many of the larger cages to give them a "natural" effect. The workmen knew nothing about snakes and how they can squeeze through small crevices. They also had no imagination. Every cage looked alike.

Second, and worse, Macdonald succumbed to the wiles of an unscrupulous animal dealer who managed to sell him so many live reptiles that every cage and many boxes behind the scenes were filled when I arrived on board. The dealer made a killing, because he literally unloaded all of his "trash," a lot of it sick, along with a few good things. They began to die off, figuratively giving me a black eye. Reptile husbandry was in its infancy in those days, and the techniques and medications that have developed so remarkably in the past few decades, were still unrealized dreams. To cap the climax, I discovered to my sorrow that, in order to make room for me on the payroll, Macdonald had forced the retirement of Robert Hess, the kindly old gentleman who had looked after the reptile house for most of his life. He was nearly 70, and it was a tragedy for him to be suddenly deprived of both his job and his major interest.

I had my work cut out for me. Fixing the rockwork was easy. I had a natural aptitude for working with cement, and I made repairs and filled all the chinks I could find. I segregated and quarantined all the obviously sick and ailing snakes and lizards. I sought the help of the zoo's Penrose Research Laboratory, where Dr. Herbert L. Ratcliffe was beginning to make a name for himself by standardizing and simplifying animal diets. He pitched in to help me as best he could. Also, Raymond L. Ditmars, who was assuredly the nation's best-known zoo herpetologist at the time, gave me helpful advice and even invited me to visit him at his office at the New York Zoological Park.

It was routine practice at the Penrose Lab to autopsy animals that died in the zoo, and by that method Ratcliffe was able to prove that most of the recently purchased reptiles were ailing before they arrived. His report was noted by key board members of the Zoological Society. I was relieved when one of them told me they understood my problem. It was a good six months, however, before I had things back in order.

In the meantime, I fixed up a small office for myself in a side room of the reptile house, using my personal rolltop desk and typewriter. Like all similar curators at the time I was bombarded with inquiries about how to take care of pet turtles and alligators, and I made many a trip to different parts of the city and even the suburbs to rescue hysterical women by catching the garter snake or tiny brown snake that had suddenly appeared in their yards.

Macdonald, as soon as he realized that I had an excellent zoo background, began to delegate me to take care of divers chores and errands for him. I guided guests around the zoo and took all the telephone calls from the public on mammals and birds as well as reptiles. In a sense, I became his lieutenant. One assignment was to greet and assist representatives of Philadelphia's press corps who wanted to get stories or pictures for their papers. Most were casual drop-ins, but one, the "Evening Bulletin's" top-rate photographer, Newton H. Hartman, kept the zoo on his regular beat, and he stopped in at least once every fortnight. Together we could always get a picture or two about something unusual that would "make the paper," as they said. Newt was resourceful and he had a reputation for being able

to create a news item out of a doorknob. With the others I often had to use my imagination, but I always managed to suggest a picture or story that was useful. Very soon, when reporters and cameramen arrived at the zoo, they went directly to my office to seek help. Macdonald inadvertently and unintentionally was starting me on my career as the zoo's press agent, a subject on which I expand a bit in the next chapter.

One Saturday morning in early 1936 Dr. Macdonald strode breathlessly into my office stating that he didn't have time to do a radio program and would I take his script downtown to station KYW and read it on the air? There was nothing to do but comply, but when I looked at my watch I discovered I must leave for the studio immediately. I wasn't even sure exactly where it was, but I arrived just in time. I was pushed in front of a microphone, and there was not a moment to review the script. I read it slowly and deliberately but ran out of copy five minutes before the program was scheduled to conclude. The station filled the gap with music, much to its consternation and my embarrassment.

After the same thing happened two weeks later, I pounded out a script of my own on the typewriter, and the next time Macdonald asked me to substitute for him, I was well prepared.

He had started the program on February 15, 1936, shortly after KYW transferred its operations from Chicago to Philadelphia. After the tenth program the show was mine, and I prepared every script from that time forward. I talked about everything under the sun, and I am sure that every animal in the zoo's collection was the subject of at least one program. Some of them, like the notorious gorilla Bamboo, repeatedly made good subjects.

To be chronologically consistent, I should, at this point, return to events of my first year at the Philadelphia Zoo. On the other hand, the radio program, entitled "Let's Visit the Zoo" and introduced by the recorded roaring of a lion, turned out to be very important, and set so many records, that it probably is best to continue with the story of its progress. It remained on the air for the incredibly long period of 33 years and eight months. It was terminated late in 1969, and then only because KYW changed its policy and became an all-news station. Our zoo show survived even longer than "Amos and Andy" did (on radio), but there was a major difference: they broadcast five days a week instead of one, and they had a commercial sponsor, which we never did.

In the later years of the show's long life, I found myself talking to the grandchildren of persons who had been in the audience toward the beginning. Although I

RC with a cockatoo during a 1936 KYW radio broadcast. Photo by Mark Mooney, Jr.

wrote all the scripts, there were occasions when other staff members read them on the air for me, as when I was away from town or the few times I was ill. Later, when it became possible, I recorded a dozen programs or more in advance when I was doing fieldwork in Mexico. "Let's Visit the Zoo" even followed me to Albuquerque when my wife and I retired to the Southwest in 1973. Once, in my dermatologist's office, a nurse heard me speak and said, "I know that voice. Were you on the Philadelphia Zoo's radio program?" More recently an elderly lady in a shop saw my name and heard me speak, and she reacted similarly.

But back to the program's early history. It became apparent almost at once that a straight talk, even in 1936, was deadly and virtually certain to make any listener turn to another station. Also, because we were extremely anxious to increase the number of visitors to the zoological garden, we needed some device to arouse interest, not only in the program, but in the zoo itself. At first we invited listeners to send us questions. That worked for a while, but it was always the same dozen or so persons who responded.

Dramatizations, even then sarcastically dubbed "soap operas," were popular at the time. So we tried using true stories about the capture, transportation, and care of animals in captivity. Soon I found myself being a playwright faced with the necessity of coming up with a new topic each week. We dramatized Sir Harry Johnston's discovery of the okapi, Martin and Osa Johnson's adventures in Borneo and East Africa, stories about catching animals, events that happened in zoos all over the world, and so on. It was great fun. My role was that of narrator, but what a time we had getting enough different voices to lend credibility to the various

adventures! We dragooned our friends and even Boy Scouts into visiting the station on Saturday mornings to take part. We even had sound effects. Shaking a large piece of sheet metal sounded like thunder. We had creaking doors, and sometimes one of us would go inside a closet to produce the effect of talking in a cave or at the bottom of a well, if we were hunting for bats or snakes. Some of the shows were truly professional, and we began to acquire a large audience.

The dramatizations lasted for five years, but eventually we were forced to quit because our talent deserted us, one by one. It was then that we hit on the device of running summertime contests with prizes of free zoo tickets for anyone who could correctly answer five simple questions. Unless the listener was disturbed, as by the doorbell or telephone, during the program, he or she had no trouble in culling the answers from the conversation I held each week with the announcer. We began modestly in 1939 with 10 contests that stimulated an average of 202 pieces of mail a week. Later, contests were offered for 30 weeks each summer until the show went off the air. In 1947 we received 18,131 pieces of mail, or an average of 604 a week. "Let's Visit the Zoo" was attracting far more mail to KYW than any other program. With the advent of television the audience dwindled, but even as late as 1967 we had more than 200 responses a week.

Giving away free zoo tickets greatly boosted attendance. The recipient seldom came alone. He or she brought along the family and friends, all of whom had to pay to get in.

During the winter months I conducted interview programs during which I talked with persons with a broad spectrum of interests, including the explorers Lowell Thomas and Osa Johnson, experts on various subjects in zoology, persons with unusual hobbies involving animals, and sometimes just plain interesting visitors who were fond of the Philadelphia Zoo. Eventually we ran out of such talent, and during the last several winters the program consisted chiefly of conversations I held with the announcer about animals or what was going on at the zoo.

The management of KYW was very helpful and liberal, and I was allowed to choose my own subjects. In retrospect, I am pleased with my conservation efforts. For example, I inveighed strongly against the use of DDT and other chlorinated hydrocarbons at a time when I felt like a voice crying in the wilderness. Those chemicals were finally, of course, outlawed by both federal and state governments. Quite naturally, the reptiles came in for their share of attention, and I think I convinced a number of persons that snakes are highly useful animals that deserve protection, instead of slaughter on sight.

There is no doubt that the KYW program was a useful tool for getting people interested in the zoo, and we were extremely grateful to the radio station for the enormous amount of free time they gave our "public service" program.

The single greatest individual benefit we derived from "Let's Visit the Zoo" surfaced when the will of a deceased elderly lady was probated. We were delighted but amused to discover that she had bequeathed $30,000 to the zoo in my honor, but with the understanding that none of the money was to be used to purchase reptiles! I never had the pleasure of meeting her, but it turned out she was an ardent listener, and she proved it by her substantial bequest. By the time we finally received the money it had increased to $37,000. We used it to help build the hummingbird exhibit to make sure that not a penny would be spent for reptiles.

My part in the "Let's Visit the Zoo" program was a case of my being in the right place at the right time. I was in my office when Macdonald marched in to dispatch me to KYW, and I was very lucky to inherit the show during its infancy. Almost everyone is interested in animals, and all I really did was to pass on to the public some of our gold mine of stories about the birds and beasts and reptiles. Happily, that also had the salutary effect of stimulating interest in paying us a visit at the zoo.

Chapter 10

The Zoo's Press Agent

Dr. Macdonald tried his best, I am sure, but he was dismissed in 1936. An accountant and office manager, named Freeman M. Shelly, was hired by the Zoo Board as Business Manager, and they put him in charge of the zoo. He took office on May 18 of that same year. He introduced new fiscal policies and found many ways to save money. Shelly was successful, so much so that certain disgruntled employees and purveyors promptly dubbed him a nickel nurser and tightwad. He proved to be an excellent choice, however, and he kept a close rein on the zoo's finances during his long tenure. There was no point in ever asking him for a raise. I never did, but when I was offered a job elsewhere a year or two later, I made sure that he saw the letter I received, and he, in turn, passed it on to our superiors. Somewhat later my salary was increased, although not enough to match the outside offer. I hadn't wanted to leave anyway, but my finesse worked. A somewhat similar ploy produced even better results a few years later.

In general, Shelly and I got along well, although we had our differences from time to time. He knew nothing about animals, and I knew nothing about accounting. He left the care of the livestock to the Penrose Laboratory, which prescribed the diets, and, when curators of birds and mammals came aboard many years later, he let us more or less alone insofar as our charges were concerned. Only once did we have any real trouble. For some reason Shelly began to pick on me and criticize things I was doing. After taking it from him for a month or so, but mindful of how I had become the whipping boy at Toledo, I had it out with him, and he stopped at once. He later was promoted to Director of the zoo, an assignment I emphatically didn't want at that stage of my career. It was a long time before I succeeded him, but he never let any of us forget that he was the Director.

But I am getting ahead of my story. Several members of the zoo board contributed rather substantially to a fund with the commendable goal of trying to get the zoo back on its feet. They engaged the services of a high-powered promotional outfit in New York to start the ball rolling. The company had a part-time Philadelphia representative, but, in my opinion, they never earned their fees. They did, however, come up with a slogan that was supposed to kick off a campaign for a "Free and Modern Zoo," but that idea died aborning. The City of Philadelphia, beset with its own fiscal problems, was not interested in the zoo, and almost every wealthy citizen had been hurt, some severely, by the Depression. The promoters did engineer a sample "Free Week" of two successive weekends and all the days between when the public was admitted free. It was a smashing success from the standpoint of numbers of freeloaders. They came in such droves and did so much damage to the zoo's physical plant, to say nothing of bombarding the animals with empty pop bottles and anything else throwable, that the aftermath was a firm and unshakable decision against any more free days. We went back to charging admission ever afterward. The fee at the time was a quarter for adults and a dime for children.

The promotional outfit was also supposed to get publicity for the zoo. Meanwhile, I was keeping up my sporadic contacts with the press, helping where I could and even suggesting a feature story from time to time. I clipped all the newspapers, and after a few months I made a comparison. The lineage and pictures resulting from my feeble, amateur efforts were almost 20 times greater than those engendered by the promoter. That was duly relayed to Shelly and the zoo board. It wasn't long before I was told officially that henceforth it was part of my job to be the zoo's press agent. I was to keep on curating the reptile collection just the same, however.

Promoting the zoo was a real challenge, particularly since I lacked any formal training for the job. What little I had accomplished could be attributed to horse sense and my knowledge of what people liked to read or hear about animals. What to do? Where to begin with my new assignment?

Horse sense won again, and I instinctively followed a hunch that paid off handsomely. At the time there were five newspapers in Philadelphia: two in the morning—the "Record" and the "Inquirer"; two in the afternoon— the "Public Ledger" and the "Evening Bulletin"; and a tabloid—the "Daily News." I knew from talking with reporters and photographers that the city editor was the boss who made the final decisions on what would be published and what would be discarded. So I visited each of the five city editors in turn and asked them what to do. I explained that I knew a little something about animals, but next to nothing about publicity. My humble approach won their respect, and, to a man, they took the time and trouble to coach me. I should prepare news releases to give them, stating all the facts, and the lead paragraph of each should include all the W's and the H: Who, What, Where, When, Why, and How. I should play no favorites. Be fair to all publications. If I gave a feature story to one, I should give the others feature stories as they became available. One of the editors cautioned me to space my news releases and not to send them out too often. "Nobody can live on a diet of spices," he said.

My first news release was scarcely earthshaking, but I gave it a slight twist. We had just received a yak at the zoo, and I used some such wording as "whereas the camel is the ship of the desert, the yak is the ship of the steppe," referring, of course, to the fact that both are domesticated beasts of burden, the yak in the highlands of Asia. All the papers featured it, no doubt just to encourage me.

So I was off and running, and the parade of zoo stunts and stories began in earnest. The motivation was to increase attendance at the zoo and thus augment our financial "take" at the entrance gates. With zoo attendance hovering around 300,000 annually we were desperately in need of publicity. The Philadelphia public, having heard so much about troubles at the zoo—the fact that it might close during the Depression and that the buildings and collection were run down—had little incentive to pay us a visit. We had to "improve our image," although that now hackneyed expression hadn't yet come into use. There was no television in the 1930s, except at the experimental Philco studio, and we had to depend largely on the newspapers for help. A good way to get space was to take some of the more manageable animals outside the zoo.

One of our first attempts was to transport a litter of lion cubs to the Warwick Hotel for a meeting of the Junior League. Pretty young ladies and lion cubs always make good picture combinations, but the Warwick Hotel unwittingly gave us front-page coverage by refusing to let the lions board a passenger elevator. They, the guests of honor, had to ride on the lift reserved for freight. The reporters hung their story on that, and we received far more space than we would have otherwise.

Another time, Temple University asked for a camel to appear at some special event. In those days we had a relatively tractable camel. He was loaded aboard a truck and transported to the campus. He participated in the ceremonies, and everything went well until time came to return to the zoo. Then he steadfastly refused to reboard the truck, with the result that two members of the zoo staff had to lead him back through the streets from Broad and Montgomery to 34th and Girard Avenue. The trip would have been tedious but uneventful except for the fact that camels cannot distinguish between red and green lights. Many a motorist had to slam on his brakes to avoid an accident.

Sometimes we could get celebrities to visit the zoo. Once, Tommy Dorsey, the famed big band leader, visited the monkey house with his Clambake Seven, a Dixieland group that was part of his musical organization. It was a publicity stunt all the way, but under the guidance of Si Shaltz, then city editor for the "Philadelphia Record," the event was billed as a test on the reaction of the chimpanzees to the jazz of the day. There was even an expert on hand, with the impressive name of Thaddeus L. Bolton, retired head of the Psychology Department at Temple University. We made all of the newspapers, and yours truly, a confirmed Dixieland fan, had a wonderful time.

Even unglamorous events were newsworthy. I arrived at work one morning about 8:30, parked, and had gotten out of my car when I heard an exceptionally loud crash. I looked up just in time to see a switching engine and its coal car being sideswiped by a long train. The engine and car were dumped on their sides, and the train braked to a halt. The Pennsylvania Railroad tracks paralleled the west (rear) side of the zoo, and someone had neglected to throw a switch or set a signal. I raced to the telephone and called the two evening papers. The morning ones were already on the street. The zoo was on the front pages again, but only because the accident occurred in our own backyard, so to speak.

Timing, I soon learned, was important. When something newsworthy happened that should be reported quickly ("spot news," they called it), I had to be sure to phone first to the papers that were then gathering their news for the day. I also discovered that there was keen rivalry between pairs of papers, the morning "Record" against the "Inquirer," for example. Each wanted the story first and any and all features available. Eventually I found myself being accused of showing favoritism. When I called the "Record" first, then the "Inquirer" was mad at me, and vice versa. The rule about fair play didn't always count, it seemed. Soon I was walking a tightrope, and I had to give careful thought in advance as to how I

RC hastening to close the service gate lest the zebra slowly trotting behind him blunder out into the traffic. Photo by Dominic Ligato of the Evening Bulletin. Although the picture is in the Philadelphia Zoo archives, the print duplicated here, a cherished memento, was presented to RC during a farewell gathering of the Philadelphia Press Photographers Association when he retired after his long tenure with the zoo. Isabelle was praised at the same time for her cooperation while she was the official zoo photographer.

should handle each news event. The zoo was always good copy, and the papers all wanted the best—for themselves. The rule was to have a story about an animal, a child, or a woman on the front page every day, even if it was only a paragraph or two.

I also learned that there often was a marked difference in how the newspapers responded to news releases and telephone calls. When they excerpted from my releases, everything was usually accurate. Telephone calls, however, could get garbled, sometimes badly. Incidentally, at that time there were two telephone systems in operation in Philadelphia and vicinity, the Bell and the Keystone. The latter was quite a bit cheaper, and Shelly told me to use it whenever possible. Soon the city desks were referring to me as Keystone Conant.

It was inevitable, I suppose, because I was the mouthpiece for the zoo, that I would sometimes be quoted about this or that, and an occasional new reporter would refer to me as the "Director of the Zoo." I was careful to apologize to Shelly whenever that happened because I knew how sensitive he was about his title. When it occurred twice in the same month, however, he took matters into his own hands and complained about it to Dr. Williams B. Cadwalader, the President of the Zoological Society. The next morning I was summoned to Dr. Cadwalader's office, and he told me, in no uncertain terms, that it was to stop at once. I explained that I reminded the city desk people over and over again

that I was the curator and that Mr. Shelly was the director. No matter. He ordered me to visit every paper and tell them, for him, that he insisted that they get things straight. I followed his instructions, but it would take no professional psychologist to predict the result. Thereafter, neither Shelly nor Cadwalader was ever mentioned in any of the five papers unless they were directly and personally involved.

Some years later I was assigned a dual title, Curator of Reptiles and Curator of Public Relations, which various and sundry wits translated into Curator of Snakes and People.

One story backfired on me. We had received a zebra from the Cincinnati Zoo in a standard wooden crate, and it was due to be placed in its yard on a certain afternoon. I alerted the papers and the newsreels, and several photographers were on hand at the stated hour. It was then that Charley Campbell, the elderly head keeper, suddenly decided to become supercautious. He wanted to liberate the animal into its shelter house instead of the outdoor yard. That would mean no pictures. Why hadn't he said so in advance, in which case I would have waited until later to inform the press? He and I got into an argument. In the meantime, the zebra became impatient. It raised its hind legs, kicked mightily, knocked out the whole back end of its crate, backed up, and was on the loose!

The zebra leaned over, sampled some of the grass

behind its intended home, strolled around a bit, and then began to trot leisurely along the adjacent walk. Suddenly I realized that the zoo's service gate was wide open and there was a real danger that the animal might go through it and blunder into the traffic that raced along the bypass street between the zoo and the adjacent railroad. I took off at once, with my assistant, Nigel Wolff, racing ahead of me, both of us intent on getting the gate shut as quickly as possible. Dominic Ligato, one of the photographers, snapped a picture of us as we ran with the zebra behind us. It made the front page of the "Evening Bulletin" the next day with a caption to the effect that "Curator flees from zebra." It took only a few minutes of quiet persuasion and manipulation to get the runaway into its outdoor pen, where it quickly settled down to eat some of the hay we had spread out for it.

It is really amazing how much interest February 2—Groundhog Day—engendered among the news media each year. Perhaps it was a response to everyone's yearning for warmer, springlike weather as the winter months drew to a close. Be that as it may, we were hard put at times to think up new ideas to please the press and later the television people when the special day rolled around. We soon learned that we should always keep at least one tame groundhog on tap, so to speak, to be sure of having it available for picture purposes. Over the years, we posed our groundhog in front of calendars, under umbrellas (so it wouldn't see its shadow), alongside man-made burrows, and so on. Several times we took the animal to the Philadelphia Weather Bureau to compare notes with the good-natured experts, who, quite frankly, had little faith in the groundhog's ability as a prognosticator.

One groundhog episode was outstanding. We received a call from one of the radio broadcasting systems asking if they could borrow our groundhog. None was available in New York City, and they wished to broadcast from Times Square. We were not averse to national publicity, of course, so we promptly agreed to send Susie, our pet groundhog, to New York.

The radio people arranged for air transport, and they reserved a seat for one of our keepers. In those days there was no Philadelphia International Airport, and the planes touched down in Camden near the overpass at the eastern end of Admiral Wilson Boulevard. Susie was put in a box, and we drove to the Camden Airport in a blinding snowstorm. When we arrived, we were met by the largest battery of news photographers ever assembled for a zoo stunt up to that time. All the newspapers and news services were represented, and so were the newsreels, whose offerings appeared in the motion picture theaters.

The plane landed despite the bad weather, and nothing would do but to have Susie pose with the plane's hostess at the gangway. We obliged, pictures were snapped by the dozens and by the hundreds of feet, and Susie behaved beautifully. The moment the picture taking was over, however, she dashed for freedom and disappeared under the belly of the plane. We all learned instantly what a whiteout must be like in the Polar Regions. It was virtually impossible to see anything, and it was 10 or 15 minutes before we rounded up Susie, and put her back in the box.

Most of the passengers thought it was great fun, but there was a congressman aboard who had an appointment in New York, and what he had to say about planes that are detained by such nonsensical things as groundhogs is unprintable.

Susie did her bit for us at Times Square, but she and the keeper returned by train. Our guess was that the broadcasting company had had enough trouble during the morning and didn't want to risk another "escape" on her return trip.

There were innumerable other zoo publicity stories, probably more than enough to fill a small book. I'll mention a few of them as this narrative progresses.

Chapter 11

Hitler's Germany

It seems incredible that I was in Nazi Germany 60 years ago, that I crossed the Atlantic by ocean liner, and that I had to give the Nazi salute and mutter "*Heil Hitler*" before I was permitted to enter any public building. Brown-shirted storm troopers blocked my way until I complied. *Der Führer* was very much in power in 1937, and his war machine was growing by leaps and bounds, with factories working around the clock turning out equipment and munitions.

Officially I was on an inspection tour of leading European zoos. I had done so well during my early efforts to promote attendance at the Philadelphia Zoo, that its Board of Directors sent me abroad for six weeks, including time at sea, to get new ideas. After visiting the *Tiergartenen* (literally animal gardens) in Hamburg, Berlin, Hannover, and Munich, I moved on to Switzerland, France, Belgium, the Netherlands, and England. Quite a crowded schedule, but I was still in my 20s and fully able to cope.

My route was laid out for me, and I had little choice about where I would go or in what order. Germany was topmost on the list. I would have preferred to visit England first, where I could at least speak the language and where I might have become acquainted with European customs, which I knew were far different in many ways from our own. But Germany it was, and I have always suspected that Dr. Cadwalader, the zoo's President, insisted on it because he wanted a map of all the good fly-fishing localities. Did he fear, if my route were altered, that he might miss out? In any event, he gave me a detailed description of what he wanted, and I made his wish my first order of business in Hamburg. It took me a full morning to get it, even though the concierge at my hotel gave me instructions on where to go, written in German, and which I handed to my taxi driver. In peacetime I probably would have had little trouble acquiring a map but, with Germany arming to the teeth, why did I want a map of any kind? My reason had to be explained, through an interpreter, who had to come from an adjacent building. I quickly learned that, away from the hotels, few people spoke English. Next a military officer was summoned and I explained that my superior was an avid trout fisherman who planned to visit Germany in the summer to try his luck. Eventually, the officer, after examining the sportsman's map with great care, decided there was nothing of military importance on it, and I was permitted to purchase a copy.

I had sailed from New York at one minute after midnight on January 7, 1937, aboard the *Europa*, a relatively new and fast ship of the North German Lloyd Line. She was positively enormous, displaced 50,000 tons and was longer than almost all of New York's skyscrapers were high. I was traveling tourist class with a private stateroom and bath slightly astern of the ship's midsection. The more luxurious first-class accommodations were forward, and the steerage passengers were crowded together aft, over the vessel's huge propellers, where the noise and vibration must have been constantly annoying. Elsewhere on the great ship, the turning of the big gyroscope helped keep her steady, and all was quiet and restful.

The passage was smooth and uneventful. I spent much of my time writing an article for "Frontiers," the magazine of the Academy of Natural Sciences of Philadelphia, but I recall a few things that interested an active young man. Food was unlimited, and I could choose anything and everything I wanted from a bewilderingly long menu. Whenever I went on deck, I saw gulls following the ship, even in mid-ocean, and dropping down to scavenge whenever anything from the galley was thrown overboard. I took a tour of the ship's engine room that was offered to passengers, and three Japanese in the party spent all their time furiously writing notes. In the evenings a German band played for dancing. At polkas they were superb but, when they tried to oompah their way through American jazz, they stank. I had an insane urge, fortunately restrained, to grab the cornet and show them how it was done. There was no trumpet, my favorite instrument, in that band.

On the fifth day we reached Cherbourg, the French port, and I had my first glimpse of Europe. Equally impressive to a dyed-in-the-wool naturalist was my first black-backed gull. It would be quite a few years before the species became common along our own east coast. After offloading passengers, the great ship had difficulty in turning around and the screws churned up masses of mud from the bottom. We remaining passengers, looking down from the rail, wondered if we would be stuck fast until high tide, but we soon pulled free and were on our way to Southampton, England, where lighters (large, flat-bottomed barges) were used to move people and freight ashore.

The next day we were to land in Germany, and I confess that I slept little during the night. How would things go? So much was *verboten* (prohibited) and there were so many restrictions that I felt uneasy. For example, foreigners entering Germany had to register every valuable—cash, traveler's checks, letters of credit, and especially passports. I was not panicky, merely concerned with doing things right. I eased my way by hiring a guide. I had met and talked with him several times aboard ship. He was a young German, fluent in English, and a trade representative in the United States for a large company. He was being forced to return, under threat of harm to his family, to take his military training and become part of Hitler's cannon fodder, and he bitterly resented it. I offered to pay his train fare if he would stay with me until I was in my hotel in Hamburg. Getting over the first hurdle would be a great help.

We docked at Bremerhaven, the *Europa*'s home port, but when we went through customs and immigration we were forced to separate; there was one gate for returning Germans and another for foreigners. I was on my own, and I made a mistake by cashing a traveler's check at a bank window I passed before my valuables were checked. I feared the worst, but, when I handed everything to the inspector, I heard him murmur "*Dummkopf*" (blockhead) as he adjusted my money card, on which every traveler's check I cashed had to be recorded as long as I remained in the country. Finally, with the red tape finished, I began to look for my guide. It took him longer to go through his formalities because he also had to be checked in by the military authorities. We headed for the nearby train station and, as we rolled rapidly toward the city of Bremen, I gazed out the window at the signs, all in a strange and difficult language of which I knew only a relatively few words and phrases, despite a self-initiated cram course. In Bremen we changed trains and went on to Hamburg, and from the station to my hotel by taxi. My friend went to the desk and said something in German to the clerk. The latter turned to me and asked, in perfect English but with a strong British accent, "Would you like a room with a bawth, Sir?"

That broke the ice for me, and as my friend bade me

RC studying a map of Europe before his trip abroad in 1937. Photo by Mark Mooney, Jr.

farewell, I realized that whenever I needed help I had only to go to the desk. I learned very soon that the concierge was the one to whom I should address questions. *Concierge* is the French word for "hall porter" and, since French was then still the lingua franca, or worldwide language, the term was used throughout Europe, and, no doubt, elsewhere. In every country I visited the concierge was fluent in several languages. He had an encyclopedic knowledge of his city and its environs, and he could get train and theater tickets, arrange for guides, and, in fact, accomplish virtually anything a hotel guest required.

Because it was fairly late I went directly to the dining room and ate my supper, after which a porter conducted me to my room on an upper floor. There I received a rude shock. The temperature was surely below 50°F and there was no way to increase it except with a tiny heat lamp in the bathroom. What's more, conditions were much the same in every other hotel where I stayed that winter. How glad I was for the longjohns that my dear mother had insisted I take with me. I wore them every day out-of-doors, and more than once to bed. I had hated the blasted things from my boyhood days, when Mother insisted on my wearing them. When I played outdoors, sometimes in the snow with my pals, who were unencumbered by such garments, they teased me unmercifully for being such a sissy.

I examined my bed. Beneath the cover was a single featherbed, a large ticking filled with feathers. I had visions of shivering all night, so I picked up the telephone and had one devil of a time trying to get through to someone who could speak English. I finally succeeded and asked for two blankets. After waiting an hour, alternately huddling in my overcoat and doing calisthenics to keep warm, I undressed and crawled into bed wearing both my pajamas and heavy bathrobe. The *Federbett* was slippery and not long enough for a tall man. Suddenly the door flew open and in marched a chambermaid who hadn't even knocked. She put the blankets over me, tucked me in, said, "*Gute Nacht*" (Good night), and marched out. I certainly wasn't accustomed to such familiarity. The next morning at breakfast, I was joined by two American men who had also just arrived. I told them how my chambermaid had entered without so much as a "by your leave." In reply they said, "That's nothing." They had been in the bathroom, clad only in their undershorts, one shaving and the other sitting on the john. The latter looked up and saw two chains hanging down, one obviously for flushing the toilet, and wondered aloud what the other was for. His companion said he didn't know but suggested, "Give it a pull and see what happens." Within 30 seconds their chambermaid came rushing into the bathroom obviously expecting to cope with an emergency.

Because I had grown up in a strictly Victorian atmosphere, it took me awhile to adjust to the freedom of the sexes. Unlike American trains, which had a men's room at one end of a passenger car and a women's room at the other, all restrooms on European trains were coeducational.

It was appropriate that the first zoo I visited in Europe was the world-famous Carl Hagenbeck's *Tierpark* in Stellingen, within the Hamburg metropolitan area. It was there that a new trend in zoo construction had its origin, a basic concept that even in the 1930s was beginning to revolutionize the way in which many types of large animals were displayed to the public. Free-sight exhibits, they were called. In short, viewers could see the animals without having to peer through bars or wire. Deep moats they couldn't cross kept the animals from escaping. The use of moats in zoos was not entirely new. They had been employed in a small way for many years, but Hagenbeck did it on a grand scale, exhibiting large carnivores and hoofed animals, their natural prey, so that they appeared to be together although they actually were separated by a concealed moat. Hagenbeck was credited with determining the maximum distance a lion or tiger could leap, which was, of course, the critical dimension in determining the widths of the moats. I was fortunate indeed to meet and be entertained by both Hagenbeck's son and grandson. The firm of Carl Hagenbeck was world renowned as a supplier of animals of all kinds for zoos and circuses. Through their agents the Hagenbecks could provide anything from a walrus or rhinoceros to a hummingbird. The exhibits in their own zoo changed as new animals arrived and others were sold, which meant that frequent visitors to the *Tierpark* obtained a

visual education on the diversity of wildlife that was unequaled elsewhere. The place was very popular in good weather, but it was cold and drizzly on both days that I explored it in detail. Large flocks of the dainty common gull had flown in from the North Sea to rest in the zoo and to glean what they could in the way of food that was distributed by the keepers to the animals on exhibition. I admired their beauty while in the company of one of the Hagenbecks, which was a mistake that was to lead to my embarrassment later.

My next stop was Berlin. All travel in Europe was by train, and, as we sped along from Hamburg, I was impressed by the profusion of truck gardens, although they were brown and idle during the winter months. It seemed that every square meter of extra space was devoted to growing edible crops. Around the edges of the towns, houses that were not close together had gardens between them. In open areas, great clusters of plots were fenced, often just by shrubbery, and each had a tool house. I learned later that the thrifty and hard-working Germans, women and children included, bicycled out from the towns on weekends and during the long summer evenings to tend their crops. It was no wonder that they were able to feed themselves to a large degree during the exigencies of war, even when, toward the end, Germany was surrounded and massive armies were closing in from both east and west.

Nazi flags had been in evidence in Hamburg, but I was unprepared for the swastika blitz that met my eyes as we entered the capital city. They were everywhere—all over the railroad station, on poles of every description, and surrounding all public buildings. Brown-shirted storm troopers with swastika armbands were also very much in evidence. Getting past them without giving the Nazi salute with one's arm extended forward and upward and saying "*Heil Hitler*" was impossible. It was perfectly obvious that *Der Führer* and his "master race" would soon embark on their attempt at world domination, and which would result in the destruction of much of Europe and the death of millions. I was an American, and I would barge right past, I told myself. I tried it only once. My way was blocked by a storm trooper who glared at me and shouted at me in German. He was joined at once by two of his fellows. There was nothing to do but yield. Afterward, when I gave the salute, I muttered, "Damn Hitler," and got away with it.

The pompous ceremony seemed ridiculous, but it was, of course, part of the propaganda designed to make Hitler's position thoroughly secure and invincible. Great numbers of Germans welcomed him as their liberator from the dominance of the western nations that had imposed the Treaty of Versailles on Germany following World War I, with its demands for huge reparations and the total crushing of Germany as a world power. Yet most of the people were friendly and kindly toward me, and some went to great lengths to help me.

The Berlin Zoo was very large and impressive. Its collection was extremely varied and truly superb, and with so many rarities that it made my head swim as I saw dozens of species in life for the first time. Several of the older buildings were designed to suggest the countries of origin of their animal residents. The elephant house had a touch of India, and the ostrich house was strongly Egyptian, for example.

Quite naturally, my greatest interest was in the reptile collection. It was housed in the aquarium, a unique building erected in 1913, in which were exhibited, on three floors in ascending order, fishes, reptiles and amphibians, and insects. On the first floor were two large galleries, one for saltwater exhibits, the other for fresh. In the great tanks arranged along the walls of each were fishes, some of them quite large. I saw my first spectacular display of anemones and my first octopus. I guessed that the salt water must be imported from far out at sea, but Dr. O. Heinroth, the director of the aquarium, assured me that it was entirely artificial, and he took me down into the labyrinth of pipes, pumps, and filters, all in operation, and showed me two rooms where food was raised for the livestock. One reeked of rotten meat and was full of houseflies; the other smelled of spoiled fruit and was thick with fruit flies.

All the reptiles and amphibians exhibited on the second floor were living in habitat cages except for the largest snakes and turtles. What an exciting display it was for me. I was used to bare cages or those provided only with small shelters and branches for climbing. Perhaps the star of the collection was a Komodo dragon, largest of living lizards, and the very first I had ever seen. Situated in the center of the building was a large atrium, the entire three stories in height and artistically banked with a profusion of tall tropical plants. It was very humid, and condensed moisture was dripping down onto the exhibit like a gentle rain. A rustic bridge crossed it at the second-floor level and permitted visitors to gaze downward at scores of crocodilians of no less than 11 different species.

The insects on the top and smallest floor were also in habitat cages, many of them with their food plants growing right with them. There were bizarre leaf insects and mantids, intriguing ants and huge beetles, and many moths and butterflies that had pupated for the winter months. Two object lessons for lazy housewives showed dining tables with the utensils and remains of a meal on each. Roaches disported on one, and houseflies

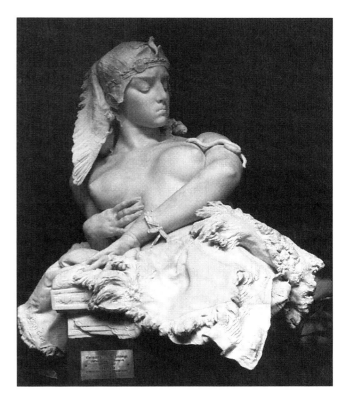

Cleopatra in the Berlin aquarium building. Photo by RC.

buzzed on the other. I was enthralled by the entire structure and its exhibits. When I descended a set of stairs to leave the building, I was greeted by a beautiful bust of Cleopatra staring down scornfully at the asp on her breast—the whole done in marble.

The Berlin Zoo was directly on an elevated railway line and a number of surface car routes. I was told that attendance exceeded 2 million annually and that the largest crowd ever recorded had been 100,000 persons in a single day. Truly, at the time, the Berlin Zoo must have been the largest and best attended in the world.

Dr. Lutz Heck, the director of the zoo, invited me to his home one evening for dinner, and there he told me about his and his brother's efforts to reproduce the ancient wild ox of Europe, the aurochs, which had been extinct for centuries. Domestic cattle with the blood of the aurochs "in their veins" had been assembled from many sources, and, through selective breeding, they now had animals that strongly resembled the species. I enjoyed meeting Dr. Heck's two young sons, who showed me their miniature railway and the first narrow-gauge electric toy trains I had ever seen. Ours were big and clumsy by comparison.

While I was in Berlin I spent an evening attending the opera, where I saw and heard Richard Wagner's "Götterdämmerung," the "Twilight of the Gods," the last of his four Ring operas. The German was far beyond me, but I was intrigued by the first revolving stage I had ever encountered. While a segment of the opera was in progress, the next set of scenery was assembled on the invisible half of the stage. The lights were dimmed severely and, whereas movement could be discerned, it wasn't until the lights were on again that the new background and human cast were fully revealed, as the next scene began.

Another German family, named Ruhe, and based in the Hartz Mountains, had gained an international reputation as animal dealers. They had taken over the zoo in Hannover rather recently, and I knew their English-speaking American representative, Heinz Ruhe. He was in Germany at the time, so I asked the concierge at my hotel to telephone him. I was able to talk with Heinz, and he agreed to meet me at the railroad station in Hannover during mid-morning the next day. I arose very early, made my train, and arrived exactly on time, thanks to the efficiency of the German railroad system. When I alighted I looked for Heinz, but there was no sign of him. I sat down to wait, but, after 20 minutes or so I began to get "antsy" and thought I had better do something. I went first to the ticket window and asked the man behind the metal grille, *"Sprechen Sie Englisch?"* (Do you speak English?) He shook his head in the negative, whereupon I pointed first to my right and then to my left. He got my message at once, indicated my right, and said, *"Der grosse Kellner."* (The big waiter.) He was pointing to the station restaurant, the sign for which I could see from where I stood. I went inside, found a tall waiter, and asked him if he could speak English. He replied in the affirmative, so I explained that Heinz Ruhe was supposed to meet me. He knew the Ruhe family, and he went into action at once. He entered the waiting room, looked around, enlisted help from a couple of other employees, and they made a thorough search, even checking the parking lot and the men's room. No Ruhe. So the waiter telephoned Heinz and told him I was at the station. I thanked him profusely and offered him a tip, which he refused, stating that it had been a pleasure to help me. His prompt action was a good example of the kindness and helpfulness I was to experience again and again from complete German strangers. Unlike the arrogant brown-shirted guards, almost everyone else did his best to help me.

Ruhe arrived in a few minutes and said he had lost track of the time. He drove me to the Hannover Zoo, which was small compared with those in Hamburg and Berlin. Many of the animals were transient, so to speak, and ready to be shipped out when buyers wanted them. It took only an hour or so to see everything, chiefly large mammals and some of the more spectacular birds. We had lunch together, and Heinz outlined his family's ambitious plans for improving the place. Whether they ever were consummated I never heard, but probably they had to be scrapped when war broke out two years later. I was driven to the company's headquarters in the Hartz Mountains, a low range of nearby hills, from which huge numbers of canaries were shipped every year. Raising canaries was a cottage industry in the region, and I remembered it, even years later, every time I saw a sign or a display of canaries for sale. All bore the designation of "Hartz Mountain Canaries."

Heinz took me back to the station, I ate on the train, and was soon back in Berlin.

Although individual Germans were very polite, kind, and helpful, I could not overcome the aura of evil that, like a metastasizing cancer, was enveloping the entire nation. It had begun to affect me mentally soon after my arrival in Nazi land. Hitler had abolished freedom of speech and freedom of assembly, anti-Semitism was rampant, and there were far too many restrictions. I had to keep constant track of my valuables, and no money could be taken out of Germany—only the amount I had brought in, less my expenses. I clung to my traveler's checks, my letter of credit, and the monetary transactions card I received when I entered at Bremerhaven, and I guarded them as closely as my passport. A friend had asked me to buy her an expensive tablecloth for which she would reimburse me upon my return. I felt nervous about it and decided to seek advice from the American consulate. I was told to avoid any major expenditures. The consular officer said I might purchase some small item, such as a penknife, but nothing of greater value. Under the Nazi regulations I was also expected to keep a list of my expenditures, but no one challenged me about them. I was prepared nonetheless, because Freeman M. Shelly, the Philadelphia Zoo's Business Manager, had instructed me to get receipts for all expenditures, other than personal ones. I really astonished him when I produced a fistful of odd-sized papers, including receipts for every meal I ate in a restaurant, in five languages—German, French, Flemish, Dutch, and English.

Most disconcerting were the inevitable check-ups on the trains. The conductor punched tickets, as expected, but he was accompanied by an armed officer in uniform who required all passengers to show their passports or identification cards, and he also selected several at random from whom he demanded all their other papers and valuables. Would I be next? None of us had what I was accustomed to thinking of as freedom. No one could leave Germany without permission, under penalty of execution, a fact that I vividly recalled each time I have seen the classic motion picture "The

Sound of Music." In the last scene the von Trapp family is making its way across the mountains, escaping from Austria. That country was still free in 1937, when I was in Germany, but Hitler swallowed it up with his *Anschluss* (annexation) the following year, and the strict Nazi rules prevailed at once.

European trains were quite unlike American ones in several respects. I was used to passenger cars with a central aisle and rows of double seats on each side. Continental trains had a passageway down one side with doors on the other side leading into compartments, each seating six persons. A notable advantage was that the window in each compartment could be lowered at station stops, and luggage could be handed out to a porter.

When I arrived in Munich from Berlin I gave a stolid, stocky, middle-aged porter my two bags, then walked down the passageway, descended the train steps, and met him outside. He asked, in strongly accented English, "Where go?" I answered, "The Hotel Gruenwald." He trudged along and kept on going even when I turned off in the direction indicated by a taxi sign. I stopped and went after him, repeating, "Taxi, taxi." He paid no attention to me, but I quickly discovered, from an illuminated sign, that the Gruenwald was almost directly across the street. He was honest and I tipped him well. As I write this, I cannot help but recall the scheming taxi drivers I've encountered in various cities, who attempted to run up miles on their meters along circuitous routes to reach a relatively nearby location. Cheating strangers was fair game in their code of ethics. It has happened to me in such diverse places as New York, Chicago, St. Louis, Los Angeles, and Singapore. Fortunately, I detected the ruse in all cases save one. My love of geography induces me to gather up maps at every opportunity, and I usually know pretty well where I am going and roughly how far away it is.

Late in 1937 a series of illustrated articles about my visit to Europe was published in "Parks and Recreation" magazine. In one, I described the last German zoo I saw:

The Munich Zoo is one of the newest zoological parks and certainly one of the most beautiful. It was founded in 1929 and built, with evident forethought, in a roomy location at the edge of the city. The grounds are level and situated in a valley through which runs a swift, crystal clear stream fed by the melting snows of the nearby Alps. Part of the zoo is wooded and, in the shady glades, cleverly planned barless paddocks are arranged for the accommodation of the animals of sylvan habitats. Here are grouped herds of the wisent, tarpan, the synthetic aurochs, and several species of deer, antelope, aquatic birds, etc.

Water diverted from the Alpine stream was circulated through moats fronting barless exhibits. There were also several buildings, including a large circular elephant house with a spacious outdoor area where the big pachyderms could exercise. One huge Indian bull, which reminded me of Babe at the Toledo Zoo, was kept in solitary confinement, but it had sired three babies, all born right there in the zoo.

The newest structure was the *Menschenaffen* (great apes) Station. It consisted of a series of buildings and patios all enclosed by a high wall, and admission was gained by paying a small fee. Chimpanzees, orangutans, and gibbons were exhibited. One large, glass-surrounded enclosure constituted the playground and dining room, with tables and chairs for 8 or 10 young anthropoids, who received special care. Attendants hand-fed or encouraged them to feed themselves with spoons, scrubbed them daily, and even brushed their teeth. Each had its own individual sleeping quarters. Outdoors was a miniature amphitheater that accommodated a few hundred spectators who watched the animals at play during warm weather. Nearby I could see the new reptile house and aquarium, which was under construction.

Wandering about the zoo was a distinct pleasure. Many of the animals seemed quite tame and would approach visitors. I made friends with a walrus which had to initiate me before our "friendship" was complete. It swam to the edge of its pool near me and complacently stared upward until I was tempted into scratching its nose. That was the signal for action. The next instant my legs were drenched with a flipperful of water.

Possibly because I was tired from the previous stops during my strenuous trip, but more likely because it was so peaceful and lovely, I spent most of my time at the zoo and did little sightseeing in Munich. I did, however, visit the famous beer hall that had become a major symbol of Hitler's *Putsch* (armed uprising) to power, where I had myself a stein of dark beer. The famous Oktoberfest was long since over, but the place was swarming with fanatical brown-shirted storm troopers, and swastikas were everywhere.

My patient and genial host was Heinz Heck, director of the Munich Zoo and a brother of Berlin's Lutz Heck. Winifred Felce, in charge of the apes station, was English, and she served as interpreter, although Heinz Heck had a fairly good English vocabulary himself. Those two people, a few of their friends, and even other zoo employees enjoyed walking through the zoo grounds during the early twilights before Germany's long winter nights, and I joined them. The weather had been chiefly cold and drizzly, but, on my last full day at

Swastikas were in evidence everywhere in Hitler's Germany—even in the remote station where RC entrained to ascend the Zugspitze, the nation's highest mountain. Photo by RC.

the Munich Zoo, the sun came out as we walked, and it illuminated the snow-capped peaks of the Bavarian Alps. Herr Heck asked me if I was going to the mountains, and I responded that I hadn't planned to do so. He said, "You go tomorrow. Good sunny day," and he urged me so forcefully that I followed his advice and had a truly inspiring adventure.

With general information from Miss Felce and details about trains from the concierge, I was up betimes in the morning headed for the Zugspitze, or Train Peak (or Mountain), whose summit, at 9,721 feet, is the highest point in Germany. As we rolled southward, truck gardens were again much in evidence, as they seemed to be almost everywhere in the countryside of Germany, but there were also woodlots and patches of forest. The day was clear and cloudless. Herr Heck had been right about the weather. When we reached the station that served the two towns of Garmisch and Partenkirchen, I left the train and made inquiries about what to do next. No language problems that time. The magic word "Zugspitze" resulted in a finger pointing immediately to where I should go. There I boarded a much smaller train of cars of a cog railroad built to stop quickly on steep grades. Once started, it moved upward across gently rolling slopes. As the track twisted and turned I could see the great wall of mountains to the south and which we gradually were approaching. One enormous shaft rose almost vertically for thousands of feet above us, and the train was headed directly for it. I strained my neck staring out the window, looking for the track that surely would be used for our ascent. None was in sight. Shortly we entered a tunnel, and a few moments later

the car tilted so that my back was resting firmly on the rear of the seat. Suddenly it dawned on me that we were climbing *inside* the mountain. How incredible! I thought about the wonder of it all through the rather long upward ride, until, at the top, the train stopped in a spacious lobby facing south and with sunshine streaming in through the windows. I found a door leading to an outside balcony and, as I stepped through it, a glorious panorama met my eyes. Snow-capped mountains stretched away in every direction as far as I could see, straight ahead and both to the left and right. A fellow visitor pointed to the distant peaks and said, "Dolomites."

A few skiers were moving about almost directly below us, but my attention quickly turned to a half dozen Alpine choughs on the balcony railings that approached me, obviously looking for food. They were coal black birds, smaller than our American crow and with brightly colored bills and feet. I did not record the colors, either in my mind or my notes, but according to Peterson's "Field Guide to the Birds of Britain and Europe" their bills are yellow, their legs red. It was relatively warm on the balcony in the brilliant sunshine, and I lingered for quite a while drinking in the fantastic and awe-inspiring beauty of the Alps.

Eventually I went inside and discovered that there was a tramway to the summit of the mountain, and I promptly bought a ticket. After a few other persons had assembled, we made the ascent. We were lifted many more hundreds of feet, and we stepped out onto a platform. We didn't stay long because there was no shelter, and a cold wind quickly chilled us.

Back in the spacious lobby I found an entrance to a restaurant and I soon warmed up with hot soup and a good dinner. My crumbs were carefully saved to give to the choughs outside. The birds came very close, but they wouldn't take food directly from my hand.

I don't recall how many times I went back and forth to the balcony, but at last I had to tear myself away from the wonderful sight and start back to Munich. The descent through the mountain was uneventful, and there was still enough daylight, when we emerged below, to admire several lovely Alpine chalets along our route. What a perfectly marvelous day it had been!

The next morning I thanked Herr Heck for insisting that I go to the mountains. I had no inkling at the time that I would see him in Munich again 30 years later. By then he had retired, but he was still living at the zoo. The new director was his nephew, Lutz Heck, who most assuredly was one of the two youngsters whose narrow-gauge toy trains I had admired in Berlin. There was a very noticeable change in 1967. By then most of the younger Germans spoke English, which had superseded French as the world language.

My next destination was Basel, in Switzerland. It was a long ride on the German train, and I was in for a worrisome experience. En route there was a scheduled stop at the Swiss city of Schaffhausen, where a small part of Switzerland jutted northward into Germany. Long before we arrived, two uniformed and armed officers came through the train and collected all of our papers and passports. The reason was obvious. With the brutal rules against leaving Germany without permission, the Nazis were taking no chances that anyone would escape by getting off the train at Schaffhausen. Politically they had no jurisdiction in Switzerland, but the train was bristling with armed guards prepared to shoot, but more likely simply to remind would-be deserters what might happen to them. Without my papers I felt naked, and I sweated it out for nearly an hour before they were restored to me after the train was back in Germany.

At the end of the trip I had to surrender my money transactions card and have my other papers and passport carefully scrutinized. The officers seemed confused over some minor point and started arguing with each other, but they eventually waved me on, and I stepped onto the soil of a free and neutral country. What a relief that was. Everything would be peaceful and unregimented from then on.

It was fairly late in the evening and I was lucky enough to get an English-speaking cab driver. On the way to my hotel we were stopped momentarily beside a large, brilliantly lighted factory where machinery could be seen and heard. I asked what it was, and the driver replied, "They're making ammunition to sell to both sides." Switzerland might be neutral, but nonetheless it was cashing in, making money from both France and Germany, which soon would be at war with each other.

Much has been written about the rise and eventual obliteration of Hitler's Third Reich, but I have never seen a convincing explanation of a question that still troubles me. The German people I met were kind and polite. The Germans could build great, speedy ocean liners, marvelous zoos, and revolving stages. They could tunnel a great distance through a solid mountain to reach the snows high in the Alps. Their genius and devotion to hard work could accomplish anything, or so it seemed. But why were they willing to accept such a tyrant as Adolf Hitler? Was it because they had always been regimented and disciplined and had blindly followed Frederick the Great, Bismarck, and Kaiser Wilhelm in earlier years? I am neither a historian nor a psychologist and am not qualified to offer an opinion. All I know is that I am fortunate to have had a glimpse of a great country before its self-destruction.

Oh, there was one other thing that I discovered after I was safe in my hotel. The German officials at the Swiss border had become so involved with my papers that they forgot to stamp my passport to confirm my exit from their country. Did that mean I technically was still in Hitler's Germany? I had no intention of going back to find out.

Chapter 12

More Prewar Continental Zoos

Concurrent with my departure from Hitler's Germany in 1937, the aura of evil vanished. My arrival in Switzerland gave me a feeling of having escaped from jail. More realistically, I no longer needed to worry about the possibility that some innocent failure to respect the Nazi demands would place me in jeopardy.

I was in Europe to inspect leading zoos, and I still had five countries on my schedule, including Switzerland. It behooved me to get on with my assignment. I devoted the next day to the Basel Zoo. Dr. Adolph Wendnagel, the director, greeted me cordially, and I was escorted through the grounds by his son, Walter Wendnagel. My first impression was of the spotless conditions. Not a scrap of paper anywhere, and the shrubs and plantings reflected careful and constant care. I was told that visitors rarely ventured on the lawns, which were separated from the walks simply by a row of stones. Guardrails, except in a few places, were conspicuous by their absence. The Swiss public obviously was what we would have called "well behaved."

Most of the buildings, which were old and of a style that was already becoming obsolete, were in excellent condition, and so were the animals. Newer structures were on the barless plan. Visitors had free-sight views of monkeys, bears, sea lions, and antelopes of several kinds. A klipspringer, a tiny antelope, met us on one of the walks, and I commented on the shallowness of the moat fronting the exhibit. As we approached, the little animal leaped back home, and I learned that it and its companions often grazed on the lawn, but they immediately retreated when any person approached them.

The bird house was of special interest. It was designed so that many of the birds could go out-of-doors at will, summer and winter. The individual large cages were separated by panels of sturdy translucent glass that admitted light but prevented the birds from seeing their neighbors and trying to fight with them. One side of the building was occupied by banks of cages piled one on top of the other, all serviced from a passageway at the rear. The emphasis was clearly on exhibiting as many different bird species as possible. There was no reptile exhibit, only a naturalistic outdoor serpentarium, whose occupants were in hibernation at the time.

Because it was my job to prepare zoo cage signs back home in Philadelphia, I admired the more complicated task of whoever had that assignment in Basel. All labels had to be in two languages, French and German. A similar problem occurred in Belgium, where signs were in both French and Flemish.

The Basel Zoo's two-story restaurant, where we had lunch, was cleverly arranged to assure maximum use. Zoo visitors entered and used the lower floor, whereas pedestrians from the street bordering the *Tierpark* were accommodated on the upper floor, where an outdoor balcony, overlooking the animal exhibits, was undoubtedly very popular during the warmer months. I was told that the restaurant did a brisk business in season.

France, the land of "liberty, equality, and fraternity," was next on my itinerary, and I approached Paris with a feeling of relief. The memories of all the *verboten* things in Germany were still very fresh in mind. I ate on the train from Basel and arrived in Paris, the "City of Lights," about 7:30 P.M. The short taxi ride to the hotel was scary, as the driver ducked and dodged through the traffic. I registered, went to my room, washed my hands and face, and then returned to the lobby. I asked the concierge, "What does one do in Paris at night?"

"Has Monsieur seen the Folies?" he asked. I responded negatively.

"Would you like to go?" My reply was in the affirmative, but wasn't it too late? He said he could still get me a ticket. He had me print my name on a piece of paper, picked up the telephone, talked with someone, and then told me to show the paper to the cashier. So far so good, but how would I get there? A taxi? No! The theater was almost around the corner from the hotel! With his explicit directions I made it with ease, bought my ticket, and was in my seat about a minute before the curtain went up.

Wow! Imagine getting to the Folies only a half hour after arriving in Paris. Had I set a record?

Josephine Baker was the star of the show. I don't

remember the French words that were illuminated on the theater marquee, but the concierge told me later that she was billed as "the American mulatto with the golden skin." At the time she was the toast of Paris. The show was spectacular, and the costumes were gorgeous, colorful, and flamboyant. "Webster's Dictionary of Proper Names" described the Folies as a music hall where spectators could conduct anatomical research.

But back to business. The next morning I visited the new zoo in the Bois de Vincennes. My first impression was of great masses of artificial rocks rising in every direction. The general plan, however, was simple and effective. Buildings were designed as winter or sleeping quarters for specific groups of animals. Except for its skylights, windows on a central court, roofs, and entrances, each building was encased in a shell of concrete molded and sculptured to resemble cliffs, ledges, and mountains. The entire zoo, in essence, was a succession of such buildings, each set down within its encircling barless exhibits, like rounded islands in a sea of walks. That impression was especially evident from the observation tower, also a mass of concrete, which I ascended by elevator, after paying a fee, and from which I took a picture. Moats and pools were of different sizes as required by the exhibits, but the landscaping and rockwork were so much alike as to be monotonous. Aside from sod and a few trees there was little vegetation, but time and growth eventually subdued the rawness and sameness of the zoo as I saw it in 1937.

The collection was large and varied, and, because of the cold, damp weather then prevalent, most of it was indoors. I welcomed the chance to be inside, where I could warm up from time to time. The emphasis was on mammals and all the major groups were well represented. I saw my first babirusas—weird-looking, virtually hairless pigs with almost vertically erect tusks, and known only from the East Indian island of Celebes (now Sulawesi) and a few nearby smaller islands.

The birds exhibited were chiefly of aquatic or flightless species, such as ducks, geese, cranes, herons, penguins, rheas, and ostriches. I failed to find a bird house, but I discovered a small building containing parrots. I also couldn't find a reptile house.

I tried to view the zoo objectively and make allowances for its newness, but the treatment I received there left a sour taste in my mouth, to say the least.

There is an unwritten law among zoo personnel to be as polite and helpful as possible toward professional visitors. At the Philadelphia Zoo, for example, whenever a representative of a sister institution—zoo, aquarium, or museum—appeared at the entrance gate, one of our own staff members would act as guide and host. Quite

often I assumed that responsibility myself and patiently showed our guests whatever they wanted to see, answered their questions, and took them to lunch if they were with us at noontime. My reception in every European zoo I visited was the same, very cordial and pleasant—except in Paris.

Before I left my hotel I asked the concierge to telephone the director's office at the zoo. He was out of town, but my name was given and the statement made that I was on my way. I taxied to the main gate and showed the cashier and his companion the letter of introduction I had brought from home. I did not expect them to read English, but our zoo's official letterhead and accompanying seal were prominent, and they were more than adequate to summon someone in authority at other zoos. Not so this time. The cashier pointed to the table of admission prices. So I shrugged my shoulders and thought, "What the heck. I'll pay my way in." I handed over the necessary sum and started through the gate. Out came the helper, who blocked my way. He pointed to my camera. There was a charge for it, too. I was surprised, but gave him more money. It wasn't enough. He indicated through pantomime and by showing me a price chart, handed out to him by the cashier, that the cost for movie cameras was five times as much as that for still cameras. I didn't have a motion picture camera, and I had to open my case to prove it. They finally gave in, and I went on my solitary way for the first and only time during all of my zoo visits in Europe.

It was midwinter and the refreshment kiosks were closed down. There was no place to eat. So about 1:00 P.M. I went back to the gate and, again in pantomime and a few scribbled French words, I indicated that I wanted to find a restaurant. There was one a few blocks away. I thanked the men and took off for lunch. About an hour later I returned to the gate and started back into the zoo. They stopped me at once. They positively refused to recognize me, even though there probably had not been a dozen visitors on that dreary day. I had to pay admission again and go through the same haggling about my camera. Once I had paid, they suddenly remembered me. Did they get a commission on all they collected?

I tried to forget the experience, but it was only one of many like it in Paris. The usherette at the Folies had thrust her leg across the end of the row of seats and would not let me pass until I coughed up a few francs. When I bought railroad tickets to go to Cleres, France, and later to move on to Belgium, both cashiers tried to shortchange me. It was the same in restaurants and the store or two I visited. People were impolite. They sometimes virtually pushed me out of the way, and arrogance was rampant wherever I went in Paris. During later years,

I learned from scores of friends and even total strangers that they disliked Parisians for those very things, and because of their attitude of superiority toward everyone else. If you weren't French you were inferior.

The other Paris Zoo, in the Jardin des Plantes, is one of the oldest and most famous in Europe. It was well established at the time of the Franco-Prussian War in the early 1870s, and many were the stories, perhaps apocryphal, about the high prices paid for hippo steaks when famine was causing as much damage as the Prussian guns.

Situated in the renowned botanical garden and adjacent to the natural history museum, where I went first, the old zoo was literally in the heart of the French capital's biological center. At the museum I was approached by a student who spoke considerable English and asked me many questions about America. We hit it off so well that he accompanied me through the zoo and vivarium, with which he obviously was quite familiar, and I treated him to lunch.

Except for a few new structures the zoo looked its age, and, whereas the animal collection was relatively large and well-rounded, the husbandry left a lot to be desired. It was untidy and unkempt, and some cages exhibited a real lack of cleanliness.

The modern vivarium was in sharp contrast with the rest of the zoo. Its aquariums and terrariums, all attractively planted and landscaped in miniature, housed a variety of both vertebrates and invertebrates, the former including all the major groups except birds. There was a fine display of tropical fishes, amphibians and reptiles, and such small mammals as jerboas and other rodents. The insects were many, chiefly bizarre, and the tarantulas and scorpions were cleverly displayed. A flat, slightly raised piece of glass had been placed in an otherwise bare cage, and the occupants instinctively crawled beneath it for shelter, but they were still readily visible.

I had one more stop to make in France: the small private zoo at Cleres on the estate of Jean Delacour, the celebrated ornithologist and naturalist. We had met the previous year, but while I was inspecting European zoos he was doing the same thing in the United States. F. E. Fooks, his gamekeeper and director, was my host.

It was foggy when I entrained in Paris early in the morning, but eventually, after I changed at Rouen and was speeding through the lovely French countryside, the sun broke through the clouds and made every moisture-laden twig and leaf sparkle. As I stepped down from the motor-train the air was balmy, and before I had walked the brief distance to the marketplace, I almost wished I had left my overcoat in Paris.

Cleres was an enchanting and picturesque village. I was absorbed at once in the quaint architecture of its buildings, but as my eye trailed from one cornice to another, I was startled to see an adult gibbon, most agile of the apes, skipping nimbly along the eaves. It was moving leisurely and receiving no more attention from the villagers than would a pigeon traveling the same route. I was soon to learn that such visits were commonplace and they exemplified the freedom accorded many of the animals in the Parc Zoologique de Cleres. I rounded a corner, stepped through what appeared to be a garden gate, identified myself, and discovered the most delightfully charming zoo I had ever seen.

The grounds were very attractive. Spacious lawns were interspersed with thickets, and a large pond and small stream occupied a portion of the zoo. There were no large buildings except the historic Delacour chateau, which had been restored after suffering major damage during World War I. Birds were exhibited in open-air aviaries, many communicating with shelters that were heated during cold weather. The pheasant collection was superb. A large number of species, many of them rarities, were represented, and they also were in marvelous condition. The more delicate birds of tropical origin lived in greenhouses.

Mammals capable of being entrusted with their liberty were free to move about at will. A high fence surrounded the grounds to prevent straying. There were 30 wallabies (small kangaroos), 20 or more blackbuck antelopes, and many muntjacs (small, slender deer), as well as cranes of several species. A crowned crane was a personal pet of Mr. Fooks, and it followed him everywhere. Our walk through the grounds became a tour of discovery. As we rounded every hedge and thicket we came upon groups of wallabies and other species mingled more or less together. The roaming birds were pinioned, and some of the ducks and geese had left their pond and were foraging on the lawn.

There were six gibbons. Three were confined to an island in the stream, but the others went where they pleased, even into the village. One of them stayed close to me and eventually climbed to my shoulder, where it remained for the better part of an hour, even though I had no food to attract it. What an enchanting novelty, but even a 12-pound gibbon can get heavy to carry after a time, and I admit I was relieved when it finally leaped off my shoulder into a small tree beneath which we passed.

The zoo was still a private estate, but it had recently been opened to the public. The admission price on Sundays and holidays was relatively low, but the amount was doubled on weekdays, no doubt to keep the number of visitors at a minimum so as not to interfere with maintenance and to give the livestock ample time to rest. When people became too numerous the animals could retreat into the thickets.

Aside from the birds, which were Jean Delacour's specialty, the collection was small, but what a fascinating way to discover many of its residents. The Parc Zoologique de Cleres was a lovely showplace.

From Paris I was off to the Low Countries, with stops in Antwerp, Rotterdam, and Amsterdam. The zoos in all three cities were noteworthy.

The most striking thing about the Antwerp Zoo was its location directly adjacent to the city's large, ornate, and roofed-over railroad terminal, which formed one of the boundaries of the zoo. The advantage was obvious. A considerable part of the zoo's admission receipts accrued from persons killing an hour or two in pleasant fashion while waiting for train connections.

When it was founded in 1843, the zoo was on the outskirts of Antwerp, but its approximately 25 acres had become entirely surrounded by buildings, some of them residences set back-to-back with animal shelters. I could not help but wonder how unsuspecting overnight guests would react to the roaring of lions or other vociferous animals.

My first duty was to call on Dr. Michel L'Hoest, the director, who assigned a very courteous English-speaking staff member to show me one of the finest animal collections I had seen. The headliner was an okapi from the Belgian Congo, the only one then living in any regularly established zoo. The various paddocks, pens, and buildings occupied most of the space in the relatively small area of the zoo, but they were so cleverly planned and laid out that there was even room for several lawns and plantings of shrubs and flowers. An arched pedestrian walkway rose above some of the exhibits, and, from it, I had a bird's-eye view of the entire zoo. In the lobby of the stately lion house were sculptured busts of all the zoo's directors, dating back almost a century, but also including Dr. L'Hoest.

An unusual exhibit was a group of camels, llamas, and yaks living amicably together. All are domesticated, of course, but in different parts of the world. My guide pointed with pride to a herd of reindeer that was thriving after being weaned away from reindeer moss onto a diet of more easily procurable food.

The collection of birds of prey was large and impressive. Pairs of each kind were in separate wire, short-flight cages fitted at their backs with wooden shelters. Shutters were arranged so they could be closed or opened, depending on weather conditions. Much of the birds' food was provided right in the garden, in the form of rats and mice, against which the employees waged a constant campaign.

The aquarium, built in 1911, included both fresh-

The city's main railroad station (left) serves as one of the boundaries of the Antwerp Zoo. Photo by RC.

and saltwater exhibits, and the closed-circuit system was renewed by water brought from the Mediterranean Sea every three or four years. The reptile collection occupied the second floor of the aquarium, but it was reached separately by ascending an outdoor ramp. No venomous snakes were included, and, much to my surprise, I learned that the Belgian public took little interest in reptiles. How very different from American zoos where the reptile houses were often crowded.

There was a small but complete museum of the native Belgian fauna. This and the administration office were in a magnificent edifice that also included a beautiful concert hall and an attractive winter garden. All the signs were in two languages, but the staff was hard-pressed at times to invent common names in Flemish for unusual animals.

During World War I, Antwerp was occupied by the Germans. Prior to their arrival, the chief meat-eating animals and other valuable species were transferred to the nearby Rotterdam Zoo in neutral Holland for the duration. Hay remained plentiful during the occupation, and the rest of the zoo carried on as usual, and there were no war-related casualties.

Bicycles were much in evidence in Antwerp, but they really swarmed in the Netherlands. They were the principal mode of transportation, and they were used by a cross section of the populace, from laboring men and women to well-dressed professionals, many carrying briefcases with them.

The first pair of wooden shoes I saw were on the feet of a keeper in the Rotterdam Zoo. Such footgear is quite practical for zoo work. Using a hose is a daily necessity in every zoo, and wooden shoes, easily washed, are just the thing for sloshing about when cages are cleaned.

Even though the keepers wore them while at work, they all changed to leather shoes before going home. Perhaps some of the people in the countryside still used wooden shoes, but I looked in vain for them in the city. I took time to wander along Holland's "highways," the canals, but there were no wooden shoes on either pedestrians or persons living or working on the many ships, mostly small, that were moored along the canals. I eventually found a good supply in a shop that specialized in selling souvenirs to tourists. I bought a pair and added them to the collection of gifts I was assembling to take home, and on which I had started after leaving Germany, where spending money on anything but trivia was *verboten*.

Kurt Kuiper, Director of the Rotterdam Zoo, took the day off to show me his collection which, as one might have expected, was especially rich in species from the Netherlands East Indies. Included were the orangutan, anoa (a dwarf buffalo), the so-called black ape, gibbon, black leopard, and several kinds of birds-of-paradise. Among the larger carnivores was a pair of leopards that recently had produced two young, one black and one spotted. There was also a handsome pair of black jaguars.

Emphasis among the perching birds was the exhibition of as many different species as possible, a policy then in vogue in zoos all over the world. An impressive outdoor flight cage accommodated many large birds. Its wire meshes were wide enough so that wild birds the size of starlings and thrushes could enter and leave at will. Atop the structure and in the adjacent trees were the nests of scores of European herons that used the zoo as their rookery during the breeding season. Other wild birds were in evidence, and I saw my first pair of hooded crows.

When we entered the reptile house I almost stumbled over a big Galápagos tortoise that was plodding its way across the public space. It and a few others of its kind spent the cold months in the lobby of the building. There were no venomous snakes. Outstanding, at least to me, was a Malayan gavial, a crocodilian, with its curiously shaped head and attenuated snout that together resembled a frying pan.

Connected with the zoo and under the same management was an excellent botanical garden with several greenhouses. One of the latter was filled with orchids, a number of them in bloom but with no protection except for the watchful eyes of an attendant. They were more or less immune to petty pilfering, but not so the miniature cactus plants, which were exhibited inside a wire cage! A crew of men was busy with pruning and tree surgery. Elimination of deadwood was an annual wintertime function, partly because of the Dutch elm disease, but also because a visitor once sustained a fatal injury when a limb fell on her.

The Amsterdam Zoo also had a splendid collection, and of so many species that I was almost bewildered trying to keep track of them all. The display of wild cattle was especially impressive because it included virtually all the known kinds, including the nucleus of a small herd of the wisent, a species nearing extinction. The wisent, the European counterpart of our American bison, is a browser (rather than a grazer) that was once abundant in the great forests of central Europe. The species had declined in numbers for centuries, and it suffered severely during World War I as armies fought back and forth through reservations set aside for it.

Dr. A. L. J. Sunier, the Amsterdam Zoo's director, escorted me and pointed with pride to many of his institution's accomplishments. Crowned pigeons and cassowaries had been hatched and raised there. A special small building was provided for a manatee that had already lived for eight years in captivity. The lions and tigers were exhibited in family groups instead of having the males confined to solitary cages. Gulls, storks, and rails occupied small ponds with profuse vegetation in parts of them, and from which the ducks, geese, and swans were excluded so they would not destroy the plants by nibbling at their roots. Many of the enclosures in the reptile house were densely planted, and visitors sometimes had to hunt to find the exhibits, a novelty then but a commonplace way of showing reptiles and amphibians nowadays. A Komodo dragon had lived more than eight years and was still thriving. A Russian sturgeon, an original occupant of the aquarium when it was erected 53 years previously, was still doing well.

An outstanding feature of the Amsterdam Zoo was its devotion to education. A branch of the city's university was right on the grounds and teaching laboratories were provided. A fine museum of natural history was also included, and its director, the eminent ichthyologist, Professor Dr. L. F. de Beaufort, was soon to do me a special favor. The two directors and several staff members gathered for a social meeting in my honor at lunch and, happily for me, all were fluent in English.

After we had eaten, Dr. de Beaufort invited me to his office where we had a long talk centering on the extraordinary wildlife of the East Indies. He was a friendly, fatherly person, and he asked me, "Have you been able to do everything in our country that you wish?" I hesitated, but then I mentioned that I had not seen a bookstore where I could purchase the classic works on the Indies by Nelly de Rooij (two on reptiles) and P. N. Van Kampen (one on amphibians). He suggested a source, but I had to tell him that I was scheduled to depart from the Netherlands that very night. I was to leave Amsterdam by train for the Hook of Holland, where I would take a steamer across the North Sea to England. He then asked me if I would be stopping in Leiden. I consulted my timetable and saw that the train would be there for about five minutes. Dr. de Beaufort picked up the telephone on his desk, put through a call, talked with someone, and then asked me if I would pay a certain amount for the three books. The price was more than I could afford. Books for my private library could not be put on my zoo expense account. He spoke again and then quoted a price about half as much. The original was for bound copies, the second for paperbacks. I nodded my head yes, and he kept the line open until we had worked out a scheme for my receiving and paying for the three volumes. When the train stopped at Leiden I was to lower the window in my compartment and display a sheet of paper with the word "Philadelphia" prominently printed on it. Someone would hand me the books.

I took great care to have the exact number of guilders in my pocket when I left my hotel in the evening. I followed instructions, and the transaction was completed. I thanked the young man who had been the errand boy, so to speak, and carefully clutched my prizes. The three books are still in my possession, although I had them bound when I became a little more affluent.

I have never forgotten Dr. de Beaufort's kindness and ingenuity. I corresponded with him until the Germans invaded the Netherlands, and again after the war was over. I offered to send him anything he might need and which might have been denied to him during the occupation. He thanked me but declined my offer. He and his family had made out fairly well despite many hardships.

After changing trains farther down the line, I reached the Hook of Holland and looked forward to setting foot on the land of my ancestors on the morrow.

Chapter 13

The London Zoo and Whipsnade in 1937
(And a Few Recollections)

Instead of making a pleasant and eager entry into England, I arrived feeling almost like a zombie after a sleepless night on the little steamer that pitched and rolled across the stormy North Sea. My "stateroom" was so tiny that I literally had to climb over my baggage to reach my bunk, which was too short for me. Several times during the night I had to hold on desperately to keep myself from being tossed out of bed.

England was the sixth and last of the countries I was to visit on my tour of European zoos. My journey had been strenuous but exceedingly interesting despite many language difficulties. I looked forward to visiting a place where I could speak with everyone, or so I thought, but my arrival in the early morning was anything but glamorous.

After having something substantial to eat (I passed up the kippered herrings), I felt a little better, but I dozed in the train all the way to London where, still half asleep, I taxied to the Hotel Ivanhoe. At last I could go to bed. But no! My room would not be ready for hours. I retreated to the warmth and quiet of the lounge hall, where large logs were blazing in the fireplace. I sprawled on a couch and slept off and on until my room was ready and a porter came to help me with my bags. Just as had been the case on the Continent, the room was very cold, and I ordered more blankets immediately. There was a sink and hot and cold running water, but, alas, the toilet and shower facilities were far down the hall. Then I made a discovery. There was an electric heater operated by placing a shilling in a slot. I activated it at once, and, although I made no attempt to check on how long the heat lasted, it seemed to demand another shilling every five minutes. Nuts! (I probably uttered a stronger expletive.) I broke out my longjohns again to supplement my nightclothes.

The travel agent who laid out my schedule and had it approved by Dr. Cadwalader, our president, had booked me into what definitely were second-class hotels. I didn't mind. All I needed was a place to sleep, and I would have been bored to death in the swank establishments where Dr. Cadwalader stayed when he went abroad. One had

to dress for dinner and behave like an aristocrat. But too many of my stays were overly brief. I would arrive in a city during the evening, stay overnight, inspect the local zoo the next day, and then move on to the next city. Distances were short, but my progress was frenetic at times. Now that I was in London, however, I would stay at the Hotel Ivanhoe until it was time to go home. Not only did I visit the two wonderful zoos operated by the Zoological Society of London, but I also went to a private game farm. Even so, there was ample time to see something of London and to do a little shopping.

My first duty was to report to the London Zoo in Regent's Park. I went by bus, climbed to the upper deck, sat near the front, and had my first taste of vehicles driving (to me) on the wrong side of the road. On the Continent the traffic moved just as it did in the United States.

Dr. G. M. Vevers, the zoo's general superintendent, greeted me cordially and made me feel very much at home. I was introduced to many staff members, and established a relationship that continues to this day. I was later made a Corresponding Member of the Zoological Society of London. Every year I still receive my membership card, which entitles me to free admission to the Society's zoos and to certain publications.

The zoo itself was extremely compact and occupied a surprisingly small area. It was divided into three unequal parts by a park drive and canal passing through it, but bridges and tunnels made it possible for visitors to move freely from one section to another. Most of the zoo was old but in excellent condition, and it was dominated, in part, by the curious Mappin Terraces rising high above the rest of the zoo. Numerous enclosures rose in series, from those at ground level for hoofed stock, to a row of bear dens set back at a higher level, with the whole surmounted by peaklike areas for the surefooted aoudads and tahrs. The terraces were arranged so that visitors could walk along the various levels to see the animals at close range, or they could turn around and view other parts of the zoo down below. The terraces somewhat resembled the ruins of a large ancient structure rather than the naturalistic crags I had seen in other zoos.

Beneath the terraces was a large, splendid aquarium, presided over by E. G. Boulenger, son of the British Museum's extraordinarily prolific herpetologist, G. A. Boulenger. A novel feature was a littoral (seashore) assemblage of starfishes, mussels, crabs, and associated animals for which artificial tides rose and fell daily.

The newer buildings included monkey and reptile houses (both erected in 1927), an ultramodern gorilla house (1933), and a penguin pool (1934). The gorilla house was unique in providing both summer and winter accommodations for a pair of the big anthropoids. During the cold weather that prevailed during my visit, the building was divided in two, half for the gorillas in a barred cage and the other half for the visiting public. A large, ingeniously designed door permitted the entire building to be converted into one huge circular exhibit during warm weather. The enclosure was so large, however, that the innermost portions were quite dark, and the almost black animals were difficult to see. That defect was pointed out to me by Sir Julian Huxley, Secretary of the Society, with whom I had the pleasure of chatting several times.

Most of the larger kinds of mammals were represented. In addition to the monkey house there was an old lion house, but many of the lesser carnivores and other small mammals lived in a dozen different installations, such as the small cats' house, the civet house, and the rodent house. Collectively, these buildings contained an astonishingly large number of species. The hoofed animals were also scattered in several different buildings as well as on the Mappin Terraces. Outstanding were an Indian rhinoceros, presented by the Maharajah of Nepal, four giraffes of three different varieties, four pygmy hippos, a pair of babirusas, a bongo and her calf, and one of the few chamois I saw during my trip.

The main bird house was crowded with cages and featured a dozen species of birds-of-paradise. The parrot collection was extensive. One special cage in the center of the building was equipped along one side with a large concave-shaped piece of glass which prevented reflections and offered perfect visibility. Even a number of hummingbirds were on exhibition. Aquatic birds were scattered through the zoo in assorted aviaries, flight cages, and pools. A special installation for cormorants was of exceptional interest to me. Those birds lived in a large cage just below the ceiling of one of the buildings, but it was subtended by a glass-fronted tank filled with water, and spectators could see them swimming and diving for food.

The new reptile house, with many innovations, including rocks electrically warmed from beneath to

Part of the Mappin Terraces in London's Regent's Park Zoo. Photo by RC.

encourage snakes and lizards to lie in full view of the public, had been designed in part by Joan B. Procter, who had served as curator of reptiles until her recent death. Acting temporarily in her stead was Dr. Malcolm A. Smith, the distinguished physician to the royal court of Siam and who had published many contributions on the herpetology of that country and other parts of Southeast Asia. It was an honor and pleasure to meet him and to have a chance to talk with him at some length. He was then working on the reptiles for the "Fauna of British India" series. I had the first volume on the crocodilians and turtles, and he told me that the second, on the lizards, had recently appeared. The very next morning I went to Red Lion Court, Fleet Street, and purchased my copy directly from Taylor and Francis, the publishers.

Acquiring books was one of my personal goals, and I discovered that the firm of Wheldon and Wesley was within short walking distance of the Ivanhoe. I browsed through all their herpetological titles, wanted to buy most of them, but was able to purchase only the few my limited personal funds would permit. I acquired G. A. Boulenger's "The Snakes of Europe" and his two-volume work on "The Tailless Batrachians of Europe." My name was added to the company's mailing list, and I became a mail-order customer from then on. In recent correspondence with Christopher K. Swann, the current Managing Director, he wrote that when I purchased those first books in 1937 he was only three years old.

The German bombing blitz of London in 1940 flattened the book district and destroyed countless literary treasures. Perhaps of most interest to herpetologists was the elimination of a large part of the limited edition (450 copies) of Charles R. S. Pitman's "A Guide to the Snakes of Uganda" and all the metal plates from which the exquisite color illustrations had been printed. Wheldon and Wesley later moved to Hertfordshire, well north of London.

I visited the Regent's Park Zoo almost every day, and each time I found something I hadn't seen before. I also had a chance to talk with a number of persons, ranging from keepers to David Seth Smith, Curator of Mammals and Birds, and James Fisher, who later would become one of the world's outstanding conservationists. I did, however, take time to go by train to the Whipsnade Zoo and Foxwarren, the private estate of Alfred Ezra, Esq., O.B.E. and Vice President of the Zoological Society of London.

Foxwarren was not open to the public and could be visited only by invitation. Dr. Cadwalader had seen that I received one, and the people at Regent's Park phoned ahead about my time of arrival. The place, near Cobham in rather open, rolling country, reminded me somewhat of Jean Delacour's estate at Cleres, France. There was a small, carefully selected variety of mammals, but the bird collection was well worth the trip. Many lived out-of-doors year-round; heated shelters were provided during the winter months. Except for one small tropical house and several aviaries there were no buildings of any size. Dense plantings were widely used and, to show me the birds, it was necessary to tempt them to come out in the open by offering food or by the attendants entering the shrubbery and flushing them out of it.

The Whipsnade Park Zoo, initiated and operated by the Zoological Society of London, was near Dunstable, Bedfordshire, and I had heard so much about it that I looked forward enthusiastically to my visit. Miraculously, it was a sunny day, and there was much to watch from the train, including the first gliders I had ever seen in action. Several were taking off from a relatively low cliff and drifting outward and downward, apparently for a few minutes, before coming gracefully to earth.

Whipsnade was the first of the large country zoos. Several others have been established more recently in places where open areas of land were relatively inexpensive to acquire. Many are under the management or ownership of a nearby city zoological park or society. A somewhat comparable and familiar parallel is the very large zoo at San Pasqual, near Escondido, in California, which is operated by the Zoological Society of San Diego.

Somehow I had the preconceived notion that Whipsnade was a barless zoo modeled on the plan that was then finding wide approbation and application in various parts of the world. That illusion was dispelled at once. Whipsnade made broad use of fences, but on such

a vast scale that one scarcely noticed them. It was an enormous place, and I heard two statements that gave some conception of its vastness. The first was that its largest paddock was greater in acreage than the entire Regent's Park Zoo, and the other was that, to follow all the walks and pathways without repeating a single one, required a 20-mile hike.

The animal collection was very large, and the majority of species were represented by herds, packs, and coveys, or at least family groups. In one large paddock I saw dozens of zebras and antelopes grazing in the midst of a field so large that it required little imagination to think one might be in East Africa instead of England. Binoculars were almost a necessity, but the lack of closeness was more than compensated for by the thrill of seeing the entire assemblage thundering across my view at full gallop.

Carnivores were shown in a variety of ways. Lions and tigers, respectively, occupied large circular and semicircular depressions, one of which was an abandoned chalk pit. Iron bars and moats surrounded them, but each enclosure was so large that one tended to forget that the animals were confined. Cheetahs occupied a large fenced run equipped with an overhang that effactually prevented their exodus. Bears lived in a wooded area that provided them with opportunities for climbing, digging, and running. The wolf woods was especially impressive. In a close-set forest of tall trees, devoid of underbrush, was an amazingly large pack of wolves. I happened to see them, just before my departure in late afternoon, as long black shadows trailed out behind them. The effect was both weird and impressive.

Without thinking ahead, I set off on foot to see as much as possible right after my arrival, and I soon realized I had walked miles before I thought to seek the center of things and introduce myself. Captain W. P. Beal was in charge, and he gave me a guide.

More or less together were houses for the larger animals, such as rhinos, elephants, and giraffes. The younger chimpanzees had their own private island surrounded by a moat. My guide took me behind the scenes to see how the animals were cared for and shifted from one cage to another in the buildings.

I discovered that there was a shuttle bus for visitors who didn't care to walk. I didn't use it, preferring instead to enjoy the succession of surprises that awaited pedestrians. Wallabies, muntjacs, female deer, Arctic hares, cattle egrets, sarus cranes, pheasants, peafowl, parrots, and wild turkeys were at complete liberty, and they came and went as they pleased. One or another was constantly putting in an appearance or suddenly coming to life at our feet. Yet all were so tame that it was easy to approach them slowly, and many took food from visitors' hands. Whipsnade really tired me out, but it was worth it.

On my way either to Foxwarren or Whipsnade, I have forgotten which, my train was so old-fashioned that I thought at once of Sherlock Holmes and Dr. Watson. Each car consisted of compartments entered directly from the station platforms. There was no long passageway down one side. Once inside the compartment you stayed there. All it contained were two wide seats, one permitting you to look out the windows to see where you were going, the other where you had been. Oh, yes, there were racks for baggage. It was fun to be traveling as Sir Arthur Conan Doyle's characters had done en route from Baker Street to some distant place to investigate a crime.

I was familiar enough with the typical British accent so that I could easily understand the well-educated people at the zoos and almost everywhere else, but there were times when I might as well have been back on the Continent. As I explored parts of London, I sometimes had to inquire about directions and, when I questioned some individuals (perhaps they were Cockneys), I had to ask them to repeat slowly what they had just said. One burly, rough-looking character, after I completely failed to understand what he was saying, stalked away, no doubt muttering to himself about the "dumb American."

There was also a new vocabulary to learn. The subway was the "underground," an elevator was a "lift," a run in a lady's stocking was a "ladder," an odd amount of money larger than a pound was a "guinea," the bathroom was the "loo," and so on, and so on. The money was almost unintelligible at times. My raincoat and hat had been sufficient protection during most of my trip, despite the almost constant inclement weather, but it poured rain so hard in England that I needed an umbrella. I went into a department store to buy one, tendered a 10-pound note, and received a jumble of change—pence, tuppence coins, crowns, half crowns, shillings, and pound notes. I shoved it all into my pocket. It would have taken me an embarrassingly long time to figure it all out.

The British eventually, and intelligently, changed to the decimal system for their money and switched to the metric system for everything else. It was difficult to understand at first, but they profited immensely by abandoning their long-established conglomeration of measurements. The new system simplified both change making and the calculation of distances, weights, and temperatures. Yet, to this day, we here in America stumble along with the archaic English system: 12 inches to a foot, 3 feet to a yard, 5 and a half yards to a rod, 40 rods to a furlong, and so on. We even have the idiotic

measurement of 5,280 feet to a mile. How stupid we are! The metric system, once learned, is infinitely simpler.

I visited the British Museum (Natural History), looked at many of the excellent exhibits, and then hunted up H. W. Parker in the Department of Zoology (Reptiles and Amphibians). He found several preserved specimens for me to examine, among them a young anaconda. It belonged to, and confirmed the validity of *Euneçtes deschauenseei*, the new species that Emmett Reid Dunn and I had described just a few months previously, based on a single huge individual living at the Philadelphia Zoo. I later corresponded with J. C. Battersby, of the same department, and even sent him a copy of the first edition of my "Field Guide to Reptiles and Amphibians." In reply I had an interesting letter. He was amazed at how colorful many of our American species were in life. Many were represented in the British Museum collection, but all were dull and faded.

One evening I visited a British nightclub with some acquaintances I had made aboard the *Europa* when I was on my way across the Atlantic, and whom I had promised to look up while I was in London. The show was tame compared with the Folies in Paris, but I learned a curious fact. The law prohibited the club from purveying alcoholic drinks. So when you left the club you purchased a bottle of your favorite beverage, and it remained in storage in your name until your next visit. It was perfectly legal to prepare mixed drinks or to pour directly from your personal bottle. It was after 2:00 A.M. when my taxi pulled up in front of the Hotel Ivanhoe, which was bolted and barred for the night. I pushed the emergency bell, and I had to identify myself as a guest and produce my passport before the watchman would let me in.

One other evening I wandered into a pub not far from the hotel and ordered a glass of stout, just for the hell of it. It was awful—like vile-tasting medicine. I stoically persevered, however, and downed it all. I sensed that several pairs of eyes were watching me to see how the American would react.

On my final day at the London Zoo I was joined at lunch in its splendid restaurant by several of my new friends. We had a gay time talking, promised to keep in touch, and we arranged for trades of animals. They were to ship a pair of muntjacs, a pair of nilgais, and another antelope, all surplus in their collection, and I would respond with animals from the Philadelphia Zoo. We traded for several years, mostly reptiles. I recall that once, when I received more than 100 prairie rattlesnakes from A. M. Jackley, South Dakota's rattler control officer, I shipped many of them to the London Zoo, which, in turn, doubtless traded them to other British or Continental reptile collections.

My tour of European zoos was over. I took the boat train to Southampton, and there I boarded the *Bremen,* flagship of the North German Lloyd Line. She was slightly larger than her sister ship, the *Europa,* on which I had made the eastward crossing, but essentially they were twins.

I was still unpacking my belongings in my stateroom when there was a knock on the door, and an English-speaking crewman asked me what I wanted him to feed my birds. My first reaction was, "What birds?" but instead of blurting that out, I asked him where they were. "In the *Hundehütte* [doghouse]," he replied. I asked him to take me to them. We climbed up and up and finally reached the topmost of the seven decks, which was open to the sky. In a sheltered spot aft of one of the ship's enormous funnels was the *Hundehütte,* a series of kennels where passengers could keep their pets until they disembarked in New York. He took me into one of the compartments and showed me a sizable crate containing a number of gulls. It bore the label of the Hagenbeck *Tierpark* in Stellingen, and tacked to the lid was an envelope addressed to me and containing a brief note reading, in essence, "Please accept these birds with our compliments." I was dumbfounded. I had forgotten all about admiring the gulls during my very first visit to a German zoo a month earlier. No wonder the Hagenbecks had asked me when I would be sailing home and on what vessel. The rascals had planned their surprise while I was there with them. I was embarrassed, but I thanked them profusely for trapping the birds for me. But that had to wait until after I was back at my home. Once I knew what "my birds" were, I instructed the crewman to give them small fishes or pieces cut from large fishes, or even small chunks of meat. They throve on the diet I prescribed and arrived safely in New York only to embarrass me again. Where was my import permit, the American authorities wanted to know. I explained the circumstances, but they kept the birds for two days before shipping them, not to me personally but to the Philadelphia Zoo. Did they think I was importing them for personal profit?

The voyage was restful. I was far more tired than I realized from my strenuous, month-long trip, during which I inspected 14 animal collections in six countries. Also, I had to admit, I had added to my own fatigue by going to the opera, the Folies, the Alps, a nightclub, and several shops, as well as doing a bit of sightseeing here and there. What an exciting and inspiring excursion it had been, and how marvelous it was for a young, inveterate zoo enthusiast and naturalist. I devoted much of my time while homeward bound to polishing my notes,

planning my report to the Board of Directors, and even getting started on the series of four articles on European zoos that were published in consecutive issues of "Parks and Recreation" magazine late during 1937.

The only untoward event was a bad storm, which caused the great ship to roll back and forth and slowed us enough so that it took a full extra day to cross the Atlantic. I suffered no distress and only had to hang on to the handrails when I moved about. I enjoyed all my meals and, in fact, had fun during them. The plate rails were in place all around the tables to keep the dishes from crashing to the deck, and it was quite a game to hang onto my plates and cup as I dined. It was rather lonesome, however. The dining salon seated several hundred persons, but on a couple of mornings there were only a dozen or so of us on hand for breakfast. How unhappy most of my fellow passengers must have been with their *mal de mer.*

It was the golden age of the great liners, which had become bigger and speedier as the years went by. There was keen competition among the British, French, and Germans. The fastest ships carried the mail. There was no overseas air mail in those days. If you had a letter that you wanted to reach its destination quickly, you looked in the newspaper under "sailings" to see which of the fast ships was next to leave, and then wrote on the envelope "Via the S.S. *Bremen,*" for example. The two speedy German vessels each had a catapult for launching a plane, when they had approached to within a few hundred miles of their destinations, to speed up the mail even further. Businessmen and others used the faster vessels in order to save days of time at sea. Both the *Europa* and *Bremen* held the record at different times for crossing from Cherbourg, France, to the Ambrose Light Ship near the entrance to New York Harbor in well under five days. The French *Normandie* cut their time by several hours, and then the "blue riband" was captured by the British *Queen Mary.* Eventually, in 1952, our own *United States* made it in 3 days, 10 hours, and 40 minutes, from Ambrose to Bishop Rock, the westernmost isle off the coast of England. Even the Italians were in the race, but over a different route. Their *Rex* sailed from Gibraltar, at the entrance to the Mediterranean Sea, to Ambrose in a little over four and one-half days. Most persons nowadays fly across the Atlantic; the few who use ships are generally seeking relaxation and pleasure. How fortunate I was to experience two speedy and luxurious crossings.

As this is written one of the great liners may still be visited. The huge *Queen Mary,* of over 81,000 tons, is moored at Long Beach, California, as a tourist attraction and hotel, and it has several fine restaurants.

The two German liners were both doomed to ignominious ends. With war imminent in 1939, the *Europa* sailed for Europe in late August but, probably under orders from the German High Command, she failed to stop at Southampton, as scheduled, and sped on instead to her home port. The *Bremen* slipped out of New York on the night of August 31, 1939, without passengers and, by heading far to the north, eluded the British fleet and reached the safety of the then neutral Russian Arctic port of Murmansk. A few months later she ran the gauntlet surreptitiously down the coast of Norway and reached the safety of Bremerhaven. A traitorous crewman set her afire in 1941, and she was scuttled. The *Europa* fared better, serving as a naval training ship at Kiel in Germany. Later she helped to repatriate American troops, and was eventually transferred to the French, who renamed her the *Liberté*. She was broken up for scrap in 1961.

It was a glorious sight to see the Statue of Liberty in New York Harbor and the spectacular skyline of Manhattan as the voyage ended. The ship's crew efficiently lined up all the baggage, including my birds, on the pier, in alphabetical order according to the name of each owner. I was soon cleared to reenter the United States. I had been away for six weeks.

My mother and the zoo's business manager, Freeman M. Shelly, met me at the pier, and we all had lunch together. We saw Mother off on the train back to Red Bank, New Jersey, and then we two men rode the express to Philadelphia. Shelly was especially polite, and he thanked me graciously for the bottle of Scotch whiskey I had imported as a gift for him. It didn't occur to me at the time that he fully expected me to be named Director of the Zoo, largely because I had been the one selected to make the trip abroad. He need not have worried that I might become his boss. I never wanted his job.

My objective had been to get new ideas in Europe. I returned with an abundance of them, and they stood me in good stead all during my long zoo career. Two, however, were destined to make so much money for the Philadelphia Zoo that the cost of my trip was small change by comparison.

First, I had noticed that almost all the European zoos operated their own restaurants and kiosks, the latter for dispensing snacks and souvenirs. Our zoo had a rather mediocre eating place that was run by a concessionaire who also managed a good restaurant in downtown Philadelphia. We suspected that the leftovers were transported to the zoo and warmed up for visitors. We

were supposed to receive 10 percent of the gross, which amounted to only a paltry few thousand dollars a year. There was no way to check on the accuracy of the receipts, and no attempt was made to improve the menus or to make the surroundings more attractive for the public. The contract was not renewed. I had suggested that we vend all food and mementos ourselves, and the Zoological Society put my idea into operation. Business really began to hum.

It took awhile to get organized, and the busy spring and summer season was far advanced before we were geared up to go. Shelly hired a professional food dispenser, and several refreshment and souvenir stands were opened. We netted well over $75,000 during that short first season. The business of purveying grew apace, and when I retired many years later we were grossing well over a $1,000,000 annually, half of which was profit. Inevitably, Shelly or one of the board members would have initiated the policy of running our own concessions, a type of business that blossomed in most American zoos during the 1940s and 1950s. So I cannot claim too much credit.

Secondly, I was greatly impressed by the Children's Pet Corner at London's Regent's Park Zoo. It was closed for the winter during my visit, but Julian Huxley showed me many pictures of it in operation and answered my questions. The thing that appealed to me most was the opportunity to have a wide variety of young domestic animals that city children could both watch and touch. Most of them had never seen a live cow or chicken. We opened our children's zoo and dubbed it the "Baby-Pet Zoo," for reasons explained elsewhere. A small fee of admission was charged. That generated revenue, but the new facility also induced families to pay their way into the main zoo so their youngsters could have the fun of being right with the animals. The installation was an instant success, and the children's zoo is still thriving to this day, even though it was rebuilt long ago and its name and policies were altered.

How extremely fortunate I was. I had thoroughly enjoyed an exciting, inspiring trip to a distant part of the world, and I came home with ideas for two major improvements that were to help enormously in getting the Philadelphia Zoo back on its financial feet. I am still proud to have been the catalyst, the one who pointed the way toward providing a strong, healthy flow of cash into a zoo that had been almost moribund during the Great Depression.

Chapter 14

Promoting the Zoo

The years immediately following my return from Europe were extremely busy ones. The Philadelphia Zoo's only hope for quickly obtaining badly needed money was to increase attendance. It was up to me to get all the publicity I could and to dream up ways of making the zoo a fun place to visit. Admission at the time was only a quarter for adults and a dime for children under 12. Nowadays that seems like very little, but a dollar went very much farther then than it does today. Also, with our own refreshment and souvenir stands in operation, there was more potential revenue for us than ever before. A family of four could easily spend five dollars, a respectable sum in those days when people were still feeling the effects of the Great Depression.

My first promotional effort was the children's zoo. There were no funds to construct one, so it was jerry-built by our own maintenance force, which included carpenters and other "mechanics." An open area southeast of the bird house was enclosed by an eight-foot board fence, and several small pens with low railings were provided inside to hold a sizable collection of lambs, calves, young goats, chickens, a turkey gobbler, and young wild animals born in the zoo that could be trusted with children. The object was to permit the youngsters not only to see them but also to pet as many as they wished. We named it, appropriately, we thought, the Baby-Pet Zoo.

A small hut was erected inside, near the entrance to the enclosure. Across its front was a broad opening surmounted by a conspicuous sign reading "Pet Bank." There, a child could borrow a small harmless animal to play with and caress, but it had to be returned to the attendants before the family left the area. The Bank's assets consisted of kittens, puppies, guinea pigs, white mice, and a few white rats. We had no way of monitoring the borrowers, but most of the animals were returned, although often with the comment, "I wish I could keep it." Our supply of white mice steadily dwindled, however, and we were forced to conclude that many of them were smuggled out in pockets, up juvenile sleeves, or perhaps even unknowingly in a mother's tote bag.

Ours was the first children's zoo in any major zoological garden in the United States, and it was an instant success. We charged a small fee to enter it, but the word-of-mouth publicity about its novelty and the joy it brought to the youngsters was an extremely valuable asset.

An unexpected dividend accrued as the result of a visit, unknown to us at the time, by J. David Stern, owner and publisher of the "Philadelphia Record." His was a crusading newspaper that had often taken us to task for our shortcomings, real or imagined. For example, when a popular animal died, even of old age, the question was asked, "Had we taken care of it properly?" The "Record" was quick to pounce on anything it could criticize. Mr. Stern had his grandson with him, and the little lad spent a magical hour in what must have seemed like a veritable fairyland as he petted the animals and made trips to the Bank. Grandpa was so charmed and impressed by the entire installation that the lead editorial in the next day's paper praised us to the sky. The "Record" never again complained about the zoo, and it became one of our staunchest allies.

The Baby-Pet Zoo was later expanded to accommodate three young chimpanzees that, with some help from two prominent board members, I talked Zoo Director Shelly into buying. I remembered how very popular young apes were in European zoos and how the superb chimpanzee show at the St. Louis Zoo had become world renowned.

Our pet zoo was doubled in size, and a roofed-over stage where the animals could play and perform was erected, and it was encased in open-mesh wire to a height of about eight feet. Along part of its rear side was a comfortable holding cage for the little anthropoids between shows. Opposite the stage the men built a grandstand accommodating about a 100 spectators.

John J. Regan took charge of the show. He was a remarkably talented keeper who had literally grown up in the zoo, beginning as a young pony boy. He had a way with animals, and he was the logical choice for showmaster. He worked out his own routines, two of which were to dress the chimps in children's clothing and help

The Pet Bank in the Children's Zoo. Philadelphia Zoo archives.

them ride tricycles, which they seemed to enjoy. After he had dressed one of the animals he would turn to the next, whereupon the first would start disrobing itself while the children in the grandstand screamed with delight.

One day, for newsreel purposes, John took two of the chimps outside their arena. Holding an active, wriggling chimpanzee is a trick in itself, let alone two, and, with the added chore thrown in of shutting and padlocking a door at the same time, John was flirting with disaster. He grabbed two chimpanzee hands, took care of the lock, and then discovered that he was holding *one* animal by both hands. The other, racing with the peculiar four-legged shuffle characteristic of chimpanzees, was headed for the boundary fence. One of the keepers and I caught the runaway just as it was vaulting over.

Lew Lehr, master comic of the old Fox Movietone News, who was famous for his "Monkeys is the Cwaziest Peoples," really capitalized on our chimps. Among other things, they launched a Victory Ship (actually a rowboat) on our bird lake during the time the United States was catching up for its lack of preparedness for World War II; they built a house with bricks and "mortar" (the latter was whipped cream); and they appeared in countless movie theaters across the land. The Philadelphia Zoo was finally getting on the map!

The Baby-Pet Zoo thrived for many years. Eventually, much to our dismay, older children began borrowing animals apparently for the sole purpose of mauling them and tossing them around. So the Pet Bank was closed. In time, the wooden structure of the entire ensemble deteriorated and was abandoned. It had served its purpose well, however, and was the first of a trio of activities that helped to bring crowds of visitors into the zoo.

Philadelphia is a northern city, and that meant the zoo had only a seven-month busy season, extending from April to October. As might be expected, our biggest days were Sundays and holidays. During the colder part of the year, visitors were few, and it was important to rekindle interest with an annual spring barrage of zoo stories and activities.

The idea for my second promotion actually originated with a group of socialites (ladies whose names were in the "Philadelphia Social Register"). They wanted to raise money for one of the local hospitals. An enthusiastic committee presented its plan to the largely socialite Board of Directors of the Zoological Society of Philadelphia. They proposed to stimulate public interest sufficiently to attract a large crowd on the first Sunday of May, in exchange for a percentage of the gate receipts. That year the first Sunday happened to be May 1, so they suggested the title "May Day at the Zoo." Their worthy cause was approved, and the women began a month-long series of stunts and activities into which they entered with vigor. The committee, like so many others that are long on enthusiasm and short on attention to details, sent news releases to the papers that failed to contain all the Ws or the H. The men at the various city desks telephoned me to ask, as they put it, "What the hell's going on?" I had to plead ignorance. The women's committee didn't even know I existed. It was an awkward situation until I hunted up and consulted with the chairlady and explained the rudiments to her.

They didn't lack for whacky ideas, the most harebrained of which consisted of delivering a monkey to the zoo in a special way. One of the ladies came to the zoo and picked up a small shipping box in which we had placed a tame monkey. She then drove it to a nearby seaplane base, where her husband (I presume it was he) put the box aboard, took off, and glided his small floatplane into the Schuylkill River just east of the zoo. There was no Expressway in those days. He landed near the Girard Avenue Bridge and taxied toward shore, and one of our men waded out to retrieve the box and monkey. News photographers were on hand, of course. The pilot was visibly nervous, and he kept looking up and down West River Drive for a possible police or park guard patrol car. Frankly, I couldn't understand his anxiety. He allowed the press to take pictures of his plane near shore, and they obviously would soon be in the papers. It was strictly illegal to land in the Schuylkill except in dire emergencies. Oarsmen practiced there, and college and amateur scull races occurred almost daily in good weather.

I helped all I could with the May Day promotion, chiefly by providing spot announcements and even giving short talks for the many radio stations in the metropolitan area. I also pitched in to supervise whenever animals were involved. Nonetheless, it was the ladies who put over the affair, although they had an unexpected lucky break. The Baby-Pet Zoo was scheduled to make its debut on the very same day. I wondered at the time how much additional money they made for the hospital because the public had that extra inducement to attract them to the Zoological Garden.

One socialite family must have owned stock in Fox Movietone News, because they were able to pry Lew Lehr loose from New York. He made a brief public appearance before retreating to a private room in the zoo to slake his thirst and regale an all-male audience, of which I was one, with a succession of off-color stories, all told in his inimitable quasi-Pennsylvania Dutch accent.

The weather that Sunday was perfect, and we had a paid-admission crowd of nearly 20,000, probably the largest ever at the zoo in a single day. (A possible exception might have been during the spring or summer of 1876 when the Centennial Exhibition, with its great crowds of people, was held almost directly across the street from the then-infant zoo.) The ladies made their money for the hospital and they'd had their fun, but nothing was said about a repeat performance. Their whopping success made me resolve to keep May Day at the Zoo as a continuing promotion. For seven additional years it became my self-imposed assignment to have a bang-up program on the first Sunday in May.

The second May Day at the Zoo was comparatively easy. It coincided with the third of our early promotions, the opening of the monkey island (more about which later). At my suggestion, Zoo Director Shelly got in touch with Frank Buck, whose book, "Bring 'Em Back Alive," became such a hit that it catapulted him into the popular conception that he was the greatest and most skilled animal catcher and shipper who ever lived. No matter that he more properly deserved the name of Frank "Bunk." His notoriety was nationwide, and he proved to be a good attraction for the zoo. He made a personal appearance wearing a white pith helmet—the symbol, in the average person's mind, of an explorer. A large crowd, surrounding the monkey island and occupying the upward slope southeast of it, watched as he pulled a rope that lifted a trapdoor on the floor of the island. Out poured 30 frisky rhesus monkeys, which soon were climbing on the ropes and rings provided for them. The crowd roared and laughed, and we knew we had another hit.

I had been warned that Frank Buck was not a good speaker, so I invited Leroy Miller, the early-morning star and comedian of radio station KYW, to participate. Shelly introduced Buck, who, after pulling the rope and

mumbling a few sentences, retired for the day. Leroy Miller took over and kept the spectators entertained with humorous comments about the cavorting monkeys that were broadcast over loudspeakers we had erected in the trees surrounding the island. The Baby-Pet Zoo was reopened for the season, and we had another record crowd, well exceeding that of the first May Day.

Subsequent May Days were more difficult, and we found ourselves working harder and harder beating the drums of advance publicity. We had posters printed, and we distributed them ourselves for use in store windows all over the city and its suburbs. We gave each store owner two free zoo tickets in exchange. We delivered thousands of small fliers to hotels, restaurants, and other gathering places. I obtained permission to have a huge banner stretched across Broad Street, a couple of blocks south of City Hall, that no one, in that very busy area, could possibly miss seeing. All the radio stations gave us free time, and I was hard-pressed preparing scripts to be read on the air.

The first May Day at the Zoo had included a photo contest with prizes for the best pictures taken at the zoo. We followed suit, and we also, with the blessing of the School District of Philadelphia, initiated an annual poster contest months ahead of time in which students in art classes vied with one another for cash prizes. The winning poster was used as the logo for all our advertising and promotional material. One year, Strawbridge and Clothier, a leading Philadelphia department store, sponsored the poster contest, and, through a friend, I was extremely fortunate in getting Benny Goodman, the ace clarinetist and band leader, to present the prizes to the poster winner and runners-up. I suggested that it would be great publicity for the store to have the ceremony on its premises. That idea was quashed instantly. Benny Goodman was then at the height of his popularity, and the young people mobbed him just as they did Frank Sinatra, Elvis Presley, the Beatles, and other musical idols in later years. I was told they would make a shambles of the store. So the presentation took place in one of the large office suites above the Earle Theater, where Benny's musical organization was playing something like four or five big-band jazz concerts to packed houses every day. Present were just the three winners, their parents and teachers, a representative of the School District, press photographers, a couple of burly policemen, Benny Goodman, and yours truly. For me, it was a thrill to talk with the famed band leader who had risen from poverty to the very top of his profession.

We worked like dogs getting out the advance publicity year after year, and during every March and April,

Isabelle with one of the stars of the Children's Zoo in 1943 or 1944. She was totally unafraid of the animals, but was cautious near dangerous ones. Frequently she took the cameras of timid news photographers to make close-ups for them, thus earning their respect and gratitude. Philadelphia Zoo archives.

and sometimes into May, we were at it seven days a week. I use the plural pronoun "we" because I had acquired a small staff.

The first to join me, originally as a volunteer, was Mark Mooney, Jr., a prince of a guy who was also a good photographer. He produced many a picture that was used for promotional purposes or in our own publications. The zoo had no darkroom, so he developed his negatives and prints at home at night on his dining-room table, with the room's single window covered with a blanket to keep out the light. We became close friends, and remained so until his death many years ago. Mark brought Phil Edwards into the organization, and the three of us did most of the work. A woman who kept track of the Zoological Society's financial investments could also type, and she became my part-time secretary.

After a few May Days and numerous other activities that involved hard work, Phil Edwards made the mistake of asking Zoo Director Shelly for a raise without consulting with me first. As I easily could have anticipated, he was turned down flat. So Phil quit. That was bad enough, but what was worse, he talked Mark Mooney into leaving with him. I was suddenly in a real picklement, to use a bit of slang. Fortunately, Nigel O'Conner Wolff was working as a temporary keeper in the monkey house. He was several cuts above his fellow workers, and he had a broad knowledge of animals. I drafted Nigel, with Shelly's approval, and he became an able assistant. But I badly needed a photographer, especially since, by that time, we had inaugurated our zoo magazine, "Fauna," and pictures were essential for it and many other reasons. Albert F. Hallowell, who occupied a lowly post in a bank, made many splendid zoo pictures

over a period of several years and had served as chairman of the judges of the annual photo contest. He agreed to take the job, especially since the salary had been raised. After Mark and Phil left, Shelly realized he had been too conservative. Another case of "locking the barn door after the horses ran away." Hallowell did well at first, but having to take pictures on assignment was not for him. He wanted to pick and choose his own subjects. So he walked out without notice a few months later. I passed the word around that we needed a successor, and I had about a dozen applicants. I interviewed them all and examined their portfolios, and I soon narrowed the field down to two: Sam Dunton and Isabelle dePeyster Hunt. Both had excellent qualifications.

By that time we had entered World War II, and many things had changed. What would happen to me? Because of my crippled hand (see "Snakebite!") I felt sure I would not be drafted for combat, but I could be assigned to a desk job to help the war effort. So I chose Isabelle, who, as a woman, was not subject to the draft and could carry on in my absence. Besides, she had been serving as the business manager of the Staten Island Zoo in New York, and she had an excellent background in zoo work. She got off to a poor start, however. Because she was a woman, she was not qualified, in Shelly's opinion, to earn the same wage as that paid to a man for comparable work. He cut the salary, and she nearly left before she started. I talked her into staying, or so I thought. I later discovered that her real reason for taking the job was her desire to escape from an exceedingly nasty, humiliating marriage on her native Staten Island. She went to work with a will and quickly became my "Girl Friday." By that time the new service building

new young stock each year. Adult male rhesus monkeys are fearsome, dangerous brutes, as many a misguided pet owner has discovered much too late.

Leroy Miller became a fixture at the opening program each year. Once, I pulled the rope and he appeared through the trapdoor dressed in a gorilla costume, much to the amusement of the children. Another fixture from the second May Day onward was the Girard College Band, whose music and uniforms added to the color and sense of excitement that prevailed on the big day. The Philadelphia Rapid Transit Company, whose Route 15 ran along Girard Avenue, provided two empty trolley cars for transportation in each direction. They stopped at the College entrance at Corinthian Avenue

had been erected, and it had a small darkroom. That was before anyone except Shelly had air conditioning, and in hot, humid weather it was difficult to work there. No matter. She managed, and very capably. Sam Dunton, my other finalist, became the photographer at the Bronx Zoo in New York. I was never drafted for anything, but I did my bit by serving with the Volunteer Port Security Force of the U.S. Coast Guard for two years.

I promised to write more about the monkey island, or the monkey mountain, as we sometimes called it. Federal funds were used to erect it by the WPA, CWA, FERA, or whatever other government relief agency was then in vogue. (Al Smith, the prominent New York politician and aspirant to the White House, referred to such combinations of letters as "alphabet soup.") There was no architect. I solicited photographs of monkey islands in other cities, and I had assembled numerous dimensions from the same sources. I drew several sketches for the foreman of the work gang, and a draftsman prepared working drawings. The result was a satisfactory and highly useful new exhibit. It consisted of a raised pile of rocks firmly cemented together, and it was replete with ropes, slides, a seesaw, and other apparatus on which the monkeys could entertain the public with their antics. It was surrounded by a water-filled moat. The monkeys could swim in it if they liked, but the outer wall was too sheer for them to climb from the water. It was completely barless, and visitors sometimes stood by the hour watching the monkeys in action. They were all males. Sex was a taboo subject at that time, and we were instructed to expose the public to it as little as possible.

Each October we caught the animals, sold them to a dealer, and then started with a fresh troop the following spring. Rhesus monkeys were then much in demand for medical research. Disposing of them annually saved us from having to provide winter quarters, and we had

while the boys piled aboard with all their instruments, ranging from piccolos to tubas and bass drums. At the zoo they moved by twos and threes to the concert area. We had long since learned that a marching group of any kind greatly disturbed some of the animals.

Several celebrities participated over the years. Lowell Thomas, the great explorer and news commentator, was one. Dainty, petite, and always charming Osa Johnson, who had spent years in Africa with her late husband filming wildlife, came twice, several years apart. During one of the war years Lucy Monroe, the "Star Spangled Banner Girl," sang for us.

We had several themes. One was an exceptionally good African village constructed under the watchful guidance of Warren Buck. He was no relation to Frank Buck, but he was a legitimate animal collector who traveled from Camden, New Jersey, every year to West Africa to return by ship with a deckload of animals, ranging from baboons and chimpanzees to small birds and snakes. He also imported crateloads of native artifacts, many of which he lent to us for the African village. Robert Riggs, the famous lithographer, also let us use a few African specialities from his extensive private collection. Through a theatrical agency we hired three talented black men who played native African instruments and dressed as tribesmen. They added a lively touch to the village.

During one of the war years we used the theme "Weapons of the Wild," and featured animal horns, a prominently displayed but descented skunk, and such well-protected animals as armadillos and turtles. Veterans of former wars let us borrow their mementos, and we had a fine display of swords and bayonets, shell casings, and even a wooden propeller from a World War I biplane. There also were patriotic posters from several wars. If you have been wondering why we worked

seven-day weeks, just imagine the logistics of assembling all those things and then getting them back to their respective owners.

The last May Day at the Zoo was the most troublesome and chaotic, but nonetheless the most successful of them all. It had been years since Frank Buck had been with us, but his notoriety was as much alive as ever. At my request, Shelly reached him by telephone, and he agreed to make another personal appearance. We also scheduled a demonstration by a tame eagle, named Águila, that Dan and Jule Mannix, good friends of mine and the zoo's, had trained in Mexico, and thus its Spanish name. Dan was in uniform somewhere in Washington, so it fell to me to hold the short straps (jesses) attached to the eagle's legs on my stoutly gloved hand, my arm supported by a wooden strut that pressed against my hip. We chose the spacious outdoor elephant house yard, around which a great many people could gather to watch. I was at one end and tiny Jule Mannix was at the other holding a lure and a piece of meat in her gloved hand. At the given signal I released the big bird

and it flew directly to Jule as planned, despite the large crowd and all the noise that could have distracted it.

That part of the show worked perfectly, but Frank Buck failed to appear. Two or three days earlier he sent a telegram to Shelly stating he had accepted a paid lecture engagement on the West Coast and could not come to Philadelphia. Nothing daunted, I enlisted the help of Warren Buck, who appeared in the traditional white pith helmet. There were mighty few people, outside of the zoo staff, who knew the difference! Shelly suggested the ultimate slap in the face for the no-show, telling me to "lay it on thick" when I did it. I made up a parcel to mail to Frank Buck that included a picture of the huge banner across South Broad Street bearing his name and copies of all the promotional material, including many radio scripts. It was quite an impressive package, and my covering letter stressed the (exaggerated) fact that we had printed hundreds of thousands of posters and fliers with his name on them, as witness the enclosed samples. Several months later I had a letter from him stating that he guessed he should have been with us instead of on the West Coast. Later he was seriously injured in a taxi smashup. He never fully recovered. His career was over, and he died at a relatively early age.

That May Day at the Zoo, Sunday, May 6, 1945, was the last. We drew an enormous crowd of almost 40,000, and the zoo's 42 acres were packed with people from one end to the other. In the interest of public safety, we

Carmichael, the polar bear, developed a routine for splashing zoo visitors on warm summer afternoons. Once wet, the innocent victims stepped back until others took their places, and then guffawed loudly when Carmichael scored again. Isabelle recorded the action with her one-shot still camera. The pictures were taken on different mornings in 1943 before visitors arrived. A keeper whom Carmichael disliked served as bait. Philadelphia Zoo archives.

had to deemphasize and spread the May Day activities over the several weekends of the entire month. We retained the annual monkey island opening for the first Sunday, however, and Leroy Miller and eventually other entertainers from radio, and later from television, became our celebrities for the day. In the meantime, we kept up the drumbeat of publicity.

In retrospect, and in the light of present-day zoo policies, our early promotions seem amateurish and frenetic, but they paid off handsomely. We garnered much badly needed revenue, and, even more important, the general public knew that the zoo was alive, healthy, and prospering. It became the goal of a great many families to visit at least once a year. Such ample encouragement permitted the Board of Directors of the Zoological Society to use its endowment funds to begin rebuilding. Until we were positive that we had wide public support, the money accruing from the invested funds was needed to keep the zoo afloat. Without such income the Philadelphia Zoo might have sunk into oblivion during the Great Depression.

Chapter 15

The Monkeys Invade West Philadelphia

Our third May Day at the Zoo (1940) was just over. We had reopened the Baby-Pet Zoo and released a new batch of 30 rhesus monkeys onto the island. Osa Johnson was our distinguished guest, and we had enjoyed chatting with her about the years when she and her late husband, Martin, made an extraordinary collection of black-and-white motion-picture films in Africa while the so-called big game animals were still present in great abundance.

I was sitting at my desk late that Monday morning going over the small mountain of paperwork that had accumulated during our preoccupation with the May Day promotional activities. I was trying my best to set priorities for tackling it when the telephone rang. A voice said, "This is the 'Evening Bulletin.' We hear a couple of monkeys are loose near 34th Street and Mantua Avenue. Are they yours?" My response was that, insofar as I knew, they weren't.

Scarcely had I replaced the telephone when it rang again. That time it was the "Public Ledger," and the alleged number of monkeys had increased to five. Before I could get out of the office to investigate, all of our daily newspapers had called. The tabloid "Daily News" was the last, and, by that time, the estimated number of monkeys was said to be a 100.

I hastened to the monkey island, where nothing seemed amiss. Many monkeys were in evidence, at least on my side of the "mountain" of rock that rose on the island's center. The only difference was that the moat had been drained because the visitors the previous day had made a "cesspool" of it with their trash and garbage. Keepers were just arriving to clean up the mess. I kept on going, exited through the zoo's south gate, and walked onward, crossing the bridge over the railroad tracks and heading for Mantua Avenue.

I found myself in the midst of chaos. Traffic was snarled in all directions. The police and fire departments had been summoned, and long ladders led up to the roofs of several houses along the streets. Amateur "Frank Bucks" were chasing monkeys across the rooftops. One animal, hotly pursued, jumped from the top of a two-story building to the concrete sidewalk below. When it

landed it merely shook itself and dashed down an alley. It was too much for a lady spectator, however. She fainted and collapsed into the gutter. She told us later she thought the little animal had killed itself.

I used a pay telephone at a corner store to summon help. Soon several keepers arrived, each carrying a stout hoop net that looked like a crabbing or fishing net, but was much stronger in every respect. Then the chase began in earnest. The men quickly caught one monkey and took it back to the island, where they released it. The rascal immediately demonstrated how it and many of its mates had escaped. The moat was still empty of water, and the monkey jumped up to an overflow drain, secured a seemingly impossible toehold, and then leaped to the rim of the barrier moat wall. It was loose again! After showing us what had happened, the animal made a beeline back to the scene of the excitement, scaling the zoo's perimeter fence with ease. Keepers were alerted to keep an eye on the remaining monkeys while they cleaned up the mess of paper, remains of picnic lunches, banana skins, hats, and other debris that the callous, thoughtless visitors had dropped into the water of the moat.

Fifteen monkeys had escaped, and it was a wonder that the entire 30 weren't scampering over rooftops. We tried our best to dissuade the amateur hunters, pointing out that monkeys could bite fiercely. Our words fell on deaf ears. Meanwhile, a large crowd had gathered, and it was augmented by the many children from the nearby Morton McMichael School who had been dismissed for the noon recess. Scarcely any of them went back for the afternoon session. They were having too much fun watching the chase.

The monkeys were adept at eluding the amateurs, and even the keepers had to work hard to round them up. One of them thrust out his net when an animal leaped down from a roof, and deftly caught it in midair. Another monkey peered into a window where a lady was taking a bath. She screamed. Still another took refuge in a delicatessen and was caught behind a pickle barrel.

So it went, in and out of houses and stores, across rooftops, monkeys shinnying up downspouts, and so on.

In pursuit of the runaway. Photo by Jack Snyder, Philadelphia Record, 1945. Philadelphia Zoo archives.

There was only one casualty, a totally unnecessary one and completely the fault of the amateurs. Several of them closed in on a monkey from several sides and it tried to escape into a chimney. It fell in and, judging from the fumes escaping from the top, was quickly suffocated.

The press was out in force, as were the newsreel and syndicate cameramen. The affair pushed Adolf Hitler completely off the front pages of the two evening papers. At the time, his *panzer* (armored) units were making an end run through the Low Countries—Belgium and the Netherlands—to avoid the supposedly impregnable Maginot Line that paralleled the French border with Germany. The monkey escapade provided comic relief during an exceedingly tense and worrisome time. It was preceded and followed by banner newspaper headlines proclaiming the astounding speed and destructiveness of the Nazi advance.

The zoo's maintenance men fashioned downward-slanting guards for all the overflow drains along the inner side of the moat, thus foiling future escapes via the same route. Nevertheless, whenever the moat needed to be drained and cleaned thereafter, enough men were on hand to keep an eye on the simians.

A few years later we had another mass escape, and again it was on a Monday immediately after "opening day." A small grandstand had been erected for a handful of VIPs, and our men disassembled it and piled up the planks for a truck to haul away. Mischievous boys, we assumed (there were no witnesses), tossed two of the

planks into the moat, and the monkeys used them as boats from which they could spring upward to the lip of the moat. Nineteen of them were gone by the time the prank was discovered.

That time, instead of staying more or less together in a troop, they scattered and moved across 34th Street to the trees between it and West River Drive. There was no Schuylkill Expressway in those days. Trying to chase them in such an arboreal habitat was hopeless. Box traps were baited and set, and four of the runaways were caught within a few hours, but otherwise we bided our time. Hunger came to our rescue. One by one the monkeys returned to the zoo looking for food, and there they were caught, some of them with ease. We even had an unconfirmed report that a visitor saw one jump voluntarily into the moat and swim to the island. Counting the active, often scampering animals accurately was almost impossible, but we later discovered that there were two holdouts. One was reported on the roof of a house not far from where the great monkey chase had occurred a few years previously.

West Philadelphia houses, like those in much of the city, were massed cheek-by-jowl in long rows, with a common wall between all adjacent ones. All had flat, slag roofs, and in sultry weather they were unbelievably hot. I know, because I lived in one of them when I was a young boy. There was, however, a crawl space between the second-floor ceiling and the roof, and a trapdoor could be propped partway open to vent some of the heat. A few residents opened theirs in spring and didn't close them until autumn.

Three experienced keepers were dispatched to the scene and, with the aid of police and some of the residents of the block, were given access to the roof where the monkey had been seen. Indeed, there it was. They approached it slowly, but when they drew close, it ducked through the only open trapdoor in the row of houses and disappeared. The smallest, youngest member of the keeper trio volunteered to go after it. He wore heavy gloves, and enough light filtered in so that he could keep his quarry in sight. Suddenly the ceiling gave way with a crash, and he and the monkey fell through to the room below, fortunately landing on a bed. Not so lucky was a girl in her late teens who was asleep on an adjacent bed. The sudden crash scared her half to death.

Catching the monkey was easy. The zoo had to pay for repairs to the house, much to the justified annoyance of our always cash-conscious Zoo Director Shelly. He persuaded the owners to sign a release absolving the zoo from any further liability.

The other holdout monkey managed to cross the Schuylkill River, probably by walking across the Spring

Garden Street bridge. It was discovered, of all places, on George Washington's hat, high up on the great equestrian statue of our first president that stands at the head of the Benjamin Franklin Parkway in front of the Philadelphia Museum of Art. The fire department erected ladders, and the press made pictures as firemen and keepers clambered around while the monkey ducked and dodged to avoid them. Jack Snyder's photograph of the runaway high up on the statue was reproduced in the "Philadelphia Record" the next morning, and the paper let us borrow a print to use in our zoo magazine, "Fauna." Because it was nearly exhausted from being chased, the monkey sat down to rest, and it was caught by a passerby who, miraculously, was not bitten.

As for the zoo staff, by that time we'd had enough monkey business to last us a lifetime.

Chapter 16

The Renaissance of the Philadelphia Zoo

If it had been up to me, I doubtless would have chosen a glamorous new animal building as the first step in our rebuilding program. Our old structures were in deplorable condition. Most of them had been erected in the 1870s. The woodwork was rotting, the plumbing was corroding, and they were horribly outmoded.

Take the lion house, for example. It was near the zoo's main entrance, and almost all visitors entered it first. In summer, with all the doors and windows wide open and the animals outside, it was tolerable. In cooler weather, however, the stench inside was almost unbearable. Many visitors turned right around and exited faster than they entered. Others held their noses. It wasn't for lack of care. John MacMullen, the lion house keeper, spent 52 years, before his retirement, washing and cleaning daily. The trouble was with the building's design. The floor of each cage was of hardwood slanted slightly to the rear, where a narrow slot, only a few inches wide, ran the full width of the cage. John, standing in front of each, used his hose to wash all the animal excrement to the back, where it dropped through the slot and cascaded onto the basement floor. Urine, under the influence of gravity, followed the same route. Once he had hosed out the row of cages, he had to descend to the basement, scoop up the mess with a shovel, deposit it in a bucket, and then hose down the concrete floor. In the meantime, the slots above him were still dripping. All day long, whenever one of the great cats defecated, John had to repeat the procedure. I spent an hour or so with John MacMullen early one wintry day soon after my return to Philadelphia, and I watched the entire performance, even down in the basement.

Surely a moron designed that old lion house. How John could stand it, day after day, was beyond comprehension, especially since there were no ventilating fans. The floorboards, over the decades, had become saturated, and they still smelled bad at close range many years later, long after the big cats were moved out. The last use of that ancient structure, before the rare mammal house was built on the same site, was in its central area,

where there was room to stage a series of zoo television broadcasts.

The elephant house wasn't much better, but I had to admit years afterward, when its new replacement had long been in operation, that the the big pachyderms—elephants, hippos, and rhinos—had strong and penetrating body and dung odors. On wintry days, when visitors dropped into my office, I could always tell when they had been to the elephant house. Their overcoats would be saturated with a smell that took quite awhile to dissipate. John King, the keeper, put the matter into sharp focus with his favorite story. He enjoyed surf fishing, and, in summer, he often took the train to the New Jersey coast on his day off. One time, when he was homeward bound, another passenger sat next to him, and a few minutes later asked John if he noticed the strange odor that permeated through their part of the railroad coach. John's reply was laconic. "I'm what you smell," he said. "I'm the keeper in the elephant house at the zoo."

Zoo Director Freeman M. Shelly decided, and convinced the Board of Directors, that a new service building should be built first. It would replace the motley assortment of run-down wooden structures where the food for the animals was prepared and tools and supplies were dispensed. He was right. It was a wise choice to put the very "heart" of the zoo in order first. So the renaissance began with the erection of the workaday service building. There, into one central location, were funneled most of the vital activities that our zoo needed to function and to grow and prosper. Deliveries of supplies, preparation of food for transport to the many scattered animal exhibits, carpenter and print shops, garages, a lunchroom for employees, and other activities were all assembled in a double-winged building.

I had little to do with the planning of the new structure, although I offered suggestions when asked, including a request for a darkroom somewhere in the ensemble. Shelly kept things to himself, and he completely surprised me by announcing, when the new complex was ready for occupancy, that I and my staff were to move into a suite of rooms on the second floor. Included were a spacious office and a private one for me, from which a small, but adequate, darkroom opened directly. What a relief to escape from the tiny, cramped quarters in the reptile house!

Wilson Catherwood, a member of the Board of Directors of the Zoological Society, willed a substantial fortune to the Society, upon his death in the 1920s, for the express purpose of making improvements in the zoo. His money was a godsend during the Great Depression. The sum was large enough so that the interest from its investment kept things going through a succession of difficult years. Finally, after we had turned the corner, so to speak, and our cash flow from admissions and sales of refreshments and souvenirs was bringing money steadily into the zoo, the Catherwood Fund was tapped to pay for the service building and also for the erection of a modern elephant house. There was even enough left over for a complete remodeling of the bird house a few years later.

We broke ground for the new elephant house in 1940 and Osa Johnson, who had traveled so widely in Africa, laid the cornerstone while she was our guest of honor during the annual May Day at the Zoo. The building, which opened a year later, featured free-sight exhibits both indoors and out. The only visible bars fronted the two indoor elephant pens and parts of the doors used by the keepers to enter the enclosures from a long work passage in the rear. There were spacious outdoor yards that included swimming pools, and the building was well illuminated by natural light. It was enthusiastically accepted by the public as a major improvement. There were large ventilating fans, but we refrained from using them in cold weather to conserve heat. Thus the accumulation of odors, but that was at a time of year when we had only a scattering of visitors.

On April 16, 1941, the zoo gates were kept closed for the first time in 67 years (except for winter holidays) while the largest animals in the zoo's collection were transferred from the old building to the new. We feared that curious visitors might interfere with the keepers' activities or endanger themselves by attempting to get close to the action.

A runway more than 100 yards long, built with strong wire on each side and heavily buttressed, was erected between the two buildings. At about the halfway point and again near the new structure, heavy wooden gates were installed, that could be closed after each animal had passed, effectively preventing it from trying to return in the direction from which it had come.

Pete, the three-ton hippopotamus, was the first to make the trek. After almost an hour, during which he

The elephant house, opened in 1941, was the first major new building in the Philadelphia Zoo in 25 years. Photo by IHC, Philadelphia Zoo archives.

spent most of the time stopping to look over the situation, interspersed with half-hearted charges aimed at the keepers trying to herd him along, he finally entered his quarters in the new house. Peggy, the big Indian rhino, followed, and drove her human escorts over the fence twice when she lunged at them. News photographers on stepladders along the route recorded the action. Burma, the baby elephant, marched smartly along, surrounded by a cordon of keepers. She marched as smartly back again when we discovered that she could get her head through the bars of the keepers' door at the rear of her pen. She returned later after suitable temporary adjustments had been made. Least trouble of all was Jimmy, the young hippo, who kept moving, slowly but steadily. Once inside his new home he made up for his good behavior by putting on a determined but futile effort to get out. The smaller animals, a tapir and a pygmy hippo, were crated and trucked to the new building.

Gentle, obedient, and tractable Josephine was moved last. She was a forest elephant, a smaller, more slender animal than the great pachyderms of the plains and more open woodlands of Africa. She had been sold to the Philadelphia Zoo many years previously as a "pygmy" elephant. Like a youngster growing up, her height was measured annually, and her steady growth proved once and for all that "pygmy" elephants were a myth, or perhaps only the invention of an animal dealer as an excuse to increase the selling price.

In previous years Josephine had provided some 175,000 youngsters (a few with their parents) with the thrill of riding on her back as she walked slowly around a small track, led by Pat Cronin, the veteran elephant house keeper. After paying a small fee, the children climbed up one of a pair of stairs between which

Frederick A. Ulmer, Jr., with a mother hedgehog and her young. He brought them to us from the London Zoo when he returned from Europe after World War II. Ulmer later (1947) became Curator of Mammals. Philadelphia Zoo archives.

Josephine stood while her passengers, about four on either side, took seats on a stout wooden saddle that was held in place by broad straps extending beneath her belly. The riding area was a relatively long way from the old elephant house, and Pat and Josephine walked it each way, halting frequently to let people pat her trunk and legs. They also invariably stopped at a refreshment stand where a treat of stale bread or buns, or sometimes cookies, awaited her going in each direction.

During their walks, Pat used an ankus, an elephant goad developed in India to aid the mahouts as they worked the great beasts when piling logs or doing other tasks requiring great strength. An ankus is made of sturdy steel tipped with a sharp point and bearing a hook at one side. It is attached to a stout stick, whose length depends on the height of the animal involved. Our ankus was blunted, and it was used only on Josephine and young elephants when they first arrived at the zoo. Pat placed the hook of the tool over the front upper corner of one of Josephine's ears where it met her skull. It rested gently in place, but, by manipulating it, he could have her walk straight ahead with him or turn left or right as required.

We anticipated that Josephine would be the easiest of all the animals to move to the new house, and she, therefore, was the last to go. Pat used his ankus, as usual, and together they walked down the long runway. They passed through the gate that provided service trucks with access to the outdoor elephant yard, and crossed that open space. All seemed well until they reached the entrance to Josephine's new home. There she balked and refused to enter. Food and treats were brought, but to no avail. Pat had to lead her back to her

old quarters. It was the same the next day and the next.

Because demolition of the old structure had already begun, the maintenance men built a wire corral in the new elephant yard, and Josephine spent both days and nights in it. The door to the building was wide open and so was the gate into the elephant pen, but she refused to enter. Keepers placed her food inside. When she was hungry she stepped in, then quickly backed out with hay or vegetables clutched in her trunk. She ate in the corral. The food was moved farther and farther inside as the days passed, but she continued to back out with it despite the longer distances. That went on for weeks, and someone offered the opinion that it might take all summer to get her established in her new home. It almost did.

The night watchmen regularly passed through the new building, flashed a light into the empty cage, and then stepped outside through the visitors' entrance. The service truck gate was opened when the zoo closed each day, so the men could walk to the corral to check on Josephine. Usually she was just standing quietly or munching hay. One dark night in August the watchman followed his usual routine, but, when he reached the outdoor pen, Josephine had vanished. A quick inspection showed she had pushed down part of the wire fence. He hastened to the telephone to summon help, and eventually reached Pat Cronin and head keeper Charles Campbell, both of whom rushed to the zoo in taxis. Neither owned a car. Together the two men, armed with flashlights and an ankus, went exploring in the dark. Josephine was somewhere in the zoo, but where?

Pat had a hunch. They went to the site of the old riding ring, and there she was, calmly eating small branches of leaves that she had pulled from nearby trees. Pat used his ankus in the usual fashion and marched Josephine back to the shattered corral and, wonder of wonders, onward into the new building and then her new pen. Charley closed the big gate behind her. They were astounded, to say the least.

The next morning we discovered marks made by Josephine's tusks where she had tried to push open the refreshment stand door through which she had been handed goodies during previous years. From there she had evidently moved on to her old workplace. Josephine apparently needed to have one final fling before she gave in and did what we wanted her to do.

The pachyderm collection was gradually enlarged, and Jimmy sired a number of young hippos after we obtained a mate for him. When a new Indian rhino came several years later, Norman Hess, an outstanding keeper, showed me a trick that I should have had enough sense to figure out for myself. Wild rhinos have a habit of depositing their fecal matter in specific places to which they may return repeatedly. When the new one arrived and had been introduced into its quarters, Norman went to the empty shipping crate, scooped up all the manure from its floor with a shovel, and put it in the pen immediately adjacent to the keepers' service door at the rear of the enclosure. It worked perfectly. Following an olfactory inspection, the big animal used the same spot and did so regularly thereafter. The keepers were able to clean with ease instead of having to venture inside with a potentially dangerous animal.

I thought at once of our earlier problem with Josephine. We should have carried some of her excrement to her new pen, thus giving her a sense of self and a feeling of being at home. How prone we are to forget that the sense of smell is of great importance to so many animals.

After the completion of the new elephant house and the boost in zoo attendance it engendered, there was a long interruption in the building program. World War II with its priorities, shortages of materials, and reduced civilian manpower put a stop to any new construction. There were other major developments, however, especially in 1947, not too long after the war was over.

One day, just prior to a monthly meeting of the Zoological Society's Board of Directors, which I routinely attended, Shelly took me aside. I knew that something important was afoot because he sat me down on a park bench in the midst of the zoo instead of talking to me in his office or mine. He explained that I no longer would be curator of the zoo. Two new curators were being appointed, as would be announced at the Board meeting. John A. "Gus" Griswold, a noted aviculturalist, was joining the staff as Curator of Birds, and Frederick A. Ulmer, Jr., who was then one of my assistants, was being promoted to be Curator of Mammals. My title henceforth would be Curator of Reptiles and Public Relations. There would be no change in my salary.

Actually, I was relieved. I had been spreading myself far too thin, to use a hackneyed expression. Freedom from having to make routine inspections in various parts of the zoo and having to cope with new crises almost daily would permit me to concentrate on my "own" animals and to get on better with my job of promoting zoo attendance.

Also in 1947, there was a personal development of extreme importance to me. Let me quote, with minor emendations, from a farewell article I wrote for our newsletter, "America's First Zoo," shortly after I retired as Director of the Zoological Garden in 1973: "It turned out that the smartest move I made during my entire zoo career was to hire Isabelle dePeyster Hunt as the zoo photographer and my general assistant. After getting used to

John A. "Gus" Griswold feeding a macaw. He was a noted aviculturalist who was named Curator of Birds in 1947. Philadelphia Zoo archives.

each other's idiosyncrasies daily in the office, we decided we could make a go of it around the clock. We celebrated our twenty-fifth wedding anniversary last year."

Isabelle and I had both emerged from extremely difficult and traumatic previous marriages, and we were determined that ours would be enduring. It was. (See the chapters entitled "A Quarter Century in Paradise.")

The zoo rebuilding program resumed with the complete remodeling of the bird house and the construction of a brand-new lion house.

The bird house was the youngest major building in the zoo. It had been erected in 1916 with the welcome contributions of three wealthy ladies. When it was new, it probably was acclaimed as the best in the world, but it was dreadfully old-fashioned by the time Gus Griswold joined our staff. It reminded me of the bird houses I had seen in Europe before the war. There were dozens and dozens of small cages and an emphasis on exhibiting as many different species as possible. The flight cage in the center of the building was also overpopulated. The

The visitors' walkway through the hummingbird exhibit, opened in 1970. Photo by Franklin Williamson, Philadelphia Zoo archives.

south wing was an ear-splitting bedlam all day long. It was crowded with parrots that seemed never to stop squawking and screaming. It had long been zoo policy to accept any psittacine bird that had outworn its welcome in a private home, and we had acquired far too many of them.

Dr. Cadwalader, President of the Zoological Society, decreed that only the curator in charge should work with the architects, a policy that I soon managed to have changed. Several board members with whom I talked agreed that the curator who would preside over each new building should have the major say in its planning, but having the architects' drawings reviewed by several pairs of curatorial eyes could be a distinct asset. So, all three of us participated, and we each made helpful contributions.

Some of the birds were removed to our ancient parrot house, where macaws and cockatoos were kept. Others were sold or given to other zoos. The shell of the existing bird house was saved, and the walls of the wings were extended to provide additional space. Everything inside was removed.

Opening day was in May 1950, and the transformation was sensational. A feeling of freedom had been achieved. Bars and wire had been completely eliminated. Most of the birds were in spacious enclosures behind glass, but the central display that greeted visitors as they entered the building had only a low guardrail separating a spectacular free-flying avian group from the public. A 20-foot waterfall, a stream, a pond, and lush tropical vegetation provided a naturalistic habitat. Gus earned an abundance of compliments on the extraordinary changes that had been wrought, largely under his direction.

The carnivore house, which opened in April 1951, was a gift from the City of Philadelphia. A million dol-

lars was appropriated through a councilmanic loan and administered through the Fairmount Park Commission on whose land the zoo was situated. We had an evening preview, which was attended by several hundred members of the Zoological Society. Each of them and other VIPs received a handsome brochure about the new building. It also contained an even dozen splendid black-and-white portraits of the animals that my talented wife, with the help of the keepers, assembled as the many cats were introduced into their new quarters. The brochure also stated: "Our Mayor, the Honorable Bernard Samuel, announced on August 1, 1946, that funds were being set aside for the building's erection. For nearly three years thereafter the zoo's Board of Directors, the Zoo Staff, and the architects labored diligently to design the finest building of its kind in the world."

At the time, the new house doubtless qualified for that distinction, and our collection of cat animals, augmented by financial contributions from many members of the Zoological Society, was the most outstanding in America. Curator Fred Ulmer worked long and hard with the architects, and his broad knowledge of the mammals of the world, and his many careful inspections of zoos in the United States and England, paid off handsomely. He personally supervised the placing of the huge boulders in the outdoor grottoes for the lions and tigers. Gus and I made a few suggestions, but Fred Ulmer deserved the real credit for the staff's contribution.

Inflation after World War II made the million dollars inadequate to do everything as planned. The bids for construction came in too high. The Society used some of its own funds to complete the tiger grotto, but equipment for a quarantine room for medical check-ups, illnesses, and pregnancies had to be omitted. Also, the basement was unfinished. It would have held a number of animals, in season, which, because of their tropical origin, had to be taken indoors each winter.

The gift from the City was a milestone of the first magnitude. It marked the beginning of a massive capital improvement program that resulted in the almost complete replacement of the old antiquated buildings. Also, much-appreciated help from several private sources gave us a number of splendid new exhibits. The renaissance of the Philadelphia Zoological Garden was under way in earnest.

Dr. Cadwalader died in 1957, and Radcliffe Cheston, Jr., succeeded him as President of the Zoological Society. Mr. Cheston's chief concern was with the zoo's physical plant. Society funds for rebuilding had been exhausted, so he turned to the City. He visited everyone in municipal government who would lend a sympathetic ear, especially the President and Chairman of the Finance Committee of the City Council. Through his efforts, the City Administration, the City Council, the Commissioners of Fairmount Park, the City Planning Commission, and the Citizens' Council on City Planning unanimously agreed that the zoo was a major civic asset. It was well managed by the Zoological Society, the participation of which saved the City potentially large sums of money. In short, the zoo deserved the City's help, and a series of grants continued for many years, through the remainder of Freeman Shelly's directorship, through mine, and even beyond.

An order of priorities was established in 1959. First, the main entrance gates at Girard Avenue would be altered to permit a much more rapid flow of visitors as they paid their admission fees to the cashiers. The historic appearance of the buildings would be retained. Next would come the erection of a rare animal house, chiefly for anthropoids, on the site of the old lion house. New small mammal and reptile houses, retaining parts of the older structures but completely modernized, would follow. All were built in due course. Private funds were generously given for the Daniel W. Dietrich Memorial Children's Zoo, which opened in 1957; the unique Impala Fountain, a memorial to Herbert S. Morris (1964); and the Eleanor S. Gray Memorial Hummingbird Exhibit (1970). Also, many fine pieces of animal sculpture were placed on the zoo grounds, largely through the cooperation of the Fairmount Park Art Association, its members and donors.

After I took office as Director of the Philadelphia Zoo on January 1, 1967, I succeeded in getting the zoo board and city officials to change the order of priorities, moving a new administration building from near the bottom of the list, where Shelly had kept it, to the top. I did it for two reasons. First, we were crowded in the historic John Penn House, which had long served as the zoo's headquarters, and it needed major repairs. Late one summer day, during a violent thundershower, part of the roof caved in and the rain cascaded down the stairs to the first floor. Second, I had long wanted to establish an educational program. I had been doing all I could for many years, despite my crowded schedule, by talking about the zoo and its animals to schools, groups of visitors at the zoo, scout troops, service clubs, and so on. I felt it was time to raise education to its rightful level. My plan was to combine the two needs, and the Educational and Administration (Ed-Ad) Building, funded entirely by the City, was opened in 1972. The African Plains were well advanced when I retired in 1973.

Thus, the Philadelphia Zoological Garden, which had so badly deteriorated and almost ceased to operate during the Great Depression, once again ranked with the finest institutions of its kind in the nation—and the world. It gave me a great feeling of satisfaction to realize that I had been in on the renaissance from the very beginning and that I had had a small share, along with so many others, in bringing about a truly remarkable change.

Chapter 17

The Delmarva Peninsula

How different the Delmarva Peninsula was 60 years ago. Except for scattered towns and a few small cities, it was almost entirely rural and lightly populated by humankind. Also, the term "Delmarva" had not yet come into general use. Some of my more scholarly friends in the Wilmington area corrected me every time I mentioned it. They preferred to call the several states by name—Delaware, Maryland, and Virginia—or to use the term "Eastern Shore."

Delmarva was isolated in a very real sense. There was no way to get across Chesapeake Bay except by boat. North-and-south-trending roads gave access to the markets and activities in Wilmington and beyond, but toward the south there was no exit except to take the long ferryboat ride from Cape Charles to the Norfolk region. For anyone who was not in a hurry, such a trip was an enjoyable boon. One could drive his car or truck aboard, have a leisurely meal in the ship's dining salon, and then relax to enjoy the scenery. There were always other boats in sight, as well as sea birds of several kinds.

The Peninsula was a quiet, bucolic oasis along the bustling Atlantic seaboard, and life moved at a slow pace. The residents engaged chiefly in agriculture. There had been some lumbering, as was attested by the occasional abandoned sawdust piles we found while exploring the area, and which had been left in the wake of the itinerant sawmills of earlier years. The Great Cedar Swamp, along the southern border of Delaware, had long since been logged. What a vast wilderness it must have been in colonial days, when it consisted of Atlantic white-cedar (*Chamaecyparis*) and bald cypress (*Taxodium*) and occupied an estimated 50,000 acres. The forest was destroyed by a catastrophic fire in 1782 that raced through it after a succession of dry seasons, but much of the area was still swampy.

Those families who lived near the coasts, east or west, derived their livelihood from the water, the home of myriads of oysters, clams, crabs, fishes of various kinds, and even terrapins, although those turtles were far less in demand than they once had been.

In time the Chesapeake Bay Bridge was built, giving access from 1952 onward to the Atlantic seacoast for hordes of people seeking to escape from the sticky summer heat of the Baltimore-Washington megalopolis. Later, the over-and-under water engineering marvel was constructed, the Chesapeake Bay Bridge-Tunnel. It opened in 1964, and Delmarva immediately became a shortcut for avoiding the heavy traffic on the western shore. The great influx of people improved the economy of the region, but it destroyed the peace and quiet, and a lot of the wildlife suffered.

As a person who spent most of his life working in zoological gardens, loved animals, and was an avid herpetologist, the change was anything but welcome to me. Happily, most of my fieldwork on the Peninsula was done well before the advent of World War II, although it continued for a few years after gasoline rationing came to an end. How fortunate I was to have been there frequently and before the great transformation took place.

In 1935 I returned to Philadelphia and began to serve as curator of reptiles at the zoo after a six-year stint in the same capacity and, later, as general curator of the Toledo Zoo. While I was living in the Buckeye State, I did fieldwork in 87 of its 88 counties that eventually led to my "Reptiles of Ohio," which was first published in 1938. Now that I was in the East again, I made an occasional foray into the New Jersey Pine Barrens, but I missed getting into the field for a definite purpose. Carl F. Kauffeld, of the Staten Island Zoo, was then investigating the herpetofauna of the Pine Barrens.

I soon discovered, however, that little work had been done on the Delmarva Peninsula. Witmer Stone, Henry W. Fowler, and Emmett Reid Dunn, all associated with the Academy of Natural Sciences in Philadelphia, had published short papers on specimens collected on the Peninsula, but no study in depth had ever been attempted. Here was a challenge for me. I thoroughly enjoyed being in the field far away from the noise, fumes, bustle, and crowds that characterize cities, but I wanted to do something worthwhile, herpetologically speaking. Documenting the occurrence of the various species, making distribution maps, and preserving voucher specimens would all add to our knowledge of the amphibians and reptiles of the area. I began to make plans for a general survey of Delmarva.

An early decision was to place the northern edge of my study area along the Pennsylvania state line, thus including all of Delaware and the eastern segment of Maryland to the Susquehanna River and Chesapeake Bay. The two Virginia counties were, of course, far to the south. A better and physiographic boundary might have been the Fall Line, but that passed right through the city of Wilmington, just as it does through many other eastern cities and towns. The Fall Line (actually a narrow zone), which is little known to most people nowadays, aside from historians and geologists, marks the outer boundary of the Piedmont Plateau where the streams flowing to the sea accelerate as they leave the hard rocks and cut into the softer strata of the Coastal Plain. In colonial days, the rapidly moving water provided power for grist and other mills, and early settlers tended to cluster near where their grain could be ground. Towns and eventually cities developed on the sites, especially if there were port facilities nearby. Trenton, Philadelphia, Wilmington, Baltimore, Washington, Richmond, and many other smaller cities are all on or close to the Fall Line.

A brief look at a road map indicated that the shortest route to the Peninsula from Philadelphia's western suburbs, where I lived, was through Chester, Marcus Hook, and Wilmington. I tried it only once. The traffic was horrendous even in the 1930s. There were no by-passes, and driving through those cities was at a crawl, with stops at virtually every corner. After a few exploratory attempts, I discovered a way around Wilmington to the west, using rural roads, and thereby cutting the time of passage by at least an hour. Time was precious, because all I could manage at first were one-day trips. Members of the Junior Zoological Society, friends, and zoo staff members, and often my young son, Skip, accompanied me, so we went on Saturdays when there was no school. All Philadelphia Zoo personnel, except Director Shelly, worked a six-day week, but I was permitted to swap my usual Friday off for Saturday so I could be in the field. We would start, whenever possible, on Friday evenings after dinner, drive 100 miles or more, and stop frequently, especially in the spring, to hear and to sample the huge frog choruses. We would then camp out or sleep in my ancient Chevrolet, and work northward the following day to get home Saturday night. The longer distances far down the Peninsula were too much for one-day trips, and had to be reserved for vacation periods or when I had an extra day coming to me for having worked on my usual day off. Cape Charles, near the

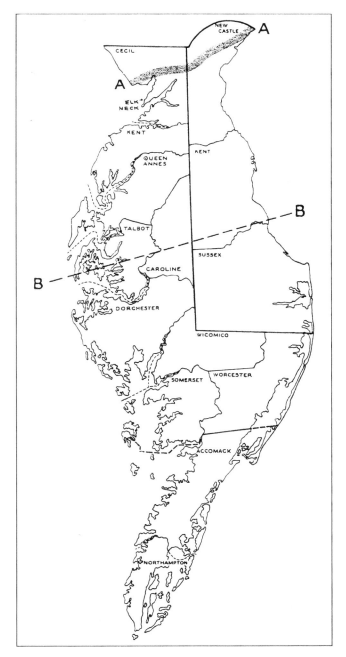

The Delmarva Peninsula, consisting of Delaware and the Eastern Shore counties of Maryland and Virginia. The dotted area (A-A) represents the Fall Line zone separating the coastal plain from the piedmont in the two northernmost counties. The line (B-B) indicates the former northern limit of pure stands of loblolly pine. Both lines influence the distribution of some of the native reptiles and amphibians. Map by Edmond V. Malnate.

southern tip of the Peninsula, was well over 200 miles from the Philadelphia area. At least a two-day trip was necessary to reach the Virginia counties, work in them, and then get back at a reasonable time on Sundays.

Just as I had done when I first began the survey of the reptiles of Ohio, I sought to learn everything I could about the area where I planned to work. The botanists had long been active on the Delmarva Peninsula, and two of them, the highly conservative Frank Morton Jones and Robert R. Tatnall, were leading spirits in the Society of Natural History of Delaware. I looked them up in Wilmington. They were polite, but I had a sneaking suspicion that they considered me as little more than a youthful upstart, until I showed them a copy of my "Reptiles of Ohio." That broke the ice, so to speak, and I was invited to give a lecture on herps at a regular public meeting of the Society. Several years later, in 1945, the Delaware Society printed my "An Annotated Check List of the Amphibians and Reptiles of the Del-Mar-Va Peninsula," which is now thoroughly outdated. They forced me to use hyphens for Delmarva, a term they were not yet willing to accept. Nor would they permit me to credit the map on the inside front cover (reproduced here) to my close friend and colleague, Edmond V. Malnate, who had drafted it with great care. They even balked at putting his initials under the map itself. We let Dr. Tatnall use the same base map in his lengthy and scholarly "Flora of Delaware and the Eastern Shore," which was published in 1946, but no credit was given to either of us. It was against their editorial policy, I assume, to let readers know who executed illustrations. By the time I gave my last lecture to the same Society, about our African trip in 1968, the arch-conservatism had disappeared.

It was obvious from the very start that there were only two physiographic provinces involved. Most of Delmarva is part of the Atlantic Coastal Plain, but the northernmost portions of both Cecil County, Maryland, and New Castle County, Delaware, are in the Piedmont. The narrow Fall Line zone separates the two. Such species as the long-tailed salamander, the slimy salamander, and the northern copperhead were restricted to suitable habitats in the Piedmont and along the adjacent Fall Line zone. Other species occurred only in the Coastal Plain. Still others were widespread and they turned up more or less throughout the entire region. We made the interesting discovery that the Elk Neck promontory that extends roughly southwest between the Elk and Northeast Rivers, and which is rocky in part, supported at least small populations of herps that otherwise were restricted to the Piedmont. Elk Neck also had strong populations of Coastal Plain species. Like the area along the Fall Line zone, Elk Neck was the home of a mixture.

A surprise that came into focus after I began plotting localities on distribution maps was another "boundary line" that appeared on no map I could ever find. In Sussex County, Delaware, and the adjacent Maryland counties to the west, the soil is sandy, a mixture of sand and other components, and it differs from the soils farther north. A number of species occurred in suitable habitats from Sussex County southward that appeared to be totally absent from the areas farther north. Included among them were the carpenter frog, the corn snake, and the red-bellied water snake.

I never did find a satisfactory explanation for the "barrier" across the center of the Peninsula. I discussed it with my friends in Wilmington, and Dr. Tatnall suggested that it more or less coincided with the northern limit of pure stands of the loblolly pine, *Pinus taeda*, as he had observed them during his many years of botanizing up and down the Peninsula. The loblollies appeared to do well in the sandy soil, so the "boundary" may have been of edaphic (soil-related) origin. Nonetheless, I showed the "boundary" on my map of the region.

A later discovery was that the American toad, which was abundant in the Piedmont and also occurred on Elk Neck, was missing altogether from the northern part of the Coastal Plain. Yet it reappeared south of the "barrier." It was the same with the copperhead. That venomous snake was in the Piedmont and along the Fall Line and, like the toad, it skipped the upper part of the Peninsula, but was present from southern Sussex County to and through the Virginia counties. The only difference was that, whereas the copperheads in the north were identifiable as *Agkistrodon contortrix mokasen*, those in the south belonged to the widely distributed intergrading population designated *Agkistrodon contortrix contortrix* X *mokasen*. But I was not to learn that until many decades later when I became deeply immersed in the study of the genus *Agkistrodon* (written by Howard K. Gloyd and Conant, and published in 1990).

Our first forays to Delmarva were short one-day trips west and north of Wilmington and to the vicinity of the Conowingo Dam, a huge hydroelectric impoundment not far from the mouth of the Susquehanna River. Just south of the dam, paralleling the river and easily accessible by road, we found a series of swampy areas that, over the years, through our own work and that of others, yielded many interesting species, including all three of the eastern turtles of the genus *Clemmys*. Of these, the wood turtle was confined to the Piedmont and Elk Neck, and the bog turtle was similarly distributed, although it turned up much later well down in New Castle County. The spotted turtle occurred all over the Peninsula, and we found it to be relatively abundant in virtually all suitable habitats. The map turtle was more or less restricted to the Susquehanna, but it also occurred along the Northeast River on Elk Neck.

I have enough interesting information about the herps of Delmarva to fill dozens of pages, but space will not permit. So I must generalize and restrict myself to some of the more important observations and events.

One of my overall memories of our fieldwork in the region was the sheer abundance of so many species. On rainy spring nights many of the frog choruses were so enormous and so deafening that one species could not be distinguished from another by ear. Sometimes there were so many frogs and toads migrating across the paved roads to the nearby breeding ponds and swales that we had to stop the car and shoo them out of the way. There were a few DORs (the designation for specimens found "dead on the road" where cars had run over them), but the traffic was so light that the attrition on the populations was negligible.

Snakes were also abundant, and it was not unusual to see large ones crossing the road in spring or autumn, even in broad daylight. One day, near Machipongo in the more southern of the two Virginia counties, Phil Edwards, a member of the zoo staff, was relieving me at the steering wheel of my car. He had never been on a field trip, and, as we found out, he went along just out of curiosity. He was driving slowly along when a large black rat snake started across the road. Both Ed Malnate, who was with us, and I saw it and yelled, "Stop!" Phil didn't see it, paid no attention to our loud voices, and, of course, ran over and killed it. I had to pickle it with formalin, using a hypodermic needle and syringe, as I did with every other DOR reptile or amphibian that was salvageable for a study specimen. I hope I can be forgiven for thinking, for an instant, about how suitable it would be to jab Phil with the needle. If he had not run over the snake it would have gone back with us for the Philadelphia Zoo's reptile house.

On that same trip, at about 10:00 P.M., as we were looking for frogs by flashlight, we discovered another large black rat snake climbing up a tall stump amidst masses of poison ivy. That one we didn't try to catch.

Because I wanted voucher specimens of frogs from different localities, and the easiest way to preserve them was at my home base later, I needed some way to distinguish where they were caught. As we moved from pond to pond, we would put a few specimens, often of different species, into a thoroughly wet collecting bag, add a handful of sodden moss or vegetable debris, and then toss in a paper note with the locality written on it. That led to problems, because the paper might be almost illegible the next morning. So I acquired a series of bronze identification tags. Each was an inch in diameter, stamped with one of the letters of the alphabet, and punched with a small hole that permitted it to be strung

RC preserving a kingsnake found dead on the road in southern Delaware on May 2, 1936. Photo by Mark Mooney, Jr.

on a small dispenser. Such tags were impervious to frog excrement and assorted debris. We would drop the "G" tag, for example, into a bag with the frogs and write the collecting data opposite "G" in a notebook.

My first deep penetration down the Peninsula, on May 2 and 3, 1936, was a memorable one. I had recently become the volunteer godfather of the Junior Zoological Society of Philadelphia, and two of the most active members participated. One was William F. "Bucky" Reeves, who eventually earned my admiration by pulling himself up from poverty to become a professional lecturer on natural history. Every Saturday he and one or two of his friends hitchhiked from distant Riverside, New Jersey, to attend the Junior Society's meetings at the zoo. The other was James "Jimmy" Emlen, then perhaps 12 years of age and a member of a prominent Quaker family. Jimmy's father, George Emlen, offered to drive us down and back and to camp out overnight. He said we should fill his car, so Mark Mooney, Jr., was invited to go along. He was then the zoo's unsalaried photographer, and through his enterprise I have a series of pictorial mementos of the trip. One includes a picture of me on my knees in the dirt pickling a DOR kingsnake.

By a stroke of good luck we explored and collected near Millsboro, Delaware, a highly productive area to which I was to return again and again as a promising stop on longer trips. South of that town was a vast swampy region that surely had been part of the site of the Great Cedar Swamp before the catastrophic conflagration of the late eighteenth century, and subsequent and repeated burns as growth was renewed. Nearby were deep woods, swamps, abandoned sawdust piles, and rustic trails leading back into prime herp habitat.

Evidently the owner resented frogs being gigged from his private pond, but he was a little awkward as a sign painter. Near Hallowood, Virginia, May 20, 1940. Photo by Edward Deal, Jr.

We caught several snakes on our 1936 trip, including three black racers, one of which I ran down personally with my hip boots flapping as I went. We had a splendid time, and I developed a warm friendship with the Emlens.

The Millsboro area yielded two amphibians of special interest. During that first excursion, Bucky Reeves and I waded into a prairielike swamp about five miles south of town. The swamp was roughly square and about a fourth of a mile across. It contained an abundance of sphagnum and clumps of cattails, and rotting logs were scattered on the surface. A brief shower stimulated a chorus of carpenter frogs, and we collected a few, the first ever recorded from the Delmarva Peninsula.

Almost exactly six years later, Nigel Wolff, of the zoo staff, and I spent an hour in the same swamp. We separated, and I turned over innumerable small flat mats of sphagnum lying on the decaying logs or on clumps of fairly firm mud around the perimeter of the swamp. I finally caught up with Nigel, and he asked, "What are you looking for?" I explained that four-toed salamanders sometimes could be found under flat mats of sphagnum. With that he reached down right where he

stood and scooped up a handful of moss and turned it over. "Is this it?" he asked. Sure enough, he had one. Ironically, it was the only four-toed salamander we ever found in the area, despite repeated visits.

During my youth, I had spent four summers serving as a counselor at a Boy Scout camp along the broad, estuarial part of the Metedeconk River in the New Jersey Pine Barrens. Along the shoreline were thick masses of floating vegetation, which accumulated in every cove or small indentation. They formed hiding places for seemingly countless water snakes, many of them in excess of three feet in length. By stalking and then patiently waiting for a head to protrude, I became adept at catching them, but almost every time I was bitten, sometimes severely. Later I began experimenting with a new technique. After grabbing a large snake by the body, I would sling it between my legs, with its head facing to the back. My heavy dungarees protected me from attacks from the rear. I would slowly draw the snake forward, tail first, through my hand until I felt the taper to the snake's head. I then grasped it by the neck, and I eventually became so proficient that I caught large snakes of several species with nary a bite.

I guess I was a born teacher, because I was always showing my young companions all sorts of things about reptiles and amphibians—where to look for them, how to handle them, and so on. One warm evening in southern Delaware we overturned a wide piece of board and beneath it was a large kingsnake. I waved back the three teenagers and my young son, Skip, and told them I would demonstrate how to catch it without being bitten. I grabbed the snake, tossed it between my legs, and began my well-practiced routine. The snake did not cooperate, however. Instead, it thrust its head back through my legs, seized my thumb in its mouth and started chewing, bringing blood repeatedly. The lad who laughed the loudest and longest was my son. And to think that I had caught many a kingsnake simply by picking it up and having it behave at once like a thoroughly tame snake that was used to being handled!

Edward Deal, Jr., was one of a succession of printers at the Philadelphia Zoo. His job was to set the type for the copy I gave him, print it on waterproof cardboard, dunk it into a preservative, and then erect the finished sign in front of the animal it described. Eddie was a city boy who had never been in the country. He heard so much about our fieldwork from the Junior Society members that he asked me, timidly, if he could go along on a trip. Talking to me about such a great favor was an ordeal for Eddie. He stuttered, and his affliction was magnified whenever he was under stress or excited. Things worked out so that he and I went down together for two days. From his reactions and enthusiasm it was quickly obvious he was having the great adventure of his life. He was then in his early 20s. He was overwhelmed by the frog choruses, especially since he had never heard a frog make a noise. He reveled in the sights and sounds and smells of rural Delmarva. He marveled as he saw me pick up a live snake from the road. But the climax did not come until the second day.

We were near Locustville on May 20, 1940, in the upper of the two Virginia counties. We had separated for some reason, but I was well within earshot. Suddenly I heard a gurgling sound punctuated by brief yells. Eddie was calling to me as best he could, but his stuttering had increased to the point that I could not make out a word. I hurried toward the noise, found him in a cold sweat, almost bug-eyed, and pointing to a large hognose snake, perhaps 10 feet from him, that was hissing and going through its amazing act. I moved in close and motioned for him to do likewise so he could watch. Presently the snake opened its mouth, began to writhe, and then turned belly up. After it was completely inert and, to all appearances dead, I turned it over with a stick and explained what was going on. I was able to show Eddie that the snake deliberately turned on its back time after time. I could not really blame him for being scared. He knew nothing about *Heterodon*, and the performance can be frightening for almost any layman. I'll admit that even I, after many years of experience, gave a start whenever I heard the first loud hiss of a hognose snake, just as I invariably did whenever a covey of quail suddenly exploded into flight virtually at my feet.

It didn't take me long to find the Rodney Boy Scout Camp on Elk Neck. It was named for Cecil Rodney who, although he was sick at the time, rode horseback to Philadelphia as fast as he could to deliver the papers that made Delaware the first state to ratify the Constitution. The camp and I immediately became mutually helpful. Scores of youthful eyes watched for species I particularly wanted from the Neck, and once or twice each camping season I would give an evening lecture on herps, using live animals from the zoo's collection. Somewhat later I discovered the Horseshoe Scout Reservation on the Mason-Dixon Line where Octoraro Creek makes a great horseshoe-shaped bend. Still later I found other camps well down on the Peninsula, but my lecturing was confined to the two northern ones. Even they were too far from home to drive back late at night and be ready for work early the next morning. After the first time or two I took blankets along and slept on a camp cot. The counselors were very helpful, as were many other persons all over Delmarva who saved specimens for me or gave me reports about unusual species they observed.

We worked hard on Delmarva, mostly in the spring and autumn when herps were most apt to be in the open or under shelters we could overturn. We crisscrossed the Peninsula, searched through or around seemingly innumerable ponds, swamps, and woodlots, and felt we were learning much about the overall distribution and abundance of the reptiles and amphibians of the region. But we also wanted to explore some of the offshore islands that extended from the attenuated Assateague, off the coast of Maryland and adjacent Virginia, all the way to Smith Island near the tip of the Peninsula. Only Chincoteague Island was accessible by car. We worked there, but we looked longingly at the other islands from the mainland shore. Visits to them had to wait. We were suddenly at war, and gasoline rationing precluded further forays down the Peninsula.

After serving for two years with the Volunteer Port Security Force of the U.S. Coast Guard, it was only natural for me to turn to the regular Coast Guard for help in reaching the islands. I knew they had stations scattered along the coast and boats for overwater transportation. So I wrote to them in Washington, explained my research project, and asked for assistance. After what seemed like endless red tape, I learned that it was up to the petty officer in charge of each post to decide whether he had the time and manpower to devote to such extracurricular activities as mine. Eventually they gave me the name of Chief John T. Mapp at Wachapreague. I had an encouraging response from him, a date was set, and, in the spring of 1947, in the company of Frederick A. Ulmer, Jr., Robert G. Hudson, and Robert Reeves, I spent several days on Parramore and Hog Islands. We stayed at the Coast Guard station on Parramore and wandered all over that rather large island. It was heavily wooded in part, with fresh- and brackish-water swales and ponds here and there. Our turtle traps yielded a surprisingly large number of snappers. Mud turtles were also common, but the only snakes we found, virtually all of them under boards or other debris, were rough green snakes (*Opheodrys aestivus*) and brown snakes (*Storeria dekayi*).

Hog Island, to which coastguardsmen took us by boat for a day, showed the devastating effects of hurricanes and erosion. A town of 100 or so residents had existed on it for nearly two centuries, but half the seaward side of the island was now underwater, and the breakers had reached the lighthouse, which had been erected half a mile from the beach. The human residents had long since departed. We found more brown snakes, and I uncovered a clutch of green snake eggs that apparently had hatched the previous season.

In October of the following year (1948), again through the courtesy of Chief Mapp, my wife and I visited the same two islands. Things on Parramore looked just about the same, but Hog Island had endured an almost total inundation on October 5. When we arrived there just two weeks later, salt water was standing everywhere except on the slightly higher ground. We found no herps, and all we could do was to take photographs of the destruction, the remains of the devastated old Coast Guard station, and dead trees, some topped with osprey nests. Subsequently we made a brief overnight visit to the small but active Coast Guard station on Smith Island, at the southern end of the chain of barrier islands. It, too, had been inundated by the recent high water, and the only herps we found were ground skinks (*Scincella*), although we saw several minks as well as skeins of geese, cormorants, and other waterfowl heading south, just as we had from Hog and Parramore.

I did not return to the islands again until 1975, when I took a trip to the East to see my elderly mother and other members of my family. James D. Anderson, of Rutgers University, with two of his students, Sally Litwin and Keith Hawthorne, drove us down the Peninsula from New Jersey to herpetological meetings at Williamsburg, Virginia. En route, Gerard J. "Rod" Hennessey, then head of The Virginia Coast Reserve Study, took us to Parramore, Hog, and Revel Islands. On the return trip James D. Lazell and I left Williamsburg early, and Rod boated us to Smith Island, where we found examples of a number of different species, including a kingsnake, black racers, and a snapping turtle. Jim Anderson picked me up later to go back to New Jersey. Things on the islands were quite different in several ways. For example, the vegetation on Hog Island was lush and thriving, and we watched diamondback terrapins laying eggs. Recovery there and on Smith Island had been remarkable during the intervening 27 years.

So, I finally had seen something of the islands which, in comparison with the mainland, have an impoverished fauna. Certain species had reached certain islands, in one way or another, and some of them were abundant in numbers of individuals. A review entitled "Barrier Island Herpetofauna" was published in 1990. Joseph C. Mitchell and Christopher A. Pague wrote most of it, but they insisted that my name be included as an author, inasmuch as I had pioneered the study, in a sense, so many years previously.

The trip down and back with Jim Anderson and the students was disheartening. The traffic was dreadful, even on roads paralleling the main highways. It was vastly different from what it had been before the Chesapeake Bay Bridge-Tunnel was opened. There were virtually no DORs of any kind, and I could not help but think how awful the carnage must have been when cars

and heavy trucks raced along the highways on the first warm, rainy nights as the frogs made their way to their traditional breeding ponds and swales. I could well remember some of the depressed acres that quickly filled with water and attracted earsplitting choruses. By 1975 they had been drained or filled to make room for more crops. Along much of the Peninsula it seemed as though there were wall-to-wall fields, to say nothing of the vast chicken farms that had hatched, forgive my pun, in many places. We hear and read so much nowadays about the sudden decline in amphibian populations. Not all of it can be blamed on air and water pollution. Destruction of habitats is surely a major factor in a great many parts of the world as the human population grows ever larger and requires greater quantities of food.

Our work on the Delmarva Peninsula spawned a number of short published contributions in herpetology, such as reporting species found in the area for the first recorded time, evidence of intergradation among ringneck snakes as well as among milk snakes, and lists for various purposes. Unfortunately, the major report on the area has not been finished. After 1948 my duties at the Philadelphia Zoo increased and, in 1951, work began on the meticulous and time-consuming text, illustrations, and maps for our "Field Guide to Reptiles and Amphibians." I had to put the Delmarva survey on hold, so to speak, but I picked up the threads again soon after my retirement and move to the Southwest in 1973. During a series of trips to the East to see my mother and others, I also managed to visit many museums, large and small, to examine their holdings of material from the Peninsula, New Jersey, and adjacent areas. Unexpected circumstances soon overtook me, however, and I was unable to press onward as anticipated. Now that I have been an octogenarian for several years, my chances of ever finishing the definitive report are tiny, at best. I still have all my records, a great bale of correspondence about the region, and a large number of ring binders filled with pertinent data and detailed notes, as well as a partially completed text. To save all this information from dying with me, I plan to make it available to trusted colleagues who can use it for their own research. How wonderful it would be if I could have another lifetime to finish all the projects that are well under way, partly executed, or in an advanced planning stage. I must say, however, that among them all, my early work between Chesapeake Bay and the Atlantic Ocean has left me with wonderful memories. What a marvelous place it was for reptiles and amphibians those many years ago!

There is another reason, cogent and highly personal, why I have happy memories of the Delmarva Peninsula. They concern Isabelle dePeyster Hunt, whom I had hired as the Philadelphia Zoo photographer and my assistant during 1942.

Because we had both suffered through disastrous previous marriages, Isabelle and I were drawn together. We consoled and advised each other. We found, over the years of our association at the zoo, that we worked well together. We made a good team. We came to depend on each other in many ways. Were we falling in love? Perhaps it was inevitable, but even before all the legal hurdles had been cleared with our respective erstwhile spouses, we decided we were meant for each other. Where should we be married when the time came?

I had taken Isabelle along with us once or twice on Delmarva trips so she could take pictures for use in our zoo magazine, "Fauna." I loved the quiet and the old-fashioned atmosphere of the Peninsula. She liked them too, and when I suggested Snow Hill, Maryland, as the place, she enthusiastically agreed. Maryland was then the Gretna Green of the Mid-Atlantic States where marriages were performed with a minimum of fuss and feathers. Neither of us wanted a formal wedding. The simpler the better.

So, with our good friend Robert G. "Bob" Hudson as chaperon, we drove down in late March of 1947 and obtained our marriage license without difficulty. We learned, however, that only a preacher could officiate at weddings in Maryland. A Justice of the Peace did not have that privilege. We had set April 10, 1947, for our wedding day, so while I was in the vicinity, I telephoned to make an appointment. I do not recall which denomination I called first, but I was immediately asked, "Have either of you been divorced?" When I replied that both of us had, the response was, "It is against the policy of my church to remarry anyone who has been divorced." I thanked him and tried the next one. The result was the same. I talked by telephone with gentlemen of the cloth who were Episcopalians, Lutherans, Methodists, Presbyterians, Unitarians, and so on, not only in Snow Hill but elsewhere in Worcester and Wicomico Counties. I think that was the lineup, but the answer was invariably the same. Finally, in despair, I blurted out, "How then does one get married in Maryland?" After a slight hesitation, a scornful voice said, "Maybe John Ditto will marry you," and the speaker cradled his phone. Inquiry revealed that the Reverend John Ditto was a Baptist minister in Pocomoke City, down near the Virginia line. I called him at once, and he had no compunctions about divorce. I told him we had our license and asked him what else I should bring. His laconic reply was, "Just the girl and a ring." I joyfully thanked him, and we arranged for the ceremony to take place at his home between 2:00 and 3:00 P.M. on April 10.

Isabelle dePeyster Hunt prior to our marriage in 1947. Photo by her brother, Livingston Sloan Hunt.

So Snow Hill was out, but perhaps we could stay there on our wedding night. There was a small old-fashioned place, the Outen Hotel, in what was then a quiet little town, and it had a spotless dining room, excellent food, and a polished staff of white-coated black waiters. The atmosphere was much like other restaurants of the Old South I had visited. Maryland had been a slave state before the Civil War, but it remained loyal to the Union. During our early fieldwork on the Peninsula, long before Isabelle arrived at the zoo, we would occasionally see a restroom at a service station or elsewhere that had not yet been painted out, and which read "Whites Only."

Young people of today have no conception whatsoever of the difficulties which existed until relatively recently. The sexual revolution was still far in the future when Isabelle and I were married. Fornication is commonplace nowadays, and few people pay attention to it unless there is a pregnancy. Not too long ago, however, being caught sleeping with a woman, other than one's wife, was a serious matter, a felony in some states. Laws were strict and penalties could be severe. We had to be very circumspect, and that is why we asked Bob Hudson to be our chaperon when we drove down to get our marriage license. He and I occupied the same room and Isabelle was by herself in the hotel where we stayed while we were en route to Snow Hill. When Isabelle and I traveled south on April 9, however, we stopped at the old Centreville Hotel, and that night we decided to take a chance and save the price of an extra room. I registered us as "Mr. and Mrs." After all, I had our license in my pocket, and a phone call to the Reverend Mr. Ditto would confirm our appointment with him on the morrow, just in case someone asked. No one did. After all, we were not a pair of eloping kids. I was 38, and Isabelle was a few years older.

Because we had ample time to reach Pocomoke City on the tenth and we were both inveterate naturalists, we decided to take both field and dress clothes with us. We drove south in the morning and stopped at Wye Mills to see and photograph the enormous, very old, and historic white oak tree. We continued through Easton and Cambridge and then to the Gum Swamp, a small sphagnum bog near the Blackwater Wildlife Refuge. There we were astounded to hear the unmistakable mating call of the carpenter frog, *Rana virgatipes*, which never previously had been recorded from Maryland. There were several males in the chorus. It was with real eagerness that I donned my old clothes, pulled up my boots, and waded into the bog. As soon as I did, the frogs became silent, but eventually I sighted my quarry. When I moved to within grabbing distance, however, they all vanished into the moss. Based on past experience I stood stock still, and, presently, a head popped up above the surface. The behavior was exactly the same as I had witnessed and exploited many times while showing visiting herpetologists carpenter frogs in the New Jersey Pine Barrens. I quickly caught two specimens, which are now in the collection of the American Museum of Natural History, and which formed the basis for a short published note that appeared later the same year in "Maryland, A Journal of Natural History." Ever afterward Isabelle teased me by saying that I always remembered our anniversary date because of the frogs.

After wandering around in the bog for a short time, and seeing a number of other herps, I changed back into my "civvies," as we called civilian clothes in those days. We drove to Salisbury, where we had lunch and I bought an orchid for my sweetheart. (She later pressed it, and it still remains in our "wedding book" after all the many intervening years.)

Finding the Reverend Mr. Ditto's house in Pocomoke City was easy. He was ready and waiting for us. He was the only witness. He read the text for the marriage ceremony, told me to put the ring on Isabelle's finger, and then to kiss her. I gave him the twenty-dollar bill he requested, and that was that. Ten minutes at the most. It was the start of an extraordinarily happy partnership that lasted "until death do us part."

After offering our thanks to Rev. Ditto we drove to Snow Hill. It was a heady ride, not only because we had just been married, but also because we were driving my brand-new Oldsmobile sedan. It was one of the first to come off the line after the long hiatus during and after World War II when new cars were virtually impossible to get. We stopped to admire the bald cypresses and other vegetation of the Pocomoke River basin, and to do a little smooching.

At Snow Hill we received an unexpected shock, but which was followed by a touching gesture of great kindness. I had carefully prepared for our wedding in advance but I had not made hotel reservations. Surely it would not be crowded in early April. It was full! No vacancies. What was worse, the lovely old dining room was closed. There had been recent labor troubles caused by agitators from the North. A union? The employees went on strike, and Mr. Outen, the owner-manager, decided to abandon his marginally profitable food service and concentrate on the hotel business. After all, he owned a diner right next to the hotel, and his guests could eat there. He was at the desk in person, and when he noted our obvious great disappointment and looked at Isabelle's orchid, and I told him we had just been married, he took pity on us. His home, almost an antebellum mansion, was right across the street. He escorted us there, showed us into a beautifully furnished guest room with a private bath, and told us it was ours for the night—for free! Perhaps he was impressed by our radiant but dignified appearance. No matter what his reasoning was, he provided us with a splendid bridal suite for the night. We had to eat our wedding supper, however, while seated on stools along the counter of the diner. We were too happy to care.

Mr. Outen trusted us, who were two complete strangers, and gave us a key to his beautiful home, which contained innumerable antiques and other treasures. How could anyone beat that for Southern hospitality!

We were soon to realize that we were pair-bonded in the true biological sense of that term. Our lives seemed suddenly to be all ahead of us. We were to be constant companions, lovers, and devoted pals for almost 30 years.

Chapter 18

The Mystery of the Black Racers

Every field-worker, regardless of his area of interest, can remember experiences that ended in frustration: the rare bird that flew off before getting a good look at it; the snake that got away, or the one that was run over and killed by the car just ahead. My cold-weather observations on the black racer, *Coluber constrictor constrictor,* seemed to offer an unusual opportunity for study, but I accomplished little, thanks to circumstances beyond my control. In short, I was annoyed. My finale with one of the snakes, however, was ludicrous, to say the least.

On February 18, 1948, as the Philadelphia Zoo's curator of reptiles, I received a call from a Chester J. McDonald who asked if I would like to have a black snake. I, of course, responded in the affirmative, and I agreed to meet him the next morning at the Sun Oil station at Ellisburg, New Jersey. There was no town to speak of in those days, only a cluster of small stores and houses, with open fields in almost all directions. Ellisburg was little more than a circle where two main highways intersected. It was convenient for me, however, because it was directly on the way from the city to Taunton Lake, in the Pine Barrens, where Isabelle and I had just bought a summer cottage.

The snake, which measured approximately 750 mm in total length, still retained slight traces of the spotted juvenile pattern. McDonald had found it out of hibernation shortly before he phoned, and said he had seen larger black snakes on both February 17 and 18. He offered to show us the place, which was perhaps a mile away, but Isabelle and I had an appointment with a workman who was helping us get our new home ready for occupancy. So we postponed an inspection of the site. I thanked McDonald, told him we could use more snakes, and gave him the customary pair of free passes to the zoo for his kindness.

March 12, a few weeks later, was a cold, blustery day with a severe wind chill, but we stopped on our way to Taunton. After receiving rather vague directions at the gas station, we eventually found where McDonald lived. It was east of the southwest-northeast-trending Kings Highway and was reached by a rough, rutted dirt lane that was probably impassable in rainy weather. The McDonalds were squatters living in an abandoned farmhouse in the midst of a rather low open area of poorly drained and abandoned fields. McDonald wasn't home, but his two teenaged boys, Bill and George, were there, and they had been saving snakes for me. There were eight of them, but the boys said they had frozen to death (the snakes, that is) in the empty parlor of their "home" during the previous night. I was shown the carcasses. Most had surely been dead much longer, because some of them were rather ripe from decay. I saved the best one to preserve as a voucher specimen. I suggested that they catch no others unless they were sure I would be able to take them off their hands promptly.

I asked the boys to show us the spot where they found the snakes. They had missed the school bus and were delighted with their unexpected holiday. So off we went on foot, but I was totally unprepared for the surprise awaiting me. Somewhat east of the McDonald house there was a ditch running roughly north and south. At the southern end of it, water welled up slowly from the openings of two terra-cotta pipes that were set below the surface of the water, and which obviously were intended to help drain the rather marshy adjacent terrain. The boys told me that the water ran continuously throughout the year, and that it never froze. When I asked them where they found the snakes, they said they were always in the water, and usually completely submerged! I could scarcely believe it, but, when we reached the end of the ditch, I was flabbergasted to see the head and neck of an adult racer protruding horizontally from the center of one of the drain tiles for a distance of perhaps four inches. The snout of the snake was held in a perfectly rigid position, and it was four or five inches beneath the surface of the water. I watched it for at least 15 minutes, and then I reached down and caught it. It was in excellent condition, and the following day at the zoo it appeared perfectly normal and active. The air temperature just a few inches above the water surface was 34°F, and the water temperature was 39°F. The boys told me they often saw snakes coming out of the tiles, and that others frequently were in the mud under the water flowing through the ditch.

Isabelle took a picture of the three of us (and the boys' dog) looking down into the pool, and another shot of one of the terra-cotta pipes. We went on our way, and immediately lamented that we didn't have a photograph of the snake emerging from the tile. To remedy that omission, we returned the next week, but no snakes were in sight, despite the warmer weather.

I was very curious about the underground hibernaculum. Was there an air pocket below the frost line where the snakes could overwinter? Did they use the tile line as a means of access to it? Could they possibly hibernate underwater? Did they lie in the water with an air space above them? Asa Pittman, the well-known snake man of the New Jersey Pine Barrens, had found many timber rattlesnakes hibernating together in soaking wet masses of sphagnum moss at Mount Misery many years previously.

How could I implement an investigation? There were many difficulties. The soil was frozen solid from the cold winter, so digging by hand was out of the question. Who owned the land, and would he permit an excavation? Time was also precious. Traditionally, our spring publicity blitz for the zoo began on Groundhog Day, February 2, and continued into May. Both Isabelle and I were deeply involved in that activity. We were so busy that, even by returning to the zoo at night, we could scarcely squeeze in our regular day off in order to work on our new home. We were very anxious to get away from our third-floor walk-up apartment near the zoo, which was in a steadily deteriorating neighborhood where several murders occurred within the first two years after we moved away.

Under the circumstances I had to put the racers and their winter quarters out of my mind. We could try again next year. We did, but when we visited the site on February 25, 1949, we found no racers, nor had the McDonald family seen any. Surely the boys would have noted them in the water if they had been there. Had something happened to the colony?

Exactly a year later, on February 25, 1950, I received a call in mid-afternoon from McDonald. He had 11 racers! I immediately left to meet him, and, with his help and that of his two sons, I sexed, measured, and marked the snakes for future identification. The last was done by clipping scales among the subcaudal scutes and recording the combinations for future identification. We used the tailgate of my station wagon as a table and, as we were working, the air temperature dropped from 36°F to 34°F. The snakes were cold and very sluggish. So were our hands after the half hour it took us to manipulate

the reptiles and record data. They ranged in total length from 870 mm to almost 1,400 mm, and all were males except the smallest. Three had incomplete tails.

After we finished, we carried the snakes to the spring around the drainpipes and put them in the water. They remained virtually inert at first, some of them upside down. Two, however, soon began to swim into a drain tile. Because the temperature was dropping, and so a raccoon or other predator wouldn't find and kill the snakes, we manipulated them all until their heads were aimed toward the tiles. All but one had "crawled" in out of sight before we left sometime about 5:00 P.M. The last one was partially concealed in mud and, presumably, it also made its way to safety. The water temperature was 41°F, and the air a few inches above the water surface was 34°F. On the way home to Taunton I listened to the radio and learned that the official low in the city was 29°F. The day had been partly cloudy and it felt really cold because of the wind chill. Why did the snakes elect to come out on that day, or had they been coming out for several days previously? McDonald had seen only two snakes. He caught one, but when he pulled the second one out of the water, it was entwined together with nine others!

My desire to get at the hibernaculum was greater than ever, but at least many of the racers were marked, and the boys would surely find some of them again. I eventually located a person who told me that ownership of the land was in litigation, but the area was destined to become a real estate development. He had no idea when, but he promised to keep me informed as things developed. I had visions of bulldozers working through the area, but perhaps I could persuade whoever was in charge to let us know in advance so that I could be present when and if they worked their way through the ditch and drain tiles.

March 31, 1951, was a clear, windy day, and I left the zoo at about four o'clock in order to stop and check on the black racer site on my way home. When I arrived at the entrance to the lane, however, I found posts and a barricade so that I could not drive in. It was just as well, because the lane was in horrible condition and was badly rutted from recent rains. I hiked down to the spring, noting, as I advanced, that the McDonald house and other buildings nearby had been vandalized. Boards and other parts of the structures had been ripped off, and obviously the place was abandoned. The McDonalds must have moved away. I never saw them again.

I examined the ditch. There were no snakes, but when I advanced to the head of it, the terra-cotta pipes were gone. Someone must have taken them, too. It seemed that it might be well for me to probe into one of the holes where the pipes had been, each of which was more or less accessible from the bank. So I removed my overcoat, suit coat, and wristwatch, and rolled up my right sleeve. It was necessary to lie flat on the ground, because the bank of the ditch was fairly steep. I probed into one of the holes with my right hand and felt something move. I reached a little further and touched the body of a snake. It tried to pull away, but I grasped it firmly. As I did so, I started to slide forward into the ditch headfirst. I spread my legs apart in a vain attempt to brake my descent, but I plunged all the way into the pool. I floundered out, thoroughly soaked from head to foot. At least I had caught the snake and, wonder of wonders, my hat had stayed on. I mopped up as best I could, bagged the racer, and put on my outer coat over my wet clothes. Then I hurried back to the car, a good half-mile away. The exercise of walking fast kept me fairly warm, and, as soon as I got into the car, I turned on the heater. I glanced into the mirror to see how much muck I had on my face and discovered that I didn't have my glasses. So I had to hike all the way back to the spring. Fortunately, they were there in plain sight. Apparently I had pulled them off my face after my bitterly cold plunge, without realizing what I had done. I had visions, on my squishy walk back to the spring, of perhaps having to probe for them in the mud. They might easily have fallen off when I slid in.

I was glad to get back to the car. The air temperature was not too bad (it registered 61°F on my thermometer), but the wind blowing on my wet clothes for the second time chilled me to the bone. The temperature of the water in the spring was 49°F.

The snake was not one of those I had marked. The next day I found that it was a male with a truncated tail. The head-body length was 1,016 mm, and the total length only about 1,100 mm. Enough of the tail remained so that any clipped subcaudal scutes would have been visible.

My hope of recovering some of the marked snakes was gone, at least insofar as help from the McDonalds was concerned. I made many telephone calls trying to learn what the plans were for the area, but I was unable to get any information. Not too long afterward the entire area was torn up for the erection of houses. Thus doubtlessly perished the colony of black racers. So also did my vague hope of having a look at their hibernaculum. How frustrating!

After my involuntary bath, I managed to stay relatively comfortable with the heater in the car going full blast, but it was a good half hour before I was home. Our garage was quite a long way from our cottage, so, between my wetness and the wind, which had turned cold, I was thoroughly chilled by the time I walked in the door. I must have looked terrible to Isabelle, but she had to wait for an explanation. I rushed to our tiny bathroom, peeled off my soggy clothes, dumped them on the floor, and then stepped into the stall shower to let the warm water refresh my body and my spirits. My dear wife brought me my bathrobe and slippers, and then we repaired to the living room couch. When she heard the full story we both laughed so hard we nearly had hysterics. The only good thing about my watery adventure was that I had the snake.

Chapter 19

Our First Long Trip to Mexico:
Part I. Monterrey and the Río Nazas

When I began to reminisce about our first excursion deep into Mexico, way back in 1949, a host of memories came to mind. Some were still crystal clear, whereas others, dimly recalled, leaped sharply into focus as I read Isabelle's detailed diary of our peregrinations, troubles, and triumphs. She kept a marvelous account, 189 pages in a five-by-eight-inch bound notebook crammed with information about all we saw and did during that autumn of 1949. What's more, her records of all the many trips we shared together during later years are a gold mine for me, an old-timer who marveled then, and even more so now, about her diligence and tenacity. How nostalgic they are for me. She omitted almost nothing except trivia and a few things that happened while I was alone, as when I was exploring rivers and swamps well away from our car.

As I contemplate our initial excursion far southward into a strange land, I cannot help but recall the many things we had to learn the hard way. How could we have been so naive as to expect to find motels or even hotels free from lice, fleas, and bedbugs in every town where we attempted to stay overnight?

Eating in most Mexican restaurants was fraught with danger. No matter how clean they looked, it was impossible to know how carefully the dishes were washed or whether some part of the meal included leftovers that had not been refrigerated properly in the warm (often hot) climate.

Boiling all our water for 10 minutes sounded simple enough, but it had to be done at night, so that our metal container could cool off while we slept. Also, it held several pots full of water, so even three took a minimum of a half hour. Many a time we returned late from the field only to face the midnight chore of getting out our gas-powered cookstove instead of falling into bed to rest our weary selves. Besides worrying about contaminated water we had a long list of foods we shouldn't eat, including dairy products of any kind.

Why did we try to see and do so much during the limited time at our disposal?

That question is easy to answer: we fully expected it might be our one and only visit to Mexico, and we wanted to accomplish all we could. Visiting the Río Nazas to look for water snakes was a must. The southernmost known locality for the west coast water snake was near Acapulco, and two Mexican subspecies of the diamond-backed water snake occurred along the Gulf Coast. We wanted to try our luck at catching some and at observing and photographing their habitats. Also, if we could possibly work it in, we wanted to see Parícutin, the volcano that was then in eruption. Those were our objectives, but we almost didn't go at all.

In 1949 I had been at the Philadelphia Zoo for 14 years and we were still working a six-day week. Isabelle, who was the official zoo photographer and my general assistant, and I had only Fridays off. Having to work on our days off was not unusual, partly because we were still slowly recovering from a zoo that was almost moribund during the Great Depression. I was in charge of publicity, and we needed every bit of it we could get, seven days a week. My boss, Zoo Director Freeman M. Shelly, was very good at saving dollars, even pennies, and I doubled in brass, so to speak, by being the zoo's public relations officer as well as its reptile curator. It was up to me to attract cash-paying visitors to the zoo. One way was through our annual Zoo Day, which was celebrated on the first Sunday in May, as explained in another chapter. We, meaning just Isabelle and I, but with all the help we could muster from other zoo employees and friends of the zoo in general, developed a special program with entertainment, a celebrity, and a deluge of publicity freely given by the newspapers and radio stations. We worked very hard, and it was normal for us to be at the zoo seven days a week all through March and April, as we sought to reawaken interest in the zoo after the long winter hiatus. We were paid no overtime, but we were allowed equal, or "comp," time, meaning that we could take off an equal number of days at a less hectic period of the year. In 1949 we each had eight comp days coming to us in addition to our two weeks of vacation. During the late summer I asked Shelly if we could possibly be away for an extra week, so we could have a month in the autumn to drive to Mexico and back, see something of that country, and do a little collecting. He knew of my interest in water snakes, but he refused to make the decision himself. He told me I'd have to get Dr. Cadwalader's permission.

Williams B. Cadwalader, M.D., was an elderly, dignified member of a socially prominent old Philadelphia family and President of the Zoological Society of Philadelphia. He maintained an office and a small practice. He was not noted for granting favors. I made an appointment to see him, took copies of my most recently published papers in herpetology with me, and reminded him about my "Reptiles of Ohio." I had given him a copy when it was published in 1938. He listened to my carefully rehearsed request, and then responded by saying, "Roger, if we let you and your wife do this, other persons on the zoo staff will want similar favors. We cannot let you go."

I felt crushed. It was my first request ever for time off, and both Isabelle and I had worked like dogs, to use an old cliché, for the good of the dear old zoo.

Much to my surprise, Dr. Cadwalader telephoned me the following morning and said we *could* be away for a month. I was truly astounded, and I thanked him profusely. I didn't learn the reason for his change of heart until several days later, and then only by chance. Immediately after my departure, Ann Rutledge, his secretary of some decades' standing and the one person he relied on for almost everything pertaining to the running of his office, had spoken up for me. She could tell from my face that I was bitterly disappointed, and she knew how hard we had worked to promote the zoo. "Why don't you let them go?" she asked. "He really didn't ask for much, and he said his wife was willing to take an unpaid leave." I could have kissed Miss Rutledge, but it was a week before I could thank her by telephone on a day when I knew that Dr. Cadwalader was out of town.

So we were off on September 17, 1949, driving an overloaded, secondhand Oldsmobile station wagon with, we later discovered, a leaky roof. After crossing into Mexico at Laredo, Texas, we drove south to Sabinas Hidalgo, arriving there at dusk. We traversed the main and seemingly only street slowly, looking for a place to stay, saw nothing promising, and then returned to the small and unimposing Powers' Café just north of town. It was run by an American family who had been there for years. We had a so-so meal, and then I asked if they could recommend a place for us to stay overnight. Mrs. Powers said that they had a couple of rooms which were still under construction, but one was habitable. She took us across the road and showed us a high-ceilinged room with one small, naked lightbulb high over our

heads. The cost was under a dollar, so we took it. After road-running in search of herps for an hour or so in the hot, drizzly weather, and finding only a few toads, a cold shower felt good. There was no hot water. There was a plus and minus for us, however. On the outside of the door screen I caught two Mediterranean geckos, *Hemidactylus turcicus*, a species that was expanding its range northward, and which is now well established in our southern states, especially in Texas. The minus was my discovery in the morning of a bedbug bite on my rump.

By chance I mentioned our stop to ornithologist R. A. Paynter, Jr., some years later, and he chuckled and said he had slept in the same room nearly a decade before we were there. He, too, had been told that the place was under construction. Evidently even the Powers family had fallen under the spell of *mañana*.

We had a passable breakfast at the café, and then sped southward toward Monterrey, Mexico's third largest city. Before I go on, it would be well to explain how poorly we were prepared to provide for our own culinary needs. We had a portable cookstove, but it was intended primarily for boiling water. We had only a few cans of food with us, and we reserved them for emergencies or times when we were far from a restaurant. We had been warned in advance that Mexican customs authorities frowned on large quantities of food and might charge us duty. The intention was probably to make visitors spend as much money as possible in Mexico. As we later discovered at Nuevo Laredo (see "Crossing the Border"), our "three-dollar tip" for an inspection, or rather for a "noninspection," would have permitted us to transport all we could use. The station wagon was so heavily loaded, however, that we would have been hard-pressed to find room even for a few more cans of food. We planned to eat at Mexican restaurants, which was a mistake. Either Isabelle or I, or both of us at the same time, repeatedly suffered from dysentery, the dreaded "D," on that long first trip.

But to return to the narrative. Eight miles south of Sabinas Hidalgo I found my first water snake, a juvenile diamondback, dead on the road, partially damaged by some unknown scavenger but quite preservable. The habitat seemed wrong. No water was in sight except for puddles left from the previous night's rain. I learned later that even water snakes wander into arid terrain during rainy weather. The Río Sabinas, or what was left of it after much of its water was diverted to supply the town, was not far away.

Farther south we saw a large, dark snake crossing the road. Isabelle, who was driving, speeded up and slammed on the brakes as we neared it, and I vaulted out of the car door on the dead run. Presently, like a baseball player

The hole beneath the bridge had to be enlarged slightly to get at the lizard. The prize, a blue spiny lizard, Sceloporus serrifer cyanogenys, *photographed in daylight. Photos by IHC.*

stealing second base, I slid head-first as the snake started down a moderate slope, but I grabbed its tail instead of the "bag." It was a splendid six-foot indigo snake that made no attempt to bite. The only damage was to my dungarees and my hide—a hole in my pants and scrapes

on my knee and wrist. At Ciénega de Flores we worked along the Río Salinas, in a different drainage system, and found two young diamond-backed water snakes.

By the time we reached Monterrey it was early afternoon and we were hungry. We were well into the outskirts when we noted a large, rather imposing restaurant called Los Arcos (The Arches). We pulled into its parking area and had ourselves an excellent meal at a reasonable price. Directly across the highway were the Regina Apartamentos and a Pemex (Mexican petroleum) station. We inspected the apartments and found them sadly run down, but they looked clean, so we took the most expensive one, with twin beds and private bath, for the equivalent of three dollars a night. It was a happy choice. Monterrey became a sort of headquarters for us on three different occasions during the same trip, and we had close access to Los Arcos where the food was good and certainly untainted, because we had no subsequent trouble from eating there.

After getting ourselves settled in, driving east from the city to take pictures of the curious Cerro de la Silla (Saddle Mountain), we were off right after dinner to cruise a quiet road in the dark. We headed north toward the airport and turned off on the road leading to Salinas Victoria. We saw toads only, but the rain had left puddles, which were largest under the many small bridges that carried the road over what presumably were usually dry arroyos. Mindful, however, of the water snake we had found dead on the road in the morning, I ventured beneath the first bridge, carefully scanned the puddle under it with my headlamp, glanced upward, and made a surprising discovery. Clinging to the masonry abutment, almost at its very top, were two beautiful adult blue spiny lizards, obviously asleep, and as easy to catch as picking grapes.

We then stopped at every bridge, perhaps a dozen of them, and I went below each one whether water was present or not. The bridges were low, chiefly of masonry, and varying from 3 to 12 feet in height from the bed of the wash to the concrete floor of the roadway overhead. We saw no snakes but, under the majority of the spans, there were more sleeping lizards of the same kind. They varied from half-grown individuals to adults approaching the maximum size for the species. Several had concealed themselves partially to almost entirely in chinks in the masonry. To extract an exceptionally large and pretty one, I enlarged the hole slightly with a hammer and stout screwdriver while Isabelle snapped pictures. Under some of the bridges there was only 1 or none, but sometimes there were as many as 5 or 6 lizards. We caught 10, examined them carefully in the daylight the next morning, took photographs, saved a pair to preserve, and liberated the others at bridges where they had been most common. We must have seen well over two dozen in all.

Bats were also in evidence under some of the bridges, clinging at night, like the lizards, to the abutments. I counted as many as 50 in one cluster. They were fairly active, and individual bats were constantly joining or leaving the groups. We caught one, euthanized it, and put it in formalin. Frederick A. Ulmer, Jr., the Philadelphia Zoo's curator of mammals, later identified it as a pallid bat, *Antrozous pallidus*, and deposited it in the collection of the Academy of Natural Sciences of Philadelphia. The next morning we found no bats at all. They must have used the abutments just as resting places during their nocturnal pursuit of insects.

Monterrey proved to be an excellent temporary base. From it we visited several streams on consecutive days, all within easy driving distance, and we found water snakes in three of them. The day we liberated the lizards we continued onward to the Río Salinas, close to Salinas Victoria. With the aid of some local lads, we found a relatively deep pool that had evidently been scoured out when a fast-flowing freshet had raced down the river after an upstream cloudburst. Gracefully draped on dead branches of a small tree was a large diamondback, but it dropped into the water and disappeared. We looked but found no others. When we stopped again in Monterrey, homeward bound after our peregrinations farther south, we took time out to visit the same locality at night, and that time I caught six of the dozen we saw. There had been more rain, and numerous males of the leopard frog complex were calling lustily nearby at the time.

Near Santa Catarina, not far west of Monterrey, we bounced over a rutted dirt road to the Cañon de la Huasteca, a place of spectacular beauty. Sedimentary rocks form horizontally, but a deformation had rotated the bedding plane so that it was almost vertical, with many huge slabs of limestone standing erect, some almost 1,000 feet high, and forming jagged patterns against the sky. A clear, swift stream ran along the floor of the canyon, but part of it was diverted into a flume to carry water, presumably to the nearby town.

In 1860 Robert Kennicott described a new species of water snake, *Nerodia couchii*, based on two specimens, one from "Santa Caterina," but in all probability from Huasteca Canyon. It was collected in 1853 by Lieutenant Darius Nash Couch, an early naturalist on leave from the U.S. Army, during which he mounted a personal field expedition on horseback through northeastern Mexico. Couch later became an important Union general during the Civil War. I wanted to know whether the snakes still survived in the canyon, and whether they differed from

RC caught the water snake, but he tripped and was soaked to the skin. Photo by IHC.

the blotched water snake, a western subspecies of the red-bellied water snake. It had been almost a century since Couch's visit.

We parked near a small house where an enterprising *campesino* (countryman) had a saddled burro for the use of visitors who wandered into the canyon. They could have the thrill of sitting astride the beast of burden for a small fee, or riding it while the man held the bridle for a larger one. If some other member of the party wished to do so, the rider could be photographed against the backdrop of the canyon wall. The *campesino* was too poor to own a camera himself.

The afternoon was cool and cloudy, and ribbon and water snakes were out and not concealed to avoid the heat as they would have been if the hot sun had been shining. I saw six *couchii* and succeeded in catching three. Five were resting in branches over the flume, which not only was fast running but also rather deep—almost up to the top of my hip boots. By stalking and then rushing, I caught two of the snakes along the flume, but, in getting the second, I lost my footing on the slippery bottom, went down, and got soaked to the skin. The largest of the three was evidently moving from the river to the flume. Isabelle spotted it, and I was

The two burros, Isabelle and the one for hire. Photo by RC.

able to get it without taking another unexpected bath.

Normally when my boots were full of water I would lie down on my back, raise one leg at a time, and let the water run out, but my wet shirt would have picked up mud and debris, so I elected to squish-squash my way along the bank of the flume looking for more snakes as I made my way back to the car. Meanwhile, Isabelle toted my wet shirt, undershirt, and sodden snake bags, plus her two cameras, struggling to keep the wet things separate from the dry. When we were back, Isabelle glanced at the burro and said that, loaded down as she was, she felt like one herself. So I pointed to her and the riding animal, and the little *campesino* nearly had hysterics when I said, "*Dos burros.*" I must admit, however, that part of his laughter may have been because of my soaked condition. After I had sat on the tailgate and emptied my boots, Isabelle climbed into the saddle and I took her picture, which we promptly dubbed "The Two Burros."

Then I had a good look at the snakes. The two larger ones were nearly uniform medium dark gray in coloration, but the smallest, about two feet in length, showed pale transverse lines such as are typical of those found on many specimens of the blotched water snake. It was obvious that my catch represented just another pattern morph of that highly variable and wide-ranging subspecies.

The next day we drove to García on the Río Pesquería. García had certainly deteriorated since the days long ago when it was called Pesquería Grande, which name was used to distinguish it from Pesquería Chica farther downstream and which long since had outstripped it in size and prosperity. García, however, was the scene of the most spectacular (and in some ways most stupid) catch I ever made of a water snake.

This one was lying in the branches of a small, bushy tree 10 feet or more above the surface of a deep pool of water in a stream which was very low with scarcely any water flowing. I was on the bank above the pool, and the snake was almost on the same level as my eyes with its head pointing toward me. I noticed, however, that the strong breeze that was blowing made the snake's perch bob up and down a bit, so when each gust of wind came I moved a little closer, screening myself as best I could. Eventually I crouched at the edge of the bank, momentarily expecting the snake to drop down into the pool. I made a desperate thrust, lunging far outward. By a stroke of good fortune I grabbed the snake with my right hand, clung desperately to the tree with my left, and found myself dangling over the pool, in imminent danger of falling in. My right foot was already submerged. To make matters worse, the snake, which I had seized near midbody, was vigorously striking at my wrist, and bringing blood with every blow. It took all my strength to haul myself up the bank, but I was soon sitting down, panting at a great rate, and examining my prize. It was a blotched water snake, slightly more than two feet long, brownish gray and with somewhat more pattern than the smallest one I had taken at the Cañon de la Huasteca. The pool, which was lined in part by small cottonwoods, and in part by a deep undercut in the bed of the stream, was probably the only place where water remained in the dry season and trees could grow. I walked along the bank for perhaps a quarter mile and saw no other pools. Once I had calmed down after catching the snake, I had time to reflect on how foolish I had been. I would not have minded getting wet, especially after my dunking the previous day, but I could easily have hurt myself if I had fallen on unseen rocks or sharp snags hidden beneath the surface of the muddy water.

On the morning of September 28 we left Monterrey and headed westward to make our all-important visit to the Río Nazas, a sizable stream, at least during the rainy season, that had emptied into a sump in a huge dry desert *bolsón* (or playa) for millennia. Yet a large water snake lived in the river as well as aquatic turtles and fishes. How did they get into that isolated desert stream system? The answer to that question I have tried to explain in the chapter entitled "Water Snakes in the Desert." I wanted to see the river and try my luck at finding at least one of the snakes myself.

We ascended the easy pass through the Sierra Madre Oriental to the mile-high city of Saltillo. The road was paved and in good condition, but far different from the excellent divided highway that now connects the two cities. Westward from Saltillo we dipped downward to the somewhat lower *altiplano* (high plateau) for the long drive to Torreón, more than 175 miles away, and almost all of it through barren, shadeless desert, the western part across the extremely arid Bolsón de Mapimí. Traffic was very light, but, surprisingly, we saw a few pedestrians, all of whom were nowhere near any visible signs of human habitation. We could not help but think what a bad place it would be to have a car break down. We eventually reached San Pedro de las Colonias, which, at the time, was a miserable place with deeply rutted, unpaved streets and not a decent house in sight. Crops were being grown near it, however, all the way to Torreón, principally corn and cotton, the latter being picked and hauled off to a gin on burro back. There was much irrigation in the general area, nourished by water from the Nazas. The region bore the curious name of the Laguna (Lake) District. There were no lakes, only a few impoundments. Doubtless the water table was close to the surface in many places, and perhaps the Mexicans were thinking of an underground lake when they named the area.

During the afternoon, when we were within a few miles of Torreón, we were astounded to see a small truck pass us that bore a rear license plate reading "U.S. Department of Agriculture"! I tried to overtake it, but it was moving too fast. Fortunately for us, however, the truck had a soft tire, the driver stopped to have a look at it, and we were able to catch up. I approached the man with a big smile and a hearty greeting in English. Wrong language. He spoke only Spanish. I said the equivalent of "please take us to your boss." He agreed, but stopped at the first Pemex station to inflate his tire while we filled our almost empty gas tank. We followed our guide to the central square and parked, and I was escorted to an office where I was warmly greeted by a Mr. C. S. Rude. Because much of the local produce, including vegetables, was exported to the United States, his duty and that of his men was to make inspections for insect or other pests before anything left the area. He gave me tips about reaching the Nazas upstream. There were good hotels in Torreón, which to our eyes seemed a rather modern city, but no motor courts where we could keep our car right with us. He did know of one in the smaller but sister city of Gómez Palacio, just across the river. He telephoned to see if there was a vacancy. There was, and the driver of the truck volunteered to escort us there, which was assuredly a wonderful favor.

We would have had great difficulty finding the place, because it was off any main road and the route to it seemed torturous. Thus, through the courtesy of a fellow American we found a good place to stay—La Cabaña Courts.

Although we paid the same price for our room, it was palatial compared with the antiquated accommodations in Monterrey. Everything was new, and there were even Venetian blinds. At the Regina, for privacy, we had to rig a blanket to cover the window. Both rooms had one thing in common, however. The water was unpredictable, although rather better in Monterrey. Sometimes there was none at all or it would run out in the midst of trying to take a shower. Frequently there was no hot water and sometimes not even cold at Gómez Palacio. Mexico was not well geared up for tourist trade in 1949 except in the large, fancy, high-priced hotels. Matters improved later, but the burgeoning human population is making matters ever more difficult, and the demand for water has destroyed a great many habitats for water snakes, fishes, and other wildlife. It can only get worse.

La Cabaña Courts had one major drawback. There was only a very small restaurant, and it suggested impending dysentery. Happily, our cases were mild.

As we prepared to take off for the Río Nazas the next morning, we were as eager as youngsters at holiday time. What was the river like? Would I find water snakes similar to the one my friend, Charles M. Bogert, wrote to me about from Mexico three years earlier? That had been my stimulus for wanting to visit the Río Nazas. After threading our way through the streets of Gómez Palacio and nearby Ciudad Lerdo, we sped along the highway in the direction of the distant city of Durango, and soon arrived at the Nazas. It was flowing freely, which meant that we were well upstream from the major impoundments that supplied water for the cities and the widespread irrigation. The river was lined intermittently by cottonwoods and willow trees that were nourished by its water. It was shallow, and the flow was moderate; it reminded us of what we would have called a creek back in New Jersey or Pennsylvania. A fisherman was setting homemade fish traps, and he let us photograph one. I donned my boots, headed for a pile of stones on a small island not far from the highway bridge, and within minutes I had caught a juvenile water snake and two narrow-headed garter snakes. The water snake was quite pale, and when it undulated as it crawled or breathed heavily the scales separated slightly to reveal the striking pink color of the skin between the scales. Although I waded upstream for an hour I saw nothing more of herpetological interest. When I returned to our car there were a dozen Mexicans, including a motorcycle policeman, indulging in the common practice of staring at us in curiosity, a trait to which we soon became accustomed. It happened almost everywhere in the countryside. I explained what I was doing, and I even asked the cop if I could use my headlamp after dark. He replied in the affirmative.

We went back to La Cabaña for a nap. The long drive of the previous day had been tiring, and I wanted to be fresh for an after-dark foray. It turned out to be an exciting one, because I caught three more juvenile water snakes and a beautiful big female, which swam directly toward me and literally right into my hands. I saw two other large water snakes but they kept well within a tangle of brush. What luck! Five water snakes in the bag, so to speak, on the very first day.

We slept late the next morning, and after breakfast I preserved specimens we had found dead on the road and which I had kept on ice. Isabelle wrote notes. It was after noon before we were back at the river. A fisherman, who lived with his family nearby, offered to guide us upstream to explore a place where he had seen several snakes. He rode with us on a rough trail for less than a mile to a small, shallow pond left from an overflow when the Nazas had been at a higher level after downpours upstream. No snakes, but I did find two baby pond sliders allied to the red-eared turtles of the United States.

Several persons at La Cabaña Courts, and even at the river itself, urged us to take the rough road on the other side of the river and drive to the Cañon de Fernandez, which was alleged to be teeming with snakes. So we eventually found ourselves wending our way beside fields of cotton, alfalfa, corn, and tomatoes, all irrigated by water sluiced from the Nazas and being worked by numerous *campesinos*. The road was in miserable condition, narrow, rutted, and punctuated with muddy seeps. A few bridges were barely one car wide, and in one place we drove across two huge timbers, firmly anchored in the opposing banks of a small arroyo, but each certainly not more than twice the width of our tires. It was a hairy, scary procedure. Whenever we stopped to make inquiries we were invariably told that the canyon was only two or three more kilometers ahead of us. We surely must have driven at least a dozen when we were stopped by a huge muddy wallow that we dared not try to cross. Even then we were assured, by a barefooted pedestrian, that the canyon was only two or three kilometers away. We had to back quite a way to turn around. We used up several hours, and our engine boiled over, all in an abortive attempt to reach an elusive

goal. Back at the highway we broke out some of our emergency rations, cooked supper, and after dark I made another try in the river. I caught only one more juvenile water snake but saw two fully adult ones, probably the same two I had observed the previous night. I was greatly intrigued with how red the heads of the large snakes looked, especially in the beam of my headlamp.

We returned the following night, and I caught another young water snake and also one in excess of what might have been called medium size. That gave me eight in all. I studied them with great care and made notes. All were quite pale, like so many other residents of arid regions, and all had a pinkish cast, the juveniles especially. It was obvious that they were related to the blotched water snake and therefore members of the *erythrogaster* (red-bellied water snake) complex. Dorsal blotches, although pale, were discernible, but the lateral blotches, which were very narrow, had virtually all the dark pigment confined to the skin between the scales. The blotches were better defined in the juveniles. The bellies were yellowish and unmarked. The heads of the two larger snakes, like the two that were still in the river, were strongly reddish, especially in the temporal region.

Eventually, when we arrived home in New Jersey many weeks later, with all eight snakes alive and well, we took numerous pictures of them, including both dorsal and ventral views. I recorded the coloration in detail on matte prints that Isabelle made for me. We kept the larger snakes alive for about two years, but I eventually euthanized and preserved the entire series in order to make scale counts and to get on with the painstaking and exacting chore of assembling the data necessary for describing the population as a new subspecies, which I named *bogerti* in honor of my friend. My paper was published in 1953. I had a good series to study. How different they were from the blotched water snake which had broad lateral blotches instead of narrow ones, and how dissimilar they were in coloration. The snake Bogert brought home was an adult male; I had caught a splendid adult female and another of somewhat smaller size, and six young of the year, all probably not more than a few weeks old.

We were destined to return to the Río Nazas several times a decade and more later, but we felt that our first experience with that fascinating desert stream was a great success. We had achieved one of our major goals.

We returned to Monterrey, stayed overnight, ate twice again in a good restaurant, and soon were on our way southward.

Chapter 20

Our First Long Trip to Mexico:
Part II. Acapulco, the Basilisk, and the Fiery Volcano

It was our first long excursion into Mexico, and we thought it might be our one and only lengthy stay south of the border. In our eagerness and enthusiasm, we tried to do too much. To compound our problem we had lingered for an extra day hunting along streams near Monterrey and another along the Río Nazas. Isabelle and I were mindful that we could be away from the Philadelphia Zoo for only a month, and we had already used up two precious days unexpectedly. We had to get moving. So we hastened southward, stopping only to sleep and to catch a few young diamond-backed water snakes (subspecies *blanchardi*) in the Río Moctezuma near Tamazunchale (dubbed "Thomas and Charlie" by the tourists).

In those days there were no roads for bypassing the capital, so we were forced to brave the life-threatening traffic in Mexico City. It was just as well, because we arrived there after dark and we had seen no overnight accommodations anywhere along the way. They were even scarce in the city. We finally found a vacancy at the second-rate Aztec Courts, where we discovered that the only food available was ham and eggs. We turned in early because it was my turn to have dysentery, and bed felt good. The next day we had another exposure to *el tráfico*, fierce and frenzied, with cars and taxis cutting in and out of line with wild abandon. We finally found the Kodak agency, where Isabelle bought more color film, but, contrary to what she had been told at home, they could not ship her exposed rolls back to the States for processing. Too much customs red tape, they told us.

We felt entitled to a good lunch after having eaten a second round of ham and eggs for breakfast. We could see the Hotel Roosevelt dining room while we were stopped for a traffic light, so we decided to eat there. No one could speak a word of English, and, for the one and only time I can remember, my use of Spanish ended in a minor gastronomic disaster. I ordered *chiles rellenos* (stuffed peppers), but the waiter misunderstood me and brought us *riñones* instead. That's the Spanish word for kidneys, which I detest, but I figuratively held my nose and ate them. Isabelle didn't mind. Actually, the

waiter did us a real favor. *Chiles rellenos* are stuffed with cheese. Was I out of my mind? Cheese was one of the things we were forbidden to eat. (See "On Staying Healthy.") Our guardian angel must have been bilingual to save us from that one!

We were soon back in the traffic, headed southward. When we were at another stoplight, I noted that the two great snow-capped volcanoes southeast of the city were vaguely visible through the smog. When we ascended the high mountain road south of the metropolis, we were delighted to find them revealed in all their awesome glory. It was a rare sight even then. Many cars had pulled off the road wherever there was space, and the passengers were all outside taking in the magnificent spectacle. We joined them.

Popocatépetl ("Popo" to virtually everyone), at about 17,900 feet, and the more northerly, attenuated, closely adjacent, and almost as tall Iztaccíhuatl (the sleeping lady) are two of the highest mountains in North America. Together they form a vast rampart towering high above the city and, with other mountains north of them, effectively block the prevailing westerly winds. In consequence, the ghostly, ghastly smog, the dreadful, almost suffocating air pollution that now blankets Mexico City, piles up to a great depth and renders the mountains completely invisible. We were extremely lucky to see them from the west, although we later had excellent views of them from the east. It was our first glimpse of the lofty transvolcanic belt, a truly thrilling experience for two easterners to whom any knob, knoll, or ridge in excess of 2,000 feet was a mountain.

Our immediate destination was the Casa Humboldt in Taxco. It had been recommended by Daniel P. and Jule Mannix, friends who had resided there for many weeks while they trained their pet golden eagle, Águila, in the ancient art of falconry and made a motion picture for lecture purposes.

Taxco was a fascinating place, all up and down, and a famous mining town ever since the days of Hernán Cortéz and his *conquistadores*. It was noted for its silversmiths and its early colonial architecture, and some

The Conants on the tailgate of their station wagon on the way to Acapulco. Photo by Richard Vieth.

years later it was designated a National Historic Monument by the Mexican government. Buildings may be restored, but all modern structures of any kind are prohibited. As a result, Taxco has preserved its charm and atmosphere, and it is still a major tourist attraction.

The Casa Humboldt, said to date from the sixteenth century, was built into the side of one of the town's precipitous hills. It was dark when we finally found the entrance on a cobblestone street. There were boardinghouse accommodations for visitors two or three floors below. The building had been named for the celebrated naturalist and explorer Baron Alexander von Humboldt, who once slept there during 1803. Appropriately, it was operated by the Baron and Baroness Alexander von Wothenau, with whom we became on a first-name basis during our second stay there.

After unloading necessities, and, on the recommendation of the people at the Humboldt, I drove the car down the street and over the curb into a fenced-in area, where I paid a small fee and was assured it would be quite safe even though pigs and chickens belonging to the resident proprietors were much in evidence. Before I had even walked back the word had spread about our arrival, and I was greeted by two young Americans, one of whom was George Holton, a photographer and son of the owner of the Twin Brook Zoo, where, as a teenager, I had my first taste of working with zoo animals. I hadn't seen him since he was a tiny tot. The other was Richard Vieth, who was making a bicycle trip through Latin America, taking pictures and expecting to write a book.

We had supper with Dick in the restaurant next door, which was called Los Arcos, the same as the excellent place we had found in Monterrey. We agreed to take

Dick with us to Acapulco the next day, even though the car was already crowded with our gear. We returned to our room, and, with Dick's help, I pickled specimens we had found on or near the road. Suddenly the water ceased to flow, a chronic problem in Mexico, but Dick knew how to turn on the reserve tank.

The next morning I retrieved the car, wiped off the decorations the chickens had left on the hood, and, after some repacking, we were off along a road that was almost never flat or straight. We snacked for lunch, but we were in storied Acapulco before suppertime. The swank and expensive hotels and their grounds were well manicured but, to our way of thinking, the rest of the town was a scummy, dreary place, and prices for everything were double what we had been charged elsewhere in Mexico. The restaurant, the best we could find, suggested possible trouble.

The people at the Casa Humboldt had told us there was an inexpensive, if somewhat primitive, motel at Pie de la Cuesta, a few miles west of the city. After receiving false directions from several people we finally found it, but the lights were out and it appeared to be out of business. The trip was not a total loss, however, because the Laguna Coyuca, the southernmost known locality for the west coast water snake, was directly adjacent. Coyuca is a long, narrow coastal lagoon with a normally shallow, but changeable, inlet from the Pacific Ocean roughly eight miles up the coast from Acapulco. The water is chiefly fresh, but I was to learn later that Mexican water snakes, at least some of them, tolerate considerable salinity. We had a brief glimpse of the water in the darkness, but it was getting late, so we hastened back to town. On its outskirts we found a small hotel, Las

Anclas (The Anchors), shortly before midnight. The lights there were also out, but my rapping on the door soon brought the proprietor, who was a Dane. He wanted 35 pesos for each of us, but that was too much, so we started haggling in a mixture of my Spanish and his strongly accented English. Possibly because he thought we might be the last customers for the night, or perhaps because I told him we had a penniless student with us, he finally agreed on a flat 50 pesos for the three of us. The place reflected Scandinavian influence. It was spotless and comfortable, but there was no running water. That deficiency was remedied by the arrival of a bucketful for us and one for Dick.

The next morning, as we were eating breakfast at a restaurant in town, I saw a fairly respectable garage where I took the car to be greased. The car was readily visible from the street, and, while the work was in progress, a man stopped and asked me in English what we had in the racks toward the rear of the car. He was, of course, referring to the sliding-drawer cages where we deposited our snake bags. He introduced himself as Morris Silverman, a former employee of the American Museum in New York. He was experienced enough to guess what we had and what we were doing. He took us in tow. At the very edge of glorious Acapulco Bay, listed by some authorities as one of the seven most beautiful bays of the world, he operated a small zoo. We inspected it, and I even traded him a couple of extra tortoises for a few snakes. Then we all went swimming and had a delightful time in the warm, buoyant water, taking turns using Silverman's facial mask to look at the brilliantly colored fishes below us. After lunch we drove again to the Pie de la Cuesta. I saw a water snake, but it also saw me and quickly slipped into a pile of rocks.

Silverman recommended the fancy Hotel Bahía, which turned out to be a real favor. The manager, Antonio "Tony" de Dominicis, spoke perfect English, was deeply interested in tropical fishes, and seemed quite pleased to chat with us about natural history in general. He gave us rooms for well under half price and made us feel at ease by assuring us that it was the off-season, and he could afford to help us financially. Dick left to visit with another American lad he had met. Meanwhile, we rested, cleaned up, and then had a splendid dinner in the hotel dining room. Tony joined us and so did Al Pflueger, of Florida, who was renowned for his skill in mounting game fishes for sportsmen. His name was quite familiar to me, but I had never met him. When we were nearly finished Dick returned, and I expressed a wish to try for snakes in the dark in the lagoon. Tony spoke right up, saying, "Let's go. That will be fun." So we off-loaded some of our gear to make room for another

passenger and away we went. While I waded in the water with my headlamp agleam, the others watched from the shore and enjoyed seeing me catch three water snakes, the largest of which bit me savagely after I grabbed it at midbody to keep it from escaping into a mat of floating water hyacinths.

It had been a truly wonderful day. I'd like to say a perfect day, but the blasted "D" had caught up with us again. Doubtless the native restaurants were at least partly to blame.

The following morning I had to spend an hour showing off our entire collection and lecturing on reptiles in general for Tony, his brother, their children, and their pet dog. Tony translated as I went along. Afterward we wrote notes and did chores until late morning, when Isabelle, who had made a rapid recovery, went swimming with Dick and Silverman for about an hour. I crawled back into bed. I ate little at lunch, but I felt well enough to drive on an abortive excursion looking for the Laguna Tres Palos east of Acapulco. Silverman said there were lots of snakes there. He went along as our guide, but it quickly became apparent that he either didn't know how to get there or had completely forgotten the way. So we returned to the hotel. After he had left, we searched for a restaurant that would feed us early. Because of the daily siesta, most Mexicans ate rather late. We, of course, wanted to try the Laguna Coyuca again soon after dark, and it was well that we went. I caught four more water snakes, and Dick, clad in Isabelle's boots, got another. We were back at the Bahía by 10:30, but we had to give a full report on the day's activities, after which we packed most everything back into the car. We were anxious to get an early start northward on the morrow.

It was a dreary day for me. I had no appetite, my head ached, and everything I did was an effort, but I managed to do some of the driving to relieve Isabelle, and we were back in Taxco by midafternoon. We had expected to drop Dick off at the Casa Humboldt and press onward at least to Cuernavaca, but I felt so miserable that we decided to stay at the Casa where we had friends and help if we needed it. I went right to bed, but I managed to eat something at Los Arcos during the evening.

The next morning I was worse and obviously running a temperature, so Isabelle asked Trixie (the Baroness) if she would call a doctor. "The best one in town," Juan Meana, M.D., arrived almost at once. His English was quite good, and he had studied at the University of Michigan Medical School. He thought my trouble might be a slight case of malaria. He prescribed milk of magnesia and gave Isabelle a prescription that I was to take every hour. With the help of one of the other guests she

We posed at the Casa Humboldt in Taxco while RC was recovering from his short but severe illness. Rosita, the dachshund, is on his lap. Photo by the Baroness Alexander von Wothenau.

quickly found a *farmacia*. By late afternoon I was able to eat with at least a trace of appetite.

The next morning I was quite sick again and had developed a bad cough. The doctor came back, took a blood sample to check for malaria, and gave me a shot of penicillin. He returned in the afternoon to report that the malaria test was negative. He prescribed a sulfa drug and also codeine for my cough. To make a long story short, I spent most of four days in bed with various combinations of fever, headache, cough, one sleepless night, and general weakness. Finally my fever broke, and during the afternoon of the fourth day I showered, shaved, and dressed, and went down the stairs for a meal. On the fifth day I felt much better. We walked around town a little and even visited the church to see its dazzling array of gold and silver in various forms, such as small statues and other religious artifacts. With the help of several of the friends we had made, we packed up and were ready to leave the next morning.

Dr. Meana's opinion was that I had a respiratory infection, a common ailment, he said, when people changed altitudes quickly. My good friend Sherman A. Minton, M.D., with whom I discussed the case years later, thought it probably was a viral infection.

During my incarceration, as I called it, poor Isabelle had to curate the livestock daily and make innumerable trips to the car in the pig and chicken yard for all kinds of things, including our boiled water that ran out all too

soon. The maid at the Casa obliged by boiling more for us. Friends had hauled most of our belongings into our room, and the spacious bathroom with its enormous tiled tub was a good place to look after the animals and to park our live turtles. Because the Casa Humboldt was a historic building, tourists trooped in now and then to look at its interesting interior appointments. Rosita, the Baroness's pet dachshund, adopted me, usually slept on my bed, and growled whenever any tourist peeped in the doorway. They gave her a bath one day, but, while she was still covered with soapsuds, she struggled loose, made a wild dash for our room, and scooted under my bed. It took four people, including Isabelle, to block her exit and haul her out and off to finish her bath. Poco, a pet spider monkey, broke his chain and was on the loose for a while. He was finally caught while eating sugar on the dining room table downstairs. Most of all I remember the "tortilla factory" in the small courtyard about two floors below our open balcony. There were no windows. Early every morning a half dozen or more women foregathered, and whereas individual ones probably came and went, the entire day was spent making tortillas, patting them flat with their hands. It was also a wonderful place for gossip, because the chatter of feminine voices, with occasional shrill laughter, drifted upward to our room all day.

My nagging worry was the severe erosion of our precious month of time. If we adhered to it exactly we might as well start homeward almost at once, with only a day or two to spare en route. I decided to gamble. I carefully drafted a letter to Dr. Cadwalader, who had given us permission to be away. I explained my predicament and I solicited help from Dr. Meana, who kindly wrote a note on one of his prescription forms that corroborated what I stated. I asked whether, in view of my misfortune, we could stay a few extra days to complete our original schedule. I also asked Dr. Cadwalader to write to me in care of the *lista de correos* (postal list) at Monterrey. We went ahead as we had planned, but we kept our fingers crossed, hoping that my letter and Dr. Meana's note might save the days, to coin a phrase.

All roads led to Mexico City. In 1949 there were no shortcuts between most of the provincial cities, and no safe ways for a stranger to bypass the city at close range without getting hopelessly lost. So we were off to the capital again, stayed overnight, and the next morning we left for Veracruz on the east coast. It was a spectacular ride, with marvelous views of the two great volcanoes from the east, and a drop down a breathtaking, zigzagging escarpment road near Acatzingo that I describe in "Potential Perils." Later we saw a small sign in English that read "Bungalows" near a turn in the road. We followed the accompanying arrow up a short hill, and discovered the truly beautiful Posada Loma, where we stayed for the night. It was close to the town of Fortín de las Flores (Little Fort of the Flowers), and the extensive gardens at the Posada were in keeping with that name. The bewildering array of flowering tropical plants was a riot of color. Everything was spotlessly clean and the food was good. We had a fairly early breakfast the next day and, when we had finished, the proprietor opened two tall curtains, and there, in all its extraordinary beauty, was snow-capped Orizaba. At almost 19,000 feet, it is the third highest mountain in North America, exceeded only by Mount McKinley in Alaska and Mount Logan in Canada. Isabelle went to our room at once to get her camera.

We drove on to the port city of Veracruz, ate at an open-air restaurant, the best we could find, and then headed south for Alvarado, where our good friend Emmett Reid "Dixie" Dunn had collected years earlier. He had seen many water snakes in pools behind the barrier dunes that faced the Gulf of Mexico and also in the ditches along the road. So we started back at night. Traffic was light and we could stop almost anywhere, but not a snake did I see, despite long and diligent searching. Once, as I walked back to the car, I noticed a pair of small mammals on the road. They seemed interested in each other, and I was able to sneak up and plant my booted foot gently on the tail of the one facing away from me. The other may have been blinded by my headlamp, but it scooted rapidly away as soon as I touched its fellow. My temporary captive turned and bit futilely at my boot. It was a four-eyed opossum, so named for the two patches of whitish fur, one above each eye, that give the illusion of an extra pair of eyes. I called Isabelle, we had a good look by flashlight, and then I raised my foot and the little animal quickly made its escape.

Shortly ahead of us was a small bridge and, mindful of the lizards I had found under such structures near Monterrey, I went under it for a look. Success again, but this time the lizards were basilisks, *Basiliscus vittatus*, large, slender reptiles that sometimes exceed two feet in total length. Adult males have a rounded crest at the back of the head, females a lobe. They have fringes on their toes that help them, juveniles especially, to run rapidly across small, still bodies of water without sinking in. In Mexico and other Latin American countries they are called Jesus Christ lizards because they walk on water. Under the bridge was a pair of adults, both of which I caught and took up to the car for Isabelle to see. I debated about taking them home with us, but feared they would not do well in transit. They were too large to

be comfortable in snake bags. So I took them back, and hooked their claws over the masonry, where they remained motionless just as I had found them.

The next bridge and its abutments were decorated with basilisks, from juveniles to half-grown ones. It seemed likely that the young ones might do better in captivity, and we had had some success in raising lizards at the zoo, so I collected an even dozen, placing two between each of the fingers of both my hands. I returned to the car and Isabelle held a snake bag upward since we both knew that lizards usually went up, catching their claws in the cloth. All were transferred from my right hand. Then another bag, and all went well until one of the lizards, reversing direction, dropped onto Isabelle's lap, dashed across the car seat, and disappeared into the labyrinth of our closely packed equipment. We thought nothing of it. We'd catch it later. Other bridges also had many basilisks, but I took no more, even though I saw in excess of 50 altogether.

A few days later, as we were once again in the mad traffic melee of central Mexico City, the lizard suddenly ran up one side of the dashboard, across it to the other side, and down, while both of us made wild grabs in a vain attempt to catch it. We saw it once or twice later when we were outside the car, but its presence inside was to save us later from what might have been a disaster.

At the time of our trip the U.S. and Mexican governments were cooperating in an attempt to wipe out foot-and-mouth disease, a deadly scourge of cattle, before it crossed into the States. Herds were carefully inspected, and even single or small groups of animals on which impoverished families depended for milk, meat, and fertilizer. Infected cattle and all their stable mates were slaughtered at once. We never learned what compensation the owners received, but the campaign was highly unpopular, and we heard that some of the inspecting officers were murdered.

The operation was widely advertised as AFTOSA, from the Spanish word for the dread disease. There were inspection stations on all the highways heading north. On our way back to Monterrey we were stopped by a uniformed officer who made us get out and walk through a large pan of liquid apparently designed to disinfect footgear. His next task was to spray the inside of the car, and I was horrified. I had no idea which of several deadly chemicals he was using and what effect it might have on our reptilian livestock. I was tempted to remonstrate vigorously, but he seemed resolute and he was armed. As I tried to tell him about our snakes and things, he opened the car door and pulled back the handle of his "Flit" gun, and was just about to plunge it forward when our runaway lizard jumped on the front seat almost alongside of him. The inspector was so startled that he slammed the door shut and almost shouted, "¡Pase, señor!" Pass on we did—at once. Wow! Were we ever thankful for the errant basilisk, which we eventually caught and pampered. It lived for a surprisingly long time at the zoo, despite the husbandry techniques then in vogue, and which seem truly archaic in the light of present-day procedures.

But to return to our journey back to Veracruz. We would need a place to spend the night. Dixie Dunn had told us to beware of thieves. He described the *posadas* (inns) of that city as having rooms with no screens, with the windows protected only by vertical iron bars. Every bed had a mosquito canopy that one pulled down and tucked in with care before going to sleep. Dixie said that the ingenious robbers had long poles with big unbarbed hooks, and that they were adept at reaching in through the bars and fishing out the occupants' belongings. We smiled at his story and promptly forgot it.

When we arrived back in the city we started hunting for our night's lodging. It was late. The hotels all had vacancies, but using one meant leaving our car on the street, exposed to possible theft of its contents or even the vehicle itself. We were discouraged, but as we drove slowly around the streets we came across the Hotel Mena Brito, which was fronted by a huge steel gate. I got out of the car, found a bell button to push, and an attendant said there was one room left. He slid the gate sideways so we could enter, and then closed it behind us. I drove along a wide alleyway and parked right by our room. When we entered, we gasped in astonishment. It matched Dunn's description exactly. An open, barred window with no screen, and a huge double bed with a mosquito canopy. Forewarned, I put all our things under the bed where they would be safe from "fishermen." We fell asleep promptly, but the miserable "D" woke us both several times to make trips to our fortunately private bathroom. Isabelle wrote in her diary that those episodes spoiled her illusion of feeling like a heroine in a motion picture with a degenerate tropical setting, such as "Rain," a movie that had recently been popular in American theaters.

We returned to Mexico City by way of Jalapa, the capital of the state of Veracruz. The road was mountainous but more easily negotiated than our route toward the coast had been. Along the way, as Isabelle wrote in her diary:

The most interesting sights were a mountain covered with a lava flow on which lichens and cactus were struggling to live among the ashen rocks. Also a lovely azure blue lake at El Limón which looked as though it was in the crater of a volcano. It was the

right shape and did not appear to have an inlet or outlet. Women were washing clothes on the shore as they do everywhere in Mexico where there is water. Just after we left Veracruz we spotted the top of Orizaba above the low cloud banks. It looked strange to see snow so close to such tropical heat and vegetation.

We were in Puebla by 4:30, and, if we hadn't been so worried about our time, which had been so badly eroded by my illness, we would have stopped there overnight. It would have been good to see the nearby extinct volcano, La Malinche, far less tall than the snow-capped peaks we had so much enjoyed, but impressive in its own right, according to the guidebook we carried. That would have been possible only in the morning, when all the mountains away from the smogbound capital were almost always clearly visible. By midday most of them were usually clouded over, as was La Malinche as we passed it. We were back at the Aztec Courts by 8:15. We tried another restaurant, ordered steaks, and then waited almost an hour before they were served, stone cold. I fear that I lost my temper, because Isabelle wrote that I bawled out the waiter in a flood of Spanish and ordered him to take everything back and have it warmed up. How we yearned for a really decent meal, and one we could eat without fear of the consequences.

The next day we had a busy morning curating the livestock, writing notes, having laundry done, and getting the car serviced at the Oldsmobile agency—an oil change, lubrication, adjusting the brakes, and tightening body bolts that had rattled loose. That was all finished just a few minutes before siesta time, which saved us a two-hour wait while everything was shut down.

We were near the Bosque de Chapultepec, Mexico City's large and famous park and where the Instituto Biología was situated. Dick Vieth had told us how to find it. I had written to Rafael Martín del Campo, then Mexico's leading herpetologist, and said we might try to look him up. We found him and had an excellent visit. His English was about on a par with my Spanish, so we had little trouble communicating. He and I visited in his office while Isabelle stayed with the car, partly to keep an eye on it and partly to leave the windows open so the interior wouldn't become overheated in the sun. Señor Martín accompanied me outside so that he could see what we had collected. I was very happy to meet him that one and only time, even though we corresponded for years, both previously and afterward.

We were up betimes the following morning, but found no place open for breakfast, and we had to drive all the way to Toluca, about 40 miles over mountain roads west of the capital, before we could eat. Then we sped westward, through the lovely old city of Morelia

Isabelle rode a horse led by an Indian boy on our pitch-dark trek across the lava fields. Photo by RC.

RC astride his mule with the smoking Volcán Parícutin in the background. Photo by IHC.

and then to Uruapan, near the active volcano, Parícutin. We hunted up the Hotel Progreso, which had been recommended to us and there, much to our pleasant surprise, we found Dick Vieth who greeted us warmly. He had spent the day climbing the peak with a Mexican geologist and had peered down into the crater, with fire bombs roaring upward all around only to fall back again or roll down the eastern side of the mountain. "What if the wind had changed?" I asked him with a shudder. He said they had studied the weather reports, took a chance, and made it both up and down unharmed. After having supper with Dick in a nearby Chinese restaurant, we retired early, poor Isabelle with the damned "D."

Up at 2:00 A.M. after too few hours of sleep, gulped down oranges and sandwiches we had bought the night before, and before 3:00 we entered a taxi with a Mexican military officer, a fellow passenger who would share the 50 pesos charged by the driver to take us to the volcano. It took an hour and a half to bounce over a miserable road to the ruined village of San Juan.

It was pitch dark, and we could see almost nothing. A warm but dirty *sarape* was hoisted over my head, and I was helped onto the back of a sturdy mule. Isabelle had the same experience, except that she had a horse. Then we started off, each steed led by a boy on foot, moving steadily onward and upward. The sky was completely overcast. But let Isabelle pick up the narrative as she related it in her diary:

It was weird riding through the night trusting to the

instinct of an all but invisible muchacho *leading my horse. Most of the time the trail went up and, after an hour the caravan, including the Mexican officer, halted by a rough shelter. We were on top of a mountain and across a valley from the famous, fiery volcano. The fumarole on its side was glowing like an open hearth furnace, and the red hot lava could be seen to move slowly down the mountainside. Clouds of dense smoke, only slightly illuminated by the fires below, poured from the main crater and periodically showers of sparks arose. The "sparks" were huge boulders, burning red, that were pushed up by the gases. Some fell outside the crater and others dropped back in. A group of six tourists had preceded us to the shelter and, although we talked with them, we could scarcely see them. I set up the color camera on the tripod and took some night shots. We had arrived about 5:30 A.M., and by 6:00 the dawn was breaking, and the brilliant glow of the volcano was diminishing. As the sun came up we could see that we were on a knoll completely covered with volcanic ash and totally black dead trees. The eeriness was increased by the coarse croaking of ravens as they flew among the burned trees and stumps. The tourists—three American couples—were full of misinformation about the volcano, so Roger explained about it, and then did the same in Spanish for our Mexican companion. Unfortunately, Roger felt miserable with a severe attack of dysentery but, as the sun warmed things up he felt a little better.*

Even though we had on our own jackets, we were glad for the additional comfort of the sarapes, dirty though they were. We lingered for two hours absorbing the spectacular grandeur of the volcano, the lava flow, and the ash-covered hills. At 7:30 we started down. Erosion had taken place on the slopes which six years ago had been covered with volcanic dust. [The volcano erupted in February 1943.] In places the trail came perilously close to the edge of chasms, cut by rainfall, and was so narrow and rough that we were glad the boys and the several horses and mules were so sure-footed. As we descended we could see the church spire, arising from the lava bed, at the buried village of San Juan. Part of its twin spire, which had never been completed also showed. The trail skirted the edge of the lava flow, which is 500 feet deep where it emerges from the volcano but gradually tapers down. The little village of Parícutin was entirely covered, but some of San Juan escaped. However, the town was abandoned and the inhabitants moved to another site. The only thing left were a few adobe walls. Roger and I had our boys take us over to the San Juan village site. We rode as far as possible, then dismounted and climbed over the jagged lava for a closer look at the church.

The entire landscape for miles around was covered with black ash, and I noted that several of the mountains within view were all about the same height as Parícutin, which eventually spewed out 1.4 cubic kilometers of lava, ash, and bombs. I wondered whether they, too, had erupted at various times in the past and then petered out when they reached a certain height and volume. The Volcán Parícutin became extinct a few years after our visit.

Norman E. Hartweg, a close friend who had done much fieldwork in Mexico, visited Parícutin soon after it first erupted in the middle of a farmer's field. He was well posted on the history of the volcano, and he said that, when he was first there, every horizontal branch and twig had ash an inch deep on it. That quickly dissipated with the first strong wind. Happily, he had told me about his visit, and that was why I was able to explain things to my tourist audience.

Back in Uruapan, we found the ice house, had lunch, and were off. We had rushed all the way from Mexico City, and now we were rushing back. By a reshuffling of our load we cleared the backseat of the car so we could take turns lying down. We pushed onward as rapidly as we could, but by 11:30 P.M. we were both completely exhausted from lack of sleep the previous night and the exertion of constant vigilance on the twisting, turning mountain roads we encountered over much of the

route. We found a place to pull off the highway beyond Toluca, and there we slept soundly, despite the loud groaning of trucks in low gear as an intermittent stream of them struggled up the steep inclines. We blessed ourselves for bringing along three blankets each. We awakened at dawn. Our altimeter registered 9,600 feet and the thermometer inside the car was exactly at freezing. Luckily the livestock, which had been insulated when we repacked our load partly around their pull-out drawers, suffered no ill effects.

In retrospect, I wonder where we found the stamina to manage that long, exhausting trip, but it surely was worth it to see the volcano in eruption.

We dropped down into Mexico City, washed our hands and faces in the Hotel Roosevelt's restrooms, ate breakfast, and took off immediately for distant Tamazunchale. We stayed for the night, but put off sleep long enough for me to catch three more water snakes in the Río Moctezuma.

One thing we especially wanted to do before we left Mexico was to visit Tampico on the east coast and meet the Villaseñors. Let me explain why. About a year previously, a charming, thoroughly Americanized Mexican couple from Cleveland, Carlos and María Moreno, and their 15-year-old son, Daniel, came to my office at the Philadelphia Zoo at the suggestion of Fletcher Reynolds, then the director of the Cleveland Zoo. The adult Morenos had been born and raised in Mexico. I eagerly asked them questions about their native land and mentioned that I hoped some day to hunt for water snakes down there. We discussed many things, but they said if ever we were in Tampico we should look up their friend, Roberto Villaseñor, who was fluent in English and had married an American. They gave us his address, and I promptly wrote to him. He responded that we must be sure to visit them, but what intrigued me most was his statement that water snakes were abundant in the lakes and marshes around Tampico.

We had originally hoped to drive up along the Gulf of Mexico from Veracruz to Tampico, but that plan was scotched when Señor Villaseñor wrote to advise us that the road between Tuxpan and Tampico was impassable. If we had been able to proceed straight north we would have gone to the volcano before visiting Veracruz.

Should we take the time to go to Tampico for a day or two, or should we press on homeward? We were already more than a week overdue. We talked about it on the way north from Tamazunchale, and we finally decided to turn off on the new road at Ciudad Valles. I hoped that I had made myself sufficiently indispensable at the zoo so that I would earn nothing more than a reprimand for being away for so long. Also, it was the slack season and zoo attendance had surely fallen off sharply with the onset of cool weather.

Eventually we neared the coast. We were ferried across the Río Tamesí, passed the oceangoing freighters on the Río Pánuco, and suddenly were at the railroad station, where we parked while I went inside in search of a telephone. Señor Villaseñor answered in person and was soon on his way to meet us. He guided us to a brand-new motel, recommended a restaurant, and said he would come back for us in the evening and take us to meet his family. We dug out clean, if rumpled, clothes and made ourselves as presentable as possible. Señora Villaseñor, Rose, was a charming American, whereas their daughter, Luisa, and son, Roberto, were very Mexican and quite intelligent as well as bilingual. We left after an hour or so, pleading fatigue. We were to return for dinner on the morrow.

The next day we had innumerable chores to do. Curating of the collection was imperative after many days of neglect. I had to preserve specimens. We had to find someone to wash our clothes and snake bags, and we had to catch up with our paper work. During the afternoon Villaseñor took us to several places where we could get close to the water. Tampico is virtually surrounded on the landward side by swamps, lakes, rivers, and canals, a literal watery wilderness, which includes the Lago Culebra and the Laguna Tortugas (Snake and Turtles Lakes, respectively). I decided to revisit some of the places after dark. Our dinner was a smashing success. We could eat everything, including the salad, because we knew that Rose had prepared it. Our compliments were truly sincere.

About 8:30 P.M. our host and Luisa guided us to the dock where he maintained his fine motorboat. The area was subject to tidal influence, and the water was up near the dock, but not over my boots. Suddenly Villaseñor saw a snake swimming at the water's surface, he shouted excitedly, and thanks to my headlamp, which probably blinded the reptile, I was able to make a wild but successful grab. It was a large adult male of Blanchard's water snake that was very pale and almost patternless. I searched the area thoroughly, but with no additional luck. The Villaseñors left us, and we returned to several of the places where we had reconnoitered during the afternoon. Still no luck. It was very hot and humid, and the mosquitoes were exceedingly numerous and persistent. We finally quit, returned to our motel, and turned in for the night by 1:00 A.M. Before we were asleep, however, a hard rain began and the temperature dropped sharply. The first *norte* (northern storm) of the season had arrived.

The following day, although sunny, was very much cooler. With Villaseñor's help and his kindness in letting a trusted boy take us out in his boat, we cruised along

several canals and along the Río Tamesí. We saw only one water snake, and I nearly went overboard in a vain attempt to catch it. The dock area greatly intrigued me. When the tide was out, the place where I had caught the snake was completely out of water but muddy. Most important, the water was brackish; boats, we were told, became covered with barnacles in a few months' time. The dockman, an employee of the boat club, said he often saw three or four snakes in a single evening. It was a new and strange habitat for me. I had always thought that the diamond-backed water snake (of which *blanchardi* is a subspecies) was confined to fresh water.

We said good-bye and profusely thanked our very hospitable friends, never dreaming we would see them again in Tampico more than a decade later, when we returned to collect in the marshes west of the city. We were off early the next morning, but made poor time because the road from Tampico to Ciudad Mante was full of holes and under repair in many places. We did better once we reached Mante and headed north on the main highway, and we were in Monterrey by 6:00 P.M. We went straight to the post office, which was still open. It was the custom for a list (the *lista de correos*) to be posted on a bulletin board with the names of persons in alphabetical order for whom letters were being held. After that was determined one went to a window, and a clerk matched the number or numbers, verified the name, and handed over the mail. There were three letters for us, one from Dr. Cadwalader, which I opened posthaste. He had received my communication and Dr. Meana's note from Taxco, he was sorry I had been sick, and we could stay in Mexico until we had completed our schedule. What a relief! We hastened to the Regina Apartamentos, tidied ourselves up, and crossed the highway to the Restaurante Los Arcos to celebrate. Several of the waiters remembered us and greeted us cordially. I think we had at least two tequila sours each, followed by a good dinner. We felt relaxed for the first time in weeks.

Since we were no longer under pressure, we slept a little later than usual. It was cloudy and quite cool. Our waiter assured us that the *norte* was early and that such weather was usually expected in January and February, not in October. Nonetheless, we took off for the Cola de Caballo (Horsetail Falls), a well-known tourist attraction where a waterfall tumbled over a cliff. It splayed outward toward each side so that it really resembled the tail of a gigantic white horse dropping down 100 feet or so. Collecting was poor, but I did pick up a few lizards and frogs and a baby ribbon snake. We went back to Monterrey, which was only 20 miles away, had dinner, and then headed in the dark for Salinas Victoria, where we had seen a diamond-backed water snake on our way south. En route, I again checked beneath bridges. Very few spiny lizards were in evidence, but with my hammer and large screwdriver I enlarged holes in the masonry, as I had done previously, and soon extracted five blue spiny lizards, now known as *Sceloporus serrifer cyanogenys,* to take back with us. Collecting water snakes was difficult around the big pool in the Río Salinas, where I repeatedly stepped into water so deep that it poured into my boots. Nonetheless, I caught six of the dozen snakes we saw. What was equally important, I collected enough leopard frogs to feed all our larger snakes.

The next morning we said farewell to Monterrey, stopped at Ciénega de Flores, picked up another water snake, and then moved on to Sabinas Hidalgo, where we braved the austerity of the Powers' unfinished accommodations, as we had during our very first night in Mexico. We decided to put up with it so we could visit the Ojo de Agua, a big spring about four miles west of the town, but the road, at the time, was exceedingly muddy. I found a young diamondback water snake under a stone in the outflow stream during the afternoon, but I decided we'd do much better at night. So we muddled back to town, took a siesta, ate at the Powers' Café, and went back after dark.

The stream had a good flow of crystal-clear water, but it petered out in a half mile or so as it was diverted for the use of the town. In the broadest part of it I caught four more diamondbacks, including the largest water snake we had seen during our entire trip, a female measuring more than four and one-half feet in total length. She swam directly toward me, but then veered off and dove downward when she was about six feet away. I was able to follow her movements in the clear water, but had to grab her near midbody, whereupon she sank her sharp teeth into my hand. I had real trouble prying her loose and then into a bag. We also picked up several adult giant toads, *Bufo marinus,* for the zoo collection, so our last night in Mexico was a big success.

In the morning we were off for home, reached Laredo, and there we ran into trouble, fortunately temporary, with both the Mexican and U.S. inspectors, as recounted in "Crossing the Border."

Our journey homeward was uneventful. I brought back a wealth of new information for my studies on the water snakes of Mexico, in addition to a considerable number of specimens. We also had many fine additions for the zoo collection, including the big indigo snake I caught when I "slid into second base" so many weeks previously. I promptly thanked Dr. Cadwalader, and he seemed to enjoy hearing about some of our experiences during the 15 minutes he could spare for me in his office.

It was a hard trip, grueling in many respects, and we were sick far too much of the time. As it turned out a decade later, however, it was a marvelous training experience for us, and was the beginning of what amounted to a full piecemeal year of fieldwork in Mexico, ranging from just a few days or a week or so, to as much as two months at a time.

When I reexamined my voluminous data on the west coast water snakes, on which I had published in 1946, and compared them with the snakes we collected near Acapulco in the Laguna Coyuca, it became obvious that the population from Colima southward was different in coloration and scutellation from the population farther north. In 1953 I described it as a new subspecies, which I named *isabelleae* for my beloved wife, without whose staunch support and presence the 1949 expedition would have been impossible. In the same paper I described *bogerti* from the Río Nazas, as mentioned previously, as a new subspecies of the red-bellied water snake complex; and *werleri,* from southern coastal Mexico, as a new race of the diamond-backed water snake. John E. Werler, who had done a lot of fieldwork in Mexico, was then curator of reptiles at the San Antonio Zoo, but he later became director of the Houston Zoo.

At the end of the paper I wrote: "Words of appreciation should be expressed to Williams B. Cadwalader, M.D., D.Sc., President of the Zoological Society of Philadelphia, who made it possible for me to spend several weeks in Mexico in 1949." I didn't dare mention Miss Ann Rutledge, his elderly longtime secretary, whose intercession on our behalf had been the main factor in our being able to go. To express our profound thanks, I eventually gave her the kiss she so richly deserved.

Chapter 21

The Philadelphia Lawyer

R. Sturgis Ingersoll, Esq., was a distinguished member of the bar, a free-thinking patrician, an outdoorsman, and a good friend despite his being 20 years my senior. He was bald, tall and lanky, almost gaunt, and he sported a waxed mustache, which he kept scrupulously pointed at each end. For several years he was the vice president of the Zoological Society of Philadelphia, but he resigned that position when he became the president of Philadelphia's prestigious Museum of Art.

Whether Sturgis's interest in snake hunting originated personally or evolved from his son Robert's enthusiasm I never determined, but he sponsored three excursions afield, all of them memorable, although one was not very productive.

Our first trip was to the Pocono Mountains of northeastern Pennsylvania in search of rattlesnakes. At that time, in the late 1930s, timber or banded rattlesnakes were common at rocky denning areas in the spring of the year. A visitor to the zoo confided that there were two dens on property he owned and that he guarded the snakes from persecution. He was willing, however, to let us take a few for the zoo's collection.

Sturgis, Bob, who was then in his 20s, and I set a weekend date and motored up from Philadelphia with high hopes, despite clear, but unseasonably cold weather. Alas, the snakes were not sunning, as hoped, and we saw only one small rattler far back in the rocks and completely out of reach. We did catch a milk snake and a black racer, so we had something to show for our trip. The truly memorable part of it was the marvelous, old-fashioned Sunday dinner served to us by our host's genial wife. Platters of chicken, gravy and mashed potatoes, and vegetables of many kinds, all so bountiful and tasty that we stuffed ourselves and then topped off with apple pie. Even in those days such sumptuous meals, except at holiday time, were almost a thing of the past. Our friend remedied our failure to find rattlers by catching two pairs a few weeks later and sending them to me at the zoo where they lived for several years.

Our second excursion was to the Okefenokee Swamp. As I wrote in 1940 in "Fauna," the Philadelphia Zoo's magazine:

> Far south in Georgia, resting on the Florida line and two score miles from the ocean lies a swamp so vast that it is one of the few places in all the eastern states that deserves the title of "wilderness." Its watery wastes flood nearly seven hundred square miles and within its confines are animals enough to delight the heart of even a well-traveled naturalist. Such is the famed Okefenokee, the "quaking earth" of the Indians.

> Gone from it now are the Florida wolf and probably the ivory-billed woodpecker, but many another rare or exciting species still makes its home in and about the great swamp. Alligators abound, black bears occur in fair numbers and panthers still frequent the dense wooded areas around its edges. Aquatic birds are plentiful, especially during the annual migrations when ducks and geese seek sanctuary in the Okefenokee Wildlife Refuge.

Less conspicuous animals, snakes and frogs especially, were then present in abundance, and they were the chief objectives of our visit.

After an overnight run on the *Florida Special* in April 1940, Sturgis, Bob, and I detrained at Jacksonville, hired a car, and drove to Folkston, a tiny village on the swamp's eastern edge. There we met our guide, Tom Chesser, who maintained a fleet of small, narrow boats, the only effective conveyances for getting about in the morass. Following his lead we waded out through a cypress swamp, arrived at a landing, and soon were witnessing a skilled demonstration of how a slender craft can be poled down a winding waterway scarcely wider than the beam of the vessel. Propelled by Chesser's skilled hands, the boat fairly skimmed down the weed-choked canal that was the only navigable watercourse from "Chesser's Island" to the swamp proper.

Poling looked easy. All one had to do, it seemed, was to stand in the stern, balance himself, and shove away on a pole. Not to be outdone, we attempted to follow our guide's example, but a winter of indoor office work and our total lack of skill took their toll. We fell overboard, developed charley horses, lost our poles, and had to admit that, when it came to supplying motive power for a boat, Chesser's 14-year-old son, Wade, put us all to shame.

From the cypress swamp the canal threaded its way through a meadow of sphagnum moss and terminated eventually in what was known as a "prairie," a vast open area covered with shallow water and studded with a myriad of little islands. There, as the two boats moved along, we saw ibises and egrets in flight, and we inspected, but were careful not to disturb, nests of the Florida crane, a subspecies of the sandhill crane.

After an hour or so of admiring the scenery, contemplating the vastness and solitude of the Okefenokee, and admiring the skill of the two Chessers, we were suddenly reminded of the purpose of our excursion. Bob spotted a cottonmouth, which promptly vanished into a mass of aquatic vegetation. Then, at Tom Chesser's suggestion, we began a systematic tour of some of the islands where, he told us, snakes were most likely to be caught.

The soundness of his advice was proved in short order. We soon discovered another cottonmouth, and in an instant we three adventurers were in hot pursuit. Instead of heading for the water, the snake retreated into a tangled thicket of vines and creepers, the kind that catch on hands and clothing and make progress extremely difficult. By surrounding the spot we brought our quarry to bay, its tail beating a lively tattoo and its mouth agape, ready to plunge its fangs into anything that came too near. By crawling on our hands and knees, we forced our way to it, pinned down the dangerous head with a stick, and seized it by the neck. A few moments later we had a live and squirming trophy in our collecting bag.

And so it went. After our adventures in the swamp, we wandered for another day over southeastern Georgia, capturing whatever we could find in the way of amphibians and reptiles. Those that were suitable for exhibition at the zoo we kept, meanwhile liberating the others.

Our most amusing happenstance befell us at Camp Cornelia, the public landing where would-be explorers of the Okefenokee hired boats and sought the services of government guides. We had been tramping in the woods nearby, and, just as we stepped into the open, we beheld a five-foot alligator lazily sunning itself on the bank of a small canal. While Sturgis took photographs, Bob and I threw caution to the winds, stalked as close as we could, and then rushed the reptile. The net result was two collectors soaked to the skin, and one alligator complacently eyeing the damage from the safety of deep water. Doubtless many another rash visitor had

rushed him, and so often that he knew exactly how to elude us. He was the most nonchalant alligator imaginable. Fifteen minutes later, when we passed the same spot, he had resumed his siesta on the shore. We contented ourselves with the knowledge that there were plenty of alligators in the zoo's reptile house anyhow!

About a decade later, at a dinner party that both the Ingersolls and Isabelle and I attended, the conversation eventually drifted to the subject of wildlife. Sturgis reminisced about our trip to Georgia, and suddenly exclaimed, "Let's go back again. That was a lot of fun." And so it was that in May 1951 we headed for the swamp once more. At the last minute some unexpected business matter prevented Bob from joining us, and his place was taken by his son, Bobbie, a nice lad of 13.

That time we went by air. Commercial aviation was still more or less in its infancy, but Sturgis elected to fly. We left Philadelphia's primitive airport, which, in comparison with today's vast and complicated facilities, looked like something one might expect to find in a tiny cow town on the Great Plains. In Norfolk, we changed planes and boarded an "airliner" seating perhaps two dozen passengers, which would take us to Jacksonville. Just before we took off I watched the pilot and copilot in the open cockpit as they linked their little fingers across the gap between them and then touched the balls of their thumbs together in a symbolic gesture of good luck. It worked. We took off in a fog, and when we emerged into the clear, hundreds of feet above the ground, another plane was almost within touching distance. Both aircraft veered instantly away from each other, and we survived.

Because I knew the Ingersolls much better by that time, I had decided to do our second trip to the Okefenokee up brown, so to speak. I invited my good friend Ross Allen, from his Reptile Institute at Silver Springs, Florida, to join us, and he accepted at once. Ross, a handsome, vigorous man, and a champion swimmer and alligator wrestler, was then at the height of his popularity. He met us in late morning at Jacksonville, and from then on, whenever we were near groups of people, we were surrounded at once by admirers seeking to shake his hand. Such attention prompted Sturgis to exclaim that Ross should run for governor.

Ross, who immediately took charge, suggested, since we didn't have a full day, that we do a bit of canoeing on the St. Mary's River, which drains the swamp to the east and forms part of the boundary between Florida and Georgia. The place he chose was still wild, little frequented by human beings, and it was easy to stay close to shore and slip up on basking water snakes. We rented canoes and then split up, with Ross and Bobbie in one headed upstream and Sturgis and I in the other drifting downstream. It was a hot afternoon, and collecting was poor. Soon Sturgis suggested we have a swim. We beached our craft and were skinny-dipping a few moments later. Stimulated by such informality, I became bold enough to seek free advice from a Philadelphia lawyer for the first and only time. I had just signed a contract with Houghton Mifflin for the first edition of the "Field Guide to Reptiles and Amphibians," and I asked what expenses I could deduct for income tax purposes. I was delighted when Sturgis replied, "Anything and everything associated with its preparation."

The next day, under Ross's guidance, we went to the landing at the edge of the Okefenokee and hired a small motorboat that barely accommodated the four of us. With it we began the long trip along the canal which had been dug to penetrate many miles into the swamp, evidently, at least in part, to permit rangers to keep an eye on the wildlife. We noted, however, that it was also used by fishermen, several of whom we passed as we putt-putted along in the first part of the canal. After we had left them behind, Ross shut off the motor and suggested that we use the paddles with which the boat was equipped. He and I took turns at the bow while the other steered from the stern toward clumps of bushes containing snags on which water snakes and an occasional cottonmouth were basking in the early-morning sun. As experienced snake hunters we simply grabbed the water snakes with our hands, but used tools to catch the two or three cottonmouths we decided were worth taking back to the zoo. We feared to let Bobbie do any grabbing lest he make a mistake. Sturgis declined taking the bow position, citing his below-par eyesight as the reason.

At one point a large cooter turtle had hauled out on a stout horizontal snag. Bobbie slipped overboard, swam slowly and carefully under the turtle, reached upward, and grabbed his prize. Like many a young enthusiast, he expressed his success with a shout and a broad grin.

We moved onward along the canal, sometimes using the motor, but paddling again wherever snakes were concentrated. We must have caught close to 50, but we threw back all except for a few we took home with us.

Eventually we arrived at the end of the canal, where a broad circular turning basin had been dredged. What a sight met our eyes. A large alligator, at least eight feet long, was on the opposite shore, basking in the sun. Ross and I slowly and silently paddled toward it. When we were perhaps 30 feet away, Ross began his remarkable and long-practiced imitation of the grunt of a young alligator. More than once I had seen him stand in front of the large alligator pen in the Philadelphia Zoo's

old and long-ago demolished reptile house, and the instant he gave the distress call grunt, every alligator in the pen would swim toward him. Now, here in the swamp, he gave the imitation call again as we paddled closer. The big gator immediately rose to its feet, waddled to the water's edge, and started swimming toward us. Ross stopped his grunting, and the big reptile disappeared beneath the water. Moments later its head surfaced less than a paddle's length from our small craft. Bobbie and I whispered excitedly. Sturgis heard us, and suddenly blurted out, "Where is it? I can't find it in my bifocals." Seconds later the gator came into focus for him, and its nearness made it look immense. Sturgis let out a shout and nearly did a back flip in his spontaneous effort to get away from the monster. Ross and I frantically steadied the boat lest we all go overboard, and the alligator sank from sight, not to be seen again. As we paddled away we all had a hearty laugh; the loudest and longest was from the Philadelphia lawyer, who quickly recovered from his scare.

On our return trip we mostly used the motor, but we turned it off occasionally when we sighted something of interest. During one of the silent periods Sturgis remarked, "I don't see how you fellows find those snakes and know instantly which ones are poisonous. I can't even see them until they're in the boat." We assured him that it was a matter of skill and practice, but we politely mentioned nothing about our younger and better eyes.

About halfway along the length of the canal there was a small, brushy island that sported a tiny dock and picnic table and where we had gone ashore on the way into the swamp to stretch our legs. This time we stopped again, and all four of us went our separate ways to relieve ourselves. Ross, Bobbie, and I leisurely sauntered back to the landing, but Sturgis had disappeared. Presently he emerged from behind a bush with a look of triumph on his face and a small snake clutched behind the head in his hands. At long last he had made a catch! We hurried to see it and Ross, speaking in a calm voice, said, "That's a cottonmouth. Put it down on the table and I'll take care of it." Sturgis did just that, instantly jerking his hands away and breaking into a cold sweat. Ross pressed the flat side of his broad-bladed hunting knife on the snake's head and then picked it up and dropped it into a bag I held open for him. It was a small cottonmouth, but it was fully capable of inflicting a painful and serious bite.

As we paddled quietly away Ross told us about a man he knew who had been bitten by a small cottonmouth and who had had a rough time of it. A few moments later Sturgis, in a stern paternal voice, said, "Bobbie, don't you ever do a damn fool thing like your grandfather just did!"

We were soon back in Folkston at a small restaurant. Ross, as usual, was quickly surrounded by admirers, but Sturgis made a beeline to the telephone to call his wife long distance and tell her about his adventures with the alligator and the cottonmouth. His day in the Okefenokee was a favorite topic with him, and he retold it often until the time of his death in 1973 when he was in his 80s.

Chapter 22

Attempting the Impossible:
Part I. Origin of the Field Guide

About four years after our marriage, Isabelle and I attempted the impossible. We set out to photograph every species and most of the subspecies of reptiles and amphibians found in the United States and Canada east of the 100th meridian. The wonder of it is that we very nearly succeeded, thanks in large part to many friends, colleagues, and even total strangers.

Why did we tackle such an ambitious project? The first edition of our "Field Guide to Reptiles and Amphibians" required it. But let me explain.

Following preliminary correspondence, Roger Tory Peterson, author of the "Field Guide to the Birds" and founder of the series of books that bears his name, arrived at the Philadelphia Zoological Garden one day in 1951, to offer me in person the opportunity to do a field guide on herps in the same general style as his bird books. I accepted with enthusiasm and looked forward to tackling what certainly loomed as an enormous undertaking. I was sure I could handle the text, because by that time I had already written the first two editions of the "Reptiles and Amphibians of the Northeastern States." But there was a king-sized problem that had to be solved as quickly as possible—the illustrations. Peterson was not only an excellent ornithologist, he was also a splendid artist who could illustrate his own books. Neither Isabelle nor I could qualify in that respect, although she was an outstanding wildlife photographer. She had been highly successful in preparing labels for the zoo's large flight cage, where a bewildering variety of birds lived together in harmony. To help visitors identify them, she photographed each kind of bird in black and white, made a print, and then hand-colored it, using oil tints.

In those days color photography was unreliable without special, costly equipment and, by experimenting, we found it almost impossible for us to reproduce colors in their true tonal values. Further, the publisher, the Houghton Mifflin Company, required us to submit our plates in camera-ready condition. Every picture had to be exactly to scale and pasted in its proper position. We quickly ruled out any attempt to accomplish that assignment with tiny color transparencies.

So, Isabelle tried her oil paints and immediately ran into trouble. Her failure to obtain a good color rendering of a coral snake will explain her dilemma. If she made a photographic print pale enough to feature the yellow, the black came out gray. Conversely, a good dark print made the yellow far too muddy. What to do? I appealed to a friend at the Beck Engraving Company in Philadelphia, which at the time was doing color printing for the "National Geographic Magazine." The Beck Company graciously permitted their expert colorist to train Isabelle in a whole new world of artistry.

A few comments on the new technique are instructive. Isabelle made black-and-white prints to the required scale and then brown-toned them in her darkroom so they resembled the pages of the Sunday rotogravure sections of the newspapers of those days. The brown retained the pattern of the animal, and to this she applied watercolor dyes exactly matching the colors in life. There was even a black dye, but it and all the others had to be used with great care. Once on the print they could not be removed. Even a slight mistake meant starting all over again with another print. With practice Isabelle became quite skilled, and we were off and running, so to speak, with our illustrations.

We took inventory and found we had suitable pictures of most of our local species, as well as many others, although quite a number had to be rephotographed in poses matching, as closely as possible, those of related kinds that would appear with them on the same plate. Often that wasn't easy, especially with a squirmy venomous snake. We did the photographing together. I posed the animals while Isabelle operated the camera. We used a plain white nonshiny oilcloth background so that our photographs would match Peterson's bird drawings as closely as possible, with no distracting items in the background. Isabelle prefocused and I tried to place the animals in exactly the right position. Some kept crawling or walking away, but many of the calmer ones eventually "froze" in place. They would even permit me to manipulate their toes and tails into better positions, if I did it very slowly and gently with a pair of forceps. Others required endless patience and sometimes ingenuity. I discovered that, if I held frogs and salamanders beneath the cold water tap for about 10 seconds, and then blotted off excess moisture with a paper towel, they would often remain motionless for at least a few seconds. I became adept at placing snakes and lizards upside down, applying slight pressure with the fingers or palm of my hand. After a minute or so I would say "now," raise my hand quickly and the supine position was retained long enough for Isabelle to snap the shutter, which automatically set off the bright flashbulb. We used that source of light for virtually all our pictures, except for a few that were taken out-of-doors. Strobe lights came into use during the midst of our labors and we experimented with them, but the results were not as good as those obtained with the bulbs. Modern automatic cameras were still far in the future.

Covering a venomous snake with a cloth bag for 10 minutes or so would sometimes calm it down, and then the bag could be lifted off gently with a snake hook. More often than not, however, the pose would be wrong, and we would have to start over again. Sometimes we placed a transparent cake cover from our kitchen over a rattlesnake and waited until it coiled itself into a usable position. We must have spent a year's worth of hours waiting out specimens that wouldn't cooperate.

The day before our departure on a long field trip to collect more herps, I received a litter of newborn copperheads. We needed a picture of one to go with that of a baby cottonmouth already in our photo collection, and the pose had to match as closely as possible. We kept at it until after midnight before we had the desired result. The exposed film went into cold storage until our return, and the baby snakes were liberated near where their parent had been caught. In the morning we departed later than planned, short of sleep, but happy about our eventual success.

Turtles were the most exasperating. We, of course, wanted to show their heads, the two feet nearest the camera, and the tail, if possible. It was usually a case of waiting them out. Because I was working fulltime at the Philadelphia Zoological Garden, it became Isabelle's unhappy chore to "turtle sit." Once placed on the posing table the turtle would often remain completely immobile for an hour or more, with all its appendages concealed by the shell. Then its snout would be extended ever so slowly until the eye appeared, just enough for it to see the photographer. Later the two front feet would be thrust slightly forward, ready for an instant takeoff. Many a time the turtle dashed away without ever exposing its head, and poor Isabelle would put the reptile

back in place and resume her seemingly endless vigil. It is a tribute to her patience and perseverance that our collection of nonmarine turtle pictures eventually included all those which appeared in the several editions of our field guide.

Softshell turtles were photographed underwater. So also was an exceptionally recalcitrant mud turtle. It wouldn't move for hours, so I placed it in a narrow aquarium that had a piece of our white oilcloth taped to the back. Even in the water it remained quiescent, only occasionally paddling to the surface for a breath of air. Eventually it stuck its head out partway and, in desperation, Isabelle snapped the shutter. The bright light from the bulb stimulated it, however, so that for a few seconds afterward it extruded its head and feet well outward from the shell. With this behavior as a clue, we decided to trick it. We rigged up another flashbulb, I set it off, and the head and feet came out as they had previously. Isabelle snapped the shutter and we had our picture.

We had, of course, alerted many of my herpetological colleagues about our needs, but we wanted to do as much of the fieldwork as possible ourselves. One- or two-day excursions were manageable for localities relatively nearby, but we knew we also would have to go far afield—which we did on a series of trips. The first was when the American Association of Zoological Parks and Aquariums held its annual conference in Miami, Florida, in November 1951. I attended it and took my vacation immediately afterward.

We drove to Key West, stopping en route to collect at various places on the long chain of islands, which at that time were still relatively wild and not crowded with wall-to-wall housing as so many of them are today. Several kinds of geckos, almost all of them introduced, were known to be established on Key West, so we worked there for several days. We explored the graveyard, abandoned buildings, and various trash piles where geckos allegedly were common, but a cold front had moved in, and the lizards were mostly in hiding. Several local people whom we met told us that they wished we would keep the "damn yankee" weather up north where it belonged.

Despite the cold—it was down in the 40s throughout most of the mornings—we soon assembled a small collection and went to work photographing it. We had brought along all our camera gear. It was our first long trip, and we thought it best to take pictures at once and not risk the possibility that some of the animals might die on the long drive homeward. On later trips we devised foolproof containers to transport our livestock in the car. It was far easier to do our photographing at home than in the field.

As things worked out, it was well that we took posed pictures on a table at Key West. I had managed to find only a single yellow-headed gecko, but, once on the table, it dashed away and quickly disappeared among the furnishings of our motel room. Despite an hour-long search we failed to find it, but we discovered it dead on the floor the next day. That accident forced me to have another look and, in a trash-strewn empty lot, I found a much better female than the one we had lost and, in addition, a handsome male. The weather had changed for the better, and those largely diurnal lizards were evidently warming up after the cold spell.

We were staying at the Hilton Haven Motel, and Mrs. Hilton, the proprietress, took a keen interest in what we were doing. She evidently had considerable influence in town, because she helped us to get on the "off limits" air base and even the submarine base, which was then known as the "Little White House." President Harry S. Truman used it as a retreat from the endless pressures of Washington. He was in residence while we were there. We were met at the military gate by an armed Marine in uniform, who had been assigned to accompany us everywhere we went on the bases searching, with only moderate success, for anoles and geckos. Later Mrs. Hilton asked if we would mind being interviewed by a reporter from the local newspaper. Because of the wonderful cooperation she had given us, we agreed. Was Mrs. Hilton a member of the famous hotel family? We should have asked her.

Another interesting person we met was Edward Fernandez, the island's cistern inspector. Because fresh water had always been a scarcity on the remote islands of the Florida Keys, rainwater was channeled from roofs into barrels and large concrete cisterns. It was Fernandez's assignment to introduce small fishes that ate mosquito larvae into the cisterns. That helped to reduce the hordes of the insect pests that we found so much in evidence on the Keys, particularly when the wind died at sundown. He showed us how frogs huddled close to the cisterns by day, taking advantage of leaks or seepages here and there. Fernandez later sent me live Mediterranean geckos by mail; we had failed to find that species, possibly because of the cold weather.

The Key West Aquarium was a godsend for us. Through the kindness of its director, William H. Kroll, we were able to obtain pictures of four species of sea turtles: green, hawksbill, loggerhead, and ridley. That completed our series of those interesting marine reptiles, except for the leatherback, but more about it later.

We made our way back along the attenuated two-lane highway that used the breathtaking, spidery, abandoned railroad bridges spanning gaps between islands.

We stopped at a motel in Homestead, which became our headquarters while we made daily trips into the Everglades National Park. At the time the region was still a "river of grass," even though the manipulation of its water supply through the use of canals was already well under way. I fear I would be sadly disappointed if I were to return to the Park today after all the many difficulties and indignities it has suffered. We had superb cooperation from the Park staff. Dan Beard, the superintendent, and the grandson of the Dan Beard who had founded the Boy Scouts in England decades earlier, executed a document that made me a "collaborator" of the National Park Service while we were there. That entitled me to use Park equipment, even boats equipped with outboard motors. We enlarged our collection and saw many things of interest, including huge flocks of spectacular water birds, such as spoonbills, wood storks, and many species of herons, as well as anhingas, gallinules, and other water-loving birds. We also saw a young American crocodile and many alligators of assorted sizes, and I caught a huge indigo snake that measured well in excess of seven feet in total length. Willard E. Dilley, Joseph E. Moore, and William B. Robertson, all excellent naturalists (the last-named a student of Hobart Smith's at the time), gave us invaluable help. Our only disappointment in the Park was our failure to see a reptile of any kind at Snake Bight, a tiny arm of Florida Bay. How good it would have been to catch a snake at a place with such an appropriate name.

We stopped at the Miami Serpentarium, where William Haast, the oft-bitten owner, gave us permission to photograph a pale, highly spotted south Florida kingsnake, then known as *Lampropeltis getulus brooksi,* but now recognized as *L. getula floridana.* It was the only live snake of the *brooksi* morph I ever saw, before or since.

On our way homeward we made two more important stops. The first was at the Ross Allen Reptile Institute at Silver Springs. Ross was a close friend of mine for several decades, and he helped us with energy and enthusiasm. His entire collection was at our disposal. He skillfully and patiently manipulated a large American crocodile into position for Isabelle to get the shot of its head that we needed, and he made a small summer house on the Institute grounds available to us, complete with a posing table to which we could take individual specimens to photograph as needed. Ross had accompanied us partway down the Florida Keys, but he had to return home on business before we went on alone to Key West.

At the University of Florida in Gainesville we visited Archie Carr and Coleman J. Goin, who were working on a book on the cold-blooded vertebrates of Florida. They badly needed illustrations, so we worked out an agreement with them. They would ship us live reptiles and amphibians, which we would photograph and, in exchange, we would make extra pictures of the same specimens for them. During the next year Coly Goin sent us box after box of "goodies," and that is why the Carr and Goin "Guide to the Reptiles, Amphibians, and Fresh-Water Fishes of Florida," published in 1955, includes reproductions of so many of Isabelle's beautiful photographs.

One other event of our 1951 Florida trip should be recorded. While we were attending the zoo and park convention in Miami, I sneaked away from the meetings one evening and went in search of *Anolis distichus,* an introduced species that was known to be established in Brickell Park. This small, almost geckolike anole blended well with the twigs on which it slept, and I managed to expend almost three hours before I found two with the aid of my headlamp. We attempted to photograph them in our room in the Hotel McAllister but, as luck would have it, one of them scooted away and disappeared behind a bureau. We literally tore the room apart in our search for the escapee, but we failed to find it. Sometime later, however, as we were undressing for bed, the lizard peered over the top of my briefcase. A lively pursuit developed, which included searching under the furniture and removing all the drawers from the bureau, one by one. I eventually caught the lizard, but I am eternally grateful to Isabelle for not snapping a picture of me crawling across the floor in my underwear.

Chapter 23

Attempting the Impossible:
Part II. Exploring the Appalachians for Salamanders

The winter of 1951-52 was a busy one, as Isabelle and I pressed forward with our effort to photograph all of the species and many of the subspecies of amphibians and reptiles known from east of the 100th meridian. We returned from our successful excursion to Florida in early December, and, because we had taken special precautions for getting our catch home safely, everything was alive and well. We rephotographed many of the specimens and thus obtained better poses than those we had gotten in the field. Also during that winter, I used an insulated box and transported snakes and turtles in my heated car to our home on the shore of Taunton Lake, in the New Jersey Pine Barrens. We were thus able to get pictures of several species in the Philadelphia Zoo collection, over which I presided as curator of reptiles.

Spring brought an opportunity for local fieldwork to obtain some of the things we still lacked in our rapidly growing collection of black-and-white negatives and prints. The warmer weather also brought a few desiderata from friends, but we had no inkling of the huge bonanza that was to come our way in April.

The 1952 meeting of the American Society of Ichthyologists and Herpetologists was to be held in Austin, Texas, beginning on the eleventh of that month, and we received word late in March that the Texas Herpetological Society was planning an extensive concurrent display of living amphibians and reptiles. Further, we learned we'd be welcome to photograph anything we wanted, and that we could take home whatever livestock we needed. What an extraordinary piece of luck! The word was broadcast well ahead of time, and many persons made extra trips afield in order to find rarities for us. The news of our project had spread far and quickly.

In addition to our camera gear, we took along a carry-on container holding empty snake bags, large and small, and an assortment of bottles with holes punched outward in their lids. After our flight to Austin and a night at a hotel, we taxied to the University of Texas, where W. Frank Blair provided us with a small, mostly empty room in the Biology Department for our use as a studio.

Isabelle visited a nearby camera shop and rented a tripod and floodlight and purchased a supply of flashbulbs.

What a sight we beheld when we inspected the live collection! Texas is a big state, and the varied assemblage of herps was positively stunning. There were hundreds of animals, and a large percentage were of species I had previously never seen in life. One, the buttermilk snake, *Coluber constrictor anthicus,* I didn't even know existed. We could scarcely wait to get at them.

We managed to photograph a few specimens before the meetings started, which was well, because I had to dash back and forth to help Isabelle whenever there was a lull. I was then on the ASIH Board of Governors, and I also, of course, wanted to hear several of the papers that were being presented. Although our progress was slow, we had decided, in advance, to participate in the day-long field trip that included a visit to Ezell's Cave, and that turned out to be an adventure.

Ezell's is a fault cave, and therefore very different from the great limestone caverns with their stalactites, stalagmites, flows of travertine, and other spectacular evidence of the long, slow interaction of carbonic acid with limestone. Ezell's Cave is near San Marcos on the Balcones Escarpment, which sharply separates the Edwards Plateau from the lowlands to the east and south. Beginning near Waco and extending southward close to San Antonio and then swinging westward to Del Rio, the Escarpment varies in height from near nothing at Waco, to 300 feet at Austin, to as much as 1,000 feet near its western end. Its summit, as a result of surface erosion, is highly irregular. The Escarpment was formed by a series of shifts in the earth's crust, which disrupted the water table and created long series of underground passageways as well as numerous fault caves. Ezell's is one of the latter. The rare Texas blind salamander, *Typhlomolge rathbuni,* a sightless ghostly troglodyte, was known to occur in the reservoir at its bottom.

The entrance to the cave was a hole on the surface of the ground among some large rocks. Our guides produced a stout rope, tied it securely, and told us we would have to descend one at a time, hand over hand, down a fairly

RC, hot and dirty, emerging from Ezell's Cave after delving into the bowels of the Edwards Escarpment. Photo by IHC.

wide and open shaft. It had been decades since I had attempted any rope climbing, but I was not to be outdone by Clifford H. Pope, who was several years my senior. About 20 others joined us. After what seemed like an interminable drop of 100 feet, but was actually much less, I arrived in an open room. Off to one side was a narrow slit in the rock, and that, we were told, was the way to the bottom. Furthermore, we were instructed to crawl down headfirst on our hands and knees. What a weird experience as we followed our leader. Having my head lower than my body felt very strange, but there was no way to go except onward, twisting, turning, and squeezing down the narrow passageway illuminated only by a few headlamps and flashlights. Eventually we arrived at a crystal-clear pool bordered by a narrow bank. Unhappily, there were no salamanders, but at least we had seen their habitat far beneath the surface.

As we stood there I had a bad turn. I suddenly remembered that central Texas had been shaken by a sharp earthquake just a few days previously. Suppose another one occurred and our escape was cut off. It didn't, and our ascent was accomplished much more quickly and easily than our descent, but I was relieved, nonetheless, when we reached the surface. None of the ladies in the party had entered the cave with us, but Isabelle, camera in hand, waited patiently so she could take my picture as I emerged from the depths.

Someone explained the ecology of the cave to us. Numerous bats roosted in the cracks and crannies of the upper part of the cave, and their guano attracted insects and many other kinds of invertebrates, some of which filtered downward to serve as food for the salamanders.

Eventually the cave became too popular, especially with teenagers, and the man who owned it and the adjacent property became fearful of a possible lawsuit if there were an accident. So he sealed the entrance with a solid barrier that remained in place for some years. Eventually the Texas chapter of The Nature Conservancy purchased the property, remodeled an old house on it for a graduate student caretaker to live in, removed the solid barrier, and replaced it with an iron grille to permit free passage for the bats, but not for would-be spelunkers or salamander collectors. William Davis, of the Southwestern State Teachers College (now University) at San Marcos, served as custodian of the cave for many years. Regrettably, the bats never returned, and the food chain was broken.

After my stint as an amateur caveman and the use of muscles I didn't even know I had, I was quite content to relax in the car that Richard J. Baldauf had provided as part of a caravan to transport the crowd of us on the field trip. My rest was soon interrupted, however, by our arrival at the large spring pool that is the source of the San Marcos River. It was covered, in part, by mats of floating algae that are the only known habitat of the tiny neotenic salamander *Eurycea nana,* which attains a maximum total length of only two inches. John C. Wottring provided us with two or three live ones a year later, and I should also mention that our photograph of *Typhlomolge* was taken of a live specimen from Johnson's Well, also near San Marcos, sent to us by John E. Werler.

Back at the university we pressed on with our photography, but it very soon became obvious that we would have far more livestock to transport home than we could possibly manage. Even the animals we had photographed had to go back with us to be sure we had good negatives after they were processed in the darkroom. Also, Isabelle would need most of the herps as models when she applied their colors to her special prints.

A friend who lived in the Philadelphia area had made the trip to Austin by train, and he volunteered to help us by taking back some of the larger specimens. There were a number of them, because we had been urged to accept extras for exhibition at the Philadelphia Zoo. While I was attending meetings Isabelle made a trip to a store and purchased a stout, zippered bag for our friend. Even with his help we were loaded down. We arrived at the airport with all our pockets, our carry-on bag, and Isabelle's camera case crammed with bags of small snakes and lizards, as well as bottles of frogs, toads, and salamanders nestled in wet paper towels. Fortunately, there were no security checks in those days. One simply ascended a movable gangway and walked into the plane. No one knew we were loaded with "creepy crawlies."

Once we had taken our seats I opened the tops of the carry-on bag and camera case so the animals would have plenty of air. All went well, and we were spared the embarrassment we experienced a few years later when, under similar circumstances, several recently collected frogs began to call loudly as we descended to land at the Philadelphia Airport. Perhaps they were stimulated by the change in air pressure. In any event, all the surrounding passengers' heads and eyes were quickly turned in our general direction. We stoically maintained straight faces and mentally blessed our guardian angel. If we were going to be put off the plane, at least it would be at our destination.

We arrived at our home base with our menagerie intact, and I worked most of the next day transferring livestock into cages, aquariums, and other, more roomy containers, because I knew it would take us quite awhile to photograph the many dozens of species. Also, I would have to keep them in good condition until Isabelle could make her toned prints to scale and then painstakingly color them by hand using live animals as models. The larger, more durable reptiles I took to the zoo to be retrieved later.

When I picked up the zippered bag from our friend a day or two later, it felt lighter than I had remembered. We hadn't listed its contents, but, as we unpacked it, we tried to recall how many of each of the larger snakes we had been given, especially mud snakes, *Farancia abacura*. Didn't we have at least two or three of them? It really didn't matter, because there was still an excellent one in a bag.

Many months later I received an item in the mail that had been torn from a page in the Pullman porters' magazine. It described how one of the men, in the small hours of the morning during the previous April, had found and killed a large red-and-black snake as it was moving down the aisle between the sleeping passengers. It could only have been one of our mud snakes. I never told our benefactor about it for fear of embarrassing him, and that is why he remains nameless. Apparently he had opened the zippered container and then some of the snake bags inside in order to have a look at the contents, inadvertently allowing one or more of the inmates to escape.

Spring was always the busiest time of year at the zoo. In my capacity as public relations officer, it was my duty to promote and make all the arrangements for the zoo's annual fiesta on the first Sunday in May, which drew tens of thousands of paying visitors. I was on a seven-day-a-week schedule until the event was over, but I worked with Isabelle in the evenings and made plans soon to devote all my time and energy on my days off toward getting on with the task of photographing our bonanza. But then disaster struck. Isabelle sprained her wrist and was out of commission, with her right arm in a sling.

A feisty rat snake, Elaphe obsoleta lindheimeri, *from the live collection assembled by the Texas Herpetological Society. Photo by IHC.*

Well, almost out of commission. She managed a minimum of household duties and, with my help, she set up the camera on our tripod so she could operate the release with her left hand. I changed flashbulbs and helped in many other ways. She was able to continue her darkroom work, but at a much slower pace than normally. Coloring prints was out of the question.

So, I was faced with the problem of keeping almost 200 amphibians and reptiles alive and healthy for the duration. For food, mice, pinkies, and mealworms were available at the zoo, but there were then no reliable purveyors of live crickets of assorted sizes. I set out a light trap for insects each night and was able to provide enough of them for most of the frogs, toads, and lizards to eat. The only casualties were the cliff frogs, *Syrrhophus marnocki;* fortunately, David L. Jameson, then a student at the University of Texas at Austin, was able to send replacements.

Isabelle's wrist slowly improved, but it was painful for many weeks. Gradually things progressed, but it was late summer before we were all caught up—and ready for more.

Despite our long preoccupation with the livestock, I managed to do quite a bit of writing, and I had long since prepared a master list of the species and subspecies that needed to be illustrated. We checked each one off when it had been satisfactorily photographed and, in most cases, colored. (A number of our subjects appeared on black-and-white plates.) The list of desiderata was still formidable, and it was apparent that our weakest group consisted of the lungless salamanders of the family Plethodontidae. I reread Emmett Reid Dunn's pioneering book on that subject and all the other literature I had available, and I also corresponded with colleagues who had worked on the various genera. I even had several personal consultations with Dunn, a good friend who served on the faculty of nearby Haverford College. Our next excursion afield would have to be to the southern Appalachians, where so many different members of the family occurred.

One very important thing had to be done first. We had to get Houghton Mifflin's approval of the color work. Several members of their staff had seen samples of the oil-tinting technique, and they agreed with us that they were unsuitable. By the summer of 1952, however, Isabelle had become quite skilled in applying watercolor dyes to her brown-toned prints. So we assembled a sample color plate with all the individual animal portraits cemented in their proper positions. We delivered it to Lovell Thompson, the publisher's general manager, at their New York branch office on September 10. We also took along several samples of Isabelle's line drawings, as well as a few excerpts from my partially finished text and a copy of the legend page that would appear opposite the color plate. Mr. Thompson liked them all, but he told us we would have to wait for final approval until the engraver had been consulted.

As we had in 1951, we devoted my vacation to fieldwork, and we departed for the southern mountains on September 19. I was armed with a long list of potential collecting stations, including type localities, where my informants thought we might be successful in finding salamanders of many taxa.

Our first stop was at the Dixie Caverns near Salem, Virginia. Clifford H. Pope and James A. Fowler had recently described a new species, *Plethodon dixi,* from there. Jim arranged for an introduction to the owner of the cave, who welcomed us with enthusiasm. In marked contrast with Ezell's Cave, this one was a normal limestone cavern, but it had been commercialized and wired so it could be illuminated for conducted tours of cash-paying visitors. The salamanders were numerous, chiefly well up on the formations, but I had my best luck collecting the few we needed by using a flashlight when the bright lights were off. They clung to the stalactites and flowstone by the natural adhesion of their moist bodies. *Plethodon dixi* was eventually synonymized with Wehrle's salamander, *Plethodon wehrlei,* but I retained it on one of the color plates because the Dixie Caverns' form looks different.

It would read like a travelogue if I were to write an account about each of our many stops and our success in getting the animals we needed as we worked our way southward. We stopped at Comer's Rock, White Top, Grandfather Mountain, Linville Falls, and at many places along the Blue Ridge Parkway, which, at the time, was quite new. On our way home we reached the summit of Mount Mitchell, the highest peak in the Appalachian chain.

Our interim destination was the Great Smoky Mountains National Park where we remained for a week ranging through its forests, searching its streams, and visiting nearby localities. Also, I wanted to see a friend of many years' standing, Arthur Stupka, who was the Park's Chief Naturalist. He had helped in advance with the formalities necessary to make me a temporary collaborator of the National Park Service, which gave me the authority to collect throughout the area. Further, the privilege included permission to carry a key to gates placed across many dirt roads to keep casual visitors from driving along maintenance roads and fire trails. Beyond the gates we were often able to penetrate into the "hinterland" for a mile or two and thus avoid the tourists who were still present in considerable numbers despite the lateness of the season.

We rented an isolated cabin where the sound of the Roaring Fork of the Little Pigeon River provided a constant musical reminder of the wilderness that was so close to us. We off-loaded our livestock, which was doing very well in coolers freshened almost daily with ice. I inspected the collection every night before retiring. We'd had such good success getting our animals home safely from other trips that we did a minimum of black-and-white photography while we were in the Park. It was so much easier to take pictures at home.

Collecting was excellent in the Smokies and, in addition, we had two memorable experiences. The first occurred as we were driving slowly through a forested area and we noticed a large black rat snake, *Elaphe obsoleta obsoleta,* crossing in front of us. Isabelle applied the brakes, but, when I stepped out of the car, the snake promptly stopped and shrank itself, so to speak, into dozens of undulations, and then "froze." Even though we walked all around it and Isabelle took several pictures, it didn't move until I touched it with my hand, whereupon it crawled away in a virtually straight line. I have never seen an explanation of such behavior in the herpetological literature, but I recalled having watched another black rat snake kink itself in a similar manner on the Delmarva Peninsula, and also a yellow rat snake, subspecies *quadrivittata,* in Florida.

The second experience occurred when we hiked upward along the trail through virgin forest to Ramsey Cascade. We started in mid-morning, but we stopped so often to admire the enormous old trees, the sparkling brook, the birds and butterflies, and such novelties as a fungus that looked like a blooming flower that it was lunchtime long before we had reached the falls. As we ate our sandwiches we reveled in the joy of being in such a lovely place, remarking to each other that it was the most magnificent forest we had ever seen. After lunch we continued upward along a steep trail, reached the beautiful double-drop cascade by early afternoon, took pictures, and then started downward, collecting as we went. That took time. There were so many seeps and so many stones and logs to turn and then to put back into place, that we were not more than two-thirds of the way down when we suddenly realized it was getting dark. We quickened our pace, abandoned collecting, and covered as much ground in 20 minutes as we had during all the rest of the way from the falls. By then it was so nearly dark that we had to pick our way with care. Isabelle turned her ankle, not badly, thank goodness, on an exposed root along the trail. Finally, when the light was almost gone, she sat down on a fallen log while I groped my way very slowly onward, with visions of having to crawl back on my hands and knees to sit huddled with Isabelle through the black, cold late September night. I knew I could find her because we both routinely carried whistles.

Miraculously, I had advanced less than 100 feet when there was our car! It was the work of seconds to unlock the door and switch on the lights. I heard Isabelle shout, and I hurried back to her with a flashlight. How thankful we were that we had been able to open the gate and drive inward a long way before parking. We were soon on our way, but humbled by our experience and with the firm resolve to keep close watch on the time in the future.

Years later, when I was visiting the American Museum of Natural History in New York, I was invited to go behind the scenes to have a look at several nearly finished large exhibits of horizontally life-sized and splendidly executed examples of forest types of North America. I lingered in front of an exceptionally impressive one and remarked, "That looks like the trail to Ramsey Cascade." A dozen eyes instantly turned toward me in surprise. That was exactly what they were trying to reproduce, and they were pleased because I had recognized it. It was a good choice. There are almost as many native species of trees in the Great Smoky Mountains National Park as there are in the whole of Europe, and the valley leading up to Ramsey Cascade must have a good proportion of them.

The Cascade trail had yielded salamanders of several species, but the most interesting were several examples of the imitator salamander, a member of the genus *Desmognathus* that has a bright reddish, orange, or yellow cheek patch that closely resembles a similar marking in the red-cheeked *Plethodon* we had found elsewhere in the Park.

While we were enjoying our fieldwork in the Smokies, we received two telegrams that boosted our morale even higher. The first wire was from Paul Brooks, the Editor in Chief at Houghton Mifflin. The color plate we had submitted was completely acceptable. Brooks followed it with a letter addressed to our home. He also returned our samples, and stated that, as Isabelle wrote in her diary, "Everything was eminently satisfactory." We rejoiced at having cleared all the technical hurdles. Our biggest remaining problem was to press on with our goal of getting live examples of all the remaining herps we needed.

The second telegram was personal. Betsy Jane Conant, my number one granddaughter, was born on September 27. We were off at once to the nearby town of Gatlinburg to send a telegram of congratulations to her proud parents, my son, Skip, and his wife, Virginia. Incidentally, when Skip was eight years old we spent the better part of a week in the Park. He and I and Art Stupka hiked daily, even to the top of Blanket Mountain, despite Skip's then short legs. Even today, almost 60 years later, he vividly recalls that trip. He found a pygmy salamander, then recently described as a new species, and he reminded me that I overturned a rock on one of the balds and found a quarter under it.

After we left the Smokies we drifted southward as we visited a variety of other localities, most of them accessible at the time only by traveling along atrocious dirt roads that were barely passable in our Oldsmobile station wagon. They included Wayah Bald in the Nantahalas, Whiteside Mountain, Bridal Veil Falls, Rabun Bald, and a surprise finale at Jocassee, in South Carolina. We managed to find motels every night, but it had grown so cold in the upland towns by early October, that I removed the livestock from the car and took it inside with us. At Highlands, North Carolina, it had dropped to 23°F inside the car when we opened it early in the morning.

Our excursion to the southern Appalachians was truly a salamander trip. We found a few snakes, lizards, and toads, but the members of the Order Caudata were preeminent. Even now, many decades later, I can vividly recall many of the thrills we enjoyed. Overturning rocks in seepage areas in the forest and suddenly exposing bright red salamanders, or even the more spectacular orange spring salamanders, was as startling as turning on colored lights in the pitch dark. A special remembrance is my finding of three large yonahlossee salamanders with their deep red unicolored backs. They were in moist forest duff at a stop we made while we were descending White Top in extreme southwestern Virginia. Many times I waded in shallow, stony-bottomed brooks, usually clad in boots, but occasionally braving the cold water in my wet shoes, socks, and jeans, as I slowly overturned small water-worn rocks. The shovel-nosed salamanders walked slowly away, but their irregular and variable coloration and pattern blended so well with the stream bottom that I had to keep a sharp eye on them lest they "vanish" even though they were still in sight. Occasionally I would uncover a large black-bellied salamander. No hesitation for them. They darted away either with or against the current, and, thrill of thrills, I twice saw large blackbellies atop wet boulders motionless in broad daylight, and in the sunshine at that! While working along brooks at night I sometimes spotted seal salamanders partially emerged from their streamside burrows, and they looked indeed like tiny seals.

In moist forest habitats there were many kinds of woodland salamanders, genus *Plethodon*, among which the red-cheeked and red-legged forms were the most spectacular. Also, I recall slowly progressing on my knees in spruce-fir forests at high elevations, carefully removing moss and chips of bark and occasionally being rewarded by finding a pygmy salamander.

The trip was an education for me, but trying to classify many members of the group properly was a major headache. The authorities disagreed, and in several cases I had to be arbitrary and side with one while earning the ire of the other. In the second edition of our field guide the classification in many cases was different, and in the third edition it was even more different. Now, thanks to studies in biochemistry, we know of species that can be identified only by highly sophisticated laboratory techniques, an obvious impossibility for an amateur herpetologist.

It was fitting that our last planned stop was near Jocassee, in upland extreme northwestern South Carolina. In 1927 Clement S. Brimley had described a new salamander from Jocassee, *Plethodon clemsonae*, named for Clemson College. It was a great rarity that had been found again only a very few times. We had little hope of getting one, but the type locality was not far out of our way, and we thought it worth a try. Quite late during the afternoon of October 5 we drove on a rough dusty road to Jocassee, which consisted of only two or three houses and an old camp. We parked near the camp, fairly close to a bridge over the Keowee River. It was growing dark and the air temperature was dropping steadily. A half hour's reconnaissance revealed nothing herpetological, so we sat on the tailgate and snacked on what little food we had with us—a bit of cheese, a few potato chips, and a soft drink apiece. We knew it was a long way to any town big enough to support a restaurant.

We had thought we were in a remote and almost deserted area, but soon after dark an almost constant stream of dilapidated, battered old cars and trucks appeared, each stirring up clouds of dust as it passed us going away from Jocassee. Then each returned at intervals of about 15 or 20 minutes. We finally decided that only a moonshiner's hideout could attract so many vehicles over such a rough back road at night.

After our snack, and because of the dropping temperature, we were about to depart when our flashlight revealed a garter snake crawling across in front of where we were sitting. If it wasn't too cold for a snake, maybe some salamanders might be out. So I buckled on my headlamp, thrust the clip on the battery case over my belt, and started along a footpath through the woods. I had walked only a short distance when I spotted a salamander crossing the path and, marvelously, it was a *clemsonae*! I had scarcely bagged it along with a handful of damp forest floor debris when I saw another, and then another, and another. They seemed to be everywhere, some walking, others motionless, and still others standing with their heads protruding from their burrows. I saw 25 in all; we had our desideratum, and proof positive that *clemsonae* was not rare at all. It was a matter of being in the right place at the right time.

There were two sequels to that discovery. Albert Schwartz, the noted authority on the herpetology of the West Indies, was at that time interested in South Carolina amphibians and reptiles. I drew a map for him and he subsequently visited Jocassee and obtained additional evidence of the abundance of the supposed rarity. Richard Highton later lumped *clemsonae* with the highly variable members of the *Plethodon jordani* complex, but I retained Isabelle's rendering of it on a color plate, along with other outstanding variations in the group, because of the distinctive silvery or bronzy lichenlike pattern in *clemsonae*.

We were a happy couple as we sped homeward, stopping only occasionally at salamander habitats, and then chiefly just to stretch our legs. Our trip had been a great success and we had assembled a collection that would keep us busy for quite a while. We would work together photographing the many salamanders, but then proceed with our individual duties. Isabelle would concentrate on her darkroom and coloring chores, and I would get on with the formidable task of writing.

Chapter 24

Attempting the Impossible:
Part III. Tying Up Loose Ends

By the early spring of 1953 Isabelle and I were caught up again, and we paused to take inventory and make plans for the coming season. Work was well advanced on our "Field Guide to Reptiles and Amphibians." Our effort to photograph all the species and many of the subspecies found east of the 100th meridian was well past the halfway mark. What animals were still needed and how best to get them? I studied our master list, on which we had checked off every animal that was finished, and I carefully correlated it with geography. It quickly became apparent that there was no remaining large single section of the country to which we could journey in the hope of collecting considerable numbers of desiderata, as we had during previous years. Thanks to our own excursion to Florida and massive help from Coleman J. Goin, of the University of Florida, the Southeast was fairly well covered, with only a score or so of species, including rarities, still missing. The huge collection contributed by the Texas Herpetological Society in the spring of 1952, and our own lengthy field trip to the southern Appalachians during the previous autumn had given us a wealth of pictures from those general areas.

We decided that our 1953 foray into the field would have to be a peripatetic one with a succession of stops in likely places. We finally settled on three general areas: (1) the Central Highlands of Missouri, Arkansas, and eastern Oklahoma, where many unusual salamanders occurred; (2) Reelfoot Lake in Tennessee, with its great numbers of turtles; and (3) the vicinity of New Orleans where Fred R. Cagle, of Tulane University, assured us that his students would be happy to go afield with us. It would be autumn, however, before I could take my vacation. Spring and summer were the busiest times of the year at the Philadelphia Zoo and I was, after all, a full-time employee of that institution.

Another device I used to acquire herps was to appeal to some of my younger friends. I drafted a seemingly endless series of carefully tailored lists, all designed to include the missing forms that might be found within 100 miles of each recipient's vicinity. This paid off well,

and, although specimens arrived at odd intervals, they, in conjunction with our own one- or two-day field trips, kept us busy all summer.

I requested that all animals be sent by the Railway and Air Express agencies, and addressed to me at the zoo, and I promised to reimburse each sender for his out-of-pocket expense. Several of our benefactors, however, ignored my instructions. Some of the animals came by mail, even snakes, which are prohibited by postal laws and regulations. Others were addressed to our home at Taunton Lake in the New Jersey Pine Barrens, where there was no express office closer than Trenton, a long drive for us. In such cases we would receive a postcard, mailed to Taunton, advising us that a "perishable" shipment was being held for us to pick up. Because we feared that packages might have been left standing in the sun or otherwise mishandled during the two or three days since their arrival, we were justifiably worried. I telephoned the Trenton express office as quickly as possible, reached a different person each time, and requested that the consignment be kept in a cool place. It seemed futile to have it reshipped to the zoo, which would have increased the charges and, more important, the risk of fatalities. I made several hurried trips to Trenton, and once, when Isabelle and I went at night, I had to bribe the agent. We had to find his house, take him to the express office, get our package, return him to his home, grease his palm, and then drive to Taunton where we arrived about midnight. I never succeeded in getting the Trenton express office to telephone me collect when anything arrived there for me. Against regulations, they said. One shipment did meet disaster. All the animals inside were dead when I finally received it, but the sender made replacements directly and correctly to the zoo after I explained what had happened.

We were off on our 1953 field trip on October 8, and we made our first herpetological stop at Columbia, Missouri. There we visited with James A. Kezer, who was well acquainted with the salamander fauna of the Ozarks. Jim had written to some of his friends on our behalf, and he gave us several hand-drawn maps to help us find obscure localities. Armed with these we headed south and visited the Devil's Bathtub, and Fairy, Marvel, and Mud Caves. In the twilight zones of these we found cave and dark-sided salamanders, and we also obtained grotto salamanders, both pigmented larvae and white adult troglodytes.

The collecting in the caves appeared to be normal, but the region outside them, after a prolonged drought, was bone dry. The dust on the back roads we traveled was so overwhelming, sifting into everything, including our eyes and the mucous membranes of our noses, that we were miserable. We headed south into Arkansas to meet Herndon G. Dowling, who was then on the faculty of the University of Arkansas. He and his student, Robert S. Chase, spent a day with us. They found two snakes of species we already had photographed, and showed us a few small, almost dry streams where some of the salamanders we needed normally occurred. Herndon, however, gave us two nice ringed ambystomid salamanders. We stayed together all the way to Mena, close to the Oklahoma line, where we rented a motel room to which Isabelle retreated to, as she put it, dedust herself. In Herndon's car, we three males ascended Rich Mountain after dark. My only reward was a nice series of the central dusky salamander (*brimleyorum*), taken where a small spring was still flowing. We returned to Mena, I rejoined Isabelle, and the two younger men drove through the night to get back to the university in time for an eight o'clock class.

The next day we headed upward to explore the long east-west-trending mountain, and we stopped first at the lookout tower. Jim Kezer had suggested that we search through a nearby pile of rotting shingles where the Rich Mountain salamander, *Plethodon ouachitae*, had often been taken. I overturned the entire pile, much of which was well on its way toward being reduced to wood pulp, but it was so dry that I had little hope of finding anything. Under the crumbling, slightly moist penultimate shingle, however, I uncovered a single specimen.

We continued westward along the crest road, and met two snakes of interest. The first was a timber rattlesnake, the only live western one we had yet seen, and we both were intrigued by its reddish brown middorsal stripe, a marking that previously we had associated only with the canebrake rattler of the southeastern states. The second was a black rat snake that "kinked" itself in the same way as the one we had found in the Great Smoky Mountains. The dust was atrocious, enveloping everything and taking forever to settle. We persevered, however, and were lucky enough to find another spring with a large assortment of the local dusky salamander, from which I made a careful selection. We braved more

dust on Caddo Mountain, but nothing further of interest turned up except for three many-ribbed salamanders that I netted with a tea strainer in a brook that still had water running in it.

Several of the friendly, helpful people we had met in the Central Highlands very kindly offered to send us salamanders after the drought was broken, and, because the entire region was so distressingly desiccated, we decided it was futile for us to continue. We moved on to our next destination, Reelfoot Lake in western Tennessee.

I was no stranger to Reelfoot. I had been there twice during the 1930s, once with turtle expert Norman E. Hartweg, who called the lake the "turtle-iest" place he ever saw. Also, Isabelle and I stopped there for a few days in 1950. The drought must have affected the lake, because I had never seen it so low. The water level must have been close to three feet below normal.

In 1934 Reelfoot Lake had seemed like a naturalist's paradise. Water snakes of several species abounded, I caught cottonmouths there, and I could see at least 100 turtle heads protruding from the water on any clear day as I rowed casually about in a boat. The entire area was virtually unspoiled by the incursions of human beings. There were a few fishing camps near the spillway, but the principal industry was turtles. Vast numbers of hatchlings were gathered and sold in the pet trade, most of them to die miserable deaths from careless handling or malnutrition. Mercifully, in more recent years, their sale has been prohibited in the United States because they carry salmonella, but large numbers are still exported to other countries. I have seen baby red-eared turtles paddling listlessly around in pet shop aquariums, even as far away as Hong Kong.

There was also a market for larger turtles. Soups and stews made from the diamondback terrapin, *Malaclemys*, of brackish coastal marshes were very popular and expensive in several eastern cities, and the Reelfoot turtles were used, in part, to increase the bulk. Cheating, perhaps, but such turtles were far less expensive than the diamondbacks. During our 1953 visit, turtles were still being trapped in numbers, some even apparently for racing purposes. By then, however, the shores of the lake were studded with motels, restaurants, and other facilities, chiefly for the accommodation of fishermen.

By far our most profitable procedure was to examine the catches of professional turtle trappers. This we did for the better part of two days, buying just the few we needed. One morning J. T. Colwick, Reelfoot Lake manager for the Tennessee Game and Fish Commission, took us to a place where two large, boxlike "turtle crawls" were swarming with adults, mostly red-ears. They were all jumbled together, and we had to remove them, one by one, with a dip net, to the bottom of our rowboat. After we emptied the smaller box I rowed out into the "channel" so Isabelle could take a picture. Checking all the turtles was a slow process and, after we had returned most of them to the crawls, I had less than half a dozen that were useful to us. The following day we hired a youngster to collect baby turtles, and I bought a number from him, including duplicates, for 15 cents each, three times the going price. We checked our list, and all we were still missing from Reelfoot Lake was an adult slider or hieroglyphic turtle, but Hudson Nichols, who was studying fisheries biology at the lake, eventually sent us two fine large ones.

Our own collecting efforts were not very successful. I found a beautifully striped adult southern painted turtle, but, in the process of catching it, managed to coat myself with thick, sticky mud from head to foot. The lake was so low and the water-filled ditches, to which large numbers of turtles had retreated, were so muddy, that our efforts were hopeless. We took a day off to rest in our motel and write copious notes about our adventures and the herps we had obtained.

Our next stop was in New Orleans, where I immediately telephoned Fred Cagle. He had already helped us by sending several sawback turtles, all members of the genus *Graptemys* and each occupying a different stream system emptying into the Gulf of Mexico. Males and juveniles bear strong spines on their vertebral scutes. No wonder that fishermen and other local people call them sawbacks. Dr. Cagle and his student field crews, largely working at night, had demonstrated that all of the sawbacks were abundant, and he described two (*G. nigrinoda* and *G. flavimaculata*) as new.

We were warmly welcomed, given several animals that were being held for us, and treated to gustatory delights. Later, Isabelle and I, both Dixieland fans, spent

A boatload of turtles, examined one by one, from the crawls in the background. Photo by IHC.

a long evening on Bourbon Street listening to several different musical combos.

We were enthusiastically joined for a day in the field by several young men under the leadership of Donald W. Tinkle. They met us, in the Tulane University truck, at our motel cabin early on a Sunday morning. One of the boys rode with us (in case we lost sight of the truck and became confused) as we sped northward through Slidell to Bogalusa. We stopped along the way at Talisheek Creek, where Don and one of the other students deftly caught a waterdog, *Necturus beyeri,* for us. Just across the Mississippi line we drove through clouds of dust (kicked up by the truck just ahead of us) to a place where a jumble of old lumber lay scattered around. The boys began heaving it aside, uncovering a profusion of herps in the process. After eating our brown-bag lunches, we drove to Varnado and then to a nearby fishing camp along the Pearl River, which was also very low. We obtained 18 species in all. Most important for us were the southern red salamander, named for Percy Viosca, Jr., and the Mississippi ringneck snake. One of the boys had carefully scouted the two localities to make sure they had been undisturbed for a long time and that they could put on a good show for us. Late in the afternoon we drove back to Bogalusa, stuffed the young men with ice cream and other sweets, and bade them farewell. They returned to Tulane, and we headed eastward for the long drive home. The next day, after passing through Mobile, it began to rain, and from then on, ironically, after weeks of braving the dust, we had almost constant precipitation all the way home—a mixture of drizzle, rain, and torrential downpours.

These reminiscences emphasize our fieldwork, which, in my younger days, was the fun part of being a herpetologist. I thoroughly enjoyed being out-of-doors, seeing new parts of the country, and finding miscellaneous

Reelfoot Lake has long been known for its abundance of turtles—hatchlings for the pet trade and large ones for racing and for human food. Photo by IHC.

herps under all sorts of circumstances. Even meeting species that were new (in life) to me at the Texas Herpetological Society display at Austin was exciting: so many bright colors, frogs and toads sitting upright and alert, snakes gracefully coiled. How different they were from the preserved museum specimens that, in so many cases, were all I had seen of them previously. And there we were, thanks to my skillful wife, making those colors come to life in a book.

Less exciting, but rewarding in its own way, was my writing of the text. Much of it went smoothly, but there were knotty problems to solve, such as the classification of the salamanders as mentioned previously. A pattern of procedure quickly evolved, however, to which I strictly adhered throughout. I would write what I could on each species or group, and then submit my copy to at least two persons who were authorities on or at least familiar with the species or genus involved. I asked for criticisms and suggestions, and I got them aplenty, but all served to improve the quality and accuracy of my text.

The most difficult paper job was the mapping. In the early 1950s there were few maps showing accurate distributions of individual species, so I usually had to assemble my own. The older generic revisions, such as those of Ruthven on the garter snakes (1908) and Blanchard on the milk and kingsnakes (1921), were hopelessly out-of-date. The newer revisions were a big help. So also were the many hundreds of spot maps sent to me, graciously and laboriously prepared, showing localities for all the species known to occur within the state or region where my benefactors were working. The two-volume "Handbook of Snakes," by Albert H. and Anna A. Wright, wasn't published until 1957, which was too late; our book was in press by then. As it turned out, it was well that I hadn't depended on their maps. Regrettably, they contained many errors, as colleague after colleague pointed out to me later. The consensus was that the Wrights had accepted too many hearsay, undocumented records. My maps, like my text, were submitted for review to all who contributed to them, and to anyone else who wished to see them. For several consecutive years I took a complete set of working maps to the annual meetings of the American Society of Ichthyologists and Herpetologists. I sat at a table that all herpetologists would have to pass to attend the scientific sessions, and I solicited criticisms and additions from anyone interested. After the maps were published, W. Frank Blair was kind enough to call them the best available to date. I was well aware, however, that there was ample room for improvement, and I predicted that their appearance would "smoke out" many unknown and unreported localities. That was indeed true, and I

had many hundreds of new records to add when I prepared the second edition. There were also many refinements for the third edition.

By the spring of 1954 our need for live specimens had become spotty. The list of desiderata was still discouragingly long, however, and it included so many rarities that it was impractical for us to attempt to seek most of them ourselves. We decided that perhaps a pickup trip would be best. I wrote to many friends and correspondents in the South and told them we would like to visit them and show them some samples of what the field guide would be like. In several cases we would be meeting them for the first time. I pointed out what we still lacked from their general vicinities and, as subtly as possible, suggested that it would be nice to pick up such-and-such specimens during our visit. My ploy worked unexpectedly well, and we prepared a promising itinerary. First to Brownsville, Texas, an area where many Mexican species entered the United States. Then we went across the Rio Grande into northern Mexico itself in the hope that road-cruising at night would yield one or two of those very same species. Our destination was Monterrey, then one of our favorite Mexican cities. From there we would work back through Texas, stopping at several places, then to New Orleans again and Mobile on the way home.

Through the kindness of the Board of Directors of the Zoological Society of Philadelphia, I was permitted to take my only spring vacation ever, and we were off on May 3. We stopped at a motel each night but, by dint of taking turns napping while the other drove, we were in Brownsville by suppertime four days later, and I was telephoning correspondents whom we had never met. Ted Beimler, who was associated with the Brownsville Zoo for many years, and Pauline James, of the Pan American College at Edinburg, Texas, both had species we needed. Rather than to risk the animals on our short jaunt to Mexico, we decided to return to Brownsville. Our good friends, newly made, were quite willing to hold them a few days longer for us. Ted accompanied us on a local field trip the following day, during which he showed us many interesting habitats in "The Valley" of the Rio Grande, and I caught several four-lined skinks.

In Mexico we obtained a *Tantilla* and two splendid male blue spiny lizards. We even devoted two days and nights to looking for *Natrix* (now *Nerodia*) to continue my work on the water snakes of Mexico, which I began in 1949, and which was published in 1969.

I hope I may be pardoned for mentioning a nonherpetological event. In Monterrey we made our headquarters in the rather run-down Regina Courts, but only because they were directly across the highway from the excellent Restaurante Los Arcos where we had enjoyed eating several years previously. I managed to consult with one of the waiters in private, and I asked him if they could provide a cake for Isabelle's birthday. He replied in the affirmative, and asked how many candles would be needed. I tactfully responded by saying that, when a lady was over 30, a single candle was sufficient.

After a day in the field we cleaned up and headed for Los Arcos. As soon as dinner was over, the waiter marched in with a big, round, beautifully iced cake surmounted by a burning candle. Isabelle was so surprised and excited that she almost forgot to blow out the candle, and, for the first time ever, she asked me to take her picture. In the meantime, all the restaurant employees, from the busboy and dishwasher to the cashier and majordomo, hovered discreetly in the background wearing broad grins. Because it was not the tourist season, other diners were few. We passed the cake around, but the employees consumed the bulk of it. The waiter didn't give away my secret, and my dear wife interpreted the single candle as symbolic of her first birthday in Mexico.

We were soon back in southern Texas. Pauline James and a student, Maurice Fox, joined us for a brief evening field trip, which included the opening of many water-meter boxes in the alleys of Harlingen, where we found tiny Rio Grande frogs, *Syrrhophus campi*. Maurice had two black-spotted newts, *Diemictylus meridionalis*, for us, and Pauline gave us a Mexican treefrog, *Hyla* (now *Smilisca*) *baudini*, that was found on the sleeve of a shirt about to be put into a washing machine. They had other goodies for us, and so did Ted Beimler. Collectively, they supplied us with an excellent representation of south Texas rarities.

Our homeward trip was a succession of triumphs, at least from the standpoint of getting the species and subspecies we still needed. At the San Antonio Zoo, John E. Werler had no fewer than nine different "new" animals for us. From Austin, Ralph W. Axtell took us on a field trip to the Edwards Plateau, and Fern and W. Frank Blair had a buffet supper for us along with a group of herpetologically oriented students, who showered us with more specimens. Also, Frank gave me some tapes of frog calls that proved invaluable when I had to describe their vocalizing. At Houston we were invited to the home of J. Patrick Kennedy, where 15 or 20 members of the Houston Herpetological Society were assembled, every one of them with animals for us. I was kept busy recording the collecting data for everything. Afterward, Isabelle passed around samples of the artwork for the field guide, and I gave a brief talk about its scope. At New Orleans there was again a large group of herps awaiting us, including rare turtles of the genus

Isabelle surveying the cake for her first (and only) birthday in Mexico. The tray, an advertisement for Carta Blanca beer, was a gift from the Restaurante Los Arcos in Monterrey. Photo by RC.

Sternotherus that Donald W. Tinkle permitted us to borrow. We had accumulated such a large herpetological zoo that we had to send some of the larger and more hardy animals by express, from both San Antonio and New Orleans, to the Philadelphia Zoo. When we left New Orleans, Ernest A. Liner followed us in his car through the pouring rain, and he and I waded in the swamps for several hours. We saw or heard 13 different kinds of frogs and toads, but none we had not already photographed.

Our last pickup was at Mobile, and in some ways it was the most exciting. In a desperate effort to get a black pine snake, *Pituophis melanoleucus lodingi*, a form known for its rarity, I had written a letter to the superintendent of schools in Mobile. H. P. Löding, for whom the subspecies was named, had been a resident of Mobile, and that seemed a good place to start. In response, I had a letter from Carl A. Watson, the forester for the county school board, who was in charge of the 22,000 acres it owned. A lively correspondence followed, and Watson wrote that, because he was constantly in the field, he might be able to help. I sent him a detailed description of the snake and its behavior and an empty snake pullman, in case he should be lucky enough to find one to send us. He was enterprising enough to report my request to a columnist for the "Mobile Press Register," who promptly featured it.

We had agreed to stop to see Carl Watson on our way to Texas, but when we arrived in Mobile and tried to telephone, neither he nor his wife could be reached. So

RC with the black pine snake, Pituophis melanoleucus lodingi, *the outstanding prize of the 1954 excursion. Photo by IHC.*

we left word that we would call again when we returned. On the way back we stayed at a motel at Long Beach, Mississippi, on the night of May 26. In the morning, I phoned Mobile and learned that Carl was in the field for the day. A call to another number revealed that Mrs. Watson had taken her school class on a picnic. What to do? We hated to drive on without at least making contact with one or the other of them, so we decided to wait. I arranged to have the car serviced, and we had a leisurely swim in the shallow waters of the Gulf of Mexico right in front of the motel. We took off for Mobile around noon, and arrived there about three hours later. When I finally reached her by telephone, Mrs. Watson told me that they had a snake that might be what we wanted. She gave me directions on how to reach their home. No one was there, but when I walked around the house, I saw a barrel in the backyard, covered by a piece of hardware cloth and held down by a couple of bricks. I rushed over, removed the covering, and, lo and behold, inside was a big black pine snake almost six feet in length. It was long and strong enough to push off the lid, and I was amazed that it had remained inside at least all day. I bagged it immediately, and we sat down to wait for the Watsons.

Our meeting with them was a joyful occasion, for all of us were excited about our success. We took them to a good restaurant for dinner, and then we heard the story of the snake's capture. A man by the name of C. G. Steadham had read the columnist's story months earlier, and when his two dogs brought a big, belligerent black snake to bay, Mr. Steadham managed to maneuver it into a 10-gallon can. He had to call the newspaper to get

Watson's name and telephone number, and the latter quickly picked up the snake. But that had been about 10 days previously! How lucky we were that it had stayed in the barrel all that time. Carl Watson called the columnist, who interviewed me by phone. Later he wrote another story about our success and how the first column had produced results.

Thus ended our extraordinarily successful trip. Our list of desiderata was greatly reduced. What's more, we were busy all summer getting everything processed.

Another of the elusive critters was the dusky gopher frog, then designated *Rana areolata sevosa*. It lived in a narrow Gulf Coastal strip from eastern Louisiana to the western part of the Florida panhandle. I knew from past experience that gopher frogs are explosive breeders that appear suddenly after heavy rains, lay their eggs, and then vanish. Once, when I was on my way to Reelfoot Lake with some young friends during the 1930s, we stayed in a tiny cabin near Paducah, Kentucky. It rained hard, we heard gopher frogs "roaring," and we caught three. The next night, despite much more rain, we searched but neither saw nor heard any. With those facts in mind, *sevosa* was high on my first list of desiderata, and it stayed there on many consecutive lists. Several persons who lived in or near the range of *sevosa* searched for it on our behalf. One rainy spring night, two groups of lights were bobbing about in a swamp near the coast. They gradually approached each other and eventually met. "What are you doing here?" one group asked the other. "We're hunting for Rana *sevosa* for Conant," was the reply. Whereupon the first group responded, "So are we!"

Finally, during our fourth spring collecting season, we hit pay dirt from a totally unexpected source. On March 23, 1955, a letter arrived from William E. Brode, of the Bay High School at Bay St. Louis, Mississippi. He had been alerted by Percy Viosca, Jr., of New Orleans, a mutual friend. Brode wrote that he had 25 or 30 live *sevosa* in a specially constructed pond, and that he was studying gopher frogs. Did we still need *sevosa*? My reply went by return mail, and within a few days four fine specimens arrived by air parcel post. Brode later wrote, "At two degrees above freezing, after five days of hard rain and during a very heavy downpour, *sevosa* crossed a dirt country road by the hundreds. We were able to hear them for a good two miles." He suspected that rain was the chief stimulus, and that, once the breeding urge began, cold weather did not matter. He even put a pair of *sevosa* in his refrigerator as an experiment, and when he opened the door a little later the male was clasping the female.

On July 25, 1955, Pauline James found a white-lipped

frog, *Leptodactylus labialis,* in Mexico during the first heavy monsoon rain of the season, and she shipped it to us as soon as she returned to the States. At last we had all the frogs and toads (the anurans), just four years after we began seeking them. We considered that a prime accomplishment because so many are seasonal. They appear suddenly after intense rain storms, breed, and then go underground, literally in the cases of many species. Trying to find such frogs and toads out of season is virtually impossible. Sheer luck at best.

On May 18, 1956, I received a telegram from John E. Werler. He had a speckled racer, and, if we still needed that species, he would be glad to send it to us. I wired back in the affirmative at once. Another desperately needed species could be removed from our list.

It took a few minutes for my excitement to subside, but I then returned to the pile of zoo work on my desk. I was still busily engaged with that when, an hour later, one of the zoo employees brought me a square, sturdy box, measuring perhaps 15 inches in all directions. He told me the express man had just delivered it. I opened the box at once, and, when I saw what was in it, I let out such a loud whoop that my secretary, Ruth Endy, and other staff members came running into my office in alarm. It was a large, perfect, and extremely beautiful speckled racer. It had been sent to me by Pauline James, so it must be from southern Texas or nearby Mexico. What a coincidence! We had waited for years to acquire that species. Here was one in hand, and another would arrive by air express, probably on the morrow.

Pauline had found the snake while investigating a beaver dam and pond about a mile from the Rio Grande in southeastern Hidalgo County, Texas. It was actively chasing young leopard frogs. She was lucky enough to grab its tail as it was disappearing into the brush at the water's edge. The snake immediately bit her, but she pluckily held on and made her capture.

John Werler's snake, which he had purchased from someone at a quite reasonable price, was of the western subspecies, *Drymobius margaritiferus fistulosus,* which ranges northward along the western side of Mexico to southern Sonora. Its pattern differed somewhat from the subspecies occurring in Texas, but no matter. With Isabelle's skill, she could easily have retouched a print for use on one of the black-and-white plates.

I wrote immediately to both benefactors and reimbursed them for their expenses. Perhaps I told them eventually about getting two speckled racers almost simultaneously, but there is nothing about it in my correspondence. In retrospect, I am sure I wanted both Pauline and John to share in our exuberance. To have mentioned the other's contribution would have tarnished their euphoria of success.

For the benefit of readers who are familiar with all three editions of our field guide and are thus aware of how much both common and scientific names have changed, I should state that I have purposely used the nomenclature for both types of designations as they appeared in our first edition, with which we were pioneering. In a few cases, however, I have also included the present-day usage.

In the end, our goal turned out to be impossible, at least within the time frame of our deadline, but we missed only two species. When one considers how many hundreds of taxa were involved, the lack of two seems almost like an infinitesimal number. We made a truly determined effort to obtain living specimens of all the necessary species and subspecies of reptiles and amphibians, and, with the deeply appreciated help of a very large number of friends and even complete strangers, we almost succeeded. The two species that eluded us were the huge leatherback sea turtle and the cat-eyed snake, which enters the United States only in extreme southern Texas.

Three times while we were hard at work on the field guide we learned about the stranding of dead leatherbacks along the Atlantic coast, two of them hundreds of miles away, a distance we would have gladly driven even to get photographs of a deceased specimen. As soon as we heard, I immediately telephoned, but I was too late. Local public health officials had ordered the removal of the carcasses from the beaches, and dismembering was already well advanced. Possibly other dead leatherbacks had washed ashore on barrier islands remote from public beaches, but word of such strandings didn't reach the news media, on which we were dependent for information. In the end, we borrowed a leatherback picture from the American Museum of Natural History. It was of a dead animal with its eyes closed and a dark streak descending from the salt gland on the near side of its head. Isabelle cleverly retouched the photograph so that the animal looked alive.

Fortunately for us, William E. Duellman was concurrently working on his doctoral dissertation, a study in depth of the cat-eyed snakes of the genus *Leptodeira*. He did considerable fieldwork in Latin America, and he sent us many living examples of a variety of species that we photographed for him. None was of the taxon that gets into Texas, but one was rather similar in appearance. Isabelle's artistic talents came into play, and she adjusted the pattern to suit. Both of the missing species went on black-and-white plates, but for the second edition we were able to borrow a cat-eyed snake from Texas to depict in color.

In addition to the leatherback picture, we also borrowed a photograph of the Tennessee cave salamander, this time from Edward McCrady, because ours had a stumpy, partially regenerated tail. Isabelle used our live one as a model for coloring a print she prepared from Dr. McCrady's picture.

Almost 3,000 live herps passed through our hands during the many years we worked on the field guide, and we illustrated some 600 of them. The great majority appeared on the color and black-and-white plates, but Isabelle used many other photographs in preparing her diagnostic and decorative line drawings. Also, I used them as guides while I was doing my writing.

Many of the 3,000 or so specimens were sorted in the field, and extras were liberated where we found them. Among those taken or sent to us at our base, some were added to the collection at the Philadelphia Zoo; others were returned to the people who let us borrow them. Other specimens, especially rarities or individuals representing range extensions, were eventually preserved and placed in museum collections, chiefly the American Museum of Natural History, where I have long been a research associate.

Given today's emphasis on rare and endangered species and the need to protect many kinds of reptiles and amphibians that are suffering severely from loss of habitat, I doubt if it would now be possible to duplicate what we accomplished in seven years, counting from the day my contract was signed in 1951 until publication late in 1958. Perhaps someone with unlimited time and patience could manage under the present conditions, but it is almost beyond imagination to contemplate the mountain of paperwork that would be required to follow all the federal and state red tape in order to stay within the limits of the law and bureaucratic regulations. Thank goodness we worked on our field guide so long ago.

Roger Tory Peterson's reaction to our project was expressed in his "Editor's Note" in the first edition, where he wrote, "The magnitude of the problem of securing live specimens of virtually every species and subspecies of reptile and amphibian east of the 100th meridian and then keeping them alive and healthy, sometimes for months, almost staggers the imagination."

We coped alone with the curatorial, photographic, and coloring work, but we were immensely indebted to scores of herpetologists, whose names appeared in the "Acknowledgments" section of our first edition. It was the younger ones who did most of the fieldwork on our behalf. To express our appreciation, we dedicated the book "To the younger herpetologists of America whose high standards of professional ethics and spirit of mutual cooperation assure them a brilliant future in their chosen field. Without their enthusiastic aid this book would have been another five years in the making."

An old proverb, attributed to the Chinese, holds that one picture is worth a thousand words. Without its profusion of illustrations our field guide would have been of limited value. Isabelle, my hard-working wife, deserves the credit for depicting the animals shown on the plates and for the great number of line drawings she contributed. Even though she protested when our second edition was published in 1975, I insisted on including the following: "This book is dedicated to Isabelle without whose talents as photographer and artist it never would have been attempted."

Speaking of the second edition, a few final sentences are necessary. Robert C. Stebbins's "A Field Guide to Western Reptiles and Amphibians" was published in 1966. He, however, terminated his boundary at the eastern borders of New Mexico, Colorado, Wyoming, Montana, Saskatchewan, and the former District of Mackenzie. That, of course, left a large geographical gap between the two books, including the western half of Texas and large parts of the states to the north, as well as portions of Manitoba and Keewatin, which latter is now part of Canada's Northwest Territories. As I recall it, the omission was not discovered at the Houghton Mifflin office until the work was in type, and starting over would have been impossible. Roger Peterson, in an effort to solve the problem, made a special trip to our wooded lakeside retreat in the New Jersey Pine Barrens and politely asked us if we would fill up the "hole." Fortunately, I had anticipated the dilemma that faced the publisher, so I'd had time to think about it in advance. We discussed the matter in depth, and I pointed out to Peterson that taking on this assignment would tie us up for several more years. We finally agreed to do it if we were given eight additional color plates, and if the title of our second edition could be changed to "A Field Guide to Reptiles and Amphibians of Eastern and Central North America." Thus, we had the responsibility for the herps in approximately two-thirds of the total territory involved; the remainder was Dr. Stebbins's.

So we had the problem all over again, although on a smaller scale. We had to obtain living specimens of a large number of additional species, a sizable proportion of which consisted of Mexican taxa that also inhabited the Big Bend region of western Texas. It took us quite a few years before we succeeded.

Chapter 25

Research, Publications, and Other Zoo Activities

The Penrose Research Laboratory played a major role in the welfare of the Philadelphia Zoological Garden, and especially its animal collection. It was established in 1901, right in the zoo, by two medical doctors, Charles B. Penrose and Cortland Y. White, professors in the Medical School of the University of Pennsylvania. Dr. Penrose eventually became the president of the Zoological Society of Philadelphia, an office he held from 1909 until 1925. His interest in the Laboratory continued unabated, and his written and financial contributions to its work and publications were substantial.

The most important routine function of the Laboratory, and one that began years prior to its founding, was conducting autopsies on every mammal and bird that died in the zoo. Careful records of the causes of death were kept, diseased organs were preserved, and microscope slides and paraffin-blocked tissues became part of the Laboratory's study museum, which, during my early years at the zoo, occupied the second floor of the Lab building. More than 20,000 autopsy records had accumulated for study and comparison by the time I retired in 1973. Information gleaned from that data bank produced profound changes in the management of the animal collection.

The Laboratory's first major accomplishment was the virtual eradication of tuberculosis from the primate collection. The necropsy protocols clearly revealed that apes and monkeys were quite susceptible to the disease, and many succumbed to it, so techniques were developed for quarantining newly arrived primates. All were tuberculin skin-tested, and they were admitted to the collection only if they were free from infection. All keepers and other employees who came in contact with the primates were X-rayed regularly to be sure they did not have tuberculosis. Meanwhile, the interior of the old monkey house, which had anthropoids on one side and monkeys on the other, was walled with plate glass, effectively shielding the living exhibits from the thoughtless visitors who tossed half-eaten food into the cages, and the morons among them who even spat at the animals.

Dr. Herbert Fox was the leader in developing the new routines, and he was Director of the Laboratory when I joined the zoo staff in 1935. He was an able pathologist, a professor at Penn's Pepper Laboratory, and highly regarded by his peers. He made many important contributions, including assembling information from the Lab's records for an authoritative book entitled "Disease in Captive Wild Mammals and Birds." It appeared in 1923, and the cost of its publication was underwritten by Dr. Penrose.

Dr. Fox was the most pompous person I ever met. He was difficult to approach and so steeped in his own work and importance that he would brook no nonsense. John Regan, the keeper who was placed in charge of the three young chimpanzees in the Baby-Pet Zoo, innocently named one of them Herbie. When Herbert Fox learned about it, he was livid. No "monkey" was going to bear his name. In Dr. Fox's eyes, I was a young whippersnapper. Viewing things as he did from his lofty ivory tower, he had no conception of what the public wanted. I was striving diligently to make the zoo a fun place to visit so that people would come and spend their money, and give us the revenue we so desperately needed in those days to keep the zoo solvent. Dr. Fox scoffed at my efforts. To him the public was a nuisance, scarcely to be tolerated.

When I began preparing the zoo's first modern guidebook, I submitted a general outline and samples of my writing to several members of the zoo's Board of Directors. They enthusiastically approved, but, through Williams B. Cadwalader, M.D., the longtime president of the Zoological Society, Dr. Fox acquired a copy, and his criticisms were scathing. My writing was much too "newspaperish," he said. The guidebook was published in 1938 and immediately became a best-seller at the zoo; it went through nine carefully updated editions.

There were a few loudspeakers mounted on trees in various parts of the Zoological Garden for the broadcasting of announcements—about lost children who had been taken to the office, automobiles in the parking lot with their motors running, and so on. I saw it as a useful tool for educating the public and telling them

Herbert Fox, M.D. Philadelphia Zoo archives.

things they might like to hear. My assistants and I set up a crude studio in a small room on the second floor of the bird house. We had a microphone, a turntable, and a collection of records. Every Sunday and holiday in season, and often on weekdays when many people were in the zoo, we played music; made announcements about when the lions, tigers, and sea lions would be fed; and called attention to the Baby-Pet Zoo and newly arrived animals. In between phonograph records we also made brief statements of general interest. For example: Did you know that the hippopotamus attains a considerably greater weight than the rhinoceros? That the cheetah, which has been clocked at 70 miles an hour for short spurts while pursuing prey, is the fastest of all quadrupeds? That a male ostrich standing erect is eight feet tall? That the anaconda is the largest of all snakes? The public loved it. I wrote all the copy, and I was constantly on the watch for bizarre and unusual information about the animals in the collection.

One day Herbert L. Ratcliffe, the Assistant Director of the Laboratory, and I were standing on the walk conversing when the Doctors Cadwalader and Fox joined us. The latter saw a good opportunity to put me in my place. He demanded to know, "What kind of rot are you broadcasting all over the zoo? You said it may take more than a week for food to pass through the gut of a sloth. I never heard of such rubbish!" Dr. Ratcliffe calmly stated, "But, Dr. Fox, that was published in the 'Proceedings

of the Zoological Society of London.'" Which, of course, was where I had obtained my information. Dr. Fox stalked off in disgust, but he never again tried to persecute me.

One of his maxims I have always remembered, and the older I get the more I realize how true it is. Dr. Fox said, "No animals are vicious. They may be ferocious, but only man is vicious."

Dr. Ratcliffe was soon making a name for himself. He became the Director of the Laboratory when Dr. Fox died in 1942. The Penrose staff had long been aware that malnutrition, resulting from improper or inadequate diets, was a leading cause of death. Here was a challenge worthy of their best efforts. Spearheaded by Dr. Ratcliffe, and with the early collaboration of Dr. Ellen P. Corson-White, a determined effort was made to develop nourishing diets for the zoo's animals. Eventually an uncooked composite mixture that contained all necessary proteins, fats, carbohydrates, vitamins, and minerals was concocted, and was promptly dubbed "monkey cake." It was prepared in large, rather deep pans, and, when cut into chunks, it resembled, in both color and general appearance, that Philadelphia culinary achievement known as scrapple.

Changing over to the new menus required time, careful observation, and study, and, in some cases, disappointment. The monkeys and apes and a large number of the other animals throve on the monkey cake, to which supplements in the form of vegetables and fruits and some meat were added. The extras were important, especially for the birds. Ground horse meat was added to the monkey cake for the carnivores, and it was successful for most of them with the marked exception of the great cats. The lions and tigers, and the others did much better on the accustomed chunks of meat, supplemented at intervals with bones on which to gnaw. Sea lions and other fish eaters continued to receive raw fish, but Ratcliffe saw to it that the fish was fresh and of nourishing species. The hay burners, such as elephants, antelopes, zebras, and deer, were major exceptions, but they also received their share of the cake and supplements. It was several years before the many varied diets had been tested and perfected, and eventually two other preparations, known as buffalo ration and meat mixture, were added to the menus as required. Monkey cake was not the whole answer to malnutrition, but it was basic to good health and long life.

In many cases the animals were reluctant to change, but, when they became hungry enough, most of them ate what was given to them. The most exasperating problems were with people and not the animals. Almost without exception, the keepers were fond of their animals and did their best for them. They were upset at first when their charges refused the new food, and they shared their lunches with them, or even brought food from home. When he discovered what was happening and how it was undermining his efforts, Ratcliffe had to scold the guilty parties, and he was soon the most unpopular man in the zoo. The employees poured out their troubles to the zoo's director, who was then C. Emerson Brown. It must have posed quite a dilemma for him. I always liked Brown because of his kindness to me when I was getting started in the zoo field, but he was not a forceful man, and he was inclined to take the path of least resistance.

Many habitués who visited the zoo regularly and frequently, among them members of the Zoological Society of Philadelphia, who enjoyed free admission, were in the habit of bringing food to give to their favorite animals. Controlling them was almost impossible. When asked politely to stop what they were doing, they retaliated by writing letters to the local newspapers, complaining that the zoo was starving the animals by experimenting with them. Others fumed that the livestock was being fed moldy scrapple. The zoo did not enjoy a sympathetic press in those days, and the controversy was long and lively. Fortunately, the Laboratory had the full backing of President Cadwalader and several key members of the board of directors. The problems gradually subsided when the animals began to prosper on their new diets.

The benefits were many. The incidence of malnutrition, as revealed by the autopsies, dropped substantially, and the animals were living longer. Another gain was a welcome reduction in the zoo's food bills. It was far cheaper to purchase the ingredients for monkey cake than to buy fancy fruits. For example, I remember when, during the 1930s, a dealer arrived with a bird for our collection and told us emphatically that it would need a fresh alligator pear (avocado) every day. That was possible in season, but avocados were then rarities that had to be imported during the rest of the year, and they could cost five dollars each in midwinter. The bird in question was quickly weaned to one of the new diets.

The success of the program catapulted the Philadelphia Zoo into the limelight, and our sister institutions were anxious to use Ratcliffe's formulas and procedures. Quite flatteringly, two zoos in Switzerland sent three key staff members, each for a year or more, to study our feeding routines. Dr. Ratcliffe was invited to visit European zoos and to recommend improvements in their dietary procedures. He taught classes in Switzerland and earned honors from the Antwerp Zoo in Belgium.

As often happens, the solving of a difficulty opened

the door for another requiring immediate attention. Stress became a major problem. Once their diets were properly adjusted, many of the animals acted more as they would in nature. The most dramatic change was among the monkeys. Instead of sitting around and moping in their cages, as they had been doing for months or years at a time, they were suddenly full of pep, so to speak, and they needed more room and different conditions to play and exercise to the full. Dominant males became very macho. Younger males were tormented and had to be removed, and sometimes entire families or groups were in a constant state of stress.

Many of our management practices had to be altered. Fortunately, the zoo's new building program offered opportunities to solve some of our exhibition problems. The small mammal house, with its numerous hiding places and its dark gallery for nocturnal animals, was a case in point. The plantings in the bird house and the hummingbird exhibit were arranged so that birds could take shelter by disappearing from view. They could fly or run behind clumps of vegetation to escape from more aggressive birds, for whom "out of sight was out of mind."

Dr. Ratcliffe had to cope with some of these problems at first, but his absences overseas resulted in others paying the most attention to stress.

Soon after I arrived at the Philadelphia Zoo in 1935, Dr. Ratcliffe and I were on a first-name basis. I respected him for his knowledge and ability, and he quickly realized that I was serious-minded and wanted very much to improve the reptile collection. He told me ruefully but good-naturedly about his troubles with the staff and the public when he was developing and testing the new diets. He came to my rescue when I could have been in deep trouble. Roderick Macdonald, who succeeded Emerson Brown as executive head of the zoo, thought he was doing me a favor by stocking the reptile house in readiness for my arrival, but he had succumbed to the wiles of an unscrupulous dealer, who, no doubt at good prices, unloaded a lot of sick and poorly nourished snakes and other reptiles. I asked Herb Ratcliffe for autopsy reports, which quickly proved that the high mortality in the collection was not my fault.

Prior to that the Penrose staff had shown little interest in reptiles and amphibians and, apparently, only the large or valuable specimens were subjected to postmortem examination. That situation quickly changed. Herb and his associates checked them all from then on, and their findings helped me in making improvements. Two major innovations, among others, produced excellent results. First, I began using pieces of heavy cork bark, convex surface uppermost, in many of the cages in the old reptile house. The snakes could coil beneath them instead of prowling endlessly in search of a place to hide or escape. The pieces of bark arched upward fairly high, and we were careful to place them so that visitors could see the snakes beneath them, so little exhibition value was lost. The second and truly profound improvement, for which Herbert Ratcliffe deserved full credit, was our purchase of premium mice, rats, and other food animals from closed colonies guaranteed to be free of disease. We had been buying cast-offs from hospitals, which had used the rodents for various tests. The improvement was little short of spectacular, and we managed to establish numerous longevity records, many of which have never been exceeded.

A few months before my departure from the zoo, Herb and his wife, Jean, made the long trip from their home west of Philadelphia to our place in the Pine Barrens, just to bid us fond farewell. They knew we would soon depart for the Southwest. It was our last time together. We had enjoyed an excellent rapport for many years, and Herbert L. Ratcliffe was blessedly different from Dr. Fox.

Herb had retired in 1969, and Dr. Robert L. Snyder, who had been the Associate Director since 1961, took his place. Both were Professors of Comparative Pathology at Penn, and both earned their doctor of science degrees at Johns Hopkins University. By the time Dr. Snyder took charge, I was occupying the hot seat as the zoo's director, and I had relatively little personal contact with him. I had to devote the great bulk of my time to taking care of the endless parade of problems created by human beings, an unhappy state of affairs that plagues every large public institution.

Dr. Snyder was deeply interested in the effects of stress on the welfare and behavior of the animals. I well remember the tender loving care he and his helpers lavished on the six young gorillas, fresh from Africa, that I bought for the zoo, and how they did their utmost to make the young apes feel at home in their new environment. He also was interested in a broad spectrum of research, and he, his students, and his associates produced many learned papers on diseases in animals, most of which were far over my layman's head. Two subjects are worthy of mention, however. First was his work with the hepatitis B virus in groundhogs, which eventually led to his being invited to visit China, where that disease was almost pandemic in some areas. Dr. Snyder had proved that the hepatitis B virus is oncogenic, that is, it causes liver cancer.

The second item had a distinct bearing on many of our present-day social problems, and I write more about that in a later chapter. It concerned Bob Snyder's experimental mouse cage and the things he learned about the residents therein.

Two pairs of mice were placed in a large wire cage with an upper floor the little rodents could reach by using a ramp. Adequate food, water, and nesting material were provided. The occupants were under close observation, and their activities were carefully noted. Everything went well until the fifth generation arrived and there were 648 mice in the colony. Then things began to happen. Large numbers huddled together, a few became recluses, fighting broke out, and many mice died, some from infections resulting from combat. Others succumbed to kidney disease. The entire colony was beset by abnormalities.

It was obvious that crowding produced many problems. By inference, crowded human beings may be expected to exhibit similar aberrancies in their behavior. Also, there is the factor, quoting Dr. Fox, that "man is vicious." I cannot help but think of the mouse cage every time I hear about senseless riots, drive-by shootings, random killings, and wanton destruction of property. Not only mice go berserk!

The Penrose Research Laboratory was a very important part of the Philadelphia Zoological Garden during the almost four decades I was associated with it, and it was also our liaison with the University of Pennsylvania. Many a student worked in the laboratory, and a sizable number of them did their research for advanced degrees right in the zoo.

Not all the research at the zoo emanated from the Laboratory, however. We three curators made numerous contributions. Gus Griswold worked out many techniques for getting his birds to breed. He was particularly successful with cranes, and he authored, among other articles on aviculture, an 18-page booklet entitled "Proven Methods of Keeping and Rearing Cranes in Captivity." Probably his best-known accomplishment was in demonstrating how to restore the pink coloration to the plumage of captive flamingos that had become almost white. He simply added carrot juice to their food.

Fred Ulmer had a phenomenal knowledge of the mammals of the world, but he also delved into the scientific literature and the preserved mammal collection at the Academy of Natural Sciences for information pertinent to articles he wrote on specific zoo animals or groups of them. He was a prolific contributor to the zoo's own publications.

I had started writing papers on herpetology before I left Toledo, and one of my first extracurricular tasks after moving back to the East was to complete my "Reptiles of Ohio," which required much burning of the midnight oil, as we used to say. There was no time available at the zoo for such an activity. Once my book was published, in 1938, I developed a keen interest in the reptiles and amphibians of southern New Jersey and the Delmarva Peninsula. I spent many an evening and day off, in season, doing fieldwork in the two areas. That spawned several papers. My chief interests were in systematics and zoogeography, although I did write several things on the care of herps in captivity, based on methods that seem archaic today. Isabelle and I began work on our field guide in 1951, and that, in a very real sense, was another scientific contribution. I went at it carefully and thoroughly, just as though I were preparing a doctoral dissertation. Eventually my interests turned to the herpetology of Mexico, on which I published many papers, including a rather lengthy monograph on the water snakes of that country. In retrospect, I wonder where I found the ambition, tenacity, and energy to turn out so much research while working full time at the zoo. Without Isabelle's constant encouragement and assistance, it would have been impossible. Not only did she manage all the mundane necessities of our lives, but she also made major contributions with her camera and artist's pen.

Back in the 1930s when I was trying my best to publicize and revitalize the zoo, my head was full of ideas. One that stayed on the back burner for a year or two was to have our own zoo magazine. The Bronx and San Diego Zoos had theirs. Why couldn't we?

Coincidental with the arrival of two large Komodo dragons, which were featured on the cover of the first issue, we began the publication of a four-page news bulletin, entitled "The Philadelphia Zoo," in December 1937. Three other numbers followed at quarterly intervals, but their place was taken in March 1939 by a bona fide, many-paged magazine on slick paper that we called "Fauna." Its circulation was small, because it was sent only to members of the Zoological Society of Philadelphia and persons in key places, including the newspapers and radio stations, who were in a position to help us with publicity. It won approval from both our board and our members. I asked for and received permission to pay a small sum for natural history articles on a variety of subjects in order to broaden our approach and styles of writing. "Fauna" became a general natural history magazine, although every issue had at least a page or two devoted to current Philadelphia Zoo news. At first I did all the layouts and editing, and Mark Mooney took the pictures, which he developed and printed at his home at night. Eventually other members of my small staff participated. I was delighted when Isabelle Hunt joined us, and I discovered she had

many artistic talents that were helpful in getting each issue ready for the press.

"Fauna" was published quarterly for many years, and it developed into a fine magazine that earned many plaudits. Our layouts were so well planned, executed, and printed that we were able to obtain articles that certain well-known authors had refused to give to other publications. Among them were Edwin Way Teale, who became a celebrated natural history writer, and Richard E. Bishop, a member of our board who was famous for his etchings of birds. I invited friends and colleagues to write for us, and many of their names will be familiar to herpetologically-oriented readers. Included were Archie Carr, Carl F. Kauffeld, Arthur Loveridge, M. Graham Netting, and Karl P. Schmidt. There were also a number of other distinguished authors, among them Professor Earnest A. Hooton, Harvard's outstanding anthropologist; Dillon Ripley, who later became the Secretary of the Smithsonian Institution; and Major Stanley S. Flower, of the Zoological Society of London.

As "Fauna" become better known we received almost a flood of unsolicited articles. We used a number of them, but most were almost more trouble than they were worth. Writers who knew little about animals had to have their facts checked and corrected. Conversely, college professors with good topics often had no idea how to present their subjects for the layman, and we had to rewrite what they wrote.

We solicited subscriptions and garnered quite a few. Advertising was considered, but the problems were too great. Our circulation was small. Agencies who could solicit ads for us demanded a third or more of all receipts, including any ads we might receive gratuitously from board members or others who wanted to help. Our production costs were fairly reasonable until prices started shooting upward after World War II. Finally, after exactly a decade, we had to abandon the magazine with regret. It had been hard and exacting work to lay out, edit, and see each issue through the press, but we were very proud of the results. My bound set of "Fauna" is one of my treasured possessions.

The magazine was succeeded by a quarterly news bulletin, almost exclusively about our own zoo. It was called "America's First Zoo," and it began with four pages an issue but, when required, it was often expanded to eight or more pages. Its publication was continuous until well after I retired.

I have already mentioned the zoo guidebook that I wrote during the 1930s. After its ninth edition, it was replaced by a handsome, 100-page publication that we called the "Philadelphia Zoo Animal Book and Guide to the Garden." It was largely a picture book, both in color

Freeman M. Shelly, Philadelphia Zoo Director, presenting prizes to James D. Lazell (left) and John Demcisak, winners of the 1953 contest on radio station WPEN. Photo by Franklin Williamson, Philadelphia Zoo archives.

and black and white, but it also was crammed with facts about the various animals. It sold, at a dollar a copy, almost as fast as we could keep it in stock. Not only was it an excellent souvenir, but it was of great value as a teaching aid. It covered all the major animal groups, whether we were exhibiting them or not. Unlike guidebooks designed for museums, any that we could compile would be out-of-date before they were printed, as new animals arrived and others departed.

The preparation of the animal book was a cooperative effort. Fred Ulmer assembled a large number of maps and charts highlighting important facts, such as the maximum known sizes of large mammals, and he also contributed many excellent drawings. Gus Griswold supplied most of the information about birds, and I took care of the reptiles and amphibians. It also was my job to handle all details and to see the book through the press. Franklin Williamson, who succeeded Isabelle as the zoo's official photographer, took many photos expressly for the book. The one that troubled him (and me) the most was the cover picture depicting a pair of tigers. I wanted to have a really eye-catching color portrait for the cover. Franklin tried, but there was always some flaw in the way the big cats were standing or looking. Finally, on the seventh attempt, he obtained the perfect picture. To attract the animals' attention, Norman E. Hess, Assistant Head Keeper, crawled on his hands and knees through the shrubbery near the outdoor tiger grotto, and the tigers, standing close together, were portrayed as they intently watched the movements of the vegetation above him.

The animal book had a truly professional appearance, thanks to the skill of Edmond V. Malnate, my close and esteemed friend, who at the time was the art director for a Philadelphia advertising agency. He laid

out all the pages. I could always count on Ed to help with the artwork for various zoo publications as well as for my own research. Not only was he talented, he also was keenly interested in herpetology. For a while he worked at the zoo, back in the early days when I needed all the help I could get to put the almost moribund zoological garden on the map. Unfortunately, Zoo Director Shelly, in one of his frequent economy moods, severed Ed from the payroll, much to our dismay. Nonetheless, Ed continued to help from time to time, even though he was paid far too little, or not at all, for his work. At least he knew that he had my deep and enduring gratitude. Sometimes his wife, Georgette, an artist in her own right, pitched in to help. The Malnates moved to Lake Pine, which was fed by the waters overflowing from our own Taunton Lake, so we were almost neighbors. For some 15 years, Ed and I commuted back and forth to Philadelphia together, using my car but taking turns driving. Ed volunteered to curate the herp collection at the Academy of Natural Sciences, and he eventually became an outstanding herpetologist with many important papers to his credit. We still keep in frequent touch, even though we live more than 2,000 miles apart.

The zoo staff was in demand for occasional radio and television shows, and we conducted weekly series in both media. There was, of course, the long-running radio program on the then NBC's KYW, which was my weekly assignment. Freeman M. Shelly, Director of the Zoo, and thus its titular head, wanted his own show, but, since he knew little about animals, it was up to me to invent some way of getting him on the air. We initiated a weekly contest for teenagers on WPEN called "What Do You Know about Animals?" The show's topic was restricted each week to a specific group of mammals, birds, or herps. Shelly would ask a question, such as "Which is the largest of the flightless birds?" and he had the answer, "the ostrich," on a list prepared in advance. When the first hand went up, he would ask the respondent to elaborate on why his answer was correct. At first I carefully prepared the questions and answers, but eventually Fred Ulmer took over. In most cases the contests went smoothly, but we were mightily embarrassed for our director when he got off the track, and it became all too obvious that the young people knew far more about the subject than he did. We could only wonder why he hadn't reviewed the topic of the day in advance.

Fred conducted a weekly television show on WFIL for more than a decade by taking various tractable small mammals to the studio. We really had our workouts, however, when first one and then another half-hour television show was broadcast every Saturday morning directly from the zoo.

The first of these, sponsored by Lit Brothers Department Store and called "Lits Have Fun at the Zoo," was on WFIL, and it, in the main, was fairly easy for all concerned. Usually we didn't rehearse much, and we never knew what some of the animals would do. When there were slipups we laughed just as hard as the home audience must have done. WFIL was pioneering in a sense. Our activities were transmitted by shortwave to the station and then relayed over the regular airwaves. There were occasional glitches. Once, just a few minutes before we were due to start, something went wrong with the transmission, and we had to commandeer every available vehicle to transport props, animals, and staff members to the station. We made it with only seconds to spare. Some of the shows were good, and, like the title of the show, we had fun.

Then along came WCAU and things changed drastically. That station was then an affiliate of CBS, the Columbia Broadcasting System, and it was actively seeking a program to compete with Marlin Perkins's "Zooparade," which originated in Chicago on the rival NBC network. We staff members were kept in the dark, but somehow a committee of our zoo board found a way to break the contract with WFIL and replace it with a fully professional network show on CBS. I was put in a difficult position, because I was in charge of zoo publicity, and Roger Clipp, the General Manager of WFIL, was so angry that he decreed no zoo news of any kind would be carried on their radio or television stations for a year. We had greatly offended a person who had been one of our best friends.

The CBS show, called "Meet Me at the Zoo," was a carefully rehearsed presentation with a no-nonsense atmosphere. A professional writer, an experienced director, and two television cameras were assigned to it, and a studio was set up in the old lion house, which was then empty. Most of the shows emanated from the studio, but we also broadcast from other sites in the zoo, inasmuch as a great many of the animals could not be moved from their usual quarters. Our network consisted of only about eight stations, but some were far away, including Honolulu, Hawaii, if I recall correctly.

"Meet Me at the Zoo" turned out to be a minor nightmare for me. Because I was an experienced public speaker and had conducted radio shows for many years, I soon inadvertently outstripped the other staff members, much to their annoyance. Fred Ulmer was an exception. He was allowed by the CBS executive, who watched us all closely, to present his own mammal programs, but I was ordered to participate in all the other shows, no matter who was supposed to be conducting them. I was needed, I was told, to keep things running

smoothly and on time, which meant that I occasionally had to interrupt when one of my colleagues became too long-winded. Zoo Director Shelly, who quite naturally thought he should be the star, was not permitted to appear on any shows, except to say a few words of introduction on the first one. The CBS executive told him he didn't photograph well, which I am sure Shelly took as a deep personal insult.

Not only did we need to have our animals in readiness, but we had to collect our props well in advance. For example, I once did a program on crocodiles and alligators. We could handle small live ones fairly easily, but they were not very impressive. Large ones were far too dangerous. To get around that problem I had to find a short film clip showing crocodiles in the field. I also borrowed the skull of a large crocodile from the Academy of Natural Sciences, to demonstrate its massive size and its mouth full of teeth. Such things were not supposed to be removed from the Academy, but they gave me permission as a special favor if I would handle it personally. So I had to go to the museum to get the skull and then take it back after the show was over. The "Meet Me at the Zoo" program eroded an enormous amount of my time, especially since I prepared my own reptile shows with great care, and even rehearsed them at home so I could get the timing down as accurately as possible. There was also the long rehearsal just before each presentation, and our half hour on the air as well. I kept a time log and found that I was spending an average of 27 hours a week on the TV show alone, and I was expected to keep up with all my other duties as well.

After about the fifteenth program I was really on the spot. The CBS executive told Shelly that they wanted me to do all the shows and to be Marlin Perkins's competitor. That was too much for Shelly. He succumbed to the green-eyed monster and told me I would have to resign from the zoo and go to work for CBS. Although I didn't mind doing TV shows if I were not under constant pressure, I balked and declined. It would have meant a substantially greater income for me, but I wouldn't have been able to call my soul my own. It was one of the wisest decisions I ever made. Just a few weeks later Marlin's show went off the air, and CBS lost all interest in a zoo program. They promptly canceled ours.

One of the best ways to keep abreast of developments in any professional field is to meet periodically with peers and colleagues. I learned that early in my career, and I joined the American Association of Zoological Parks and Aquariums (AAZPA) during its 1930 meeting in St. Louis. There were then less than a score of members, and the zoo organization, at the time, was a subdivision of the American Institute of Park Executives. Even during the Great Depression I managed to attend several meetings, including one in Toronto, Canada, from my base in Toledo, but I had to miss those that were held far away because of the expense. Nonetheless, I remained active and served as zoo editor of the Institute's journal, "Parks and Recreation," for two decades. I attended meetings when I could, and I even labored mightily twice, but years apart, as a member of the local committee when Philadelphia was the convention city.

Unhappily, friction developed with my boss, Zoo Director Shelly, chiefly, I assume, because I had a head start on him, in both the organization and the zoo business in general. He attended all the AAZPA meetings, but I was permitted to go only if I paid my own expenses, which I did a few times. Eventually, the zoo board authorized a trip a year for each of the three curators. I regularly took part in the meetings of the American Society of Ichthyologists and Herpetologists, Fred Ulmer went to those of the American Society of Mammalogists, and Gus Griswold visited one or the other of the several gatherings of aviculturalists or ornithologists.

In the autumn of 1946, just before he was to leave for St. Louis to attend the meeting of the AAZPA, of which he was the chairman, Shelly came down with a strep throat. Instead of canceling his trip, he telephoned and instructed me to pick up his tickets and go in his place. That was a great kindness on his part that I very much appreciated. The trip involved a long train ride on the Pennsylvania Railroad's *Spirit of St. Louis,* some 20 hours in each direction, in a cramped roomette. I could walk up and down the aisles, though, which I did, and I visited with a few friends from New York and Pittsburgh who were on the same train.

When I arrived at my destination and explained to other members that their chairman wasn't coming, no one knew quite what to do. It was the first meeting after a hiatus during World War II, when many such gatherings were curtailed. To make a long story short, I was drafted to preside over the meeting of some 50 members. Fortunately, I had been thinking about the organization while I was on the train, and I was able to prepare a last-minute agenda. All went well but, much to my embarrassment I was elected, virtually unanimously, as the new chairman. I was also renamed as the zoo editor of the magazine, and, to cap the climax, I was elected one of the six governing members of the American Institute of Park Executives. As one colleague put it, I wound up winning the top spot in every office available. Anyone who knew the background could appreciate Shelly's chagrin at having sent me off to St. Louis in his place. I managed to attend all the Institute's meetings, at my own expense, but my subsequent presence at AAZPA gatherings was sporadic.

In 1948 Shelly was invited to participate in the meeting of the International Union of Directors of Zoological Gardens in Paris, France. He was elected a member and went every year to a different city in Europe, and he eventually became the Union's president, in which office he served with distinction. In my opinion it was the most wonderful thing that happened to him during his long professional tenure. He at last had the recognition and prestige he craved and really deserved. In a sense, it was also a godsend for those of us on the zoo's staff. He learned that many of the problems he had faced at home, and had difficulty understanding, plagued all zoo administrators. He even had the kindness to apologize to me for having complained years previously to President Cadwalader when I was inadvertently given the newspaper title of "Director of the Philadelphia Zoo." His new friends had had similar troubles. His association with the world's distinguished zoo directors was a liberal education for him, and he became a much better boss for us all as a result of it.

Before leaving the topic of special activities at the zoo, I must devote a few paragraphs to the Junior Zoological Society. Beginning in the mid-1930s, several teenaged boys began visiting the zoo regularly on Saturday mornings. All were interested in natural history, but the chief lure was the fun of taking part in activities in a place that appealed to all young people. The boys banded together and called themselves the Junior Zoological Society.

Probably because I've always been interested in youngsters who have a leaning toward natural history, it was normal for me to become their sponsor. For many years I met with them regularly on Saturdays for an hour or more, and we had a wide variety of programs. Sometimes I talked about animals, although not often. Chiefly it was the boys themselves who boned up on special topics, such as "How big do elephants get, and how long do they live?" or "How come there are members of the camel family and members of the tapir family on opposite sides of the world?" There were many guest speakers, some from Penn and Temple and the Academy of Natural Sciences, and sometimes out-of-town friends or colleagues who happened to be available on a Saturday morning.

During May Day at the Zoo and other celebrations the boys were assigned to staff members as assistants for the day. They ran errands in the zoo, helped put up decorations, and aided in dozens of different ways. I sometimes took two or three of them with me on field trips to the Delmarva Peninsula or southern New Jersey, and I taught some of the most reliable how to make scale counts on snakes, and thus enlarged my data bank for future studies.

The program was worthwhile, if only because it kept the boys off the street corners on Saturday mornings. Many acquired an avocation they continued to pursue all their lives. Although it was difficult to keep things moving month after month and year after year, I am really proud of what so many of them accomplished. A number went on to important careers, among them three medical doctors, a veterinarian, five college professors, the general manager of the local SPCA, a well-known wildlife photographer and lecturer, and a top-flight radio announcer at one of New York's most prestigious stations. The last named got his start in broadcasting when he temporarily took over while the regular staff member he was assisting left for lunch. They were a great bunch of lads, I enjoyed their company, and it is still a source of deep satisfaction for me that I helped so many of them to reinforce their hobbies, and that so many of them went on to professional careers.

Chapter 26

Two Great Apes: Bamboo and Massa

Nowadays every first-class zoological garden exhibits gorillas, sometimes in large family groups that live in elaborate, naturalistic quarters. Young are born among them so frequently that new arrivals receive little attention except locally.

It wasn't always so. When I was just getting started in the zoo business, gorillas were a great rarity. In a very real sense the Philadelphia Zoological Garden was the pioneer with captive gorillas. To understand why, let me quote a few excerpts from an article I wrote for our zoo magazine, "Fauna," way back in 1939. It was about Bamboo, the first gorilla to live for any length of time in the United States.

Prior to 1927 tragedy stalked in the wake of every gorilla brought to America. Not one lived a single year. Pneumonia and ennui took their toll. So consistently did the rare apes succumb that some authorities concluded our climate was not suited to them, others ventured that gorillas could not endure captivity.

Then came Bamboo. There were those who shook their heads. "We will give him a few months," they said, "but he won't last. None of them do." And frankly Bamboo was not much to look at on that memorable August day in 1927 when he became the prize boarder of the Philadelphia Zoo. He was quite a baby, tipped the scales at eleven pounds and fitted snugly inside the ventilated suitcase that served as his Pullman.

With him on his day of arrival, and occupying another valise, was a young female chimpanzee who was destined to be one of the greatest factors in the successful rearing of Bamboo. Her name was Lizzie, and she was a mischievous ape who, like most of her kind, seemed blessed with boundless energy. She and the infant gorilla became pals at once; they lived, ate, and slept together. Most of every day they played, and Bamboo's chances of sulking or pining away in a corner were almost nil from the start. Lizzie led the way, invented simian games, and so teased her cagemate that he was forced to run and romp, getting the exercise that every growing animal needs.

No pampered heirs of doting parents received more lavish care than the little apes. Day and night someone was on hand to attend their needs. Their diets, health, and appetites were studied daily, their coats were groomed and, under the kindly, but exacting care of keeper Jimmy McCrossen, they grew and prospered.

Eventually even the scoffers were forced to admit that Bamboo might be the exception, and they joined the admiring throngs which came almost daily to watch the leading, if still juvenile, citizen of the Zoo. Anthropologists and psychologists studied the antics of the young gorilla and compared him with his fellow apes—and with Man. Photographers found him an engrossing subject and more than one artist and sculptor used him as his model.

In time, Bamboo's features changed. His skull lengthened and the beetling brows of his race made their appearance. He grew in size and weight and finally there came a day when he'd had enough of Lizzie's dominance. Although he had long outstripped her in bulk, he acceded to her leadership until the day—no one knows just how or why—he decided he had his own life to lead. A few cuffs put Lizzie in her place and, whereas the two continued to play together, she never again took the liberties which had been her wont.

The investigators on the staff of the Philadelphia Zoo's Penrose Research Laboratory made a very important contribution to the successful rearing of Bamboo. They had carefully studied the incidence of tuberculosis among the captive primates, and, as one result of their findings, stout panes of plate glass were erected in front of all the indoor ape and monkey cages. Not only was Bamboo thereby protected from that dread disease, but he also was immune to the bombardment by the public, which previously tossed all manner of objects into the barred cages, including food that had been in people's mouths—apple cores, for example. Other senseless or sadistic persons spat into the cages or even tossed glowing cigarette and cigar butts to the animals.

To give the little apes additional exercise, Jimmy McCrossen took them for walks in the monkey house yard, and that is where I first met them. Despite my pre-occupation with my courses at the University of Penn-sylvania, and my desperate efforts to earn every cent I could, I managed to get to the zoo a few times during my college years. Through the kindness of one of my biology professors, I had an introduction to C. Emerson Brown, the zoo's director. He greeted me cordially, and, when he learned I had worked at the Twin Brook Zoo and knew a little something about zoo management problems, I was more than welcome. He escorted me to the monkey house, introduced me to Jimmy McCrossen, and I had the wonderful privilege of holding Bamboo's hand in one of mine and Lizzie's in the other, as I took them for a short walk just as Jimmy did. What a thrill for an aspiring young zoologist! Mr. Brown gave me a half dozen free passes to the zoo, so I wouldn't have to surren-der a quarter at the gate for admission after any of my long hikes up 34th Street from the Penn campus.

As Bamboo grew in size and strength, the walks were restricted and only his keeper was allowed with him. Eventually even those came to an end. Tragically, Jimmy McCrossen was killed by a speeding automobile when he left the zoo late one afternoon to board the Girard Avenue trolley on his way home.

Later, as Bamboo became very much stronger, a large outdoor cage was constructed of concrete and stout steel bars. It was connected to his indoor quarters by a tunnel equipped with a sliding door, which could be secured by a padlock. His inside cage could be entered for cleaning and scrubbing while he was locked out-doors, and vice versa.

Outside, the public promptly resumed its bombard-ment, using all manner of objects, even stones and gravel. Finally, for the protection of all the apes in out-door cages, including Bamboo, a 10-foot fence of heavy quarter-inch-mesh hardware cloth was erected all around the outdoor yard. That effectively cut off most of the missiles, but on busy days the monkey house keepers and guards had to patrol the outdoor area in an effort to make the visitors behave. If they weren't watched, some people would lob heavy items over the wire fence, hoping they would hit the animals. The human species can be really vicious at times.

Bamboo was the star of the Philadelphia Zoo's collec-tion. As an example of how much attention he attracted, I quote the following from an article written by Har-vard's renowned anthropologist, Earnest A. Hooton, that was published in "Fauna" in December 1943:

One beautiful spring morning, about ten years ago, I arrived in Philadelphia to attend the annual

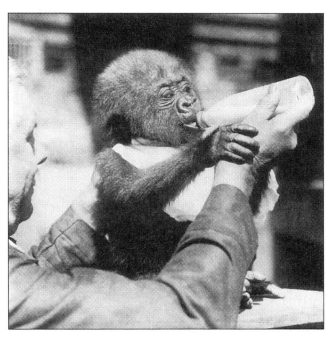

The infant gorilla, Bamboo, soon after his arrival in 1927. Keeper Jimmy McCrossen gave him his bottle. Photo by Newton H. Hartman, The Evening Bulletin. Philadelphia Zoo archives.

meeting of the American Philosophical Society. This is the oldest learned body in the United States, having been founded by Benjamin Franklin. When I reached the hall, I took a look at the program of tech-nical papers and at my various scientific friends and acquaintances there assembled. Then I whispered to Dr. Charles B. Davenport, eminent geneticist and anthropologist of the Carnegie Institution of Wash-ington, "Let's sneak out and go to the zoo to see the gorilla."

We sneaked. Neither of us had ever seen a live gorilla, and we would not have missed the opportu-nity, even if Darwin himself had been reading a paper at the meeting of the Philosophical Society.

Bamboo made such an impression on Dr. Hooton that, during a later visit, he made a statement to a news-paper reporter which rated the front page and was also transmitted by wire to other papers all over the country. He said, "The most interesting and worthwhile object or person I have ever seen in Philadelphia was a gorilla named Bamboo at the Philadelphia Zoo."

Bamboo became a mischievous rogue as he grew older and stronger. He had a stout steel drum and a length of telephone pole that he could roll around in his outdoor cage. He developed a habit of throwing things—whatever he could get hold of, including pieces of food and sometimes even his own dung. He became

Bamboo, the holy terror. He was an enormously strong and frightening brute when he grew up. Photo by Franklin Williamson, Philadelphia Zoo archives.

adept at holding his head so that it looked as though he were staring in a different direction, whereas his eyes were intently watching human visitors outside the fence. Most of what he tossed landed harmlessly against the wire mesh, but it was disconcerting, to say the least, to have something thrown right at you unexpectedly, even though you were safe behind a barrier.

Early during my assignment as the zoo's press agent, I thought how wonderful it would be if a scale could be mounted in Bamboo's cage so that every time he stepped on it visitors could see how much he weighed. I wrote to Hubert D. Bennett, the president of the Toledo Scale Company, and reminded him about how he had marooned Reeve Bailey and me overnight on Green Island in Lake Erie. (See "The Ohio Reptile Survey: Part I.") I explained that we needed to weigh Bamboo and asked him if he could help. He could, and his response was prompt. His welcome gift was installed, but there was a major problem. The scale's platform should have been mounted flush with the reinforced concrete floor when the cage was built. The Toledo Scale men braced their

apparatus carefully, and for several weeks it functioned well, and we learned that Bamboo was approximately 435 pounds of bone, brawn, and viscera. He, however, had all day to tinker with the new object in his cage. Eventually he managed to work something loose, and then it was only a matter of minutes before he wrecked the scale, much to the consternation of all concerned.

The annual birthday party for Bamboo always attracted a large battery of news photographers. We had no idea when his real birthday was. He was surely well under a year old when he arrived at the zoo, but information on his origin was sketchy, and it reached Emerson Brown third- or fourthhand. Probably his mother was shot and killed, and he was nursed by native tribeswomen until he was old enough to sell to an itinerant animal collector. So we arbitrarily made August 5, the date of his arrival at the Philadelphia Zoo, his birthday.

The first party was a mild affair. The newsmen were allowed inside the wire fence and were permitted to aim their lenses between the big bars of Bamboo's cage, but they were sternly admonished to keep out of his reach. He had very long arms. While the big ape was indoors, the keepers prepared a birthday cake composed of the standard zoo food mixture that contained all the essentials of a balanced diet. Bananas, standing on end, served as "candles." The outdoor cage was securely locked, the tunnel door was opened, and Bamboo came rushing out. When he saw the cake he stopped, stuck a finger into it, and then picked up a banana, peeled it, and calmly ate it. Moments later his huge hand scooped up the cake and flung it full force at one of the photographers. The others snapped their shutters, but the unfortunate victim had to duck to save himself and his camera.

The next year we arranged a more elaborate party, and the press got even better pictures. In addition to the cake and "candles," we provided a watermelon, of which the big ape was quite fond. The procedure was the same, and the cameramen lined up to record the action. They got it, and fast. Bamboo fired the whole watermelon at them. It smashed against the bars, and several of the men were royally splattered with wet pulp. The following year they all showed up wearing raincoats and rain hats.

The most exciting and exhausting zoo event I can remember occurred on April 27, 1947. For me it started when the telephone rang in my office, and Head Keeper John Regan shouted, "Bamboo is loose!" and hung up. I dispatched Fred Ulmer, who was then on my public relations staff, to pick up one of our high-powered rifles, and then he and I drove to the monkey house in my car. Bamboo was loose in the outside yard. The keeper, occupied with his morning chores, had forgotten to lock the tunnel between the indoor and outdoor cages. He had finished his outside cleaning, set down his pail and shovel, and was stepping out of the cage when the big ape came dashing through the tunnel. He dropped into his cage, jumped out into the yard, seized the keeper, and carried him off like a sack of meal under his arm. The man screamed and Bamboo promptly bit him, but the commotion attracted the attention of Regan and another employee, who appeared at the service door. They shouted at Bamboo, who dropped his burden, and the keeper scrambled to safety. Regan then rushed to the telephone and called me.

When we arrived on the scene, Bamboo was having the time of his life. He was racing up and down inside the yard, pulling up the sign holders and scattering them like tenpins. A few other animals that were locked in their outdoor cages were cringing near the roofs of their enclosures, screaming at the tops of their voices.

We had trained Bamboo to be afraid of water, and squirting a syringe filled with warm water was usually sufficient to send him scurrying. Our first thought was to hook up the fire hose, but we were afraid to use it for fear he might dash away so rapidly that he'd go through the outside wire fence. Even a high-school football fullback could have breached it with little effort. No one ever dreamed that one day it would be the flimsy barricade that prevented a full-grown gorilla from escaping into the zoo proper.

We tried lobbing oranges into Bamboo's cage, a fruit of which he was inordinately fond. He was having too much fun to pay attention to them. Next we tried the old circus man's trick of appearing with several large harmless snakes. Baboons and monkeys will usually run from snakes, and many a carnival or circus employee has succeeded in getting such primates back into their cages by that simple procedure. But Bamboo showed no interest in the snakes, one way or the other.

Finally it dawned on us that Bamboo, who had spent his entire life since babyhood inside a set of iron bars, thought the wire fence was another solid barrier. We decided to risk using the hose, and I gave the order to turn on the water. Bamboo ran from it, headed straight for his cage, and leaped inside. But the keepers were so excited they managed to wrap the hose around a tree, and the pressure dropped to a trickle. Bamboo came dashing out of his cage again!

We knew, however, that we had the problem solved. A few seconds later the stream was played on him again, and he returned to his cage, passed through the tunnel, and entered his inside cage. Bill Maloney, who had just returned from serving in the U.S. Navy, was stationed inside. He slammed the door shut and locked Bamboo in. Then we all collapsed.

How thankful we were that we didn't have to shoot Bamboo. Fred Ulmer had the high-powered rifle from the lion house. I assigned the monkey house rifle to a trusted keeper, and gave them both orders to shoot to kill if the big ape crashed through the flimsy outside fence. We could take no chances. He was a dangerous animal, and if he killed or seriously injured a zoo visitor we would have been severely condemned. On rare occasions, keepers have been killed by their charges, and the public tolerates such disasters. Keepers, like policemen and firemen, take risks. But to have a visitor attacked would be an inexcusable tragedy. That was why we had rifles in all buildings containing dangerous animals.

The zoo was already open to the public the morning that Bamboo escaped, and a class of youngsters was just outside the wire fence when their teacher was heard to exclaim, "Look, children. They've let the gorilla out in the yard to exercise." She and her charges were hurried into the safety of the monkey house. Several announcements were made over the zoo's public address system for visitors to take shelter in the various buildings. It was a relief to give them the "all clear" signal about a half hour later.

After we had caught our breath, I decided on my next step. Because many people already knew that Bamboo had been out, and because we had sent the injured keeper to a public hospital, I decided to call the press and tell them what had happened. They treated the story lightly, and more or less played down the potential danger.

Zoo Director Shelly was away when the event took place, but when he returned and heard the full story, he promoted William J. Maloney to keeper in charge of the monkey house. It was well deserved. In later years Bill served as superintendent of the Daniel W. Dietrich Memorial Children's Zoo and as head keeper. During my directorship I promoted him to the newly created position of Superintendent of the Animal Collection, to be responsible for all the livestock under the supervision of the several curators.

Bamboo lived for many more years. He remained untrustworthy and downright ornery, yet he seemed to mellow in some ways. He became a silver-backed gorilla. Keepers noticed that, when he was indoors, he would spend hours staring sullenly into their room. They were mystified at first, but soon realized that he was fascinated by the rock-and-roll music emanating from the small radio they kept turned on most of the day. They paid closer attention and discovered that Bamboo had a favorite tune, a zoologically appropriate one entitled "Running Bear." We gave the story to the news media, and it was picked up from coast to coast. He was referred to as "the gone gorilla" and the "swinging ape."

Massa in his old age. He died when he was 54 and still holds the longevity record for gorillas. Philadelphia Zoo archives.

Bamboo's reputation as a tough character remained, however, and during the Korean War the zoo received a letter signed by 28 members of the Intelligence and Reconnaissance Platoon of the 187th Airborne Regimental Combat Team. They asked for a picture of Bamboo as "the boy we would most like to have with us on a combat patrol."

During 1959 Bamboo showed signs that he might have sustained and then recovered from a heart attack. On January 21, 1961, he was found dead in his indoor cage. An autopsy revealed the cause as coronary disease.

So our famed but notorious star passed away at the age of approximately 34. He had fooled the experts and survived, despite dire predictions. I thumbed through the zoo's voluminous collection of newspaper clippings, and found a headline from the "Philadelphia Inquirer," dated October 9, 1927, two months after his arrival as a baby. It read: "Only One of His Kind in America. Bamboo, Year-Old Gorilla Now in Philadelphia Zoo, Costs His Keepers Five-Dollar-a-Day Insurance Premium, While Learned Scientists Crowd About to Study Him, Fearing He Soon May Die."

And now for the story of Massa. Roderick Macdonald was the managing director of the zoological garden

when I returned to Philadelphia in 1935 after a six-year stint at the Toledo Zoo. He was kind to me, gave me the "Let's Visit the Zoo" radio program, which survived for almost 34 years, and encouraged me to work with the press. Unfortunately for him, he made a bad decision that was largely responsible for his dismissal in 1936. In brief, he bought a mate for Bamboo, a gorilla named Massa. The $6,000 purchase price, a princely sum in those lean days as the Great Depression waned, was approved by the zoo's board of directors, but we discovered within two days that Massa was actually a male. That fact was duly reported to Dr. Macdonald. He was stunned, but he ordered us to keep quiet about it. "No one will know the difference," he said. That was where he made his mistake. He should have demanded an accounting from the seller, a lady who had thought for years that Massa was a female. Actually, the genitalia of gorillas are difficult to see, and other persons had made similar errors, among them the famous explorers, Martin and Osa Johnson, who provided the San Diego Zoo with a pair of gorillas that turned out to be two males.

After Dr. Macdonald left, it fell to my lot to report the mixup in sexes. The newspapers made much of it, and the tabloid "Daily News" used a screaming headline, which, if I remember correctly, read "Massa Aint No Lady!"

Massa was destined to live in the zoo until he was about 54 years of age, thus surpassing Bamboo's longevity record by two decades, and becoming a character in his own right. He earned the vicarious affection of innumerable zoo visitors, and his annual birthday party attracted large numbers of visitors even though it occurred on almost the last day of the year when the weather could be cold and stormy.

The American Association of Zoological Parks and Aquariums passed a resolution in 1956 commending the Philadelphia Zoological Garden for its outstanding success in maintaining gorillas in captivity.

Frederick A. Ulmer, Jr., who served as the zoo's curator of mammals for more than a quarter of a century, carefully researched Massa's early history and reported the results in "America's First Zoo," the zoo news bulletin that succeeded "Fauna." I wish I could reproduce what he wrote so well in its entirety, but space will not permit. I must condense it and excerpt from it instead.

Massa was captured when his mother was speared to death by angry tribesmen because she and a band of other gorillas raided their *shamba* (native garden). The mother was carved up for the stew pot, but the infant ape was suckled by a native woman along with her own baby. Eventually Massa reached a West African seaport, where he was purchased from an animal dealer by a Captain Phillips, the skipper of a freighter that plied between New

York and Africa. He also bought six young chimpanzees and took them all to Mrs. Gertrude Lintz, of Brooklyn, whose dedicated mission was to rescue such waifs as Massa and nurse them back to health. Almost always such newly imported arrivals were in poor condition. All six chimps were sick and Massa was almost dead from pneumonia. Mrs. Lintz worked day and night with them, and finally had them all in good condition. Massa would not eat solid food, however, so she chewed for him and transferred her "cud" from her mouth to his, probably as his own mother would have done.

Mrs. Lintz was convinced that Massa was a female, and she acted in good faith. Years later, in corresponding with Ulmer, she continued to refer to the animal as "she." Massa arrived at her home in September 1931. Late in 1932 she received another young gorilla that had been horribly burned on its face when a disgruntled sailor, fired by Captain Phillips, tossed a vial of acid at the animal. Mrs. Lintz managed to salvage, as Ulmer put it, "the pitiful wreckage of a baby gorilla," which she named Buddy. He was badly scarred, however, and his lip curled up in a perpetual snarl. Later he was sold to the Ringling Brothers, Barnum and Bailey Circus, which gave him the name of Gargantua the Great and publicized him all over the country.

The two young gorillas had the run of part of the Lintz house. Massa learned to imitate human actions, and became adept at scrubbing the kitchen floor. Ulmer wrote:

One morning Mrs. Lintz entered the room so quietly that the gorilla, now weighing more than a hundred pounds and incredibly powerful, did not hear her. Mrs. Lintz slipped on the wet floor and fell, dumping a pail of water over Massa. The startled gorilla, thinking it was being attacked, turned with a roar on the defenseless woman, and bit her savagely. Fortunately her cries were heard by a young woman friend in the next room, who courageously rushed in, seized a heavy iron skillet and brought it crashing down on the gorilla's head. She stunned the animal long enough for Mrs. Lintz to crawl to safety. It took some seventy stitches to close the wounds.

The intelligent gorilla quickly realized it could defy its mistress, no matter how sternly she commanded obedience, and, although she was very fond of the ape, she reluctantly decided to part with it. And so, on December 30, 1935, the strapping anthropoid arrived at the Philadelphia Zoo, in a station wagon driven by Mrs. Lintz herself.

In anticipation of Massa's arrival, Lizzie, the chimpanzee who had been Bamboo's constant companion for so many years, was transferred to another part of the

building. Massa was put in the cage next to Bamboo. A special door made of a solid sheet of steel had been installed between them that, when opened, was just large enough for Massa, but through which the much larger Bamboo could not follow. On August 25, 1936, the two apes were allowed together for the first time. Bamboo was about nine and weighed nearly twice as much as Massa, who was about five years old. Here is Ulmer's account of what happened:

Once the door was opened, Massa did not hesitate, but charged through the opening, clouted Bamboo on the head, and followed up with a pinch and a little hair-pulling. The big gorilla, amazed at the effrontery of the intruder, roused himself and jumped at his tormentor. But Massa quickly scurried back to the safety of his own cage, where he made faces at Bamboo. In all, the gorillas engaged in some seven tussles, and, after about two hours, each retired to a neutral corner to catch his breath. Most observers gave Massa the decision as victor in the "battle." After five days of fisticuffs, the gorillas were separated for good, and since then Massa has lived in solitary splendor.

The behavior of these great apes was comical and very human at times. Each was extremely jealous of the other and watched closely to be sure his rival did not receive more food or attention. Bamboo, when annoyed, charged across his cage toward his rival, slamming the steel door and bars so hard the building trembled and, at the same time, uttering a loud, derisive noise that was unmistakably a "Bronx Cheer." Massa was a great chest-beater from early childhood, and he would reply to Bamboo by standing erect and beating a rapid tattoo on his barrel-like chest. The older gorilla had a strong distaste for water, so the pool in his outdoor cage was never filled. But Massa, in his adjacent cage, enjoyed bathing on hot summer days, and he took fiendish delight in scooping the water from his pool and tossing it all over his protesting neighbor.

After Bamboo died, the zoo acquired two quite young gorillas, Fern and Bamboo II, and they were placed in Bamboo's old cage. The keepers spent much time playing with them and giving them their bottles. Massa, who was still living next door, obviously was upset by all the attention the newcomers received, and he lost his appetite and developed diarrhea. When the little gorillas were moved and replaced by a group of lemurs, Massa quickly recovered. Obviously, jealousy played a big part in the emotional behavior of gorillas, to say nothing of a "macho" attitude in the presence of another male.

Massa was never the ruffian that Bamboo had been.

Nonetheless, he was an impressive animal, and he commanded the attention of visitors, whom he often entertained by standing up and beating his chest with his hands in approved gorilla fashion. Once, when Zoo Director Shelly was showing Massa to distinguished visitors at close range in the monkey house yard, he turned his back, and Massa reached out and yanked down his topcoat, neatly ripping it almost in two and forcing Shelly's knees to the ground. He was a dangerous animal and could not be trusted.

During my administration Massa developed abscessed teeth and a veterinarian, Dr. Wilbur Amand, extracted them while the animal was anesthetized. More tooth trouble followed, along with a number of other more or less minor health problems, and Massa was beginning to look quite old. When the younger apes were moved to the rare mammal house in 1965, Massa and the two elderly orangutans, Guas and Guarina, were left in the old building for fear they might be too severely traumatized if they were crated, moved, and introduced into a new environment after residing in their old quarters for almost all their lives. When the time came to raze the ancient building, however, Massa had to go. He was prepared by introducing him to his transfer box, where he was fed and to which he often retreated when he wanted to be alone. The move to the rare mammal house on June 2, 1983, was achieved without incident.

Meanwhile, Massa's birthday (actually the anniversary of his arrival at the zoo) was celebrated annually, and, as he added year after year to the longevity record for captive gorillas, the crowds increased. On his fiftieth anniversary, in 1980, he made news all over the world. Barbara L. Beamer, then the Manager of Public Relations for the Philadelphia Zoological Garden, pulled the zoo publicity stunt of the century. She hired a steeplejack, had him dress in a gorilla costume, and then climb up the huge statue of William Penn surmounting the tower of Philadelphia's City Hall. The similarity to the motion picture "King Kong," in which the giant gorilla climbed New York City's Empire State Building, was perfect. Through a clipping service, "Bobbie" Beamer received items from almost 400 cities in the United States alone, as well as from England, France, Japan, and a few other faraway places. On the day of Massa's party there were 27 radio interviews from as far west as Honolulu and up to the tip of Maine. She also made the "Johnny Carson Show" and the ITV in London. A picture of the event appeared in the newspapers in Albuquerque, where I am living in retirement, and I sent her two clippings and a letter of congratulations. Her inspiration far eclipsed my own attempts at zoo publicity so many decades earlier.

Massa lived for four more years. He died during the night following his fifty-fourth birthday party. When I wrote this, in 1993, Fred Ulmer told me that Massa still held the longevity record for gorillas.

Chapter 27

Unsung Heroes of the Philadelphia Zoo

The Board of Directors of the Zoological Society of Philadelphia consisted of civic leaders, prominent citizens, and a sprinkling of naturalists. All served without pay, and they deserved enormous credit for their sustained devotion to the zoo and for the time and effort they expended on its behalf. I was deeply indebted to many of them. I wish I could mention them all, but my space is limited.

When I arrived back in the East from Toledo in 1935, almost all of the board members were listed in the "Philadelphia Social Register," and a majority of them had served for many years. Williams B. Cadwalader, M.D., for example, had been a member long before he was elected President of the Board in 1926, and he held that office until his death in 1957. Other presidents and officers also served for many years. The board was self-perpetuating. New members were nominated and elected, and they contributed their time, expertise, money, or all three.

As a young and brand-new employee, I had little contact with the board at first, but that soon changed. After I had demonstrated my enthusiasm and my ability to get the zoo into the newspapers, I was invited to attend the meetings of the executive committee, and, later, the monthly board meetings. Frank B. Foster, a wealthy and energetic member, took a liking to me, and I was a guest at his home on several occasions. I have long suspected that he had a large part in making my 1937 trip to Europe possible. Several members of the Tyler family were very active. Sidney F. Tyler served as treasurer, and his brother, George F. Tyler, Jr., much later as president. Their sister was married to Harry F. West, a senior editor at J. B. Lippincott, and he helped me launch our zoo magazine, "Fauna," and gave me much advice about editing.

Dr. Cadwalader was a patrician of the old school. He was quite conservative and never made snap decisions, but he was always willing to listen to his peers and associates, as he demonstrated when he permitted Isabelle and me to spend a month in Mexico. R. Sturgis Ingersoll, Vice President of the Board, became a good friend and even went snake hunting with me several times. (See

"The Philadelphia Lawyer.") Radcliffe Cheston, Jr., succeeded Dr. Cadwalader as president in 1957, and I enjoyed a close rapport with him that began in humorous fashion.

Throughout my entire career at the Philadelphia Zoo I worked on weekends. Warm-weather Saturdays and Sundays and the holidays were our busiest times, of course, and the days when problems involving visitors were most apt to develop. I was almost always the troubleshooter and the one called upon to cope with emergencies.

After Isabelle resigned her position as zoo photographer to devote her time to illustrating our field guide, she occasionally accompanied me to the zoo on Saturdays. She was still preparing signs for the bird house. With Gus Griswold's help, she photographed individual birds, made black-and-white prints, and then hand-colored them. When posted in the bird house, they made it possible for visitors to identify the birds in the displays where many different species lived together.

One Saturday afternoon she was busy coloring and I was putting together the dummy for an issue of "America's First Zoo," wielding my scissors on proofs supplied by the printer and pasting columns and paragraphs into position. Suddenly a voice sounded loud and clear at the door of my office: "My, aren't we industrious."

It was Mr. Cheston. The dignified rascal had tiptoed up the long flight of stairs to the second floor of the service building and then down the hall. He presumably was expecting to find me "goofing off" on a dull and quiet afternoon, but he was pleased to discover us hard at work instead. He lingered for a full hour while we chatted about a broad spectrum of subjects. Ever afterward he trusted me unreservedly, and he called on me for help on many occasions. One day, a month or two before my retirement, I invited his daughter, Sydney, and her husband, Antelo Devereux, friends of long standing, to a private farewell luncheon in the boardroom of the administration building. I told them about Mr. Cheston's "spying" on me, and Sydney said, "That sounds just like my father."

During the period while Mr. Cheston was the zoo's

Presidents of the Zoological Society of Philadelphia

Williams B. Cadwalader, M.D. (right), with Mayor Bernard Samuel in 1951. Photo by IHC, Philadelphia Zoo archives.

Radcliffe Cheston, Jr., with a young llama. Photo by Franklin Williamson, Philadelphia Zoo archives.

George F. Tyler, Jr., President from 1965 until 1972. Philadelphia Zoo archives.

John G. Williams was the last President under whom RC served. Philadelphia Zoo archives.

president, Isabelle and I resumed our fieldwork in Mexico. The National Science Foundation was then encouraging studies on the fauna and flora of the Tropics in various parts of the world, and some of my herpetological colleagues suggested that I apply for a grant. I followed protocol and consulted Zoo Director Shelly first. He was noncommittal and told me to see Cheston. The latter accepted the idea with enthusiasm, and, when the first of my three consecutive grants was approved, Radcliffe Cheston, Jr., was the first to offer his congratulations. He generously permitted me to take an annual leave of a month, during which my salary was paid by the NSF. That much time, added to my month's vacation and whatever comp days were due to me for having worked when I was supposed to be off, gave us ample opportunity for long field excursions to Mexico during late summer and early autumn. I was still very busy each spring promoting zoo attendance, but I could be spared late in the zoo's busy season. The overhead paid to the zoo by the NSF was first 10 percent and then 15 percent, quite a contrast with the large percentages granted to universities in later years. I carefully kept my own fiscal records on the use of the grant money. Shelly graciously audited them for me, and he signed the checks that were due for various expenditures. Not only did the NSF take care of my salary, it also paid our expenses while we were in the field. When I retired a decade later, the zoo board passed a resolution generously giving me all the overhead money, to be used for purposes germane to my research. I used it for field trips to Chihuahua, Durango, and Zacatecas after we had retired to Albuquerque. The American Museum of Natural History, which published my monograph on the water snakes of Mexico in 1969, gave me enough copies so I could present one to each interested board member. Thus, they were assured that I was serious about my research, and that Isabelle and I had not used my grants as an excuse to take long, unproductive vacations.

Unhappily, Zoo Director Shelly had no such close association as I enjoyed with our President. Soon after the assassination of John F. Kennedy, Mr. Cheston telephoned me at the zoo and demanded, "Where's Shelly?" My response was, "I don't know." Next he said, "He's supposed to be working. His secretary doesn't know where he is and neither does his wife. I just talked with her at their home. Now, where is he?"

I could only repeat that I didn't know. Next Mr. Cheston asked, "Will the zoo be closed tomorrow on the day of mourning for President Kennedy?" I said that I hadn't heard, and to that he responded, "Should we close?" I reminded him that I couldn't make any decision inasmuch as I was not the director. Then he told me that

he was the president and he was ordering me to tell him what we should do. My suggestion was to call the other Philadelphia cultural institutions—the Museum of Art, the Academy of Natural Sciences, the Franklin Institute, and so on—to learn what their plans were. "Good," he said. "Telephone them and call me back." All were closing for the day, and when I reported that to him, Mr. Cheston gave me my instructions. "Close the zoo and notify the press and broadcasting stations immediately."

With the help of our zoo telephone operator I alerted the staff, and we arranged for the keepers to follow the feeding and abbreviated cleaning schedules we used on winter holidays when the zoo was also closed. I was careful to tell everyone that I was acting under Mr. Cheston's orders. I tried to reach Shelly by telephone at his home in the evening, but with no success. Predictably, he was furious, especially when he arrived at the zoo the next morning and discovered it was closed.

He avoided Mr. Cheston at every opportunity, and I repeatedly found myself in the middle, and acting, during Shelly's frequent absences, under direct instructions from the president. In a sense I was running the zoo part time, and I think my track record during that lengthy and difficult period was why Mr. Cheston was a prime mover when the search committee insisted that I take over the directorship when Shelly retired at the end of 1966.

I didn't want the job. After witnessing all the aggravations Shelly had to suffer, his bouts with an aggressive labor union, and the daily problems requiring decisions and actions, I had long ago decided the job was not for me. Some of the board members had hinted from time to time about my taking over, but I made it clear that I wasn't interested. Like almost everyone else, I guess, I thought I was underpaid, but Isabelle and I were getting along satisfactorily. Royalties were coming in from our book, Isabelle was selling occasional batches of photographs, and I did a bit of extracurricular paid lecturing.

When I was summoned to meet with the search committee, I made every excuse I could think of. I pointed out that I knew nothing about accounting. No matter. They would hire a business manager. I had never negotiated with a labor union; they would find someone who could. I lived in New Jersey, and several cities, New York included, had recently required residency within the city limits for all employees. I was not paid directly by the City of Philadelphia, they said. The committee made so many concessions and countered my objections so skillfully that I began to feel like an ungrateful idiot. I finally capitulated, but as soon as the meeting was over I began to wonder what I was in for. How strenuous would my responsibilities be?

George Tyler succeeded Radcliffe Cheston as president, and under his regime the Society's by-laws were changed to limit the terms of service of the board members. When Mr. Tyler relinquished his own seat some time later, in accordance with the new requirements, he appropriately stated that he was "hoisted on his own petard."

The last president under whom I served was John G. Williams, a noted Philadelphia attorney who had the highest and most awesome I.Q. of anyone with whom I ever worked. Our association was amicable throughout. He and his wife, Phyllis, became our good friends, and we attended dinner parties at each other's homes. Twice, when I had the unpleasant task of discharging key staff members, John volunteered to meet with us and did most of the talking, thus saving me much unpleasantness. When I learned that he had died of cancer in 1987 I could not hold back my tears.

Many other board members became good friends, and they helped me in a variety of ways. John F. Lewis, Jr., once came to my rescue. At the board meeting following the escape of Bamboo, the gorilla, Dr. Cadwalader chided me for giving the story to the newspapers. Mr. Lewis quickly pointed out that, under the circumstances, I was fully justified. Visitors had seen Bamboo running at large in the monkey-house yard, and we had sent the injured keeper to a public hospital. The event was already common knowledge. My action was actually favorable for the zoo. Instead of treating it as a sensation, the press presented the event in a matter-of-fact, even humorous, manner. Dr. Cadwalader realized that I had acted properly, and gracefully withdrew his complaint.

When our magazine "Fauna" was being published, we handled all the preparations for distribution ourselves. I personally took each heavy quarterly mailing to the post office. There was a substation that stayed open fairly late, and I could drop it off on my way home. But there was always considerable other mail that needed to go off at once. The list of recipients of our news releases grew to large size, and there were always letters about animals and so on. When it became known that I stopped every day, the zoo's business mail was soon shunted onto my shoulders. Frankly, it became a burden, having to find a place to park near the post office during the evening rush hour. I appealed to Zoo Director Shelly to see if we couldn't get a large mailbox placed near the zoo. His attitude was that it wasn't necessary. I was doing a good job.

For many years, in May, when our many shrubs and flowers were at their finest, the monthly meeting of the Board of Directors of the Zoological Society of Philadelphia was held at the zoo and followed by a tour of the grounds and new exhibits. Afterward, all the members and a few invited staff members went to The Rabbit, a private club in an old historic building in Fairmount Park. There we were served a traditional dinner of deliciously prepared roast mutton. Some of the board members drove their own cars, but Mr. Lewis didn't have one. He asked if he could ride along with me, and I, of course, was pleased to have his company. I apologized, however, for having to digress quite a way in order to drop off an unusually large amount of mail at the post office. En route, he asked me if I had to make the trip often, and I answered, "Almost daily, but on my way home." Although it was a year or so since I had asked Shelly for help, Mr. Lewis suggested that it would be a good idea to have a large mailbox right outside the main zoo entrance at 34th Street and Girard Avenue. I replied that it would be wonderful.

The following morning, shortly after I arrived at work, I was astounded to be summoned to the gate. The Philadelphia Postmaster, in person, was waiting for me to show him and an assistant just where I wanted the new mailbox put! I had forgotten that John F. Lewis was a leading Democrat who contributed generously to every campaign. In those days the Postal Department was under political control. After I drove Mr. Lewis home following the dinner party, he had telephoned the Postmaster at his residence.

I was delighted. I called Mr. Lewis and thanked him profusely, but the next day I had to call him again and ask him, please, to explain to my boss what had happened. I had been unjustly accused of going over Shelly's head to get a mailbox.

Mr. Lewis did me another great favor in 1949, when we celebrated the Philadelphia Zoo's Diamond Jubilee (75th anniversary). Opening day had been on July 1, 1874. I wished to have as spectacular a show as possible, but also one that would be in keeping with the event. How better than to do everything in an old-fashioned way? Isabelle and I and about two dozen other employees were costumed in clothes of the Gay Nineties, including three men in uniforms like the old Keystone Cops used to wear. We hired a small German oompah band, a talented barbershop quartet dressed for the part and sang songs of days long gone, and an enthusiast rode his high-wheeled bicycle in the spacious yard outside the zoo's dairy barn. Also, Isabelle and Fred Ulmer rode an old-fashioned tandem bike. With help from friends we had borrowed several vintage automobiles, but where on earth were we going to get horses and carriages? Mr. Lewis knew someone who had a collection of old vehicles, and several were loaned to us along with horses to pull them. I have no proof, but I feel positive,

To observe Old-Timers' Day, commemorating the zoo's 75th (diamond) anniversary in 1949, many of the employees dressed in costumes of the Gay Nineties. Isabelle is at extreme right; Roger is near the center. Photo by Franklin Williamson, Philadelphia Zoo archives.

even to this day, that John F. Lewis, Jr., actually rented them for us and paid the bill out of his own pocket.

A decade later, in 1959, we had a similar ensemble of old-fashioned effects for Old-Timers' Day, which was part of the centennial celebration of the issuance of the charter creating the Zoological Society of Philadelphia by the Commonwealth of Pennsylvania. I appeared in a white suit and top hat, a respectable gentleman's costume of the nineteenth century. I also was wearing a full beard that I had grown while Isabelle and I were in the field in Mexico, from which we had returned about a month previously. It is debatable who had the most fun—the large crowd that visited the zoo to participate in the festivities or those of us who had a part in the pageantry.

James S. Hatfield, Chairman of the Building Committee, and I worked closely together, and we met regularly once a week while the small mammal and reptile houses were under construction. His architectural firm, Hatfield, Martin & White, designed both buildings, and Mr. Hatfield supervised their progress. Both were opened to the public during my administration.

Among the naturalists who were members of the Board, I had known Witmer Stone for quite a few years. He was long associated with the Academy of Natural Sciences and was the recipient of scores of honors and awards from learned societies on both sides of the Atlantic. I was deeply grieved by his death in 1939. Dr. Stone was an all-around naturalist, but his chief interests were ornithology and botany. After his retirement he kept his voluminous library at his home, and it grew so large that he had bookshelves built along the staircase, and he sometimes had to step up and down to find the volume he was seeking. An amusing anecdote was often told about his enormous collection of dried and pressed plants, all carefully prepared for study. Mrs. Stone, in speaking to a friend one day, said, "We have 20,000 plants in our house," and the instant response was, "How do you ever find time to water them all?"

Rodolphe Meyer de Schauensee, the distinguished ornithologist who wrote many long and authoritative books on the birds of such diverse regions as Colombia and China, was a curator of, and conducted his research at, the Academy of Natural Sciences of Philadelphia. One day in 1946, in its library, he picked up a recently published copy of the "American Midland Naturalist," in which I had a review of the Mexican west coast water snake, then known as *Natrix valida.* That was several years before I began fieldwork south of the border. Mr. de Schauensee complimented me on my thoroughness, and he was so impressed that we quickly became good friends.

Richard E. Bishop readily acceded to my request to reproduce a number of his beautiful etchings of birds in "Fauna." Joseph W. Lippincott, who wrote many excellent stories about animals, was another good friend, but I never quite forgave him for his bitter hatred of snakes. Richard W. Foster, who was a vice president of the board when I left, was a son of Frank B. Foster and the owner of the Rittenhouse Book Store, and he helped me with library problems. Other board members, including Maurice Heckscher, James M. Large, Henry D. Mirick, James D. Winsor III, and Richard D. Wood, Jr., offered their friendship and gave me useful advice. Contrariwise, some members of the board sought information from me about animals of various kinds. At least two longtime members were regular listeners to my weekly radio program, "Let's Visit the Zoo."

When the board sought to broaden its membership

Head Keepers of the Philadelphia Zoological Garden

Patrick Menichini as a young keeper was always eager to pitch in whenever or wherever help was needed with the animals. Photo by IHC. Philadelphia Zoo archives.

Head Keeper John J. Regan, with Pandora, the chimpanzee he raised from infancy when her mother deserted her. Real affection developed between John and the little ape, and he often kissed her. One day Mrs. Regan visited the zoo and saw the bussing. John claimed, with a twinkle in his eye, that his wife never kissed him afterward. Photo by IHC, Philadelphia Zoo.

Norman S. Hess examining the teeth of Limpopo, the young hippopotamus. His talented widow, Ann, is still working with the animals. Philadelphia Zoo archives.

William J. Maloney weighing a young orangutan. Bill rose through the ranks to serve in several key roles. Philadelphia Zoo archives.

base, I suggested Frank Palumbo, a renowned Philadelphia restaurateur and philanthropist who had donated many expensive animals to the zoo collection. He also, at least once annually, entertained the entire zoo staff, from janitors and laborers to the "top brass"—and their spouses—giving us all a free dinner, all we wanted to drink, and the best seats in the house to watch such

top-flight entertainers as Jimmy Durante. John Williams and I visited Mr. Palumbo at his restaurant in South Philadelphia late one morning to tell him he had been nominated to sit on the zoo board. He was delighted and insisted that we stay for a gourmet lunch as his guests.

Robin Roberts, ace pitcher of the Philadelphia Phillies and now a baseball Hall of Famer, also became a member of the board. He and I had fun reminiscing about some of the games I had seen or heard on the radio when Robin was in his prime.

Before I left the zoo, a few ladies had become board members, and they were just as interested and devoted as the many men with whom I had been associated. Most unfortunately, I had little opportunity to work with them. In all fairness, I probably should have added "and Heroines" to the title of this chapter.

How extremely lucky I was to have such a cooperative, sympathetic, and influential Board of Directors to back me up. By the time I departed in 1973, I was on a first-name basis with most of them, and I deeply appreciated their willing and enthusiastic ears whenever I had zoo business to discuss.

There were other heroes of the zoo: the dedicated curators and keepers; and the men who rose through the ranks, eventually to acquire supervisory positions. Several among them assuredly deserve mention in these recollections.

John A. Griswold, Curator of Birds, was a pioneer aviculturalist who fathered many innovations that helped to revolutionize his profession. He also had an eye for beauty, as witness the Eleanor S. Gray Memorial Hummingbird Exhibit, which he, in large measure, envisioned and created.

Frederick A. Ulmer, Jr., Curator of Mammals, qualified in similar respects. His zoo monument was the small mammal house which reflected his imagination and his intimate knowledge of the requirements of the animals that resided in it. Also, because he started to work at the zoo in my department after World War II, he was of constant help in publicizing the zoo through his writings and television appearances.

Both curators are mentioned repeatedly in the chapters about the Philadelphia Zoological Garden.

John J. Regan's life was the zoo. He never worked elsewhere. He started as a lad leading riding ponies around a ring, but he soon graduated to the bird house and became its keeper. He also would have made a good publicity man. He never failed me when a reporter or news photographer suddenly appeared at the zoo, and I was hard-pressed to think of a new angle involving one or more of the animals on which they could hang a story or photograph. John was full of ideas, and he helped me repeatedly during the days when I was becoming the zoo's press agent. He eventually was appointed Head Keeper, a position he held for many years.

William J. "Bill" Maloney, who had recently returned from the U.S. Navy after World War II, was so calm and capable the day Bamboo, the rambunctious gorilla, got loose, that Zoo Director Shelly promoted him and put him in charge of the old monkey house. Bill distinguished himself in many ways during his 44 years of service—as Superintendent of the Daniel W. Dietrich Memorial Children's Zoo, as the leader and lecturer of the School Bus for Animals program, and later as Head Keeper. Whenever animals had to be moved, shipped, or required extra attention, especially after Fred Ulmer retired, I thought of Bill Maloney as my strong right arm. While I was Director of the Zoo I promoted him to Superintendent of Animals, a rank just below curatorship. When he retired in 1986, long after I did, his title was a little fancier—Superintendent of Animal Services.

Patrick Menichini and Norman S. Hess also occupied the position of Head Keeper at various times during the many years I was at the zoo. All of these men served with distinction that earned them accolades and commendations.

Once, when Isabelle and I were in downtown Philadelphia for an evening social function, we had arranged to remain overnight at a hotel. When I awakened very early the next morning it was snowing hard, and two inches or so had already accumulated. Since there was foul weather gear in our car, and it was equipped with snow tires, I left Isabelle at the hotel and I drove to the zoo, arriving well before the employees checked in for work at the time clock. Several of the key staff members were already on hand, but it was amusing to watch the faces of the employees when they found me standing in the booth where they punched in.

All the older ones were on time or 15 minutes late at the most. The next generation was all present and accounted for within an hour, but the youngest employees, with a few exceptions, didn't make it at all. The predicted 8 to 10 inches of snow apparently was too much for them. It was easy that day to sort out the conscientious men and women from those who thought of the zoo as just a place to collect their paychecks.

I can state, categorically, that the zoo was never closed. The public was excluded on winter holidays, but work inside the grounds went on just the same. It is relatively simple for a school, an office, or many entire businesses to close down, but we had a moral obligation that transcended any vagaries of the weather. We had animals to feed, and their welfare and comfort required attention every day of the year.

Head Keeper Pat Menichini unquestionably shortened his life because he knew his presence was needed at the zoo during one of the worst winter storms I can remember. The snow was so very deep that all public transportation except the subway and elevated trains was at a standstill. Pat lived several miles from the zoo, but he arose extra early and walked all the way, sometimes through waist-deep drifts. Then came the long, hard grind in caring for the outdoor stock. Mountains of snow had to be shoveled, and ways found to get food to the animals through the deep snow. Much of our hoofed stock lived in paddocks equipped with shelters. Few had accommodations in those days where they could be locked indoors when storms were imminent. The same was true of such animals as the wolves and bears. Large numbers of waterfowl had no shelters at all, only their wings beneath which to tuck their heads. The daily chores were enormously magnified as Pat and his co-workers did their best to feed the animals and make them as comfortable as possible. That night he slept on his desk. The following day was a little easier, and, when it was over, Pat hiked home, tired but confident that everything was in order at the zoo. Just a few days later he suffered a severe heart attack. After a long convalescence he returned to work on a limited basis. Another attack, a fatal one, followed. He was only 45.

Any public institution, be it a zoo, museum, or whatever, needs a loyal, dedicated cadre of enthusiasts to assure its success. We certainly had such an indispensable asset for America's First Zoo—from our distinguished board members to the men and women who worked daily with the animals, giving them the equivalent of tender, loving care.

Chapter 28

Mexico of Yesteryear:
A Prelude to Many Memorable Field Trips

My first trip to Mexico was as a typical tourist, when I was driven across the border at Tijuana in what, at the time, was still called Lower California. It was a dirty, dusty town with scarcely any paving. I had read about the miserable Mexican border towns, and Tijuana surely matched the description. There were numerous souvenir shops, saloons, liquor stores, and a variety of tourist traps. A few boys were hawking tickets for the local bullfight and others were acting as pimps for their "virgin sisters," all in understandable but strongly accented English. What impressed me most was the enterprising men who had painted black stripes on their riding burros to resemble zebras. One could sit in the saddle and have his picture taken for a flexible sum, meaning whatever could be wheedled out of the American tourist. After we had walked down a street and back, in far less than an hour, I was happy to return to the States. But I had entered Mexico. That meant I had been in another country, a total of nine, including Canada and the six I had visited in Europe. Big stuff!

I was to discover in later years how very different most of Mexico was from the Tijuana I saw. What an extremely interesting and beautiful country it really was. A culture and conditions far different from our own—in music, dress, and architecture; abject poverty contrasted with untold wealth; glorious mountain ranges and giant snow-capped volcanoes (even an erupting one); a myriad of kinds of cacti and other prickly plants; and magnificent tropical beaches.

All that was a decade and more away, however. I was in Tijuana in the autumn of 1939. Hitler's blitzkrieg was under way, but most Americans felt far removed from the murderous chaos that was engulfing Europe as the Nazis swept all before them. It would be awhile before we, too, became involved.

I was on my first trip to the American West, on a railroad Pullman tour across the Great Plains and western mountains, which were all new to me. My prime scheduled stop was at the San Diego Zoo. I knew Belle J. Benchley, then the General Secretary of what was destined to become one of the world's greatest zoos.

The herpetologists, however, were just names to me. I met C. B. "Si" Perkins, Curator, and Charles E. "Chuck" Shaw, his student assistant, for the first time. I marveled at the many species of reptiles, most of them new to me in life, that were on display in their exhibit, and there were many other kinds behind the scenes. Si and Chuck took me in tow, so to speak, and it was one of them who drove me to Tijuana. More important, they and Charles R. Schroeder, D.V.M., who later became the world-renowned Director of the Zoo and the great San Pasqual Animal Park, took me on a field trip. Late one afternoon we drove east, crossed the Coast Range, and then road-cruised far into the night all the way to Benson's Dry Lake, stopping for every herp we saw on the paving, dead or alive. My hosts had great fun testing me, making me identify each species. I passed with good marks, however, because I had read all the papers Laurence M. Klauber had published up to that time, and I was fairly familiar, through his text and illustrations, with much of the herpetofauna of San Diego County. Most regrettably he was out of town, and I didn't meet him until many years afterward.

A few days later Mrs. Benchley offered me the use of her car, and I drove all the way to Yuma, Arizona, and back, collecting lizards here and there. What an adventure! I was absorbing the magic of the desert, seeing for the first time enormous sand dunes and stark, barren, rocky ranges in the rain shadow of the high mountains. I was enjoying a whole new natural world, all vastly different from the humid, well-watered, and heavily vegetated East that I knew so well.

I mention all this because during my 1939 trip I made my first venture into arid country. It whetted my appetite for more, a desire that was to be satisfied in large measure years later during the long series of field trips that eventually took me and Isabelle, my devoted wife and co-worker, into every state and territory of Mexico, as well as the Federal District. We spent by far the greatest amount of our time in the countryside, where wildlife was present and often abundant. We avoided cities whenever possible, although we did have

The Conants cooking supper on a portable gas-powered stove near Villa Corona, Jalisco, August 14, 1964. Photo by IHC.

to visit them occasionally to stock up on supplies and to have our vehicle serviced.

Just when I first became interested in Mexican herpetology I cannot recall, but it received considerable impetus when I did an early study, based entirely on museum specimens, of the Mexican west coast water snake. I began writing papers on water snakes during the 1930s, and by the 1940s my interest in that group of serpents had gelled, and I began working intensively with them. The Mexican emphasis and my extensive field work south of the border were sparked by Charles M. Bogert, then the Chairman of the Department of Herpetology of the American Museum of Natural History. He wrote to me from the field in Mexico during August 1946, that a large water snake had just been collected in the Río Nazas, a stream that for untold millennia had emptied into a sump in a huge, barren, bone-dry playa or *bolsón*.

What was a water snake doing in an isolated stream far from any other suitable habitats for members of its group? It couldn't have crawled across the desert. How did it get into the Nazas? Geological history suggested the answer, but studying the problem took us to the Río Nazas many times, and also to the equally intriguing Río Aguanaval in the State of Zacatecas. Details about our work in that general region are recorded in another chapter on "Water Snakes in the Desert."

To make a long story short, my interest was sufficiently aroused so that Isabelle and I made a series of field trips to Mexico to study the water snakes of that largely arid country. Because several species of garter snakes (*Thamnophis*) occupy the "water snake niche" over a large part of the Mexican plateau, they also became of prime interest to me.

Our first and last trips to Mexico we paid for ourselves, but the bulk of the fieldwork was supported by the National Science Foundation, from which I had three grants providing for activity during six different years. Not only were our traveling and living expenses provided, but the NSF also paid my salary for a month each year so that I could take a leave of absence from the Philadelphia Zoo. That time, when added to my annual month's vacation, made it possible for us to spend many consecutive weeks in Mexico. We chose the summer and autumn months, when reptiles were most active. May and June are very dry over most of Mexico, and often windy, and the landscape is desiccated and brown. We tried to be in the field at the onset of the rainy season, usually in July, when amphibians appeared, sometimes in great numbers, and garter and other snakes suddenly emerged to gorge themselves on frogs and toads.

Our transportation was by automobile, and we somewhat eased the long drill from home on the East Coast to the Mexican border by taking turns sleeping while the other drove. Sometimes we kept going until late evening, when vacant motels became more and more difficult to find. On our first two long trips we used station wagons that had racks of drawers built into the back to accommodate our catch, much of which we transported home alive. When all our gear and clothing were piled inside, however, there was precious little room left for us, let alone for a tent or sleeping bags. During those trips we stayed in Mexican motels, but most of them were poor. All too often, when night came, we were far away from the better ones recommended by the American Automobile Club. In 1959 we tried sleeping for a few nights in the car, but we were miserable. Our big problem was that we needed to be in the field in some remote locality near a stream or *ciénaga* (marsh) at dusk, but there were no accommodations for people near such places. We knew we would need to seek a different type of vehicle for our fieldwork.

Fortunately, Volkswagen introduced its new Kamper at the Philadelphia Automobile Show during the winter. It was revolutionary at the time. The German Westfalia Company had outfitted a standard Volks microbus, with its sliding side door, with just about everything except the kitchen sink. Even so there was running water and a plastic washbowl. A tank contained 20 gallons, and a small electric pump supplied water to a bowl or any other container. There was a built-in table and benches that assembled into a bed at night, a commode, a clothes closet, a hatch in the roof for letting out the heat (an essential in the desert), numerous shelves and compartments for clothing and equipment, and a tent that attached to the vehicle with a separate little room to assure privacy when the commode was in use. To all this we added two plastic ice boxes that would keep ice for as much as four days under ordinary conditions, and a cookstove and lantern powered by bottled gas. We were at once mobile and self-sufficient. We could camp anyplace anytime. Even with the roof luggage rack, however, our collecting apparatus and materials for preserving specimens took up too much space, and we found ourselves wishing at times that we were the size of African Pygmies. Isabelle likened our lifestyle to "living in a closet." Matters were particularly difficult in the rain, because nothing could be laid on the ground, and we had to play three-dimensional musical chairs in order to get and serve meals and make up the bed for the night. We were frequently plagued with rain at suppertime, and, since we had resolved never to cook inside the car for fear that some grease might catch fire, I spent many an evening holding the front apron of my poncho over the stove outside the car as the raindrops fell.

Our Kamper was almost an ideal vehicle. Like a turtle, we carried our house with us. It was the forerunner of a plethora of campers, including larger and better ones made by Volks. It was small enough to maneuver almost anywhere, and it was economical to operate. The main trouble was that it had only a 36-horsepower engine, and that made things difficult in hilly country.

Before I attempt to record some of our adventures, troubles, and successes south of the border, I think it would be well to mention our general impressions of the country, its atmosphere, and its people.

The scenery, away from the cities and larger towns, was gorgeous. Almost always a mountain (or many) was in sight, even on the desert flats. Driving along highways traversing any of the sierras was often a thrilling experience. Around the next curve might be a breathtaking vista, a hairpin turn, or a sheer drop of hundreds of feet, with no guardrail. Many of the roads, decades ago, were not well graded, and often a newly paved stretch on which one could get up good speed gave way without warning to deep potholes that necessitated careful maneuvering. Driving a car anywhere on Mexican highways required constant vigilance and the ability to anticipate sudden changes.

Most of the paved roads had no shoulders and no place to pull off so one of us could run back to pick up a dead snake. We had to be very wary about stopping to catch a live one lest we be rammed from the rear.

There were then two hazards that have now been largely eliminated: (1) the *vado* (ford) that was paved but dipped downward, sometimes sharply, and which was a place to negotiate with great care, or not at all, when water was running through it; and (2) the *puente*

angosto (narrow bridge) that usually was only one vehicle wide. Fortunately, there were almost always warning signs well in advance of such obstacles.

By comparison, the paved highways in Mexico are now vastly improved in general, according to several friends and other travelers who have driven on them recently.

The unpaved roads were invariably bad, except in a few places near towns where gravel was used and treated to a scraping now and then. We traversed many a back road on our way to springs or streams, and our progress was always slow, but that had its advantages. We often saw lizards or snakes we would have missed if we had been bowling along. There was almost never any traffic on those roads, and we could stop whenever we wished to admire plants or rock formations.

Mexico has changed in many ways during the past several decades, and, from the standpoint of itinerant naturalists, most of the changes have been bad. The matter of personal safety is a case in point.

From the late 1950s through the mid-1960s we camped out all over rural Mexico, stopping anywhere and at any time that suited our purpose. Sometimes we simply pulled off the highway, getting as far away from the (usually) light traffic as possible. Quite often, because my principal objectives were semiaquatic snakes, we would stop near a stream and, where a road crossed a permanent body of water, there was usually a settlement, ranging in size from a village to a tiny cluster of houses. In such cases I made it a point to talk to one or more of the people, asking politely if we could camp nearby for the night. The answer was usually "Si. ¿Como no?" (Yes. Why not?), or something similar, and the attitude was quite friendly. Then I explained that I was a "professor" studying snakes. In the case of most Americans, mere mention of that word produced a shudder or a look of revulsion. Not so with the Mexicans. They expressed interest, but not surprise. I always told them what I expected to do. I would wade in the stream after dark with a lamp attached to my head so I could see any snakes or other herps that might be on the prowl. Occasionally a boy or two would volunteer to accompany me, but very often I went alone. Isabelle stayed with the vehicle, and sometimes I would be away for as much as two hours. Never, in all of our travels, was either of us molested in any way. It took only a few minutes for the word to spread through the settlement, and everyone knew what we were doing. We felt perfectly safe, far safer indeed than we did in our own country.

Nowadays such casual camping could be suicidal. Reports of robberies, even murders, are all too frequent. In recent years some of my personal friends have been relieved, at gunpoint, of their money and cameras, even

During their peregrinations in Mexico, the Conants saw numerous unusual sights, including many that no longer exist. The beautiful El Salto (The Falls) in the Río Naranjo was a mecca to which busloads of people came over rough roads to see fresh water in abundance. Alas, a year or so after they were there on August 7, 1960, the water was diverted to a power plant and the falls ceased to exist. Photo by IHC.

when camping well away from any visible settlement. Others have had their cars stolen. Crime has mushroomed in Mexico just as it has in the United States.

There have been many other changes. We almost never saw trash. Every piece of paper was fuel, and a tin can was a utensil. People simply did not throw such things away. But when I was back in north-central Mexico in 1976, litter had become visible, at least in and near cities.

During our fieldwork we found many clear and beautiful springs and small to large *ciénagas*, all with an abundant local fauna and flora. Now all too many of them have been destroyed. The water has been channeled away for irrigation or other human uses, and some of those near cities have become depositories for raw sewage. In both cases the snakes and frogs, turtles and dragonflies, and all the other wildlife have disappeared. Such habitat destruction is even worse than our own thoughtless ravaging of wetlands.

There was some smog here and there in the larger towns, but even Mexico City was not too bad, at least in 1949, when we actually saw the snow-capped Popocatépetl and Ixtaccíhuatl, which, with other mountains, form a huge and lofty rampart east of the capital. Nowadays the air pollution in Mexico City ranks among the world's worst.

The exchange rate during most of our fieldwork was 12 pesos to the dollar. Years later it rose to more than 3,000 to the dollar, but in late 1996 it was roughly 8. The

Mexican peso is now a floating currency that may vary from day to day.

During the 1960s we could bring our catch home across the border with relative ease. I carried letters, updated annually, from the United States Fish and Wildlife Service, Department of Agriculture, and Department of Health, Education, and Welfare, stating that there were no laws prohibiting the importation of reptiles and amphibians. Now there are numerous restrictions, so many regulations, and so much red tape that trying to do what we did is impossible.

The Mexican government required collecting permits, and I would make application to the proper authorities in Mexico City a few months ahead of each trip. I sent references and abstracts outlining my research, and, some weeks later, I received a *permiso* (permit) to collect reptiles and amphibians. That was a valuable piece of paper—in Spanish, of course, that I used to identify myself on several occasions. Many of my friends and colleagues, especially those who lived relatively close to Mexico, also applied for and received *permisos*, and they made excursions of a month or several weeks to Mexico every summer to do largely what we were doing. They made general collections and salvaged and preserved specimens killed on the road and, in most cases, what they brought back eventually went into research collections in museums or universities. Our general knowledge of the distribution of species of Mexican herps increased rapidly in those years.

Now such activities have ceased entirely. Mexican collecting permits have become expensive and difficult to get, and there are so many restrictions in conjunction with them that it is scarcely worthwhile to attempt any herpetological research in Mexico unless one has unlimited time and funds. No specimens may be taken out of Mexico without special permission and the payment of a substantial fee. In the meantime, the smuggling of large numbers of reptiles and amphibians for the pet trade goes on apace. The smugglers take risks, to be sure, but legitimate and conscientious herpetologists who might wish to follow in our footsteps, and who carefully try to obey the laws and regulations, are severely penalized. Yet the number of specimens researchers brought back in former years, including those found on the roads that would have been scavenged by vultures and other carnivorous birds and mammals, was very small in comparison with the huge numbers now being smuggled.

A few paragraphs on the climate in Mexico may be of interest. The weather on the plateau was always pleasant—if one allowed, by doffing or donning sweaters, for the daily changes in temperature that are typical of high desert climates. It could be cool, often cold, at night, but warm or even hot during the afternoons. As an example, we camped one night in mid-September south of Rodeo, Durango, at an elevation of 4,650 feet. When we awakened soon after dawn, the temperature was 44°F, by mid-morning it had doubled to 88°F, and in early afternoon it was 100°F. Because of the chilly evenings and cold nights, we soon learned the value of the Mexican *sarape*. One's head goes through a slit in the middle, there is a warm blanket down one's chest and back, but one's hands and arms have perfect freedom at the sides to do things.

A pleasant peculiarity of dry desert weather that must be experienced to be appreciated occurs when one steps out of the sun into full shade, and the temperature seems suddenly to drop by 10 to 20 degrees.

At low elevations it was hot and sultry, and the humidity, which, except in rainy weather, was usually low in the uplands, became an important factor. Many of the snakes we sought were most abundant in the lowlands, so we spent considerable time enduring the enervating, sweaty weather. We avoided daylight travel, staying in the shade or within our motel, if we were using one, and venturing forth about sundown to patrol the roads. That, unhappily, coincided with the departure of truck drivers from the cities and larger towns so they, too, could avoid the sweltering heat of the daytime. Inevitably, they ran over many snakes, some of which we salvaged to preserve for future study. The traffic sometimes was rather heavy, and we had trouble keeping out of the way of speeding trucks on the narrow roads when we wanted to pick up specimens, dead or alive. It was particularly bad west of Tampico, on Mexico's east coast. Snakes of many species, but mostly water snakes, swarmed in the marshes traversed by the highway extending west from the city. On some nights the carnage was heavy. Twice we found more than 50 dead snakes within a distance of a few miles, most of them mashed flat by the heavy trucks' big tires. Edmund D. Keiser, Jr., during a drizzling rain about 3:00 A.M. on August 17, 1967, counted 124 dead snakes on the road east of El Ebano on the Tampico highway. Obviously the snakes did not mind the high humidity, but when, coupled with the high heat, it became unbearable for us, we could retreat to the uplands.

Purposely I have postponed comment on the people of Mexico until last. They varied in temperament as human beings do everywhere, and their attitudes toward gringos depended, I am sure, on their past experiences with visitors from the United States.

The Americans who arrived in such tourist centers as Guadalajara, Monterrey, and Mexico City in their big cars and sneered at the poor roads, the dust, the poverty, and virtually everything else, left a mighty poor impression with almost everyone. They became targeted prey for cheating. Prices went up on everything, especially since very few of them understood Spanish. We were both surprised and delighted when we discovered that they had to pay, sometimes heavily, for their snobbish, superior attitude toward everything Mexican. We despised them but were grateful that they never visited the rural areas where our interests lay. The typical small villager never came into contact with them, and the country folk remained friendly and unspoiled. Our attitude was always that we were guests in their country, and we constantly behaved as such. Also, we had another advantage. We could speak their language, even though we were not fluent in it. In short, we met them as equals and treated them as friends.

In time, we came to have almost a vicarious affection for them. They helped us so much and were so pleasant and understanding. I can best describe our feelings by quoting from a letter I sent to an influential friend in Philadelphia from Jocotepec, Jalisco, on July 24, 1965, during our last year of support from the National Science Foundation:

Greetings from Mexico! Not the Mexico of the tourist, but primitive, bucolic Mexico. We know little of the sparkling sands and clip joints of Acapulco or the somber art and night spots of Mexico City, but the countryside, the volcanic mountainscapes, the thirsty desert—"that ees very deeferent, Señor."

During our wanderings in pursuit of the serpent we have penetrated to some of the more remote parts of this picturesque republic. And in so doing, despite all his shortcomings, we have come to respect the paisano, the peón, *or, in European parlance, the peasant. He may own merely a shirt, a pair of trousers, and* huaraches *to guard his feet from the thorns and, oh yes, the indispensable* sombrero, *but he is a gentleman in all matters affecting the itinerant Gringo. He is a font of information on where the snakes may hide, where the water holes may be and, given a chance, will work hard for hours for a pittance. He is self-reliant, living off the country and doing a little gardening and, where available land is at a premium, planting his corn on a slope so steep he literally can fall out of his field. His wants are few, and he supplies them. He accepts no dole, but is grateful for any few pesos he can earn. He is proud and independent even though he lives in what, to American eyes, is the most abject poverty.*

His government, mindful of the self-respect that comes from working, encourages labor. If an axe or machete *will do, why use a power saw? Why dig a ditch by machine when there are so many laborers willing to work?*

There is much of the pioneer spirit here—the desire to make one's way in life and a willingness to accept one's lot that seems almost to have vanished in our own land of extraordinary plenty where luxuries of a decade ago are now a must for virtually everyone. Perhaps Mexico has heard of automation but, if so, it's in the cities, perhaps in the big manufacturing plants. Oh, yes, and on the highways. Modern road-building equipment is used in construction, but repairs and all subsidiary roads are products of hand labor.

We think that during our many trips to Mexico we have absorbed a little of the color of a great nation that has solved many of its problems, a country with a program and currently one of the most stable

governments in Latin American. Coupled with our adventures in the wilderness and our snake hunting, we think it might be fun some day to write a book about rural Mexico. It would take time, of course, but maybe I should think about it after I retire from the Philadelphia Zoo.

But perhaps that would be too late! Mexico, which has copied so much from the "colossus of the north," might get some modern notions, such as unemployment insurance and relief checks. Gone would be the hand labor, the personal initiative and self-reliance, and in their stead would come indolence, schemes for beating the government, and the inevitable rise in crime.

We think Mexico has something we could use— the desire for a man to be a man, instead of a parasite on the tax-payer. ¡Viva la republica!

Chapter 29

Crossing the Border

We crossed from the United States into Mexico and back again many times, but inevitably as we approached the border we steeled ourselves for bureaucratic red tape, never knowing whether our passage would be easy or fraught with difficulty. It was always an adventure, sometimes pleasant, but sometimes so maddening that we were almost ready to say, "Never again."

In general, our entrances into Mexico were relatively smooth and efficient, whereas reentering the States could be tedious and exasperating. We soon learned that the difference was based on "visitors" versus "returning citizens." We noted that Mexicans who had been in the United States received close and often rigorous inspections that were usually worse and far more thorough than most of those we experienced on our way home. Radios, other electronic devices, parts for automobiles, miscellaneous machinery such as typewriters, and a long list of other items that were expensive in Mexico were restricted, and it was understandable why many returning citizens became temporary smugglers. Many Americans also fell into that category after buying gems in Querétaro or pre-Columbian artifacts that, under Mexican law, could not be exported.

All this we learned eventually, but our first entry into Mexico, in 1949, was in the role of greenhorns. We were driving an overloaded Oldsmobile station wagon with free space only in the front seats, and a wooden rack, built at the rear, and on the shelves of which we hoped to place many well-filled snake bags.

Fearful that crossing an international boundary with a heavily loaded car might lead to difficulties, especially when we returned, I ventured into the U.S. Customs office (at Laredo, Texas) and started asking questions. I had made inquiries back in Philadelphia, but some of the answers there had seemed rather vague. No one was sure about the rules governing the importation of live reptiles and amphibians, either at home or in Laredo. I showed them my papers from the various government agencies, however, and they "guessed" that I would probably be OK. How wonderfully reassuring!

There was nothing to do but go onward. We started to cross the bridge over the Rio Grande, and were stopped briefly by U.S. Customs men who wanted to know if we had any foreign-made equipment. We informed them that Isabelle's cameras had already been registered and showed them our document to that effect. We were told we could bring back items bought in Mexico up to a value of $100 each if we stayed two weeks, or $400 each if we stayed longer, but "be sure to save all your receipts for our inspection." We asked about liquor, and, because I had mentioned Philadelphia, we were told emphatically that Pennsylvania did not permit its residents to bring back a single drop, obviously because liquor sales were a state monopoly. I called attention to our New Jersey license plates, and we learned we could return with a gallon apiece.

We continued onward to the Mexican customhouse and there, for the first time, we went through a routine that seldom varied over the years. First we had to show our health certificates, which certified that we had been vaccinated for smallpox. Our tourist permits, obtained from the Mexican consulate in Philadelphia, were inspected and stamped. Then I had to show the official title for my car and sign papers swearing I would take it out of Mexico and not sell it there. Then I was given a permit to take the car anywhere in their country.

Next came baggage inspection. The persons ahead of us had their suitcases and packages taken inside the customs building, where each was opened, given a cursory examination, and then a yellow sticker was attached to each piece. We were approached by a sleepy guard in an ill-fitting and tattered uniform. He walked up to our car and peered through the windows at our huge load, which was piled to the roof with equipment and personal belongings. He turned to me and blandly asked, "You pay three dollars for inspection? Two dollars for the *jefe* [chief] and one dollar for me?"

We were greatly relieved. It was certainly worth three bucks not to unpack the car. At the man's request I opened the tailgate, and he made bold white chalk Xs on three or four of our largest pieces of baggage. That seemed to be the system. We never saw yellow stickers again, but chalk marks were made in a similar manner on all our subsequent trips. As I handed him the three dollars he gave us a large red *turista* sticker to attach to our windshield. We were finally off, but a few miles south of Nuevo Laredo we were stopped by customs guards. All they wanted to do was to see our car permit and cadge cigarettes from Isabelle!

Because our 1949 trip would be our first deep penetration into Mexico, I had tried to anticipate every possible problem we might encounter. Not only did I visit the Mexican consulate, but I also invited the chief consular officer, his wife, and their two children to be my guests at the Philadelphia Zoo. They came one Saturday afternoon, and I gave them a personally conducted tour as well as a dozen free tickets of admission so they could come again and bring their friends. During the course of their visit we talked about many things Mexican, and one question I asked was whether any sort of permit was necessary for catching and exporting herps. The consul promised to check on it for me, and a few days later I received a list, in Spanish, of all the game animals of Mexico on which there was a closed season for hunting. The only reptile or amphibian was the iguana. I telephoned to thank him, and he said I would have no trouble. Unfortunately, he was wrong.

After a long and successful trip we arrived back at the border weeks later with a rather large collection. Although I didn't know it at the time, it included two type specimens for new subspecies that I would eventually describe. We surrendered our car permit and tourist cards, but, during a cursory inspection of the contents of the car, the bags of snakes were discovered. I was asked to show my *permiso* (permit) for collecting in Mexico. I replied that no permit was needed. Then an argument began that soon exhausted my Spanish. A volunteer interpreter offered to help, and, since both the customs man and I had been waving our arms while we argued, a small crowd had gathered. I reiterated what the Mexican consul had told me, and stated that the only protected reptile was the iguana, and we had none. More arguing ensued, and we were told that our collection would have to be confiscated! I was dismayed. In reply, I said, "I thought you would be happy to have me take snakes out of Mexico, and you would get rid of them."

When that was translated into Spanish the crowd roared with laughter. The customs man threw up his hands in surrender and walked away. What a close call! A chance remark of mine had saved the day. The next time I made sure by getting in touch with the authorities in Mexico City, and in due course I received an official *permiso*.

We continued on our way, crossed the Rio Grande

into Laredo, and arrived at the U.S. Customs station. We were required to state that we were American citizens, which was quite obvious. Next we were told to pull over in the shade alongside a long bench. A very polite agent asked to see our health cards, and, once he saw that we were OK for smallpox, he told us to take everything out of the car and put it on the bench. A laborer of unquestionable Mexican ancestry assisted us—for a fee, of course. When the car was half empty, the agent said that was enough, and he proceeded to have a careful, although random, look at what we had. He even poked into various things in the car. All went well until he encountered our livestock in the wooden rack. When he asked what was there, I replied, "Snakes, mostly water snakes." I opened one of the bags so he could look inside, and I showed him our letters and papers. He said that the man who was in charge of imports of plants and animals was off for the day, which happened to be a Sunday, and he would have to consult with his chief. So off he went with all our papers for what seemed like a very long time, while we had visions of having to wait where we were until the morrow when the specialist would be on duty.

Eventually our agent returned, and explained that he had convinced his boss that water snakes were perishable. It seemed there was a regulation permitting the passage of perishable goods through customs, even on Sundays. We were extremely grateful to him, and I would have gladly given him a generous tip except that such gestures are strictly prohibited on the U.S. side of the border. We thanked him profusely instead. Thus ended our first return trip through customs. All our livestock arrived home safely in New Jersey, and our gallon each of tequila.

Once on a later trip I accidentally (stupidly is the proper word) left the title for the car at home. I didn't miss it until we were in Texas, and there was nothing to do but try to bluff our way through. When I arrived at the desk where Mexican automobile permits were issued I laid down my current car registration card on top of a five-dollar bill. The agent didn't even look up at me. He slipped the banknote into his pocket, recorded the numbers from my card, and handed it back along with a permit. *Propinas* (tips) were a way of life on that side of the border.

During our many trips to Mexico we crossed in one direction or the other at all the principal checkpoints from Nogales, Arizona, to Brownsville, Texas. Although we sometimes had minor delays elsewhere, Laredo was the place where we were most apt to have problems.

More than a decade after our 1949 trip, while we were sponsored by the National Science Foundation and were driving our Kamper, we crossed back into the States at Laredo and encountered the only surly customs inspector we ever saw. He was obviously an exhibitionist, a big, burly young character, in uniform, but packing two pearl-handled pistols, one on each hip. He swaggered when he walked, and he looked like a gun-toting extra in a low-budget western movie. In a loud voice and with sweeping gestures he instructed us to, "Take it all out."

I placed the ladder on the side of the Kamper, which gave access to our bulky top load, then turned to him and said, "Point to anything you'd like to inspect and I'll get it out for you, either here in the car or from the roof rack. It took us a solid day to pack and to fit everything into place. I'm not going to take it all out, especially since we are both exhausted from a very long field trip." At least he listened to me, but then he almost bellowed, "Take it all out! If you're tired hire this guy to help you." He pointed to a Mexican laborer standing nearby. By that time I was getting a little annoyed, and my response was, "I don't want him getting our things all misplaced." Whereupon I sat down on the bench and he glared at me. "Have it your way," he said, "but you're not going anywhere until you do what I say." He marched away.

Isabelle sat down next to me. At least a half hour passed, and then an older, obviously long-experienced agent appeared and asked me what was the matter. I told him what had happened, showed him my papers, and stated again my offer to get anything out that he wished to examine. He gave us a wry smile that told us, more than anything he could have said, that he was well acquainted with the behavior of his younger colleague.

"What have we up here?" he asked, and then climbed up the ladder and peered under the canvas cover at our rows of bottles filled with pickled specimens. I explained what we were doing and showed him some of the live snakes, which I kept in an insulated compartment beneath the rear seat of our little dining area that could be quickly changed into a bed. He showed real interest, but, because it was his duty, he asked us to open several containers. Then he said he was satisfied and we could go. We were delighted that my resistance had paid off and that we didn't have to repack the car, into which scores of objects were fitted together like the parts of a three-dimensional jigsaw puzzle. It

would have taken us hours to put everything back.

During our long drive homeward we thought occasionally of our unpleasant experience, and we developed a scheme for beating the rap, so to speak. We resolved to put it into action on our trip the following year. It worked so well that we repeated it thereafter every time we returned from Mexico.

We would drive close to the U.S. border in the evening, perhaps 10 or 15 miles away, pull off the road, and camp there for the night. We would arise early, as we always did when we were in the field, drive the rest of the way, and arrive at the U.S. side as close to 7:30 A.M. as possible. The guards had been on duty since midnight, and we postulated that they would be tired and ready to go off at 8:00. We were right. Our every passage from then on was relatively swift and easy. Also, we had the salutary advantage of immediately hunting up an American restaurant, where, after many weeks, it was safe to drink milk and water that we didn't have to purify first. Also, we could order a good old-fashioned American breakfast that would be prepared by someone else. What luxury!

Once when we crossed early we had an amusing experience. We were asked, as usual, if we were American citizens, and were then instructed to pull over by the customary off-loading bench. A young inspector in his 20s came to us, and I asked him where he wanted to start. "Let me see your health certificates," he replied. He looked at them, but scanned mine longer than the guards usually did. He then asked, "Are you a herpetologist?" I replied in the affirmative, and, with unexpected eagerness, he asked, "Gee, would you autograph my book for me?" I said, "Sure," and he hurried off to his locker and returned with a copy of our field guide. Both Isabelle and I signed it for him.

Perhaps the best way to describe his reaction would be to say that he was ecstatic. Then suddenly he realized that some of his colleagues might be watching him, so we received what probably looked like a thorough inspection. He poked into and at things here and there, but most of the time we had a lively conversation about snakes and snake hunting. He was happy and so were we. He even shook hands with me on the far side of the car where he was hidden from the customs office.

That was certainly the most pleasant border crossing we ever had.

Chapter 30

On Staying Healthy

Appropriate subtitles for this subject might be "Avoiding the Aztec Curse," "Montezuma's Revenge," or just plain "Turista," all of which euphemistic expressions were, and still are, in vogue among American visitors to Mexico. Traveling in the Tropics or subtropics anywhere in the world requires careful attention to what one eats and drinks. There are too many unaccustomed "bugs" to contend with, ranging from different strains of colon bacilli and numerous viruses to the more serious hepatitis, amebiasis, salmonella, and other problems that may require medical attention. If the traveler remains in one place he may develop an immunity to some of these, but our itinerant wanderings brought us into contact with new alimentary hazards almost daily. When we were doing fieldwork in Mexico we had a list of taboos for preventing dysentery. Our first (1949) trip was a particularly touchy one, and we learned so much through personal discomfort that all of our subsequent excursions were far more pleasant.

The rules, in brief, were: Drink no water unless it has been boiled or treated. Drink no milk and eat no dairy products of any kind. Eat no salads in restaurants. Carefully wash, with treated water, all raw vegetables and fruit, and do not eat any of them unless you have prepared them yourself.

Water was our most important concern. We were told to boil it for 10 minutes or treat it with halogens (chlorine or iodine). Bottled water, opened at the table by a waiter, was presumably safe, but our limited funds did not permit us to eat in the expensive places that served bottled water. We had Halazone tablets with us, but, when used in the proportions recommended, the overwhelming taste of chlorine was intolerable. News about Globaline (iodine capsules) reached us before we left home in 1949, but much too late to get in touch with what we were told was the one and only source at the time. Boiling water, as I have mentioned elsewhere, was a confounded nuisance. During all our later trips we used Globaline and found that the taste of iodine was not too bad. Its use was quick and safe (except for some very resistant protozoan cysts): one capsule to a quart of water, wait for 10 minutes, and then shake well. We, of course, used the cleanest-looking water we could find, and we never took it from a stream or pool, although that was also said to be permissible.

It was surprising how many travelers we saw who failed to take even the most simple precautions. Even at the Restaurante Los Arcos in Monterrey, where we ate many times without a trace of trouble, we touched neither the water nor the ice that was usually floating in each glass. Several times, however, we overheard other Americans ask whether the water was safe to drink. The reply was always in the affirmative, with the explanation that it was pure mountain water from the nearby highlands. That was good enough for the tourists, but we had seen cattle defecating in those very streams, so we abstained.

There were two items on our original drink list that gave us a change from the either tasteless or bad-tasting boiled water: beer and carbonated beverages. We tried beer, and, whereas Isabelle tolerated it well, it promptly put me to sleep, especially right after lunch. That meant Isabelle had to do the driving during the hottest part of the day, when the glare of the sun caused additional discomfort.

Coca-Cola and other soft drinks were available in many places, especially in the small *cantinas* that sold beverages and snacks, the latter mostly homemade. We often saw such miniature stores perched at the edges of sidewalks in the cities and even, occasionally, in smaller towns. Sometimes one would appear seemingly in the middle of nowhere, at a crossroads in the desert, for example. They had two drawbacks, however. First, the drinks often were not iced, so we had to plan ahead and put two or more at a time in our portable ice boxes. Second, a deposit was required on all bottles, and sometimes it was as much as or even more than the drink itself. When we turned in used bottles, the pouring rim was invariably inspected. If it was chipped, it was rejected. I recall, one time at the *alameda* (central square) in the city of Oaxaca, watching an elderly blind lady who operated a small *cantina*. She felt the top of every empty bottle very carefully with a finger to make sure it wasn't chipped before accepting it. Evidently the drivers who delivered the soft drinks were instructed not to take any damaged bottles, and even a peso or two would have been an important loss to such an impoverished person.

During our many travels in Mexico we visited two bottling plants, one by accident, and saw how spotless they were and what great care seemed to be taken to keep the fluids sanitary. With that in the back of our minds, we discovered Squirt during the early 1960s which, in those days, was not carbonated. We had been driving for hours across the Chihuahuan Desert toward the city of the same name. The temperature was well over 100°F and the relative humidity less than 10 percent. When we finally entered the city we were really parched, and we stopped at the first restaurant we saw, ordered something to eat that was not on our blacklist, and also two large ice-cold bottles of Coke. After downing them I noticed a tall green bottle on an adjacent table, and I asked the *señor* sitting there how he liked it. His reply, prompt and to the point, was that it was the best thing he had found to quench one's thirst. So we tried it, and drank two bottles each. Thereafter, whenever we could find it, we always had Squirt with us during our fieldwork. I had seen ads for it on billboards in Philadelphia, even one near the zoo, but after reading its slogan, "It's in the Public Eye," I subconsciously treated it as a joke. Later we discovered that Squirt makes a good mixer with tequila.

Avoiding dehydration was important, especially for me. Isabelle almost always stayed with the car, and often some critter would come crawling, walking, or hopping past her that she could catch and surprise me with when I returned. I was the member of the partnership who did the rock turning, hiking, climbing, and, worst of all, wading in water in my hot, clumsy hip boots. In the lowlands, where most of the water snakes lived, I perspired profusely. One hot evening in August 1961, along the Río Armeria in Colima, not far from the Pacific Ocean, I set out at dusk to wade along the stream and also the canal that carried water to a nearby settlement. It looked like ideal habitat, but not a snake did I see. I kept doggedly at it, exploring every bit of shoreline, but, after perhaps an hour and a half, I began to feel very tired and faint. I headed back, crossed the Armeria, which was then quite shallow, and almost staggered up the gentle slope to our Kamper. I suddenly realized that my skin was dry. I sat down and asked Isabelle to get the water bottle from one of our ice boxes, and I drained it dry, a full quart. I bathed my face and head from our wash water-tank, but I still felt thirsty. Within an hour I drank every drop of liquid available. No harm resulted, but I apparently had used up my entire reserve of expendable body moisture.

RC filling styrofoam boxes with ice (hielo). Icehouses were always on back streets in the larger Mexican towns, but were nonexistent in most smaller settlements. Ice was trucked to some of them, however, where it was stored underground, and covered with straw. The easiest way to find ice was to ask a boy and let him ride with us to the icehouse. Photo by IHC.

Despite our efforts to consume ample liquids while we were in the field, we invariably lost weight during every long expedition. Once we were back in the States and could drink the water without fear of problems, we quickly regained several pounds.

Milk and all its products were forbidden. One winter between trips to Mexico the newspapers carried a story about a group of doctors in Mexico City who had issued a warning to residents that many types of cheese were dangerous, presumably because of brucellosis. The main thing I recall about our abstention from milk is that Isabelle liked cream in her coffee, but she had to give it up for many weeks during our first long trip in 1949. Once we had crossed the border toward home she eagerly looked forward to having cream again and poured a generous amount into her cup. She took one sip, made a face, and exclaimed, "It tastes awful." For the rest of her life she drank her coffee black. As for me, I have never cared for coffee, and what caffeine I imbibe comes from tea and soft drinks.

During our earlier trips we ate dry bread or spread jam or mayonnaise on it that we brought from home. Then, in the early 1960s, we learned that at least one brand of oleomargarine was safe, and it made a much appreciated improvement in our daily diet. Good bread was available in Mexico, and we particularly liked Pan Bimbo and the rolls made by the same company.

It was a simple matter to push aside salads when they were served with restaurant meals. As a matter of fact, we had little trouble with fruits and vegetables. We avoided leafy varieties, such as lettuce and cabbage, which were grown with organic fertilizers and probably in some places with night soil (human excrement). Instead, we concentrated on those that were self-wrapped, so to speak, with tough skins. If they were unblemished we needed only to wash them well in our treated water. They included oranges, melons, and *aguacates* (avocados, but I like the Spanish word for them so much that I'm impelled to use it). Bananas with completely unbroken skins we could eat as they were, peeling them as we went. Tomatoes, squashes, and cucumbers could be treated easily. We even discovered a new vegetable, *choyotes*. It looked and tasted like squash, but grew on arbors and hung down over our heads when we inspected a small plantation of them.

I recall our first venture into an old-fashioned *mercado* (market), where each vendor occupied his own stall and sold his own specialties, which doubtless varied with the season. I wanted a half dozen of the small lemons—green and much more like limes to our way of thinking, but which they called *limones*. The man ahead of me bought six for 50 centavos, but when it was my turn the price had increased to five pesos, 10 times as much. An argument ensued in Spanish, and, since I knew what the previous customer had paid, the vendor eventually gave up and grudgingly let me have mine at the same price. What bothered him most, I am sure, was his disappointment at not being able to cheat a gringo.

Once we acquired our Volkswagen Kamper in 1960, our culinary problems eased at once. After our unhappy experiences from eating in Mexican restaurants during earlier trips, we decided to do most of our own cooking. Our new vehicle had a multiplicity of cabinets and cubbyholes in which we could stash canned and dehydrated food. We also took along powdered milk. We knew that tips would doubtless get us through customs on the Mexican side of the border, especially since we were nearly as loaded as we had been when our station wagon was inspected for three dollars, two of them for the chief. It meant that we could feed ourselves at any time or any place. Most convenient was our ability to have supper close to a remote, isolated aquatic habitat where I could start searching from dusk onward. Only when we were in cities having our car serviced, or when we became so gamey that hot baths were a necessity, did we use Mexican restaurants. Most of them were at good motels, but only those recommended by the American Automobile Association, whose inspectors had checked them with care. As a result of our sweeping changes in policy we stayed well and were rarely ever bothered by ailments of any kind. Also, we soon learned about a number of additional foods we could buy and use in Mexico, and we frequently stopped at the *mercados*, some even on the sidewalks in smaller towns, to stock up on fresh fruits and vegetables.

We became better prepared for serious illnesses as the years went by. Proof of vaccination for smallpox was always required when we were crossing the border in either direction. Before leaving home we received inoculations for typhoid and typhus. At first we used Atabrine, a drug of questionable value, we were told, against malaria. We soon graduated to chloroquine (Aralen), and, despite the many mosquito bites we sustained, we remained free from malaria. I was particularly susceptible to those blasted insects, because I did a lot of wading in swamps. I wore long-sleeved shirts, turned up my collar, donned a cap above my headlamp, and doused myself with insect repellent. For a year or two we used Entero-vioform to keep our digestive tracts in order, but it, too, was controversial, and we soon abandoned it. We rarely had diarrhea.

Virtually everyone has had at least a touch of dysentery, and we all know how embarrassing it can be, especially if the onset is sudden or violent. But hold on a minute! If you dislike what Isabelle called the "latrine school of humor," I suggest that you skip the next few paragraphs and go on to the following chapter.

After we acquired our Kamper in 1960, we were always prepared for the worst. The commode could be used even while the car was in motion, as once happened when we were speeding along a busy throughway. There were curtains at every window, which we invariably closed at night, and, when drawn, provided privacy even during the daytime. Our first two trips, however, were made in station wagons that lacked such amenities. When necessary we took to the bushes, but what to do on the open desert? A truck driver provided us with the answer. He simply walked 100 feet or so away from his vehicle, turned and faced the highway, squatted down, and let nature take its course. No one paid the slightest attention to him.

One day, during our first long Mexican trip in 1949, we were in open country and Isabelle was driving. I knew I was in for trouble, so I asked her to slow down when I saw a small, rather open copse of scraggly, thorny growth ahead. Even though there was a small house across the road, it offered the only shelter in sight. She stopped, and I hastened along a path that ran back into the brush. I had scarcely dropped my pants when a Mexican came charging after me. When he saw my predicament, he slowed down but kept right on coming, while I muttered, "*Estoy enfermo*" (I am sick). Did he have some sort of contraband along the path that he thought I might discover, or was he just curious because I had seemed to be in such a hurry?

Another time, in an area devoid of virtually all vegetation

except grass and other very low plants, I was more than 100 yards from the car and the road. Only a nearby railroad track offered any shelter, and mighty little at that. I crossed the tracks and squatted down in a slightly shallow place just far enough away to be clear of any passing train. One was coming, not especially fast, and it was still some distance away. I anticipated that my back might be seen only by the engineer and fireman if, indeed, they happened to be looking straight ahead. Unluckily, it was a passenger train with an observation car attached at the rear. As it passed I was clearly visible to a man standing on the platform. When he saw me hunkered down close to the ground, he smiled and waved. In response to his friendly gesture, and because I was greatly relieved to note that there were no ladies with him, I waved gaily back.

We invariably carried toilet paper in our pockets for just such emergencies. It was as indispensable as a loud whistle, in case one of us should become lost.

Chapter 31

Water Snakes in the Desert

During our numerous field excursions in Mexico, we sporadically spent many days hunting for water snakes in the desert. That sounds ridiculous, but it's true, although admittedly, an explanation is in order. How do water snakes survive in arid country? Indeed, how did they get there in the first place?

Before attempting to answer those questions, let's first consider the reptiles themselves. I was particularly interested in what are known, herpetologically, as natricine snakes. Collectively, they are a wide-ranging group, with many kinds across the northern continents and northern Africa, and even in West Africa and Australasia. At one time a large proportion of them were placed in the scientific genus called *Natrix*, but rather recently that composite group was partitioned by several specialists, and the largest and heaviest of the New World members are now assigned to the genus *Nerodia*. In arid parts of the United States and Mexico, several species of garter snakes of the genus *Thamnophis* (also natricines) are locally called water snakes, because they, too, frequent streams, marshes, and other wet habitats. To use a term that seldom is heard nowadays, certain garter snakes occupy the "water snake niche." They, like the true water snakes, became one of my major objectives.

The three following paragraphs are abstracted and emended from an article I wrote in 1960 for "America's First Zoo," the quarterly publication of the Philadelphia Zoo:

Our local water snake, Nerodia sipedon sipedon, *so often mistaken for the venomous cottonmouth of the South, is frequently seen along streams, either basking in the sun or prowling in search of frogs or fishes. Mexican water snakes have similar habits, but since they can survive only where water is permanent or at least semipermanent, they are confined to rivers in the drier parts of Mexico. And the great heat of much of the region requires that basking be largely limited to the early morning hours or to cloudy days and that most hunting for food be done at night.*

Explaining how the water snakes reached the rivers is far more difficult, especially since the streams are far apart and separated by inhospitable tracts of desert where aquatic or semiaquatic animals would literally dry up and blow away. Further, there are a number of rivers on the great central plateau of Mexico that never reach the sea. They rise in the mountains toward the west, flow eastward or northeastward, and dissipate their waters onto desert flats. Yet, at least two of those rivers are populated with water snakes.

It is to the science of geology that we must turn for our answer. Evidence from several sources clearly indicates that arid Mexico, as well as our own Southwest, were far more blessed with rainfall at several times in the past than they are at present. Forests flourished and streams gurgled in many areas that are now occupied by open deserts and dry arroyos. Aquatic or semiaquatic animals could use many avenues of travel that are closed to them today. It is logical to assume that during one or more pluvial periods the streams, which are now characterized by their interior drainage, were able to flow far to the east or north to join other streams from which they received their aquatic fauna. Unfortunately, geological investigations in Mexico have not yet advanced to the point where we can trace many former drainage patterns with accuracy, but we can at least make some guesses, and the more we learn about the animals in the isolated rivers the better we can match them with those in streams that do reach the sea. Here was a fascinating field for investigation that was reinforced by the fact that animals in isolation tend to change, developing new habits and physical characteristics that differentiate them from their nearest kin. We know, for example, that the water snake inhabiting the Río Nazas, a major stream of interior drainage, has become altered enough from its more eastern relatives to be recognized as a separate subspecies.

Our first visit to the Río Nazas was in 1949, when Isabelle and I made our initial long trip to Mexico. Charles M. Bogert had written to me from the field in 1946 about the discovery of a large water snake in that stream, and his communication was the original impetus for my studies in depth on Mexico's desert rivers.

The Río Nazas is formed by the Río de Ramos and the Río del Oro, which drain large portions of the western uplands of the State of Durango. At the confluence of the two streams, a huge dam, the Presa Lázaro Cárdenas, named for a former president of Mexico, was built to control the flow of water. Previously, there had been severe floods, coincidental with the summer monsoon season, followed by long periods of low water. Tunnels at the base of the new impoundment could be opened or closed, and the flow of water available for use in the so-called Laguna District downstream could then be kept more or less regular throughout the year. Irrigated agriculture is widely practiced around the trio of cities of Torreón, Gómez Palacio, and Ciudad Lerdo. Prior to early settlement, the Río Nazas emptied into a playa in the western part of Coahuila in the now very arid Bolsón de Mapimí. It went nowhere, so to speak, and its waters sank into the ground or evaporated in the Laguna Mayrán, which has long been a dry lake.

The water snake, a slider turtle, and many species of fishes in the Río Nazas have strong affinities with the same or closely related taxa in the Rio Grande, the Río Bravo del Norte of the Mexicans, which forms the southern boundary of Texas. Seth E. Meek, the ichthyologist who published an important treatise on the fishes of Mexico in 1904, was the first to note their similarity. He postulated that the Río Nazas once flowed northward to empty into the Rio Grande near the present common boundary of Chihuahua and Coahuila, but no one, even yet, knows just where it might have been. The Mexican geologist A. R. V. Arellano offered the alternate suggestion that the Nazas may have flowed eastward. I also heard the theory expounded verbally that the Nazas may course underground and then surge upward through the great springs that characterize the Bolsón de Cuatro Ciénegas, well to the northeast in Coahuila. The main difficulty with such a supposition is that the springs were still flowing steadily when we visited the area twice during our Mexican explorations. The Nazas, however, had been harnessed and its water used for irrigation for a very long time before we arrived.

We explored the Nazas as thoroughly as we could, considering how few of the primitive roads were within walking distance of its banks during the 1960s. In three places I succeeded in finding the large water snake I described in 1953 as a new subspecies, *Natrix* (=*Nerodia*) *erythrogaster bogerti*: at La Goma, the town of Nazas, and a half mile or so below the Presa Cárdenas.

That huge earthen, stone-faced impoundment was protected by a concrete relief dam near the small village

The Presa Lázaro Cárdenas, a large dam named for a former president of Mexico. Tunnels (one visible to the right and just below the dam) can be opened to permit water to flow to the cities downstream during the dry season. Photo by IHC.

of El Palmito. Its spillway was lower than the main dam and, in times of flood, water would pass over it. Many years later, in 1976, I revisited the area in the company of James D. Anderson and three students. I was astounded to discover that a catastrophic flood had swept away the relief dam, which was then being replaced by a new structure. The cause was Hurricane Naomi, which swept ashore in the Mazatlán area in September 1968, and dumped an enormous amount of rain onto the watershed feeding the Nazas. When the dam gave way, the ravine below it eroded to a depth of 10 meters (about 33 feet), and the high primitive road along which Isabelle and I had camped 16 years previously had completely vanished, as proved by photographs taken before and after.

How well I recall my first foray along the Nazas below the big dam. Normally, I made an effort to survey a stream during daylight hours to reconnoiter the terrain, fix landmarks in mind, and plan the evening's peregrinations before the landscape was swallowed in a sea of blackness. Such was not always possible, however, and the day we reached the remote Presa Cárdenas we spent so much time getting acquainted and seeking permission to collect that the brief tropical twilight had long since passed by the time we ate our supper. Since field time is always precious and not to be wasted, I decided to work the river anyway, and I carefully aligned our car with a pumping station down the cliff below us where a light was burning brightly. It would be my beacon on the return trip. The going was hard, largely because several rocky headlands jutted out into the streambed, and I had to clamber over them despite the impediment of

The Conants with their Kamper near the source of the Río Nazas in Durango, September 11, 1960. Photo by IHC.

hip boots and a large flashlight in addition to my head-lamp. Two hours later, when I returned, I saw the light glowing in the distance and oriented myself to keep it just to my left as I worked upward toward the car. I climbed and climbed up the steep mountainside, but found no road, and finally the realization was forced upon me that there was no road, no car, and that I obviously was lost. Fortunately, I could still make out the light far below me, so I half stumbled and half slid down the slope and eventually arrived at a small house. There I explained my predicament, and the *señor* of the household very kindly arose and dressed, even to his sombrero, to guide me back to base.

The next morning, when I surveyed the mountain up which I had struggled, I could not help but wonder what would have happened if I had kept going and crossed the crest where nearly 100 miles of wilderness lay ahead of me. I was not alarmed about my own safety, for my early Boy Scout training was still vividly remembered, but I could imagine my frantic wife, through whose mind

would have raced all sorts of dreadful thoughts as she organized a search party. Thereafter we resolved to undertake no nocturnal excursions without first reconnoitering during the daylight.

The original light? I discovered that the workmen in the pumping station had gone home shortly after my departure, switching off the electricity and thus erasing my landmark.

Although we continued to visit the Río Nazas whenever we were near it in the Chihuahuan Desert, and at as many places as possible, I had long known that there was another desert river in Zacatecas, the Mexican state south of Durango. It also drained western highlands. I read all I could about it, and learned that officially it was called the Río Aguanaval, but that various sections of it bore different names. The main stream was known locally as the Río Florido, Río Medina, or Río Nieves; and, below its confluence with its tributary, the Río Sain Alto, it was called the Río Trujillo. How confusing, but Mexican geography was often difficult to follow. The names of towns, rivers, and other features were subject to change, sometimes to commemorate the activities of some local hero. Also, the available maps of Mexico of the period did not always agree.

After we visited the region we discovered that the Río Aguanaval was smaller and far less important than the Nazas. Its water was sluiced through streamside canals for the irrigation of crops, and, except during monsoon-stimulated floods, it seldom flowed past the town of Río Grande in Zacatecas. It previously had emptied into the now dry Laguna Viesca. Also, it formerly had been a part of the Río Nazas system, and had apparently joined that river through a gap east of the Sierra de la Peña later utilized by a railroad connecting the city of Torreón with Saltillo.

It took little imagination for me to guess that the Aguanaval might also support a water snake. My supposition was confirmed when Richard B. Parker, then a student at the University of Michigan, collected three on July 21, 1957, and sent them to me for examination and study. That whetted my appetite to have a look for myself, and, two years later, Isabelle and I were at Parker's locality, which was near the town of Río Florido where the highway bridge crossed over the stream.

The river was in flood after a heavy rain the previous evening. I searched along a small impoundment, but had no luck until I returned to the river itself, where I found a large female water snake that had just been killed by someone. It was not seriously damaged, and would make an excellent study specimen. I had scarcely picked it up and was having a good look at it when a *campesino* approached and promptly asked me what I was doing with the reptile. I gave him my stock statement about how I was a *profesor* studying snakes. Always previously the Mexican countrymen had accepted that explanation. If that was my business, that was fine with them. But this fellow stumped me by asking why I was studying snakes. How do you explain to an uneducated *peón* that water snakes probably reached the desert rivers during pluvial periods of the Pleistocene or earlier? I had to think quickly, so I invented an answer. I said, in Spanish, of course, "Some kinds of snakes are venomous but others are not." To this he nodded in the affirmative, so I continued with, "I'm trying to find out why." That satisfied him completely.

We tried collecting at night, but it was too cold at the high elevation of 6,700 feet for the serpents to prowl. During the early morning, two days later, we returned to the town of Río Florido. From the highway bridge, we could see that the water level in the river had dropped considerably. We pulled off the road, and I donned my boots, scrambled down to the water's edge, and made my way toward a place, less than 100 yards from the highway bridge, where a sizable clump of bushes overhung the stream. A dozen or more garter snakes, *Thamnophis melanogaster*, were stretched out on the branches, warming themselves in the sun. While I was concentrating on catching a few of them, an adult male water snake swam right past me, and I grabbed it with ease. A prize indeed, and within 15 minutes of our arrival. A comparison of it with the female I had preserved indicated that both looked different from the water snakes that occurred in the Nazas. They obviously were members of the red-bellied water snake complex, but perhaps they, too, had differentiated. I had to wait until the following year to acquire a large enough sample to confirm my assumption.

We then had our Volkswagen Kamper, and we could stop wherever we wished instead of having to find a place to spend the night, as we had done when we were traveling in our station wagon the previous year. We drove downstream more or less parallel with the river from the highway at Río Florido all the way to Río Grande, meantime stopping to reconnoiter at numerous places. We found no suitable place to camp near Río Grande, so we retraced our route and selected a spot near Rancho Grande where the Río Medina, as it was called there, passed through a small dammed area that held water in reserve during the dry season. I had time to set my turtle traps before one of the daily evening thundershowers struck. They invariably dropped the temperature, and we were soon so cold that crawling into our sleeping compartments and piling on blankets was a welcome way to get comfortable.

We were up early the next morning, and, after breakfasting, I walked to the small concrete dam. I was both astounded and delighted to find seven large water snakes out in the open, sunning themselves all fairly close together after the cold night. I moved fast and furiously, and, since the serpents were not yet fully warmed up, I managed to catch them all. At one point I had a snake in each hand, my foot on another, and a fourth had captured me by burying its teeth into the fleshy side of my palm. How extremely lucky to get such an excellent sample. The adults from the Río Nazas were pale and pinkish, whereas the ones I had just caught were much darker and far more distinctly patterned. I was later to discover that there also were differences in scutellation.

My surprise and success were not over yet, however. Six of the seven snakes were gravid. We returned to the United States briefly at El Paso, Texas, and from there I shipped them home by air express. All gave birth to healthy litters later in the year.

The Rio Nazas near its source.
Giant cypresses flourish where
water is plentiful. Photo by IHC.

The seventh snake, also a female, we kept alive with us, and, as we searched stream after stream in Chihuahua, to which we returned, we showed it to people we met along the rivers. None of them had ever seen a *culebra* (snake) like it, and their negative responses helped me to confirm my rapidly developing conclusion that, except in the Nazas and Aguanaval systems, there were no water snakes in the western part of the Chihuahuan Desert. Toward the east, water snakes enter the desert in the Rio Grande and Pecos River drainage, as well as in the Río Salado-Río Sabinas system in Coahuila. There they are in contact with the main portions of the ranges of their species, or were until very recently.

During a trip two years later to the same section of the Río Medina near Rancho Grande, we saw many more water snakes, so the samples I had taken apparently had little effect on the population. The water was much higher, and the snakes were therefore much more difficult to catch. I hired two men, probably in their 30s, who obtained two adult males for me, one dead and the other alive and in excellent condition. Because I paid them a few pesos for their efforts, they promptly dubbed me *El Patrón*, their employer.

With my wealth of material I was able, in 1963, to describe the Río Aguanaval water snake as a new subspecies, which I called *Natrix* (=*Nerodia*) *erythrogaster alta*, a name I selected because of the high altitude at which that taxon occurred.

The presence of the desert rivers could be detected from a distance as we drove through the arid terrain they traversed. They supported gallery forests. Any river

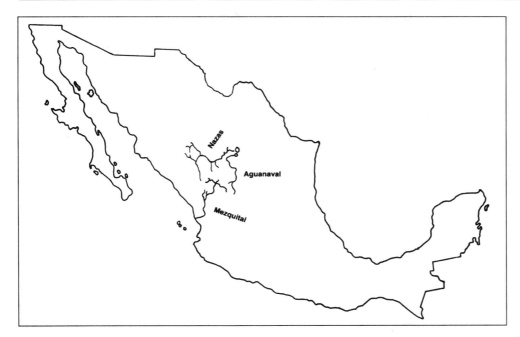

The old Río Nazas was once a major stream system that originated in the highlands of western Mexico and terminated in the Rio Grande somewhere along the Texas border. The remnants of the old Río Nazas are split into three parts. The main stream of the Nazas and its tributary, the Río Aguanaval, emptied into desert sumps in presettlement times. Now, most of the water is used for human activities. Volcanism truncated some of the southernmost tributaries, and they were captured by the Río Mezquital, which discharges into the Pacific Ocean. Map delineated by IHC.

that flowed permanently through even the most arid Mexican countryside, even if it slowed to a trickle during the dry season, was bordered, in the 1960s, by a long, narrow line of willow or cottonwood trees or both, which were nourished by the stream itself. If water were in greater supply, giant cypress trees might also flourish. The forest was often only one tree wide on each bank, but, collectively, they formed a long, undulating gallery marking the exact course of the river, and making its presence visible in open country from miles away. In some places the rivers widened, sometimes supported small swamps, and, in extreme cases, almost forests of trees. Dam construction expanded the habitats for water snakes, especially around the resulting impoundments.

Late one afternoon we drove along a primitive, well-rutted road upstream from Río Florido so I could look for natricine snakes the following morning. It was quite cold at night, and I was unsuccessful the following day, but we awakened very early, and I espied a dawn rainbow, a unique experience for us. Isabelle was still groggy from sleep, but she obtained a good picture. The only problem was that the lens cap from her camera fell off unexpectedly, dropped into the miscellaneous gear piled in our Kamper, and we didn't find it until we unpacked at home weeks later. Isabelle took good care of her photographic equipment, and she was greatly annoyed with herself. She told me that, if I wanted her to take any more pictures at daybreak, I should wait until she was fully awake. I didn't get her up early again until some years later when we were back at the Posada Loma at Fortín de las Flores in Veracruz. I was up not

too long after dawn, pulled on my clothes, and stepped outside our cabin. The rising sun was brilliantly illuminating the snow-capped Pico Orizaba, Mexico's loftiest mountain. I also noted that a massive cloud bank was approaching and that it would soon blot out the summit. So I gently awakened my wife, and she obtained good photographs before the clouds spoiled the view. That was the daily sequence during the rainy season—clear in the early morning, but "socked in" later in the day. It was the same with the two towering volcanos farther west, Popocatépetl and Iztaccíhuatl. They were readily seen from their eastern side, but neither one can now be viewed from smog-bedeviled and heavily air-polluted Mexico City.

My research on the two desert rivers, the Nazas and the Aguanaval, revealed a highly interesting situation that is worthy of comment. A million or more years ago, the highlands west of the city of Durango drained into an ancient master stream, the Old Río Nazas, that flowed all the way to the Rio Grande bordering present-day Texas. Some of the fishes living in the headwaters of mountain streams of the State of Durango are derived from and have their closest relatives in the Rio Grande, even though they have been cut off from it for a very long time. Just when and where the break occurred was obscured by subsequent volcanism in the region, but the upper Durango portion of the Old Río Nazas was truncated and captured by the Río Mezquital, which flows to the Pacific Ocean. That explains the curious phenomenon of fishes peculiar to the Rio Grande occurring today in Pacific drainage. Even Meek, in his 1904 report on Mexican fishes, was aware of that

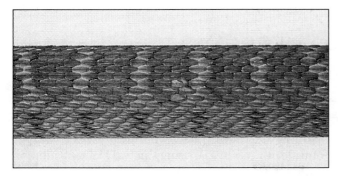
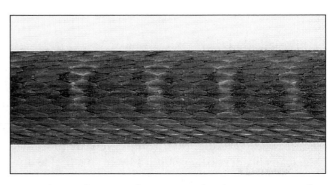

The two water snakes that live in the desert. Left: the Río Nazas form, Nerodia erythrogaster bogerti. *Right: the Río Aguanaval subspecies,* Nerodia erythrogaster alta. *The upper pictures show the entire snakes; the lower ones their body pattern details. Photos by IHC.*

anomaly. Since his day, other ichthyologists have confirmed the strange distribution.

Stream capture, incidentally, occurs when two running bodies of water coalesce, and the water of one is diverted into the other. This may happen where a stream eroding headward on one side of a divide taps into tributaries of a stream on the opposite side. Other causes include earthquakes, volcanism, and tectonic events. In any case, the indigenous organisms of the captured stream are free to enter a new drainage system.

While I was studying the natricine fauna, including the garter snakes, it soon became apparent that the various vertebrate groups had not all ascended the Old Río Nazas at the same time. The fishes no doubt were first, and they must have become well established before they served as a principal food for the carnivorous natricine snakes. *Nerodia erythrogaster*, the so-called plain-bellied water snake, subsequently arrived in both the present Nazas and Aguanaval systems long before the two rivers were separated. It must have been a great while ago, because the populations in the two rivers have had sufficient time to evolve into quite distinctive subspecies. The turtle, *Pseudemys* (= *Trachemys*) *scripta*, apparently arrived in the Nazas later, but in ample time to differentiate into a separate subspecies (*hartwegi*). It may not have reached the Aguanaval. There is, however, some evidence that it may have been in a wet portion of Laguna Viesca, where the Aguanaval once emptied, until recent times.

All this I had in mind when I returned to the Río Nazas, in the rainy season, for the last time during our 1960s fieldwork. At one point, as I explored the river, I walked across the Chihuahuan Desert a short distance from where our car was parked. I stepped into the welcome shade of a tenuous gallery forest that was only two or three trees wide. I waded across the shallow water, which was scarcely a foot deep and certainly not more than 30 feet wide, and then I entered the narrow gallery forest on the other side. With a few more strides I was back in arid terrain. In that brief moment of time, a fraction of a minute, I had crossed a lifeline that made it possible for water snakes to live in the desert.

Chapter 32

San Blas, Nayarit

In its heyday, a long time ago, San Blas, Nayarit, was an important seaport on Mexico's Pacific coast, but its prominence had long since waned. Heat, humidity, and somnolence characterized it during our visits, and there were few visitors except for fishermen, tourists who sought a glimpse of tropical jungles, and naturalists. Time was when galleons from the Philippines made San Blas a regular port of call, but there was little to recall its former glories during our visits. The crumbling ruins of the old Spanish customhouse still stood, but amidst the debris there was a living reminder in the form of a tiny lizard, a gecko with the apt scientific name of *Gehyra mutilata*. Touch one by the tail, and that member is instantly detached to writhe about and attract attention while the rest of the animal scampers to safety. It mutilates itself, in a sense, but, like so many other lizards, soon grows a new tail. But this is an Oriental reptile that evidently secreted itself in cargo, made the long voyage to Mexico, and escaped in San Blas to populate a tiny segment of the New World.

Motorists during the 1960s reached San Blas by way of a paved road that dropped off seaward from the main Pacific Highway. It wound its way downward, meanwhile crossing three streams without benefit of bridges. During the dry season it was a simple matter to drive across the *vados* (fords), for there were broad ribbons of concrete stretching from one bank to the other, but during the summer rains, when one stream or another might be badly swollen, traffic often came to a standstill. Near San Blas the road traversed a small mangrove swamp, and a side road branched off to Playa Matanchen, where there was a "black" sand beach and a tiny fishing village. Clearly there was little at San Blas at that time to attract the average tourist, but for the naturalist it was almost a tropical paradise.

During one of our visits we arrived at the village in late afternoon, drove to Matanchen, and ate our supper while parked in what scanty shade we could find. As was our wont, we were preparing to cruise the road immediately after dark in search of any reptiles or amphibians that might venture onto the paving. This is a tried-and-

true method of the herpetologist, for many secretive *animalitos*, as the natives call them, leave their hiding places soon after dusk to forage for food. They stand out prominently in the headlights of a car, and an agile collector equipped with a flashlight or headlamp can often catch rarities that are seldom encountered by day. Back in the old days, the running board of an automobile was a convenient place to stand, for the instant the driver stopped, the collectors could hop off in pursuit of their quarry. Modern cars lack such luxuries, but even so it is still possible to catch many a specimen, especially if it is momentarily dazzled by the glare of the headlights.

Just at sunset we stopped at the road fork in the midst of the mangroves and were treated to an unexpected sight. To the west, brilliant shades of red, orange, and yellow ranged the sky above the Pacific, but, to the east, gathering storm clouds hung black and ominous over the mountains, their somber hues relieved now and then by great jagged streaks of lightning. Unknown to us, the mangroves were a nighttime rookery, and great skeins of birds, approaching chiefly from the vast swamplands to the north, began to settle into the trees. They came by the thousands: egrets and ibises garbed in white; cormorants and other ibises clothed in iridescent black; anhingas, or snake birds, with long serpentine necks; and huge flocks of great-tailed grackles. We were enthralled as we watched them against the flaming western sky and listened to their loud calls and bickerings as they settled down, jockeying for choice perches and squabbling with one another.

But soon it was time to depart, and, as the brief twilight faded rapidly, we hit the road. We elected to drive first into San Blas itself, or rather to its outskirts, where we turned around and rolled slowly eastward with Isabelle at the wheel. Moments later we spied a Mexican swinging mightily with his machete at something at the road's edge. We both shouted, "Snake!" Isabelle stepped on the gas, drew abreast, and braked to a sudden stop as I jumped out and dashed around the car. The man was at first startled and then astounded when I grabbed the snake by the tail. It was a boa constrictor, roughly four feet in length. The *campesino* did his best to warn me that this was a very dangerous serpent and that I was taking my life in my hands, but I knew, of course, that boas have neither fangs nor venom, and that an able-bodied herpetologist could easily catch and bag a snake of such dimensions, heavy-bodied though it was. Fortunately, the man was so afraid of being bitten that he had tried to hit the snake with his machete stretched at full arm's length, and the only damage he had done was to make a tiny nick on the reptile's skin.

We were scarcely under way again when the rain came, heavy at first but then diminishing to light showers that continued intermittently for an hour or more. Almost like magic small frogs appeared all over the road. We caught a few to check on what species they were, and then we started snake hunting in earnest. We found a baby boa and then an *Imantodes*, an extraordinarily attenuated snake with a body so long and slender that at first glimpse it seemed no thicker than the wool Grandma used to knit us heavy sweaters. We also picked up a curious blind burrowing snake that was either flooded out of its retreat by the rain or was taking advantage of the wet terrain to seek a new hiding place. A cat-eyed snake, a species equipped with fangs in the rear of the mouth, was eating a frog right on the road. When we first saw it we thought its head had been crushed by a passing vehicle, because its mouth was stretched so wide in the process of swallowing that it looked flat and misshapen.

After driving some six miles we turned around and retraced our course, and noted immediately that there were many dead frogs on the paving. Some, no doubt, had been crushed by our own wheels since there were far too many to avoid them all, but a few other cars had passed as well, and all had taken their toll. We were soon to discover that the dead frogs played an important role in the ecology of many of the nocturnal predators of the region.

Back near the road fork we found a raccoon feasting on frogs. Although we patrolled the same stretch of highway no less than six times the raccoon was always in the same vicinity. By the time we left, it had apparently collected all the dead frogs along a stretch of almost 50 yards. We saw no fewer than seven opossums that somewhat resembled our native species but were more slender and rattier looking, and surprisingly active. They had long black tails with white tips. An armadillo scurried across the road, and it, too, was moving much faster than we had thought possible. Most interesting, however, were two coatimundis, long-snouted members of the raccoon family, that held their long tails stiffly erect as they scouted out the dead frogs with their long, wig-

gling rubbery noses. Probably we saw more wild mammals during that one night than at any other one time in Mexico. It is truly a wonderful place for wildlife. On a previous trip to San Blas I caught a glimpse of a jaguarundi, a small, slinky wild cat that is widespread through the American Tropics.

Near the fork we found two water snakes, both small but important because they added to the sample size I needed to study the remarkable variation in coloration and pattern that obtained in that particular region. One was eating a frog on the road; the other was being eaten by a land crab, and we arrived too late to get a perfect specimen, for part of the head had already been devoured.

After the frog bonanza had been virtually all consumed by the various scavengers, collecting petered out, and we headed for the highlands. Everything was soaking wet, and we realized we probably would have to drive some distance to find a dry or even semidry campsite for the night. All went well until we approached the first of the streams. There ahead of us were all the cars that had passed us while we hunted. The heavy rain had filled the streambed, and the racing torrent made passage impossible. We were marooned for the night.

We turned around and drove very slowly, looking for a place to pull off the road. Most Mexican roads had virtually no shoulders and, since there were few side roads or even lanes leading into *ranchos*—at least that were passable by motor vehicles—we knew our chances were slim. In time, however, we found a place where, with careful maneuvering, we could pull off onto a rocky area in the midst of a sea of sticky mud. Isabelle stayed inside the car, but I had to get out to guide her as she moved the car into position. Cleaning my shoes was an impossibility, so I sat down at the side door of the car, took them off, and wrapped them inside a newspaper for the night. Making a bed while kneeling on top of it is not easy, but Isabelle had done it before, and we managed quite comfortably inside our Kamper for the night. We were awake at dawn, and, although the sun dried things a little, we could escape the mud only by carrying our campstove onto the paving, where we cooked breakfast right on the road. There was no traffic, of course, with the highway blocked by the flood.

After breaking camp we drove back to the ford and waited there for hours in the hope the water would subside. It did, to some extent, but crossing under our own power was still out of the question. Finally, in desperation and with considerable apprehension, we hired an enterprising Mexican with an ancient, beat-up truck to tow us across. Only a small amount of water entered through the Kamper's side door, but, since we were being pulled by an old frayed rope, we sighed with relief when we safely achieved the other side.

So it was while traveling in the wilds of Mexico long ago. There would be too much water or not enough, a paucity of bridges, or some other unexpected contingency with which to contend on short notice. While annoying at the time, they all contributed to our feeling of adventure and exploration.

Chapter 33

Off to Baja California

We were delayed so long by the flooded river on the road from San Blas that we barely completed the lengthy drive to Mazatlán before closing time.

Mazatlán, for us at least, was the gateway to Baja California. This interesting tropical port on the Pacific coast with its fine harbor has long been an important town and is often ballyhooed as a mecca for fishermen and sun worshipers. Few of either were in evidence during the hot summer weather prevailing during our visit in early September 1961, but the array of fancy hotels and motels bespoke a wintertime clientele. Mazatlán is a lot closer to California than Acapulco, and doubtless the prices for visitors were much lower than the outrageous ones we were charged in the latter, more elegant winter resort.

Mazatlán was merely a means to an end in our plans, for we were to board a steamer there and sail across the open Pacific and the lower end of the Gulf of California to La Paz, a trip of some 300 miles in all. Arrangements for our passage had been made by mail many weeks in advance, and a telephone call, placed a few days previously, had confirmed the fact that we should be at the shipping broker's office before closing time at 6:00 P.M. on Tuesday. So we drove as fast as we dared with our heavy load, and made it with minutes to spare. There was sufficient time, however, to obtain the necessary information. We were to be at a nearby office to pick up our tickets early on the morrow, when arrangements could be made to store our specimens, extra gear, and the roof rack in a warehouse until our return. We would sail sometime during the morning.

Off we went to a motel, where we repacked our equipment and made last-minute adjustments. We were up betimes, ate a hasty breakfast, and dashed off to the market for fresh vegetables for our larder. After a trip to the icehouse to refurbish our two styrofoam containers, we went to the warehouse and off-loaded our gear, picked up our tickets, paid the freight for our Kamper, and were soon at the quay. There was our ship, the *Mexicali*, a coastwise tramp steamer built in an American shipyard and acquired by the Mexican merchant marine sometime after World War II. She

seemed seaworthy enough, but she also looked tired and dirty. Cargo was still being loaded, so we drove into the scant shade provided by the pier housing and sat down to wait. Hours went by and the shade vanished as the sun climbed high. Impatiently I went aboard and found the mate, who told me it would be some hours yet and that we had best go somewhere for lunch. This time we ate leisurely, for we knew that the Mexican siesta was soon to follow and there would be no activity until it was over.

At 6:00 P.M. the ship was still being loaded, and, in response to my inquiry, the mate suggested that we come back *mañana*. So—hot, tired, and discouraged—we retreated to the interior of the air-conditioned motel where we had stayed the previous night. We were somewhat startled when the room clerk showed no surprise whatever that we had returned.

We were back at the quay early but not too bright, for the sad fact was beginning to emerge that no arrangements for our trip had been made in advance, despite our letters and telephone call, and we were at the mercy of the crew, the stevedores, the shippers, and, most of all, that extra something known in Mexico as *mañana*. "*Mañana, Señor.* Perhaps tomorrow all will be finished and we shall sail. Come back in the morning."

To impatient *norteamericanos* (North Americans, to use the Mexican term for us) the thought of having to sweat through another day of inactivity seemed unbearable. We voiced our disappointment to each other and cursed the cartographer who had drawn a dotted line on one of our maps from Mazatlán across the water to La Paz and labeled it "Ferry Service." Ferry service indeed! That fellow should have stuck to marking highways on his confounded road map instead of disillusioning prospective voyagers like ourselves.

After a swim in the chlorinated water of the motel pool we felt a little better, and decided to improve our time by doing some night collecting along the coast road. Ever mindful of the fact that road hunting is always best at twilight and for an hour or two afterward, we drove northward and pulled off into a convenient abandoned quarry. As we cooked and ate our supper, we watched the parrots squawk past in twos or threes or small family parties as they headed for their night-time rookery.

The collecting wasn't bad. We picked up several frogs and toads, and, at the Río Quelite, which was rapidly subsiding after overflowing its banks, I managed to catch five water snakes. They made quite an impression on the beer drinkers in the little roadside *cantina* perched on the rocky bluff overlooking the river. The same men had assured me that there weren't any snakes, when I stopped to tell them what I was doing, just before I descended to the water with my headlamp bobbing this way and that.

In the morning we returned to our well-used spot by the *Mexicali*. That was Thursday. We did the same on Friday, and again on Saturday. But things looked a little better on Saturday. One of the hatches was battened down and there were signs that the seemingly endless loading operations might soon terminate. In early afternoon our turn finally came, and, while Isabelle manned both still and movie cameras, I tried to supervise the job. The boom was lowered above the Kamper, the stevedores drove it onto a pair of heavy rope slings, one for each pair of wheels, the winch went into action, and our precious vehicle, tilted at a disheartening angle, was slung aboard. Then came the process of waltzing it into position on the deck and chaining it fast. We went aboard and lowered the car windows to let in some air. Despite the heat (did you ever try sitting on a broiling deck with the torrid heat shimmering upward in the afternoon tropical sun?) we watched with enthusiasm as the men closed the hatches. Even the fact that they had just piled fireworks virtually beneath us didn't matter. We would soon be off. Fireworks? Oh, yes. They were set pieces in the form of the bull, *el toro*, and they were going across the water to La Paz, capital of southern Baja California, for the upcoming Independence Day celebration on September 16. We watched with pleasure as the booms were lowered and all seemed in readiness. Moments later, however, there was a great shout from the dock, and we turned to see a huge truck overloaded with king-sized bottles of a soft drink whose very name still stirs up unpleasant memories whenever I see it. There would be a delay. Up went the booms, off came the hatch covers, and we stewed and fretted for another three or four hours while the soda pop was taken aboard and the tedious preparations for departure were repeated.

We finally sailed at dusk, and as we cleared the harbor the *faro* (lighthouse) was blinking its light against the black sky of an approaching thunderstorm.

The tramp steamer Mexicali *that transported us across the great rolling waves of the Pacific Ocean to near the southern tip of Baja California. Photo by IHC.*

The instant we passed the terminal jetty the sea struck us with great force on our port beam, and we dipped to such a dizzy angle that Isabelle and I scrambled out of the Kamper lest we go overboard with it. Fortunately, the chains held, but the waves were so great, after sweeping 6,000 or 7,000 unobstructed miles across the Pacific, that we were apprehensive and didn't dare spend the night in the Kamper lest we meet with a watery disaster. Sleep was impossible, although I did manage to doze a little as I lay propped up against a great pile of sacks of onions on one of the hatch covers.

We were deck cargo. Period. There were no cabins or staterooms, except for the one occupied by our high-toned *capitán*, who behaved as though his command were an ocean liner. The deck passengers had a spot behind the smokestack sheltered from the wind and covered by a thin screen to ward off the great heat of the sun during the day. We looked it over and found that our fellow passengers, mostly residents of La Paz going home and numbering about 20, were not sleeping either. They were very much awake, bracing themselves constantly to keep from being tossed off their benches. We retreated to the deck and snuggled down again among the onions.

It is well that we ran our own commissary, even on shipboard. There was no provision for meals unless one bribed the cook in the crew's quarters to fry an egg or something. I made an early-morning inspection of the galley and found it so unsavory that my appetite momentarily left me. I managed with difficulty to open the rear of the Kamper while I cast a weather eye over the side where the only protection for us and the vehicle was a frayed rope strung through the stanchions. Some guardrail!

After a sandwich we began to feel human again, and we took stock of our surroundings. We were now in the

Hoisting our Kamper aboard. Isabelle was so nervous at seeing our house on wheels hanging from a rope sling at a dizzying angle that, for once, she didn't focus carefully! Soon men were maneuvering the car into position before it was chained to the deck. Photos by IHC.

lee of Baja California, and the huge rollers that had tossed us back and forth all night were behind us. In the distance, as a gray line, we could see the coast of the long, gangling peninsula that hangs down from the California mainland for hundreds of miles like the tail of some huge, antediluvian monster. Sea birds sailed overhead, and every now and then a flying fish broke the surface and hung above it for a few seconds. We were enjoying ourselves at last, for the first time since we boarded the *Mexicali*. But then that early-morning urge caught up with us. Where had they hidden the head on this vessel?

We found it, but the less said about it the better. A single toilet for all the passengers and crew. The paper had already run out. (Thank goodness we carried our own!) It wasn't too bad in the morning while it was still cool, but by midafternoon that noisome little room was unbearably hot and a veritable torture chamber.

During the afternoon we passed through the channel between the Baja mainland and the Isla de Cerralvo and had our first fairly close glimpse of what was then a remote frontier. Cerralvo, a sun-baked, barren, and desolate island, was studded with rocks and cactus. One of the passengers, with disdain in his voice, muttered, "*chivos*." That means goats, and they probably were the only thing of value on the entire island, insofar as he was concerned. But I, thinking about the many interesting snakes and lizards, even new species, that were constantly being found on the many islands, large and small, of the Gulf of California, wished I could go ashore for a day or two.

As the *Mexicali* moved closer inshore and details of the coast became clearer, our thoughts turned to the history of this wild, parched land. We wondered if we could work our way along the primitive roads to the nearby mountains, which were our objective. Almost every part of the Baja Peninsula is arid and dusty, save when the infrequent rains turn the dirt roads into quagmires. Horses and burros are more dependable methods of transport than automobiles. Fortunately, the Chevrolet Motor Company saved us many long explanations after we returned home, for that was the period when they sent a fleet of trucks down the peninsula and back as an advertising gimmick, and all our friends had seen the horrible roads, rocks, dust, and sparse vegetation on their TV sets while sitting in the comfort of their homes. It was far easier for us to sail from Mazatlán than to try driving down that endless peninsula road.

We wondered what was in store for us. First we'd land at the sleepy little town of La Paz, which was so far from the daily noise and hubbub of the modern world that it was a lure for many a person who wanted to get away from it all. In La Paz we would find many modern conveniences, not unlike those of the Mexican mainland, but once we left it we were on our own.

As we rounded the headland and entered the beautiful bay we could see great numbers of man-o'-war birds coasting far above our heads on motionless wings as they rode the thermal updrafts. The shore was more rocky and barren than the island had been, and, even with binoculars, it was difficult to see any green vegetation. It looked more like a lunar landscape, or so we imagined, than anything we had ever seen.

Far ahead we could make out the town and several other ships like our own in the harbor. As we approached, our thoughts quickened and we planned what we would do. First, a hotel and a hot bath and some cooked food. Then we would have the car washed to remove the coating of salt accumulated from the spray, buy fresh fruits and vegetables, and soon take off.

But our daydreaming was due for a rude awakening.

La Paz had only a small quay that could accommodate three ships of the Mexicali's size and two or three smaller ones. When we got nearer, we saw that the quay was jammed with vessels unloading, while others lay at anchor awaiting their turn ahead of us. We were to ride in the roadstead and near dockside for two more exasperating days before we could get the Kamper ashore.

A few days later, while checking a road map published by a different petroleum company, we made the discovery that, on it, there was a dotted line labeled "Weekly Boat Service." At least that cartographer was honest. It had taken us exactly one week, including loading time, to get from Mazatlán to La Paz.

Chapter 34

The Classic Loop Road

During my volunteer Coast Guard days of World War II I spent many a hot summer day and night sweltering on the decks of steel ships, and I swore, once the conflict was over, never to do it again. Yet there we were in the La Paz harbor doomed to endure two mortal days roasting under a tropical sun on the *Mexicali's* stove-hot stern. We whiled away the time loafing in our Kamper and reading whodunits. We always carried several with us just in case we encountered a long waiting period.

Early on the second day our vessel tied up alongside the *Aries*, a ship of similar size that was moored to the pier. A gangplank was laid down between the two vessels, and I was able to go ashore and find an icehouse with the aid of a taxi driver. With an ice box functioning again and chilled drinks available, our situation became a little more tolerable. In late afternoon the *Aries* moved out and we tied up at the dock, but our hopes of getting the car off were dashed. The stevedores had quit for the day! So we packed a few necessities in a tote bag, securely locked the car, went ashore, and walked to a nearby hotel. As Isabelle wrote in her diary, "after two baths apiece and a good dinner" we began to feel almost human again.

La Paz was a free port. There was no customs inspection, no duty to pay, and both gringo and Mexican could walk directly ashore. But it wasn't free if you had a car or other freight arriving by boat. In that case you paid double!

At Mazatlán, on the mainland, the stevedores collected a fee for loading our Kamper aboard the *Mexicali*, and we expected a similar charge for unloading at La Paz. But we were not prepared, mentally or budgetwise, for what actually happened.

Once dock space was available, the workmen lowered our vehicle onto the pier, and we breathed a sigh of relief. After paying them we advanced to take possession, only to be brushed aside by a swarm of men who promptly pushed the car 100 feet or so along the pier to the edge of the paved street. There they surrounded it and refused to budge until we handed over an exorbitant fee. It did no good to protest. That was the law of the port. If the *señor* wanted his car, he had better pay up. So, grudgingly, we parted with our money. We discovered later that every item transported by ship cost double for unloading, and that was certainly one of the main reasons why prices for everything in La Paz were far higher than in mainland Mexican towns. When I talked with some of the local merchants, they shrugged their shoulders and said they had no choice. If they wished to stay in business they kept their mouths shut.

After getting ourselves and much of our gear freshened up and arranging to have the salt washed off the car, we spent the rest of the day seeking a way to ensure prompt boat passage back to the mainland. Not that we wanted to run away. Not at all. But with the exasperating *Mexicali* experience fresh in our minds, we thought it well to make sure of our line of retreat. The only other way out of the Cape Region in those days was up the long, torturous road to Ensenada, close to the California border. Anyone who attempted the trip had to carry all his own gasoline and water, and the road was impassable in many places except for large, powerful vehicles. Tackling such a journey with our little 36-horsepower Kamper was unthinkable.

We were also spurred on by a chat with a young American couple who were to leave the next day. They had sailed a small boat all the way to La Paz from Los Angeles. It was great fun, but they knew that tricky currents and strong winds would be against them if they tried to reverse their course. They didn't dare attempt it. They had been told in the States that they could put their small craft on the deck of a steamer, like the *Mexicali*, which would take them home cheaply and quickly. That all sounded fine until we discovered they had arrived at La Paz in early May, but no northbound ship had called at La Paz until we arrived in mid-September. They were tired of living on their small craft after more than four months, meanwhile having to fish to keep themselves alive because their money had run out. We hoped they had saved enough to pay for fares and freight, to say nothing of the two unions.

Inquiry revealed that two or three times a week a

The canal where RC caught his first Baja California water snake. It was basking in the brush overhanging the water. Photo by IHC.

The prize, Natrix *(=*Nerodia*) valida celaeno. The scientific name of this species is in dispute. Some authorities would place it with the garter snakes (*Thamnophis*), but recent research suggests that it may be a water snake after all. Photo by IHC.*

much smaller boat, with a capacity of one automobile, made the run from La Paz to a port across the Gulf of California with the euphonious name of Topolobampo. The vessel was so small that no matter how crowded the quay, it could always berth. Without a doubt, the agent told us, it was the most reliable service between the Cape Region and the mainland, if one planned far enough in advance. Luckily, there was a vacancy, so we booked passage for a crossing a week later, took on water, ice, and stores, and headed our Kamper south for the great adventure.

The classic loop road ran south on the eastern side of the Cape Region to the port town of San José del Cabo, across the southern extremity to land's end at Cabo San Lucas, and then northward paralleling the west coast and back to La Paz. It had been traversed by parties of biologists and geologists at intervals for many years. Herpetologist Alan E. Leviton, of the California Academy of Sciences, along with experts representing other disciplines, established a base at La Paz during the winter of 1958-59. From there they made two complete circuits of the loop road. Al thought we would be able to negotiate the route in our Kamper. We did, but just barely!

Baja California is one of the driest places in North America, except during the rare and sometimes violent storms, called *chubascos*, that dump torrential rains severe enough to wash out roads and even entire villages. Normally the long, gangling peninsula receives little precipitation except along the loftiest spines of its mountainous backbone. There, at the higher elevations, moisture-laden clouds, sweeping inland from the sea, condense and drop enough rain to support forests. The lower mountains get far less rainfall, and, on the east side, toward the Gulf of California, the weather may be bone dry every day of the year. In the Cape Region at the far south, however, the climatic pattern is

somewhat different and, below La Paz, there is more rainfall, especially in the mountains. There were no roads into the uplands and, because we lacked time to penetrate them by a pack train of mules or horses, we contented ourselves with visiting the small streams that issue from the lofty central massif at such places as Agua Caliente and Boca de la Sierra. In them I hoped to find the water snakes that were the object of our expedition. I knew that Joseph R. Slevin, of the California Academy of Sciences, had collected a large series of specimens at Agua Caliente way back in 1919. A few others had been found occasionally in more recent years, but did the "cape water snake" still survive there? What was the habitat like? How did these snakes differ from those of the same species on mainland Mexico, from which they had been separated for millions of years? I was hoping to collect a few myself. I especially wanted to get at least one healthy adult specimen home alive so that Edmond V. Malnate, my friend, artist, and colleague, could portray it in watercolor to complete the plates he was preparing as illustrations for my contemplated "Water Snakes of Mexico."

That was the background for òur penetration into a region that, in 1961, was still a frontier, a place where a mishap could lead to disaster.

It was charitable to refer to the loop as a "road." Most of the way there was *no* road. We bumped our way across bare rocks, over sand flats, and through deep dry ruts left by trucks that had managed to plow their way across muddy stretches during wet weather. True enough, there were a few small sections that could be called roads near the few tiny villages through which we passed. In the vicinity of San José del Cabo there was gravel, but for much of the way we followed what we sarcastically called "goat trails." There were a number of small hills to climb, often so rocky that we had to ascend them slowly. Invariably our 36-horsepower engine stalled. We had to back down, retreat as far as possible, get a running start, and let the car rock violently as we bumped our way upward. There were no road signs, and, when we came to a fork, all we could do was to follow the side that looked the most traveled. Twice we made the wrong decision and had difficulty finding a place to turn around in order to go back.

Happily, we were able to gas up at Santiago during the morning of our second day. We were serviced from an old-fashioned dispenser, the likes of which we hadn't seen in many a year. It was surmounted by a large glass container marked with lines indicating the number of liters. The gasoline was pumped upward by hand to the required amount, and then allowed to flow by gravity into our tank.

During mid-afternoon we reached Agua Caliente, a small cluster of run-down adobes and shacks, and, much to our surprise, found a Mexican who had lived in San Diego for many years and spoke perfect English. I inquired about the dam and hot springs that were supposed to be nearby, and he directed us to them and assigned a boy of about 10 to guide us. The dam was two miles west of "town" over an atrocious rutted lane, and we had to ford a shallow, very rocky stream to reach it. We drove on as far as we could and found ourselves close to a small, almost new concrete canal. It was about three feet both across and deep, with sloping sides, and roughly U-shaped in cross section. Crystal-clear water was flowing along it and onward to the settlement. The boy and I walked about a half mile along the canal and eventually arrived at the Presa del Chorro (the dam of the jet) which formed a small impoundment near the end of a rocky arroyo descending from the adjacent highlands. It, of course, was the source of the water in the canal. The name "Chorro" was derived from small jets of water issuing from rocks at one side of the pond, which our "Lower California Guidebook" described as "hot springs." They gave Agua Caliente its name. Except for two small jets, the "springs" were inactive during our visit.

I returned to the car and dismissed the boy with a small bag of candy and two pesos. I also asked him to catch and hold any amphibians or reptiles he might find, and for which I would pay him at the regular price of a peso for each snake and 50 centavos for each frog or toad.

We decided to stay right where we were for the night, and, since it was already late afternoon, Isabelle was getting our vehicle in shape and thinking about supper. I trudged off with a bucket to get water for washing, and, almost as soon as I reached the canal, I spied a large water snake sunning on a clump of vegetation. If ever I

had "buck fever," it was then. I carefully put down the pail and, no doubt with my hands shaking, rushed the spot. The snake dropped into the canal and it was a simple matter to grab it. I returned in triumph, the snake in one hand and a half-filled bucket in the other. We were both overjoyed. After all the exasperating roads and long delays, we had finally succeeded. What's more, I had then personally collected every kind of water snake known to occur in all of Mexico.

I returned to the canal and found several more specimens. Including those I collected the following morning, we had an even dozen, most of them large adults. We were ecstatic. But there was still the job to do of learning all I could about the habitat and the snakes' behavior. After dark I walked the length of the canal, searched for a long time at the Presa, and then went back to camp, but saw not a single snake. It was warm, and nights were usually the best time to hunt. In the early morning I caught six in the water of the canal. I took the cloacal temperatures of each with a quick-recording thermometer, and discovered that, whereas two had exactly the same temperature as the water, the others were all cooler. They obviously had just emerged from their nighttime retreats, which presumably were underground. Along the canal there were many red-spotted toads, *Bufo punctatus*, from fully adult sized to recently transformed juveniles. A fairly small snake I caught later in the morning disgorged a toad, and my examination of previously preserved material, including the large series obtained by Slevin in 1919, showed that red-spotted toads constituted the principal food of the cape water snake, at least at Agua Caliente. I saw no fishes in either the canal or the impoundment, and that was confirmed by several of the local people whom I asked. I had thus established two facts, one about food and the other that the snakes were diurnal.

As usual, our Kamper, a type of vehicle that none of the natives had ever seen before, attracted much attention, and the families living in two or three nearby shacks came to stare. While the *señor* was gone (meaning me), the women ventured close, and they saw Isabelle open a can with our rotary, hand-cranked opener. They left, but returned a few minutes later, each carrying several empty cans, some of them already rusting and all with the jagged edges that result from using an old-fashioned can opener. Isabelle obligingly ran them all through our little machine, giving each a smooth top, and earning smiles and thanks. Empty cans were then valuable utensils in Mexico, especially in such remote places as Agua Caliente.

We were packed well before noon and bounced our way back into town. There we were stopped by our youthful guide of yesterday carrying a can full of red-spotted toads, 18 of them, and demanding payment. I gave him 10 pesos, which was probably more money than he had ever earned at one time. I thanked him, but, once we had driven out of sight, I turned several loose at a damp spot along the road. Both Isabelle and I had picked up a few the night before from among the many that came close to our camp light to forage for insects.

A small crowd gathered while I was paying the boy. Entertainment was a rarity in Agua Caliente, and everyone had long since learned that a gringo and his *señora* were camped near the dam. We had to open our vehicle and show them how the dining area made up quickly into a bed, and that we had running water and almost all the other comforts of home. As we were closing up, we heard a middle-aged woman extend her greetings in English. We were startled, but when we tried to talk with her she refused to give her name and said only that she was from Boston and "had come down here to get away from it all." What possibly could have transpired to make an obviously well-educated American retreat to live in such a primitive, isolated place? An affair of the heart? A criminal offense? We wondered.

We drove on southward and soon came to the turnoff to Boca de la Sierra, which, wonder of wonders, had a sign pointing to it. A short while later we were in the village, just in time to eat our lunch and be stared at by a score of persons, most of them boys. From among them I recruited two to take me to the impoundment across the Arroyo San Bernardo, which our guidebook said was about a mile west of the town. When I started off I found that I had six guides instead of two, and all of them, I felt sure, would expect a *propina* (tip).

The water made a rather shallow but respectable pond, and as soon as we arrived I spotted a young water snake swimming a few yards away. In fact, I saw five in all, each about the same size, but, even with the boys' help, I succeeded in catching only two. That was enough to establish that the species still occurred there. My guides asked if I wanted to walk along the canal which, of course, I did. Their canal was quite different from the one at Agua Caliente. It was a narrow, straight-sided aqueduct measuring approximately a yard deep and wide, with a concrete base and vertical sides of masonry. It carried water down to the village and a few nearby fields, and was apparently used only for a short time each day. Water was rushing down the canal when we arrived in our car, but a gate at the dam had been closed some little time before the boys and I reached its almost level upper course. It was virtually empty of water but still quite wet. Under a patch of algae, I found another water snake, this one of medium size. Just before mak-

ing the catch, I looked back along the canal and saw a six-foot whipsnake probably doing what I was—looking for water snakes, or, in its case, any other provender it could find. The posterior part of its body was resting on the bank, but the remainder of its length was in the canal, with the head probing first in one direction and then another. It was gradually working its way toward us. How fortunate that we were ahead of the whipsnake, for it probably would have found and eaten my prize.

Back at the car I found Isabelle beset by flies and children. The youngsters kept bringing her things, among them lemons, unidentifiable fruits and vegetables, and large live rhinoceros beetles. She said that all the time I was gone there were three young children (not always the same ones) sitting on the sliding-door edge of the Kamper. It was far too hot and humid for her to close up the car. I rewarded my guides, paid a pittance for each beetle, and we then drove off. After a mile or so we stopped and had a cold drink. Also, the time had arrived for a decision.

Now that we had achieved our objective, prudence dictated that we turn around and head back to La Paz. San José del Cabo was very much closer, however, and we knew it was a fairly sizable port. So we continued southward. In town, we freshened our ice boxes, filled our tank with potable water (to which we added iodine just the same), and bought gasoline with a higher octane rating than had been available at Santiago. I asked the service station attendant and a policeman about the road up the western side of the Cape Region. Both agreed that it was no worse than the one on the eastern side which we had just traversed. So we opted to continue around the loop. Perhaps the spirit of adventure made us go onward, but there was also the chance that we might find something of interest, even a stream descending from the mountains.

It behooved us to get out of town, however. The next day was September 16, a national holiday in Mexico commemorating the Grito de Dolores—the shout from the village of Dolores, Guanajuato, when Father Miguel Hidalgo y Costilla issued the cry in 1810 that called for independence from Spain. Flags were flying all over San José, we could hear bands practicing, and a few unshaven, unkempt men, each clutching a bottle, were getting a head start on the celebration. We returned to the countryside and found a suitable place to spend the night about nine miles west of town.

In the early morning we headed on westward and found that the road, through rolling sand dunes, was not too bad most of the way to Cabo San Lucas. We stopped to take pictures of the huge *cardones* and also of the chain of rocks that reminded us of the almost vertical plates rising from the back of the dinosaur *Stego-saurus*. The rocks marked the "land's end" of the Baja peninsula.

At the tiny village of San Lucas we inquired again about the "road" running northward to Todos Santos, and were assured that it was open. So off we went. The "goat trails" resumed almost immediately, and for miles we struggled along, almost never getting out of first gear. There had been more rain on that side of the Cape Region than on the east, and, although everything was then well dried out, our progress through the ruts was slower than ever. As we topped a small hill we could see a vast stretch ahead, at least a mile wide, where a huge flood from what must have been a king-sized *chubasco* had raced downward from the mountains, carrying everything before it. We would have to cross what looked like a barren plain, but there were ruts left by trucks that had traversed it while it was still wet. We had no choice except to follow them, but they were so deep and potentially dangerous for us that I had to use our shovel repeatedly to fill in the worst ones. It took us an hour to cross what must have been an impassable morass after the storm.

We resumed our bumpy northward trek, and finally reached the outskirts of Todos Santos in very late afternoon. We found a place to pull off, had a soft drink, and sat still for a while to calm our nerves. It had been a harrowing experience. We had stopped for a half hour about noon to eat lunch, and I had collected a few lizards, but otherwise we had been traveling all day. We had driven 60 miles in about 12 hours, an average, even allowing for stops, of not much better than 5 miles an hour. After we left San Lucas and until we reached the small settlement of Pescadero near Todos Santos, we had seen only one person, the driver of a truck that passed us as it headed south. On the east side there had at least been some traffic. We had seen several trucks and even a bus. What would have happened to us if our little Volkswagen Kamper had broken down? We were all too forcefully reminded of that about a year later when we started on another trip to Mexico. We were crossing Delaware, not too far from home, when the engine quit and we had to be towed into Dover for major repairs!

After a brief rest we entered Todos Santos and discovered that everyone was drunk, or so it seemed. As we slowly picked our way through the town looking for a gas station, at least half a dozen men thrust a bottle of tequila toward me and invited me to have a drink. I had no intention of swigging from bottles used by others, but neither did I want to offend a patriotic Mexican. So I invented an excuse and told them, in Spanish, that my doctor had forbidden me to drink. That satisfied them. Eventually we discovered a gas pump with a Chinese attendant who, although tipsy, was able to fill our tank.

We drove on northward and found a camping spot a few miles out of town. The road, although suffering from an overabundance of potholes, was gravel all the way to La Paz and could easily be driven on the morrow. We cooked supper and enjoyed a glorious sunset, and, just before dark, a great-horned owl landed on a large yucca directly across the road from us. While we watched, it dined on the large rodent it had caught.

Before retiring we broke out our own bottle of tequila and celebrated—not for the Grito de Dolores, but because we had escaped unscathed from the wilderness.

Chapter 35

The *San Jorge* and Topolobampo

Back in La Paz, one of the first things we did was to check on our reservation for the boat trip back to the mainland. Everything was in order. We looked forward to the voyage, because it would be made during daylight hours and the crossing should be smooth. We would be in the Gulf of California all the way, and not be exposed to the surging Pacific rollers that had plagued us when we made the longer trip from Mazatlán. We could not foresee, of course, the amusing experiences and minor exasperations that awaited us at the dock at Topolobampo.

We weren't to sail for several days, which gave us a chance to get caught up with all sorts of things. Our trip south had not taken nearly so long as we had anticipated. Amazingly, we had camped out for only four nights during our circuit of the Cape Region's nightmarish roads. It seemed like a fortnight, but it had been a great adventure, and we were proud of our success. The cape water snake would be depicted in both color and black and white in my forthcoming review of Mexico's water snakes.

Since we were back in civilization, so to speak, we were able to do many things. Cleaning up the Kamper and ourselves, including our personal laundry, took hours; we found mail from home at the post office; and we wrote copious notes and a few short letters to friends and relatives back in the States. I also had many specimens to preserve, a time-consuming job. There were no casualties among our livestock. All the toads, snakes, and lizards had withstood the jolting, doubtless because the bags and bottles containing them had been on stacks of foam rubber pads.

The extra time also gave us a chance to sample the herpetofauna near La Paz. Most of that was accomplished by cruising after dark along the paved road that ran first southwest from town, then westward, and finally swung toward the northwest. It had been built to transport cotton, wheat, and other agricultural products. The traffic was light, and it consisted solely of loaded trucks proceeding toward the port and empty ones returning. The crops were grown by irrigation. The paved road ceased beyond the fields, and the route farther north was even worse, we were told, than the one we had traversed to the south. And, lest we forget, all water and gasoline had to be transported in one's vehicle!

We road-cruised for three consecutive evenings, and assembled quite an assortment of herps, most of them alive, although several others that had been run over were in good enough condition to preserve. Included were four rattlesnakes, two each of the Baja California rattler, *Crotalus enyo*, and the southernmost subspecies of the red rattler, *C. ruber*. Most interesting to us was the cape gopher snake, *Pituophis melanoleucus vertebralis*, a far-western subspecies of the pine snake which, at the time, was still common in our Pine Barrens back home in New Jersey. We also found a few of the smaller desert snakes and an assortment of lizards, most of them by day. All are now in the study collection of the American Museum of Natural History in New York. We also completed the list of Cape Region amphibians. There are only three. We had found the red-spotted toad, *Bufo punctatus*, at numerous places along and near the loop road; and I had collected the Pacific treefrog, *Hyla regilla*, at Boca de la Sierra. The males were not calling at the time, but I was quite familiar with their vocalizations. Hollywood has used them, over and over again, for sound effects for jungle and swamp scenes no matter in what part of the world the plot is supposed to be unfolding.

The last of the trio of Cape Region amphibians was Couch's spadefoot toad, *Scaphiopus couchii*, which we had encountered in many places in mainland Mexico. Unwisely, I picked up the first one by hand and I soon had a strong allergic reaction, with sneezing and my nose running as though it never would stop. After that I placed a wide-mouthed bottle in front of each spadefoot we found, and touched its rear end with a small stick, and it obligingly hopped inside for me.

La Paz was a free port when one entered it, but getting out was quite another matter. It was worse than the usual border crossing into Mexico from the United States. On Wednesday, the day before we were to sail, the ship's agent suddenly appeared at our hotel and said we must come at once with him to the customs office. I had to show all our papers, both those in English as well as in Spanish, the most important of which were our Mexican tourist permits and my *permiso* to collect amphibians and reptiles. The officers were quite friendly and, after a brief chat, they gave us permission to sail. We were instructed to be at the dock at eight o'clock the next morning.

We were there promptly, and immediately were surrounded by men of the first union, who demanded that we open up the car and unpack everything so they could haul it into the office for inspection. After fighting them off, chiefly in loud Spanish, I went into the customs office and showed my *permiso* once again, and the officer in charge sent word out to the union not to open the car. Inasmuch as we had already paid the union, they let us pass, but then there was another argument about getting the Kamper on the boat, the *San Jorge*, translated as St. George. It was a small vessel, moored parallel to the dock, and it reminded us of the excursion boats that operated in bays and sounds along our East Coast and in the Great Lakes. There was no derrick for loading freight. The only place for our car was across the forward part of the deck, a short distance aft of the bow. The space was so narrow that, once aboard, our front fender protruded slightly over the starboard side and the rear fender hung over the port side.

The second union laid down two planks, from the dock to the deck, and their chief then advanced to drive the car on board. I balked. I wasn't about to let anyone but myself move our precious vehicle in such a situation. How familiar was the man with Volkswagens? What if he touched the accelerator instead of the brake? The car would go overboard into the bay. A hot argument ensued, but he finally surrendered when I suggested that he sit in the front seat beside me while I drove. He climbed in and said, "*Es igual*" (It's the same thing). If ever I moved a car with great care it was then, literally inch by inch. A crew member kept close watch and signaled me so that I knew exactly when to stop. The car was firmly chained to the deck, and I paid off the union chief for laying down the two planks and featherbedding as my passenger.

I hadn't even had time to sigh with relief when a young man wearing some sort of uniform demanded our tourist permits and walked off with them without any explanation. I followed. We would be in trouble without them, and I wanted to keep them in sight. It turned out that the immigration authorities had to prepare a list of passengers, foreign as well as Mexican, and it had to be signed by the officer in charge before the ship could sail. I was gone quite a long time, and, since the mail and all the other passengers except me were aboard, Isabelle began to worry. "By this time I was getting very

nervous," she wrote in her diary. "I was debating with myself what to do—sail with the car or wait for Roger." I soon appeared and we were together again. After all that, we, unaccountably, didn't leave for another hour.

The trip was truly enjoyable. We watched the rugged coast north of La Paz and skirted around the equally rugged Isla Espíritu Santo. Except for a slight swell the sea was calm. The *San Jorge* was a sturdy little ship and it moved right along. There was much to see—many flying fishes, dark brown boobies, pelicans, and gulls. Most exciting were four large sea turtles, none close enough to identify by species, however. The weather was clear and we both acquired more sunburn than we should have.

Just before dark we passed Isla Ajithueca, a very large rock rising far out of the water almost at the entrance to Topolobampo Bay. A dolphin played close to the ship, diving and later surfacing to blow. We could distinguish its long, sleek body and dorsal fin even in the rapidly fading light.

The seaward and south side of Topolobampo Bay is more or less surrounded by a series of rocky hills, the main mass of them high and extensive enough to earn the designation *sierra* on Mexican maps. The town of Topolobampo itself was on one of the lower hills.

By the time we docked, around 7:00 P.M., it was dark, and our mooring was illuminated by a series of lights mounted on poles. As soon as the gangplank was lowered, incidentally right next to our Kamper, a customs inspector came aboard to check the baggage of the returning Mexicans. When he had finished with them, I showed him our *permiso*, and he said we were OK. Moments later an immigration official told us we would have to report, with all our papers, to his *jefe* (chief). I donned my headlamp, dug out two flashlights, and locked the car, and we followed a young man who offered to guide us. We started to climb up and up and up a steep path, getting more winded with every step. When we arrived at the bottom of a long concrete staircase, Isabelle sat down to rest. I asked how much farther we had to go, and I was told we were only halfway, but our guide thought it would be all right if I went on alone. So Isabelle decided to sit it out. I climbed onward and upward with the young man, and eventually reached a small building within which the middle-aged *jefe* sat scowling behind a battered old desk. As soon as I laid down my papers he demanded to know why the *señora* wasn't with me. I told him that the climb was too long and steep for her. He started to get ugly, and I finally said, "She is too old to come way up here." He fussed and fumed but finally used his rubber stamp, and I departed. It was a long way down in the dark without the guide, who actually was going home when he accompanied us upward. When I reached Isabelle and told her what I had been forced to say, we had a good laugh. To satisfy the ego of a two-bit bureaucrat, all foreigners had to hike almost to the top of the town.

The men of the unloading union had long since left for the day. I asked the captain what we should do. He advised us to wait until morning. He said he could send someone to summon the union, but it would take at least an hour for them to assemble, and they would charge 300 pesos instead of the customary 80. He gave us permission to sleep in our car. So, very belatedly, I managed to get into our ice boxes. They were accessible only from the back end of the Kamper, which still overhung the water. We had a cold supper washed down with icy soda pop. We didn't want to cook on the deck, and the coffee in the ship's galley had run out.

We retired, but we didn't go to sleep. Crew members and others kept coming and going and talking, and the gangplank, as mentioned, was right next to us. Finally, all of the crew went ashore and, insofar as we knew, we were the only persons still aboard. We were just dozing off when suddenly we heard a very familiar sound, well in the distance but unmistakable. I asked Isabelle if she heard what I did, and she replied, "It's a lion roaring. You'd think we were back at the zoo." Before we finally fell asleep we heard it perhaps half a dozen times. What was an African lion doing on mainland Mexico's west coast? The mystery was solved in the morning when a member of the crew told us there was a circus in town.

I awoke sometime after midnight and almost instantly realized that something was very wrong. I pulled on my socks, pants, and shoes, and stepped onto the deck. The *San Jorge* was listing heavily to starboard. The dock lights were still on, and I moved off to investigate. I soon discovered that the ship was caught, along parts of its starboard side, under the edge of the dock. The Gulf of California is a long, narrow body of water noted for its strong tides. The tide was rising, and the more it rose the more the deck tilted. The *San Jorge* was riding steadily higher in the water, but far from evenly. Here was a dangerous situation. Imagine the thoughts that raced through my mind as I contemplated it. How much higher would we be lifted, and would it be sufficient, eventually, to turn the ship on its side? Or would it break loose from the dock before such a disaster occurred? Were we doomed to have our expedition terminate at the bottom of Topolobampo Bay? I groped my way through the ship as best I could, but no one was aboard. Then back to the dock, but I was helpless to do anything. I hastened back to the car, awakened Isabelle, and then I leaned on the car's horn button. Maybe

The labor unions were strong in Mexico. The men laid down two planks for us to drive off the San Jorge, *and charged us 80 pesos. Photo by IHC.*

someone in the town above us might hear it. Nothing happened. Should we gather up our valuables, including our precious water snakes, and go ashore?

We were still pondering what to do when two crewmen appeared, singing and a little high from partying in the town. I rushed to show them the problem, and they instantly realized its seriousness. They found a sturdy plank on the dock and tried using it as a lever, but to no avail. So they attacked the wooden dock with a pair of the ship's fire axes, chopping steadily until the dock gave way and the San Jorge righted herself with a great rocking that quickly subsided. The two sailors grinned at us, and bade us *"buenas noches"* as they disappeared toward the stern of the boat.

Isabelle and I sat on the floor of the Kamper by the side sliding door with our feet on the deck. It took us awhile to calm down, but, once we did, we began to laugh gently, meanwhile smiling at each other. How typically Mexican! Not enough fenders put over the side of the ship. No guard posted. No night watch, to use the nautical term. Everyone had gone to town, and, once the problem had been licked, the two men showed no concern about the damaged dock. *Mañana* everything would be all right. We relaxed and slept until dawn.

We managed to eat and take care of other personal matters before the union arrived, which it did promptly at 8:00 A.M. Fortunately, the tide had changed and the deck was almost level with the dock. The men, 10 of them, laid down two planks, and I drove off the boat. No argument that time, but, since I had become a little annoyed with unions, I demanded a receipt. On a scratch pad I wrote, in Spanish, "80 pesos received from Señor Conant," and the *jefe* scribbled out his name. I gave him a 100-peso note, and, in return, he handed me a wad of filthy, tattered paper 1-peso notes, all scrunched together. He probably expected me to put the wad in my pocket. Instead, I counted while he watched. There were only 10 pesos and therefore he had shortchanged me by a similar amount. While his men and several members of the crew looked on, I called him a *ladrón* (thief) and waved the receipt at him. He reluctantly gave me the other 10 pesos in coin. Here was one gringo who could count.

Probably I became suspicious because single-peso notes were so rarely seen. Coins were almost always used for small denominations. I was willing to bet then, and I still am, that members of the union had saved every old peso note they could find just to trick some unwary person who transported his car across the Gulf. In retrospect, it was a paltry sum. Eighty pesos divided among 10 men was little enough, even though they had done practically nothing to earn it. The peso was then worth about eight cents in American money, but, on the other hand, almost everything was cheap in Mexico in those days. If I hadn't caught the *jefe* red-handed, so to speak, I would have been inclined to give him the full 100 pesos. Life was hard for the laboring men and their families.

Isabelle, ever practical, the bookkeeper of the family and the former business manager of the Staten Island Zoo, added up our expenses, including the last 80 pesos. The total cost of our trip from the mainland to the Cape Region and return was $305.25, or, as she put it, $20.35 each for 15 water snakes. That seemed like a lot in those days, but, compared with price lists for rare snakes that I receive nowadays, the cost for ours was almost trivial.

We drove away but stopped before we were out of sight of the dock, and got out of our car to have a look at the high, rocky promontories in the early morning sunlight. We also took a last look at the *San Jorge.* Several years later we were told that, during a fog or storm, she had rammed the Isla Ajithueca, near the harbor's mouth, and then had sunk like a stone.

As we drove toward the large town of Los Mochis we realized we had been fortunate to have stayed aboard overnight. The paved road passed through a large swampy area, and there was no place we could have pulled off to camp for the night. We stocked up on food and ice in the town and then turned north to have a daylight look at the Río Fuerte and the Río Sinaloa, where I had collected water snakes in the pitch dark two years previously. We then headed south, stopping at the Motel Tres Ríos in Culiacán overnight, and then on to the Motel Flamingo in Mazatlán. We were far behind with many things: curating the live collection; pickling specimens; getting cleaned up; writing our notes, which were far in arrears; and retrieving our top load from the warehouse where we had left it. Putting it back on top was a chore. First the roof rack, which had

Few people realize how enormous a cactus can grow. These are giant *cardones, the most massive of all the species in the Sonoran Desert, and known occasionally to attain a height of 20 meters (65.6 feet). They surely dwarfed Isabelle. Photo by RC.*

to be fastened with great care, and then all the bottles full of preserved specimens and divers other things, including turtle traps. All had to be lifted while I stood on a small removable, folding ladder built just for that purpose. We finally had a good night's rest, which we both agreed we badly needed.

As we readied our Kamper in Mazatlán for the long trip home, our thoughts turned to our recent strenuous excursion around the bottom of Baja. It had started at the dock in this very port city, we had achieved our objective, and we were back safe and sound. What an adventure! And one that, most assuredly, we would never attempt again. Such trips were for young people, and we were a middle-aged couple. But what memories we had, and what tales we could tell about our most difficult fieldwork in all of Mexico. We had seen and conquered one of the last frontiers.

As I write these memoirs, more than 30 years later, I am both amazed and appalled about what has happened to Baja. Luxurious ferries have replaced the Mexicali tramp steamers for the crossing from Mazatlán to La Paz, and anyone can now drive from Tijuana, at the California line, to San José del Cabo and many other places with ease. The circuit we made with such difficulty can be negotiated on paved roads in just a few hours. In late 1973, Mexico's then President Luis Echeverria stood on the twenty-eighth parallel, the boundary between the State of Baja California and the Territory (now State) of Baja California Sur (south), and dedicated the new 1,061-mile highway slicing through the length of the peninsula.

Gone now is the solitude and much of the charm,

although few of the present-day swarms of tourists venture far from the paving. Much of the primitiveness has vanished, however, at least in the areas we visited. In its place has come a steady influx of sightseers with all their noise, demands, and trash. Some of the travelers are doubtless enthralled by the majesty of the desert, and they seek out the quaint remains of the old villages, admire the chain of rocks at land's end, and pose their spouses, as I had done, with the giant *cardones*. They linger, take pictures, and profit intellectually by their experiences. All too many, however, don't give a damn about such things. All they do is race down the peninsula and then back again just to say they did it.

How glad I am that we went when we did.

Chapter 36

Potential Perils

Collecting in Mexico in the 1960s was not all fun and games. There were times when Isabelle and I came perilously close to being in real trouble. Not from *bandidos* (bandits), thank goodness. We were never molested. We always behaved as if we were guests in someone else's home, and we were treated politely, but also with curiosity. After all, we spent most of our time in the countryside where most gringos never ventured. Besides, we had a "house on wheels," one of Volkswagen's first, pioneering Kampers, and the *campesinos* had never seen one. Neither had most *norteamericanos*. Our only unpleasantness occurred when we twice encountered *borrachones* (drunks) who, like so many of their besotted counterparts throughout the world, acted belligerently. Coping with them was no problem. We simply drove away.

In the main, the roads offered the greatest hazards. I have mentioned elsewhere how we might be bowling along on a well-paved road and suddenly, without warning, come upon a stretch full of deep potholes through which we had to thread our way with care. Most roads had no shoulders, and often the paving was perched along precipitous cliffs with no guardrail.

During our first long trip to Mexico, in 1949, we left Mexico City and passed through Puebla on our way to the Atlantic coast, little dreaming we soon would be creeping down a seemingly sheer, 3,000-foot cliff on the face of which engineers had carved a narrow, zigzagging two-lane road. It was paved, but it was so scary that passing any vehicle, especially a big truck ascending the escarpment, made our hair stand on end, to use an old cliché, particularly when we were on the outer half of the road. I was driving and I didn't dare take my eyes off the paving. Isabelle cast a few quick glances downward at the abyss along whose edge we were so precariously moving. She almost regretted it. Once we were safely at the bottom, we had to pull off the road to calm down before we could go on. Frankly, I asked her to please take the wheel for a while.

That almost sheer drop near Acatzingo (Acultzingo on some maps) was an outstanding engineering achievement. We were to traverse it twice more during our extensive Mexican peregrinations, once up and once down, but both times it seemed wider than during our first descent. A new, unexpected wrinkle had been introduced, however. When a truck's lights were on, it meant we should respond by putting on our lights and then driving on the left (wrong) side of the road, thus allowing the big and often lengthy vehicle to make a wider sweep at the outer side of the hairpin turns as it struggled upward in low gear.

I have neither been back since the 1960s nor talked with anyone who has driven recently in that part of Mexico, but current maps show a toll road, so there probably has been considerable improvement or perhaps even a new road altogether. Undoubtedly there is a constant stream of traffic in both directions flowing back and forth from Puebla and other cities on the plateau to the lowland cities and towns and onward to Veracruz.

In the early 1930s, long before the road was built, Edward H. Taylor and Hobart M. Smith, while conducting herpetological fieldwork, unwittingly drove near the edge of the cliff, during a dense fog, seeking a place to camp for the night. They didn't realize how close they had come to disaster until the fog lifted the next day, and they could stare in amazement at the lowlands far beneath them.

It wasn't until 1961 that Isabelle and I tackled another potentially very dangerous road, and the one from which, most assuredly, we had the most spectacular views of any we ever traveled. It had only recently been opened, it had taken 18 years to build, and it clung to the rim of one of the gigantic barrancas of western Mexico. Some of those great gorges equal or even exceed our own Grand Canyon in depth.

We started upward in early afternoon from the town of Villa Unión on the Pacific Coastal Plain south of Mazatlán and, except for a gas station at the tiny settlement of El Palmito, we were virtually in the wilderness for more than 100 miles, most of it uphill. Because the road clung to the northern edge of the barranca and we were driving eastward, we were in the outside lane and thus cliff-hanging almost all the way. There were very few places where we could pull off to stop and admire the scenery, take pictures, have a snack, or simply rest. As evening approached we began to worry about finding a place to camp. We had no desire to drive that road after dark. Luckily, the paving crossed a small promontory overhanging the gorge on our right, and it had been quarried to grade level for road-building material and fill. It was a perfect place to spend the night.

To capture the flavor of that interesting but nerve-wracking trip, I have excerpted and slightly edited several sentences from Isabelle's diary:

The road rose gently through the first 20 miles on the Coastal Plain, then began to steepen. We crossed some vados *(fords) where water was flowing across the paving, some of it swiftly but not over our hubcaps. We saw a coatimundi cross in front of us. The road was an engineering marvel. About 130 miles were new. The last 60 miles, from El Salto to Durango, had been paved for a long while, and it was badly in need of repair, as we discovered when we drove over it. As we ascended it got cooler and we donned sweaters and eventually our sarapes. At our campsite it was 62°F at 8:30 p.m. and 58°F when we awakened in the morning. Quite a change from the sultry, more than 100-degree lowlands in which we had been traveling, boating, or waiting for weeks. After breakfasting and stowing our gear, we climbed up the back of the quarry to look at the magnificent view. The mountain peaks rise so sharply in this range (Roger calls it a* barranca) *that one looks virtually straight down for one or two thousand feet. Driving on the road is rather frightening. It is narrow, only two lanes, and there are no guardrails. Fortunately there is little traffic—trucks, buses, and an occasional car.*

We would have enjoyed lingering in the highlands of the Sierra Madre Occidental near El Salto, because it was refreshingly cool and also prime garter snake (*Thamnophis*) country, but we had a schedule to meet. We would be back another year to explore the area.

Once, we made an abortive attempt to reach a freshwater lagoon along the Pacific coast near Puerto Angel. We started in our Kamper from Oaxaca de Juárez, on the plateau, and Charles M. Bogert accompanied us in his own field vehicle with a married couple of friends. The road was paved southward to Miahuatlán, but, from there onward we had 100 miles of dirt road to negotiate along knifelike ridges with sharp drops on either side, and then the long, steep, sinuous descent down the escarpment to the coast. In some places, during afternoon thundershowers, we could see the cliff-edge road eroding away on its outward

The Kamper on the floor of an abandoned quarry, the only place we could find to spend the night safely along 100 miles of cliffhanging highway with no guardrails. Photo by IHC.

side. We wondered whether there would be enough room left for us to pass on our return trip. I was to learn later that William E. Duellman, heading for Puerto Escondido on the same or an equally primitive road slightly farther west, managed to get around a mudslide, but the Mexican truck following him failed to make it and vanished down the mountainside. With such hazards and those caused by reckless driving on the paved highways, it was no wonder we saw so many handmade crosses along the roadsides erected in memory of those who had lost their lives.

It was impossible to drive and much too far to walk from Pochutla in the Coastal Plain to the lagoon we sought. So, I never did find out whether the west coast water snake, which was abundant near Acapulco, occurred that far southeastward. We managed to get back up the escarpment road without incident, and we picked up a number of interesting herps on the way. I caught my first live *Loxocemus bicolor*, the curious snake which, at the time, bore the common name of New World python. I also found a turtle that James F. Berry and John B. Iverson later placed in their new species of mud turtle, *Kinosternon oaxacae*, with my female specimen serving as the allotype (the designated animal of the opposite sex from the one on which the species is based).

Once back in Miahuatlán we were even further reminded how close to the wilderness we were. We needed gasoline, but there was no pump. Instead, a large funnel was inserted in the neck of our gas tank, a filtering cloth was fitted into it, and the gasoline was poured in from a hand-held five-liter can.

Our closest brush with death was at Culiacán, capital of the Pacific State of Sinaloa. It was a major bottleneck on the coastal highway during the years when we were doing fieldwork in Mexico. There is now a toll road passing over the Río de Culiacán for vehicular traffic, but no such luxury existed when we crossed the river. There was a fairly long ribbon of concrete, scarcely two lanes wide, across the streambed, but it offered safe passage only during the dry season. We were always there in the wet one, when reptiles and amphibians were most active. Two streams, the Río Humaya and the Río Tamazula, converged at the city to form the Río de Culiacán, and, if it rained hard upstream in either or both during the monsoon season, there soon would be a flood of water racing across the concrete *vado*. In such cases traffic was diverted to a one-track railroad trestle on which planks had been fastened. Traffic would be southbound for an hour or so and then reversed. Once, we had to cross on the planks and there was no guardrail on either side. A little scary, but not too bad inasmuch as we drove slowly. Another time, water an inch or two deep was flowing across the *vado*, and we had a safe although watery crossing.

The third time, we nearly came to grief. Traffic was using the *vado*, but muddy water, almost hubcap deep, was racing across it. We were southbound, so we were in the more dangerous downstream lane. We were proceeding at a cautious speed, but I had to give way for a huge overloaded truck coming from the opposite direction. As it passed I could see the Mexican drivers behind it waving wildly for me to move to our left. As I turned the steering wheel, I glanced down—we were right at the rim where the water was cascading over the edge in a broad waterfall. Another inch or even less would have precipitated us into the turbulent torrent below and among the jagged rocks protruding above the surface.

All this happened in what seemed like a split second. We survived and made it across safely, but I was shaking when we reached the other side, and I had to get out of the car and walk around before we could go on. Isabelle was as white as the proverbial sheet. Even today, so many decades later, I shudder every time I think of how close we came to a horrible death.

I don't recall the exact words we used, but I'll never forget the sentiment we expressed. That night, when we embraced and kissed goodnight before crawling into our separate sleeping compartments, I whispered, "We nearly got it today." Isabelle whispered back, "It wouldn't have been so bad if we both had died, but . . . ," and she paused. We both knew that life wouldn't be worth living without the other. We hugged each other tighter than ever.

Our little Kamper, to which Isabelle referred in her diaries as *la casita* (the little house), was showing the effects of the rugged treatment it had received. We had

driven it over the roughest imaginable roads, even the open desert, through mud, and across shallow, rocky streams. We had overloaded it unmercifully. Our personal gear was at a minimum, but our collecting equipment took up a large amount of space, and it was heavy. We had several turtle traps, nets, snake pullmans, hip boots, a shovel and pick ax, a 20-gallon tank of water, and two portable ice boxes. Also, there were at least two dozen gallon bottles and several large cans for pickled specimens, and they became heavier as we progressed. I preserved all study specimens and road kills worth saving in formaldehyde in the field, and I had to add water (and its weight) in diluting that chemical to its proper strength. Any animals that were destined for the zoo collection back home were kept alive in various containers on a bed of foam rubber under the backseat of the car, which we discovered was the only relatively cool place. It remained so, even if we were on the desert for days at a time. On top we carried a luggage rack that was secured by metal clamps holding fast, if rather precariously, to the water run-off gutter on each side of the car roof. A folding ladder enabled me to climb up to get at the top load, which had a zippered canvas cover. Also, we carried enough canned goods with us to do all our own cooking, an absolute necessity in the remote places we frequented. Dehydrated dinners were a help, but many of them were so tasteless that ketchup was indispensable. Obviously we had a very heavy load.

We kept the *casita* in as perfect condition as we could. Our local Volks agency checked it out thoroughly before each of our Mexican expeditions. We followed the lubrication and check-up schedule recommended by the manufacturer as closely as we could. Instead of letting it sit all winter, Isabelle used it every Wednesday for her weekly shopping expedition to Marlton or Medford, the then small country towns nearest to our home at Taunton.

There was one major improvement. Volks came out with a new, much better motor that was desirable in several ways, notably in power and speed. It became standard equipment in their new vehicles, but if we wanted to buy one separately, it would be at what we thought was an unfair premium price. The Kamper was our car and our contribution to the research. We hadn't asked the National Science Foundation for a field vehicle. I consulted with our local Volks people as soon as I heard about the new motor, and they said they would see what they could do. Many months later a new van with a body similar to that of our Kamper was parked head-in against a high brick wall, which collapsed and smashed in the front end of the vehicle. After the insurance company made its inspection, the Volks agency bought the wreck. The motor, which was in the rear, was unharmed, and it was transferred to our car. What a difference it made, but its presence as our source of power created a new worry. Everywhere we stopped for servicing at Volks agencies, both in the United States and Mexico, some mechanic was sure to ask whether the transmission had also been changed. It had not; our local agency said it wasn't necessary. Nonetheless, the numerous inquiries and some shaking of heads made me fret at times, wondering if we might find ourselves stranded in some remote place far from help.

We had little trouble during our next excursion with *la casita*, but in 1964 things went wrong with a vengeance. En route, in Mississippi, Isabelle was driving. Suddenly I heard an odd noise, and I asked her to stop and pull off the road. We had a flat tire on our rear right wheel. I had to work on a downward slope because the road shoulder was quite narrow, and, whereas I managed to jack up the car, I couldn't raise it far enough to remove the wheel. I needed help, so I hitchhiked back to the town through which we had just passed and found a service station. With their professional equipment they soon had our spare on the wheel. I followed them back, but when they checked the tire it was a total loss. The walls had collapsed. There was nothing to do but buy a new one.

We kept on going, all the way to Yucatán, then back and across the Isthmus of Tehuantepec and eastward to the Guatemalan border. We returned through Oaxaca and on westward to many of the isolated lakes of the transvolcanic belt before heading home.

Quite a trip for an ailing *casita*. It was punctuated by eight flat tires and the purchase of another new one. Three times the motor wouldn't start in the morning. We were towed into town twice, once into Villa Corona from the scene of one of our most amusing experiences (see "*El Baño* (The Bath)"). That time a taxi driver managed to get our motor started. Other Mexican amateur mechanics had to help us more than once. We stayed fairly well on schedule even though things kept going wrong. Before we left Mexico, however, our transmission quit in part, and we couldn't get into low gear. I had to hire *muchachos* (boys) to give us a push so we could start off in second. On the way home across the States we had to park on a grade whenever possible, so gravity would start us rolling. Traffic lights were a problem, and we tried to gauge them so we wouldn't have to make a full stop. Several times, with Isabelle at the wheel, I had to push the car myself, and then jump in while it was moving.

Once we were home the transmission was finally replaced and the motor was rebuilt in part. We used the *casita* for several trips afterward, including excursions to the Big Bend of Texas in conjunction with the second edition of our field guide. But the Kamper was wearing out and nickel and diming us to death. Buying new parts and having them installed, wheel bearings included, were expensive. We finally traded it in, during the spring of 1969, after one last memorable all-day jaunt through the byways of the still nearly deserted New Jersey Pine Barrens, with Marlin Perkins as our guest.

The 1964 trip, despite all the mechanical troubles, was a memorable one, herpetologically speaking. We found many interesting and valuable study specimens and made two unexpected discoveries. On our way southward down the eastern side of Mexico we camped in the cloud forest near Teziutlán, and I caught an obviously pregnant garter snake of the little-known species called *Thamnophis sumichrasti*. I kept her alive until she had her young. Eleven of them bore the spotted pattern of the mother, but the other 10 had the rectangular dorsal blotches of what had been known as a different species, *Thamnophis phenax*. Thus, *T. phenax* was simply a pattern morph of *T. sumichrasti*. I gave my information to Douglas A. Rossman, who had long worked on the garter snakes, and he published the results of my discovery in the journal "Herpetologica" in 1966.

The other unexpected find was a dwarf boa, *Ungaliophis continentalis*, the second known record for the species from Mexico. It was dead on the road near Teopisca, Chiapas, but in virtually perfect condition. I published a note on it in the same journal, also in 1966.

There were a few other, more or less minor, mechanical happenstances on that trip that I will mention briefly. During a visit to the remote area below the Presa Cárdenas (the Cárdenas Dam, named for a former president of the Republic) and the source of the Río Nazas, I discovered that our fan belt had split longitudinally and probably would break long before we could hope to reach a professional mechanic. So I installed a new one, a chore I had never previously attempted. We carried a spare along with other emergency parts, such as spark plugs, distributor points, and headlamp bulbs. We moved the car to a shaded but open place and, with the Volkswagen manual at hand, I managed it, clumsily but satisfactorily in the end. In the midst of my labor, however, a small keystone piece of metal went flying off, and my heart sank. Without it we were helpless. Isabelle, who was watching me, saw where it landed, and went over and picked it up, thus saving the day.

We weren't so lucky when we were camped near the Volcán de Colima, a slightly active volcano in western Mexico. Our propane cookstove needed attention, and a part popped away while I was trying to adjust it. We never did find it, even though I cut down every blade of grass and other vegetation for a distance of several yards all around as we searched for it. We had to limp along on one burner instead of the customary two. We made a special trip into Guadalajara to the Sears Roebuck store in an effort to find a replacement. They didn't stock any field stoves. We had bought ours originally at the Sears store in Camden, New Jersey.

Another time we had stopped at a *supermercado* in Guadalajara to stock up on supplies, but, when we returned to the car, the accelerator failed to function. We learned later that the cable connecting it with the motor, in the rear of the Kamper, had snapped. I hailed a taxi driver and asked him if he could tow us to the Volks agency, which we had visited on a previous trip. He explained that it was against the law for a taxi to pull or push a car through the city. With a generous *propina* in mind, however, he would maneuver us through back streets. So we were given the first of a series of strong pushes that enabled us to roll half a block, and sometimes right through an intersection if there was nothing coming. We had the hazard of only one traffic signal but, after making sure no policemen were in sight, our benefactor shoved us through on a green light. We finally reached our destination, and he had surely earned the substantial *propina* that was accepted with an enthusiastic "*Muchas gracias.*"

Never, in our travels all over Mexico, did we encounter *bandidos*. They supposedly were around, but, as we heard during our first (1949) trip, if they were caught by the police or military, they were summarily executed. Kraig Adler and David M. Dennis came close to witnessing such an event in December 1969.

Those two cofounders of the Ohio Herpetological Society, which eventually became the Society for the Study of Amphibians and Reptiles, were in Guerrero in southern Mexico not too far from Chilpancingo. They were on a collecting trip driving along a narrow dirt road toward the Cerro Teotepec, and were approaching the small logging town of Puerto del Gallo. Unexpectedly, they had to stop for a military convoy coming from the opposite direction. Three jeeps were filled with officers, and two canvas-roofed trucks carried soldiers. Despite language difficulties they learned from the colonel in command that his men had just disposed of some *bandidos*. That was confirmed when they reached the town and an American resident informed them that the bandits had been executed in full view of a small crowd as an object lesson for the witnesses.

Several years after we terminated our Mexican fieldwork, Howard W. "Duke" Campbell told me about a harrowing experience he had on a paved road over which we had traveled several times. It was well after dark. He was driving his panel truck with his wife at his side and their youngsters asleep in the back. Suddenly, well ahead of them, they spied a vehicle with its lights on that was standing motionless across the middle of the road. Duke did not even slow down and, with more nerve than I ever could have mustered, he kept right on going. At the last possible moment, the crosswise car pulled out of the way, and Duke barreled through, but the car turned and took off in pursuit of them. It was a wild ride, all the way into the outskirts of Guadalajara, where they found a truck stop with several big rigs lined up parallel to one another. Duke pulled in beside them and asked the nearest driver if it was safe. He hastily explained that *bandidos* had been chasing them. The driver said, "*Tengo pistola*" (I have a pistol), and motioned Duke to stay where he was. They were there all night. The children slept through the entire adventure.

How different our friends' experiences were in comparison with the quiet, peaceful trips a few years earlier that Isabelle and I enjoyed over a period of more than a decade.

Chapter 37

El Baño (The Bath)

Whenever possible during our Mexican fieldwork, we tried to make camp by late afternoon so there would be time for at least a cursory examination of the stream, lake, or pond where we expected to hunt for aquatic snakes by jacklight after dark. To borrow the language of the criminal, "casing the joint" ahead of time could often prevent mishaps and such misadventures as the one when I was almost completely lost at night in the Chihuahuan Desert (see "Water Snakes in the Desert").

Late one afternoon in mid-August of 1964, we arrived at the head of the Laguna de Atotonilco, a lake that is strongly alkaline and also much shrunken from its former size. The increasing desiccation of the Mexican landscape, a process that has been waxing and waning for thousands of years since the Ice Age, has greatly reduced the lake in depth and area. Concurrently, the shrinking has concentrated the salts that are leached from the surrounding hillsides and are flushed downward by the infrequent but violent storms that are common to this and other arid parts of the world. Although its water is far from fresh, the Laguna de Atotonilco supported an apparently large population of the strongly aquatic Mexican garter snake at the time of our visit.

As we approached, we could see the lake a half mile south of the highway. Several small, obviously freshwater ponds adjacent to the road looked even better as reptilian habitats. Isabelle, who was driving, stopped our Kamper, and I trudged off along a dirt secondary road on foot in search of a campsite. Perhaps 100 yards to the north, at the base of a small hill and well screened from the highway by dense thickets of thornbushes, I found an abandoned paved road, or rather a fragment of one. That was ideal. No matter how hard it might rain during the night—something we always had to consider—we would have traction in the morning to get our car under way. Evidently this had once been part of an older road, for nearby was an abandoned inspection station, where truck drivers stopped to show their papers. Someone had erected a wire fence, stout and cattle-proof, but with a stile, across the end of the paving. Beyond it, hidden by a large tree and rock, was a

tank of water perhaps 10 by 20 feet in breadth and length and a few feet deep that sported a miscellaneous collection of floating algae and other vegetational debris on its surface. Probably the concrete-walled tank had been a source of water for the inspectors, but the area now seemed deserted. It looked like an excellent spot to camp for the night.

After plodding back through the dust, I imparted the good news to Isabelle and we carefully drove to the paving. The first task was to police the area, for cattle and burros had long made use of it, and the innocent beasts, unaware that their droppings wouldn't fertilize macadam, had left their marks. It was simple enough, however, to fashion a primitive broom from the thornbushes, and that, with our trusty and oft-used shovel, made the cleanup swift and easy.

We backed the car into place, broke out the stove, which we set up close to the thorn thicket, and soon had supper under way. But our solitude didn't last long. We should have expected what was coming. The dirt road, up which I had reconnoitered, turned out to be a main route to the hamlet of Villa Corona a mile or two away. First came boys on bicycles, then women toting great loads on their heads, and finally a small herd of cattle and some goats. These with their *vaqueros* had been out to pasture all day, munching on the lush grasses that grew around the ponds and a nearby large ravine. Probably because the *campesinos* have become accustomed to tourists, especially in this region near the city of Guadalajara, with its large American colony, most of them paid little attention to us. A few stopped and stared briefly, but most gave us scarcely a glance. But they left us a legacy—their flies. Those pestiferous insects, of several species and each more proficient than the next at the art of biting, came to stay just as they never fail to do every time a herd of *ganado* (livestock) passes by an open, occupied car.

Keeping the flies off our food became a major concern, and my vigorous preoccupation with the swatter probably kept me from noting our visitor. It was apparent, when I first spotted him, that he had been there for some time, for he was sitting on the ground a few feet away absorbed in a Mexican comic book. It seemed strange that he would tarry so close to us, and as he sat there, never looking toward us all through our meal, we became a little uneasy. Presently he rose to his feet, circled around our vehicle, squeezed himself between our camp stove and the thorns, and disappeared over the stile. Isabelle and I stared at each other and half whispered, "What is he up to?"

It wasn't until the dishes were washed and dried and put away that I discovered his purpose. We could hear voices, not too clearly, and I realized that a boy had joined our strange visitor and the two of them were talking. By moving closer and listening intently I could hear what was said, and, when I realized what was going on, I had great difficulty in restraining myself from bursting into laughter. Our man was taking a bath in the water tank just out of sight behind the tree and rock.

After I was sure from the conversation that he was nearly dressed, I stepped over the barrier and offered our apologies for blocking the road to the *baño*. He greeted me with a big smile and assured me it was nothing.

A half hour later, when the sun had dropped close to the horizon, it was time to prepare for wading in the nearby pond. I unpacked my headlamp and snake bags and donned my hip boots, but it was so warm that I thought I'd wait until the last minute before pulling them up all the way. I dropped into one of our camp chairs to rest for a few minutes and idly stared across the road, where I was rather startled to see a mustachioed *campesino* sprawled on the ground. Behind him and some distance away his *señora* was scrubbing away at their laundry close to a small spring. I smiled, but my overture at friendliness was not returned, so we ignored each other. Perhaps 15 minutes had passed when I suddenly became aware that a large black snake was crossing the road perhaps 25 or 30 yards away. I was instantly off in pursuit, my boots flapping wildly. By diving at the rapidly disappearing snake I managed to grab its tail at the very edge of another thorn thicket, and there we were in a dead heat for the moment. I was prone on the ground, hanging on to the tail, but the snake had so

entwined itself amidst the vegetation that I couldn't pull it out. Isabelle rushed to the rescue and, with my penknife, cut away enough of the thorny growth so I could thread my catch from out of its retreat. We stood there admiring the reptile, a six-foot indigo snake, and for a moment were unaware that the *señor* with the mustache had joined us. He was quite excited, and I had to explain why I had caught the snake, that I intended to take it back to the zoo, and so on. That broke the ice, and the old gentleman then asked me politely if he and his wife could use the bath!

With my best Castilian manners I doffed my hat, bowed at the waist, and muttered the Spanish equivalent of, "Certainly. Be our guests!"

He beamed, but, just as he turned to go, there was a sudden clap of thunder as the daily evening, sometimes violent, electrical storm approached. He paused, stared toward the heavens, thought for a moment, and then with a look of disappointment said, "*Mañana.*"

Isabelle and I chortled for a long time after we watched the Indian couple trudge away, and as we reflected on how our choice of a campsite had inadvertently cheated them out of a bath.

Our *campesino* friends, bless them, had solved one of the basic problems of rural, arid Mexico—the scarcity of water for bathing. The small ponds, where I waded after dark in my search for snakes, were too shallow and muddy for such purposes, and the alkaline waters of the lake were also useless, with or without soap.

At daybreak the next morning it was quite chilly, and we both agreed that surely no one would wish to use the *baño* at that early hour. But we were wrong. Two men came by, and one of them even borrowed a cake of soap from us.

When I absentmindedly stowed some of our gear in the wrong place, Isabelle called my attention to it, and I replied that doubtless I was distracted because my mind was on my new job of "keeper of the bath"!

We were glad to get away from the place, or thought we would be. When we were all packed, we climbed into the cab of our Kamper, but the motor wouldn't start. No amount of tinkering did any good. Finally, we had to be towed ignominiously into Villa Corona for help.

Chapter 38

Fancy Seeing You Here!

It was hot on the Chihuahuan Desert that September afternoon in 1960. The temperature must have been at least 40°C, which translates to 104°F. Also, the humidity was high for that part of the world. The rainy season was nearing its end, but the late-afternoon clouds that produced the almost daily thundershowers, usually just as we were trying to cook our evening meal, had not yet begun to form. The sun shone down mercilessly, and there was no shade in sight. We were driving roughly westward from Ciudad Camargo, in Mexico's State of Chihuahua. Our objective, as usual, was to hunt for natricine snakes (water snakes and their allies), and Lago Toronto, a small lake shown on our road map, seemed a likely place to look, especially at night. The lake was formed by a dam across the Río Conchos.

As we rounded a curve or reached the crest of a hill, I have forgotten which, we noticed an unexpected haven—a grove of trees. Isabelle was at the wheel, and she automatically slowed as we approached. There was a double-wheel track leading into the beckoning copse, but it was blocked by a rope stretched between two posts. I hopped out of the car and released the rope at one end, she drove into the welcome shade, and I replaced the barrier. With the car parked beneath a tree, I immediately placed the short ladder on the side of our Volkswagen Kamper, climbed up, opened our roof-rack load, and handed down our two folding aluminum chairs.

We had scarcely seated ourselves when a truck passed, then stopped and backed up. "University of Utah" was emblazoned on its side. I was up at once and lowered the rope again, the truck parked under another tree, and I greeted John M. Legler, turtle expert of the faculty at Utah. We had visited with him and his family in Salt Lake City. With him was Raymond Lee, a mammalogist. It was time for the old "Fancy seeing you here!" routine. Neither John nor I had known that the other was in Mexico.

We chatted for a few moments and quickly decided we had found a good place to camp. The lake and the river were not too far distant. John wanted to set his turtle traps and Raymond his for small mammals. They

drove a little farther in so we would all have privacy during the night. As I took my temporary leave of them, I turned to face a small, irate, feisty, elderly Mexican sporting a pair of drooping handlebar mustaches. He ordered us all to get out—at once!

My Spanish quickly had a good workout. I gave him my oft-repeated speech about how I was a professor, that we were looking for snakes, and that I had a *permiso* (permit) from the authorities in Mexico City. Isabelle hastened to get it from my briefcase. It was a formidable document. I had fastened colored ribbons and a large "gold" embossing seal to the envelope to make it look all the more impressive. With as graceful a short bow as I could muster, I presented the *permiso* to the angry man and suggested that he read it. He opened the envelope and unfolded the paper, which was in Spanish, of course. He began to read, and very soon large beads of perspiration appeared on his forehead under the brim of his sombrero. He struggled onward, doffed his hat, wiped his forehead with his sleeve, and said, "*Mucho trabajo*" (A lot of work). His education had apparently been minimal, and he seldom had to read anything. He quickly gave in and accepted my statements. Besides, I had my *señora* with me, and he was, after all, a gentleman. Had we known that he would object, I assured him, we would have asked his permission to enter the miniature woods.

But what about the others, in the truck? I told him that they, too, were professors, but he couldn't believe that. They were far too young! Actually, both were professors (probably associates), whereas I was not. I considered myself legitimate in claiming that title, because the Spanish word *profesor* also means "teacher" and, as a curator and lecturer, I surely qualified as that.

The old gentleman calmed down, the "boys" joined us, and we discovered that John Legler's thirtieth birthday was on the morrow. That called for a toast. Isabelle broke out our bottle of tequila, the young men opened their bourbon, which they preferred, and the Mexican had a full jigger from our bottle. He downed it, made a face, muttered, "*Muy fuerte*" (very strong), and refused

We camped in a rare copse in the Chihuahuan Desert, along with friends from the University of Utah (left). Photo by IHC.

a refill. It turned out that he, years earlier, had planted many of the trees, which were nourished by a small permanent desert stream that suddenly appeared from underground, flowed for perhaps 100 feet, and then vanished back into the earth. He also had a tiny flower garden. He lived across the road and considered the copse more or less as his, even though property was sketchily defined in rural Mexico, and water rights, we had been told, were the exclusive property of the government. Our sympathies were strongly with him, however, and he became quite friendly toward us. He even picked two of his precious zinnias and presented them to Isabelle. Later, he brought his grandchildren to see our snakes and turtles.

We found a small stream descending from a cascade a mile or so away, and we decided to concentrate our efforts there. The Utah collectors did fairly well, but the snake hunting was poor. We found only a single garter snake and a rat snake, and Raymond Lee caught the latter.

When we parted the next day, Isabelle and I continued on to Lago Toronto but found it was too new to be productive. The construction of the dam had greatly disturbed the bed of the river (the Río Conchos), and the edge of the lake was still too devoid of vegetation to provide a suitable habitat for snakes.

The Conchos, in a very real sense, forms the boundary between the United States and Mexico. That statement may seem strange but, as I write this, it is indeed the Río Conchos that flows along our southern boundary and onward to the Gulf of Mexico near Brownsville, Texas. The explanation is simple, but I checked it out personally, just to be sure.

The Rio Grande is one of the major streams that developed after the orogeny that uplifted the Rocky Mountains. It has its source in the mountains of Colorado and flows southward across New Mexico. In former years it

continued eastward and eventually flowed into the Gulf. Nowadays the waters of the Rio Grande are tapped for agriculture and for the use of the towns along its course, and they help to recharge the aquifer on which the City of Albuquerque depends. The large reservoirs, Elephant Butte and Caballo, store much of the river's water farther downstream. The demands of two large cities, however, El Paso and Ciudad Juárez, the latter on the Mexican side, normally use every remaining drop of the Rio Grande. The river ceases to flow beyond them, except during unusually rainy seasons or following an exceptionally rapid melting of the snowpack in Colorado and northern New Mexico. Each of the several times that I have checked on the river beyond El Paso, one could walk across dry shod. Theoretically, one could hike along the riverbed, except for occasional seepages and the trickling input from minor tributaries, from the vicinity of El Paso to Ojinaga, Mexico, a distance of roughly 200 miles.

At Ojinaga, the Río Conchos, a former major tributary of the Rio Grande, enters the channel where the main river used to flow, and goes on its way to the Gulf of Mexico. In summary, the Rio Grande now normally flows from Colorado to El Paso before it dries up, whereas the Río Conchos, with its several tributaries, flows from the highlands of northwestern Mexico to Ojinaga, and then to the sea.

The burgeoning population and the concomitant need for more and more water make it virtually certain that many additional dams will be constructed, and the impounded water will be solely for the use of humankind. The Río Conchos eventually may cease to flow and thus will no longer serve as an international boundary. If so, the term "wetbacks" for Mexicans trying to sneak across into the United States would become an archaic anachronism.

After our return to Ciudad Camargo, we headed south, stopped, hunted, and camped at various streams or dams, and eventually reached the Río Nazas near El Palmito. En route we encountered the Utah men several times, but finally parted company with them six days after our first meeting.

Dr. Legler had an interest that closely paralleled mine. The slider turtle inhabiting the Río Nazas system had differentiated from its related subspecies, just as the water snake in the same basin had evolved from other forms of the red-bellied water snake. I described *Natrix* (=*Nerodia*) *erythrogaster bogerti* in 1953, but Legler's preoccupation with his turtle fieldwork and other studies caused him to delay publication until 1990, when he described the Nazas form as *Pseudemys* (=*Trachemys* of many authors) *scripta hartwegi*. It was named in honor of Dr. Norman E. Hartweg, a leading earlier student of turtles. I was pleased to discover that Legler chose a turtle I had trapped in the Nazas on October 2, 1961, as the type specimen. Years later, at almost the identical spot, and while in the company of James D. Anderson and three students, I trapped an enormous female *hartwegi* that had a carapace with a straight-line length of 308 mm (12.25 in.). After making notes and measurements and taking photographs, we liberated the turtle back into the Nazas. The river at that point was, in all probability, a safe habitat. It flowed steadily from water released from the nearby big dam, the Presa Cárdenas, to ensure a continuous supply to the Laguna District well downstream.

It was our practice, Isabelle's and mine, to visit archaeological ruins whenever we passed near them during our numerous peregrinations through Mexico. After all, we worked day and night and put up with the exigencies of camping out. So we felt justified in taking an hour off, now and then, to do a little sightseeing.

When we were in Yucatán in July 1964, we stopped one morning at the famous Mayan Chichén Itzá. We saw the pyramid, the "Castillo," the ball court, and the other ruins that were still standing. When we returned to our car a panel truck was parked near us and it was hand-lettered "John Doe's Herpetological Expedition" on the side. (I use John Doe because I don't remember the owner's name.) Presently, two young men arrived, I introduced myself, and we had a lively conversation for a few minutes. Then one of them said, "This place is sure full of herpetologists." I asked why he made that statement, and he told us they had met three Americans interested in snakes at Nuevo X-Can just over the Yucatán state boundary line, in the then Territory of Quintana Roo. We were told later that a group of shady characters, who were evidently engaged in something illegal, had started a small settlement close to X-Can, Yucatán, but across the line where they were out of reach of the state authorities. Hence the "Nuevo."

We had decided to cross the Yucatán Peninsula in any event, and the two X-Cans were right on our way. We arrived during the afternoon and made inquiries about anyone who (we guessed) might be buying snakes, dead or alive. Everyone knew where they were, and presently we found an abandoned road-building camp that was a palatial place to stay in comparison with some of the miserable sites we had used during our travels. There were four thatch-roofed buildings with low, waist-high sides, and raised on stilts. Three occupied hammocks, each protected by mosquito netting, were hanging, and all was silent. Earlier, as we were driving eastward, I had recalled that the National Science Foundation had

asked me, a few months previously, to review an application for a grant submitted by T. Paul Maslin for fieldwork on the peninsula, and I had heartily recommended it. So I wasn't surprised to see a University of Colorado truck parked nearby. I hesitated to disturb the obvious siesta, but one of the group suddenly poked his head out of his netting. I asked, "Is this Paul Maslin's outfit?" The answer was "Yes," and out stepped Jack McCoy, one of Dr. Maslin's students who later became the distinguished herpetologist at the Carnegie Museum in Pittsburgh. Also with them was Gary Knopf, another student. They all stirred from their hammocks and greeted us warmly, but they obviously were embarrassed by their unkempt appearance—unshaved faces, soiled, skimpy, sweaty clothes, and other signs of fieldwork. We told them not to apologize. We would have looked much the same, except that we had spent the previous night in a motel.

After chatting awhile, Isabelle and I drove on to Puerto Juárez and had our first glimpse of the Caribbean Sea. The Isla Mujeres glimmered in the hazy distance. The town itself was just a collection of shacks. We bought ice, gasoline, and two large bottles of beer as a treat for our friends, and were back at Nuevo X-Can before dark. What a transformation. All three had shaved and donned clean clothes, no doubt for Isabelle's benefit. We all ate together. While Isabelle and Paul cleaned up, chatted, and adjusted their cameras, the two students took me road-cruising for a couple of hours, but we had no luck. How I wish I could have found a cantil, *Agkistrodon bilineatus*, because of my great interest in its genus. When we returned, we downed our beer, and then to bed. Our Kamper was parked nearby.

Our friends from Boulder decided to move to another location. As usual, in all parts of Mexico, the residents of both X-Cans came to stare at the gringos, especially the young people who had been catching snakes and lizards for a small reward for each specimen. They acted as though they were full-fledged members of the Maslin expedition. There were at least two dozen persons in our audience at suppertime, and almost as many at breakfast.

We packed up, said our farewells, and were off on our way back across the Peninsula shortly after 9:00 A.M. We rolled along for quite a distance without incident, when all of a sudden our car began to buck and the engine stalled. We were right on the road. Like so many Mexican highways in the 1960s there was no shoulder, only a rather steep embankment. There was no place to push our car out of the way. Fortunately, there were very few passing vehicles. Soon a jeepload of Mexicans pulled up behind us, and they offered to help. One was a mechanic. He tried everything he could think of, and finally concluded, perhaps a half hour later, that we were out of gas. Miraculously for us, the University of Colorado truck came along. Our friends had a reserve five-gallon can of gas. I tipped the would-be helper, gas was poured into our car, and off we went to stop at a service station in Valladolid. There we filled up, replenished the five-gallon can, and said "many thanks" and then "good-bye" all over again.

How in the world could we have run out of gas? We had filled up at Puerto Juárez, and I had watched the attendant. Years earlier I had learned to keep an eye on gas pumps. It was a favorite trick to allow the gauge to remain where a previous customer had paid for it, add the required amount in one's car, and then soak the unwary for the entire amount. I am convinced that the fellow who cheated us at Puerto Juárez used some sort of legerdemain to send the gasoline to a container of his own and not into our Kamper. Or perhaps he had tinkered with the gauge on the pump so that it registered even though no gasoline was passing through it. How he did it, I'll never know. Our tank had no leak in it.

Two nights later we were back at the Hotel Margón in Coatzacoalcos, Veracruz, which we had used several times as a base for excursions to the adjacent lowlands and across the Isthmus of Tehuantepec and to Chiapas. The desk clerk, who knew us by sight, told us that a man from Philadelphia was looking for us. It turned out to be David Cutler, a well-known birder whom I had met a few times. He wanted to add some Mexican birds to his life list. We had dinner with him, and he ate and drank everything, saying that he didn't bother with the various precautions that physicians and tourist agents talked about. He was a chastened young man when he came to us the next morning to see if we had anything with which to combat dysentery.

We met two other Americans in Taxco, back in 1949, but they were only chance acquaintances. George Holton, son of Oliver W. Holton, who gave me my first zoo job, had been a tiny lad when last I saw him. Dick Vieth went from Taxco to Acapulco with us, and it was a real pleasure to run into him again at Uruapan near the Volcán Parícutin.

We met Chuck Bogert and his wife, Mickey, in Mexico several times, both at Lake Chapala and far south in Oaxaca, but our visits with them were planned ahead of time. There was one exception, however. On our way home in 1959, we stopped overnight at Zacatecas, which boasted only one motel. We had carried our livestock and a tote bag or two into our room. When I went out again to get something else I noticed that a car had pulled in across the court, and Mickey Bogert, with her

back more or less toward me, had the trunk open and was leaning into it. I walked over and asked, "*¿Quisiera ayuda?*" (Do you want help?), and to that she replied, "*No, gracias.*" She then turned to face me. Because I had grown a beard to add a little authenticity to the old-timers' pageant we were to have at the Philadelphia Zoo after our return, she was a little slow recognizing me—until I spoke again. Chuck had told us she was on her way to Chapala to join him, but we certainly hadn't expected to see her in Zacatecas! We had dinner with her and the lady with whom she was traveling.

In 1969 we were working in the Big Bend region of Texas, trying to fill in the gap between our field guide and the western one written by Robert C. Stebbins. We were there for a month, and, after two weeks, it became necessary to drive the 100 miles to Alpine, from our headquarters in the Big Bend National Park, to get additional food supplies. As we walked along a street in the town, I noticed a sign on an office reading "Kenneth K. Otto, Certified Public Accountant." I did a double-take and went inside. I asked if Mr. Otto was in, and with that he appeared at the door of an inner office.

"Did you study accounting at the University of Pennsylvania?" I inquired.

"Yes," he replied.

"Did you have a roommate who played the baritone horn with you in the band?"

"Yes," he repeated, and with that I extended my hand and said, "Hello, Kenny. I'm Roger Conant."

We had a nostalgic reunion. In addition to his CPA he had earned a law degree, but he had moved to a dry climate because of a health problem. It had been more than 30 years since we had seen each other.

During the late summer and autumn of 1968 we spent seven glorious weeks in Africa. One night we stayed in the tent camp at the Amboseli Game Reserve. It was in Kenya but faced Tanzania, where giant Mount Kilimanjaro, the highest peak of the so-called Dark Continent, towered far into the sky. Meals were served in a large tent, and Isabelle and I had just finished our supper and were walking out when we met Leonard J. and Carol Goss coming in with their two children. He was the Director of the Cleveland Zoo. That was another time for "Fancy seeing you here!" Or was it? They were having a look at the fabulous African wildlife, but they were actually on their way to attend the conference of the International Union of Directors of Zoological Gardens in Pretoria, South Africa, just as we were. We should have expected to see zoo people. In fact, when we boarded the airplane in Nairobi to fly to Johannesburg, there were several zoo directors aboard who had flown down from Europe.

I've had other chance encounters far from home. With my present wife Kathryn, I had short, pleasant, totally unexpected visits with Walter and Eleanor Auffenberg in both Madras and Bombay, in India, during our trip to the Orient in 1984. Three years later we were eating lunch in a hotel on Hong Kong Island when a man walked up to our table and asked, "Are you Dr. Conant?" It was Charlie McDaniel, one of our neighbors in Tucson.

Chapter 39

Nostalgic Memories of Mexico

As I assemble these recollections, memories of our fieldwork in Mexico are major components. How Isabelle was awakened very early one morning when a small boy thrust a wet toad into her hand. How we discovered an enormous colony of garter snakes sunning themselves on the rocks at water's edge along the century-old causeway crossing the Lago de Cuitzeo. How I stumbled onto one of the legendary "balls of snakes" during an evening near Magdalena. How we fought off the old man who filled our gas tank, at the remote La Zarca, to stop him from wiping our windshield with a dirty, oily rag. The piecemeal year my devoted wife and I spent working together in the countryside of Mexico still stands as the quintessence of fun, adventure, and excitement during a busy lifetime.

Here I record a miscellaneous assortment, presented in no special order, of some of our experiences during those truly wonderful days of 30-odd years ago.

In the early 1960s any town of consequence in Mexico had at least one *mercado*. Not a supermarket, because that modern innovation had scarcely as yet penetrated south of the border. They were old-fashioned markets, like those in vogue during my youth, and, indeed, even in Philadelphia's Reading Terminal Market throughout my long period of service in that city's zoo. Stalls were occupied by men or women who featured their own produce, meat, fish, handicrafts, and a variety of other saleable items. Some of the Mexican markets were small, but the large city of Monterrey sported a huge one where one could buy anything from a carrot or lemon to goatskin rugs or heavy, handwoven *sarapes*.

It was outside the latter *mercado* where we met the first of the enterprising boys who wheedled pesos from tourists. We parked outside, and four lads, all about 10 years of age, approached. Each pulled down one of his lower eyelids, and said, "Watch your car, meestair?" I designated one, and, sure enough, when we returned an hour later, he was sitting on our front bumper. Other boys, equipped with buckets of water and filthy rags, wanted to wash the car. At Pemex gas stations they courted tips by wiping off our windshield, which they invariably smeared if I let them do it. At some of the larger, more popular stations there might be a half dozen boys, all vying for the job. In such cases I would guard the front of the car as our tank was filled, and then I would toss several coins as far as I could. As the boys scrambled after them, we would drive away. The old man at La Zarca was the worst. His miniature Pemex stop was in the middle of nowhere, and his tips were therefore few. We had to fill up with him several times for the long round trip to the distant Río Nazas and its dam, the Presa Cárdenas. I finally told him I would pay him *not* to wipe the windshield.

We often had help with our fieldwork. In the interest of good public relations and to assure our personal safety we found it expedient to make friends with the natives wherever we camped. In the remote districts nearly all of them were Indians, the men clad in simple shirts and trousers, often barefoot but never without a sombrero. They readily accepted the fact that here were a "professor" and his wife catching snakes for study. Many of them cooperated with a will, especially after they saw us handle a snake or two and we offered a small reward for specimens in good condition. One group of Indian boys in Nayarit fell to with such enthusiasm that we had an abundance of material from their locality, and I had to sneak back to their village by the river at night to liberate a score of turtles we didn't need, but which had to be purchased to maintain goodwill. In another tiny Indian village we left some snake bags behind and announced we would come back the next day to buy any snakes or lizards they could catch or provide in good condition. We knew that they would use their slingshots, and that I would probably have to preserve most of their "catch" at once.

When we returned as promised, near dusk, the appearance of our vehicle caused great excitement, and small boys converged on us from all directions, their bare heels flashing as they first ran to their adobe huts to gather up their treasures. Chances are that the few pesos they earned represented their total cash income for the summer. It was also profitable for me, because

210

they provided a good series of whiptail lizards, *Cnemidophorus*, a genus that was then under intensive study by several herpetologists. My "pickled" specimens from a remote part of Mexico, which I promptly gave to the American Museum of Natural History, were more than welcome.

Adults were a little less enthusiastic about handling snakes, but one elderly Indian came into camp at night dragging a six-foot boa constrictor at the end of a rope fashioned from a vine. It was quite dead, having been run over on the road, and it was far too large to preserve in any container available to us, but we paid him two pesos for it, and he went away happy and satisfied.

Any expedition to a primitive part of the world, even a man-and-wife team, inevitably finds itself in close contact with the native peoples, and talking with them and learning about their thoughts and habits is one of the most interesting experiences that can accrue while in the field. Whenever we stopped near villages we were at once the center of attraction. Sometimes the entire population would turn out to gaze at us and our house on wheels. After a few minutes the curiosity of most adults would be satisfied, and they would leave us. But not so the children, and often a male loafer or two. They remained to stare—by the hour. At first it was disconcerting, but we soon grew so used to it that we thought nothing of eating, washing our faces, brushing our teeth, and doing a multitude of other daily chores for an audience of one to a dozen or more.

Because we had our "house" with us, we were often asked, "Where are your children?" We parried that question by replying, "*Somos abuelos*" (We are grandparents).

From among the boys we recruited our collectors, but sometimes their eagerness was almost painful. One morning, near a river in Zacatecas, Isabelle awakened early to discover that several children had been waiting patiently for some sign of life in our microbus. They rushed up at once and a boy handed her a large toad, for which they demanded payment at the prearranged price of 20 centavos (almost two cents). While she groped for her pocketbook she nudged me awake to find a bag in which to deposit the specimen. She commented afterward that she could think of better ways to be awakened than by having a wet toad thrust into her hand.

The children remained to stare at us. We dressed behind the car curtains, but, when I opened the sliding side door, I could see a girl of seven or eight holding a baby. The infant was sucking on a piece of tortilla, which it dropped onto a nearly dry cow pie. The sister-nurse picked it up and restored it to the baby's mouth. Oh well, such primitive living may have helped the sibling-in-arms to develop early immunities.

On the few occasions when our path took us back to villages where we had been during the previous year, we were greeted as long-lost friends. When we helped the people they repaid us in kind, as was forcefully impressed upon us in Durango at the Río Melones, a beautiful mountain stream that flows through a deep gorge surmounted by volcanic rocks. To reach the water it was necessary to drive down an exceptionally steep and rocky dirt road from the highway that crossed the valley via a high-level bridge. We were using our station wagon on that trip. Sometime after our arrival at the bottom, a truck came down, but, when its native driver attempted later to start his motor, it was obvious he was out of gas. After some hesitation he approached us for help, and we obligingly drove him to a nearby town where he purchased a few liters of gasoline, although in the process we barely made it up the steep grade. Our friend departed after getting his truck running, but we remained so we could search for snakes after dark.

Late that evening we started up the rough road again, confident this time that we could drive fast enough to maintain our forward momentum, for headlights stabbing through the darkness would warn us of any cars approaching on the highway. Alas, as we reached the very crest of the grade, our own headlights picked up a string of mules and wagons passing through the night. We hesitated for an instant, lost our headway, and stalled. Backing in the blackness to the bottom of such a horrible road for a fresh start was out of the question, but when we tried to go forward, released the hand brake, and let up on the clutch, we immediately stalled again. After a few such attempts young men began appearing from nowhere. They placed rocks under our rear wheels and put their shoulders against the car. We inched ahead, stalling repeatedly, but finally, with great sighs of relief, pulled out on the paved roadway. My hand went to my wallet immediately, but not a person would accept the smallest tip. We had befriended one of them during the afternoon, and they were happy to save us from a bad predicament as a small token of their gratitude.

Whenever we drove at night, as, for example, to avoid the high heat of the desert, we progressed slowly, seldom exceeding 30 miles an hour, and usually going much slower. We carefully watched the road, and rather often we saw snakes or toads on the pavement. Sometimes they were alive and active, but more frequently they had been run over, later to form food for foxes by night or vultures by day, or to be picked up by itinerant herpetologists like ourselves. Surprisingly, many of the defunct specimens were in sufficiently good condition to be preserved for future study. By watching diligently for specimens on the road we accumulated an imposing

lot of rarities and range extensions for the use of fellow naturalists. Also, some of the toads we picked up, as well as the more common species of frogs, when we could get them, made it possible for me to feed our traveling serpentine menagerie fairly regularly.

Sometimes at night we were thrilled by the sight of other animals, most often rodents. We also saw kit foxes and jaguarundis and the more familiar raccoons and opossums, and even a four-eyed opossum, a curious member of the group which gets its name from a light patch of hair above each eye. Almost every night when we were encamped in near-wilderness areas we heard the yapping of coyotes, usually within an hour after sundown. Many times we saw coyotes on the open plains and deserts, and once, thrill of thrills, a half-grown puma ran across the road in front of us during the late afternoon. It sat down under a Joshua tree to watch us pass, but we slammed on our brakes, and it took to its heels as we squealed to a stop.

We normally didn't take firearms with us, but at Lake Pátzcuaro in Michoacán, we needed something to shoot with, and needed it badly. That high, isolated lake is almost completely bordered by tall stands of rushes that are impenetrable by boat, and great floating mats of dead rushes of the same species sometimes extend 50 feet out into the lake. On the mats we saw large numbers of basking garter snakes, *Thamnophis eques*, a species that looks and behaves like a water snake. They were inactive at night, and since we could neither walk upon nor maneuver a boat through the rafts of vegetation without alarming every living thing, the snakes might as well have been in the next state insofar as orthodox methods of collecting were concerned. Obviously we needed a gun, so we hired a gunner and stepped 100 years back into history.

The weapon was a muzzle-loading carbine of a type

that was still widely used in rural Mexico. First we poured in a measured amount of black powder and then tamped down a wad that we manufactured ourselves from rope ravelings. Then came the birdshot, followed by another wad, and the whole was tamped tight with a ramrod. Then the percussion cap was applied, and the carbine was ready to fire. The teen-aged lad who manned it was a crack shot, and we soon had all the specimens I wanted. Dead reptiles don't flee, and we could work our boat far enough into the floating rushes to lift the snakes off with a pole.

Mexican plumbing was often an enigma, even a nuisance, especially in some of the smaller hostelries we patronized after a week or so of camping in the boon-

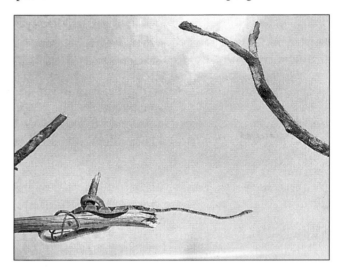

docks. Although our Kamper was outfitted to make us almost self-sufficient, it was good to have a hot shower now and then.

The most common problem was the water faucets. In the 1960s, most of them had been imported from the United States, where the letter "C" stood for cold and "H" for hot. In Spanish, however, "C" meant *caliente* (hot), and "F" was for *frío* (cold). The American manufacturers supplied faucets with an "F" on them, but there were frequent mixups. The Mexican plumbers, many of them unskilled "do-it-yourselfers," apparently paid little attention to the letters. We encountered every possible combination, even including a "C" on both hot and cold. To make matters more confusing, the hot water was often on the right instead of the customary left side. We quickly learned to test temperatures very carefully.

Another custom, which we never quite understood, was mounting the toilet directly adjacent to the shower. There were no tubs. Even when there was a shower curtain, which there often was not, the john was bound to get wet. The water spattered on the floor and sometimes flooded the entire bathroom if the drain was sluggish.

Most exasperating of all was to have the hot water turn cold all of a sudden, or, even worse, stop running altogether. I can recall two times when one of us had to go to the Kamper and draw a small pail of water to rinse off the other.

We tried our best to stay at places recommended by the American Automobile Association, but its list was skimpy, compared with the lengthy one of today. Not every town boasted a hostelry qualified to meet the specifications of the AAA inspector. Sometimes, even at recommended hotels and motels, plumbing troubles developed.

Josefina L. Myers was a godsend, and we met her by

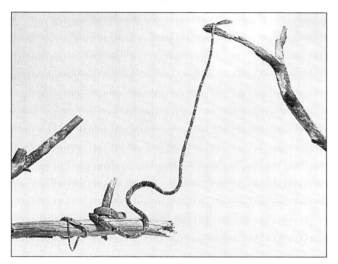

sheer chance. Late during the afternoon of August 27, 1961, we were nearing the Lago de Chapala, by far the largest lake in Mexico. It is more than 50 miles long and at an elevation of almost 5,000 feet. We knew we probably could find overnight accommodations at the bustling resort of Chapala, but we wondered if there might be someplace closer. Isabelle was at the wheel, so I dug out our AAA tour book and was surprised to find that the Granja Azul (the Blue Farmhouse) was listed from Jocotepec at the western end of the lake. We had trouble finding it, because darkness descended and it was well outside-of-town. It had several spotlessly clean cabins, to one of which we were promptly escorted. What an oasis from noise. It was very quiet. No sounds of human voices. No blaring jukeboxes that were so commonly heard. Mexico was a noisy country in general.

The next morning we discovered that we were in beautifully kept grounds, and we had breakfast in a spacious, very clean dining room. There we met Josefina, a lady of 77, who managed the place for the owner. It was adjacent to a large, impeccable bottling plant where

Roca Azul (Blue Rock) mineral water was prepared for sale all over the country. At the time we were the only customers, and Señora Myers introduced herself in perfect English, and asked if she could sit with us. She had lived in Indiana for many years but, when her American husband died, she returned to her native Mexico. She was eager to converse in English, and she helped us in all sorts of ways. She assured us that the water, which came from deep wells, was safe to drink. A new brand of Mexican margarine was also safe, she told us, and it was to relieve us from having to dab mayonnaise on bread and rolls to alleviate their dryness. We carried small jars of mayonnaise with us, but as soon as one was opened we had to keep it on ice. Ditto the margarine, which we bought at the first opportunity, but what an improvement it was.

Josefina told us about a weaver in Jocotepec, named Mendoza, who was noted for his white (actually light gray) *sarapes*. His was a cottage industry with carding equipment, spinning wheels, and looms right in his house. As so often happened, we had to make inquiries before we found him. A boy climbed into the front seat with us, and acted as our guide. We bought some of Señor Mendoza's beautiful products, and two of them are still used as large throw rugs in the master bedroom of our home in Albuquerque.

The food at the Granja Azul was excellent, and we would have liked to have tarried for several days, mean-

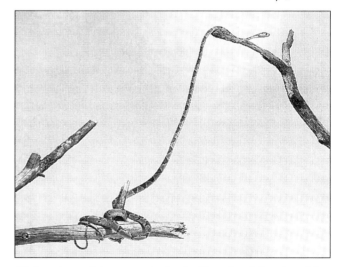

We found two of the extremely slender blunt-headed snakes of the genus Imantodes *on roads at night during our wanderings in Mexico, but Isabelle's best photographs were of an adult* I. cenchoa *about a yard long from Panama. They show how it could hold itself stiff and rigid, seemingly indefinitely. The snake hooked its neck over the upper branch, moved slowly forward, and gradually transferred its body and tail to the upper perch. These pictures were used in* Life *magazine and several other publications.*

time snake hunting in and near the lake, but we had a schedule to meet. We were destined to return twice in later years, however, and the last time Josefina arranged for us to rent a cottage in Jocotepec, where we stayed for a month in 1965. From there we made excursions to several nearby lakes and rivers and short camping trips to the hot, humid lowlands of the Pacific coast. At "home" behind the waving fronds of banana trees it was always springlike. Our maximum-minimum thermometer recorded up to 76°F, and down to 64°F, the total range of temperature for the entire month. The place had a living room and bedroom, a kitchenette, and a tiny bathroom. Early each morning a small boy arrived with a great bag of corncobs, used them to fill a primitive heater under a tank of water, and poured on a bit of *petróleo* (it looked like used crankcase oil to me). He then lit it with a match. That gave us hot water, enough for one shower or to wash the dishes. We could also heat our own water in the kitchen.

We kept in touch with Josefina, exchanging Christmas cards and an occasional letter with her until she was 88. The last four years we wrote in care of one of her nieces. After that there was no response, and we concluded that she had died.

The Cuatro Ciénegas Bolsón (basin) in Coahuila had an extraordinary assemblage of aquatic and semiquatic organisms, both vertebrate and invertebrate, that attracted the attention of many systematists and zoogeographers. There were amazingly strong evidences of endemism (species known only from and restricted to the immediate area), which indicated that the basin had been isolated from outside influences for a very long time. Cuatro Ciénegas means "four swamps," which is a misnomer. Actually, there were a considerable number of clear springs welling up through the very arid, treeless gypsum desert floor. The outflowing water from the springs formed many small marshes, or *ciénagas*, as well as a few short streams. Before settlement times the water never left the basin, and most of it evaporated into the atmosphere. The fauna included the unique aquatic box turtle, *Terrapene coahuila*, and water snakes, the subjects of my major interest.

Early during the twentieth century the waters of the *bolsón* were tapped for use in the steel mills of Monclova, many miles to the east. A serious erosion of the environment began almost at once. Canals were dug, and the water was channeled through them and existing streams, or parts thereof. Many of the organisms living in the Río Salado-Río Sabinas system, which empties into the Rio Grande well south of Laredo, Texas, were able to work their way upstream, thus breaching the unique isolation of the basin.

We first visited the area in 1960, and, in the Río Nadadores, the stream flowing through the eastern portal of the Cuatro Ciénegas Bolsón, I caught a number of blotched and diamond-backed water snakes, as well as a ribbon snake more than a meter in total length. Douglas A. Rossman subsequently chose it as the type specimen for his new subspecies, the arid land ribbon snake, *Thamnophis proximus diabolicus*.

We drove onward to the tiny town of Cuatro Ciénegas, where we received vague and inadequate instructions on how to find one of the "swamps." We started along a dirt road, but before we reached a crossing, a freight train stopped with the locomotive blocking our passage. We waited in the broiling sun for half an hour, and then I walked over and asked the engineer how long he expected to be. He replied that he didn't know, but he looked back along each side of his train, blew his loud whistle, and obligingly backed up the whole string of cars for us!

We were gone an hour, traversing a horrible road, and we failed to find any indication of water. When the going became virtually impossible, we retraced our route and found that the train was still where it had been. We crossed the tracks, and Isabelle thought she should take a picture of me and the engineer together. So I climbed up into his cab with him. He asked why we had gone to the other side of the tracks and, rather than try to explain our true objective, I simply told him that we were taking pictures. I gave him a generous *propina* for his kindness. An hour later, on the road leading out of the *bolsón* and which was paralleled by the railroad, we stopped while trying to find a round-tailed horned lizard, *Phrynosoma modestum*, which had literally vanished by flattening itself on the ground. We heard the train whistle, glanced up, and saw the engineer waving at us. We waved back, and he blew his whistle in response. His train soon disappeared through the eastern portal of the basin, through which we passed soon afterward.

Two years later we returned to the Cuatro Ciénegas Bolsón, armed with an excellent, although preliminary map showing the location of the many springs, or *posos*, as they were known locally. The map had been drafted by Wendell L. Minckley and Robert R. Miller, who very kindly gave me a copy. We also had instructions to hunt up José "Pepe" Lugo, the little town's "water commissioner." He had helped other visiting naturalists, and he joined us with enthusiasm, first stopping to gather up his swim trunks and face mask for peering under water. He took us to Becerra, a rather large pond formed by springs, and which served as the recreation area for the townspeople. They had erected a small building with

Pepe Lugo (left) and RC setting turtle traps in Becerra, one of the large ponds formed by upwelling in the harsh gypsum desert of Cuatro Ciénegas, Coahuila. We caught several turtles, but Becerra was drained to supply more water for the steel mills of Monclova about a year or so later. Photo by IHC.

two separate changing rooms, and there was also a concrete picnic table under a ramada to supply a tiny amount of shade. Concrete steps led down into the pond, which had a sandy bottom and was well populated with fishes and turtles. We changed and went swimming. The water tasted slightly salty, and it was tepid. The moment we stepped out of it, however, the strong winds cooled us rapidly through evaporation. My traps, which Pepe helped me set, yielded several sliders, now known as *Trachemys scripta taylori*, an endemic subspecies, and also two softshells of different kinds. One was *Trionyx* (=*Apalone*) *ater*, another endemic, but one that was already on its way to oblivion. It was interbreeding with the spiny softshell that apparently invaded the *bolsón* by moving headward from the Río Salado, evidently using the canals, probably soon after they were constructed. It was quite likely that the water snakes also arrived via the same route.

We camped at Becerra, but decided to avoid it on the next day, a Sunday, when we knew it would be swarming with people. Pepe told us about the Poso Escobeda, which was not too far away, and where, he said, people almost never went. We drove over a very bad road to reach it, and, when we arrived, we found no shade whatsoever. Only a small, broken-down old building with no roof, and a scraggly single tree visible some distance away. Escobeda was an almost circular, crystal-clear spring, much like some of those we had seen in Florida. It was salty, however, even more so, we thought, than Becerra. I learned much later that it was 30 meters

(almost 100 feet) in diameter and 8 meters (about 26 feet) deep. On that afternoon of July 7, 1962, the temperature was 110°F and an ovenlike breeze was blowing hard. Because I wanted to look for water snakes at night in the overflow that had been channelized years earlier, Isabelle and I endured the heat. We managed by swimming in the tepid water in our shirts and underwear, and then sitting on newspapers in the Kamper with all the doors, windows, and the roof vent wide open. Evaporation cooled us, but we had to swim at least once each hour. The ordeal was worth it, because after dark I caught a large blotched water snake that later gave birth to young, and, in the beam of my headlamp, I also saw an unusually large diamond-backed water snake across a broad swampy spot where I couldn't get at it.

While we were in the *bolsón* we trapped successfully for sliders in the Poso San Marcos, and we watched aquatic box turtles swimming and walking on the bottom of small streams fed by some of the springs. We found the Río Cañon, a freshwater rivulet that flowed from a spring north of the town of Cuatro Ciénegas, and supplied the needs of the residents.

We were enthralled by the uniqueness of the area, and I subsequently read all I could about it and the many new species, especially among the molluscs and fishes, that had been or were still waiting to be described in the scientific literature. We heartily endorsed the suggestion, from several colleagues who specialized in other disciplines, that the entire *bolsón* should be set aside and protected as a living laboratory for years of intensive study.

RC bagged a black-bellied garter snake, Thamnophis melanogaster, *just as the wind blew the container open. South shore of the Lago de Cuitzeo, Michoacán, August 16, 1960. Photo by IHC.*

Alas, it was not to be. More canals were dug, and even Becerra was drained in December 1964. Thus was destroyed the recreation spot that was so important to the people who lived in that very hot and dry environment. The needs of industry were far more important than the welfare of a comparatively small number of desert dwellers. Who cared what happened to the unique species of the *bolsón,* which had a greater concentration of endemism than any other place in the Western Hemisphere? What good were they, anyway? Unhappily, that is the attitude worldwide of vast numbers of human beings who have no knowledge of our biological treasures, and care not a whit about the future. It is not solely a Mexican viewpoint. I've heard that same stupid question asked, *ad nauseum,* in the United States for decades.

An important spinoff of our intensive concentration on water snakes was a burgeoning interest in the garter snakes, *Thamnophis,* that shared the same habitats. They were much wider ranging than the water snakes, and often occurred in quite small bodies of water. With my deep interest in zoogeography, as well as herpetology, I began to specialize, at least secondarily, on the three species of *Thamnophis*—*eques, melanogaster,* and *rufipunctatus*—that behaved like water snakes. Indeed, all were called water snakes, or *culebras de agua,* on the respective sides of the border. During our last two years of support from the National Science Foundation, we devoted most of our time to them.

The Lago de Cuitzeo was once a large lake, second in

size in Mexico only to the Lago de Chapala. Unlike the latter, which is regularly recharged by the Río Lerma, the largest tributary of the Lago de Cuitzeo had long been tapped as the water supply for the City of Morelia, the capital of the State of Michoacán. What water remained, and also that from another tributary, was largely diverted for agriculture. As a result, the lake had shrunk to a fraction of its original size, and the remaining water was quite shallow and concentrated along the lake's southern shore. The lake bed was so nearly flat that we drove right onto its dry northern side, and used it as an excellent campsite during both of our overnight visits. The altitude was sufficiently high for us to need all our blankets.

In the early morning, after one of our stops, we drove to the southern end of the lake, and I began lifting rocks and finding a few specimens of *Thamnophis.* When we turned our attention to the eastern side of the century-old causeway that crossed the lake from north to south, we witnessed the sight of a lifetime. Hundreds of garter snakes, of two species (*eques* and *melanogaster*), were sunning themselves on the rocks at the water's edge! Never, ever, anywhere, had we witnessed such a vast aggregation of reptiles, all in sight in the open at the same time. When we peered over the stone balustrade along the causeway, some of the snakes took alarm and retreated into cracks in the masonry below us. They vanished even more rapidly when I climbed down and tried to walk along the rough uneven rocks.

There was an abundant supply of small fishes to serve as food for the snakes and to support a minor industry. I excerpt the following from Isabelle's diary of August 5, 1964:

> *The lake is very shallow and the fishermen wade out with a flat-bottomed, dugout canoe and a long net of very small mesh. They catch tiny fish of three sizes, then spread them out on the shoulder of the causeway to dry. This takes 24 hours and, if it rains, the fishes must be gathered up to keep them dry. They are respread when the sun shines. The dried product is sold in Morelia to be used with tortillas in making tacos and enchiladas, and some are also canned. A kilo [2.2 pounds] sells for 18 pesos [or $2.25 in American money, at the then-current exchange rate]. Roger was told that these little fishes are more in demand than the Pátzcuaro white fish, which are larger.*

We discovered that garter snakes were also abundant in other isolated lakes, or what was left of them, but we never found such huge numbers as we did at the Lago de Cuitzeo. There are many stories I could tell about our experiences with *Thamnophis,* but I'd have to write two or three more chapters to do so. One encounter was so unexpected and so exciting, however, that I must set it down on paper.

When I was a lad living with my grandparents, I had a farm-raised uncle who delighted in regaling me with misinformation about snakes. He knew all the stories. How they "charmed" birds, how they rolled like a hoop, and how they wouldn't die until sundown. Another of his tales was about balls of snakes, and how they would pile up, always squirming toward the center of the pile. I was to learn from personal observation and notes in the literature that such congregations of serpents have a sexual basis, as many males seek to mate with one or more receptive females. During fieldwork in the United States, I had seen up to a dozen water snakes (*Nerodia*) clustered together on two occasions, but certainly not in balls. They were all males except for one female in each case. Nonetheless, I was unprepared for what happened at Magdalena, Jalisco, on the evening of August 30, 1961.

We had heard that there were lots of snakes near that town, so when we were in the vicinity we pulled off the highway onto a dirt side road, and I walked down a small hill to reconnoiter. I peered into a culvert, and it was literally crawling with large garter snakes. I ran back to the car, grabbed a longer collecting hook, excitedly told Isabelle there were at least 20 in the culvert, and asked her to bring a bag and to come and help me. It was a long reach downward, but I succeeded in hooking out one of them, which Isabelle promptly captured when it landed near her. The others vanished into the adjacent drainpipes.

As so often happened during our sojourns in Mexico, boys seemed to be drawn as though by a magnet whenever gringos did something unusual. Three teenagers appeared almost at once, and they knew a place nearby where they had seen many snakes. They were right. All were Mexican garter snakes, *Thamnophis eques*. The odds were good that we could do better at night, so I thanked and rewarded our guides, and we found a place to pull off the main road a mile or so west of town.

After fixing and eating supper, and attending to various chores, we headed back at dusk. We should have known. Two of the boys were waiting for us. I must have said something to tip them off that we would return. We took them along, and because they had seen me grabbing the snakes with my bare hands, they followed suit, and soon had caught several more.

We worked upstream in a fairly broad irrigation ditch in which water was flowing slowly. One boy walked along each bank and I waded up the middle, knee-deep in my hip boots. Meantime, Isabelle, depending on the brilliant starlight, drove the darkened car along the traffic-free road paralleling us. We worked our way toward a small bridge that crossed the canal. During the afternoon, we had noted a ledge beneath it on which the water was shallow. The boys were quite excited. I had loaned each one a flashlight, and they searched eagerly and caught two or three snakes along each bank.

When we neared the bridge and my headlamp strongly illuminated the ledge, I gasped with astonishment. There was a huge ball of large garter snakes right in front of me.

I shouted, "*¡Espere!*" (Wait!), but there was no holding back the boys. They rushed in, getting soaking wet in the process, and, because my chance of making careful observations on the slowly writhing snakes was lost, I literally fell on the pile. I seized two snakes in each hand and there were four more under me. The boys accounted for a few others. Once we had disturbed them, the other snakes beat hasty retreats in all directions. Isabelle and I independently estimated there were at least 50 snakes in the ball. It was perhaps two feet wide and half as high.

How much better it would have been if we had been alone! The snakes were probably so intent on their sexual activity that I could have made copious notes. There even might have been time for Isabelle to get out and assemble her camera and the flashbulbs we used in those days. From my position in midstream I could easily have obtained pictures. I was deeply disappointed. The eight snakes I caught were all males, but the boys had dumped their catch in with the others taken previously, which, in all probability, included both sexes. When I checked their bags, both males and females were present.

I lost a marvelous opportunity, and I regretted it, but my folklore-loving uncle had been right on one point. There were such things as balls of snakes.

We walked back along the same ditch in August 1964, but we saw nothing spectacular. In the company of James D. Anderson and his student, Robert Giacosie, we also were there on July 7, 1965, coincidental with the first heavy rain of the season. Frogs and toads of many species were emerging from estivation in great numbers on the nearby flats, and scores of snakes were gorging themselves on the sudden bonanza.

Our memories of Mexico were legion. We traveled so far and did so much—in every state and territory and in the Federal District. We often talked about our adventures and reviewed Isabelle's pictures together, even during her long terminal illness. Now she has left us, but I still have her precious diaries. She was an ace reporter for the "Staten Island Advance," a daily newspaper, during her early adult years, and her descriptive prose is a joy to read. She commented in depth about the *campesinos* and *indios* we met—their behavior, their curiosity, and their poverty. She truly caught the flavor of rural Mexico of the early 1960s. As for us, she often hilariously remarked about our less desirable campsites and unexpected hardships.

Her writing brings to mind a multitude of cherished recollections of our fieldwork together, often under harsh and difficult conditions. How we drove across roadless deserts or in the mud. How we always cooked our meals outside the car, even in the pouring rain, so there would be no chance of starting a fire inside. How losing our vehicle in some isolated spot might be fatal.

How we fought clouds of flies and mosquitoes. How we tried to find a modicum of privacy in the countryside, where our very arrival was an event of importance to people who almost never saw a foreigner, let alone a house on wheels. What a stout companion she was. She ran the camp, although I worked hard and did all I could to help. In a very real sense she made our trips and my research possible, just as she made an extremely important contribution to our field guides. What a pal, what a soulmate, what a devoted wife.

Isabelle is and always will be the shining star in my own nostalgic memories of Mexico.

Chapter 40

Closing the Gap:
Part I. Off to Trans-Pecos Texas

"A Field Guide to Reptiles and Amphibians of the United States and Canada East of the 100th Meridian" was out at last. It was number 12 in the Roger Tory Peterson Field Guide series. Isabelle and I received our first bound copies, sent from Houghton Mifflin in Boston, on October 6, 1958. How eagerly we scanned them, her color plates first because they were the core of the book. Then we leafed from page to page, checking Isabelle's drawings and rereading many of the phrases and clauses I had written to help readers remember how to distinguish between various pairs of confusing species.

We were proud of what had taken us seven years to produce. But how would it be received by the public? A good clue was the large number of advance orders the publisher had received. We began to hope that maybe, just maybe, there might be enough sales to recompense Isabelle for abandoning her salaried position at the Philadelphia Zoo to devote more than five years full time to the book. I, of course, continued to work daily, and my contributions were made chiefly on days off, during vacations, and often far into the nights. The field guide received excellent reviews, and I was pleased that I had written the text and planned the layouts as meticulously as though I were writing a scientific treatise. Our book was most assuredly not a hurry-up potboiler. We had done our best to make it as perfect as possible.

What a relief it was to be finished at last. Now we could turn our attention and spare time to other things. Our dream home, which we dubbed Hyla Holler, was being built while we were reading proofs. We did most of the finishing—laying floors, painting, paneling walls, and a myriad of other chores—ourselves to save expense. Then came my grants from the National Science Foundation which permitted us to do fieldwork in Mexico during six long and several short trips to virtually every part of that fascinating country. The field guide, except for the welcome royalty checks, was far from our minds.

A few years later, however, the editors pointed out that we should begin thinking about a second edition.

We knew it would have to be updated. Several new species, especially salamanders, had been described, and a number of additional tropical herps had become established in Florida. It would not be too much trouble to revise the field guide, or so we thought. But then a bombshell hit us full force.

That bold statement needs explanation. Robert C. Stebbins, of the University of California at Berkeley, had written several books and papers on western amphibians and reptiles. In addition, he was a superb artist. It was only natural that Peterson, another accomplished artist, should pick Stebbins to do a companion volume to ours on the herpetofauna of the West. We cooperated in many ways, even letting Stebbins use the outline maps we had drafted for our own book, in order to provide uniformity. But a serious problem arose that stunned Houghton Mifflin. They didn't discover it until the western book was far advanced through the press, and it was much too late to make major changes. Dr. Stebbins, as he had done in his earlier contributions, set his geographic limit to coincide with the eastern boundaries of New Mexico, Colorado, Wyoming, Montana, and Saskatchewan. Thus, he did not meet the 100th meridian line, the western boundary for our book. That left a huge region without a field guide, including the western half of Texas and parts of all the states north of it. The rich herpetofauna of Trans-Pecos Texas, with its strong Mexican affinities, would be almost a "no-man's-land" for field guide readers.

There was consternation in Boston. How to make up for the discontinuity? Would we be willing to fill the gap when we did our second edition? The first suggestion from Houghton Mifflin was for us to illustrate the missing herps on four black-and-white plates, write accounts about the taxa portrayed, and make the new text and pictures an appendix to our second edition. Admittedly, that would have been the cheapest escape from the dilemma, but we firmly refused to do it that way. I pointed out that pictures of scores of species of many different groups would have to be jammed together in very small size to fit onto four plates, that several of the Big Bend herps were very colorful, and that an appendix would simply advertise and magnify the omission.

Other schemes were suggested, and many letters flowed back and forth. There were even some long-distance telephone calls, which were quite expensive in those days. Finally, after considerable discussion, Houghton Mifflin agreed to do our second edition properly, and in keeping with the dignity and reputation of their field guide series. It would be an entirely new book, the animals of the hiatus would be included in their proper places with related species, and we would have eight additional color plates. Also, the title would be changed to "A Field Guide to Reptiles and Amphibians of Eastern and Central North America." After all, we would be covering the herpetofauna of 61 percent of the conterminous 48 states, as well as more of Canada to the north. That is why our second edition is so much thicker than the first.

Roger Tory Peterson arrived at Hyla Holler on December 1, 1966, for an overnight stay, and we ironed out most of the remaining difficulties. Our wish to have a handsome new book had finally been granted. I took care to point out to Peterson that it was going to take a long time to prepare the greatly expanded second edition. Most important, we would have to acquire live specimens of all the many additional taxa so we could photograph them. Also, within a month I would become Director of the Philadelphia Zoo, and my new responsibilities would cut deeply into my research time. He said there was no hurry. He seemed to be pleased because, in essence, we were rescuing Houghton Mifflin from what might otherwise have been a bad reflection on its staff.

Early during our negotiations with Houghton Mifflin I compiled a long list of the reptiles and amphibians that lived in the hiatus area that would need to be included in the new edition. Eventually I sent the list to a number of colleagues who lived in Texas or had worked extensively in Trans-Pecos Texas. I also solicited the help of persons in Florida who were familiar with the recent introductions in that state. They added more species to my list, and eventually I had to adjust a majority of the old plates, and lay out eight new ones. Many of the old ones were reorganized, as, for instance, to bring all the rattlesnakes and all the garter snakes together on two plates of each. As I advanced with that chore it became more and more obvious that Isabelle and I really had our work cut out for us.

Once the word spread that we were expanding the scope of our second edition, live specimens began to dribble in from friends and colleagues. We managed to photograph and color them, just in case we failed later to obtain additional specimens of the same taxa. As soon as I could, I wrote the text for them and mailed copies to experts on the species involved, asking for their criticisms and comments. I even started work on some of the additional distribution maps that would be needed.

In order to explore the possibilities and to prime ourselves for what was to come, we spent my month-long vacation during 1966 driving to and from the Big Bend National Park, and trying our hand at fieldwork within and near its borders. The location was ideal, and the splendid cooperation of the Park staff inspired us to return again, in 1967 and 1969.

We arrived at Panther Junction, the Park Headquarters, on September 18, 1966. Chief Naturalist Roland H. Wauer graciously took us in tow, helped me with the paperwork to obtain my "collaborator's permit" so we could collect, and promised to show us many parts of the Park. He then took us to the K-Bar Ranch, which was to be our residence and laboratory, rent free, for the duration of our stay. "The accommodations surprised and delighted us," Isabelle wrote in her diary. "There were four rooms, one a kitchen with an electric stove, a refrigerator, sink, hot water, a bathroom with shower, two rooms full of cots, and an air-conditioner in the fourth room. The front porch, overlooking the Sierra del Carmen [across the Rio Grande in Mexico], was shady after 10:00 or 11:00 in the morning." Perry Brown, Superintendent of the Park, had his men bring us a truckload of more substantial furniture for our comfort and convenience.

The Big Bend National Park had once been a state park, and prior to that it was rangeland where cattle eked out a meager living and ate or trampled the native vegetation, thus greatly altering the local ecology. Under National Park Service administration, such use came to an end, and, at the time of our arrival, the shrubs and grasses were making an excellent comeback. The K-Bar, which had long been a rancher's house, was behind a hill and well out of sight of casual tourists and visitors. It was kept intact to serve as a temporary residence for naturalists working in the Park. It afforded privacy, which was important while we were working and taking photographs of the species and subspecies we needed. The only problem was that "civilization" was 100 miles away, in Alpine or Marathon, and we had to drive a long way for food and supplies. Gasoline and a few staples were available in the Park, but we had to make the trip "to town" every 10 days or two weeks. We had been warned in advance, however, and we arrived well stocked with assorted comestibles.

It was obvious from the beginning that we would

The old K-Bar Ranch house in the Big Bend National Park where the Conants spent a month in each of three years while working on the second edition of their field guide. Photo by IHC.

have to do much of the fieldwork ourselves. It would help not only in getting the necessary animals, but also in giving me a broader background for writing my text. We were well acquainted with the Chihuahuan Desert, which we had visited many times during our recent peregrinations in Mexico, and the Big Bend was part of that extremely interesting region.

It was good to get back into the desert again, and we pursued our fieldwork with vigor and enthusiasm. Also, just as it had on many previous occasions, our presence encouraged local herpetologists and their students and friends to search diligently for the animals we needed while we were in the vicinity. In addition, they were familiar with the local terrain and could suggest habitats we should explore.

Ro Wauer had been keeping live specimens for us that he and the rangers found during their recent activities. Even some of the laborers in the Park caught snakes and lizards for us. James F. Scudday, of Sul Ross State College (now University), and his students, Charles E. Babcock, Jerry A. Johnson, and Samuel Sykes, brought us rarities. They also accompanied me in chasing lizards and searching the roads at night. The late summer of 1966 had been rainier than usual, and snakes were frequently seen crossing the pavement after dark. We spent almost every evening, sometimes well into the night, driving on the few paved roads. Rattlesnakes were especially in evidence. The first one we found was a blacktail, *Crotalus molossus molossus*, and what a beautiful snake it was. We took it and another handsome one back to the Philadelphia Zoo with us. All the other rattlers, mostly diamondbacks, *Crotalus atrox*, I picked up with my snake hook and carried well away from the road. We didn't want them to serve as targets for others who might be tempted to run over them.

Our most startling discovery was a Trans-Pecos copperhead, *Agkistrodon contortrix pictigaster*, that had just been hit by the car ahead of us and was still writhing in its death throes. I couldn't believe my eyes. A copperhead in the middle of the desert? How incredible. I carefully marked the locality, which was 17 miles north of Panther Junction, by tying a white rag around a yucca, so we could return to the same spot on the morrow to have a good look at the terrain in the daylight. In my field book I wrote that the habitat was a broad desert flat and "the mountains were far away. We checked the dominant vegetation and it consisted chiefly of creosote bush, but there was a sprinkling of lechuguilla (a dwarf agave), and a few yuccas."

Years later, when I was studying *contortrix* in detail for the Gloyd and Conant monograph on *Agkistrodon*, I learned that Trans-Pecos copperheads had been found several times in similar exceptionally dry-looking habitats. Although there was no water visible on the surface, it was possible that there were mesic habitats underground, to which the snakes had access through cracks and crevices in the substrate.

During our nocturnal drives in the Park, we noted cars patrolling the roads just as we were doing. From their actions, including their efforts to avoid us, we assumed they were poachers. The colorful and highly variable gray-banded kingsnake, *Lampropeltis alterna*, had suddenly become popular with snake fanciers, and was selling at the time for $500 each, a fantastic price for a small snake back in those days. Other Trans-Pecos presumed rarities were also bringing high prices. I heard of a copperhead that sold for $300. A year or so later Sam Sykes caught a fine adult lyre snake, *Trimorphodon biscutatus vilkinsonii*, that he shipped to us by air express so we could photograph it and Isabelle could apply its colors to a print from life. Sam insured it for $800 and he asked me to return it to him with the same coverage.

We did quite a bit of exploring in 1966, our first year in the Big Bend region. Besides seeing much of the Park, we visited the Davis Mountains, and drove west through Terlingua and Lajitas to Redford and Presidio and beyond. Later, on our way home, our curiosity got the better of us and we visited Langtry and had a look at the saloon museum of Judge Roy Bean, the "Law West of the Pecos" in pioneer days.

Our most interesting stop, en route to the Big Bend, was at the Monahans Sandhills—in Texas but close to the southeastern corner of New Mexico. Some of the dunes were covered with low vegetation, and others were open and in motion when the wind blew. The lure for us was that a disjunct population of the sagebrush lizard, *Sceloporus graciosus*, had been reported from the

Sandhills, far from the main habitat of that wide-ranging western species.

During our many excursions into Mexico I had often used a noose at the end of a pole to catch lizards, but I had never developed that method to anything approaching perfection. Since lizards of many kinds would soon be our quarry, I decided it was time for me to become really proficient. We stopped at Weatherford, Texas, on our way west, and I bought a fishing rod equipped with a ferrule, so that it was easy to separate into two parts to stash away in our vehicle, but could be quickly restored to its full length. I had brought some stout nylon thread with me, and also a small chunk of paraffin that I kept in my pocket. A noose was permanently tied to the small end of the fishing pole, but I waxed the thread before each use, so the loop would be rigid and ready to drop over the head of an unsuspecting lacertilian.

We arrived at the Sandhills late one afternoon and, during a short evening road cruise, we were delighted to find a sagebrush lizard that had been run over but was still in good enough condition for me to preserve. We needed a live one, however. The next morning was cool and cloudy, but the sun gradually came out, and I was able to noose several side-blotched lizards (*Uta*). Isabelle found a sagebrush lizard, and watched it run away and bury itself in the sand at the base of a clump of brush. She called me and I discovered that its tail was visible, which made it easy to catch, since I knew the lizard's exact location. So we had our first real prize, a female specimen of a rarity. After lunch it was warmer, and we prowled through the stabilized dunes. We eventually found a male, but he was active and wary. We managed to get him between us, and, as he stood still, probably keeping his eyes on two large potential enemies, I slipped the noose over his head, gave a quick jerk with my pole, and I had him. What luck! Part of my first day's catch with my new tool. We learned later that the dunes lizards are extremely elusive and quite difficult both to find and to catch. Our pair were in patches of dwarf shin oak, *Quercus havardii*, and sand sagebrush, *Artemisia filifolia*.

William G. Degenhardt and Kirkland L. Jones later described the disjunct populations from the Texas Sandhills and the Mescalero Sands of southeastern New Mexico as a new race of the sagebrush lizard. Recently, Hobart M. Smith and several associates proposed that the "dunes" lizard be considered a distinct species, *Sceloporus arenicolus*. It certainly looks different from the sagebrush lizards found far to the north and west. Dorsally, specimens are virtually unicolored and closely match the sand of the dunes.

Chief Naturalist Wauer and his wife, Sharon, planned to hike up into the Chisos Mountains, the highest range in the Park, to spend a weekend at the ranger cabin at Boot Spring. They invited us to go along, but Isabelle thought the trip, a total of more than 10 miles, all up and down, would be too much for her. I accepted the invitation, however, and J. Wesley Phillips, a seasonal ranger, accompanied us. The Wauers stayed at the cabin, but Phillips and I made the round trip together. During our ascent a long string of horses passed us. They were ridden by tourists led by a guide, and were bound for the South Rim of the Chisos, which offers spectacular views far into Mexico. While we were chasing a lizard during our descent in the afternoon, the same string of horses passed us, slowly that time, because most of the tourists were walking. Saddle sores and stiff legs develop quickly when one attempts a long horseback ride without being used to it.

Boot Spring is well named. Standing completely free and at some distance from the mountain wall is a large stone column rising 50 or 60 feet that is shaped like a boot, with a well-defined heel and toe at its summit. Nearby I caught two western black-necked garter snakes, *Thamnophis cyrtopsis cyrtopsis*, in a small arroyo through which a gentle stream was flowing. I didn't need it for them, but I was carrying my trusty snake hook with me. It was a golf putter that one of the mechanics at the zoo back home had ground down to the standard L-shape for me. Phillips toted my fishing pole with its lizard noose. We used the tools occasionally, my hook chiefly to overturn rocks. The return trail ended in the Basin, a bowl-shaped area at the foot of the Chisos that was a headquarters for tourists. There were cabins to rent, a lodge that served food, and many places for camping. As we walked along, Wes Phillips with the lizard noose over his shoulder and I with my snake hook over mine, we passed fairly close to two men, who were sipping highballs. When they saw us, one of them said, "Would you look at that! They told us the nearest golf course was 100 miles away, and that there was no fishing except in the river." They had recognized our tools, but had no idea how we used them. We managed to keep straight faces, but when we were out of sight and sound we had a good laugh.

Isabelle drove over from the K-Bar Ranch to the Basin to meet us on our return, which Ro Wauer had estimated might be about 3:00 P.M. We were late. She wrote in her diary, "I waited and waited and paced back and forth. Roger and Wes showed up at 4:30. We went into the Basin Lodge for a cold drink, and the concessionaire said I might as well have gone on the hike. I had walked almost as much with my pacing."

That was my devoted wife! We were always concerned about each other whenever we were apart for long periods of time, especially when one of us might be at risk in the field.

Our 1966 stay in the Big Bend region was highly successful in point of numbers of specimens acquired for the field guide. When we left for home we had roughly half of all the taxa we needed to illustrate. We had made friends who would continue to help us, and we looked eagerly forward to returning the next year.

Chapter 41

Closing the Gap:
Part II. Back to the Big Bend

We were back in the Big Bend National Park on August 28, 1967, and were quickly reensconced at the K-Bar. That old ranch house had been kept intact, in repair, and improved by the Park administration to provide living quarters and a workplace for visiting naturalists pursuing specific projects. Ours, of course, was to obtain live reptiles and amphibians to photograph as we pressed on with the preparation of the second edition of our field guide in the Peterson series. A large majority of the many additional species and subspecies we needed were indigenous to Trans-Pecos Texas, which has a strong representation of Mexican taxa.

Isabelle and I had stayed at the K-Bar during the previous autumn. It was roomy and comfortable, and it had long since been modernized by the installation of electricity and running water. Happily, it had recently been reroofed. We had abundant rainfall during our first few days of residence in 1967, but it made the air redolent with the pleasant, pungent odor of wet creosote bushes. The K-Bar also offered the delightful dividend, at least for herpetologists, of having live lizards, usually *Sceloporus merriami*, occasionally wandering across the floor. They evidently found chinks in the walls or squeezed under the screen doors. One day we had an entirely different kind of visitor, a very old lady wearing an old-fashioned sunbonnet, the likes of which we hadn't seen since we were children. She wanted to look at the place, because she had lived there for many years before, as she put it, the government took it away from her and her late husband. She was surprised by all the improvements, and pointed them out to her companion-chauffeur.

During our 1966 visit we had explored not only in the Big Bend National Park, but also throughout much of the surrounding region. With the help of Park staff members and several persons from Sul Ross State College at Alpine, especially James F. Scudday, we had acquired a large number of the herps we needed, but our list of desiderata, especially for lizards, was still lengthy.

Originally we had planned to devote my month-long vacation in each of three consecutive years to collecting

and photographing in and near the Park, but things didn't work out that way. A golden opportunity arose in 1968 that we couldn't afford to miss. The International Union of Directors of Zoological Gardens met in Pretoria, South Africa, and, because I was a member of that organization, the Philadelphia Zoo Board permitted me to go with all expenses paid. Isabelle accompanied me, of course, but because we were so far away from home and already on the spot—well, sort of—we enjoyed my vacation that year in East Africa. So, our third trip to the Big Bend region was postponed until 1969. Also, we played hooky, so to speak, during our 1967 excursion by taking the fabulous train trip across Mexico and down through one of the great barrancas to the Pacific coast. While we were at it, we tarried for several days at the tiny former railhead of Creel, Chihuahua, to sample the herpetofauna of the Continental Divide. (See "The Great Barrancas.")

When I laid out the first edition of our field guide I congratulated myself that I had only two species of whiptail lizards, *Cnemidophorus* (cnemis), with which to contend. Now, with the new territory we unexpectedly had acquired, there were nine. Actually there were 10 kinds, including the two easily recognizable geographic races of the racerunner, *C. sexlineatus*. Telling the various cnemis apart was difficult, and it very often required having the lizard in hand so that minute details of scutellation could be checked. We approached our coverage of the whiptails, both text and illustrations, with some trepidation. For years there had been much controversy, often bitter, about the classification of the admittedly difficult genus *Cnemidophorus*. But as Charles H. Lowe wrote in the "Biology of Whiptail Lizards" (published in 1993): ". . . good discrimination of the taxa was achieved during the period 1950-1970." That was precisely the time span when we were preparing our two editions (published in 1958 and 1975). The discovery of parthenogenesis (development of an unfertilized egg) and the confirmation of several all-female kinds of whiptails brought about drastic changes, and the classification of the cnemis began to make sense.

Several experts helped us, notably Richard G. Zweifel, and Isabelle made a series of detailed drawings showing unique variations in the scutellation that are useful in distinguishing one kind from another. Jim Scudday was also studying cnemis, and he pointed out differences to me that were very helpful.

All that was extremely useful, but first we had to catch our lizards, alive and unharmed. There are several different whiptails in Trans-Pecos Texas, all of them capable of running and dodging with bewildering speed once they are warmed up. I tried using my noose, tied to the end of a fishing rod. I had become proficient with it, and I caught several kinds of lizards with ease, but only one whiptail, and it solely by chance. They were difficult to approach, and often they ran under clumps of vegetation. They would stand quietly and let me get close to them, but threading my rod and noose through a maze of twigs and leaves was impossible. Noosing was also a challenge, because the necks of whiptails are only slightly narrower than their heads, and they could easily slip out. T. Paul Maslin, one of the early students of *Cnemidophorus,* told me, some years later, that he had fairly good luck by keeping the rod or pole in motion until his free hand could grab the lizard.

While we were in residence in the Big Bend National Park I constructed pitfall traps, which consisted of large cans or wide-mouthed bottles buried with their tops at ground level. Around them I set a ring of small stones, on top of which I placed a flat stone or board, hoping that lizards and other herps would seek shelter beneath the cover and fall into the container. I never caught any whiptails, but I did get a few lizards of other kinds, as well as toads and hundreds of camel crickets and other insects.

Our greatest success with cnemis resulted from using a drift fence. Jim Scudday purchased a 100-foot roll of quarter-inch hardware cloth about 18 inches wide for me at a store in Alpine, and brought it down in the company of some of his students. Together we stretched it out in the Park's Grapevine Hills. We buried wide-mouthed bottles near each end of the barricade and one in the middle. We waited quietly at a distance until foraging lizards reentered the area they had deserted while we assembled the apparatus. We then spread out in a line and walked slowly forward, driving our quarry before us. When the lizards reached the fence, they ran right or left along it and dropped into the bottles. We caught a nice series of marbled whiptails, *C. tigris marmoratus,* from which we chose the ones best for photographing. We used the fence successfully during each of our three visits to the Big Bend. It was held in storage for us at the Park, so we didn't

RC with James F. Scudday and some of his students from Sul Ross State College setting a drift fence for lizards in the Grapevine Hills. Photo by IHC.

have to haul it all the way to the East Coast and back.

I learned a lesson the very first time we used the fence: Never reach down into a buried pitfall to grab a cnemi. It will run up your arm or sleeve before you know it. An active one can get away every time. One of us held a snake bag flat and firmly across the top of a bottle while another squeezed a hand under it to probe for a lizard. That worked fairly well, but the best method was to scrape away the dirt from around the top of a buried bottle, screw on the lid, and then take it back to the K-Bar. An hour's sojourn in the refrigerator was sufficient to make any active herp handleable.

Jim and his students were adept at using wide rubber bands, which they shot from their fingers with considerable accuracy. That helped a lot, but many of the stunned lizards sustained serious injuries or succumbed a few hours or days later. In such cases, I preserved them for the study collection at the American Museum of Natural History in New York, with which I have been a research associate for many years. I made no attempt to master the rubber band technique, because I knew I couldn't do it. I lack a left thumb due to the bungling of the attending physician who treated me for rattlesnake bite, from a smallish *Crotalus mitchellii,* when I was only 20.

Sometimes an active lizard could be captured by a group of collectors working together, if they more or less surrounded the reptile and closed in from all sides. Of the many different species I personally caught, by far the easiest was the round-tailed horned lizard, *Phrynosoma modestum.* It normally flattened itself against the substrate, remained motionless, and its camouflage helped it avoid detection.

On rare occasions I was just plain lucky. Here are a few examples:

Early one cool morning I overturned a rock and found a relatively sluggish blue-tailed cnemi, *C. inornatus,* under it.

Once, at night, we discovered a beautiful adult male greater earless lizard (now known as *Cophosaurus texanus*) virtually hugging the paving of the road, apparently seeking any residual warmth that might mitigate the chill of a cool breeze.

At dusk, with the light nearly gone, we stopped our car near the fallen remnants of an old building, and I started searching through a pile of rotting boards. One yielded a real prize lying motionless beneath its shelter: a twin-spotted spiny lizard, *Sceloporus magister,* the first of only three we obtained during our stays in the Big Bend region. It was even larger than the handsome, robust, crevice spiny lizard, *Sceloporus poinsettii,* several of which we found.

A large collared lizard, *Crotaphytus collaris,* was standing motionless on the paved road one morning. Instead of scampering away as we approached, it stood its ground, facing us and with its mouth wide open. Isabelle was at the wheel of the car, so I hopped out and walked slowly toward it. When I was close enough I made a quick grab. Even then, it didn't try to run. Instead, it clamped its jaws shut on one of my fingers as I seized it. Ouch! They can pinch painfully hard. Why didn't the mountain boomer, to use its alternate vernacular name, run away? Usually they raced off with a speed that sometimes would accelerate enough for them to assume bipedal locomotion, like a miniature dinosaur.

Such lucky breaks were unusual. Hunting lizards normally required a combination of alertness, agility, skill, determination, and often quick thinking.

One day we drove to the Black Gap Wildlife Management Area, a large tract northeast of and adjacent to the Big Bend National Park. At their headquarters I introduced myself, explained our objective with a copy of our first edition in my hand, and politely asked if we could do some collecting. The response was, "Nothing doing." We were informed that I would need a permit that had to be issued in Austin, the state capital. There was also an implication that only Texans need apply. So, that was that, for the moment at least. I later appealed to colleagues in the Lone Star State who interceded for me. When we returned to the Big Bend in 1969 I had a permit that had been mailed to me at the Philadelphia Zoo before we left home.

My interest in the Black Gap Area was because of the recent startling discovery of a new species of lizard, the reticulated gecko, *Coleonyx reticulatus.* The only known specimen was found dead there in a snap trap set for small mammals. It eventually turned up in several places in Brewster and Presidio Counties, as well as in Durango and Coahuila, well south in Mexico, but too late for us to get a live one to photograph. We examined the type specimen, and Isabelle made a diagrammatic drawing of the dorsal scalation that clearly showed how it differed from the smaller, relatively common Texas banded gecko, *Coleonyx brevis.*

Despite our disappointment during our first Black Gap visit, we had a pleasant surprise at the end of the road. Instead of heading back to the Park, we drove in the opposite direction, toward the Rio Grande, intending just to have a look. When we arrived, we were surprised to find a small but sturdy bridge, so we crossed into Mexico. Nearby was the small settlement of La Linda, which appeared on no maps available to us. Aside from a few small dwellings there was one large building, which we later learned was a fluorite processing plant. That mineral was mined in the vicinity.

Soon we came to a tiny *aduana* (customs station) manned by three guards. We paid them 60 cents as a toll for crossing the bridge, and immediately began conversing in Spanish with them. They told us about La Linda, and, when we inquired, they said it was "OK" for us to hunt lizards and snakes. We drove a few miles southward over a gravel but well-graded road, parked in the midst of some rocky hills, and spent a lively hour pursuing lizards. A gusty wind kept blowing the noose on the end of my fishing pole so that it turned the wrong way just at the crucial instant when it should have passed over the lizard's head. I caught several, however, of two species: the tree lizard, *Urosaurus ornatus,* and the canyon lizard, *Sceloporus merriami,* but the latter was of a different subspecies than the one that was so abundant in the National Park. When we returned, the guards wanted to see what we had. We obliged, showed them the lizards, and I even demonstrated how I caught them. They were so pleased to be relieved from the tedium of manning the *aduana* all day, with little to do, that they refused to let me pay the toll to recross the bridge.

I was not so naive as to think we might find a reticulated gecko in a few hours in the Black Gap Wildlife Management Area, but, when I presented my permit on our second visit, biologist Sam Brownlee took us in tow. He drove us in a pickup truck to several tanks where there was an abundance of water. I caught several black-necked garter snakes, *Thamnophis cyrtopsis,* and, with the aid of my traps, three yellow mud turtles, *Kinosternon flavescens,* all of which went back to the zoo with us. We found nothing that we still needed for the field guide, and I didn't pursue any of the species we already had photographed. The trip gave us a chance, however, to see the area and to note how much wildlife the tanks of water attracted. There were many frogs of the *Rana pipiens* complex, and several birds that seemed out of place in a desert. Included were herons of two species, a kingfisher, and a sora rail. Except for the rail, we had seen the other kinds along rivers and wet places in other parts of the Chihuahuan Desert. The tanks were depressions filled with water, and they evidently had been constructed in earlier days for the use of cattle. I estimated that the largest we saw may have been a fourth of a mile long and about a third as wide.

Much of Trans-Pecos Texas lies due south of New Mexico, and one would expect it to be on Mountain time, like the state to the north. Not so. All of Texas was on Central time except El Paso and its immediate environs. As a result, in the far western Big Bend region, the sun rose and set an hour later than one might expect. That gave us long evenings waiting for dark so we could set forth on our nightly road cruising. Also, it meant that we often didn't return home and to bed until midnight, so we slept later than usual. After the morning chores were finished we often sallied forth at about the time the lizards were becoming active, I with my fishing pole, noose at its tip, and Isabelle with her camera. We ranged outward from the K-Bar, hiking along the lower parts of Panther Ridge, exploring nearby shallow gullies, and having a look at rocks standing upright here and there.

We found half a dozen species of lizards nearby, of which two kinds were abundant. The canyon lizard, *Sceloporus merriami,* was usually well above the ground on rocks and with its general coloration approximating that of the background. It was not particularly wary, and would let us approach closely if we moved slowly. If we came too close, it would run around the rock and out of sight. If we stood stock-still, it was quite likely to reappear, extending its head and neck far enough to have a look at us. Noosing them was easy, and I caught many a canyon lizard, examined it carefully, and then returned it to its home rock. Their behavior reminded me of the painted turtles and carpenter frogs back home in New Jersey. Those species occupied a watery, vastly different habitat, but when they were approached slowly and were not too badly frightened, they would almost always appear again close by.

The other abundant species, the greater earless lizard, *Cophosaurus texanus,* taught me several things about its behavior and its pattern and coloration. It was larger than the canyon lizard. It would run speedily away from us for 15 or 20 feet or so, and then stop on a stone or open place and slowly wag its tail back and forth, reveal-

ing the black bars across its undersurface. It was strictly terrestrial and was most often seen on the rocky flats where vegetation was low and relatively sparse. Catching it without help was virtually impossible.

The southwestern subspecies (*scitulus*) of the greater earless lizard, the one indigenous to the Big Bend, is really colorful. Jim Scudday told us that, in the spring breeding season, males are so brilliantly hued that local ranchers know them as "the lizards with the pink shirts and green pants."

A good field mark is the pale-bordered dark stripe along the rear of the thigh that is conspicuous in females and young, but much less so in adult males. It was easily seen when the lizard faced away from us, especially if we used binoculars for a close-up look.

We also strolled near the K-Bar during the long twilights. Herps of any kind were seldom in evidence at that time of day, but we enjoyed the birds and would occasionally see a small mammal. Also, piglike collared peccaries, or javelinas, as the Mexicans and Southwesterners call them, were around and, during our 1969 visit, we frequently disturbed a sounder (herd) of 12 or 15 of them while we were walking. They would be lying quietly together in the shelter of vegetation or rocks but would dash off, making considerable noise and clashing their large canine teeth, whenever we came upon them suddenly. In front of the K-Bar sat a small concrete basin, its rim virtually flush with the ground, providing for birds and other wildlife. We filled it with water every morning. Once at midday we found it being utilized by the javelinas. The largest boar of the group was luxuriating in the pool and occupying most of its space. The others had difficulty getting a drink. We watched them for perhaps 15 minutes as they sauntered around at close range. Isabelle took snapshots of them through the window. We didn't dare open it or the front door, because we knew that would make them dash away at once.

For most of my life I had lived and worked chiefly in the Northeast and the Midwest. In both regions lizards were few, in both numbers and variety of species. The fence lizard was common enough in the New Jersey Pine Barrens and a few other places I'd frequented, but lizards composed only a meager part of the herpetofauna. How different it was in western Texas. There, they were by far the most readily seen of the native vertebrates, excepting perhaps for a few kinds of birds. Our three periods of residence in the Big Bend National Park were an eye-opener for me, insofar as lacertilians were concerned. I learned so much about them, and about so many different kinds. In addition to those I've mentioned, I caught and watched many others, but there is not sufficient space to discuss them all in detail. We knew from our many wanderings in Mexico that it, too, has a large and exciting lizard fauna, but we saw it only casually during our peripatetic travels south of the border. In contrast, we were actually living with lizards at the K-Bar.

Speaking of Mexico, I must record the startling discovery we made well west of the Park. The Big Bend was sparsely settled. Great fenced ranches occupied most of the terrain. There were a few named localities near or along the road more or less paralleling the Rio Grande, some left over from old mining operations. During the 1960s such places as Lajitas and Terlingua were virtually deserted. Presidio, according to the road map, seemed to be the most important, but it appeared to us to be well on its way toward becoming a ghost town. Numerous abandoned buildings were falling apart; cacti, yuccas, and other desert plants had invaded the old fields; and the downtown area boasted only a handful of amenities, including the small Oil Flyer Restaurant and a third-rate motel.

Out of curiosity we crossed the river from Presidio into Mexico and were astounded by Ojinaga. Unlike the nearly moribund Presidio, it was a thriving town. There were parks replete with flowers, and a profusion of shops. It reminded us of some of the enchanting little cities we had visited far down in Mexico. It even had well-stocked *farmacias*. The people in Presidio had to visit Ojinaga to buy medications and many of the other necessities of life.

What a revelation! We had crossed the border at many places over the years. On the U.S. side there were important cities. Opposite such places as El Paso and Brownsville, however, were what tourists characterized as dirty, sleazy Mexican settlements through which they had to pass en route to destinations farther south. The Presidio-Ojinaga combination was just the opposite. By far the better town was on the Mexican side.

Our third and last trip to the Big Bend National Park, in 1969, was different in several ways, some good and some bad. First, we had traded in our Kamper, so we flew to the Midland-Odessa Airport in western Texas and hired a car. The agency had promised me a small compact, but all they would give us when we arrived was a huge monster of a vehicle, no doubt the one for which they could charge the highest rental fee. It was useless for negotiating back roads in rough country, but I will admit there were times when we appreciated its air-conditioning.

Second, when we arrived at the K-Bar Ranch we found it was already occupied by two students who had their gear and clothes scattered all over the building. We

The Chihuahuan (Big Bend) mud turtle we worked so hard to get. Photo by IHC.

had to share the place with them for two weeks. That meant far more housekeeping for us, especially Isabelle, because the boys were just camping out, and their standards of neatness and cleanliness were far below ours. We got along with them, but we sorely missed the privacy we had enjoyed during our two previous visits.

On the plus side, William G. Degenhardt, of the University of New Mexico, and his wife, Paula, were in the Park for a long stay, and they had an excellent field car, a British Land Rover. They spent a lot of time with us, and took us to many places where I wouldn't have dreamed of trying to drive the "monster." Also, Bill had his turtle traps with him, and they proved to be a godsend, as we shall see. We discovered that a considerable variety of foodstuffs had become available at the store in the Park, which saved us at least one long trek to Alpine or Marathon, each about 100 miles away.

So things tended to even out. Our friends in the Park and at Sul Ross State College rallied round and helped us as enthusiastically as ever. So did the students, Ted L. Brown and William Butler.

There are not many turtles in the Big Bend region. Some of the species included in our original field guide live in the Rio Grande or other places where there is water, but we hoped to include three more kinds on the plates in the second edition.

The desert box turtle, *Terrapene ornata luteola*, was soon acquired. We found several. They were so much like the ornate box turtle in general appearance, however, that we decided a black-and-white figure would do as an illustration. So my talented wife prepared a semi-diagrammatic drawing showing how the radiating yellow lines on the large scutes are much more numerous in the western subspecies.

We also wanted a water turtle of a species that had undergone changes in both its generic and common names. In our second edition I called it the Big Bend turtle, *Chrysemys scripta gaigeae*, but it is now placed in the genus *Trachemys* and is called the Big Bend slider. I had trapped a few in and near the Rio Grande during both of our first two stays in the Park, so I had a good chance to study live specimens before turning most of them loose. We concluded that, since we already had a black-and-white figure of its head, we didn't need to show the entire animal. Its distinctive cephalic markings and its restricted range—the Rio Grande drainage system—were enough to distinguish it from any of the other turtles with which we were concerned.

The third species proved to be a tough nut to crack, if I may be pardoned for creating an unintentional pun. I had written that cliché before I remembered that both turtles and nuts have shells! When Bryan Glass and Norman E. Hartweg formally described the Big Bend mud turtle, *Kinosternon hirtipes murrayi*, in 1951, they knew of only two localities for it: at Marfa and on a ranch 37 miles south of Marfa, both in Presidio County, Texas.

In search of that species we drove to Marfa, during one of our earlier trips, and made local inquiries about turtles in any springs or swampy areas of the general area, but no one we asked could help us. We tried driving southward from Marfa on dirt roads, but we soon had to stop when it became obvious that a four-wheel-drive vehicle or truck, with high clearance, would be needed to negotiate the primitive roads of the area. Our little Volkswagen Kamper failed to qualify, of course. So I turned my attention to localities closer to the Rio Grande. I tried trapping in the river itself, in nearby ponds and impoundments, and in small streams flowing into the river. We drew a blank everywhere we tried. So, during the hiatus between our 1967 and 1969 visits to the Big Bend, we concluded it was hopeless, and Isabelle made drawings of the plastrons of both the Big Bend and yellow mud turtles, showing how the pectoral scutes were widely in contact in the former species and only narrowly touching in the latter. That, we thought, would have to serve as our illustration.

One day in 1969 when we were both doing fieldwork in the Park, Bill Degenhardt and I were chatting about the local herpetology and the matter of mud turtles came up. We decided to make a trip to Ojinaga, across the Rio Grande in Mexico, to try trapping in the Río Conchos, a major tributary. Because Isabelle and I had visited the site previously, we knew that the "monster" might bog down hopelessly in the mud, so Bill offered to use his Land Rover. It would be a long, hard trip, and the two students wanted to go. Paula Degenhardt went with us, but Isabelle elected to stay at the K-Bar. It was well that she did, because we were away for almost 14 hours, and her presence would have made us rather crowded.

I had mailed three of my collapsible turtle traps to the Park before we left home, and Bill had four of his own.

We set all seven traps in sluggish parts of the Conchos, and then spent two hours hunting snakes and toads while we waited. When we pulled the traps we were overjoyed. Mine had not caught a single turtle, but in Bill's were three spiny softshells and two of the long-sought mud turtles. Now we could include a picture on the musk and mud turtles plate in our field guide. Bill was pleased because he had designed his own traps, whereas mine were patterned after those of a turtle expert. When we trapped elsewhere, Bill's traps proved superior again.

Over the next few years more information about the mud turtles came to light. In 1971 Frederick R. Gehlbach found two colonies of the Big Bend mud turtle approximately 30 and 46 miles south of Marfa. He was in the region while assembling information for his book on changes in the boundary region from Texas to California during the previous century. The more northern colony was almost certainly the type locality for *murrayi*. He also was able to demonstrate conclusively that Marfa was the shipping point rather than the spot where the "Marfa" specimen was collected. Incidentally, I highly recommend his book, which bears the intriguing title of "Mountain Islands and Desert Seas," for anyone interested in the natural history of our Southwest. It was published in 1981 by the Texas A&M University Press.

Several years later, Jim Scudday and Dennis J. Miller, under contract with the U.S. Fish and Wildlife Service, made an exhaustive survey of *Kinosternon hirtipes murrayi*. They found relict populations in several spring pools along Alamito Creek, but none in the Rio Grande. They also discovered that the name used virtually unanimously by residents of the area was "Chihuahuan mud turtle," and they recommended that it be accepted as the standard common name for the subspecies. I wish I had known that before the second edition of our field guide was published in 1975. It is far more appropriate than "Big Bend mud turtle," the name I used. After all, it ranges widely through the Mexican state of Chihuahua and extends only marginally into Texas.

Before leaving the subject of the mud turtle and its aquatic habitat, I should mention something about the impact of mankind on the flora and fauna of the area. The insatiable quest for water in arid regions on both sides of the border has resulted in drastic changes. The water table has been lowered enough to dry up many springs and *ciénagas* (marshes), with a concomitant extirpation of wildlife adapted to moist conditions. Many streams in the general area once supported tenuous gallery forests along their courses, but the trees were felled in numerous localities to serve as fuel for smelting valuable ores. With their removal, many of the riparian plants and animals disappeared. As I mentioned in "Fancy Seeing You Here!," most persons are unaware of it, but the Río Conchos becomes the Rio Grande at Ojinaga.

On our way home late that night from our Río Conchos foray, we found three Trans-Pecos rat snakes, *Elaphe (=Bogertophis) subocularis*, on the road or its shoulders. The Degenhardts were especially interested in them, inasmuch as they were studying an ectoparasite, a tick, found in nature solely in that species. As we drove along, my thoughts went back to the historical past and my early predecessor, Arthur Erwin Brown. He was the herpetologist who was head of the Philadelphia Zoological Garden, as I was, but long before I was born. It was he who first described *(Coluber) subocularis* way back in 1901.

In addition to our success with lizards and turtles, we also acquired, either on our own or with the assistance of our eager helpers, several snakes we needed. Getting some of them, however, was often a matter of chance encounters as they crossed the road. Among others, we added the Big Bend and mountain patch-nosed snakes, of the genus *Salvadora*; the striking red phase of the western coachwhip; and three different kinds of *Tantilla*. Incidentally, I will never again use the disagreeable name of "blackhead" snake for any member of that genus. Black-headed snake is much more suitable and acceptable.

We continued diligently to search the Big Bend region for the herps we still needed, and we made a pleasant several-day excursion to the Davis Mountains with Jim Scudday and his wife, La Ferne. Through the cooperation of the Park authorities and our enthusiastic helpers, our list of reptiles and amphibians needed to illustrate our second edition was greatly reduced. We were deeply grateful to everyone mentioned above, and especially to Chief Naturalist Roland H. Wauer, who did so much to help us. We also were indebted to David A. Easterla and Felix Hernandez III, seasonal ranger-naturalists. William W. Milstead, who was deeply interested in the Chihuahuan Desert, visited us two or three times, and I learned much from him about the area.

Our new reptile house at the Philadelphia Zoo was under construction, and we were permitted to collect and ship a large assortment of cacti that would be stored in the zoo's greenhouse and later be used to enhance habitat exhibits in the new building. Ro Wauer taught me how to identify the many different species. For my part, I reciprocated in a very small way by giving an illustrated lecture during each of our visits, Isabelle's and mine, for the Park's staff members, their families, and visitors. The subject was exclusively reptiles during

The "corkscrew snake," actually a regal ringneck snake, not only twisted its tail to show the red underside, but also arranged its body in symmetrical loops. Photo by IHC.

1966 and 1967, but in 1969 the topic was Africa, including mention of snakes we saw during our long visit to that continent. A highlight was a picture of a boldly lettered sign at the outskirts of a town in southern Africa which bore the name "Big Bend."

We left the Park for the last time on September 16, 1969, drove our big vehicle back to Odessa, and slept there overnight. The next day we took off for home. We changed planes in Dallas and had a good, but brief, visit with Gerald G. Raun and James B. Murphy, who came to meet us and gave us two gray-banded kingsnakes for the Philadelphia Zoo collection. It was a most welcome gift, because we still needed to photograph that species.

Our visits to the Big Bend National Park were interesting highlights in our busy lives and crowded schedules. How we enjoyed the wildlife, the companionship, and the solitude. Besides the many wonderful herps, we also were intrigued by the other vertebrates. Among the birds, the scaled quail were always a joy to see, and the *paisanos* (roadrunners) were invariably comical. Among the mammals, we saw mule and white-tailed deer, pronghorns (near the Park), peccaries, ring-tailed cats, skunks, jackrabbits, kangaroo rats, numerous other small rodents, and bats. The coyotes serenaded us almost nightly with their loud gregarious yapping. Our greatest disappointment was missing out on seeing the puma and her cubs that occasionally appeared in the evenings, during a period of some weeks, in the upper part of Green Gulch where the road twisted into The Basin.

The mountains were gorgeous, and the K-Bar had been oriented so we could watch the sunrise over the Sierra del Carmens in Mexico in the mornings and see them colorfully illuminated by the setting sun in the evenings. Perhaps it was because we were desert rats at heart that the Big Bend appealed to us so greatly. Even yet, I think of it as my favorite national park, and I have seen a lot of them.

It would be another two or three years before we acquired all the taxa we needed. We eventually got them all, except for the ever-elusive leatherback sea turtle. In the end, we had to use the same picture we had borrowed previously from the American Museum of Natural History. How similar our efforts were, but less hurried than when we were "Attempting the Impossible," as chronicled in three previous chapters.

Chapter 42

The Great Barrancas

During the late 1950s and early 1960s, when we were visiting Mexico annually for many weeks of fieldwork, Copper Canyon, or the Barranca del Cobre, to use its proper name, was a legendary, inaccessible place in southwestern Chihuahua. Only a few outsiders equipped with large four-wheel-drive vehicles had ever braved the so-called road to get to it. They had to carry all their own gasoline, water, and food, and they had to be able to extricate themselves from deep mud or sand, and take care of breakdowns and other emergencies. It was not for us, of course, with our little Volkswagen Kamper. We never expected to see the Barranca del Cobre, but then came the Chihuahua al Pacífico railroad. It not only reached the renowned canyon, but plunged right down into it on a cliff-hanging engineering masterpiece that conveyed passengers and freight all the way to Los Mochis in the western lowlands. Would we ever ride on it?

Our opportunity came in 1967. We were back in the Big Bend National Park seeking live herps to photograph for illustrations in the considerably expanded second edition of our "Field Guide to Reptiles and Amphibians." The previous year, while we were pursuing the same objective, we had learned that one could board a train in the prosperous little Mexican city of Ojinaga just across the Rio Grande from the decaying Texas town of Presidio. Why not take some time off and treat ourselves to the train trip of a lifetime? We did, but before relating our experiences, let me first mention something about the great barrancas of western Mexico. The Spanish word *barranca*, which translates as "gorge," is in common use in our Southwest.

The *altiplano* (high plateau), the vast interior plain of much of Mexico north of the transvolcanic belt, is flanked by two mountain ranges, the Sierra Madre Oriental (east) and the Sierra Madre Occidental (west). That is an oversimplification, because there are also small, isolated mountains and other topographic variations on the *altiplano*. Not all of it is flat by any means. Toward the west, the area with which we are concerned, the Sierra Madre Occidental is not very impressive. It

seems but little higher in many places than the *altiplano* itself. When viewed from the other side, along Mexico's western Coastal Plain, however, the range is a spectacular, deeply dissected escarpment.

The western Sierra rose as the result of an outpouring of vast amounts of volcanic material over a period of millions of years, dating well back in the Tertiary. Since then, erosion has created many deep canyons that rival and even exceed our own Grand Canyon in both depth and width. The Barranca del Cobre, the largest of them all, is a complex of several huge gorges that collectively form a void four times larger and 280 feet deeper than the Grand Canyon. The railroad, which previously had its terminus southwest of Ciudad Chihuahua at the miniscule village of Creel, was not completed until 1961.

Isabelle and I had already seen much of Mexico. It seemed fitting to top off our adventures south of the border by experiencing one of the world's great chasms.

Ojinaga was our point of departure for the train trip across Mexico. Sanborn's Travel Agency, which specialized in schedules and accommodations in Mexico, had a tiny office in Presidio, attended on appointment by a lady resident of the town. That was where we made our reservations and bought our train tickets.

We prepared carefully for our excursion. We would be on our own, and our jim-dandy Volkswagen Kamper, with all its varied equipment and cubbyholes full of possible necessities, would be left behind in Presidio. Besides blue jeans, heavy footgear, and other field togs, we would need more presentable clothing, especially since I needed to get my collecting permit validated in Ciudad Chihuahua en route. Also, because we would be at a fairly high altitude in mid-September, we took along our heavy *sarapes*, which had served us well in several upland parts of Mexico.

The carpenters at the Philadelphia Zoo built me a sturdy, but lightweight, carrying case equipped with shelves on which I could carry bottles and ventilated cans for any livestock we might catch and wish to bring back with us. There was also room for a canteen, iodine capsules for water purification, first-aid supplies, and various odds and ends. On the bottom shelf I had a small bottle of formaldehyde and all the necessary tools for preserving any salvageable specimens we might find dead or injured. My fishing pole, with its lizard noose, came apart and was easily stowed. The only awkward item was my golf putter made into a snake hook. Our baggage was rather bulky, but we wanted to be ready for anything and everything.

On September 6, 1967, we left the old K-Bar Ranch, our headquarters in the Big Bend National Park, about 9:30 A.M. and drove west toward Presidio. Isabelle had made sandwiches, and we estimated we would reach Closed Canyon at about lunchtime. We had already walked inward for quite a distance in that narrow cleft in the rock wall, which runs all the way from the road to the Rio Grande, or so we were told. Aside from a single canyon lizard, *Sceloporus merriami*, we saw nothing of interest, and, probably because the atmosphere was so claustrophobic, we didn't stay long. Nevertheless, it was a good place to pull off the road while we ate our lunch, changed our clothes, and repacked. Our plan was excellent, but we nearly came to grief. I'll let Isabelle tell the story, which I quote from her diary:

> When we turned off the highway we found the canyon road badly washed out in places, and we couldn't get down all the way to park. Roger started to back up and then pull into a smooth side road when, suddenly the car gave a terrific lurch and the front end hung up in the air. He had driven too close to a washout on the right side and the right rear wheel had gone into a deep ditch. This was certainly the worst calamity that had ever befallen us in all our years of driving over rough roads. It was impossible to extricate the car by ourselves.

The fault was entirely mine. I thought I had ample room, but I should have asked Isabelle to get out and guide me, a routine we had carefully heeded, no matter which one of us was driving, during our many years of travel in the wilds of Mexico.

We had passed a road crew a mile or so before we arrived at the Closed Canyon turnoff, so I hitchhiked back and sought their help. The men were eating when I arrived, but, as soon as they finished, they responded to my pleas, and I rode back with them. They piled up stones under our right rear wheel to make a crude ramp, fastened a heavy tow chain to the hook on the frame of our Kamper, pulled with their truck, and had us back on the level in a jiffy. We were both shaken by the mishap, but the men refused to accept anything in the way of a gratuity. They knew they had our grateful thanks. We were also grateful that the Kamper didn't seem to be damaged.

Happily, there were no other untoward incidents on that trip. We ate and changed our clothes and were in Presidio early enough to visit some students at the local Texas A&M research station. We had a substantial snack at the Oil Flyer Restaurant, and then drove to the home of the Sanborn's agent. She provided a parking space for the Kamper during our absence, and then telephoned for a taxi in Ojinaga to come get us. The driver took us to the Oficina de Migración to have our tourist permits stamped, and then drove us out of town to the railroad station. He explained in Spanish that it was situated close to where the Mexican tracks could meet those on a bridge that crossed to connect with the Santa Fe Railroad on the American side. We were aboard before 5:00 P.M., moved our watches back an hour (to Mountain time), and we soon were off.

The train had comfortable seats that reclined like those in airplanes. The windows were exceptionally wide, they had just been washed, and visibility was perfect. It was a Fiat (Italian) train, and we were riding, now that the barranca link was finished, on the last major railroad to be built in North America. The scenery across the Chihuahuan Desert was more or less monotonous, but there were distant mountains, and the few little towns through which we passed reminded us of our travels in rural, arid Mexico. It was dark when we arrived in Ciudad Chihuahua, and we didn't have dinner until we reached the Hotel Fermont at 9:30 P.M. (10:30 stomach time, according to Isabelle).

The next morning we went looking for the office of the Fauna Silvestre (the wildlife department), which had to validate my collecting permit. It turned out to be quite a chore. First we were directed to a large government building several blocks from the hotel. It was the wrong place. We were shunted across the street, but that was also incorrect. An obliging clerk, however, made several telephone calls, and he finally was able to tell us where to go. The office we wanted was in an unimposing edifice, on the second floor above an auto repair shop. The *jefe* (chief) didn't arrive for half an hour, and then he was too busy to see us. So we cooled our heels in a dingy waiting room for the better part of an hour before a typist prepared the profusion of copies of forms that had to be sent to all the agency's representatives in the State of Chihuahua. What red tape! The Mexicans must have visited Washington, D.C., and discovered how things are done in our officialdom. In previous years it had been a simple matter for me to obtain a collecting permit that was good anywhere in Mexico. All I needed to do was to write a letter outlining my field plans and stating the purpose of my research.

With the morning shot, to use a bit of slang, we lunched at the hotel, and then, because we knew we would have a long hard day on the morrow, we took a nap. A band playing music awakened us. It was in the park next to the hotel, so we pulled two chairs up to our fourth-floor window and had front-row seats. When the band finished, we were treated to an acrobatic exhibition by a group of *voladores* (high flyers). I take the following from Isabelle's diary:

> There was a large crowd of people on the sidewalks and in a nearby church plaza. Soon five men in ancient period costumes started doing a sedate dance under a pole at least 50 feet high with a tiny platform on top. One of the men played a peculiar instrument, a small reed with a little drum at the end of it on which he beat with a stick. One by one the men climbed almost to the top with the aid of a rope. The last was the man with the musical instrument. The climax came when the other four men launched themselves into space and were lowered to the ground by slowly unwinding ropes as the whole top revolved. Meantime the musician played and danced on the platform, which was no larger than his two feet. He came down last, using a rope.

There were other performances, too, and we presumed that the local merchants had hired the acts to drum up business. After all, Independence Day, September 16, was only a little more than a week away. How like our own vendors, who commercialize every holiday, even religious ones.

The following morning we were up at 4:30, had breakfast, and were waiting with our baggage when a Sanborn's man picked us up for the trip to the station. Our reserved train seats were on the shady side, which was a help on that bright, sunny day. First we crossed a rolling landscape but, as we climbed gradually higher, the desert vegetation gave way to juniper and pine. We stopped at a few small settlements, including Creel near the Continental Divide, where we planned to stay for several days on our return trip. It was a tiny place, but its environs, partially forested and with picturesque rocks and ridges, looked mighty inviting to a dyed-in-the-wool pair of naturalists. We surely would have fun exploring when we came back.

The next stop was at the upper end of the Barranca del Cobre, where we detrained for 15 minutes to have a look at the beginning of the great chasm. The broad steps down to the viewing point were lined with Tarahumara Indians selling tortillas, fruit, minerals, and even live chipmunks.

The ride down to the coast was worthy of all the superlatives that can be heaped upon it. A 1994 advertisement for the Discovery Tours of the American Museum of Natural History summed it up succinctly:

MEXICO'S COPPER CANYON BY TRAIN
A rail journey through Mexico's mammoth and scenic Copper Canyon, or Barranca del Cobre, is one of the most breathtaking journeys in the world. Over four times the size of the Grand Canyon, Barranca del Cobre is a natural marvel best experienced along a rail route itself considered a marvel of engineering. Explore a remarkable region that has long been home to the Tarahumara, an isolated people whose ability to traverse rugged terrain on foot is legendary.

Breathtaking, indeed. We found ourselves frequently moving along narrow ledges on steep or almost vertical precipices. We crossed long and spidery trestles, and in one small section of the route, near Témoris, the track made a bewildering series of switchbacks and hairpin turns. We passed through 86 tunnels, if we counted correctly. What scenery! Vast panoramas across to the opposite wall of the great barranca, waterfalls, boulder-strewn streams, and an ever-changing series of rock formations. What a trip. We didn't hesitate to recommend it to anyone.

We were in Los Mochis, a sizable town on the Coastal Plain at 7:30 P.M., set our watches back another hour to be on Pacific time, and we ate and slept in the Santa Anita Hotel.

The next morning we accompanied a small group of fellow train passengers on a Sanborn's tour to Topolobampo. That was where we had made our landfall aboard the steamer *San Jorge* in 1961 after we drove our Kamper to the southern tip of Baja California (see "The Classic Loop Road"). What an adventure that had been. There was no paving in those days, and we sometimes found ourselves negotiating what could best be described as goat trails. When our 1967 tour arrived at Topolobampo, we saw the steamer *Viosca*, which took over the run to La Paz after the *San Jorge* sank. Our group boarded a cabin cruiser for a trip on the bay, and we again saw boobies and dolphins, which had delighted us six years previously. It was a nostalgic day for us.

In the evening we got down to business again. I hired a taxi in Los Mochis, and we did some road-running in the dark. The driver, who spoke no English, soon entered into the spirit of things, and he helped us to spot toads on the paving. Most had been mashed flat by passing traffic, light though it was, but I collected four live *Bufo mazatlanensis* and a small *Bufo marinus*. The

A Chihuahua al Pacífico *train stopped at Creel's tiny station after winding its way upward through the vast Barranca del Cobre. Photo by IHC.*

only snakes were both dead: a garter snake, *Thamnophis cyrtopsis collaris*, which I pickled; and a speckled racer, *Drymobius margaritiferus fistulosus*, which was in such poor condition that I left it for the next scavenger that might come along.

The following day, September 10, we rode the train upward and were met in the late afternoon at Creel by Señor Ricardo Dominguez Quezada, with whom I had corresponded before we left home. He had the only accommodations for visitors in the entire town. He led us across the tracks to his Hotel Nuevo and to our room, which was spotless but definitely primitive, even to lacking a toilet seat in the miniscule bathroom. He remedied that omission by transferring one from another room. Meals were served in the back of a small general store, La Tiendita Super, by his wife who, as Isabelle put it, had five and one-half children, because she was obviously pregnant.

Señor Dominguez was a former schoolteacher who was kind enough to correct my Spanish now and then, but he had become an entrepreneur, and he earned our admiration. He had done much of the work on the motel and store himself, and he had the vision to realize that Creel, situated on the scenic railroad and close to the Barranca del Cobre, offered an excellent opportunity for future tourism. His *tiendita* had a variety of goods for sale. Among the customers were Tarahumaras, who obtained such things as salt and pieces of cloth in exchange for violins they handcrafted themselves, which Dominguez sold to tourists. We bought one and a bow, and Isabelle, who had been exposed

to the violin when she was a girl, coaxed a tune from it.

It was cold at night in Creel, which was at an elevation of 7,325 feet and close to the Continental Divide (8,056 feet). So we were mighty glad we had brought along our heavy *sarapes*. The outdoor temperatures dropped into the 30s (36°F one morning), and the only heat in our room was from a wood-burning stove that went out during the night. There was hot water, but we had to let it run for a full five minutes before it began to get warm.

Our host had an almost brand-new Chevrolet Carry-all that seated 14 people. In it he transported us to several nearby places over the miserable dirt roads, including the main one from distant Ciudad Chihuahua, which was blocked by a gigantic boulder that had crashed down during a storm. One destination, where he left us to our own devices for a few hours, was at the Laguna Arareco, a perfect gem of a lake. It had been formed by a small dam, but was a marvelous facsimile of an Alpine tarn, nestled among rocks and completely unspoiled by mankind. Even the road on which we had traveled was out of sight. There I found nine of the garter snakes I had named *virgatenuis* in 1963, as a new upland race of the wide-ranging Mexican garter snake, *Thamnophis eques*. My new subspecies had a very narrow, light blue middorsal stripe and a venter to match it in color. Small fishes, many of which I saw in a shallow place near shore, were probably its principal food. One snake, however, was swallowing a small frog, a member of the *Rana pipiens* complex.

While we were eating the lunch Señora Dominguez

Not today or maybe not for months to come will the main road to Chihuahua be passable. Photo by IHC.

had fixed for us, we were surprised to see a *campesino* come along the road. After we exchanged greetings, he pointed to my fishing rod and told us there were no *pescados* (edible fishes) in the lake. Fortunately, I didn't have to explain the use of the pole, because a mountain (Yarrow's) spiny lizard, *Sceloporus jarrovii*, suddenly appeared on a nearby rock, and I was able to demonstrate how I used my noose. That started a lively conversation. He said there were many lizards around, but that snakes were scarce. I showed him my garter snakes, and they astonished him as much as watching me catch a lizard with a fishing rod.

Señor Dominguez suggested an all-day trip to see another great barranca. It was a bit expensive because we were his only fares, but it surely was worth it. We traveled southward in comfort along a sinuous, up-and-down road on a round trip that was 75 miles in each direction. In addition to the money he made, the vehicle was so new that our host was enjoying driving it. He had installed a group of *cornetas* (horns) that played a musical chord, but they were loud enough to be heard by an approaching car or truck. He demonstrated their use repeatedly as we rounded curves and approached blind spots.

The dirt road was only a single lane, but it was fairly well graded because it was used to transport ore to the railroad for shipment. There were occasional pull-offs for passing, but getting by most of the big ore trucks was a matter of squeezing and maneuvering. As we moved steadily southward we met and passed a dozen or more that were almost overflowing with ore and proceeding at a moderate pace. We eventually reached the rim of the Barranca de Batopilas, toward whose head the trucks crawled slowly upward from someplace far below. Our driver told us it was the deepest of the great canyons, and, indeed, when I used my binoculars and

braced myself against a rock for steadiness, I could make out no details of the road and the tiny village at the bottom. It was assuredly the most precipitously awesome chasm we ever saw, and Isabelle and I were no strangers to the Grand Canyon. There was a noticeable difference, however. Winds from the Pacific carry moisture eastward into the barrancas, and the brilliant rock colors, so spectacular in Arizona, are muted by sparse vegetation (lichens?) that produces a generally grayish panorama. We had noticed the same phenomenon during our trip by rail through the Barranca del Cobre.

Whereas the full trucks took their time coming up, the drivers, having off-loaded at the railhead, drove back as fast as they could. Although it was still broad daylight, our *cornetas* were used even more frequently than they had been earlier in the day. Once, we rounded a curve and met a truck coming toward us at a fast clip. Only the reflexes of our driver and the one in the truck saved us from a violent head-on collision. They both literally stood up on their brakes, and we came to a bone-jarring stop that threw Isabelle and me out of our seats. Only a few feet separated the two vehicles. The truck driver had obviously been drinking. We decided the best way to describe the daily routine was to say that the drivers came up loaded with ore, and returned loaded with tequila.

During that all-day trip we stopped where a bridge crossed the Río Urique. The gorge through which it passed at that point was not particularly impressive, but it is the Urique that carved much of the Barranca del Cobre farther downstream. Eventually it joins the Río Fuerte, which flows into the Gulf of California.

On our way back to Creel, during the afternoon, we stopped two or three times to look for herps. The Arroyo de Basíhuare, 12 miles by road south of the town, had considerable water flowing through it, and some boys, who were throwing stones into it, told us they had seen snakes. Upstream were many large water-worn rocks, sharply angled above a pool that was about three feet deep. There we saw three more of the blue-striped garter snakes. I caught one as it swam by, well below the surface, and I nearly went in headfirst when I grabbed it.

The next snake, which I caught nearby, produced considerable excitement. It was a narrow-headed garter snake, *Thamnophis rufipunctatus,* and, when I plucked it from the water with my bare hand, there was a chorus of excited yells from Dominguez and the boys: "*¡Cuidado! ¡Es muy peligroso!*" (Take care! It is very dangerous!) Those exclamations were followed by, "*¡Es un pichicuate!*" (It is a *pichicuate!*) So I had caught a legendary snake, one of a variety of

The pichicuate, *allegedly more deadly than the largest rattlesnake. It actually was a narrow-headed garter snake,* Thamnophis rufipunctatus. *Photo by IHC in our home studio.*

species to which the same colloquial name was given.

Many years later, while I was working on the Gloyd and Conant monograph on *Agkistrodon* and its allies, the word "*pichicuate*" surfaced again. That time it was used for the formidable *Agkistrodon bilineatus*. I did some research and found that the appellation "*pichicuate*" was loosely given to any usually grayish, triangular-headed, presumed venomous snake. The *pichicuate* was alleged to be more dangerous than the largest rattlesnake. The name obviously derived from folklore rather than from any knowledge of the anatomy of the snakes themselves.

We made a few forays on foot from the Hotel Nuevo. Creel, at the time, was scarcely more than a swelling along the railroad, and it could be inspected easily in 15 minutes. There was a tiny train station, structures for the storage of ores and timber, and equipment for loading them onto railroad cars. A fairly liberal sprinkling of houses, storage sheds, warehouses, and a church completed the meager ensemble. One day I walked along the railroad tracks for more than a mile and made a startling discovery. They were twin ribbons of steel without a single break in them. It was my first experience with welded rails, and I wondered how they worked. When I was a boy, I sometimes would walk along the railroad tracks that passed through Red Bank, New Jersey, where I spent most of my adolescence. They consisted of long steel rails spiked to the wooden crossties, but there was a gap between each rail and the

next to allow for expansion in warm weather and contraction in cold. As the trains moved along there was a steady clickety-clack as the wheels rolled over the gaps. But at Creel there was not a break in the long, continuous rails. Since then I have encountered the same type of equipment in Europe and at home. I even found that welded rail runs through Philadelphia's 30th Street Station and onward, in opposite directions, to New York and Washington. Surely the law of contraction and expansion had not been repealed. Over a period of many years, I asked several engineers for an explanation, but I stumped them all.

I finally received the information I wanted indirectly, through "Iron Age," a magazine devoted partly to railroading. When metallurgic research showed that the special alloys used in modern tracks have a minimum of expansion and contraction, welded rails were tried. They worked well in Europe, where we saw them in Mexico, and in much of the United States, but in very hot regions they sometimes buckled and were responsible for railroad wrecks. Fairly recently the old-style rails were being replaced by the welded type not far from Grants, New Mexico.

Behind the Hotel Nuevo was a 300-foot hill surmounted by a large white statue of Cristo Rey (Christ the King) similar to ones we had seen on elevations countless times near small Mexican settlements. We discovered there was a footpath to the summit, so one afternoon we climbed upward accompanied by 10-year-old Juan Dominguez. Isabelle remained at the base of the statue, taking in the view of the little town and the wilderness beyond it with both her eyes and her camera. Juan and I went exploring. The hilltop was relatively flat and sparsely covered with second-growth pine, but there were several stone piles through which we began to search. Under a flattish rock I found a real prize, a twin-spotted rattlesnake, *Crotalus pricei,* a rather small snake marked with pairs of dark spots along its back. I pinned it down gently with the basal half of my fishing rod and picked it up, holding it in back of its head in the approved fashion with one hand and supporting its weight with my other. Then I suddenly realized that I had no place to put it. My snake bag was thrust through the back of my belt. Despite knowing that I had a *víbora* (venomous snake), Juan not only extracted my bag but also held it open while I dropped in the snake. The same hilltop yielded a garter snake, *Thamnophis cyrtopsis cyrtopsis*; a fairly young mountain skink, *Eumeces callicephalus*; another *Sceloporus jarrovii*; and three treefrogs, *Hyla eximia,* a species that ranges widely through western and southern Mexico and into our own Southwest. I gave Juan five pesos (then worth about 65 cents) as a reward for his help. When we neared the bottom of the hill on the way back, he started running and raced all the way home to spread the news that I had caught a live *víbora*. He dutifully gave his mother the five pesos, but he stirred up so much interest among the Dominguez's friends and neighbors that I had to show off the snake for them. We gathered in a small lounge in the Hotel Nuevo, the spectators at a safe distance from me. I fished out the garter snake with my hook, and then I upended the snake bag and gently "poured" the rattler into my wide-mouthed gallon bottle, and screwed on the lid. The bottle was placed on a table, the crowd was cautioned not to touch it, and soon Señor Dominguez had everyone lined up to have a close-up but brief look at the unusual serpent. In the crowd was a rather elderly Tarahumara, in native costume, who, with gestures, informed us that it was good to eat. He and Dominguez told me that the native name for it was *chachámuri*.

That prize went back with us to the Philadelphia Zoo, and I felt sure it would be a first for the reptile collection. I was wrong. We had exhibited one way back in 1902 that had come from Colonia Garcia, a lot farther north of where I found mine, but still in Chihuahua.

We were far more intrigued by the Tarahumara than we ever had been by other native tribes. They were a strong, virile people, but most of them were extremely shy. We saw them occasionally in Creel, but the moment Isabelle's camera appeared they vanished. There were a few exceptions: the vendors at the stop before the train began its descent into the barranca, the elderly man who came to see my rattlesnake, and another whom Dominguez knew. For a handful of *dulces* (wrapped candies) and a pack of cigarettes he let Isabelle take his picture, but his family remained well in the background. Twice we saw men resting with one foot raised and held against the knee of the opposite leg, a stance also used by primitive people in other parts of the world. Each man had a load on his back supported in part by a tump-line passing across his forehead.

Dominguez, with whom we spent considerable time on our excursions from Creel, told us a lot about the Tarahumara. The caves in which they lived were mere rock overhangs walled off with stones at the outer edge. In cold weather a blanket covered the gap through which they entered and exited. Their clothing consisted of a white tunic, the equivalent of a loincloth, a band around their heads, and a pair of *huaraches* (sandals) or no footgear at all. I asked how they dressed during the winters, and was told it was the same. I then inquired about the depth of the snow, and our host told us that sometimes there was a meter (slightly more than three

feet) on the ground. How incredible! We admired their physiques and stamina.

Recent information indicates that the Tarahumara are now the largest native tribe in Mexico. They have a vast rugged region in which to live, roam, and retain their traditional customs. Dominguez told us that they thought nothing of climbing up and down the nearly sheer walls of the Barranca de Batopilas. Their footraces, during which they kick a wooden ball for long distances for days, are legendary. Incidentally, among my most treasured possessions is one of their balls, which I found in a relatively flat, open area a few miles south of the town.

Our departure from Creel was on September 13 at 8:00 P.M. We slept fairly well in a Pullman car in which I had reserved a compartment, and we were back in Ojinaga at 7:00 the next morning. We hired a taxi to take us to Presidio, but, of course, we had to stop first for U.S. Customs inspection. It was perfunctory, except that I had to show my Mexican collecting permit and list all the livestock I was taking back to the zoo. We soon retrieved our Kamper, ate breakfast at the Oil Flyer, and then drove back to Ojinaga. There we used up our remaining pesos buying gifts for friends and relatives, as well as a bottle of tequila each. When we met the Customs man again on the American side of the Rio Grande bridge, he told us we were in luck. The Texas tax man wasn't there. We were delighted, because we were thoroughly disgusted with the local law that required everyone to pay a tax just to haul alcoholic beverages across Texas. We thought it was a holdup. The tax, during earlier years, was more than we paid for our full bottles in Mexico.

My first chore in Presidio was to visit a service station and have the Volkswagen placed on a lift and inspected for any damage that might have resulted from our near disaster at Closed Canyon. Neither the mechanic nor I could detect anything wrong. We then bought food and ice. During the noon recess from school we found Wayne Baize, who had custody of several live reptiles the Texas A&M field crew had caught for us. Among them were three checkered whiptail lizards of the *Cnemidophorus tesselatus* complex, which were very welcome. We had not yet photographed any member of that group and didn't know where we might get one.

Once we were out of town we changed from our "good" clothes into dungarees and were ready for fieldwork. All we did on our way back to the Big Bend National Park, however, was to guide a fairly large western diamondback, *Crotalus atrox*, into a large clump of cactus well off the highway. We were back at the K-Bar in time for supper.

The trip to Creel and the great barrancas was a truly marvelous experience. We had ridden the train both down and up over the most rugged route we ever traversed, and we had sampled a bit of the herpetofauna of the highlands of southwestern Chihuahua, a dozen species in all. That wonderful journey would remain in our memories as long as we lived. We didn't know it at the time, but it was the last trip we ever made to Mexico together.

Things are different now. Most important, the Mexican government created the Parque Nacional de Barranca del Cobre, embracing 7,350 square miles, to preserve the vast canyon complex and its environs, even Batopilas and its precipitous gorge. Tourism blossomed. Auto excursions such as we took, as well as several others, are available, and there are two motels in Creel worthy of listing by the American Automobile Association. Further, the road is now paved all the way from Ciudad Chihuahua to Creel. That town is no longer isolated, and can easily be reached by automobile. The wonderful train trip is still the main attraction, and travel agencies soliciting business strongly stress the marvelous scenery and the spirit of adventure.

According to information I have received from Dennis J. Miller, Executive Director of the Chihuahuan Desert Research Institute, Presidio has come to life and is now one of the fastest-growing towns in Texas. Ojinaga is connected by paved roads not only with Ciudad Chihuahua, but also with Ciudad Camargo to the south. There is no longer passenger service from Ojinaga, so one must board the Chihuahua al Pacífico in the state's capital city. The implementation of NAFTA, the North American Free Trade Agreement, bids fair to make both Presidio and Ojinaga important links between the two countries. How very much has changed in almost 30 years!

Chapter 43

The Difficult Years

My youthful ambition had been fulfilled. I had reached the top. I was the director of a zoo. Not just any zoo, but one of the most important in the nation, and the oldest. It was enjoyable to contemplate the wonder of it all, but my reverie lasted just one day. The zoo was closed on New Year's Day, as usual, and I was at home. The next day, January 2, 1967, I met the first of a multitude of problems.

Emergency repairs were needed in the old kangaroo house. The labor union had a grievance it wanted settled immediately. Virtually every staff member had been saving a long list of problems that needed attention, knowing it would be useless to take them up with my predecessor, who would so soon be out of office. There was a stack of unopened mail that apparently had accumulated for several weeks. Numerous other items, if I even could remember them, are too unimportant to mention, but that first week was a rough one. It was almost the same every week, year after year. Some problem or crisis developed almost daily. There were routine matters that could not be neglected, and all too often there was some crank, usually a zoo visitor, who had a complaint that he insisted on taking up with the boss. None of the persons I deputized to listen to him would do. Sometimes I felt like a juggler trying to keep a dozen balls in the air all at once.

As the zoo's director, I had to give up my comfortable small suite of rooms in the service building that Freeman M. Shelly had so kindly provided for me many years previously. I had to move into his rather small office on the second floor of the historic Penn House. That wonderful old structure had been built in 1785 by John Penn, grandson of William Penn, the founder of Pennsylvania. The younger Penn purchased 15 acres, then well outside the City of Philadelphia, and created a country estate clustered around his house, which he christened "Solitude." At that time there was a small, separate kitchen behind it, and also quarters for servants. An underground passageway, connecting with Penn's wine cellar, gave access from the kitchen to the basement of Solitude. The grounds were beautifully landscaped, and the house was near the Schuylkill River. Friends sometimes rowed up from the city to attend Penn's dinner parties.

Solitude, which measured 26 feet in both length and width, was described as an exquisite box, built in neo-classical style. Inside a narrow entrance hall, a staircase with a handsome hand-wrought iron railing ascended to the second floor. Behind it was a large drawing room with a fireplace and a decorative Adam ceiling imported from England. Upstairs were two small bedrooms and Penn's library, which measured 15 feet square. That would be my office.

Penn returned permanently to England in 1789. Solitude was rented for a while, but it steadily deteriorated and was acquired by Fairmount Park in 1867. In 1874, when the zoo first opened its gates, the house became the administrative headquarters, and so it had remained for the better part of a century. For the first few years of the zoo's existence the reptile collection was exhibited in the drawing room on the first floor.

The Penn House remained virtually as it always had been except for the installation of such modern equipment as a furnace and radiators, electric lighting, and a telephone switchboard. But it was decaying badly. The wood was rotting here and there, the roof was not in good condition, and repairs seemed to be needed constantly. In short, the "exquisite box" was totally inadequate as the headquarters of a large and now modern zoo, but it was all we had.

My office, Penn's former library, was equipped with bookcases and also cabinets above the doorways, all fronted by small inlaid panels of glass. They revealed a motley array of rolls of old building plans and dusty objects of many kinds. I had them cleaned out, and Isabelle, my good wife, made curtains that we installed directly behind the glass. We retired the large picture of the extinct dodo that had hung for many decades above the mantelpiece, and we eventually introduced a few modern decorations. Among them were prints of Rena Fennessy's beautiful portraits of Africa's giant cats, which we bought in Nairobi, as well as bird prints by

Solitude, the country home of John Penn, William Penn's grandson, served as the administrative office of the Philadelphia Zoological Garden for almost a century. Philadelphia Zoo archives.

Basil Eads that had been part of an exhibition in Philadelphia. My office now had a slight personal touch, and I held sway there for several years. It was nostalgic for me. In it I had first met C. Emerson Brown, who had helped me to get started professionally in the late 1920s. There I had consulted innumerable times with Directors Macdonald and, especially, Shelly. Even the weekly staff meetings were held in it, with extra chairs brought in from outside for the occasion.

My longtime secretary, Ruth G. Endy, had her desk and typewriter in one of the bedrooms. The business manager and his assistants occupied the first floor and the second upstairs bedroom. The switchboard operator was ensconced at the base of the stairway.

In general, I had inherited an excellent and highly competent staff that included many men and women who were hardworking and dedicated. I appreciated their help and counsel. Alas, there were others. As an example, I will mention only one. The superintendent of maintenance, whom I will call "Smith," was a splendid construction man. When something needed to be built, he was eager and enthusiastic; he could even prepare his own working drawings, and the results of his efforts were first class. As a maintenance man, however, he was a dismal failure. He could trip over the same hole in the paving a dozen times and never see it. Giving him

verbal orders was useless. He ignored them, along with most of my written instructions.

I would have fired Smith, but my hands were tied, so to speak. He was a friend of an influential board member who had gotten him his job at the zoo some years previously. Every time Smith thought I was badgering him, he complained to the board member. So I put up with Smith, but used the device of telling the board member about the worst maintenance problems. In such cases they were fixed promptly. Smith retired a few years after I did, and he had the gall to tell some of my friends on the staff that I had been a lousy director who never understood anything about construction and maintenance. Obviously Smith was determined to defy me and to take orders only from his board friend, who otherwise was an able person and who had long since earned my great respect. Such is life. Sometimes I had to work around problems instead of meeting them head on.

An unexpected chore developed in our search for a good man to handle public relations for the zoo. I was far too busy to cope with that assignment on a daily basis, as I had done for decades. We hired a succession of persons, but they didn't last. One had no imagination; another insisted on writing news releases in complicated gobbledygook with its involved and obscure

Zoo Director Roger Conant in his office in the Penn House in 1970. Photo by Ken Kawata.

verbiage, such as was then popular in government circles. City editors began telephoning me to ask why they couldn't receive straightforward news about the zoo instead of wordy conundrums that had to be decoded. Another man, who was well recommended to us, had plenty of imagination, but the title of Director of Public Relations went to his head. He soon began to behave like Smith. He disregarded longstanding zoo rules and defied me, and I had to step in several times to untangle messes he had created. I finally had to dismiss him. He had anticipated what was coming and, on the day he left, he sent out a previously prepared news release to about 200 recipients, including small neighborhood newspapers as well as all the broadcasting stations throughout the huge Philadelphia metropolitan area. He had dreamed up a long list of things that he claimed were wrong with the zoo, basing them on half-truths and sheer fabrications. Further, he used zoo stationery and zoo postage stamps for mailing the release. His secretary, who had been party to his farewell plot, had the good sense to resign, thus sparing me the unpleasantness of firing her.

That affair created quite a furor. The newspapers played down the accusations and even stressed the fact that the culprit had used zoo stationery to vent his spleen. The city editor of the "Philadelphia Inquirer" told me that, if he had been on duty at the time, not a line would have appeared in his paper. It is axiomatic, however, that the media love controversies, and that meant both sides of the story had to be presented to their audiences. So I had to prepare a rebuttal, which was easy. I had a ready answer for all of the ex-employee's specious claims. A couple of examples will suffice. He stated flatly, in the release, that our guards, who patrolled the grounds in uniform, were all so old they would collapse if they ever had to run for any reason.

Actually, just a few weeks previously, a teenaged boy had stolen a cash box from a small temporary souvenir stand and sped out the exit turnstile with it. One of our younger guards took off in pursuit and caught up with him some 50 yards away. He held the would-be thief until the park police arrived in a patrol car.

Another accusation was that we failed to take good care of the animals. In response, I invited both of the two Societies for the Prevention of Cruelty to Animals (the Pennsylvania SPCA and the Women's SPCA) to send a representative to inspect our livestock. They found nothing wrong, and that fact was duly reported by the news media.

Despite my ready response, I was on the run for days as I defended the zoo and its staff on many television and radio stations. Embarrassingly, Isabelle and I were entertaining houseguests from the Frankfurt, Germany, Zoo, at the time. She had to take them in tow alone during the daytime and show them our institution. Fortunately, she knew it well, because she had served as official photographer for a decade.

The former employee had his revenge for getting sacked, but he cut his own throat in the process. The dirty trick he played on us was not forgotten, and he never again obtained a public relations job. His reputation had been tarnished beyond repair. In the meantime, Richard H. Cooper moved into the vacant position.

Having to cope with oddball (warped?) personalities was probably just part of my job, but treachery was another matter. I suppose that a power struggle can develop in any organization, but why two staff members would try to unseat me was beyond imagination. I was well entrenched, my reputation was good, and I had the strong support of the zoo board, the City Council, and many persons in high places. I had worked for the zoo for three decades, and it wouldn't be too many years before I retired. None of that mattered. One of the two plotters wanted my job—now! I was suspicious, but not really concerned. Snide remarks were aimed at me and about things I had done or hadn't done, and they surfaced almost always when I was away from the zoo, especially when I was off on a trip. One that almost amounted to an accusation was relayed to President George F. Tyler, Jr., but, when he challenged me about it, he quickly accepted my explanation. Matters almost came to a head when a good friend, and staff member, inadvertently overheard the two conspirators discussing their next move. I was informed at once, and I consulted with John G. Williams, who had succeeded Mr. Tyler as President. Mr. Williams advised me to ignore the matter for the present but to keep my eyes and ears open for further developments. As I had assumed, he assured me that my position was secure. The aspirant to the directorship went out of his way to snub me at every opportunity. Aside from that childish annoyance, I lived with the problem. He did not succeed me when I retired, and I don't think he was even considered for the position.

An unexpected phenomenon surfaced immediately after I took office, when a number of employees exhibited a marked change in attitude toward me. Some had been close friends who had long brought their troubles to me for discussion and counseling. Only a couple of them continued to do so. The others approached me, as they had Shelly, only when they thought it necessary to report to management. I was always ready to discuss matters with them, but my heavy schedule necessitated appointments made in advance. That canceled much of the closeness I had enjoyed with them. I was now the boss instead of a confidant.

For years I had been friendly with virtually all the employees, and I exchanged small talk and pleasantries with most of them, even the janitors and laborers. Now as I walked around the zoo they turned their backs on me. I tried to start conversations with some of them, but their response was stony silence. I failed to grasp the reason, but an explanation was soon forthcoming. Some four or five employees had refused to join the union, but they had to pay dues nonetheless if they wanted to keep their jobs. That was the way the law was written, and it was strictly enforced by the city administration. One of the holdouts decided, since he had to give part of his salary to the union, that he would attend a meeting or two to learn what was going on. He reported to me that the workmen, my erstwhile friends, were ordered to turn their backs on me as a means of harassing management. They had behaved the same way toward Shelly, but I was unaware of that. Personally, I thought it was poor psychology on the union's part. Such actions tended to stiffen management's attitude and make it less willing to yield to their demands.

I let our business manager and personnel officer cope with the union on a day-to-day basis. Both had been hired to fill the positions which the zoo's board of directors had promised when they talked me into taking the directorship. I held myself in readiness to make final decisions. There was at least one grievance every week, and sometimes many, and all of them took hours to iron out. Their complaints often seemed silly. Someone had picked up a shovel, for example, when it was the duty of another union member to handle such a tool. We were compartmentalized, with each man or woman restricted to the narrow limits of his or her job description. Gone was the spirit of camaraderie that had so

long prevailed. I could not help but think back to the long-ago day when, as a youth, a keeper and I, the zoo's young cashier, had helped the construction men erect a steel cage front at the Twin Brook Zoo. We would have been in deep trouble if union rules had then prevailed.

Several years previously the Teamsters' Union had tried to organize the zoo employees. They were voted down by a small margin, but, as several men told me at the time, the zoo was ripe to be organized by labor because of Shelly's constant efforts to keep salaries low.

When the State, County, and Municipal Employees Union entered the arena there was no stopping them. They had the support of City Hall. They were well entrenched when I took over, but I had virtually no contact with them until I was the boss. Then I had to learn fast.

One insidious union maneuver was known as "bumping." Seniority counted first and foremost. The person who had belonged to the union the longest got the best job in his category, if he wanted it. Thus, a keeper with seniority who was good with a hose, broom, and shovel, for example, could "bump" another keeper out of his job in the bird house, even though the keepers in that position required long periods of training and experience to master the complicated diets of the many different types of birds.

One year we had a bad summer. It seemed to rain every weekend, and that meant the loss of 10,000 or more visitors each inclement Sunday, along with all the money they spent on admissions, souvenirs, and refreshments. In the early autumn the board took cognizance of our sizable deficit, and told me to lay off the four or five union members with the least seniority. That news set off a violent storm of protest. The union demanded help from City Hall. Mayor James H. J. Tate credited the union with having pushed him over the top in a close election. He owed his office to them. Almost immediately after the layoffs were announced, no fewer than three highly placed persons in the city administration telephoned me and angrily objected. The gist of their messages was that, if I laid off the men, the zoo would not get an additional penny from the city as long as Jim Tate remained in office, and he had two or three more years to go. At the time we were receiving capital funds for our new buildings, and the city treasury also made up whatever our usual small deficit might be. I immediately got in touch with President Tyler. He consulted with the board's Executive Committee, and they agreed we had no choice but to capitulate. In a sense, we had a loaded gun pointed at our collective heads. In all fairness, however, the city found some excess money somewhere that was later appropriated for the zoo, so things worked out well financially in the end.

We had several strikes that forced the zoo to close down for a day or more. Supervisory personnel had to take over the feeding and watering of the animals, and I had to look after the reptile collection. One day, a truck arrived at the service gate with a week's supply of fodder for the livestock, and the pickets refused to let it in. I was summoned to the gate, but the men were adamant. Visions of screaming headlines popped into my head. "Strikers Starve Zoo Animals" was among them. All I had to do was to telephone the newspapers and other news media outlets to give the union a nasty black eye. Wisely, I held off and went to check on how negotiations were proceeding. I learned that a final agreement appeared to be imminent. I went back to the gate and told the truck driver to take his perishables to the Women's SPCA. Within an hour a settlement was reached, the pickets deserted their posts, and the SPCA made delivery back to us without incident.

The zoo had been a fun place to work before the union took over and made things much more difficult for those of us who were charged with its care and operation.

Another difficulty I encountered was the erosion of my time off. Because they knew I was adept at handling problems caused by visitors, the board asked me to continue working on weekends as I had done for decades. I was agreeable, but it seemed as though everyone forgot that I was supposed to be off on Thursdays and Fridays. Innumerable times I had to drive into the city from our quiet retreat in the New Jersey Pine Barrens to attend meetings, City Council hearings, and divers other matters of importance, thus disrupting my alleged days of rest. Also, there were many evening functions where I had to appear as the head of one of Philadelphia's leading cultural institutions. Because of my decades-long radio program and my frequent appearances on television, I was too well known for my own good, and I had to participate in far more extracurricular activities than were required of my predecessor. Admittedly, some of the evening meetings were fun and interesting, especially when I was invited to bring Isabelle. Far too many of them, however, were boring, and I felt sure, many a time, that I had been invited by an ambitious chairperson who wanted to have some "distinguished scenery" (meaning me and other business and institutional heads) on the speakers' platform. I manfully did my best to accept such requests. I will confess, however, that I sometimes pleaded previous engagements, even though they were excursions into the Pine Barrens, sometimes with visiting herpetologists.

There was a bright side to being head of the zoo. Not

everything was toil and trouble. Among other things, I was free to travel to zoo conferences and scientific meetings, and many of them were in foreign countries. Isabelle and I both liked to visit distant places and to learn about customs and activities different from our own.

In the autumn of 1967, shortly after I had moved into what I called "the hot seat," I received an invitation to attend the annual meeting of the International Union of Directors of Zoological Gardens at Barcelona, Spain. That was the same organization Freeman M. Shelly had served so well and of which he was eventually elected president. Upon his retirement he became an honorary member.

In the meantime, three other excursions to far places had already been planned for my first year in office. The American Association of Zoological Parks and Aquariums, of which I had been a member for 37 years, was scheduled to meet in March in Mexico City with the Hispanic Zoo Association, which included zoo directors from Spain and the many Spanish-speaking countries of Latin America. The American Society of Ichthyologists and Herpetologists was to convene in San Francisco in June, and attending it would give me a chance to see both the zoo in that city and the famous Steinhart Aquarium. Also, I could include a side trip to San Diego to visit the splendid zoo in that city, which I hadn't seen in many years. Because Isabelle and I were under contract with Houghton Mifflin to produce the greatly expanded second edition of our field guide, I had to spend my month's vacation, in late August and early September, in the Big Bend National Park and its vicinity. There I would have the help of the Park staff and of James F. Scudday and his students as we searched for live specimens to photograph for reproduction in the book. Then back home and off to Spain and other parts of Europe in October. I wonder how many miles Isabelle and I traveled in 1967? There is not enough space to write about all those excursions, but I'll try to hit a few high spots.

We were due to fly to Mexico City on March 9, but I had an unexpected telephone call the previous day. Richard J. Baldauf, an old friend, told me I had been elected a Distinguished Honorary Fellow by the Texas Academy of Science in recognition of my contributions to the herpetology of that state. Could I be at the Academy's banquet at College Station, Texas, on March 17 to accept the award? I thanked Dick profusely, but said I would have to call him back. I immediately telephoned President Tyler and asked him if I could have an extra two days to fly to Texas A&M University from Mexico City and then home. Mr. Tyler congratulated me and said to go by all means, especially since the date dovetailed so perfectly with the Mexico City meeting. Also, he graciously told me to add the extra plane fare and incidentals to my expense account. Dr. Baldauf was delighted to know I would be present.

My part on the AAZPA program was to give a brief lecture on our fieldwork in Mexico, using many of Isabelle's color slides for illustrations. Since there were a number of Hispanic persons in the largely American audience, I threw in a few Spanish words here and there, but I made no attempt at a general translation. Later on the same day, we were all bused to the zoo in the Bosque de Chapultepec. Isabelle and I had found it to be rather run-down when we visited it two years previously. What a transformation! A small army of painters had arrived a couple of days previously with buckets of bright green paint. Everything was fresh and green, even some of the animals. There was a bear, for instance, with vertical green stripes on the side of its body that resulted from leaning against the bars of its cage before the paint had dried. Several other of the larger mammals were similarly decorated.

The registration fee for the conference was $100 for the two of us. We received a fat portfolio containing the usual collection of program material, places of interest and good restaurants in Mexico City, and so on. We went through ours with care, and noted that attendees were to see the Ballet Folklórico at the Palace of the Fine Arts. On the scheduled evening we were walking across the Alameda, a city park between our hotel and our destination, when I noticed that several friends were holding tickets in their hands. I asked them where they got them, and they said in their portfolios. I responded that there were none in ours, which provoked both laughter and sympathy. "You won't get in," some of them said. We kept on going, however. When we reached the Palace they presented their tickets and went inside. I hung back with Isabelle until there was a lull, whereupon I approached the attendant and said, "*Nuestros billetes son perdidos, pero tengo recibo*" (Our tickets are lost, but I have a receipt). He noted our badges, and saw that they were similar to those of the delegates preceding us. I pulled our registration certificate from my pocket and I pointed out, in Spanish, that I had paid $100 for it. He could not read English, of course, but he was impressed by the amount. "*Momentito, señor*" (Just a minute, sir), he said and opened a nearby door and called to someone. He resumed his assignment of collecting tickets, but presently an assistant manager appeared, and I showed him my receipt and gave him the same explanation. He, too, was impressed and he motioned us to follow him. He conducted us to box seats, just about the best in the house, with a marvelous view of the stage and the superb performance. Some of our friends in the general audience spotted us, and their jaws popped open in amazement. When they asked later how I managed it, I replied with a slight touch of braggadocio, "I can speak Spanish." Then I went on to explain my ploy of using my hundred-dollar receipt.

We had a personal matter of business that required attention while we were in the capital. We visited the Dirección General de la Fauna Silvestre, met the *jefe* (chief), Dr. Rodolfo Hernández de Corzo, and gave him a copy of our field guide, autographed by both of us. In exchange he issued me a collecting permit for use in Mexico during our later trip to the Big Bend region.

As soon as we arrived in Mexico City, I had asked the American Express office to get us tickets to College Station, but it took them until our very last day to find the place on their route maps and to arrange for us to fly to Dallas and then on to our destination. When we picked up our tickets we took a few hours off from the zoo meetings to visit the truly magnificent Museo Nacional Antropología, in which there were replicas of many of the ancient ruins we had visited during our travels throughout Mexico. They were reproduced, at least in part, to scale. It was a thrill to see so many of them under one roof.

The visit to the California herp meetings, as we called them, was interesting and instructive, but, surprisingly, two trivial matters come first to mind when I think about that trip now. Because the planning for our hummingbird exhibit was under way at the Philadelphia Zoo, we spent considerable time with K. C. Lint, Curator of Birds at the San Diego Zoo. I carefully studied, and Isabelle took many photographs of, his outstanding spacious outdoor hummingbird enclosure. One evening he and his wife, Marie, invited us to have dinner with them at a steak house. While we were chatting we discovered that they, like Isabelle and I, were Dixieland jazz fans. We spent the entire evening with them at Mickey Finn's, which was built and operated like an old-fashioned speakeasy of Prohibition days. There was an excellent Dixieland band, including a musician who used a valve, rather than a slide, trombone. In between the several sets, silent movies of Charlie Chaplin and the Keystone Cops were shown. It was delightfully nostalgic, and especially so when we discovered that Mickey Finn's was on a half-hour radio network program, and we could listen to the same band at home once a week.

At the ASIH meetings we all lined up in rows for the annual group picture in front of the California Academy of Sciences, in Golden Gate Park. The wind was blowing in strongly from the Pacific, and my hair was constantly falling down over my face. It convinced me that my barber's scheme of training hair from one side of my head to cross my bald pate was futile. I was bald, so why not get rid of that affectation? I did, as soon as I was home, and thus emulated W. Frank Blair, the Texas herpetologist, who had reached the same conclusion.

Our experiences in the Big Bend and a never-to-be-forgotten train trip from the Chihuahuan highlands down to the west coast of Mexico are discussed in other chapters. So also (in an anecdote) is the day we spent on the Mediterranean island of Mallorca (Majorca in the English geographical lexicon).

Our trip to Barcelona was memorable indeed. I was welcomed by everyone, and that meant most of the great zoo directors of the world. There were several Americans, and the meetings were conducted largely in English, although translations into Spanish, French, and German were available by donning earphones and pressing the correct button. The Barcelona Zoo was a good one and it featured the already famous snow-white gorilla, Copito de Nieve (Little Cup of Snow), that had been found as a baby in Río Muni, then a small Spanish colony on the west coast of Africa. We were entertained, taken to many interesting places, and wined and dined. I apparently made a good impression because, from then on, I was a regular member of the IUDZG.

In Barcelona my Mexican Spanish received considerable criticism. It seemed as though every taxi driver, doorman, and porter sought to correct me. I write this phonetically, but what they said was, "Not sinko sentavos,

Señor. It is think'-oh then-ta'-vos." We were in Catalonia. Who was the king who lisped and whose subjects learned to lisp so as not to offend him? I had been taught Castilian Spanish in high school, but all my lisping sounds had long since vanished from my vocabulary.

From Barcelona we went on to Zürich, Basel, Munich, Stuttgart, and Frankfurt to see their famous zoos, and especially their reptile exhibits. While we were in Munich we digressed so that I could take Isabelle to the Zugspitze, where the cars climbed upward inside the mountain. I had traveled the same route just 30 years previously.

That European excursion enabled me to learn many new things that were invaluable in planning our own exhibits. President Tyler surprised us and earned our enduring gratitude when he told me that the zoo not only would pay my expenses, but also Isabelle's. He was aware of the enormous contribution she had made to publicizing the zoo during her 10-year tenure as official photographer and my general assistant. Normally, when Isabelle went with me, which she almost always did, we paid her way ourselves.

In 1968 we had an extremely lucky break. The IUDZG meeting was in Pretoria, South Africa. Not only did we attend, but I also took my month's vacation in East Africa en route. Our adventures during that wonderful visit to the mecca of so many naturalists are detailed in two chapters entitled "The Trip of a Lifetime." We traveled a lot while I was the zoo's director, and that was the most pleasant part of my administration.

Chapter 44

Hoodlums, Vandals, and Other Problems

Most people visited the Philadelphia Zoological Garden to have a pleasant day, to enjoy the out-of-doors and open space, and to see the animals and their capers. Many went there for an annual outing. They were welcome, and we did our very best for them. On the other hand, there was a hoodlum-vandal element that caused us endless trouble, and there were others who, through mischief or accident, managed to get into difficulties.

Our biggest problem was to protect the animals from being targets for anything throwable. It was only in the monkey and reptile houses that most of the exhibits were behind glass. Wire-fronted cages were also fairly safe, but the animals in open pens or paddocks had no protection except what we could provide through the vigilance of the guards and keepers. We carefully removed all loose rocks and pebbles, but we could not prevent visitors from using things they had with them. The usually inert alligators were bombarded with pennies, and sometimes nickels and dimes, in attempts to make them move. Every year $100 or more accumulated, although it was collected piecemeal during each periodic cleaning and scrubbing of the pool. On the minus side, some idiot, long before my time at the zoo, tossed a ball into the open mouth of a rare and valuable pygmy hippopotamus. It lodged in the poor animal's windpipe and quickly killed it. Legend had it that, when he heard the news, Zoo President Charles B. Penrose, M.D., for whom the Penrose Research Laboratory was named, exploded by saying, "The zoo is a wonderful place, and it would be perfect if we could keep the goddamned public out of it."

During the pop bottle years we were our own worst enemies. The sale of refreshments in several locations in the zoo, which I had so strongly recommended when I returned from Europe in 1937, was a great success, but for the first few years the soft drinks were dispensed in standard glass bottles. It was a cumbersome method, but well suited to our constantly fluctuating requirements. On warm Sundays and holidays we needed vast quantities of bottles, whereas when it was cool or on rainy weekdays the demand was slight.

The bottles were placed in tubs full of cracked ice, and, on busy days, even with a relay of tubs, the refreshment stand people were hard-pressed to cool them fast enough. No one had yet invented easily opened cans to hold soda pop. We placed empty-bottle crates at strategic locations, near the stands and alongside benches where visitors paused to rest and have a drink. Few of the crates were used. Most of the bottles were tossed into the shrubbery or flower beds, shoved under benches or into odd corners, or just dropped on the sidewalks to become pedestrian hazards. Far, far too many were thrown at the animals, however. After a busy Sunday the hippo pool looked as though the entire German U-boat fleet was present in miniature. The necks of pop bottles, partially filled with water, protruded above the surface like tiny periscopes. Probably most of them had bounced off the tough hide of Jimmy, the big male hippopotamus. Theoretically, only a direct hit in an eye could hurt him. Periodically we had to clean out the large bird lake. It was drained and the muck removed from the bottom along with as much as two huge truckloads of bottles that had been thrown at the ducks, geese, and swans. Believe me, there were many days when the entire animal department, including yours truly, felt like echoing Dr. Penrose's sentiments.

Our reserve supply of ice for the soft drinks was stored in great blocks in the mortuary room of the Penrose Research Laboratory. The room was rather large, however, and there were shelves at the rear where the carcasses of animals that died in the zoo could be kept chilled pending autopsy. The ice was piled as far from them as possible, just inside the door.

One day an ailing kangaroo was found lying virtually moribund in its pen, and it was transported to the Laboratory and given a shot to put it out of its misery. It was laid on the floor in the back of the mortuary. Sometime later the delivery man arrived with a huge cake of ice on his shoulder. As he opened the door, the kangaroo, which had suddenly come to life, hopped toward him, and our entire day's supply of ice shattered on the floor.

Eventually, automatic equipment guaranteed to

dispense ice-cold soda pop all day long became available. Zoo Director Shelly, after what many of us thought was too long a delay, finally found some machines that he thought were within our limited budget. They were installed in each of several refreshment stands. What a relief! Paper cups were impossible to throw for any distance and with any force.

Then a new problem developed. After the zoo closed for the day, honey bees gathered at the then open-air stands, and crawled up inside the faucets. The first cups filled each morning were full of bees, all struggling to escape from the sticky, wet mess. The personnel who operated the stands had to cover the mouths of the batteries of faucets each day before they went off duty.

We also sold zillions of hot dogs on buns, and visitors could add their own mustard from jars with paddles on the counter of each stand. One year, Gus Griswold, the Curator of Birds, was raising a pair of young rheas, tall South American birds that look like small ostriches. He suggested at a staff meeting that he turn them loose to mingle with the public just as he did the peafowl and several ducks that were at liberty on the zoo grounds. It sounded like a good idea and, once the birds had their freedom, many visitors were at first startled and then enthralled by their encounters with the strange-looking birds. We were all quite pleased with the results, but then the rheas discovered the mustard. They gobbled it up with gusto. The attendants had to hide the jars and paddles under the counters and make them available to customers only on demand. The resourceful rheas then would wait until someone bought a hot dog. Youngsters were their most frequent victims. The birds would reach their long necks over the victims' shoulders, snatch bun, hot dog, and mustard, and then run off to eat them. That didn't happen too often, so we made good with duplicate hot dogs, and visitors had an amusing story to relate to their friends and neighbors, who we hoped would visit the zoo, pay their way in, and then spend more money on food and souvenirs.

There are two other stories to tell about those same two rheas. One day a group of 10 or so youngsters arrived at the zoo with an older girl in charge who could not have been long out of her teens. As an object lesson in responsibility, she gave one of the boys all the coins for their homeward-bound carfare, and instructed him to put them in his pocket and guard them well. They toured the zoo for a while, and then, like most youngsters, the boys began to play, rolling in the grass and wrestling with one another. All the coins fell out of the boy's pocket, and the rheas, lurking nearby, raced over and gobbled them down before the startled youngsters realized what was happening. A short time later a tear-

ful group of kids arrived at the zoo office. The leader explained their predicament. Someone with access to the petty cash box remedied the situation.

The rheas adapted well to outdoor conditions, and the weather remained mild until Thanksgiving. Just before the holiday, one of the two birds disappeared and was never found. The zoo grounds were searched with great care on the assumption that a vandal might have killed or injured it, and it could be lying concealed, perhaps under the shrubbery. Not so. One of the keepers jokingly, but possibly with at least a small grain of truth, suggested that the only way to discover the culprits was to find an oven in some nearby West Philadelphia home that was big enough to roast a rhea for a holiday feast.

During my first few years at America's First Zoo the public was reasonably tidy. Suddenly, soon after we entered World War II, people began to throw trash, banana peels, and other garbage from the homemade lunches they brought with them, and it landed almost anywhere. The baskets and bins we provided might contain a few pieces of paper, but, for each item properly disposed of, there were literally thousands dropped on the ground. On Monday mornings after busy Sundays, the zoo looked as though there had been a snowstorm. All hands in the maintenance department, including the higher-salaried mechanics, had to abandon all other assignments in order to clean up the enormous mess. I even pitched in to help a few times, when I had no pressing duties waiting for me at the office. One visitor wrote a scathing letter to the editor of one of the Philadelphia newspapers complaining about the filthy zoo. The response was an excellent editorial absolving us and placing the blame squarely where it belonged— on the public's bad manners.

In a sense, we got off easily in comparison with the National Zoo, in Washington, D.C., where it was traditional for hordes of people to visit on Easter Monday each year. Admission was free, and it was a holiday. Every animal that could be was locked inside its shelter. All exhibition buildings were bolted shut, with all the livestock inside. Even with large police details, however, vandalism was rampant. Why do people en masse behave like pigs and barbarians? Years later, experiments with mice in the Penrose Lab and elsewhere gave us an inkling about what weird and horrifying episodes can occur when people are crowded together.

Speaking of Easter, it was in the late 1950s or early 1960s that a phenomenon developed suddenly that gave our paid attendance a spurt, but worsened our headaches. All at once it became the fashion for teenagers, dressed in their Easter best, to arrive at the zoo in early afternoon. They presumably had been to

Other birds could be mischievous. Leona Griswold unexpectedly lost her cap one day while she was working in the toucan enclosure. Photo by Franklin Williamson, Philadelphia Zoo archives.

church to learn how to be good, but they came to the zoo in an opposite mood, and they created havoc. They crossed guardrails, broke off branches from our trees and shrubbery to have sticks to poke at the animals, jumped into the open-air bird pens and enclosures, chased the birds around, raided our flower beds, and even got into fights with one another with knives. On that first Easter, I hastened to the telephone to ask for more police help, but the park guards could spare only two men because of unexpected mischief elsewhere in Fairmount Park.

For each Easter Sunday following the first melee, I arranged in advance with the park guard superintendent for a squad of men, some in plain clothes, to be on hand. They kept a patrol van at the zoo, and many a time it was filled with culprits and driven to the Park lockup. I checked annually at the trolley car stop in front of the North Gate entrance and, from about 1:00 P.M. onward for a couple of hours, every car arriving in either direction was crammed to the doors with teenagers, mostly boys, all of whom got off at the zoo. Easter Sunday was surely our most worrisome day of the year.

For more than a dozen years we had a naturalistic, barless, outdoor reptile pen and pool in which we kept surplus turtles and young alligators. Visitors would stop to look, but an occasional small boy would step down into the two-foot-deep perimeter moat to have a closer look. One day a pair of mischievous lads caught two small gators, each perhaps 18 inches long, surreptitiously opened the door to the women's restroom, and pushed them in. They hovered nearby and were rewarded by seeing and hearing their victims emerge precipitously and sometimes screaming. I was summoned to catch the alligators, but the boys ran out the turnstile exit and disappeared.

Another time a teenager took a large red-bellied turtle out of the pen. He probably concealed it beneath his jacket, and carried it to the South Gate entrance, where an elderly attendant worked alone for the benefit of visitors who made use of the small parking lot directly adjacent. He kept everything carefully locked, and would admit no one into the small office except zoo employees. The boy went to the side where admission tickets were sold and where he could be heard through the narrow area below the plate glass window. He held up the turtle and said he wanted to present it to the zoo. Unthinkingly, the man opened the locked door and promptly received a savage blow to the forehead with the turtle's shell as a weapon. He was badly cut and knocked unconscious. When he came to, the day's receipts, his reserve bag of change, and the boy had vanished. The turtle, its shell undamaged, was on the floor. That scoundrel was ingenious, and he was never caught.

Wherever crowds gather there almost invariably is the problem of lost children. They wander off while their parents are talking or concentrating on exhibits or activities. The results range from real trauma to humorous situations. We had our share of both at the Philadelphia Zoo.

My most memorable experience with lost kids occurred after the close of our first really busy day, which was May Day at the Zoo, May 1, 1938, when we had 19,569 visitors by actual count. We were unprepared for the aftermath. The amount of minor damage was unbelievable, several staff members were still counting money by hand at midnight, and I took over the lost child chore. I found myself, about 8:00 P.M., in the ticket office at the North Gate entrance with 17 young boys and two dogs. I had no direct phone line. The operator in the Penn House had to help me. I started with the oldest lad and asked him his name. He also knew where he lived, but he didn't know his phone number. That was easily ascertained, however, by consulting the telephone book. After a short delay I had his mother on the line, and was she irate. "So that's where he is. You tell him to come home immediately!" To which I replied, "That's more easily said than done, lady. He has no money for car fare, and I refuse to take the responsibility of putting him on a trolley car. He is too young to travel alone." There was dead silence for a moment, and then she said, "OK. I'll send his big brother after him."

An hour later I had managed to get in touch with two more sets of parents, but the remainder of the restless mob seemed hopeless. "I want a drink of water." "I hafta go to the bathroom." "This dog's licking my face." "I wanna go home." They all knew their first names or nicknames, but that was all. I even went through their pockets looking for names and addresses. None was over nine years of age, and the youngest couldn't have been more than five. Finally, in despair, I called the park guard office, and they sent over a paddy wagon. I was relieved when they told me not to hesitate to call them if we ever had lost kids on our hands. Parents eventually got in touch with the police when they couldn't find their offspring.

During a busy Sunday a few years later, one of our uniformed guards found a little boy of about six wandering along by himself. In the prescribed manner he asked, "Are you lost, sonny?" In reply the lad said, "No. I'm at the zoo." Then after a short pause, he added, "But my mother's lost."

One Sunday morning when the Penn House was still the Philadelphia Zoo's administrative headquarters, I was working in my office on the second floor, when the telephone operator asked me if I would come down to help solve a problem. A boy of perhaps seven or eight had been brought in by a guard. He had not answered any questions. What to do? I sat down beside him on a bench and tried my luck. Still no response. On a hunch, I switched to Spanish, and his face lit up at once. He was a member of a large Puerto Rican family that had come to the zoo en masse with his eight or nine siblings. I chatted with him for a few minutes, showed him where the bathroom was, and found him a picture book of animals to look at. When I went to lunch an hour later he was still there. Before I returned I checked with the operator and asked if his parents had come. No. So I bought him a lunch and carried it back with me. To make a long story short, the boy was in the office all day, except for when I took him for a walk, holding his hand as a precaution, as I made my usual Sunday inspection of the grounds and crowd. Finally, at 4:30, I called the park guards, and they came for him. His parents, with such a large brood, had failed to make a head count when they left the zoo for home.

Eventually, on busy days, we constructed a temporary "kiddie pen" by forming park benches into a square, inside of which the "strays" were entertained by one of the hostesses from the children's zoo with a rabbit or kitten or two. Mothers, often tearful and almost frantic, could retrieve their offspring, sometimes with hugs and sometimes with scolding admonitions never to wander off again.

In the mid-1960s another unexpected problem developed. During the evenings of busy Sundays and holidays, when almost all visitors and employees had left for the day, boys from across the Pennsylvania Railroad tracks, along the rear side of the zoo, would climb over the fence. That was no mean feat, because the zoo grounds were protected by brackets extending outward that carried three parallel strands of barbed wire. Such an arrangement was strictly illegal, but the authorities tolerated it because they knew the zoo was sometimes the victim of vandalism. Once inside, the boys raided the refreshment stands, which by then had been enclosed. They did several hundred dollars' worth of damage by breaking in to steal a relatively few dollars' worth of candy, ice cream, or other items. Soon they learned to bring along pieces of old carpet or flat pieces of heavy cardboard, which they laid over the barbed wire to ease their passage across it. They came week after week during the spring and summer seasons.

A few days after I became the zoo's Director, I took steps to terminate such destruction. I consulted with my old friend Robert G. Hudson, who was then the Managing Director of the Women's Society for the Prevention of Cruelty to Animals. He found us two tame but ferocious-looking German shepherd dogs and an excellent trainer. About 20 of us, myself included, took the obedience course. We learned how to handle the dogs, how to make them sit, and how to hang on to their leashes when they were all set to run after a trespasser. They could bark furiously and they looked downright dangerous. Unlike the Bronx Zoo, in New York City, which had similar and even more severe problems, we never used attack dogs that were trained to seize and hold hoodlums.

In accordance with legal requirements, we posted signs at specified intervals inside the fence that were readily visible from outside. They stated that the grounds were patrolled by guard dogs. When warmer weather arrived, we were all set. One of the zoo's guards or keepers would walk a dog each evening along the rear fence. That year and each subsequent one, not a single boy climbed into the zoo over our back fence, insofar as we knew. The pilferage stopped.

I was often an impatient guy, and I have long wondered

why it took my predecessor so long to get rid of the pop bottles and to purchase apparatus for cleaning up the trash in the zoo. Why didn't he take steps to protect the refreshment stands from the weekly raids? He was noted for his skill at saving money, but there surely were limits. Perhaps he hoped that public manners and morals would improve, but I, as a professional biologist, had long since learned that human beings, when crowded or en masse, tended to behave like uncontrollable savages.

It was the consensus, among those of us who looked after the livestock, that taking care of the animals was easy compared with trying to cope with the public.

Chapter 45

Our Accomplishments

It sometimes happens, when an institution acquires a replacement director, that he serves as a new broom, sweeping aside many long-established policies and forcing his own imprint on everyone, even to the extent of discharging longtime employees. I was determined that nothing of the sort would happen in my case. After all, many of our key staff members had played a substantial part in the zoo's renaissance. Further, I would retire in a relatively few years. Upsetting the applecart, to use an old saw, was the farthest thing from my mind.

There were, however, many improvements I could make. Some I had been thinking about for years and had even suggested to Zoo Director Freeman M. Shelly, only to have them vetoed. Now that I have reviewed some of the problems and unexpected headaches that developed after I took office, I should discuss some changes and innovations that I introduced.

There were a few things I could do almost immediately to remedy longstanding problems. First, I reformed the weekly staff meetings. To me, it seemed almost criminal to tie up all the highest-paid employees for hours at a time, but that had long been the practice. We assembled in Shelly's (now my) office at 10:30 A.M. and often we were still at it until well past noon or even 1:00 P.M. Both my predecessor and I had been instructed by our superiors to have weekly meetings of minds, so to speak, but why waste so much time on them? I recall that, one day, some of those present wrangled for over an hour on how to collect the manure from the elephant house, a formidable problem to be sure, but one that could be better solved by an on-site discussion. I streamlined the staff meetings at once. I let my colleagues discuss a subject for five minutes or so, and then I instructed the person who brought up the subject to study the problem, consult with others, and submit his recommendations at the next meeting. That saved a lot of time, and it also had the salutary effect of discouraging the reporting of trivial matters. The staff member who brought them up soon realized he would be stuck with the problem of solving them himself.

A little later I brought in guard dogs, which, when our busy season arrived, stemmed the exasperating flow of fence hoppers bent on mischief inside the zoo. (See "Hoodlums, Vandals, and Other Problems.")

I had always been security conscious. Maybe it stemmed from my Boy Scout training. Or the U.S. Coast Guard. When I joined the Volunteer Port Security Force during World War II, I was assigned, during my watch, to check on all safety devices on the piers we were guarding, and that included hydrants, hoses, fire extinguishers, alarm bells, and everything kept under lock and key.

At the zoo I was always making sure all the cages were locked, which annoyed some of the keepers until, on rare occasions, I found something amiss, much to their embarrassment. The night watch concerned me. There were only two guards, and, while one made the rounds and punched the time clocks in the various buildings, the other stayed at the switchboard to await any alarm call from his partner. I would have liked to add another man, but I failed to convince anyone that it was necessary. At least I could beef up the system we had. I gave each man a walkie-talkie, so that when one was patrolling the grounds well away from any telephone, he could communicate with his partner. I also required them to carry whistles which, when loudly blown as though to summon help, might scare off trespassers. Most important, I visited Park Guard Headquarters, which was not far from us in Fairmount Park. All of the officers and most of the men of that splendid force knew me by sight, and I was generous with free zoo passes for the entire corps. I explained how thinly we were guarded at night, and they promised to see that a patrol car circled the outside of the zoo grounds every hour or so.

One night, not long afterward, one of our watchmen rounded the corner of a building and saw a strange automobile pulled into the recess where trucks waited at the service gate for someone to unlock the barrier. What was it doing there at 2:00 A.M.? The watchman backed away quietly, went to the nearest telephone, and asked that a call be put through to the park guards. Before he could get back to within sight of the gate, a patrol car had arrived. Two men were changing a tire. Nothing was wrong, but the extremely prompt response of the guards was a real morale booster for the watchmen.

Philadelphia, like so many other big cities during the 1960s, had its share of riots, burnings, and lootings. Entire blocks of houses were destroyed by arsonists. Things had been quiet for quite a time when the park guards alerted me about a tip they and the city police had received. The two groups of officers worked closely together. Small bands of hoodlums planned to start riots in three widely separated parts of the city simultaneously. Police Commissioner Frank Rizzo arranged to have two buses filled with police waiting just a few blocks away from each of the targeted areas. As soon as the rioters went to work, they were completely overwhelmed by the police, and the planned uprisings died aborning.

The general destruction of property and disrespect for law and order worried me. The zoo was inadequately guarded, especially insofar as sheer vandalism was concerned. What might we expect in the mental climate of that period? Our ancient giraffe house, which was very largely constructed of wood, was a tinderbox, and so close to the street that a firebrand could easily be hurled into it from outside the fence. So, while the menace continued to be acute, a half dozen of us took turns supplementing our meager night force from closing time until midnight. I took one of the guard dogs with me and patrolled chiefly near the boundary fence. I kept the leash short and talked to the dog when we approached any of the more nervous animals in their outdoor paddocks, so they could easily hear as well as smell us coming and wouldn't bolt. I even visited all the zoo's restrooms. They were never locked, and they were ideal places for someone bent on mischief to hide. I let the dog go into each one first, knowing it would bark if it detected anyone.

A few weeks later the park guards felt it was no longer necessary to continue our patrols. They were an elite corps, chartered by the Commonwealth of Pennsylvania, and they had police powers anywhere in the state. I personally thought it was criminal when Frank Rizzo, after he became mayor, absorbed them into the city's regular police force, thus bringing an end to their long, distinguished service as an independent body of law-enforcement officers.

One thing I wanted to do very badly was to improve the zoo's exhibits by introducing some of the modern techniques that were revolutionizing animal displays in many of our sister zoological gardens. Fiberglass was coming into wide use as a means of replicating realistic suggestions of natural habitats.

After I was well settled in my new job, I broached the subject to President George F. Tyler, Jr. He was very much interested, and he even drove me and Fred Ulmer, our Curator of Mammals, to the Bronx Zoo in his own car to look at what they had been doing. Particularly impressive was the addition of the basal portion of a huge tropical African tree, made of fiberglass, that had been installed in the mandrill cage. It even had buttresses beneath which the highly colored baboons could pass if they wished. The tree had transformed a routine cell-like cage into an exhibit of outstanding interest. I received the green light to look into hiring exhibit experts of our own.

Even earlier, James S. Hatfield, Chairman of the board's Building Committee, had discovered Mervin Larson at the Arizona-Sonora Desert Museum during one of his visits to Tucson, Arizona. Larson was skilled in making all sorts of objects from fiberglass, and he was engaged to prepare a large number of naturalistic exhibits for our new small mammal house. They included the inside of a cave for vampire bats, a prairie dog exhibit where those social animals could be seen both below and above ground, and an African veldt scene for meerkats. In fact, virtually every exhibit in the new building was designed to look like the animal's natural habitat. What a vast contrast in comparison with the way our animals were exhibited in the other buildings. The small mammal house was an instant hit with the public.

Larson fabricated the various fiberglass units in Arizona, using the building plans as guides for dimensions, shipped them to Philadelphia, and then he came east to install them. It seemed to me that we would be better off, financially and in many details of design, if we could produce our own fiberglass work in-house. Mr. Hatfield agreed and so did President Tyler. We had already ordered some graphics exhibits for the hummingbird exhibit from an outside source. Again, why not do such things with our own people in the future?

Finding a good fiberglass artist wasn't easy. I interviewed and examined the work of several, and I finally hired Kenneth D. Dills, a genius who could create anything using the new techniques. Although he did all of the wonderful backgrounds in the new reptile house, and many other things, I consider that his greatest accomplishment, during my time at the zoo, was creating the huge tree in the hummingbird exhibit. It was so lifelike and had so many bromeliads and other plants growing on its widely spreading branches that many visitors couldn't believe that it wasn't real. The plants, installed by Charles W. Rogers, Jr., the staff horticulturalist, were real enough. Charles did all the tropical planting in the hummingbird exhibit, in addition to his regular duties of supervising the plantings throughout the entire zoological garden.

I eventually hired additional skilled personnel for the new Exhibits Department, and soon we were able to provide our own graphics in many different parts of the zoo. Also, many objects made of fiberglass began to appear in cages here and there. I quote the following from the December 1972 issue of our quarterly zoo magazine, entitled "America's First Zoo":

> The Zoo's Exhibits Department pitted its technology and skill against the brute strength of our six young Gorillas when the Apes moved into their remodeled enclosure in the Rare Mammal House. The lush jungle habitat became home for the Gorillas after it passed a durability test by our Chimpanzees, who lived in the enclosure for a short while. The Gorillas, who now occupy three adjoining enclosures in the Building, seem to enjoy sitting in the trees and swinging from the fiberglass branches.

The new exhibit was far better done than the base of the huge tropical tree that we had driven to the Bronx Zoo to see, but in the meantime, they, too, had been improving their techniques.

Construction on several major projects was well under way when I took office. Five were completed and a sixth was finished in part when I retired. Another was rapidly taking shape. We were nearing the end of the renaissance of the Philadelphia Zoological Garden.

The small mammal house was opened to the public on May 14, 1967. Its naturalistic habitat backgrounds made it unique, and it compared favorably with the best of similar structures in other zoos. Fred Ulmer worked hard and long with the architects, who incorporated many of his ideas and called upon him constantly for advice. Then he had the assignment of obtaining the animals for it, all to be on hand before opening day. Among other things, he had to find living vampire bats and liquid blood with which to feed them. Not an easy chore, especially since no animal dealer we knew had ever listed them for sale.

The Zoo Safari Monorail, which gave visitors a bird's-eye view of many of the outdoor exhibits, was opened in May 1969. It was quite expensive to erect, but it was financed by a concession that shared the revenue derived from rides with the zoo. On busy days the cars were crowded. At other times it was a good management tool. I rode it at least once a week, and I often spotted places that needed attention. One day, while I was on such a tour of inspection, an idea popped into my head. There was nothing much for riders to see in the extreme southern part of the zoo. Why not develop an outdoor exhibit against the slope leading up to the boundary fence? That was the origin of the wolf woods project. I brought up the subject at a board meeting, but the opinion was expressed that there wasn't enough space to do what I envisioned. President John Williams made a special trip to the zoo, rode the monorail with me, and saw clearly that the project was feasible. He quickly convinced the doubters. The first and larger of the two units of the wolf exhibit was completed before I retired. The work for it was done entirely in-house. Our superintendent of maintenance, who caused me so much trouble, was very good at construction, and the Exhibits Department did an excellent job in giving the area a quasi-natural appearance.

The Eleanor S. Gray Memorial Hummingbird Exhibit was opened to the public early in 1970, and it was so beautiful and superbly done that it deserved every superlative in the dictionary. It was planned, designed, erected, furnished with graphics and many naturalistic backgrounds, including the man-made giant tree that dominated its center, and then finally planted throughout, with tender, loving care. In a sense, the exhibit was a monument to a score or more of people who contributed their skill and knowledge to its completion. Curator of Birds Griswold was the moving spirit throughout the three-year construction period, but he was quick to give credit to all those who had a part in it. The entire exhibit was privately funded. Many persons contributed, some for the purchase of birds, and a substantial sum was provided by J. Maurice Gray, in memory of his wife. In order to prevent crowds from becoming too dense, and also to discourage vandals and hoodlums who, unhappily, seemed always to be with us, an admission fee of 25 cents was charged to enter the exhibit.

The international zoo meeting (IUDZG) was held in New York in the autumn of 1969, with the Bronx Zoo serving as host. With the permission of its Director, William G. Conway, I invited the delegates, their spouses, and guests to spend a day at the Philadelphia Zoo. They traveled by bus in both directions. We had lunch in the lobby of the bird house alongside the large planted and landscaped area where the birds were at complete liberty. Afterward, we entered the hummingbird exhibit, which was nearing completion. There were no birds in it as yet, but they, too, would be completely free, and they could fly, if they wished, over and around the public. As the delegates made their inspection, they were obviously greatly impressed, and there were superlatives in several languages. I wish I could have translated them all.

The small mammal and reptile houses were among

the projects funded by the city. There was also an auxiliary list for further improvements, including the African plains exhibit, to be done in two phases, new bear dens, and replacements for the old monkey, kangaroo, and antelope houses. The order of priorities had been changed from time to time. At the very bottom was a new administration building, and my predecessor, Freeman M. Shelly, had kept it there for years, although I think it may have occupied the penultimate position once or twice. We were still ensconced in the old historic Penn House, and we were finding it more and more inadequate. Then came the day when an unusually violent wind and thunderstorm wrecked part of the roof, rain poured in, and we had to scramble to rescue the files and other records from water damage. I was in my office at the time, but I hurried out to help get things under cover. Something had to be done. We could not go on indefinitely in the old building.

I lost quite a bit of sleep worrying about what to do and thinking about ways and means to provide a better place for us. After much cogitating, I came up with a plan that I thought offered an ideal solution. Why not construct a combination administration building and educational center—all in one? I kept my idea to myself until I had studied all the angles.

The zoological garden had long been considered an educational institution. Just visiting the zoo was a learning experience. We supplied information about the animals on signs placed in front of each cage or paddock. They identified the animals, and, for advanced students, they even included the scientific names. There was a brief statement about the animal's region of origin—Africa or South America, for example—and, in the case of an unusual animal, its pet or nickname. "Jimmy" appeared in the case of our large male hippopotamus. He was quite a character. When he was young, he chased the zoo's tame, free-roaming ducks out of his pen, only to tolerate them when he grew older, by letting them use his broad back as a resting spot when he lazed in the water of his outdoor pool.

Speaking of signs, I once overheard a small boy who had stopped in front of an outdoor pen where our female camel, named Sheba, was on exhibit. He turned to the elderly lady with him and asked, "Grandma, what kind of animal is that?" She walked as close to the guardrail as she could, adjusted her bifocals, read the sign, and then said, "That's a Sheba." The youngster responded by saying, "Gee, it looks like a camel to me."

I took over the preparation of signs very soon after I arrived at the Philadelphia Zoo, and they became more elaborate over the years. Later, Curators Gus Griswold and Fred Ulmer prepared the copy for birds and mammals, respectively, for me to edit and fit into the available space. Color photographs were used for most of the bird signs, especially when several different kinds were living together. Eventually, graphics with maps and special messages were added in many places.

School visits were very popular, particularly in the spring. Teachers came with their classes, usually accompanied by a mother or two to keep an eye on the youngsters. We had a special low admission rate for them. Unless they were carefully disciplined, the children could be unruly and boisterous, however. In fact, we had to cover the smooth walls and ceiling of the lion house with acoustical tile to deaden the dreadful noise their shrill voices and laughter created. The attitude of the teachers varied considerably. A few, once their classes were inside the zoo, would announce, "Now, children, we have two hours before our buses return for us. Be sure to be back here at the gate by half-past eleven." Then they sat and chatted in the shade while the kids ran wild and got themselves into all sorts of mischief. We finally had to insist that the teachers stay with their charges. We especially appreciated the ones who came equipped with a long rope. The children lined up along it and were required to hold it with one hand the entire time they were in the zoo.

The Daniel W. Dietrich Memorial Children's Zoo, with its many domestic and young wild animals, was an outstanding educational unit, but it was idle and partly empty during the winter months. Why not take part of it to the schools, at least during cold weather when it was closed to the public? By appointment, way back in 1959, I took William J. Maloney, then Superintendent of the Children's Zoo, and one of the hostesses, along with a few tame animals to the office of Paul E. Long, Director of Audio-Visual Education for the School District of Philadelphia. They gave a demonstration of how they would handle the animals and talk about them in a classroom. Mr. Long was delighted with the presentation, and he said his department would sponsor our activities. Also, his people would take the responsibility for scheduling talks for elementary school auditoriums twice each day, one in the morning and the other during the afternoon. Reservations poured in so fast, when the plan was announced to the teachers and principals, that within three days the zoo program was booked solid for the winter.

Armed with that information I approached the zoo board, and several of the members chipped in enough, out of their own pockets, for us to purchase a Volkswagen bus. I had it professionally painted with colorful birds and mammals, and with the legend "School Bus for Animals" prominently displayed. The program was

Four important zoo person-
ages (from left): Kevin J.
Bowler, Assistant Curator of
Reptiles; Virginia Pearson;
Stephen R. Wylie, Assistant
Curator of Birds; and Jeanne
Segal. The two ladies, with a
few friends, organized the
zoo's Docent Service. Photo
by Franklin Williamson,
Philadelphia Zoo archives.

in demand every slack season, and it had the ancillary advantage of advertising the children's zoo both at the schools and on its trips to and from them.

As a moneymaker, "talking storybooks" were installed at strategic locations, so that visitors could hear about the animals as well as see them. I prepared many of the messages that were used on them. Visitors operated the metal boxes by inserting a key they had to buy in advance. The same key operated all the boxes. Mr. Shelly arranged for their installation. Unhappily, the mainte-nance by the concession company was not good, and we had too many silent boxes most of the time.

All these activities were definitely educational, but I had long dreamed of a truly professional program with many participants.

Eventually, I formulated a mental master plan and drew a few rough sketches. The building I envisioned would be two stories high, with the zoo's business offices upstairs, and classrooms and an auditorium on the ground floor for easy access by schoolchildren. The structure would be close to the zoo perimeter fence so that persons on business visits would not have to walk a long way through the grounds to reach the office. For personnel to inaugurate the educational program, I hoped that Paul Long would be able to assign a teacher or two to us, as he did to other cultural institutions in Philadelphia. I also had in mind a volunteer group of

docents (guides) whom we could train to take school groups through the grounds, telling them about the animals, conservation, and the protection of our natural environment as they went. Such volunteer programs were already proving successful in several other zoos.

I discussed my plan with President Tyler, then with the board's Building Committee, and finally at a regular board meeting. My report was received with enthusi-asm. Everyone knew about our problems with the Penn House, and a combination of an educational center and administration offices, both in one building, was accepted as a novel addition for the zoo. I had won the first round, so to speak, and I was deeply grateful to have the backing of the board.

Next I had to convince the city officials, and that wasn't easy. I visited several of them in their offices, and all advanced the argument that more animal exhibits, or "crowd pleasers," as some of them put it, would be better for the zoo. They would attract more people and increase our attendance and revenue. In rebuttal, I pointed out that we were already getting in excess of a million paid admissions each year, and that on pleasant spring and summer Sundays and holidays our 42 acres were crowded to capacity, and people had to stand in line, sometimes for long periods, to get into certain build-ings. The condition of the Penn House was a futile argu-ment. None of them had ever been inside it. In short,

The 25th anniversary of the "Let's Visit the Zoo" weekly radio program in 1961. From left: RC; Isabelle; Richard Paisley, station manager; and Robert Benson, program director. Photo by IHC.

they were lukewarm at best about changing the order of the priorities. Unexpectedly, I acquired a powerful ally in the person of Robert W. Crawford, City Recreation Commissioner and later President of the Fairmount Park Commission, technically our landlord. He enthusiastically endorsed my plan and pointed out that a historic edifice like the Penn House should not be used for a workaday business office and subjected to such constant attrition as the traffic of our own feet and those of divers business visitors, seekers of lost children, or people desiring information. Further, he liked the educational idea. His opinions and influence got things moving.

When I appeared before City Council, several of the Zoological Society's officers and board members were present to back me up. I was asked to outline my plan for the new building. I stressed the educational angle, and it was immediately obvious that it appealed to the councilmen far more than the administrative advantages we would derive from the new structure. One councilman asked me a pointed question: "You are asking the City of Philadelphia to finance the new building, but would you also expect to use it for suburban schoolchildren?" My answer was, "Yes, but we must schedule all class visits in advance, and the Philadelphia schools will always have priority." That satisfied him, and several other councilmen nodded their approval. They passed the bill, and we were off and running. Construction began in 1970.

Accompanied by Henry D. Mirick, the architect for the Ed-Ad Building, as we soon began to call it, I visited administration offices in other zoos, including Milwaukee, where we had an unexpected adventure. We studied that zoo's new offices and also its large open paddocks. We soon would have to think about our own African plains. Our host, George Speidel, Director of the Milwaukee Zoo, drove us to the airport in late afternoon so we could catch our plane back to Philadelphia. When we arrived at the ticket counter, Mr. Mirick and I discovered that the plane would be about 90 minutes late. I remarked that I guessed we had better telephone our wives so they wouldn't think we'd been hijacked or something. I called Isabelle and she agreed to pass the word along to Mrs. Mirick. Then the two of us walked to a newsstand to buy some reading matter to help occupy the long wait. As we were paying, we were surrounded by two policemen and four or five other armed guards, who marched us to a small room off the waiting room lobby. We were asked to identify ourselves. We had our driver's licenses, and I explained who we were and our mission at the Milwaukee Zoo. Could we prove that? George Speidel, of course, was the best person to vouch for us, but he was lost in heavy traffic at that time of day. I finally found a zoo membership card in my wallet, and that helped a little. After giving us a lecture on security and telling us never to use the words "hijack" or "bomb" in an airport, they let us go. Time-wise, we were right at the initiation of the tight security that followed a rash of hijackings to Cuba.

Because the Ed-Ad Building did not require special construction for livestock and the attention of the Exhibits Department, it was designed and constructed quite rapidly. Mr. Mirick came up with a novel plan whereby, at the touch of a button, two flexible partitions, one on each side, followed tracks sidewise in the floor of the auditorium, and separated it into two large class-rooms. Two groups could thus be accommodated at once, or, when more room was needed, another touch of a button restored the auditorium. Work was completed in 1972, and we began moving into our spacious new administrative offices on the second floor in March.

Once the Ed-Ad Building was assured, I called on Paul Long, and he assigned an excellent teacher to us. Linda Jennings joined us at the beginning of the fall school semester in 1972, and staff members helped to orient her with an abundance of facts about the live-stock in our care. Tame animals from the children's zoo were available for her talks and demonstrations to the classes that came to the zoo under the aegis of the school district. Technically, each child had to pay admission at the reduced group rate, so I sought and obtained a grant from the Ludwick Institute to take care of that detail. The Institute generously renewed the grant on an annual basis.

Meanwhile, I was wrestling with the problem of how to organize a docent service that would require dozens, and eventually scores, of volunteers. How to recruit them? At that point Jeanne L. Segal entered the picture. She came by appointment one day early in 1971 to see

The plaque erected in RC's honor. Photo by Franklin Williamson, Philadelphia Zoo archives.

me and ask what she could do to help the zoo as a vol-unteer. She was so eager and enthusiastic that I out-lined the proposed docent program for her. I was in luck. She and her friend Ginny Pearson enlisted the help of seven other persons, and our zoo staff assisted them by giving a series of talks about the animals. The two women took charge and organized the Philadel-phia Zoo's Docent Council. By the time the full-scale educational program began in the autumn of 1972, after the Ed-Ad Building was in operation, the docents were already taking children for tours of the zoo. The Docent Council grew and prospered, and my latest information is that it now has more than 200 members.

My dream had come true at last. I thought back to the time in 1930 when an ambitious but callow youth deliv-ered a paper at an AAZPA meeting entitled "The Educa-tional Duty of the Zoological Park." Even at that early age I had the designation of "Educational Director" for the Toledo Zoo. The trouble was that I was the entire education department, and I had a plethora of other duties to perform. During the following 40-odd years I had done my best to teach everyone I could about ani-mals, conservation, and the plight of the many species that are threatened by the loss of their habitats or other causes originating from the rapid and enormous increase of the human species throughout the world. My longtime radio program had been an excellent vehi-cle for spreading the word.

Now we had an honest-to-goodness educational pro-gram involving many well-qualified persons. We were taking the zoo to the schools. The School Bus for Ani-mals program began its thirteenth season in November under the supervision of Robert M. Callahan, who was then the Superintendent of the Children's Zoo. Formal classes in the Ed-Ad Building, with Linda Jennings as teacher, began on October 12. The Docent Council, which had its headquarters in the Penn House, had

The main entrance to the new reptile house at the Philadelphia Zoo. Photo by Franklin Williamson, Philadelphia Zoo archives.

grown large enough to start taking prescheduled school groups on tours of the zoo by November 29. The autumn of 1972 was most assuredly one of the high points of my long zoo career.

Quite a few months previously another important event had occurred—the opening of the new reptile house. It turned out superbly, but it had received a truly massive amount of attention. After all, I was also Curator of Reptiles. Surely no other building in the entire zoo had been so long in the planning stage. That began shortly after I arrived back in Philadelphia in 1935. We were then confronted with the formidable problem of trying to keep temperature-sensitive amphibians and reptiles in an old building that was a drafty, chilly barn in winter and a steamy, breathless hothouse during torrid summer weather. The keepers and I began making notes, they mentally and I on paper, about what we would like to do if we ever had a new building or refurbished the old one.

When the time came for a brand-new reptile house to take its place on the city-funded rebuilding program, I worked long and hard with the architects, who were led by James S. Hatfield. I carefully reviewed my notes, and I thought about innumerable details. A great many of these were incorporated and committed to linen drawings and later to blueprints. We tried to include every necessary requirement for keeping the collection in excellent condition. Certain sections of the building were designed as cool quarters and others as warm, depending on the species to be exhibited. We tried to make everything easy to keep clean with a minimum of work. A considerable number of the cages were interchangeable modules, molded from fiberglass. Thus, we could substitute a new exhibit for an old one with little effort. Each of the keepers' work spaces was snake-proofed so that, in the unlikely event that one should fall to the floor, there was no place for it to hide or escape.

It required almost three years to erect and install everything in the building. Our emphasis was on natural habitats. The Exhibits Department spent a full year working in it after the construction men were finished. There were cliffs and rock ledges, waterfalls and pools, fiberglass replicas of the huge prickly pear cacti of the Galápagos Islands, and innumerable other background features to lend authenticity to the exhibits. Two spacious enclosures, containing pythons and anacondas, each had an aquarium glass front so the big snakes could be seen lying in the water, which they did much of the time. The signs and graphics were elaborate. Also, there were audio aids. Visitors could push buttons permitting them to hear the roar of an alligator, the buzz of a rattlesnake, the mating calls of male frogs in early spring, and so on.

The dominant feature of the new reptile house was a replica of a tropical river with crocodiles in the water or hauled out on the bank. Several times daily there was a realistic thundershower. First came the sound of distant thunder, then the lights were slowly dimmed as though a heavy black cloud were passing overhead. The thunder grew louder and louder and was accompanied at intervals by lightning. Suddenly there was a brief but torrential rain, and then the storm receded into the distance. Throughout the sequence a vocal message was giving an ecological review of the rhythm of nature in tropical rain forests. The public was fascinated by the realism of the program.

The storm was controlled by a switch in the keepers' workroom, and I could turn it on for VIP visitors. Unhappily, the complex electronic equipment had bugs in it that took us quite awhile to correct.

During a special preview, one of the members of the Zoological Society remarked, "Why, it's just like our exquisite hummingbird house. Of course, you can't walk right in with things like you do with the birds, but you can get a lot closer to cobras and crocodiles than would be safe in the wild." The member was right. She could gaze at a rattlesnake, eyeball to eyeball, and within easy striking distance of the snake's fangs, without any danger, thanks to the stout pane of glass between her and the snake.

The public space in the new building was air-conditioned. Outside the main (west) entrance was a large bronze sculptor's rendering of *Hadrosaurus foulkii*, the first dinosaur skeleton discovered in North America, and the first to be publicly exhibited. Appropriately, it was looking in the general direction of Haddonfield, New Jersey, where its fossilized remains were unearthed in 1858.

The new reptile house was an outstanding success, and President Williams described it as *the* showplace of the zoo. The board wanted to dedicate the building to me, but they couldn't because the principal funding had come from the City of Philadelphia. They compromised by dedicating the exhibits to me. Those had cost $200,000, which sum was expended from the funds of the Zoological Society.

History was about to repeat itself, although I didn't know it at the time. At the Toledo Zoo, way back in the early 1930s, I had helped design a splendid new reptile house (see "Miracle at the Toledo Zoo"). Very soon afterward I departed for Philadelphia, leaving the new exhibit gem for someone else to manage and enjoy. I was soon to leave my post as director of America's First Zoo, and to take an early retirement after an unexpected personal disaster that changed my whole life.

Chapter 46

The Trip of a Lifetime:
Part I. East Africa

Africa! What excitement and interest that very word engenders in the mind of any true naturalist or student of wildlife. Even as a boy I had dreamed of someday going there for a visit. Great herds of hoofed animals, elephants, rhinos, hippos, giraffes, lions, cheetahs, hyenas, and a host of other species. The last remnant of the great Age of Mammals!

Somehow my dear mother managed to save a few of my father's sectional bookcases and a number of his books, even though she was widowed when I was 12 and we were having a difficult time finding enough money to buy food. Among the lot was the six-volume "Library of Natural History," edited by Richard Lydekker and published in 1904, which I still have. How I devoured those books as a boy, reading about the creatures of the wild and marveling at the abundance of engravings that served as illustrations. I recall thinking that the picture of the gelada baboon portrayed the most hideous beast imaginable. Later, when I saw the animals in life, I realized that many of the illustrations were distorted caricatures.

My dream of going to Africa never left me, but the opportunity didn't arrive until 1968 when, as the head of the Philadelphia Zoo and a full-fledged member of the International Union of Directors of Zoological Gardens, I attended a meeting of that organization in Pretoria, South Africa. The zoo paid all my meeting and travel expenses and also for a two-week post-conference tour of Kruger National Park and the white rhinoceros country of the Natal. What a marvelous chance to make my dream come true. But *there was more*. I was permitted to take my month's vacation in East Africa.

Isabelle went with me, of course, and since we both felt it probably would be our only chance, we decided to do and see everything possible, even though we had to pay for her trip and for all our expenses during my vacation time. It was worth every dollar we spent. As she succinctly put it, "We saw so many animals that it seemed as though all the zoos of the world were turned loose." And what magnificent photographic opportunities, but more about that later.

What fun we had planning our trip! We knew we should rest for at least a day in Europe, both going and coming, so why not take an extra day or two for sightseeing in the two great centers of the ancient world: Rome on our way to Africa, and Athens on our return? Little was known about jet lag in those days, but frequent fliers warned us that long flights could be debilitating. With the aid of a travel agency we arranged our schedule in detail. We even included the luxury of having our own car and driver for our safaris in Uganda, Kenya, and Tanzania. Joining a tour or using a vehicle occupied by other people was not for us. Just when you are focused on a perfect shot, some unthinking tourist can jab you with an elbow or jiggle the vehicle badly and spoil the picture.

We flew from New York's Kennedy Airport to Rome. After two full days in that storied city we were off to Entebbe, Uganda, and then to Nairobi in Kenya, our departure point for the Serengeti Plain and the Ngorongoro Crater in Tanzania. When we returned to Nairobi we flew to Johannesburg. We would return home with brief, transient stops in Nairobi and Khartoum en route to Athens. Then to London's Heathrow Airport and directly back to Philadelphia.

After reviewing the available information—my still vivid memories, Isabelle's detailed diary, and miscellaneous notes and keepsakes—I found I had so much that I could almost write a book on our African trip alone. It wouldn't lack for truly superb pictures either, mostly taken by my talented wife. In this narrative, however, I can hit the high spots and mention a few things of lesser importance as well.

Isabelle was an accomplished photographer, so we were well equipped for taking pictures. She bought us two identical Pentax cameras, several lenses, and what seemed like a huge supply of film, mostly Kodachrome, but also black and white. Color was best, of course, especially for slides to be used in lecture programs, but we needed pictures for "America's First Zoo," our in-house publication, and for other purposes. We had an excellent exposure meter that Isabelle took to be professionally checked before our departure. There were no automatic cameras then, and no zoom lenses on small, hand-held equipment. We returned home with some 2,500 pictures. We both manned a camera and sometimes, during the excitement of seeing something unusual or interesting, we each grabbed the one nearest at hand. There was no time to record who took which photograph. I probably exposed some "jim-dandies," but I insisted that all the good results were Isabelle's.

We didn't take a tripod, because it would have been an annoying encumbrance during most of our journey. An ingenious homemade device served just as well. It was a simple beanbag that Isabelle stitched together before we started. It was flat and easy to carry when it was empty, and when filled it rested on the windowsill of a car with the window cranked down, and made a firm base for a camera. We expected to buy dried beans in the first African town we entered, but none were for sale. Cracked corn worked just as well.

We left New York before midnight on September 20, 1968, and it was daylight when we emerged over the Mediterranean Sea east of Spain. From my window seat I could see Corsica and Sardinia, and a few moments later I identified Elba, the much smaller island where Napoleon was exiled for a time. We landed outside Rome at an airport where chaos prevailed. We found our bags quickly, however, had no baggage inspection, passed speedily through the rest of the red tape, and then threaded our way through the milling crowd to a waiting bus. It conveyed us to central Rome, where we hired a taxi to take us to the Hotel Forum. We felt like zombies after crossing six time zones during the previous night, so we went to bed at once. We awakened in time, however, to walk a block or two in daylight to the Roman Forum, where, we were told, the Roman Senate met many centuries ago.

I quickly learned that many of the waiters, policemen, and others could understand me if I spoke Spanish slowly and precisely. That was an asset. On foot, by taxi, but chiefly aboard a sightseeing bus, we managed to see a lot of Rome in addition to the Forum. We took pictures of and threw coins into the Tivoli Fountain, saw the Colisseum from the inside as well as out, and admired the impressive monument to Victor Emanuel II. We taxied to the Rome Zoo, and were disappointed. It was in a beautiful setting, but it was dirty and untidy, and there were at least a half dozen decaying snakes in full sight in the reptile collection. I smelled them the moment I opened the door to the building.

We found the Vatican to be majestically impressive. Saint Peter's Cathedral, the physical seat of Catholicism, is a truly magnificent structure, and we soon had aching necks from staring upward to see Michelangelo's masterpieces. Our guide led us to a lower floor where we saw the tomb of Pope Paul XXIII, who had died several years previously. He had been embalmed by a master mortician, because his hands and face still looked life-like. His remains were surrounded by a huge bower of fresh flowers.

As soon as we returned from the bus tour to our hotel, we learned that we had to vacate our room for newcomers by 1:30 P.M. We took that in hasty stride, and discovered a near catastrophe in the process. The handle and lock of one of our large, heavy suitcases had pulled loose. How to cope? The concierge summoned a hotel mechanic, but he could do nothing more than to supply a full skein of rope. One of the porters wrapped the suitcase like a mummy, with a plethora of knots. It was travelworthy, but we would have to get it fixed in Africa; there was no time to go shopping for a new one.

After a night flight and crossing two more time zones, we arrived in the morning at Entebbe, Uganda. It lies on the north shore of Lake Victoria, second in area only to our own Lake Superior among the great freshwater lakes of the world. It was pouring rain. We were met by a Mr. Mulindwa, of the United Tour Company, who drove us to the Lake Victoria Hotel, where we had breakfast and went to bed as soon as our room was ready. When we awakened, about 3:00 P.M., the rain had stopped and, since we'd been told the Entebbe Zoo was only a short walk from the hotel, we decided to pay it a visit.

As we emerged from the entrance we met Bill Hoff, of the St. Louis Zoo, and his wife, Lynn, who were leading a party of tourists and were soon due to leave. Isabelle wrote in her diary that "Lynn presented us with a pair of elephant [tail] hair bracelets and which are supposed to bring good luck if they are a gift. One wears the bracelet on the left wrist until one shoots an elephant—then it can be transferred to the right wrist." As soon as she had photographed ("shot") an elephant two days later, she moved the bracelet to her other wrist. I followed suit soon afterward.

The Entebbe Zoo was small, and most of the simple pens and cages needed repair. The collection was not outstanding except for four spotted-necked otters, a species we had never seen previously. As Isabelle described them, "They were lively and sleek, and their white necks were spotted with brown. One lazy fellow reclined on his back with a front foot in his mouth, like a child sucking its thumb."

The biggest thrill on that, our first day in Africa, was in having a large hornbill fly over our heads as we walked back to the hotel. Isabelle likened its flight to that of a pelican—"flap, flap, flap and then soar." There

Isabelle, our car and driver, Abdulla Hassan, during our safari in Uganda. Photo by RC.

were other ornithological goodies, some of them in trees near the lake, including a strikingly patterned fish eagle, ibises, colies (mouse birds), a hamerkop (hammerhead), and several brilliantly hued kingfishers. They whetted our appetites for getting off on our safari, but we wisely retired early to rest for the vigorous adventure that would begin on the morrow.

Our driver from the United Tour Company arrived for us at 8:00 A.M. in an almost new Peugeot. Because Uganda, like all of East Africa, had been under British control for a long time, the car had a right-hand drive. I sat in the left front seat, and Isabelle had the back to herself and her camera gear. It was a good arrangement, because it gave her access to both rear windows on which she could rest the beanbag and one of the cameras. Our driver's name was Abdulla Hassan. He was intelligent, knowledgeable, and considerate of all our needs and desires. His home was in the Sudan to the north, and he was a Muslim. That gave him the privilege of having four wives, but he said he could only afford two, now that he had sired seven children. We were extremely fortunate to have him as our daily companion throughout our visit to Uganda.

He took us first the short distance north to Kampala, the capital, which turned out to be a poor shopping center. We wanted to buy safari jackets with many deep pockets, and I also needed a broad-brimmed hat. No jacket was large enough for me, but Isabelle found one that fitted her. No large hats. No beans. The local mini-supermarket had cracked corn.

Not too long after we left Kampala we stopped briefly for an important ceremony. We crossed the Equator and entered the Southern Hemisphere for the first time. By the side of the paved road the Ugandans had erected a large white circle about 10 feet high and across the top of which were emblazoned the words "UGANDA" and

"EQUATOR." At the bottom of the circle were white blocks with the black letters "N" and "S" on them. They straddled a yellow line wide enough so that Isabelle could stand on it with both feet. I took a picture of my inseparable pal for an important memento.

Then we were off, westward bound for Queen Elizabeth National Park. Our route passed mainly through inhabited country, at least for the first half or so of the trip. Banana plantations and women in colorful costumes were much in evidence. A real treat for me was to see Watusi cattle, a type of ruminant we were prohibited from importing into the United States because of the tight rules formulated for keeping the dread hoof-and-mouth disease out of the country. They would have been wonderful zoo exhibits because of their huge horns, which are not especially long, but are amazingly broad close to their heads. We stopped at the village of Mbarara for lunch, and thus met our first African place-name that began with an "M" that was followed by another consonant. Its pronunciation, we learned, started with a mumbled "M" or "umh" followed by the rest of the word. We had difficulty with such names.

Once we were under way again, the countryside grew steadily wilder, and we saw waterbucks and Uganda kob antelopes in the distance. A sudden drenching rain shower, punctuated by the lively tattoo of hail on the car roof and bonnet (hood), slowed us a little, but it was merely sprinkling by the time we reached the entrance portal to the Park about 5:00 P.M. Abdulla took us directly to the Mweya Safari Lodge, where we were given a small comfortable cottage with a porch that overlooked Lake Edward, which lay below us at the foot of a small escarpment. We could see many hippos and pelicans, and, when I walked to the edge to peer over, a marabou stork with a 10-foot wingspan flew upward virtually in my face. It was so large and impressive that I could not have been more startled if it had been a pterodactyl. Outside the compound, and not more than 50 yards from us, a big bull elephant was standing. Dark fluid was seeping down the side of its cheek, which reminded me instantly of Babe in musth, the always dangerous male elephant I had known all too well at the Toledo Zoo so very many years ago.

Boy, oh boy! What thrills. What would happen when we set off again in the morning with wild animals all around us? The answer was, "plenty."

Bright and early, soon after we left the lodge, we found two spotted hyenas so engorged with food that they scarcely raised their heads. One finally stood up, and gave us a chance for a picture or two. Then Abdulla took us to a large pond where there allegedly were 100 hippos floating at the surface, their eyes, nostrils, and ears all elevated above the water by the configuration of their heads. We counted up into the 50s, but couldn't make out the more distant ones. We learned later that it is normal for a hippopotamus to remain in the water all day, and to venture forth to feed on the dense succulent lakeside grasses and other vegetation at night. The big animals probably learned to do that ages ago to escape from primitive men armed with spears, a habit that was reinforced by the arrival of guns of various kinds. Water was abundant in western Uganda, which has a profusion of lakes. We were in a western branch of the Great African Rift, about which we were to learn more later.

Like all other travelers who go on safari for the first time, we discovered quickly that a car driven slowly and skillfully can approach almost any kind of animal, certainly close enough for picture taking. Large animals, especially lone bull elephants, rhinos, and a few others, had to be treated with caution, and with the motor running for a quick getaway. The ground was fairly flat, but holes, rocks, and eroded stretches had to be avoided. Apparently the smell of gasoline and oil masks the scent of the car's occupants, mankind—the archenemy of wildlife. A few years previously it had been the fad for wealthy sportsmen to kill, and then have mounted, as many different heads of African mammals as possible. Times have changed, and big-game hunting is no longer in vogue. The sheer proliferation of people is attacking far too many kinds of animals in another, far more serious way. I refer to taking over their habitats for a great variety of usages—farm lands, settlements, and industry, for example. Such dismal thoughts were far from our minds that morning in September 1968, however. We were far too interested in what we were seeing.

Abdulla drove us across the plain to a small herd of eight elephants, including cows and two babies, and we really burned up the film. We found another small herd of elephants, and our skilled driver also took us close to a sizable group of African buffaloes, the majority of which were brown instead of black, their normal coloration.

Presently we noticed several vultures perched high in a dead tree, and that could be a sign of only one thing. There must be a dead animal nearby. We soon found it, a young buffalo, and shortly afterward we saw the lioness that had made the kill and her three hungry cubs. They played hide-and-seek with our car for a short time, but we did get a few pictures. From Isabelle's diary: "This was one of the most exciting mornings I can remember!"

We were supposed to take a boat trip during the afternoon through the Kazinga Channel, the narrow waterway that connects Lakes Edward and George. Because we were late getting back for lunch at the lodge,

we found that the relatively small launch was already packed with tourists, and there was no room for us. We were disappointed, but it turned out to be a blessing. We spent most of the afternoon writing postcards to friends back home and tending to other chores. While Isabelle washed and rinsed some of our clothing (with soap powder she had brought from home on the advice of friends), I tackled the formidable task of untying the scores of tight knots the chap in Rome had used when he wrapped our large suitcase with rope. I found that a fourth as much rope was all that we needed, but I saved the rest for a possible emergency.

We took the boat the next morning, and there were only three other passengers, which was much to our liking. What a profusion of wildlife, and what an obliging captain. He wore ragged shorts and no shoes, but he had a regular skipper's cap. Whenever we wished, he stopped the boat and turned off the engine, thus eliminating the constant shudder and shake that probably would have blurred our pictures. I quote again from Isabelle's diary:

Hippos were the most prevalent animals. We saw hundreds. They would be in groups of a half dozen to a dozen or more. Usually, when the launch approached them closely enough to take pictures, they would all submerge. But we did get a few shots. One of the most interesting animals to us was the profusion of monitor lizards, many of them of large size. We must have seen ten or a dozen, all near or in the water. They were wary, but we managed to get a few pictures of them. Buffaloes, waterbucks, bushbucks, fish eagles, goliath herons, white and pink-backed pelicans, snake birds, marabou storks, saddle-billed storks, cattle egrets, hammerheads, and elephants were among the things we photographed.

We saw only three elephants. They were together and were huge males. The skipper ran the boat ahead of them and pushed the prow against the bank and waited for the elephants to approach us. One big tusker, who was in musth, walked so close to the launch that he could have reached Roger or me with his trunk. Knowing elephants, as we do, we were a bit scared. But the monster just stared at us, pulled up some buffalo grass a few feet from the prow, and plodded on.

Roger and I both took pix like mad, using both cameras, all four lenses, both in color and black-and-white. I had to reload both cameras while afloat.

We lunched at the Mweya Lodge, and then took off northward and eastward for distant Murchison Falls National Park, where we were supposed to spend the night. The going was slow, however, along the narrow gravel road, which passed at first through flat terrain, but became hillier as we advanced. We also had gotten a very late start, inasmuch as we had devoted the morning to the boat trip. We realized we were behind schedule, but Abdulla knew of a place where we could stay overnight near Fort Portal. Unexpectedly, that was a lucky break. After a torrential shower, the weather cleared, the clouds lifted, and we had a brief but excellent view of the lofty Ruwenzori Mountain Range from the hotel. We were to learn that almost all the high mountains of East Africa were obscured by clouds at that season of the year, except during occasional periods of sunshine. The substitute accommodations were OK; we liked our room, but not having to share it with a swarm of large termites.

Early in the morning we pushed onward, stopping now and then for pictures. Among the highlights were many elephants, one herd of which blocked the highway for a while; huge termite nests containing literally tons of dirt brought to the surface and piled up by the insects (some of the mounds were twice as tall as I was); and our passage through a dead forest. During a recent period of drought, when there was little vegetation available, elephants had stripped off all the bark to eat, and there stood the stark, naked, vertical skeletons of trees that used to be, their unstripped upper dead branches still rising skyward.

Before mid-afternoon we reached the Victoria Nile River, and our little car was ferried across by a small motor launch. It had a capacity of two vehicles, but ours was the only one. The river was wide and flowing with a strong current. Once we were on the north side, Abdulla took us to the Paraa Lodge, the visitors' headquarters in Murchison Falls National Park. (*Paraa* means "hippo" in the native dialect.) Our room was on the second floor, and from the window we could see many lizards moving up and down the outer stone walls of the structure. I borrowed some stout thread from Isabelle's emergency sewing kit, went outside, found a short pole, attached the thread as a noose, and soon had two, both agamids, members of a family that is widespread in the Old World. Just then a fairly large elephant came around the corner of the building, and I beat a hasty retreat. Two lodge employees, in a truck, opened the near door and beckoned me to get in with them.

The following morning, which was bright and clear, we had another exciting boat ride, chugging up the Nile close to the shore, where the current was far less rapid. We were aboard a fairly large launch that was packed with 36 people, many of them Germans. Photography wasn't easy with virtually everyone elbowing his way in front of fellow passengers with cameras at the ready.

The wildlife was superb, however. We saw at least a dozen large crocodiles sunning on the riverbank, each 10 feet or more in length, and one which must have been close to 15 feet. Most had their mouths open, and we saw small birds plucking leeches from inside them. I spent too much time watching through my binoculars, while poor Isabelle vied with the other photographers.

The skipper, as had the one in the Kazinga Channel, stopped his motor when photo opportunities were good, but he didn't even slow down when we passed a pair of open-bill storks. Admittedly, they are not striking in appearance, with their dark plumage and height of about three feet, but they have an extraordinary anatomical peculiarity of interest to zoologists. The cutting edges of their long, stout bills curve away from each other, leaving a gap when closed. We could see this clearly as we passed, but we had no chance to take pictures. That morning, besides the crocodiles, we photographed buffaloes, antelopes of several species, a troop of baboons, vervet monkeys, a mother hippo with her baby, both out of the water, and a large elephant with no tail. Had it once come too close to a crocodile?

The launch, named the *Nyati*, which meant buffalo, chugged a long way up the river, but shallow water, laden with rocks, prevented us from going close to Murchison Falls. We could see the clouds of spray, however, that marked the site between two rocky hills.

Our return trip, aided by the rapid movement of the water, was much speedier, and we were soon at the dock, where Abdulla and our Peugeot waited to take us to the lodge for lunch. Isabelle, in her diary, noted that, "Out of all those pushy tourists, not one tipped the Captain. Roger did and was asked to sign the log, as he had also done on the Kazinga Channel boat."

After lunch we set off on a "game drive." That meant cruising along the dirt roads until we saw something of interest. Abdulla knew where to look, and he never hesitated to drive cross-country to get close to the various animals. Near the Albert Nile, in the northwestern part of the Park, we suddenly spotted a trio of white rhinos, the first we had ever seen, in or out of a zoo. That species had been almost extinct, and, in fact, the northern subspecies, at which we were looking, still teeters on the brink. Our well-informed guide told us that a half dozen rhinos, for their protection, had been brought into the Park from across the river where a remnant colony still existed. We saw two adults. Both were females, and one was a mother closely tailed by her quite bulky offspring. They were well within camera range, and Isabelle exposed a color slide showing a cattle egret walking in step with one of the rhinos. (Actually, it was out of step, militarily speaking, but their legs were fully extended as though marching.)

Hartebeests were numerous near the Albert Nile. Two males were in combat on the road. When we stopped they paused to look at us, but soon knocked horns again. We were also lucky enough to photograph a large bustard, probably a kori. On the way back a sizable snake was on the road, but it crawled quickly off into the brush. I guessed it was a cobra.

From the narrowest part of the north end of Lake Albert, we were close enough to see, with our binoculars, into the neighboring country to the west. The same had been true near the Mweya Lodge far to the southwest, and possibly also when we glimpsed part of the Ruwenzori Range, which is on the international boundary. Once that territory was known as the Belgian Congo. When we were in Africa in 1968, it was the Republic of the Congo. Now it's Zaire.

Our last full day in Uganda started off with a bang. Abdulla drove us to nearby Murchison Falls, and we finally had a close-up view of that mighty cataract in the Victoria Nile. The water roared over a narrow lip of rock in a huge torrent that sent up enormous clouds of spray when it hit the bottom 118 feet below. That was what we had seen from the launch. The sun was shining brightly that last morning, and, when we looked behind us, there was a splendid rainbow fronting the mist.

The rest of the day was dull compared with the recent fun and excitement, but we had to drive back to Kampala, where the United Tour Company had booked us for the night into the swank, almost new Apolo Hotel. We felt embarrassed entering it in our rumpled field clothes. We bid Abdulla good-bye with genuine regret, but we thanked him profusely and gave him a generous tip for all his kindnesses and efforts on our behalf.

We were up very early the next morning to be driven to the Entebbe Airport to catch an early plane to Nairobi. Unexpectedly, Abdulla was at the wheel. He was supposed to have the day off, but no other driver was available. It gave us a chance to bid him a fond farewell again and to enlarge his tip.

At the airport we learned a lesson. Neither in New York nor Rome had our baggage been overweight, but this time it was, heavily so. I had to hand over the equivalent of $35 for the short trip to Nairobi. A faulty scale? A dishonest attendant who slipped some or all of the extra money into his pocket? Ever afterward, whenever we checked in at an airport counter, Isabelle sat or stood well away with her heavy camera case at her side, and I joined her *after* I had the boarding passes. We always took that bag aboard as hand luggage. It contained too much of value to risk it among the checked baggage.

In all fairness, I cannot continue without expressing my profound regret for the disaster that was soon to engulf Uganda. Winston Churchill, who traveled widely through many parts of the so-called Dark Continent, referred to Uganda as the "Pearl of Africa." Even though our experiences there were limited, we were inclined to agree with him. We enjoyed Uganda immensely. All seemed so calm and peaceful. The lodges and other accommodations were well managed, and the food they served was good. We were particularly pleased by the profusion of wildlife and the efforts being made for its conservation, even though the motivation was doubtless, at least partly, to increase tourism. Also, it was our first stop, and we had by far our best driver.

Sadly, Uganda went down the drain, so to speak, just three years after we left, when a demented despot named Idi Amin seized control and chaos descended. We had reports that the huge crocodiles we saw along the Victoria Nile were all poached for their hides or shot, just for the hell of it, by Amin's armed henchmen. The destruction of the game and many of the birds was devastating. The small colony of white rhinos was surely wiped out, and their horns sold for aphrodisiacs or other senseless purposes. It was eight years before Idi Amin was ousted in 1979, after allegedly putting more than a quarter million of his fellow countrymen to death. He escaped to Libya and the protection of Muammar Gadhafi, another notorious dictator.

Poor little Uganda. Its marvelous wildlife, which we enjoyed so much, was reduced to low ebb. No longer did the animals tolerate the close approach of cars. They fled instead. Time has a way of healing, however. As this book goes to press, Uganda is once again being advertised by travel agencies as a wildlife utopia.

The plane trip to Nairobi lasted only about an hour, but the visibility was nil, save for the snow-capped summits of distant Mounts Kenya and Kilimanjaro, which protruded above the dense cloud bank. We had to stand in line for almost an hour to pass through immigration, but customs was quick and without trouble. We were supposed to be met by a representative of the United Tour Company. With the aid of a porter, we eventually found her, a girl who knew so little about what she was doing that she must have been new on the job. She took us to the Norfolk Hotel, which had been recommended by friends at home as the gathering place of people on safari.

Our first order of business was to get our broken suitcase repaired, and that was soon accomplished. Nairobi, which was visited by far more tourists than Entebbe or Kampala, was an excellent shopping center. I bought a broad-brimmed hat and a first-class safari jacket. We even purchased a set of prints of Rena Fennessy's beautiful paintings of the heads of Africa's four great cats—lion, lioness, cheetah, and leopard. As I write this, in 1995, I can glance upward from my easy chair and see them, neatly framed and hanging in a row on the wall of our living room in Albuquerque. For several years, the same pictures graced my office at the Philadelphia Zoo. Wisely, we had them shipped by mail from Nairobi to our home at Hyla Holler in New Jersey.

We would be at the Norfolk for several days. They were busy ones as we visited places of interest in and near the city and met with friends, all the time unaware that just a few days later we would be hovering on the brink of disaster.

One morning we walked to the Museum and Snake Park. We met the director, Dr. R. Carcasson, and discovered that his secretary was Mrs. Cecil Webb, whose late husband had known Fred Ulmer, our Curator of Mammals, when Fred was stationed in England during World War II. We were introduced to James Ashe, the Park's reptile curator, who showed us around his domain. It was small and unimpressive, and the cages were filthy and literally stank. He claimed the snakes survived better under such conditions! A deep pitlike exhibit, into which I descended with Ashe a few days later to take pictures, contained a few cobras, boomslangs, and a mamba.

Ashe was able to help me with my live lizards. I had caught several more with my bare hands at the Paraa Lodge in the early morning as they sunned themselves on the east side of the building. He had formalin, so I preserved them, and let them steep in the fluid until we returned a few days later. I then wrapped them in rags soaked with the preservative, placed them in a tightly sealed container, and mailed them home. They came through in good shape, and are now study specimens at the American Museum of Natural History.

We had other things to do. Soski Piroeff, a wealthy big-game hunter and President of the Philadelphia Safari Club, was in Nairobi with his wife, Rose, and we had a pleasant dinner with them, carrying on a lively conversation about Africa's teeming wildlife as we ate.

John Seago, an ethical animal dealer, took us to his compound near the city, and showed us the excellent care his animals were receiving. He also introduced us to several notable persons, among them two distinguished veterinarians, Tony and Sue Hartshoorn. They were deeply interested in the rapidly developing technique of shooting large animals with darts containing tranquilizers. It was revolutionizing some of our most dangerous and arduous chores with the livestock at our zoo back in the States. We later were to do the Hartshoorns a major favor. We also met George Adamson, and he drove us back to our hotel to save us taxi fare. A year or so later, his wife, Joy Adamson, author of the best-selling book "Born Free," gave a lecture for the Philadelphia Safari Club in the lion (carnivora) house at our zoo.

John Seago had lunch with us at the Norfolk and then took us for an hour's ride northward in his car to show us beautiful Lake Navaisha. There were hundreds of birds, mostly out of camera range, and innumerable islands of reeds and papyrus near the shore. The three of us boarded a dory with an outboard motor that was started by one of the attendants at a small marina. John took the helm. We were still in the channel leading to the lake when the motor died. Four young men in a boat stopped long enough to get it going again. We continued cruising close to the vegetation and then the motor quit again. Our host began tinkering with it, but couldn't get it started. Meanwhile, a steady wind from the east was blowing us along. I began grabbing reed stems in an attempt to slow our progress, but my efforts scarcely helped us hold our own. John's back was turned as he faced the outboard, so I yelled, "We're being blown into the open lake!" It was far too wide to see the other side. John was startled. He began seizing stems as I was doing. Between the two of us, working desperately, we made slow progress against the wind but finally reached a large clump of papyrus that was strong enough for us to get good grips and a chance to rest for a few minutes. But let Isabelle tell the story, as recorded in her diary:

> There was no paddle or oar aboard. . . . For two hours we pulled and pushed (with a couple of crooked sticks we found floating) until we could see the marina. I say "we," but Roger and John did the exhausting work while I trimmed ship to keep us on an even keel. I was glad we had brought the bush jackets as they covered the camera cases and kept them dry. Everything else, including ourselves, was wet. A black boy on a nearby island finally saw Roger waving his undershirt, and he paddled over to us. He came aboard and had the motor going in no time and drove us ashore. He apparently was one of the marina boys.

Seago was mightily embarrassed, and I was deeply chagrined, because I had used boats often enough to know that an oar or paddle must be aboard in case a motor ceased to function. We were both exhausted.

The gravity of our predicament wasn't driven home until we were back at the Norfolk and able to review our adventure in perspective. It had been late afternoon, and there were no boats visible on the open lake. Would we have been missed if the wind had driven us into the broad watery expanse? What wildlife might we have encountered? Hippos and crocodiles? Suppose we had been blown across? Lions? Hyenas? We were unarmed. Later we learned that Navaisha, at 6,200 feet elevation, is the highest lake in the Great African Rift, and the only major body of fresh water in the central part of it. That altitude probably would have precluded the presence of warmth-loving crocodiles. It could get really cold at night; frost occurred at times. We also learned that sudden wind shifts and gusts churned up waves that easily could have capsized our little cockleshell of a boat. It was awhile before we had all those facts, but we were shaken nonetheless. We were mighty glad to be safe in bed at the hotel a few hours later.

The Norfolk was an old hotel, but it was in good repair. Apparently it had been built when all of East Africa was British. A humorous yarn about the proper Englishman held that he always had his bathtub with him, even if a porter had to carry it when he went exploring in wild places. The Norfolk had bathtubs but no showers. Ours didn't look too clean, and, since we had learned long ago in Mexico to guard our health carefully in strange countries, neither of us would use it. There was plenty of hot water, so I borrowed a large pitcher from housekeeping. That did the trick. I poured warm water on Isabelle as she stood erect, she soaped herself well, and then I rinsed her off. Then she did the same for me.

One afternoon, by prearrangement with the United Tour Company, Robert Makoha came to meet us. He would be our driver for the long trek across the Serengeti Plain and during stops on the way back through Tanzania and southern Kenya. He was a pleasant young man, but he lacked the warm personality of Abdulla. He was studious, and, when we stopped to take pictures, sometimes series of them, he opened a textbook on the German language instead of telling us about the animals and staying alert to move the car when necessary. We admired Robert's industry and mentally wished him luck. Most of the German tourists we had seen in the field or in Nairobi were rotund and pushy, well-heeled financially but slow to do any tipping.

Robert took us to Nairobi National Park for the afternoon. It was a small reservation crowded with vehicles full of tourists. It held an amazingly large number of animals, many kinds of which we had not seen in Uganda. We photographed giraffes, zebras, gnus (wildebeests), kongonis, impalas, Thomson's and Grant's gazelles, and two jackals for the first time. We were also able to get close enough to several warthogs to obtain good portraits of them. Some leaned on their elbows as they moved forward while foraging. We were astounded at how well the animals tolerated the approach of vehicles.

A mother cheetah, another first for us, and her four cubs, were literally surrounded by cars. So also was a small pride of lions having a nap. From within the Park we could see many of the taller buildings in the city of Nairobi. What an extraordinary tourist mecca.

A few days later we started off on our long journey. Most noticeable to us was the marked difference in habitat. In the parts of Uganda we had visited, water had been a major factor, and species that lived in or near it were very much in evidence. Now we were on an open plain with trees spaced well apart or in clumps here and there.

We had a paved road for a while as we drove west from Nairobi, but soon we were off on a dirt track. Our vehicle this time was a Land Rover designed to operate in rough terrain. It had a roof hatch that could be opened when we were stopped, and both of us could take pictures at once, as we stood in the rear part of the car. When it was closed, however, and I sat in the back as we rolled along, I was too tall to see the landscape without leaning down or kneeling. We took turns occupying the rear. Robert drove very fast, and we were bumped and bounced by the primitive road. When we asked him to slow down, he replied that we would have to move as rapidly as possible if we were to reach the Keekorok Lodge, in the Masai Mara Game Reserve, by 12:30 P.M. It was the only place on our route to have lunch.

After eating, we turned south, crossed the border into Tanzania, and headed into the Serengeti, a vast, partly rolling high plain across which, in earlier days, millions of game animals, accompanied by their predators, had moved more or less north and south following the seasonal rains. It was long described as *the* wildlife spectacle of the world. The early explorers, even up to the time of Carl E. Akeley and Martin and Osa Johnson, saw it in its heyday. Much had happened since then, however. Although the area had been designated a national park, the boundaries were invisible lines. All the wildlife in the Park was allegedly protected, but there were far too few wardens to enforce the rules. Hunting and poaching were continuous, farms were encroaching around the edges, and the cattle of the Masai people competed for grass with the native grazing animals.

The Grzimeks, outstanding German father and son naturalists (see the vignette on Bernhard Grzimek), had proved a few years before our visit that the migration is not a great single mass movement. Some types of grass are palatable, whereas others can grow hip deep and remain untouched. The animals often circle. They crop the grass virtually to the ground, and then return later when it has grown to two or three inches and they can crop it clear again. We saw nothing of the migrations, but there were considerable numbers of animals in the Serengeti, far more than enough to keep our cameras busy.

Speed was no longer an element in our time schedule, so we stopped to take photographs at least a half dozen times before we reached the Seronera Safari Lodge in late afternoon. The accommodations there were tents, each with a small satellite, roofless tent behind it with bathroom facilities. We had comfortable cots in the main tent, whose canvas floor was continuous with the sides, so that snakes and other creepy crawlies were prevented from entering in the dark. Our bathroom consisted of a commode and a very large overhead tin can with holes in it. When we filled it with water and pulled a cord, the can tilted, and an erratic spray descended. I used the makeshift shower, but Isabelle wrote that she was "chicken." After all, the water was cold. So that we wouldn't have to venture outside the tent in the dark, I moved the commode inside with us. During the night we heard lions roaring in the near distance and even the whoop of a hyena a little farther away. It was quite a contrast with the luxurious facilities we had enjoyed in Uganda. The food served in the lodge was good, however.

Not far away was a large, rather high jumble of rounded granite rocks. "Lizard habitat" popped into my head, and, sure enough, a short time later I found and photographed a beauty. It was nearly a foot long, bright red from the tip of the snout to its waist, including the forelimbs, but then abruptly changing to dark blue on the hindquarters and tail. I saw others, caught one by hand, and had a chance to examine it closely. Almost instantly it became a medium dark gray all over. It was a male rainbow lizard, *Agama agama*, a species noted for its ability to change color.

The rock pile was also the abode of at least three dozen hyraxes, small mammals roughly the size of our American woodchuck or groundhog, but anatomically very different. The hyrax is most closely related to the elephant. The management fed them on table scraps, so they were accustomed to people and were easy to approach.

We were off in the Land Rover right after breakfast. It was to be an exciting day, marred only by too many small buses full of tourists who appeared whenever we found something of interest. We and they watched three cheetahs that were intently gazing at a herd of Thomson's gazelles (Tommies). There was no immediate action, so we moved off and Robert took us to a small gallery forest in a rather wet area where there was a row of fever trees, so called because early explorers who camped near or under them sometimes came down with malaria. That, of course, was long before anyone knew that mosquitoes were the vectors. Their larvae need water in which to mature. The name "fever tree" stuck, however.

A handsome male leopard was stretched out on a limb fast asleep. Just below him, a small antelope carcass was draped over another limb, hauled up there, no doubt, in the leopard's mouth as it climbed. The strength of those big cats is amazing. Soon a female leopard appeared, climbed the same tree, and also napped. Later, she dragged the kill off the limb, dropped it to the ground, and disappeared with it into some nearby tall grass. A half dozen safari wagonloads of people pulled up alongside of us, all burning up film as we were.

Later, Robert found some giraffes we could photograph without competition, and also a sleepy male lion with a full belly. Isabelle wrote, "We shot him until he flopped down prone in a most unphotogenic pose."

We returned for a late lunch and a short rest, and then took off again on a game drive in another direction. Not far from the lodge we discovered three more cheetahs, an adult pair and a half-grown one. The attention of all three was riveted on a herd of Tommies quite far away. All of a sudden the female took off with incredible speed (cheetahs are known to reach 70 miles an hour), she caught up with the herd, cut off two Tommies, and an instant later seized one of them in her mouth. The young cheetah went to join her, and the two began feasting. They were soon joined by the male, who cleaned up the remains. Our car and several others were clustered around at close range, but the speedy cats paid no attention to us. Afterward, Isabelle wrote, "It was an exciting piece of nature in the raw."

Weeks later, when we were home, we told friends about that amazingly fast chase. Some of them had been on safari in East Africa several times, but had never witnessed such action. We congratulated ourselves for having been in the right place at the right time.

After supper, Isabelle looked after the cameras. It was the dry season, and dust was everywhere and it seeped into everything. We had been forewarned, and we kept all our photographic gear carefully covered, except for the cameras and lenses in immediate use. Even so, it became Isabelle's daily, and sometimes twice-daily, chore to use her camel's-hair brush to clean off the lenses and other exposed parts.

Following our second night at the Seronera Lodge, we headed southeastward and found many things of interest on our way. I spotted a pack of 10 hunting dogs, and Robert drove across the plain to get close to them. They were on the move, so we had to take our pictures while both they and the car were in motion. A little later we saw a black rhinoceros with a half-grown young one.

Robert said we should not go too near them. Black rhinos are notoriously nearsighted, and it is impossible to predict whether one might charge or run away. We moved in as far as he thought was safe, used our long lenses, and did very well. Those same lenses enabled us to get good photos of vervet monkeys and dik-diks. A male ostrich was walking down the rough road ahead of us, followed by 15 tiny chicks. They turned off onto the plain before we were close enough to portray them well.

We also turned off to see the Olduvai Gorge, where members of the Leakey family made anthropological discoveries of major importance. A guide at the Gorge conducted us over the dig.

We reached our destination, the Ngorongoro Crater Lodge, by late afternoon. Just before our arrival, we saw a large herd of zebras in a valley almost surrounded by hills. We stopped long enough to estimate that there were more than 300 of them. What a sight!

The Great African Rift indicates that the continent, as we know it today, will eventually be torn asunder, just as titanic subterranean forces broke up and distributed pieces of Gondwanaland eons ago. South America, Antarctica, Australia, and India, as well as Africa itself, were all once part of that vast supercontinent in southern latitudes. The Great Rift extends from Lebanon, in the Levant, all the way to Tanzania and Mozambique, and it manifests itself in a variety of ways. The Red Sea and the Gulf of Aden are part of it in the north, where the Rift has sunk below the level of the oceans. Southward, it extends across East Africa as a deep trench, roughly 30 miles wide, with precipitous escarpments on both sides. Its depth varies, but, for a considerable distance, the floor of the Rift is 2,000 feet below the surrounding landscape. Evidences of the trench peter out in the vicinity of Lake Nyasa in Mozambique. The Rift Valley has branches extending outward at angles, notably the one occupied by Lakes Tanganyika and Albert, the latter of which we had seen in Uganda. Quite a scar on the face of the earth. The Rift is roughly paralleled on both sides by evidences of the volcanic action that occurred while it was forming. Craters are numerous and, in a few places along its route, the sodium carbonate (washing soda) that spews out during eruptions is so abundant that it has turned sizable bodies of water, especially Lake Natron, into treacherous caldrons of the corrosive chemical. There are many volcanoes, great and small, along the Rift's route, some nearby, some farther away, and some 30 of which are in various stages of activity.

We crossed the Great Rift in several places and saw its associated lava and other evidences of volcanism. The most spectacular, from the standpoint of a zoologist, is the Ngorongoro Crater, which Bernhard Grzimek, late Director of the Frankfurt Zoo, in Germany, called the greatest zoo in the world. But let me explain.

The Ngorongoro Crater is all that remains of a long-extinct volcano, but one of such stupendous magnitude as to stagger the imagination. Actually, it is a caldera, which, by definition, is a crater vastly larger than the original volcanic vent. Calderas are formed by the collapse of the floor of the crater or as the result of supreme violence. We were told that Ngorongoro is the largest caldera on the face of the globe. Consider its dimensions. It is nearly round, 12 miles wide at its broadest and 10 miles at its narrowest. There are an estimated 80 to 100 square miles on the surface of its floor. It is surrounded by nearly vertical walls that are 2,000 feet high, and the summit of the rim is 7,500 to 8,000 feet above sea level. It contained, at the time of our visit, a fairly large salt lake, a few smaller freshwater sumps, a considerable forest, and an abundance of grassland, along with a huge assemblage of wildlife of the same species that lived outside the caldera.

We descended the face of the escarpment on a steep, narrow, breathtaking "road" that could be negotiated solely by four-wheel-drive vehicles, like our Land Rover. A similar one-way upward climb at another place on the cliff wall was our exit.

During our brief visit we saw, of course, only a very small fraction of the animals living in the Crater. Our trip into and across several parts of Ngorongoro lasted from mid-morning through mid-afternoon, but we saw a good sample of the abundance of many species. There were large herds of zebras and gnus, a sprinkling of Tommies and elands, the latter the largest of all the antelopes. A solitary black rhinoceros let us approach close enough to get good pictures of it. We also saw three lions and several vervet monkeys. All in all, it was not a very large number compared with the many species of mammals that we knew lived within the confines of the Crater, including elephants and hippos. What we did see, and the large number of reported species, raised a question in our minds. How did hoofed animals, especially such ponderous pachyderms as rhinos, hippos, and elephants, get into the Crater? The sheer walls, insofar as we could see with our binoculars, were unbroken all around the vast enclosure.

Birds are a different matter, with their power of flight. We saw many of the same species we had encountered elsewhere, as well as some new ones. Most conspicuous were hundreds of flamingos, flying or standing beside or in the shallow water of the lake. Many were puddling, standing with their heads upside down and separating food from the salty water with their efficiently constructed bills. We also saw a woolly-necked stork, and

An inquisitive waterbuck with an attendant herd of zebras and gnus. Photo by IHC.

a few colorful passerines came close enough for us to photograph them while we were quietly eating our sandwich lunch. So did vervet monkeys, all hoping for handouts from visitors.

The king-sized conundrum continued to intrigue me. Descending the escarpment would have been possible for monkeys and baboons and perhaps the sure-footed cats. Maybe there were spots along the precipice where rocks had tumbled inward to serve as stepping-stones downward. I could not rule that out, but I continued to mull over the problem, even as I was falling asleep that night. In my musings I envisioned the following scenario: After volcanism subsided, the vast caldera must have been bleak and empty of life. It probably took a very long time to cool. Pioneering plants, their seeds and spores blown in from outside, came first, and eventually vegetation carpeted the entire floor. A lake formed. The mammals, especially the large, heavy, and long-legged ones, must have arrived much later. I decided that time must have been an important factor. As the centuries marched onward through the millennia, opportunities probably arose, now and then, for animals to blunder from the rim down into the caldera. But that was not very scientific thinking.

If it were not for the pressure of trying to complete a few cherished projects during my declining years, I would enjoy researching the geological history of the region. I have always tried to think in terms of geology as it applies to the distribution of animals. Zoogeography has been one of my chief interests for as long as I can remember.

Our accommodations at the Ngorongoro Crater Lodge were excellent. There was plenty of hot water and a gas heater to repel the nightly chill of the high altitude. The food was good, and we ate two novelties. The first was zebra leg, which was tough and without much flavor. The next evening we were served wildebeest steaks, and they were tender and tasty. I asked about the source of the meat, and we were told that the animals had been shot when they entered nearby farmlands. The management was prepared to salvage them quickly. Better to eat them than to let the carcasses rot. From the rim of the Crater, through our binoculars, we could see vast farms off to the southeast.

Our next destination was Lake Manyara National Park, which is occupied in part by another body of chemically charged water. As advertised, lions were lying on stout branches of large trees, an anomalous habitat for the so-called king of beasts. There were so many trees that it was difficult to see the wildlife, let alone photograph it, but we made several attempts. We were amused by the antics of a large troupe of baboons, which we watched for quite a while as they moved about.

On our way out of Tanzania, mostly on paved roads, we stopped in the sizable town of Arusha for lunch. After crossing back into Kenya we were in the Amboseli Game Reserve, and we transferred onto a dirt road where every vehicle stirred up clouds of dust. We headed for the lodge, which turned out to be virtually all tents, including the mess hall and bar. The setup was similar to that which we had occupied at the Seronera Lodge in the Serengeti. There were cots for us and a satellite, open-topped wall of canvas for cold-water ablutions and elimination. There was no electricity, but the tent was equipped with a Coleman lantern. This time, however, we had a novel experience. Shortly after dawn, four vervet monkeys dropped from the tree above us, moved along the ridgepole, urinated over our "bathroom," slid down the sloping side of the tent, and tried to get in, apparently searching for food.

The tents faced south toward mighty Kilimanjaro, an exceptionally massive volcano and, at 19,342 feet, Africa's tallest mountain. Most of the time it was obscured by clouds. On our second morning at Amboseli, we arranged to be awakened at 6:00 A.M. just in case the monkeys decided to land on someone else's tent, and rouse them early instead of us. The summit of Kilimanjaro was clear, although a little hazy, and we managed to get fairly good photographs. Just as had been the case with so many of the Mexican volcanoes we had seen during our years of fieldwork in that country, the great African mountain was soon again enveloped in clouds.

Game animals were not so common as we had found them elsewhere. Possibly because of the drought? We spotted a herd of 18 elephants, accompanied by a big bull in musth, and we saw several black rhinos. We also saw waterbucks of a species different from the kind we had met previously. Most enjoyable were several graceful, long-necked gerenuks, but they were too shy to let us approach them. Lions were seen in several places, and we were intrigued by the weaver birds, whose elaborately constructed, ball-like nests, each with a hole for the parents to enter, were numerous in many of the more isolated trees.

We were in Masai country, home of those tall people and their omnipresent cattle, which they bled for blood to drink, as well as using their milk. Members of the same large tribe had also been present on the floor of the Ngorongoro Crater with their herds—which, of course, competed with the wild grazers for the grass. Some of the young men carrying long spears and guarding the animals were quite handsome. None of the older members of the tribe would qualify for a beauty contest, however. They had a curious habit of piercing their earlobes, letting the holes increase in size until they were grotesque, to say the least. They used them to carry anything that would fit. Beads and ornaments were common in both sexes, and we saw one young man who had a full pack of cigarettes stowed in one of his earlobes. In former times the Masai shunned all outsiders and lorded it over the other tribes. Civilization was influencing them, and we were able to photograph several after we gave them a few shillings apiece.

While we were at Amboseli we met John G. Williams, the British naturalist who wrote "A Field Guide to the Birds of East and Central Africa" and "A Field Guide to the National Parks of East Africa," both of which we had purchased while we were in Nairobi. Williams, who apparently was leading a party of tourists, very kindly

autographed both books (on October 11, 1968), and chatted with us a while. I deeply regretted that I had not had time to study his books in detail, so I could talk intelligently about them. That deficiency was nullified when I told him that we were the author and illustrator of "A Field Guide to Reptiles and Amphibians" of eastern North America. He immediately took over the conversation and queried us in detail about our work.

As we were leaving the large dining tent one evening, we passed Leonard J. Goss, Director of the Cleveland Zoo, his wife, Carol, and their two children who were coming in. All we could say was "*Jambo*," the Swahili word of greeting. We knew we'd see them soon again in South Africa.

The time had come for us to return to Nairobi and terminate our fascinating sojourn through East Africa. En route, the most interesting interlude was the discovery of a large, almost four-foot-long, pale snake that was dead on the road. It was in good shape, without a single apparent blemish, unlike so many snakes that are mashed or torn when they meet their fate in traffic. As an inveterate collector how I yearned to preserve it and send it home. That was impossible, however, because we were to leave on the morrow, and there would be no time to visit the Snake Park and take care of it properly. So I coiled it in a lifelike position and photographed it. The species was *Rhamphiophus oxyrhynchus*, the beaknose snake. How I regretted having to leave a perfect specimen for a vulture or other scavenger.

We were in Nairobi before noon. We checked with the United Tour Company to be sure we would have transportation to the airport in the morning, and then Robert drove us to the Norfolk Hotel. We thanked him for his help, and I gave him a generous tip. We cleaned up after all the dust and tent camping, packed our gear and clothing, and worried about the discouragingly large mound of things we would have to hand-carry to Johannesburg. Then we relaxed over dinner with friends, our reminiscenses creating a final fond farewell to East Africa.

Chapter 47

The Trip of a Lifetime:
Part II. South Africa

We knew we were going to the land of apartheid, but we didn't expect to meet it head-on in Nairobi. The reason was that no communications of any kind were permitted with South Africa by the black nations. No letters, no telephone calls, no telegrams. South Africa was completely ostracized.

The Hartshoorn veterinarians had asked us if we would be willing to carry a few technical journals and similar documents with us, and then mail them to their colleagues when we arrived in South Africa. We agreed, and they gave us rands, the unit of currency we would need to buy stamps. Another acquaintance made a similar request. Unfortunately, the word spread, and we were astounded, when we returned to the Norfolk Hotel from our safari, to find many fat envelopes and packages waiting for us, some rather heavy, all neatly addressed. The hotel cashier had a number of rand notes with instructions to give them to us. There was enough mail, we estimated, to overflow a sizable suitcase.

We were all too mindful of what had happened to us in Entebbe, when we were charged a large sum for overweight baggage. What to do? We quickly decided to hand-carry all the extras. So we donned our wide- and deep-pocketed safari jackets, put our raincoats over them, and stuffed everything we could into our garments. We still had two fat packets left over, which I tied with some of the rope I had saved for an emergency. It was quite a load, but we managed to balance ourselves. At the airport, Isabelle, with the two packages and her camera case, stood out of sight while I got our boarding passes. I checked our regular bags, and I sighed with relief when there was no surcharge. We had gotten away with it, but we still had to stagger on and off the plane. Unexpectedly, we had help from friends, who carried some of the packages for us. There were two American zoo directors, with their wives, on our Lufthansa plane, and two Germans, including Bernhard Grzimek, whom I greatly admired for the work he and his late son had done to help protect African wildlife.

When we arrived in Johannesburg we were met by a staff member of the Pretoria Zoo, who arranged red-carpet treatment for us. No baggage inspection, and only a cursory glance at our passports. We were whisked into a small bus and then driven some 30 miles directly to the Boulevard Hotel in Pretoria, the administrative capital city of the Republic of South Africa.

Our vacation was over, and it was time to get down to business. We were in Pretoria to attend the annual meeting of the International Union of Directors of Zoological Gardens (IUDZG). It was the first time that organization had ever met in Africa, and the local authorities were determined to do it up brown, to resort again to a bit of slang. They had an elaborate program planned for us, and they picked the exact time of year (mid-October, their spring) when the jacaranda trees would be in full bloom. Thousands of those South American trees had been planted all over the city, and their lavender blossoms were omnipresent.

We had the usual meetings—discussions about new techniques for exhibiting animals, concern about worldwide conservation, and so on—all very important issues for zoo professionals. There were many social functions as well. Tours of important buildings and the Pretoria National Zoo, receptions and banquets, and the like. We were received by the Lord Mayor of the city dressed in his full regalia and carrying a stout mace. Ditto the Administrator (Governor?) of the Transvaal. Also, we were taken to an impressive hilltop edifice, the equivalent of our White House, for a reception and cocktail party hosted by the Honorable B. J. Vorster, Prime Minister of South Africa, and his wife. We arrived there in late afternoon, and, when we went outside to the terraces, we were greeted by a virtual sea of lavender flowers. It was an unforgettable sight and experience.

The morning after our arrival, I had to register for the meetings and sign up for the tour to Kruger National Park and the white rhinoceros country in the Natal. Then I went right into formal sessions. Dear Isabelle volunteered to get rid of our postal impedimenta. She managed to walk to the post office, which fortunately was not far away, to dispatch everything.

Her diary doesn't state how many trips she made getting rid of the heavy pile. It must have been several.

Our host was David J. "Frank" Brand, Director of the National Zoological Gardens of South Africa in Pretoria. He was very likable and a highly competent executive. He and his staff did everything possible to entertain us and take care of our needs. We must have numbered close to 60, including wives and a few youngsters. When we departed for two weeks in the field, he accompanied us in his own car, so he would be mobile and able to run errands, if any became necessary, or if an emergency arose. We were all deeply indebted to him. We learned that he was fluent in both English and Afrikaans, a language that originated with the Dutch settlers in the seventeenth century. No one could hold an important office in South Africa unless he or she could converse with ease in both. All signs, notices, and other printed matter were given twice, with either English or Afrikaans appearing first. Frank also did well in German, as we were to learn later.

It was hot and dry in South Africa, and the clothing we had worn at the high altitudes in East Africa was too heavy for comfort. The dryness helped, because Isabelle was able to wash our lighter clothing and let it drip dry. We inquired about what the weather conditions would be for our two-week field trip, and we were told it would be mostly hot. We might encounter some rain the second week in the Natal, where the prevailing winds blew in from the Indian Ocean. I, along with several colleagues, bought a safari suit. It was light in weight and consisted of a pair of dress shorts and a short-sleeved jacket that I could substitute for a shirt. Both were well supplied with pockets, and they proved to be ideal for the warm climate. Mine was light green, and, when I looked recently, it was neatly folded in one of my bureau drawers, unused for decades. Isabelle wore blouses and slacks. We took along our regular safari jackets in case we should encounter a cool spell— also our blue jeans to wear while we were in the field. I had my swimming trunks. We were traveling light at the zoo people's suggestion, because they told us that space would be at a premium. The remainder of our belongings we packed into our regular suitcases, which we checked at the Boulevard Hotel.

I had a nagging worry that I tried to eliminate before we departed on our long trip. The previous year, when we attended the IUDZG meeting in Barcelona, Spain, I had learned to check our departure reservations as soon as possible. Ideally, that was done before we left the airport for our hotel, or at least by telephone the following morning. Our arrival in Johannesburg among a party of VIPs precluded any opportunity there. So I tried

to phone from Pretoria, with no success. The long-distance service was poor, and when I inquired at the hotel desk, they agreed that it was sometimes impossible to get through. Occasionally it was easy. Even though I tried again, I had no luck, so I asked the hotel people to confirm our reservations when the line was open. To make doubly sure, I also asked one of Frank Brand's assistants at the zoo to do the same thing. Both promised that they would have confirmation for me when we returned.

Thirty-seven of us departed on the morning of Saturday, October 19, aboard a new air-conditioned luxury bus. But let Isabelle continue the narrative from her diary:

The air conditioning wasn't adequate, the windows wouldn't open, and we sweltered all day. Our seats were on the sunny side. Several private car loads followed us. . . . The photographers in the crowd made so much fuss about the bus windows not opening that Dr. Brand assigned some of us to ride in the private cars in the cavalcade. Roger and I and Dr. Nouvel [Jacques Nouvel, Director of the Parc Zoologique de Paris] went with a Mr. Graphorn. He had a terrific cockney accent that was hard to follow, and he was a lousy driver. He would usually stop when we wanted to photograph, but would jockey the car back and forth so that we never knew when we could get a steady shot. The first thing he did was to slam into the back of Brand's car because he wasn't watching the road. Brand's rear bumper was damaged, but Graphorn's "bonnet" was loosened and wouldn't close tightly. As we drove along, the hood flew up and cut off our vision. Mr. G. found a strap and tied it down and we proceeded.

After lunch we rested awhile and then we all went out again. As the afternoon progressed, Mr. G. decided we had better speed up to return to camp by 6:00 P.M., the time when the Park closes for the day. As he was doing 50 miles per hour, the strap on the hood broke and it flew up again, bending it more out of shape than before. In order to drive back to camp Roger used his web belt to fasten the hood down and it held. Talked Mr. G. into getting a piece of wire so Roger could have his belt back.

Isabelle put that last bit mildly. Graphorn insisted that I give him back my belt when I removed it from his damaged car and returned it to my waist. He became very nasty when I refused. I asked him how I was supposed to hold up my pants, but that fell on deaf ears. A bystander at the camp volunteered to find a piece of wire, and we beat a retreat toward our cabin. It was a relief to get away from Mr. G. What a shock to be racing along on an uneven, pebble-strewn dirt road at 50, and to have the

hood fly up in our faces. Graphorn slammed on his brakes, but the car skidded through a U-turn and headed in the opposite direction.

Months later, at home, I received a letter from Frank Brand stating that when Graphorn rammed his car, he (Brand) had suffered a back injury, and he was suing for damages. Frank asked me to send him a deposition describing the accident, which I did and had properly notarized. He won the suit. We never did learn why Mr. G. was with our cavalcade in the first place.

The excerpts above from my late wife's diary were written on two separate days, but I have kept them together to point up how wise we were to hire our own private car and driver during our wanderings through East Africa. Taking pictures on the crowded bus was exceedingly difficult, and being rushed around by an erratic driver wasn't much better. I will say, however, that Dr. Nouvel took our misadventure in stride. He was rather taciturn at first, and, like most loyal Frenchmen, he conversed only in his own language unless he was forced to speak English. He was fluent in the latter, however, and as the day wore on he became less and less reticent. Neither Isabelle nor I spoke French.

After leaving Pretoria, we reached the famed Kruger National Park about 5:00 P.M. after a few stops—for lunch, to visit restrooms, and to take pictures of scenery. Each time we were all glad to get out of the hot bus. There was a delay in receiving room assignments, and we were advised to wait inside our vehicles. There were panhandling monkeys and baboons outside, and some of the latter were large ugly males that could and would bite. One big baboon climbed up on the hoods of all of the cars in our retinue, one after the other, and the occupants kept all their windows tightly shut. When staff members in uniform appeared, the simians beat a hasty retreat.

Kruger National Park is in the extreme northeastern

corner of the Republic of South Africa, and it is bordered on the east by Mozambique, which was known as Portuguese East Africa during the time of our visit. The Park is irregular in shape. It extends southward from the Limpopo River for 200 miles and varies in width from 25 to 50 miles. Altogether, it encompasses an area of about 8,000 square miles. It was named for S. J. Paulus Kruger, one of the founders and a former president of the Transvaal Republic. He was a national hero of the Boers, the descendants of Dutch and Huguenot settlers in South Africa who fought a bloody and bitter war with the British at the turn of the present century.

In 1968, the Park had 12 rest camps with bungalows and restaurants. During our first night there, we stayed at the Pretoriuskop Camp, and were billeted with

Reginald and Hilda Greed. Reggie was the Director of the Bristol Zoo in England. We had our own rooms, but shared a bathroom. After that, Isabelle and I were assigned to private quarters.

To celebrate our arrival, the Park staff tendered a barbecue for us. There was much singing afterward, a lot of it directed toward Charles and Maxine Schroeder, who, we discovered, were celebrating their first wedding anniversary. Charlie was the Director of the San Diego Zoo. According to Isabelle's diary, "Roger managed to buy a small cake and one huge candle." It reminded me of the time, years earlier in Monterrey, Mexico, when I arranged to have a cake baked for Isabelle's birthday. This time, however, the only candle available was a large one designed to furnish light at night if the electricity went off.

We stayed in Kruger Park for six nights in three different camps, as we gradually moved northward as far as the Oliphants Camp on the Oliphants River, which was almost in the vertical middle of the great wildlife reserve. We were in the Transvaal veldt, a mostly flat to gently rolling plain, partially wooded, at least along the few watercourses. Animals were abundant in some places but definitely scarce in others. Our transportation varied. One day we reboarded the bus, another we were transferred to Land Rovers and similar vehicles, but most of the time we rode in Frank Brand's car. Wilhelm Windecker, Director of Germany's Köln (Cologne) Zoo, was in the front seat and Isabelle and I with our camera gear were in the back. I suspect we were so honored because Brand quickly recognized that, among all the persons in the entourage, Isabelle was the most dedicated photographer. It was a doubly advantageous arrangement, because our host was well informed about the wildlife of the Park, and we learned many

things that would have escaped us otherwise. Frank was willing to answer all our questions, in both English and German, and he would stop anytime for picture taking. That was all to the good and deeply appreciated. On the other hand, the weather prognosticators back in Pretoria were in error. It was cloudy most of the time, cool to cold, and it even rained or drizzled occasionally.

One morning, our hosts and South Africa's leading veterinarians put on a thrilling demonstration for us by tranquilizing and immobilizing a large adult wild elephant. As I have mentioned previously, great strides were then being made in the development and perfection of the new technique. The demonstration was a splendid way to show us how it was done, and it also was entertaining, especially for the many women in our party.

In Land Rovers and similar vehicles we were taken to a brush-covered area near the Lower Sabie Camp. A large tusker had been hanging around in the vicinity. Soon after our vehicles were all in sight, scattered

though they were, a helicopter appeared and circled over and around the big beast. At exactly the proper moment, a vet aboard shot a dart into its rump. Nothing happened for a minute or two, but then the elephant began to sag, its front legs bending and its forequarters moving downward. By means of a bullhorn, we were told we could leave our cars, and many of us moved in for a close look. I had one of our cameras, and I was able, even though it was raining, to obtain a series of pictures that could be titled "Going, going, gone!" Just before the elephant eased flat onto its belly, one of the veterinarians rushed in, grabbed its trunk, and tugged it out nearly straight so the animal could breathe. Otherwise the heavy skull might have pinched it shut, or at least partly so. We were permitted to walk all around the animal. Isabelle, wisely, stayed in the car, not only because of the rain, but she also knew photo opportunities would be slim, and that I could manage alone at close range.

The antidote was then injected, and we were all told to get back into our cars and move away. They didn't want the elephant to be disturbed while it was still groggy and getting back on its feet, which we saw it do, and then walk away. We reassembled at a cluster of buildings at the camp. There we learned that the dart, with its load of tranquilizer, had been driven through the pachyderm's thick hide with a powerful crossbow, the deadly weapon that decided the course of history during the Middle Ages. The one the vet used was so powerful that the string had to be drawn back with a long, stout lever. The men demonstrated how to do it as several of us took pictures.

A large elephant, shot with a dart full of tranquilizer, slowly sags to the ground. Just before the last picture was taken, a veterinarian seized the trunk and pulled it out nearly straight so the animal could breathe. Photos by RC.

A crossbow, aimed by an archer in a helicopter, drove the dart through the elephant's tough hide. The crossbow was so powerful that it had to be cocked with a special long lever. Photo by IHC.

The drug used on the elephant was called M99, the antidote was M5050, and those names were all we heard from our skilled hosts. Many years later, through the good efforts of friends, I learned that the technical names are eterophine hydrochloride and diprenorphine hydrochloride, respectively. How much easier for lay, non-medically oriented persons to stick with M99 and M5050.

A little later, our hosts planned a buffalo drive for us. We remained in our vehicles along a dirt road, some of them off on the veldt on either side, and we were cautioned to stay well back from where the action would be. The same helicopter used for the elephant demonstration was able to assemble about 200 of the big black ruminants in a loose milling mass. Apparently the sound and sight of the chopper, a giant noisy "eagle in the sky," caused the buffaloes to shy away from it. The skill of the pilot brought them together. Finally the whirlybird, at low altitude, flew toward the herd, and the animals began to run away from it. They crossed the road, but too far away for good pictures. It was impressive, however, to see the wide river of black buffaloes as they galloped across in front of us.

Two other notable events occurred while we were in the Park. When we were in a Volkswagen bus with several other people on the only really clear day we had in the Kruger, our driver kept a close watch on an exceptionally large group of elephants perhaps a quarter of a mile from the road on which we were driving. He didn't tell us how he divined it, but he slowed the car almost to a crawl and said, "I think they are going to stampede." He was right, because presently the herd started to run

parallel to the road, not too rapidly, and the smaller animals were able to keep pace with the big ones. As we drove along parallel to them, other elephants, loners and small groups, joined them, and soon there were almost 200 animals, all moving at a rapid pace. The driver had no explanation for the phenomenon, and we soon had to leave the unusual sight so he could keep up with his schedule to meet others at a predesignated time. The herd was too far away for our small cameras to record the event photographically.

On the evening of October 23 at the Oliphants Camp, Isabelle and I had dinner with visiting company. Marlin Perkins was in South Africa with a film crew to obtain photographs of hippos for his ever-popular "Wild Kingdom" television program. He knew the zoo directors were in the Park, and he drove over to greet us all. We were also joined by Captain Jean Delacour, the distinguished ornithologist, whose wonderful little zoo at Cleres, France, I had visited way back in 1937. The four of us enjoyed a lively conversation. Marlin was an old friend, of course, and Delacour had been living in the United States. He had an office at the American Museum of Natural History, where I had visited him several times, and he was acting as an adviser for the New York (Bronx) Zoo.

Our stay in the Park was over. We boarded the bus for a five-hour drive to the relatively large town of Nelspruit, near the southwestern corner of the big wildlife reserve. It took that long because we were a 100 miles north, and the dirt roads were neither intended nor maintained for speeding along.

After lunch the party broke up. The majority of the group would be returning to Pretoria and from there onward to wherever their destinations might be. We all said fond farewells, one of them to Pierre A. Fontaine, a good friend of long standing. We had celebrated his birthday while we were together at one of the rest camps. Sadly, we never saw him again. We were aghast when he told us that he and his wife, Jayne, were flying straight home, all the way to Dallas, Texas, where he presided over the zoo and aquarium. They would have no rest, except for napping on airplanes and sitting in various airports during layovers. The trip was too much for him, and he died a few weeks later. How smart we were to stop off in Europe, both coming and going. I have practiced the same policy ever since, tarrying for a day's rest before or during long trips. Prior to taking off for the Orient, Europe, or South America, in recent years, Kathryn and I have habitually spent a night on either the West or East Coast, giving us a chance to sleep well and to slow down after the exigencies of final packing, closing up the house, and attendant chores.

Fifteen of us, in addition to Frank Brand in his car, and our drivers, took off in another direction, headed for the white rhinoceros country in the Natal. We had two Volkswagen buses, but the seating arrangements were different and more roomy than those in buses of the same make with which we are familiar in the States. We were about to enjoy a rare treat, because we were headed first for Swaziland, a kingdom whose black sovereign had ruled for a great many years. It was an independent nation, but closely allied to and under the protection of South Africa.

We soon left the paving and began winding our way up and down almost mountainous dirt roads. It was picturesque territory and quite a change from the veldt we had so recently left. The border with Swaziland closed at 4:00 P.M., but the lead bus driver, who was supposed to know the route, chose the wrong fork in the road. He didn't realize his mistake until we had gone at least a dozen miles. We turned around, but that delay, in addition to halting to change a flat tire on the other bus, made us have to race to beat the deadline. It was 4:01 by the clock in the customs station when we arrived, but the South African agents took pity on us and persuaded their Swaziland colleagues to do the same. So there we were in a tiny country that none of us from the Northern Hemisphere had ever expected to visit. Frank Brand included it on our itinerary as a special highlight, a treat to punctuate our journey.

Mbabane, the capital, was not too far from the border. It was a fairly modern city, not unlike some we had seen in South Africa. We went to the Swazi Inn, which was a little on the swank side, but we ate all together in a private dining room where no one noticed our rumpled field clothes. Most of the 15 people in our group were Europeans. There was also a Canadian. We and Robert Bean, Director of the Brookfield Zoo, were the only Americans. Tadamichi Koga, Director of the Ueno Zoo in Tokyo, Japan, was also with us, and he took a liking to the Conants. He often ate at our table, and while the tire was being changed, he removed my camera from my shoulder and took a snapshot of us against a background of Swaziland hills. Isabelle thought it was "very cute of him." His English was not at all bad, but we knew only one word of Japanese, which he taught us: Ohio means "Good morning" in his language.

In the courtyard of the Swazi Inn there was a swimming pool that looked unused and rather unkempt, and had low weeds growing all around it. That was a boon for me, because after dark I heard the voices of many anurans emanating from the general vicinity. I borrowed a strong flashlight from one of the Volks drivers, and in just a few minutes I had samples of five kinds of frogs and toads. Before we retired I caught a gecko on the window drape in our room. With almost boyish enthusiasm I thought to myself, "I wonder if any other American herpetologist ever collected in Swaziland?"

After our night spent just outside Mbabane, we drove southward through rain and fog; the weather improved by 10:00 A.M., but remained overcast. En route we were entertained, as Isabelle recorded, when we "came upon about 20 Swazi tribesmen in hunting costume—spears, beads, and fur shields—who put on a dance for our cavalcade by the roadside. Brand paid them, but whether or not it was prearranged I don't know." She continued with, "Lunched at a sleazy hotel in Gollel on the border just before we went back into South Africa. It did not take long to have our passports stamped before proceeding south in the pouring rain." We were in the Natal, the home of the Zulus, the fierce tribe that was in conflict for years with both the Boers and the British.

The Lake View Hotel, near the St. Lucia Estuary in Zululand, was to be our headquarters for five consecutive days. What a relief. We would not have to pack every night for a change of venue the following morning. There would be daily excursions to keep us busy.

The first day we were the guests of the Natal Park Board, which took us to see the estuary. There were four small motorboats to accommodate us, and we cruised northward for 13 miles through the rather narrow estuary to the much wider and more open St. Lucia Lake. It was sunny, but the wind was high, and our hosts thought it would be dangerous to risk our small boats in the high waves, so back we went. In the estuary we saw sunning crocodiles and two herds of hippos, as well as many birds. When we returned to the landing we made sure to photograph the warning sign, which read:

> <u>DANGER</u>
> THESE WATERS CONTAIN CROCODILES,
> SHARKS AND HIPPOPOTAMI.
>
> <u>GEVAAR</u>
> HIERDIE WATER BEVAT KROKODILLE,
> HAAIE EN SEEKOEIE.

Just for the fun of it, I include the Afrikaans version of the warning. Such two-language signs met us seemingly everywhere.

During the afternoon the Park's people took us for a land tour of the area, but it poured rain most of the time. We were disappointed to miss having our first glimpse of the Indian Ocean. There was no way to get close by road, and we didn't want to get soaked by walking in the downpour across the dunes and spit that largely blocked contact between the estuary and the sea.

We were in rhinoceros country, and we were soon to witness an amazing series of events. The South Africans, through strict control of poaching and their recently initiated "Operation Rhino," were destined to save the white rhinoceros from oblivion. They eventually made the species available in numbers for zoos and wild animal parks and reserves all over the world.

Among the large land mammals, the rhinos have long been the most endangered and of the gravest concern to conservationists. There are five living species, two African and three Asian. Their numbers, and the territories to which they were earlier indigenous, have shrunk drastically since the days of exploration and settlement by the European colonial powers.

The main enemy of the rhinos is the absurd belief, in some Oriental countries, that rhino horn is a powerful aphrodisiac that will restore virility. Even small pieces brought—and still bring—fabulous sums. Unscrupulous dealers encouraged natives in both Africa and Asia to slaughter the animals, remove just their horns, and sell them for more than they could earn during a year of hard labor. What a great temptation! Even during the 1990s we still see ugly pictures of the carcasses of dehorned black rhinos rotting away. Another use for the horns, about which general knowledge became widespread only in recent years, is in Yemen, where having a scabbard of rhino horn for one's long knife is a mark of distinction.

Those of us who think of the future and what sort of world our progeny will inherit, are well aware that the rhinos deserve every bit of protection they can get.

Not far from the St. Lucia Estuary, where we were staying, were two game reserves, Umfolozi and Hluhluwe (the latter pronounced rather like Castilian Spanish, viz. "thlu-thluwe," as near as we could manage that tongue twister). Compared with the enormous Kruger Park, the two game reserves were tiny, little more than dots on a map. Yet, as a result of careful husbandry by the authorities, each supported a thriving colony of white rhinos. The two reserves were only a little more than 10 miles apart. The rhinos, unaware of man-made boundaries, often wandered off the reserves, and damaged the crops of the neighboring Zulu farmers. It was chiefly within the "corridor" between Umfolozi and Hluhluwe that Operation Rhino was conducted. It consisted of the immobilization and then the revival of the wandering animals, using M99 and M5050, the same two drugs that were employed during the elephant demonstration we had witnessed

in Kruger Park. Once they were knocked out, the rhinos were prepared for transportation to a holding *boma* (pen) where they soon became tame. Their temperaments were vastly different from those of the truculent black rhinos. From the *boma* the captive white rhinos could be shipped elsewhere. They had been reintroduced into the other South Africa reserves and parks, and eventually in some of those in the black nations. In the latter cases, however, the rhinos went first to a neutral country and then back to Africa! Since our visit in 1968, white rhinos have been shipped all over the world, and they are now the most common species of rhinoceros in zoos and game parks. When Isabelle and I were in the Great Wild Animal Park near Escondido, California, in 1971, a herd of 20 had recently arrived, even though the park was still under construction. From that nucleus, scores of young have been born and raised.

The success achieved with the big pachyderm points out what can be done, through careful planning and supervision, to save a rare animal from almost certain extinction.

We arose early, breakfasted, were off by 7:45 A.M., and were driven over rough dirt roads until we were close to the Hluhluwe Reserve, where we met rangers at a predesignated point. As soon as all of us had arrived, they used their walkie-talkies to alert men on horseback who had located two rhinos, each more than half grown. They had been waiting for us, and they then fired darts into the animals' rumps. We were told to wait for almost a half hour so the big beasts would not be disturbed while being sedated. Our party split in two. Our rhino was down on its knees, and it was really immobile, not even blinking its eyes. We could examine it closely, and some of our more venturesome friends climbed on its back to have their pictures taken. I noted and photographed many large ticks that formed a partial ring around each eye and also around the anus. Their presence seemed strange. Were there no oxpeckers in that part of Africa? I was told later that those birds are local and uncommon in the south. When we were in East Africa they seemed almost omnipresent. They are smaller than our robin, and their feet are adapted for clinging to the hides of large animals, including domestic cattle. They climb all around, searching for ticks and other ectoparasites, and are virtually ignored by the host animals.

Presently, a large Operation Rhino truck drove up and backed fairly close to the rhino. Several small trees had to be felled for its passage. Two ramps equipped with rollers were lowered, and a large crate slowly descended. It was equipped with guillotine-type doors at each end. Several tribesmen moved it close to our rhino, and raised the near door.

The animal was facing away from the crate, and just ahead of it was a small ravine which a truck could not negotiate. No problem. Several men, including rangers and veterinarians, rolled the rhino onto its back, and swiveled it around until it faced the crate. They then rolled it back onto its knees. A rope was placed around its neck, and the loose end was passed through the crate and then through a hole in the closed door at the opposite end. One of the vets administered the antidote, and soon the big mammal rose groggily to its feet. Men pushed from behind while others pulled on the rope. In a very short time the rhino was in the crate, and the guillotine door was lowered behind it. A winch pulled the big box, with its heavy load inside, up onto the bed of the truck, and the vehicle soon departed for the *boma* a half hour's drive away.

We stopped for a quick cold lunch en route to the *boma*, and by the time we arrived our animal had walked out of its crate into a small holding area. Nearby was a pen made of logs that held several rhinos of similar size. They had been brought in some weeks earlier, but already a man was working right among them. The new drugs provided a unique way to catch rhinos.

The demonstration was planned and executed for our benefit, and how much we zoo directors learned from it. We had witnessed how rhinos could be immobilized from a safe distance by injecting darts loaded with tranquilizers. Timewise, we were there almost at the birth of one of the most useful tools in the zoo business—the ability to put dangerous animals quietly to sleep when they had to be moved. While the process was under way, Isabelle and I each shot a 36-exposure roll of film. What a wonderful set of pictures we obtained!

The next day we visited the Umfolozi Reserve, and we saw several rhinos walking along the distinct trails they had created to get from one part of the preserve to another.

An unexpected dividend for me was frog hunting. October is springtime in South Africa, and there had been a lot of rain. Frog voices were numerous at night, but none resembled the calls of the North American species with which I was familiar. The good-natured driver let me borrow his flashlight again, and even put in a new battery for me. I used it every evening while we were at St. Lucia, and I caught several kinds of frogs and toads and a skink. Even while we were still in Swaziland, I decided I would try to take some of the frogs home alive for the zoo, since our trip was nearing its end. I kept them in plastic bags, and rinsed them off with fresh cool water several times daily. Frank Brand told me there were no restrictions about taking them.

Among our large series of pictures of Operation Rhino was one of RC crouched by the drugged animal. It was truly inert; it didn't even blink its eyes. Hluhluwe Reserve, South Africa, October 27, 1968. Photo by IHC.

A few died, and I managed to get them pickled, but I arrived home with two live species of toads, five of frogs, and the skink *Mabuya varia.* We even found time, despite our busy schedule as soon as we were home, to make black-and-white photos of all the species for our extensive collection (many thousands) of reptile and amphibian portraits. Some of my imports survived at the Philadelphia Zoo for quite a long time, and as they died off I preserved them and, as usual, presented them, along with the dates and localities where they were collected, to the American Museum of Natural History. The most interesting of the lot were three blaasops, or rain frogs, of the genus *Breviceps*, which, like the much bigger Mexican burrowing toad that barely enters the United States in extreme southern Texas, inflate themselves with air when alarmed. They looked like tiny balloons when I caught them, with the tip of the snout barely protruding. I also found a beautiful reed frog, *Hyperolius*, belonging to a large and widespread African genus, whose members show even more colorful variations than our own treefrogs, *Hyla*.

Our party moved on to the large port city of Durban, and we were billeted at the Four Seasons Hotel, a really fancy place. We were a shabby, motley crew in our field clothes. On the way to our rooms we passed the spacious dining room, and I noted a sign near the door that read "Gentlemen Are Obliged to Wear Jackets and Neckties." Inquiry revealed that we would be eating there, so, after we were settled in our room, I walked down and asked questions. My safari jacket was acceptable, but my blue jeans were definitely not. Pants of that type were worn by black laborers, and were definitely objectionable in a fashionable, all-white dining room. So were shorts, which no doubt were considered infra dig. I had no necktie. There was nothing to do but go shopping. I bought a pair of cheap dress trousers, but, to get legs that were long enough, I had to take a pair that were five or six inches too wide around the waist. My belt held in the excess. Getting a necktie was no problem. Isabelle's khaki slacks were OK. Dr. Windecker had to buy a jacket, and Bob Bean borrowed a coat from one of the drivers, who were staying elsewhere. We assembled together in advance and entered the room as a group. What an odd assortment we were. I think that everyone in the place turned to gawk at us, including the Hindu waiters. A pox on the people in Pretoria who told us that field clothes would be ample throughout our trip!

We had a day at liberty in Durban. I found a tailor who altered my new pants so that they almost fitted. We took a taxi to the Snake Park, which was small but excellent. The manager, Ray Parker, gave me some extra formalin to supplement my meager supply for preserving specimens that died. We walked along the waterfront and had a look at the aquarium, which was long on big tanks with many large aquatic exhibits, including marine turtles and sharks, but short on small tanks and colorful fishes. Later, as Isabelle wrote in her diary, "Our first swim in the Indian Ocean this afternoon. At least Roger swam and I waded, getting my jeans wet in the process. My bathing suit was too heavy to bring, and anyway the surf was so rough and the undertow so strong that I probably wouldn't have enjoyed it. The beach was only a couple of blocks from the hotel and our windows overlooked the ocean."

We left Durban on November 1, en route back to Pretoria, but we were to have one more delightful stop. For a while we rode along the east side of the Drakensberg (Dragon Mountains). We crossed that range at Reenen Pass, where, we were told, the wind sometimes blew so hard that it overturned high-profile vehicles if they were moving too fast. By early afternoon we reached Golden Gate Highlands National Park, in the Orange Free State, and were assigned to exceptionally good rooms in a brand-new installation. The chief ranger joined us and led us on a tour of the park. The elevation was 6,100 feet at the lodge; the highest point within the area was 8,700 feet; and, according to Isabelle's diary, "This was a fantastic place full of vistas of rolling hills, red and yellow rock faces, and outcroppings in various sizes and shapes." Some of the colorful rocky cliffs inspired one of our European colleagues to remark, "It's just like the American cinema." No doubt he was referring to some of our "Western"

movies that were popular on both sides of the Atlantic.

Isabelle continued, "We saw springboks, blesboks, zebras, elands, and white-tailed gnus, all in numbers. They were shy and the long lenses were needed. There was one exception—a tame eland that the ranger had raised—and we were able to get close to it."

Just at sunset we arrived at an overlook, and saw and photographed a group of cliffs and a small peak highlighted in bright yellow, the source of the name "Golden Gate." What a gorgeous picture they made.

After dark I went frog hunting again where I heard a chorus calling. They were in a small pond, and I felt a little uneasy about grabbing them in the water. I knew about schistosomiasis and that it was transmitted by organisms in aquatic environments. Fortunately, the elevation was high enough to be out of the range of the pandemic parasitism. The frogs were later identified as members of the genus *Ptychadena* of the big frog family Ranidae. The other frogs and toads I had caught in the lowlands were all out in the open, not in water.

The next day we returned to Pretoria and the Hotel Boulevard. The very first thing I did was to check on our plane reservations on Scandinavian Airlines via Nairobi and Khartoum to Athens, Greece. The hotel people said that everything was OK. To make sure, I double-checked with the zoo office, and they reported the same. We were to leave by air on November 4 at 5:30 P.M. Our long stay in Africa was almost over, but we had two more special functions to attend. The following morning we travelers were invited to the Brands' home for tea. They lived in a nice house in one corner of the zoo, and afterward we and Dr. Koga roamed through the various exhibits once again.

We all thanked Frank Brand for providing such a marvelous program for us. It was, in fact, the most lengthy and elaborate ever attempted in conjunction with a meeting of the IUDZG, at least up until that time. Usually the gatherings centered on the host zoo and its vicinity, and ancillary trips were advertised on which parties or individuals could go on their own. Brand and his associates, however, planned and executed an extraordinarily interesting postmeeting adventure for us. Imagine the logistics of getting us to various places on time and making sure that meals and lodging would be ready and waiting for us. Also, think of the marvelous cooperation Frank had from the authorities in demonstrating how to immobilize huge beasts with M99 and then restoring them with M5050. There were also the visits to the Kruger and Golden Gate National Parks. No other host zoo director, to my knowledge, had ever attempted such a complicated excursion. Also, Frank Brand went with us so he could help whenever he was needed. Isabelle got something in her eye that left it irritated and uncomfortable, so Frank made a special trip in his personal car from St. Lucia to Mtubatuba, the capital of Zululand, to get a bottle of eye lotion for her. What a marvelous host and "prince of a guy." We gave him our heartfelt thanks in person, and I followed up later with an official letter on Philadelphia Zoo stationery.

On our last night in Africa we were transported to the suburban home of C. K. Brain, Director of the Transvaal Museum. Two other herpetologists were also present: Vivian F. M. FitzSimons, a prolific writer, former director of the museum, and son of F. W. FitzSimons, the pioneer authority on South African snakes; and an up-and-coming young man named Wulf D. Haacke. Wulf very kindly shipped my preserved specimens to me, and carefully identified them all. Among them was a Natal green water snake, *Philothamnus natalensis,* we found dead on the road. Mrs. Brain served us a buffet supper, and afterward we had a long, delightful chat about herpetology.

On our last morning in Pretoria we took several things to the post office and mailed them to ourselves, including a small suitcase full of dirty clothes for which there was no time to launder. We also visited a bookstore and I purchased a copy of Roberts's "Birds of South Africa." I wanted to read about the species we had seen in our travels, such as the rollers, barbets, and hornbills, including the large and curious ground hornbill. I gave the store enough money to mail the book. We had all we could possibly manage in the way of baggage.

We were unaware that the longshoremen in the United States were in the midst of a long strike, and not a single cargo ship was being unloaded, not even the mail. We were home four months, well into 1969, when our things finally arrived, all in good condition, including the book, my preserved specimens, and our dirty clothes.

Right after lunch on November 4, we taxied to a terminal and rode the bus to Jan Smuts Airport in Johannesburg, where we arrived at 3:15 P.M. (according to Isabelle's diary). We engaged a porter and sauntered up to the Scandinavian counter, where I presented our tickets. The agent demanded to know where we had been. They had held our plane for us for an hour, and it had taken off just six minutes ago!

We were flabbergasted. I pointed to the departure time on our tickets, and I was told the schedule had changed as of November 1. What had gone wrong? Had the SAS attendant forgotten to mention the change, when (and if) the hotel and zoo people had called? Had someone lied to me? We never did find out, but we were in a picklement.

What to do? The SAS people reluctantly relinquished our fares to South African Airlines, which had a plane leaving for Rome that evening. Through SAA we reserved seats on Olympic Airlines from Rome to Athens. We would get to Greece after all, but it cost us a lot of extra money, and took almost all our cash. We should have brought along more traveler's checks; we had used all we had after surrendering the last one to the South African line. I had paid our hotel bill in Athens for three nights before we left home. I was carrying a letter of credit for $2,000, but I didn't want to use it except for some dire emergency. It was the Philadelphia Zoo's money.

In early evening we took off on our way north, but over an unanticipated route. We flew to Luanda, in Portuguese Angola, to refuel. The airport was under heavy guard because of intertribal warfare that was to last for decades. You may recall that Fidel Castro eventually sent large numbers of Cuban troops to assist the side that favored Communism.

We headed north-northwest for a very long overwater flight. We couldn't pass over any part of black Africa. If the plane had been forced to land for any reason, it would have been seized and there would have been real danger for the crew and probably the passengers. We had to cross the Gulf of Guinea and go around the great northwestern bulge of the African continent. In an emergency we could put down in the Cape Verde, Madeira, or Canary Islands, I presumed, but we landed safely in Lisbon, Portugal, soon after dawn. A little later we went on to Rome, where we discovered that the Olympic Airlines flight on which we were booked had been canceled!

We arranged to get on a later plane that would arrive in Athens about dusk, but we had something like eight or nine hours to wait in the Rome Airport. What a dreary prospect. We managed to doze a little, we read paperbacks we had brought with us, and I watered the frogs in the men's room. Fortunately, the flight from Johannesburg had many empty places, and we managed to sprawl out on three seats apiece. With the armrests pushed up we were fairly comfortable, except that I had to bend my long legs at the knees to fit. We were lucky to have gotten quite a bit of sleep during the night. There was no dearth of blankets and pillows. Our luggage, checked through to Athens, was, happily, at the Olympic counter in Rome and would accompany us to Greece.

The weather was beautifully clear. In midafternoon we flew southeastward along the coast of Italy, crossed the instep of its foot-shaped southern extremity, and then turned eastward. Soon a vast galaxy of islands and peninsulas came into view, and we descended to the Athens Airport in the fading but colorful light of the sunset behind us. Our long delay in Rome was forgiven in the glory of that spectacular arrival.

The very first thing we noticed were the signs in Greek letters. At one time I recognized all of them, and I could even recite the alphabet, but that was long ago. The old saying "everything is Greek to us" was eminently true, but our cab driver recognized the name of the Hotel Amalia, and he delivered us to the door, almost a day after our scheduled arrival. I went to the concierge at once and explained our predicament. He consulted with the people at the main desk, and they finally agreed to my suggestion that they let the money I had sent them for three nights be divided into two nights' lodging and the food we would consume in their restaurant. What a relief. We had so little cash that we ate only a frugal snack in the Rome Airport.

With the help of the concierge I checked on our reservations for our departure to London. Then we went to bed and slept the clock around, a full 12 hours.

By using a rubberneck wagon (tour bus) and through the versatility of a lady guide who repeated everything in five languages, we saw quite a bit of Athens. Isabelle wrote:

> *The tour took us through the archeological museum, which was interesting and very well presented, the ancient Temple of Zeus, where we could get out and take pictures, the original Olympic Stadium, and a look through the barred gates of the Royal Palace (the king and queen are now exiles in Rome). Roger took pictures of the guard dressed in ancient, traditional Greek costume. Then to a Byzantine Greek Orthodox church. The last and best place was the Acropolis, with the Parthenon and other ancient buildings, but the stop was nowhere near long enough.*

After a late lunch and a rest, we went for a walk and peered into store windows. Isabelle admired a silver snake ring. We went inside, asked for it, and I handed the manager my credit card, the only one internationally honored in those days. His English was not bad, and he asked immediately, "Don't you have any American money?" I told him no, and that we had spent nearly everything we had. His response was that he could give us a much better price if we had cash. He was reluctant to accept my card, but he finally did after we picked out a few souvenirs that would remind us of Greece. "I don't like them," he said. "They take too long to pay me."

The next morning we arose at 3:45 A.M. and departed by bus (with no breakfast) for the airport. At that early hour there were no porters, and we had to struggle by ourselves with our all-too-plentiful baggage. We were delighted to find Reggie and Hilda Greed aboard. They

were on their way home to Chester, England, from Nairobi. We maneuvered to sit together and had fun reviewing our recent South African excursion. They had been with us for the two full weeks after the formal meetings. As we approached the Alps, the clouds parted and we were treated to a vast panorama of snow-clad peaks that were the color of strawberry ice cream in the light of the rising sun. We flew directly over Mont Blanc in France. Everything beyond was an unbroken sea of clouds. Reggie wistfully remarked, "Good-bye, sun. We'll see you again at home sometime next spring or summer." We had a two-hour wait at London's Heathrow Airport, but the lounge was new and comfortable. The plane from there to Philadelphia was crowded and "we spent a miserable eight hours," as Isabelle put it. We landed in late afternoon and quickly passed through customs, even though I had to identify myself as the director of the zoo in order to import my live frogs. Fortunately, one of the men recognized me. I had cleared incoming shipments for the zoo with him at their local headquarters. Ed Malnate, our good friend and neighbor, met us. He drove us to Marlton, where we stopped to pick up a huge pile of accumulated mail and where we also spent the very last of our money buying a little fresh food. We were soon home, and Isabelle wrote, "Dear old Hyla Holler looked mighty good to us. It was about 6:00 when we arrived but it was 1:00 A.M. according to the time we had left Greece. We had taken 21 hours to reach home."

We were back on Thursday, November 7, and we expected to sleep late the next day. Our biological clocks didn't cooperate, however, and we were up extra early. We had hoped for a day of rest and leisure. Instead, the battery was dead in one of our two cars. After starting it with jumpers, I took it to town for a quick charge. Isabelle went to the bank and then laid in a week's supply of groceries. We skimmed through the mail, sorting out due or overdue bills, and took care of a multitude of chores. No time to rest. The next day, a Saturday, I was back at the zoo facing a small mountain of accumulated problems, all demanding my personal attention. On Tuesday, Isabelle put up 100 jars of cranberry sauce for gifts and for the coming holidays. The berries were at their very best, and that job could not be delayed. What energy we had in those days!

I mention all this because it was some time before we could sit quietly and reminisce about Africa objectively, and reflect on what we had seen and done. It had been a superb trip, and it more than matched my rosiest boyhood dreams. What vast numbers of animals we had seen, and of so very many different kinds. What thrills we'd had—huge crocodiles at close range, leopards asleep in a fever tree, a cheetah racing at incredible speed to catch a gazelle, an elephant and rhinos being sedated and revived with the new wonder drugs. And, how many close friends we made. Our Christmas card list, which already included more than 500 names, had to be supplemented with a couple of dozen more.

What had we liked best? We both voted for Uganda to top the list. Other highlights were views of the great African Rift and its accompanying volcanism, the Ngorongoro Crater, the unexpected visit to Swaziland, capturing white rhinos, and, especially for me, a chance to sample a bit of the South African herpetofauna. It was also wonderful to have brief looks at Rome and Athens, the centers of two long-gone civilizations.

We both admitted to having felt a little odd in South Africa, the land of apartheid. Over the years we had heard many tales about the segregation of the races in South Africa and the problems it engendered. The pragmatic protocol was that whites were superior, and blacks were fit only for manual labor and tasks befitting their inferior abilities. In the eyes of most of the rest of the world, such an attitude was demeaning and archaic, and all too reminiscent of slavery. But that's the way it was when we were there in 1968. South Africa, completely and thoroughly hated by the black African nations, was at least tacitly accepted elsewhere. The Portuguese worked closely with it. Their two big colonies, Angola (Portuguese West Africa) and Mozambique (Portuguese East Africa), served as buffers, along with Rhodesia, between the black countries and the land of apartheid. There were several black-ruled enclaves, in and adjoining South Africa, including Swaziland, which were in essence protectorates of the all-white government. There were also the so-called black townships, which supplied labor pools for the large cities and the gold and diamond mines.

Our hosts, as would be expected, did not expose us to the seamy side of racial segregation, but we witnessed two events that made us realize that separation was the law of the land. One was mild, but the other was a vivid example of the hatred it created.

When we returned to the Boulevard Hotel after our fortnight's trek, we were assigned to the same room we had occupied previously. When we entered, however, we found that it contained three single beds instead of two. Inquiry revealed that the housekeeper was expecting a group of boys from Vienna, Austria, and thought we had departed for home long ago. The extra bed would have to be taken out because it partially blocked the passage to our bathroom. Its removal would be a simple matter, we thought. Not so. A white female supervisor arrived with two small black men—Bantus, they called them. The men picked up the bed, one at each end, and, in trying to exit, they banged the bed against the door jamb. The same thing happened on the second try and again on the third. At that point the woman, asserting her authority, bawled them out unmercifully. She could have saved a lot of energy if she had taken the trouble to show them how to center their burden as they passed through the door. The men obviously had never moved a bed before, and they seemed quite nervous when they entered the room. They were grossly out of place.

The other racial incident occurred on the streets of Durban, and it involved two young men, both probably in their early 20s, one white and the other black. The white boy, driving a car, cut into a side street while going much too fast and slammed into a black boy riding a bicycle. The white jumped out and berated the black for getting in the way. The black was not hurt, but his bicycle, probably his pride and joy and doubtless his only means of transportation, was badly damaged. The white's car was scarcely scratched. The black said nothing, but his face betrayed his hatred and the injustice of the event. The arrogant white boy drove away cursing his victim.

Despite the racial tensions, South Africa was a modern and prosperous country, in many ways a match for the highly industrialized and progressive nations of Europe and elsewhere. We saw our first ever nuclear reactor in the distance as we passed through Witwatersrand on our way back to Pretoria. Isabelle would rejoice with me if she could know that apartheid came to an end not too long ago. As for me, a zoo director and dedicated conservationist, I shall never forget how South Africa saved the largest rhinoceros of them all, the white, or square-lipped, species, from extinction. Or the great care it was taking of its wildlife in its many parks and game reserves. We had seen only a fraction of the many sanctuaries the government had set aside and was carefully protecting. I was very favorably impressed.

Above everything, it had been a photographic trip for us. Isabelle began at once to send film, a few rolls at a time, to one of the Kodak color-processing centers in a distant city. In those days they were the only source of quality development. And what a chore she had sorting and labeling 2,500 pictures. We selected some of the best for showing to friends and relatives, and in my paid lectures. How wonderful it was to hear the compliments of several prominent naturalists, who, on seeing our photos, said, "The National Geographic Society couldn't have done better." My talented wife deserved almost every bit of the credit.

Chapter 48

The New Jersey Pine Barrens

How extremely lucky we were, Isabelle and I, to spend 25 of our 30 years of married life residing on the shore of Taunton Lake, in New Jersey's fabulous Pine Barrens. By day we were in Philadelphia, with all its noise, bustle, confusion, traffic, and pollution. At night we were in a different world—a world of peace and tranquility, with wildlife all around us. We enjoyed the Pine Barrens immensely, and also the thrill of "getting away from it all" on a daily basis. When we first moved to Taunton Lake in 1948, the two of us could hike all day through the woods on old sandy roads and trails without seeing a single other person. Yet, our home was only 16 miles, as the crow flies, from Philadelphia's City Hall!

Admittedly, less nature-oriented persons than we were thought of the Pine Barrens as a boring, sandy waste. On weekends, en route from the city to New Jersey's profusion of summer resorts, hordes of people raced down either the Black or White Horse Pike or along the few other paved roads to the seashore, and the sooner they passed through the pines the better they liked it. Few ever penetrated the region otherwise, and scarcely anyone, except fellow naturalists, had any idea of the treasures it held.

How did such a near wilderness manage to exist so close to the big city? The reason was the deep mantle of sand and gravel, which, in pioneer days, occupied an almost undisturbed 1,164,000 acres, roughly a fourth of the entire state of New Jersey, but concentrated in its southern half.

Where did the sand come from? I had read about it, of course, but I learned firsthand about its geological history through the simple expedient of digging cesspools. But I had better back up for a moment and explain why I was wielding a shovel.

Our dream home was under construction in 1958. We had accumulated enough cash to hire a contractor to do the heavy work. The rest we expected to finish with our own labor, including the digging of cesspools. The first excavation was to be eight feet deep and six in diameter.

As I dug downward I noted that the three or four surface inches consisted of a fairly tough tangle of roots, decayed leaves, and other vegetational debris. Once that barrier was passed, however, the spade cut sharply through a few inches of almost white sand. Then, almost abruptly, the sand turned yellow and remained that color to the bottom of the hole.

Why the change? The explanation is complex and involves soil chemistry and the action of rainwater. The white silica sand of the Barrens is intimately mingled with clay that gets its yellowish color from admixed iron oxide. Water, percolating gradually downward, leaches out the iron compounds and carries them with it, and the process is speeded as the water takes up acids formed by the decay of plant material. Removal of the iron pigment reveals the whiteness of the silica and gives the undisturbed bare surfaces of the Barrens their characteristic snowlike appearance. It is within the underlying yellow area that the iron compounds are precipitated out. If such action is abundant enough over a long period of time, a hardpan of iron oxide, variously called limonite or ilmenite, will form—the source of the iron ore mined in colonial times.

As my digging proceeded, pockets of pebbles, smooth and well rounded, appeared here and there in the otherwise uniformly clean sand. They looked waterworn, as though they had tumbled down a mountain stream. That supposition was confirmed a few days later when I met Horace G. Richards at the Academy of Natural Sciences of Philadelphia. Dr. Richards, an outstanding geologist who had spent a lifetime studying the record of the rocks, explained that the mantle of sand that covers the area occupied by the Pine Barrens was deposited long ago by rivers that flowed from the mountains to the sea. With the sand came pebbles. The Appalachians once were even higher than the Rockies of the American West, and, as they were eroded downward in many stages to their present heights, the resultant debris—prodigious quantities of it—was carried downstream, much of it toward the Atlantic, and much toward the interior lowlands from Canada to our southern states.

That explained the presence of both the sand and the

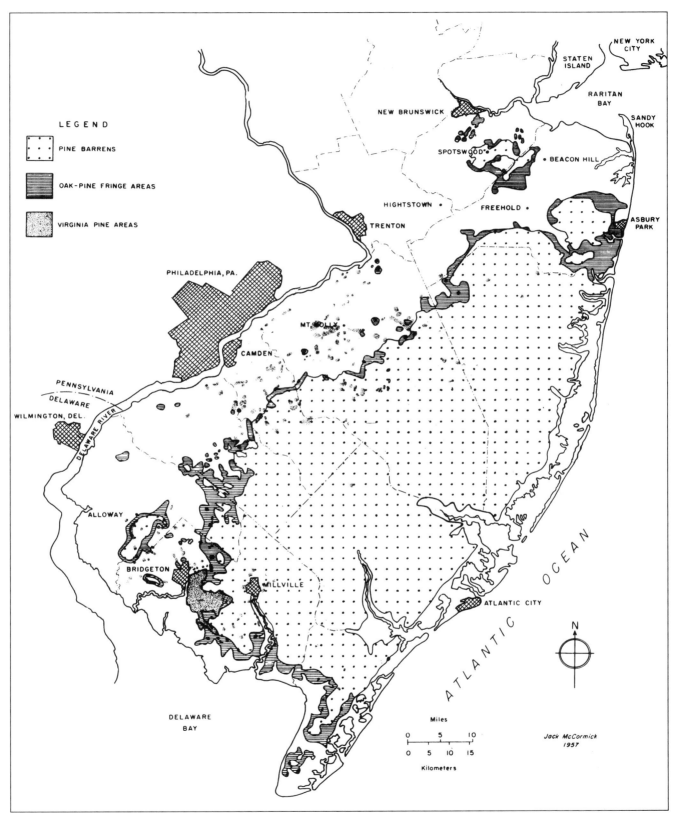

The New Jersey Pine Barrens with their fringe areas as they were before interference by humankind. Map delineated and used with the permission of Jack McCormick.

pebbles, but, while digging a few days later, I exposed a large stone, six inches in its long diameter and weighing almost a pound. How could it have been transported by water? Dr. Richards had a ready answer when I queried him. Sizable stones become imbedded in ice during the colder months, as anyone can readily observe while winter hiking along a mountain stream. Before the spring thaw is complete, freshets pick up chunks of ice and float them downstream, and stones and pebbles trapped in the ice travel with it. Geologists call this ice-rafting.

We were in for one more surprise before I reached the bottom. Chunks of black flint appeared, some of them half the size of a golf ball. Dr. Richards told me that comparable pieces of black flint are known from mountains in Pennsylvania and northern New Jersey. Here was more evidence that our sand and its contents had been transported from the uplands. It had been spread, perhaps deltalike, over a broad area by at least one, or, more probably, several, ancient rivers.

Additional black flints came to light, and so did more large, well-rounded stones. Because digging takes time, especially when you are near the bottom of a hole and occasionally have to rest from the effort of tossing shovelfuls of sand over your head, I had ample time to think about what Dr. Richards told me. I also recalled that Emmett Reid Dunn, Haverford College's distinguished herpetologist, once pointed out that certain of the reptiles of the Pine Barrens, notably the wood turtle, the red-bellied snake, and the timber rattlesnake, may have entered the region by following streams southeastward from the highlands. The Schuylkill River flows in that direction, and so, in part, does the Delaware.

A theory concerning the origin of the Pine Barrens that was long generally accepted, held that the area was once an offshore island surrounded by and derived from the sea. Aside from the evidence we found in our own backyard, there are other reasons why the sea island theory is no longer tenable. The sands of the Barrens contain no marine fossils, which would be expected if the area had been submerged beneath salt water. Further, remnants of fossil trees have been found, as has lignite, a brownish black material with the texture of the original wood still discernible. Both of these indicate a nonmarine origin of the sands. Dr. Richards also pointed out that, if the Pine Barrens had been an island, we would expect to find young (Pleistocene) marine fossils on all sides of the region, but that definitely is not the case.

The Pine Barrens, although markedly changed in many places by development and the destruction of the original vegetation, once extended virtually unbroken from just west of Asbury Park to the upper part of the Cape May peninsula, and, except for a tenuous coastal

strip, from the sea far westward into Burlington and even into Camden and Gloucester Counties. Outlying patches occurred apart from the main mass in several places, but some, notably near Spotswood in Middlesex County, were drastically altered by mankind a long time ago. The approximate original full extent of the Pine Barrens appears on the acompanying map.

The sandy mantle of the Pine Barrens, which is hundreds of feet thick in some places, was long considered to be a useless waste, except for such purposes as road building and glass making. Certainly it is worthless for general farming, as many a would-be settler learned to his sorrow. The sand and gravel act as a gigantic filter, and soil nutrients produced by the decay of vegetation are quickly leached downward by the abundant rains of the region. So also are fertilizers. Only two crops are commercially exploitable—cranberries and blueberries.

During colonial days a number of small towns appeared within the Pine Barrens as the early settlers sought to earn a living by manufacturing glass or paper, or by smelting iron from the hardpans of iron oxide, using wood from the forest for fuel. Such industries were short-lived, however. Cannonballs were made there for General Washington's army, but the subsequent discovery of iron ore and coal farther west doomed the activities in the Barrens. We often took friends to see some of the ruins that still survived from earlier days, and suggested they read such historically oriented books as "Forgotten Towns of Southern New Jersey" and "Iron in the Pines." Some of the older settlements and crossroads had curious names, among them Slabtown, Ong's Hat, Mount Misery, Hog Wallow, and Double Trouble. A few towns, Chatsworth notable among them, survived into modern times, as the residents eked out a living by picking berries, gathering sphagnum moss, cutting white-cedar poles, and doing a little lumbering.

At the time we departed for the Southwest in 1973, the sand and gravel cap of the Pine Barrens was receiving increasing attention as a major aquifer. It contained the largest untapped source of pure water remaining in the populous Northeast. Its potential in that respect had long been recognized. In an effort to purvey water to Philadelphia, Joseph Wharton, the financier for whom the University of Pennsylvania's Wharton School of Finance and Commerce was named, gradually assembled 100,000 acres in the Barrens during the second half of the nineteenth century. He was thwarted when the New Jersey Legislature passed a law prohibiting the exportation of water, but his holdings, long known as the Wharton Tract, remained in his family's possession until they were sold to the state for conservation and recreational purposes during the 1950s.

The unique character of the Pine Barrens is not confined to its geology, its aquifer, and the nature of its surface. The flora and fauna of the region have attracted the attention of naturalists for centuries. We knew that long before we began living at Taunton, but it was impressed ever more firmly on our minds as we escorted our decades-long parade of nature-oriented guests to many parts of the Barrens. Some of our visitors were almost as excited as children at Christmas as they found and photographed species of plants they had seen or read about only in books.

The most conspicuous tree of the Barrens is the pitch pine, *Pinus rigida.* That evergreen, which varies in size and shape and may attain a height of 50 feet, was once so abundant that John W. Harshberger, Professor of Botany at the University of Pennsylvania, estimated in 1916 that there might be more than seven billion of them in the Barrens. They constituted a chiefly open forest through which a person could walk with ease, except where the understory, often of scrub oaks, was too dense to penetrate. In some places there was little brush, and the woods seemed almost parklike with the large trees well separated.

The pitch pine is highly resistant to the forest fires that are of frequent occurrence in the region. A tree may be burned black, but a large one, unless it is killed outright by a very hot crown fire, will soon sprout new needles from its trunk and larger branches, and within a few years will look almost as good as ever. Charcoal persists on the bark almost interminably, however, as many a wearer of light-colored clothing has learned to his dismay after unthinkingly leaning against a blackened tree. Following the severe wind-fanned fire that swept across the back of our property in 1965, most of our pine trees were black sticks against a macabre background that looked like a scene from Hell. Five years later, all the big trees had recovered. The smaller ones, which had been killed back to the ground, had sprouted new shoots, and from three to a dozen small pines were growing where one had stood before. This sequence of events was a clue to the origin of the dwarf forests, locally known as the Plains, that occupied large areas in the eastern part of the Barrens and could be seen from the highway while driving to the seashore. The repeated and frequent fires of the region acted as gigantic lawn mowers, and, as the pines on the Plains struggled to recover, more and more grew from single original root systems, with subsequent dwarfing.

In the final analysis, the pine forests owe their survival to fire. Oaks constitute the climax vegetation of the area, and they would eventually top all but the tallest pines if it were not for the fact that they are slower than pines in recovering from burns. The dominance of the oaks and other deciduous trees may be seen in areas that have long been protected from fires, such as near the dam at Taunton Lake, in the general vicinity of where the old Taunton Forge was situated in colonial days.

For the many botanist friends who visited us, the bogs of the Barrens were a major lure. There, often with Witmer Stone's great work on the plants in hand, they sought and examined rare or unusual species. Carnivorous kinds, which live, at least in part, on insects, were represented by the pitcher plant and three species of sundews. The pipeworts, golden clubs, and gentians were special treats to be studied and photographed with care. And for the phytogeographer there were the species far out of their ranges, such as the diminutive curly grass fern that occurs in many of the sphagnum bogs in the Barrens but is otherwise unknown south of Nova Scotia. Conversely, a large number of southern plants reach their northern limit in the Pine Barrens. Almost every bog of any size was once surrounded, at least in part, by Atlantic white-cedars, *Chamaecyparis thyoides,* but the dense stands of those valuable trees, which were a unique sight and asset of the region in earlier days, had all but vanished

Isabelle sitting on the bridge rail alongside the old swimmin' hole. Photo by RC.

before the lumberman's ax and saw, except in a few protected areas.

We explored the Pine Barrens so well and so often that we could easily guide our visiting guests to the places that interested them most. We knew where the rare plants grew. We could lead them to many of the bogs and marshy swales that dotted the area, or to larger bodies of water if desired. We even knew where the best swimming holes were.

The surface streams, lakes, and ponds of the area are tea colored, a hue originating from tannic material that may be colloidal and which leaches from roots of the swamp vegetation. The waters are acid on the chemist's scale, and they greatly affect the habitats and limit the types of plants and animals that can live in contact with them. The water table is close to the surface in most parts of the Barrens, but so great is the downward percolation and so rapid the desiccation of the top layer of sand that a vertical distance of just a few feet may result in a remarkably different habitat. The pine snake, *Pituophis melanoleucus,* the eastern representative of the species that includes the bull and gopher snakes of the arid West, is at home in the dry surface sand, where it burrows in search of hiding places and the rodents on which it feeds. Only a few feet away, in a shallow pond with floating or slightly emergent vegetation, may be the carpenter frog, *Rana virgatipes,* a species admirably adapted for an aquatic life. That amphibian and the Pine Barrens treefrog, *Hyla andersonii,* are finely tuned to the acidic waters, and neither occurs elsewhere in New Jersey. Their habitat is easily damaged or destroyed. They disappear quickly when there is ditching or draining, or when pollution poisons the pools in which their tadpoles develop. There were many other reptiles and amphibians of interest in the Pine Barrens, among them the secretive scarlet snake, *Cemophora coccinea;* the corn snake, *Elaphe guttata;* and the pine snake, mentioned above. Other species—such as the kingsnake, *Lampropeltis getula;* the hognose snake, *Heterodon platirhinos;* and the timber rattlesnake, *Crotalus horridus*—occurred both in the Barrens and outside them, the rattler just barely beyond their edge.

Carl F. Kauffeld's vivid tales about his success in finding snakes in the region were chronicled in his book, "Snakes and Snake Hunting," published in 1957, and they brought large numbers of ardent collectors into the Barrens who literally tore habitats to pieces, notably the area around Crossley. While looking for snakes hiding under shelters, they ripped up the wooden ties along the abandoned railroad line we had once used, when we were on my way to Grandmother's house in Red Bank when I was a boy. The collectors roamed the roads and woods, some seeking personal pets, some hunting for the market. Other forces were also at work to damage the fragile ecosystem of the Pine Barrens. As the years went by, we noticed, more and more frequently, that vandals were littering the sandy roads with masses of debris and garbage. Others raced their motorcycles along the sandy roads and through the open woods, destroying colonies of rare plants in the process.

What was badly needed was some agency to protect a large part of the unique Pine Barrens in perpetuity. Toward that end the National Park Service authorized a survey of key portions of the region, and its representatives interviewed many persons. One even visited my office while I was serving as Director of the Philadelphia Zoo. The Park Service recommended the creation of a national monument to preserve and protect a large tract, but Congress never funded the plan, and a unique opportunity was lost, in all probability forever.

Several efforts to protect parts of the region have occurred in recent years. In 1978 the Pinelands National Reserve was designated by Congress, but it was left to the State of New Jersey to implement the federal bill. The State Pinelands Commission was established to regulate land use and permit increased human activities, while also attempting to retain existing conditions—a patently impossible long-range goal. Because local communities are also involved, it has slowed some of the destruction of the Pine Barrens. In the meantime, the Pinelands Preservation Alliance, composed of several conservation organizations, is doing its best to protect as much of the area as possible. Probably several enclaves, including state parks, will survive in the foreseeable future, but, like the more accessible parts of so many of our national parks, they may be literally trampled to death by the constantly increasing hordes of human beings who visit them.

By the early 1970s Isabelle and I were becoming increasingly disturbed by the avalanche of people invading southern New Jersey, and the proliferation of real estate developments, which were creeping toward us like a gigantic amoeba that eventually would engulf everything in its path. Long gone were the many open fields and the small dairy farm we passed en route to the city and back as we commuted. Thousands of new houses were appearing, seemingly everywhere, including within the borders of the Pine Barrens themselves. Some of the promoters hit upon the bright idea of buying cranberry bogs, flooding them, and selling lots as waterfront property, even when the depth was scarcely enough to float a canoe.

We could see what was coming, and so, when Isabelle's health took a disastrous downturn, it was not too difficult to give up our cherished dream home, especially when, coincidentally, our taxes skyrocketed. Unlike the people who bought what the developers were peddling, we had excellent bona fide waterfront property.

I have been back to the Pine Barrens a few times during recent years. There are new houses at Taunton Lake, but the general character of that nostalgic paradise remains much the same. Elsewhere, including many of the places where we used to tramp through the silent woods, there are now innumerable houses and people, along with noise pollution and all the other abominations of civilization. How disheartening! Certainly the Pine Barrens as we knew them are rapidly disappearing. The character of the vegetation will also change in time. Fire ecology maintained the Barrens for countless centuries and enabled the pines, because of their rapid recovery, to predominate. With so much property crammed and scattered through the woods, forest fires are now fought with vigor. It takes little imagination to envision a time when the name "Pine" Barrens will no longer be applicable.

Speaking of that, the word "Barrens" itself is a misnomer. Barren of what? Productivity for agriculture, perhaps, and that, no doubt, is how the name originated. But for anyone who appreciated the out-of-doors and wildlife, and who understood the need for open space in the crowded East, the region was anything but barren. How extraordinarily fortunate we were to reside in that unique part of America while so much of it was still in pristine condition.

Chapter 49

A Quarter Century in Paradise:
Part I. Taunton Lake and Hyla Holler

My discovery of Taunton Lake was a by-product of my service with the Volunteer Coast Guard during World War II. Matthew F. Van Istendal, Jr., an attorney who stood the same watches as I did on the Philadelphia waterfront piers and ships, told me about it and telephoned one of his former schoolteachers, Bertha Weeks, who had a cottage on the lake. He put in a good word for me, and I rented her place for six weeks during the summer of 1945. Taunton Lake was in the solitude of the New Jersey Pine Barrens, far away from the noise and bustle of the city, although only 25 miles by road from the Philadelphia Zoo.

What a joy it was to be there. It gave me a chance to escape from the sultry heat of my lonely room in a boardinghouse near the zoo, where I had retreated to escape from my devastating first marriage. Our personal physician and my attorney ordered me to leave or risk at least a nervous breakdown, or, at worst, a complete collapse.

Also, Taunton was a wonderful place for my mother, who was then in her 60s. She, too, lived alone, but in Red Bank, in north-central New Jersey. As a schoolteacher she had the summer off with no pay. If she were with me, she wouldn't have to work at the reception desk of a seashore hotel for her food, lodging, and a small stipend, as she had been doing for several summers.

In the cottage, Mother and I had separate rooms, and there was ample space for a guest or two. With such an ideal vacation spot, we had an abundance of visitors. Friends from out of town were always welcome, and so were some of my fellow employees at the zoo. Nigel Wolff and his wife, Dorothy, and Isabelle dePeyster Hunt were among them. Even Howard K. Gloyd, an esteemed herpetological colleague, came from Chicago to stay with us for a while. We had a wonderful time during my vacation and days off, swimming, canoeing, hiking, and exploring the Pine Barrens along the white-sand roads and trails of that great neowilderness.

Mother thought it was the best summer she'd had for a great many years, so I said, "Let's fix it so we can come back again." We cleaned up everything, and Isabelle,

who was with us at the time, pitched in to help. We borrowed a vacuum cleaner from one of the neighbors, scrubbed the sinks and tiny bathroom, washed windows, and, just before we left, I wiped up the entire linoleum floor on my hands and knees, using a bucket of warm soapsuds and a large rag.

Several days later, after giving her ample time to inspect her property, I telephoned Miss Weeks and asked if we could come again next year. She replied, "You certainly can. I went over expecting I'd have to clean up after you, but there was nothing to do. No other tenant ever left it so spotless."

So we were back in 1946 for a full two months and, with gasoline rationing finally at an end, we drove all over the Pine Barrens. What an extraordinary region it was, almost completely devoid of people, except in a few tiny towns, and with an abundance of wildlife and interesting plants everywhere, especially in and near the many bogs and ponds.

We returned in 1947, but there was a major and, for us, a glorious difference. By then, Isabelle and I were man and wife. We decided we wanted to live at Taunton year-round. After our marriage I had moved in with Isabelle in her small third-floor walk-up apartment in Philadelphia. It was near the zoo, but across the railroad tracks. The neighborhood was decaying rapidly. So, early in 1948, we bought a cottage close to Miss Weeks's place, at a reasonable price, even though it had only a tiny piece of land around it, and we knew it would require a major effort to make it livable during the winter. Mother was invited to be with us whenever she wished, and she came, but for shorter periods. She had a new interest—William G. Borner, whom she would marry several years later.

Isabelle and I went to work with enthusiasm and an abundance of hard labor. We did everything we could ourselves, but we had to hire professional help to insulate the walls and ceiling, and to install a kerosene furnace in the basement with a steel grille in the floor of the living room to allow the heat to rise.

We had our eyes on a spacious spot farther up the lake,

Our publisher, the Houghton Mifflin Co., asked for a publicity picture to use in promoting the field guide we were writing and illustrating. So we went to our Hyla Holler property, before the house was built, with a pine snake and camera. Photo by Don Corvelli.

however. It was on a small peninsula between the estuary of Piney Run and the main lake. The land had been burned more than a decade earlier, but the pine forest, with its understory of oaks, had made an excellent comeback. On it was a small hollow descending to the lake. When we sat at its foot on the lakeshore on spring evenings, we could hear the Pine Barrens treefrogs, *Hyla andersonii,* calling ("hollering") in chorus in the nearby Sylvan Pond. We put the two together, the hollow and the frogs, and thus was born the name Hyla Holler, where we hoped someday to build our dream home. In the meantime, we thought of our little cottage as a stopgap, or just the 'Gap for short.

We had no illusions about building a house anytime soon. It would be awhile, probably at least two or three years before we could manage that. We bought the land at Hyla Holler, however, about three acres, at a price we

could afford, and we had a small dock built at lakeside. Those acquisitions exhausted our financial reserves. We saved every cent we could, and we found other ways to implement our income. I developed a lecture, using pantomime, about humorous events at the zoo. It went over so well, when I first delivered it at a women's club meeting in suburban Philadelphia, that I suddenly found myself in demand. I must have spoken before virtually every similar organization in the metropolitan area during the next two years, and, at $50 a talk, it soon mounted up. Isabelle found a market for many of the photographs she had taken on her own.

We continued to make improvements at the 'Gap, because two important events forced us to live there far longer than we expected. The first was our field guide. After signing the contract with Houghton Mifflin, it became imperative for Isabelle to have a dark-

Isabelle adjusting her camera at the top of the steps leading down to our dock. The basement of the 'Gap was entered through the open doorway. Photo by Franklin Williamson.

room at home. We hired local professional builders to shore up the cottage, excavate a basement under it, and construct work spaces for us.

The Korean War, which broke out in 1950, was our second problem. It did not affect us at first, but it was not long before shortages of building materials developed. In a sense, the delay was a blessing. It enabled us to accumulate enough money so that we eventually built a much larger and far better home than we had anticipated. As it worked out, we lived at the 'Gap for 10 years, and then at Hyla Holler for 15—a quarter century in all, in a wildlife and lovers' paradise. What magnificent memories come racing back as I think of our truly wonderful years at Taunton.

During our decade of residence at the 'Gap, we concerned ourselves with two prime objectives. The first was to get the place repaired, livable, modernized, and tailored to our needs. The second, of course, was working on our ambitious field guide project. Isabelle resigned from the zoo in 1952 to devote full time to illustrating the book, but my efforts necessarily had to be concentrated during my evenings, days off, and vacation periods. We were a busy, busy couple, but we

still found time to relax, to exercise and swim, and occasionally to devote a half or even a full day to wandering around the Pine Barrens. During hot weather what a joy it was to have a brief, refreshing dip in the lake before dinner. On my days off, weather permitting, we almost always managed to spend at least an hour or two pruning and clearing brush on our Hyla Holler property. Our future home was very much on our minds, whenever we could spare the time to think about it.

We realized, of course, that building in the Pine Barrens proper was fraught with potential danger. Wildfires raced through large portions of the forest after long periods of dry weather. We would have to take every precaution, and make our dream home as fireproof as possible. It had to be built of masonry, and, if at all possible, we wanted to have our valuables, library, and work areas underground where they would be safe. A lot of thought would go into the planning. So it was that, late in 1957, with the plates, maps, and text for the field guide already at the Houghton Mifflin office in Boston and with only proofreading yet to do, we were able to begin concentrating on the next major step in our blissful connubial life.

To whom should we turn for help? We surely needed professional advice. It was our esteemed friend Edmond V. Malnate who pointed the way for us. Ed and his wife, Georgette, and their son, Chip, were frequent visitors at the 'Gap. They liked the quiet and serenity of the Pine Barrens. Eventually, they bought a waterfront lot and built a house at Lake Pine, the next body of water downstream from Taunton. They moved in on July 2, 1954. Soon Ed and I began commuting back and forth to the city together several days each week. When the time came for us to build, I naturally turned to him to learn how his home had worked out. They had then been in it for more than three years.

A contractor named Walter Claypool had erected it, no problems had developed, and Ed highly recommended him. So we made an appointment to discuss our needs and safety precautions with Claypool, and he inspected the site we had chosen. A week or so later he arrived at the 'Gap with a huge bundle of house plans, and he suggested that we study them and see if one might be suitable for our requirements. He said he could make adjustments in shapes and sizes and building materials, and thus save us the expense of an architect. We finally picked one that offered possibilities, and Claypool agreed with our requested alterations. The entire house, walls, and partitions would be made of cinder blocks, and there would be a large and deep excavation that would open into the hollow. We would have a suite of work rooms, chiefly underground, and a thick concrete slab would cover the ensemble. Our living quarters would be above it. A stairway would give access between the two floors. The result was a magnificent house, which I'll describe in more detail later. Walter Claypool gave us a firm figure on cost, and we signed a contract with him for what, in view of the great inflation that has occurred since, seems now like a ridiculously low price. We had almost enough money, and we were assured we could borrow the rest.

Isabelle and I staked out the approximate location on October 31, 1957, and about a month later surveyors did it professionally. We all decided that, since it was so late in the season, we should wait until the following spring to break ground.

That event, which we looked forward to with great anticipation, was scheduled for March 20, 1958. When we awakened that morning we discovered that a snowstorm was in progress. The heavy, wet snow stuck to the power lines leading in to Taunton from Marlton, a distance of about four miles, and soon great accretions of snow, to a thickness of about six inches, formed on the wires, breaking them between every pair of poles. We lost power for days, which meant no electricity or water. A year or two earlier we had installed a new gas stove powered by a large, heavy cylinder of propane. Our neighbors had smilingly chided us, saying that we surely were old-fashioned to put in gas again. Electric stoves were ever so much better and cleaner. Guess who came to our house to cook their meals during the power outage! We dipped water out of the lake to flush the toilet.

Finally, ground was broken on March 28. A bulldozer, for which we had created an entrance path, to save our best trees from damage, excavated mountains of sand. A lot of it was used for backfill after the foundations were completed and the cinder blocks forming the outside of the house were above ground level. But it left us with huge sandpiles. We found use for them, but what a lengthy chore it turned out to be. Taunton Lake has a black muck bottom. Each year, usually in April, the water was drained out of the lake by opening valves at the dam. With the water down, residents could clean their beaches, repair their docks, or spread fresh sand. We undertook the laborious task of shoving the muck as far out into the lake as possible. I then built a series of ramps, and we began moving our mountains of sand to the lakefront, and constructing a spacious beach. Although we had started in a small way long before the bulldozer came, we didn't finish until May 1959. Isabelle kept track; the tally is still in her diary. We transported a total of 1739 wheelbarrow loads to the dock. When the water was up, we tossed shovelfuls as far out into the lake as we could. We had help. My son, Skip,

We worked long and hard wheeling sand from the huge excavation for our basement to the lakeshore. It was helpful for making a broad smooth beach. Photo by IHC.

moved a lot of the sand, and so did my Uncle Harold and his brother-in-law, Harry. On our biggest day, when I hired a helper, we moved 335 loads.

The year 1958 was a busy one. Work on the building of Hyla Holler began the day after the bulldozer left. As the structure took shape, Isabelle kept a record with a series of photographs. The proofs for the field guide came in batches, and, as soon as one arrived, we dropped everything in order to cross-check the galley sheets against the original manuscript. Terry Baker, of the Houghton Mifflin staff, flew down from Boston with the plates so he could go over them with us. Also, 1958 was the first of my three years as secretary of the American Society of Ichthyologists and Herpetologists. In those days the secretary had to send out the bills and collect the dues, a procedure that is now taken care of elsewhere. In my day, however, it was a dreadfully time-consuming chore.

We did all the work we could ourselves at Hyla Holler. I dug two cesspools, one six feet in diameter and eight feet deep, and learned a lot about Coastal Plain geology in the process. (See "The New Jersey Pine Barrens.") I had help with a third cesspool and also with the big hole in which to bury the fuel-oil tank for our furnace.

On August 18, an unusually heavy rain filled a dam to the brim far upstream in our watershed, and it overflowed and finally burst, sending a great surge of water downstream that took out dam after dam. Fortunately, the very large and high dam held, the one that created Centennial Lake, the beautiful body of water just above us. The relief culverts that were set in place below the summit of the dam breast, however, poured torrents of water into Taunton Lake, and it rose over all the docks and swept away everything movable that was not rescued promptly. It was a Saturday, and I was up early to go to the zoo at just about the time the water began to rise rapidly. I felt like Paul Revere as I sallied forth and ran to waken our late-sleeping neighbors, and urge them to get to their docks at once to save their chairs, canoes, and odds and ends.

In September, Hyla Holler was nearly finished except for the vast amount of work we had reserved for ourselves—painting, carpentry, facing the fireplace with stone, laying tile on all the floors, and the myriad other things we could do. We knew, of course, that it would take us a very long time to complete everything, but we were enthusiastic and not afraid of hard work. Besides, it was our pride and joy, our dream home.

On September 15 a moving van conveyed all the big and heavy items from the 'Gap to Hyla Holler, and we spent our first night in our unfinished house. We were so thrilled and excited that we had trouble getting to sleep.

Three weeks later we received the first copies of our field guide from Houghton Mifflin, and we reviewed them with care and pride. Just to think! Two extremely important events in our lives occurred almost simultaneously!

Hyla Holler was isolated during the summertime. Not another building was visible. There was a house across the lake, but we could make it out, vaguely, only when the leaves were down during the winter. We were on a peninsula and, at its tip, about 200 yards away, was the beautiful summer home of Vladimir K. Zworykin, the genius who invented the scanner that made television possible. He had escaped from the Russian Bolsheviks during his youth, and had risen to the position of Vice President of the Radio Corporation of America. He and his wife were quite friendly, but never intimate, neighbors. After we had been settled in for a year or two, and he had noticed how clean and tidy we kept our house, garage, and grounds, Dr. Zworykin, in his strongly accented English, complimented us by saying, "You nice people. You like the order." It would be some years before there was any further building on our sandy access lane, Piney Run Trail, but, before we left in 1973, there were three additional homes, one under construction, and more to come. Our solitude was evaporating.

I should mention a few words about the 'Gap. We were lucky enough to rent it as soon as we moved out, but the tenant stayed only a few months. We listed the place with two real estate agencies, hoping it would sell, but it was too small and too oddly arranged to appeal to potential buyers. So we had a succession of tenants with long hiatus periods in between. Frankly, the 'Gap became a nuisance. When it was empty I had to check on it weekly, and in the fall I had to turn off the water and

drain down the system. All the tenants caused problems, mostly by leaving trash, doing minor damage, or providing us with a day's cleanup work in their wakes. Our worst one, a woman in her 40s, paid her rent through the end of January 1961. On January 31 it turned bitterly cold, and, on a hunch, I decided to make a special checkup. I knocked loudly several times, and then let myself in with my key. There was an undated note in the kitchen reading, "I have found a better place to live," followed by her initials. The house was icy cold. She and her belongings were gone, and she had let the fuel run out for the furnace. The water pipes were frozen!

Maurice Schwinn, an excellent handyman and cabinetmaker, as well as a good friend and neighbor, came to my rescue. With the aid of his blowtorch we thawed out the copper tubing and replaced a few split pieces, before draining out all the water. The old adage "It takes all kinds of people to make a world" is certainly true. Why hadn't the blasted woman alerted us? There was a telephone where she worked.

Happily, we finally sold the 'Gap on June 20, 1962, to a young German couple who thought it was a delightful place to live.

We seldom lacked for company at the lake. Friends and colleagues were always welcome. Taunton had so many attractions that sometimes we were almost overwhelmed. Every bed, couch, and cot might be occupied, and some guests even brought sleeping bags they could place on the sandy substrate outside. The Conants were known as hospitable people.

Most important of all were relatives. My son, Roger Karl Conant, known to everyone as Skip or Skippy, and his charming, vivacious wife, Virginia, were frequent visitors. Their family grew, and after a few years there were four adorable little girls with them. Betsy, the oldest, when she was still a tiny tot, began calling my wife "Nanabelle." All my other granddaughters followed suit, and Isabelle, to them, was their beloved and affectionate grandmother. Their real grandparent, my ex-wife, became a recluse after her parents died.

Swimming, canoeing, and just having fun were the treats when visiting Taunton. After we moved to Hyla Holler, we kept a big box full of what were known as "Grandpa's toys," for which the youngsters made a beeline as soon as they arrived. They played for hours, but we would still be picking up marbles, jacks, jackstraws, and pieces of jigsaw puzzles a week or more after they left. Taunton was also a great place to escape heat waves in summer. Skip was a great fisherman, and he and his buddies caught many a large pickerel in the lake.

After calm freezeups during the winter, the lake became a huge skating rink, an irresistible lure for Skip, who was a superb skater. One day, after we had lived at Hyla Holler for several years, Skip brought friends along and they set up an impromptu hockey game. In chasing the puck, Skip skated too close to the shore in front of the house, and he went through thin ice up to his neck. He climbed the steep bank in record time, skates and all, and rushed into the house shivering mightily. He had to borrow clothes from me, but, as soon as his skate straps were dry, he was back on the ice.

Isabelle had two darling nieces, Isabelle (named for her, but called Izzy when she was small) and her younger sister, Turrell, or Terry. Izzy was about Skip's age. She had come to Philadelphia to visit Isabelle several times before we were married, and, since she spent each day at the zoo, I had the opportunity to become very fond of her. She and Terry were frequent visitors when we were at the 'Gap, and, later, when we were in residence at Hyla Holler, Izzy's two daughters, Sue and Ellie, took their places as our fun guests. Isabelle's brother and sister-in-law drove down occasionally from Staten Island.

When the plates for our field guide were well advanced, I invited or inveigled every herpetologist I could to visit the 'Gap to see and criticize them. Anyone who came to Philadelphia was fair game, and even those I learned might be in New York or Washington. For example, Karl P. Schmidt interrupted a trip to Europe to oblige me. He flew down from New York; I met him at our airport, took him home to see the illustrations, and he stayed overnight. We had to arise very early the next morning to get him back in time for a return flight to New York, so he could catch his transatlantic plane. Our guest book, a cherished memento of those long-ago years, includes the signatures of virtually every herpetologist of the period who was interested in eastern herps.

Browsing through it brings back many memories. To save space, I'll mention only two. On July 16, 1955, Richard E. Etheridge wrote in the remarks column, "A wonderful escape from the U.S. Navy." He was serving aboard a destroyer that put in to the Philadelphia Navy Yard for complex structural work that required several weeks. He came to the zoo, and I took him home with me several times—whenever he had leave from standing watches and other duties. What a contrast Taunton was with the waterfront. I had served there in the Coast Guard during World War II, and I knew that metal ships were like ovens in hot weather. Also, the water in the Delaware River estuary stank. Seasoned sailors, who had been around the world, said that the Port of Philadelphia was the smelliest they ever encountered. Taunton must have seemed like Heaven to Dick, and it

We greatly enjoyed the picture windows on the east side of Hyla Holler that gave us a good view of the lake. Photo by Edward J. Freeman, Philadelphia Inquirer. Courtesy of Urban Archives, Temple University Libraries.

came with the added bonus of having someone with whom to talk herpetology. From Guantánamo Bay, Cuba, his ship's next port of call, he sent Isabelle a handsome, handcrafted solid mahogany tray that she greatly appreciated, and which I still have. Thomas M. Uzzell, Jr., was another sailor who had a chance to visit Taunton, but he came during the winter.

The stream of visitors continued after we moved to Hyla Holler. There were dinner parties for distinguished guests, and several rather large gatherings of friends and herpetologists. The combined floor space of our basement work area and our living quarters above it was many times that of the 'Gap's.

Downstairs, Isabelle had a large and well-appointed darkroom, the best she ever worked in. We had a truly large study with many-shelved bookcases along three of its four walls. There was also a roomy, walk-in fireproof vault, a small laboratory with running water, and a spacious storeroom, which housed our furnace and had an alcove with a toilet. Another amenity, which could be shut off by a fire door when not in use, was a shower room where we rinsed off after swims in the lake. It was roomy, and Isabelle and I could easily wash each other's backs, just as I presume most other married couples did. Access to our living quarters, above the concrete slab that served as a fireproof ceiling for the basement complex, was a stairway with a stout fire door at its base.

We had a beautiful big living room with picture windows, two overlooking the lake and two with a view of the gently sloping hollow that gave the place its name. There was a dining alcove, and an efficient kitchen that faced on the yard where we had our bird feeders in wintertime. It also gave us a good view of the generous pile of scrap lumber that we purposely left, after Hyla Holler was built, to serve as a temporary shelter for wildlife visitors, chiefly small mammals, snakes, and fence lizards. We each had our own bedroom, but we shared a bathroom. A third bedroom with twin beds was adjacent to a half-bath, so that guests could have privacy.

Our only weak feature was the peaked roof. We had hoped to have it completely fireproof, but the cost was positively prohibitive. So we settled for fire-resistant composition shingles. Beneath the roof was an insulated crawl space that was equipped with a huge ventilating fan that made it possible to blow out the warm air at dusk. The hot air passed through louvers at each end of the roof, and the cooler evening air was drawn through the screen doors and windows.

It was a wonderful and efficient setup, and we were mighty proud of it. Our hearts and souls were in it, as well as countless hours of hard personal labor.

We were particularly pleased with our fireplace. The mason had roughed in a steel Heatalator, but we faced it with stone ourselves. I had long had an interest in and an aptitude for masonry, and I enjoyed it. We bought Indiana sandstone of three different blending colors and three different widths. I had to cut and chip the edges, and fit it all together, piece by piece. The floor of the living room was still a bare concrete slab at the time, so we brought in a steel wheelbarrow and Isabelle mixed the cement in it as I progressed. Because I could work only on my days off, it was a month before we finished. The mason, Frank Buccialia, who had erected the cinder blocks for our house and stuccoed them on the outside, came to see it a few days later. He stood in front of it for a full five minutes, his arms akimbo, and then announced, "I couldn't have done better myself."

I was proud of my handiwork, and Isabelle was proud of me. Months later, however, when I asked her what she would like for a birthday present, her prompt response was, "A cement mixer."

With so much space at Hyla Holler we had many gatherings of guests. First was a house-warming party for close friends, then we invited our neighbors from around the lake, and finally zoo staff members. When our piecemeal relief map of Mexico was assembled later, on the one blank wall of the study, it was an impressive sight. It was 7 feet high and 11 feet wide. We had a map-warming party for our herpetological friends, and almost the entire staff of the Department of Herpetology of the American Museum of Natural History drove down to participate. When one of the herp organizations met with the American Association for the Advancement of Science in Philadelphia, immediately after Christmas, we invited really large groups on each of two evenings at Hyla Holler. The first time, in 1962, there were 25. In 1971 there was a total of 43, including us and two young zoo staff members who volunteered to help. One supervised the parking of cars and the other served as bartender.

At the time of the 1971 party, we were nearing the end of our work on the second edition of our field guide. My work maps for the many species and subspecies were nearly finished, and I invited all knowledgeable guests to offer comments, which they did by attaching notes with paper clips to the individual map pages. As I recall it now, they collectively gave me well over 100 range extensions and/or minor emendations. Many of them had worked in Mexico and, when they discovered that we had an ample supply of José Cuervo tequila *añejo*, they polished off seven or eight liters of it. During our annual field trips in the 1960s, we were able to bring back the equivalent of a gallon apiece every time. What a treat for the guests who hadn't tasted tequila for many a year.

Speaking of parties, beginning in 1958, shortly after we moved to Hyla Holler, Thanksgiving dinner there became an annual tradition for family gatherings.

Until Isabelle was stricken, in the spring of 1972, we continued to make improvements both in the house and on the grounds. Tiles—asphalt in the basement, and thick cork over the concrete slab floor upstairs—were laid very early after we were in residence. Stepping-stone walks with cement between the components paved the way from the garage to the raised patio by our entrance door. They did double duty, because they also kept us and visitors from tracking sand into the house. One of the last things we completed was a lower stepping-stone patio on the "holler" side of the building that led to the door giving access to our shower and basement suite. We built a cactus garden alongside it. The hardier species stayed out-of-doors year-round, but there was also ample space for potted ones that were transferred indoors for the winter.

Over the years our property gradually increased in size. For protection we bought the long, narrow lot immediately adjacent to the south side of Hyla Holler. It

Thanksgiving Day at Hyla Holler, 1963. Back row, from left: Isabelle, my mother, George Phillips; middle row: my daughter-in-law Virginia Phillips Conant, Skip, RC, Marian Phillips; front row: granddaughters Nancy, Cathy, Betsy, and Carol. Photo by IHC.

previously had been owned by a private party who built such a monstrosity of a dock at the lakeshore that we feared we might be saddled with sloppy neighbors too close at hand for comfort. We also bought three smaller lots across Piney Run so we would have the head of that small estuary locked in, so to speak. At first, we had to drive or walk a rather long way around by road to get to them. We dubbed the new area Chigger Holler. Isabelle was particularly susceptible to those pestiferous itch mites. Unless she routinely and carefully used a repellent, she might get 100 bites just by walking through the uncleared masses of vegetation, dead and alive, that had accumulated since a fire burned through the area many years previously. Soon we had a footbridge built so we could cross directly and with ease to the new property. Downstream from the bridge was the open shallow water of the estuary, but on the other side we had a small sphagnum bog, where spotted turtles lived and bred. The insectivorous pitcher plant and sundews were also present. At the edges, many cranberries grew and ripened every year.

That reminds me of how Isabelle made whole-berry cranberry sauce each autumn. She knew how to do it to perfection. She bought premium berries, but to them she would add and stir in the few dozen I managed to gather from our bog. Thus, we could say they were our berries. She averaged 100 jars every year, most of which were given to her family and mine for use with the winter holiday feasts. After I became the Director of the Philadelphia Zoo, we also gave a jar to each person on the staff. The union members, who constituted the bulk of the employees, got none. Not after they were trained by their leaders to snub management at every opportunity.

For exercise and because we loved to work in the woods, we tried to keep our acreage in good condition. We carefully maintained the path to our little footbridge, and we constructed another one almost to the far end of Chigger Holler. There, overlooking the water, I built a crude, rustic bench, and another on the Hyla Holler side of the bridge. On either of them we could sit to rest, watch birds, enjoy the solitude, and occasionally see a green snake, *Opheodrys aestivus*, of which there was a small resident population.

When they appeared voluntarily, we encouraged the native plants, many of which were typical of the Barrens. Among them were teaberries, bearberries, and pink lady's slippers. After I became dexterous with mattock and ax, I grubbed out literally scores of old stumps.

Our grounds were a showplace for casual visitors. Professional botanists often came, notably John M. Fogg, Jr., Provost of the University of Pennsylvania and the possessor of an encyclopedic knowledge of plants on a world-wide basis. Edward S. Thomas, one of the last of the great all-around naturalists, drove all the way from Columbus, Ohio, several times with his wife and daughter, Buffie, just to see and photograph rare Pine Barrens bog plants. They and others taught us the names of a great many of the local species, and we soon were able to identify them ourselves.

Among other things, we learned that we had seven kinds of oaks, of the genus *Quercus*, living on our property. The white oak, *Quercus alba,* was the most abundant. Black and post oaks were well represented, but there were only two or three each of the chestnut and blackjack oaks. On the other hand, there was an abundance of chinquapin and scrub oaks, the two scrubby species of the understory. The latter bore the scientific name of *Q. ilicifolia*, because its leaves rather resemble those of the holly (*Ilex*). Among the three species of pines indigenous to the Barrens, we had only the pitch pine, *Pinus rigida*, at Hyla Holler. The other two—the shortleaf pine, *P. echinata*, and the Virginia pine, *P. virginiana*—occurred sparsely around the edges of the woodlands near the 'Gap.

Something that always astounded visitors who came at the right time in spring was the profusion of mountain laurel, *Kalmia latifolia*, at Hyla Holler. Some years the pink-tinged white blossoms seemed to be everywhere. It was a novelty to almost everyone to find a supposedly upland shrub growing in the flat Coastal Plain Pine Barrens.

We were enjoying our "estate." After mingling with great throngs of visitors at the zoo and braving the commuting traffic, which grew worse month by month, it was a joyful relief to get home to the peacefulness of Hyla Holler. We enjoyed company, but we were happiest when we were alone. We hated being apart, and we looked forward to my days off, when we could work, play, or explore together, often taking picnic lunches to some distant part of the Pine Barrens.

All was not rosy in paradise, however. Inevitably, problems arose, and the most ominous long-term one was a sudden tax increase in the spring of 1961. The nonprofit Taunton Lake Company, of which I was a director, owned all the unoccupied land bordering Taunton Lake, a large amount of waterfront property. The township, basing its increase on the numerous new homes in the Medford Lakes area, raised the tax rate many-fold. To have paid what they demanded would have wiped out a fair fraction of the nonprofit company's

Isabelle mans the camera and RC poses the animals in their home studio. Photo by Edward J. Freeman, Philadelphia Inquirer. Courtesy of Urban Archives, Temple University Libraries.

capital, and it would have taken all of it within a very few years. We had no income except interest on our funds and from the sale of lots. We were all reluctant to sell and to crowd our quiet lake with a swarm of newcomers. What should we do? We finally decided to bring suit against the confiscatory bombshell. The matter was settled out of court, and the township reduced its demand by 40 percent. We were still in trouble, but the problem wasn't quite so acute.

Concurrently, our own taxes were raised substantially, and we could foresee a time coming, hopefully still many years away, when we no longer could afford to live at Hyla Holler. It was a heartbreaking development, but we realized that, when it came time for me to retire in 1974, we might have to give up the nearest thing to paradise on Earth that we had ever enjoyed.

There were a few other upsetting events. I have already mentioned the flood when I had to emulate Paul Revere to alert our neighbors. Potentially, that had been a dangerous situation, but the Centennial Dam held, and Taunton escaped serious damage.

During the mid-evening of March 13, 1964, our electric lights began to flicker on and off so badly that I

Hyla Holler from across the lake. The house was nestled among the trees. The dark clouds were from a roaring forest fire, the thing we dreaded most. Photo by Larry Miller, a teenaged neighbor.

went outside to see if I could detect any trouble. I did. I could see flashes of light emanating from the new McCamy house 100 yards south along Piney Run Trail. I realized instantly that an electrical fire was in progress, so I hurried back to the house, telephoned our small local fire department, and then ran to see what I could do. It was well that I went, because, when I was about halfway there, I saw what looked like a small ball of fire drop from between two power poles, and it instantly set the dry debris beneath it ablaze. I was still stamping it out when the fire engine arrived. The "ball of fire" severed the electrical power to the house, and the men soon had things under control. The interior was gutted, however. Everything inside was black, even the walls and ceiling.

McCamy brought suit against the electric company, and, a few months later, I was summoned to appear in court to testify as the only witness to what happened. McCamy won his suit.

On Saturday, May 15, 1965, I went to the zoo alone. Isabelle often accompanied me on one or both weekend days, but that time she stayed home to take care of some paperwork that could best be done at her desk. In very early afternoon one of the zoo keepers called and said he had just heard on the radio that there was a bad forest fire at Centennial Lake, over in Jersey. I tried to telephone Isabelle, but there was no answer. So I informed the zoo operator I was leaving. Before I could gather up my things and don my hat, the phone rang. It was Ed Malnate calling from Lake Pine. He wanted to know if

Isabelle was with me. He and his son had discovered a fire along the Berlin Road that, propelled by a strong wind, was burning toward Hyla Holler. They would do what they could to check on Isabelle. I raced home in my car, hitting over 70 miles an hour where the traffic was light. When I reached the edge of Taunton I saw a huge column of black smoke rising high in the sky in the general direction of home. My heart sank, but the safety crew let me pass the barricade. My usual route, they said, was closed because there had been a fierce fire on both sides of the paved road. So I had to go a roundabout way.

According to her diary, Isabelle heard the fire siren about 12:30, and within a half hour she could see dense smoke approaching from the northwest. She hurried to close all our fire doors and the windows. Then she went outside to see what she could do. She hooked up our yard hoses and was wetting down the grounds, probably just at the time I tried to telephone her. She said that Piney Run Trail filled with men and older boys carrying Indian pumps, backpack tanks filled with water and bearing short hoses to direct a stream at the base of flames. Two pieces of fire-fighting apparatus also arrived. Soon Dr. Van Istendal, a dentist and the brother of my Coast Guard buddy, Matt Van Istendal, came with two teenagers. They set up our ladders and began wetting down the roofs of our house and garage. A plane dumped slurry at the fire's edge. Mercifully, the wind shifted, and the men were able to gain control as the flames moved away in another direction. The fire was stopped 100 yards from our house, and we couldn't see a single bit of damage from any window or from the walk on the west side of the building. But our back acreage, especially Chigger Holler, was burned as black as a scene from Hell.

When I finally got through all the barricades and pulled into our driveway, it was all over. Poor Isabelle was exhausted, both mentally and physically. We flew into each other's arms. We had been spared, and our safety precautions, both in planning and building Hyla Holler, had not been put to a fiery test.

Larry Miller, a teenaged lad who lived across the lake from us, took a picture that showed our house against a huge wall of smoke. The "Central Record," the Medford weekly newspaper, used it on the front page. Larry let Isabelle borrow his negative, and our moment of peril is reproduced with these recollections.

I worked until dark hauling buckets of water to put out hot spots. To add insult to the injury of having our woodland so severely burned, a crew from the New Jersey Fire Service arrived with a huge, heavy plow to dig deep ditches all around the still intact edge of the burned area. That was to prevent any possible subsurface spread. The driver seemed to take fiendish delight in knocking down as many of our live trees as possible. He even went through the patch of pink lady's slippers we had so carefully tended. I was furious, but it was the law, and I could have landed in the clink if I had attempted to stop them.

A careful inspection the next morning revealed the full extent of our loss. We had a difficult time finding the badly burned remnants of our bench in Chigger Holler, the part of our property that was the most seriously affected. The ground litter, which we had just begun to haul away, was all black ashes, and ankle deep in spots. The fire-resistant pitch pines, *Pinus rigida*, were still standing, but their trunks and branches had turned to charcoal. Most of the oak trees, all of them smaller, were also still erect. We knew, based on our visits to various previously burned parts of the Barrens, that the pines would recover, but the oaks were dead, except for their root systems.

The fire, under the influence of the wind, leaped across Piney Run, but, as we were told by members of the fire crew, it slowed appreciably when it reached our core Hyla Holler property. We had long since picked up all the inflammable debris and trimmed away all the dead branches. Periodically, on drizzly winter days, we had burned our piled-up accumulations of such material, after getting a permit each time from the local fire warden. What we had done was comparable to the preventive burning advocated by foresters. The difference was that, instead of using fire to clear away combustibles on the ground, we had picked them up by hand. Even to this day I think that our careful husbandry of our woodland close to home saved us from serious damage. A comparison with what happened on our neighbors' properties supported that conclusion. On our acreage the fire was stopped a long way from our house. It burned to within 10 feet of the McCamy residence, where it was halted only by the heroic efforts of the firefighters. On the Zworykin land it advanced all the way to Piney Run Trail.

Part of our footbridge was burned, but Maurice Schwinn soon replaced the charred planks. Our small bench was also damaged, but I was able to repair that myself. My biggest, most exasperating chore was filling in the ditches the state fireplow had so deeply gouged.

A curious, unexplained phenomenon was the sudden appearance of great swarms of tiny flies hovering above the warm, blackened surfaces for several hours after the burn. A few days later brackens grew up seemingly everywhere.

The fire was almost certainly incendiary. Arsonists, possibly young people, may have wanted to stir up some excitement on a dull spring Saturday. The woods were ripe for a conflagration. They were very dry, and the wind quickly fanned small flames into big ones.

We left for our last sponsored trip to Mexico less than a month after the fire. Even in that short interval of time, however, the pines had started to sprout new needles. When we returned in mid-August they superficially looked normal, except that many needles were growing directly from their trunks and large branches. Those needles eventually fell off. New growth appeared around the bases of most of the otherwise dead oaks, and some of the lesser vegetation had sprouted anew and was fresh and green. We were happy to find that the blackness we had left was now greatly subdued.

We had a backyard laboratory during the next few years, where we could observe the results of the fire ecology that kept the pines dominant in the Barrens. At the bases of most of the oaks, numerous new stalks, up to a dozen around each one, started growing from the underground root systems. We gave up trying to resuscitate Chigger Holler, except to maintain a path through it. On our "home" property, however, I eventually felled all of the dead oak trees and shrubs, and encouraged the strongest of the new shoots by pruning away the weaker ones. It was truly amazing to see how quickly virtually everything recovered. It would be a long time, however, before the oak trees became really large again.

The northern copperbelly (front) and the Lake Erie water snake, two now endangered natricine snakes, described as new taxa after their discovery during RC's survey of Ohio. From a watercolor painting by David M. Dennis. Courtesy of the Society for the Study of Amphibians and Reptiles. (See Chapter 4.)

Nearly vertical limestone rock slabs in the Cañon de la Huasteca, near Santa Catarina not far from Monterrey, Mexico. A deformation had rotated the bedding planes so they now stand erect. Some are almost 1,000 feet high and form jagged patterns against the sky. Photo by IHC. (See Chapter 19.)

Isabelle with gardenias, October 17, 1949. All the ladies who were guests at the Posada Loma received a daily bouquet. Photo by RC. (See Chapter 20.)

Isabelle holding the large indigo snake that RC figuratively had to "slide into second base" to catch. It was our policy, whenever possible, to make a daily inspection of any livestock we carried with us. Photo by RC. (See Chapter 19.)

Snow-capped Orizaba. The great quiescent volcano, at almost 19,000 feet, is Mexico's highest mountain. Photo by IHC. (See Chapter 20.)

The Volcán Parícutin at dawn on October 21, 1949. Photo by IHC. (See Chapter 20.)

Isabelle on the tailgate of our Oldsmobile station wagon as she opened one of the wooden drawers built to hold bags of live reptiles. At Ross Allen's Reptile Institute, Silver Springs, Florida, November 29, 1951. Photo by RC. (See Chapter 22.)

Periodically, while working in the field in Mexico, it was necessary for RC to take time out to preserve reptiles and amphibians found dead on the road. Many were in excellent condition and could be salvaged for study specimens. Injecting them with formalin and writing out tags recording the species name, date, and locality where found was a tedious task. Photo by IHC. (See Chapter 28.)

The huge Nazas River slider that RC, James D. Anderson, and several students trapped during a return trip to Durango in 1976. Like the water snake of the same isolated desert river, the turtle has differentiated into a new subspecies. Photo by RC. (See Chapter 38.)

RC catching a Mexican garter snake near Lago Cuitzeo, Michoacán. The area, when we visited it, was swarming with garter snakes of two species, especially along the causeway crossing the lake. Photo by IHC. (See Chapter 39.)

Isabelle on the Equator in Uganda. Photo by RC. (See Chapter 46.)

The barranca of the Río Batopilas, claimed by our guide to be the deepest of Mexico's great chasms. We did not undertake the long, tortuous road, with its innumerable switchbacks, to the town of Batopilas at the bottom. The narrow single-track dirt road to the rim of the canyon from Creel was an adventure in itself. Photo by IHC. (See Chapter 42.)

An extremely rare northern white rhinoceros marching along precisely out of step with a cattle egret. In Uganda, 1968. Photo by IHC. (See Chapter 46.)

Piney Run, the estuary of Taunton Lake that bordered the west side of our Hyla Holler property. The autumn foliage in the Pine Barrens was always colorful close to the various watercourses. Photo by IHC. (See Chapter 49.)

The footbridge that gave us access to Chigger Holler across Piney Run. Photo by IHC. (See Chapter 49.)

RC and Kathryn J. Gloyd in front of their home in Albuquerque with a copy of the Gloyd-Conant monograph on Agkistrodon. Photo by Kraig Adler. (See Chapter 53.)

A Sri Lankan hump-nosed viper, Hypnale nepa, from the National Zoological Gardens of Sri Lanka. Photo by Louis W. Porras. Courtesy of the SSAR. (See Chapter 55.)

A Malayan pit viper, Calloselasma rhodostoma, from southern Thailand photographed by RC at the Singapore Zoo, November 9, 1984. Like the cantil, Agkistrodon bilineatus, of Middle America, Calloselasma lives only in areas that have a pronounced annual dry season. Courtesy of the SSAR. (See Chapter 54.)

An adult hundred-pace viper, Deinagkistrodon acutus, at the snake farm in southern Taiwan. Photo by RC. Courtesy of the SSAR. (See Chapter 58.)

Kathryn sitting on a statue of a lion in Colombo, Sri Lanka, with the Indian Ocean behind her. Photo by RC. (See Chapter 55.)

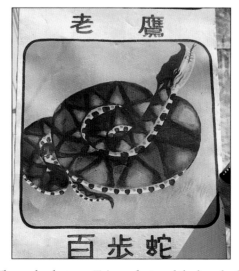

The snake shops on Taiwan featured the hundred-pace viper on their advertising signs. Photo by RC. Courtesy of the SSAR. (See Chapter 58.)

RC and Kathryn with their Indian guide, Rafael, en route to the tower where an uneven wooden stairway winds upward around a giant ceiba tree above the canopy of the Ecuadorean rain forest. Colorful macaws and toucans flew past the lookout at close range. Photo by Bill Ward. (See Chapter 60.)

The huge bull sea elephant expanded its proboscis just as a wave rolled in. Photo by RC. (See Chapter 61.)

Kathryn and RC in front of a breeding colony of southern sea elephants on the Peninsula de Valdés that juts into the South Atlantic Ocean in southern Argentina. Photo by Ana Jones. (See Chapter 61.)

RC on his 86th birthday, May 6, 1995, in front of part of his extensive cactus garden at his home in Albuquerque. Photo by Martha R. "Mickey" Bogert.

Herps Named as New Taxa Honoring Roger Conant:

Desmognathus fuscus conanti, *by Douglas A. Rossman. Photo by Jeff Boundy.*

Bolitoglossa conanti, *by James R. McCranie and Larry D. Wilson. Photo by James R. McCranie.*

Agkistrodon piscivorus conanti, *by Howard K. Gloyd. Photo by Ed Cassano. Courtesy of Louis W. Porras*

Lampropeltis triangulum conanti, *by Kenneth L. Williams. Photo by William W. Lamar.*

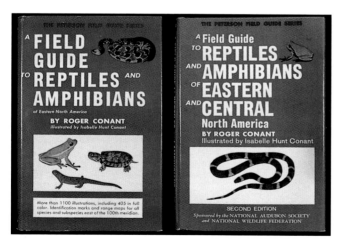

Dust jackets of the first two editions of the herpetological field guide in the Roger Tory Peterson series. (See the chapters entitled "Attempting the Impossible" and "Closing the Gap.")

Pine Barrens treefrog, Hyla andersonii. Its loud mating call formed part of the inspiration for naming our dream home in the New Jersey Pine Barrens Hyla Holler. From a watercolor painting by Tom R. Johnson, a treasured gift to RC.

Chapter 50

A Quarter Century in Paradise:
Part II. The Wildlife and Our Personal Happiness

How can I begin to describe our animal neighbors and all the fun we had watching them? We were nature-oriented, to be sure, and Taunton was a virtual utopia for us.

Our two lakeside residences occupied different habitats. The 'Gap, with several other cottages and a few houses not far away, was within an enclave that had long been protected from fire. It was near the dam that impounded the waters of the lake, and close to the long-extinct Taunton Iron Works, which functioned spasmodically during the late 1700s, and was a stagecoach stop in pioneer days. Large deciduous trees were dominant, although a sprinkling of tall pines shared the canopy with them. Many kinds of birds and a few mammals favored that habitat but shunned the more open and considerably less diverse vegetation of the Pine Barrens proper, in which Hyla Holler was situated. Yet some birds, such as the brown thrasher and the rufous-sided towhee, preferred the Barrens. So did the ruffed grouse, which we heard "drumming" occasionally in the spring. One even came walking through our yard one day. With our two different environs we had two views, as it were, of the warm-blooded vertebrates. We saw many more species than we would have if we had spent the entire quarter century in just one of them.

The birds were most conspicuous, of course. We operated bird feeders every winter. At the 'Gap I built a well-drained open box for the windowsill directly adjacent to our indoor dining table. Because we had storm windows, the only access to the box was from the out-of-doors, and I had to go out each morning to replenish the food supply and, all too often, sweep or shovel away the snow that had fallen during the night. The sparrows and juncos, which habitually search for seeds on the ground, required just as much attention as the birds that came to the window box and the suet feeders I installed nearby.

When we moved to Hyla Holler in 1958, I hung an elaborate commercial feeder by a wire from a tree. It was supposed to foil the gray squirrels, which it did not. I still had to sally forth daily to strew seeds. I clad myself to suit the weather. Many a time, on cold mornings, I pulled on socks, a pair of pants, and knee-high rubber boots, wrapped myself in a jacket or heavy coat over my nightclothes, donned a pair of gloves and a hat, and ventured outside, even when the temperature was below zero. Almost at once the birds descended en masse, and they put on a lively show for us while we were eating breakfast.

Over the years we saw all the usual winter residents, such as chickadees, titmice, white-breasted nuthatches, brown creepers, blue jays, and woodpeckers. There were also special visitors, often including evening grosbeaks, pine siskins, and purple finches. Red-breasted nuthatches came daily some winters, but were conspicuously absent during others. Also, we saw many migratory transients in the early spring.

Only one bird ever stumped me. It was a ground-feeding sparrow at the 'Gap. It had faint streaks on its breast, but it failed to match any species I knew. At my earliest opportunity I made a trip to the Academy of Natural Sciences of Philadelphia, where the Delaware Valley Ornithological Club maintained a synoptic collection of bird skins to assist anyone confronted, as I was, with an oddity. My bird was a Lincoln's sparrow, a western bird far out of its range, but one that turned up occasionally in the East.

Most of our surprises came among the waterbirds, and we noticed them especially after we moved well up the lake to Hyla Holler, where there were almost no other human dwellings at the time. During a series of early springs we saw a wide variety that apparently had dropped into the lake toward nightfall, but which sometimes stayed for a day or two or even longer. Among them were the common loon, pied-billed, horned, and Holboell's (red-necked) grebes, bufflehead, canvasback, American and Barrow's goldeneyes, ring-necked and ruddy ducks, common merganser, blue-winged teal, snow and Canada geese, and the whistling (now tundra) swan. One year a wild mute swan was in the lake for weeks, and once we saw an osprey grab a fish with its talons. When the water was down for any reason, we might see great blue herons, egrets, and shorebirds of several species, including a spotted sandpiper teetering on our dock. Great horned owls serenaded us with their five-syllable notes during their winter nesting season, and one spring a saw-whet owl was around. Our list would have been greater if we had been avid bird-watchers with binoculars constantly dangling from our necks. All the birds mentioned above were seen or heard from our residences. We didn't have to go looking for them.

One warm spring day, while we were clearing brush from our future Hyla Holler homesite, we were resting, lying on our backs on the ground and staring up at the sky, when two bald eagles soared past not more than 50 feet above us.

In a sandbank near the 'Gap, a pair of belted kingfishers excavated a hole just large enough for them to pass through, but they also cleared a spacious chamber inside. I peered in periodically at night with a flashlight for brief glimpses, and I saw the eggs, the hatchlings, and eventually the full-fledged young, which, with their parents, filled the entire space.

Whippoorwills arrived in April every year, and their loud, penetrating calls seemed to blend perfectly with our woodland retreat. They seldom kept us awake, but one night, during a full moon and after a particularly difficult day at the zoo, sleep did not come easily. Sometime after midnight I went out on the patio that served as our porch at Hyla Holler. I never did see the calling male, but I discovered he had a regular route with four different stops, from each of which he called "whip-poor-will" several times. One was near the house, but one of the others was across the lake, which was relatively narrow opposite us.

It was among the small mammals that we numbered the rascals and comedians. At the 'Gap we put our trash and garbage in a 20-gallon metal can near the back door. As soon as our new garage was finished, a few weeks after we moved to Hyla Holler, I placed the can behind it, almost touching the wall. A few days later, when I went out to leave for the zoo, the can was lying on its side and its contents were strewn around on the ground. I had to stop, pick everything up, and then go back into the house to wash my hands. The next morning it was the same, and the next and the next. So I instituted a watch and sat indoors, by the guest room window, where I could see anything that might happen. Luckily, I had enough moonlight to witness the events that transpired. Presently, a large raccoon appeared, walked up to the can, stood upright, placed its paws upward, and began rocking it back and forth. Soon the can had moved outward a few inches, whereupon the ingenious animal

forced its way into the narrow space, raised its paws to their full height, and, with its back braced against the garage wall, gave a mighty shove. The can crashed to the ground and the lid flew off. Moments later two other raccoons appeared, and they all pawed through the mess, eating off and on as they went. After that the garbage can was kept inside the garage, close by the rear side door that gave us direct access to the interior.

The experience taught us a lesson. Thereafter, we placed all unused tidbits of food in the feeding area near the pile of leftover lumber scraps we had purposely retained as a hiding place for transient wildlife. Chicken and steak bones, melon rinds, and a large variety of other items, once consigned to the garbage, became food for our visiting nocturnal menagerie. In the morning all traces were usually gone. Over the years we saw several opossums and skunks, as well as many raccoons, picking up the scraps and carrying them away. Our darkened kitchen, with its window facing toward the yard, was an ideal observation post. Only once in our many years of residence did we see a rat, and I trapped it in short order.

We moved into Hyla Holler on September 15, 1958, but it wasn't until a week later that work started on our cinder-block, two-car garage. We were soon able to put both cars inside, but the concrete floor had not been poured. The contractor and mason were so busy erecting other houses at nearby Lake Pine and elsewhere, that we had a sand floor all winter. When the garage doors were pulled down there was a wide space beneath them that was an open invitation for our critter friends to venture inside. We often found raccoon tracks on the hoods of the cars. Much more important, a pair of adorable little red squirrels moved in, running easily up and down the rough cinder-block walls. They climbed over the top, dropped down into the hollows inside, and built a nest of twigs, leaves, and other debris from the forest floor, including small pine cones that they transported under the doors. They were doing no harm to us, so we let them alone. Next spring, they surprised us with four cute little squirrels, which ran around the yard in the company of a parent. At first they retreated to the garage every night, but when the weather warmed they found outdoor quarters. They were always back during the daytime, however, to feast on our largesse. It was well that they were gone, because the garage floor was finally poured, and there wasn't enough room left beneath the doors for a worm snake to crawl through. Incidentally, I found one of those diminutive serpents, *Carphophis amoenus,* on the concrete apron at the front of the garage when we came home late one summer evening in a rainstorm.

A young red squirrel. Several families of these lively little rodents were reared in our garage. They kept us amused for years. Photo by IHC.

We had an early cold snap the next autumn, and, when I started off to work one morning, I noted a white patch at the bottom of our dark green side access door. I leaned down for a good look. It had been gnawed. On a hunch, I went around to the front of the garage, and, sure enough, one of the large doors had also been gnawed. The squirrels wanted in!

I left the small door open for the day, but, after supper, I opened the standard up-and-down sliding window at the back of the garage. It was a simple task to nail a piece of two-by-four to the sill, wide side down, but leaving room at one end for a red squirrel to pass. I then lowered the window and fastened it so it couldn't be raised. The squirrels caught on at once, and used the opening as their means of ingress and egress. They were our annual wintertime guests for many years, and we even gave them an occasional burlap bag they could shred for nest material. They or their offspring must have been with us for the better part of a decade before they finally disappeared.

They were great fun to watch. They were perky and lively, and they seemed to think the place belonged to them. We enjoyed seeing them chase the far larger pestiferous gray squirrels, nipping at their heels as they pursued them. We had an active yard during at least part of every day.

In 1960 we traded in our beautiful, wood-paneled Oldsmobile station wagon, which had reached the venerable age of 10 years, and for which parts no longer were available. In exchange we acquired our Volkswagen Kamper that we would take repeatedly to Mexico and the Big Bend National Park in Trans-Pecos Texas. All winter it shared the garage with our rodent guests, except on most Wednesdays, when, weather permitting, Isabelle made her pilgrimage to Medford or Marlton, then both small towns, to lay in our week's supply of groceries and other necessities. We figured that the Kamper needed a bit of weekly exercise to keep it functioning. I had to use our other car to commute to the zoo.

Five years later, in 1965, we departed for Mexico on our last expedition sponsored by the National Science Foundation. When we were crossing southern New Mexico, a slight noise developed that sounded as though it might be in a front wheel. Because El Paso was not too far away, we decided to stop there at the Volks agency. The mechanics diagnosed the trouble as a broken front shock absorber, replaced both of them, and we soon were on our way. The noise was still present, so we went back. Because it was late in the day, they asked us to bring the Kamper in the morning so they could make a thorough inspection. We were at their shop before 8:00 A.M., and, after considering all the possibilities, they decided they had better have a look at the steering mechanism. To get at it, a rather large flat pan, more or less under the front seat, had to be removed. Up went the car on a lift, and a stocky, swarthy mechanic of undoubted Mexican ancestry began removing a series of bolts from under it. All of a sudden he shouted, " *¡Caramba!*," followed by a string of other expletives in Spanish. When he pushed the pan aside he was showered with a bushel of twigs, leaves, forest floor debris, and shredded burlap. The red squirrels! The little rascals had evidently found a way to get onto the pan and had built a nest there, and we had transported it for 2,000 miles. As soon as a steering knuckle was replaced, we were off. Long after we crossed the border, Isabelle and I were still chuckling about the industry and audacity of our self-invited pets.

The gray squirrels, on the other hand, were frustrating nuisances. They were greedy, gobbled down large quantities of expensive seeds, monopolized the feeders, and kept the birds from getting at them. They persistently returned a few minutes after we chased them away. They were neither too annoying nor too numerous at the 'Gap, and usually a sharp rap on our window glass would make them jump down to the ground. At Hyla Holler they were intolerable. My expensive special feeder, suspended by a wire from a limb, was not squirrel-proof as claimed. They shinnied down the wire. I fashioned a wide, flat rat guard and attached it halfway down the wire. That stopped them for a while, but they soon learned to make prodigious leaps from the trunks of nearby trees. They outsmarted me over and over again, so I declared war on them.

I bought a live trap, which I baited with peanut butter. Within an hour I had caught one of the pests. He had a crumpled ear, perhaps the result of a fight or accident. I put the trap in the car, drove a mile or so away, and turned him loose. Two days later he was back, with his battered ear to identify him. I tried hauling captive squirrels much farther away. Maybe they, too, came back, but no matter how much I tried to thin out their population, others replaced them. Finally, in desperation, I took them to the zoo, hauling them, inside the trap, in the rear of the Volkswagen squareback we owned at the time. I felt sure that moving them across the Delaware River would prevent any return. There was ample room for them at the zoo, and Fairmount Park was directly adjacent. One winter I transported 37, one at a time, but I was still doing battle with them the winter before we said a sad, sad farewell to Hyla Holler.

There is a third kind of squirrel in the Pine Barrens, but we saw it only at the 'Gap. We had a pair of flying squirrels, and I erected a feeding box for them on a large tree right by our screened porch. They would come, just as it grew really dark, to eat the cracked nuts we put out for them. If we sat quietly on the couch nearby, often with guests cautioned to remain soundless and to make no sudden movements, we could see them faintly with eyes that had become adjusted to the darkness. What dainty little creatures they were. They never flew for us, beating instead a very squirrel-like retreat up the bole of the tree.

One of the greatest thrills I ever experienced occurred on the night of May 8, 1958. Hyla Holler was under construction, but progress was by fits and starts, with many things done rapidly at times, but very little at others. The men were trying to work on too many jobs at once. I had been at the zoo all day, and we cross-read proofs for our field guide in the early evening. Isabelle decided to retire early, but I drove the mile by road around the lake to see what, if anything, had been accomplished. Nothing, apparently. So I drove slowly back, my thoughts on the proofs. I had nearly crossed the Taunton dam when two otters appeared on the road. In the glare of my headlights, one stood erect in that curious stance they assume as they look around. I stopped, and a few seconds later it dropped down on all fours and the pair waddled off to the water. Never before had I seen an otter so close except in a zoo. What a delightful experience. I moved on, started up the

slight incline from the dam breast, and, lo and behold, there was another otter standing erect on the road. I was so bursting with excitement when I reached the 'Gap that I just had to tell my soul mate all about it. Fortunately, she was still awake, but even more fortunately we were destined to see otters many times from Hyla Holler. What lithe, beautiful creatures they are. We often saw them playing with one another in the lake, eating fishes on the ice during winter, and once two of them even hauled out on our dock.

March 15, 1968, was a red-letter day. I was at home, and we both had been working steadily in our downstairs study at Hyla Holler. In midafternoon we decided to take a break, go upstairs, and sit in our easy chairs overlooking the lake for a few minutes. I went to the kitchen sink to get a drink of water, and I was astounded to see an otter on top of our pile of scrapwood. I called to Isabelle, who hurried over, and we both saw the otter go down beneath the pile, only to emerge a few seconds later holding a cub in her mouth by the scruff of its neck. The cub was an albino! Mother otter and her burden vanished over the steep bank in front of the house. We speculated that recent heavy rains had perhaps flooded out a waterline den, and that our woodpile had served as a temporary nursery. Months later, Alice Yerkes, a good friend who lived close to the 'Gap, telephoned excitedly to ask if there was such a thing as a white otter. She was the last to see it. We never learned whether it survived through the hunting and trapping season.

On the 1961 anniversary of Pearl Harbor Day we suffered an unexpected disaster at Hyla Holler. It was one of my regular days off, but we didn't discover the damage until it was time for our mid-morning Coca-Cola break. We were aghast. Several of our carefully pruned trees, directly in front of the house, were leaning at crazy angles, and the largest of them was flat on the ground.

We put down our glasses and hurried outside, and the word "beavers" popped into both our heads as we went. Sure enough. The trees had been gnawed off during the night. There were piles of wood chips, and some of the trees hung as by a thread, where another slice or two with the rodents' sharp, stout teeth would have severed them. The stump of the largest was standing free with a sharp point upward, as though it had passed through a very large, worn-out pencil sharpener. If it made a crashing noise as it fell, we failed to hear it. Our sleeping quarters were at the far other end of the house.

We finished our break, but then I donned blue jeans, field shoes, and a heavy jacket against the chilly day. Some 200 white oak trees had been cut, and the boles of most of them hauled away. Some were sizable but all were relatively young, since they had grown back subse-

We were astounded to discover many of our white oak trees cut off and others leaning. Beavers had been at work during the night. Photo by IHC.

RC standing on a small island that remained when the lake was drained. He and Fred Ulmer assembled a pile of tree boles and branches 10 feet high and 20 feet across, all taken from the beavers' storehouse. Photo by IHC.

quent to a fire of perhaps 20 years previously. Branches, haphazardly gnawed off, lay strewn about. Most of the damage was on the Zworykins' property, and a week or so later I discovered a beaver lodge just above the waterline in the high bank on their land. The rodents apparently had dug deeply, about halfway between our house and theirs. At least no logs stuck out.

We learned, when spring came, that every magnolia tree growing close to the water's edge was gone, and then the animals had started on the white oaks. If the onset of the invasion had occurred earlier in the year, it probably would have been discovered by one or more of the canoeists or rowboaters who maneuvered on the lake. Powerboats of any kind were strictly prohibited. All the people at Taunton, like ourselves, were bitterly opposed to noise pollution.

I called the New Jersey Game Department and they promised to send an agent on the morrow to assess the situation. In the meantime, we strung wire netting around our best remaining trees, and that saved them from attack. It was obvious that the beavers, unlike most of the rest of our wildlife, were not welcome and would have to go. Plans were made to catch and remove them farther into the Barrens, where there were no human residents whose property they could destroy. The traps didn't work. Not a single beaver was caught. I tried my best, armed with my headlamp and a powerful flashlight, to see them at night, but I had no luck. My only success was in hearing the loud slap several times, as they slammed their broad tails down against the surface of the water.

When the lake was drained down partway for the annual spring cleaning, I decided to tackle the beaver lodge. Fortunately, I had the able and enthusiastic assistance of Frederick A. Ulmer, Jr., the zoo's Curator of Mammals. He was eager to see what the inside of a beaver cache looked like. He and I worked "like beavers" all day long, removing huge masses of sticks and small to medium-sized logs, and carting them to a nearby small island in the mud of the lowered lake. Before we finished we had a pile roughly 10 feet high and 20 feet in diameter. What a huge amount of damage the animals had done. The pile was burned before the lake was restored to its normal level. The beavers disappeared and never came back.

To reach the 'Gap when we drove home from Philadelphia, we passed through the remnants of old Taunton, a small cluster of buildings erected long ago and in various stages of disrepair. We then crossed the dam breast of Taunton Lake, and were home two minutes later. We paid little attention to the old village, although a caretaker was in residence.

One evening we strolled down across the dam about dusk, and saw bats emerging through the broken windowpanes of the top floor of one of the buildings. They probably roosted in the attic during daylight hours. On my next day off, I obtained permission to enter, borrowed the key, and went exploring. The stairs and other parts of the old structure were still sound, and thus I had no trouble reaching the top floor. There, just as I had guessed, were bats, about 100 of them, clinging to the rough masonry of the chimney and nearby rafters. I didn't disturb them, but I alerted Fred Ulmer the next day, and invited him to have a look at his convenience.

Together we examined the colony, and Fred, a dedicated mammalogist, returned a week or so later with a supply of tiny numbered aluminum bands to attach to a wing of each bat along the bony structure that supported it. The principle exactly matched the banding of birds—to determine how long they live and where they go. Fred thought it was likely that they might hibernate in one or more of the caves of eastern Pennsylvania, which he and some of his colleagues explored. The Taunton colony consisted of little brown bats. We wrestled a ladder up the stairs, and, with its help, we managed to catch and tag many of the animals. On June 28, 1950, Isabelle accompanied us, and she took several photographs. When more than one of us was present, we invariably disturbed the bats and many of them flew off onto the rafters in other parts of the attic. So, she was able to portray only part of the colony. Fred came back to the building several times, and also to look for other bats when I learned about another abandoned old house a few miles away. In addition to the little brown species, we met three other kinds of bats at Taunton: the big brown and red bats and the pipistrelle. I found one of the three kinds lying dead on the ground, and the others managed to find their way (one each) onto the porch of the 'Gap and the garage at Hyla Holler, where I caught them alive. Fred identified them for me.

During our quarter century at Taunton we saw or heard 26 kinds of wild mammals. If we omit the alien Norway rat, we had an average of one species for each year. Many were common, and we were aware of them daily, but several on the list that I kept were seen only once. Such was the case with the red and gray foxes, both of which were at the very edge of the Barrens, but quite close to Taunton. A mink appeared once on the ice near the Hyla Holler dock, and I liberated a muskrat that managed to get into one of the traps set for the beavers. The latter, of course, I heard but failed to see. We had quite a menagerie of wild four-legged critters. White-tailed deer, by far the largest of them, were never seen at the 'Gap and were a rarity at Hyla Holler. But we often found their tracks in our back acreage.

When it came to reptiles and amphibians, we eventually acquired all the species indigenous to the Pine Barrens. Not all were on our property, but most of the others were not very far away. My interest in herps was well known to all the residents of Taunton Lake, and many a snake, turtle, and frog was caught and brought to us, mostly by boys. There were two young buddies of 9 or 10 who came running to our doorstep whenever they found something of interest. We always thanked them profusely, commented on their skill in finding things, and placed their catch in a cage or other container

and admired it in their presence. If Isabelle was alone, she saved everything until I came home; then, after an inspection, I surreptitiously liberated most of them where the kids said they caught them or in other suitable habitats. A few of the choice specimens went to the zoo, and all the dead or badly injured ones were preserved for future study.

Sometimes Isabelle was called upon to make captures herself, usually water snakes that had fallen into a swimming pool. Yes, some of the wealthy people who eventually built homes at Centennial and other nearby lakes had private pools. They wanted to swim in clear water, not the strongly brown-tinted kind that was characteristic of all Pine Barrens lakes. (See "The New Jersey Pine Barrens.") Isabelle always took a snake hook and box with her, but she was surprised one day to find a baby timber rattlesnake floating in a pool. She lifted it out with her hook and deposited it in the box with care. It lived at the zoo for a great many years, and grew into the most handsome rattler of its species I ever saw. Incidentally, there was a colony of those same rattlesnakes only a few miles from us that apparently hibernated in a sphagnum bog.

When they learned about Isabelle's rescue of stray serpents, the editors of the "Philadelphia Inquirer" paid her to write an illustrated article about it for their Sunday supplement. It was entitled "Here's the Snake Lady, Mama."

Two summer camps, operated, respectively, by the Boy Scouts and the YMCA, were only a few miles from Taunton, and they became good sources of herps, especially since I sometimes gave talks on reptiles and amphibians at evening campfire gatherings. I occasionally had telephone calls from one of the camps when they found something unusual, and Douglas A. Rossman, who later became a distinguished herpetologist at Louisiana State University, came over to visit us from Camp Ockanickon in 1954 when he was staying there prior to starting his college career.

Over the years I personally found all the Pine Barrens species. The last one was the scarlet snake, *Cemophora coccinea*. One appeared in the headlights of my car, during the evening of May 21, 1959, as it crawled across the Centennial Lake dam. It was the only one I, personally, ever found in the Barrens. The species was unknown from New Jersey until 1935—which, incidentally, was the year I started work at the Philadelphia Zoo. During our 25 years of residence in the Barrens I managed to assemble only 25 records for that secretive fossorial snake, an exact match for the number of mammals I listed.

During the entire time from when I joined the zoo staff until we left for New Mexico in 1973, I kept careful records of all the reptiles and amphibians found in southern New Jersey and on the Delmarva Peninsula, and I plotted the localities where they were found on maps. I even worked on the herpetology of those two areas after I retired. I searched the collections of a dozen museums for additional records when I made trips to the East to visit my family and elderly mother. The ambitious reviews I had planned for both regions have not been finished, and I can only wonder, at this late time in life, if they ever will be, at least by me. (I surrendered the time I had expected to devote to them and other projects in order to complete the lengthy manuscript for "Snakes of the *Agkistrodon* Complex" that I promised Howard K. Gloyd I would finish for him.)

In retrospect, I regret having spent virtually no time getting to know the fishes of the Pine Barrens. My interest in them, I fear, was almost all utilitarian. Small fishes that could be seined from the shallow water near our Hyla Holler dock were excellent fodder for the water and garter snakes we brought back from Mexico, many of which I kept alive for long periods for observation and study. We caught swamp darters, and the young of eastern creek chubsuckers and the pumpkinseed. I am sure of the identity of those, because I preserved a small series of each and sent them to Reeve M. Bailey, Curator of Fishes at the University of Michigan. There was also the chain pickerel, many of which Skip caught in the lake, cleaned, and prepared for the frying pan. That was the crop with which I was acquainted, except for one very special nocturnal fish.

The water by our dock at the 'Gap was only about breast deep, but, a relatively short distance farther out, it was over our heads. After swimming we would often stand by the dock to rest before climbing out or returning to deep water. That was fine during daylight hours, but not at night. Why? Bullheads, the rather chunky catfish of the genus *Ameiurus*.

If we stood still in the water at night, it was usually only a few seconds before the fish were nibbling at our legs. Not biting, but examining us with their fleshy lips. At first it was disconcerting, and I wasn't sure what was going on until I set a fish trap and caught two of the bewhiskered bullheads. After that, I paid little attention to them, but they bothered Isabelle and many of our guests who wanted to swim in the dark. The solution was to keep constantly in motion, which kept the fish away.

We discovered the bullheads during our first summer at Taunton, in 1945, but it wasn't until quite a few years later that I had a fun idea. Could I catch one by dangling my bare feet in the water as I sat on the dock at night? I armed myself with a short-handled crab landing net and put the idea into action. In less than a minute I had

caught a bullhead. When it was at my toes I swung the net quickly and accurately.

My trick was a good way to entertain summertime visitors. One night, when my first two granddaughters were old enough to be active and interested in everything, and they didn't have to be in bed by dark, I made an announcement: "I think I'll see if I can catch a fish with my feet."

The anticipated response was, "You can't catch fishes with your feet, Grandpop. You need a hook and line." They, of course, had seen their daddy, Skip, land fish of several kinds. Doubting though they were, they were quite willing to go down to the dock with me. There I told them to be still and quiet and just watch. Very shortly I had a bullhead in my net and, with the aid of a flashlight, the youngsters had a good look at it. An instant later they were running up the steps to the cottage screaming, "Grandpop caught a fish with his toes!" Skip and Ginny, their mother, were wise to my routine, and they and Isabelle were all smiles when the kids arrived in our living room still extolling my accomplishment.

So much for the fun provided by our wildlife neighbors. But what about us, a pair-bonded couple, deeply in love and happiest when we were alone with each other? We worked, played, and lived together as one. We were each other's alter egos.

We cherished the benison of the quiet and solitude of Taunton and the great near-wilderness in which we lived. Also, it was quite dark at night and, as an amateur astronomer, I could point my tripod-mounted telescope at the moon, the four large satellites of Jupiter, or any other celestial display in the sky, weather permitting, of course. It was well worth the long drive back and forth to the zoo, and the often maddening traffic. At home we were in a completely different world. Unlike many persons who thrive on crowds and prefer multiple companionship, we reveled in our personal paradise.

Our lives were a paradox in one major way. At the zoo—Isabelle worked there with me for 10 years—we spent a large part of our time and energy inducing people to visit the place. Until I became its director in 1967, I was public relations chief as well as curator of reptiles. Even after I moved up into the "hot seat," it was my duty to promote attendance, which grew from less than 300,000 paid admissions a year when I first arrived to 1.25 million before I retired.

Our day off each week was on Friday. Later, long after Isabelle resigned from the zoo, I also had Thursday, when the staff forced Zoo Director Shelly to give us all a five-day week. Thus, I was free on days when most other people had to work. Every summer we made at least one trip to the seashore for a saltwater swim and fun in the surf. The beach was virtually deserted on weekdays, whereas on weekends even space to lie flat on the sand was often at a premium. The Pine Barrens, almost completely devoid of human presence, except in a few small towns, retained their beauty and solitude, at least on weekdays. By the 1960s picnickers, snake hunters, and goons bent on vandalism invaded some parts of the Barrens on Saturdays and especially on Sundays. During the rest of the week most of the area was as deserted as ever. How wonderful for us who liked to be by ourselves in an enchanting world where we might see or find something of interest at every turn of the sand roads.

One early spring day, when the weather was unseasonably warm and our romance was new, we drove from the city on our day off to see if any snakes were out yet. That was our excuse. With no particular objective in mind, we found ourselves moving slowly along the sand road paralleling one side of the then-unpopulated Centennial Lake. We discovered an intriguing narrow peninsula jutting out into the water, well above but still within easy sight of the dam breast and the paved road that surmounted it. I pulled my old battered car off from what was little more than a trail and stuck a pair of clean snake bags under my belt, and we walked out through the shrubs growing on the spit of land. There was no sign of any wildlife, so we sat down on the sand of a narrow beach. It was hot in the sunshine, and a few moments later we exclaimed simultaneously, "Let's have a swim." No sooner said than done. We stripped, had a short invigorating dip, took a few dozen strokes, and then laid the snake bags flat on the sand to sit on while we dried.

Suddenly there was a loud yell. We both dove for the bushes, but as soon as we were out of sight, we peered back at the road across the dam. Not a soul could we see, but we hastily started to draw on our clothes. We both turned to look up the lake, and, just as we did, the loud yell was repeated, this time behind us. We then concentrated on the water, and soon heard the noise for the third time. It was a loon, moving on the surface and giving voice to its weird quavering call, which we had never heard before. What a relief! Evidently the bird had stopped during its northward migration. We were to see and hear several more of its kind when we moved to Hyla Holler many years later.

Ever afterward, when we were alone, we referred to Centennial as "Loon Lake," smiling as we recalled how a wild bird made us think we'd been caught in an embarrassing situation.

Once we were living at Taunton, our swimming was largely confined to home. We discovered that the tea-colored water absorbed heat rapidly, and in midsummer the upper few inches could be tepid, almost uncomfortable. It was much cooler below, so we learned to stand by the dock at the 'Gap and scoop up handsful of water toward the surface to refresh ourselves. At Hyla Holler, I would swim out to the channel of the meandering stream whose sandy banks persisted, as we could readily see when the lake was lowered periodically. When I stood on the sand the water was just up to my neck, and I followed the same procedure of bringing water from below to the surface. It was always cool in and near the stream channel. There were no natural lakes in the Pine Barrens. All were formed by man-made dams across various streams of the region. Many of the lakes, including both Taunton and Centennial, had previously been commercial cranberry bogs.

There were natural swimming holes in a few places, however, and the best one was near the old Martha Furnace. The water spilled over what we took to be a layer of hardpan, and it was deep below it and formed a sizable pool before flowing downstream to the Wading River. Few people knew it existed. It was secluded, and we utilized it on hot days when we were exploring the Barrens in the general vicinity. On August 7, 1951, we made a day of it. Isabelle packed a lunch, I put cold soft drinks in our small car icebox, and we had our own nudist colony. We were in and out of the water, walked along the nearby sandy trails, and enjoyed the unique freedom of being unimpeded by clothing of any kind. No one came near us all day. There was only one problem. We got too much sunburn.

Our life together progressed serenely despite our constant hard work, both physical and mental. We were accomplishing many things, and we were happy with our progress. Probably because we were always in contact with many people while doing our zoo work, we picked up numerous infections. Later, when I was commuting without Isabelle, I often unknowingly carried germs and viruses home with me. No matter. When either of us was under the weather, we had our close friend and dearly loved and respected physician, Louis Spitz, to pull us through. But he retired in 1968 and moved with his wife, Ruth, to Florida. The doctor to whom we turned, partly because his office was near Taunton, left much to be desired.

We had our share of sadnesses and emergencies. Who can escape them? We both attended many funerals of mutual friends, and I, alone or with Fred Ulmer, went in memory of zoo board members, the older of whom gradually died off. The most dismaying and mournful catastrophe was the sudden death, on May 5, 1957, of Isabelle's brother, Livingston Sloan Hunt, who was only in his early 50s. We knew he had a bad heart, but losing

From left, Asa Pittman, Howard K. Gloyd, and RC on the steps of Pittman's home deep in the Pine Barrens, September 5, 1945. Photo by IHC.

a close relative, especially one with whom my sweetheart had shared a happy childhood, was a dreadful personal blow for her and therefore for me.

My first onset of prostate trouble occurred in the summer of 1966, and I stayed overnight at Jeanne's Hospital in northeastern Philadelphia for tests. I had a good urologist, Dr. David S. Cristol, who had been recommended by Dr. Spitz. On April 17, 1971, I felt lousy all day and I was running a temperature. I called our new general practitioner, and he advised me to drink lots of water, which was the worst possible thing to do. By midnight I was in agony, unable to void any liquid. I called Dr. Cristol at his home, and he ordered me to leave immediately for Jeanne's Hospital. I was so doubled up with pain that I wakened Isabelle, and she drove. We took off for a virtually unknown part of the city. After crossing over to Pennsylvania, we got lost, but we eventually found a prowl car, and it guided us to our destination. The cops even stayed until I had been catheterized, and thus relieved. There was no place where Isabelle could spend the rest of the night, so she started home alone. She lost her way, and it was almost 4:00 A.M. before she telephoned that she was back at Hyla Holler, and I could relax and go to sleep. Once my fever subsided, two days later, Dr. Cristol decided to operate, and I was reamed and relieved of most of my prostate.

I was quite awhile convalescing, and Isabelle drove me to the zoo on each of the first few days when I

returned to work. It was not long, however, until I was back in stride, and we were able to resume our usual interests, including our love of the Pine Barrens. My mother had been sick again, so we soon drove over to see her. That required passing the place, just off the main highway, where the Upton railroad station had once been. Whenever we did so we invariably thought of a friend of former years.

When he was living, we almost always stopped to see Asa "Ace" Pittman when we were crossing the heart of the Pine Barrens on the paved road that led to Lakehurst and onward to Red Bank, where my mother lived. Ace was a "Piney," the name given to permanent residents of the Pine Barrens, who did odd jobs, such as picking berries in season, gathering sphagnum moss, and occasional lumbering. He was also a snake man. People from all over the area brought him snakes, and he sold them to supplement his income. Through reading and frequent contact with persons interested in herpetology, he had acquired an excellent working knowledge of the subject, at least the local aspects of it. He lived near the highway with his wife in an old small frame house, and he always had several live snakes on hand. We would look at his collection and chat awhile, and I usually bought a few snakes, sometimes to send to distant zoos that wanted pine or kingsnakes or other local species for their public displays.

Pittman was an interesting character, and twice,

when Isabelle was with her family on Staten Island, I spent the day with him, tramping through the woods near his home and listening to his stories. He had been born in 1879 almost within a stone's throw of the long famous, but now probably defunct, Mount Misery rattlesnake den. His interest in serpents began when, about 1912, he and his wife saw a rattler sunning itself and "he allowed he'd catch it." He did and, while exploring the surrounding area, he found 30 additional rattlesnakes by scraping away masses of sphagnum and digging into the roots of shrubs around a spring where the snakes had obviously hibernated while lying in the water. In the flowing springwater beneath the sphagnum they were protected from freezing during the winters. J. Wendell Burger reported Pittman's experience and some observations of his own in the journal "Copeia" in 1934. Ace died on January 9, 1955, at the age of 76. A forest fire burned his house to the ground in 1964. During his lifetime he sold thousands of snakes, a fourth of them rattlers, and he was never bitten by a venomous one.

We had many surprises and minor adventures during those golden years in the unspoiled Pine Barrens.

The husband of our cleaning woman uncovered a red "lizard" while clearing a ditch in a fallow cranberry bog. He put it and some muck in an empty tin can, and his wife phoned to ask if I wanted it. I drove over to their place and, miraculously, I had the first mud salamander, *Pseudotriton montanus,* ever found in New Jersey. Emmett Reid Dunn, the authority on the lungless salamanders, confirmed my identification. The habitat at the exact site of the capture was in sandy soil in, but close to the edge of, the Barrens. The species normally occurred in muddy habitats, insofar as we knew, so being on sand was new information.

One late spring day, with Isabelle at the wheel, we drove slowly along a back road, and I espied the head of a green snake protruding from a hole in a tree 6 feet above the ground. I still don't know how I managed to spot the snake from 15 or 20 feet away.

By doing a little detective work, interrogating residents, and writing a few letters, I solved the mystery of how the spiny softshell turtle, now *Apalone spinifera,* arrived in the Maurice River system at the western edge of the Pine Barrens, hundreds of miles from its normal range. I learned that four adults from Indiana were turned loose in Kean's Lake, at Elmer, New Jersey, way back in June 1910. They had multiplied, prospered, and spread.

Then there was Butch Cramer's place. He was an old recluse. Several of us who were afield together, during our first summer visit to Taunton, discovered him and his environs, a couple of miles or so south of the lake.

He lived in a tumbledown shack, but the lures for me were a small boggy pond nearby, the piles of old rotting boards, and the frequency with which many kinds of snakes turned up there. I was to catch a young rattlesnake there at night many years later. The bog filled with water in the spring, and it was an excellent place to hear and find the Pine Barrens treefrog, *Hyla andersonii,* the first part of the name Hyla Holler.

The best secretary I had during the manpower shortages of World War II was Catherine Barnett. She became quite familiar with frogs, at least on paper, because I was always giving her letters to type about them and other herps. When her husband returned from Okinawa, some months after the Japanese surrendered, she told him about them, and they both expressed a desire to see and hear the frogs in the flesh. One spring day, we made spur-of-the-moment plans for an evening excursion to Butch's place in the Barrens. I was living alone in the boardinghouse near the zoo at the time, but I still had my ancient Chevy, which I had used for fieldwork in Ohio when I was based at the Toledo Zoo. Fred Ulmer and his wife, Kathryn, joined us, and so did Isabelle, who had visited the spot when Mother and I spent our first summer at Taunton. The weather was auspicious. A light rain, almost a drizzle, was falling. When we arrived at our destination, then on a virtually deserted gravel road, the frogs were calling loudly. What's more, there were at least a dozen males right on the road. With our flashlights, we could see them clearly and even watch their throats expand into a bubble as they called. We all imitated the sounds they made, a nasal "quonk-quonk" repeated many times. What an opportunity, even for me, to witness such a herpetological event under ideal conditions.

All of a sudden a drenching rain descended upon us. We raced for the car, but we were soaked to the skin before we were within its shelter, the three women in the back and we three men up front. Fortunately, there were clean snake bags available, and the girls decided to disrobe in part, wring out their wet clothes, and dry themselves as best they could. We males were given strict orders not to look around, and to tilt the rearview mirror. Perhaps 10 minutes later, still in pouring rain, we drove away. On the highway back to the city we found a restaurant that was open, and, since the rain had slackened, we stopped for coffee and hot chocolate to warm ourselves.

What an amusing adventure, and one we never forgot. (The Ulmers, as I wrote this in 1994, vividly recalled it.) The next morning I drove my sodden car to the zoo and wisely made an inspection after I parked it. In the back, in plain sight, I found a feminine garter and a piece of unmentionable clothing. I hid them quickly. What was I, living alone and hoping eventually to be granted a divorce, doing with female undergarments in my car?

My decree came through on November 8, 1946. Isabelle and I were married on April 10, 1947, and much of our life together is chronicled in these two chapters about our "Quarter Century in Paradise."

Ours was an idyllic union. We were always thinking about each other, and we were determined to have a happy life, forever. We never quarreled, and I cannot recall a single time when either of us raised a voice directed at the other. We disagreed at times, but we always settled our differences amicably. Isabelle admired my ability to communicate verbally or through my writing, my leadership, my patience in getting along with my peers and superiors, and also my research. Once, when an acquaintance asked why I wasted so much time studying snakes and writing papers about them, she hastened to my support by saying, "You don't recognize the scholar in Roger." Isabelle was my constant companion, and, even when we were middle-aged, we thought nothing of walking hand-in-hand or with our arms around each other in public.

For my part, I never ceased to be amazed by the multiplicity of her talents and the skill with which she pursued them. Everyone who knew her recognized her outstanding ability as a photographer and artist. Living with her gave me an insight into how very many other things she could do, and do well. For example, she was an accomplished seamstress. She made her own blouses, altered the suits and dresses she bought, and kept my wardrobe in perfect repair. She crocheted thick, soft bathroom mats. We purchased truly lovely, heavy, hand-woven material in Mexico, and she made, and backed with reflective fabric, huge drapes to cover our four large picture windows at Hyla Holler. I hung the traverse rods on which to suspend her beautiful handiwork.

Isabelle was also a good cook, although she often resented the time she had to spend at it. She cleverly developed delicious casseroles that she could prepare in advance. When company arrived, she would put one in the oven to heat while she joined in the preprandial highball and conversation. With the table set in advance, and salads and desserts laid out on plates, in or out of the refrigerator, she needed only a few moments to have everything ready to eat.

From the very beginning and almost until the time of her death in Albuquerque in 1976, Isabelle assumed the responsibility for many household duties. She paid all the bills, kept all the books, supervised the cleaning women, and did most of the shopping, thus giving me

more time for my studies. She did it voluntarily and cheerfully. Her experience as business manager of the Staten Island Zoo stood her in good stead.

As my share, I pitched in constantly to help. I washed windows, did the dishes on a daily basis, attended to innumerable chores, and assisted in keeping everything in order, indoors and out. When we were alone I frequently brought home take-out meals, and I often arranged for us to eat out to save her time and energy, especially on the days when she accompanied me into the city.

We were frequently preparing surprises for each other. Many a time I arrived home to discover that she had polished two or three pairs of my dress shoes, or had treated my ankle-high field boots with neat's-foot oil. Most thoughtful of all was the evening I found she had made me a half-dozen flannel nightcaps to cover my bald head as I slept on cold nights.

When business took me into town in late afternoons, and I could go home directly from there, I stopped at the Reading Terminal Market and bought her favorite treats, such as crabmeat or freshly shucked raw oysters. During the harvest seasons I stopped at roadside stands on the drive home to buy fresh-picked asparagus, corn, tomatoes, and other goodies. How we missed those products of the Garden State when we moved to the Southwest! On every excuse for an occasion, I took her flowers, a bottle of liquor, or chocolate maple creams or pralines, the only sweets, besides ice cream, that she liked. Our deep love for each other was neverending, and it was apparent to everyone who knew us well.

While reading Isabelle's diaries as I prepared these memoirs so many years later, I burst into tears several times. Consider such entries as the following:

"Roger had his beard shaved off and I was so happy to see his dear, handsome face again after two months." (While the two of us were in Mexico in 1959, I grew a beard so I would look authentic for our Old-Timers' Day celebration at the zoo.)

"The surprise of my life came when we finished our dinner. In walked the waiter with an enormous cake. . . . He put it down in front of me, and I was so astounded I didn't know what to say. Roger, the sweet, thoughtful cutie-pie he is, had arranged for it the night before without my knowledge. Collecting my wits I blew out the candle—just one because it was my first birthday in Mexico." (We were at the Restaurante Los Arcos in Monterrey, in 1954, while looking for rarities we still needed to photograph for our field guide.)

"Two letters from Roger—oh happy day!" "Two more letters from my beloved." "He is back and I am happy again." (I had flown to Amsterdam in the Netherlands to attend a meeting of the International Union of

Directors of Zoological Gardens, but chiefly to say farewell to my colleagues from all over the world. That was in 1972, but because of her recent operation, the doctors wouldn't permit her to accompany me. I sent her an airmail letter every day while I was abroad.)

After my sweetheart was stricken, we carried on as best we could, she to the limits of her ability, and I with a heavy heart as I worried constantly about her.

Is it any wonder that our life together was one long perpetual honeymoon?

Chapter 51

Disaster and Departure

Things were going very well at the zoo. It was early in 1972. The building program was advancing splendidly, and the marvelous new facilities were nearly ready for the educational program I had dreamed about for so long. Also, the spectacular new reptile house would soon be opened to the visiting public. It was no time to feel complacent, however. There was still much to do. The first phase of the African plains exhibit was under construction, and there were more projects to follow. I felt that we were "on a roll," to borrow a bit of slang. America's First Zoo was now a first-class institution, and I was grateful to all the very many people who had helped it to achieve that distinction.

Personally, things were also going very well. On May 26, 1971, I received a signal honor. The University of Colorado, at Boulder, awarded me an honorary degree: an Sc.D., or Doctor of Science. My longtime and esteemed friend Hobart M. Smith was the prime mover, but he was aided by T. Paul Maslin, also a professor on the Boulder campus. People, usually strangers, had addressed me as "Doctor" for years, a sort of courtesy title. Now I was the real thing, but I took care, when new zoo stationery was printed, to follow my name with "Sc.D. (Hon.)," which was standard procedure for those holding such a degree. We were enjoying our lovely home in the Pine Barrens, our work was far advanced on the second edition of our field guide, and Isabelle and I were as deeply in love as ever. We were, however, already making plans for my retirement, which would come in 1974, the centennial year of the opening of the Philadelphia Zoological Garden. I'll admit that, in the quiet serenity of our home, we had a minor feeling of euphoria based on our progress and recognition.

Suddenly, in May 1972, there was an ominous and heartbreaking development. We discovered that Isabelle had cancer. She was faced with the emotional and physical trauma of a mastectomy.

She had begun smoking when she was 12 years old. She hid it, of course, from her parents. Children were not supposed to indulge, but the majority of adults did. We thought nothing of it. I smoked for years, and I always had a box of Wheeling stogies in my desk drawer at the zoo. Those were the sinuous cigars that look a little like snakes. I used a pipe, burned many a hole in my vests from falling tobacco embers, and once I was up to two packs of cigarettes a day. I quit "cold turkey" in the early 1940s, however, assisted by a stubborn respiratory ailment that caused me to cough violently and was greatly aggravated by smoking. How lucky I was to have dropped the habit so long ago. Isabelle, on the other hand, had kept it. She was a heavy smoker when she joined the zoo staff in 1942. She was then almost a nervous wreck after just escaping from the heartless monster who was using her as little more than a plaything rather than a wife. She was drinking eight cups of coffee a day and far too much hard liquor. Once she reached the security of her new job, well away from her tormentor, she began to cut down. First, she reduced the caffeine and settled on three cups of coffee a day. Her alcohol consumption dropped to a reasonable level, but her smoking continued. When the medical statistics showed overwhelmingly that smoking is hazardous, she cut the number of cigarettes in half, and then to a quarter, and she switched to filter tips. Like so many millions of other unfortunates, she was unable to kick the habit completely. As soon as she lost her breast, she quit, but by then it was too late. After that she would let no one smoke in the house. Her sense of smell returned, and she voiced the opinion that smoking stank, literally and figuratively.

Her convalescence was slow and complicated. She needed me, and I contrived to be with her much more than my very busy schedule really warranted. We did not lack for sympathy. Her hospital room was almost cluttered with cards and flowers. Less than a week after her operation—which, ironically, occurred on her birthday—I had a special function to perform. We had a large evening dinner party in the lobby of the rare mammal house, and I had to initiate an appeal for help to construct new bear dens to replace our ancient bear pits. Despite my aching heart, I presented the program, replete with numerous color slides of the splendid barless and naturalistic bear exhibits that had proliferated in so many other zoos. Many board members and their spouses, social leaders, and prominent Philadelphians were present, and I don't think a single one failed to express his or her sympathies and wishes for Isabelle's speedy recovery.

About two weeks later, chills and a high fever developed, and it was back to the hospital again. Isabelle's incision had become infected close to her armpit.

It was my practice, during both of her incarcerations, to telephone her two or three times from the office each day. I would leave the zoo as early in the afternoon as circumstances permitted, so that I could be with her until the early evening. Visiting hours were over at 8:00 P.M. and, except for the first two nights, I was ordered to leave at that time. "Be sure to phone when you get home. I won't be able to sleep until I know you're safely there," she said the first evening when I left early. The traffic was light at that hour, but it still required more than a half hour to make the journey. I called as soon as I was in the house, only to be stonewalled by the hospital operator: "We are not permitted to ring patients' telephones after eight o'clock," I was told. I tried to explain, but to no avail. I waited for about 10 minutes and then called back, and that time got a different operator. "Hello," I said. "This is Doctor Conant speaking. Please put me through to the nurses' station on the third floor." Seconds later I was talking to one of the nurses on duty. She delivered my message to Isabelle while I waited for her to come back and report that her mission was accomplished. I had to use the same subterfuge every evening, but I gave Isabelle a supply of free zoo tickets to hand out as tokens of appreciation to each of the several ladies who conveyed my goodnight message. They varied from evening to evening, of course. That was the only time I ever pretended that "Dr. Conant" meant an M.D.

Isabelle improved slowly but steadily, but she never regained the level of energy she had enjoyed prior to her hospitalization. We both fervently hoped that the cancer was now arrested, but there was always the sinister specter that it might have spread. She was able to resume work on the illustrations for the field guide, and soon could drive her car. Her illness was a dreadful blow to us both, and, admittedly, it was a severe mental setback for me. All of a sudden, the drive and enthusiasm that I had maintained for decades for promoting and improving the zoo slipped into low gear. With my beloved wife threatened, my job became secondary. She and I devoted much time and thought to what we should do, and we reached the conclusion that I should take an early retirement. If the board would let me, I would leave at the end of May, my birthday month, in 1973 rather than in 1974. We said nothing to anyone. I didn't want to weaken my authority at the zoo, and I didn't want to start rumors or even infighting over who might take my place. Also, there were many things I wanted to do before I left. First and foremost was my great desire to spend time breaking in the new reptile house and the educational center-administration building, both of which had opened just a few months previously. There were also lesser things I wanted to finish. As far as we personally were concerned, we began making plans and preparations for our retirement to the Southwest.

We had made up our minds, about two years previously, that when the time came, we would leave the humid East. We both liked a warm, dry climate, and we knew from spending so much time doing fieldwork in the Chihuahuan Desert, in both Mexico and the Big Bend region of Texas, that the open areas suited us well. We had toyed with the idea of moving to Alpine, Texas, 100 miles north and west of Big Bend National Park, but the town was so small that it had only a single doctor and a single dentist, and the sole cultural activities centered around Sul Ross State College, now a university. William G. Degenhardt, a friend of long standing and who had been working on lizards in the Park, suggested that we visit Albuquerque before we made a final decision. Bill was on the faculty of biology at the University of New Mexico, and he felt that some way could be worked out for making me a research associate, thus giving me a base for my herpetological interests. We took Bill's advice and liked what we saw, and we knew that Barney Gardner, one of my oldest friends from Toledo days, also lived there. Thereafter we stopped in Albuquerque whenever we were on trips to the West, and in June 1971, we bought 65 acres of chiefly forested land in the Manzanito Mountains east of the city. Later we acquired an additional adjacent 5 acres. So we already had a base in New Mexico, but it was too far from civilization for an aging couple. I, too, had been hospitalized in the summer of 1971 with a prostate problem. We needed a house in the city, near stores and medical help.

In the meantime, things had deteriorated in southern New Jersey. Urban sprawl was engulfing the area. When we first moved to Taunton Lake, it took me about 35 minutes to drive to the zoo, a distance of 25 miles each way. By 1972 I was lucky to make it in an hour on weekdays, both going and coming, because of the heavy traffic and the steady influx of people into the constantly proliferating new subdivisions. On Saturdays and Sundays I could still manage it in 35 minutes. Many new houses were appearing in the Pine Barrens, and it seemed only a matter of time until we would be swamped with humanity, and the peace, quiet, and wildlife of our woodland retreat would be threatened and eventually gone. The taxes on our waterfront property skyrocketed, and the prognosis was such that we realized we soon would be unable to meet expenses. Our house was much too large for Isabelle, in her weakened condition, to look after, even with the help of our faithful cleaning lady, who came once each week. Also, Isabelle was having trouble negotiating the stairs from our suite of offices in the basement to our living quarters above. So, despite all the wonderful years we had spent at Taunton, the last 15 of them in our dream house, it was time to leave. We started by shipping my bulky scientific library, which required 107 large double boxes. Unless we were away from home, we endeavored to mail two or more boxes each week by library rate, which at the time was only six cents for the first pound and two cents for each additional pound. Bill Degenhardt stored the boxes in cabinets in the spacious range for herpetology in the biology building.

John G. Williams became President of the Zoological Society in April 1972. He and his wife, Phyllis, were already good friends of ours. After Isabelle and I had worked out more details, I went to his office to discuss my future at the zoo. We had a long talk. He praised me for all the things I had done over the years, and then said, "Isabelle is not only your wife. She is your life. You do what you think is best for her."

So the die was cast, and plans for our departure developed rapidly. We began giving away excess items, we pushed on with work on the field guide, and we even made some quiet inquiries about the future sale of our house and the seven adjacent acres of woodland that we owned.

One of the things I especially wanted to do was to say farewell to my professional colleagues, many of whom I thought I might never see again. The international zoo meeting was in Amsterdam in early September 1972, and I decided to go, but the doctors would not permit Isabelle to accompany me. They said the trip, particularly the long hours in the air, would be too much for her. So for the first time since our marriage 25 years earlier I made a long trip without her. Isabelle stayed at home, but she slept at night at the cottage of one of her lady friends at Taunton.

I managed to write to her in my hotel room in Amsterdam every night, no matter how tired I was. Because of her Dutch ancestry, I addressed her as "Miss dePeyster" or "My darling Dutch wife." She saved all those letters, and they are still among my keepsakes. It

was heartbreaking not to have her with me to see the land of her ancestors. I tried to make up for it by telling her in full detail about all I saw. It was an interesting visit, especially when we went on a bus tour to see something of the countryside. I was exceedingly fortunate to have Dr. A. C. V. van Bemmel as my seat companion. He was the former director of the Rotterdam Zoo and his English was perfect, without even a trace of an accent. He was able to explain things to me in far more detail than any professional guide could possibly have done.

Isabelle was enthralled when I explained to her how the Netherlands (the very name means "low country") has achieved marvels for centuries by reclaiming land from the sea. The Dutch created polders (tracts of low land that formerly were under water) by building huge dikes around large sections of the Zuider Zee. When the area was completely encircled, the water was pumped from the inside, using the great windmills for which Holland is famous. The resultant exposed land was well below sea level. The frequent rains of the region soon diluted the residual salt, the brackish water was pumped out from time to time, and in a few years the polder was ready for the planting of crops or the grazing of cattle. During the tour, our bus crossed a bridge over a canal and then dipped down into a polder that was celebrating its 350th anniversary. More polders were under construction. The Zuider Zee had been blocked off at its northern (seaward) border, and the remaining body of water was rechristened the IJsselmeer, or lake of the IJssel River. Huge electric pumps replaced the windmills, a number of which were saved, however, as national monuments.

When it came to traveling on much shorter airplane trips in the United States, the doctors were willing to let Isabelle go. My final AAZPA meeting as a delegate from the Philadelphia Zoo would be in Portland, Oregon, in October. En route we digressed to Albuquerque and went house hunting. After three days spent inspecting a dozen homes, we finally bought an excellent house with a yard more than large enough for the building of a fireproof room attached directly to our living quarters. That, of course, was for the accommodation of the library and our other valuables. A bank, grocery store, and large shopping center were within easy walking distance.

The announcement of my early retirement was made at my home base before I left for Europe, so it was no secret in Portland that we were saying good-bye to people we had known for years as a result of attending other AAZPA meetings. The Portland Zoo was disappointingly small, but it had been breeding and raising elephants, a novelty at the time. We managed to see

Mount Saint Helens in the far distance from our hotel, but that, of course, was long before it blew its top. At the final banquet, where prizes and accolades were handed out, I expected someone to mention my active role in the organization since 1930, but no one did. That recognition was to come later, when I received the prestigious Marlin Perkins Award for my "unstinting service to AAZPA and excellence as a professional zoo man" among other things.

Soon after our return, the search for my successor began with a request to me from the board to suggest the names of possible candidates. I prepared a list of zoo directors in other cities, some of whom were invited to Philadelphia for interviews, and each of whom we entertained at our home for the night he was in town. Ronald T. Reuther, the Director of the San Francisco Zoo, was selected to take my place.

We continued work on our field guide, and Isabelle was able to finish the color plates. What was the last animal to be received alive to photograph and then render into color? Believe it or not, it was the spotted dusky salamander, *Desmognathus fuscus conanti,* from Douglas A. Rossman, who had described that new taxon in my honor way back in 1958.

On November 16 we received some disturbing news. My mother, then almost 91, had suffered a series of mild strokes. After going it alone for years as a teacher, she had married William G. Borner, who was quite a bit younger than she was, although she didn't tell him that. He was a pleasant, amiable chap until he reached his eightieth birthday, when he suddenly announced that he was going to do as he "damn pleased," whether anybody liked it or not. He became difficult from then on, and Mother inadvertently fueled his fire. Like all married couples they occasionally had differences of opinion, and she, in trying to make her point, would say, "If Roger were here I am sure he would agree with me." That always raised Bill's hackles, and he started referring to me as "The Hero," meaning Mother's hero. It was all too reminiscent of the nickname "Hero" that my male high school classmates had given me when I became an Eagle Scout after earning my lifesaving merit badge.

I went to Red Bank, where Mother still lived, but in Bill's house. She had a slight speech impairment and limited use of her right arm and hand. Within a relatively short time she pulled through, while Bill loyally took care of her. Mother's condition, however, brought into sharp focus another serious problem we might have to face. Isabelle's parents had died many years previously.

The winter of 1972-73 passed quietly. I worked with Kevin Bowler, Assistant Curator of Reptiles, who would soon take my place. I had held the title he would receive

for almost 38 years. We finally managed to get the thundershower working well, and the live collection was flourishing under Kevin's supervision. We were deeply grateful to him and to Stephen R. Wylie, the assistant to Gus Griswold, the Curator of Birds. One or the other of those two young men had driven us to the Philadelphia Airport or picked us up on our return from a trip many times. I also devoted much of my time to educational activities, meeting with Linda Jennings, the school district's teacher, and with Jeanne Segal and others about the docent program.

In February 1973 I had a stunning and totally unexpected surprise. Word came from the University of New Mexico that I had been appointed an Adjunct Professor in the Department of Biology. During our previous visit to Albuquerque, Bill Degenhardt took me to meet Paul Silverman, the Chairman of the Department, and we had a short but pleasant visit. Bill deserved much of the credit, but I also detected Hobart Smith's "fine Italian hand" once again. Silverman mentioned that Hobart always spoke highly of me when he (Silverman) was associated with the University of Colorado. First a doctor and now a professor! How incredible.

On April 15, 1973, Ron Reuther arrived in Philadelphia and was our houseguest for a couple of nights. A few days later the change in command was announced to the news media, and there was a reception for the two of us. It was attended by an amazingly large number of persons, including many of our board members, the zoo staff, the heads of Philadelphia's cultural institutions, and representatives of the city administration and the police department, with which I had worked so closely. Surprisingly, the city councilmen recessed their meeting at City Hall, and came to the zoo in a body to say farewell and to thank me for what I had accomplished during my long association with the zoo. It was a very touching and emotional affair for me, especially since I found myself with an armload of framed citations and metal plaques from various Philadelphia organizations.

I spent the next two weeks introducing Ron Reuther to key personnel at City Hall and the press and TV and radio stations, and I did my best to indoctrinate him into the routines that were necessary to keep the zoo moving forward. Doubtless he would change some of them once he was firmly in the saddle. Then I left the scene, as it were, although I remained on call in case my help should be needed. Several times, until my official retirement on May 31, I was at the zoo to assist and to attend various functions.

The staff and their spouses had a "roast" for me during which I was teased and kidded about my various idiosyncrasies. (See the anecdote entitled "The Roast.")

The zoo's Board of Directors held a farewell party for us at the Racquet Club, and almost every member was present, as well as the directors of other zoos. It was another touching affair, and I came away with the 13-volume English edition of Bernhard Grzimek's "Animal Life Encyclopedia," a collective gift from the board members. Grzimek was long the director of the Frankfurt Zoo, and his series of television programs made him the best-known naturalist in Germany.

We also attended farewell parties of the Safari Club and the Wilderness Club, and the latter made me their medalist of the year. The News Photographers Association also entertained us at Frank Palumbo's restaurant, and I was presented with a framed picture taken years before by Dominic Ligato in which I appeared to be running away from a zebra that was loose in the zoo.

We invited all the members of the zoo staff who had not yet been to our home, and they reciprocated by asking Jim Finn, the manager of the zoo's refreshment department, to provide snacks for the get-together and to assign one of his assistants to help with the serving and the cleaning up afterward. They all had a good time, and there was so much food left over that we were eating it for days.

After so much partying, we were exhausted, especially Isabelle, whose energy was low and who had days when she didn't feel well and was able to work only a few hours, and sometimes not at all. She tired easily and required far more rest than had been her wont. Nonetheless, we had to get on with several major projects. One was to finish the field guide and to deliver everything to Houghton Mifflin in Boston before we departed for the Southwest. The plates and line drawings were complete, with all the captions affixed in place, but we still had the maps to do. I roughed them all out, cut them to fit the allotted spaces that I had drawn on the plates, attached them securely, and turned them over to Isabelle so she could apply the stippling, hatching, and other patterns that showed the ranges of each kind of animal. Some maps required multiple patterns, as many as 8 or 10 in a few cases.

Then we had to face the staggering problem of packing for our big move. I was glad for the extra time I had acquired by leaving my office soon after Reuther came aboard. I did all the heavy work, and I pitched in to help Isabelle in many different ways. Richard G. Zweifel, Chairman of the Department of Herpetology of the American Museum of Natural History, drove down from New York twice with his wife, Fran, to transport large loads of preserved specimens from the work collection I maintained at my home. Raymond B. Cummins helped

This cartoon served as a frontispiece in a bound book of letters presented to RC at the roast in conjunction with his retirement as Director of the Philadelphia Zoo in 1973. The legend in Spanish on the serpent means "water snake made in Mexico," in reference to our extensive fieldwork south of the border. Drafted by the Art and Exhibits Staff of the Columbia Zoological Park, Columbia, South Carolina.

me pack more than 100 gallon bottles, chiefly full of natricine snakes, which were crated and sent to the University of New Mexico. I expected to work on them during my retirement. I should probably admit that I was eager to start devoting a large part of my time to herpetology. How much more pleasant that would be than having to cope with vexing problems day after day.

I had gone to Red Bank, a distance of some 80 miles, a couple of times to check on Mother. On June 24 she telephoned in the early morning to tell us that Bill, my stepfather, was very sick and in great pain. She had a telephone number for Bill's son, who was in Indiana on a trip. I managed to reach him, and he promised to start for Red Bank immediately. He was the only person who had any real influence with his father, who had become more and more cantankerous with the passage of time. To make a long story short, Bill Borner had stoically endured constant, severe pain for weeks and had refused to go to a doctor. Eventually he was forced to enter a hospital. An operation disclosed a huge gallstone and a badly infected gallbladder that had ruptured into his digestive tract. He was in very serious condition. The doctors put him into intensive care, and it was touch and go whether he would survive. He did, but his convalescence was lengthy.

I at once brought Mother to Taunton. She was feeble, both mentally and physically, and she was with us virtually all summer. I drove her to Red Bank once a week to see Bill at the hospital, where he remained for quite a long time. She was too weak to make the round trip in one day, so we stayed overnight at their house and returned in the morning. That, of course, meant a serious erosion of my precious time. I helped all I could, but Mother needed so much care that it was very hard on Isabelle, who had almost all she could do to keep herself going. Bill was finally discharged and sent by ambulance to a nursing home near his son's residence in far northern New Jersey. Mother wanted to see him off, so it was back to Red Bank again. We were very thankful that Bill had pulled through, but what were we to do about my poor dear old mother? I finally found an excellent protective care home at Hazlet, near Red Bank, and one of Mother's younger teacher friends agreed to keep an eye on her and report any changes to me. Mother, in her more lucid moments, realized that Isabelle was not physically able to look after her, and besides, she assured us emphatically that she wanted to stay as near Bill as possible.

Happily for them both, by the time Bill was able to return to his home, Mother had improved somewhat, and the two of them could live together again, with the aid of a housekeeper.

Mother died in a nursing home in 1975. I flew east to the Newark, New Jersey, Airport, hired a car, and drove to Red Bank to attend the funeral. There I was joined by my son, my daughter-in-law, and two of my granddaughters. Poor Mother. What a difficult life she had. I couldn't help thinking about our early struggles when the loss of my father left us virtually penniless. How long it took her to become self-supporting, while I lived with relatives during so many years of my school days. She had always dreaded old age, and I remembered that, even when I was a boy, she had said repeatedly, "Don't ever let them put me in a nursing home." How thankful I was that her mind was completely gone and that she never knew where she spent the last months of her life.

In spite of the unexpected difficulties, we completed work on the field guide on September 1, 1973. On the tenth, using our Volkswagen bus (we had long since traded in our Kamper), I drove to Boston. Kevin Cleary, a teenage son of one of our good friends at Taunton, went along with me as a relief driver. I had four suitcases

filled with the text and artwork on which we had labored for years. The color plates were irreplaceable. We stopped overnight at a motel just outside of Boston, and Kevin and I took turns watching the treasures. We ate separately, so that one of us was always on guard. The next day Isabelle flew to Boston, arriving at the Houghton Mifflin office not too long after I had delivered everything safely. I sent Kevin back by train to New York, and from there by public bus to the terminal a few miles from Taunton. Isabelle and I lingered in Boston for a couple of days to go over things with the editor and artist, and then we made the long drive home together. The relief of knowing that the publisher now had the field guide bolstered Isabelle's morale. She even did some of the driving, and we managed to stop off for an hour at Hazlet en route to see my mother, who was quite comfortable and well cared for.

Now all we had to do was finish packing. What a colossal chore. We had a gigantic garage sale that was mobbed with customers for two whole days, a Saturday and Sunday.

We had already sold our adjacent acreage, but the purchaser of our house had trouble getting financing. The economy was in a slump, and, rather than to put ourselves off schedule, we accepted a mortgage larger than we had anticipated. The closing was on October 16. It took two full days—until 10:00 P.M. on the second one—to load the huge moving van that would transport all our things to New Mexico. Isabelle's pale blue Volkswagen squareback, which I am still driving, became part of the load, and it looked tiny once it was inside. The neighbors prepared dinner for us, but we ate separately so that one or the other of us would constantly be on hand to guide the moving men when necessary. A week or so previously a large number of our friends and neighbors had assembled in a home across the lake to bid us fond farewell.

With the house empty, we went to the Holiday Inn in Moorestown for the night. Isabelle would take a limousine from there to the Philadelphia Airport where she would enplane for Denver and then fly on to Albuquerque. Neither of us thought she could stand the roughly 2,000-mile drive. Kevin Cleary and I undertook that, and, by dint of keeping at it for long hours and with one of us napping on the wide backseat while the other drove, we managed to reach our destination in an incredible three days.

At last Isabelle and I were ready to begin our new life in the Southwest. But what an exhausting spring and summer we had endured getting everything taken care of before we could move!

I had finally left the Philadelphia Zoological Garden, which had been a dominant part of my life for almost four decades. My main concerns now were Isabelle and getting our new home in order, but I did look back, now and then, to the difficult early years, the renaissance, and our various accomplishments. After we were well established in our new and pleasant home in Albuquerque, I occasionally laid awake at night, and my mind would drift back over my long career in the zoo business. The Twin Brook Zoo had been my springboard, and the Toledo Zoo gave me six years of valuable training. It was at Philadelphia, however, that I really could expand and put my enthusiasm to work. I had played an important role helping to resuscitate that ailing institution, and in dreaming up ways of popularizing it, thus bringing in much-needed revenue.

I had served under three administrations, including my own, and during the terms of four board presidents, each unique and resourceful in his own way. I had helped wherever and whenever I could. I had written speeches, reports, and other assignments for Dr. Cadwalader, Mr. Cheston, and especially Zoo Director Shelly. I had counseled all of them, openly when requested, but sometimes subtly when, in my professional opinion, they were making mistakes that might be detrimental to them and the rest of us. I had especially done my best for Shelly, a lonely man who was often unsure of himself. I had featured him every time I could in our zoo publications. I arranged an elaborate celebration for his twenty-fifth anniversary at the zoo that kept him busy and in the public eye all day long. When it was over, he thanked me, and he was kind enough to remark that someone should have thought of my twenty-fifth, which had occurred about a year earlier but passed unnoticed. The possibility of featuring such events seldom occurred to anyone else. I had to be the behind-the-scenes mover and shaker.

I saw myself as the power behind the throne. Although I was not in command, I was the one who initiated and implemented many things that contributed to the zoo's popularity and growth. In retrospect, I realized I had a large part in making it once again one of the world's great zoological gardens. I had done my best, and that, to me, was my greatest achievement. How proud I had been, however, when the zoo board literally forced me to take the top job. And how wonderful it was that I, almost single-handedly, brought about the erection of the educational center and administration building that made it possible for me to fulfill my decades-long ambition to establish a real, honest-to-goodness educational program.

I guessed, during my nocturnal musings, that maybe, after all my hard work, I had really accomplished a few useful things during my long zoo career.

Chapter 52

Twilight

We loved our new home in the Southwest. It was a ranch-style house. No stairs to climb. Only two steps upward to enter it. We had a spacious backyard that was still large even after our new fireproof library had been erected in it. Like all the adjacent properties, the yard was surrounded by a cinder-block wall just high enough to ensure privacy. We were in a quiet neighborhood that had been designed so that no through traffic could enter it. Yet, a bank, a grocery store, and the huge Coronado Shopping Center were only three or four blocks away. We soon knew we had chosen wisely and well.

The huge moving van that contained virtually all our goods and chattels was delayed by flat tires and a minor accident that, fortunately, did no harm to our possessions. It required a week to make the trip, which was a real help, because that gave us time to make a few preparations. Isabelle washed shelves and the bathrooms and unpacked the few household items that had come out by car with me. I busied myself with an unexpected chore. The builders had done a marvelous job with the library, but the thick concrete ceiling slab, which had been cast in place, had a layer of powder on its undersurface. I took a broom to it and raised such a dust storm that I choked as I made my way into the library to turn on the built-in exhaust fan. After sweeping away all the dust that would come loose, I left for the hardware store to buy sealer and paint. Meanwhile, Isabelle borrowed a stepladder for me from one of our new neighbors. Oh, my aching arms, even with a roller! I finished a double sealer coat before the van arrived, and I also drew lines on the floor with chalk, marking the exact places where all the heavy items should be placed—tall steel bookcases, correspondence files, an old safe, and a large map cabinet.

We were soon settled in. All my books and the many bottles full of preserved snakes made the trip safely. There was much to do in the house and yard, of course, and we were mystified as we kept finding empty liquor bottles tucked here and there in out-of-the-way places. We soon learned that the former owner, a widow, was an alcoholic. She had agreed to stay on in the house until we arrived, paying us a small token rent. She didn't. The house had been painted and slicked up when it was offered for sale, but, once we had bought it, all housekeeping ceased. For example, the lint in the dryer had not been removed since heaven knows when, and the exhaust system was packed tight with it. That was a minor matter, however. Bill Degenhardt found a graduate student and his wife who needed a place to stay. They moved in, cleaned up the pigpen, and earned our gratitude for putting our house back into livable condition.

We also loved our land in the mountains. Almost immediately after we bought it in 1971, we had to hasten back to the East, so we had no real chance to explore it. So, the next time we were in Albuquerque we were as eager and restless in our motel beds as a couple of kids waiting for Santa Claus. We were up betimes to see our new "toy," and when we discovered mistletoe growing on the trees—well, Christmas Ridge it was ever afterward.

With the aid of a topographical map we learned that we owned half a mile of limestone ridge with a maximum elevation in excess of 7,000 feet. Most of the property was clothed with juniper and pinyon pine, but we also had a mountain meadow sloping down from the crest, and it was bordered at one edge by a "gold mine." That's stretching things a bit, but the land was prospected for uranium after World War II, and we picked up amethysts and topazes (not of gem quality) in the tailings. It was in Torrance County, New Mexico, which had a population density of 1.6 persons per square mile, in contrast with New Jersey's almost 1,000. From the spot where we thought it might be nice to build a small cabin or set up a used trailer, we could see three mountain ranges, including the Sandias with their 10,000-foot crests. What a wonderful playground. I was all over it from one corner to the other, and Isabelle accompanied me, except where there was rock climbing to do. She still tired easily.

She stayed behind at the car one spring Sunday when graduate student James S. Jacob and his wife, Angela, were with us. The two young people and I followed a rocky cliff that rose a short distance away from our property. We were hoping to find rattlesnakes, but Jim suddenly said, "Well, look at this!" We did, and there, in a small crypt in the rock wall, less than 20 feet from us, was a full-grown bobcat standing stock still, except for jerking its tail ever so gently. None of us, of course, had a camera. We watched for a full five minutes. We turned our backs, then I whirled around instantly, or so I thought, but the cat had vanished and was not seen again. Some weeks later, Isabelle and I were returning from Christmas Ridge in midafternoon by a route different from our usual one, when another adult bobcat crossed the road in front of us and leisurely walked down a nearby open arroyo. We had just as good a look at it as we did at several lions when we were in Africa. We often heard coyotes yelping in chorus, and we found evidence of porcupines and badgers on our property, but the most exciting and gratifying discovery was the relative abundance of the short-horned lizards, *Phrynosoma douglasii*. It was truly a wonderful place, and very different from the flat, sandy New Jersey Pine Barrens.

We learned that the taxes were delinquent on the 5 acres we bought some time after acquiring our original 65. Before we left the East I had great fun telling our friends and neighbors about it. I would say, slowly and deliberately, "We had to pay a delinquent tax fine on five acres of our mountain property out in New Mexico, and it cost us 68 [here a carefully timed pause] cents." It was delightful to see the amazement on their faces. Such a ridiculously small amount was unbelievable.

At least once a week in warm, dry weather we drove to Christmas Ridge for a picnic lunch. It was only 28 miles from home through beautiful Tijeras (Scissors) Canyon and then across upland meadows where we invariably saw mountain bluebirds, those exquisite symbols of happiness. The climb up the rough, rocky road to the crest of our ridge was the only difficult 100 yards of the entire trip. I cleared a shady parking space on our property, and from there we hiked off in all directions.

Once we had settled into our new environment, we counted our blessings. First, I had gained a full day each week. It had taken me an hour, and sometimes much longer, to commute from our home to the zoo and then another hour or more to get back. Multiply that by five days, and I was spending a minimum of 10 hours a week fighting traffic. What a relief to escape from that rat race.

Second, we were both free from deadlines, appointments, and other demands on our time, mine especially. We could set our own pace and do as we pleased. What a marvelous change for the better.

Third, by subscribing by mail to the "Albuquerque Journal" a full year before we moved, we knew we were

in a pleasant dry climate where the humidity was far lower than in the East, and where it often dropped below 10 percent, sometimes even below 5 percent. The winters were mild, except for an occasional brief cold spell. What little snow there was quickly melted when the sun came out, except in shaded places. Summer temperatures of 100°F were rarities, but the low humidity made them tolerable. Also, during clear weather, it often dropped 30 degrees at night, which made for good sleeping. Our house checked in at 5,500 feet, slightly more than the "mile high" advertised by Denver.

Most important of all, we had a full year together that we would have missed if I had not taken an early retirement. Isabelle and I had spent a lot of time alone together, especially on my days off and when we were traveling, but now we had each other all day, every day. How truly marvelous.

There was a fiscal problem, however, with which we had to contend. We were short of cash. A year before my retirement I had to state my preferences regarding my pension. Should it be structured so that a large portion of it would remain for Isabelle if I should predecease her? And did I want my payments to begin as soon as I retired at age 64, but at a much lower rate than if I waited until I was 65? These were problems that all zoo employees eligible for pensions had to face. No one can predict the future or foresee possible fatal accidents, so making the decision was a gamble. We talked it over at length and with great care. Isabelle's recent operation had given us a sharp warning, but she insisted that the full amount should go to me. Otherwise, my pension (*ours* as long as we both survived) would be much lower. In essence, she was telling me she probably wouldn't live as long as I would. She was several years ahead of me in the journey through life. Also, she knew that if she became ill or incapacitated, I would never desert her.

When I was 30 years old, all four of my grandparents were still living, and their ages, when they eventually died, were 97, 93, 92, and 84. So we knew that I probably had inherited considerable longevity. We decided to delay my pension until I was 65. The zoo's business manager thought I was crazy, and didn't hesitate to tell me so: "It will take you 10 years to get caught up. Start when you're 64 and get all that's coming to you." Now that I am in my late 80s, I most assuredly have won the bet. The zoo board made me a consultant at a dollar a year, which meant that I retained my major medical health insurance under the zoo's group policy during my sixty-fifth year. Isabelle was already on Medicare.

We had other resources, some of which we could use, but there were others, including a sizable tax-deferred annuity I had accumulated, that we didn't want to touch. At my request, the zoo had been paying part of my salary into it for a number of years. So we avoided all the expenses we could, lived frugally, and depended on the royalties from our field guide. That was not quite enough, so we began cashing government bonds, one of which we had purchased each month for quite a few years. The financial pressure ended when I turned 65, and began receiving my Social Security and my pension, both at the same time.

We had another, totally unnecessary problem. The Houghton Mifflin Company, publisher of our field guide, had a brand-new copy editor, and she was assigned to work on the text we had delivered to them in September 1973. For some unknown reason, maybe because she thought it was expected of her, she proceeded to rewrite virtually all of my copy. For example, she changed place-names, and I had to photocopy pages from the postal register to send to her proving that my spellings were correct. She made unintelligible messes of some of my sentences. She quibbled about inconsequential details. In short, I had to fight with her every step of the way, making her put everything back virtually the way I had it originally. She did find a few misspellings and minor errors, and for that I was grateful, but the waste of my time was infuriating. Matters were so bad that I telephoned her boss in Boston and protested. He was sympathetic, but he told me to keep on going. They wanted a book that was as letter-perfect as possible. Time did not matter. They were in no rush to get the book on the market. That at least boosted my morale, but the net result was that it required 22 months for the field guide to go through the press, from the date of submission to the actual publication. In contrast, the first edition passed "through the mill" in just half that time— 11 months. I never learned what happened, but not too long after our second edition was in print, the copy editor was no longer with Houghton Mifflin. Isabelle, of course, worked right with me, cross-checking copy and, later, reading both galley and page proofs.

We didn't lack for friends in Albuquerque. There was my Toledo pal of long ago, Barney Gardner, and his wife, Virginia, and Bill and Paula Degenhardt. The faculty and graduate students in the Biology Department at the University of New Mexico welcomed me, and many of us became good friends. So did several of the neighbors. There were also the Bogerts, Chuck and his wife, Mickey, who lived in Santa Fe.

It took us awhile, however, to build up our personal staff, something that every couple or family needs. First, we had to find a good doctor. The Gardners recommended Thomas B. Gibbons, M.D., who was accustomed to caring for older patients. He became a good

friend, and he and I quickly were on a first-name basis. The real estate agent who sold us both our home and Christmas Ridge suggested a good accounting firm, and they, in turn, directed us to an excellent attorney. The agent at Northwest Mutual Life, which held both my annuity and my life insurance policies, was very helpful. He pointed out that my library, which had appreciated considerably in value over the years, should be willed to some eleemosynary organization. If I did not do so, my 10,000 reprints of scientific papers might be evaluated by the Internal Revenue Service at a dollar or more each, thus adding considerably both to the amount of my estate and to the taxes to be paid on it. We had soon accumulated our circle of helpers and we knew who to call when we needed a plumber, electrician, painter, or appliance repair man.

Isabelle seemed to be improving in the dry climate. Also, she had the stimuli of a new home, a new environment, and a complete change in our lifestyle. She was even able to help me switch a pair of the heavy (but still empty) steel bookcases in the library. One of them suffered minor damage in moving, and we thought it best to put the scars out of sight. She reveled in that experience and wrote in her diary, "It's great to be a 'Powerful Katrinka' again." We had high hopes for her complete recovery, although there were days when she didn't feel well. Nonetheless, she kept up the housework while our cash was low, and she vacuumed, dusted, and took care of other necessitities on a regular and frequent basis.

Our first winter in the Southwest passed pleasantly. We visited and often had meals back and forth with our many friends. We were invited out for Thanksgiving and New Year's dinners, but, on the day we had celebrated so enthusiastically for decades, we decided to take it easy and to pay a visit to Christmas Ridge as an appropriate gesture. The weather turned bad, unfortunately, so we stayed home and enjoyed a fine, big steak, a welcome relief from turkey.

I visited the university frequently, did considerable research on my snakes, and developed a rapport with several of the graduate students. In the meantime, the copyedited script for the field guide began coming back piecemeal. I plunged into the unwelcome chore of putting it back the way I submitted it, and I took pleasure in bombarding the editor with letters and documents showing how wrong she was.

One thing Isabelle and I had planned for our retirement was to visit as many of the western national parks and monuments as possible. We had seen most of the eastern ones, but the West was peppered with them. We set off for Durango, Colorado, on May 28, 1974, stayed in a motel, and spent the next day exploring Mesa Verde

National Park. It was all very interesting, especially the spectacular cliff dwellings, but by early afternoon Isabelle had tired so much that she preferred to stay in the car to look at things from a distance, while I got out for a closer view. Our return trip took us to the Four Corners Monument, where four states all come together, the only such point in the entire country. We could stand in Utah, Colorado, Arizona, and New Mexico atop the sturdy horizontal plaque set firmly in concrete at the exact spot. We then turned south past the towering Shiprock and through the Navajo Reservation to Gallup, where we stayed overnight.

By the time we were home Isabelle was not feeling well. For the next few days she puttered around as best she could but slept much of the time. I, in my amateur way, took over the culinary duties. A good idea, I found, was to visit fast-food restaurants and bring home our suppers. On June 4 she was so sick that I called Dr. Gibbons and took her to his office. He checked her pulse, which was racing, listened to her lungs, and told me to take her at once to the hospital. We were not to go home first, not even for her nightie or toothbrush. She had pneumonia, and she had quite a stay before she was discharged. I spent most of every day with her, but I went home to sleep. She was delirious one night and telephoned me in the small hours of the morning to make sure I knew where she was. Early during her hospitalization, tests were made to determine which antibiotics should be used. Several other tests were made simultaneously. Tom Gibbons, a conscientious physician, sat down and studied all the results. He asked me to come to his office. He stunned me by telling me, as gently as possible, that the tests indicated that Isabelle had multiple myeloma, or cancer of the bone marrow. So that damned, dreadful disease had metastasized after all. As I held back the tears with great difficulty, I asked him what the prognosis was. He referred us to the only oncologist in the city, but a man who had a good reputation. Chemotherapy would doubtless help.

I went home, broke down, and cried harder and longer than I ever had since childhood. I needed a full hour to compose myself before I could go back to my beloved sweetheart at the hospital.

The specialist confirmed the multiple myeloma. There was no question that he knew his business, but he was a cocky little man who thought nothing of keeping a room full of elderly patients waiting for hours on uncomfortable chairs to suit his convenience. He was merely annoying at first, but Isabelle soon grew to despise him and invented an unflattering nickname for him. Nonetheless, we respected his ability, and, in the final analysis, we had no one else to whom we could turn.

We were told there were three procedures available in the way of chemotherapy that could be employed, one after the other. We never learned their names, but the first one the doctor used was the most effective. For it to function, however, Isabelle's blood levels had to be built up in advance. In part that would be accomplished by medication, in part by blood transfusions. Once she had taken a course of treatment she perked up and, whereas she was not strong and continued to tire easily, she led a more or less normal life. She drove her car and often went shopping alone, and for a while we were quite encouraged. I was able to leave her occasionally in order to fly east to see my elderly mother and other members of the family. While I was at it, I paid visits to various museums to gather information on their holdings of herpetological material from the Delmarva Peninsula and New Jersey. During my first trip or two, Isabelle telephoned one of our kind neighbors every morning at 8:30 to report that she was OK. Eventually, I hired carefully selected helpers to stay in the house at night with her while I was gone. I kept in touch by telephone every other evening.

During periods when she was feeling better, I even managed to make a few field trips down into Mexico with some of the students, and also with Isabelle's great-niece, Sue, and her husband, Peter Brooks. They had never been in Mexico, and we had a three-night camping trip, which they thought was great fun. When I was in Albuquerque, I either stayed home or told Isabelle exactly where I was going so she could call me in any emergency. For exercise, I constructed an elaborate cactus garden in our yard, using large blocks of limestone that I hauled down from along one of the roads leading up to Christmas Ridge, which we continued to visit at frequent intervals.

Eventually, the first type of treatment lost its effectiveness, and the doctor shifted to the second, but it apparently was worthless in her case. He had to move on to the third and last. With Isabelle's bone marrow involved, her immune system was seriously affected. She was susceptible to all sorts of infections, and that became quickly evident whenever she began to feel weak and poorly in general. Then it was back to the hospital, where the doctors, Thomas B. Gibbons among them, pulled her through, and she would feel good again. In time, she seemed to be hospitalized almost at monthly intervals, yet in between times she was cheerful and kept going as best she could. I had hired a cleaning lady to come every week as soon as Isabelle first became sick, and later I engaged a part-time housekeeper who also could cook. Through it all, Isabelle's mind remained clear. Her eyes were bright, her ears were keen, and her voice was as strong as ever. When she talked by telephone with friends or relatives in the East they could scarcely believe how sick she was. The stereotype of an ill person is one with a weak and feeble voice. The big change was in her appearance. She aged 20 years in 2, and when we managed to attend the international zoo conference (IUDZG) in Colorado Springs in 1975, many of our friends scarcely recognized her.

There were two highlights that she enjoyed immensely. One was our acquisition of a cute, coal-black little peekapoo, a cross between a poodle and a Pekingese. Her name was Sugar, and she became imprinted on Isabelle and was her constant companion. In fact, when I left on one of my trips to Mexico, Isabelle was holding Sugar. I kissed my wife good-bye and the dog bit me, I guess because she thought I was attacking her mistress.

Isabelle's seventy-fifth birthday was on May 17, 1976, and I decided to do it up brown, just as I had with so many events at the zoo some years previously. I sent notes to people we knew requesting a "card shower," and I arranged, with the help of some of the students, for a reception at our home in the afternoon for the neighbors and other guests. Here is what she wrote about it in her diary: "My 75th birthday—a beautiful, sunny, warm day. More than 80 people (80!) sent me cards. We had an open house in the afternoon and about 40 people came and went. We served beer and soft drinks, dips, crackers, snacks, etc. Phyllis [one of the neighbors] made me a 3-tier birthday cake decorated with rosebuds and squiggles. It was a memorable occasion and I enjoyed it very much. Also I felt quite well."

In preparation for the party she hand-printed two large, colorful signs to display in the house. They read "Thank You for Not Smoking Indoors" and "Ashtrays Outdoors." The card shower was a success, not only in quantity but also in quality. Those of our friends who were artists even made special cards and drawings for her. It was, without a doubt, the most glorious day of the twilight that was descending upon us.

Our trips to see the oncologist continued. One morning after the usual long wait in his office, we entered his inner sanctum and discovered that he had a bad cold. He was seeing terminally ill patients, some of them apparently far worse than Isabelle, but he never thought to wear a surgical mask to protect them. Isabelle, of course, caught his cold immediately and she was soon back in the hospital. We added the word "stupid" to our description of him.

November 2, 1976, was election day. Gerald Ford and Jimmy Carter were running for president. We went to the poll and voted, and then we were off to a supermarket with our part-time cook and housekeeper to buy a week's supply of food. Isabelle's morale was good. She

was bright and cheerful all day. In the evening while we were watching the election returns, however, she suddenly screamed and began moaning loudly. Her right arm hurt her terribly. It was the very first time during her long illness that she had felt any pain. Examination revealed a large, ugly red blotch on her upper right arm, near the middle of the humerus. I gave her the prescribed sedative as often as allowed, but she was in pain all night. No more sudden dreadful onsets, but a nasty, constant ache. I catnapped on the couch in her bedroom, but we were both awake most of the time. To comfort her, I snuggled in bed with her, as we did daily, but it only aggravated her pain whenever I touched the right side of her body.

At dawn I called an ambulance, and I rode beside the driver to the hospital. They reached the specialist by telephone well before 8:00 A.M., but he didn't come ambling in until after 9:30. In the meantime, the effects of the sedative had worn off and she was in acute pain. Without even attempting to lower his voice or to take me aside, he announced, "There's nothing I can do except to give her a shot." What a thoughtless jackass! She heard him clearly. The shot was a strong one, because she never regained full consciousness. In the hall I asked the little man what caused the red blotch on her arm. His blunt reply was, "Her arm broke, and all her other long bones will also break." In short, she would become a vegetable, but she was spared that dreadful indignity. She died in my arms during the afternoon.

What ghastly thoughts passed through my mind during those final hours. In my bitter agony I couldn't help but think, "Chalk up another victim for the greedy tobacco trust!" Ever since her operation in 1972 she had lived with the knowledge that she had shortened her life and greatly reduced its quality by being a slave to nicotine. I thought of the good times we had together, of how hard we had worked, and of all the far places we had visited. She had been a crucial part of my life. I had dedicated the second edition of our field guide to her, but I owed her far more than that. Without her love, backing, and companionship, I would have fallen far short of accomplishing all the many things I did. She was indeed my soul mate and dearly beloved wife. I mourned her deeply, and, even now, two decades after her death, I still miss her and think of her every day.

Isabelle's body was cremated, but she meant so very much to me that I couldn't just let her death go unnoticed. So I arranged for a memorial service at a funeral home on November 6, 1976. Dr. Clifford S. Crawford, Chairman of the Department of Biology at the University of New Mexico, very kindly agreed to read her eulogy. I assembled facts about her life for him, typing them while peering through a veil of tears. He put my sentences into his own words and added several things of his own. Some 60 people were present, a truly remarkable number, I thought, considering the short time we had lived in Albuquerque. From a secluded room where I could see but was invisible to those in attendance, I listened and silently wept. Angela Jacob held one of my hands, and Sally Litwin, a graduate student whom both Isabelle and I admired, held the other. Under the title "The Passing of a Great Lady," this is what Professor Crawford had to say:

Isabelle dePeyster Hunt, a lineal descendant of Johannus dePeyster, the first Burgomaster of Manhattan, was born to wealth in Staten Island, New York. Such virtually now extinct species as in-servants, including a governess for the two children, cared for the family's every need. Isabelle grew up in a tradition of grace and leisure, attended a private school, and was educated and groomed to be a lady in the full concept of the word Lady *as it was held by society in those days.*

When she was an adolescent, financial reverses struck the family and they eventually were reduced to humble circumstances. Their problem was complicated by a stroke that incapacitated Isabelle's father. There was no such thing as applying for Relief from federal agencies in those days and, even if there had been, the family would have been far too proud to accept something they would have considered as charity. So she went to work, and eventually served as a reporter for the "Staten Island Advance," a daily newspaper. Because of her contacts among the still wealthy people of the community she soon became Society Editor and for a long time was the paper's bridge expert. In 1936, after the Staten Island Zoo was founded, she accepted a position with it as Business Manager and Publicity Director. There she made such a name for herself that she was a leading contender for a vacancy that existed, for a photographer and publicity assistant, at the much larger Philadelphia Zoo, with which Dr. Conant was long associated. Roger, with a smile on his face, once told me that it was almost by accident that he chose her over several male candidates. World War II was then sapping the country's manpower, and he reasoned that a woman would be far less vulnerable and could carry on in his absence if he were drafted into some sort of war-related activity.

Again using his language, "After working together daily for four or five years and getting used to each other's idiosyncrasies we decided we could make a go of it around the clock." They would have celebrated their thirtieth wedding anniversary next spring, and theirs has been a truly solid and loving marriage.

Isabelle Hunt was without a doubt the perfect partner for Roger. She was his alter ego and constant companion, not only in their daily activities, but also in their travels through all 48 conterminous states, to Europe several times, and to East and South Africa. During the many long field trips that took them into every state in Mexico, she cheerfully assumed the arduous task of keeping the camp running and doing all the catering so her husband could spend the absolute maximum of time seeking the reptiles and amphibians he needed for his studies. She carried the same devotion into their home where she kept everything in order and was constantly planning ahead. For example, the very day before she died, she went shopping briefly with Roger, and she urged that they get on with plans for their annual unique holiday greeting card. She also wrapped and labelled, with the intended recipients' names, the cranberry sauce she had made and which she intended as Christmas gifts for many of her good friends in Albuquerque.

This wonderful lady's greatest contribution was made with her camera and talented artist's pen. She accepted her assignment as the Philadelphia Zoo's photographer with enthusiasm, and she dressed in slacks so she could climb into cages for close-ups of the animals, and that was in a day when such garb for working women was severely frowned upon. Her pictures helped to make the Zoo famous as one of the best and largest in the world. She made the wire many times, a term used in newspaper parlance for outstanding photographs that are sent by wire to publications all over the nation. Through it all she worked under difficult conditions in a miserable darkroom with no air conditioning during sultry Philadelphia summers and often under great pressure to meet deadlines. An indication of the esteem with which she was held by the Philadelphia press photographers corps was their frequent requests for her help even to the point, on several occasions, of asking her to take pictures for them. Some were afraid of the animals.

In the field of herpetology she and Roger, over a period of many years, amassed an unsurpassed collection of nearly 10,000 black-and-white photographs of reptiles and amphibians. Prints were made available free of charge to their colleagues, and as a result her beautiful portraits of these interesting animals have graced a large number of technical publications. I think that most, if not all, of us are familiar with the colossal task she undertook and so successfully completed for their "Field Guide to Reptiles and Amphibians."

Isabelle was raised to be a lady in the traditional sense, but despite many difficulties she became a lady of great talent and renown, as a professional and distinguished artist, to say nothing of her love and devotion to her husband and her family. She was never a mother, but she was the patient and revered "auntie" and "Nanabelle" of many nieces and nephews and step-granddaughters as well as scores of youngsters who grew to love and respect her.

She was a lady to the last, and after Roger told her a week or so ago that I had offered to conduct this memorial service, she sent me a most gracious note thanking me for the great favor I would be doing them.

To me, talking about her and sketching her accomplishments has been a real privilege, despite the sadness of the occasion. Isabelle dePeyster Hunt Conant was truly a Great Lady who made her mark in the world.

Chapter 53

The Promise

Isabelle's life was over, and so, it seemed, was mine. Gone was my warm, affectionate, and constant companion of three decades. Gone was my alter ego (the "other I" by dictionary definition), the one I had consulted about everything from trivia to serious problems. Gone was the one person I trusted implicitly, a feeling that was mutually shared.

I scarcely slept my first few nights as a widower. My mind was constantly on my staggering loss. It was true that Isabelle had been ill physically for a long time, but her mind was keen and alert to the very end, and we could still talk about all kinds of things. Now the house was silent. I thought of how much she had accomplished, and of how enormously I was indebted to her. Several times as I tossed in bed I recalled what she had said to a group of students in my presence just a few days previously: "When I go, it's going to be awfully hard on Roger." She had never spoken truer words. I felt lost and crushed.

The neighbors, many of the students, and the Barney Gardners rallied round, and I was invited out to dinners and lunches. I plunged into my research on the herpetology of New Jersey, the Delmarva Peninsula, and adjacent areas, which I had kept up for decades despite my preoccupation with the Philadelphia Zoological Garden and the work on our "Field Guide to Reptiles and Amphibians." When I concentrated on the research, I could put aside my anguish, but the moment I stopped it all came rushing back.

I took care at once, of course, of necessities, preeminent among them notifying a host of friends about her death. The telephone, with friends doing the calling for me, was used in several cases, but otherwise the news was largely dispatched by mail. We had been preparing our highly personalized holiday greeting, and the envelopes for sending it had already been printed. With the help of a student they were addressed, and I inserted a copy of the "in memory" folder furnished by the funeral home, which also included Tennyson's "Crossing the Bar." Most of the few hundred recipients thought they were getting our annual card, only to discover that our familiar envelope brought sad news instead. There was an immediate outpouring of messages of sympathy, and, for weeks, I received a dozen or more daily. There were innumerable expressions of love and admiration for Isabelle. One of the communications that I best recall came from Bill Duellman, who commented that he would always remember the middle-aged couple who attended herpetological meetings and other events arm-in-arm or hand-in-hand like a couple of newly wedded youngsters. Another touching tribute was a large bouquet of flowers and a special card from the Philadelphia News Photographers Association, in gratitude to Isabelle for all the help she had given them years earlier when she was the zoo's official photographer.

The flood of messages finally did me in. I had to get away from the house with all its poignant reminders of my beloved wife. I thought of flying to the East to visit my son and daughter-in-law, but there were nubile granddaughters at the time whose comings and goings were doubtless keeping their home in a state of bedlam. What I needed was peace and quiet, and not a little morale building. Among those who were notified of Isabelle's death by telephone were the Gloyds, in Tucson. When Howard Gloyd heard the news, he choked up and was unable to speak, so his pretty and charming wife, Kathryn, took over. I managed to talk with her briefly without breaking down, and she graciously told me to let them know if there was anything they could do for me.

When I had to escape from the scene of my sorrow, I telephoned the Gloyds and asked if I could visit them for a week or so. The answer was an emphatic *yes*. So I packed my bag, left the house in the care of Ana Guevara, a student whom Isabelle liked very much, and flew to Tucson.

Dr. Howard K. Gloyd was undoubtedly my closest professional colleague. We had first met during 1929 or 1930, when he was a graduate student at the University of Michigan and I was the curator of reptiles at the Toledo Zoo. Our rapport developed rapidly as we visited back and forth. In our youthful enthusiasm we envisioned

Dr. Howard K. Gloyd holding a preserved hundred-pace viper in his laboratory at the University of Arizona. Photo by Donald B. Sayner.

preparing a monograph on the snake genus *Agkistrodon*, which includes the copperhead, cottonmouth, and the cantil of Middle America, as well as a number of species in Asia. He was already working on the rattlesnakes, the subject of his doctoral dissertation, which, in expanded form, later appeared as the classic book "The Rattlesnakes, Genera *Sistrurus* and *Crotalus*." We published several papers together over a period of a few years, but my departure for the Philadelphia Zoo in 1935, and his in 1936, to become Director of the Chicago Academy of Sciences, caused our project to slow to a crawl. By the time he left Chicago in 1958, to join the faculty of the University of Arizona, I was swamped with zoo responsibilities, so I withdrew from the project. Nonetheless, I kept in frequent touch with him, sending him data and even live specimens, some of which fortuitously arrived at the zoo from Korea. With the aid of grants from the National Science Foundation, he forged ahead with the work on his own, aided by his students. He accumulated an enormous data bank of tens of thousands of file cards while he carefully indexed

the literature on *Agkistrodon*. There were also thousands of scale-count data sheets. All were typed or written by hand. (There were no computers in those days.)

We knew the Gloyds well, and the last trip Isabelle and I made together was to visit them in Arizona early in 1976.

When I arrived in Tucson I was warmly welcomed. It was good to see my old friends again, but Howard obviously was in trouble. He did not look well, and he seemed tired and listless. I soon learned that he was suffering from bone cancer which, as the doctors put it, affected every bone in his body. It was devastating to find my esteemed colleague so sick and with such a heartbreaking prognosis. He had to rest a lot, but we reminisced about old times, and, in an effort to cheer me up, he and Kathryn (Kay) played some of his fine collection of Dixieland records for me. They knew that I, as they did, enjoyed such happy music and that I had loved to play it myself in days long gone. In their presence, my personal grief was mercifully suppressed, at least for the time being.

After some hesitation, I found the courage to ask Howard how he was coming with the *Agkistrodon* monograph. He replied, "I'll never be able to finish it." Then I inquired how much he had completed, and his answer was, "About 90 percent." To that I responded, "I'll finish it for you." I was not prepared for his reaction. He broke down and cried, but his tears were of relief. His hard work of many decades would not die with him. He knew I was capable of bringing the project to a successful conclusion, and that I would do my best to complete it.

That promise, although I didn't know it at the time, was to turn my whole life around.

The next day, Howard, or H.K., as we affectionately called him, began talking with me about *Agkistrodon* in detail, but he tired so quickly that we could pursue the topic for only an hour or so at a time. While he rested, I began to read his manuscript; before I flew back to Albuquerque I had perused it all.

At the end of January I returned to Tucson for a long stay, during which I concentrated on getting started with many ancillary items, such as setting up tables to summarize the scale counts, preparing a checklist and keys for the identification of the various taxa, constructing a glossary, and pressing on with several other facets to which H.K. had given much thought but had not yet committed to paper. I urged him to assemble a list of persons who had helped him, so their names would not be omitted from the acknowledgments. Also, we talked at length about the manuscript itself and the proposed illustrations.

In the midst of my visit we celebrated his seventy-fifth birthday, for which he received a shower of scores of cards, some of them elaborate original artwork. He suspected my fine Italian hand, and I confided to Kathryn that I had written to all of his friends I could think of, reminding them of the milestone in his life and pointing out that he was sick.

It quickly became apparent that Kay was worn out and operating on her nerve, so to speak. Not only was she taking care of H.K., but she also had her elderly parents to supervise. She had induced her father and mother to move to Tucson where she could keep an eye on them. Her father had bought a small condominium a few years earlier but, by the time I arrived, he and Kay's mother had gone to live in a protective care home. Both had been ill and required Kay's personal attention. Her mother died on the last day of February.

It was quite obvious that I shouldn't add to Kay's burden by being a guest in their house, but all three of us realized that time was of the essence, and that H.K. and I should consult together as much as possible. He had his ups and downs and was hospitalized off and on. So on my next trips to Tucson I stayed at a motel, and used H.K.'s car for transportation. To save me from that considerable expense, however, Kay persuaded her father to let me use his condominium, which I eventually bought from him. I took Isabelle's small car to Tucson, but commuted back and forth by air. I finally had a base in Arizona.

In the early spring the Gloyds flew up to Albuquerque to pay me a visit of several days, and they went with me to inter Isabelle's ashes, in a burial urn, in the cemetery where mine will join hers one of these days. During their visit I arranged for H.K. to have quiet chats of not more than an hour with students and colleagues. He greatly enjoyed talking about pit vipers, his favorite topic.

Stimulated by my reentry into the project, H.K. completed and published a paper he had long contemplated, in which he described four new taxa of the *Agkistrodon* complex from Asia. His erection of *Deinagkistrodon* as a new generic name for the hundred-pace viper of China and Taiwan was published posthumously, but he saw and approved the final proof. Also, he saw the advance flyer announcing the republication of his classic work on the rattlesnakes, by the Society for the Study of Amphibians and Reptiles, although the book did not appear until after his death.

The year 1977 was punctuated by two near disasters for me. First, Ana Guevara, who was living in my house, telephoned in early May to say she had surprised a burglar during the afternoon. He had put on the safety chain inside the front door, thus blocking anyone from entering, but the noise she made trying to get in alerted the intruder, and he escaped through the

RC examining copperheads in the herpetology range at the University of New Mexico in 1982. Student photo.

bedroom window he had jimmied to enter. He had taken only my best bolo ties and a small turquoise necklace of hers. I had my 1976 Volkswagen campmobile in Tucson at the time, so I started home early the next morning, and drove the entire distance in one day, some 465 miles, instead of stopping for the night in Deming en route. It was well that I persevered, because about 10:00 P.M. I discovered that a man was working on the front door lock, and a large truck was backed into my driveway. I switched on the porch light, the would-be burglar ran to the truck, jumped in, and it raced off down the street as though the devil himself were after its occupants.

I called the police, but they could do nothing about a drab, unidentifiable truck with its license plate covered. What a frightful shock it would have been if I had arrived home to find an empty house!

How lucky I was to have foiled the robbery. Isabelle's heirloom heavy sterling silver tableware, beautifully crafted and at least 100 years old, was worth several thousand dollars alone. It was at the time when the Hunt brothers were trying to corner the silver market, and the value of the metal was exceptionally high. I shipped the 12-place setting to Isabelle's great-niece, Susanna Brooks, so as to keep it in their family.

After getting estimates and weighing the advantages and disadvantages of a burglar alarm system, I arranged to have heavy steel grilles placed over all the doors, windows, and skylight. Escape hatches were provided in the bedrooms and kitchen in case of fire. I felt, of course, as though I were living in a prison, but it had its advantages. I knew that my house would be safe while I was away, and today, with hooliganism and lawlessness mushrooming, I am glad to spend much of my time inside my own roomy cage.

The other near disaster was more serious, because it involved me, and not property. Late in the year I learned that I had prostate cancer. After a series of tests, I underwent surgery in a Tucson hospital and was then stuffed, seemingly endlessly, with female hormones that eventually forced me to undergo a double mastectomy. Nonetheless, I was grateful to be saved from the prostate scourge that kills so many men. But then I was told that I, too, had bone cancer. The immediate prospect was that I probably would soon be dead. The doctor continued, at regular intervals, to order expensive bone scans, for which Medicare paid, thank goodness. There was no change, and I pressed on as rapidly as I could with the *Agkistrodon* monograph.

Eventually I sought medical counseling in Albuquerque, and, after more scans, the diagnosis of bone cancer was proved to be faulty. I had Paget's disease, a relatively benign ailment for me. Far too many years had passed, however, before I knew that I didn't have a life-threatening problem hanging over me.

In the meantime, I had continued my commuting, flying most of the time, since I had a car in each of the two cities. Dr. Gloyd's health continued to deteriorate, and he was hospitalized several times. I pitched in to help as much as I could. I took care of the Gloyds' yard, serviced their evaporative air cooler, washed windows, made minor repairs, and ran many an errand for which Kay had neither the time nor the energy. When H.K. was in the hospital I took Kay to him every day, and, at his request, picked her up late at night and saw her safely home. I had the feeling that I was needed and wanted, which was the very best way of pulling me out of the deep depression into which I had fallen when Isabelle died.

Howard's terminal hospital stay lasted more than a month, and Kay remained with him the entire time, sleeping on a cot in his room and literally being on 24-hour duty with him. I spelled her daily and stayed with him while she went for short walks around the grounds, when she had a dental emergency, and when she needed to go to the bank or back home for changes of clothing. I fed Kay's cat, monitored their house twice daily, and was on call whenever needed. The end came on August 7, 1978, when H.K. passed quietly away. I remained in Tucson, so Kay would not be alone, until one of her sisters came to keep her company. In the autumn I flew with Kay to Kansas City, rented a car, and drove her to Ottawa, Kansas, which is near the rural cemetery where H.K.'s parents were buried, and where he had requested that we take his remains. Later, Kathryn had a tombstone erected for herself alongside his.

It became obvious that, if I were to press on efficiently, something had to be done to reorganize H.K.'s extensive library and the banks of files and ring binders containing his enormous number of data cards and scale-count sheets. When he retired at age 72 from the faculty of the University of Arizona, everything had been moved to their home, where space was limited. Unhappily, the students who assisted with the transfer managed to make a jumble of the wooden boxes containing his huge reprint collection, instead of arranging them in alphabetical order. Finding a specific paper was a time-consuming chore. My small condominium, which still contained a great many things that belonged to Kay's parents, was totally inadequate to hold everything. So, after consulting with Kay, I bought a much larger condominium, to which she, with tender, loving care, personally transported his library and all the satellite files and records. Eventually she moved in with me. We were married at a quiet ceremony in Albuquerque shortly after Christmas in 1979.

Neither of us had any illusions regarding our relationship. I knew I never could replace H.K. in her memories and affection any more than she could replace Isabelle in mine. With my full consent, she chose to retain the name Kathryn J. Gloyd.

With Kathryn's help, both in looking after me and as a professional science librarian, the *Agkistrodon* monograph was finally finished, and publication was in 1990. H.K. would be proud of it. In fact, he would be astounded if he could see the book of more than 600 pages that bears his name followed by mine. I did a large amount of additional writing and updating, and I considerably expanded the scope of the work. His greatest surprise, however, would be the 33 color plates. He never dreamed there would be even one.

We were proud and happy that such a book had evolved from the enormous data bank he had so painstakingly assembled over a period of decades.

Chapter 54

Off to the Orient

My several trips to the Orient had their roots, incredible though it may seem, in Costa Rica in Central America.

Howard K. Gloyd, my esteemed colleague, had departed from this mortal world and, as I pressed resolutely forward with the monograph on the snake genus *Agkistrodon* and its allies, it became apparent that the cantil, *A. bilineatus*, needed further study. Many more specimens had found their way into museum collections than had been available when Dr. Gloyd prepared his preliminary draft on the species several years earlier. His study culminated, however, in his description of the population from the Yucatan Peninsula as a new subspecies that he called *russeolus* because of the somewhat reddish tinge of the dorsal pattern. He had predicted to me that there might be another race in the far southern part of the cantil's range, which terminates in Costa Rica.

Naturally, I wanted to have a look for myself, and when Louis W. Porras invited me to accompany him and Gordon W. Schuett for a fortnight in Costa Rica, I accepted at once. Louis had been born in San José, he had an intimate knowledge of the herpetofauna of his native land, and he was completely bilingual. He was a perfect guide.

Our visit was during the winter of early 1982, and I was astounded to see, for the first time, what a tropical deciduous forest looked like when all the trees were bare and the annual drought was at its height. In the rainy season it was a veritable jungle, as I had noted when Isabelle and I were in similar habitats along the west coast of Mexico during late summers. The dryness, so apparent in Costa Rica, clinched my belief that the cantil lived only in areas with a lengthy dry season, often of many months' duration. All the localities for the species, when plotted on my work map, fell within or very close to areas that received no rain for extended periods of the year.

We found no cantils during our exploration of the Parque Nacional de Santa Rosa, but Louis returned later during the year and caught an adult male that eventually became the holotype of *Agkistrodon bilineatus howardgloydi*.

A year or so later, when I plotted the locality records for the Malayan pit viper, *Calloselasma rhodostoma*, of southeastern Asia, it became clear that it, too, lived only where there was a dry season. The thought flashed through my mind about how helpful it would be if I could have a look at *its* habitat. If I could manage such an ambitious goal, I definitely also should see something of the places where other members of the complex lived. Then, too, I would have a chance to meet Asian herpetologists. Neither Dr. Gloyd nor I had ever set foot in the Orient, to which many different members of the *Agkistrodon* complex are native. The more I dreamed about a trip to the Far East, the more I wanted to go. Because Louis Porras had been such a stout companion in Costa Rica, I asked him if he would like to accompany me. We made some tentative plans, especially to include Thailand and Sri Lanka en route, and Louis discovered that, if we went right on around the world, the airfare would be considerably cheaper than if we flew directly back home. I began to build up hope, but then Louis sold his business (he was a purveyor of live reptiles) and went west to reestablish himself in Salt Lake City. He was unable to be away for a long period of time. I was keenly disappointed, but I asked Kathryn if she would like to go. She would. Thus began a series of journeys that took the two of us to the Orient four times and to Europe twice before the *Agkistrodon* monograph was published. We became world travelers. I rationalized about the considerable expense, and told myself that I was plowing my royalties from my "Field Guide to Reptiles and Amphibians" back into herpetology.

Our first trip across the Pacific was in 1984, but, before I recount some of our experiences overseas, I should explain that age was creeping up on me. I was 75 years old, and I had grown accustomed to taking an hour's nap each afternoon. My hearing had deteriorated, and, along with it, had come Ménière's syndrome (a recurrent and usually progressive group of symptoms including deafness, ringing in the ears, dizziness, and a sensation of pressure in the ears). My first experience with that ailment was frightening. I had driven home from the University of New Mexico, and as my car entered my driveway, everything began to whirl around me. Instinctively, I stopped and pulled on the hand brake, but, when I tried to go to the house, I couldn't stand up. I had to crawl on my hands and knees to the front door, and, once inside, all the way to my bedroom on all fours. I began to disrobe so I could get into bed, but I had to stop in order to vomit and then immediately squat on the john to empty myself at the other end. One would have thought I was seasick. In bed, the room seemed to revolve around me, but I did manage to telephone a neighbor who had a key to my house and who was kind enough to put my car in the garage. I was in bed for 24 hours, unable to eat anything, although I managed an occasional sip of water.

When I was back to normal, I consulted Dr. Gibbons, who had helped so much during Isabelle's terminal illness. He prescribed Antivert, but that useful medication had to be taken in advance. How was I to know when a seizure might be coming? It took awhile for me to discover that any unusual stress might trigger an attack. The first experience was by far the worst, but during the following year I had a few less severe episodes, including one in Costa Rica when, much to my embarrassment, Louis Porras and Gordon Schuett each had to take one of my elbows and almost carry me across the street, like a common drunk they had found in the gutter. Probably I should "knock wood" as I write this, but I have not had an attack in many years. I carry Antivert with me habitually and take it routinely. I do have a balance problem, however, that becomes severe only when I am very tired. I cannot travel long distances alone.

Armed with the knowledge of my weaknesses, our plans for visiting the Far East were adjusted accordingly. I would have a wheelchair waiting at the termination of each long flight, and we would use business class on all except short hops. Frankly, I had not been aware of business class until the travel agent suggested it. Amazingly, it was only a little more expensive than the usual tourist class, but each seat was wide and comfortable, and the other amenities were almost the equivalent of first class. Business passengers on Singapore Airlines had to climb a circular staircase, and the seats were in the bubble atop the giant airliner, directly aft of the pilots' cabin. Visibility from the windows was perfect, and beside each pair of seats was a cabinet for stowing carry-on luggage. The stewardesses were in Oriental costumes, and they were kind and thoughtful. The food was superb. We flew on the same airline many times, and we agree with the frequent fliers who annually vote Singapore Airlines the best in the world. What's more, that wonderful carrier was affiliated with American

Airlines, and every mile we flew on Singapore was added to our American Airlines AAdvantage tally. No wonder we piled up enough frequent flier miles to travel to South America years later for free.

The wheelchairs were a great success. After any long flight I would climb into one and hold our hand luggage on my lap, and an attendant would wheel me along, while Kathryn walked at my side. He knew exactly where to go, so we didn't have to look for signs (which were often in a foreign language). We made rapid progress, and at the immigration desk or window we often went through a special gate and had our passports stamped immediately, even if there were 100 people waiting in line. We were taken quickly to the baggage claim area, our suitcases were retrieved, and we moved almost as rapidly through customs. Then to a bank in the airport lobby to change a small amount of money, and onward to a taxicab stand to be driven to our hotel. The porter, who often was bilingual, would tell the driver in the native language where we were to be taken. I always tipped our attendants, even though Singapore and other foreign airline people told us it was not necessary. Not so in the United States, where tips were expected. It was always a shock to come back from overseas, because American porters were often surly instead of being friendly and helpful. Incidentally, we noticed everywhere we went in Europe or Asia, and later in South America, that baggage carts, usually bearing conspicuous advertising signs for local businesses, were free to passengers. At home we had to rent them or hire a porter.

Quite by accident I acquired an extremely valuable paperback book at the Denver Airport about a year before Kay and I started on our annual series of long trips. "Overcoming Jet Lag," written by Ehret and Scanlon, and published by Berkley Books, New York, outlines the plan used by our military forces, so that troops sent to far places will arrive ready to fight and not feeling like zombies. It is a matter of controlling one's diet, especially the use of caffeine, for three days before departure. I could well recall how miserable Isabelle and I had been, in earlier years, when we flew across the Atlantic and wanted only to drop into bed to sleep for hours right after our arrival. Kay and I went "by the book," and we had no such troubles.

But enough of procedures. I should get on with our first crossing of the Pacific. We left San Francisco on Singapore Airlines bound for Hong Kong, with a stop en route at Honolulu. When we landed there, well after midnight, the pilot announced that one of the plane's four engines had quit halfway from the mainland, and we could not go on without repairs. We had to lay over in Honolulu. We were given free hotel and meal vouchers.

The next night we resumed our trip on another plane, and we arrived in Hong Kong the following morning, a day late.

We were booked into the Airport Meridien Hotel, part of a chain of French hostelries. It was right at the airport in Kowloon, across the harbor from Hong Kong Island but still a part of the British Crown Colony, so we needed no taxi. When we arrived at the registration desk, a comedy of errors unfolded. First, they could find no Conant in their computer. After a long, careful scrutiny they discovered a Roger "Ponant" with my passport number, but then the clerk said, "You had a reservation for last night. You are responsible for payment of it, but we have no rooms available for tonight."

My heart sank, but since the man spoke clear, fluent English, I explained what had happened. I told him that in Honolulu, sometime between 3:00 and 4:00 A.M., a very sleepy person, temporarily representing Singapore Airlines, had canvassed all the passengers from our plane, asking where we had reservations to stay in Hong Kong, so the various hotels could be notified. Somehow she listed us as going to an all-Oriental hotel, which turned out to be in a sleazy part of the Colony. The "Ponant" reservation had been sent weeks earlier by our travel agent, but evidently someone at the Meridien had punched the wrong key on the computer.

After all that, the clerk called an assistant manager and related my tale to him in Chinese. He asked me to wait a minute, but he soon returned, saying, "We have one room that nobody wants. We can let you have it for half price." I asked him what was wrong with it, and he showed me the key. It was number 1313!

I accepted the offer, and it turned out to be an excellent room. It was high up and afforded a perfect view of the airport's long landing strip, which extends far out into Hong Kong Harbor. Actually, it was the best room we ever had at the Meridien, and we were destined to stay there four additional times during later years. The hotel had a wonderful dining room and fantastic breakfasts, featuring some of the finest fruits we ever tasted. Just for the fun of it I took a picture of our "double trouble" key. Late in the day, someone from management telephoned and told me they had checked with Singapore, and the airline admitted its responsibility. He told me they would not expect me to pay for the night we missed, but, under the circumstances, they would charge us the full rate for room 1313.

We had planned to spend two days in Hong Kong, but now we had only one. We tried to jam everything into our single day, which was a mistake. We crossed on the Star Ferry to Hong Kong Island where mobs of people were walking fast in every direction, like ants rush-

Double trouble. Photo by RC.

ing out of their hill in warm weather after the top was burst open. We visited two snake shops in a vain attempt to find a pit viper I could photograph. Both shops had cobras, kraits, and a variety of nonvenomous snakes. Most were in filthy cages, and some were badly emaciated. When I called their appalling condition to the attention of the English-speaking Chinese in charge, he merely shrugged his shoulders and pointed to a pile of dried snake carcasses on an upper shelf. I learned later that, when a snake died, it was eviscerated, and both the internal organs and the bones were dried and saved for sale as Chinese folk medicine. How insanitary and how utterly worthless in the eyes of an Occidental herpetologist. A boy arrived with two or three live snakes in a bag to sell to the shop. Another came to buy a cobra, and we watched as its mouth was propped open and the attendant snipped off the fangs, and apparently part of the bony structure, with a pair of cutting pliers. People can be cruel.

Outside one shop, baby red-eared turtles, *Trachemys scripta elegans*, were swimming listlessly in a bare aquarium. American vendors, deprived of their home market because of the prevalence of salmonella bacteria among baby turtles, were selling their luckless living wares in every foreign outlet they could find.

Kay wanted to visit a Chinese-type department store just to see what it was like. To make a long story short, I was ready to drop by the time we were back at the hotel. I felt faint and discovered that I had a very rapid, thready pulse. I performed the breathing exercises Dr. Gibbons had prescribed for that symptom, and, after napping for an hour, I felt a little better, so we had a light supper, after which I promptly fell asleep. In the morning my pulse was normal, which was a good thing, because we were scheduled to leave for the city-state of Singapore.

Our southward flight between the two great Oriental cities was uneventful. We saw the coast of Vietnam en route and flew over atolls in the shallow South China Sea. Finally, after almost 60 years, I was about to visit Singapore, as I had told my mother I wanted to do when I was a teenager.

What an extraordinary city! Absolutely clean. No smog, no cigarette butts, no trash, no spittle on the sidewalks or in the gutters. There was a law against jaywalking, and flowers were in bloom everywhere. All arriving passengers were given a card that read: "Penalty for trafficking in drugs—DEATH. No exceptions." We taxied to our hotel and took a nap that lasted four or five hours, probably because we were catching up for our lack of sleep when we were up all night en route to and in Honolulu.

We managed to do many things during our two-day stopover in Singapore. I telephoned Bernard Harrison, Director of the Singapore Zoo, and he agreed to meet us in the afternoon. When I asked him whether there was any original forest (snake habitat) in nearby West Malaysia, he said it was too far away to drive, but suggested that we visit the Bukit Timah (Tin Hill) Nature Reserve, an area of 75 hectares on a high, steep hill not far from our hotel. We did, but found it rough going. Nonetheless, I was able to get a good feel for primeval equatorial forest with its huge, buttressed trees. Bukit Timah and a much smaller area in the botanical garden were all that remained of the original forest on the island. All the hills otherwise had been denuded and cut away, and the dirt loaded on trucks, and hauled to the shore and dumped. In that way Singapore had enlarged its area considerably. Back in Rudyard Kipling's day it was possible to sit on the porch of the old Raffles Hotel and watch the passing ships. At the time of our visit, that historic hostelry was something like a half mile from the water.

Mr. Harrison was a good host, despite the short notice we gave him, and even though he was very busy preparing to open a new exhibit on the morrow. He turned us over to his reptile curator, Francis Lim L. K., who helped me to get some good photographs of two Malayan pit vipers in their collection. The zoo was quite young. It opened in 1973, the year I retired from the Philadelphia Zoo, but it already had a well-rounded collection. Most interesting to me was a breeding colony of 19 orangutans.

The second day we devoted to sightseeing, by taking professional tours. In the morning we visited Sentosa Island, which lies just south of and belongs to Singapore. It featured cultural and recreational activities. We crossed Singapore Strait by ferry, and had a good look at the Coralarium, with its fine display of living corals and fishes. Then we went on to a wax museum, where the surrender of the city to the invading Japanese was dramatically depicted, as well as the capitulation of the Japanese to the British and their victorious allies. We toured Sentosa by monorail, and then returned to the city by a tramway slung on cables across the strait.

Our tour ended in front of the Raffles Hotel, from which we were to set off on another journey during the afternoon. So we had a light lunch in the venerable old building and we each drank a Singapore Sling. Neither of us liked it!

Our postmeridiem excursion took us across a narrow strait into Johore Bahru, the southernmost part of West Malaysia. A giant, bearded Sikh, wearing the traditional turban, was our guide, and he got us and our fellow passengers across and had our passports stamped quickly, ahead of the hundreds of local inhabitants waiting to get out of Singapore for the weekend. We saw the palace of the former Sultan of Johore, witnessed the cutting of a rubber tree's bark so that the latex oozed downward into a collecting container, and stopped at a large and impressive cemetery where hundreds of service people were interred. The tombstones indicated that the cemetery's occupants were from many parts of the old British Empire, and many had been killed as they fought to keep the Japanese from swarming in from the north to capture the city. During that day we did nothing concerned with zoos or herpetology, but we did absorb a great deal of the flavor of the Orient.

The next day we were off to Thailand and Malayan pit viper territory. We landed on the island of Phuket, from which the great herpetologist George A. Boulenger had reported our venomous objective way back in 1903. The species is now called *Calloselasma rhodostoma*. In early days Phuket was known as Junk Ceylon Island, a rather romantic name for which I have not found an explanation. At the time of our visit in 1984, the area was being developed as a resort, and at Patong Beach, on the shore of the Andaman Sea, small swarms of Germans and Scandinavians were soaking up the sunshine in an absolute minimum of swimwear. Their presence was a help to us, however, because the growing popularity of the island had induced the Thai government to establish an airport. It was still rather primitive when we were there, but it gave us access to what once had been prime viper habitat.

The morning after our arrival I engaged a taxi to drive us to a "primeval" forest at Nam Toke Tone Sai, a small, well-kept natural park where conditions were probably similar to those that once prevailed over much of the island. I was not so naive as to think we might see a viper, but I took many habitat photos and, later in the day, of the forest rising on the hillsides near the beach. The maps I consulted later showed that the area is subject to an annual dry season of two to three months.

Memories of Phuket come to mind as I write this. Several Buddhist monks, clad in saffron robes, barefooted, and carrying their begging bowls, were active along the streets of the town of Phuket in the morning. They were the first we had seen. At dinner, back at our hotel, we were supposed to have fresh pineapple as a side dish. It didn't arrive, so, when the waiter brought me the check, I asked him about it. He knew enough English to understand me, and his face betrayed that he had forgotten to serve it. He motioned for us to wait, and perhaps 15 minutes later he returned with two large bowls, each containing a whole pineapple that had been cut up. Although we both felt rather full, it was so delicious that Kay and I ate all of it. We agreed that Thai pineapple is "out of this world."

We flew on to Bangkok the next day, and we had an excellent view of the knifelike mountain ridges that separate the long, tenuous, southward-extending parts of both Thailand and Burma. In sharp contrast with the openness of Phuket Island, the capital had an abundance of smog, heavy traffic, and millions of people. We arrived late in the day at our hotel and decided to take it easy, although we digressed for an hour to visit a noisy, well-patronized bazaar right next door. Before we fell asleep that night, I mused to myself that we were in Siam where two distinguished herpetologists were once known to the royal family: Malcolm A. Smith, the British doctor who gave them medical care; and Edward H. Taylor, who did fieldwork and later published his findings on the reptiles and amphibians of Thailand.

A few months before we left on our trip, I learned about the Siam Farm and Zoological Co., Ltd., in Bangkok. An American named Merel J. "Jack" Cox was in charge of the reptiles, and there was time for an exchange of correspondence before our departure. I asked the concierge at our hotel to telephone the Farm to let them know we had arrived. Within the hour Cox returned my call and said he would come to meet us. We chatted at length and had lunch together, and he took us to inspect the live collection at the Queen Saovabha Memorial Institute, run by the Red Cross and where snakebite serum was made. They had numerous cobras and kraits, but their few vipers were not in good condition. Mr. Cox told me there were better Malayan pit vipers at the Farm, which we would see on the morrow. He worked part time there, but earned the bulk of his living teaching English. He was fluent in both languages, and he had married a Thai woman who was

then in the hospital with their newborn baby girl. I expressed curiosity about a man who was hanging around the Institute, and Cox explained that he was hoping farmers or others might bring in snakes. If the Institute didn't buy them, he would. The man's brother ran a restaurant where they served snake!

The next morning a Mercedes-Benz with a chauffeur came to take us to the Farm, which was actually an animal dealer's compound in the old tradition. Its extremely large and varied collection was especially rich in birds, including a wealth of psittacines from many parts of the world—for example, two dozen hyacinthine macaws and dozens of loris and cockatoos—and also numerous toucans, a score of crowned pigeons, and a wide variety of other kinds. The mammal collection was less extensive, but it included a splendid pair of Bengal tigers and a really tame clouded leopard. The reptile collection was small, but it was expanding under Cox's direction.

We were introduced to the owner and operator, Komain Nukulphanitwipat, whom everyone called Mr. Dang, thank goodness. He was relatively young, but grossly overweight, and a workaholic, constantly busy at his desk or consulting with visitors, as we could see from our several stays in his air-conditioned waiting room. He was an autocrat, and we did very little that day or the next except things he planned for us.

After we inspected the collection, which included many rare species we had never exhibited at the Philadelphia Zoo, Mr. Dang took us and Jack Cox to lunch at a restaurant right on the bank of the muddy Chao Phraya River, on which there was considerable boat traffic. We were out-of-doors, but a roof shielded us from the sun. Our sumptuous seafood meal included a number of unidentified delicacies. It became obvious while we ate that Dang was a trencherman, a clue as to why he was so fat.

After lunch, Dang escorted us to the Pata Department Store, which had a zoo, with many more rarities, on its roof. The Siam Farm maintained and supplied it. What an interesting novelty. It was open air, there was no accumulation of odors, and everything was spotless. On the floor below, a large male gorilla was on exhibit in a stout steel cage behind a wall of glass.

We were introduced to the owner of the store and his wife, and, because I had once been the executive head of a large zoo, I was asked to sign their guest book and to fill an entire page. I complied, mentioning that it had taken me 38 years at the Philadelphia Zoo to meet, in life, many of the kinds of animals I had seen at the Farm and the Pata Zoo just that day. Dang had assembled a remarkable collection indeed. The animal I admired most was a large adult Malayan pit viper in perfect condition, which Dang promised to have sent to the Farm for me to photograph. We were driven back to the hotel in one of Dang's fancy cars, but the traffic was so horrendous that it was long after dark when we arrived. We tumbled into bed after an exhausting day.

The next morning Jack Cox picked us up at the hotel and took us to the Farm. With his help I photographed three rather smallish vipers, but the large one from the Pata Store Zoo had not yet arrived. We looked over the reptiles together, but then he departed for a meeting, telling us he would see us at our hotel the following evening.

It was hot and humid, so Kathryn and I retreated to the air-conditioned waiting room. Dang was not in sight. We sat and read magazines, and I looked at books from the reading rack for an hour and a half. By 1:30 we were so hungry that I asked an employee if we could have a few of the bananas which were outside in bunches waiting to be given to the animals. The man asked us to wait a few minutes, and presently a hot meal arrived, the main course first, then soup, followed by dessert. Dang walked in while we were eating, but he didn't even glance in our direction from behind the plate glass that separated his office from us.

As soon as we finished eating we were told that the big pit viper had arrived. So on a full stomach and in the sweltering, enervating heat of a Bangkok afternoon I set forth to use my camera, fortunately in the shade.

What a firecracker of a snake it turned out to be, especially with the temperature so high. It was about a yard long and one of the feistiest snakes I had ever worked with. It was in a cloth bag, which an attendant untied, and then slowly slid the snake from it into a large plastic pail. I had only Jack's snake hook with which to manipulate it, and I wished it were a foot longer. I had set up a background of sand and leaves on a table, and I gently lifted the snake onto it. Instantly it struck at me, and so forcefully that it slid forward and dropped to the floor. During the hour I was photographing the snake, it struck several times, and twice more landed on the floor. In between times it was quiet, and I was able to manipulate it gently with the snake hook into better poses. It frequently flattened itself, as I had seen many natricine (water and garter) snakes do both in the field and in captivity. The short, narrow tail was quite noticeable during the flattening process, so I was sure it was a female. After I maneuvered the snake back into its bag, I asked one of the English-speaking boys watching me, from far more than a safe distance, if it had come from Bangkok. He told me the Farm's own collector had found it at Surat-Thani, which gave me a new locality for my distribution map.

RC manipulating a Malayan pit viper into a more photogenic pose. Photo by Merel J. Cox at the Siam Farm and Zoological Co. in Bangkok, Thailand.

After the lengthy photo session was over, I was soaking wet and almost exhausted, so we returned to the waiting room while I recuperated. After about a half hour I asked one of Dang's employees if he would call a cab so that we could go back to our hotel. His response was, "The driver will be here in a few minutes, and he will take you." The "few minutes" turned out to be well over an hour. After I had seen the driver pass by the window several times, I began pacing slowly up and down. Dang took the hint and sent for his chauffeur, and we were escorted, far too rapidly for common courtesy, to the car. Despite his rudeness, I thanked Dang profusely for his cooperation. It was all too obvious that, at the Farm, he was the dictator, and he expected everyone, even visitors, to bend to his will. Because of the traffic, it was late when we got back to our room. No nap again.

Dang, through his hard work and ability, had become an obviously wealthy man. Despite all he had accumulated, however, he was felled a few years later by a massive stroke.

We had only one more day in Thailand, and we decided to spend it sightseeing. We signed up with a tour company to visit the Royal Temple complex in the morning, and a crocodile farm, outside the city, in the afternoon. The Temple was extraordinary, with beautiful, fantastic, and even grotesque architecture enhanced by millions of tiny mirrors set into the walls of the buildings. The statues and structures were so many, unusual, novel, and unreal that it would have taken us several days to examine them all. I took many pictures and was soon on the verge of heat exhaustion. I stepped into an open, but roofed, stoa to get into the shade, but I was promptly told, in quite good English, that if I wanted to stand in that sacred place I would have to take off my shoes!

The crocodile farm specialized in raising the reptiles for their hides, and most of the 30,000 said to be there during our visit were not on exhibit. Nonetheless, there were many on display. The bulk of them were Siamese crocodiles, but there were also a few salt-water crocodiles. The most interesting for me were about 35 or 40 false gavials, *Tomistoma schlegeli,* a species I had seen in life very few times previously. The rest of the place was a tourist trap, with elephant rides, a mediocre elephant show, and a character who yanked a large, phlegmatic Siamese crocodile by the tail and posed for pictures while holding its jaws apart and placing his head near, but not within, the huge, tooth-rimmed mouth. A young English-speaking guide tried to pass off the false gavials as American alligators.

When we got back to our air-conditioned hotel late in the afternoon, I dropped onto the bed, fully clothed, and instantly fell asleep. A little later, Jack Cox brought us coconut milk prepared by his wife, and invited us to visit his home. He realized, however, that making the trip would be too much for us. I thanked him profusely for all he had done for us in Bangkok, and, because he was a good correspondent, we became warm pen pals. He helped me with some important facets of the *Agkistrodon* project, and I was able to reciprocate in a small way with his studies on the snakes of Thailand. I didn't see Jack again for almost nine years, when he brought his family on a visit to the United States.

Chapter 55

Sri Lanka and India

Sri Lanka (long known as Ceylon) was our next stop after Thailand. We planned to stay there for about 10 days. Not only was it the home of the small, curious hump-nosed vipers (*Hypnale*), one or possibly two of them endemic, it was also an especially interesting island because of its varied topography. Besides, I had two excellent contacts who had offered to help. Lyn de Alwis, whom I had met at an international zoo conference, was the Director of the National Zoo at Dehiwala at Colombo, the national capital. We were also to see F. Ranil Senanayake, grandson of the first premier of Sri Lanka after it received its independence from Great Britain in 1972. Ranil was an authority on the flora and fauna of the island. He had received his Ph.D. from the University of California at Davis, basing his dissertation on the curious distribution patterns of the freshwater fishes of his homeland. He also had an excellent knowledge of the herpetology of Sri Lanka. So, as we winged our way from Bangkok to Colombo, I had high hopes of adding to our (Gloyd's and mine) limited knowledge of the hump-nosed vipers. In that I succeeded, but events over which I had no control prevented me from accomplishing one of the things I especially wanted to do.

After having our passports stamped and declaring how much money we were bringing into the country, we stepped into the main foyer of the Colombo Airport and saw a man holding a sign on which was printed "Dr. Conant" in bold letters. I had often seen such signs when arriving in airports, but it was the first time it happened to me. He represented our hotel and escorted us to a taxi. It took us 40 minutes, much of it driving at quite a rapid speed, to reach our destination. It was good to know that we needed to allow at least an hour from hotel to airport when we left for India more than a week later.

The view from our top-floor hotel room was magnificent. We were on the shore of the Indian Ocean, and the waves broke continuously against a large cluster of rocks near us, splattering them with a constantly changing curtain of water. There was a lighthouse nearby, a paved walk paralleled the beach, and we saw a few large

ships moving in and out of the harbor to the north. After enjoying the panorama for a short while, we napped. When I awakened, I discovered that my pulse was thready and racing again, as it had been in Hong Kong. Three strenuous consecutive days without a nap in sultry Thailand had taken their toll on the septuagenarian. Although I didn't feel well, we went to the coffee shop for soup and tea, and then back to bed. I slept for 10 hours.

A message came from Senanayake that he was in the mountains, but would be back shortly. Lyn de Alwis wanted me to meet Sarath Kotagama, an expert on the biota of the Sinharaja (Lion) Forest fauna, but, when I told Lyn I had been sick, he advised me to rest all day and telephone him on the morrow.

While I took it easy I studied the map of Sri Lanka for at least the tenth time. "The Pearl of the Orient" is shaped indeed like a huge pearl dangling from the eastern tip of the Indian subcontinent. The two land masses are separated from each other only by a chain of islets and shallows, collectively known as "Adam's Bridge," which precludes circumnavigation of Sri Lanka by any watercraft except of the shallowest draft. The main island itself consists of three superimposed peneplains. A peneplain is a large, flat land mass produced by erosion. The lowermost peneplain covers much of Sri Lanka, especially in the north and east, and extends from sea level upward for a few hundred feet. Uplifts have elevated a large part of the southwestern portion of the island into a second peneplain about 1,000 feet higher, and a third and innermost one from 3,000 to 4,000 feet above the second, with peaks in excess of 8,000 feet. The general topography is similar to that of the Western Ghats along the Malabar (lower western) coast of India, of which Sri Lanka, geologically, is an extension. Precipitation, of course, is most abundant in the highlands, and there is considerable erosion on the third peneplain. De Alwis had suggested that we plan our visit during the winter monsoon. Sri Lanka has a fauna and flora similar to that of the Western Ghats, as well as a goodly number of endemic animals and plants, and I looked eagerly forward to seeing as much of it as possible.

After my rest I felt quite able again, so we were off to the zoo the next day. Lyn greeted us warmly and invited us to have a native-food dinner with him and his wife the next evening at their home. The zoo's animal collection was quite varied and in excellent condition. It featured a pair of sable antelopes and a group of kudus, including a magnificent male. There were eight Indian elephants, probably all from the island where the great pachyderm still lives under protection. There was also a pair of African elephants, and the male was a splendid but relatively small, streamlined forest elephant, a rarity in zoo exhibits. The reptile house was well stocked and featured many Sri Lankan snakes and lizards, and crocodiles of several kinds. Of chief interest to me were five hump-nosed vipers, the first I had seen in life. They were all of the common species, *Hypnale hypnale*, and I photographed three of them.

While we were at the zoo we met Dr. Kotagama, who said he would pick us up at our hotel at 7:00 A.M. on November 22, Thanksgiving Day. That was no holiday in Sri Lanka, of course, but it seemed appropriate to be looking for the rare *Hypnale nepa* on that day. He assured me that the Lion Forest was one of the best places to search for that endemic hump-nosed viper.

On the appointed day we were up at 5:00, we prepared drinking water to take with us, and the hotel coffee shop sent up the well-wrapped lunches we had ordered. We had scarcely finished getting everything ready when, as they say in baseball, the roof caved in. The daily English newspaper was pushed under our door, and there, in banner headlines, we read that an islandwide curfew was in effect for the next 24 hours. Tamil terrorists, who had been causing serious trouble, had slaughtered many policemen in the northern part of Sri Lanka near Jaffna. No one would be permitted on the streets or roads during the curfew. We hadn't yet had time to absorb the full impact of the shock when the telephone rang. It was Dr. Kotagama, canceling our excursion. He said he could probably get a permit to drive, but we would be stopped by police or the military at every crossroads, and it might take us until nightfall just to get to the forest. He was sorry, but his schedule was full, and he would not be free again until after our departure for India. Thus evaporated my chief hope of seeing *Hypnale nepa* in the field.

We ate some of our lunch for breakfast. I made notes, Kay took care of our accumulated laundry, and, for exercise, we were permitted to walk on the hotel grounds, but not on the street. What a dreary and discouraging day. I wandered into the dining room after one of the walks, and found that the kitchen staff was hard-pressed to prepare meals, because the delivery trucks weren't allowed on the road either. There would be something for lunch, but we would have to take potluck. I offered them my sympathies and said anything would be acceptable. We were there about 1:00 for a snack, and we had just finished eating when three hotel guests, well-dressed American women, walked in and loudly announced, "Here we are, all ready for our Thanksgiving turkey dinner." We were ashamed of them. How stupid they were not to realize it was no holiday in Sri Lanka, and that turkey probably never graced the menus. They surely deserved the title of "Ugly Americans," which is so often applied to overbearing tourists. I took it upon myself to explain things to them and even to show them a newspaper about the curfew.

The dreariness of the day was broken by a telephone call to our room. It was Ranil Senanayake. He was in the lobby of our hotel, and he had gotten a permit to travel. I went right down to meet him, and we plunged at once into a lively conversation. It was quickly evident that he had a very broad knowledge of the Sri Lankan fauna and flora, and he had some very cogent remarks about hump-nosed vipers.

Before I go on, I should mention a few facts about those unusual snakes. As I have said, there are two species, *Hypnale hypnale* and *H. nepa*. Both have uptilted snouts, but in *nepa* there is also a tiny protuberance, or wart, at the very tip that consists of a cluster of extremely small scales. Howard K. Gloyd had described a third species, which he called *Hypnale walli*, but he thought that it might actually be a variant of *nepa*.

Ranil, based on his studies, told me he believed that the endemic *nepa* had been on the island since the Miocene, millions of years ago, when Sri Lanka was attached to the Indian mainland and animals and plants could move freely back and forth. After the subsequent separation of the two bodies of land, the species *hypnale* became well established in the Western Ghats of India. From there it invaded Sri Lanka by way of a land bridge in the Pleistocene, during part of which epoch the sea level was far lower while so much of the world's water was tied up as ice in the great glaciers. At that time *hypnale* entered Sri Lanka and spread over much of the island. The endemic *Hypnale nepa* lived in the moist forests, many of which are now being destroyed by lumbering. When the trees come down, *nepa* is unable to survive, and the invader, *hypnale*, moves in. *Hypnale nepa* was becoming more rare all the time. Here was exciting information to be investigated for the big monograph on the genus *Agkistrodon* and its allies.

Ranil Senanayake went all out to show us as much of the highlands of Sri Lanka as possible, and he devoted the better part of three days to driving us through the region. As we moved along he explained the topography and geology, and pointed out habitats of the two vipers and other animals. I took many pictures. We stayed at a hotel the first night but visited his mountain home the next day, where his charming wife prepared a fine native noonday dinner for us, and we met their two boys. Then we were off to the highest part of the island. After a long drive followed by supper, Ranil took us to his family's ancestral summer home at Nuwara Eliya (pronounced "Nor-eel'-ya"), high up on the third peneplain. It dated from well back in colonial days, and, although it had indoor plumbing, it was rather primitive. A servant brought us a jar of hot water and towels just before we retired. It was cold at the high elevation, but we slept fairly well. When we awakened in the morning I tried to recall what I had read about customs in British colonies, so I put our empty water jar just outside our door. Within minutes an elderly gentleman, who had been in the employ of the family since 1922, brought us tea, and more hot water arrived.

In a very real sense we slept in a historic house. Ranil's grandfather was the first prime minister of Sri Lanka, and other members of the family had also served in official capacities. The hallway was lined with photographs of several generations, and, in the sitting room, there was a picture of family members posed with Queen Elizabeth II. It was the Sri Lankan equivalent of sleeping in George Washington's house.

Our motor tour continued in Ranil's vehicle. We dropped back down to the second peneplain, admiring, as we went, the spectacular waterfalls descending from the third. Ranil left us about noon at a hotel in Kandy, the ancient city where the Temple of Buddha's Tooth is situated and where the elaborate and colorful ceremonies each year attract many tourists. We profusely thanked our kind and gracious host. He deserved most of the credit for the enthusiasm with which I plunged into a detailed study of the hump-nosed vipers when Kathryn and I returned to our home base.

After resting overnight, we took the train from Kandy to Colombo, enjoying the scenery and the abundance of birds as we rolled along down to and through the lowlands.

Before we left Sri Lanka we visited the national museum, and, through the courtesy of Mrs. Thelma Gunawardane, I examined its preserved collection of *Hypnale*, while Kay acted as my secretary. We also met Anslem de Silva, of the University of Peradeniya, near Kandy, and with whom I was later to have a long and

Our first and only experience with the fakir business. For a fee the boy removed the lid of his basket and the cobra raised the forepart of its body and spread its hood. RC, playing a toy flageolet, had performed the same trick for television years earlier at the Philadelphia Zoo. Photo by RC.

important correspondence on subjects pertinent to the hump-nosed vipers.

I was disappointed not to have encountered any *Hypnale* during our travels, but Lyn de Alwis, until his retirement, and then S. B. U. Fernando, completed an exchange. Through the kindness of Louis Porras, a number of American snakes, including a few rattlers that I purchased, were sent as a gift to the Sri Lanka National Zoo. In response, again through Louis's expertise with import regulations, we received several live specimens of *hypnale* and two of *nepa*. Louis even photographed some of them for me.

Two minor items linger among my memories of Sri Lanka. First, while I was walking in Kandy I saw a troop of rhesus monkeys rummaging through a large trash pile in search of food. They were the only wild simians of that species I ever saw. Second, right outside our hotel in Colombo and on the walk paralleling the beach, two boys had set themselves up in the fakir business. Each had a basket with a removable lid and a live cobra inside. For a fee they would remove the lid, the snakes would pop upward with their hoods spread, and the boys would play on flageolets just as I had often seen men do in pictures and movies taken in India. I could not help but wonder if the two snakes had been defanged like the one we saw undergoing crude surgery with cutting pliers at the snake shop in Hong Kong.

Poor Sri Lanka. It endured agonies during the years immediately following our departure. A small minority of Tamil separatists resorted to terrorist activities in a vain attempt to force the much larger Singhalese population to partition the island into two separate countries. They bombed and badly damaged the power plant in Colombo, blew up an airplane at the airport, committed wholesale murder, and, recently, wrecked the capital's business district with a powerful bomb in a truck. Ranil Senanayake and his family, who could have been prime targets for assassination because of their ancestry, fled the country and vanished. Who could blame them? But what a brutal and humiliating experience for them. Their patriotic family had donated much of its land to raise money to get Sri Lanka started as an independent nation. The Senanayakes deserved a far better fate. They really and truly loved their country.

On our arrival in Madras, India, from Colombo, we underwent tight security measures. All passengers alighted from our Air Lanka plane right onto the tarmac and were immediately surrounded by soldiers carrying rifles. We were then marched into a building and subjected to a hands-on personal inspection, presumably in search of weapons or whatever the Indian authorities considered contraband. When we were released, there was a wild stampede, with courtesy thrown to the winds, as the Asians raced to the immigration and customs lines. We avoided such behavior, so we were almost the last to pass through the required formalities. That didn't surprise our host, who knew the impatient habits of his countrymen.

We were met by a charming young Tamil named Shekar Dattatri, who rode with us in our taxi to our hotel, and who later escorted us to the Madras Snake Park and the Crocodile Bank.

Months prior to our departure from home, I had written to Romulus Whitaker, who conceived and established the Snake Park, asking him whether there were any living hump-nosed vipers (*Hypnale*) or Himalayan pit vipers (*Agkistrodon himalayanus*) in his collection. He replied that there were several *Hypnale hypnale*, but he knew of no live captive *himalayanus* anywhere in India. He suggested, however, that if I would send what seemed like a paltry sum, he would dispatch someone to the far northwestern state of Jammu and Kashmir to hunt for that species. I did, and Shekar and a friend who was fluent in the Hindi language made the long trip by train. Shekar presented me with a handsome set of color slides of *himalayanus*, and also some of a hump-nosed viper with one of her babies, which he had taken. His pictures filled my needs for *himalayanus* completely. We would have liked to have seen the Himalaya Mountains, the loftiest in the world, but Romulus and Shekar had saved us from considerable expense and loss of time.

We had only a short stay in Madras, but, through the thoughtfulness of Shekar, we met and chatted with T. S. N. Murthy, and met briefly with Jeff Lang, an American researcher on crocodilians. We also had tea with Walter and Eleanor Auffenberg, who happened to be in Madras. Walter was an old friend of mine. We didn't see Romulus Whitaker because he was in the field in New Guinea.

We saw cattle, goats, and water buffaloes that were permitted to wander freely in the streets of Madras, and we watched from our room window as the animals placidly stood in the midst of the very busy street. Cows, lying on the pavement, were chewing their cuds right in the midst of heavy, horn-blaring traffic that had to dodge around them. Shekar was quite amused because the livestock was eating the paper posters advertising the coming national elections. All this was a new experience for us. Also, we had vegetable burgers, substitutes for beef, which is taboo as food in much of India. We ate them, but told ourselves that once was enough. We were out of luck. They were served for lunch on the plane from Madras to Bombay!

All was chaos at the Bombay Airport, which was 25 miles north of the city. Our fellow passengers were pushing, shoving, and elbowing others out of the way, and most of them had an incredible amount of baggage. The delivery belt jammed repeatedly, and it had to be stopped while attendants untangled the resulting jumbles. Our luggage was almost the last to appear. By that time, every cart was engaged except for one with only three wheels. After I struggled out with it, all the regular taxis had departed. A lad of perhaps 12 took two of our bags, and we followed him to a car, whose driver wanted an exorbitant fee to transport us southward. We haggled, and he finally reduced his demand by a third, whereupon I relented.

The ride into Bombay was extremely depressing. We passed through a seemingly endless stream of human misery. Thousands of people had only old woven mats or cardboard boxes for shelter. Their clothing consisted of rags, and everyone seemed emaciated. Some looked like walking skeletons. There were no sanitary facilities. A long, shallow ditch, paralleling the highway, was the only latrine, and it was being used by people of all ages and both sexes, with no effort to seek privacy. The stench, augmented by the exhaust fumes of hundreds of vehicles racing pell-mell, was overwhelming, especially in the hot, very humid atmosphere. Our vehicle slowed to a crawl, and for at least 15 minutes we crept along until we came to a place where policemen were squeezing two lanes of traffic into one. A human corpse was lying on the road, and someone had spread a filthy sari over it. As we drew closer to the city proper traffic lights appeared. Whenever we stopped, we were immediately surrounded by beggars, each exhibiting some disability—a crippled, sometimes badly twisted limb or a missing one; starving babies; blind, elderly companions; and so on, all of them pathetic. After we exhausted our few coins, the driver suggested that we close the windows whenever we stopped and, as he put it, "ignore the low-caste dregs of humanity." Friends who know India told us later that the slum we passed through was on a par with those in Calcutta, the worst in the world!

With the human population burgeoning at a frightening rate, and predictions of billions more of us within a relatively short time, are we all to be reduced to similar desperate conditions?

It took us nearly two hours to reach our hotel. I paid our driver the amount on which we agreed, plus a tip, but he started yelling that I had cheated him. Because similar disturbances were probably commonplace, the hotel porters ignored him and ushered us into the plush lobby of the Oberoi Towers. What an extraordinary contrast with the utter poverty through which we had just passed! Well-dressed businessmen from many nations were much in evidence along with their well-groomed women, and there were numerous Indians among them. An Arab, hooded in a burnoose and with the black ring (ägäl) around his head, was standing to one side. We were told that Saudis from the extremely arid Arabian Desert rented rooms by the year, but visited chiefly during the monsoon season, when they could stand outdoors in the rain. Such a privilege was unattainable when they were at home.

Our room was on the seventeenth or eighteenth floor, and what a view we had. Our window faced south, toward a sea of skyscrapers. We could imagine that we were in New York. Off the southern tip of the narrow peninsula on which the city is situated, a flotilla of small warships was at anchor. Most interesting of all, at least for a naturalist, were the Brahminy kites, rapid, graceful flyers, and some of which passed close to our window.

We visited the Bombay Natural History Museum, where I wanted to buy a copy of the recently published "Reptiles of India," by J. C. Daniel, director of the museum. We were asked to wait, and then were told to climb a very long series of stairs to the upper floor, and to take seats at the top. Presently, someone came out of an office into which we were conducted. There sat the

Auffenbergs, grinning at us. They had been consulting with Daniel. He autographed a copy of his book, I paid him the advertised price for it, and we had a brief chat during which he gave me permission to look at the museum's preserved snakes of the *Agkistrodon* complex. We and the Auffenbergs repaired to a spacious basement room, and, while I looked at snakes, Walter examined monitor lizards, of the family that includes the Komodo dragon. Afterward, all four of us went to lunch in the nearby Taj Mahal Hotel, but we had to duck and dodge our way through the speeding traffic. There were no pedestrian crosswalks. All the drivers seemed to go as fast as possible, and apparently vehicles had the right of way. Even in the enormous slum through which we passed, cars raced along and people had to jump out of the way—or else! Incidentally, there were no cows in or near Bombay. They would have been quickly reduced to beef burgers by the frenetic traffic.

P. J. Deoras, of the Haffkine Institute, whom I had met and entertained years earlier when he visited the Philadelphia Zoo, kindly served as our guide. In return, I offered to give an illustrated lecture on herpetology, especially rattlesnakes, for the Institute's staff. Among other things, Deoras guided us to the Borivili National Park, not many miles from the Bombay Airport. We also had the company of Humayun Abdulali, a congenial and entertaining ornithologist who brought along binoculars for us to use, and who helped me to identify 40 species of birds. He told us that four or five leopards lived in the reserve and were sometimes seen in the very early morning walking along the narrow paved road on which we were riding in his car. How incredible to have such large carnivores so close to teeming Bombay. The great cats were isolated, however, and there was no chance for gene flow with others of their kind.

We appreciated Deoras's help, but I was rather provoked when he scheduled my lecture, much against my wishes, on the very day of our departure from India. I had stressed in our advance correspondence that I wanted to rest on that day. Also, I had asked for the privilege of a half hour to myself before I spoke, because I knew that my slides would have to be loaded into their projector, which turned out to be of truly ancient vintage. Instead of giving me time, our host rushed through the Institute and made us look at many things of little interest to us. In the meantime, their projectionist transferred my slides. He did fairly well. Only one was upside down, but three or four were out of order.

The lecture itself was ludicrous. Five or six times in the midst of it the electricity went off, leaving the screen blank and my microphone inoperable. Someone from the audience had to make a trip each time to the fuse box (or whatever) and then return. There was no way for me to control the slides, except to say, "Next, please." The operator was either hard of hearing or didn't understand English very well. Sometimes the next slide would appear much too soon or we would go back to the one just shown. I have never given an illustrated lecture under such trying conditions, but a hard core of the audience listened and watched with rapt attention. While I answered questions, the projectionist put my slides back in the box in an exasperating jumble. After I finished, one of the staff members made a short complimentary speech, and Kathryn and I had long, stringy flower leis put around our necks, accompanied by applause. Then to the director's office for pictures and refreshments, which consisted of one bottle of orange soda each.

When we got back to the hotel in early afternoon I was exhausted, especially since dysentery had caught up with me for the first time during our long trip, and just prior to my lecture! I needed a good nap, but, to get it, I had to engage our room for a full extra day, even though we were to leave Bombay that night. The Oberoi Towers, to which our travel agent assigned us, was a very expensive place, and I began calling it "Robber's Roost" as soon as we discovered the exorbitant prices they charged in their coffee shop. To add insult to injury, when we finally checked out, the cashier claimed we had not paid for our first night, although the money had been sent far in advance by our travel agent. Fortunately, I had a copy of the voucher with me, but, even so, we had a long, bitter argument before I finally convinced the cashier's supervisor, and then hers! I felt certain they were just trying to squeeze more money out of me.

What deplorable conditions we found in India. Hordes of human outcasts, cheating and schemes to extract every rupee possible from visitors, and great wealth contrasted with the worst imaginable poverty. I should also mention that I paid for all our transportation, except when we were in Abdulali's car in the national park. Deoras had to come from some distance to our hotel, but I reimbursed him for every expense.

We were a little tired of India, despite our pleasant stay in Madras, and we looked forward to boarding the Swissair plane bound nonstop to Zürich. The trip to the airport was another nightmare. We retraced our route through the slum, but it was dark and we were spared seeing much of the human misery we had witnessed previously. Other taxis and trucks, and a few private cars, were darting in and out of line to get past one another. Both a Hindu and an Islamic holiday were in progress, and parades forced us to take several detours. We saw some of the gaiety, in the form of ferris wheels

and bright lights over bazaars, before we left the city proper. Finally, shortly after midnight, we were settled in our comfortable business-class seats on our way out of a country we didn't ever want to see again.

We tarried in Zürich for a few days, staying at a hotel in the city, but visiting with René Honegger and his wife. He had worked as a sort of apprentice for a couple of years at the Philadelphia Zoo, and we became good friends. We were very glad we had shipped our heavy clothes to him before we left home. It was cold in Switzerland in December, and we had just left the sweltering Tropics.

We visited the splendid Zürich Zoo, with its unique modern exhibits designed by Heini Hediger while he presided as director. He had retired, but he came in from the country to visit with us. Dr. Peter Weilenmann, the new director, hosted us all for a splendid lunch in the zoo's restaurant. Kay and I took the train to Lenzburg to see if we could find the old Drei Sternen (Three Star) Hotel, which Kay's mother's family had owned a century previously. We did, and we were graciously shown all of it that she wanted to see. I gave my same lecture at the University of Zürich one evening. The projector was superb, and so were all the other accommodations. I even had time to run through the slides to refresh my memory. The projector was set up in a classroom that held perhaps 25 students, but so many people came that the movable doors into two adjacent classrooms had to be opened to accommodate the crowd. The lecture went without a flaw, and I was greatly flattered to see many friends and acquaintances whom I had met at one time or another. Hans Wackernagel, who, like René, had spent a long time learning the feeding methods at the Philadelphia Zoo, came over by train from Basel, and several friends from southern Germany drove to Zürich to hear me. Many of us assembled at the bar in our hotel after the lecture was over. It was all very heartwarming.

We were transported by Swissair to Chicago's O'Hare Airport with a stop at Boston en route. As soon as I was in my wheelchair I was jolted back into reality. The skycap who pushed me was surly and unsmiling, and he didn't even thank me when I gave him a generous tip. We stayed overnight at an airport hotel before continuing on to Tucson the next day. The twin beds in our room had been made up after the departure of the previous guests, but the bathroom and floors had not been touched. I called housekeeping, but no one could be bothered to help us. We made the most of a bad bargain, but that hotel was the filthiest place in which we had stayed during our entire trip around the world. Welcome home!

Chapter 56

Around the World the Other Way

Phileas Fogg traveled "Around the World in Eighty Days" (Jules Verne's classic 1873 novel), but, in 1984, thanks to the efficiency of jet planes, we did it in 43, despite stops of 2 or 3 days each in such places as Singapore, Bangkok, and Bombay, and 10 in Sri Lanka. Fogg, however, had traveled in the opposite direction, and because he had crossed the International Date Line from west to east he gained a day. We lost one.

In 1985 I presented papers at the annual meetings of the Societas Europaea Herpetologica in Praha (Prague), Czechoslovakia, and the Sino-Japanese Herpetological Symposium in Guangzhou (Canton), the People's Republic of China. The two meetings were chronologically almost concurrent but the one in Prague was slightly earlier, so we went there first after a brief visit with friends in what was then West Germany. We flew against the sun instead of with it, and we gained back the day we had lost in 1984.

Our first stop was a pleasant and leisurely two days with Peter and Renata Kisser, who owned and operated the excellent and well-stocked Reptilien-Haus at Uhldingen in Germany's summer resort belt on the Boden See (Lake of Constance). We found it surprisingly warm there. Renata had visited with us both in Tucson and Albuquerque, and they insisted we stop to see them. They drove us from Frankfurt, where our plane landed, southward within sight of the Vosges Mountains in France and across the Black Forest through beautiful countryside. They treated us royally, and Peter took us by ferry steamer to Mainau Island, where exquisite floral displays were maintained by the Swedish royal family. When Peter drove us back to Frankfurt we thanked him profusely for all his help with the Gloyd and Conant *Agkistrodon* monograph, in the form of photographs taken by his friend, Hanspeter Fülleman, and the many specimens he gave me that had been withdrawn from the Dresden Museum. Thus, our 1985 saga started off well. But we were a bit apprehensive about our next stop, our first venture behind the Iron Curtain.

We flew to Zürich, stayed overnight, and the next day landed at Prague for the European herp meetings at which I was to speak. We knew immediately when we stepped into the airport that we were in the land of "Big Brother."

Once, decades earlier, in my capacity as curator of reptiles of the Philadelphia Zoo, I was asked to visit Moyamensing Prison to rescue a medium-sized boa constrictor that had been confiscated from a girl who was serving 30 days for dancing publicly while clad solely by the snake. The moment the turnkey closed the ancient lock behind me, I felt trapped. I had a similar feeling after the hour we spent passing through the tight security control at the border of a nation that had been violently invaded by the Russian military juggernaut and its allies. Our passports were stamped, and the top sheet of each visa, which bore the officially required personal photo, was removed. Our baggage was not opened, but just ahead of us a curtain was yanked across and a returning citizen was obviously searched to the skin. A huge, surly woman wearing an ill-fitting uniform waved us through, and we stepped into Communist territory.

We had been warned not to take so much as a kopek out of the country when we left, and to exchange American money only at official banks. One was in the airport lobby, so I bought a few Czech crowns. When we ventured outside it was raining, but we were sheltered by a marquee. Two other couples were waiting for taxis, but when one arrived it came directly to us. Americans, no doubt, gave higher tips. The driver's English was excellent, and he told us that members of his family lived in Cleveland, Ohio. He wanted me to pay him in dollars, but, mindful of the strict rules, I used crowns instead. I did not wish to run afoul of the Czechoslovakian "gestapo."

The driver deposited us at the Hotel Park Praha, but when we went to the desk we were told that our reserved room wasn't ready. We "evil capitalists" had to sit for hours in the lobby while Czechs and a whole busload of East Germans, all good but probably enforced Communists, went immediately to their rooms. When we finally were permitted to register, our passports were taken from us to be sent to the Prague police headquarters for scrutiny. We were given tourist cards in exchange.

The hotel was fairly new, but our room was neither tidy nor really clean. In the bathroom a pipe descended from ceiling to floor, and its base was surrounded by a dozen or more old dried mop strings that no one had bothered to pick up. The hotel employees, all Czechs, hated the Communist regime forced upon them, and they did as little work as possible in protest. The chambermaids spent most of the day sitting and smoking in a small service room. The waitresses literally threw the plates on the counter of the lunch room. The food, in general, was not very good. The people expressed their dislike for their captivity in these and a variety of other ways. No one smiled. How overjoyed they must have been when the Berlin Wall finally came down, and they were liberated from the brutal Russian bear.

We had been required to send money in advance to pay for our room and meals at the hotel. To eat, we were given a small handful of coupons that were good only in the hotel's dining or lunch rooms or in the souvenir shop. We had a surplus when we left, which Kathryn exchanged for some really fine crystal necklaces as gifts for friends. The headwaiter, who lorded it over the dining room, especially at breakfast time, cheated us royally by demanding double the number of coupons required. I tried to argue with him, but he managed his skulduggery under the pretext that he couldn't understand English. I heard him speaking it, however, on the day we left.

We arrived in Prague a couple of days before the meetings began. For exercise, we walked a few blocks from the hotel, visiting a nicely wooded park and a curious, to us, cemetery, where the amount of land used for burial was at an absolute minimum. We also passed a Kultural Center, which seemed more facade than substance. We were warned that we must be back in the hotel before dark. From our bedroom window at night we could see that the streets were dark and completely deserted. Lights were visible at corners here and there, but they were faint. Police patrols, no doubt, made sure that no trouble would start at night.

Under all these unusual conditions, I felt constantly on edge, although the situation was somewhat alleviated when our passports were returned to us two days later. One evening, as we were eating our supper, I noted, out of the corner of my eye, a pair of military-looking trousers stop at our table. My first thought was, "What have we done wrong now?" I looked up with apprehension, but was relieved to discover an old friend, herpetologist Rudolfo Ruibal and his wife, Irene, who were also staying at the hotel. We had a pleasant time chatting with them.

The headquarters for the meeting were at Charles University. After registering and greeting Zbyněk Roček, the chairman of the gathering, we began to meet persons whom I previously had known only through correspondence. Among them were Wolfgang Böhme, Ilya Darevsky, Göran Nilson, and Ivan Rehák. Several American friends of long standing were also present. We discovered that most of the delegates were staying at the university (Katjetánka) dormitories, which probably would have been better than the stern, official hotel. I disliked dormitories, however. During earlier years in the States I had discovered that dormitory residents were noisy and their carousing often lasted until the early morning hours, thus robbing us of sleep. Because it was Sunday and the formal sessions had not yet begun, we joined perhaps a dozen others at a *restaurace* across the street. We, personally, drank little, but huge mugs of beer were popular, and the crowd, including many resident Czechs, overflowed onto the sidewalk outside. It seemed that social drinking on Sunday afternoons was one form of relaxation that the Communists permitted their vassals to enjoy.

The meetings were held in widely scattered places in Prague, and some were concurrent. I was scheduled to speak at an old monastery called Emauzey, which was now a historic landmark, and not a place of worship.

Despite the absence of a light on the lectern I managed to give my paper without too many glitches, and the audience was kind enough to applaud it well. When the afternoon session had concluded, everyone left in a body for the four- or five-block hike to the subway. Kathryn was wearing fairly high heels, and she was unable to keep up with the group. We would have been in dire trouble if it had not been for the kindness of Joseph Butler and J. C. Reid, who had come all the way from Nigeria to attend the meetings. They knew my name, but they were strangers to me until they rescued us by hanging back and keeping us company. Butler even took my heavy camera case and carried it for the old man. We saw our colleagues well ahead of us as they disappeared down a set of steps into the subway. Traffic blocked us from catching up with them, but Reid, thank goodness, knew the way to Katjetánka. After we walked down to a landing and I paid a crown for each of us, we descended far underground on two escalators, one below the other, to the subway station proper. Obviously it had been designed to double as a bomb shelter to be used when the wicked American capitalists, according to Communist propaganda, shot off their intercontinental missiles. We rode to about the third station, escalated back to the surface, and then took a bus the rest of the way.

Our plight would have been hopeless if we had been alone. Getting a taxi to stop on the street was impossible, as we learned the following day. Such vehicles were permitted to pick up passengers at the airport or at hotels, but apparently not elsewhere. We attended the sessions at Emauzey the next morning, participated in the group picture, but tarried a bit to talk with a colleague whom we would not see again. Everyone else had left, so Kathryn and I walked to a busy intersection where we were sure we would be able to get a cab. Nothing doing. I gestured at quite a number of empty ones, but none would stop. An hour later, in despair, we walked back to Emauzey and discovered the proper way to engage a taxi. An attendant telephoned for us and asked for a cab. Ten minutes later an official called back and asked if we had called for a taxi. He was told yes, whereupon one was dispatched. What miserable, inexplicable red tape! It was the same when we left Katjetánka after the Society's banquet. My friend Ivan Rehák, who was a Czech, knew what to do. He phoned for us and received the call that came in return.

The next day we departed, and therefore missed a long bus ride through the countryside of Czechoslovakia. The meetings in China were coming up all too soon, and we wanted to have a day of rest after the long flight through a plethora of time zones from Zürich to Hong Kong. What a relief it was to be on a Swissair plane escaping from the tight restrictions and taboos of an Iron Curtain country. Our sympathies were all with the poor Czechs, Slovaks, and other Eastern Europeans who had to endure the tyrannical practices for several more years, until the sudden and complete collapse of Russian Communism. We were lucky, because we were soon back in Zürich.

Swissair, no doubt because we were on the economical around-the-world fare, seated us right over the wing. I could see nothing of the ground without looking backward over my left shoulder. I soon had a king-sized stiff neck, but I managed to see Belgrade and Sofia as we passed over those Balkan capitals. Also, and with a bit of a thrill, over Istanbul, Turkey, and the Sea of Marmara, from which I could see the Bosporus and into the Black Sea. We crossed arid Anatolia and clipped the northeasternmost tip of the Mediterranean Sea at the Gulf of Alexandretta. Presently we were over Syria. I soon noticed that a fighter plane was accompanying us a few miles away and to our rear. I wondered whether all foreign planes were tailed until they crossed the opposite Syrian border. By the time we were over the great Arabian Desert it was getting dark, and my neck was

able to resume its normal position. We stopped in Bombay after midnight, passed over soggy and poverty-stricken, but invisible Bangladesh, and landed in Hong Kong about midday. Back again in the familiar lobby of the Airport Meridien Hotel. We hoped to have a full day of rest on the morrow.

That evening we had a telephone call from Japan. Our esteemed friend Richard C. Goris wanted to make sure we had arrived, and he urged me to get our railroad tickets from Hong Kong to Canton (Guangzhou) as soon as possible. On our way to breakfast, I stopped at the concierge's desk, and one of the young men told me to apply at the travel agency office in the small complex of shops in the basement dining area. No one was there. I called the agency's telephone number repeatedly, but with no success. At about 10:00 A.M. I went down in person, only to find a sign reading "Will Return After Lunch"! I left a note asking that I be called as soon as possible. About 3:00 someone phoned. The voice said it would see what it could do, but it wasn't until well after 4:00 that I was told it was impossible to get tickets. I sped to the concierge, explained my problem, and one of the young men who knew me by sight said, "Nonsense." He grabbed a telephone and spoke in Chinese at some length. He then told me that if I could get to the Chinese Travel Agency office by 5:30 they would have our tickets and entrance papers ready. While he wrote a note in Chinese for me to show to a taxi driver, I used the house phone to tell Kathryn I would be away for a while. Most fortunately, I had both our passports and our entrance visas to the People's Republic of China in my pocket, so I didn't have to rush back to the room for them. My benefactor's note must have stressed the need for speed, because we took off with wild abandon in very heavy traffic. It was a Friday afternoon, and the eve of a three-day holiday!

We arrived at my destination just two minutes prior to the deadline. I had to take an elevator to an upper floor, and when I stepped from it I was dismayed to see that a steel grille had been pulled across the office entrance. The guard behind it could speak no English, but when I showed him the message to the driver, he motioned for me to wait. He came back with a girl who escorted me to the counter. She already had our names and hotel room number written out, kits with customs forms (China and Hong Kong), and even the tickets with our names on them. What a wild cliff-hanger of an experience. I learned later that, if things hadn't worked out, we could have taken a boat to Canton instead.

My old friend Hajime Fukada, who had visited Isabelle and me at Taunton many years previously, was president of the Herpetological Society of Japan.

Unhappily, he was ill and his doctor would not permit him to make the trip to China. Dick Goris was elected to serve as leader of the Japanese delegates in his stead. The next morning we met Dick and his 14 Japanese companions at the railroad station. The younger ones helped us stow our baggage in the passenger car reserved for non-Chinese travelers. It was new and modern, but I was disillusioned when I tried later to use the restroom. The facilities consisted solely of a fairly wide slot in the floor and a roll of toilet paper. All waste matter went down onto the railroad ties, as well as any loose coins in one's pockets!

In a few hours we were at the station in Canton, where we were met by the eminent herpetologist Zhao Ermi and several others, including Pan Jionghua, who was soon to retire as president of the South China Normal University. He was a charming little man who could speak no English but smiled constantly and kept saying, "Ho-ho-ho." There were only four Americans at first, and all of us had been invited because we had helped Professor Zhao in one way or another. We were Kraig Adler, Kenneth V. Kardong, and the two of us. Somehow or other Kathryn's name badge and credentials were labeled "Johns Gloyd," for her middle and last names. All the foreigners, including Jean Garzoni, a Swiss, were assigned to the VIP building, a modern air-conditioned structure where everything functioned well except our bathroom sink, which leaked and produced a swamp on the floor.

Our first meal in China was both a revelation and a shock. We had bowls of soup and porcelain spoons. Our Oriental friends were issued chopsticks, but we had brought two forks with us. Our table was round, seated 10 persons, and was equipped with a large lazy Susan laden with mostly unrecognizable foods. We tried them all, including squid, softshell turtle with the bony parts still present, and a long stringy vegetable somewhat resembling spinach. Whenever our bowls were empty, we used our porcelain spoons, chopsticks, or forks to transfer more food from the lazy Susan. Theoretically, the buccal germs from all 10 diners were transferred to everyone else. No wonder the American doctors sent to China to cope with a cholera epidemic during World War II were in despair. Most of the Chinese refused to break with tradition, and that was that. We had no trouble, but we felt squeamish at every meal.

A dozen students who were proficient in English were assigned to us, both to assist us and to practice their language skills. We were soon joined by three other Americans: Oliver Johnson, who had been studying salamanders in China; and Jack and Susana Frazier, who were working on turtles under the auspices of the

Smithsonian Institution. The students had abundant practice with their English, and, because they had been taught to revere the elderly, and I was the oldest person present, I came in for more than my share of attention. Our room on the third floor was reached via an outdoor circular staircase, and the students insisted on helping me up. One was welcome, two were tolerable, but sometimes I would have four at my elbows. I'd designate two and wave the others away.

The VIP building was directly adjacent to a small lake. Twice we saw turtle heads protruding above the surface, and a water snake of the genus *Enhydris* was cooperatively coiled a large part of the time on a snag readily visible from the staircase.

As had been the case in Prague, the meetings were conducted in English. What a change since my first trip abroad in 1937, when French was the lingua franca! Most of the Japanese were more or less fluent in English, but, for the Chinese, we were asked to give copies of our papers in advance to a designated person to study overnight. When I gave my presentation I would read a sentence or two and then pause until what I had said was repeated orally in Chinese. No such device had been used in Czechoslovakia, because of the many languages involved, but everyone spoke in English. That was fine in theory, but the accents of some speakers were so strong that we could scarcely understand them.

As a pleasant interlude we went for an evening cruise on the Pearl River, the stream passing through Canton that widens into a broad estuary toward Hong Kong. How amazingly different from conditions in Czechoslovakia. The streets were brightly lighted, and so were many shops. Couples and groups of young people were walking along, some arm-in-arm, singing as they went. On the boat we were entertained by an accordionist and a guitarist, and all of our national groups were encouraged to sing. We few Americans obliged, but we soon ran out of songs we all knew. Nonetheless, it was an enjoyable experience, and in sharp contrast with the grim, foreboding darkness of Prague at night.

An outstanding feature of the symposium was a bus trip to see the Seven Star Crags. We were off at 6:00 A.M. En route we stopped at a biological station in the mountains and visited an old Buddhist monastery, from which we descended on foot through a forest with trickling rills that reminded me of places I had visited in the American Appalachians. Bennie Huo, one of the English-speaking students, very kindly attached himself to us, and I used his shoulder to steady myself as we walked down the rough, rocky terrain. My balance problem was slowly worsening as my hearing deteriorated.

About noon we arrived on the outskirts of the City of

The American contingent to the Sino-Japanese Herpetological Symposium singing on an excursion boat on the Pearl River at Guangzhou (Canton), the People's Republic of China. From left: Kraig Adler, Richard C. Goris, Kenneth V. Kardong, RC, Jack Frazier, Kathryn, and Susana Frazier. Photo by Tsutomu Hikida.

Zhaoqing. Because buses were prohibited on the streets, we had to walk a dozen blocks or so to a hotel where a banquet had been prepared in our honor. On arrival we were all parched, and Kay and I each downed two or three bottles of soda pop before we felt hydrated again. The banquet must have been some sort of city affair, because the mayor and a dozen or more officials formed a receiving line, and we had to shake hands with all of them. Afterward, with Bennie to handle the language problem, we taxied to a small restaurant where we could rest and which was close to where the bus would pick us up. Then we were off to the Seven Star Crags.

The unique tower karst formations of southern China and adjacent northern Vietnam have been pictured innumerable times in travelogues, artwork, and geology texts. They sometimes occur in isolation, but often in groups, extending vertically upward for hundreds of feet. Some have caves in them that have yielded spectacular fossils. Others have caves beneath them through which water may pass. The towers are mostly of limestone, notable for the ease with which it erodes in the presence of even slightly acid water. One hypothesis for their formation is that huge flat, deep blocks of limestone developed vertical cracks down which water percolated, continuously widening the distance between adjacent towers over the millennia. Regardless of their origin they are picturesque. It was a treat to see them at close range and to visit one, inside of which a footbridge crossed a small flowing stream.

During our return trip to Canton we reached an impasse where a truck loaded with huge rocks had overturned, blocking the only usable lane in a section of

highway under repair. We had to retrace our route and take a longer way back to our base. In short, our trip lasted 14 hours, and we were all exhausted and yearning for a shower on our return. That was not to be. Another banquet awaited us. It was all cooked and ready, and we were told to be in the dining room in less than half an hour. The feast ended with songs, and I was persuaded to sing a solo a capella despite the lateness of the hour. We were not in bed until midnight. What a day! Several persons complimented me on my endurance, but they didn't know that I slept most of the next day.

As a very special privilege, our group of delegates was permitted to visit Hainan, the large island south of mainland China. We flew in a body to Haikou, the principal city, and arrived in late afternoon following a brief but heavy rainstorm. Our hosts were surprised, because Chinese pilots did not fly in bad weather, but it had been clear when we left the mainland. We flew in American-made planes, which, presumably, were equipped for instrument landings, but we were told that Chinese airports lacked the complementary instruments. We were assigned to quarters and somewhat later were treated to another elaborate banquet that was also attended by government officials. It was a memorable affair, notably because a waitress arrived with a large tureen of soup in which a whole cooked chicken, sans feathers, was floating. The girl stirred the soup vigorously, and the bird disintegrated. I was served one of the feet in my bowl. I wondered who got the head. Alas, toward the end of the meal our forks disappeared, and Kathryn had to go out in the kitchen in an attempt to retrieve them. We would have been in real trouble had we been forced to use the traditional chopsticks. Our forks were lost, but Kay emerged with two others, also of stainless steel, but stamped "China" and which eventually became souvenirs.

Our room was in a new and very modern complex that obviously had been built for an anticipated influx of tourists. Capitalistic experiments were being tried in southern China, notably near Hong Kong. The rooms were grouped in the midst of an extensive flower garden. Just as in other tropical regions, there were geckos on the walls in the evening waiting for insects to be attracted to the lights. I found a supple wand such as I had used in Africa almost two decades earlier. With it I thought I could bring down a gecko from far above my head if I concurrently jumped upward. I tried it only once, because I nearly fell over backward. My blasted balance problem precluded any further attempts. One night later, in another part of the island, as we were descending a long set of stairs after our supper, we noted a large gecko high up on the wall, far out of reach. Kraig Adler took a wide elastic band from his pocket and sent it flying from his cradled fingers. It hit and stunned the gecko, which fell just as Ken Kardong opened his hand and caught it on the way down. It was a perfect demonstration that was roundly applauded by our Oriental colleagues. Kraig and Ken could not have done better if they had rehearsed for a week.

One of our young Japanese friends remarked that we certainly had luxurious quarters for our stay in Hainan. His English was quite good, and, in response to my comment of surprise, he assured me that we would be making trips out from Haikou for the next few days. He was grossly misinformed, and we nearly had a catastrophe as a result. The next morning we walked the 100 yards or so to the bus that was waiting for us. I was carrying only my shoulder bag containing my heavy camera and an assortment of film and lenses. Kathryn had her handbag. When we boarded the bus a chorus of voices asked where our baggage was. We would be away from Haikou for several days. Jack Frazier and Kathryn rushed back to our room and threw everything into our hand luggage in record time, but even so we held up departure for at least 15 minutes, meantime feeling mightily embarrassed. It was a shame that Bennie wasn't with us. He would have known exactly what the plans were.

We circumnavigated the island by bus, traveling around the perimeter in a counterclockwise direction. We saw the Gulf of Tonkin, which lapped the shore of Vietnam on the opposite side. We ventured into the mountainous interior of the south to stay for two nights at a primitive research station, where our beds consisted of thin mattresses over pieces of plywood and a light blanket for each of us. Between nights we were taken into wild country where the younger Japanese members of our group collected many unusual species of herps. Lunches were provided, but liquids were in short supply, and we were all parched from the sultry heat. Our personal bottle of iodinized water was used up all too soon. We were in a heavily forested region where, according to the Chinese biologists, such mammal species as the pangolin and gibbon still survived. The aborigines of the region were permitted to hunt game. We saw one carrying a flintlock rifle.

Our tour took us to the Border of the Earth, a rocky promontory at the southern end of the island, and then on to another tourist complex that was still under construction but where our accommodations were not too bad. Except for an occasional brief shower, the weather had been good throughout our stay in China, but as we drove up the east coast back to Haikou, a storm was brewing. Dick Goris suggested that a typhoon might be coming; not one of the vast destructive storms like our Atlantic hurricanes, but still severe enough to keep the Chinese planes grounded. He was right. We were taken to the Haikou Airport, but our flight had been canceled.

We returned to our hotel, where we were informed that we were now on our own. The local committee would fly us back as soon as possible, but the symposium, for which we had paid a fairly large sum, was over. We would have to pay for our lodging and food. The first was easy, but the menus were incomprehensible, and none of the waitresses knew a word of our languages. All the Chinese members of our party stayed at another hotel, so the many who knew English could not help us. We Americans sat at one table in the restaurant of the fancy complex, the Japanese at others, and Dick Goris alternated among us. We resorted to pointing at food on the tables of other diners, but we finally had excellent help from a bilingual man who lived in Hong Kong and who was also waiting to leave Hainan.

Finally, after two days, the Chinese pilots decided it was safe to fly, but by that time three days' worth of passengers had accumulated. Professor Pan evidently had some influence, because all the foreign herpetologists were scheduled to leave in the early afternoon. Except for him, Professors Zhao and Ding, and a few other leaders, all the Chinese delegates had left on the long ferry ride from Haikou back to Canton as soon as the weather began to clear.

The small room at the airport that served as a ticket counter and for the immigration and customs personnel was jammed with people. It was hot and sticky from the sultry weather, and it reeked with the odor of profusely sweating bodies. Many persons were trying unsuccessfully to get seats on our plane. The processing was agonizingly slow. After almost an hour, I was beginning to feel the pressure and must have shown it, because Susana Frazier, Jack's feisty Argentinian wife, grabbed my arm and pushed through the mass of humanity, with Kathryn at my heels. I was guided behind the counter and plunked down on the only chair in sight. Courtesy to the aged came to the fore again, and we were quickly escorted through the red tape. All went well until an armed guard found two packages of Tums in my pocket. Those neatly wrapped antacid tablets admittedly looked a little like cartridges, but, when I pointed to my mouth and rubbed my abdomen, he understood and smiled. We had to wait for the rest of our group, but at least we were able to sit in a spacious waiting room where a welcome breeze blew away all traces of the fetid odor in the lobby. The flight back to Canton was uneventful.

Because of the delay on Hainan, some of the members of our party had to go right on. Their belongings had been piled in a bus and transported from the university to the Canton Airport. Several were going to Chengdu, Sichuan, and their plane was awaiting our arrival from Haikou. So there were hasty good-byes from those of us who would be returning to Hong Kong on the morrow. Kay and I were bused back to the university and, to our relief, food was chosen for us both at supper and breakfast the following morning. Its quality was far below what was served to us earlier, but at least it wasn't very expensive.

We had accumulated considerable extra baggage. Many of the Chinese delegates, apprised in advance of the work on *Agkistrodon*, brought me books and papers—far more than enough to fill the two handmade briefcases Kay and I received when we arrived, as well as a sizable cardboard box. Laden though we were, our baggage loomed small in comparison with Jean Garzoni's. He was from Lausanne, spoke French and a little English, and he had been collecting under a special permit for weeks prior to our arrival. While getting to the train platform he had to carry as much as he could some 50 feet or so ahead, and then return twice more to move the rest. Kathryn and I pitched in and helped him, and we transported many of his boxes, bags, and cases short distances forward along with our own. His material was finally placed in a baggage car, and we all repaired to the passenger coach reserved for non-Chinese travelers. When we arrived in Hong Kong, I went along with Garzoni, mindful of his limited English, and found an employee who provided a four-wheeled, hand-pulled cart that would carry all Garzoni's

things. We accompanied him to the customs inspection, where he had to produce numerous documents to clear his possessions, especially the many live reptiles he was taking with him. Among the latter were two rather large 100-pace vipers, *Deinagkistrodon acutus,* that he had captured personally in Anhwei Province. One of them eventually arrived in the laboratory of Beat Schätti, in Zürich, where it was photographed by Harry Sigg, and I am indebted to both of them for some superb pictures that were reproduced in the monograph.

We were soon back in the Meridien Hotel and, after washing up, we headed for the dining room for some western-style food, which tasted mighty good after our "guess what this is?" meals in China.

Instead of the four or five days we had planned to spend in Hong Kong, we had only two because of being marooned on Hainan. Besides wanting to rest after our strenuous two weeks, we had much to do. Repacking required a lot of time. A sizable box of our possessions that we had left at the Meridien while we were in China had to be consolidated with our other things, plus the many books and papers in Chinese. We inquired about mailing them, but the costs were so high that we decided to carry everything with us. Since we were traveling business class we were allowed 90 kilograms each, which was more than ample, but we had eight items on which to keep an eye.

We also went shopping. One of the bellboys recognized us when we arrived, and, after he conveyed our mound of things to our room, he asked if he could help us in any way. In response I asked him how to find a map store and several other places we wanted to visit. He offered to go with us and suggested we meet him about 4:15 P.M. at the McDonald's fast-food place up the street from the hotel. By that time he had gone off duty and was out of his uniform. He knew Kowloon, on the mainland of the Crown Colony, quite well, and he was an excellent guide. He even took us on the subway during the rush hour, which we never would have attempted alone. We bought several maps, some luggage, a few pieces of clothing, and even an inexpensive Citizen watch, the first I ever had showing the date and day of the week. My faithful Hamilton had stopped running while we were in the People's Republic. Our benefactor managed to flag a cab for us despite the crowds near a general market and the light rain that was falling. We dropped him off near his home on the way back to the hotel, and I offered him a generous tip, but he refused to take anything, saying it had been his pleasure to help us. His name was Kwok Siu Lun, but, like so many Orientals who are in frequent contact with travelers, he assumed an English name that was easily remembered. He called himself Aaron, pronounced "R'-on." We were to see him again another year.

Our visit to Communist China had been an interesting and exciting adventure. We made many friends and learned much about a nation and culture very unlike our own. From an American viewpoint, things seemed to be looking up. The destructive Cultural Revolution, initiated by Mao Zedong in 1966, was over, and he was dead. One noticeable hangover, especially apparent to naturalists, remained, however. Birds were scarce or absent almost everywhere we went on the mainland. We were told that was the result of a decree to kill them all because they ate seeds and thus stole food from the peasants. No thought was given to their role in the control of crop-eating insects. In contrast, we saw quite a number of birds on Hainan Island. Also, children were more numerous there. They were few in Canton and its vicinity. The government's policy of permitting only one child to a family seemed to be working, in the attempt to reduce China's enormous billion-strong population. The experiments with capitalism and the obvious preparations for tourists seemed commendable, to us. At the time we were in the country it appeared that great changes were on the way. Recent informants tell me they still are, despite the massacre some years later at Tian'anmen Square in Beijing.

We were deeply grateful to Zhao Ermi (now Er-mi Zhao) for inviting us, and I was grateful to several others, both Chinese and Japanese, who helped me in one way or another with the *Agkistrodon* monograph. Richard Goris was a tower of strength, not only in stature and ability, by acting as leader of the foreigners, but also by keeping an eye on me, the oldest of the delegates. We also formed a warm friendship with Hidetoshi "Toshi" Ota, who was then a student at Kyoto University. Both he and especially Goris were extremely kind and helpful when I was stricken in Tokyo the following year. I still correspond occasionally with Goris and Zhao, and also, Aaron, Bennie, and Toshi.

From Hong Kong we flew to Taipei in Taiwan, the other, but free, China. There we had a pleasant and informative visit with the able herpetologist Shou-hsian Mao, of the National Defense Medical Center. Because we returned to Taiwan in 1987 and I have much more to write about that beautiful island, I have reserved the details about our first visit for a later chapter.

When we were leaving Taipei to fly to Japan, our trip fell apart. At the airport the attendant at the counter thumbed quickly through our passports and then went through them again more slowly. She then asked, "Where are your Japanese visas?" I responded, "The travel agency told me we didn't need any." She picked up the telephone and asked a man, evidently a supervisor, to come to the desk. With him I wheeled our great load of baggage to a small office, and he gave us the bad news. We could apply for visas in Taipei, but it might take a week or more to get them. Our only alternative was to ask for 72-hour "shore" passes, but for them we needed proof that we were scheduled for departure within the prescribed 72 hours. Kay and I quickly consulted. In essence, our trip was over and our planned 10-day stay in Japan had to be abandoned. The man made reservations for us on a Japan Airline flight leaving Tokyo for Anchorage, Alaska, in three days. We boarded the plane for Japan disheartened and discouraged, feelings that were heightened by one delay after another. Something that required an hour's time had to be done to make our plane airworthy before we could take off for Tokyo's Narita Airport. The shore pass line was long and moved at a snail's pace. It took us far more time than usual to retrieve our baggage and pile it onto one of the free carts.

We finally pushed the load out to the main lobby and found poor Dick Goris, who had waited for hours to meet us. We told him our sad story. He was sympathetic and tried to make up a little for our disappointment by pointing things out to us during the long drive from Narita into the city. He showed us mamushi (*Agkistrodon blomhoffii*) habitats, Japan's Disneyland as we passed it, and indicated an ingenious device to discourage speeding. Mounted at intervals were machines that took pictures of speeding cars that included the license plate numbers. The guilty party received a copy in the mail along with an order to pay a fine or else! Dick showed us parts of the city, including the renowned Ginza District, and he deposited us at the Fairmont Hotel, well out of mid-city, and across from a moat surrounding the Emperor's palace. We apologized to him profusely and promised we would try to come back next year. He was able to stay with us for only a short time, because he had a very long drive in heavy traffic to get back to his home near Yokohama.

Perhaps it was because we were so disturbed by our bad luck, but I let down my guard. Surely in Japan everything would be spick-and-span. I took a deep swallow from the water carafe in our room before I realized it tasted bad. Something was wrong. Had the chambermaid forgotten to change it? Whatever the cause, I was soon making frequent trips to the bathroom, which, thank goodness, had modern flush plumbing. I could not help but think of some of the more primitive facilities we had been obliged to use while we were in Communist China and the likes of which, I soon found out, were still present in a great many places in Japan. The next day, in a small publication in English, about what to do and where to go in Japan, the matter was neatly summed up as follows:

How To Use Japanese Style Lavatory

The chances are that sometime during your stay in Japan you will find yourself having to use a Japanese-style lavatory. It is not made for sitting down, but don't despair.

The receptacle is usually on a raised floor. The opening is rectangular with a sort of hood over one end.

Climb up on the raised floor and stand flat-footed astride the opening with your face towards the hood. Then bend down into a crouching or squatting position, making sure that your rear is over the opening and not protruding beyond it.

The position may not be comfortable but it is sanitary because no part of your body comes in direct contact with the fixings.

In the case of the male, he urinates by standing on the lower floor and aiming for the opening. Please aim carefully.

Our flight to Anchorage was relatively short, but we crossed the International Date Line en route. We arrived in the morning and the Japan Airlines flight continued on directly to Frankfurt, Germany, by flying over the North Pole or close to it.

Our visit to Alaska was not a happy one. The hotel selected for us by our travel agency was inferior, and it had been built in sections with stairs in odd places. It was supposed to have a bellboy, but we never found him, and we had to wrestle our voluminous baggage up and down the steps by ourselves. The desk clerks were almost surly, and when we opened the door to our room, we found that it had not been made up, and the stench of stale tobacco smoke was stifling. I quickly opened the window, tossed out the overflowing contents of two or three ashtrays and let the place air out despite the 50-degree temperature outdoors. A maid delayed her lunch to make us comfortable, and she was the only person I tipped in the entire establishment.

Neither of us had ever been in Alaska and, for me, it was my fiftieth state. The weather was clear and cold, and during the afternoon we could see Mount McKinley, North America's highest peak, which crested at over 20,000 feet. During our short stay we saw several drunken bums, one in the gutter, heard another cussing out a policeman in the foulest language imaginable, and saw two cops escorting a hoodlum from a store he had attempted to rob. Anchorage was a frontier town, which was further emphasized by the presence of many Indians and Esquimaux who had arrived there for some sort of conference. Along with our walks and observations, my dysentery caught up with me again, and it didn't respond to any of the remedies we carried with us.

We had to go to an airline office to have our schedule changed. Our departure was in the early morning, and the sun rose and turned all the snow-clad mountains and even faraway Mount McKinley rosy pink. We stayed overnight in Seattle but were back in Tucson, our starting point, late the next afternoon. In the morning I paid a visit to the travel agency that had forced us to return unexpectedly early.

Chapter 57

The Tokyo Disaster

We were disgusted, of course, with the travel agency for ruining our visit to Japan. When I walked into their office to demand an explanation, they were astounded to see me back a full week earlier than expected. The owner herself had prepared our tickets and other details. When I asked, politely but firmly, why she had sent us to Japan with no visas, she still didn't know they were required. To make a long story short, she subscribed to some type of liability insurance, and she offered us a free round trip to Japan by way of apology. She didn't mind when I said we'd have to wait until next year. We were certainly not prepared to take off again right away! Also, I had other commitments that needed to be honored.

So we planned an ambitious trip in 1986. Japan first, on to Taiwan to see a recently established 100-pacer (*Deinagkistrodon*) farm, and then to the island of Java, to examine the historic specimens of the Malayan pit viper (*Calloselasma*) in the museum in Bogor. I spent much time making preparations and reservations and writing letters to people we planned to visit. All was set, and on May 12, 1986, we departed from Tucson.

We always made it a point to spend a day and night in the city of our long-distance departure in order to catch our breath, shake down our luggage, follow the regimen for overcoming jet lag, and to get a good night's sleep. It was well that we had the day of ease in Los Angeles, because an ailment caught up with me that I had experienced only once before, some months previously in Albuquerque. I discovered small welts in and near my armpits. To my dismay, I was getting the hives again. Soon I itched in a dozen places, but I knew that trying to scratch was hopeless and would only aggravate the agony. I napped during the afternoon and wakened to find great red welts on my chest and back. In other places where I had itched in the morning, my skin was perfectly clear. The blebs came and went within a few hours. I was in bed by nine, still itching, even though I had taken my first dose of Prednisone, the medication my internist had prescribed for my hives. When I awakened soon after midnight, all the welts had disappeared.

A few blebs were present the next morning, and I suspected I was in for another itchy day. I hoped my trouble would go away as quickly on this trip as it did in Albuquerque. There it had lasted only four days.

We boarded our Singapore Airlines plane for Tokyo, and, when we arrived at Narita Airport, I climbed into a wheelchair, as I did after every long flight. Our passage through customs was perfunctory. Then to a bank to buy yen, after which my attendant pushed me out to the curb where we had to wait for the bus to the Narita Holiday Inn. We were to stay there for the night, resting before making the long trip (60 miles) into Tokyo.

I awakened in the morning with a bad case of the hives, but accepted it in stride and ate a hearty breakfast. We took the bus back to the airport and there transferred to the TCAT bus, the English designation for the main air station in Tokyo. On the way I developed a severe abdominal pain, but Kay thought it was because I had consumed too much fat (bacon and butter) with my breakfast. When we reached the Fairmont Hotel, I felt so lousy that I went right to bed. I telephoned Dick Goris, and he recommended a group of English and American doctors who operated the Tokyo Clinic. We made an appointment for 11:30 the next morning. Later, we went to the hotel dining room, but I had no appetite. Just broth and ice cream. Then back to bed, the pain returning sporadically.

At the clinic, Dr. J. H. T. Marshall examined me, pressing my abdomen here and there and checking blood pressure and temperature. He had nothing specific to recommend, but gave me a prescription. He promised, however, to telephone us on the morrow. As soon as we were back at the hotel, I went to bed again. We visited the dining room for supper, but after some soup I felt very sick, and I was escorted back to our room by the headwaiter, who held my arm all the way. Once in our room, I made a quick dive to the bathroom sink, and vomited with explosive force. The hotel people, who were genuinely concerned about me, consulted with Kay, and at about 9:00 P.M., moaning with pain and doubled up, because my legs were too long for a

Japanese-sized ambulance, I was on my way to the Police Hospital, the only one open at night. Several doctors poked my abdomen, and, although I pleaded by gestures for a sedative, I was given none. Finally, after what seemed an eternity, I was wheeled into another room for a series of X-rays. Nothing showed, but one doctor, in very poor English, asked if I still had my appendix. I answered in the affirmative. Finally, I received a shot in the arm and the pain slowly receded. Sometime between 1:00 and 2:00 A.M. Kay and I returned to the hotel. Throughout the excursion to the hospital we were accompanied by an English-speaking junior hotel executive, who had picked up many thousands of yen at the front desk before we left. He paid all the bills, but Kay reimbursed the hotel with traveler's checks in the morning.

I slept after our return from the hospital. When I wakened at dawn the pain was still present, but its severity fluctuated.

What could be wrong? Was it my appendix? Gallbladder? An intestinal obstruction? When Dr. Marshall called, Kay recounted our nocturnal experience to him, but he still could not pinpoint the problem. He said he would be on duty on Sunday (the next day) and to call him if anything developed. I stayed in bed all day, managed to squeeze down a little bouillon and custard, but was miserable with pain and weakness.

There was no change the next morning, so Kay called Dr. Marshall, and he agreed to come to see me at the hotel. A house call, so to speak, and an extremely important one as it turned out. It was noonish when he came, and, after another examination, he called his colleague, Dr. Fujii, on our room telephone and announced, "I have an old man here with a surgical abdomen." The "old man" managed a wry smile, despite his pain and misery.

So it was off to the hospital again, but this time to Tokai University's Tokyo Hospital. There we met Dr. Koichi Fujii, who had trained in St. Louis and spoke idiomatic American English without a trace of an accent. He turned out to be an excellent surgeon, which was a godsend considering what developed later. He and his students put me through all sorts of tests, one of which I could watch on an electronic screen. I could see my gallbladder, but, although it was somewhat enlarged, it seemed not to be involved with my trouble. My pain was still severe, although spasmodic. Dr. Fujii finally recommended opening me up in order to see what was the matter. We agreed that he should, so they prepared me for the operating room and went to work, for over three hours. The operation over, I came out of the anesthetic and Dr. Fujii encouraged me to stand up

and take a few steps, which I did. Then to my hospital bed where I dozed and awakened somewhat later in a private room which, I noted, was even more spartan than the simplest I had seen in the States. Also, the bed had been designed for a Japanese, not a six-foot American. I had to keep my knees bent most of the time. If I stretched out, lying flat on my back, for example, the covers came up only to my chest. By the time I was discharged, six days later, I feared that my feet were permanently numb. It was days before I had much feeling in them.

When Dr. Fujii and his team opened me up, they found a dreadful mess. My appendix was necrotic, and so was the cecum. There was a great amount of yellow pus. Several loops of my small intestine had grown fast to the body wall. That suggested I might have had a ruptured appendix years ago that had somehow healed enough for me to function normally. Could it have been when I was under constant sedation while suffering from tetanus (lockjaw) way back in 1929? I would have felt no pain at that time. In any event, Dr. Fujii cut away a lot of my gut, and anastomosed healthy tissue at each end of the mess. That he did an excellent job was evidenced by my recovery and return to good health.

The nurses were excellent. They were prompt in answering my call bell, and nothing was too much trouble for them. When I needed to go to the bathroom they often went down on their knees to put my big slippers on my feet. The size of them provoked smiles, even giggling, as they had in China the previous year. At first I slept a lot and had no desire to read or do anything else. My trips to the bathroom were infrequent, and Dr. Fujii, upon hearing about it, questioned me closely, and I reported my prostate trouble (the old man's disease), which dated back almost two decades. Also, I told him I was on diuretics. He seemed satisfied, but he ordered that a catheter be inserted that, with frequent changes, I had to endure until I was back in Albuquerque weeks later. (What a damned nuisance!)

My appetite was poor at first, and it was not helped by the Japanese food that appeared on my meal trays—all sorts of strange items and concoctions. Most unusual of all was my breakfast one morning. Staring up at me was a fried egg with a bright orange eye resting on a bed of spinach, the entire ensemble stone cold! By that time my appetite was improving, and I ate it all, but during the early part of my hospital stay I nibbled only a little, which was, of course, reported to Dr. Fujii. He commented that, even though I might not like institutional food, I must eat in order to gain strength.

It quickly became clear to me that he was an intellectual with an exceptionally high IQ. When he discovered I was associated with a university we had many lively conversations on a variety of topics. He stopped in my room every evening, sometimes for as much as 20 minutes, no doubt chiefly to practice his English.

Dick Goris arrived for a visit as soon as I was able to socialize. He was followed by other visitors. Hidetoshi Ota came by train from Kyoto and stayed in Tokyo overnight with a friend so he could visit me twice. He had dinner with Kay and taught her how to use the subway to get back and forth between the hospital and the Fairmont Hotel. Michihisa Toriba, of the Japan Snake Institute, appeared at my room carrying a curious bamboo vase with a spray of dwarf iris from his family garden. In late afternoon he and Kay went back to the hotel. She expected to take him to dinner in the Fairmont dining room, but he asked if there was a Japanese restaurant in the building. There was, and he hosted her with money that Dr. Yoshio Sawai, the director of the Snake Institute, had supplied. Kay gave him a lot of my film, with which he agreed to photograph the living members of the *Agkistrodon* complex at the Institute. (He assumed that responsibility with splendid results. He later sent me more than 200 slides, and he did much better than I would have done. In exchange, I sent him a photocopy of Emelianov's Russian-language "Snakes of the Far Eastern District" (1929), from Dr. Gloyd's library, along with English translations of the text on the vipers, the introduction, and the conclusions of that work. Toriba felt well repaid for his kindness.)

I was scheduled to leave the hospital the following Saturday morning. After I checked out, we took a taxi to the Fairmont, where we arrived in midafternoon. Some sort of formal function was in progress, with well-dressed Japanese couples clustered around the dining room entrance. As we crossed the lobby toward the elevator, I looked at the desk, and was delighted to see the "top brass," five men in striped pants and tails, bowing to me in welcome after my harrowing ordeal. I waved to them, which produced broad smiles. Kay had kept the desk posted daily about my progress.

We spent a week in the Fairmont Hotel while I convalesced. It was a relatively small hostelry, but with a splendid dining room and good food. Its location was ideal, directly opposite the Emperor's palace grounds, which were wooded and separated from the nearest streets and buildings by a broad moat. Directly in front of the Fairmont there was a narrow park paralleling the moat and supporting a large number of huge Japanese cherry trees. Photographs showed that they were a riot of blooms in early spring, but they were in full leaf during our stay in May. Many waterbirds frequented the moat, and there were numerous passerines as well. Because we were on the sixth floor we had a grandstand view of the area. Dick Goris had recommended the Fairmont when we were in Tokyo briefly the previous year. It was vastly better than the downtown hotels, from which only buildings and heavy traffic would have been visible.

Although I spent most of the first day or two in bed, I was up looking out the window as much as possible. It was difficult for me to sit comfortably, but I could tolerate being propped up with pillows in a chair for a short time, which gradually lengthened each day as I grew stronger. From the chair I could look out the window, and on Sunday the weekend boaters were there in force. There was a fleet of 70 small white rowboats in the moat, all neatly aligned on weekdays in groups of 10. Few people used them during the week, but they were all out on Sunday. It was amusing to see them bump into one another as Japanese swains, unaccustomed to oars, took their girlfriends for boat rides.

Dick Goris went all out to help us. At the hospital he had given me a book on Japanese birds that was written by a member of the royal family, but which he had translated and organized for the publishing company for which he worked. The illustrations were from old paintings, and some of the birds were grotesquely portrayed but interesting nonetheless. The book included a long chapter on birding in Japan with descriptions of many of the islands and bird habitats. I was impressed with how cold Hokkaido, the large northern Japanese island, really is. Yet the mamushi (*Agkistrodon blomhoffii*) lives there, and it also occurs on Sakhalin, which the Russians stole from the Japanese in the closing two weeks of World War II. Later, Dick brought us a modern field guide in English and two pairs of glasses—binoculars and opera glasses—with which we could watch the birds in and around the moat. For sedentary observers, we ran up a fair list: little egret, intermediate egret, common shag (cormorant), little tern, glaucous gull, Pekin and spot-billed ducks, jungle and carrion crows, gray and European starlings, house swift, dove (species?), and azure-winged magpie. The last was by far the most attractive. A pair apparently had nested close by, and sometimes we saw as many as three at once.

On Sunday afternoon we watched a televised baseball game, which was about the only thing on Japanese television that was intelligible to us. There was one huge American player with a full beard, and when he hit a home run with the bases loaded, the crowd cheered with a mighty roar.

At first we had to live via room service, which was costly, but I was not able to go to the dining room until late in the week, and even then it was quite an ordeal. The confounded catheter was uncomfortable and I was unsteady on my feet, although I walked a lot back and forth in our room. On Monday, May 26, we taxied to Dr. Fujii's office, and he removed my "stitches," which consisted of what looked like a large brass zipper. It came off readily and I scarcely felt it. A new experience for me. Fairly late in the week we had to taxi to a branch of the Mitsubishi Bank to get a draft with which to pay the clinic, and some of my traveler's checks were needed. We were out for over an hour, and I was exhausted by the brief excursion. We had a difficult time flagging a taxi to return to the hotel, but a well-dressed Japanese man saw we were in trouble, and quickly got us a cab. On Friday, May 30, we were back at the clinic where Dr. Fujii changed my catheter. When we said farewell to him I told him that the name of Dr. Fujii would always stand as high in our minds as Mount Fujiyama, Japan's sacred mountain. He was quite pleased, but he deserved it. I was lucky to have been in the care of such an able surgeon. We often thought of what might have happened if the onset of my emergency had occurred while we were in the mountains of Taiwan or the hills of Java. I would surely have come home in a box or a crematory jar. Dr. Fujii told us the operation had been virtually in the nick of time.

When I was functioning again, I had much telephoning to do. I had to call Dr. Mao in Taiwan to tell him we would not be able to visit him, and I asked him to cancel our hotel reservation and the appointment he had made for me with an acupuncture doctor who was to have a try at helping my failing hearing. I talked by long distance with the travel agent in Tucson and asked her to make reservations for us from Los Angeles to Tucson and then to Albuquerque. Also, she was to call Candice R. Corley, my secretary, and ask her to write, on my behalf, to my contacts in Java stating that we would be unable to visit them during 1986. We talked with Toshi Ota several times, and also Dr. Hajime Fukada, who, unfortunately, was hospitalized in Kyoto.

Soon after my operation, we were flabbergasted to receive a registered letter from Dr. Fukada containing 50,000 yen, the equivalent of $300 U.S. A note that came with it stated that the money was a gift. What on earth was I to do about it? I didn't want to offend him by returning it. As soon as I was able, I consulted with Toshi by telephone, and he called back the next day and told me he had talked with Dr. Fukada, and that, inasmuch as the latter had been our guest (Isabelle's and mine) for four nights at our home on Taunton Lake, he had planned to pay our hotel bill when we arrived in Kyoto, where we had expected to visit him in his hospital. I conveyed our thanks to Dr. Fukada when next I telephoned him, and, sometime later, after our return

Dr. Richard C. Goris and his wife, Yukimi. Photo by RC.

to the States, I added an equal sum of my own money and gave the entire amount to the Society for the Study of Amphibians and Reptiles as a donation in Dr. Fukada's honor. I wrote to tell him, and so did Henri Seibert, the SSAR's treasurer, and the old Japanese gentleman was greatly pleased.

The staff of the Fairmont Hotel went all out to assist us. Nothing was too much trouble. I was constantly helped and escorted around the building, the chambermaids and bellmen inquired daily about my progress, and we were better treated than we ever have been in any hostelry anywhere in the world. I told Dick Goris how pleased we were, and his wife, Yukimi, said that the Fairmont evidently was like the country inns of Japan that are noted for their hospitality. When we left the Fairmont, half a dozen staff members lined up on the curb by our car. I shook hands with them all, and they bowed low to the guest who had met with such bad luck. After we were home I sent a letter to the manager of the hotel thanking him and his employees for all they had done for us. He had it translated, assembled the entire staff, and read aloud what I had written.

In a very real sense, Dick Goris saved my life. He recommended the clinic through which I acquired the services of Dr. Fujii, and he constantly did both of us many favors. On Sunday, June 1, he drove all the way from his home near Yokohama to our hotel—a very long trip by automobile through heavy traffic. He brought Yukimi with him, so we were finally able to meet her. She is a charming Japanese intellectual, and Dick deeply appreciates her and his luck in having such a fine and valued partner. She helps him with his translations and also with their menagerie of live reptiles, mostly snakes and geckos. Dick even brought two live snakes with him in the car so that I could have a look at them—a mamushi from Korea and a tiger water snake, *Rhabdophis tigrina,* that he had caught near his home that very morning. That snake, long thought to be harmless, had recently been found to have toxic saliva, and there have been a few fatalities as the results of bites.

Dick and Yukimi had lunch with us at the Fairmont and then drove us to the Narita Holiday Inn near the airport, a distance of more than 60 miles from Tokyo in the opposite direction from their home. He is a wonderful friend, and he cheerfully gave up his Sunday to help us. Trying to make the long trip by taxi and then the TCAT bus would have exhausted me far beyond my then feeble endurance.

The next morning, the hotel bus took us to the airport, and there we had to arrange with Singapore Airlines to return to the States by first class. Dr. Fujii insisted on it so that I could lie down during the long flight to Los Angeles. The extra cost was staggering, almost $1,000 for the two of us, but Kay charged it to Visa and I reimbursed her later. The flight was uneventful. The service was superb, and we were wined and dined almost ad nauseum. We have used Singapore Airlines several times, and we are permanently numbered among those who think it is the best airline in existence. We had put Swissair almost on a par with it until several snafus occurred when we used it from Zürich to Hong Kong in 1985.

We started from Japan on the second, and because we crossed the International Date Line it was still June 2 when we arrived in California. After an interminable wait for a wheelchair, a rather surly porter appeared with one. He took us outside the airport to a place where we could get the bus to our motel, and although I tipped him handsomely he refused to wait so I could sit in the wheelchair. He had to eat his lunch! So I sat uncomfortably on our baggage until the bus came almost a half hour later. Welcome back to America! Just about the same as our miserable return reception in Chicago in 1984. We stayed overnight at the Holiday Inn, and were soon back in Tucson, where we walked outdoors into a temperature of 106°F. Two days later we returned to my home base in Albuquerque where I completed my convalescence.

We knew before we left on our several trips abroad that Medicare is worthless outside the United States, so I bought travel insurance from Health Care Abroad, whose advertisement Kathryn had found in a copy of the "New Yorker." A policy has to be taken out for each trip, and for a specific number of days. Without it, my financial loss would have been substantial. Health Care Abroad is affiliated with other insurance companies, and they had three offices: in Washington, London, and Singapore. After I was stricken, Kay, through the Fairmont Hotel operator, called the office in Singapore and reported my troubles and gave them my insurance number. They immediately sent us their Tokyo representative, a quite capable young lady, and she took over. My hospital bill was paid by Europ Assistance, one of the affiliates. We paid the doctor, but I was later reimbursed by Health Care Abroad for the clinic bill, our cabfares from the hotel to the clinic and back, all prescriptions, and for the extra charge for my first-class fare back to the States. They did not reimburse us for Kay's first-class fare. Because the yen had jumped in value (it had increased by a third in relation to the dollar since the previous year, 1985) the costs were very high. My hospital bill was in excess of $6,000 U.S. Including the reimbursement, my "Tokyo Disaster" cost almost $10,000. In addition, our hotel bill exceeded $3,000, and that I had to pay personally.

Without Kay I would have been sunk. She handled all the details, acted as nurse and errand girl, and did all manner of things to get me back to health. Actually, she enjoyed Tokyo and felt quite at home there, negotiating the subway back and forth to the hospital, shopping for many things, including fruit (what we got was sour and unripe), and mingling with the hotel staff and other Japanese, all of whom were most helpful. A number of them were people we had met in China the previous year.

An afterthought—were the hives associated with the deteriorating situation in my abdomen? I asked Dr. Fujii, and he thought they probably were.

So we had been to Japan twice, with bad luck both times. I had seen the Narita International Airport, the high-speed highway from it to Tokyo, the moat around the Emperor's palace, and the ceilings of two hospitals and our room at the Fairmont. Not much else—not the historic city of Kyoto, the bullet train, Mount Fujiyama, or the Japan Snake Institute. It would have been nice to go back later, but the value of the yen had skyrocketed so badly that the cost was prohibitive. Such is life. One cannot do everything he would like.

Chapter 58

Taiwan and Java

We had struck out twice in Japan. We would have been delighted to go back later, but the crippling financial problem was steadily growing worse. Prices over there remained virtually the same, but the dollar was being devalued in relation to foreign currencies. By early 1987 the yen was so high that we couldn't afford another trip, much to our sorrow. We never did achieve our objectives in Japan, but, thanks to Dick Goris and several Japanese friends, I had an abundance of photographs and data about its mamushis.

If things had gone as planned in 1986, we would have continued on to Taiwan and Java, two islands inhabited by one each of the two egg-laying members of the *Agkistrodon* complex. So we made them our goal in 1987 instead. We had visited Taiwan for a few days in 1985, and, since I skipped writing about it in a previous chapter, I will digress a bit to review our earlier stay.

We flew in from Hong Kong, and as we rode by bus from the airport into Taipei we noticed a huge, very ornate, multicolored building that we guessed must be a government edifice. We were astounded to discover that it was the Grand Hotel, our destination. It was positively awesome and in perfect repair. Bright red stone columns a meter in diameter supported the upper floors. The main lobby was so vast and impressive that I thought immediately of the Vatican in Rome, which Isabelle and I had visited in 1968 on our way to Africa. The central ceiling consisted of an intricate series of carvings, so ingeniously executed as to suggest the work of some Chinese Michelangelo. The extremely broad and high staircases had beautifully carved marble balustrades with marble lotus buds at the level of every few steps. At every turn we found new and exquisitely designed foyers and sitting rooms. From the exterior we could see that the Grand Hotel was 10 stories high surmounted by two pagoda-like roofs, an actual rather steeply pitched one with marginal upward flares and another lower, similarly shaped one, with a floor between them. The underside of each roof was ornamented with intricate designs, rather like the superb assemblage in the ceiling of the vast main lobby. The components were brightly painted

and looked as though they had been done yesterday. What a chore it must have been to keep them that way! The underside of the upper roof was a very long way above the ground! The roof and the flaring subroof below it were covered with gleaming yellow tile. What's more, there was an impressive ornate entrance gate some distance from the main structure, and there was an annex (where we stayed) whose much smaller lobby was only slightly less fancy. The outdoor grounds were cleverly landscaped, even to having some of the shrubs trimmed in the shape of animals. What an extraordinary complex! Surely it ranked among the man-made wonders of the world.

My first thought, after settling into our room, was to telephone Professor Shou-hsian Mao, who had kindly offered to show me a habitat of the 100-pace viper, *Deinagkistrodon acutus*. According to popular legend, one could walk only 100 paces if bitten by that snake. Professor Mao came to our hotel the next day with a student, Jie-shen Hwu, and he took us to his office on a military base, where he had to obtain clearance for us at the gate. He showed me some of his publications, chiefly in English, and then escorted us to see large plastic containers filled with preserved snakes, including many *Deinagkistrodon*. All were in formalin, and the fumes soon drove us out of the room.

After lunch we taxied to the railroad station and boarded a train in first-class seats that Mao had reserved for us. The ride was spectacular. The eastern half and more of Taiwan, as well as most of the south, is very mountainous, with more than 40 peaks topping 10,000 feet. Yushan, at 13,100 feet, is higher than Japan's Fujiyama. On the east coast a number of the mountains are almost sheer cliffs plunging into the sea. From Taipei the railroad heads east and slightly north to avoid a mountain range. It then turns sharply south and runs along the coast. At times we were on a narrow coastal plain skirting the Pacific Ocean. At others we followed a narrow ledge and then passed through one long tunnel after another, where there was no space between the mountains and the sea. The slopes were very steep and

Dr. Shou-hsian Mao, our guide and benefactor on Taiwan in 1985 and 1987. Photo by RC.

were mostly densely forested except where numerous landslides had occurred. We were told it had taken seven years to build the railroad.

Our destination was Hualien. We stayed at a hotel, and we were up in time, the next morning, to see the sun *rise* over the Pacific; quite a novelty. A great many Americans have seen the sun *set* over the Pacific, but few have had the privilege of experiencing what we did.

The student, Hwu, had grown up in or near Hualien, and he became our guide. A friend of his provided an air-conditioned car—for the use of which I paid, of course—and we were soon driving south at a fast clip through a fairly broad coastal plain that was heavily cultivated. We passed through several small towns, and just beyond the village of Kuang-fu we turned inland toward sloping hills backed by tall mountains. We took a dirt road partway up Ma-Yuan Mountain, but the going was rough. When the car scraped bottom we got out and walked. It was a rather gentle slope, but we climbed a good half mile to a point where the road dipped down again. Within this general area, at about 1,000 feet elevation, Hwu had found *Deinagkistrodon*, and he said that members of the local aboriginal tribe said it was a common snake. The general terrain was partially forested. Several large rock outcrops surrounded by natural vegetation were pointed out to me as places where the 100-pace viper took refuge. We saw none, even though Hwu crisscrossed a hillside where he had found the species previously.

After an hour or so of looking around and taking

pictures, we headed back, stopping in Kuang-fu to buy soft drinks and to look at a snake shop with no *Deinagkistrodon*. There was a painting of such a snake on a sign outside, however, that I photographed. Back in Hualien we found another shop that had two 100-pacers. One was about half grown, and the other measured about three feet in total length. Out of curiosity I asked Dr. Mao to inquire about the price of the big one, and I was startled to learn that they wanted the equivalent of about $500 in U.S. money. The species is highly valued for its use in traditional Oriental medicine.

As a farewell gift, Mao took us and two students for a special treat—a Peking duck dinner. We had a big lazy Susan on our table, as is usual in most Chinese eating places; the hors d'oeuvres consisted of miscellaneous unidentified vegetables. Next, the roasted duck was brought for Dr. Mao to inspect and approve. Then it was taken away and dismembered. The waitress brought a plate full of strong-tasting cylindrical onions, a bowl of black goo that looked like thick soy sauce, and a stack of small "tortillas." These ingredients were followed by a plate full of pieces of duck skin, each about the width of a hen's egg or larger. Mao took the lead. He placed a "tortilla" on his plate, smeared an onion and then a piece of duck with the goo, placed both on the "tortilla," rolled up the concoction, and bit a piece off the end. We all followed suit. Presently slices of duck meat arrived, and they were eaten in the same fashion. Finally the pièce de résistance was placed on the table— the duck's head on a plate. It had been neatly split (with a cleaver?) right down the middle vertically so we could eat the brains!

On our next visit, in 1987, we flew directly from Los Angeles to Taipei, and Dr. Mao took us to see a snake farm where an attempt was being made to raise *Deinagkistrodon* commercially. The offspring, when they reached large size, would be sold for high prices, especially for their gallbladders. After riding a bus south through the flat lowlands of western Taiwan, we stayed overnight in Kaohsiung. In the morning we took a bus to the small inland town of Chiashian, where we disembarked and were met by S. D. Huang, promoter of the farm, with his Renault. He drove us to a farmhouse to which a snake holding pen was attached.

I was taken immediately to see the snakes. They were chiefly in a large, circular concrete enclosure about 30 feet in diameter, one portion of which was occupied by an entranceway where Huang and the farmer, Yeh Chao Ping, donned leather boots. I was wearing heavy leather high-top shoes. There were two wire doors from waist height upward above a concrete wall, which we had to straddle to get inside the pen. The outer walls were also of concrete and were more than 6 feet high. The roof was supported by small beams. Some sunshine penetrated through screening overhead, but mostly the pen was shaded. The flooring was of unfinished concrete around the edges, but stumps and logs had been assembled in the center. There also were a number of square flat boards propped up on one side to provide shelters for the snakes. Low, rather sparse vegetation grew here and there. It was very muddy in spots from a recent rain. The snakes avoided the wet places and were mostly lying around the perimeter of the enclosure on the slightly elevated areas of unfinished concrete.

I saw about 25 *Deinagkistrodon acutus* while I was in the serpents' den, most of them coiled or stretched out in the open. A few were under the shelters. All were alert and well aware of our presence. Some changed their positions as we approached, and one large one, a yard or more in total length, uncoiled but did not crawl away. I photographed at least a dozen different snakes, using my 100-mm lens and strobe light, while Huang and Ping guarded me with their snake hooks. Huang said there were about 40 of the vipers on hand, ranging from perhaps a foot and a half in length to several large ones measuring three feet or more. All seemed to be in excellent condition, but we found part of a snake rotting in one place, and the men showed me the skeletal remains of another that had died. I wondered why they hadn't removed the dead snakes and also the dead chicks (for food), three or four of which had not been eaten.

The *Deinagkistrodon* farm was short-lived. Its operators were unable to raise the young that hatched, all of which succumbed, probably to a viral infection. How lucky I was to see the place when I did.

Back in Taipei I tried acupuncture for my bad hearing, and it worked rather well. (When I returned to Albuquerque I continued such treatments at monthly intervals, but it eventually became obvious that the nerve could no longer be stimulated.)

Dr. Mao took us to see "Snake Alley" in Taipei, and it was a revelation. There were many live snakes, but no venomous ones of any kind at the time. There were also many other small animals, mostly dried and in large glass jars, including flying lizards (*Draco*), seahorses, starfishes, and other invertebrates, all of them elements used in traditional Oriental medicine.

There were a number of live snakes, and a customer could select one, the attendant would kill it and remove the gallbladder, and the buyer would promptly swallow the organ and wash it down with a glass of rice wine. Allegedly it would cure a variety of ailments, ranging from earache to impotence. Several recently killed snakes were hanging by their necks waiting to be dried

RC and Kathryn in front of the monument to Chiang Kai-shek, Taipei, Taiwan. Photo by Hsein Yu Cheng.

or otherwise processed. Treatments were not cheap. Dr. Mao wanted to buy a couple of live snakes for his herpetological research, but he refused to pay the high prices charged for them.

Despite all the miraculous advances in modern medicine and surgery, there is still a big market for serpents and parts thereof in the Orient, even in such advanced countries as Japan. Venomous species are especially in demand, and the attrition on their natural populations is enormous. There is much on the subject in the Gloyd and Conant monograph on *Agkistrodon*.

When Chiang Kai-shek and his legion of anti-Communist followers retreated from mainland China to Taiwan in 1949, they commandeered every boat that would float. Quite remarkably, they took with them a vast treasure trove of Chinese antiquities that are now assembled, labeled in both English and Chinese, in an impressive museum. We visited it and also saw the great monument to Chiang while we were in Taipei.

After thanking Dr. Mao profusely for all his help, we flew to Hong Kong for a short stay, and then on to Singapore, where we spent two nights in the historic old Raffles Hotel.

Our final destination was Java, the only place, along with small satellite islands, where any member of the *Agkistrodon* complex occurs south of the Equator. We landed at Jakarta, the capital of Indonesia, and then were driven south to Bogor to visit the historic museum that the Dutch founded and operated during their long occupation of the East Indian archipelago. Dr. Boeadi was our host. Like so many of his countrymen, he had only a single name. He allowed me to remove all the museum's preserved specimens of the Malayan pit viper, *Calloselasma rhodostoma*, from their bottles so I could examine them carefully and make scale counts and measurements. With the data from some of them, I was able to show that this egg-laying snake is absent from Borneo.

Like the cantil, *Agkistrodon bilineatus*, of Middle America (Mexico and Central America), the Malayan pit viper lives only in areas that have a dry season, sometimes long and severe, and during which it estivates. With the arrival of the rainy season it becomes active again, and mating apparently occurs soon thereafter. Neither species occurs where a dry period is lacking. Like the Lesser Sunda Islands, Java is seasonally under the influence of hot desiccating winds from the nearby great Australian deserts. It has a dry season, and is still inhabited by *Calloselasma*.

Boeadi took us for a tour by primitive, three-wheeled jitneys to wooded places near Bogor where Malayan pit vipers had been seen or killed. They even occurred in the famous botanical garden, in whose rest house we stayed. The sweltering heat at night was relieved only by a small electric fan set up at one side of our high-ceilinged room. Because of its constant cloud cover we never did see Mount Salak, where Thomas Barbour collected many vipers early in the century. We were lucky enough, however, to peer out a window of the Museum Zoologicum Bogoriense just as a monitor (*Varanus*), four feet in length, walked by in the grass on the ground below us.

There are swarms of people and great numbers of children everywhere in Java, which is largely Muslim. Even in heavily wooded country areas we found many houses, and scores of residents came to stare at us. When we returned to Jakarta, we passed the Iranian embassy, which had a large portrait of the Ayatollah Khomeini as part of its facade. Our English-speaking cab driver, with whom I had carried on a lively conversation all the way from Bogor, said, "We dislike that man. He is a bad Muslim. All he wants to do is kill people."

Bogor, a city of three million, has a horrible air pollution problem, caused largely by the hordes of mopeds and jitneys. On our first night in that city we had to walk rather a long way to find a restaurant where we could have supper. When we returned to the botanical garden I had to lie on the bed and pant to replace the polluted air in my lungs with the much purer air of the very large, beautifully planted area. Incidentally, we passed a Kentucky Fried Chicken place en route to the restaurant. It brought memories of home, but within easy housefly range of it was an open sewer, a ditch with a slowly running current of water saturated with stinking offal. No thanks!

Chapter 59

The Last Continent:
Part I. Venezuela

Just why South America was the last habitable continent on which I set foot is difficult to explain, even to myself. Logically, it should have been one of the first. It is relatively close, and my Spanish is good enough for me to get by anywhere on that continent except in Portuguese-speaking Brazil and the Guianas, Dutch (now Surinam) and French.

I was born in North America, and I visited Europe as early as 1937, and several times afterward. Isabelle and I immensely enjoyed our superb seven weeks in East and South Africa in 1968. With Kathryn I had ventured to New Zealand and Australia in 1980—with, and at the urging of, William M. Clay, an old friend from my Toledo Zoo days. Work on the *Agkistrodon* monograph was responsible for several trips to the Orient and southern Asia.

After the monograph had been published and Kathryn and I had caught our respective breaths, we checked our accumulated frequent-flier mileage, and found that we each had enough for two free trips to South America, at least to the three countries of Colombia, Ecuador, and Venezuela. Happily for us, Singapore Airlines was affiliated with American Airlines, and the miles we accumulated crossing and recrossing the Pacific Ocean were added to our total.

We selected Venezuela as our first goal. Colombia was out because of the violence and terrorism generated by the drug cartels, which sometimes boiled over from Medellín to Bogotá, the capital, where American Airlines had its terminus. I had come close to visiting Venezuela when I was invited to participate in the First International Ophidian (snake) Congress. But that was back in 1976, and the doctors advised me not to go. They were right. My beloved wife, Isabelle, died at the time I would have been in Caracas. I never would have forgiven myself if I had been away and unable to comfort her during her terminal agonizing ordeal. Another reason for my interest in Venezuela was its proximity to Puerto Rico. I had never visited any of the West Indian islands, and American Airlines flew directly from Caracas to San Juan and permitted users

of accumulated mileage to tarry there for several days.

We arrived in Venezuela one night in mid-April 1991. It was well after dark, and I had been warned about *bandidos* and others who were all too eager to take advantage of elderly travelers. I was 82 at the time. My Spanish stood me in good stead, however. As might have been expected, boys picked up one each of the four bags we had checked through on the plane, and they took off separately in the general direction of the taxi line. I stopped them, selected one boy, and told the others to scram despite the dirty looks cast in my direction. We were able to find a middle-aged taxi driver who was honest, and who carried us to our hotel safely and directly.

The airport was virtually at sea level, but we started climbing steadily toward Caracas, a vast city partly on a mountainside at about 3,000 feet. Suddenly, as we rounded a curve in the road, we were greeted by a sky full of lights, which our driver told us was Caracas. The many hillsides looked as though they were decorated with millions of tiny white lights for the Christmas holidays.

We stayed at the Residencias Anauco Hilton, a sort of annex to, but far less expensive than, the fancy Hilton almost directly across the street. Because we were mentally exhausted from more than a solid year of meticulous and time-consuming proofreading, we spent quite a bit of time resting in our room, although we made forays, both morning and afternoon, exploring the vicinity. An interesting discovery was that the hotel office opened directly into an underground labyrinth of shops and stores, some swank, some sleazy, and including a supermarket, a post office, and tourist traps loaded with cheap to expensive souvenirs. It would be no exaggeration to state that anything anyone needed was somewhere in that maze. The complex extended for blocks in parallel rows and cross-connecting promenades, and one could quickly get lost if he failed to remember turns, twists, and landmarks. The walkways were crowded with pedestrians on weekdays, but far smaller numbers were present on Sunday. They were replaced, in part, by young men sitting here and there with shotguns in their hands or within ready reach. They were guards, of course, but we wondered how they could avoid hitting innocent people if they shot at a thief.

We patronized the *supermercado*, where we could buy cookies, fruit, and soft drinks at very reasonable prices, and which we used for noontime meals instead of paying restaurant high prices. Included in our peregrinations were walks to the main Hilton and to the nearby natural history museum. The displays, in general, were good, but there was no air conditioning, and it was so stiflingly hot inside that we didn't tarry long.

On Sunday morning we took a tour of the city on a sightseeing bus. "Rubberneck wagons" are the best way, of course, to see a lot in a small amount of time. We picked the right day. There was only one other passenger, so we were spared crowding, and the expedition was at a leisurely pace. We passed through slums, one where shacks and hovels were perched on precipitous hillsides, and another on flatter ground but replete with trash and two dead dogs. We also saw an affluent part of the city far above the noise and bustle. A highlight was in an imposing government building where we visited the Oval Room, a national shrine featuring spectacular murals depicting patriots under the leadership of the great liberator, Simón Bolívar, who led the fight for independence from Spanish rule.

As we rode along in our bus I was intrigued by great sluiceways paralleling some of the main streets and down which water raced because of the steep grades. I thought at first that they must be used to drain rainwater, but we soon learned otherwise. They were open sewers from the homes, offices, and any other buildings with plumbing and flush toilets. The entire mess cascaded into the Caribbean Sea. All the beaches nearby were badly polluted. When we left by air for Mérida, in western Venezuela, our plane skimmed low over the coastal waters before beginning its climb toward the highlands. The surface of the sea was pockmarked with masses of toilet paper and other offal. What an atrocious way for a large and otherwise modern city to dispose of its sewage! I cannot think of a word sufficiently strong to describe such a loathsome practice.

Our hotel room in Caracas had one of those insidious minibars, such as we had encountered many times during our travels. It was stocked with liquor, wine, soft drinks, snacks, and other tempting tidbits. Take anything from it, and its absence shows up on your hotel bill at three to five times the normal retail price. We thought of minibars as ancillary rackets, but probably they were helpful to persons who didn't want to leave their rooms for a late-night snack or who wished to engage in revelry of one sort or another. We never took anything from a minibar, but, since they were refrigerated, we found them handy places to store our own cold drinks and perishable items. Several times the minibar inspector knocked on our door while we were in our room and, with our permission, checked to see what might be missing. After about the third visit he remarked that we had removed nothing, to which I responded, "*Hay mucho más barato en el mercado*" (They are much cheaper in the market), and that provoked a broad smile.

To us, Caracas was just another big city, but the small community of Mérida was quite different. It was in the western highlands of Venezuela about a mile above sea level and thus at roughly the same altitude as Albuquerque. It was nestled in a small valley surrounded by mountains, with the Andes towering on the west. The landing strip was so short that our plane had to hit it squarely and brake almost instantly.

We were met by smiling, bearded young Enrique La Marca, a member of the faculty of the University of the Andes and a former student of Hobart M. Smith, one of our eminent senior American herpetologists. Enrique helped us with our baggage, took us to his car, and then told us that the Hotel Mintoy, where we were supposed to stay, was too close to the university. The students, like their counterparts in many parts of the world, had been rioting during the spring holidays, and he feared we might be exposed to the tear gas the *policia* were using to quell youthful exuberance. Instead we went to a quiet, old-fashioned *posada* (inn), a nostalgic experience for me, as I stepped back in memory to similar rather cramped quarters where I had stayed years previously in Mexico and Costa Rica. Our room cost less than $18 a day, with a small extra charge for breakfast and dinner when requested.

Because I am so tall I really need a double bed to myself. There was only one in the entire establishment, and Kay had to occupy the lower level of a double-decker combination in the same room. The place was clean, and all the furniture, doors, closets, and cabinets were handmade. The *posada* had a central atrium with many plants, and it was all open to the out-of-doors, but covered by a tight, ramada-type roof because of the frequent rains.

The washbowl in our quarters had only one faucet— cold, of course. There was hot water in the shower, and the toilet was clean and appeared adequate. Alas, it would not take paper! Kay used it first, and it overflowed on the floor. After sounding the alarm, so to speak, two men came running, one with a mop and the other with a plumber's helper. We were asked, please, to put all soiled paper in the basket, which was equipped with a disposable plastic bag. All was well thereafter

By the time we reached the summit of the tramway visibility was approaching zero. Photo by Enrique La Marca.

except that, after a lifetime of dropping paper into the hopper, we forgot a couple of times, and we had to fish it out with a wire coat hanger. We were not alone with the problem. Twice while we were at the *posada* we saw the same two employees hurrying with mop and plumber's helper to the rooms of other newly arrived guests.

Enrique was a wonderful and informative host. He took us to his home and introduced us to his lovely wife, Dexy, and their three boys ranging in age from a babe-in-arms to a gentlemanly lad of about eight. He drove us to several places of interest in the surrounding countryside, sometimes with his family. We made a brief inspection of an undisturbed *páramo*, a high plain at about 10,000 feet with dwarf vegetation, much of it growing in rosettes. Most unhappily, the daily cold fog soon moved in, enveloping and obscuring everything, and we hastened back to the car lest we become lost in the whiteout.

On Friday, April 26, we experienced the highlight of the entire trip. Enrique picked us up at 7:30 A.M. and drove us to the base of the *teleférico*, a tramway with cars slung on cables, similar to the one in Albuquerque. The *teleférico*, however, was in four stages, with a station at each where one changed cars for the next upward ride. At the topmost station the elevation was 4,765 meters (15,629 feet). Because of my age and the rarified atmosphere, Enrique thought we should not ascend higher than the top of the second stage. We rested at the end of each of the first two, and I took pictures of the city of Mérida far below, as well as shots of the mountains

nearby. I did so well at the second stage that we agreed to go up one more. Before arriving at the third station, the forest stopped and a *páramo* type of vegetation took over. Much of the ground was bare, with rocks, cliffs, and huge boulders much in evidence. Before we reached the end of the third stage wisps of clouds began to obscure the highest peaks. We rested awhile, and then both Kay and Enrique thought it was safe for me to go on. I was not panting, but I kept my activities and movements to a minimum. So we went all the way to the top, and the highest we have ever been except in an airplane!

It was cold, and everything outdoors was enveloped in heavy fog. It was windy, however, and occasionally we caught glimpses of the white marble statue of the Virgin of the Snows through the mist. Both the top station and the statue were on Pico Espejo (Mirror Peak), close to Pico de Bolívar, which, at 16,411 feet, is the loftiest of the Venezuelan Andes. Soon after we arrived, a group of young men with backpacks and climbing equipment entered the station. They had ascended Bolívar to its pinnacle after sleeping in the basement of the topmost station the previous night to get an early start. They looked and admitted they were half frozen.

Soon we were on our way back. We sat in the rear of each tram car as Enrique explained the alterations in the vegetation. We saw the frost line above which it freezes every night, and where low *páramo* plants prevailed. Below the line, trees appeared immediately, and the undisturbed climax forest continued far down the precipitous slope of the mountains. Lower down, agriculture had once been practiced on grades so steep that it seemed impossible for a farmer to maintain his footing. There the replacement vegetation was in various stages of succession and quite different from the virgin forest. The most conspicuous newcomer was the cecropia tree, *Cecropia santanderensis*, which was tall and sported large, pale gray leaves that could be seen for long distances, even from our *posada* far below.

The tramway was a marvelous method for seeing the high mountains, and surely the only way for elderly visitors. Our pleasant memories of that lofty trip were interrupted, however, by an involuntary shudder when Enrique wrote, some months later, telling us that a cable had broken on the highest sector; a car had crashed to the earth early one morning, and its two occupants were instantly killed. Enrique and his class from the university had ridden the *teleférico* to its summit just a short time previously. How fortunate we were to have been to the top before the disaster! But we could not help but think, what if?

In late 1995, Enrique informed me that the *teleférico* hadn't yet been repaired. Not being able to get to the top has been a blow for tourism in Mérida, because the tramway was the highest in the world, and it was a mecca for mountain lovers and climbers.

After leaving Mérida we returned to the main Venezuelan airport, but, instead of climbing upward to Caracas again, we went by taxi to La Guaira, farther east along the seashore, and were lucky to find a vacant room at the Sheraton Macuto Resort Hotel. It was swank and expensive, but we decided we could stand it for one night. We had saved a lot of money on lodging during our weeklong stay in Mérida. Our room looked right out onto the Caribbean. The pollution was farther to the west, and a few people were bathing. Pelicans, cormorants, and even an Amazon-type parrot flew past our windows; swallows kept landing somewhere above us, and we could see man-o'-war (frigate) birds soaring overhead. We were there most of the afternoon, and we had time the next morning to walk along the beach and the adjacent paths through tropical vegetation that included two immense strangler fig trees. Carib grackles, with their deeply keeled tails, foraged in the outdoor restaurant area, and Kay put both her hands and, inadvertently, one of her shoes into the waters of the Caribbean Sea.

Our departure from the airport was as ludicrous as it was annoying. As two (presumably rich) *americanos*, we were shunted through a succession of lines, and our bags were picked up by a parade of different porters, who carried them forward a short distance and then expected a tip. It took us at least 20 minutes to pass through the gauntlet, have our passports stamped with a loud bang, and enter the waiting room for our plane to Puerto Rico.

We stayed in San Juan for three nights, taking sightseeing tours by day, including one to the only tropical U.S. national forest, El Yunque (the anvil), named for the shape of the mountain on which it is situated in part. Because we had taken our one and only permissible stop in San Juan on our return trip, we had to travel all the way to Albuquerque in three consecutive stages. En route to Miami we passed over several of the Bahama Islands. They, of course, are the highest parts of plateaus that were drowned in large part when the glaciers melted at the end of the Ice Age. I knew they were tenuous, but it was interesting to see how little dry land many of them have. The weather was bad in Texas, and the Dallas-Fort Worth Airport was closed and opened several times during the day. So we were delayed, and didn't arrive home until 11:00 P.M. after a 20-hour day.

My list was complete at last. I had visited all the habitable continents, and all those where living reptiles and amphibians exist. Antarctica, with its covering of ice, snow, and great glaciers, is not included, nor do I ever expect to see it in person.

Our brief sojourn in South America and the speed with which my Spanish came back to me, whetted our appetites to see more of the "last continent," and we looked eagerly forward to using our other free trip, courtesy of American Airlines, to see as much as possible of Ecuador in 1992.

Chapter 60

The Last Continent:
Part II. Ecuador

Ecuador, which embraces an area roughly the size of Colorado, is one of the smallest countries in South America. Only Uruguay and the three Guianas rank below it. What Ecuador may lack in dimensions, however, is more than made up by its extraordinary diversity and its incomparable features that serve as a lure for naturalists. The most important are: (1) the Galápagos Islands; (2) a long series of towering volcanoes, including the loftiest active one in the world; and (3) a generous slice of the Amazon basin rain forest that remains in virtually pristine condition.

We were scarcely back from our 1991 trip to Venezuela and Puerto Rico when I began thinking about Ecuador and making plans for our visit the following year. Information about the Galápagos Islands was easy to acquire. Howard L. Snell, a member of the faculty of the Department of Biology at the University of New Mexico, had been doing research in the islands for several years, and he and his wife, Heidi, were able to answer all my questions in detail and to supply pertinent literature about visits. Not that I was ignorant about the archipelago and its reptilian and other treasures. I had read avidly about the region ever since I acquired a copy of William Beebe's "Galápagos: World's End" for five dollars when I was a teenager. I had always wanted to visit the area, but the years went by and here I was, an old man with a balance problem associated with my deteriorating hearing. No matter. I would go and do what I could.

Most people travel to the islands by boat, but that was out of the question for me. Boats rock and toss, and I would need to hold on to a rail or some other stationary object every moment, lest I fall and break a bone—not an acceptable prospect for an octogenarian. Also, only a few of the islands permit dry-shod landings. On others one must wade ashore, sometimes on sand, but frequently on hidden, uneven rocks. Our best bet was to fly, so Heidi Snell made plane reservations for us when she was in Quito, the capital, some weeks before we arrived.

Trying to find some way to see the volcanoes was not so easy. From travel agencies I obtained a variety of pam-

phlets and leaflets about Ecuador, and, after perusing them with care, I decided our best plan would be to go southward by train from Quito to Riobamba and back. There were pictures in the travel literature of the outstanding peaks that would be visible en route, but I was not so naive as to expect we would be able to see all or any of them. I had spent enough time in tropical regions to know that, whereas high mountains might be fully visible at dawn, they often quickly cloud over except on those rare days when atmospheric conditions are perfect for observation. We would have to take our chances. I learned that a tour car was attached to the rear of certain of the regular trains, and dining facilities and restrooms were available. That sounded wonderful after the several long-distance bus tours I had made over the years, hungry, thirsty, and with miserable or no bathroom facilities. I called the Metropolitan Touring agency in Dallas, only to learn that the special cars were no longer in use.

It was then that I talked by telephone with my esteemed friend William W. Lamar, who is ever ready and willing to help in any way he can. Bill had been in the field in South America many times. When I mentioned my troubles in planning our trip he said, "Let me put you in touch with Doug McMeekin. He is in business in Quito and he is sympathetic with all naturalists." I thanked Bill, he dispatched a fax message to Ecuador, and then things happened fast and with ease. I talked with Doug by telephone, we exchanged letters and faxes, and everything fell rapidly into place. A trusted cab driver would take us down the InterAmerican Highway along what the great explorer Alexander von Humboldt called the Avenue of Volcanoes. In Quito we would stay at the Hostal los Alpes, which Doug highly recommended and where he made reservations for us. Also, he broke the red tape, so to speak, by finding open dates for us to visit La Selva, far down the Río Napo in the Amazonian rain forest. What a relief to have an able, knowledgeable person to smooth the way. Planning from then on was a breeze.

Because it was readily apparent that our trips to the

islands and the Amazon basin would be strenuous, at least in part, I decided that Kathryn and I had better plan for rest days between our various excursions. We would spend the entire month of June 1992 in Ecuador.

After a quiet rest stop in Miami, following our flight east from Albuquerque, we boarded our plane for Quito. For some unknown reason, we arrived at our destination 40 minutes ahead of the scheduled time. We taxied to the Hostal los Alpes, and were scarcely in our room when the telephone rang. It was Doug McMeekin. He had very kindly gone to the airport to meet us, but we had already departed because of our early arrival. He wanted to know if we were OK, and he promised to send a messenger in the morning to conduct us to his office.

Our room was in a small, almost separate building from the main complex of the Hostal, and we were very glad that each of the twin beds was provided with four blankets. Quito is more than 9,000 feet above sea level, and it gets cold at night. We shivered our way into bed. Later, the management gave us an electric heater to reduce the chill in the room.

The Hostal los Alpes was inconspicuous, on a side street, almost completely hidden by trees and shrubbery. We discovered, after eating breakfast in its dining room, that it was also almost a miniature museum. Curios hung on the walls, and numerous cabinets contained small artifacts, mostly of Ecuadorian crafts. It was spotless, and, as we found out later, a corps of maids worked all day long to keep it that way. It was well furnished, and there was a fire burning in one of the sitting rooms at night. What a difference from the *posada* we had occupied in Venezuela in 1991. The manager-owner, Don Claudio Facchinei, a cordial, middle-aged Italian, provided two boons for us, a lockbox in his office where we could keep our valuables, and permission to leave most of our bags and baggage in our room during our journeys afield.

Doug McMeekin greeted us cordially at his office, and it was quickly apparent that he had spared no effort to make sure we could do and see all we wanted in Ecuador. He would accompany us on the first leg of our trip down the Avenue of Volcanoes to La Ciénega, where we would stay overnight, and he had engaged a taxi driver to take us onward the next morning for a flat fee (no meter). Doug knew that our arrangements were already in hand for our flight to the Galápagos Islands and for our trip to the Amazon rain forest (the Oriente), but he said not to hesitate to call him or any of his bilingual staff members if we needed help, or if any problems developed. He then introduced them to us, and we met Ximena Reyes, a well-informed young lady on whom I was to call, more

than once, to help us over rough spots. Doug had even bought us tickets for the Ballet Folklórico, apologizing for the short notice, because the show was performed only on Wednesdays, which was that very night. I told him I expected to reimburse him for all his out-of-pocket expenditures, and he agreed to give me a statement before we left the country.

After we chatted awhile, Doug took us to a very good restaurant close to his office, where we had a noonday dinner. Then he sent us, with his messenger, to a money-changing place where we were granted his discount. On Doug's advice I cashed $400 worth of traveler's checks and in exchange received 576,000 sucres in 5,000-sucre notes, which made a roll big enough to choke an elephant! Each dollar was the equivalent of 1,440 sucres. The advantageous exchange rate meant that, away from tourist centers, prices for most things were quite cheap.

The Ballet Jacchigua, to give it the proper name, was held in the national theater, with a cast of 40 or 50 persons. We thoroughly enjoyed the show. The costumes and dancing were superb. As a musician in my youth, I was particularly intrigued by the seven-piece band that stood at the back of the stage. There was a bass drum and two guitars, but all others were native instruments consisting chiefly of horns, flutes, and pipes of various kinds. The theme was based on the ancient Incas, the coming of the cruel Spaniards, and the blending of the two cultures.

On Friday, Doug drove us, in his own vehicle, to La Ciénega, about two hours south of Quito. An unexpected feature of the landscape was the profusion of eucalyptus trees, which, Doug told us, were introduced from Australia in about 1840. They are used for firewood and lumber, and we saw several plantations of them. La Ciénega was the site of an old hacienda, dating back to Spanish colonial days, and it served as a quiet hotel with good food. It was set in the midst of well-kept grounds that included an old church, still in good repair.

In the morning we bid Doug farewell, and he returned to Quito. We continued south in a bright yellow taxi driven by Bolívar Buenaño ("Goodyear" in translation). We were also accompanied by Gonzalo Carrillo, Doug's bilingual teenaged protégé. It was good to have him with us, but we didn't really need an interpreter. I sat in front with Bolívar and we conversed in Spanish as we rode along, and I felt the language flowing back into my mind and being expressed by my tongue. Both young men complimented me on its improvement during the trip.

We could see little of the high mountains because of a cloud cover that broke only partially from time to time.

Another disappointment was in seeing only a single llama, and it was too far away to photograph. Those beasts of burden are abundant in Peru, we were told, but Kathryn and I did not venture into that country because of the turmoil and danger generated by the Shining Path guerrillas, then at the height of their power. The signs along the road, the half-finished and then abandoned buildings, and the occasional horse or cow loose on the highway all reminded me of the many trips Isabelle and I had made to Mexico decades earlier. We passed through several towns on the railroad route that I naively had thought we might see from a train. Most of the people were in European-American garb, but a great many others wore native dress, with heavy loads on their backs and no tumplines.

Eventually we began descending steadily into the valley of the Río Pastaza, a swift stream with mountains rising on both sides of it for 1,000 feet and more. The slopes were steep, precipitous in places, yet most were either cultivated or grazed by cattle, some to the very top. There was some attempt, here and there, at terracing or the use of retaining walls, but a great many of the fields had no protection from erosion except for parallel, crosswise cultivation, similar to the contour plowing practiced in the United States. In many places farmers could literally fall out of their fields.

The entire region we traversed is volcanic. The relatively few flat areas, the jumbled masses of rocks, the numerous landslides, and the hills, crags, mountains, and especially the towering peaks are all the result of the subduction of the Nazca tectonic plate as it plows slowly but relentlessly beneath the South American continent. I had read somewhere that in 20 million years, more or less, the Nazca plate will have moved eastward enough so that the Galápagos Islands will disappear into the magma.

In time for lunch we arrived in Baños, a small town frequented by tourists, and we registered at the Hotel Sangay, named for one of Ecuador's active volcanoes. After eating and a siesta, Bolívar drove us for more than an hour down through the gorge of the Río Pastaza on a perilous dirt road that hung on the edge of a series of cliffs. What's more, there was considerable traffic—only a few cars, but many trucks and even buses. We were told it was the main road from Baños down to the lowlands of the Oriente.

At many places the road was wide enough for only one vehicle. Cliffs rose above us, and sometimes we drove under them where they were concave. In one place water was falling from the rocks above, and the taxi was deluged as we passed through. There were many blind curves, each of which had to be approached

with caution lest there might be another vehicle coming from the opposite direction. I certainly would not want to drive under such conditions, but Bolívar managed with great skill. After all, he lived along that very road, and he had to drive far down it to get home!

There were many photo opportunities—of the river, numerous waterfalls, some quite large, cliffs, and many great landslides (*derrumbes* in Spanish). Occasional pull-off places where the road was wider enabled us to get out to see the view. Eventually Bolívar turned his taxi around, and we braved the narrow road in the opposite direction—no guardrail and sheer drops of hundreds of feet seemingly inches away from the wheels of the car. We returned to Baños for the night.

The next morning we breakfasted early and, because the weather was essentially clear, we started back at once in the hope of seeing some of the snow-capped mountains. It was a good decision. Although they were far from us and seemed quite small in the camera's viewfinder, we were thrilled to see three of the great ones—Chimborazo, Cotopaxi, and Tungurahua. Chimborazo, at nearly 21,000 feet and in three lobes, is the highest mountain in Ecuador. All were partly obscured by clouds, especially Cotopaxi, but, by waiting for a few minutes, I was able to obtain what were no better than fair pictures. Cotopaxi and some of the other volcanoes that we didn't see are still active, and they could "blow" at any time. Like the Icelanders and the people near Mount Etna, on Sicily, a large part of the Ecuadorian population could be exposed to disaster at any time.

We drove onward toward Quito, and reached there in early afternoon after passing through the town of Machachi, where Güitig mineral water is bottled for the entire country. The road climbed to 11,000 feet, and on either side were *páramos* that had long since been ruined by cultivation or grazing. I had hoped to see a primitive one, such as we missed photographing in Venezuela the previous year, when the fog moved in just as we arrived.

Back at the Hostal los Alpes we enjoyed a few rest days, except that we were traumatized by rather severe bouts of dysentery. We wondered where we had acquired "the Inca curse," and finally blamed it on the food at Baños. I spent most of two days in bed, and I had to telephone Ximena for help. I was supposed to pick up our plane tickets to the islands, and it had to be done in person, since I was using traveler's checks to pay for them. Because of my indisposition, Ximena persuaded Gonzalo Cerón, an executive of the Darwin Foundation office in Quito, to bring the tickets to me, and I signed my checks while sitting up in bed. Señor

Cerón was a young, suave, handsome *latino*, and his fine manners and good looks made quite an impression on Kathryn.

For exercise, in Quito, we trod the sidewalks in several directions from the Hostal los Alpes. The cement walks were uneven and broken in many places, with depressions, some deep, and even sharp rises where the roots of trees had pushed up blocks of paving. Open manholes were a particular hazard. We saw two different places where there were deep holes into which one could tumble, and neither was protected by barriers or warning signs. Perhaps Ecuadorians do not bring suit, as would be the case in our own country. In Quito it was a case of "watch your step" wherever you went. So I carried my cane, a folding one that I bought before we left home. It fitted into my shoulder bag and could be taken aboard airplanes.

During a rest period we took a short bus trip to the Mitad del Mundo (Middle of the World) a few miles north of Quito. The very name of the country, Ecuador, means "equator." A truly impressive monument straddled the line. It was roughly four stories high, vertically rectangular in shape, and surmounted by an immense globe of the world. On the way to the entrance there was a continuous row of narrow stones that were laid exactly on the Equator. If you walked to the right you were in the Northern Hemisphere, to the left in the Southern.

Inside the building we were whisked to the top floor in an elevator, and we stepped out for a panoramic view of the surrounding countryside. On one steep mountainside farming and grazing had been practiced at some time in the past, but erosion had devastated everything.

To descend the monument it was necessary to walk down flights of stairs. There were about a dozen landings, and, at each, one of the Ecuadorian tribes was featured. Most were native, but one was a group of African Negroes. A map showed where in Ecuador each group lived. Large photographs, some of mural size, carefully selected costumes, and artifacts, including tools and blowguns, illustrated the various cultures and their activities. We thought the entire museum was very well done, and that it gave visitors a good overview of the nation's people.

Ecuador's Galápagos archipelago is fabulous by any imaginable yardstick—for its volcanic origin, the giant tortoises and other strange reptiles, the curious birds, and how the wildlife influenced Charles Darwin in developing his theory of evolution. Literally reams of printed copy have appeared about the islands during the past century, much of it involved with the decimation of the great herds of giant tortoises.

To summarize briefly, back in the days of the sailing vessels, ships, particularly the whalers, were at sea for months at a time, fresh food was a constant problem, and scurvy was a dreaded menace. There was then no refrigeration. It became the practice for the ships to visit the Galápagos Islands, and to take aboard as many live giant tortoises as possible. In the vessels' holds they would live for long periods, up to a year by some accounts, without food or water, and they could be killed and butchered, one by one, to provide fresh meat, which was claimed to be quite tasty. Inevitably, the tortoises became scarce on some islands and were completely extirpated on others. Charles Haskins Townsend, of the New York Aquarium, laboriously checked the logbooks of many New England whaling vessels during the 1920s, and found that hundreds of thousands of tortoises were removed. His results were far from complete, however, because he surely missed some logbooks; and buccaneers, crews of naval vessels, and others also removed tortoises over a long period of time.

Nowadays, the entire archipelago is an Ecuadorian national park. A staff of wardens patrols the islands, and carefully controlled tourism is a big business. We had to pay $40 each (in dollars; sucres not accepted) for permission to make our visit. Conservation and restoration have moved to the fore, and the internationally funded Darwin Research Station on Santa Cruz Island is playing a major role.

We left Quito in the early morning of June 11 and flew to Guayaquil, the largest city, principal port, and financial center of Ecuador. Because it is on the coast, the weather was hot and humid, but we soon transferred to another plane for the 600-mile trip to the "enchanted islands." Ever since I first read "Galápagos: World's End" I had used the English names for individual islands, but each one now bears a Spanish designation. I gave up trying to remember which was which, and carried a conversion map with me. We would be landing on Baltra, or South Seymour in the English terminology.

During World War II Baltra served as a U.S. Air Force base. It was small and flat, and a long runway covered a large part of it. The Ecuadorians repaired the landing strip and erected a small terminal from which tourists began their boat trips of the islands or crossed to a much larger island to the south.

I approached Baltra with a feeling of exultation. I was about to visit a naturalist's paradise about which I had dreamed for more than half a century. We had scarcely landed when we were met by Cynthia Jaramillo, the Darwin Research Station's public relations officer, who was extremely helpful and treated us like VIPs. She and the driver of one of the station's trucks found our baggage, and soon we were on an ancient bus for a short

The ferry that conveyed us across the channel from the flat Baltra Island, where our plane landed, to the rugged and very much larger Santa Cruz Island on which we stayed for almost a week. Photo by RC.

drive to the south end of the island, where we took a *ponga* (ferry) across the wildly beautiful Canal Itabasca, a narrow arm of the Pacific, to the north shore of Santa Cruz Island (Indefatigable in British parlance). Once across, we climbed aboard a roomy pickup truck, stowed our baggage in the back, and all four of us squeezed into the front seat. We drove for something like an hour and a half across the island, enjoying the strange vegetation and carrying on a lively conversation. Cynthia was completely bilingual. There were very large *Opuntia* (prickly pear) trees in the lowlands, but, as we climbed toward the center of the island, which receives more rainfall, the growth became much more lush and deciduous trees were in evidence. We finally reached the small town of Puerto Ayora on Academy Bay, and were taken to the Galápagos Hotel, where we were to stay for several days.

Our room was superb, the best one in the house for visiting zoologists. We were on the corner of the hotel complex with a splendid view of Academy Bay, and with the Pacific on one side and the town and part of the bay on the other. In the immediate foreground were masses of small to medium-large lava rocks extending down to the nearby low-breaking waves of the sea. The rocks were crawling with wildlife. Most conspicuous and most exciting for me were the marine iguanas, *Amblyrhynchus cristatus*, of all sizes from hatchlings to large adults. Bright red and orange crabs stood out conspicuously against the black lava. The tide was down, and birds of several species foraged among the wet rocks. We saw lava herons with their bright yellow or orange feet and legs, lava gulls, ruddy turnstones, and a great blue heron that stood stock-still for an hour wait-

ing in vain for a small marine iguana to poke out its head. Brown pelicans were much in evidence, and so were frigate birds soaring far overhead. Yellow warblers and Darwin's finches were extremely abundant. What a curious mixture of birds. Pelagic ones, of course, but others endemic and many with origins on the American mainland.

After an exciting series of observations on the wildlife we napped. At 7:30 we were in the hotel dining room as dinner guests, along with Cynthia, of the new director of the Darwin Station, Dr. Chantal Marie Blanton, a slim, vivacious lady. We had a very interesting conversation, and it was after 10:00 before we headed for bed. It had been a long, hard day.

The Estación Científica Charles Darwin was farther along the shore, 100 yards or more, but the road leading to it was blocked by a picket line of strikers. No one could pass except members of the station's staff. The strikers were Ecuadorian government employees, chiefly wardens who patrolled the archipelago. They claimed they were underpaid, and we heard later, after the strike was over, that they had won salary increases. The men had the sympathies of the station personnel, but the entrance was effectively blocked so that no tourists could pass. The station was one of the showplaces of the islands, and it was included on virtually all commercial tours. Apparently, however, the news of the strike had been suppressed on the mainland. One of the guests at the Hostal los Alpes came back from the Galápagos in high dudgeon because his tour company failed to advise him and his companions in advance that they could not enter the station grounds. There was much to see there, and it was the only place where the presence of giant tortoises was guaranteed. Finding them elsewhere could be sheer luck.

The ladies had told us at dinner the previous evening that they had a secret way to get us in. It proved to be an end run by sea. About 10:30 the next morning a small boat with an outboard motor came to pick us up. The trip was short but choppy. Cynthia met us at the station's dock and took us first to the air-conditioned library to talk with students who were working on two species of geckos, one endemic and the other introduced. I promised to send them books on hatching and rearing geckos.

A small museum was devoted to the tortoises, their early destruction, their extinction on some islands, and their current status and distribution. I learned that there are five volcanoes on Isabela, largest by far of the Galápagos Islands. The giant tortoises around each volcano are different from those around the others. Speciation is already under way. One group, the most northern, I think, is now extinct as a result of eruptions, but their shells are available for study. As the tectonic plate carries Isabela and the much smaller Fernandina eastward from over the hot spot on the ocean floor, the large island may break up into smaller ones, perhaps with one extinct volcano and a different race or species of tortoise on each. Fernandina currently has one inactive volcano, with a lake in its crater.

We moved on to the nursery, where tortoises, hatched from eggs at the station, were growing large enough to be repatriated to their own islands. Many groups of various sizes were represented, and, collectively, there were hundreds of tortoises. As babies they frequently fall victim to predators, including birds and introduced rats, but, once they attain some size, they are safe from most things except accidents. A considerable number have been repatriated on Isla Española (Hood Island), and there is now evidence that the reintroduced tortoises are reproducing.

When rangers of the Ecuadorian Park Service find eggs on the islands, they bring them to the station for incubation. No eggs were present at the time (because of the lengthy strike?), but we were shown one small tortoise which had hatched about 90 days earlier and still bore its egg tooth. Inspecting that area was a great privilege. Ordinarily, visitors are excluded.

We continued onward to see adult tortoises. The going was rough. I had borrowed a bamboo walking staff from the hotel, and I moved with great care, but twice I stumbled on protruding rocks in the roadway. Each time, willing hands grabbed me at once. Five very large tortoises were in one big rocky pen, but most visitors had to look at them from some little distance away. We were permitted to go closer, and I had to struggle over sharp, uneven rocks to get there. I had lots of help, however. The five tortoises cannot be repatriated, because it is impossible to determine which island they came from originally, but they are a great attraction for visitors.

A boardwalk had been constructed to a rocky pen holding Lonesome George, the last survivor of the species that once inhabited Pinta (Abingdon) Island. Two females of a closely related taxon were living in the enclosure with him, but he had not yet accepted them.

In another pen, large and densely planted, a pair of tortoises were in copula, and we were told they might remain that way for 18 hours or more. The female, which was much smaller than the male, kept struggling to move forward, but the male extended his long neck so that his chin pushed her head back into her shell and effectively halted her advance. How difficult sex is for tortoises!

It was wonderful to see the efforts of the Estación Científica Charles Darwin to restore the fauna and flora

The unique marine iguana was represented by scores of individuals near our room in the Galapagos Hotel. This and other large ones occasionally walked across the grass or paving; juveniles frequented rock piles near the ocean that were clearly visible from the window of our room. Photo by RC.

of the islands as nearly as possible to their original condition. The international interest and support it has engendered was demonstrated the next day, when a delegation from Spain arrived to talk with Dr. Blanton about lending its financial support to the work of the station.

We spent the next two days—the entire weekend—drinking in the beauty and wonder of the natural paradise in which we found ourselves. Our corner room had two large windows, facing roughly to the south and west, through which we could see much wildlife and its varied activities. We couldn't have wanted a better observatory. Also, on the night of June 13 the full moon rose and the ocean was illuminated by myriad sparkling moonbeams on the low waves. Before dawn the next morning, the moon was on the other side across Academy Bay, but the reflections were far fewer on the more quiet waters. We walked around the spacious grounds of the Hotel Galápagos, watching the birds and the little lava lizards, *Tropidurus*, and taking many pictures with my lightweight "boob" camera—one of those self-focusing gadgets you aim and just press the button. (My far more reliable Canon, with its macro and telephoto lenses, tubes, and filters, and which I had laboriously hauled all over the Orient, was left at home. The camera gear seemed to grow much heavier with each passing year, and I no longer could cope with it.) We even walked over to Puerto Ayora, the tiny town on the bay.

Our return trip to Baltra was by an ancient public bus, which was loaded with passengers and their baggage. Willing hands helped me up and down the uneven stone steps as we boarded and disembarked from the *ponga* across the Canal Itabasca. Our plane arrived from the mainland just as we approached the runway. An hour later we departed from the "enchanted isles" a full 15 minutes ahead of time. All the passengers were accounted for, so why wait? The return to Quito was uneventful, except that Kathryn, who imbibes far more liquids daily than I do, became dehydrated. That difficulty was quickly dissipated when she consumed two pots full of herb tea that Hugo, one of the Hostal's waiters, brought to our room unsolicited.

Before leaving the subject of the Galápagos Islands, I should add some general comments. The archipelago is isolated and has few resources. A small amount of agriculture is practiced in the highlands of Santa Cruz; there are a few farm animals and some fruit trees. Most foods and other commodities must be transported from the mainland, and there are supply ships that make regular crossings. Lumber, concrete, and many other things must all be imported. Prices are thus higher, and shortages may occur at intervals. Fresh water has always been in short supply, and I recall reading that there were mighty few places where the old-time whaling vessels could obtain it. Modern science has solved the problem, at least at the Hotel Galápagos. It had its own reverse-osmosis desalinator, which produced pure fresh water suitable for drinking and making ice. The station had not yet acquired one, but hoped to have one soon. In the meantime, rainwater was collected in cisterns or purchased from natives who gathered it in the highlands of Santa Cruz, where precipitation is greater. For washing, the hotel supplied heavily chlorinated brackish water, which was useless for working up a lather. Both the hotel and the station had their own electrical generators. Government generators supplied the town with electricity, but "juice" was available only from 6:00 A.M. until midnight.

We discovered while in the hotel and at the station that Ecuadorians have a clever, sanitary way of kissing. They put one of their cheeks against the cheek of another and simultaneously make a sound like a kiss. No lips meet, no germs are exchanged, and, of course, no lipstick. We both kissed Dr. Blanton and Cynthia Jaramillo good-bye in that manner.

As promised, once we were home, I sent books to the station to help with the research on the geckos of the Galápagos archipelago. Later, Thomas H. Fritts, of the U.S. Fish and Wildlife Service, who attended a meeting in the islands, brought back a magnificent gift for me from staff members of the station. It was a lifelike tortoise with its head and neck extended and a carapace almost six inches long. It had been beautifully carved from manzanita wood by Fausto Llarena, a park warden

who has been active in the rearing program for many years. It replicates the type of giant tortoise found on Pinzón (Duncan) Island, and it is now an outstanding feature in my collection of wood, bone, and stone animals picked up on our travels to many faraway places.

After returning from the islands, we rested in Quito for a couple of days and then headed for an extraordinarily different habitat.

Amazonia! The greatest rain forest in the world, historically encompassing a third of South America. A land of towering trees, some more than 200 feet tall, and within whose canopy much of the action takes place. The rain forest has an enormous biodiversity, including tens or perhaps hundreds of thousands of species—chiefly invertebrates and plants—still unknown to science. What a vast and extraordinary habitat about which so much has been written and recorded on film. All my life I had dreamed about seeing it, and the moment had finally arrived. The very word "Amazonia" gave me as great a thrill as hearing "Galápagos Islands."

We boarded a plane in Quito on Monday, June 22. It was an old-fashioned craft with Rolls-Royce engines mounted like outriggers that effectively blocked any view of the countryside, except when I strained to look straight downward. I could see the deep ravines dividing the capital city into many parts. Presently we rose above the lofty Andes Mountains, and then began the steep descent into the Oriente, the eastern part of Ecuador.

As we flew I could not help but think of the plight of the great rain forest, which is being felled at a staggering rate, especially in Brazil, where 5,000 square miles of it is leveled annually. What an immense loss. As we sarcastically put it, just to make a fast buck selling chiefly wood, meanwhile destroying one of the earth's grandest natural resources. What effect will the loss of so many trees have on our global environment? On the absorption of carbon dioxide? On the innumerable species not yet discovered and described? Perhaps to lose them forever. The brush from the trimmings is burned, and the soil, infertile and shallow, can supply only a limited amount of traditional agriculture. Despite such gloomy musings, Kathryn and I were about to see one of the best parts of Amazonia firsthand. Commendably, in Ecuador, the rain forest was still virtually untouched, and we would experience it in its natural state.

It was cloudy in the Oriente, but when our plane dropped below the overcast, we beheld a vast green sea of vegetation, relieved only by a few muddy streams. We landed at Coca, whose real name is Puerto Francisco de Orellana. Oil from underground deposits was being pumped nearby, but that activity, as yet, had had little effect on the rain forest. Our baggage was loaded on an ancient bus, and, with a handful of other passengers, we slowly chugged our way across the tiny town to a primitive dock, where we were helped aboard a small vessel shaped like a dugout, but actually a planked boat. It was open all around, but a thatched roof above our heads offered some shelter. We were on the Río Napo, one of the principal tributaries of the Amazon, mightiest of all the rivers on Earth. A powerful outboard motor drove us downstream, but, even with the strong current of the broad river helping to push us along, it took two and a half hours to reach our destination, La Selva (literally, "the forest").

Entrepreneurs had built it, a jungle camp, on the shore of a picturesque lake to give visitors a base from which to explore with professional guides. Accommodations were rather primitive, but there were such amenities as hot meals and flush toilets. Walks, floored with rounded slabs of wood, slimy with mold because of the constant dampness and frequent rains, were laid on the ground or raised on stilts and crossbars above the soggy earth. While walking on them I had to watch with great care where I placed each foot, lest I slip and fall. From the rickety dock on the Río Napo, we walked a full half-mile on such a planked walkway to a point where real dugout canoes awaited us and our luggage. Indians employed by the owners were on hand to help all guests, and one of them took my arm and carried my shoulder bag, in which I always keep such things as my camera, binoculars, medications, and other necessities.

Our dugout crossed the lake, and we disembarked and climbed upward on more slippery slabs that made me grip the handrail firmly. We arrived in the social center of the complex of La Selva, a large thatch-roofed room with a small bar at one side, chess and checker boards, and damp, limp books, with which guests could amuse themselves between excursions into the jungle. Nearby was the dining hall and another slab walk to private quarters.

We were assigned to thatch-roofed *cabaña* number 3. There were two single beds, a small table, and a rack for our bags, all made of rough wood and other primitive materials. The bathroom held a high sink with one faucet, a square shower with a drain set in the floor, and a ridiculously low toilet that was more suitable for a six-year-old lad than a six-foot-tall octogenarian. There was no electricity, and the water was pumped from the lake and was, therefore, undrinkable. Our two flashlights and a kerosene lantern would furnish illumination during the 12 hours of darkness that prevail near the Equator. For drinking we had two bottles of Güitig mineral water.

I was so weary when we arrived in late afternoon that

The porch on the rustic cabaña *we occupied at La Selva in the Amazonian rain forest in Ecuador. One afternoon a troop of squirrel monkeys cavorted in the trees and bushes only a few feet away. Photo by RC.*

I flopped on the bed, tucked the mosquito netting into place, and slept for more than an hour. We were summoned to dinner by the blowing of a conch horn or similar instrument at 7:00 P.M., and we had to make our way along the elevated and highly uneven boardwalk by flashlight. Fortunately, there was a handrail on either side. I had to be careful, because there were steps up and down here and there that could easily be overlooked in the dark.

We stumbled along to the dining hall. The tables were illuminated by more kerosene lanterns, and it was barely possible for us to see our plates and what we were eating. The soup, entrée, and dessert were good, however. We began to get acquainted with our fellow "explorers" and those who had come earlier, some 20 or so people in all. We were fortunate that there were so few. The day after we left, a capacity crowd of 42 was due to arrive, and we were told it would be the same all through July and August, the vacation months in the States and Europe.

We were briefed about the morrow's activities, which would feature lengthy hikes along jungle trails. That sounded rather strenuous. I pointed out that Kay and I were elderly, so the chief guide assigned us, and we alone, to Bill Ward, a young American assistant.

We elected to tour the lake in one of the dugouts. A young Indian named Rafael also became our constant companion for the remainder of our stay. He used a paddle to maneuver the craft slowly close to the shore, and his sharp eyes spotted a number of things we otherwise would have missed. Among them were three red howler monkeys at long range. We closed in a bit, and I was able to pick them up in my binoculars. Other interesting mammals were a flock of nine long-nosed bats that flew rapidly just above the surface of the water after we approached a log, part of which protruded horizontally just a few inches above the surface. Bill said they habitually clung beneath such objects during daylight hours. We saw many birds, most of which Bill identified, and all of which I was able to see clearly through the binoculars. The biggest surprise was five hoatzins at close range. The hoatzin is an avian anomaly. It is a slender, small-headed brown bird about two feet in length with a long, loose crest and stiffly shafted feathers. The chicks are virtually naked on hatching, and they have two well-developed claws near the tip of each wing, which they use for climbing; the claws disappear in two or three weeks. The hoatzin lives only in shrubby trees bordering streams or lakes, such as the one on which we were "dugouting," and it occurs only in northern South America, including much of the Amazon Basin.

There was an almost constant parade of strange birds, and I wished my son, Skip, an accomplished birder, could have been with us. On our list were many I had only read about: yellow-rumped cacique, russet-backed oropendola, violaceous jay, white-winged swallow, tropical kingbird, lesser kiskadee, silver-billed tanager, crimson-crested woodpecker, greater ani, screaming piha, red-capped cardinal, black caracara, macaws of two species, and white-eyed parrot.

After our siesta we donned rubber boots that extended upward to our calves. Kay's were OK, but mine, the largest pair available, were tight and uncomfortable. I decided to use them rather than my sneakers, however, in order to avoid bacteria and biting organisms. We boarded a dugout and headed for the end of the lake, where we stepped ashore and I was more or less hauled up a slippery bank. We walked along a muddy trail and soon came to a place where a seemingly endless horde of leaf-cutter ants was streaming along holding pieces of leaves above them. An equally large horde of "empty-handed" ones moved in the opposite direction. Bill said the parade in both directions was continuous night and day, except during and right after heavy rains when their pheromone trail was washed away. The leaves went to nourish the fungi colonies that the ants maintain underground to feed their young. Nearby was a colony of tiny bees such as, Bill said, was invariably present near the nests of leaf-cutter ants.

When we dressed in the morning we had doused ourselves with insect repellent. Evidently my profuse perspiration rinsed most of mine away, because I acquired scores of chigger bites on our afternoon excursion. Kay must have retained her repellent, because she had virtually none. Despite this nuisance we thoroughly enjoyed our leisurely sunset excursion on the lake. After supper I paused to admire the sky. The stars were bril-

liant, and I quickly found Scorpius and the Southern Cross, with Rigil Kent and Hadar, the two first-magnitude stars, pointing to it.

The next morning, clad in our rubber boots, we walked the long muddy trail to the observation tower, a structure with nearly 100 steps. Some of the steps were narrow, and some wide, but all were higher than the stair risers we were accustomed to using. It was a hard climb, especially for me in my tight boots.

The uppermost level, where Kathryn, Bill, Rafael, and I stood virtually motionless and silent, was level with the canopy, the top of the rain forest where much of the activity occurs. The tower was built around a giant ceiba tree whose summit protruded well above the canopy.

Within minutes a magnificent pair of scarlet macaws flew by at eye level only about 50 feet from us. Later they (presumably the same pair) flew back, and just as close. What a thrill it was to see them. We always had the species at the zoo, but there they were, completely wild and free. From our aerie we also clearly saw, although farther away, a white-throated toucan—another thrill.

The descent from the tower was easier than I thought it would be, but the long hike to it from the lodge and back was an ordeal. The mud was ankle deep in spots, and there was much slipping and sliding where the trail went up and down small rises. By the time we were back my feet hurt badly, and, after suffering foot, leg, and ankle cramps during the following night, I resolved not to use the boots again.

We were so weary from our long early-morning trek that we attempted nothing but rest during the afternoon and a little bird-watching from our quarters. I was asleep when Kathryn woke me to see the monkeys. A troop of about 20 squirrel monkeys was very close to our *cabaña*, and some were as clearly visible as if we were watching them at the zoo. They were feeding on seeds from long, dependent pods. Some leaped across an open space that I estimated to be 15 or 20 feet wide. They dropped slightly in altitude but instantly grabbed vegetation to break their falls. One had a baby on its back. We watched them for at least 15 minutes before they moved away.

Many of the guests went off on a long, boot-clad hike through the jungle the following morning, but we took another dugout canoe ride around the lake instead. Rafael slowly paddled our craft, while we kept our binoculars at the ready. We stayed out most of the morning, saw many more birds and, near the shore farthest from the lodge, a troop of about a dozen cebus monkeys, one with a baby clinging to its back.

It was disappointing not to find any reptiles or amphibians, but the footing was so insecure that I dared not watch anything but my feet as I moved along. Bill Ward and Rafael found a few specimens of *Bufo typhonius* and an unidentified *Eleutherodactylus*, which they showed me and then liberated. Nary a snake nor lizard, but a few turtles were basking.

During the last afternoon we packed everything we could, because we knew we would be up and away very early in the morning, while it was still pitch dark. We would have to tuck in our nighttime necessities in the morning, but we wanted to have a minimum to do by flashlight and kerosene lantern, if it was still working. One night it had gone out before morning.

We were up before 5:00, and the Indians soon picked up our bags. As luck would have it, our flashlight, which we had carefully recharged in Quito, quit and was useless. A battery-powered one still worked. We made our way to the dining hall over the slab-covered walkway, slowly in my case. I didn't want to fall at the last minute. We were served tea or coffee and hard buns, and then we went down the difficult long series of steps to the dock, where I was helped into one of the dugouts. As we were paddled to the end of the lake we could see the waning moon and many stars. It began to get light before we reached the half mile of treacherous walkway to the river landing. Rafael stayed immediately behind me as I walked along. Twice he grabbed my arm as I teetered, and once, where a huge root had forced the walkway upward, he hung on to me as I made my way across the sloping, slippery slabs. Fortunately, it was becoming lighter and lighter and I didn't have to use the flashlight at all, although I clung to the staff that had been cut for me. Kathryn made out OK, but she, of course, was slowed by my progress. Finally, we arrived at the boat landing. I made my way down the uneven steps and various impedimenta, and was helped into the large, so-called dugout. Because Kay and I were the last of the passengers, we were off almost at once. The boat ride upstream, against the strong current of the Río Napo, took an hour longer than going down.

Our trip back to Quito was uneventful, except that our plane was very late, but it took us squarely over Cotopaxi, and I could look down into the crater of the mighty volcano. What a thrilling trip it had been to experience the primeval rain forest. We shuddered as we thought of how rapidly it is being destroyed in other countries.

We returned to the Hostal los Alpes with less than two days before our departure for home. Kathryn, who is an excellent packer, managed to stow things so well that we discarded the sturdy box we had thought we might need. The next morning we transferred to the Hotel Colón Internacional, where food and taxis were available at all hours. It was a large, first-class hostelry, and, except for walks outside, we spent the day there, but retired early in preparation for rising at 3:30 A.M. We were at the airport shortly after 5:00, and it was already crowded. We had to run a complicated gauntlet—checking tickets and baggage, paying the departure tax of $25 each (no sucres), passing through the safety checkpoint, having the immigration inspector stamp our passports, and finally boarding our plane. We taxied onto the tarmac for takeoff, but promptly returned to the terminal. A sharp-eyed attendant had noticed something leaking. It proved to be from a generator, and, although repairs were attempted, the flight was aborted, much to the consternation of many of the passengers. We didn't care. We would take our day of rest in Quito instead of Miami, especially since we would be the guests of American Airlines. They gave us vouchers for free meals and a night's lodging at the Colón.

The next morning we repeated the early venture, and were suddenly extremely grateful for the delay in departure. As we walked out to the plane we gasped at the magnificent spectacle confronting us. The previous day had been cloudy, but it was now beautifully clear, and Cotopaxi was revealed to us for the first time in all its awesome grandeur. Not a bit of it was obscured by clouds, and it seemed to rise from the very edge of Quito, even though it was many miles away. I had asked for seats on the right side of the plane, and, when we had gained a little altitude, we had a marvelous view of the whole mountain chain from Chimborazo to the south all the way to the Colombian border to the north. What a rare and wonderful panorama as our last parting glimpse of the fascinating country where we had spent a month absorbing something of its extraordinary diversity.

The flight went smoothly. We crossed the southwesternmost corner of Colombia, traversed the Pacific to the Gulf of Panama, and then flew directly above the Panama Canal. Onward we went across the Caribbean, over Cuba, and into Miami, where we stayed overnight and then on home to Albuquerque the next day.

Our month-long trip enabled me to accomplish two lifelong dreams: to visit the Galápagos Islands, and to catch a glimpse of the Amazonian rain forest, with the bonus thrown in of traversing the great Avenue of Volcanoes. The going was difficult at times, but I persevered with the help of a great many kind persons who were willing to lend a hand to the old man. It is well that we allowed ample time for resting between excursions. It gave us both a chance to relax and prepare for the next adventure.

Our airfare cost us nothing except a small fee each that was charged to meet some regulation. We traveled on accumulated mileage resulting from our many journeys to Europe and the Orient while progressing with the work on the *Agkistrodon* monograph. Financially, we would not have been able to make the trip otherwise. Our expenses in Ecuador were low, except at the Hotel Colón and on the domestic airline (TAME). The sucre is worth very little, and it is constantly shrinking in value.

Despite the difficulties I had clambering over the sharp, uneven rocks of the Galápagos, and slipping and sliding in the rain forest of the Oriente, the trip was worth every penny. I will admit, however, that such ambitious and arduous travel is best undertaken when one is under 50!

Chapter 61

The Last Continent:
Part III. South of Capricorn

A subtitle for this chapter might be "Stumbling through South America from Paraguay to Patagonia." Both Kathryn and I were on canes. A year earlier she had undergone hip replacement surgery, and, when we took off for South America in 1995, she was walking well but not with long strides. My balance problem and my recent recovery from a very sore heel (plantar fasciitis) also had to be considered. Hence our canes, which also served as our "safety nets." We knew that, in Latin America, sidewalks are often broken and full of booby traps for the unwary. That proved to be especially true in downtown Buenos Aires, where huge throngs of people and racing traffic multiplied the possibility of accidents.

Two graduate students whom I knew well at the University of New Mexico were closely associated with Paraguay. Aida Luz Aquino, or Lucy, as we called her, was born there, and she currently is Directora of CITES (the International Convention on Commercial Trade in Endangered Species) in Paraguay. Lee A. Fitzgerald, whose interest in Paraguay dates from 1980 to 1982, when he served as a Peace Corps volunteer, had amassed an almost encyclopedic knowledge of the wildlife of the country. Also, he was engaged in an intensive study of the life history of the tegus, the large lizards of the genus *Tupinambis* which have long been the source of exotic skins for the leather trade. What legislation might be needed to ensure a permanent sustainable yield? Lee was still working on that important research under the aegis of the World Wildlife Fund.

Both of those young people had long urged me to visit Paraguay. Their invitation, along with the fact that Kathryn and I both had accumulated many additional frequent-flier miles on American Airlines while visiting family and attending conferences, prompted us to go. It would be a final travel fling for two elderly people.

While we were at it, and so far from home, why not venture farther on southward to see the wildlife of Patagonia, whose marine components are the same or similar to those of nearby Antarctica? We had crossed the Tropic of Capricorn on previous excursions to other parts of the world, but our 1995 destinations would all be south of that line.

As we always did on long-distance journeys, we took a day to rest, this time in Miami, before boarding an all-night flight to the far south. Our plane stopped first at São Paulo, Brazil, where a large number of passengers disembarked. After refueling we headed west to Asunción. Lee Fitzgerald and his student, Guillermo "Memo" Terol, met us and took us to the Gran Hotel, which once had been the ornate country home of Madame Lynch, the paramour of dictator Mariscal López. We were there for two nights and were astounded at the large number of babies we saw, virtually all accompanied by American mothers. It seemed that Asunción was a noted place for adopting children, but the process was lengthy and could be heartbreaking if anything went wrong. After selecting a child, the prospective foster mother had to wait four months to see if the natural mother was still willing to give up her offspring. Our guess was that it could be an expensive procedure—a lengthy stay in Paraguay, lawyers' fees, and probably a consolation gift for the true parents.

We soon moved to the much less expensive Hotel Castillo, which was comfortable, quiet, and secure, and not far from Lucy Aquino's office. One of her associates found it, Lee inspected it in advance, and it became our headquarters during our stay in Paraguay. The Castillo was unique in that it had been built around, but was separate from, an elegant home. It was in the form of individual rooms and small suites designed by the owner and operator, Helmut Anzberger, an elderly, industrious German who kept everything in perfect order. We had a spacious room, with a small bath, and meals were available in the Anzberger residence. We supplemented those with noontime snacks of fruit and cookies purchased at a nearby store.

Lucy had a reception for us at her home, and there we met a dozen young people who were associated with her office or studying various facets of the natural history of Paraguay. We subsequently visited with them individually, and Lucy permitted some of them to ferry us to various places in cars belonging to her department. Everyone was enthusiastic and helpful. We learned much about their activities, and we inspected the natural history museum, which was in the early stages of development.

One of the outstanding features of Paraguay that I especially wanted to see was the Chaco, a region noted for its fauna and flora. Actually, the Chaco extends through parts of three countries, far south into Argentina and, to the north, into Bolivia. The ownership of the upper part was disputed by Bolivia and Paraguay for the better part of a century, and it resulted in a war between those two countries in the early 1930s. Under the terms of the peace treaty, Paraguay kept about two-thirds of the contested territory.

In Paraguay, the eastern part of the Chaco is swampy in part but subject to lengthy wet and dry seasons influenced by the prevailing winds sweeping in from the east. The western part is much more arid. With few human residents and soils unsuited for agriculture, the Chaco has an amazingly abundant and varied fauna. The native vegetation is low, but it includes palms of moderate height, and another dominant tree that is allied to the mesquite of our own Southwest. Cattle raising is the chief activity.

Lee Fitzgerald and Memo Terol spent almost a full day driving us through the Chaco. They were on the way to their study sites northeast of the small city of Concepción where, they hoped, Guaraní Indians would be holding live adult tegus for Lee's research. An advantageous way of obtaining specimens was to buy them at a higher price than the Indians could get by selling the reptiles' skins. The highway through the Chaco, with little traffic and paved most of the way, was a much longer but quicker route than following the road along the Río Paraguay, with its twists and turns through many settlements.

It was truly a memorable day for us, as we saw what for us was a brand-new habitat. The weather was clear, and by afternoon it was so hot that we appreciated our vehicle's air-conditioning. It hadn't rained for three or four months, and almost everything was sere and dry. Places that the young men told us were full of water during the rainy season were empty. They stopped to visit some Indians who had two large tegus for them, which they promised to buy on the return trip. There was no point in lugging them along in all the heat in the truck compartment at the rear of our specialized field car. Memo spoke Guaraní, a useful asset.

We saw birds flying now and then, mostly crested caracaras and savanna hawks, but it wasn't until we reached a rest stop in late morning that I had a real chance to use my binoculars. They picked up a field flicker, a woodpecker similar to our North American flicker, but skinnier and which, as Lee told us, spent much time on the ground foraging. As I was watching it I noticed a medium-sized snake, belly up, that had apparently been run over. Neither Lee nor Memo knew what it was, but they preserved it and took it to Emilio Buongermini, who was working on the herpetology of Paraguay. He identified it as *Liophis almadensis*. It was the fourth known specimen from the country. We had seen a much larger, badly mashed snake on the road soon after we crossed the Paraguay River from Asunción. It was a five-foot false water cobra, *Hydrodynastes gigas*, a snake that spreads a hood much like that of a cobra, but is no relation to that venomous snake.

There was a stretch of road roughly 25 miles long, not far from Concepción, that was unpaved and, as our hosts well knew, it was a slippery, muddy, treacherous challenge to any driver when it was wet. As we traversed it after the long drought, it was so dry that every passing vehicle deluged us with dust that effectively blocked our view for quite a few seconds. It was near the eastern end of that unpaved stretch of road that we hit the jackpot and enjoyed an hour-long orgy of birdwatching. The reason? A stretch of road a mile or so long still had water, some of it deep, on both sides. It was an oasis that attracted waterbirds and other species from miles around.

We had seen a few of the spectacular jabiru storks flying in the distance, but at the hot spot there were nearly a dozen, and one was standing so close, when we made a brief stop, that binoculars were superfluous. The stork's huge bill, naked head, and upper neck were coal black, and so were the legs. In contrast, the body, wing, and tail feathers were white. The only exception was a small patch of red around the neck where the black and white feathers otherwise would have met. How big it was! It stood four feet high. The jabiru has one of the greatest wingspans of any Neotropical bird.

There were so many birds that Memo, who was driving slowly, had to stop again and again as one or the other of us, Lee included, saw something different. Black and turkey vultures we had seen many times, but the lesser yellow-headed vulture was new. There were two kinds of caracaras, both the widespread crested one and the yellow-headed; the latter also new to us. I saw several unusual but familiar birds that I had encountered elsewhere during my travels, including limpkin, wattled jacana, and snail kite. The kite seemed to be common all over the part of the Chaco we visited. The most intriguing avian novelty was a pair of black-and-chestnut eagles. They are huge birds, and, when they flew upward from beside a water-filled ditch, the bright russet of their underparts made a resplendent splash of color. Maguari storks were present, and so was a giant wood-rail, very much larger than any rail Kathryn or I had ever seen in the United States. I spotted a "black" ibis, only to discover that its proper name is green ibis (very dark green) after I bought a field guide quite a bit later in Buenos Aires. We also saw two very large woodpeckers, crested and with brilliant all-red heads.

Traffic was light, but when a vehicle passed and the great cloud of dust blew away, scores of doves dropped down onto the road, apparently to pick up seeds brought to the surface as the vehicle passed over the hard-packed dirt road. There were two kinds: picazuro pigeons and eared doves. Along with them was a scattering of red-crested or Brazilian cardinals, which I had first met as cage birds at the Twin Brook Zoo, where I worked soon after graduating from high school.

We also saw cowbirds and blackbirds, southern lapwings, black-headed parakeets, yellow-billed caciques, and white monjitas, or little nuns. Despite their small size, slightly larger than our warblers, the monjitas could be seen at a considerable distance. Their plumage was snow white, except for their wings and tail tips, which were black. Also present were two kinds of ovenbirds, both of which are far larger and belong to a different family than the species of the same name at home in the States. They receive their name from their handiwork, or rather billwork. One kind makes large rounded mud balls on fenceposts that look almost like miniature *hornos*, the ovens that are a prominent part of many of New Mexico's pueblos. The nest is inside the mud, which soon dries to a stony hardness, and has an opening that permits access to the interior. The other kind of ovenbird uses sticks and twigs assembled in globular fashion and attached to trees.

Along the same stretch of road we found a few animals that had been run over and killed weeks or months earlier, and were desiccated, almost skeletonized. Included were an armadillo, a giant anteater, and a seven-foot yellow anaconda.

Disrupting the euphoria engendered by the abundance of wildlife in the Chaco was a somber note, an almost frightening one. Much of the area, especially along the road, had been burned, and we passed one roaring fire that was fiercely consuming not only the plants and litter on the ground, but was also leaping upward into the taller vegetation. Thousands of palm trees had been burned. Almost all the Chaco that we could see from the highway had been blackened. The fires were set presumably to promote a quick growth of grass for the cattle as soon as the rains arrived. Many of those domestic animals were in evidence, from small groups to sizable herds. Fires were burning all over the agricultural lands in the eastern part of Paraguay, not just in the Chaco. We saw a profusion of them from our plane window as we descended into Asunción.

Probably the practice of burning is traditional. Perhaps it served a salutary purpose in earlier days when the human population was smaller. Nowadays, with the world's natural resources fast dwindling, why should so much vegetation go up in flames? Why should great quantities of carbon dioxide be added to the atmospheric burden? The odor of smoke was omnipresent, faint to almost choking, both in the eastern Chaco and in the town where Kathryn and I would be staying for a couple of days.

Soon we crossed the Río Paraguay on a high bridge, and Lee took us to a small hotel in Concepción. We stayed there for two nights, rested and explored a bit on foot, and then flew back to Asunción, a half-hour's ride.

Lee and Memo returned with more than 20 tegus and went to work with them immediately in a makeshift laboratory outside Lucy's office. We watched as they timed the big lizards' running speeds after warming them up in an oven to their optimum activity temperature. They subsequently made another foray, that time into the western part of the Chaco, and increased their total acquisition to 42, a record number of specimens for a month's research. After collecting their data, Lee and Memo turned almost all of the reptiles loose in their natural habitat.

Two days after our enjoyable excursion in the Chaco the rains descended, and we were hotelbound for several days, during which I wrote copy for these memoirs and for the daily journal I keep during long travels. On a cloudy, misty day Lucy took us into the lovely hill country east of Asunción, stopping at native homes to buy freshly baked goodies and to see a large pottery display. Against my better judgment, I bought a pottery turtle, which, thanks to Kathryn's careful attention, survived to arrive home without having its outstretched head and neck broken off.

We visited with the students, and I entertained a group of them with accounts of my adventures while working with Isabelle on our field guides and with Kathryn in the Orient on *Agkistrodon*. We exercised by walking in the courtyard of the Hotel Castillo and hiking to the small store a few blocks away. Meanwhile, I wrote postcards we had bought in Concepción. None was in sight in a novelty store. I had to ask for them, and a boy extracted a cardboard box stored under the counter. It contained only a few mediocre ones.

The lack of postcards and my attempts to cash traveler's checks revealed that Paraguay is not geared up for tourism. None of the three hotels where we stayed had cards or postage stamps for sale, and none would accept our American Express traveler's checks. Cards, stamps, and exchange banks were all available in downtown Asunción, where the traffic, crowds, and air and noise pollution were almost overwhelming. Silvia Frutos, a completely bilingual young lady associated with Lucy's work, took us twice to a large bank in the city's center. I have never seen such a simple transaction expanded into a complex procedure. It seemed as though three or four vice presidents had to examine my credentials; the page of my passport bearing my picture was photocopied; and after all that they would give me only $300 worth of guaranis, the local currency, at a time. Silvia later took me to another bank where she was well known, and the red tape was at a minimum. She had learned her English as a girl when her father, a doctor, interned at a hospital in Wilmington, Delaware.

We never did get to the post office to mail our postcards. I gave them to Lee, and he passed them along to one of our young friends, who took care of them properly. To thank everyone for their great kindness to us, I hosted a dinner at a popular restaurant.

Two days later we were off to Argentina, but in a confusing, roundabout way. To explain why, it is well to delve into a bit of South American history. During the Triple Alliance War, from 1865 to 1870, Paraguay suffered grievous losses as Argentina, Brazil, and Uruguay ganged up on it. Lee told us that 75 percent of all males in Paraguay lost their lives during the conflict, and that, during the final days of the war, regiments of women and older children confronted their enemies. In the end, Paraguay lost much of its territory to Argentina and Brazil.

Did those two large foes set their common boundary on opposite sides of the Río Iguazú so as to shut off their vanquished victim completely from spectacular Iguazú Falls, the largest and most awesome waterfall complex in all of South America? A study of a map of Argentina reveals a long northeastward-extending appendix that stops at the river. In any event, there was no way for us to reach the Falls from Paraguay except by passing through Brazil. That gave us pause. Long before we started off, several friends asked if we were going to avoid Brazil, because of the rampant crime there. We had heard several reports about tourists being victimized in Rio de Janeiro and other cities. According to all I could learn before we left home, however, we had no choice. If we wanted to see the Falls, we would have to take a long bus ride from Asunción, cross into Brazil, and then wend our way by another bus or taxi to the Argentine. I mentioned the problem to Silvia, and the next day she had an excellent solution for us. There was air service on Varig, a Brazilian airline, from Asunción

to Foz do Iguaçú. A travel agent visited me at our hotel, and through him we solved the dilemma. One of their representatives would meet us in Foz and hold up a sign with the name "Conant" printed in large letters on it. He would drive us to the Hotel Internacional, where we had reservations. We learned later that the bus from Asunción left at midnight and took six hours to make the trip! How much simpler it was to fly!

The hotel, a big, modern one, was not far from an airport where tourists from Buenos Aires arrived to see the Falls. We had to exchange our vouchers, obtained through American Airlines, for tickets on Aerolineas Argentina. Cut-rate vouchers were honored only if they were purchased outside their country.

From the lobby of the Internacional we could see the Falls in the distance with great clouds of mist hovering above them. There was no way to get closer except to walk, and we were on canes! I soon learned through a travel agency that there was a paved road on the Brazilian side that gave close access to several viewing points of the Falls. An Argentinian girl who spoke quite a bit of English came for us in a car with a male driver, and we were soon back in Brazil without so much as a stop at the border. Agency cars were well known to the inspectors, and tourists were driven back and forth at will. We had several excellent views of the falling avalanches of water, but it was cloudy and the plethora of rainbows, supposedly present on sunny days, was missing.

The Falls are not a broad continuous sheet of descending water. Instead, they are interrupted at many places by jutting masses of rock. One stupendous drop is higher than Niagara Falls. The area was heavily commercialized by the Brazilians. There was an elevator down to a lower level for a better and adrenaline-raising view, which we used, and there were walkways and boats on which spectators, clad in oilskins, could approach close to the natural wonder. Those we didn't use, nor did we take a ride in a helicopter to view the spectacle from a variety of angles.

About a dozen coatimundis were panhandling among the throngs of visitors. Several persons tried to pet them, a potentially dangerous practice, but the coatis merely veered away and sought more food on the ground or from hands or fingers, probing everywhere with their long snouts. It was almost impossible to get photographs of them without showing parts of their benefactors.

After seeing all we could, we were driven back into Argentina and taken to the airport, where our bilingual guide helped us in getting our new tickets for our destinations farther south.

The next day was clear and sunny, and we went for a walk near the hotel. While Kathryn investigated a few small shops, I concentrated on the black birds we had seen from our hotel window the previous day. They were red-rumped caciques, gregarious builders of pendulous nests resembling those of orioles.

We were at the airport by noon, and we were surprised to see how many passengers were waiting for the flight to arrive. Soon a huge Boeing jet appeared and a swarm of people deplaned; when we were ensconced in our seats, we could see that it was full for its trip to Buenos Aires. I was at a window and was able to watch the unfolding panorama on the ground as we sped along. It was swampy but cultivated in part. Near the capital, the surrounding suburbia extended outward for a great many miles in every direction except north. There we could see the broad estuary known as the Río de la Plata, across from which, but completely out of sight, was Uruguay. I could not help but think back to the time during World War II when the German pocket battleship *Graf Spee* was driven into the broad bay by three small British cruisers, the *Ajax, Achilles,* and *Exeter*. The *Graf Spee* was scuttled by its crew off Montevideo.

We stayed two nights in Buenos Aires. By day we braved the heavy traffic and hordes of pedestrians, and finally found a large bookstore where I bought the English translation of "The Birds of Argentina and Uruguay." We were glad to get back to the safety of the hotel. The big city streets were no place for two elderly persons hobbling along on canes.

On Wednesday, October 11, we boarded a plane for Patagonia, far to the south. We were glad to get away from mobs of people and to a place where wildlife still occurred in numbers.

It was raining when we left Buenos Aires, but the skies cleared as we winged southward, and we had a marvelous view of the Península Valdés, which we soon would be exploring, at least along its edges. It looked wild and deserted except for a few primitive roads.

For safety's sake, Kay and I were always the last to leave an airplane when it landed. That was especially prudent when we arrived at the small city of Trelew in southern Argentina. When we boarded the plane, we had to climb up one of those long stairways that are rolled into place. That was bad enough, but going down was worse. Once the parade of passengers bearing loads of luggage was over, flight crew members could then take our elbows and help us. So we were the last to enter the airport. A pleasant lady in her late 40s approached us and said, "I am Anna. Are you Mr. Conant?" I replied in the affirmative, and she responded by saying, "I'm your guide and I'll be with you during your visit here." She really meant it, because she and her driver, Carlos, were our constant companions day and night on the

peninsula and again for a day when we drove well south in Patagonia.

As soon as Carlos had loaded our baggage into the trunk of "Taxi 13," as he called his sturdy Volkswagen sedan, Ana (to use her Spanish name) gave us some news. Just a few days earlier there had been a deluge of rain, a most unusual event in that arid part of the world. Evidences of it were all around us in the form of large puddles, temporary ponds, and even submerged sidewalks. The road south from Trelew was impassable, so they decided to take us first to the peninsula well north of town. Before we departed, however, Ana instructed Carlos to drive to her home, where she picked up a lightweight but well-insulated jacket, fresh from the dry cleaners, for Kathryn to wear over her own coat. That act of kindness set the stage for an odyssey during which Ana and Carlos treated us with as much care and thoughtfulness as if we had been close relatives. Without question, they were the best and most alert guides we ever had anywhere in the world.

It was mid-afternoon when we headed northward. The landscape was a monotonously barren steppe. No trees. No tall bushes. It resembled the parts of Arizona where creosote bushes and other xeric vegetation prevail. I recalled, in fact, that the creosote bushes, of the genus *Larrea*, originated in southern South America. Barbara Timmermann and others studied those plants both in the south and the north, and were able to establish approximately when they arrived in the deserts of our own Southwest. They concluded that seeds, temporarily attached to the legs of migratory birds, had transported the plants to a suitable habitat far to the north. (See the vignette on William Franklin Blair.) There we were, right in the area from which our abundant and redolent creosote bushes had come. I asked Carlos to stop the car so I could examine one of them at close range and try for a picture.

The Península Valdés, which extends well eastward into the South Atlantic Ocean, is roughly 50 miles wide and 60 miles from north to south, yet, it is attached to the mainland by only an extremely narrow isthmus. It, too, had only low vegetation. There were no trees except those that had been planted as windbreaks around a tiny sprinkling of haciendas. Sheep farming was the local industry on the windswept peninsula, and we saw numbers of the wool-bearing animals. In fact, many of them ran stupidly across the road in front of us, playing follow-the-leader instead of dashing away onto the adjacent steppe.

We soon traversed the isthmus and headed for Punta Delgada at the southeasternmost corner of the jutting land mass. A lighthouse surmounted the sheer bluff down to the sea. Near it were several small buildings that once belonged to the Argentine Navy but had been bought by an able entrepreneur and transformed into accommodations for nature-oriented tourists. The Lighthouse Lodge, as the complex was called, was our destination.

It was a long ride over gravel roads, and the light was fading behind us as the day neared its end. Nonetheless, we were thrilled to see seven lesser rheas—tall, long-necked, long-legged, flightless birds that resemble the African ostrich. They were all females walking almost in single file. Had they laid their eggs? If they had, the males would be sitting on the nests. It was springtime in the Southern Hemisphere. We also had a fleeting glimpse of three or four maras, but we were to see a family of them two days later at close range. Most conspicuous of the wildlife during that ride were the many kelp gulls, almost exact counterparts of the black-backed gull of northern waters both in size and appearance.

When we arrived at Punta Delgada we were astounded by our room; it was the most tastefully appointed quarters we had during our entire trip. The bedding, curtains, and everything else were virtually new. Also, it was furnished with a portable radiator, filled with oil, and powered by electricity from the generators of the *faro*. Excuse me. By that time I had slipped so easily into Spanish that *faro* popped into mind much quicker than lighthouse, the English equivalent.

The dining room was in one of the nearby buildings, and getting to it posed a problem. There was a narrow path through the sand that was flanked on both sides by masses of low-growing vegetation that resembled the ice plants of the California coast. The night was pitch black. No moon. Getting to dinner would have been an ordeal in the strong gale, if our guides hadn't gripped us each by an arm and led us to the entrance to the dining room. There was only a scattering of guests, but the place seated 80 and could therefore accommodate a busload or two of tourists for lunch. The food was good; all of it had to be trucked in from the mainland.

We didn't get off until 10:00 the next morning, after a hearty breakfast. Ana said there was no need to hurry. We drove steadily northward paralleling the east coast of the peninsula. It was October 12, and we, like Columbus, made wonderful discoveries.

The first thing of special interest was a tinamou, a skulking bird that was adept at keeping a low bush between itself and our car. We finally managed to get it in view with our binoculars. I didn't recall ever having seen one before, either in or out of a zoo. Tinamous are rather nondescript grayish birds of which there are some 40 species. They are chickenlike in general form

and size, but their heads are small, and they seldom fly. The one in sight was an elegant crested tinamou. We would see many more of that species, singly or in pairs, in southern Argentina.

Our first stop was a few miles north of Punta Delgada. Carlos pulled the car off the road, and we got out and walked to the edge of a cliff by the sea. Well over a 100 feet below us were about two dozen *lobos del mar* (southern sea lions) lying on the beach. It was not a breeding group; their season would come later. They were twice the size of the familiar California sea lion.

Farther on we arrived at a wildlife sanctuary, the Reserva Natural Caleta Valdéz (Valdéz Cove). After a strenuous descent almost down to the beach, we reached an excellent overlook above a colony of elephant seals that were nearing the end of their breeding season. Wooden steps helped us and also a rope strung between stanchions. I managed it alone, but Kathryn was accompanied, every step of the way, by faithful Ana. Looking down, at close range, at about 50 of the great marine mammals, I could deduce much of their sequence of activities, with which I was familiar from reading.

They were southern elephant seals, close relatives of the northern elephant seals that Isabelle and I had seen at long range on the Los Coronado Islands off the Pacific coast of northern Mexico way back in 1959. The huge males, known sometimes to reach lengths of 22 feet and to weigh three tons, have an inflatable proboscis on the snout, which, combined with their immense size, earns them the adjective of "elephant." Unlike sea lions, which can swing their hind limbs forward and shuffle along fairly rapidly on land, elephant seals are slow and inept ashore, and they roll or slide whenever possible.

In the spring or early summer they assemble on beaches for their annual breeding ritual. The males battle among themselves to acquire harems of as many females as possible. A dominant bull in a really large colony may have 20 or more. The lesser males have fewer, and fully vanquished ones have none. Disappointed males are known to lurk offshore, ready to seize and kill any pup that may enter the water alone and unguarded. The females are much smaller; their pups are born soon after the fighting is over. The young are quite dark, whereas the adults are brown or gray. Each pup stays close to its mother until it is weaned. A few weeks later, the females mate again.

Much of this was revealed to us as we gazed downward, enthralled by the panorama on the beach below. Three huge males were with their respective harems of six to eight females, each accompanied by a calf. An unsuccessful male was in the sea, among the breaking waves, ready to grab any stray pup. Just to the north of the group three large males were lying alone, and Ana told us that their females and young had departed. A dead calf was lying on the sand and was being gradually dismembered by great skuas, the marine avian predators of Antarctica and its adjacent waters.

All was tranquil as we watched the fascinating scene. Suddenly scores of teenagers came dashing down to join us. A ranger slid down the sand to keep them on the ridge where we stood and prevent them from going onto the beach among the huge beasts. Most of the kids raced right back up again and piled into the two sightseeing buses that had transported them, apparently from Trelew. They had made the long trip, they had seen what they came to look at, and that was that. A half dozen of the young people did linger for a few minutes, watching as we did. I hoped they were "A" students. At least they were willing to look and learn.

I moved slowly back and forth taking pictures with my lightweight automatic Ph.D. ("Push here, dummy") camera.

We tarried at our vantage point for well over a half hour before we began the struggle upward through the sand. Then we continued northward. Soon Carlos pulled the car off the road, and he and Ana prepared our lunch, a full meal, including hot soup, that they delivered to us on trays and wrapped in cellophane. What a meal. It was so huge that I couldn't eat all of mine. Our two guides were certainly doing our trek up brown. Afterward, I wandered around looking at a small, tranquil lagoon between us and the sea, and I spotted two species of grebes, the familiar pied-billed species and a great grebe, which looked more than twice as large as the smaller kind.

Elegant crested tinamous were numerous, especially along the roadsides. Carlos, who was driving, had keen eyesight, and he spotted many long before we did. Ana was also very alert. None of the tinamous flew; nor did most of the smaller birds we saw. The wind was so strong that they would have had difficulty getting back to where they took off, unless they walked. At one point we had an excellent view of a herd of guanacos, about a score of them, all with beautiful orange-brown coats. They are the dainty wild relatives of the domesticated llama. We also saw a lone male rhea. At Punta Norte, at the northernmost tip of the eastern coast of the peninsula, I found and identified, with the help of my recently acquired book, a Patagonian mockingbird. There was supposed to be another colony of sea elephants along the beach, but their season was over. Only two large bulls remained, one in the surf, the other basking.

A small museum in the tiny settlement featured photographs of the slaughter of the southern fur seals, a common practice for obtaining their skins until they were protected by law in 1958.

In late afternoon we headed back south to Punta Delgada against a wind that grew stronger seemingly by the minute. Nonetheless, we saw more guanacos, some of which crossed the road in front of us. In the lee of a small hill we watched a southern lapwing as it foraged on the ground, and Carlos found us a burrowing owl standing erect near its underground retreat. The wind blew storms of dust, but it also helped to dry the innumerable ponds and puddles left over from the deluge of a few days previously. In quite a few places we were forced to leave the road and follow newly created tracks across the steppe to avoid extensive temporary ponds that blocked our passage. Just before we reached the lighthouse complex we saw four rabbits, of a species that was introduced from Europe long ago.

Back in our room before dark, we napped after the long but wonderful day. When it was time to go to dinner, the wind was so fierce that I don't think either of us could have made it if it hadn't been for our sturdy guides.

We had another late start from Punta Delgada in the morning, that time with our bags packed and in the trunk of "Taxi 13." We soon pulled off the road and Carlos drove across the plain to a spot where he and Ana knew a pair of maras had young. The mara is a terrier-sized rodent that is sometimes called a Patagonian hare. Soon we saw the family at easy binocular range, an adult pair and two young. As we approached, they ran slowly away and the two little ones scurried out of sight behind low bushes. The female stayed close to a fence-post, and the male sat down on its haunches perhaps 50 feet away. Presently the two young reappeared. They walked to their mother, who was sitting erect with her back against the post, and we watched them nurse for several minutes.

Our first scheduled stop for the day was at Puerto Pirámides, where there were high sand dunes that allegedly looked, from well out in the adjacent gulf, like pyramids. There were southern right whales close to shore, and from a vantage point, away from the tiny town, we could see the spray ascending from their blowholes and watch their flukes rise out of the water when they sounded. On a rock ledge a single male sea lion was sunning itself. Ana said that by next December there would be a large breeding colony on the ledge, which the animals reached via a sloping ramp that gave access directly to deep water. We were then driven to another vantage point where a large telescope had been erected and a ranger was present. The scope was pointed toward an offshore island on which gregarious birds of many species regularly nested. We were able to make out the vague outlines of two blackish birds, and we were assured they were Magellanic penguins. An exciting new bird for us, but they were too far away for us to have a good look at them.

During the day we saw a gray Patagonian fox and also a skunk. The latter took its time moving away, and we were astounded to note that instead of the usual black-and-white coat, this one had pelage of white and pale brown. We continued on to Trelew, and checked in at the hotel where we were supposed to have stayed the night we arrived in Patagonia, instead of driving north to Punta Delgada. We thanked our guides profusely, and they promised to call for us at 10:00 the next morning and take us on the most exciting part of our trip—to see the huge penguin colony. The road south was now passable.

From our hotel window we had a good look at Trelew, a city settled by the Welsh more than a century previously. It was a small city, but much larger than we had anticipated. There was a profusion of shops and even a supermarket. Some six or eight multistoried buildings, stark and unfinished, composed part of the view. When we asked about them later, we were told that the hoped-for tourists had not materialized as fast as anticipated. The builders had to quit when they ran out of money. Everyone in town hoped they would be in use in future years.

Saturday, October 14, was our last day afield, but what a superb way to end our journey almost to the bottom of the world. Carlos stopped at his home to pick up a warm pullover for me that protected not only my bald head, but also my nose, if I wished. Ana had a couple of errands to do, and she also took me to the local post office to buy stamps for the additional cards I had written to friends and relatives.

Soon we were off for our farthest penetration south of Capricorn, to Punta Tombo, where the Magellanic penguins have their greatest concentration. There are 17 species of penguins; a few kinds are large, but most are small. As we drove along I recalled a long-forgotten event involving a pair of penguins received at the Philadelphia Zoo ever so long ago. Curator of Birds Gus Griswold placed them in a pen with a large pool in Bird Valley. Later, when the keeper emptied the pool to clean it, the penguins literally went down the drain. Two or three days later someone discovered them on the Schuykill River, which runs right past the zoo. Gus and the keepers eventually caught them. What a fast underwater ride they must have had on their way to the river. Luckily, their exit was through a large, century-old drainpipe that had once carried excess water from the ravine that crossed the zoo grounds. We had no record of it, and didn't even know

that the outlet from the penguins' pool entered it. At first, we feared the birds were lost in the city's sewer system.

Soon my thoughts turned back to the birds at hand. We stopped briefly along the road near a large, prosperous-looking hacienda, but where the recent rains had created two small ponds. Another great grebe and a pair of silver teal. Like others we had seen, the hacienda was surrounded by large trees that were planted long ago. Such headquarters for sheep ranching are invariably situated where there is a reliable spring, strong enough to supply the needs of the entire establishment and its sheltering trees. Fresh water is scarce in that arid part of the world. Trelew and other towns are supplied by the Río Chubut, which flows eastward from the Andes. South America tapers and becomes narrow in the far south, and the high mountains are not far away.

After stopping to eat the lunch served by our guides, we moved on and reached the great penguin colony in early afternoon. At the refuge there was a cluster of small buildings with rangers in attendance. We passed through the portal, and drove slowly along a narrow road, and I suddenly realized there were penguins all around us. They were lying in burrows they had dug in the sandy soil, some very close to the wheels of our car. Moments later we pulled into a large parking area, and our explorations, which lasted for more than an hour, were on foot.

There were penguins everywhere, some standing erect in their inimitable way, others lying in their shallow burrows. The excavations were just large enough to accommodate two parent birds and, later, their single chick, or sometimes two. There were single eggs visible in several of the excavations we saw. The burrows protected the birds from the fierce winds, which were strong enough to bowl us over if we weren't careful. Two burrows were in the sides of short rises in the ground, and thus their residents were protected above and on all sides except one.

In general, a single bird was in each burrow, presumably incubating or, in a few cases, resting alongside a large snow white egg. The other parent stood upright nearby. When we looked around there were penguins in every direction, 50 to 100 of them in our field of view, and, with our binoculars, we could see them in the far distance. Many of them had a very long walk to and from the ocean. They didn't stand in seried ranks like the penguins of the Antarctic ice sheets do. Those we were visiting took advantage of the sandy substrate, and kept their eggs in the burrows. No need to put them on their feet as their more southern relatives do.

Some of the penguins' pathways were clearly defined, and an overpass for human traffic had been constructed above and around them so as not to disturb the birds unduly. Some were going toward the sea and some away, most often singly but sometimes in twos or threes. A small shallow inlet was available to them, on which some were bobbing up and down and preening. When the young hatched, the adults would go fishing not only for themselves, but also to fill their crops with food that could be regurgitated into the mouths of their young.

Perhaps the most amazing thing about the penguins was their tameness. We were within inches of some of them. If any of the ambulatory ones felt we were approaching too closely, they simply walked away, slowly but with dignity.

I was anxious to have photographs of us with the penguins to show to friends and especially my bird-watcher son. Ana manned my camera. Once I was very close to a bird, but it started to turn away from me. I put down the tip of my cane in the sand close to it, hoping the impediment would encourage it to remain in place. The penguin promptly bit it!

Accompanying signs indicated that part of the colony was under intense study through the cooperation of the New York Zoological Society (now the Wildlife Conservation Society). Colored ribbons were attached to the low bushes near or above the sets of burrows that were being monitored. Although travel agencies have long advertised that there are a million or more penguins in the colony, censuses conducted over a period of years indicate that, whereas there once may have been a half million birds, the present number is less than 400,000 and, unfortunately, is steadily declining.

What a thrill for us, however, to see, enter, and enjoy such a tremendous congregation of unusual birds. The Magellanic penguin is noted for the handsome black-and-white pattern on its head and body. Our experience there was the highlight of my bird-watching career, although I make no claim to be an expert.

We would have lingered longer, but it was very cold and windy, and the shelter of the car was welcome. Ana admired our interest and enthusiasm. She said that the average tourist spent 10 minutes looking at the penguins and then was quite ready for the long drive back to Trelew.

Our own return was punctuated by two events. Carlos spotted a small armadillo at the side of the road. He stopped the car, dashed out, hurried into the low brush, seized the animal by the tail, and then brought it to us. I had to reload the camera to photograph it, because I had used up all the exposures on the previous roll on the penguins. The other event was a flat tire, which Carlos changed in record time.

Our return trip was pleasant, but when we neared

Three residents of the enormous colony of Magellanic penguins at Punta Tombo, Argentina. Photo by RC.

Trelew we skirted around it and headed west to Gaimán, another town settled by the Welsh. We had one more function to perform. We were to have tea together as a pleasant farewell with our gracious hosts. First, we drove around the town a bit and looked at the well-preserved stone buildings that the settlers from Wales had erected a century or so ago. Then we crossed the Río Chubut. Along a nearby canal, through which water was racing, we entered an impeccable teahouse where we all stuffed ourselves with scones, cakes, and cookies. The place would have done justice to any of its counterparts in Britain. Soon we were back at our hotel, too full even to think about supper. We retired early and slept the clock around. At least I did.

The next morning we repacked and readied ourselves for the long trip home. Mindful of the fact that the restaurant in our hotel in Buenos Aires did not serve an evening meal, I marched, cane in hand, against the stiff wind, to the supermarket three blocks away. There I bought fruit and cookies on which to snack in lieu of an evening meal when we were back in the capital city. I wrote notes to Ana and Carlos, his in Spanish, and we enclosed some money as tangible evidence of our appreciation for all they had done for us. I had already paid the travel agency for our wildlife excursion, but they had performed well and far beyond the call of duty.

Juan Carlos Soffio had long since given me his business card for his "Taxi 13," but we still didn't know Ana's last name, even though I had asked her twice. They came for us in early afternoon to take us to the airport. While we were waiting, Ana bought a thin leather bookmark for each of us, and on each she wrote her name and address. She was Ana Jones. What a clever way to reveal her Welsh ancestry!

We rested for two days in Buenos Aires, and then flew business class on American Airlines to Miami. After a sumptuous dinner on the plane, we slept for several hours. There was more resting in Florida, and then we traveled home to Albuquerque. We had spent a full five weeks traveling almost half a world away.

In planning the trip I had built in a number of rest days, so we could recuperate after strenuous excursions and the many days when there was no time for the luxury of my customary afternoon nap. In a few places it was hard going for us, but we made it. No accidents and no health problems. We had seen a profusion of wildlife, and the trip, to my way of thinking, was second only to the glorious seven weeks Isabelle and I spent in Africa photographing animals way back in 1968. Kathryn and I needed help everywhere with our luggage, and we used wheelchairs for the long treks through large airports. But we were home safely with our heads full of wonderful memories that will linger as long as we live.

It is easy for me to imagine a cynic saying, "What's the matter with that old Conant idiot? Taking his wife so far away on a rugged trip. And with both of them on canes!"

My reply would be that I wasn't ready to give up yet. After all, I was only 86.

Chapter 62

Memories of Faraway Places

Because we enjoyed traveling, Kathryn and I managed to visit several out-of-the-way or distant places, including: on the spur of the moment, New Zealand and Australia; Iceland en route to Europe; and Trinidad and the Dominican Republic, in conjunction with our birthdays. All offered memorable experiences.

William M. Clay was a graduate student contemporaneously with Howard K. Gloyd at the University of Michigan. Although Bill switched to ichthyology after he became professionally employed at the University of Louisville, Kentucky, he wrote his doctoral dissertation on water snakes (*Natrix =Nerodia*). Thus, his herpetological interests coincided with mine and we had much in common. We eventually drifted apart, but, after Bill retired, he planned a visit to Tucson so we could get reacquainted. Before doing that he telephoned, one day in 1980, and said he and his wife had signed up for a tour to the Antipodes, and he urged us to go with them. We finally agreed, even though I was not long out of the hospital after another bout with my blasted prostate problem—the old man's disease! Because it was an alumni tour, Kay and I had to pretend we were graduates of the University of Louisville.

We met in Los Angeles and boarded a Pan American clipper for the long trip across the Pacific. We made a scheduled refueling stop in Honolulu, the first time either Kay or I had been in Hawaii, and from there flew across the International Date Line and landed in Auckland shortly after dawn.

We toured on sightseeing buses and, at two of our stops, I had a chance to see examples of the bizarre avian fauna of New Zealand. At the Auckland Zoo I beheld my first live kiwi, and then, in the natural history museum, a mighty moa, one of the largest and heaviest birds that ever existed. It survived into historic times, but is now extinct, although its remains are fairly well represented in several collections. I distinctly recall that we were in Auckland on Good Friday through Easter and Easter Monday, four days in a row when all the stores were closed, much to the consternation of the ladies of our party of about 30, who could do no shopping. What a

splendid long holiday for the husbands, who otherwise would have had to provide the funding!

We moved on to the South Island for a few days' stay in Christchurch. The field guide to the birds of New Zealand that I purchased confirmed my understanding that the land bird fauna was greatly impoverished. A number of Australian birds had been introduced accidentally, or even intentionally, in earlier years. When we flew from Christchurch to Sydney, Australia, we passed over the snow-capped New Zealand Alps, our only glimpse of them during our visit, which was continually marred by cloudy weather.

On the island continent of Australia, we stopped in Melbourne and Sydney. I had tired so badly that I spent the first day in Melbourne in bed, but I recovered enough by nightfall to indulge my amateur interest in astronomy. With the aid of a chart of the stars of the Southern Hemisphere that I carried with me, I quickly found Hadar and Rigil Kent, the first-magnitude pair that point to the Southern Cross. The latter was disappointingly unimpressive—three fairly bright stars, but the fourth one quite inconspicuous. How proud I was a few days later, however, during an afternoon and evening cruise around the large and beautiful Sydney Harbor, one of the great bays of the world with its opera house topped with sculptured sails. I was able to point out the Southern Cross to the other members of the party well before the captain of our yacht got around to doing it.

Descriptions of the loss of a northerner's sense of direction south of the Equator and our picnic with the greedy kookaburras are recounted under "Our Topsy-Turvy World."

Our trip to the Antipodes taught us a lesson. Never travel with group tours—most of them are organized for younger people. "Have your luggage out in the hall to be picked up at 5:00 A.M." "Have your breakfast early and be ready to board the bus at 6:00 A.M." Ever afterward we traveled by ourselves and set our own pace.

Being with Bill Clay and recapturing some of the happy days we spent together in Ann Arbor at the University of Michigan, and on the Lake Erie islands when he was a graduate student, was quite enjoyable. Alas, it was also a farewell. Bill collapsed outside our hotel in Sydney. He recovered, at least in part, but died from a heart attack in Louisville before we had an opportunity to get together again.

My deep interest in geology had much to do with our visit to Iceland. The Mid-Atlantic Ridge, where magma from the Earth's interior rises and continues to force the tectonic plates apart, emerges on the surface in Iceland. What an extraordinary opportunity to see geology in action, so to speak. So, when we flew to England to attend the First International Congress of Herpetology in 1989, we elected to cross the Atlantic by Icelandair, with a stop in Reykjavik en route eastward, and a day in Keflavik while homeward bound.

What a strange and fascinating island! Volcanism is everywhere in evidence: old lava flows, steam jets spouting from hillsides and from the ground, and the small satellite island called Surtsey that popped up in the ocean during a fiery eruption in 1963. The steam jets are a blessing of which the Icelanders have made excellent use. Homes, offices, and other structures are heated by steam piped into Reykjavik, the capital, and presumably other towns as well. The steam also supports very large greenhouses where vegetables of many kinds are grown, thus helping to reduce the vast amount of importation necessary to sustain the human population. Costs are high in Iceland and it is a cold country. Its northern shoreline almost touches the Arctic Circle, but the climate is moderated by an arm of the Gulf Stream. Yet there are two huge glaciers in the interior of the island.

When we stopped at Keflavik on our way home we saw awe-inspiring motion pictures of several recent eruptions. It gave us the impression that trying to reside anywhere in Iceland might be a gamble, but the fissures from which most of the lava pours forth, thus relieving the pressure underground, are well known.

Our tour of one of the most interesting parts of Iceland was a never-to-be-forgotten experience. We took a sightseeing bus and were extremely fortunate in having a very well informed lady of about 60, who spoke flawless American English, and explained everything in detail as we rode along and made numerous stops.

Once our vehicle was in the countryside we were impressed by how green the landscape was. The hillsides, as well as the more level places, were bright green. At various stops we confirmed that mosses were responsible for the color, although short grass grew in some places. Trees and shrubs were completely absent—well, almost. Twice, in small sheltered ravines,

I found a few stunted trees whose crowns reached my knees. All were representative of Nearctic genera. In Reykjavik there were occasional trees perhaps 15 feet or so tall growing in sheltered places.

We stopped at one of the vast steam-heated greenhouses, and then moved on to a gorge and falls through which a torrent of water from a distant glacier was racing. Next there was an active geyser; that name has its origin in Iceland, even though in the United States it is applied to Old Faithful and others in Yellowstone National Park. After lunch in a private home, we cut across country to Thingvalleer, the site of early Icelandic parliamentary meetings. The level of the land once dropped something like six feet while the delegates were in session. There we found a classic graben, a geological term that means "ditch" in German, and one that is featured in such books on geology as Steven M. Stanley's "Earth and Life through Time." In fact, we walked through the very place Stanley illustrated, a fairly broad graben wide enough to permit a truck to pass, and with high walls of lava on either side. Iceland is growing, in an east-west direction, at an average rate of about three-fourths of an inch a year. As the graben drops, the lava rises beside it, but seldom concurrently, thus pushing the tectonic plates apart. We had the unique experience of having one foot on the Eurasian Plate and the other on the North American Plate.

Alfred Wegener, who developed the theory of continental drift, did much of his early fieldwork in Iceland, and he died while working in Greenland. Which brings up the point that the two islands are grossly misnamed. That was done on purpose, we were told, so as to encourage early settlers to go to the larger of the two then Danish islands. Iceland is green, whereas Greenland is largely covered by enormous glaciers. Incidentally, Iceland gained its full independence in 1944.

Early in 1993, armed with American Airlines senior citizen coupons, I gave Kathryn a choice. With the coupons we could fly to any part of the conterminous 48 states, or to San Juan, Puerto Rico. The latter is a good jumping off place, and I suggested, to celebrate her seventy-fifth birthday, that we go on to Jamaica, the Dominican Republic, or Trinidad. She picked Trinidad without hesitation.

That fairly large island was long a colony of Great Britain, but is now, with Tobago, an independent nation. Both islands are on the South American continental shelf and thus, technically, are not part of the West Indies, with which they frequently are linked.

Hans Boos, a native Trinidadian, was a great help to us. Our plane from San Juan to Port-of-Spain was late and did not arrive until midnight. Nonetheless, he was there to meet us and to drive us to our hotel. We inspected the splendid small zoo of which he was Curator, and took him to dinner to help celebrate Kay's birthday, and he drove us to the Asa Wright Nature Centre, of which he was vice president.

We spent most of our time at the Asa Wright sanctuary, in the mountains of northern Trinidad. It is a very active ecotourism establishment visited by birders and naturalists from all over the world. Except for the headquarters complex, foot trails, and rocky road leading into the place, everything there has been left untouched, and the tropical vegetation was lush and quite strange to us. We were billeted in an old mansion that had a veranda overlooking a broad, unspoiled valley. Feeding trays and sugar water were lavishly provided, and it was quite possible, as advertised in the promotional literature, to add 20 or more species of birds to one's life list before breakfast. Many kinds of hummingbirds and tanagers were abundant, and so were bananaquits. Toucans, tropical woodpeckers, motmots, and many other species frequently appeared. It was truly a birdwatcher's paradise. Of herpetological interest were a very large *Iguana iguana*, a sizable tegu, *Tupinambis teguixin*, and several lizards of the genus *Ameiva*.

The Nature Centre was recently expanded. When we left Trinidad, we hired a taxi to take us to a hotel close to the airport for a very early morning departure. En route the driver stopped at Simla, the tropical retreat and research station of the late William Beebe, of the New York Zoological Society. It had long been unoccupied, but the buildings were still in fairly good condition. The walls bore printed copies of quotations from Beebe's writings, including the famous one about how another heaven and earth must pass before an extinct species might ever appear again. Under the leadership of Zoo Director/President William G. Conway, the property and the surrounding extensive jungle-clad hectares were deeded over to the Asa Wright Nature Centre.

From the Centre we left after lunch one day with a party of 30 or so to visit the Caroni Swamp, in the lowlands on the west side of the island fairly close to the small capital city of Port-of-Spain. Near the swamp we stopped to see jacanas, yellow-hooded blackbirds, many shorebirds, and the ubiquitous cattle egrets.

We climbed into a large flat-bottomed boat with a strong outboard motor to push us along a canal leading into the swamp. En route, the boatman pointed out a potoo, a weird bird that clung to the stump of a tree and looked exactly like a dead branch. Farther along, a tree boa, *Corallus enydris cooki*, bright yellowish tan and about four feet long, was coiled on a horizontal branch in a mangrove jungle. What a thrill for a herpetologist!

By late afternoon we were deep in the swamp. About sundown we tied up to a long stake driven into the mud and waited for the scarlet ibises to come in to roost for the night. For anyone not familiar with that species, it has a long, down-curved bill and is clothed in bright red feathers. It is the size of a small chicken, and its long legs are well adapted for wading in shallow water as it searches for food. By day the flocks stayed along the western coast of Trinidad, but before dark they arrived to spend the night on one small mangrove-covered island more than 100 yards from our boat. They came in groups of a dozen or so, or sometimes in long skeins of 30 to 50, a gorgeous sight as they were illuminated by the setting sun. Kathryn counted up to 1,000 of them and then stopped. We estimated that there were 1,200, more or less, and they all went to one small island and none to similar nearby islands. As Kathryn described the scene, it resembled a squat Christmas tree decorated with poinsettias.

What a sight! I am no stranger to gregarious waterbird rookeries. I have seen them in many places in the United States, along the coast of Nayarit in Mexico, and especially in Africa, but the scarlet ibis display topped them all.

In the spring of 1995 Kathryn reciprocated, much to my delight, by offering to take me somewhere for my eighty-fifth birthday, just as I had taken her to Trinidad the previous year. Where would I like to go? I quickly chose the island of Hispaniola. Second only to Cuba in area in the West Indies, it has a fascinating herpetological fauna. Fieldwork was out of the question for me with my balance problem, but I could use my binoculars and see at least some of the island's galaxy of lizards.

We flew again to Puerto Rico, tarried there for two days, and then made the short air hop to Santo Domingo, the capital of the Dominican Republic. Two things struck me sharply as we taxied to our hotel from the airport. Litter was everywhere and in quantity, and we saw not a single land bird. Later, by making inquiries in Spanish, I learned that small birds are targets for slingshots and other missiles, and that they are often eaten in the more poverty-stricken parts of the nation.

Our hotel overlooked the Caribbean, and ships at anchor waited in a nearby roadstead for docking and offloading facilities. Man-o'-war birds seemed always to be soaring overhead. That scene, at least, was splendid. The small waves coming ashore were badly polluted, however, with offal carried seaward by a nearby stream that passed through small villages. Memories quickly came to mind of Caracas, Venezuela, where we had seen raw sewage being sluiced into the southern side of the same sea.

There wasn't time to explore the island as a whole, even superficially, so on the advice of friends I arranged for us to be driven westward to Barahona, where we stayed for a few days. Most interesting of our experiences in that area was our drive all the way around the long, narrow Lago Enriquillo, the largest lake in the West Indian archipelago. Geologically, the lake was created when two land masses conjoined as the result of tectonic action in the distant past. We were informed that it lies somewhere between 100 and 130 feet below sea level, and, since it is in a closed valley and receives the runoff from the surrounding hills, it has thrice the concentration of salts common to the oceans. The lake's surroundings are rather arid, and large tree cacti and other xerophytic vegetation were much in evidence. The region has national park status, and it looked little disturbed except where a few small villages approached or reached the shore. The American crocodile, *Crocodylus acutus,* breeds on Isla Cabrito, a large island in the lake, and flamingos overwinter there in numbers. We saw none of those birds in May, but, as I stood on the beach near a small cantina, a warden came ashore with two recently hatched crocs in a bucket. Inspecting the area was an outstanding experience for me, even though I had to tote a cane to avoid tripping and to counter sudden onsets of balance loss. It was a bright sunny day, and we could see mountains in the distance.

We were close to the Haitian frontier, which country was then in turmoil some months prior to the landing of the U.S. Marines. Our driver took us to the border, where security was tight, and we saw a long string of heavily laden trucks waiting their turn to carry foodstuffs from the Dominican Republic into the neighboring, French-speaking country. Contraband? We saw none, but it could have been hidden beneath the huge bales and crates of comestibles.

On our return, and before we began the long drive along the north side of the lake, we passed through the rural village of Jimaní where poverty was rampant. The homes in the outskirts of the tiny town were thatch-roofed huts with openings for entrance and apertures built for looking out. There were neither doors nor windows. Goats and chickens wandered in and out of the dwellings at will. I asked the driver to stop so I could photograph one of them. When I turned around, I saw a more photogenic hut on the opposite side of the road. So I stepped across the paving, raised my camera, and saw children running as I peered into the viewfinder.

After I had snapped a picture and reboarded the car, Kathryn asked me if I had seen what had happened. The moment I crossed the road, a mother came rushing out of the house, and she beckoned and called the

The native hut, in the western part of the Dominican Republic, where a mother frantically called her children inside when RC appeared with his camera. May 11, 1994.

children to dash home. We thought little of it, and didn't mention it again until we were having dinner, back in Puerto Rico, with Richard Thomas. He is an authority on the herpetology of the West Indies, and he has been on the faculty of the University of Puerto Rico for many years. He explained that it was a common belief in the region that strangers kidnapped children in order to eat them! He told us that he once had a narrow escape while doing fieldwork alone in Haiti. He was suddenly surrounded by men with sharp rocks in their hands, demanding the return of the child he had stolen. After opening the doors and trunk of his car and the lid of his large icebox, and allowing the men to make a thorough inspection, he convinced them he wasn't guilty. He had been in a tight spot, and he was shaken by the episode.

It seems incredible to blasé Americans that such a superstition can be prevalent in this day and age. In the midst of our plenty, we tend to forget that ignorance and voodooism are still with us.

The people we saw near Jimaní exist under meager, primitive conditions. There is no poverty level for them and, if they ever achieved the one currently prevalent in the United States, they would think they were filthy rich. They have truck gardens, and the men find seasonal work cutting sugarcane and harvesting bananas and other tropical fruits. Their only assets (?) are an abundance of offspring. In neighboring Haiti, the average woman gives birth to 6.4 children during her reproductive years. How similar to the poverty and primitive conditions Isabelle and I saw in rural Mexico while we were doing fieldwork there 30 years earlier. More mouths to feed and a concurrent constant and alarming shrinkage of resources as the human population continues to explode.

We saw relatively few herps or other diurnal vertebrates, except in the national park and the spacious botanical garden in Santo Domingo. In both those havens birds of several species were relatively abundant. There they were protected from slaughter for the sparse amount of protein their little bodies could provide for human diets. A variety of anoles (*Anolis*) and whiptail lizards of the genus *Ameiva* were much in evidence in the same sanctuaries. While I watched through binoculars, I saw an *Ameiva* make a quick and successful grab for a butterfly that alit on the ground about six inches from it.

During our trip, we especially enjoyed listening to the vociferous calls of the coqui, a tiny frog, considered as the natural history symbol of Puerto Rico, where we stayed for several days. In the outdoor garden of our motel in San Juan, where the humidity was augmented by a fountain, several males serenaded us with their loud calls. Richard Thomas supplied the scientific name, *Eleutherodactylus coqui,* for them in 1966, when he discovered that there were two sibling species on Puerto Rico. There was a name for an upland population, but a formal designation for the much more widespread little frog was lacking, so he described it as a new species. It was a unique opportunity for us, as casual visitors, to hear the loud calls of an anuran that had been named by our dinner guest.

Ancillary Essays

The story of my adventures, travels, troubles, and accomplishments is now complete, or almost so. I think I have hit all the high spots and a few of the lows. Yet, as I assist the manuscript on its journey through the press, I keep thinking about additional experiences or fun things that might be added. But I have written enough. Too much, really. What I had originally contemplated as a collection of chapters to be read one or two at bedtime and then set aside is now a heavy book.

I've enjoyed assembling my recollections, and I hope you found them of interest and worth a chuckle here and there.

The many friends and colleagues who urged me to record my peregrinations through a long and busy life stressed my obligation to review the many changes I've witnessed as the years and decades passed. Many are mentioned in what you have already read. I should in all fairness, however, chronicle in some detail the extraordinary evolution of my duo of special interests— zoos and herpetology. Hence, the first two of the four following essays.

In the third essay I look a bit into the future. Social change is inevitable; humankind has become the dominant species of earth because of it. But the proliferation of crime in recent years, much of it senseless and bizarre, and the rate at which we are using up our natural resources frightens me. Perhaps my being a great-grandfather, and maybe soon a "great-great" one, has had something to do with it. How will those young people fare in the years to come? The number of human beings has increased so enormously that I fear the worst. Few people are aware of the catastrophic problems that are looming on the horizon. One of the several reviewers who was kind enough to send me critical comments on "Breed and Greed" thought that every intelligent person should be made to read it. I am sure you will.

The final essay consists of the musings of an old man thinking about the very many changes that have occurred since he was a boy. There are also a few more comments about the future of the many wild animals that are diminishing in numbers almost everywhere at an alarming rate.

Zoos Then and Now

Present-day animal activists would be justifiably incensed, even infuriated, if they could see some of the zoos I visited when I was a young man. Far too many of them were haphazard assemblages of animals, inadequately housed, improperly fed, and often under the supervision of a political hack who obtained his position as a reward for being a good vote getter. The keepers were laboring men, adept with broom and shovel, but many of them couldn't answer more than the simplest questions about their charges.

A majority of the zoos—menageries would be a better name for them—were orphan adjuncts of city park departments. They provided "recreation" for the visiting public, who, far too often, bombarded the animals with garbage left after lunch baskets were emptied, with sticks and stones, and anything else throwable.

Some of the zoos, chiefly those in larger cities and so few that they could be counted on the fingers of two hands, had graduated into what I call Phase I of the three phases of zoo progress that I witnessed during my professional career.

In the few better zoos, the outer perimeters were fenced or guards were employed to curtail vandalism, especially at night. Cages, pens, and paddocks were built to house the animals but, in comparison with the beautiful modern zoos of today, they were quite primitive. So also were such important procedures as the care of the animals and attention to their diets. Professional veterinary practice of the day was confined to domestic stock. When called upon to treat a wild beast or bird, the visiting vet had to extrapolate from what he had learned during his training. There also were problems with food. Animal dealers, for example, had two kinds of diets for their winged merchandise: concoctions for "soft-billed" birds and others for "hard-billed" birds. Those served well enough to get the stock to the customer alive, but they were far from adequate for an extended period in captivity. The meat and fish fed to the animals were often of poor quality, selected for their cheapness. It was common practice for zoos to send a truck to the local produce market to gather up fruits and vegetables that had been discarded as unsalable for human consumption. I was destined to be a close witness of the revolution in zoo diets, but more of that later.

Even some of the better zoos were still in the process of emerging from the inadequacies of the past. It was my privilege to work in two of them, first at the Toledo Zoological Gardens for 6 years, and then for 38 years at the Philadelphia Zoological Garden. Many of the chapters in the main text of these recollections are concerned with those two splendid institutions, and I shall refer to them from time to time.

One of the first requisites of a good zoo was to rid itself of political control as far as possible. At Toledo, a few years before I arrived, early in 1929, the Toledo Zoological Society was founded, and through its officers, a Zoological Board of Management with nine members became responsible for the operation of the zoo. Four persons were chosen by the mayor, and four by the Society. The mayor himself was the ninth. In practice, only two or three of the city people ever attended board meetings, whereas all Society members made it a point to be present. Thus, the city had little to do with the zoo's day-to-day procedures, even though it owned the zoo, and paid me and the other employees from public funds. Similar agreements with municipalities helped other zoos to move on to better things.

America's First Zoo, the Philadelphia Zoological Garden, had a unique history in many ways. The Zoological Society received its charter from the Commonwealth of Pennsylvania on March 21, 1859. Its objectives included "the purchase and collection of living wild and other animals, for . . . public exhibition at some suitable place in the City of Philadelphia, for the instruction and recreation of the people."

Plans were made to open within a few years as a full-fledged zoo, and an architect was sent to the London Zoo to study its animal buildings. The Civil War greatly delayed progress, but the Philadelphia Zoo finally opened on July 1, 1874, with several state-of-the-art buildings and a large and varied collection of animals. It was owned and operated by the Society under a perpetual lease of ground from Fairmount Park. The Society passed through good times and bad, but it still operates the zoo today. The city, for many years, absorbed the annual deficit, and it contributed substantially to the extensive rebuilding program during my tenure at Philadelphia.

At Toledo, massive help came through the WPA and other works projects during the Depression years. (See "The Miracle at the Toledo Zoo.")

I have mentioned the widely different histories of the Toledo and Philadelphia zoos in some detail, because I know them best. There were many other scenarios. Rich men contributed some of their resources to start a zoo. Politicians, particularly those who had young children, realized the potential value of a zoo, and they introduced legislation that resulted in the creation of such institutions. In other cities, proposals on public ballots were approved. Even to this day, many zoos are financed, at least in part, by public vote. The National Zoo in Washington, D.C., originated under the auspices of the Smithsonian Institution, partly as a depository for rare or unusual animals brought by visiting foreign potentates as special gifts to American presidents. Some zoos today are supported by states, counties, cities, or public trusts. Others are entirely independent.

Every zoo has had a different history, of course, but groups of public citizens calling themselves zoological societies, friends of the zoo, or other suitable designations are auxiliary mainstays. They raise money for the purchase of animals and new exhibits, and serve as buffers against the spoils system (i.e., reward your political allies with municipal jobs).

The emphasis during Phase I was on exhibiting as many different kinds of animals as possible. Sometimes there were pairs or even groups of the same species, and occasional births of young. There was rivalry among the various zoos to acquire rarities, and to build up lengthy lists of mammals, birds, and reptiles.

In 1937, I discovered that the same was also true of European zoos when, much to my utter astonishment, I was sent abroad by ocean liner on a fact-finding mission, less than two years after I transferred to Philadelphia from Toledo. During a month of intensive study and travel by train, I visited 14 zoos in six countries. The European zoos were mostly much older than ours and more interesting. I must admit, however, that my itinerary did not include smaller cities, whose facilities may not have been on a par with those in the larger population centers. I did, however, visit two small but excellent private animal parks. (See the three chapters beginning with "Hitler's Germany.")

Just as was the case at home in America, European zoos often had long rows of cages and paddocks serving as quarters for individual birds or mammals. There were also innovations, however. Munich had an ape house where young chimpanzees and orangutans went through their daily routines under the care of young ladies who dressed them, ate at table with them, brushed their teeth, and treated them almost as if they were human children. Anthropomorphism to be sure, but the public loved it. Berlin combined its aquarium, on the ground floor, with fine displays for reptiles and insects on upper floors. Amsterdam had university facilities for the study of zoology right on the zoo grounds. London's Regent Park Zoo featured the Mappin Terraces, with a number of animals on exhibition at fairly high levels, their quarters built above an aquarium. They were so arranged that visitors had an overview of almost the entire zoo. Whipsnade, in the country and well outside London, was the first of the large captive wild animal parks. It included a paddock larger than the entire London Zoo.

Of all the European zoos I visited, one was an outstanding exception, and more or less the birthplace of my Phase II. Carl Hagenbeck, an able and internationally recognized animal dealer, created a zoo at Stellingen, a suburb of Hamburg. Originally, it was built to accommodate animals from all over the world until they could be sold. The display was so popular with the local public, however, that Hagenbeck became an entrepreneur.

After determining the maximum distance a lion or tiger could jump, he built outdoor exhibits surrounded, at least in part, by dry moats across which the great cats could not leap. The Germans called the results freesight displays. There were no bars or heavy wires through which to peer. Hagenbeck's next step was to exhibit zebras and antelopes, the natural prey of carnivores, directly behind the lions, but separated from them by a hidden moat. Spectators had the illusion of seeing the various mammals much as they might appear in Africa.

Moats had previously been used for small animals, but Hagenbeck elevated the technique to a spectacular scale. Even well before I visited Europe, moats had arrived in American zoos, notably in St. Louis and Detroit. I was delighted to have seen the very place, however, where Phase II, moated exhibits, received their greatest impetus. Nowadays, moated enclosures are featured in one way or another in virtually every zoo worldwide.

Phase III deemphasized the practice of exhibiting large numbers of species. Instead, zoos began showing family groups and encouraging captive breeding. More or less coincidental with the proliferation of Phase III, the use of fiberglass in a wide spectrum of colors came

Dr. Herbert L. Ratcliffe, Director of the Penrose Research Laboratory from 1942 to 1969. His painstaking studies on nutrition revolutionized zoo diets. Philadelphia Zoo archives.

into general use. We began placing animal pairs or families in indestructible replicas of their natural habitats. What a difference that made! Individual exhibits came alive. By that time I was Director of the Philadelphia Zoo, and I was able to hire Kenneth G. Dills, one of the best of the fiberglass experts, to head our Exhibits Department. Our zoo soon became a showplace. Such diverse species as hummingbirds, vampire bats, rattlesnakes, and gorillas all lived in simulations of their places of origin. Phase III exhibits continue to be very popular.

I promised to discuss the revolution in zoo diets, and, to do that, I must return to the early days of the Philadelphia Zoo. As recorded in the chapter entitled "Research, Publications, and Other Zoo Activities," the Penrose Research Laboratory was established right on the zoo grounds in 1901. Its first triumph was the elimination of tuberculosis from the primate collection. Later, because the necropsies revealed that large numbers of animals were dying each year from malnutrition, studies on diets rose to the fore. Much careful research and planning established the correct proportions of proteins, carbohydrates, fats, vitamins, minerals, and so on, necessary for animal health.

Dr. Herbert L. Ratcliffe, who later became director of

the Laboratory, implemented a new feeding program based on three preparations compounded daily, known, respectively, as monkey cake, buffalo ration, and meat mixture. At first, virtually all the mammals and birds shared one or more of the several combinations, although their needs were supplemented with hay for the hoofed animals, fresh fruits and vegetables for monkeys, apes, and birds, and meat or fish for the large carnivores and sea lions. The results were watched with great care, and the daily rations were altered when required. Most of the new diets worked well, although many of the animals were slow to accept them at first, and they were met with outright scorn by most of the keepers. The new regimen went into effect in 1934, the year before I arrived back in Philadelphia from Toledo. There was much public opposition to the new foods. Dr. Ratcliffe soon had to face the wrath of the traditionalists and pragmatists who stoutly maintained that his "experiments" would kill more animals than they would save. For a description of some of the problems that developed, see the chapter mentioned above.

Considerable experimenting was required to get everything right, but after the new foods were adjusted and accepted by the birds and mammals, good things began to happen. The death rate from malnutrition dropped dramatically and the birthrate increased substantially. Many of the zoo's residents, the monkeys especially, became lively instead of moping around, and they began to display behaviors similar to those of their wild relatives. Dominance developed, and males had to be separated to prevent fighting and peck-order injuries. An unexpected salutary development was the cutting of food bills almost in half. There were no more expensive, fancy foods. Funds thus became available to purchase the most nourishing fish for the sea lions, and also to improve the reptile collection. We began buying food animals, such as mice, rats, and guinea pigs from closed colonies that were guaranteed to be free from infections. No more using cast-off mice from hospitals or research institutions. The condition of the snakes and other inhabitants of the reptile house improved immensely.

Incidentally, we used strictly fresh horse meat in those days. Live horses, elderly but still in good health, were purchased or donated, and they were slaughtered right in the zoo's own Commissary Department. Their meat was quickly refrigerated and normally used within the next day or two. If the horses belonged to the military, regulations required that an officer witness the execution, and then report, in writing, that government property had been disposed of properly.

After the success of our diets became common knowledge, they were copied by those other American

RC in distinguished company. Delegates to the meeting of the American Association of Zoological Parks and Aquariums in St. Louis during the autumn of 1930 included, from left: William M. Mann, Washington, D.C.; W. Reid Blair, New York; George P. Vierheller, St. Louis; RC, Toledo; Edward H. Bean, Chicago; and Heinz Ruhe, animal dealer from Hannover, Germany. Photo by Hugh S. Davis.

zoos that were not too proud to follow our lead. Nonetheless, most of the others began making changes devised by their own staff members. Three young men from Swiss zoos came to Philadelphia, for periods of a year or more, to study and practice the new procedures. Since those early days, diets have been improved in a great many different ways, but the corner had been turned, and Dr. Ratcliffe received a gold medal from the Antwerp Zoo, in Belgium, for his pioneering work.

Since my retirement in 1973, many new zoos have become established, older ones have been modernized, and all are now dedicated to the conservation of wildlife. For example, New York's famous Bronx Zoo changed its official designation to the International Wildlife Conservation Park. Also, although it was founded a century ago as the New York Zoological Society, the governing body is now the Wildlife Conservation Society. It surely has the largest and most far-flung commitment of any zoo organization. It manages not only the great zoo in the Bronx, but also what was formerly the Coney Island Aquarium and New York City's several lesser zoos, except the one on Staten Island. Further, it has Wildlife Conservation Programs in 45 nations. Quite a conservation empire.

Virtually every zoo and aquarium has "adopted" one or more endangered or threatened species to maintain and breed in its collection. Zoos exchange animals or borrow them from one another for breeding purposes, and many births have resulted. In a few cases—the

Siberian tiger, for one—there are now more individuals living in captivity than survive in the wild.

Many highly successful improvements in zoological gardens and aquariums occurred under the aegis of the American Association of Zoological Parks and Aquariums (AAZPA). That organization, founded in 1924, was originally affiliated with the American Institute of Park Executives, largely because so many animal collections at the time were under the umbrella of city park departments. The AAZPA eventually became independent, and, today, almost every respectable zoo and aquarium in the United States and Canada is on its roster of members. Quite recently, its name was changed to the American Zoo and Aquarium Association and its initials were shortened to AZA.

The AAZPA was responsible for many commendable innovations. For example, zoos began policing themselves. Each member institution had to be accredited—i.e., inspected by its peers and its inadequacies corrected before it received the stamp of approval. A code of ethics was established for professional zoo and aquarium personnel. Species Survival Plans (SSPs) were organized. By definition, an SSP "is an AZA cooperative breeding and conservation program designed to maintain a genetically viable and demographically stable population of a species in captivity and to organize zoo- and aquarium-based efforts to preserve the species in situ." Courses in zoo management procedures were and are conducted, something that was sadly lacking when I first aspired to participate in zoo activities as my life's work.

I joined the AAZPA in the autumn of 1930 during a meeting in St. Louis, and I am now the oldest living member in point of service. Only about a dozen persons attended that gathering, and half of them were park superintendents who had zoos under their wings. I was active in AAZPA affairs during my entire zoo career, and I served for two decades as editor of the Zoo Section of "Parks and Recreation" magazine, published by the Park Executives. I was also elected secretary and eventually chairman (= president) of the AAZPA, and I was proud to receive the Association's Marlin Perkins Award for outstanding service.

During the past few decades, zoos and aquariums have become wonderlands—beautiful to see, and superb educational institutions, many of them offering "hands-on" opportunities for children. Innovations are legion. Among the most popular are the large tropical rain forest exhibits with living trees and other vegetation covering large areas populated by a variety of animals, including mammals, birds, reptiles, amphibians, and even fishes and invertebrates. The longer the visitor lingers and studies each of those great habitat simulations, the more animals he or she is apt to find. Some exhibits even feature the sounds of the jungle as well as its sights. What a far cry from the miserable menageries that existed when I was young!

The veterinarian profession has made enormous strides in recent years. If I remember correctly, only the Bronx Zoo, in New York, had a full-time veterinarian when I first started. Most zoos now have one or two well-trained men or women on their permanent staffs, or a competent vet or clinic on call when needed. Several veterinarians now specialize in the treatment of reptiles and amphibians. How wonderful it would have been to be able to seek the aid of such persons those years long ago when I and other curators of reptiles were struggling just to keep our collections alive. And what a boon they are to the still burgeoning herpetoculture industry.

Antibiotics and other wonder drugs have also made a big difference in veterinary practice. So have new surgical procedures and techniques for helping animals to bear young. Artificial insemination in wild animals and the transfer of embryos from natural to foster mothers of a different species would have been categorized as science fiction not too many years ago.

The caliber of zoo and aquarium employees, at least among those responsible for the care of the animals, is vastly superior in comparison with the persons who were in charge in the early part of the century. Most keepers nowadays are intelligent, well versed in their responsibilities, and able to respond to almost any question a visitor may ask. They are often college graduates, and many of those in curatorial positions have advanced degrees. Both at Toledo and in my earlier days at Philadelphia, virtually all zoo employees were men. Now women play a large part, and some of the female zoo keepers are able to supply the extra tender, loving care that can be so important to baby animals or even older ones that may be temporarily ill.

Another great change has occurred as well. When I first entered the zoo profession, many zoos were free, including the one at Toledo. Municipalities or other governing bodies picked up the tab. Admission, if one was charged, was low. When I returned to Philadelphia in 1935, the rates were a quarter for adults and a dime for children. Foodstuffs, gasoline, and most other commodities were also quite cheap in those days, and the wages seem miniscule in retrospect. Now, after decades of inflation and rising prices, the cost of admission to zoos and aquariums has skyrocketed. According to the AZA directory for 1994-95, the fee for adults averages from $5 to $8; it is less for senior citizens and small children. Some institutions are much more expensive to enter. For example, and again using the directory, the figures for adults are $11.50 at the National Aquarium in Baltimore, $13 at the San Diego Zoo, and $17.45 for the San Diego Wild Animal Park. The cost is even higher in privately owned parks, such as Busch Gardens in Florida, and the Sea and Marine Worlds. Among the large, important zoos, only those in St. Louis and Washington, D.C., and the Lincoln Park Zoo in Chicago are still free.

Most zoos now, either directly or through their supporting organizations, operate their own sales of food and souvenirs, and thus garner much-needed revenue to help defray expenses. Let us consider what a family of five—a father, mother, and three children—may have spent for a zoo visit then and now. After we took over the management of our own concessions in the late 1930s, the hypothetical family could comfortably enjoy a day's outing at the Philadelphia Zoological Garden for $5 or less. Nowadays, $50 might not be enough, especially if they buy food and souvenirs, or enter the Treehouse, or ride the Monorail. With inflation omnipresent, prices inevitably will creep ever higher.

Rising costs and the loss of income from public funds have forced virtually all zoos and aquariums to seek financial help from other sources. Referring again to my two "alma maters," the Zoological Society of Philadelphia is now on its own with only reduced help from the city and other public sources. In Toledo, (through Lucas County, Ohio), the electorate has repeatedly and consistently voted for a tax levy to help support the zoo. The Oklahoma City Zoo is unique in receiving part of its income from a one-eighth of a cent sales tax charged citywide.

Aside from raising admission prices and profiting from sales on the zoo and aquarium grounds, the most viable and helpful asset is now a large membership in zoological societies, friends of the zoo, or comparable organizations. Memberships are not new. Back in the 1950s and 1960s we had a few thousand at Philadelphia, and we thought we were doing well. Each member received 20 free tickets, and we had a special Members' Day of fun, instruction, and entertainment for them once a year, usually in the spring.

The scope of present-day memberships far eclipses our experiences of yesteryear. Some zoos now have tens of thousands of members, and there are ongoing events for them year-round. To mention a few, there may be special tours of the zoo or parts thereof, lectures and behind-the-scenes excursions conducted by curators or other staff members, fun courses for children, evening parties open to members only, and gala, beautifully decorated nighttime fiestas during holiday seasons. Members feel they are important, and attendance at the various affairs is excellent and enthusiastic. Also, large cadres of dedicated members contribute their help, and often their cash, toward such goals as acquiring new animals or mates for those already at hand, or new exhibits. They can be a driving force when proposed financial help for a zoo or aquarium appears on a ballot, or when, as is the case at Toledo, the levy comes up for renewal.

Adopt-an-animal programs were just getting under way when I hung up my zoo hat and retired. Public-spirited citizens are asked to provide for the financial support of their favorite animals by giving an annual sum that can be deducted as a donation for income tax purposes. Such programs are now widespread and popular.

Some zoo societies sponsor safaris to Africa, or other parts of the world, to see wild animals in their natural habitats. A zoo staff member accompanies the party as an escort, but a travel agency handles most of the details. The zoo receives a commission for each participant.

Many other fund-raising devices are used successfully in different cities. Band or symphonic concerts, Zoo Nights or Weekends, summer activities and instruction for youngsters, and even Runs for the Zoo are included. New ideas, with fees involved, continue to be tried, and, if they are successful, they are copied by sister institutions.

A great many zoos and aquariums have docent programs, in which well-informed and well-trained, often retired, volunteers take school classes, groups of Boy and Girl Scouts, or other organizations on conducted tours, telling them about the animals. They are also prepared to answer questions. Because I had always been interested in education in zoos, I was proud, with the help of volunteer Jeanne Segal, to organize what eventually became the splendid Docent Council of the Zoological Society of Philadelphia. It has prospered and now includes hundreds of individuals. Docents today, and not only in Philadelphia, are staunch supporters who take great pride in their respective institutions.

The modern zoo or aquarium, well operated and dedicated to education and conservation, is a distinct civic asset. It is an interesting and beautiful attraction, and a wonderful destination for a pleasant family outing. Almost everyone is interested in animals. Television shows about them enjoy large audiences. But there is no substitute for seeing them in the flesh and experiencing firsthand the sights, sounds, and even smells of live mammals, birds, herps, and fishes.

Aquariums, many of which were early adjuncts of zoological parks, are now almost all exclusively independent. Like zoos, they have grown and modernized, and have become splendid showplaces. Thanks to Murray A. Newman, Director Emeritus of the outstanding Vancouver Aquarium, I learned that Chicago's John G. Shedd Aquarium was one of the first to be completely on its own. Newman's institution was the first to keep killer whales in captivity for any length of time, and the first to introduce wide use of graphics and an extensive educational program with docents and university affiliation.

Insofar as popularity is concerned, I quote the following from the AZA: "Based upon the increasing number of visitors to zoological parks and aquariums, it continues to be correct to state that more people visit North American zoological facilities annually than the combined number of persons attending professional football, baseball, basketball, and hockey games."

The conservation contribution of zoos and aquariums is extremely important. With their careful breeding programs and modern techniques, they have the potential to keep many species of animals alive indefinitely through succeeding generations. What a difference from the sad days when the passenger pigeon and the Carolina parakeet both became extinct upon the deaths of their last single survivors in the Cincinnati Zoo in the early years of this century. Two beautiful and once abundant birds that were obliterated by the persecution of mankind.

The raising of animals for eventual liberation into the wild is often expressed, but that hope is marred by problems and potential disasters. Two apparently successful examples are the restoration of the nene goose to the partial protection of the Hawaiian national parks, and the Arabian oryx to desert lands controlled by conservation-minded Islamic potentates. On the other hand, zoo-raised Morelet's crocodiles, released in their natural habitat in Mexico, were soon poached for their hides. The recent experiment, not zoo-related, of raising black-footed ferrets, training them to catch and eat prairie dogs, and then releasing them resulted in catastrophe. Apparently coyotes killed them all. Shouldn't they also have been trained to avoid predators? It is not easy to prepare captive animals for the exigencies of the wild. There is also the risk of introducing pathogens into wild populations. Captives may be immune to bacterial and viral diseases, but they may pass them on, with fatal results, to their free-living kin.

Habitats are being destroyed at an alarming rate through the greed, ignorance, and sheer numbers of the all-dominant human species. Will there soon be any safe places to liberate animals, large ones especially, with much hope of success? Predictably, many kinds of animals—mammals, birds, reptiles, amphibians, fishes, and other creatures—will survive only in captivity after their natural populations become extinct.

Herpetology Then and Now

Although zoological gardens and aquariums have undergone extraordinary transformations for the better during my lifetime, I view the changes that have occurred in herpetology with mixed emotions. There have been numerous improvements, to be sure, especially in husbandry, and many veterinarians now specialize in the care of reptiles and amphibians. On the other hand, such progress has been counterbalanced by restrictions on collecting and fieldwork and a confusing array of new techniques, each claimed by its practitioners to be the best suited for reclassifying the various taxa.

I refuse to become involved in the imbroglio that is plaguing a lot of the scientific literature. Instead, I will compare various facets of the discipline, on the basis of before and after.

Fieldwork

When I first became interested in herpetology at the age of 12, and for many decades afterward, there were no restrictions. We could collect anything and everything we wanted. We respected private property and wildlife sanctuaries, but otherwise we enjoyed a freedom that seems almost unbelievable in comparison with the morass of legal restrictions that prevail today.

I kept a few reptilian pets during much of my boyhood, but, as I reached more mature years, especially after my pilgrimages from Toledo to the Museum of Zoology at the University of Michigan, my personal fieldwork zeroed in on two objectives. First, I was always on the lookout for prime live herps that would make good exhibits for the zoos where I worked. Second, I sought specimens for study purposes, either for my own projects or to further our collective knowledge of the variation within the many species I encountered. There was also the important goal of adding information about the distribution of reptiles and amphibians. I have always been deeply interested in zoogeography and the natural ranges of various species of animals, and on a worldwide basis.

During my active fieldwork, which tapered off in the late 1960s, I preserved a great many voucher specimens.

They went into the study collections of several different museums, but chiefly the American Museum of Natural History, with which institution in New York I have been privileged to serve as a research associate since 1948. I even pickled herps found dead on the road, if they were not too badly damaged or decayed. I also salvaged snakes that had just been shot or beaten to death by that archenemy of wildlife, mankind. Such already dead herps often filled gaps in the known ranges of the species they represented. The institutions I chose as depositories for my material are well endowed and well curated, and the specimens are available indefinitely for qualified students and specialists. There was one exception, but it was eventually rectified, as mentioned below.

For the uninitiated, a museum specimen is not just a snake or toad in a bottle of alcohol or formalin. Each preserved individual bears a numbered tag, and information about it is carefully catalogued. Included are the date of collection; the locality where it was found, stated as accurately as possible; the collector's name; and often pertinent data on the habitat, the conditions under which it was found, and so on. When I was active in the field, I carried detailed maps with me in my car so that I could pinpoint localities with reasonable accuracy. The advent of the Global Positioning System (GPS), designed originally for military use, has made a big difference. A handy receiver aimed at the sky can pick up radio signals from 4 or more of 24 satellites circling the earth, and provide a readout that gives the latitude and longitude within a radius of 50 meters. The GPS has the added advantage of permitting the user to return to the same spot to check on seasonal changes or to make other observations.

Although I picked up herps wherever I happened to be—on several different continents, in fact—my main efforts were concentrated in Ohio, New Jersey, the Philadelphia area, the Delmarva Peninsula, and Mexico. Most vigorous of all was my work done in Ohio. During the early 1930s, along with a number of dedicated and enthusiastic young companions, I visited all parts of the state. The resultant report, "The Reptiles of Ohio,"

'WAY BACK WHEN

Roger Conant, Zoo curator, started in business at the age of 12 in the attic of his home at Red Bank, N. J.

Cartoon from "The Evening Bulletin" in 1947. Courtesy of The Bulletin Company.

which was published in 1938 and again with a lengthy revision in 1951, forms the database for the lizards, snakes, and turtles of the Buckeye State. The Ohio conservation authorities encouraged and assisted me. Property owners thanked us for removing "varmints," and I was able to work out, with considerable accuracy, the distributional patterns of the various species on the basis of the physiographic regions in Ohio. The results of my work in New Jersey, southeastern Pennsylvania, and Delmarva reside in 30, many of them fat, three-ring binders, largely unstudied and unpublished, but available to my successors or other interested persons. Joseph C. Mitchell has promised to complete the Delmarva report if my time comes before I can do it. Regarding my

fieldwork in Mexico, I published hundreds of pages in various papers, mostly concerned with the water snakes, which were eventually summarized in a major contribution of some 140 pages, supplemented with an abundance of Isabelle's illustrations.

My extensive preserved collection from Ohio remained in limbo for 46 years. I was not permitted to move it when I transferred from Toledo to Philadelphia in 1935. My superior at the Toledo Zoo, who was also my chief reason for departing, was totally unsympathetic. The collection was virtually ignored, but fortunately it was kept in a light-free room, and there was a minimum of deterioration. It was transferred to the American Museum well over a decade ago through the good offices of William V. A. Dennler, Executive Director of the splendid Toledo Zoological Gardens.

The study collections to which I contributed are the permanent backbone of herpetological knowledge, the basic evidence from which innumerable scientific publications have been spawned. Without them—both the specimens and the publications—I would not have been able to write the text or draft the range maps for the field guides that Isabelle and I so meticulously prepared. The museum collections substantiate the history of the discipline and give us a glimpse of what conditions were like years ago, before the human population destroyed habitats and eliminated the animals through greed or ignorance. I could describe many instances, but I will mention only three.

1. Sixty years ago water snakes were incredibly abundant on the Lake Erie islands, where they had an endless supply of food in the form of small fishes. They also had a plethora of flat rocks to hide under. Now, the shores are lined with summer cottages, and the snakes are slaughtered relentlessly in the belief they are venomous "water moccasins." They are now virtually extinct on the larger islands. (See the chapter entitled "The Ohio Reptile Survey: Part I.")

2. Strip-mining for coal in Ohio and adjacent states destroyed vast areas of natural habitats. All vegetation and the upper layers of soil were removed from far in excess of 1,000 square miles to facilitate the digging of coal with giant machinery. Wildlife that couldn't flee, including millions of herps, especially salamanders, was annihilated. Milton B. Trautman, in the second (1981) edition of his "Fishes of Ohio," mentioned the monstrous "Big Muskie," a machine as tall as a 32-story building and whose bucket could remove 220 cubic yards of soil or coal in a "single bite." It and other mechanical diggers left huge scars on the landscape of eastern and southeastern Ohio. The same was true in Pennsylvania and West Virginia. Although, by law, the diggings had to

be covered over, the original habitats are gone forever. What manner of fauna and flora occupied the area before it was obliterated? Aside from photographs and the writings of competent naturalists, only museum material, and the publications based on it, make it possible to reconstruct the historical background.

3. During the 1960s, Isabelle and I collected semi-aquatic natricine snakes (water and garter snakes) in and near many small streams in Mexico that supported tenuous gallery forests along their banks. Now the water has been diverted into villages for human use, and the trees have been felled for firewood. The entire riparian fauna and flora that thrived along the former streams has vanished. The specimens we obtained in such localities can now be equated with the treasures of antiquity. They can never be replaced.

Snake Hunting and the Law

During my active collecting days I was never overzealous. I never knowingly destroyed even small colonies of herps, and I took only what I needed for my studies, and samples of other species for the use of fellow herpetologists. I wanted everything that passed through my hands to be useful. Even most of the specimens I kept for exhibition in the zoos were preserved when they died. Their collecting data were in my files. Unhappily, I cannot say the same for some of my acquaintances who seemed unable to resist grabbing everything in sight. I tried to be conservative, and the sum total of all the voucher specimens I carefully preserved amounted to only an infinitesimal fraction of the enormous numbers of amphibians and reptiles that were killed during the strip-mining. The mine owners no doubt netted a tidy profit, but at what a colossal cost to wildlife and natural habitats.

An unexpected phenomenon developed in about the middle of the present century. There was a sudden surge of interest in snake hunting and in keeping them in captivity to exhibit to friends as novelties, or just to "show off." Keeping snakes in private homes had long been popular in western Europe, especially in Germany and the Netherlands. Perhaps a European influence was part of the stimulus, but the publication of several books, beginning in about 1948, was a major factor. Several field guides and handbooks appeared, including ours in 1958. Also, there was the well-written and entertaining book by Carl F. Kauffeld entitled "Snakes and Snake Hunting," published in 1957. It, probably more than any other volume, engendered a great burst of collecting. Most unfortunately, many of the readers of that book let their enthusiasm run away with them. They tore the area around Crossley, in the New Jersey Pine Barrens, literally to pieces in their eagerness to find the pine snakes and kingsnakes that Kauffeld wrote about. Wealthy young people in New York City hired buses to take them to Jasper County, South Carolina, another haven for snakes that Kauffeld eloquently described. Snake hunting became the rage.

Not only were snakes and other kinds of herps sought as personal pets, but commercial collectors saw a way to cash in, and they put additional pressure on local populations of the more desirable species. Something had to be done to slow the unhappy turn of events.

There had long been laws and regulations concerning reptiles, but most of the early ones were not for the benefit of the animals. In colonial days men were employed to kill rattlesnakes, and bounties on slain rattlers were paid in many places and for a great many years. Hogs were penned around the openings of hibernacula to kill and eat the snakes as they emerged in the spring. Early in the present century, the Fish Commission of the Commonwealth of Pennsylvania gave a medal to any boy who could prove he had killed 10 water snakes. They ate fish and thus "stole from the fisherman."

On the plus side, North Carolina, in 1905, was the first of the Atlantic seaboard states to enact a closed season and a minimum size limit for the diamondback terrapin, considered as a gustatory triumph when carefully and laboriously prepared for gourmet meals. Gradually, other reptiles, as well as amphibians, were protected. Arizona, in 1952, was the first state to protect a venomous reptile, the Gila monster. A flood of rules and regulations proliferated in response to the collecting and pet-keeping craze. The Federal Lacey Act, passed in 1900 and chiefly concerned with birds, was reenacted in 1969 as part of the Endangered Species Conservation Act, and it included provisions to protect amphibians and reptiles. It also provided a way for controlling the importation of herps from outside the United States, and from one state to another. Permits are now required from the government of the country of origin, as well I know. I did a small amount of sporadic fieldwork in Mexico during the 1970s, but I was prepared with the necessary documents when I returned home.

Now all 50 states are on the bandwagon, even Alaska. The regulations are complex and often differ vastly from one state to another. They may include stipulations on what species of herps and how many of any one kind may be kept in captivity. They may also spell out housing requirements. Venomous snakes, large constrictors, and crocodilians are considered public nuisances in some states, and they may be strictly controlled or even prohibited. Permits may be required to collect and keep certain species, and to conduct any kind of scientific investigations.

There was a time when a youngster could pick up a hoptoad or garter snake and take it home for a few days or longer. Now parents had better be aware of the rules. A book of 240 pages and entitled "A Field Guide to Reptiles and the Law," by John P. Levell, was published in 1995 by the Serpent's Tale, Natural History Book Distributors. You had better consult it or get in touch with your state authorities before you so much as pick up a herp, even just to look at it or take its picture. An enforcement agent may be lurking in the bushes.

Putting the brakes on indiscriminate collecting was essential, but the legislation designed to do it has created turmoil. Quite obviously, legal beagles and not biologists had a hand in promulgating many of the various facets. Also, bureaucrats have taken advantage of the situation. A notorious scam of several years ago involved the enrollment of a federal agent in a California college class in herpetology. He participated in a field trip to neighboring Mexico, then faked a broken leg so he would be evacuated back to the States in advance of the rest of the party. When they arrived at the border, he was standing there, in uniform, ready to make arrests for any specimens in their possession for which they had no Mexican permits. The watchdogs in most cases have done their duty well, but some of them have made exorbitant claims about breaking up huge smuggling rings without being willing (or able?) to offer proof. They were subsequently accused of fabricating nonexistent situations in order to make their work seem more important. Was their motive job security for themselves?

The Gauntlet

Before the advent of air service, imported animals arrived by ocean freighter after long voyages. Shipments were large, sometimes assembled over a period of months in advance. Because an attendant had to accompany the livestock, to feed and water it, small shipments were impractical. The birds and mammals received ample attention, but all too frequently the reptiles were neglected. No effort was made to feed them, and water was often overlooked, even for the entire duration of the voyage. I was well aware of that problem, because an animal dealer, on several occasions, asked me to unpack the venomous snakes he received. They were always far too numerous for their containers, and invariably many were dead. I salvaged some of the carcasses, and they were autopsied at the Penrose Research Laboratory at the Philadelphia Zoo. Most had died from renal failure resulting from the lack of water. The fault did not necessarily lie with the

on-board attendant, however. The following scenario usually prevailed:

Natives of Africa, for example, caught live snakes, lizards, and frogs, and kept them without food and with only a minimum of water until an itinerant trader came along to buy them for trifling sums. He, too, might hold the herpetological livestock for long periods. If he received an order for a dozen turtles of a certain species, he might have only six or eight, and there might be a long wait for the others. He, like the natives, took poor care of them. Air travel eventually expedited matters, but a recent investigation revealed that the practice of holding specimens for long periods without proper care still prevails.

There was a way for obtaining good attention for herps, however, and that was to employ a conscientious member of a ship's crew to look after them. The London Zoo knew such a man, and we traded reptiles and amphibians with them for several years by using the same small ship and crewman. On one special occasion I had a container built with a sheet-metal pan at its bottom that would hold about an inch of water. It was a large and fairly deep box, and in it I piled an abundance of wet sphagnum moss. The top of the container was of wire hardware cloth, and a cake of melting ice was kept on it, replaced as often as necessary by our special agent. There was also a wide, cleated ramp so that the herpetological voyagers could move up or down to seek warmer or cooler temperatures as needed. With the use of that contraption I managed to get nearly 100 plethodontid (lungless) salamanders, including many of the brilliantly colored species from the southern Appalachians, to the London Zoo without a single loss.

Even after air service became available, the situation scarcely improved. The shipping rates were so high that unscrupulous foreign jobbers crammed as many animals as possible into the shipping crates or boxes. Even small monkeys and birds suffered the same fate, and many were so crowded that they could scarcely move. Some shipments arrived with all the occupants dead or with only a few survivors, and those in poor condition. The same was true of herps, and still is. There have been a number of recent instances when badly injured, even dead, turtles were found packed in boxes like so much cordwood, or even stacked on their sides. What pitiable innocent victims of cruel, greedy people.

One reptile, more than any other, has been exploited for profit on an unprecedented scale—the red-eared slider, *Trachemys scripta elegans*, a widely distributed turtle in the central and southern parts of the United States. The young, with a sprinkling of other species of the map turtle complex and the southern painted turtle, have long been sold by the millions as novelties. During most of my career as curator of reptiles at the Philadelphia Zoo, all pet shops had them and even a variety of other stores. They appealed to impulse buyers. The little turtles were cute and colorful and (supposedly) made good pets for children.

My personal experiences with the pitiful little "orphans" were literally heartbreaking. Many hundreds of them were donated to the zoo over the years, virtually every one in an advanced state of malnutrition. Their eyes were swollen shut and their shells were soft from lack of calcium. We had to explain to the donors, often parents whose children were already weeping about giving up their pets, that there was nothing we could do except to put them painlessly out of their misery.

I annually devoted one of the "Let's Visit the Zoo" weekly radio programs to the care of baby turtles. I also wrote pertinent copy on the proper way to feed and care for them, and we distributed it widely. I fear that my efforts did little good. The vendors, with mighty few exceptions, didn't give a damn whether the little turtles lived or died. They just wanted something to sell. Also sold were small parcels of dried ant pupae under the guise of being turtle food.

Close friends reported two perfectly horrendous experiences to me. Robert G. Hudson, who spent almost every Saturday morning at the zoo when he was an active member of the Junior Zoological Society, eventually became an agent for the Pennsylvania Society for the Prevention of Cruelty to Animals. During a routine inspection of a pet shop he discovered a large aquarium containing little water but hundreds of baby turtles seven layers deep. Those on top were alive. Those below were all dead, the bottommost ones rotten and stinking. I seldom entered pet shops, but when I did I almost invariably found dead turtles. When I identified myself, the proprietor of the shop was nowhere to be found. Unfortunately, I lacked the police power that enabled Bob Hudson to impose a heavy fine.

Norman Hartweg, a leading student of turtles during his academic career, visited Reelfoot Lake, in western Tennessee, several times. It was noted for its enormous numbers of turtles, and he went there to study them. On one trip, in the 1930s, he found several adult females, still alive but dying, whose plastrons had been hacked open, probably with a hatchet. Their eggs had been removed to be hatched "in captivity" to supplement what must have been an already huge stock of babies to be shipped for sale. How greedy and depraved can a supposedly civilized human being get?

In 1965 medical research documented the frequent occurrence of *Salmonella* bacteria in hatchling turtles

Juvenile red-eared turtles, Trachemys scripta elegans, *are still sold by the millions as novelty pets. The vast majority die early deaths, chiefly from malnutrition. Nowadays they all go overseas because their sale is prohibited in the United States. They can carry* Salmonella *and can be potentially dangerous for children. Photo by Tom R. Johnson.*

sold as pets. During that year Mary L. Anderson, a dedicated and public-spirited person who was appalled by the health risk to children and the carnage among the little turtles, became deeply interested in the problem. She went to Washington and discovered that federal agencies knew little or nothing about the situation. After being advised to get in touch with the Centers for Disease Control, she learned that the CDC was trying unsuccessfully to solve the problem by using various chemicals in the turtle breeding ponds, and was conducting extensive research on the subject. Meantime, sales were increasing, reaching 15 million turtles annually and causing 280,000 cases of illness a year, mostly among children.

In 1971 Mrs. Anderson successfully influenced her Congresswoman, Leonor Sullivan of Missouri, to introduce a bill calling for federal regulation of the turtle trade. Similar bills were offered by two other members of Congress, but they languished in committee. Senator Edward M. Kennedy then introduced a resolution calling for action by the Health, Education, and Welfare Department within 30 days. It was successful in requiring the issuance of a document certifying an absence of *Salmonella* bacteria before turtles could be shipped. In most cases, however, by the time the turtles arrived at pet stores the bacteria were present.

The turtle vendors then came up with the asinine scheme of selling individual turtles in covered sterile bowls, but with the recommendation that the little reptiles be placed in water for a short time each day. Meantime, Mrs. Anderson kept the Animal Welfare Institute, the Consumers' Union, and the Humane Society of the United States aware of what was happening. The three organizations were finally successful in getting the Food and Drug Administration to issue a total ban on the sale of turtles with shells less than four inches long. The ban is still in effect as this is written.

With their domestic market cut off, the vendors began selling red-eared baby turtles overseas. In 1984, when Kathryn and I were in Hong Kong, I visited two snake shops in the futile hope of finding a live member of the venomous *Agkistrodon* snake complex to photograph. In front of one shop was an aquarium with several baby red-ears swimming listlessly about in the water. Since then, the foreign market has grown to seven million turtles shipped in 1994 to 39 different countries.

I am told that large numbers of adult red-ears are assembled from many parts of the range of the subspecies, and turned loose in ponds maintained by the turtle "trust." How long they live or how often they breed under such crowded conditions is unknown. Obviously, a heavy toll is being taken on wild populations: breeding stock is removed and thus fewer eggs hatch in nature.

Meantime, red-eared turtles have escaped or been liberated in a great many places where they normally do not live, including numerous localities in the United States, as well as in Europe, Asia, and South Africa. They are now breeding and seem to be well established in both domestic and exotic places. Like the Norway rat and the house sparrow, red-ears are spreading over a large part of the world as a result of manipulations by humankind. Unless foreign governments ban the importation of baby turtles, they surely will continue to be sold indefinitely as long as it is profitable.

Like all naturalists who have a sincere interest in animals and their welfare, I cannot help but think of the sacrifice of such vast numbers of little turtles as a loathsome racket.

Other turtles are now being exploited. As an example, when the European Economic Community banned the importation of European tortoises from one country to another in 1984, there was an immediate demand for American box turtles of the tortoiselike genus *Terrapene*. More than 200,000 individuals were exported from the United States during the five-year period of 1986-90. Since long before anyone can remember, it has been traditional in many British families to have a tortoise as a house pet.

In years gone by, the herps acquired from commercial sources did indeed "run the gauntlet." How many died in the country of origin, in transit, or even after they reached the stores? It must have been a huge fraction of the vast numbers of individuals involved.

Happily, the situation has changed. It is now possible to buy herpetological livestock in splendid condition, snakes especially, since they have become the "in thing." They are available from herpetoculturalists who raise them in captivity and give them first-class care. Intelligent pet shop owners are now getting much of their stock from such sources. Even so, poaching in the wild will doubtless continue.

Herpetoculture

The keeping of live reptiles and amphibians in private collections has proliferated in recent years at a phenomenal rate. It is now possible to breed and raise herps with relative ease. Advances in rearing techniques, and the increased number of veterinarians who specialize in the two groups, make many aspects of captive husbandry seem easy.

Nowadays, reptile shows, often sponsored by regional herpetological societies, are common, and they attract thousands of visitors. Vendors sell their wares at prices running into hundreds and even thousands of dollars for single specimens! Apparently, it is possible to earn a handsome living by breeding snakes and other herps. I have even heard the claim that it has become a billion-dollar business. But that may be mere hyperbole.

An offshoot of the popularity of captive herps is the veritable avalanche of popular, well-illustrated books, pamphlets, and articles on individual species, genera, and popular groups such as geckos. Most are instructive and useful, but some are so poorly written or rushed into print that they qualify as examples of what my old friend Howard K. Gloyd called literary diarrhea.

Herpetoculture is not herpetology. Far from it. Herpetoculture is the equivalent of breeding and raising cats, dogs, and other domestic animals. The emphasis among many herpetoculturalists is concentrated on breeding aberrant herps—those with rare anomalies of coloration and pattern—in order to produce strains that do not occur in nature. Their originators then invent fancy names and sell them as high-priced rarities. For example, some "Arabesque pythons" were recently offered at $10,000 each. The profit motive is readily apparent in such high-priced monstrosities; "freaks" would be a better term for them. Think of how our progenitors created new kinds of dogs that bear virtually no resemblance to their wolflike ancestors. Herpetoculture seems to be heading in the same direction, although, admittedly, many breeders try to produce good examples of well-known and popular species.

Herpetology, on the other hand, is the study of reptiles and amphibians in nature as the various species have evolved without interference by humankind. Herpetology includes the study of classification, demography, behavior, natural distribution, ecology, and relationships to the ecosystem of which they are a part.

The term "captive-bred" is widely used in herpetoculture, and, theoretically, such specimens are the only ones offered for sale at the shows. That may be true, but there is some evidence to indicate that the parents may have come from the wild, and sometimes in violation of state laws. There has also been an influx of herps from other countries. Nearly two million reptiles annually have been legally imported into the United States in recent years. No figures, of course, are available on the number arriving illegally, but smuggling, particularly from Mexico, continues apace. The recent confiscation of some two dozen world-endangered aquatic box turtles, *Terrapene coahuila*, is ample proof that get-rich-quick artists are active below the border. Also, despite all the rules and regulations, there is still much poaching in the United States. It is impossible to police all reptilian habitats. A notorious, despicable criminal, whose machinations are well documented, openly defies herpetologists and the authorities, as he continues to exterminate the timber rattlesnake in the northeastern states and elsewhere for both profit and sheer arrogance.

It is difficult to evaluate herpetoculture. It is a lucrative business, and it makes reptiles and amphibians of a great many species readily available for pet fanciers. Doubtless, it also helps to ease the pressure on wild populations. It is easier to buy snakes than to go afield in search of them, especially as habitats are being destroyed wholesale in order to provide food, fiber, and shelter for the ever-increasing human population.

Much has been said about herpetoculture making it possible to liberate surpluses to supplement wild stocks, but that is a highly controversial subject. How will animals accustomed to the quiet and safety of captivity and to receiving food from people behave under natural conditions? Will they carry unsuspected infections into wild populations that have no natural resistance to them? How many herps will a natural habitat support? And how long will any habitat last before it is destroyed by developers and others? The manipulation of animals by human activities has caused serious problems, notably through the introduction of animals that become dreadful pests once they are liberated. The brown tree snake, *Boiga irregularis,* quickly became a menace and soon exterminated many species of birds when it was thoughtlessly released on the island of Guam.

Perhaps the greatest benefit derived from herpetoculture, aside from making so many species abundant in captivity, is its commendable contribution to conservation. The Mid-Atlantic Herpetological Show, held in Baltimore, uses all of its considerable profit to buy and preserve rain forest and tropical deciduous forest in Costa Rica. Tim Hoen, the enthusiastic promoter of that annual show, expects soon to have purchased a full square mile of tropical forest!

Systematics and Nomenclature

Most of what I first learned about the technical aspects of herpetology I absorbed from the faculty members of the University of Michigan and their students. In the early 1930s I drove to Ann Arbor from Toledo at every opportunity. Everyone was kind to the aspiring young zoo curator. They answered my questions, and guided me in the principles of taxonomy and the classification of amphibians and reptiles. I quickly learned the rudiments.

The system was based on the tenth edition of the "Systema Naturae," written in Latin by Carolus Linnaeus and published in 1758. He was a great Swedish naturalist whose work helped to overcome the chaos that prevailed as zoologists of many different European countries studied and described not only their own local fauna but also the material brought home by explorers from various parts of the world.

I was well aware that every species has a two-part scientific name, which is always italicized when written. The first part is the genus, a group of closely related species, and which is always spelled with a capital initial letter. The second part is the name of the species itself, and always written with lowercase letters, even if the name was given in honor of some person: *Phrynosoma ditmarsi*, not *Ditmarsi*, for example. There are one or more genera in each Family. Higher categories are Order, Class, Phylum, and Kingdom.

The Michigan people clarified many things for me. How a carefully preserved specimen should be selected as the type (the holotype) of a new species, and how it and all other available material of the same species should be described in detail, including the geographical origin and other pertinent data. All specimens involved must be deposited in a museum collection so they are available for examination by subsequent investigators, especially those who might question the validity of the new species. The law of priority prevailed. If the same species was described twice, the name first proposed in print was the proper one to use. The International Commission on Zoological Nomenclature interprets the rules, makes lists of valid species, settles disputes, and serves as a sort of supreme court. When criticizing someone else's work, polite language should always be used.

I learned many other things later, of course. Systematics is concerned with biological history, studying the origins and the evolutionary relationships among living and extinct organisms. Taxonomy is the science of classi-fying organisms and naming them. Zoological nomen-clature is the language of zoology. The typographical approach, in vogue worldwide during the days of my pilgrimages to Michigan, called for putting a definite specific name on every specimen available. It was fol-lowed later by the "new systematics," which allowed for specimens that were intermediate in one characteristic or another. They were intergrades between subspecies. In such cases, trinomials are used; for example, *Elaphe obsoleta obsoleta*, for the black rat snake, with the spe-cific name doubled because it was the first member of the complex to be described. Other geographic races of that species are chiefly yellow, orange, or strongly pat-terned with spots and blotches.

The subspecies is a useful concept for distinguishing wide-ranging but clearly different forms of the same species. I made use of subspecies in my field guides. Isabelle illustrated—in color or black-and-white pho-tographs, or in diagrams—how to distinguish one kind from another. In some cases the range of a subspecies had been cut off from the main range of the rest of the species by some vicariant event, such as the invasion of glaciers during the Pleistocene or the changes in climate and habitats they created. Yet the disjunct subspecies was still closely related to the other members of the species. These were the concepts I used in our field guides.

A valuable reference for me was the classic work by Ernst Mayr and his associates entitled "Methods and Principles of Systematic Zoology," published in 1953 by the McGraw-Hill Book Company.

A bewildering array of new concepts and techniques has developed in recent years, each with its own, often complicated jargon: electrophoresis, cladistics, molecu-lar biology, and so on. Each offers promise in proving relationships, but many of the students of one or the other are positive that their approach is the only accept-able one, and everyone else is wrong. Some proponents of the new approaches in herpetology even scoff at sub-species, insisting that they be abandoned altogether. Some extremists characterize natural history as juve-nile, even nonsensical. As a result, there has been a del-uge of papers, many of them abusive and acrimonious, incomparably different from the politeness that previ-ously prevailed. Papers on the new practices fill many of the pages of the leading herpetological and other scien-tific journals. Natural history notes on various species or groups, which the same journals long accepted, are now relegated to local, state, or regional newsletters and bulletins, or to the few pages in the "Herpetological Review" reserved for such contributions. The Interna-tional Herpetological Symposium counterattacked by

inaugurating a new first-class journal called "Herpeto-logical Natural History."

Hopefully, some good and universally accepted con-clusions will eventually result from the complex and widely differing new techniques. Some of their separate champions admit that we are in the midst of a transi-tional stage in systematic biology that may last for a great many years. Even one who strongly opposes the use of subspecies has urged that we keep the names of subspecies in mind pending some possible far-in-the-future solution.

Patently, the matter will not be settled in my lifetime, now that I am on the near side of 90, so I have adopted the personal policy of sticking with the old system. Whatever may eventually be worked out will probably be a product of the twenty-first century.

Under the new techniques, the animals must be taken into the laboratory and subjected to highly sophisticated procedures. Tissue, blood, or DNA is extracted and studied. The living animal may be of little or no impor-tance. I have heard it said that some of the persons who conduct such research would not recognize the reptile or amphibian from which their samples were derived if they saw it in life.

Imagine trying to write a field guide based on such techniques. For an exact identification the animal would have to be caught, taken to a specialist, killed and then studied with high-tech equipment. Nonsense. No ama-teur would wish to do that, and under many of the new rules and regulations, he would be breaking the law if he did. The old-fashioned field guide, such as Isabelle and I prepared, remains by far the best approach. It has helped many a budding herpetologist to focus his professional interest on the subject. Also, it is practical for the use of youngsters, Boy or Girl Scouts, or the casual naturalist who just wants to know what species he has found.

It should be borne in mind that our field guide is essentially a tool for identifying the various taxa by their general appearance, coloration, pattern, and scutella-tion. It was never intended to be a checklist of currently valid species and subspecies, although some people have treated it as such. Nowadays, scientists, using one or more of the new techniques, are learning subtle things about relationships, especially among the more difficult complexes of species—those that do not fit the man-made rules of classification. I do not deprecate their efforts in the least, but it is disturbing to witness the belligerent attitudes of some of them toward their peers who do not agree with them.

Before leaving the subject of herpetology, then and now, I should mention how attitudes have changed. In my youth, most herps were treated with scorn, fear, and sometimes sheer hatred, snakes in particular. Most people now realize that all animals are components of the ecosystem and, in general, should be let alone, unless someone in a newly built subdivision finds a rattlesnake in his backyard.

Recently, an intelligent person told me he didn't like the illustration of a terrarium in my field guide. He said that all animals should be free, including herps. Obviously, he had succumbed to the propaganda of the animal rights activists. If they want to protect wildlife, why don't they attack every subdivision before it is built, or prevent the destruction of every habitat? I see no harm in keeping a wild-caught specimen for observation or to let young people become acquainted with it at close range. Captive-raised material is best for such purposes, however. Proper care and feeding are essential. Such information is available from herpetoculturalists, in published literature, or at zoos and aquariums. Recent discoveries indicate that longtime captive herps should not be turned loose, because they may introduce unsuspected pathogens into wild populations that have no resistance to them. For example, it is now illegal to liberate pet gopher tortoises in Arizona. Hundreds have been found dead, presumably after being infected by released captives.

Other unthinking persons criticize scientific collecting for specific purposes. They don't know, or refuse to admit, that such projects receive careful scrutiny, are reviewed by peers, and require special permits.

Another important item is the survival of the great collections of preserved specimens that are so essential to sound science. They are the great treasury of animal life of the world before it was widely disturbed by humankind. In recent years museum holdings have been stoutly defended in various publications. There also, however, have been several laments about irreparable losses. Many universities, where systematics no longer is taught, have wisely transferred their collections to big endowed institutions. Others, however, are letting their material deteriorate out of narrow-mindedness, jealousy, pique, or simply neglect. Too many funding agencies are ignorant about the collections' true value. Money is often lacking to keep them properly curated.

Is it any wonder, in view of all the above, that I have mixed emotions about the current status of herpetology?

Breed and Greed

Perhaps you are a thinking person who cares about the future and what kind of world your descendants will inherit. If not, you may find this chapter depressing. It is not pleasant reading. In it, I summarize some of the thoughts of demographers and other scientists that have come to my attention, as well as mentioning a few of my own personal experiences. For delving into the frightening subject of too many people, I recommend "The Population Explosion," by Paul R. and Anne H. Ehrlich, a Touchstone Book published by Simon and Schuster in 1991. It is still among the best of several influential books on the subject.

The future looks grim. With the world population of human beings already approaching six billion and expected to double in about 50 years, what can we expect? More crowding, more stress, food and oil shortages, and, unless we mend our ways, a complete collapse of civilization as we know it. Little imagination is needed to envision gangs of predators, armed with assault weapons, in search of food. Woe betide anyone who attempts to stop them.

A preview of what was coming was developed almost under my nose, so to speak, while I was the director of the Philadelphia Zoo. Studies conducted in our Penrose Research Laboratory, under the leadership of Dr. Robert L. Snyder, included an experiment on stress. A cubic cage made of hardware cloth, with two levels, each measuring 40 square feet, and with a ramp leading to the upper, was built for mice. Two pairs were introduced. They soon increased to 12, then to 36, which begat 108. Conditions were not crowded and the mice wandered about freely on both floors. But when the fifth generation filled the cage with 648 mice, things began to happen. The old-timers were dominant, the others submissive. Large numbers of the latter huddled together, like sheep before a dog. A few became recluses, climbing to cage supports near the ceiling. The older animals kept the population on the first floor to about 25, but the second floor was packed with all the others. Many died from fighting or from physical malfunctions caused by the crowding. Fertility dropped to almost

zero on the upper floor. Many of the offspring died from neglect or because their nests were disturbed.

Whenever people complain about the great increase in crime, the rise of gangsterism in our cities, the senseless shootings at or from moving vehicles, or the spraying of bullets in buildings or schoolyards, my mind turns automatically to the mouse cage. The stress of crowding is doing to us what it did to the mice, albeit in other ways.

Is there any way to lessen the problem of overpopulation? Is it too late to make a significant difference? The Communist Chinese have made some inroads by restricting families to one child, and for their efforts they have earned the wrath of the rest of the world. People seem to think that producing children is an inalienable right. Most of the persons with whom I have discussed the subject heartily agree that there are far too many human beings, but there is a tendency to "let George do it." Let someone else worry about it. Recently a lady with whom I talked spoke volubly about the need to cut down on the hordes of humans still unborn. A few minutes later she was bragging about how many children and grandchildren there were in her family. Although I make no claim to being a demographer, I believe we reached the point of no return during the early days of the present century, perhaps about the time of my own nativity in 1909.

Coitus is as normal a human behavior as eating, sleeping, or defecating. In earlier days a strong sex drive was a valuable resource. It could result in big families with many hands and strong backs for daily chores. Also, before the advent of modern medicine, survival was uncertain, and large numbers of children died in infancy. Procreating was then an asset, but times have changed. Smaller families are now in vogue, at least among the more advanced nations. Recent statistics show that the average American family currently has about two children. Only a generation ago it was six or more. Part of the decrease is doubtless economic. Steadily rising costs of food, clothing, and education make intelligent adults follow the precepts of Planned

Parenthood. Providing a good life for two children is an attainable goal for working parents under present conditions. Even numerous members of religions that encourage large families realize that contraceptives are a necessary part of modern life.

In many undeveloped countries conditions are vastly different. The people of Somaliland, which was much in the news not long ago, are an example. They have virtually nothing. Their ancestral lands, desertified by drought and overuse from attempts to grow food and graze livestock, yield little, and abject poverty is their lot. The only fun they can have is coitus, with its resultant orgasm. Nine months later there probably will be another mouth to feed. Such additions to the human race, although born to live in misery, put little strain on our rapidly vanishing natural resources. We Americans, on the other hand, along with the Japanese and many Europeans, consume vastly more with our high and wasteful standards of living. America has long been scorned as the "throw-away society," which discards more than it uses.

The world's resources are already shrinking badly. The seemingly inexhaustible fisheries of the Grand and Georgian Banks in the North Atlantic Ocean are now virtually gone. The great fishing fleets of New England remain in port. Alarmingly, similar depletions are reported from all the great fishing areas of the globe except the Indian Ocean, which is now being overexploited. Sportfishing will no doubt continue in favorable waters, but it contributes little in the form of edible assets, whereas constantly greater quantities are needed to help feed the growing hordes of people.

Our crops may soon be imperiled. Our topsoil is washed into rivers and then into the sea at an alarming rate. Also, there is fear that underground aquifers, such as the Ogallala beneath the grainfields of the Great Plains, may fail from overpumping. Scientists point out that food and petroleum are closely linked. Fertilizers are chiefly made from oil, and half the world's known petroleum reserves are now exhausted. The United States may soon be hard-pressed to feed its own people, and will have to abandon the enormous exports of grain that have helped to offset the negative balance of trade, a constant source of worry for economists. What a far cry from the days of our ancestors who farmed small areas and depended on their livestock's manure to fertilize the soil.

Will it become necessary to grow much of our food by hydroponics in regions where rainfall is abundant? Must we stop feeding grain to livestock to produce tasty protein, and force ourselves more and more to become vegetarians?

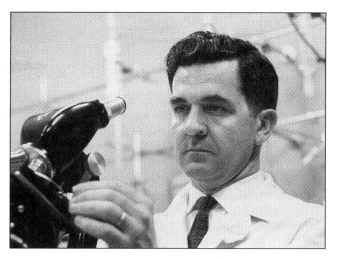

Dr. Robert L. Snyder, who succeeded Dr. Ratcliffe as Director of the Penrose Laboratory. Dr. Snyder devised and supervised the experiment to determine what happens when there are too many mice.

Speaking of water shortages, the plight of Tucson, Arizona, is a good example of impending disaster. That city, in the Sonoran Desert, has been pumping "fossil" water from underground reserves for a great many years, water that accumulated over a long period of geologic time. The water table has dropped hundreds of feet. The recently completed Central Arizona Project, considered as a boondoggle by its critics, conveys water from the faraway and already badly depleted Colorado River, but it is of poor quality by the time it trickles into Tucson. Despite conservation campaigns, designated watering days, and the use of recycled water on golf courses, far too many people go right on using water as though there were no tomorrow. Many of them are retirees from the East or the Midwest who simply cannot live without the green lawns they left behind them. Using water for swimming pools makes more sense, because of the great summer heat. But the precious water is limited. Is Tucson doomed to become the largest ghost town in modern history?

Water is in short supply throughout most of the Southwest. The large cities of California tap every conceivable source, except when they are deluged with rain. Even eastern cities can feel the pinch. The reservoirs supplying the great New York megalopolis have been dangerously low more than once. The burgeoning, runaway human population demands more and more water. It also wastes and pollutes it. The time may soon come when potable water will be in short supply in far too many places, notably in urban centers.

Wood is another cause of concern. Do you remember the television pictures of the swarms of people who fled from Rwanda during the genocidal war in that small country? Did you see any trees? Even bushes? All had been consumed for firewood. Similar shortages plague scores of undeveloped but densely populated regions of the world. Even the mighty Himalayas at the north of India, Nepal, and Pakistan are being denuded along their accessible lower slopes. Women and older children must trudge for miles every day to find the firewood and fodder they need. The resultant erosion is devastating, and the silting of dams along the great rivers is a cause of grave concern.

The large island of Madagascar, off the southeast coast of Africa, is almost a basket case. It is more than 90 percent deforested, and much of its surface now has the color, consistency, and sterility of a red brick. What a pity, because Madagascar is the home of a unique fauna and flora that survives, almost exclusively, on reservations that are inadequately guarded. The native islanders poach the remaining woodlands for firewood and other products, plant and animal, just to survive. What will become of the many species of lemurs, the incredible aye-aye, the fossas, the tenrecs, and other seriously endangered species?

So that wealthy American, European, and Japanese people can have fine furniture, and so that choice kinds of wood are available for other purposes, the great rain forests of the world are being destroyed at a fantastic rate. With them is going the greatest concentration of biodiversity on the face of the globe. How many useful drugs and other boons, potentially available in plants and animals, are being lost along with the forests? In Brazil the devastation is exacerbated by the government. Because it is confronted with vast slums, rivaling India's, that exist in São Paulo, the nation's largest city, it has been the policy to ship off as many people as possible to Amazonia. There they cut down the trees, but the soil beneath the great forest is thin and quickly washes away under the impact of torrential tropical rains. Farming becomes impossible.

Meantime, our own American forests are in peril. The spotted owl, an endangered species protected by law, is a despised symbol to lumbermen. It will put many men out of work, they say, if we protect the forests that are its habitat. How many years will it take, at the current rate of depletion, to run out of big trees, and thus spell the doom of the entire industry? Some of the large corporations plant trees for future use, but it takes years for them to grow, whereas the steadily increasing avalanche of human beings demands more and more lumber now. Can we possibly keep up with the needs of a rapidly expanding population?

Prices for wood have been constantly increasing.

Recently I had to replace two wooden gates in the wall surrounding my home in Albuquerque. I was able to buy two steel gates, installed, for less than the wood cost alone, to say nothing of the price of labor to build new gates. Steel is replacing wood in many ways in new house construction.

As I write this, the cost of printing paper has just jumped by 30 to 50 percent, and the price paid for old newspapers is at the highest level ever. Pulpwood is the basic ingredient for all paper. Inevitably, as our billions of people increase in numbers, there will be a shortage of toilet paper. Are we to be reduced to ablution, as I was in Bombay in 1984? The director of the scientific institution where I was about to present a lecture, told me to use water to cleanse myself after I sustained a sudden violent onset of dysentery. There was no paper available!

I could mention other shrinking resources, but perhaps I already have gone into too much detail. So many things are dwindling. How can we conserve them?

Recycling, in which so many of us now participate, is an excellent step in the right direction. It has become big business for several commodities. Corrugated cardboard boxes, paper for printing, and even personal stationery are now products of recycling. Reusing metal from cans saves the energy required to extract iron and aluminum from raw ores.

New technologies will doubtless help in many ways. Surely someone or an able think tank will develop a method of burning coal to keep its by-products out of the atmosphere. Some progress has been made by outlawing the chemicals that have eaten a great hole in the ozone layer that protects us from too much ultraviolet radiation. Global warming is a major challenge. Can we prevent its hazards? In time?

Let's look at petroleum, which is used for so many things including plastics, fertilizers, and energy. How can we conserve it? How can we cut down on its use? Are you willing to give up your big car, if you have one, for a much smaller vehicle with far greater fuel efficiency? Are you willing to pay three or more dollars a gallon for gasoline, as Europeans do? Will you take mass transportation to get from your home in the suburbs into the city where you work? Or will you continue to drive in alone, adding to the traffic gridlocks that plague every big city and its environs? Our automobiles are now more efficient than they used to be, thank goodness, and new technology will improve them more and more. But just think of how we guzzled gasoline for decades, meantime polluting the air.

Petroleum conservation must be practiced on a worldwide basis to be effective. Otherwise, our efforts would go for naught. You surely remember what happened when Saddam Hussein's army, in retreat after losing the Gulf War, set fire to more than 100 gushing oil wells in Kuwait. Probably just for spite and arrogance, but what a disgraceful waste!

Population control would likewise require cooperation on a global scale. In view of the longstanding ethnic hatreds in so many places, would that be possible? I think not. Each separate group would seek its own goals, and the rest of the world be damned.

A nuclear war, a possibility that was omnipresent as the Soviet Union and the United States faced off with intercontinental ballistic missiles, would certainly decimate the human population. There is still the distinct possibility that some demented and greedy dictator will obtain nuclear weapons. Even an all-out conventional war would wipe out a great many of us, but traditionally the birthrate rises following major engagements.

Pestilence is another possibility. The Black Plague, sweeping through Europe during the Middle Ages, killed a large percentage of the population. Will AIDS do the same? The Ebola virus that recently caused much concern in Zaire and neighboring African countries is a latent but potential killer. The Hanta virus, in the southwestern United States, might be another. What pathogens currently lurk in limbo that may suddenly become widespread because of the speed with which we can travel by jet plane from one distant part of the world to another?

An asteroid or a really large chunk of interplanetary space junk striking the earth might spell our doom. A similar event may well have been what extirpated the dinosaurs—sending up hurricanes of dust that circled the globe for years and prevented plants, the basic foodstuff of us all, from growing.

An episode on one of television's "Star Trek" type programs involved a visit to an overcrowded planet where millions of people were killed off periodically to make room for the others. A brutal way of controlling our population explosion would be to use similar tactics here on earth, but it would take an Adolf Hitler or a Joseph Stalin, operating on a global scale, to do it. Are we to be reduced to euthanizing people when they reach their sixtieth birthday? Their fiftieth? Older people already receive short shrift from younger ones, most of whom seem to be in a hurry. That I know from personal experience, even when I am hobbling along on a cane. Several times I have heard the equivalent of "Get out of my way, you old fool."

Humankind is anthropocentric. What happens to people is all that matters in the mind of the average person. Listen to radio or television news reports when natural disasters such as earthquakes, volcanic eruptions, hurricanes, or floods occur. So many people were killed and so many injured. Almost never is there mention about the effects on other organisms that share Planet Earth with us. Wild animals don't count. Who gives a thought about them or how their habitats have been ravaged?

We should. What is causing the frightening recent crash of amphibian populations, notably frogs, in various parts of the world? Is it because we have damaged the ecosystem? Because we have so badly polluted the water in which their tadpoles develop? Is their plight a harbinger of what may someday befall us?

The prevalent attitude is to lead our lives as best we can. Our daily problems take all our time and attention, and we give little thought about the future. Predictably, such behavior will continue until the final inevitable crash occurs, and it may come suddenly. Consider the standard classroom example. Imagine a pond into which a lily pad is introduced. It and each of its daughter lily pads are able to reproduce themselves in 24 hours and fill the pond in 30 days. How long will it take for the pond to be half full? The answer is 29 days. There is still abundant open water one day. None the next. As quick as that. Will our indispensable resources collapse that fast? Even one of them?

The population problem is a very serious one. To put its awesome possibilities for disaster into perspective, let us dwell a bit on the history of Easter Island.

That tiny speck of land in the eastern South Pacific Ocean is 2,000 miles from South America and 1,400 miles from Pitcairn Island, the nearest other habitable speck. It was discovered by the Dutch explorer Jacob Roggeveen on Easter Sunday in 1722. He described it as a wasteland of withered grasses and burnt vegetation. The impoverished inhabitants had small, leaky canoes and only chickens as domestic animals. They didn't know that other people existed, although their legends told that their ancestors visited a reef nearly 300 miles away. Most astounding were more than 200 massive, hand-carved statues in human form, the largest of which were 33 feet tall and weighed 82 tons. They were still standing in 1770, but by 1864 all had been pulled down by the islanders themselves.

Only recently has the dreadful tragedy of Easter Island come to light. Teams of anthropologists, archaeologists, and palynologists, using modern techniques for dating their findings in kitchen middens and pollen cores, put together the following scenario:

About 1,600 years ago Polynesians, in their great outrigger canoes, found Easter Island, which at that time was a virtual utopia. They managed to land despite the fact that the island is surrounded almost entirely by high cliffs. Their new find was well forested, there was a great rookery of seabirds, and it had a rich volcanic soil. Some of the land was cleared to plant the few crops known to those primitive people, or at least those they brought with them. Fishing from the top of the high, rugged shoreline was difficult, so tall native palms were felled to make additional seaworthy vessels. In them the islanders hunted porpoises, which supplied their protein needs, as confirmed by the abundant presence of bones in the middens. The colony grew and prospered, and carvers began creating the great stone statues. They were moved from quarries and mounted on stone bases solely by human muscle power, evidently using rollers and ropes. Amid the prosperity, the population paid no attention to its renewable resources, and they continued to cut down the tall trees until all were gone. When their craft wore out there was nothing with which to replace them. Lesser vegetation was burned for cooking. Food became scarce, and warring clans came into existence. They knocked off the heads of the stone statues representing their enemies, and even pushed entire statues to the ground. A number of statues seem to have been modeled after people who were gaunt, suggesting that starvation was beginning to take its toll. Eventually the people turned to cannibalism.

Easter Island and its tragic history represent a microcosm of Planet Earth. Are we to follow in their wake? How many decades remain to us? The islanders used up their resources and were unable to escape from their small world. We cannot escape from ours either, and our already awesome numbers will double all too soon. Is the end of our world to come by breeding ourselves out of existence?

Whereas "breed" applies to the major part of our present predicament, "greed" is also a very important factor.

Evidence of greed is all around us. Con and scam rogues abound. Their chief victims are the elderly or naive people who hope to make a fast buck. Thieves have always been with us. Human beings, in general, are greedy. The Ten Commandments took into account many of our shortcomings. Prime examples of greed include the following:

Unscrupulous surgeons who perform unnecessary operations, or doctors, often in connivance with hospital administrators, who keep terminally ill patients alive as long as possible, often for months, in order to milk Medicare.

Lawyers who take on impossible cases yet emerge with handsome fees. Many of them now advertise. Those who did that during my youth were branded as completely lacking in ethics. We derisively called them "ambulance chasers." Obviously some of them still are.

Many real estate developers play greedy tricks on prospective home owners. They sell land on top of city dumps or soggy marshes, caring not a whit about the consequences. Vast parts of our wetlands were destroyed by developers, although environmental impact statements and laws now help to curb some of their greedy machinations.

All too many top executives of large corporations are myopic about everything except the bottom line. They must show a profit no matter how it is achieved. They have exploited precious resources, polluted air and water, and dumped hazardous wastes into streams and ponds or buried them where they contaminated groundwater supplies. It was a long time before legislative reforms restraining such practices were put into place.

Too many of our elected representatives at all levels—national, state, and local—seem to be interested in little besides lining their pockets or getting themselves reelected.

Greedy labor unions, all too often led by racketeers and embezzlers (remember Jimmy Hoffa?), make preposterous demands. Their employers, in order to gain labor peace and keep their profits high enough to satisfy stockholders, give in to them. There are experts who blame unions for the high rate of inflation that plagued us during the heyday of the labor movement.

People who have other assets but hide them, or who are too lazy to work, manage to get on relief rolls or garner food stamps, thus cheating government agencies and all of us taxpayers.

The frightening and disgraceful condition known as drug addiction, which affects so many people, spawns the nadir of greed. Unscrupulous cartels, avaricious politicians, covetous couriers, and street pushers all compete for being the lowest of the low. Yet, the goal of making a quick and often huge profit goads them on.

For a naturalist, the saddest greeds are those that affect wildlife. Great fortunes were made many years ago by the sale of pelts of wild animals to satisfy the demands of the fur trade. The relentless slaughter of whales, almost to the point of extinction, was pursued by a few greedy nations that refused to abide by the international compact that sought to conserve the largest animals that ever lived on our planet. The poaching of elephants for ivory. The massacre of rhinos for their horns. How disgusting and how needless. Fortunately, ivory is now banned on a worldwide basis. Traditional cure-alls, including the use of rhino horns as supposed but worthless aphrodisiacs, remain prevalent in the Orient. They result in the deaths of animals of many different kinds. Can we ever control such practices?

Doubtless you can think of other examples of greed.

I certainly can. Planned obsolescence is one. Making automobiles and various appliances so they will soon wear out and force us to buy replacements. Another, a criminal act against wildlife, occurred when greedy shrimp fishermen blocked a busy port with their boats in protest against the use of excluders on their nets. They didn't care how many sea turtles they drowned. Their only interest was in making money. Many of us quit eating shrimp after that episode.

The honest, dedicated, caring doctors, lawyers, and fishermen outnumber their greedy colleagues, but there are enough of the latter to produce a strong effect on our problems. Worst of all are those who willfully waste precious resources, especially those that are not renewable.

BREED and GREED. Two short, important words with only their first letters changed. Yet, how much they explain about our deeply troubled world.

Some Final Thoughts

Am I ever glad that I lived when I did. I have seen so many things vanish or change so radically that they are now scarcely recognizable. I have done a host of things that could not be repeated today.

Take the New Jersey seashore, for example. There were resorts, such as Atlantic City, Asbury Park, and Cape May, but much of the coast between them was once wild, with long stretches of sand dunes and sparkling, spotless beaches. As a boy, I walked along them for miles without seeing a soul or any of the works of mankind, except an occasional ship well out at sea. Now homes and summer cottages, in seemingly endless rows, are piled above the dunes and even in front of them. They stand as targets for any hurricane that may come along. The beaches are polluted and, in the recent past, with garbage and hospital debris, even used hypodermic needles that made barefoot walking hazardous.

During my first crossing of the continent in 1939 by train, and even a decade later when Isabelle and I made our initial flight together to California, there were vast areas of virtually untouched land. Nowadays it seems as though almost every tillable scrap of terrain is under cultivation of some sort. Farms and fields, even in desert areas, nourished by irrigation in parched landscapes, are visible from airplane windows. Hilly, well-wooded regions are crossed by primitive roads, and, on some long flights, it is difficult to find large, undisturbed tracts. Thank goodness that we have so many national parks and monuments, wilderness areas, and steep mountain regions that are not yet despoiled with signs of civilization.

I can remember ever so many things of long ago, enough to fill many pages, but I'll tick off just a few:

I saw the Florida Everglades when they were still a "river of grass," and waterbirds of an incredible number of species were extremely abundant.

I explored the Florida Keys when, except for Key West, they were wild and in nearly pristine condition, and only a few tiny towns existed. Now houses and cottages line them cheek by jowl.

I wandered for hours through the wilds of peninsular Florida with its biological treasures. That was before its priceless natural habitats were covered with wall-to-wall orange groves and great amusement and sports centers. Few Northerners had ever heard of Orlando in those days.

I reveled with my small son in the wonders of the Great Smoky Mountains National Park before it was opened to the public.

I visited many national parks and didn't have to compete with great throngs of people waiting for entrance, camping spaces, or restrooms.

Isabelle and I spent a month in each of three years in the Big Bend National Park, and it seemed as though we could see forever in the clear Texas sky. Now, air pollution from the industrial centers of Monterrey and Monclova, and a coal-fired generator at Piedras Negras, all in Mexico, are contributing, along with activities in Texas, to produce a most discouraging curtain of smog, sometimes greatly reducing visibility.

For 25 years Isabelle and I were enraptured by our woodland retreat at Taunton Lake, well within but near the edge of the New Jersey Pine Barrens. The Barrens were almost a wilderness during much of the time of our residence, and we enjoyed them to the utmost. Now, overflow from the Philadelphia megalopolis has engulfed large portions of the Pine Barrens and threatens eventually to swallow them all.

Those changes and innumerable others were wrought by mankind. Exploitation of wild places was long condoned, even encouraged as our mandate. Development meant profits and broader tax bases. Why not use a vacant piece of land? Why not start a new project, even if it meant despoiling something else nearby or even far away? Diversion of water for crops and other human uses has almost destroyed the Florida Everglades. No one gave a thought to long-term results of disturbing ecosystems that had developed over eons.

Now, finally, there are restrictions, administered by the Environmental Protection Agency and its counterparts in the many states. Other advanced countries have legislated similar protection, but vast portions of Planet

Earth are still being exploited without regard for the consequences. That and the ever-increasing numbers of people mean less and less room for wildlife. Scarcely a week passes without my hearing about animals that are in trouble as a result of human interference. It worries me, and I have reviewed some of the problems associated with it in the chapter entitled "Breed and Greed."

Bears worldwide are now at risk. Poachers kill them so their body parts can be sold to Asians at high prices for use as traditional medicines or exotic foods. Even our North American black bear is a victim; its paws and gall bladder are particularly in demand. A surprisingly large number of carcasses have been found, especially in Canada, with only those organs missing. Not all the pilfered parts go overseas under various guises to evade the law; there is a demand for them even in large Asian centers in some of our American cities. Many animals in various parts of the world are killed and their organs sold for use in the traditional Oriental pharmacopoeia. Rhino horns and tiger bones rank high on the list of desiderata.

A unique living fossil, the rare tuatara, is also at risk, but for another reason. As the only surviving member of the reptilian Order Rhynchocephalia, it represents a special prize for collectors. There is evidence that living specimens were recently removed from the tuatara's supposedly inviolate sanctuaries on islands in the Cook Strait between New Zealand's two mainlands. The poachers are tempted by the fabulous sums, alleged to be in the tens of thousands of dollars, paid by wealthy, unscrupulous reptile fanciers.

Another dastardly theft of a rare reptile was reported by Ellin Beltz in her "herPET-POURRI" column in the "Bulletin of the Chicago Herpetological Society" for June 1996. The victim was the extremely endangered ploughshare tortoise, *Geochelone yniphora;* 72 juveniles and 2 adult females were stolen from a captive breeding program in the Amphijoroa Forest Park in Madagascar. Half the work of a decade-long conservation effort on that ravaged island was undone.

The criminals who supply poached or stolen rarities for the pet trade, including birds, often arm themselves with spurious documents or employ subterfuges to protect themselves from law enforcement agents. Even when they're caught they usually get off with fines or light sentences, mere slaps on the wrist in the opinion of conservationists. Many of us would rather see them locked in jail and the key thrown away. What a despicable racket they have in their attempts to get rich quick. But such activities go on and on, and the affluent buyers are just as guilty.

Much concern is expressed about shrinking habitats, but little is done to preserve them. For an up-to-date review of the problem, I consulted with Gary K. Clarke, a good friend and former director of the Topeka Zoo, who now is devoting all his time to conducting parties of tourists on photographic safaris to various parts of Africa. I asked him specifically about Uganda, which Isabelle and I had enjoyed so much way back in 1968, but which was later pillaged by the mad dictator, Idi Amin, and his henchmen. In the two places where we had stayed, the Queen Elizabeth and Murchison Falls National Parks, the wildlife has made a comeback, but the areas between and surrounding them are now devoted to agriculture. Uganda and much of the rest of Africa is filling up with humanity, and woe betide any animal that may attempt to forage in a *shamba* (native garden) or plantation outside the park boundaries.

In a very real sense national parks and reservations are becoming isolated oases, and inbreeding looms as a serious problem, especially in the smaller preserves. The Borivili National Park near Bombay, India, which Kathryn and I visited in 1984, is a good example. One of the former officers of the Bombay Natural History Society, who was with us, told us that four or five leopards were still in residence at the park, but there was no chance for their small group to receive new blood from outside under natural conditions. The next nearest reserve is far away, and there are millions of people in between.

Gary Clarke told me that the mountain gorillas also face a precarious future. The government of Rwanda has protected them for years because they are a lucrative tourist attraction. People who approach slowly and quietly are able to get quite close to them. Natives, however, sneak into the great upland forest reserves to collect firewood and set wire snares to trap duiker antelopes and other small mammals. Several of the gorillas have lost hands after getting caught in such snares. In view of the turmoil that recently occurred in Rwanda—the genocide, the hordes of refugees escaping to Zaire and then returning to Rwanda—can any wildlife be safe for long? With starvation facing the tribesmen and their families, nothing edible has a chance, not even rats or insects.

The slaughter of black rhinos for their horns goes on apace despite efforts to protect them. Clarke said that the experiment of removing horns from live animals to make them worthless has been a failure. Would-be horn hunters, who do their stalking at night, ever alert for the presence of game wardens, may find a hornless rhino, but they kill it anyway. They don't want to risk trailing the same animal again for no personal gain.

Clarke also said that domestic cattle are competing with wild grazers for grass and water in a great many parts of Africa.

The worldwide ban on ivory and objects carved from it stopped the slaughter of elephants. They are still not safe, however, because in many places their numbers must be thinned out periodically lest they literally eat themselves out of house and home. Once the African elephant had a very large part of the continent over which, collectively, it could roam. Now it is being more and more restricted to reservations. Too many of the big pachyderms can cause much destruction. I am mindful of the dead forest Isabelle and I saw south of the Nile River where the great beasts had stripped the bark from the trees to keep themselves from starving.

We are now in the midst of a period of mass extinctions. There have been several of those during the geologic past, of which the demise of the dinosaurs is the best known. Although we are not sure just what caused their sudden disappearance, perhaps the most widely accepted theory is that an asteroid struck the earth, throwing up vast clouds of dust that lingered and obscured the sun and prevented plants from growing; the carnage was quick and enormous.

The present period of extinction, slower but accelerating, is a man-made one. It began with the ascendancy of humankind, *Homo sapiens,* the "wise one," to give us our proper scientific name. When our numbers were small we did comparatively little damage. But when we formed clans and tribes and invented deadly weapons, our food gathering became much more efficient. Even large animals could be killed by flint-tipped lances and throwing sticks. Fossil remains of very large mammals, now extinct, are abundant. Mammoths standing 15 feet at the shoulder, bison as big as modern elephants, beavers almost as large as the black bear, and giant ground sloths, with their predators, such as the so-called sabre-toothed tiger, all inhabited North America not long ago. Human beings evidently swarmed across the Bering Land Bridge from Asia, possibly several times, at or near the end of the last major glaciation, roughly 10,000 years ago, and they found rich hunting grounds. With their weapons they eventually pursued the more solitary species to extinction. Herd animals were driven over cliffs, and their meat was removed after the victims had fallen to their deaths. The North American mammalian fauna of historic times is only a remnant of the impressive sample of the great Age of Mammals that once lived here. Similar events took place in Eurasia. The invention of firearms has also taken a heavy toll.

Early exploration by several European nations resulted in more extinctions. Take the case of the dodo, for example. Occupants of sailing vessels, at the mercy of winds and perennially short of fresh food, made short work of the dodo when they reached the small island of Mauritius in the Indian Ocean. The flightless birds, members of the pigeon family but as large as turkeys, could be easily knocked in the head. The situation was similar on other islands. The early mariners were unaware that the birds had evolved under insular conditions with no natural enemies to avoid. They were thus completely unafraid of men with sticks. The sailors described the dodo as stupid, and "dumb as a dodo" found its way into our language.

The great auk once lived in cold northern waters. Like other alcids it congregated ashore in large colonies during the breeding season. Because it was flightless it was easily killed, and it was slaughtered in vast numbers for its flesh, oil, and feathers. The last living great auk was seen in 1842. The Welsh called it *pen gwyn,* in reference to the white on its head, and the Welsh name, by a curious quirk of misnaming, was transferred to similar seabirds of the Southern Hemisphere, the penguins.

The list of birds and mammals extirpated by humans is a lengthy one. I will mention just a few. The passenger pigeon, which once numbered in the billions and flew in flocks so vast that they darkened the sky, is extinct. The last one died at the Cincinnati Zoo in 1914. It was a colonial nester, and virtually all the large trees were occupied by innumerable nests for miles and miles on end. They were easily netted for the market. The Carolina parakeet, considered a nuisance because it ate ripening fruit, and in demand as a cage bird, suffered the same fate. The last survivor also died in the Cincinnati Zoo, in 1918.

The quagga, with its head and neck striped like a zebra but resembling a plain gray horse posteriorly, was killed off after the settlement of its homeland in far southern Africa. The last live one, a captive in the Berlin Zoo, succumbed in 1875. Steller's sea cow, first discovered in 1741 on an island off the coast of Kamchatka, was an easily obtained source of food for Russian traders and fur hunters. It was exterminated scarcely more than a quarter century later, by 1768.

The list is not restricted to warm-blooded vertebrates. Many kinds of reptiles and amphibians have also been obliterated by mankind. Frogs of many species are disappearing in an alarming and disheartening way, possibly as a result of air or water pollution or the hole in the ozone layer, or combinations of these and other causes.

Who knows how many animals, especially invertebrates, are disappearing as the great rain forests of the world are felled? Most of the organisms, including plants, haven't even been identified and described in the scientific literature. Many doubtless contain valuable chemicals of potential pharmacological and anti-carcinogenic value, but these, too, are disappearing before their potential can be assessed.

Zoos everywhere are trying their best to breed rare and endangered animals, hoping in many cases to liberate them eventually in their natural habitats. But the habitats are disappearing as human needs require more and more space. Also, recent research in Arizona suggests an ominous possibility. When rattlesnakes caught alive are transported to state parks or other wild state lands, the snakes tend to prowl constantly and never become assimilated into the local populations. Would that also happen with birds and mammals? Will strange newcomers be accepted into herds or family groups?

Against such a background it is easy to understand the sadness, even the anguish I feel when I see animals of so many kinds jeopardized by the proliferation of humankind and its works. The list of threatened and endangered species grows ever longer.

There are a few bright spots, however. Some species have made comebacks when they received protection. The ban on DDT and allied chemicals allowed the bald eagle, osprey, pelicans, and certain other birds to become numerous again. And the laws against killing alligators paid off, almost too well. Some of the big reptiles become nuisances, and even dangerous, when well-meaning but poorly informed people feed them. I mentioned the success with the white rhinoceros in "The Trip of a Lifetime: Part II. South Africa." Such achievements are commendable, and they demonstrate how much can be done by careful planning and strict enforcement.

On the other hand, atrocities are perpetuated by sneaky, greedy, two-legged varmints who have no compunctions about poaching even endangered animals to satisfy the egos of wealthy clients, who look upon animal rarities as status symbols. The raid on the tuatara colony is a case in point. In the same category, but closer to home, belongs the small bog turtle, *Clemmys muhlenbergii*, which, despite laws and strong efforts to protect it, continues to be a victim of greed.

During my more pessimistic moments I cannot help but think that, despite all our conservation efforts, we are only fighting a rearguard action as the human juggernaut plows steadily onward, destroying wildlife, and eventually itself.

Enough of lamentation. I could continue, almost indefinitely, bewailing what is happening to our fellow organisms on this small planet. But I have written enough on that subject.

Enormous social changes and customs have also occurred during my lifetime. I can recall when merchants gladly waited on their customers and catered to their needs and wishes. That was good public relations on their part. Now, unless we are wealthy, each of us as individuals must seek out and do everything for ourselves, such as visiting a supermarket, a large store of any kind, and even pumping our own gasoline.

Service station attendants everywhere used to fill our tanks, wash the car windows, check the oil and water levels, and, on request, even the tires. When we paid, they tipped their caps and said, "Thank you." We didn't even have to get out of our cars unless we wanted to stretch our legs. Tips were not expected.

There was a human operator in every elevator. No need to hurry in or out or to guard against a sliding door that threatened to cut you in two.

Medical doctors came to your house to care for you in any kind of emergency, no matter the time of day or night, or how bad the weather. Now you must go to a hospital. If you have to call an ambulance you must be prepared to pay the fee before you are loaded aboard. Pity the shut-ins and people who are alone. When I was a lad of about 13 and living with my grandparents in Red Bank, New Jersey, my grandfather, Morris H. Rogers, went to see a sick friend in Eatontown, a small nearby village. Because it was on a weekend and not a school day, I went with him. First we walked the mile or so to downtown Red Bank, and then took a trolley car. When we stepped down from it, we had well over a mile of very dusty road along which to walk. We had scarcely arrived at the friend's house when the doctor, who had left his horse and buggy at the curb, came in to see his patient. The latter's wife introduced Grandpa and then added, "This is his grandson, Roger." Somewhat later, when the doctor came downstairs from the sickroom, he asked, "I once knew a person whose name was William Williams, but is this young man Roger Rogers?"

We laid out sheets of sticky flypaper or used short hanging rolls of Tanglefoot to combat household insects. We didn't pollute the air and endanger the lives of birds and other animals, including ourselves, by spraying our environs, even from big trucks and airplanes with deadly DDT and other chlorinated hydrocarbons during the days when they were the chemical industry's panacea for insect pests. Rachel Carson's classic "Silent Spring" was spawned by that near catastrophe, and her book had much to do with having such compounds outlawed.

It was possible for decades to eat raw oysters, clams, and mussels with impunity. No need to worry about toxic man-made pollution.

"Shave and a haircut, two bits," made sense, because that was all my father had to pay at the barber shop when I was a small boy.

Until very recently, when you telephoned a large

business, a human being answered the phone. Now you get a recording that tells you to listen to a long, complicated "menu" and to push certain buttons.

The politeness, the mores and morals, that were drilled into us as children seem now largely to have vanished except among middle-aged and older people. We respected the ladies, doffed our hats to them, and never told off-color stories in their presence. Nowadays, both on campuses and elsewhere, four-letter Anglo-Saxon words frequently issue from the mouths of young people of both sexes.

We used to dress for any special occasion—a dinner out, a party, or even to visit friends or relatives. We wore our best at dances and other social functions. Somber dress was a must for funerals. Nowadays most of us look like slobs. Torn and stained dungarees are the "in" things. I recall how deeply shocked I was when I attended a funeral service for a young friend a few years ago. Slobs outnumbered the more dignified mourners, and some even wore ragged shorts, scuffed shoes, and shirttails hanging out.

It used to be safe to take evening strolls, even for young girls, but not any more. It had been my custom, after Isabelle died and I was alone, to walk almost the full mile around our quiet little backwater neighborhood, the so-called Village Manor, after eating my supper. One autumn, after daylight saving time had come to an end, I went out just the same, even though it was dark. I was at the opposite side of the Manor when I became aware that a car without lights was keeping pace with me as I walked along the sidewalk. It was a panel truck entirely covered with a thin layer of dry mud that effectively hid its details. There were two round holes in the coating, one for the use of the driver and the other on the passenger's side. Suddenly I heard the car door start to open, and I had visions of being mugged. There were no lights in the nearest houses, and trying to run, at my age, probably from a young man, was hopeless. Frankly, I was scared. Just then a car came around the corner and illuminated the scene. What a piece of good luck! The panel truck door slammed shut and the driver gunned his motor and shot ahead. I noted as the vehicle passed me that the license plate was similarly coated. As I hurried on my way, I thought first of how the use of a hose for only a minute or two could eliminate the disguise. Then I thought of my own safety. I had no money with me, but I had my keys, and the hoodlums, a driver and at least one passenger, could have forced me to let them into my house where they could have stolen whatever they wanted, and perhaps left me dead on the floor.

When the police were informed, they said, "We're lookin' for those guys." Now, with crime so rampant, I don't go out alone at night. I feel safe at home in my roomy cage with stout bars on the doors, every window, and the skylight. The crooks have freedom. I'm the one who's locked in a cell.

It must be obvious to the reader that I was happiest when I was in the field with my close friends, and especially Isabelle, my constant companion and devoted pal. It seems as though I've traveled a zillion miles on foot. Except for a pair of binoculars suspended from my neck and, in earlier days, a snake bag thrust over my belt and a snake hook in hand, I was unencumbered. In more recent years, as Kathryn and I toured the world, I toted a camera. My greatest thrills came, not from watching sporting events or mixing in crowds, but from exploring wild places, finding unusual snakes or salamanders or spotting a rare bird. I was a bird watcher but not a dedicated one. I've kept no life list, but I ran a bird feeder every winter when we lived in the Pine Barrens and recorded the various kinds of avian guests.

Basically I wanted to get away from people. That's a desire shared by many—backpackers who follow the trails or plunge off on their own in designated wildernesses or other wild places, or sunbathers who seek the deserted beaches that are fast disappearing. Almost everyone likes to get away from it all occasionally, to be alone to think or to do something special.

It was natural, no doubt, for me to shun crowds in my leisure time, especially when it was my job for decades to attract as many people as possible to the Philadelphia Zoo. Then, once they came, I had to cope with the multitude of problems they created when they were present en masse. My interest in wildlife, however, dates back to my boyhood years. With such an early start I seemed almost destined to enter the zoo profession, and to stay in it for 45 years. But on my days off and during vacation periods, I was usually as close to nature as possible. How marvelous it was for me and Isabelle during our quarter century in the New Jersey Pine Barrens. All we had to do was to look out the windows to see our wild neighbors, and any walk, even a short one into our back acreage, was sure to produce something of interest.

Let me repeat my opening statement— "Am I ever glad that I lived when I did." Just think of all the advantages I've enjoyed. If I had been born well back in the nineteenth century, there would have been no radio or television, and only primitive automobiles with tires so unreliable that at least one of the four was sure to go flat on any long trip, say of 15 or 20 miles. There would have been no airliners to whisk us far away in record time. No central heating. No flush toilets. No hot running water. Instead, a bath in a wooden washtub in the kitchen on Saturday nights. What luxuries we enjoy today by comparison!

I've had a good life despite the loss of my father at an early age, a disastrous first marriage, and the many problems I've had to cope with. I've seen so much and done so many things that they even amaze *me* when I stop to think about them.

Like most old people I can remember details of long ago with clarity, clear back to my boyhood. When I was six, certainly not more than seven, I earned my first money. I shoveled the snow off the walk of our neighbor's row house, and he gave me a whole nickel! Mother was my pal, and she took me to see all sorts of things— the circus, parades, and even thrice to the opera with tickets a friend gave her. We also went once or twice each summer to Willow Grove Amusement Park in suburban Philadelphia. We had little money to spend on rides and the merry-go-round, but, for a dime or maybe 15 cents each, we could enter the large concert pavilion and listen to some of the best music of the era, including Victor Herbert's orchestra. Six great musical organizations participated in turn, each for two or three weeks. The last and best was the immortal John Philip Sousa and his great band. He always closed his concerts with the "Stars and Stripes Forever." How I thrilled to the martial strains, and how glad I am, even today, to realize that I saw the great March King in person several times.

The zoos I worked in were fun and sure to pose at least one challenge every day. What an exciting profession I had entered and one that offered so many opportunities. At Toledo I was given extra days to add to my regular day off so that I could make a detailed survey of the reptiles of Ohio in all parts of the state. How proud I was to be sent to Europe by ocean liner to study zoos less than two years after I transferred back to Philadelphia. I was still only in my twenties. On zoo business I traveled to many parts of the United States, to Mexico, again to Europe, and then to Africa.

What a lucky sequence of events brought Isabelle dePeyster Hunt into my life. I picked her to fill a vacancy at the Philadelphia Zoo solely because she was a woman and not subject to the draft. She could have carried on for me had I been required to serve in some World War II activity. She later became my wife and was with me in Europe and Africa. The National Science Foundation underwrote a full year of fieldwork for us in Mexico, although it was piecemeal and spread over six years. That study took us into every state of Mexico and the capital, and, with my devoted wife at my side, it was the acme, the very quintessence of the fieldwork we enjoyed so much.

Research on the *Agkistrodon* monograph took Kathryn and me twice around the world and twice more to the Orient. And the frequent-flier mileage we earned provided us with three trips to South America. In all I have been in 48 countries and either flown over or looked into 37 more—85 in all. How incredible! The highlights of my many trips were in Mexico, Africa, China, and Patagonia, far south in Argentina.

Surely, however, the golden years of my life were the quarter century that Isabelle and I resided in the New Jersey Pine Barrens at Taunton, with wildlife all around us. It was there, too, that our field guides were conceived and executed, and where we photographed hundreds of live herps. Also, at Taunton I wrote many of the papers associated with my becoming a professional herpetologist. What fond memories I have of the 'Gap and, especially, Hyla Holler.

During my long, active life I have met and worked with a great many wonderful people, and I have made a multitude of friends, both lay and professional. How grateful I am to so many persons. Yet, as I think about them and others, I'm reminded of two delightful old Irish maxims.

Murphy's Law maintains that if anything can go wrong, it will. That has happened to me time and time again, just as it has to everyone else.

On the other hand, I have had to contend with a small sprinkling of arrogant nincompoops and know-it-alls, exhibitionists, incompetents who sought to aggrandize themselves at the expense of others, scheming, treacherous, or jealous scoundrels, charlatans, and various other obnoxious characters. They and their ilk are examples of the Kelly Hypothesis.

You don't know what the Kelly Hypothesis is? It states that there are more horses' asses than there are horses.

Yes, I've picked some lemons in my time—while I was working at the Philadelphia Zoo, in my personal life, and when a doctor insisted for years that I had bone cancer, leading me to expect that I would soon follow Isabelle to the grave. How can you judge a person in advance, no matter how good his or her personality, reputation, or references may be? You have to work with, live with, or closely supervise people to understand their idiosyncrasies.

Such is life. Everyone's career is filled with ups and downs of one sort or another. Not everything can be perfect or to one's liking.

Now that I've reached my twilight years, I'm beset by most of the problems of old age—aches and pains, cataracts on my eyes, hearing aids in my ears, partial plates in my mouth, and too many pills. Arthritis is beginning to plague me, and so are brief memory lapses.

I'll be thinking about something of interest or importance and unknowingly, but automatically, put something away in the wrong place. Or I will lay down some papers and then wonder where they are.

Thank heavens I'm not alone with such problems. Younger people tell me they occasionally have the same troubles. I do it so often, however, that I force myself to double-check all important things. I make sure to put each outgoing letter in the right envelope, and that I file books, letters, and miscellaneous papers correctly in my library. What a waste of time having to police my own activities. But that goes with the territory. My elders have been telling me about the vagaries of old age for many a year.

It's time now for me to settle down. I'll take it easy, as many friends keep advising me to do. I'll give up the work ethic, or being a workaholic, as some people call it. I've done enough. I will enjoy the things I like, give away keepsakes that I can't take with me, and make sure my affairs are in order. I've written my life story, so I'll call it quits. I thank every one of you for your help and the honors you've conferred on me. They are deeply appreciated.

So, I'm now retired. It's not easy to slow down, but I'm getting there. Isabelle left me a legacy of whodunits—detective stories—shelves full of them. Stories by Agatha Christie, Mignon G. Eberhardt, Erle Stanley Gardner, Ellery Queen, Rex Stout, and a great many others. She devoured them all during her long terminal illness. There was nothing wrong with her eyes up to the very end. Now I'm starting to work on the books in earnest.

During a recent telephone conversation with a good friend I learned that the International Herpetological Symposium will soon have its next meeting in Costa Rica. How much fun it would be to visit that beautiful little country again. But I'm through. I'll just think about it instead of going.

I know that a number of my projects, some of them half finished but laid aside because of more pressing matters, would be worth looking at again. But I can't do everything. Let them go.

A message arrives urging me to attend the Third World Congress of Herpetology in Prague in the former Czechoslovakia. Golly, how many friends would I see there, from all over the world, probably for the last time? How different it would be from the Prague that was smothered behind the Iron Curtain and made me feel as though I was in jail when we attended a meeting there in 1985. It's intriguing to contemplate such an adventure. But I've given up.

An invitation comes to take part in another old-timers' meeting.

Oh, what the hell. I can't just loaf. I've still too many things to do. How many frequent flier miles do Kathryn and I still have available?

An Assemblage of Anecdotes

It probably is impossible for anyone trying to recall the events of a busy life to remember everything, or, for that matter, to fit many items that come to mind into the general text. So he or she winds up with a collection of interesting or amusing anecdotes that are, in themselves, worth recording. Here are a few that are left over, so to speak. I present them in no special order.

Boa Constrictors on Stage

Answering questions about snakes and other reptiles and amphibians is one of the duties of any curator of reptiles. In the early days when I had more time, I tried personally to answer as many letters and telephone calls as I could. Later we developed a mimeographed set of instructions on the care of small turtles, lizards, snakes, and amphibians that we could mail to pet owners, and we were tied up on the phone only long enough to jot down their names and addresses.

One day a man called and said his boa constrictor was sick. Trying to diagnose a snake's trouble by telephone is as difficult as a doctor's attempting to prescribe for a patient by using the same means of communication. But I offered to try. The symptoms were vague. The snake wasn't feeding properly. It seemed listless. It didn't respond to attention. My first inquiry was about warmth. Was it exposed to temperatures in the 80s at least a few hours daily? His response was no, but he asked if basking in the sun would help. I said it would, provided care was taken not to let it remain in the sun too long. That ended the conversation.

Later during the day I received calls from the Philadelphia newspapers advising me that the star performer at the Shubert Theatre, which was then a burlesque house, had been arrested for sunning her pet snake on the sidewalk in the center of town. It turned out that the man who called me was her manager, and he had told the press that the zoo's "expert" had recommended sunshine for the snake. Obviously he was seeking publicity, and I

was his innocent foil. The young lady in question appeared on the stage "dressed" in the boa constrictor.

To add insult to injury, when I passed the Shubert Theatre later in the week, I saw a large blowup of one of the newspaper stories with my name in letters several inches high! The manager was a rat. He didn't even offer me a ticket to the show.

It was on account of another boa that I found myself in jail. No, I wasn't serving a sentence. I was summoned by the police to Philadelphia's ancient Moyamensing Prison several years before the Shubert Theatre incident. Another stripper and her snake were there. The girl was serving time for indecent exposure, but the jailers were afraid of the snake and wanted to get rid of it as quickly as possible. So I went after it. I was met at the prison gate and escorted inside, and the turnkey closed a massive lock behind us that reminded me of one I had seen in a movie about the Middle Ages in Europe. I had an instant impression of what it was like to be in the lockup. I was glad to depart, a short time later, with the snake, which, I discovered, had Scotch tape wrapped around its head so it couldn't open its mouth to bite.

Times have changed. In today's climate of tolerance, such exposure of human skin attracts little attention. During the period about which I write, however, the punishment was usually up to the judge. It gradually relaxed from a jail sentence, to a fine, to a warning, and then nothing at all. The Shubert girl, I heard, was released to dance with her snake the same night. What a lot of free publicity at my expense!

The Eagle Escapade

Daniel Pratt Mannix IV was a professional writer and a good one. Soon after my return to Philadelphia following my stint in Toledo, he called on me at the zoo, introduced himself, and sought some information about animals. Fortunately, I was able to help him, and we eventually became good friends. He married Jule

Junker, a member of a prominent Philadelphia family. Dan was interested in falconry and taming animals, and he and Jule spent several months in Mexico, where they acquired a golden eagle they named Águila ("eagle" in Spanish). The bird soon became tractable and it was a feature during the lectures they gave back in the States. Águila was the big, impressive bird that flew from my gauntleted fist to Jule's across the spacious elephant house yard as a special feature of our last May Day at the Zoo in 1945.

Águila was a boarder at the Philadelphia Zoo during much of World War II. Dan Mannix was in uniform somewhere in Washington and Jule, like all patriotic noncombatants, had volunteered for some war-related effort. Their eagle occupied one of the relatively small aviaries that housed other birds of prey—one owl, hawk, or eagle in each, near the old parrot house. We were glad to help, especially since the Mannixes had done so much to assist us in promoting the zoo. But we nearly had a disaster!

One day the relief keeper, who was small in stature, entered Águila's aviary. Instead of stepping inside and quickly closing the service door behind him, the man leaned down to pick up something. Águila, noting the considerable gap above the keeper, took off, sailed through the opening, rose above the nearby trees, and disappeared.

When the news reached me a few minutes later, I was horrified. How could we hope to retrieve that valuable bird? The Mannixes had spent months of hard work training Águila in the ancient art of falconry. Exhibiting him, and his ability to fly from one to the other, was of major importance during the lecturing they did to earn a living. We must retrieve him at all costs, but how? I thought of alerting the press, hoping that some reader might see him and call us, but I wanted to spare Dan or Jule or both from the devastating shock of reading about the escape in a newspaper. It was a story that would surely "make the wire" and be used all over the country. At the time I didn't know how to reach either of them by telephone.

I summoned Head Keeper John Regan, a resourceful animal man who had risen to the occasion, to put it mildly, when other unexpected problems developed. Together, in my car, we rode through Fairmount Park, stopping frequently to crane our necks upward looking for the errant eagle. A half hour or so later, discouraged and worried, we returned to the zoo and went to my office. Presently the telephone rang. It was a park guard, and he told me that, near an isolated guardhouse across the river from the zoo, there was a big bird in a tree that kept looking down at him.

After a quick consultation with John, he dashed off to get a large net, while I hastened to the commissary and had the butcher cut me a chunk of horse meat, long and narrow and weighing perhaps two pounds.

When John returned, we took off again, crossed the Girard Avenue Bridge, and soon found the guard, who happened to know me by sight. He immediately pointed, and there, well up in a large tree, was Águila, staring directly at us. We concealed the food behind us, and John and I moved to a large, nearby open lawn. I grasped the net and John started swinging the attenuated piece of meat, whereupon Águila, to use the falconers' term, stooped to the lure, seized it in his talons, and dropped to the ground. John grabbed one wing and I seized the other. We kept the wings spread so our hands were out of reach of his sharp beak, and he held tightly to the food he had grabbed. It was the work of only a few moments to ensnare him in the net and convey him to the car. I thanked the guard profusely, and we soon had Águila back in his aviary, still grasping his meal, which he proceeded to eat leisurely. His talons were enormous, and we had no gauntlets to protect our wrists, and that was why I asked for a long piece of meat.

It took us awhile to relax and to thank our lucky star that Águila had been so well trained. As soon as he escaped, he apparently flew across the Schuylkill River, but he was so used to people that he went no farther. Did he think the park guard was another keeper, possibly with food? The uniforms were almost identical.

It was a long time before I told the Mannixes what happened.

The Adventures of Rani

Jule and Dan Mannix had another trained pet that was far larger and more spectacular than Águila, their golden eagle. It was a cheetah, a beautifully spotted cat of the species which, because of its great speed, was long trained for the chase by Old World potentates. The Mannixes made motion pictures of it racing after jackrabbits, and it was tame enough to accompany them, on a leash, when they lectured. The only trouble was that they gave it the wrong name.

They acquired the cheetah when it was young. Animal dealers frequently had them for sale. There were no lists of endangered species in those days, and the craze for wearing coats made from the pelts of spotted cats had not yet come into vogue. I blame Jacqueline Kennedy for that. It had disastrous results on wild felines. Too many wealthy women sought to emulate the First Lady, and great numbers of spotted cats were slaughtered in the wild to supply the demand.

Jule and Dan thought their cheetah was a female, so they called it Rani, a diminutive of Ranee, the title given to a Hindu queen. Sex is difficult to determine in young cats, however, because the testicles of males require considerable time to descend with the scrotum. Rani's were characteristically slow, and it was awhile before his owners realized they had bought a male instead of a female. But the name Rani stuck, despite his sex.

Several of us from the zoo had met Rani at the Mannixes' lectures and elsewhere, and we were enthralled by his beauty and tractability. He was not allowed to enter the zoo, however, except in the service building on the zoo's outer perimeter, where my office was situated for many years. There he would not come into contact with any of the animals in the collection. In addition to the strict quarantine that was in effect regarding outside animals, there was also the possibility that he might frighten some of them. I was all too mindful of the time a large stray dog managed to enter the grounds. It "spooked" a zebra, which dashed wildly away and slammed into the rear fence of its pen, breaking its neck.

The year 1949 was a busy one at the zoo. We had been celebrating the Philadelphia Zoological Garden's Diamond Jubilee, its 75th anniversary, off and on all year. The final event was a tribute to the zoo from another of the city's venerable institutions, the Academy of Music. The annual series of children's concerts began on December 17 with the world premiere of "Adventures at the Zoo," a piece with words and music about a fanciful trip made by jungle animals that built a ship with which to reach the North Pole. After numerous adventures that even took them to Antarctica, they arrived at and were made at home in the Philadelphia Zoo. Alexander Hilsberg, the talented assistant to Eugene Ormandy, conducted. The presentation would not be complete, however, without the participation of live animals. Among those requested were Rani and a penguin. The Mannixes graciously agreed to let Rani take part, but at the time we had no live penguins at the zoo. Curator of Mammals Fred Ulmer solved that problem by borrowing a mounted one from a friend.

On the scheduled morning we had quite a menagerie backstage, consisting of most of the tame animals in the zoo's collection. During an appropriate pause in the music, and on cue from the stage manager, the parade of the animals began, and proceeded smoothly. There were several small mammals in the arms of keepers in full uniform. Macaws and cockatoos sat on the shoulders of others. Under the guidance of Head Keeper John Regan, Pandora, the young chimpanzee who was born at our zoo, wheeled the stuffed penguin across the stage in a toy wheelbarrow. The hundreds of children in the audience screamed with delight.

Rani was saved for last. He walked quietly on stage with Jule holding his leash, and then looked at the sea of juvenile faces from which a shrill, earsplitting wave of noise was emanating. That did it. Obviously frightened, he dropped to the floor, and remained there until Fred and Dan Mannix carried him across the stage and into the wings. There he quickly recovered, although he remained nervous. While all that was going on, I made my way through much impedimenta around the back of the huge musical shell in which the world-famous Philadelphia Orchestra performed. I thought my help might be needed. I saw that Jule was holding Rani's leash, but at that very moment someone opened the stage door from the outside and Rani, with Jule hanging on desperately, streaked out onto Locust Street. Fortunately, he stayed on the sidewalk and thus avoided the peril of passing traffic.

There was a ground-level parking lot immediately behind the Academy of Music, and in it stood a station wagon, a type of vehicle in which Rani was accustomed to riding. With great presence of mind, Jule opened the door, and he leaped inside. By sheer luck the car was ours, Isabelle's and mine, so there was no problem. No irate car owner to complain.

On another occasion, Rani appeared on a television show in downtown Philadelphia. The Mannixes brought him to the zoo afterward, and asked me if I would look after him while they toured the zoo and then went out to do some errands before returning to their suburban home. So I had the beautiful cheetah's company in my office for several hours. He was completely housebroken. We merely shut the door so he wouldn't wander into the hall. Mostly he reclined quietly on the floor, but he occasionally got up, put his paws on the windowsill and peered out. He also would walk over to my desk chair so I could scratch his ears and pat his head. Two or three times my secretary buzzed me to let me know I had visitors. After I picked up the phone and learned who the visitors were, I told her to send them in. Imagine their surprise on finding a large leopardlike cat waiting to greet them. Any fear they may have had was instantly dispelled, however, and they were soon scratching Rani's ears as I had been doing. Meantime, no doubt, they were thinking of what they would tell their friends about their unusual, exciting experience in my office.

The Greenhall-Conant Feud

Arthur M. Greenhall was a longtime good friend. I first met him while he was a graduate student at the University of Michigan at Ann Arbor and I was employed by the Toledo Zoo. He was slim and dapper, of medium height, and reminded me a bit of a dignified Charlie Chaplin. He had a deep interest in herpetology, and especially the Tropics. I admired him because he had accompanied Raymond L. Ditmars to Panama on several field trips, for which he paid his own expenses. I saw Arthur many times at Ann Arbor, and he made a number of trips to Toledo to see me.

One weekend, when he was free from schoolwork, he came to Toledo and discovered that I was about to depart to attend a special meeting of the Toledo Naturalists Association at Port Clinton, Ohio. He asked if he could go along with me, and my response was, "Sure. I'll be glad to have company." We were served a banquet, which was followed by a boring, long-winded speaker. Without thinking, I reached into my coat pocket and fished out a small metal object I had forgotten was there. Someone had given me a palmist's symbol of a human hand, divided by grooves on the palm side that delineated the several parts that fortunetellers used to point out various characteristics. I was idly looking at it as the speaker droned on, when my nose began to itch. I used the metal hand to scratch, with the thumb touching the skin of my nose and the rest pointed right at Arthur. He smiled and then almost broke into convulsions as he sought to deaden the noise in his napkin. Inadvertently I had thumbed my nose at him. On our way home we both had a good laugh about it.

That was the start of the long-lasting Greenhall-Conant feud. The next time I was in Ann Arbor, I returned to my car from visiting the Museum of Zoology and found a piece of paper stuck under my windshield wiper that bore a drawing of a hand with the thumb at right angles to the rest. It happened again later, and I reciprocated by enclosing similar drawings every time I wrote to Arthur. The nonsense continued even after he left Ann Arbor. Two grown men acting like a couple of schoolboys, but we each had many chuckles about it.

Arthur departed for yet another trip to Panama, and I obtained his address either from him or Ditmars' secretary. I had a bright idea that was to end in an unexpected saga. I bought a pair of white work gloves, stuffed one with straw so the thumb stuck out stiffly, found a suitable stout box, nestled the glove in tissue paper, and mailed it to him in Panama. As luck would have it, he was far out in the field when my box arrived, but since a

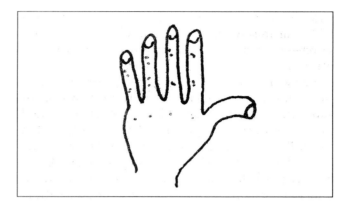

A postcard message from Arthur Greenhall.

runner was being dispatched with accumulated mail and required supplies, my package went along. How far the runner had to travel by canoe and through swamps and jungles to find Arthur I never learned, but he made delivery out in the wilderness. By sheer chance Arthur received it on his birthday!

It was a long time before he got even with me. He worked at several zoos—including Detroit and Portland, Oregon—before finally obtaining a permanent berth at a zoo associated with the Royal Victoria Institute Museum in Port-of-Spain, Trinidad, where he served for many years. We kept in touch sporadically, but one day he arrived unannounced at my office in Philadelphia carrying a sizable parcel. After exchanging greetings and chatting for a few moments, he told me to open the package, which he had plunked down on my desk. Inside was a flower pot full of dirt into which Chinese back scratchers had been thrust. A dozen carved hands surmounted the whole. He had given me "a pot of palms," as he put it. I still have one of the back scratchers. The last time I saw Arthur, back in the 1970s when he was at the National Museum in Washington studying vampire bats, he greeted me with another of his drawings of a hand on a small piece of paper.

Where's the Cobra?

The day the cobra disappeared, many decades ago, is one I'll never forget. Pete Branca, the keeper in the Philadelphia Zoo's reptile house, and I had to find and catch it.

A business appointment had taken me into town for lunch, and, when I returned, Pete was frantically trying to get in touch with me. An Indian cobra, one of the most deadly residents of what we facetiously called "Murderer's Row," had vanished from its cage. Pete had wisely cleared the old building of visitors, but it was with real misgivings that the two of us began our search—every nook and cranny was a potential lurking place.

First we inspected the cage. Nothing seemed amiss—the lock was in place, and there were no breaks or gaps anywhere through which even a snake could make its way. We soon convinced ourselves the cobra was still inside the cage, but how could it have penetrated the seemingly tiny chinks in the rockwork that had been installed many years previously by the WPA, under Dr. Macdonald's direction, to suggest a natural habitat background? Figuratively and literally we could leave no stone unturned. So, with hammers and cold chisels, we went to work on the rock pile. Half an hour later we knew where our missing cobra was—in the rocks, but gliding ever downward ahead of us in the honeycomb of stone and mortar. It took another half hour to reach the bottom of the pile, catch the snake, and transfer it to another cage. Then two tired and freely perspiring men sighed with relief and sat down to catch their breath.

That adventure reinforced a basic tenet I have observed ever since I took my first zoo job way back in the 1920s. Never touch anything alcoholic until the day's work is done. I had refrained during the lunch meeting, and was glad I did. It also taught me to do any and all cage decorations myself or to inspect every potential serpent's den personally and with great care before a snake was moved in.

Snakes have an uncanny knack for finding openings through which to escape and, if the full truth were known, there is probably no zoo in the world (which exhibits serpents) that has not had one disappear, at least for a while. That possibility has caused several zoo directors or boards of management to restrict their respective collections to nonvenomous species. In Hawaii, which has no terrestrial snakes except the harmless and diminutive introduced Braminy blind snake, *Ramphotyphlops braminus*, the Honolulu Zoo was long prohibited from having snakes of any kind. That regulation was subsequently relaxed, however, to permit a single male each of two different nonvenomous species to be exhibited, a policy that is still in force, as I recently reconfirmed.

We had our troubles in the old reptile house at the Philadelphia Zoo, which was perennially in need of repair. In newer buildings, including the one I designed in collaboration with the architects and which was opened in 1972, the keepers' work passages behind the scenes are sealed off from the public. But, through human error, snakes do get out at rare intervals.

Hound Dawg

August 2, 1960, was a hot, sunny day on the Chihuahuan Desert. By late afternoon we were looking for a place to park our brand-new Volkswagen Kamper for the night. We had entered Mexico at Piedras Negras, opposite Eagle Pass, Texas, during the morning, and had spent the day searching for streams and ponds, even as far away as beyond Múzquiz, without much success. In the early evening we returned to a place near San Juan de Sabinas where the road passed over a small dam across the Río Sabinas. It looked promising for investigation after dark. There was a grove of trees nearby and, to quote from Isabelle's diary,

> In the shade was a juke-joint, a sort of poor man's nightclub where one can drink beer or Coke and dance to canned music, all of it the Mexican version of rock 'n roll. It was pretty awful, but we expected that after dark people would go home and the music would cease. The manager said it would be O.K. for us to camp nearby, so we pulled up on a level spot as far away from the jukebox as possible, maybe a hundred yards. We kicked away tin cans, broken bottles, and other litter, got out the stove, and cooked dinner.

It was dark by the time we finished eating, and I knew I had better get out along the river as quickly as possible while the water snakes were becoming active. So I donned my boots, strung snake bags through my belt, and apologized to Isabelle for leaving her with all the mess to clean up. She was well aware of water snake habits, however, and urged me to get going. The collecting was good. I found two species, the blotched and diamond-backed water snakes, as well as several frogs. A boy joined me, and I sent him with money to rent a rowboat from the manager. We crossed the small pond created by the dam, and headed for a swampy area where I could hear cricket frogs calling. I managed to catch a few, despite the very bright moonlight that doubtless enabled them to detect me as I approached. All of this took time, and it was well after 10:30 P.M. when I returned to our car, well satisfied with the evening's catch.

While I was gone, poor Isabelle had heated water, washed and dried the dishes, and stowed everything carefully away. Then she made up our beds for the first time in the field, which took far longer than it did later, after she was well-practiced with that chore. She was handicapped by the darkness, although the moonlight, filtering down through the trees, helped some. She didn't dare turn on the inside car lights for fear of running down the battery. We hadn't yet unpacked our propane-powered lantern, which was buried under other equipment. Although she was cheerful, as she always was with me, she couldn't help but complain when I returned, saying, "I only finished a short time ago. It's so awfully dark that I had to feel my way along."

I looked at her and said, "Why don't you take off your sunglasses?" After she recovered from the shock of realizing she was still wearing them, we both had a good laugh. But it didn't last long. The blasted jukebox was still loudly blaring away. What was worse, it kept repeating the same recording over and over again. It must have been meant to attract anyone who passed along the road, but there was no traffic, and I had seen only two customers when I passed the cantina-pavilion earlier. After putting up with the noise for a while longer I walked over, bought a couple of bottles of beer so the manager, who was then all alone, would have a bit of business, and asked him if he could turn down the music. As a special favor he silenced the speaker nearest our side of his place, but not the one aimed at the road. We finally got to sleep. The noise ceased during the night, but it started again at dawn. It wouldn't have been so bad if the tune had been melodious. We both grew up in the big band era and, like many of our contemporaries, we disliked rock and roll.

What was the record played ad nauseum? A Mexican shouting Elvis Presley's "Hound Dawg" in Spanish.

Flea Palaces

During the early 1930s I spent much time in the field assembling material and information for my "Reptiles of Ohio," which was first published in 1938. I traveled all over the state with a variety of companions. Two who were often with me were Malcolm Kenneth Murphy, a chap older than I was and who was greatly skilled in catching water turtles, and Barney Gardner, a lad of 14 or 15 who was adept at overturning rocks and logs and finding snakes and other herps beneath them. One spring weekend, after a strenuous day and evening, we sought a place to sleep in the tiny Ohio River town of Gallipolis, and took a room in the only hotel we could find. It turned out to be a flea palace. The only way to escape the ravenous insects was to get into bed, crush the pests on our legs between our fingernails, and hope the tormentors would stay on the floor. They didn't. They were already in the bedding, and we couldn't shake them out. They wakened us at intervals all through the night, and we must have been a haggard and sorry-looking trio when we hunted up the only

restaurant in town that was open soon after dawn on a Sunday morning. We were the only customers.

Murph and I had the standard ham and eggs and a hot drink, but Barney, with the perversity of a teenager after a bad night, couldn't make up his mind. The waiter, who obviously was also the cook, pointed out the items on the short menu, but with no success. He then suggested some fruit, and, after considerable hesitation, Barney finally announced that he guessed he could eat half a cantaloupe. But instead of going to work on it right away, he just sat and stared at it. After a few minutes he asked if there was any ice cream. The waiter nodded in the affirmative, and then Barney asked, "What kind ya got?" "Vanilla, chocolate, and neapolitan," came the reply. "What's neapolitan?" After having it explained to him, Barney said, "I think I'll take that."

Meantime, Murphy, whose nerves were still a little raw, glared over at the half melon with its scoop of fancy ice cream, and said, "Ye gods, what a mess! Why don't you pour some ketchup on it?" "Good idea," replied Barney, suddenly coming to life, whereupon he did just that and ate the conglomeration with gusto.

Many years later, Isabelle and I were on our way for fieldwork in Mexico. It was a very long and tiring drive from our home in New Jersey to the international border. We averaged 300 miles or more every day but, even though we were using our Volkswagen Kamper, it was far easier and quicker to stop at motels at night than to try finding a suitable campsite. I remembered the night, decades earlier, when Barney and I tried to find a place to park my old Chevy somewhere in Chillicothe, Ohio, while we slept in the car. The police took care of that by making us stay right in front of the station house where they could keep an eye on us.

Isabelle and I, who took turns at the wheel, had put in a long day, and we were anxious to stop for the night. Let me quote, with minor emendations, from her diary entry for Sunday, August 13, 1961:

We reached Nacogdoches, Texas, at 9:15 P.M. and found motels scarce. The best one had no vacancies, but we looked at two more and chose the one that seemed the less ancient. It was reasonably priced and looked O.K., so we moved in. We had made a mistake. The place was infested with tiny fleas. At first we thought we might have picked them up when we stopped in a wooded area to exercise a bit and to look for specimens earlier in the day. We bug-bombed the car with our pyrethrum spray, the room, and our clothes. The pests remained very numerous in the room, however, so we decided we were not responsible. The place was simply "lousy." The fleas seemed only to get on our lower legs, so we brushed them off and leaped into bed. The real problem came in the morning—how to get out without taking any fleas with us. We dressed in our shorts so we could knock off any that clung to our legs. Apparently we were successful, as we found only two after we were under way. For us this was a unique experience. We've fought all kinds of bugs in our travels, but never fleas before. We renamed Johnson's Motel the Villa Pulgas ("fleas" in Spanish).

The only saving grace was a hilarious bedside lamp. An old standing telephone had been wired with a pipe attached that had a bulb and shade sitting on top of it. My genius of a husband discovered how to turn on the light. Quite simple. Just lift the receiver! The curiosity was funny in itself, and we giggled over it and practiced turning the light on and off. But Roger had me in hysterics when he settled down to sleep. He said, "When you're through talking, hang up!" I laughed so hard I couldn't say "Good-bye," but I hung up and the light went out.

The inventor (tinkerer?) who had changed a telephone into a lamp must have had great fun when he did it. We wished he had addressed some of his ingenuity toward battling fleas instead.

The Geographer

My earliest exposure to geography came during the First World War. There was a map every day on the front page of the newspaper showing the position of the trenches in France. There were occasional other maps, and I began cutting them out of papers and magazines. My father, noting my keen interest, bought me a small atlas, and that was followed by a jigsaw puzzle, copyright 1915, of the United States with each state cut out along its own boundaries. There were exceptions among the small ones. The five lower New England states and Long Island, New York, were on one piece, New Jersey and Delaware were attached to Pennsylvania, and Maryland and West Virginia to Virginia.

How do I remember all this? Acting on a hunch, as I started writing this, I rummaged through a back corner of my library, and there I found the jigsaw map in two boxes bearing my mother's handwriting. What's more, not a single piece was missing. Maps of the U.S. possessions were printed around the border—Alaska, the Hawaiian Islands, Porto (not Puerto) Rico, and the Philippine Islands. In my youth I could put the map together in far less than a minute, and I could even assemble it face down. At first that presented a slight

problem, because Colorado and Wyoming are both the same size and shape. I soon remedied that by putting a tiny spot on the back of Wyoming that is still visible three-fourths of a century later. How nostalgic it was for me, as I put the map together again, possibly for the last time, one morning near my eighty-fourth birthday.

I knew the states so well that I became a cartographer when I was six or seven. Mother found some fairly large sheets of paper, and I drew a map of each of the 48, added and printed out the capitals, each approximately in its proper position, and then colored each map. I must have used up many crayons, because some of the maps were quite large. Mother was so proud that she had a clothesline show in our living room with all of them displayed, and she invited friends and neighbors in to admire my handiwork.

Oddly enough, none of my devotion to maps and geography rubbed off on my dear mother. She must have been exposed to the subject when she went to school, and doubtless passed the course, because she was a good student. But then she promptly forgot all she was taught. I realized later that geography and history bored her, and I soon learned not to ask her questions on those topics, because they invariably embarrassed her. Grandma trained her and her three sisters to be housewives. In those days there were few professional opportunities for women. Mother was an excellent cook, a good seamstress, and a tidy housekeeper, and she had ample time to be a tutor and pal for her young son, her only child.

I must have been in about second grade when the teacher asked how many states we could name. Two other youngsters were called on first, and they managed to think of about 10 or so between them. Then it was my turn, and I rattled off all the rest, or so I thought. But the teacher mentioned two I had missed, and that upset me. So I promptly memorized them in alphabetical order. I can still recite them that way, but with a little hesitancy, since I must remember to insert Alaska and Hawaii in their proper places.

My own children, Skip and Susan, learned the states quickly, and I invented a game that helped to keep them from getting restless on long motor trips. I gave them each a blank outline of the United States, and, when they saw a license on an automobile from a different state they had to fill in the state in question on their own maps. At first we had a key map with all 48 labeled for reference, but soon the children were on their own. It worked like a charm, it was educational, and it included the stimulus of competition. At every rest stop they looked at all the parked cars before going to the bathroom. I recommend the game to harassed parents traveling with school-aged children.

My interest in geography enabled me to become a good zoogeographer, a student of the distribution of wildlife, and it helped me with my zoo work and as a herpetologist. There are no tigers in Africa, for example, and no penguins in the North Polar regions. Rattlesnakes occur only in the Americas, cobras only in the Old World. What's more, I studied the reasons for what seemed like peculiar patterns. I welcomed the universal acceptance of plate tectonics in the 1960s, which did so much to explain seeming anomalies.

My dear, saintly mother was worried about us during one of our long Mexican trips. Isabelle and I arrived in La Paz, near the southern tip of Baja California, after a miserable time aboard the tramp steamer *Mexicali*. We went to the local post office, and found several letters for us, including one from Mother. It read, in part, "We've just been watching television and saw the awful hurricane that hit the coast of Georgia. I hope it's nowhere near you."

She had addressed the letter to La Paz, which was thousands of miles from Georgia—across the Gulf of California, the full width of Mexico with its two high mountain ranges, one east and one west, the Gulf of Mexico, and part of the southern United States. We couldn't refrain from laughing, even though we were well aware of Mother's total ignorance of geography. I wrote back saying, "Don't worry. We are a long way from the hurricane." I never had the heart to tell her how silly her statement sounded. Yet, despite her aversion to the subject, she carefully saved my puzzle map, and she gave it to me when she began to fail during her old age.

Some people really dislike geography, and that I understand, but I am dumbfounded by the lack of knowledge of young people of today. Have they completely stopped teaching the subject in most schools? According to the polls and tests conducted annually, we seem to be bringing up generations of geographical illiterates!

All in the Line of Duty

Because of my association with zoos, I was often called on for advice, special activities, and even emergencies. Many are mentioned in the chapters about the zoos where I worked, but a few others are worth recording.

Take the case of Clarabelle. She was a trained sea lion and one of the stars of the popular Baby-Pet Zoo, which was closed during the winter months. The young chimpanzees received off-season care from Keeper John

Isabelle playing ball with Clarabelle. One winter the trained sea lion occupied an empty pen in the elephant house. Photo by Riccardi.

Regan, but who was going to look after Clarabelle? Her several tricks, such as balancing a ball on her snout, tossing it to someone, and, when it came back, catching it again on her snout, all had to be practiced at least two or three times daily lest she lose her skill. We wanted her to be sharp and ready to take the stage again in the spring. We solved that problem by having maintenance men install a sizable pen and a large tub, in which she could almost completely submerge, in the basement of the Philadelphia Zoo's service building. My office was on the second floor. A keeper came in once a day to swab up.

Isabelle and I volunteered to keep Clarabelle in trim, and we took turns walking down the many steps to the basement to put her through her paces. After each rehearsal we threw her two or three fishes as a reward. That was well before our marriage, and we were on a six-day week with different days off, so Clarabelle did not miss a single rehearsal.

There was only one problem. How, in the days before modern detergents, did you get the smell of raw fish off your hands in order to greet a distinguished guest a few minutes later? Rubber gloves seemed like a good solution, but our very money conscious zoo director refused to spend the money. What? Buy two pairs of gloves, of different sizes? We were just piqued enough to stick with soap and water.

Once, I had to appear in court as an expert witness. Like many other teenaged lads, a boy had a small collection of harmless pet snakes in the basement of his home, which was a unit in one of the innumerable row houses that characterized much of Philadelphia. All went well until a large black rat snake escaped and crawled through an opening for a pipe into the house next door. When it was discovered there, pandemonium broke loose. The luckless serpent was slaughtered, and it didn't take the neighbors long to discover where it came from. They filed a complaint against the boy's parents for maintaining a "dangerous public nuisance" in a private home.

The snake collection was given to the zoo, and I was asked to do what I could to ease the tense situation. When the hearing came up in magistrate's court, I was summoned to appear, and I testified that no venomous snakes were involved. The case was dismissed. The snakes had been removed, and nothing dangerous had been present, anyway. The family was given a stern warning, however. What was I paid as an expert witness? Nothing. All I received was the knowledge that I had befriended a lad who joined the Junior Zoological Society of Philadelphia and later became one of its active members.

One day there was an emergency in Camden, just across the Delaware River. A monkey had severely bitten someone, and the family wanted to get rid of it as quickly as possible. There was no Animal Control Department in Camden, and the family didn't want to call the police for fear that their pet would be shot. Because I lived in New Jersey and passed through Camden on my way home, I volunteered to pick up the monkey. I took a portable cage with me and, in case I had a problem, a stout net and a pair of very heavy leather gloves.

The people lived in a row house. They had bought a cute little monkey a few years previously, but it had grown large and dangerous. Someone had built a spacious cage for it against the wall of a room, and the monkey was fed, watered, and petted through the stout wire of the enclosure. The floor was also of wire, and cleanup was achieved by mopping or wiping up whatever soaked through the newspapers spread on the floor below the cage. The odor was pretty bad. In any event, I was confronted by a large male rhesus monkey with sharp canine teeth and a nasty temper. Probably I should have waited for help, but I studied the situation and thought I could manage. We opened the cage door a crack, and the monkey rushed at me, but I confronted it with the steel hoop of the net and yelled at the same time. It retreated and cowered on the cage floor, where it was easily netted. With my heavily gloved hands, I encircled its neck and put it in my cage, which a member of the family pushed shut as I gingerly withdrew my hands. They knew how dangerous the monkey was. One of the younger members of the family had been badly bitten while trying to pet it.

The zoo had no need for such a monkey, and we disposed of it to an animal dealer. We had, however, earned the gratitude of a beleaguered family and chalked up another bit of favorable public relations for the zoo.

When the old Philadelphia Aquarium, long a landmark on the east bank of the Schuylkill River just beyond the dam below Boat House Row and not far from the zoo, was closed, a commercial chain, the Aquarama, stepped in to fill the gap. The company erected a large building in South Philadelphia that was a real showplace. On November 27, 1962, a short while before it was opened, Frank Powell, the director, asked me if I would stop in to give him some advice about a large anaconda that had just arrived.

Isabelle and I had planned a big evening, and she had come in to the zoo with me that day. We had changed into informal party garb before the call came. So, in the late afternoon, we drove down to the Aquarama in all our finery. Frank took us to see a large, circular tank, open at the top and with glass sides around which spectators could circulate while looking at a fine display of large fishes. Frank said, "My curator, who is a good showman, wants to put a 12-foot anaconda in that tank as a special feature. I don't know anything about snakes, and I'm a little worried about it."

My immediate reply was, "It won't work, Frank. An anaconda cannot live permanently in water. It needs a large place to haul out and, besides, it would be out with the public in no time."

"That's what I thought," he said. "Would you like to see the snake?" I replied in the affirmative, and he led us to a heavy, cube-shaped wooden crate that measured over two feet in all directions. He summoned a man with a hammer and crowbar to pry open the lid. Inside was a large anaconda, one of the great constricting snakes, and it almost completely filled the box. It was lying quietly, with its head atop its coils, and I leaned over to have a better look. Just then there was a loud, unexplained shout, and we all turned to look for its source. I must have inadvertently moved my left hand, because the snake struck and grabbed it in its capacious mouth. Experience and self-control saved me. I held perfectly still, and within a few seconds the snake opened its mouth, freed me, and pulled its head back into the box, which the attendant slammed shut. The normal instinct would have been to yank away, but that could have resulted in many deep lacerations from the big serpent's long, sharp teeth. If I had not kept my cool I would have had a nasty bite. As it was, I had a series of puncture wounds which produced a flow of blood.

The Aquarama people were really upset: "Ye gods, it bit you!" "Let me send for a doctor." "Shall we call an ambulance?" "What should we do?" Isabelle and I were the only calm persons in the group.

I told them not to worry. I squeezed the puncture wounds to make them bleed more, thus hoping to wash out any possible infection. Then I held my hand under the cold-water tap, and the bleeding quickly ceased. After drying my hand with a clean paper towel, I applied iodine and had them bandage my hand with a roll of gauze from their first-aid kit. I suffered no ill effects except for a sore hand for a few days. Frank Powell was more convinced than ever that he wanted no anaconda in the big tank.

Isabelle and I went to dinner and then to the Latin Casino, where we were entertained by Earl "Fatha" Hines and his all-star Dixieland band, featuring the incomparable trombonist Jimmy Archey. We had brought along a record that they had made at the Hangover Club in Chicago a few years previously, and a copy of which my close friend and colleague Howard K. Gloyd had given us. The band members knew Gloyd as an outstanding tympanist, and they all autographed the record for us. I still have it. We had a marvelous evening. The only trouble was that I had to resort to gestures and cries of "Bravo." My hand was too sore to applaud in the usual way.

Los Coronados: Mexico's Northernmost Offshore Islands

We decided to play hooky. Isabelle and I were in San Diego attending the annual meeting of the American Society of Ichthyologists and Herpetologists. That was simple enough, but I was also the organization's secretary, and I found myself with a discouragingly large pile of scribbled notes when the formal sessions ended. I had to get them into presentable condition to send to my secretary back at the Philadelphia Zoo. Isabelle and I would be heading far south into Mexico almost immediately for the first of our field trips sponsored by the National Science Foundation. I knew nothing of shorthand, and jim-dandy tape recorders had not yet come into general use, so I had many hours of work ahead of me. I should have paid attention to duty, but, instead, off we went, adventure-bound, on a short cruise, no less. We had signed up for a postmeeting trip many weeks in advance.

Carl L. Hubbs, the doyen of ichthyologists and then with the Scripps Institution of Oceanography at La Jolla, California, had arranged for a small fleet of boats to take a group of us to a tiny archipelago in Mexican territorial waters. The herpetologists would be put ashore to hunt for reptiles, and the ichthyologists would anchor nearby to pursue their aquatic interests.

Isabelle recorded the details in her diary, as she always did when we were on trips (and even at home), and I have supplemented my memories with quotations from her writing, like the following:

The boat trip to Los Coronados—seven miles off the Mexican coast and just below the international boundary—was scheduled to leave at 8:00 A.M. We were on time, but there inevitably were stragglers. Three boats were in the flotilla—the Orca *which could carry 40 people, a smaller vessel called a T-boat, and a still smaller one of cabin cruiser size. We were assigned to the* Orca. *We soon sighted Los Coronados. There are four islands, one north, two middle (all small), and one south much larger and the only one on which it is possible to land. About 20 people wanted to go ashore. We boarded the smallest vessel, after the* Orca *anchored in a lagoon on the north side of the south island, then transferred to a skiff, with outboard motor, which had been lowered from the deck of the* Orca. *The skiff took in six of us at a time to the beach—actually a rocky ledge—and we all had to jump ashore. A large building dominated the spot. It had been planned originally as a hotel, but had never been finished. It was occupied by the Mexicans who were there to guard the island and protect the sea lion and elephant seal rookeries.*

There was a garrison of about six soldiers, all with their wives and families. That, we were to learn later, was a common practice wherever small groups of Mexican military men were stationed in out-of-the-way places. How could they manage without their *señoras* to cook for them?

Once all 19 of us were ashore, with a lunch provided by the *Orca's* galley, the *jefe* (the "chief," but actually a corporal or sergeant) appeared and asked for our papers. Dr. Hubbs had given us a copy of his collecting permit, so we were prepared, or so we thought. The document was in Spanish, of course, and when he read it, the *jefe* told us that it was for marine life only and we would either have to leave or stay on the shoreline! A couple of us who knew a little something of his language tried to plead with him, but to no avail. Finally, we asked him if we could eat our lunch in a better place. He grudgingly agreed and escorted us to a flat, fairly shady place behind the building.

We tackled lunch almost at once, even though it was quite early. As we ate, we looked longingly upward at the steep hill above us. What manner of herps lived up there? The lunch was enormous, and we suspected that the ship's cook had given us everything that was left over after he had provided for all the other "voyagers." We had something like eight loaves of bread, almost a gallon of mayonnaise, a huge bag of lettuce, an abundance of sliced ham and cheese, and a big basket full of assorted fresh fruits. After we had eaten, the pile looked almost as high as it had when we started.

Suddenly I had an idea. With two other men, we gathered up all the food that was left, made our way into the building, and soon found the chief's quarters. He was absent, but his *señora* was there, and she gratefully accepted our burdens, which we called, in proper Spanish fashion, a *regalito* (a small present). What a bonanza! They were isolated, and our gift of fresh food would be a welcome relief from the tortillas and beans that probably made up the bulk of their regular diets.

We rejoined our group, who were all sitting or lying sprawled out on the ground to rest until we were ordered back to the sheer rock shoreline. Presently the *jefe* appeared, a broad grin on his face. All regulations had been suspended, and he personally would guide us to wherever we wished to go!

Here Isabelle again takes up the tale:

The island is composed of several steep peaks and all the terrain is either up or down. We had to climb over the first ridge before the low scrub and cactus vegetation could be seen, because a few weeks ago the natives had burned the hillside to kill the snakes! They killed mostly lizards, as far as we could see, and it was heartbreaking to see so many "cooked" lizards lying around. The men managed to catch some of all five lizard species occurring there—four kinds alive and one "cooked." One of the women saw a rattler, but her calls were unheard by the hunters. We saw sea lions and elephant seals [on the narrow beach on the seaward side and far below]. We also had seen flying fish on our way across. The ichthyologists came back on the boats after 2:00 P.M., and we had to transfer from the land to the Orca *in the skiff and climb up a ladder dangling over the side to board the big vessel. On the way back I climbed to the crow's nest for a bird's-eye view, but saw no more flying fish or sea lions.*

Because we had been out of the country, the U.S. authorities at the dock on the mainland had to go through the formalities, but they settled on asking each one of us if we were American citizens.

It had been a wonderful excursion, and we had seen an offshore bit of Mexico that we never would have visited on our own. Also, thanks to the abundant provender, what might have been a difficult situation had a happy ending.

About my delinquency and dereliction of duty? We got up early the following morning, a Sunday, and with Isabelle's help and a rented typewriter, I roughed out the minutes of the meetings, inserting here and there lists and outlines given to me by other officers and committee chairmen. We didn't finish until 11:00 P.M., taking time out only for meals, but all was ready to mail before we left. My secretary put everything into readable shape while I was gone, and the results, much of it in small type, occupied 10 pages in "Copeia," the Society's journal, for 1959.

That's not the end of the story. Isabelle exposed four rolls of film while we were on the islands or going to or from them. Back in those days there was no profusion of places to have color film developed, and she had to send her rolls to the Eastman Kodak processing center. I think it was in Washington, D.C. The slides came back in due course, but every picture was bright blue with no other color discernible. Kodak sent us four new rolls of film to make up for their mistake, but there was no mention of subsidizing us to go back again. Worst of all, one of the sets of slides we received was of an all-blue family with young children visiting some such place as Fort Ticonderoga. Did they get her set of slides depicting blue lizards?

The Oldest Snake

A male ball python, *Python regius*, died of liver disease a few years ago at the Philadelphia Zoological Garden, after setting the longevity record for a snake of any kind. It was a serpent I knew well. In fact, I purchased it myself from Warren E. Buck, an animal dealer of Camden, New Jersey. Buck, who was no relation to the notorious Frank Buck, made more or less regular trips to West Africa, chiefly to what was then the French Cameroons, to collect mammals, birds, reptiles, and African artifacts for sale in the United States. The snake began its long residence at the Philadelphia Zoo on April 26, 1945. It was on exhibit in the old reptile house until that building was demolished in 1969 to make way for the erection of a much larger state-of-the-art structure on the same site. Thereafter, it was held behind the scenes in the new reptile house as an old-age pensioner until its death on October 7, 1992, after almost 47 and one-half years at the zoo. It was of young adult size when we received it, and it grew relatively little in length or weight after it was in our possession.

One Saturday in the late 1940s, the ball python disappeared from its cage. When the keepers reported its absence, we made a thorough search of the building,

The ball python, Python regius, *that lived in the Philadelphia Zoo for nearly 47 and one-half years. Photo by IHC.*

especially the passageways, which were sealed off from the public. The assumption was that one of the keepers had left the door open by accident. On rare occasions other harmless snakes had escaped, and once, during the late 1930s, a rainbow boa, *Epicrates cenchria*, was found after it had been loose in the old reptile house for more than a year. It was in excellent condition and evidently had thrived on the house mice that we tried unsuccessfully to eradicate. We used traps only, because I was firmly opposed to having poisons of any kind in a building where valuable livestock resided. So we didn't worry about the ball python. Eventually it would turn up. The old building was honeycombed with pipes and obsolete impedimenta in which a snake could hide indefinitely.

Two or three weeks later, again on a Saturday, a green tree boa, *Corallus caninus*, disappeared, and I became suspicious. I telephoned the newspapers and told them I suspected a "snakenapper" was on the loose. The Sunday papers published front-page stories about the missing reptiles, describing each in detail from information I gave them.

When I arrived at work the next day, Monday morning, the two missing snakes, an assortment of native species, a chastened boy, and his stern father were all waiting on the zoo's doorstep, so to speak. I escorted them to the reptile house, turned the livestock over to the keepers, and then took boy and father to my office. The latter was a Baptist minister, and the boy, who was under 16 years of age, had lied to him, stating that a friend had given him the two fancy snakes. The father, of course, was very upset and the boy contrite. As punishment his father decreed that he must give up his entire reptile collection.

The lad, of course, was the "snakenapper." He had

taken the two constrictors home by public transportation, secreted under his windbreaker jacket. Like a professional criminal, he had "cased the joint" in advance and discovered that, right after lunch, the keeper on duty went to the basement to stoke the coal fire with which the ancient structure was heated. So he had at least 15 minutes when zoo employees were not around. He also discovered that the door separating the public space from the keepers' room and passageways was unlocked, and he could get behind the scenes with ease. Thus the keepers, in part, were also at fault. They had strict orders to keep that door locked at all times. It was important to our security because, in those days, many of the cages containing nonvenomous snakes had tight catches but no locks.

I explained to the preacher and his son that the story about the missing snakes had become public knowledge, and I was obligated to let the papers know that the reptiles had been returned. In the hope of avoiding embarrassment to them, especially the father, I asked them to accompany me to the various newspapers, of which there were four or five at the time. I drove them downtown in my car, hunted up the city editor at each paper, and explained the circumstances. They all agreed that, since the boy was under 16, they would not use his name, nor would it be necessary to mention the name of the minister. The latter was greatly relieved. All the papers published the story and gave it an amusing twist. The cartoonist at one of them portrayed a small boy sitting in an elevated train with a rather large snake under his jacket.

So, all was well. We had our snakes back, including the ball python that was to live for so many additional years. Father and son remained anonymous. But there was a punchline yet to come.

The preacher, a few years later, was the person who united my son, Skip, and my daughter-in-law, Virginia, in holy matrimony.

Our Topsy-Turvy World

Have you ever visited the Southern Hemisphere? I address that question to those who have lived, as I have, most of their lives in North America, although it would be equally appropriate for residents of Eurasia.

We all know that the seasons in the two hemispheres are reversed. When it is winter with us, it is summer in southern latitudes. But did you ever stop to think that

Easter is celebrated in the autumn down there, and Christmas during the summer? No snow for Santa's reindeer! Even if you are aware of these things, you will be in for some surprises the first time you venture into the Southern Hemisphere. Let me tell you about mine.

In 1968 Isabelle and I spent many weeks in Africa, and we crossed the Equator in both Uganda and Kenya. The sun was directly overhead there, so we didn't notice any real difference, but when we were far down, in South Africa, I had my first surprise, and it was a stunner.

The weather had been cloudy and rainy, but that was good, because it brought out the frogs and I did a small amount of collecting of what, for me, was a brand new herpetofauna. I well remember my delight at finding my first live reed frog, *Hyperolius*. What a lovely little anuran, and so suggestive of some of our American treefrogs. I caught seven kinds of frogs and toads in all, including a few of the curious and amusing blaasops, or rain frogs, *Breviceps*, which, when alarmed, puff themselves up to resemble small, dark ping-pong balls with the snout and four legs protruding slightly. I was warned, however, to catch everything well out of water to avoid schistosomiasis, an often deadly infestation, common in the Tropics and Subtropics, that is caused by parasitic, elongated trematode worms, that live in natural ponds and puddles. By dint of buying plastic bags and paper towels, which I could wet and change frequently, I managed to get most of my catch home alive for the Philadelphia Zoo. All are now preserved in the collection of the American Museum of Natural History.

But I digress. To get back to my surprise, it was on the evening of November 3 when we were driven south from Pretoria by C. K. Brain, Director of the Transvaal Museum, who took us to his home, where his good wife served a supper for a gathering of herpetologists. I was delighted to meet Vivian F. M. FitzSimons, author of the authoritative "Snakes of Southern Africa," which had been published in 1962. The book was dedicated to his father, F. W. FitzSimons, one of the great pioneers in the study of snakes and their venoms. Also present was Wulf D. Haacke, an articulate, up-and-coming young man. We talked for quite a while after dining but, when we stepped outside to return to our hotel in Pretoria, the sky had cleared. I glanced up toward the stars and promptly blurted out, "Orion is upside down." Indeed it was, and it startled me to see that well-known constellation overturned. It was the first time I realized that viewing the heavens from far southern lands meant everything was in reverse. I confirmed that after returning home and studying my star charts.

In 1980 Kathryn and I were on a tour to the Antipodes, and our bus stopped near the entrance to Sydney, Australia's, spectacular bay. As we watched, a naval submarine was putting out to sea, but it seemed to be heading west, whereas I knew that the bay opened into the Pacific Ocean on the eastern side of Australia. How come? It took me a few moments to think and to turn around and face into the sun, which was to the north and not toward the south as it always was at home. When I was properly oriented the geography fell promptly into place.

While we were in Australia, Harold G. Cogger and his wife took us for a drive through the countryside and for an outdoor picnic lunch. He is the author and illustrator of the monumental work on the "Reptiles and Amphibians of Australia." As we rode along I mentioned my mixup in directions, and he told us that he had similar difficulties when he was traveling in the Northern Hemisphere. Everything was topsy-turvy to him.

Harold took us on a long, enjoyable ride from Sydney to the Hawkesbury River area, and there, at the Biological Station of Sydney University, we found a picnic table and benches. No sooner were we seated and enjoying the lunch Mrs. Cogger had prepared for us, than we were joined by three black-backed magpies and seven kookaburras that eagerly snatched and swallowed everything we discarded, even chicken bones. The kookaburra is a giant kingfisher, better known, at least in zoo circles, as the laughing jackass because of the raucous noise it makes. Some of them even perched on the edge of our table, literally at our elbows. It was a thrill for me to have them so close and so unafraid. Harold Cogger didn't share my enthusiasm, however, because one of them once played a dirty trick on him. He was photographing a rare reptile out-of-doors, and was just about to snap its picture, when an unseen kookaburra swooped down, seized the rarity, swallowed it, and flew away. What hazards a hardworking herpetologist must endure at times as he pursues his profession!

By the time we visited Java in Indonesia, in 1987, I was prepared in advance. We landed at Jakarta, the capital on the north side of the island, but we spent most of our time at Bogor, which was well to the south. When we returned to Jakarta, we were heading north and, as expected, the sun was in our faces as we drove along. Java is not far south of the Equator, but enough so that we experienced conditions as they exist for residents of the Southern Hemisphere.

Uncle Hal

The following amusing essay about an eccentric relative is a contribution from my son, Skip, who is a talented writer and raconteur.

*   *   *

Harold Conant, or Uncle Hal, was a free spirit who marched to his own drumbeat. He was actually my Dad's uncle and my great-uncle. I was often tempted to do this article for the *Reader's Digest's* "My Most Unforgettable Character," but never got around to it.

My earliest recollections of Uncle Hal were the letters I received when I was a young boy. They were half in prose and half in poetry, covering a variety of subjects, from his property acquisitions in New Hampshire and Massachusetts to philosophic discussions of life in general. The letters were absolute treasures and should have been saved, but unfortunately they weren't.

When I was 10 or 11 years old, a large package arrived just before Christmas from his home in Lexington, Massachusetts. It was addressed to me and contained, of all things, a live, young rooster. He had decided I needed a pet. The next few mornings my new pet awakened the family at two or three in the morning with his "cock-a-doodle-doo." Finally, the third day it disappeared, and I was told it had been taken to the zoo as a permanent exhibit. It wasn't until years later I found out my poor rooster provided hors d'oeuvres for a hungry boa.

I was probably 14 or 15 before I got to meet Uncle Hal for the first time. After that, there was an occasional visit, usually when he was returning from a winter in Florida.

However, one visit in particular stands out among all the others. I was in my early 30s at the time. My wife, Ginny, and I had four young daughters aged 11 down to 5. As I recall, it was a Saturday morning in mid-April when the phone rang. It was Uncle Hal. He was on his way home from Florida. Could he stop to see us? His brother-in-law, Harry, was with him.

Uncle Hal was in his mid- to late 70s at the time. His beloved wife, Mae, had passed away several years earlier. Harry had lived with Harold and Mae for many years.

Anyway, I told him, "Yes, we'd love to see you ... where are you now?" His answer was, "Just the other side of Baltimore." I then gave him directions to our house.

At that time there were no interstate highways, and travel time from the Baltimore area was about two and a half hours. Based on that, his ETA should have been about two in the afternoon. Well, two went, three went, dinnertime went, and still no Uncle Hal.

Harold A. Conant (arms akimbo) and his brother-in-law in front of the huge sandpiles left by the bulldozer that excavated the basement of Hyla Holler. Photo by IHC.

Ginny and I were supposed to play bridge with our neighbors that evening. At the time we couldn't afford babysitters, so an evening out was a few hours with our neighbors two doors away. We would call home every hour or so to make sure the girls weren't killing each other. Our date was for eight, so we decided to walk down and keep an eye open for Uncle from our friend's house.

When we were halfway down the block, we noticed an ancient car making its way up the street. Behind the car was a home-made trailer that was filled to overflowing with everything imaginable. It was a scene right out of the "Grapes of Wrath." A closer look revealed it was Uncle Hal and Harry. I managed to flag them down and directed them into our driveway. After the initial greetings, I asked them why it had taken so long. Well, it turned out that "the other side of Baltimore" was Frederick, Maryland, a good hundred miles to the west. I also found out later that Uncle Hal never drove over 35 miles per hour.

Shortly after arriving, Uncle Hal opened the back door to the car. The back seat was almost as bad as the trailer, but Hal managed to pull out an old suitcase. I asked him if it was his night things. He replied, "No, it's my money." It seems, when the banks failed in the late 1920s, he had lost some money, and never trusted the banks after that. From then on he carried all his cash, stocks, and bonds around in his old suitcase.

We offered Hal and Harry some dinner, but they had stopped to eat, and just wanted to go to bed. We got them settled for the night and proceeded to our neighbors for an evening of bridge.

Early Sunday morning I heard a tapping at the bedroom door. A glance at the clock showed it to be a little after six. Our kids used to like to romp in our bed Sunday mornings, and I figured it was one of the girls. Quickly throwing on a pair of slacks, I opened the bedroom door. It was Uncle Hal. "Can you give me a hand with my dogs?" he asked. "Your dogs?" "Yes, I have my dogs with me and they have to be fed."

Shaking my head, I followed him to the car. He opened the trunk and out bounced two large black and tan hound dogs. He quickly leashed them, but they still managed to drag him to the azalea bushes next door. Both lifted their legs and released a night's accumulation. I thought the bushes were going to die right in front of my eyes. Then, before I realized what he was doing, he had tied the dogs to two utility poles on our street. One was next door and the other was halfway down the block. Both dogs were now baying full-lung as if they had just treed a raccoon. I quickly explained to Hal we had to do something fast or the neighbors would be calling the police. We unleashed the two dogs and took them to my backyard where we secured them to two trees. Once they had been fed and watered, they laid down and went back to sleep.

With that, Uncle Hal said, "Good, now we can feed the cat." "The cat!" I exclaimed. After a little searching, he found the cat's cage buried under all the junk in the trailer. He cautiously opened the door, but the cat was too fast and shot out of the cage like it was jet-propelled. It headed down the driveway and up the street with the two of us in hot pursuit. I was amazed how fast Hal could move for a man in his 70s. The cat finally turned down the driveway two doors up, but by the time we got there, it had disappeared off the face of the earth. After looking around for a couple of minutes, we heard the cat meowing. It had crawled up through one of the cars parked in the driveway and was under the hood. With that, Hal headed up my neighbor's sidewalk toward the front door. "Hal, where are you going?" "I've got to have this fellow open his hood so I can get my cat." "Uncle Hal, it's 7:00 A.M. Sunday morning and nobody is up yet." With that, he went back to the driveway, crawled part way under the car, and lay there calling, "Here, kitty, kitty." Finally, the cat crawled out, somewhat greasy, but none the worse for wear.

By this time, Hal's slightly retarded brother-in-law, Harry, was up. He took an immediate liking to Ginny and followed her around the rest of the morning. In spite of having company, Ginny still had the chores of a housewife with four kids to attend to. She would be putting in a load of wash and hear footsteps shuffling up behind her. She would turn around and there would be Harry. "You're a nice lady," he would say. "You're like my sister, Mae . . . do you know my sister, Mae?" Or he would show Ginny the watch Hal had given him for his birthday. He must have shown Ginny that watch four or five times.

The girls fell in love with Uncle Hal. He told them funny stories and read to them. My observant second oldest daughter, Cathy, came to me and said, "Dad, he has a black shoe and a red sock on one foot and a brown shoe and green sock on the other foot." I explained to Cathy that Uncle Hal was not poor, but was thrifty. He hated to throw anything away that wasn't worn out.

We had a nice dinner together about 2:00 P.M. because Hal wanted to leave around 4:00 P.M. We were all in the driveway saying our goodbyes. I was standing on the driver's side when I noticed the folding top to a baby coach bolted over the top of the window. "Uncle Hal, what the heck is that for?" I asked. He explained that he liked to drive with his elbow and his arm out the window. However, on sunny days he often got badly sunburned on his elbow. On bright days he simply pulled the baby buggy top down and solved his sunburn problem. Now that's "Yankee ingenuity."

Uncle Hal continued to drive to Florida each winter until he was well into his 80s. He finally passed away in his early 90s. There were several other visits, but none quite as much fun as that first one.

I'm sure a long visit would have been trying for all of us, but the short visits were like a breath of fresh air in our regimented lives. Hal was indeed a free spirit who marched to his own drumbeat.

The girls are grown up now, but still talk about Uncle Hal from time to time. I, for one, will never forget this gentle soul nor the messages for life contained in his letters, and I certainly will never forget the hound dogs, the rooster, or the rest of his menagerie.

Roger Karl "Skip" Conant

* * *

Harold A. Conant was my father's brother. The two men were extremely unalike. For example, my father, whom I lost when I was 12, was always well-dressed, whereas Harold's appearance was what we would call "casual" nowadays. His wife, my Aunt Mae, kept a tidy household, but Hal's domain, the basement and workroom, strongly resembled Skip's description of the contents of the trailer he pulled behind his elderly car.

Hal's home was in New England, but he had a small shack in Florida where he spent each winter. He always used our place at Taunton as a waystop, even when he also visited my son and his family, and he came whether he was headed south or north. Once, long after he was widowed, he had to be hospitalized in Florida for a few days. He wrote me a letter and drew a map giving me detailed instructions on how to find and dig up his suitcase full of valuables, in case he should die. I could add much more, but it would be anticlimactic after Skip's excellent account of a memorable visit.

Herpetological Memories of a Day in Spain

Who would have thought our one-day excursion to the beautiful Mediterranean island of Mallorca would result in the acquisition of a herpetological specimen of exceptional interest?

During the autumn of 1967, Isabelle and I flew to Barcelona to attend an international zoo conference. At that time the airlines charged premium fares for overseas weekend flights, so, although the meetings didn't start until Monday, we elected to leave New York's John F. Kennedy Airport late the previous Thursday evening. Friday we spent sleeping and adjusting to jet lag, but by Saturday morning we were ready for sightseeing. After visiting a travel agency near our hotel, we found ourselves airborne again, this time to the port city of Palma on Mallorca (called Majorca by the English), the largest of Spain's Balearic Islands. There we spent a delightful late afternoon and early evening sitting in comfort on the outdoor balcony of our hotel room watching the movements of boats ranging from tiny sailing vessels and fishermen's craft to sizable liners. We were enthralled as the sun slowly sank and myriad lights appeared, seemingly everywhere.

In the morning we hired a taxi to take us for a tour of the island—as much of it as we could see in the relatively few hours available. Our driver regaled us in rapid-fire Spanish, but his Castilian accent and my lack of fluency in the language resulted in frequent misunderstandings. Like so many persons, Americans included, he resorted to shouting, apparently in the belief that loud words would better penetrate what he must have thought was my thick skull.

He took us first to the usual tourist stops—historic buildings and an old church, through which he led us to look at religious paintings. I soon convinced him that we were much more interested in the countryside, and presently we were passing through a region of wall-to-wall olive and almond plantations which rose in tiers

and were separated by a series of man-made rock walls. The ensemble reminded us of pictures of rice culture in the Orient on sloping hillsides. Except for seabirds, wildlife was conspicuously absent. Even wall lizards, of which there are so many kinds in the Mediterranean region, were missing. (I learned later that they were probably extinct on the island, although they still existed in numbers on smaller islets that had not been so badly disturbed by man.)

We eventually reached the north coast, and our driver obligingly stopped at numerous overlooks, some with ornate, even castlelike, watch towers where one could rest in the shade and quietly watch the sea. The water, despite its apparent considerable depth, was crystal clear, and we could easily see the bottom.

After a brief and singularly unappetizing lunch at the seaside Puerto de Soller, we headed cross-country back toward Palma. On the way we had to climb a small rocky ridge, and about halfway up I spotted a dead snake on the road. I asked the driver to stop, but he could see no obvious reason for doing so, whereupon I gave him a dose of his own medicine by shouting "*Alto*" (Halt) repeatedly at the top of my voice. He finally got the message, but not before the car had rolled a long way beyond the DOR serpent. I ran back and picked up a rather slender brown snake, about a foot and a half long, of a species I didn't recognize. It had been hit and killed, but it was in excellent shape, so I took it back to the car. The driver was unimpressed, but Isabelle asked me what I was going to do with it. I responded without thinking, "Pickle it, of course," and that set off an amusing and rather lengthy chain of events.

I instructed the driver to return to the hotel from which we had checked out in the morning, hoping to get ice to keep the specimen in good condition during our return to Barcelona. I explained my needs to the doorman, and he soon returned with a lowball glass with a couple of ice cubes in it, saying it was the best he could do. After putting the snake under the ice we drove to the airport while I held the glass clutched in my hand, meanwhile feeling like an idiot. Once arrived, we learned our plane would be late, so we sat in the main waiting room and bought ourselves a beer and a snack. That gave me an idea. I asked the bartender if he had an empty bottle I could have or buy. Nothing was available except beer bottles, so I told him what I wanted, and soon he and I were busily making ice chips by wrapping ice cubes in towels and pounding them with empty beer bottles. We filled our own bottle half full, and then I threaded the snake through its neck, much to the consternation of the barflies who had been watching us work. After piling in more ice chips, I gave the bartender a generous tip, we stashed the bottle in Isabelle's camera case, and we were back in our hotel in Barcelona soon after dark.

So far, so good, but how to keep the snake in good shape overnight? After all, it was Sunday, and all the stores were closed. Then I had an inspiration. I telephoned room service and requested that a champagne ice bucket be brought to the room—with ice but no champagne. In due course it arrived, and I, unwisely, put our beer bottle into it while the young waiter looked on. He was trained not to ask questions, but he lingered so long and his curiosity was so obvious that I volunteered the information that I had a small, dead, perfectly harmless snake that I wanted to preserve on the morrow. That did it. Soon every employee of the hotel knew what we had. Our room received special attention in the morning as a sizable parade of chambermaids and other attendants swept and washed, tidied up and vacuumed, wiped the walls and polished the mirrors as they sought to have a look at the crazy *Yanquis* with the snake. Despite their interest, most of them refused to look at the animal even when we offered to show it to them, although a few of the less timid were willing to view it from across the room.

Fortunately, word did not filter upward to the management. We were neither asked to leave nor told to get rid of the snake. It was just as well. We were staying at the Ritz, to which we had been transferred because the brand new Diplomatic Hotel, that was supposed to be the zoo conference headquarters, was not yet ready for guests. The Barcelona Ritz was just about as plush and tony as its namesake in Manhattan.

It was then that my real work began. In between conference sessions, I went to the local *farmacia* and, after explaining my purpose to the druggist, he sold me an ample supply of 90 percent ethyl alcohol and a hypodermic syringe and needle without even raising an eyebrow. (Imagine trying to buy grain alcohol in the United States without a prescription or permit! And how lucky I was that the drug craze had not yet swept through Europe and America. I have often wondered how quickly the police might have arrived, given today's circumstances.)

Back in the room, I quickly diluted the alcohol to approximately the proper strength and injected the snake, but then I realized I had nothing in which to put my, by then, well-earned specimen. So it was down to the street again, but this time to a grocery store where I bought a bottle of stuffed olives in a small, widemouthed bottle. Those I poured into the tumblers with which our bathroom was furnished, and put them on the mantelpiece. For the next two days Isabelle and I were nibbling olives every time we passed by.

At last my prize was taken care of, but I couldn't help feeling a little shamefaced about devoting so much time and energy to what probably was a common snake. But, after years of fieldwork in the United States and Mexico, I was an inveterate collector, and it was against my principles to abandon any amphibian or reptile that could be salvaged.

After the meetings were over, we left Spain for a tour of zoos in Switzerland and Germany. Our route took us to Zürich, Basel, Munich, Stuttgart, and Frankfurt, after which we headed homeward with a short stopover at London's Heathrow Airport.

In Frankfurt I had planned to meet Dr. Konrad Klemmer, an English-speaking colleague, at the famous Senckenberg Museum. After exchanging pleasantries and talking awhile about herpetology in general, I mentioned our find on Mallorca. Klemmer almost exploded. "What," he said, "you found a snake on Mallorca! Not a single snake has been taken on that island for more than a decade. You have a rarity indeed. I know, because I've been working on the herpetology of Spain for many years."

So I gave him the specimen, which he accepted with great thanks. It was an adult, measuring 550 millimeters in total length, of *Macroprotodon cucullatus*, a small rearfanged species that is widespread across northern Africa but which, in Europe, occurs only in the southern half of Spain and Portugal and on the Balearic Islands. Klemmer told me that it probably fed on the gecko, *Tarentola mauritanica*, which had managed to survive on Mallorca even though the wall lizards had disappeared.

Talk about luck! And how glad I was that I had persevered and brought home the bacon, so to speak. The snake is now number 64656 in the Senckenberg collection.

Zoo Visitors, Good and Bad

Despite our problems with hoodlums and vandals, the large majority of visitors to the Philadelphia Zoo were thoughtful and orderly, and some even did us real favors. They brought lost children to the office, put their trash in the containers we provided, and called the attention of guards and keepers to people who were feeding the animals.

Yes, we had to put up "No Feeding" signs. When the Philadelphia Zoological Garden, America's first fullfledged zoo, opened to the public on July 1, 1874, visitors *were* permitted to feed the livestock. They often brought edibles from home. That practice continued until the 1930s, when proper diets became the goal of the zoo's Penrose Research Laboratory (see "Research, Publications, and Other Zoo Activities"). Like children, many of the animals, notably the monkeys and apes, would stuff themselves on busy weekends with peanuts, popcorn, and other goodies and refuse to eat their scientifically prepared food the next day. At first we erected signs reading, "These animals are on a special diet. Please do not feed them." They were of little use. Visitors either didn't see the signs or failed to read them. Or they brazenly did as they pleased.

Some of the livestock was behind sheets of plate glass, notably in the monkey house, but that only protected them when they were indoors. During warm weather, when they were permitted to use their outside cages, the public could still bombard them with food. That's what prompted us to erect the high fence of small-mesh hardware cloth around the ape side of the building which, mercifully and most unexpectedly, was the flimsy barrier that prevented Bamboo, the big gorilla, from escaping into the zoo.

Eventually we had to get tough. "DO NOT FEED THE ANIMALS" appeared on signs all over the zoological garden, and we enforced it as best we could. Many an obstreperous rowdy was escorted out of the zoo for persisting in breaking the rule. As new exhibition buildings were designed, the use of glass panels to separate the animals from the public received major emphasis.

One of the kindest among all our millions of visitors was an elderly lady who brought us a real surprise. During 1937 we received two fully adult Komodo dragons, the largest of all living lizards, after nearly a year of negotiations and transportation. The government of the Dutch East Indies even then was protecting those wonderful reptiles, but a number were captured, under its supervision, for distribution to several zoos. They were rested and exercised at Batavia and Amsterdam en route, but they spent three and one-half months, waiting or on shipboard at sea, in crates scarcely larger than themselves. They had been fed on eggs, and that was all they would accept when they arrived in our hands. We wanted to switch them to a better diet, so we tricked them. We filled empty eggshells with the laboratory's meat mixture, which included all the ingredients of a good, healthy diet. By putting two stuffed halves together they resembled a whole egg. Our scheme worked, and the huge reptiles accepted the substitute diet at once. Because it was a good human interest story, I sent out a news release that was featured in all the newspapers. One mentioned that the zoo might be hard-pressed to get enough empty eggshells. Several of us brought shells from home for a week or two, but by that time the lizards were eating the mixture right out of a dish.

The two large Komodo dragons for which we needed dry, empty eggshells. Photo by Mark Mooney, Jr., Philadelphia Zoo archives.

Months later one of the keepers phoned my office and asked me to come to the reptile house. I arrived to find a lady with two big shopping bags full of eggshells she had carefully washed, dried, and saved for us. I thanked her profusely, praised her thoughtfulness, and gave her a number of free zoo passes for herself and her friends. The shells, of course, went into the garbage, but not until some weeks later, just in case she happened back to see how the dragons liked her gift.

Many kind persons donated animals to the zoo, most of them native species such as opossums and raccoons. Because the people had gone to a lot of trouble to bring their gifts to the garden, we usually accepted them, even though we might liberate them the very next day in suitable habitats. We could not take monkeys, however. Our space for them was limited, they would have to undergo a lengthy period of quarantine, and the chances were overwhelming that they would not be accepted by any established group of their own species. Fred Ulmer even wrote an article for our zoo publication entitled "So You Want a Pet Monkey?" He pointed out that cute, cuddly baby monkeys soon grow up into ferocious and highly dangerous adults.

Many reptiles and amphibians also were donated, very often to have us identify them. Many had been killed but were still preservable. Among the approximately 100 "copperheads" brought to the zoo during my 38-year tenure, only 2 really were. The others were milk, water, or hognose snakes, all of which superficially resemble the venomous species. The steady flow of herps was a gold mine for my studies, because the keepers or I carefully recorded the exact localities in which each had been found.

We normally sent or gave a pair of free passes to each

donor. That word got around, however, and one day a small group of young urchins, dirty and muddy, arrived at the gate, each bearing a tin can with a small salamander in it that they had found in Fairmount Park. They demanded free admission in exchange for their gifts. I was summoned, I thanked them, and decided from our conversation that they were earnestly interested and probably would not get into trouble in the zoo. So I let them in, but I warned them not to try the same subterfuge again.

Among bad visitors I include all those who stubbornly refused to abide by common sense and the policies we established for their own protection, as well as that of the animals. Two examples will suffice.

First, during the early 1970s the stupid fad of going barefoot everywhere developed among many teenagers. Some came to grief with cut, infected, or broken toes, and there were even amputations. Although we had disposed of soda pop bottles decades earlier, broken glass invariably appeared on the zoo walks on busy days. People brought fragile things from home, including babies' bottles that they dropped and left for us to sweep up later. So we placed signs at the gates indicating that shoes were required in the zoo. One Sunday a guard brought a barefooted girl to the office. When she paid her admission at the gate, her unshod condition was not noticed in the crowd. I carefully explained to her why we had the rule, that someone might sue us, and so on. She was arrogant and assured me that if I put her out she would scream and struggle all the way to the exit gate. To avoid an unpleasant scene, I finally typed out a release absolving us of any liability if she hurt herself, and I made her sign it. It probably had no legal standing, but hopefully it made her more cautious about where she walked.

Second, a group of four or five men arrived at the main gate on another Sunday afternoon. One of them was blind and he had his seeing-eye dog with him. The guards had stopped them because we had an ironclad rule that no dogs or other pets could be brought into the zoo. The sudden appearance of a dog frightened many of the zoo's residents, and pets could always bring infections or ectoparasites, such as fleas, into the animal collection.

I went to the gate and explained the reason for the rule. The dog could not come in. I was promptly told there was a city ordinance that permitted seeing-eye dogs to go anywhere. As a compromise I offered them a zoo automobile, driven by a uniformed chauffeur who would take them wherever they wished to go in the zoo. A burly spokesman called me an obstinate boob and worse, and told me I would hear from their lawyer the next morning. I kept my cool, but the speaker became

more abusive. We were at an impasse. Just then, one of the cashiers, who had been on a 10-minute break, passed the guardhouse and instantly sized up the situation. She stopped and said, "I think that dog needs a drink." She, bless her heart, found a bowl and filled it with water, and the dog eagerly lapped it up as she patted its head. One of the other members of the group said, "I guess they do take good care of their animals."

That did it. The dog remained in the guardhouse, the group rode in style at slow speed through the throngs of visitors, and I told the cashier to take the next day off as a reward for her quick thinking.

Language Problems

One morning while we were cooking breakfast, we discovered that "la casita" (the little house), as Isabelle called our Volkswagen Kamper, had a flat tire. We had camped for the night in Durango, Mexico, near the Río Nazas, along which I hunted repeatedly in search of water and garter snakes. I changed the heavy wheel with the flat on it and planned to have it fixed in nearby Rodeo. We had expected to stop there in any event, to pay our respects to Señor and Señora José Refugio de Fierro who had befriended us on previous visits to the little town. The notorious bandit Pancho Villa, we were told, had been born somewhere in the vicinity.

Mentally I prepared and rehearsed what I was going to say in Spanish to the mechanic in the small Pemex service station in Rodeo. I even checked our dictionary to make sure that the word for "tire" was *llanta*.

After stowing our gear we drove directly to the gas station, where I uttered my carefully rehearsed request to repair our flat tire. The reply was startling: "If it's got a tube in it, I can fix it." The swarthy Mexican was fluent in English, and he told us he had lived in Kansas for 30 years. He applied a hot patch, and we were soon on our way. Tubeless tires were relatively new, and many repair shops, even in the United States, did not yet have the special equipment for removing and installing them.

Twice when I was carrying on brief conversations in Spanish and struggling to remember the correct verb forms to use, the Mexicans asked, "Would you mind if we talked in English?" How unexpected to find someone who could speak our language far out in the boondocks of rural Mexico.

My Spanish never was fluent. I could almost always make myself understood, but I frequently had difficulty following rapid-fire responses. Isabelle watched their gestures, and often she was able to help me with details.

We studied Spanish together at home during the winter months, and she eventually became proficient enough to get along on her own when she was with the car and I was off hunting. As I read through her diaries, I often noted that Spanish popped up in them repeatedly. Our efforts to speak their language were much appreciated by the Mexicans, and we were often complimented on being able to converse, even though our efforts at best were amateurish. Sometimes my gringo accent was at fault, as when my order in a restaurant in Mexico City was misinterpreted for kidneys, which I detest.

During our "maiden" trip with our new Kamper in 1960, our 20-gallon tank of water lasted until we reached Saltillo, well down in Mexico. It had to be filled with potable water. Fortunately, the adjective "potable" is spelled the same way in both English and Spanish, but I guessed correctly that it was pronounced in the latter language with the accent on the penultimate syllable. I would need a hose with which to fill the tank, so I referred to our small traveling dictionary and saw that the word for "hose" is *calcetín*. At a Pemex gas station I asked them if they had *agua potable*, and I was assured that they did. Then I asked for a *calcetín*, but all I got was a blank stare. Off to one side was a hose for filling car radiators, so I pointed to it and asked what it was called in Spanish. The answer was "*manguera*." After replenishing our water supply, I went back to the dictionary, and looked in the Spanish section first. "*Manguera*" was indeed the word for a water hose, but what about *calcetín*? That was a sock (stocking)! The Mexicans had two words for the different kinds of "hose," but in English a single word doubled for two very different things. I had been confused, but I pitied the Spanish-speaking person who was trying to learn English, which we had been told was one of the most difficult of Occidental languages to master.

During World War II, when I was serving in the Volunteer Coast Guard, our commanding officer discovered that I knew a little Spanish, so I was delegated to talk with the sailors when necessary. Philadelphia was a neutral port, and we were often assigned to Spanish and Portuguese ships while they unloaded their cargos of cork, almonds, olives, and brandy. Most of the time I used the same few words: "*Se prohibe fumar*" (No smoking). Very often the seamen would sneak a few drags on a cigarette deep down in the holds or on the fantail. For security reasons smoking was strictly forbidden.

One day I was completely stumped. I had the day watch, and when I went on duty I noticed an American flag flying upside down on a Spanish freighter. For the life of me I could not think of how to say, "Turn it over." So I resorted to drawing two flags and pointed out that one was *correcto* whereas the other was not. The mistake was quickly rectified.

My worst faux pas occurred when I was the director of the Philadelphia Zoo. Kenneth G. Dills, our highly talented exhibits manager, was married to a charming and vivacious lady from Spain. One day she visited the zoo with their daughter who, as I recall, was not quite a teenager. I invited them all to have lunch with me in the zoo's small private dining room reserved for special occasions. After we finished eating, our conversation turned to Spanish food, and I mentioned that during several of the trips Isabelle and I made to Mexico, we visited a restaurant in Saltillo where we enjoyed roast *cabrito* (kid or young goat). They agreed that it was delicious when properly prepared. I then said, "Let's see if I can remember correctly. *Cabrito* is a kid, *cabra* is the adult female, and the male is a *cabrón*." Instantly there was a deathly silence, and neither Ken nor his wife would look at me. Ken quickly changed the subject.

I knew something had gone radically wrong, so I took Ken aside the next day and asked him what had happened. He replied that it didn't matter. He and María, his wife, had laughed about it later, and their daughter was too young to understand. I pressed him for an explanation, and he said that in Spain the word *cabrón* was strictly taboo and was never mentioned in polite company. "You see," he said, "over there, a *cabrón* is a man who rents out his wife as a prostitute."

Live and learn.

The Roast

A good subtitle for this remembrance would be "Cowboy Hats and Bolo Ties." They were my personal trademarks during my last decade or so of service at the Philadelphia Zoological Garden. My use of them evolved gradually. First, I was getting balder and balder, and it became imperative that I wear a hat. Ironically, it was at just about the time when most men abandoned headgear, consciously or subconsciously emulating the hatless newly elected president, John F. Kennedy. Second, I wanted a broad brim. I detested the silly hats that were in style for a while. The crown part was all right, but the brims were only about an inch wide. So, I bought a western hat while we were returning through Texas from one of our Mexican trips. We flattened the turned-up sides so they wouldn't be so conspicuous. Later I bought a real LBJ (Lyndon B. Johnson) hat, and two or three others of different shapes and colors. They were great for walking around the zoo, which I tried to do for at least 15 minutes every day, or even up to an hour or more on Sundays and holidays, when there were throngs of visitors on the grounds. The big hats protected my head and shielded my eyes from the sun and, because of my height, all the employees could see me coming. No one was loafing when I approached.

Bolo ties came a little later. For the uninitiated, they consist of sliding ornaments ranging from attractive polished stones to sophisticated Indian-crafted designs of turquoise and silver. Their variation is limitless. Two parallel slots on the back permit the insertion of a stout, braided cord that goes around one's neck under a collar. The ornament can be pulled up tight, or it can be lowered on hot days when an open-necked shirt is an advantage.

Hot, sultry Philadelphia days were just as enervating and uncomfortable as any I ever encountered in the Tropics. So, I wore bolo ties at the zoo, unbuttoned my collar, and felt well dressed, in keeping with my position in the zoo hierarchy. For the times when I had to go downtown for a formal meeting, I kept a necktie in the glove compartment of my car. At the parking garage, I would don the tie and slip the bolo into my pocket. The procedure was reversed when I returned to the zoo. A coat or jacket, incidentally, was a requirement for businessmen in those days. Casual clothing like that which has now invaded most strata of society was severely frowned upon. It was impossible for a man to enter many restaurants or certain other places unless he was wearing a coat and tie.

All this is a prelude to the real purpose of this anecdote. To commemorate my retirement, the staff of the zoo, accompanied by their spouses, put on an evening of fun and a "roast" for me. I had long known that such events were invariably given only for persons who were liked, respected, and who would enter into the spirit of things no matter how unusual their idiosyncracies might be.

Such an affair would have been totally inappropriate for my predecessor, Zoo Director Freeman M. Shelly. He made a fetish of being dignified, and, if we had teased him, for example, about his penny pinching, he would have walked out in high dudgeon. So our farewell party for him was low key and conducted during business hours. I gave a short speech about his many accomplishments—how he had arrived at the zoo when it was virtually bankrupt, and how his business acumen had helped to nurse it back onto its financial feet. We gave him a handsomely carved elephant of a size suitable for a mantelpiece, and everyone shook his hand and congratulated him.

When it came time for my farewell on March 2, 1973,

At the fun-poking roast for RC, when he retired as Director of the Philadelphia Zoo, he received a king-sized western hat. Photo by Franklin Williamson.

things were very different. The program began with a slide lecture on "The Life and Times of Roger Conant." The first picture was of me in baby clothes, the next as an ambulatory infant, then a well-dressed lad of about four, followed by me as a youth and a young man. Obviously the originals were made available by my beloved wife, who was sitting next to me. I reached over and squeezed her hand.

Then came a long series of pictures of me engaged in zoo activities, which had been abstracted from the photographic files that Isabelle had started many years previously, and which Franklin Williamson expanded and kept in perfect order after he succeeded her as the zoo's official photographer. There were also doctored pictures calculated to produce laughs. My face appeared on the body of a chimpanzee, my head on a tortoise, and a large rubber snake occupied the seat of the toilet in the private, tiny washroom adjacent to my office. My string ties, of course, were mentioned prominently.

Several of my trusted lieutenants burlesqued a staff meeting. All were wearing hats, one a gigantic lightweight contraption put together by Ken Dills, the talented head of our Exhibits Department. The wearer of the huge headpiece imitated me. Afterward, the hat was not only presented to me, but it was placed on my head so that Williamson could get a picture. Another gift was a huge whistle, also made of lightweight material, designed to twit me about my insistence that staff members carry whistles when they mingled with the crowds on busy days. More than once help had been needed to control unruly hoodlums. A whistle was the quickest way to summon assistance and to give pause to the miscreants. Also, I received a huge comma cut from a piece of plywood. That was in reference to my being a demon editor who insisted on reviewing all copy about the zoo that was to be printed or sent to the news media. I discovered later that the speaker, who showed the slides and who was the one who did most of the writing, had misspelled two words on the very first page of the copy he prepared for his presentation. I should have expected it.

I was teased about many other things, such as my insistence on punctuality at meetings and formal events. Because people often stole small potted cacti, I kept the room locked in the zoo's greenhouse where our large and varied collection of such plants was kept. We used the cacti in rotation in the reptile house and elsewhere as cage decorations. So one of my gifts was a single small potted cactus in a cage that was secured with four sturdy padlocks. (The four locks are still in use at my Albuquerque residence.)

On a more dignified side, I was given a splendid "Times Atlas of the World" and a book containing large copies of all the slides used when the program began. Also, there was a bound book of 164 letters of congratulations and best wishes from colleagues and friends. Virtually all the American zoos and aquariums were represented, as well as a surprisingly large number of zoos from all over the world. A special section included letters from the heads of organizations, such as the Smithsonian Institution in Washington, and the mayor of Philadelphia.

The program concluded with a series of African tribal dances by a large troop of barefooted young black people who were just starting to gain fame and prominence in the Philadelphia area. They gave a superb performance, and received a long standing ovation.

Isabelle and I had a lot of fun laughing at the things the staff had chosen to tease me about. But the evening was sad in some ways, because it was our last contact with many close friends who had done their best to make my administration a success.

A totally unexpected surprise that had nothing to do with the "roast" came through the kindness and courtesy of the Honorable Joshua Eilberg, a delegate from Pennsylvania in the House of Representatives. He read a statement in Congress about my retirement that rated 63 lines in the "Congressional Record," dated April 19, 1973.

The Musician

Someone gave me a cavalry bugle when I was a lad. It was small and high-pitched, and try as I would I could get nary a sound out of it. That is, until one of my fellow Boy Scouts who was taking music lessons showed me how to pucker my lips. Even so, my little bugle, with its very small mouthpiece, remained difficult to play, and I never did really master it.

Somewhat later I acquired an ancient regulation bugle. Battered and tarnished though it was, I quickly coaxed the regulation calls from it, starting with the slow cadence of "Taps" and working up to the staccato tempo of "First Call" and "Reveille." My grandparents, with whom I was living at the time, were very tolerant of my practicing, but I did retreat to the cellar at first. Eventually I was proficient enough to become the official bugler, a many-times-daily chore, during all four of the summers at the Boy Scout Camp where I served as a counselor.

An adult friend who wanted to encourage me gave me a cheap trumpet he picked up in a hock shop in New York. I soon mastered the fingering. That meant I was off and running, and, once I learned a tune, I could follow the music. With a sister-and-brother team who played the piano and violin, respectively, and with a chap who had a saxophone, we became the Sunday School orchestra at the Methodist church in Red Bank, New Jersey, where my grandparents were members. We played mostly hymns. They were easy, and we hastened through them at our semi-monthly practice sessions so we could play jazz, the popular music of the day. We were soon quite good at it, but it got us into trouble.

One Wednesday evening we were asked to play for a special prayer meeting in the church basement, led by an elder or deacon or whatever his title was. At least 100 persons were present, including a dozen and more of our classmates. They tarried after the older people had departed and asked us if we could play some jazz. We quickly assented, and several couples were soon dancing. After about the fifth or sixth tune the minister came down the stairs, gave band and dancers a spirited bawling out, and told us to desist and depart at once. Most of us didn't know it, but the Methodist church frowned on dancing at the time.

I atoned for that sin some weeks later by playing a difficult solo at a church social. It was one of those pieces written exclusively for the trumpet, and I practiced interminably to master the runs and trills, which required supple fingers, a good embouchure, and triple tonguing. When I finished, the audience applauded loudly and some even cheered. The minister frowned. Such goings-on in his staid, conservative edifice!

Several of us played in the Red Bank High School orchestra. While I was working at the Twin Brook Zoo, I joined a pickup band that met weekly at a neighbor's home where there was a piano. By that time I had saved enough money to buy a brand-new Buescher trumpet, silverplated with goldplating inside the bell. There were five or six of us, and, probably because my instrument was the loudest when I didn't use a mute, I became the leader. When I left the zoo and returned to school to cram the third year of Spanish into a single semester, so I could matriculate at a university, I sometimes mentioned *mi orquesta* when I had to compose sentences during oral drills in class. Came the night of the senior play. Even though I was an alumnus, I was in the audience, and I was both startled and embarrassed to hear over a loudspeaker, "Will Roger Conant please come backstage?" I obliged, and everyone stared as I walked from the center of the auditorium to the steps in front that gave access to both the stage and the work space in the rear. I learned that a dance was planned when the play was over, but the leader of the orchestra hired for the occasion had just telephoned to say that they couldn't make it. Could I get my group together on short notice? I said I'd try. How did they know to ask me? One of the students in the Spanish class remembered what I'd said.

With the help of the school telephone, I managed to reach everyone, but then I had to go home to get my trumpet, music stand, and sheet music arranged for an orchestra. I had to "hoof it," and it was a mile in each direction. High-school students never dreamed of having cars in those days. I used Scout's pace—50 steps walking and then 50 running—en route, but I just walked fast on the way back, burdened by my equipment and the knowledge that I shouldn't arrive out of breath. I made it, and not too long after the play was over the dance began.

That gave our group a reputation, and we played occasionally for private dances until I left to attend the University of Pennsylvania. The band was paid anywhere from $15 to $25 for an evening, which we had to split among us. Technically, that made us professional musicians.

Frankly, I was not a musician. I had an excellent tone and could produce some really sweet melodies on my trumpet, but I never learned to read music. That lack was painfully impressed on me when I auditioned for the Penn band and failed miserably. The officer in charge liked my tone, however, and assigned me to play

the baritone horn. The band was part of the ROTC (Reserve Officers' Training Corps), which gave me credit for the required physical education course. I was issued a euphonium, an instrument with two bells that permitted me to shift from bass to treble clef. Once I became accustomed to using it I stayed with the bass, because it was hard on the lips to make the transition. A classmate, Kenneth K. Otto, was issued a regulation baritone horn, and we became good friends. We marched and played at all the home football games. Other athletic events were optional, but I was so hard-pressed for time to earn money that I never went. The band's only excursion away was to Harvard. We were all in uniform, we entrained to New York, and from there took an overnight boat through Long Island Sound to Fall River, Massachusetts, and then again boarded a train. We didn't get much sleep. Our bunks were tiny, and I had to keep the big euphonium with me. I was glad it wasn't a tuba.

I grew up and played in the big band era, and I was delighted, when Isabelle joined me, to find that she was just as enthusiastic about that wonderful music as I was. We had many a private jam session at home in the Pine Barrens, blowing and singing along with top tunes, using our record player. It was our kind of music, and we mourned when it began to fade away, and resented its being replaced by rock and roll. The moment the bing-bang, often tuneless new style of music came on radio or television, we turned it off or switched to another station. I still do, and so does Kathryn.

Most happily, I was privileged to meet a number of the big band leaders or hear them play in person. Tommy Dorsey and his Clambake Seven came to the Philadelphia Zoo to play for the monkeys and apes. Benny Goodman presented the prizes for one of our zoo poster contests. As a privileged KYW "honorary" staff member, I received a ticket to watch Benny's hour-long big band broadcast from the station's largest studio. Ditto Jan Savitt. For several years the annual Philadelphia News Photographers' Ball featured a big-name band, and I can recall shaking hands again with Tommy Dorsey, as well as with Ben Bernie and Kay Kyser. I also heard Horace Heidt and Count Basie. Even during the Great Depression I managed an hour at Toledo's Trianon Ballroom, but I am not sure who I heard. I think it was the Dorsey brothers, Jimmy and Tommy, before they parted in 1935. Paul Whiteman and Vincent Lopez were the two great jazz leaders during my adolescence and before the big bands really got started. I never met Lopez, but Whiteman, as an old man, became a fixture on the staff of Philadelphia's radio station WFIL, and I had a chance to tell him how much I had liked his music.

Isabelle and I never did hear Harry James, except in a movie, but our personal theme song was his "You Made Me Love You." "I'll See You in My Dreams" eventually rated high, especially with me, after cancer took her out of my arms in 1976.

Dixieland was a big favorite, too, and we went to hear the artists whenever we could. Trumpeter Louis Armstrong was among those we liked best, and so was trombonist Jack Teagarden. We made many stops in New Orleans, especially on our way to and from Mexico, and invariably gravitated to Bourbon Street. Often we were with the Gloyds. Howard, an outstanding tympanist, had entrée into even the most crowded nightclubs, because the stars knew and liked him, and they could persuade the management to extend special favors. One night in Chicago he managed to gain entry for almost a dozen of us at the jam-packed Blue Note. We also went with the Gloyds to hear pianist Art Hodes and his combo once when we were in the Windy City. During a herp meeting in New Orleans, Howard took us, his wife, Kathryn, and Joseph R. Bailey for a tour of Bourbon Street. We listened to Sharkey Bonano for a while, but found Paul Barbarin, his drums, and his band far superior. While on our own in the Vieux Carré we always stopped in to hear trombonist Bill Williams, and once The Dukes of Dixieland.

Whenever a Dixieland group came to Philadelphia or its vicinity we tried to catch a session or two, even though my busy zoo schedule often required my presence at after-dinner functions. I'll never forget our delightful evening with Earl "Fatha" Hines and his group a few hours after the anaconda bit me. Or the night we spent with our close friends the Malnates at the Rendezvous, in downtown Philadelphia. Jack Teagarden was leading the sextette of musicians, which included Toni Parenti on clarinet, Ray Baduc on drums, and Pops Foster on bass. We saw how "Big Noise from Winnetka" was produced. Pops fingered his bass fiddle while Ray hit the strings with his drumsticks. I first met and chatted with Henry Cuesta in the men's room at the Latin Casino, near Camden, while he was playing with Teagarden. He later became Lawrence Welk's star clarinetist.

Our most memorable night of Dixieland was on December 5, 1957. As Isabelle wrote in her diary, "We had the *experience of a lifetime!*" December 5 was one of our private holidays, which we almost always celebrated in some special fashion. Despite the fact that it was snowing hard and the broadcasting stations were urging everyone to stay home, we set off, depending on our snow tires to get us through. We had dinner at a fancy restaurant and then drove to the Red Mill to hear Jack Teagarden with a new combo, which included the talented pianist Don Ewell. For three hours we were the only customers, and did we have a ball with the band! They played all our favorites and blues numbers, and we had a marvelous conversation with them all. About midnight another couple braved the storm, but we stayed until closing time at 1:00 A.M. How sorry I was that I didn't have my trumpet with me so I could say I played with Jack Teagarden!

While Howard Gloyd was director of the Chicago Academy of Sciences, he had a piano moved into the basement, and during part of each year there were weekly jam sessions. Each of the six musicians had a Ph.D., and they called themselves the Academic Cats.

Whatever became of that wonderful old music? It's seldom heard anymore except now and then at some special function. Howard Gloyd accumulated a superb collection of 2,200 Dixieland records, mostly breakable old 78s, but including some long-play 33s. He amassed books, photographs, autographs, and numerous other memorabilia. Kathryn plans to give it all to the American folk music collection at the Library of Congress.

As for me, I have our (Isabelle's and mine) much smaller collection of records of big band music, which I occasionally sample when my tired old eyes rebel at reading in the evening. There are also reruns of "The Lawrence Welk Show" which, thanks to the miracle of recorded television, are aired weekly on our PBS station. I seldom miss them when I am home, but I always wish there was less singing and more band music to hear.

More than 15 years after Isabelle died, Kathryn and I were sitting in a TAME (Ecuadorian) plane in Guayaquil, waiting to take off for the Galápagos Islands, when one of the attendants inserted a cassette to provide music until we departed. Soon an exquisite trumpet rendering came on of "I'll See You in My Dreams." I listened, of course, but didn't realize at first what was happening. Suddenly I became aware that tears were coursing down my cheeks. I was in the window seat, so I stared out, blew my nose, and soon composed myself. My love affair with my late devoted wife will no doubt continue until my mortal remains are placed beside hers in Albuquerque's Sunset Memorial Park. Kay's will go to the rural cemetery near Baldwin, in eastern Kansas, where Howard K. Gloyd's ashes are interred.

Where is my trumpet now? I still have it as a keepsake, but I haven't blown it since I played carols during my beloved Isabelle's last Christmas Eve on Earth.

The Vignettes

It is more than likely that I may seem like an iconoclast to some readers of these vignettes. All are about persons now deceased, and most of whom I knew well. I have stressed my experiences with them rather than to write biographies. In applicable cases, I have included mention of some of their problems, disappointments, and foibles, as well as their accomplishments and contributions to herpetology or zoo management. Formal obituaries tend to record only the best side of departed persons, and to overlook some or all of their weaknesses. One of my correspondents declared that the average obit treats its subject as a saint. That I have studiously tried to avoid.

The early herpetologists who wrote popular books, Clifford H. Pope and Carl F. Kauffeld, for example, tend to be remembered, and even Raymond L. Ditmars, whose first book was published before I was born. In the zoo field, the name of Edward H. Bean is perpetuated through the annual awards made by the American Zoo and Aquarium Association for the breeding of rare animals in captivity.

In communicating with younger, latter-day herpetologists, herpetoculturalists, and zoophiles, I have often been astonished to discover that many of the names that appear below are completely unknown to them. I hope my brief accounts will serve as introductions to some of the greats of yesteryear, who they were, and what they did. Their dates of birth and death appear in parentheses.

My interactions with my colleagues and superiors at the Philadelphia Zoological Garden, most of whom are also deceased, are chronicled in the main text of these memoirs, and I have made no attempt to prepare vignettes about them.

There are many other persons about whom I might write, but space is limited. Also, to be honest and consistent, some of them had problems I am reluctant to mention. The hubris exhibited by a few would be impossible to record politely.

The caricatures that accompany some of the herpetologists appeared in the first issue of "Ichtherps," dated September 15, 1939, and were distributed at the annual meeting of the American Society of Ichthyologists and Herpetologists, held at the Field Museum of Natural History in Chicago. The artists who drew them are unknown. "Ichtherps" was followed later by "Dopeia," and both were lampooning publications that poked fun at various herpetologists and ichthyologists who were active at the time.

The vignettes are assembled in alphabetical order, the herpetologists first, followed by the zoo personalities.

Herpetologists I Have Known

ENSIL ROSS ALLEN (1908-1981) had charisma. He was an extremely likable person, handsome, and with a splendid physique and a ready smile. He was an athlete and a powerful swimmer, and he had one of the deepest and most abiding interests in herpetology I ever encountered.

Ross was born in Pittsburgh, Pennsylvania, in 1908. His family moved to Winter Haven, Florida, when he was 16, and there he assembled a reptilian menagerie. After graduating from high school and attending Stetson University for a year, he transferred his animals to Silver Springs, and his collection became the nucleus of what later was named, at the request of others, the Ross Allen Reptile Institute. There he held sway for 46 years.

He had been milking snakes and selling the venom for some time, but at Silver Springs he made the extraction process pay double by doing it in front of cash customers, largely tourists, who were fascinated by the process and by his down-to-earth talks about the snakes and other exhibits. For decades he was the chief supplier of diamondback rattlesnake and cottonmouth venom, but he greatly stepped up production prior to America's entrance into World War II, when Wyeth, Inc., of Philadelphia, was called upon to produce large quantities of antivenin for troops on training maneuvers in the southern states.

Because he was such a powerful swimmer, Allen early learned how to capture alligators in their natural environment, wrestling them to the surface and then onto the shore. Handling 'gators became a natural part of his demonstration at the Reptile Institute.

Ross enrolled as a Boy Scout at an early age. He retained interest in that organization throughout his life and received several of scouting's highest awards. One was given for his leadership and woodsmanship during a cross-Florida trek, from Daytona Beach to Yankeetown on the Gulf of Mexico, with eight boys, during which they lived exclusively off the land. They made the 153 miles in 13 days. Allen was 54 at the time.

Ross and I were close friends from the time we first met in the 1930s, and he did many favors for me. In 1951, at my request, he gave a snake-milking demonstration at the annual conference of the American Association of Zoological Parks and Aquariums in Miami. Afterward, he and I and Isabelle collected herps together on the northern Florida Keys. During that trip he told me, "I know I'm not college material and I'm a poor writer, but I love herpetology and want to do everything I can to further it."

Several times Ross came to the Philadelphia Zoo to help in promoting our attendance. When we had to move the animals from the old reptile house in order to build a new one on the same site, I asked him to help with the crocodilians. I had watched and admired his skillful way of tying their mouths shut before they were even aware of what was happening. The news media turned out in force, and, once again, we were on the front page.

When Ross was in or near Philadelphia he stayed with us at our home in the New Jersey Pine Barrens. One morning we arose early and drove to New York, where we were to present a television show for the American Museum of Natural History. Ross and I received a token fee for our services, that seemed rather meager after being told that each show cost $10,000 to produce. I knew that TV required a number of cameramen and technicians, but I hadn't thought about a union.

It took several hours to get everything set up and to rehearse, and it quickly became evident that the members of the stagehands' union well outnumbered the TV crew. We were not allowed to touch anything—until it was time to move the tightly locked snake boxes into position. We told the supervising steward where they were to go. "Not us," the men blurted out. "We're afraid of snakes." Ross and I had to do it ourselves! The make-up man did nothing all day long except pat a smidgin of colored powder on my bald pate so it wouldn't shine into the cameras. No wonder the show cost what seemed to us like a small fortune. When we were on our way home, Ross remarked, "Those stagehand guys sure have a racket for themselves."

Ross was always full of fun and wry humor. Once he spoke to a men's club where I was present, and he passed around a small box containing a strange-looking dark brown object. It was a piece of coprolite (fossilized dung) presumably from an alligator.

Eventually, public interest in venom extraction and alligator wrestling waned and Ross reluctantly left Silver Springs. For a time he was associated with the Sarasota Jungle Gardens and then with the Alligator Farm at St. Augustine. Above all, however, he wanted his own place, a lifelong desire that came close to fulfillment. He was determined to prove there was still a place for the old-time showman, and that poisonous snakes and 'gators had not lost their glamour. He designed his dream exhibit, and construction was under way when rapidly declining health, because of cancer, terminated his career in 1981.

Ross Allen had a legion of admirers, thanks to his long career at various Florida institutions and his many appearances on television. We always thought of him as an outstanding herpetologist who was distinguished from all others in his own inimitable way.

MIGUEL ALVAREZ DEL TORO (1917-1996) was a distinguished naturalist and the authority on the biota of Chiapas, Mexico's southernmost state. He was born in Colima but moved to Tuxtla Gutiérrez, the capital of Chiapas, in 1945. There he founded the Instituto de Historia Natural and became an able and outspoken conservationist. His stationery long bore the slogan *"¡Comprende! Estás matando la humanidad al destrozar la naturaleza."* (Know this! You are killing mankind by destroying nature.) His letterhead featured a drawing of the rare and unique horned guan superimposed on an outline map of Chiapas.

Isabelle and I met Don Miguel and his vivacious wife while we were engaged in our extensive fieldwork in Mexico, once in 1962 and again in 1964 when our routes took us through Tuxtla. He had established a small but excellent museum, and he, himself, was the taxidermist, artist, and preparator of the dioramas and other exhibits, talents that he continued to employ throughout his life. In addition, he had a charming little zoo devoted to the animals of Chiapas. He certainly was the most eager and capable Mexican wildlife enthusiast I ever met. We developed a mutual respect that led to a lengthy, if intermittent, correspondence. He sometimes wrote to me in Spanish, but in later years it was all English, albeit with his syntax not always letter-perfect. (He did far better in English, however, than I ever did in Spanish.)

Both of our all-too-brief visits with Álvarez were punctuated by herpetological events of note. In 1962, after presenting him with an inscribed copy of our field guide to reptiles and amphibians, he gave me a half-grown all-black beaded lizard for the Philadelphia Zoo collection. It was a generous and most welcome gift. I had never seen one previously, and it represented a new subspecies, described by Charles M. Bogert and Rafael Martín del Campo in 1956 as *Heloderma horridum alvarezi*, in honor of our host.

During our 1964 visit I showed him a small snake we had found dead on the road but in excellent condition near Teopisca in east-central Chiapas. Neither Don Miguel nor I could identify it, but once I was back in the States I learned that it was a dwarf boa, *Ungaliophis continentalis*, and only the second one known from Mexico.

I always regretted that I never returned to Chiapas to see the new institute that he established on a 100-hectare wooded tract south of Tuxtla Gutiérrez. The animals had much larger quarters, and Álvarez applied all his expertise to organizing the new museum. He reported to me that he and his conservation allies had difficulty in obtaining the land, which was coveted by would-be developers. The new establishment bears his name, and I have heard that it is the best anywhere devoted to a local fauna and flora.

We exchanged many letters and publications, and I was able to ship him a number of reptile volumes for his personal library. He sent me his books for years, including all three editions of his "Los Reptiles de Chiapas." My last communication with him was during the summer of 1995 when he responded to my regret that he had been unable to attend the meeting of the International Herpetological Symposium in Denver, to which we both were invited, with all expenses paid. He explained that he no longer undertook lengthy trips alone and he hated big airports. He was still the head of the institution he had founded, but he added, "I am getting old."

During his lifetime Álvarez was the leader in establishing wildlife reserves in Chiapas, and he won many honors from conservation organizations in several different countries. He also was the recipient of two honorary doctoral degrees from universities in Chiapas.

Although his interests embraced all the biota of his adopted state, it was to Miguel, as a leading herpetologist, that I appealed for help when I was working on the monographic review of the snakes of the genus *Agkistrodon*. Álvarez knew a lot about the cantil, *A. bilineatus*, which he had encountered in the field many times both in Colima and Chiapas. He gave me an abundance of information, and it was he who finally solved a conundrum that had long plagued the herpetological community.

What was the origin of the word *cantil*, which, from the Spanish, translates as a "cliff" or "precipice"? I had long queried herpetologists for clues, but whereas several were offered, none was conclusive. I began to think that perhaps the answer was hidden in the language of some native tribe that lived in the same region as the venomous snake. Álvarez wrote to me on August 12, 1981, that he, at long last, had the answer. In a new vocabulary of indigenous languages of Chiapas he had found that the Tzeltal word for the snake was *kantiil* from the two components of *kan* for yellow and *tiil* for lips, or yellow lips, which was clearly in reference to the yellow or yellowish stripes traversing the labial scutes on each side of the snake's head. I was elated and immediately suggested that I write a paper on the subject in English, which I would seek to have published under his name. He declined and insisted that I undertake the writing alone inasmuch as I was the person who was working with *Agkistrodon*. I saw to it, however, that he received full credit for the discovery.

In the spring of 1982 Miguel Álvarez del Toro

suffered through a major catastrophe that came close to wiping out all he had accomplished and planned at his new site. On May 5, 1982, he wrote to me about it at length, and I repeat his account of the entire frightening series of events, only changing his prose to idiomatic English. Here, in essence, is what he wrote:

> *The zoo and museum are almost finished, but we almost lost everything because of the volcanic eruption which you may have heard about. At least we lost many animals and trees, and almost suffocated ourselves. Many people left the city, but I could not leave behind my work of so many years.*

> *It was all terrifying, but an interesting experience. The volcano called Tzitzunal exploded suddenly one month ago after being dormant for over a thousand years. Heavy ash fell at Tuxtla for 15 days, and it was very difficult to breathe and see. In fact, for three days there was no daylight at all. It was strange to walk at noon with a flashlight in hand. Nearer the volcano, towns were totally covered with sand, ash, and rocks to a depth of six meters, and only the church towers protruded. So far, no one knows how many people were killed. The ground is so hot that no one can walk on it.*

> *I call the entire thing an ecological disaster. In a radius of 20 kilometers around the volcano no life of any kind survived. It was an evergreen forest and now it looks like a moon landscape. Even as far away as Tuxtla I think some 75 percent of the fauna was killed. At a small reservation we have some 30 kilometers from Tuxtla there were numbers of dead birds, small and large mammals, reptiles, and insects and the vegetation was gray.*

> *At the zoo many of the animals died. We lost all hope for several days, but fortunately, the rains were soon to come, and we have had two big storms that washed the vegetation, and new leaves are now starting to grow. We survived, but we are still fighting the ashes that cover everything, and when the wind blows they are everywhere.*

I treasure the last book that Don Miguel sent to me. It is his " *¡Así era Chiapas!*" (This is the way Chiapas was.) In it he wrote about the wonderful tropical wildlife as it existed before, as he wrote in a letter, "it became hard to interfere with the politicians and businessmen who care for nothing except to get more and more money, even though the world might explode."

He inscribed that wonderful book "*Con afectuosos recuerdos*" (With affectionate memories), and he signed it in February 1986.

What a warm, lasting friendship we had for decades although we lived so very far apart.

THOMAS BARBOUR (1884-1946) was a big man, and a very generous one. He was heavyset, well over six feet in height, and an impressive person to meet. The story was told that, when he and two equally large companions, one of them the towering Josselyn Van Tyne, ornithologist of the University of Michigan, walked down the main street of a Panamanian village, the natives rushed out of their homes to see *los grandes americanos*.

As a member of a wealthy family, Thomas Barbour had unlimited monetary resources, and he used them to good advantage among herpetologists and to advance the science itself. He added enormously to the collection of the Museum of Comparative Zoology (MCZ) at Harvard University, and over which he presided for a great many years. He anonymously financed or helped to finance the education of a number of young people, he paid for field trips and even expeditions, and he personally subsidized publications, large and small. He even underwrote the printing of two of my early papers.

In 1936 I visited my Uncle Harold in Lexington, Massachusetts, and, while I was in the vicinity of Cambridge, I went to the museum. Dr. Barbour greeted me cordially and very soon with great enthusiasm, because I had with me a preserved snake of the genus *Alsophis* from Bimini in the Bahama Islands. A friend had given it to me alive, but it had soon died at the Philadelphia Zoo. Dr. Barbour told me that *Alsophis* was unknown from Bimini. I doubtless had a new subspecies, he said, and I should describe it at once. He insisted that I examine and take scale counts on all pertinent material from other West Indian islands in the MCZ collection. He even suggested a name for the new form. Because of my previous contact with the more conservative herpetologists at the University of Michigan, back in my Toledo days, I did not rush into print. I consulted with others and even borrowed some *Alsophis* from the British Museum for comparison. Once the paper was finished, I sent it to Dr. Barbour and, in what could not have been more than a fortnight, I received a package containing a generous supply of copies of the printed paper describing *Alsophis vudii picticeps*. He had published it for me in the "Proceedings of the New England Zoölogical Club," which, I believe, was his privately funded journal and an outlet for such papers as mine. In 1943 he accepted a longer paper on the milk snakes of the Atlantic Coastal Plain, on which I had worked for a year, and it was in print within a very few weeks. I learned later that he had shown the same type of kindness toward many other young herpetologists. No wonder he was looked upon almost as a godfather.

For several years, when cold weather approached in the autumn, Dr. Barbour traveled southward by train, making stops at the New York, Philadelphia, and Washington zoos before continuing on to Florida, Cuba, or the Antilles for the winter. He never let me know in advance when he was coming, but, once he was at the zoo, he looked me up, and I always found time to spend several hours with him while we "did" the reptile house and looked at newly arrived birds and mammals.

The herpetology of the West Indies was one of Tom Barbour's great interests. He and some of his wealthy friends who owned yachts worked out an agreement that was mutually beneficial. By doing fieldwork wherever they went ashore, they substantially augmented the MCZ collection, as well as adding to our knowledge of the many insular species, their distributions, and their relationships to other kinds on neighboring islands. Cruises through the enormous and diverse archipelago with Dr. Barbour aboard were designated as formal scientific expeditions of the MCZ, and the expenses involved were deductible for income tax purposes.

Tom Barbour wrote many papers, the best of which were in collaboration with others, including Archie Carr and Arthur Loveridge. His several lists of Antillean reptiles and amphibians were important references for anyone interested in the herpetofauna of that area. Some of his other solo contributions, however, suffered from triviality and lack of detail and thoroughness. His dependence on others was glaringly revealed when he attempted to compile the fifth edition of "The Check List of North American Amphibians and Reptiles," by Stejneger and Barbour. Dr. Leonhard Stejneger, who had been the authority and moving spirit in all the earlier editions, was in his 90s and unable to render much help. Barbour delegated much of the updating of the fifth edition to his paid assistants. Many omissions and errors resulted, and as soon as it was published and came under the scrutiny of the herpetological community, Barbour received numerous lists of addenda and corrigenda, including one from me. He immediately began sending out printed corrections, but there were too many for him to cover them all, and he soon ceased trying.

As a popular writer, Barbour did much better. His "Reptiles and Amphibians, Their Habits and Adaptations," first published in 1926, is an interesting and quite useful book. In my opinion, "That Vanishing Eden, a Naturalist's Florida" is probably his best work. It was a lament for what he had seen happen to a biologist's paradise during his lifetime, as wildlife was decimated and in some places even extirpated by the relentless advance of civilization and the influx of people from the northern states seeking a more equable

climate. He died in 1946, and he would be horrified by what has happened since then, especially in southern Florida: in the vast, festering megalopolis of the Miami area; the almost wall-to-wall settlement of the Keys; and the desecration of the Everglades as a result of water manipulation.

Thomas Barbour's greatest contribution to herpetology was through his checkbook. In general, he spent wisely and well, and he helped a lot of us in many different ways. We were deeply grateful to him.

WILLIAM FRANKLIN BLAIR (1912-1984) began his professional career as a mammalogist. He received his Ph.D. from the University of Michigan under Lee R. Dice, and then served in the U.S. Army as a captain during World War II. He returned to Michigan, but soon obtained a position in the Biology Department of the University of Texas. He was destined to remain there the rest of his life, most of it as a full professor. He shortened his name to W. Frank Blair for his many books and papers.

Predictably, his first contributions were on mammalogy, but his interests soon broadened, and he took students with him to various parts of the state, as he continued his studies on "The Biotic Provinces of Texas," issued in 1950. He encouraged his young people to follow their own interests, and they published a number of reports—several in herpetology—with massive help from Frank, but under their names, not his.

He seemed always to be surrounded by students. He and his wife, Fern, were childless, and the presence of the young people may have filled a need. The Blairs conducted an open house at their home every Tuesday evening during the academic semesters. The interest and companionship engendered by the weekly sessions attracted students in biology who were not directly under Frank's wing. In all, he supervised 49 Ph.D. and 51 master's students, as well as many postdoctoral fellows. It was an extraordinarily impressive record for a person who, at the same time, was conducting research on his own and editing important books. On top of all that, with his wife and several students, he made a painstaking study of the colony of *Sceloporus olivaceus* living on the 10-acre tract that he and Fern called home, and which they willed as a wildlife sanctuary in perpetuity. The results of their observations were published in 1960 as "The Rusty Lizard, a Population Study."

I first met Frank at a meeting of the ASIH in Austin in 1952, where Isabelle and I were struggling to photograph some of the huge bonanza of amphibians and reptiles that enthusiastic members of the Texas

Herpetological Society assembled and donated toward the production of our field guide. He made a room near his office available to us, and later he encouraged students to send us examples of species we had not yet recorded on film. Twice we passed through Austin on a Tuesday, on our way to Mexico or back, and both times we were invited to attend the weekly session. What a stimulus those gatherings were to a number of young men who were later to become well-known herpetologists on their own. The names of Ralph W. Axtell, Alvin G. Flury, David L. Jameson, John S. Mecham, William W. Milstead, and William F. Pyburn come quickly to mind, and there were many others who were imbued with Frank's enthusiasm and attention to detail.

In the early 1950s Frank become interested in vocalization in male frogs and its role in mate selection. With all the students he could commandeer, he was quickly off to any locality in Texas where heavy rains were reported and where resultant large choruses of anurans might be heard. With the help of tape recorders and sonograms he was able to show that the calls of males of the same species differed, depending on whether they were alone or sympatric with other species, a phenomenon now called character displacement. He also initiated experiments in hybridization among anurans. He soon became the leading authority on the behavior of frogs and toads.

Frank edited "Vertebrate Speciation," published in 1961 and containing papers from a symposium he initiated. That was followed in 1972 by "The Biology of the Genus *Bufo*," a compendium on toads written by more than a dozen authorities. Another important work that revealed Frank's versatility was "Vertebrates of the United States," intended as a college text and to which he contributed the section on mammals. His brother, Albert P. Blair, wrote the part on amphibians; Fred R. Cagle did the reptiles; Pierce Brodkorb the birds; and George A. Moore the fishes. Many of Isabelle's photographs accompanied the two sections involving herpetology. This useful book appeared originally in 1957, and a second, less-well-printed edition followed in 1968.

Frank eventually turned his attention to parallels in the fauna and flora of the farflung Americas, especially in the more xeric regions of the two continents. He served as chairman of the U.S. National Committee for the International Biological Program. In that capacity, and aided by his fluency in Spanish, he was in frequent contact with colleagues in Latin America. He undertook a tour of South America to confer with biologists and others, seeking their cooperation. In "Big Biology: The US/IBP," published in 1977, he gave his personal evaluation of the program as he saw it. In general, the participation of the Spanish- and Portuguese-speaking nations was far from enthusiastic. Along with suspicion that the "Colossus of the North" was trying to gain some advantage for itself, Frank encountered a plethora of petty jealousies and governmental bureaucracies. Apparently, most of the worthwhile research was accomplished by his own students or those he personally recruited in South America. One of the latter was Barbara N. Timmermann, an English girl who had long lived in Argentina. Because I am more or less a desert rat at heart, I was particularly intrigued by her findings, in collaboration with others, about the creosote bush, *Larrea tridentata,* an abundant component of the vegetation of our southwestern deserts. The ancestors of that redolent plant came from arid regions in South America. They arrived in the north as seeds, temporarily attached to the legs of migratory birds, and proliferated in the new habitat. Timmermann and the other scientists concluded that plants of the genus *Larrea* reached the Mojave Desert about 9000 years ago, the Chihuahuan Desert about 13,000 years ago, and the Sonoran Desert sometime in between. It was a thrill for me to find representatives of the genus in the cold Patagonian desert when I finally managed to reach that distant part of the world during my twilight years.

Frank Blair, a modest and unassuming man of boundless energy and enthusiasm, was the mentor of a small legion of students who came under his influence and then went on to blaze trails for themselves in various facets of natural history.

FRANK NELSON BLANCHARD (1888-1937) was a paradox. He had a splendid reputation as a herpetologist, and his outstanding knowledge, especially of the serpents, was indisputable. It enabled him to write his illustrated dichotomous key to the snakes of the United States, Canada, and Lower California, which was published by the Macmillan Company in 1925 in a small book that is now a collector's item. He also produced a succession of scholarly papers, and he was an excellent correspondent whose letters inspired younger men, myself included.

Meeting him was another matter. Because I respected him, I paid him visits several times during my pilgrimages, in the early 1930s, from the Toledo Zoo to the University of Michigan, which was then the nation's capital of herpetological systematics. Unlike everyone else I met there, Blanchard was never cordial. Once he even chewed me out for what he thought was a misidentification, even though, as a special favor to him, I had taken several live snakes to Ann Arbor with me that I thought he might like to see. Later, William M. Clay, Blanchard's own student, and I proved him wrong.

It would be difficult to imagine a person who was more ill at ease with others. In his classes he sat on a stool and squirmed all through his lectures. His negative personality turned many people off. My close friend and colleague Howard K. Gloyd looked eagerly forward to seeing Blanchard and undertaking his doctoral work with him, but he nearly went home in despair after their first meeting.

Gloyd eventually became Blanchard's most distinguished student, and the two of them planned to write a manual on the snakes of North America. Blanchard was most familiar with the ophidian fauna of the East, and Gloyd with that of the West. Their plan included a field trip of several months' duration that took them to the South and then west to California. Gloyd was an old hand at fieldwork and camping out, but Blanchard was not. The latter worked in the field chiefly near Ann Arbor and at the "bug camp," or summer school, at Higgins Lake, both in Michigan. He could go home every night. He approached the long excursion with apprehension and, during it, several ludicrous situations developed that Gloyd delighted in recounting to his friends.

Their field vehicle was a panel truck filled with all their gear. Before they departed, Mrs. Blanchard, Frieda, a character in her own right, stuffed every nook and cranny with cookies on which Dr. Frank nibbled all day long. When mealtime arrived, Gloyd would suggest, as they moved along the highway, that they stop to eat. Blanchard was rarely hungry. When they had to camp out, the noises of the night, which were unidentifiable and thus frightening to his ears, kept him awake and made him more nervous and irritable than ever. Camping was not for him.

When they passed through Tombstone, Arizona, Gloyd, just for the fun of it, went into the Silver Dollar Saloon to have a single glass of beer and to put his foot on the rail where divers desperadoes of days long ago had put theirs. Blanchard stayed in the truck, and, because he had read somewhere that drunkards had "tunnel vision," he wouldn't let Gloyd drive for three days.

At New Orleans they visited with Percy Viosca, Jr., a self-taught naturalist who had a good working knowledge of much of the wildlife of Louisiana. He took them on a field trip through the swamplands, during which they all were clad in boots. Blanchard was driving the van with their guide in the seat next to him when suddenly, in his southern drawl, Viosca yelled, "Doctah Blanchard, stop the cah. Stop the cah." Dr. Frank slammed on the brakes, and "Poicy," as he called him-

self, dashed off into the swamp and disappeared. Blanchard and Gloyd looked at each other, both wondering, "What did he see? Did a snake crawl off the road?"

After a few minutes they heard Viosca calling from somewhere close by, "Doctah Blanchard, Doctah Blanchard. Please come he-ya." Blanchard obliged, waded into the swamp, and soon found "Poicy" squatted down. He said, "Would you please reach up and hand me some of that there Spanish moss? That's the toilet paper of the South, ya know." Blanchard did as he was asked, and then splashed his way out of the swamp, completely disgusted. Meantime, Gloyd, who had heard everything that was said, was close to hysterics, but he had to stifle his laughter before the disgruntled, badly insulted, and grim-faced professor returned to the van.

Despite his idiosyncrasies, we and many others admired Blanchard for his research and writing. His classic monograph, "A Revision of the King Snakes: Genus *Lampropeltis*," published in 1921, was a major contribution. The snake manual was never completed. We were saddened by Blanchard's death in 1937, at the age of 48, of a strep throat, an ailment that now can usually be controlled with antibiotics. His lengthy review of the ring-necked snakes, *Diadophis*, appeared posthumously under the editorship of Dr. Gloyd.

CHARLES MITCHILL BOGERT (1908-1992) was a close friend of 50 years' standing. "Chuck," as he was known to all his friends, was extremely helpful to me. He served as my mentor when I was seeking to make scholarly contributions to the scientific literature. He never failed to make the facilities of his department at the American Museum of Natural History available during my many visits to that institution in New York, and we carried on a lively correspondence for decades. He wrote to me from the field in Mexico in 1946 about finding a water snake in the isolated drainage system of the Río Nazas in Durango and he, more than anyone else, kindled my interest in Mexican fieldwork. We developed a close rapport that overrode a curious quirk of his nature that sometimes, without warning, made him critical and even abusive toward others. It may have been a subconscious defensive behavior that apparently had originated in his early childhood. I quickly learned to ignore it, but, unhappily, others often did not, and he made a number of enemies as a result.

Chuck's productivity was enormous. His works included a number of lengthy, exhaustive tomes on diverse subjects, as well as many shorter contributions, and he was unquestionably a pioneer with his studies on the temperature requirements of lizards and vocalization in anurans. I had the utmost respect for Chuck, and I mention his occasional unfortunate negative behavior, and how he could maintain a stubborn streak, solely as a prelude to writing about what, to me, was an interesting journey into northwestern Sonora.

Early in January 1974, Chuck invited me to accompany him to Kino Bay on the Sea of Cortéz (the Gulf of California) and then on a trek northward to find the Seri Indians, known for their beautiful carvings of animal motifs in ironwood. He drove his Chevrolet Blazer and, en route in both directions, we stayed overnight at the Southwestern Research Station of the American Museum of Natural History near Portal, Arizona. Was it ever cold! We piled on all the blankets we could find, and I even added a straw mattress from an empty cot. The weather moderated as we moved southward, and bright sunshine prevailed. We found a first-class motel near the waterfront at Kino that also boasted a good restaurant. The next morning we headed north, and, at the edge of the small settlement, we passed through a large group of *indios* hawking a variety of Mexican curios. We moved onward into the desert, although scarcely a trackless one, for there were tire marks leading in all directions. By keeping an eye on the coast and, a little later, on the Isla Tiburón (Shark Island), we were able to follow a fairly distinct track leading northward, although it forked and reforked at frequent intervals.

What a desert! It was unique in my experience, because it was one of the few places where the ranges of four of the giant cacti overlap—the enormous cardón, the saguaro, the organ pipe, and the old man cactus. It was a weird landscape, to say the least.

We eventually reached El Desemboque on the Bahía Tepopa and found Seri Indians. Chuck bought quite a few of their fine carvings to take back to friends, but I contented myself with a *ballena* (whale). Unexpectedly, we found two Americans, Edward Moser and his wife, Bible translators who were living among the Indians in a primitive but fairly comfortable dwelling. They graciously invited us to lunch, after which Chuck launched into a long discussion with the Mosers on their work and on Mexico in general. About 3:00 P.M. I suggested that we ought to get started back. It was winter, it would get dark early, and we had a veritable wilderness of 50 or 60 miles to traverse with no signposts or landmarks to guide our way. Chuck told me not to worry. Finally, when twilight began to descend, he agreed to get going.

We promptly lost our way, and, in the rapidly dwindling light, we suddenly found ourselves in a frightening quagmire where seawater had flowed and then ebbed over a broad, flat salt pan. It was as slick as grease, but, by putting the vehicle into four-wheel drive, we

managed to slip, slide, and skid onto firmer ground. We then headed south (we hoped), but it was inky dark, and guessing which wheel tracks to follow was a distinct gamble. I suggested that I thought we were angling away from the coast but Bogert, who subconsciously had drifted into one of his negative moods, told me to shut up. I did for a while, but, as an amateur astronomer, I kept watching the sky. Presently Sirius, the dog star, rose directly ahead of us. Stars rise in the east, of course, so I told Chuck we were heading inland. He paid no attention to me and stubbornly stuck to his course, but very soon the wheel tracks we were following terminated alongside a small house in which a light was shining. I opened the car door and jumped out. "Where are you going?" Chuck demanded. My response was, "I'm going to find out where the hell we are." He yelled for me to come back, but I ignored him and went to the door, knocked, and then asked in Spanish, "Which way is Kino?" The *campesino* came out to the car with me. I was right. We had to turn around and go back, but our informant told us which forks to take. Chuck's Spanish was better than mine, so we both understood it all. His obstinancy suddenly evaporated, and we made it back to the motel just before 10:00 P.M. and, miraculously, the dining room was still open. I was starved and I bet Chuck was also, but he said nothing.

How typical of Bogert. I could think of others who might have been with him and who would have been as mad as the proverbial wet hen because of his behavior. As for me, I took it in stride and thought about what a wonderful story the adventure would make. Chuck was his usual cordial self during all the rest of our trip.

FRED RAY CAGLE (1915-1968) was an outstanding herpetologist, an inspiring but exacting teacher, and an able administrator. He was also a good friend who cared not a whit that I was bereft of academic credentials. I was an enthusiast deeply involved in research, primarily with water snakes and turtles at the time. That was good enough for him, and he went all out to help in a variety of ways, even to lending me his field truck whenever I was in New Orleans and wished to sample the herpetofauna of the adjacent swamplands.

My correspondence with Fred began in early 1942, but I didn't meet him in person until Isabelle and I visited Tulane University during October 1947, one of the several stops we made during our long honeymoon trip. We had been married in early April, but we were badly needed during the Philadelphia Zoo's busy spring and summer seasons. So we postponed our nuptial excursion until autumn when we could be away for a full month. Fred knew approximately when we would arrive, and he had saved a major surprise for us. He drove us to the New Orleans Airport and, in a four-seater Grumman Widgeon manned by an experienced pilot, he took us for a wide-ranging, two-hour flight back and forth across the vast Mississippi River Delta. We flew at 1,000 feet, more or less, which was low enough for us to have excellent views, even through a thin haze, of that extraordinary watery wilderness. What a thrill and what an education for us!

Later, on that same trip, we went to a swamp at Frenier Beach near the shore of Lake Pontchartrain where I collected a few examples of an abundant population of almost coal-black cottonmouths. From that locality, at an earlier date, Fred and a student, Allan H. Chaney, had sent me a small series of water snakes, one of which I designated as the type of a new subspecies I described in 1949. That was the yellow-bellied water snake, *Natrix* (=*Nerodia*) *erythrogaster flavigaster*. I wanted to see the habitat, and Isabelle took photographs of it.

Fred Cagle, who was to produce many excellent papers on turtles, had been a student of the outstanding cheloniologist, Norman E. Hartweg, under whose aegis he earned his Ph.D. at the University of Michigan. Fred previously had been at Southern Illinois University, at Carbondale, from which he received his baccalaureate and where he also served for a while as director of the museum. His active fieldwork in that region, although largely concerned with turtles, was not confined to them. He assembled information for an important review, published in 1942, on the "Herpetological Fauna of Jackson and Union Counties, Illinois." He also described the physiographic features of the area.

Among Cagle's most important contributions were two parallel papers with almost identical titles. The first, dated 1953, was "An Outline for the Study of a Reptile Life History." The second, on amphibians, appeared in 1956. They were excellent guides at a time when life history studies were seldom pursued.

Soon after Fred arrived at Tulane and became aware of the amazing abundance and diversity of the local herpetofauna, he made elaborate plans to survey Louisiana's amphibians and reptiles in depth. With grant money he bought a boat, vehicle, and other equipment, and he organized field crews of three to six male students, who amassed an extensive collection. Other interests, especially his steady movement up the administrative ladder, in addition to his early and untimely death, prevented him from completing his ambitious undertaking. His material formed a strong nucleus, however, which, supplemented by their own extensive studies, was available for Harold A. Dundee

and Douglas A. Rossman when they were compiling their book on the amphibians and reptiles of Louisiana, published in 1989.

Cagle's field crews ranged widely across the Southeast, especially as his intense interest in the turtle genus *Graptemys* reached full fervor. In addition to the wide-ranging forms, it soon became apparent that many of the separate river systems emptying into the Gulf of Mexico supported different taxa. In 1954 he described two new species, *Graptemys flavimaculata* and *G. nigrinoda*, the yellow-blotched and black-knobbed sawbacks, respectively. So that Fred could reproduce them in "Tulane Studies in Zoology," Isabelle photographed and hand-colored a print of each for him, using the same water-color dye technique she employed for our "Field Guide to Reptiles and Amphibians." Other persons eventually continued Cagle's work on the genus, including the description of the appropriately named *Graptemys caglei* from the San Antonio-Guadalupe River system of south-central Texas. As recently as 1992, Jeffrey E. Lovich and C. J. McCoy added two more species to the list.

My contacts with Fred Cagle were chiefly during the early years of our respective careers. Isabelle and I were always welcome in New Orleans, and, with his charming wife, Josephine, we feasted several times on shrimp, "crawdads," and other local delicacies at their home. Fred and his students were major contributors in our search for live herps to photograph for our field guide.

Only once did Fred pay us a visit, and that was on July 26, 1951, when he came to the Philadelphia Zoo and went home with me on a hot day to have a refreshing swim before supper. He stayed overnight with us at the 'Gap, our first home on Taunton Lake in the New Jersey Pine Barrens. As a proper and thoughtful guest, he presented Isabelle with a gift. It was a "turned turtle," a porcelain, life-sized, more-or-less allegorical specimen lying on its back, with its head turned upward. The tail was also upturned, and it was attached to the undershell, or plastron, which was removable. Fred had filled the body cavity with round white candies (crystallized cream filberts, or "mothballs") that looked for all the world like a large clutch of eggs soon to be laid. The turtle is still on my curio shelf, but the "eggs" disappeared decades ago.

In later years our encounters with Fred declined as we each became more and more involved with administrative work. We saw one another occasionally at meetings, and Isabelle and I were in an elevator with him on April 23, 1953, when he suddenly collapsed and fell to the floor. A first-aid maneuver, applied by a fellow passenger who had been an army medic during World War II, restored him, but Fred took to his hotel bed for two days. We monitored him, but he forbade us to notify Josephine for fear of worrying her. The sudden onset in the elevator was suggestive of what was to come. Fred died on August 8, 1968, as a result of a massive aneurysm, at the height of his career, when he was in his early 50s. By that time he had risen to the position of Tulane's Vice-President for Institutional Development.

If Fred R. Cagle had lived and continued to exhibit his drive and broad spectrum of academic interests, he assuredly would eventually have become the President of Tulane or some similar institution.

ARCHIE FAIRLY CARR, JR. (1909-1987) had a brilliant mind and he was one of the great herpetologists of the twentieth century. He was also a gifted writer who could vividly and entertainingly describe his observations and adventures in the language of the layman. Much of his prose flowed like poetry, and he won several literary medals, all of them richly deserved.

Archie, the son of a preacher, was born in Mobile, Alabama. The family moved, in turn, to Fort Worth, Texas, and Savannah, Georgia, in keeping with the practice of their church in those days. The last change of venue, at least in Archie's case, was to Florida, for which he developed a passionate love. It was his home ever afterward, except for four years of residence in Honduras and two in Costa Rica, where he studied and wrote about the indigenous biota. He also honed his idiomatic Spanish, in which he was already fluent. He taught regular courses to students in Honduras.

Like so many of us, Archie kept a pet menagerie of amphibians and reptiles during his boyhood years. Turtles were always represented, and they were the chief subjects of his research and conservation goals. Eventually, the name of Archie Carr became almost synonymous with sea turtles. Speaking of his name, it was shortened in steps. His early contributions to the herpetological literature bore his full name; later it was reduced to A. F. Carr, Jr., and soon he became known simply as Archie Carr.

From my correspondence file I discovered that my first contact with Archie was in 1935 while I was still at the Toledo Zoo. That same valuable source of information divulged many other interesting facts, which had become hazy in my memory. When Mark Mooney and I were assembling pictures of live turtles for Clifford Pope to use in his popular book entitled "Turtles of the United States and Canada," Archie sent us representatives of several species from Florida that we needed. Later, I was solicited by the National Science Founda-

tion to review Archie's series of applications for grants to further his work on sea turtles and the development of his monumental studies centered in large part on the green turtle nesting beaches at Tortuguero in Costa Rica. I think I was supposed to remain discreetly anonymous, but I confess that I told Archie I had done my best to help him. In my file is a short note, dated February 18, 1960, in which he wrote, "Any time *you* have been on my panel you can know perfectly damn well that I got my grant."

Early in 1959 I was asked to write a letter on Archie's behalf. The University of Florida wanted outside support for its intention to bestow a distinguished professorship on Dr. Carr, which would enable him to concentrate on research and the graduate program, and relieve him of routine curricular duties. My rather lengthy response included the following paragraph:

> *Perhaps more than anything else, I admire Archie Carr's ability to write for the public. Here is an astute scientist, respected by his peers (and envied by many of them) who has the gift of penning sparkling prose that can arouse the interest of the layest of the lay, and at the same time command the attention of his most erudite colleagues. One of the greatest tributes I have ever seen given to any professional zoologist occurred during the meeting of the American Institute of Biological Sciences at Gainesville [Florida] in 1954. There Dr. Carr, in a vast auditorium, held a distinguished audience spellbound simply by reading to them "The Passing of the Fleet," a chapter from his charming book, the* Windward Road.

Archie knew how to address a crowd. He knew exactly which words and phrases to stress, and he was as smooth and polished as any television anchor person. He received a tumultuous standing ovation after he read his chapter.

Two personal interactions with my esteemed friend remain vivid in my memory, and always will. First, by sheer chronological coincidence, Isabelle and I were beginning our campaign to photograph great numbers of amphibians and reptiles for the first edition of our field guide, just as Archie Carr and Coleman J. Goin were getting started on their guide to the cold-blooded vertebrates of Florida. They badly needed pictures, so we made an agreement with them. They collected living animals of a great many species, including rarities, and Coly Goin shipped them to us. When we took photographs for our own use, we exposed additional negatives for them. Their kindness saved us at least one, perhaps two, long collecting expeditions to the Southeast. In return they had the illustrations they needed. The presentation copy of a "Guide to Reptiles,

Amphibians, and Fresh-Water Fishes of Florida" that we received in 1955 bore the inscription "For Isabelle and Roger Conant with our regards and gratitude," signed by both authors. In the preface to their book we rated a long paragraph mentioning our offer and how helpful it was to them. They both knew from us, in person, how important the exchange of animals for pictures was for our project.

My other never-to-be-forgotten incident involved the Time-Life Nature Library book on "The Reptiles." Archie wrote the text in his flowing, eloquent style, and I was greatly honored to be invited to write the introduction for it.

As I became more and more involved in administrative work, and Archie's calendar filled with meetings, reports due, and excursions to places near and far in pursuit of turtles, our communications became less and less frequent. My correspondence file yielded two more items, however, that are worthy of mention. One concerns a turtle, and the other a monstrous emasculation of one of Florida's scenic wonders.

The Indo-Pacific ridley, *Lepidochelys olivacea,* a pelagic turtle with an enormous range, entered the Atlantic Ocean long ago, probably by rounding the Cape of Good Hope. It crossed over, presumably from West Africa, and formed nesting colonies on Trinidad and in the Guianas. Stray individuals had appeared along the shore of Puerto Rico and the northern coast of Cuba, and I sought Archie's advice about whether I should include the species in the second edition of our field guide, just in case that exotic sea turtle should turn up along the coast of Florida. He responded enthusiastically in the affirmative, and outlined an additional morphological character for distinguishing it from our own ridley, *Lepidochelys kempii,* which occurs chiefly in the Gulf of Mexico, but also wanders north along our Atlantic coast.

Although he never mentioned it to me directly, I don't think Archie ever forgave me for not using his revised terminology for the plates, scales, and bony elements of turtle shells. He introduced the terms in his "Handbook of Turtles," which was first published in 1952. I took a long, hard look at the subject, consulted with other students of turtles, and finally decided to use the older, conservative nomenclature. Hindsight suggests that I might have been better advised to follow Archie's lead. If I had, it is likely that his terms would have long ago come into vogue. At the time, however, Isabelle and I had no inkling of what an enormous and totally unexpected impact our field guide was to have on young herpetologists. One of the designations Archie used was "lamina" (plural "laminae"), for the

epidermal pigment-bearing (outer) plates of the carapace. In response to my letter on the Indo-Pacific turtle he reminded me, ever so subtly, by referring to my "laminal count" where I had used the number of "costals" instead.

Despite his heavy schedule, Archie took time out in 1965 to write to us at Taunton telling us about the proposed Cross-Florida Barge Canal, which would destroy the magnificent, unspoiled Oklawaha River. He needed help. It was doubtless only one of many letters he sent to his friends and colleagues.

Reeve M. Bailey and I had drifted down that beautiful stream in a rowboat, with many stops to look, swim, and explore, on a perfect day way back in June 1930. We caught a few snakes, chiefly the brown water snake, *Natrix* (=*Nerodia*) *taxispilota,* and we saw several alligators and many birds and turtles that were new to us. There was no sign of human occupancy or interference in that wilderness, except for a tiny, nearly invisible dock along one side of the river. That day still rates high in my memory.

I was incensed by the news in Archie's letter. The Oklawaha was to be destroyed by a stupid political boondoggle. Was no part of Florida safe from human interference? Isabelle and I, with help from Fred Ulmer and other friends, circulated petitions to be signed and sent to the governor of Florida. We wrote letters disclaiming against the "rape of the river," and urged that the project be halted.

Marjorie Harris Carr, Archie's wife, alter ego, and the mother of his five children, took up the figurative cudgels and organized the Florida Defenders of the Environment, and for years, even after Archie's death, carried on the battle. She and her many associates were successful in stopping the asinine project, but only after severe damage had been done to the Oklawaha basin. As I write this, the chief remaining obstacle to its complete restoration, a man-made impediment to free flow known as the Rodman Dam, still stands. A handful of fishermen, by putting pressure on a local politician, are blocking the removal of that worthless obstruction.

One of my great regrets is that I never visited the turtle nesting beaches at Tortuguero. We had a standing invitation from Archie, and, as we entered Ciudad Cuauhtemoc on the Guatemalan border during one of our grant-supported field trips to Mexico, Isabelle and I were sorely tempted to drive onward through Central America to Costa Rica. But *el Tapón* ("plug," "stopper," or "cork"), the landslide-plagued road through steep mountains, was closed, or so we were told. In any event, we would have been reluctant to spend grant money just to visit the scene of one of Archie Carr's greatest triumphs. He, with his fluent Spanish, had single-handedly succeeded in getting the authorities to give the beaches national park status, and to permit the exhaustive and highly productive research that served so importantly in saving the green turtle, *Chelonia mydas,* from oblivion. Then, too, our time was short. I worked for the Philadelphia Zoo, and I had to be back on duty on a pre-designated date.

DORIS MABLE COCHRAN (1898-1968) was one of the kindest and most helpful herpetologists who ever lived. Like so many ladies, especially unmarried ones, she was attracted to teenagers, and she welcomed them, as budding herpetologists, and encouraged them in every possible way. By the time I first met her I was well into my 20s, but whenever I arrived at her office, she dropped her own work to assist me. She was at the U.S. National Museum, so designated at the time, and a division of the Smithsonian Institution.

Doris had a heavy workload. Dr. Leonhard Stejneger, her immediate superior, had become an administrator, and she was directly responsible for the amphibian and reptile collections. She had only a single helper, a man who, although conscientious and a faithful worker, had no knowledge of herpetology. She called him Barry, but I never did learn his last name. To accommodate the level of education of such assistants, a system was devised whereby individual specimens could be retrieved from the collection room by their alphabetical and numerical designations. Thus, G76, to pick a hypothetical example, would mean bottle 76 on shelf G. Bottles of similar size were grouped together. Doris's records of individual specimens bore the appropriate letters and numbers, and, when a loan was requested, she would give Barry a list, and he would assemble the bottles and help her pack their contents for shipment. When loans were returned, the process was reversed. The system, of course, precluded any attempt to store specimens in systematic order.

Insofar as I know, Doris never had a secretary. She typed all of her own correspondence and manuscripts and such business matters as loan sheets to be signed. A large number of her communications to me, and which are still in my archival files, were written in longhand, especially during the later years of her life.

When I started examining USNM specimens for my herpetological studies, I began finding errors and discrepancies. I called each to Doris's attention as it arose, and in so doing I learned much about the history of the USNM. During the early years, when Spencer Fullerton Baird was struggling to process the collections that were

arriving, often rapidly, from various explorations of the American West, the Mexican Boundary Survey, and elsewhere, government clerks, paid at the rate of 15 cents an hour, were assigned to attach tags to specimens and to record data. Like Barry, they were not trained scientists, and their work was purely mechanical. I found that digits sometimes were transposed, as, for example, when I was working on *Elaphe vulpina.* Barry quickly located the snake numbered as *vulpina,* but it was identifiable as *E. obsoleta.* By trying various combinations of the same digits arranged in other sequences, we eventually found the *vulpina.* The tags had been switched; that is, attached to the wrong snakes.

During the mid-1940s I attempted my first paper on Mexican herpetology with a review of what was then designated as *Natrix valida,* the Mexican west coast water snake. The paper was based entirely on museum specimens. My fieldwork south of the border did not begin until 1949. I ran into a problem that Doris helped me to solve. The cotypes of Edward Drinker Cope's *Tropidonotus celaeno* consisted of seven specimens in the USNM and two at the Academy of Natural Sciences of Philadelphia, all accompanied by paper tags bearing Cope's original label "No. 351." Doris told me that, after Cope's demise, Dr. Stejneger went through the large collection of specimens at Cope's home, where he had done so much of his work. Stejneger returned some of the material to the National Museum, and some was sent to the Philadelphia Academy. Unfortunately, the splitting of series of specimens with the same field data, some in one museum and some in another, has caused frequent confusion.

Despite her heavy workload, Doris managed to publish many papers and articles of her own, well over 100, counting popular and semipopular contributions. Her principal interest was in frogs, and among her publications were the "Frogs of Southeastern Brazil" and "Frogs of Colombia," the latter with Coleman J. Goin as second author. Both are long and thorough works, aggregating more than 1,000 printed pages. Among other things, she wrote a wartime handbook on venomous snakes for the use of the military, but her most successful book was "Living Amphibians of the World," which was translated into many foreign languages. Several of her papers, the scientific ones especially, she illustrated herself with pen-and-ink drawings. One day I mentioned that I had better find an artist who could portray some of the perplexing pattern variations of the water snakes from near the southern tip of the Baja California peninsula. Her instant response was, "Let me do them for you," and I gratefully accepted her offer.

Doris Cochran was a gracious lady who invariably

placed her duty to help others, as a federal employee, ahead of any other interests. Her personal accomplishments, in addition to her stewardship of the USNM herpetological collection, were many, and not all devoted to research and science. On her own time she was an active devotee of handicrafts of many types, notably spinning and weaving. Personally, I recall her with affection and gratitude. I was greatly distressed when she died very shortly after her retirement from the museum in 1968.

RAYMOND LEE DITMARS (1876-1942) was by far the best-known American herpetologist during the early part of the twentieth century, largely because his name frequently appeared in the newspapers. To many persons, especially the lay public, the name Ditmars was synonymous with snakes. As a former "New York Times" reporter, he knew what constituted a good story, and he also had a flare for the dramatic. In his day, the two large pit vipers of the American Tropics, the bushmaster and the fer-de-lance, were almost legendary, at least insofar as their occurrence in zoo collections was concerned. He made several trips to Panama in search of them and other reptiles, amphibians, and insects that would make good exhibits for the Bronx Zoo's reptile house. Invariably when he returned by ship from such excursions, he was met by a battery of reporters and news photographers eager to record the results of his quest. On one occasion the word "fer-de-lance" was misinterpreted, and a story was printed about how famed curator Ditmars brought home a colony of "fertile ants" for the zoo.

Once he transported a king cobra on the train with him, and the news leaked out, much to his embarrassment and the consternation of the railroad company. I was luckier than he was when I carried a small "fer-de-lance" (an unidentified species of the *Bothrops* complex) in my lower berth from St. Louis to Toledo. Both snakes were securely confined, of course, but no one except Marlin Perkins knew about mine.

As a writer, Ditmars authored a series of popular volumes, and his "Reptile Book," first published in 1907 but reprinted many times, became the bible for many of us with a serious interest in herpetology. It rapidly went out of print, however, and it was quite a few years before I could afford the price of a secondhand personal copy. It was the only well-illustrated work on the subject that was available to herpers for many years, but it suffered from following a nomenclature that soon became outdated. Among the scientific names were *Ophibolus*

instead of *Lampropeltis, Eutaenia* instead of *Thamnophis, Cistudo* for *Terrapene,* and so on. It was a long time before Ditmars could convince Doubleday, his publisher, to permit him to write a complete revision, which eventually appeared as the "Reptiles of North America." The new book followed the technical names in Stejneger and Barbour's checklists, many of which are still in vogue. Ditmars's other books, such as the "Reptiles of the World" and "Snakes of the World," as well as several on his adventures in the field and at the zoo, had a wide readership.

Ditmars visited me while I was still at the Toledo Zoo, and we posed together for a publicity picture in which I pretended to swab out the mouth of a tree cobra, *Pseudohaje,* he was holding. When I went to work at Toledo, and again when I moved back to Philadelphia, his fine Italian hand assisted me in getting established. His reputation as the leading reptile curator was unchallengeable.

Raymond L. Ditmars had a way with young people that made him their hero, an oracle to whom they could turn whenever questions about animals came to mind. He knew how to phrase his statements in the language of the layman, and his lifetime of caring for reptiles, writing books about them, and appearing on the lecture platform placed him in a unique position. He could present reptiles in their true light at a time when they suffered from a severe stigma they certainly didn't deserve. He made friends wherever he went, and his patience in answering questions, even the most commonplace, endeared him to the public. Although he lacked formal training, he participated in a number of research projects, and he assumed a leading role in helping to provide a commercially produced serum for treating snakebite.

One day when I was in his office at the Bronx Zoo in the late 1930s, we were engaged in a lively conversation about snakes when the head keeper rapped gently on the door and said, "Doc, there's a couple of kids out here who want to see you for a minute." Ditmars politely asked me if I minded, and, when I indicated that I surely didn't, he told the keeper to bring the young men in. They were about 17 years of age, painfully shy, and their manner of speaking suggested they were from south of the Mason-Dixon Line. They haltingly introduced themselves and said that they had corresponded with him, and just wanted to meet him. After shaking hands, one of the lads said, "Doctah Ditmars, ah ain't gonna wash mah hand for a whole month now that it's held yours."

It became fashionable for certain professional herpetologists to criticize Ditmars, and even to call him a charlatan. A notable exception was Emmett Reid Dunn, who often used and recommended to others the lists of genera, the number of species in each, and their general distribution that appeared in the "Reptiles of the World." Ditmars's information was not always correct and up-to-date, but he had a wide audience. Many of his critics, some of whom produced important papers on systematics, had the unhappy disadvantage of writing for only a small group of their peers. Ditmars doubtless had his faults, but he was the great popularizer of herpetology, and he helped me personally many times. He died in 1942 at the age of 66 from causes stemming from a chronic weak voice. It doubtless resulted from lecturing to large audiences and having to speak very loudly back in the days before microphones and loudspeakers.

EMMETT REID DUNN (1894-1956) was a genius, but an impetuous one at times. I had heard much about him during my many pilgrimages to the Museum of Zoology at the University of Michigan, when I was associated with the Toledo Zoo. I knew he was a great enthusiast and that he had a phenomenal knowledge of reptiles and amphibians in general. He was also the author of "The Salamanders of the Family Plethodontidae," a classic work that opened up a whole new facet of herpetology for many of us. I looked eagerly forward to meeting him when I joined the staff of the Philadelphia Zoo. He was on the faculty of Haverford College, and he lived with his wife, Merle, in nearby Bryn Mawr.

Dunn worked during the years when part of the measure of a herpetologist's professional standing was based on his ability to find and describe new species. Each kind was distinguished solely by its morphological peculiarities. In short, one looked at the material at hand and compared it with other specimens of its own group, and, if it seemed unique, gave it a name. We were still a long way from having to discover new species by sophisticated laboratory techniques, such as have come into vogue fairly recently.

I can remember twice when Dixie, as Dunn was known to his close friends, let his enthusiasm run away with him. The first involved two large anacondas on exhibition in the old reptile house, over which I presided. He paid me a visit soon after my arrival at the Philadelphia Zoo. While we were touring the building, he stopped, looked long and steadily at the two big snakes, and then announced that they represented two new species. I was startled, of course, but his excitement was so contagious that I momentarily forgot the cau-

tious approach which the people at the University of Michigan had sought to instill in me. He invited me to be the junior author and left it up to me to put the paper together. I read everything I could about anacondas, which wasn't much. I looked for other specimens, and found two large skins at the Commercial Museum, an old Philadelphia institution. Anacondas were scarce in collections, no doubt because the preservation and storage of such large reptiles presented curatorial problems. Counting scales and making measurements on live anacondas was difficult, especially on the larger of our two, which was more than 13 feet in total length. The head scales were easy. I simply waited until the snakes were close to the plate glass surrounding their respective cages. But I had to requisition a large group of keepers to hold each as straight as possible while I counted such things as ventrals, subcaudals, and dorsal scale rows, and ran my flexible tape down the back and under the tail of each. Dunn added a number of facts to what I had written, and our paper was soon published, along with photographs of the two big constrictors. To the best of my knowledge, it is only recently that the anacondas are being studied in depth. It seems clear now, however, that the larger of our two snakes was simply an aberrant common anaconda, *Eunectes murinus.* The other, which we named for Rodolphe Meyer de Schauensee, the distinguished ornithologist who had brought the two snakes back from an expedition to South America, apparently is a valid species, *Eunectes deschauenseei.*

Not so, however, was a most unusual frog that Dunn described in 1943. He found it in a preserved collection while he and Merle were in Bogotá, Colombia, for a year or so during World War II. I have always suspected they were there for some hush-hush reason associated with the war, but I have no proof, and they avoided my questions when they returned. During their absence I acted as one of Dixie's helpers. He wrote to me repeatedly for copies of papers on neotropical herpetology, and I was sometimes hard-pressed to keep up with him. I had to borrow books from the library of the Academy of Natural Sciences, take them to the zoo, and have my secretary copy the pertinent pages word for word. No handy photocopying machines in those days.

But back to the frog. Dunn wrote, in part, that "it was a single male of a tree-frog so extraordinary that I could scarcely believe my eyes (and I am a long-time 'aficionado' of tree-frogs). It is unquestionable [sic] new to science, and may appropriately be called *Hyla phantasmagoria* sp. nov. [new species]." It had enormous hands, feet, and toe discs. Alas, Edward Drinker Cope had described the same species 57 years previously, as

William E. Duellman found during his exhaustive studies on the hylid frogs. It's correct name is *Hyla miliaria*. Again, Dunn's enthusiasm had run away with him. Despite his occasional impetuosity, however, Dixie described many species that have stood the test of time.

Over the years, I was a visitor, every month or two or three, to the Dunn home, usually during the evenings, and sometimes also for dinner. I was constantly impressed by the depth of Dixie's knowledge and his ability to answer my innumerable questions promptly and lucidly. He and Merle regaled me with tales of their experiences in Costa Rica and Panama, where they went on field trips at almost annual intervals. I urged him to assemble at least a checklist of the known species, and I even envisioned a general work, which he probably could have put together with ease. I offered to serve as his secretary and record what he had to say. It was all too obvious, however, that he had succumbed to the "describe new species syndrome," and other things had lower priorities.

Once, when we were on a brief evening field trip together in nearby New Jersey, we listened to and collected what is now known as *Pseudacris triseriata kalmi*, the New Jersey chorus frog. Dunn insisted there were two species involved, because we heard two different calls. It was not yet generally known that frogs can have a variety of notes, such as an alarm call as well as a mating call. He carefully separated the frogs with one call from those with the other, but when he returned to the laboratory he couldn't tell them apart. He did not pursue the topic, even though his search for new species was never ending.

One of the Dunns' major, but virtually unknown, contributions to herpetology was their curating of the collection at the Academy of Natural Sciences, which was rich in types and historic significance. It had long been neglected because there was no curator directly responsible for it. The Dunns devoted at least one day a week for almost a decade to the formidable chore of rearranging and labeling the collection and preparing a card index. Dixie also identified, and the two of them catalogued, a large number of specimens that had accumulated over a period of many years.

Dunn was a heavy smoker and drinker; Merle also indulged but to a lesser extent. Haverford College was a Quaker school, and using alcohol was very much frowned upon. Each evening the shades in their house were carefully lowered. Once I aided their smoking habit. During the war years there were many shortages, cigarettes among them. One of their local store owners received a shipment, and he alerted his best customers. On a certain evening at 8:00 P.M. he would dole out one pack of cigarettes to each person on a first-come, first-served basis. The Dunns asked me if I would accompany them, because they knew I had quit smoking and I would give them my pack. I obliged them, even though it required a long drive from my home to theirs. So I contributed in a small way to Dixie's downfall. Excessive nicotine over a period of years, augmented by too much alcohol, formed a deadly combination. One day in 1955 I was invited to their home for lunch, and I was stunned when Merle announced, in Dixie's presence, that he had throat cancer. My more or less regular visits ceased, but I saw Dixie several times subsequently until he entered the hospital for a long terminal stay. About a week before he died on February 13, 1956, at the age of 62, Merle telephoned me and asked me to visit his hospital room. She looked gaunt after her long vigil as his constant bedside companion. As for him, his appearance was truly dreadful. The doctors had fashioned a sizable hole in the side of his neck through which he was both breathing and being fed. I bid him farewell, but I have never forgotten that ghastly experience. What a horrible way for an esteemed friend to leave this world!

HOWARD KAY GLOYD (1902-1978) was unquestionably my closest herpetological colleague. We first met in 1929 at the University of Michigan, where he was a graduate student. I, as the very young curator of reptiles at the Toledo Zoo, made frequent pilgrimages to Ann Arbor. There I visited with the distinguished authorities on amphibians and reptiles, who were then on the faculty, and particularly with their students, who were much closer to my own age. Howard Gloyd and I became fast friends. We were destined to publish several technical papers together, one of which, a lengthy monograph on *Agkistrodon*, had a gestation period of almost six decades.

How long ago those days now seem and how ambitious we were and how many different schemes entered our youthful heads. We published two short papers together while he was still in school, one of which was the description of the broad-banded copperhead, *A. contortrix laticinctus*. Soon afterward he startled me by proposing that we monograph the entire genus together, on a world-wide basis. Although we both knew a lot about the North American forms of the group, we certainly didn't realize what we were getting into insofar as the Old World taxa were concerned. I facetiously remarked that maybe the "Gloyd and Conant" combination might someday come to rival the author combination of "Baird and Girard," which appeared in a large part of the herp literature during the last few decades of the nineteenth century. He often twitted me about it, but I think he sometimes hoped it just might come to pass.

Over the decades we were each other's most voluminous correspondents, we met whenever possible, and when the going got rough, we often turned to each other for help, like affectionate siblings.

Howard, or H.K., as his close friends addressed him, was born on February 12, 1902, at De Soto, Kansas. His father, Winfield Scott Gloyd, was a skilled harness maker, but the very nature of his profession required frequent moves. Once all the horses in the general area were properly caparisoned for work, the family had to move on. So they had a variety of addresses in Kansas over the years.

H.K. early developed an interest in natural history, which was greatly encouraged by his mother. Birds were his first love, but he also became an accomplished taxidermist. By his late teenage years, his work—including a mounted swan, eagle, and coyote—was displayed in the window of a store in Wellsville, Kansas, where the Gloyds were living at the time. Young Howard was an excellent student, and, after receiving bachelor's and master's degrees from Kansas institutions, he aspired to seek his doctorate at the University of Michigan under the chairmanship of Frank N. Blanchard, then a leading authority on North American snakes. H.K. had corresponded with Blanchard, but he was totally unprepared for their first meeting. Blanchard was an austere and unfriendly person, characteristics that were not revealed in his seemingly cordial letters. Howard was dismayed at first, but he persevered and became Blanchard's most distinguished student.

Blanchard's classic dichotomous key for the identification of the snakes of the United States, Canada, and Lower California had recently been published (in 1925) and, after H.K. had proved himself in the eyes of the master, they decided to write a handbook on snakes of the same general area. Toward that end they undertook a field expedition of several months in late 1935 and early 1936, chiefly through the South and West. Blanchard was so extremely timid and unsure of himself in the field that, in later years, Howard took pleasure in regaling his friends about some of the ludicrous situations that developed. That project, unfortunately, never reached fruition, because of Blanchard's sudden demise at the age of 48 and Howard's acceptance of the directorship of the Chicago Academy of Sciences late in 1936.

A few months after Gloyd's death in 1978, I wrote a rather lengthy review of his life and accomplishments that was published in the "Herpetological Review." I quote the following, with slight emendation, from that account:

I admired H. K. for all he did at Chicago despite the many difficulties he had to face and the slender resources at his disposal. The Academy, although it had a long tradition as a respected scientific institution, was tiny compared with the massive Field Museum, and it had little financial support from local citizens. Many people thought one natural history museum was enough. Funds were always short. The staff was inadequate. He had both a board of trustees and a board of scientific governors with which to cope and whose members represented diverse personalities and interests. The effects of the depression years had to be endured, although help, provided through such agencies as the WPA, enabled the Academy to catch up with some of its deferred maintenance and to undertake a few new activities. One of those was printing and, with hand-set type and a primitive press operated by an old-time journeyman printer, H. K. accomplished wonders. He edited and even wrote a fair portion of several journals, including the Academy's Bulletin and Special Publications, the Chicago Naturalist, and Natural History Miscellanea. The last named he developed into a nationally recognized and widely used outlet for short papers, chiefly but not confined to herpetology. The early issues of the now venerable journal, Herpetologica, were set by hand and printed at the Academy. With it all, Gloyd found time to complete his long work on the rattlesnakes, the broad nucleus of which was based on the material he assembled while preparing his doctoral dissertation at Michigan.

Nathan Smith Davis III, M.D., who had been President of the Chicago Academy of Sciences for 18 years, died in 1956. As so often happens when a strong leader succumbs, a new clique among the trustees gained power and basic policies were changed. Gloyd wisely avoided open conflict, and he left Chicago in 1958 to become a faculty member at the University of Arizona. He was no stranger to the Southwest to which he had repeatedly made field trips for decades. He was, in fact, very much at home and relished being in a warm climate far away from the wintry blasts from Lake Michigan. And finally, after a long struggle as an administrator, he achieved the profession for which he was most admirably suited—teaching and interpreting vertebrate zoology, zoogeography, herpetology, and the natural history of the desert.

Gloyd was fascinated by the pit vipers, a group with which he first became acquainted during his youthful years in eastern Kansas. He discovered that both the copperhead, *Agkistrodon contortrix*, and the timber rattlesnake, *Crotalus horridus,* were abundant in the valley of the Marais des Cygnes-Osage River system. Sometimes the overturning of a single large flat rock in the spring of the year would reveal a half dozen or more snakes, including nonvenomous species as well as one or both of the two pit vipers. He caught a great many copperheads and maintained them in captivity, but the rattlesnakes were his favorites.

The culmination of Gloyd's intensive years of study was the publication, on May 5, 1940, of his "The Rattlesnakes, Genera *Sistrurus* and *Crotalus,*" by the Chicago Academy of Sciences. It was a book of 270 pages and 31 plates, and it sold for $2.50 a copy! With its detailed descriptions of the many taxa, discussions of variation and affinities, synonymies, lists and carefully drafted maps of locality records, and a generous bouquet of illustrations, mostly from photographs that Gloyd took himself, the book quickly became *the* authority on rattlesnakes. It was soon out of print, but the Society for the Study of Reptiles and Amphibians considered it of such great historic value that it was reprinted in 1978. It includes introductory matter about both Dr. Gloyd and rattlesnakes written by Hobart M. Smith and Herbert S. Harris, Jr. It quickly went out of print again. Sadly, H.K. died before it was off the press, but he was aware that it was well under way, and he took great interest in the introductory matter, advance copies of which were available to him.

During his lifetime, Howard Gloyd described 19 new taxa among the Crotalinae, including eight kinds of rattlesnakes, one in the genus *Trimeresurus,* and the others for members of the *Agkistrodon* complex. His proposal of the new generic name *Deinagkistrodon,* for the hundred-pace viper of Taiwan, mainland China, and northern Vietnam, was also published posthumously.

Conversely, new snakes in the genera *Crotalus, Elaphe, Heterodon,* and *Sonora,* as well as three species of insects, bear the designation *gloydi.* After I reopened studies on the cantil of Middle America, I obtained many additional specimens and was able to confirm Gloyd's prediction that there might be another recognizable race of the species at the extreme southern end of the range. I named it *Agkistrodon bilineatus howardgloydi* in his honor. Oddly, it already bore a distinctive vernacular name, and was known by the Spanish-speaking inhabitants as the *castellana.*

It was interesting, although regrettable in some ways, that there were two giants in the field simultaneously. While Gloyd was earning his outstanding reputation in the Midwest, Laurence M. Klauber was emerging as an authority on rattlesnakes in California. They exchanged information and were always polite, but there was a wariness and reserve that precluded any close cooperation between them. It was tacitly agreed that Gloyd would concentrate on the genus *Sistrurus* and the eastern forms of *Crotalus,* whereas Klauber would work on the taxa of the West. Klauber's personal financial resources enabled him to hire help for scale counting and other time-consuming research chores. He was thus able to do many things that were beyond the reach of Gloyd. There was no National Science Foundation or similar large fund-granting agencies in those days.

Because I transferred to the Philadelphia Zoo in 1935, the year before Gloyd moved to Chicago, our work on the snakes of the *Agkistrodon* group advanced only slowly. We did manage to publish a few short papers together, one of which included the description of the Trans-Pecos copperhead, *A. contortrix pictigaster.* In 1958, about the time that H.K. left to join the faculty of the University of Arizona, I resigned from the project. My administrative duties had multiplied, and my research had become focused on the water snakes of Mexico. Isabelle and I were destined to spend the piecemeal equivalent of a full year exploring a great many Mexican streams, lakes, and other bodies of water. My withdrawal had the salutary effect of making it simpler for Gloyd to apply for grant money. Fortuitously, we both received our grants from the National Science Foundation on the same day, his for work on *Agkistrodon,* and mine to explore the hinterlands of Mexico.

We kept in close touch, and I continued to help H.K. with data, and I even sent him a sizable series of live vipers of the group from Korea that arrived unexpectedly at the Philadelphia Zoo. A few weeks after Isabelle died, in November 1976, I could contain my grief alone no longer, so I visited the Gloyds in Tucson. I was horrified, when I arrived, to discover that H.K. had an advanced case of bone cancer. A day or so later I summoned up the courage to ask him how he was coming with the monograph. His reply was, "I'll never be able to finish it." In response I said, "I'll do it for you," whereupon he broke down and wept tears of joy. He knew I could complete the job on which he had labored for so many years. His detailed information on 6,200 individual preserved specimens, and the huge data bank that he had culled from the voluminous literature, would be used after all.

He had worked like the proverbial Trojan for decades. There were no computers in those days, and the information he so laboriously compiled was stored on 3x5 file cards, tens of thousands of them, most of which he typed himself. There also was a separate 8x11 sheet for every specimen examined; I had done a few hundred of them myself. Each sheet was filled, sometimes on both sides, with detailed scale counts, measurements, and pattern and color notes. Almost all of these he wrote by hand after he had spot-checked on the scale counting done by students and others whom he had hired with his grant money. What a colossal chore he had undertaken. In any event, he knew that my promise would ensure the completion of the vast project he had envisioned a half century previously. My efforts and the problems I encountered are reported in some detail in the introductory matter of the lengthy "Snakes of the *Agkistrodon* Complex: A Monographic Review," by Gloyd and Conant, which was published in 1990 by the Society for the Study of Amphibians and Reptiles.

H.K. was a friendly, likable person who was always ready and willing to talk with his friends, his peers, and their students. He was a good raconteur, and he readily shared his broad knowledge of wild organisms, plant and animal. He was also talented in many ways. He was a splendid woodworker, and he built many pieces of furniture of cabinetmaker quality. He invented the snake pullman, the type of shipping box we used for fieldwork and for sending venomous snakes to colleagues, or, in my case, to other zoos. It featured a false screened lid beneath the regular wooden one, so the serpents could neither escape nor strike upward when the box was opened. Thus, the recipient could see where the snakes were before attempting to remove them. At first he made his pullmans from dovetailed wooden boxes that had originally contained small arms ammunition. He had them handy because of his great interest in firearms, which he often used, especially with dust shot to collect lizards. Gloyd also was an excellent photographer, and he devised a way of eliminating shadows in his finished snake portraits.

Of all his talents, the one that he enjoyed the most was being a musician. He was an accomplished tympanist, and he played the drums in high school and the colleges he attended, in marching bands, and, later, almost the entire gamut from symphonic music to Dixieland. The latter "happy music" was a special favorite, and many times Isabelle and I joined him and his charming wife, Kathryn, to hear the best Dixieland artists in Chicago, and twice in New Orleans when we were attending meetings there. For a decade, beginning in the late 1940s, there was a weekly jam session in the basement of the Chicago Academy. There the Academic Cats held forth with a full complement of Dixieland instruments, with H.K. on the drums. Each of the players held a Ph.D., and they performed so well that some of the great professionals occasionally sat in with them.

During his career, Gloyd earned a number of honors in Greek letter societies. He was a Fellow and Fifty-Year

Member of the American Association for the Advancement of Science, and was listed in "American Men of Science" and "Who's Who in America." He also received an honorary doctorate from Ottawa University, where he had taught when he was quite young.

Howard Gloyd was married twice, first to Leonora K. Doll, from 1925 to 1947, and by whom he had two children, Helen Katherine and Roger Scott, the latter named for me and his grandfather, W. Scott Gloyd. His second wife was Kathryn J. Stephenson, to whom he was married for almost 31 years. A few years after H.K. died, Kathryn and I were married; she continues to use the name Kathryn J. Gloyd.

NORMAN EDOUARD HARTWEG (1904-1964) was a turtle expert and one of the graduate students at the University of Michigan with whom I developed a close rapport when I was an enthusiastic stripling at the Toledo Zoo. He and I talked turtles, studied turtles, and hunted them in the field together. We became close friends, visited back and forth, and, once, when a blizzard blew into Ann Arbor, he and his devoted wife, Margaret, offered me shelter for the night. We had "turtled" all day, but changed the subject after supper by playing cribbage, at which I had phenomenal luck, beating him time and time again.

Hartweg had a most unusual nickname: Kibe. Its origin dated from his childhood in Warren, Pennsylvania, where the neighborhood youngsters played an outdoor game called "kibe," which was akin to hide-and-seek. Somehow that word became attached to him, and Margaret said that no one except his mother ever called him Norman. His middle name, Edouard, stemmed from his French ancestry.

Kibe and I did a little fieldwork together in southern Michigan and adjacent Ohio, but we also made two excursions much farther away from our respective bases. The first was in April 1932, when we and several colleagues planned to try our luck collecting in the Pymatuning Swamp region, which was then being clearcut so it could be flooded to form the large reservoir that now straddles the Ohio-Pennsylvania line not too far south of Lake Erie. My friend Malcolm K. Murphy, who was adept at catching turtles, drove from Toledo with me; Charles F. Walker came up from Columbus, Ohio; M. Graham Netting came from Pittsburgh; and Kibe drove all the way from Ann Arbor. We had agreed to meet in Linesville, a small town east of the swamp.

We arrived at various times during the morning. Murphy and I promptly set out on foot along a rough road through the swamp, and Kibe, who came a little later, took off in another direction to set his turtle traps, which were legal in Pennsylvania but not in Ohio. We assembled at a restaurant in Linesville for lunch, but it was far from a festive occasion. Hartweg, while wading in the swamp, had found a human corpse clad in overalls and long dead. He was badly upset, and his composure was further shaken by having to report the discovery to the police. Our lunch was interrupted by the arrival of two state troopers seeking directions on where to find the body. Even though we went afield again during the afternoon, Kibe's ordeal was still not over. The police couldn't find the place, and he had to take them there in person. As Netting recorded in his journal, the troopers had looked only on one side of the road, thinking that no sensible person would have entered the other side. The body was not more than 10 yards from the road.

What we had expected to be an enjoyable and memorable weekend was spoiled by the gruesome discovery. It was memorable, to be sure, but we soon scattered. Hartweg left for Warren to visit his family, Murphy and I went back into Ohio to try our luck there, and the others pursued their own interests.

The corpse was that of a woman, and she had been killed some months earlier with a hatchet or similar instrument. Identification was made through dental records, but we never did learn whether or not the murderer was brought to justice.

Our second excursion was much farther afield. Kibe invited Murphy and me to accompany him, in April 1933, to Reelfoot Lake in western Tennessee, which truly had an immense and varied turtle population. With us were Wesley Clanton, then a student at Michigan, and Kibe's brother, Herbert. Unlike our previous field trip together, this one was fun, extremely productive, and it started off with a real belly laugh. Somewhere en route to Reelfoot, Murphy demonstrated his technique for catching a basking turtle, by stepping into water on the dead run, turtle net in hand, and promptly disappearing from sight. What we all had mistaken for shallow water was quite deep. The Mississippi and its tributaries were passing through an exceptionally large spring flood.

During his lifetime Kibe had more than his share of frustrations. He planned a taxonomic review in depth of the painted turtles, *Chrysemys,* as the subject for his dissertation. In the midst of his studies, a paper was published at the Field Museum that, in essence, skimmed the cream off any conclusions he might have reached. He continued with his review, but Helen T. Gaige, then in charge of herpetological graduate studies at Michigan's famed Museum of Zoology (UMMZ), told me how unethical she thought it was, especially since the senior author of the unexpected paper surely must have been aware of what Hartweg was doing.

The kinosternid turtles were Kibe's major interest, especially after he received his Ph.D. The group includes not only the mud turtles, *Kinosternon,* and the musk turtles, *Sternotherus,* but also other genera in Middle America. He described a number of new taxa, but a thorough review of the group was impossible. Dr. Leonhard Stejneger, of the National Museum, with the intention of doing the turtles to round out Edward Drinker Cope's huge opus on the "Crocodilians, Lizards, and Snakes of North America," published in 1900, transferred all the types, unique specimens, and many others to his private office. There they languished for a great many years. No one else was permitted to see them. So Kibe's efforts were blocked. After Dr. Stejneger died at the age of 92, it was discovered that he had made very little progress, and apparently had done nothing at all with the kinosternids.

Because turtles of that group were widespread and well represented in Mexico, a very large part of Kibe's postdoctoral fieldwork was done in that country. He traveled widely, visited the Volcán Parícutin not long after its sudden eruption, and ventured to far places, including Yucatán and the Isthmus of Tehuantepec. He added considerably to the UMMZ's holdings of Mexican material, and published a number of papers on a variety of topics. Like so many Americans of the period, he had been bitten by the "Mexico bug," the desire to visit and work in a region that had an extraordinarily diverse herpetofauna. Isabelle and I were also bitten, but not until after we had finished our field guide, which appeared in 1958.

Kibe remained at Ann Arbor, and eventually became a professor of zoology and curator of herpetology and assistant director of the UMMZ. For many years he had been interested in establishing a close working relationship with an institution in the Tropics to further field studies in biology. He found that a university in Chiapas was interested, but all authority for dealing with matters involving the United States was vested in Mexico City. So Kibe spent considerable time there, staying at the Hotel Geneve, often with Margaret, while he waited patiently for a call from Enrique Beltrán, Director of the Mexican Institute for Renewable Resources, who was trying to help by acting as a liaison with the authorities who could make the decision on Hartweg's proposal.

Luckily for us, Kibe was in Mexico City in 1960, where Isabelle and I were privileged to visit with him for a few days in August. He knew the best places to eat, and we dined together every evening in restaurants that served excellent food, and which we never would have found on our own. He had to stay by the telephone every morning, but one afternoon we went shopping, visiting more than a half dozen bookstores. I eventually found and bought the two-volume report on the hydrology of Mexico by Jorge L. Tamayo. It was germane to my own research in Mexico on water snakes, and it remains one of the more interesting (amusing?) pairs of books in my personal library, inasmuch as the first volume was bound upside down in its outer casing.

Kibe had two living treasures in his hotel bathroom. One was a narrow-bridged musk turtle, *Claudius angustatus*, the only living one I ever saw. There was also a giant musk turtle, *Staurotypus triporcatus*. I eventually caught a large example of the latter one night in Tabasco.

Poor Kibe. He remained in Mexico, but the time was not propitious for negotiations with gringos. Communists rioted at the Universidad Nacional Autónoma de Mexico, and he was even accused of being one. Nothing came of his efforts. What excruciating frustration he must have endured. He was to triumph elsewhere somewhat later, however. He was the prime mover in founding the Organization for Tropical Studies in Costa Rica, and was its first president.

Kibe also served as president of the American Society of Ichthyologists and Herpetologists in 1960 while I was the secretary. He and I, Margaret, and Isabelle shared a suite in the Conrad Hilton Hotel in Chicago during the meetings.

Kibe died when he was only 59. Pancreatic cancer destroyed him in just seven weeks. He succumbed on February 16, 1964. I was shocked. I felt almost as though I had lost a brother, and I was unable to hold back the tears, especially when I wrote a long letter of reminiscences and sympathies to Margaret.

At least I was able to do one thing for him in appreciation for all the help he had given me over the years. Coleman J. Goin and I published a short review on the spiny soft-shelled turtles in 1948, and we named a new subspecies *hartwegi* in his honor.

CARL FREDERICK KAUFFELD (1911-1974)

inspired a small legion of young herpetologists. He had a pleasant personality, he wrote in a free and easy manner, and he even had considerable skill as a pen-and-ink artist.

A number of those whom he influenced went on to enter the professional fields of zoo management, academia, or medicine, including William G. Degenhardt, Carl Gans, Charles Hackenbrock, Richard Highton, and John E. Werler. Many of the others became avid and even destructive collectors. In their eagerness to catch

snakes, they literally tore apart and destroyed many of the choice habitats Kauffeld described in his books. That, of course, aroused the ire of conservation-minded herpetologists. On the other hand, human impact, in one way or another, has now destroyed or seriously altered almost all of the habitats about which Kauffeld wrote, from the Pine Barrens of southern New Jersey to South Carolina and Arizona.

Kauffeld was born in Philadelphia to parents of German descent. During his high school years he haunted the Academy of Natural Sciences, where he worked for a time as a volunteer in entomology. He also frequented the zoo, where he became the friend of Robert Hess, also of German ancestry and who served as the reptile house keeper for 42 years. Young Carl was permitted to go behind the scenes and even to assist in the care of the collection, an experience that helped prepare him for his later career in the husbandry of captive reptiles. He continued his interest in the Philadelphia Zoo and often stopped to see me when he was in town to visit his parents.

In 1936, with the opening of the Staten Island Zoo, Kauffeld found himself in possession of a dream job. The zoo was housed in a single large building, a full half of which was devoted to reptiles, whereas the other half was divided among the mammals, birds, and fishes. His association with the Staten Island Zoo continued until his death. During most of that time he served as its curator of reptiles, but he also was its director for the last decade of his life. His reptile collection was noted for the longevity records it established, and for the completeness of the series of rattlesnakes on exhibition. Several times it boasted examples of all species and subspecies of rattlers known to be indigenous to the United States.

Fieldwork was almost an obsession with Carl Kauffeld, and he escaped from the ever-growing and oppressive megalopolis of New York at every opportunity. The nearby Pine Barrens were an excellent retreat, and he never lost interest in the area, assembling notes and distribution maps that were never organized and published. I was to continue his work there, and I did for a long time, but circumstances prevented me from completing it after my retirement and transfer to the American Southwest. While in search of rattlesnakes and, to his mind, lesser herps, he made many excursions to the South and to Arizona, and in 1940 he undertook a long collecting trip, often over primitive roads, as far south into Mexico as its capital. During World War II he served in the Army Medical Corps.

Although he made several technical contributions to the scientific herpetological literature, almost all of Kauffeld's writings were in a popular vein. He was a regular contributor to the "News Bulletin" of the Staten Island

Zoological Society (later renamed "In Animaland"), and to the newsletters of various amateur societies. His highly readable books entitled "Snakes and Snake Hunting" (published in 1957) and "Snakes: The Keeper and the Kept" (1969) had a profound influence on a vast number of ardent young herpetologists, but also on market hunters.

Kauffeld had three great weaknesses that got him into trouble. He was a notorious womanizer, a heavy drinker, and almost a chain-smoker. He once told me he would rather be dead than not be able to smoke. He got his wish. He continued, despite emphysema and the added burden of an oxygen tank, and died at the early age of 63.

LAURENCE MONROE KLAUBER (1883-1968)

was the most productive and respected amateur herpetologist of the twentieth century. He was an engineer by profession, and he eventually rose to the presidency of the San Diego Gas and Electric Company, and later served as chairman of its board. Herpetology with him was strictly an avocation, but he became involved in it in a big way.

Klauber's boyhood interest in reptiles was rekindled when Harry Wegeforth, M.D., founder of the San Diego Zoo, sought his help in identifying some of the snakes living in the zoo's collection. Klauber, with the aid of several professionals, quickly learned the herp fauna of southern California, and proceeded to write about it. As his expertise improved and his interests broadened geographically, he kept right on writing, and he eventually produced some 100 titles, many of which, because of their thoroughness and the new information they contained, were classics of their day. To further his studies, Klauber assembled a superb study collection of some 35,000 preserved specimens, mostly snakes from the United States and Mexico. Because he had seemingly unlimited funds, Klauber was able to hire promising young students to make scale counts for him and to take care of various mundane procedures. He also built up a library of 1,500 volumes and nearly 20,000 reprints. Both his collection and his library eventually were deposited with the San Diego Natural History Museum.

Laurence Klauber was instrumental in adding two novelties to herpetology, one trivial and the other profound. He may not have been the first person to introduce either, but his papers vaulted them firmly into common practice. In his travels on behalf of the power company, he had often noticed dead snakes on the paved roads of southern California, especially in the early mornings and, since most of them were pale in coloration, they were readily visible on the black macadam. So he began running the roads at night, collecting and carefully recording information on the serpents he found, dead or alive. He showed that some species, previously alleged to be rarities, actually were common and simply had not been sought during the cool hours of the night. He began using the acronym DOR (for "dead on the road"), and that abbreviation soon appeared in divers publications of other herpetologists. Much more scientific was his introduction of sophisticated statistics and graphics into the study of variation among snake populations. His training as an engineer no doubt prompted that approach, which later became, with various refinements, an integral part of innumerable contributions to herpetology.

Rattlesnakes were Klauber's major interest, and his studies and publications on them made him the leading authority, challenged only by Howard K. Gloyd, who also devoted much of his attention to rattlers. At that time, those venomous snakes were considered as vermin, to be slaughtered wherever they were found and as quickly as possible. They were in the same class as other so-called pests: coyotes, gophers, and prairie dogs among others. Bounties were paid in a great many states for dead rattlesnakes or parts thereof. Prairie rattlesnakes, *Crotalus viridis*, occurred in huge numbers around denning areas throughout much of their range. South Dakota even had its own rattlesnake exterminator, A. M. Jackley. We acquired many live ones from him during 1944 at 75 cents each to educate and entertain the visiting public on Sunday afternoons at the Philadelphia Zoo. We extracted venom from the snakes while people watched, and we then gave it at once to Sharpe and Dohme. That ethical drug house was hard-pressed to provide enough antivenin (snakebite serum) for our troops on training maneuvers in the southern United States. Quite a few of the men were bitten.

With his financial resources, Klauber was able to acquire and carefully preserve great numbers of rattlesnakes that otherwise would have been turned in for bounties or left to rot after being hacked or beaten to death. The large series he obtained from the same or nearby localities were ideally suited for his statistical calculations on variation and growth.

Now that the true role of predators in nature is better known, the "vermin" animals have many friends in the much more conservation oriented society that prevails today.

Klauber's greatest work was a massive 1,476-page, two-volume treatise entitled "Rattlesnakes/Their Habits, Life Histories, and Influence on Mankind," published in 1956 and partially revised in 1972. Isabelle and I were highly flattered when he requested a picture from our files in order to complete his series of portraits of all the various rattlesnake taxa. He used her photograph of the mottled rock rattlesnake, *Crotalus lepidus lepidus,* with due credit, in his book and also on the dust jacket of volume two of the first edition.

My efforts to meet Laurence Klauber seemed jinxed for an incredibly long time. Our correspondence dated back to April 1929, and he was helpful to me, a young beginner, in many ways. I studiously read his papers, so that, when I first visited San Diego in 1939, I was ready and able to identify the specimens we found when several members of the zoo staff took me on a field trip and tested my knowledge.

During my years at the Toledo Zoo, in the early 1930s, I visited the University of Michigan and its galaxy of leading herpetologists and their students whenever I could. During one such trip I learned that Klauber was due to arrive by train that very evening for a session at the university's Museum of Zoology the next day. I stayed late and waited at the station so I could drive him to his hotel, but, when the train arrived from Chicago, he was not aboard. A sudden and unexpected business appointment had forced him to alter his plans. I could not wait over, because I had to be at work in Toledo early the next morning.

Each time I was in San Diego, I tried to meet with him. We managed to talk at some length on the telephone more than once, but he was always burdened with lunches and dinners with associates or social activities stemming from his high position in the Gas and Electric Company. Finally, on Sunday, July 10, 1955, while Isabelle and I were visiting the city for several days, he drove us from our hotel to his beautiful home overlooking San Diego Bay and Point Loma. He escorted us to his huge collection in the basement and, later, while we were sipping highballs, he showed us several of his literary treasures, which included a strong representation of books dating back 100 years and more. We, of course, had a lively conversation.

How strange that we knew each other so well through correspondence, but met only a single time, and then only for a few hours!

ARTHUR LOVERIDGE (1891-1980) was neat and

meticulous. Not even a naval officer with white gloves could have found a speck of dust in his working quarters. His many papers were written with care, and he gave me copies of his reprints, even when they were in short supply. He said that I might need them to identify reptiles and amphibians received at the zoo. I did.

Loveridge was born in Wales in 1891, and he accu-

mulated a personal, carefully curated museum of the local fauna at an early age. After attending the University of South Wales and working in the Welsh National Museum, he applied for and received the curatorship of the natural history museum in Nairobi, British East Africa, when he was only 23. He found the collection in chaos, but promptly set it in order and soon was receiving a steady stream of new specimens.

In 1915 Loveridge joined the African Mounted Rifles, whose objective was to clear the enemy from neighboring German East Africa. Patriotism may have been a factor, but his enlistment also permitted him to get into the field for months at a time. He gathered up everything in sight, caught snakes that blundered into the tents of his brothers-in-arms, popped beetles into his killing bottle while under sniper fire, and worked far into the night with his trained native helpers preserving the menagerie that came his way. A regiment once waited while a chameleon was photographed on a rifle; he borrowed a general's car and chauffeur to rescue a collection of preserved snakes from a German's abandoned house; and once he prompted his sergeant to demand, "Is this a war or a bloomin' museum expedition?"

When the campaign was over he continued at the Nairobi Museum, but in 1921 he became an assistant game warden in the former German territory and was often called upon to trap or gun down lions that killed or injured tribespeople.

When Loveridge died, I wrote an obituary that was published in the "Herpetological Review," and I quote the following from it:

> *Loveridge was always resourceful, an asset that carried him through numerous tight spots during his many years of field work. An amusing example of his ingenuity occurred when he returned to his base in the far interior and was handed a telegram asking him to be in Mombasa, Kenya, in less than a week to meet his fiancée and be married by her uncle who was coming from Scotland for the occasion. Hurriedly, he sought emergency leave, packed his gear and transported it halfway across Tanganyika by rail, and then caught the twice-weekly train to Dar es Salaam on the coast. The ship he had hoped to board had left an hour before his arrival and another was not due for a fortnight. Nothing daunted, he virtually commandeered a sailing dhow to take him to the island of Zanzibar, fifty miles away, where oceangoing vessels were more apt to call. He rounded up the score of passengers who had not expected to leave until the following day, expedited their passage through the local health and other official formalities, and hired a tug to tow the dhow through the*

winding harbor channel to open water. With sails set, progress was excellent at first, but they were soon becalmed on the wrong side of Zanzibar. Loveridge talked the captain into having him rowed ashore where he hiked through a downpour to the nearest telephone, summoned a taxi, and soothed the customs officer who was perturbed by his unauthorized landing. Such singleness of purpose deserved its reward. A French liner arrived unexpectedly the next day and Loveridge landed at Mombasa in ample time to wed his fiancée, Mary Sloan, whom he affectionately called Queenie.

In 1924 Loveridge transferred to Harvard's Museum of Comparative Zoology, where he served with distinction until his retirement in 1967. He not only curated the large collection assembled by Thomas Barbour, but he also added impressively to it on his own, chiefly as the result of five long separate expeditions that he made during the period from 1926 to 1949, inclusive. All were to forested regions of East Africa, from Uganda and Kenya to Mozambique, and reports about them appeared in the bulletins of the MCZ. In addition to his prolific scientific contributions, Loveridge was a talented writer for the layman. He began by penning accounts of his adventures for popular magazines, such as the Philadelphia Zoo's "Fauna." Later, he produced four excellent books in the same style, among them "Many Happy Days I've Squandered" and "I Drank the Zambezi."

Loveridge and his wife retired to St. Helena Island in the South Atlantic, and, because we were both good correspondents, I came to know him better when he was far away than I did when he was at Harvard. He finished several long publications. Fortunately, I was able to help with various references he needed and to answer many questions. Also, in support of a hobby that began when he was a boy, I sent him a steady stream of postage stamps from my incoming mail, adding as many stamps as possible to each letter without exceeding the weight allowed by the post office.

Despite all the "roughing it" that Arthur Loveridge did for so many decades, he remained the proper Briton. I well recall that, at a small farewell luncheon at Harvard, he announced that the time had come to drop the formality. "Hereafter," he said, "I'm going to call you Conant." And so he did for many years, until we switched imperceptibly to first names.

He kept in touch with the world from his isolation on that tiny island by conducting a vast correspondence with friends and colleagues, each letter logged by number. His last one mailed to me, in late 1979, was No. 6,812! Loveridge died in 1980 when he was almost 89. What a productive, interesting, and useful life he had led.

ROBERT FRIEDRICH WILHELM MERTENS (1894-1975) was one of the world's great herpetologists. He was associated with the Natur-Museum und Forschungs-Institut Senckenberg in Frankfurt, Germany, from 1919 until his death in 1975. He took charge of the herpetological collection in 1920 and enormously increased its size and importance. He became the director of the museum in 1947, a post he held until his retirement in 1960, after which he remained on as a research associate. He was an able and prolific writer with almost 800 contributions on scientific subjects to his credit, in addition to hundreds of popular articles and book reviews. He traveled widely, especially in the Tropics, and often produced popular books about the things he saw during his peregrinations.

I did not know Mertens well, but I include him in these recollections largely because of two things: his stature as a herpetologist and the extraordinary parallel of his death to that of Karl Patterson Schmidt.

My first contact with Mertens was soon after World War II when, at the suggestion of M. Graham Netting, I wrote to him in Frankfurt. Graham knew that I was trying to build up my library, and he thought that Mertens might respond to a request for reprints. Two large heavy packages eventually arrived from Germany containing copies of scores of Mertens's papers, ranging from his exhaustive three-part work on the monitor lizards to short contributions on herpetoculture. He kept a large and varied live collection of amphibians and reptiles at his home. Unbelievably, his publications during the war years were printed on excellent coated paper, much in contrast with our own, when due to scarcity, printing paper of almost any kind was largely unavailable in America.

I met Robert Mertens only twice: once at a meeting of the American Society of Ichthyologists and Herpetologists, but he also did me the honor of spending a day at the Philadelphia Zoo in 1949. He duly recorded the visit in his book "Zwischen [between] Atlantik und Pazifik" about his trip to the United States, complimenting the zoo on its fine collection of animals in general, and including photographs of two wood turtles and a large Blanding's turtle I gave him to take home for his personal menagerie.

When the National Science Foundation provided funds for the ASIH to bring distinguished foreign colleagues to attend its fiftieth anniversary meeting, it was up to me, as president, to send out the invitations. Mertens politely thanked me, but he refused to come because he was deeply offended by what he considered to be an unfair review, in the Society's journal "Copeia," of his book entitled "Schildkröten, Krokodile,

Brückenechsen" (Turtles, Crocodilians, and the Tuatara), which he coauthored with Heinz Wermuth.

After his retirement, Mertens still had many papers he wished to finish and, in order to concentrate on them, he decided to see no one, except in emergencies. I advised him that Isabelle and I would stop at the Senckenberg during our 1967 tour of European zoos, including the excellent one in Frankfurt, and asked if he could spare the time just to say hello. He stuck to his decision and told me to see his assistant, Konrad Klemmer, instead. While we were in the museum, I saw Mertens pass through one of the larger halls, but I made no attempt to accost him, even though I felt sure he had seen me. Later, I had a nice note of apology from him.

On August 5, 1975, he was bitten by a twig-snake, *Thelotornis kirtlandii*, an African rear-fanged snake, which had long resided in his private collection. Instead of dying rather quickly, as Karl Schmidt had done, he lingered for almost three weeks, and he, too, kept an account of the effects of the bite, which did not yield to treatment in the absence of a specific antivenom. One of the last entries in his diary could be translated as "An appropriate end for a herpetologist."

MORRIS GRAHAM NETTING (1904-1996) was a good friend—a herpetologist, an able administrator, and a dedicated conservationist. I greatly admired him, and he helped me in many ways, particularly during the days long ago when I was engaged in my survey of the reptiles of Ohio.

Almost all of Netting's life was associated with Pittsburgh, Pennsylvania, and especially with the Carnegie Museum of Natural History. He was proud of his home city and advanced its fame and reputation at every opportunity. During one of my earliest visits to Pittsburgh he accompanied me on that city's funicular railway and told me, while we were at its summit, what had been done and was still being done to erase the stigma of "the dirtiest city in America." Its vast steel industry was notorious for the soot and air pollution it produced. Netting wrote the "Geography of Pittsburgh," which had a circulation of 100,000 copies. Decades later he was a founder of the Western Pennsylvania Conservancy, an organization that accomplished wonders largely under his leadership.

At the Carnegie Museum, Netting gradually rose through the ranks. First he was a volunteer, then little more than a clerk in the bird department at 25 cents an hour. Later he was Assistant Curator of Herpetology, then full Curator, Acting Director, Assistant Director, and finally Director, a post he occupied for 21 years. He

never deviated from his ambition to rise to the top, and he endured many hardships to achieve it.

When I left Toledo to return to Philadelphia in 1935, the effects of the Great Depression were still with us. On my trip eastward I was invited to be an overnight houseguest in a large, roomy structure that belonged to his wife, Jane's, father. There they raised two children on the meager and inadequate salary he earned at the museum. Money was so tight that they fed me on spoon bread, and shared what little else they had in their larder. I went to bed hungry.

During his younger years Netting was an active field herpetologist. In the late 1920s and early 1930s he collected in Venezuela and also in Central America and the Caribbean. Later he concentrated, chiefly on salamanders, in western Pennsylvania and West Virginia, but also far south through the Appalachians. He once told me that while he was in the Tropics, he avoided dairy products, just as Isabelle and I did during our many excursions in Mexico. He had found that avocados, which could be washed and prepared in person, were a welcome relief from a butterless diet. We followed his implied advice and fully agreed with him.

Among the salamanders he found a new species, which he named *Plethodon richmondi*. That was for Neil D. Richmond, whose duties, from 1951 to 1974, included curating and enlarging the Carnegie Museum's herpetological collection, which in bulk, diversity, and importance, is now recognized as one of the ten greatest in the country.

Our late colleague, N. Bayard "Bike" Green, of Marshall College, in Huntington, West Virginia, formally described another new salamander from the Cheat Mountain system as *Plethodon nettingi*.

"M. G. Netting," as the official list reads, was secretary of the American Society of Ichthyologists and Herpetologists from 1931 through 1947, and he subsequently served that organization for a two-year term as president. He was also awarded an honorary doctorate from Waynesburg College, Pennsylvania, in 1950.

Netting was always neat and dapper (except in the field). His carefully trimmed narrow mustache and small goatee were his hallmarks, and they helped to make him stand out in a crowd despite his small stature. He signed his name as "M. Graham Netting," and from my correspondence files (a full four inches thick in his case) I learned that I first wrote to him in 1931, but we addressed each other as "Dear Conant" and "Dear Netting" for six years before we were on a first-name basis, with "Graham" for him. I didn't know what the "M." stood for until I had reason to look it up sometime later. He was always proper and even pompous at times.

While Graham was curator of reptiles, he always greeted me warmly whenever I arrived in Pittsburgh. Not so after he became director of the museum! Late during 1956 Isabelle and I made a tour of midwestern herpetological centers seeking final corrections for the distribution maps for the first edition of our field guide. I wrote to Graham in advance, and we arrived at the time he had suggested. Although we could clearly see him from the hall, and he obviously was aware of our presence, protocol took precedence. We entered his secretary's office and introduced ourselves. She picked up the telephone, talked with him, and then escorted us to his inner sanctum.

Once Graham was invited to attend the annual banquet of Philadelphia Conservationists. During the cocktail hour and afterward he carried on a lively conversation with us and some of his other friends, and we invited him to sit with us. When the president rapped his gavel, however, signaling that we should be seated, Graham immediately deserted us and marched to the head table, where he was ensconced in a place befitting the head of a famous institution.

Graham was soft-spoken, but he could deliver blistering speeches calculated to arouse interest in conservation. He was ahead of us all in realizing what the future would be like, in view of the enormous increases in the human population. He wrote in 1966, "Now we have the better life. A car in every garage and a junkyard heralding every town; more leisure to fish, and fewer waters that can grow fish; and more miles of concrete to speed us to vacation spots more crowded than the neighborhoods we have just left."

Netting was an excellent writer when, as he put it, "I have time to work slowly and carefully." I was grateful to him for providing several articles for publication in our Philadelphia Zoo magazine "Fauna." Also, as I thumbed through our voluminous correspondence, I noted how much he assisted me with things herpetological even after he was burdened with the complexities of being a chief administrator. I was also impressed by how much we respected each other and how quickly he published a paper of mine in the "Annals of the Carnegie Museum" after I had accumulated solid evidence that the red-bellied turtle, *Pseudemys rubriventris*, was a native member of the Pennsylvania herpetofauna.

Two of Graham's greatest accomplishments come quickly to mind as I write these words. He set up an international program under which young students, especially those from third world countries, could visit the Carnegie Museum to study its holdings and receive training in collection management. He also created the Powdermill Nature Reserve in the Ligonier Valley, of Westmoreland County, which he considered as his most important achievement. He talked two members of the Mellon family into donating 2,100 acres of largely forested land to be set aside as a sanctuary in perpetuity for education and research. It was to the quiet and serenity of Powdermill that he retreated with his wife when he retired as director of the Carnegie Museum of Natural History in 1975.

I last saw Graham in 1991 at Penn State University. He had come as an invited, honored speaker to talk about me at the symposium that was given in my honor. We had a pleasant private visit, but it was marred by the news that Jane had recently died. When he left our hotel, I picked up his suitcase and offered to take it to the automobile waiting for him. He insisted on carrying it himself. He was still able and strong-willed. Just ten days later he sustained a debilitating stroke from which he never recovered, and through which he had to live until he died five years later.

We kept in touch, and I sent him several parts of my manuscript for this book, notably vignettes of persons he had known. I tried to telephone him, but my poor hearing combined with his speech impediment made communication impossible. He managed to write to me on a few occasions. One of his attendants, who could type, prepared letters from his dictated comments, and he signed them shakily with his left hand.

How sad an end for a close friend who had accomplished wonders during his long and active life.

CLIFFORD HILLHOUSE POPE (1899-1974) had the extraordinary opportunity of doing fieldwork in China for several years during the 1920s. After he graduated from the University of Virginia in 1921, he learned that Roy Chapman Andrews, leader of the Central Asiatic Expeditions of the American Museum of Natural History, was looking for an assistant. Pope applied, was the successful candidate, and was soon on his way to China.

At first, he expected that he would have to stay with Andrews much of the time, but, in his own words, "it soon became evident that there was nothing to hinder my working alone and independently as a collector of reptiles, amphibians, fishes and mammals. With a special fondness for reptiles and an ever increasing interest in amphibians, I naturally spent most of my time and energy on herpetology."

Pope hired native helpers to travel with him and taught them the techniques of preparing specimens for museum research collections. He learned to speak Chinese, and considered it one of his most important assets. He worked in several parts of China, and he later reported on many of his findings. Of special importance were his technical treatises on the herpetofauna of Fukien Province along the east coast and the home of an extremely rich source of study material. Eventually he returned to the American Museum, and worked there for a number of years, and he seemed assured of a permanent position. He produced the classic and voluminous work entitled "The Reptiles of China," a book of more than 650 pages that was published in 1935. It gained him considerable prestige in the herpetological community, but it also led to his downfall. He was elected president of the American Society of Ichthyologists and Herpetologists, but his success and popularity earned him the wrath (jealousy?) of his boss at the museum, the brilliant but autocratic and always suspicious Gladwyn Kingsley Noble. Suddenly, in the midst of the Great Depression, Pope found himself without a job and with a wife and three small boys to support.

Pope turned his major efforts toward popular writing, for which he had a proven and exceptional talent. His first book, "Snakes Alive and How They Live," published in 1937, was a success and sold steadily for many years. Even while he was working on it, however, he was planning a book on the turtles of the United States and Canada. That was when our paths crossed, and I was able to do him a major favor that got me into trouble with *my* boss.

I had better explain, and thus set the stage for what followed. We were still wallowing in the depths of the Depression. I had joined the Philadelphia Zoo staff only two years earlier as curator of reptiles, but I had discovered that I had an aptitude for public relations, and I was spending considerable time, chiefly by radio and the newspapers, bringing the zoo to the attention of potential admission-paying visitors. I was greatly helped by Mark Mooney, Jr., a friend of about my own age who produced truly excellent photographs of animals that we could use for promotional purposes. Mark was strictly a volunteer, and his only income was from odd jobs.

One day, Mark and I were in my tiny office in the old, archaic reptile house when Clifford Pope dropped in for a visit. In the course of our conversation, he mentioned his plans, and said that he expected he'd have a difficult time getting photographs of turtles for illustrations for his contemplated book. Mark and I offered to help him. It would be fun, it was a worthwhile project, and it would be a credit to the zoo. So we started off on the proverbial shoestring. Clifford was able to buy a little film, and I chipped in from my own meager resources. Mark had no darkroom, but he improvised

one at home and worked at night. We photographed all the many different turtles in the zoo collection, and we borrowed others from friends and even other zoos. I posed the reptiles and Mark manned his camera.

My boss was an accountant who was hired as the zoo's business manager, about a year after my arrival, and his instructions were to pare down every expense. The zoo's finances were at their lowest ebb. When he heard about the turtle project soon after we started, he summoned me to his office and demanded an explanation. I gave it to him, but he wanted to know why we were doing it for an outsider and with no monetary benefit to the zoo. I pointed out that the zoo would get prominent mention, but he would have none of it and ordered me to desist at once. He even complained about my time. I was an employee and, as such, I was paid to work for the zoo and not Mr. Pope.

So, after thinking it over and taking into account the fact that my boss was even newer at the zoo than I was, I called the wealthy, influential member of the zoo's Board of Directors who had been instrumental in sending me to Europe on a fact-finding mission. I told him what had happened, and he immediately telephoned my boss, authorized what we were doing, and even helped us with enough money to buy ample film and chemicals for Mark's activities. My action earned me no brownie points with my boss. The ups and downs of our personal relations over a period of decades are recounted in the main part of this narrative.

Clifford was terribly upset, no doubt because of what had happened to him when he fell out of favor with *his* immediate superior. That was why, in the acknowledgments section of the turtle book, my boss, who had been promoted to general manager, was mentioned prominently. The real hero was Mark Mooney, who donated many months of his time. When Pope's book appeared in 1939, we saw that Mark had taken pictures, developed the negatives, and made prints for 80 of the 99 photographs used for illustrations. Every pertinent caption contained the phrase "Courtesy of Zoological Society of Philadelphia," and thus the zoo's part was more than adequately mentioned. Clifford's publisher, Albert A. Knopf, was more than happy to give us all a copy of the book, including my boss and our benefactor on the Board of Directors.

When Pope was in the Orient, Karl P. Schmidt, of the American Museum staff, worked up the collections being received from China. Even though Schmidt soon returned to his native Chicago to organize a department of herpetology at the Field Museum of Natural History, he continued his study of the Chinese material through a special agreement with Roy Chapman Andrews. Three important technical papers, based in large part on Pope's beautifully preserved specimens, were published almost simultaneously in 1927 in the "Bulletin of the American Museum of Natural History," with Schmidt as author.

Karl and Clifford were good friends, and Schmidt was greatly incensed about Noble's summary dismissal of Pope. When Karl moved up into the position of Chief Curator of the Department of Zoology, it left an opening at the Field Museum for a herpetologist, and Schmidt saw to it that Clifford was chosen to fill the vacancy. The Popes moved to the Chicago area in 1941.

Once he was back at a research institution, Clifford resumed his interest in salamanders, he initiated studies on snakebite treatment, and the development of a rattlesnake's rattle. He also wrote a report on copulatory adjustment in snakes. Meantime, he continued his popular writing, including many contributions to the Field Museum's publication for its friends and lay membership. He also produced "Amphibians and Reptiles of the Chicago Area," a popular, well-illustrated book of 275 pages.

Stark necessity forced Pope to make an important decision after he had been at the Field Museum for more than a decade. He had joined the staff so late in life that he could not qualify for a full pension. So he resigned and devoted his time to writing, a more lucrative way of making ends meet. He produced "The Reptile World, a Natural History of Snakes, Lizards, Turtles, and Crocodilians," "Reptiles Round the World," and "The Giant Snakes." All of them were also published independently in England. Pope also wrote a great many specific accounts for encyclopedias and other books of facts.

Despite Clifford's hard work and the efforts and patience of his wife, Sarah, affectionately known to us and their many other friends as Sally, money was always tight. We often wondered how they managed, especially with three boys to raise. They were forced to be frugal, and we participated in an embarrassing example of it in 1956. Isabelle and I were at Higgins Lake, the site of the summer research station of the University of Michigan, to attend the annual meeting of the American Society of Ichthyologists and Herpetologists. We entertained Clifford and Sally Pope at a restaurant in a nearby small town. That was fine, but Pope insisted on reciprocating. After we were seated and were examining the menus, Clifford suddenly exclaimed, "These prices are too high." I suggested that we go Dutch, each couple paying for themselves, but he said, "No" emphatically and conducted us to another eating place nearby. That event served to increase our admiration for the Popes and what they had accomplished under great fiscal difficulties. Despite their struggle just

to live, Clifford's popular writings made him the best known of contemporary herpetologists, and a worthy successor to Raymond L. Ditmars, who had been *the* great popular authority on reptiles at an earlier period.

The Popes eventually retired to Escondido, California, and, when I inquired by letter in the early 1970s about how he was enjoying the West Coast herpetofauna, he responded that he had given up chasing lizards. His senior years were better suited to collecting cactus. At least it didn't race away when he approached.

Clifford H. Pope made a double major contribution to herpetology. He produced a long list of scientific publications, and he also knew how to interpret reptiles for the lay reader. He was one of the few scientists able to write clearly and lucidly for both professional colleagues and the general public.

KARL PATTERSON SCHMIDT (1890-1957) had a phenomenal knowledge of the herpetological literature on a world-wide basis. He published on the reptiles and amphibians of such diverse places as Chile and China, Indochina and Iran, Navassa and New Zealand, Yemen

 and Yucatán, and at least a score of others. He described many new species in a variety of genera, and painstakingly reviewed the status of individual taxa, notably among the coral snakes, one of his specialties. He was also interested in zoogeography, ecology, fossil herps, and, in fact, virtually all phases of natural history. He served as the editor of several scientific journals, including "Copeia," and participated in field trips to many far parts of the world. His two great contributions on the Belgian Congo, written at the American Museum of Natural History very early in his career, established his reputation, which continued to flower all his life. He also wrote, frequently with coauthors, a number of popular books and articles, and two technical tomes: "Ecological Animal Geography" and "Principles of Animal Ecology."

My first contact with Schmidt was when I wrote early in 1930 to ask if he would like some snakes from Ohio for the Field Museum. His enthusiastic response was the start of a lengthy correspondence that was soon on a first-name basis, and included many letters from both of us that closed with "affectionately." We commiserated with each other about our pet gripes, and neither of us hesitated to offer constructive criticism of each other's writing. He helped me with my research, and even read my long manuscript for the "Reptiles of Ohio" well before its publication. It was he who suggested the inclusion of a small inset map, showing the entire range, to accompany each of my larger Ohio maps that were spotted with the localities from which each species was recorded. In fact, he helped with virtually everything I wrote prior to his death, including the first edition of Isabelle's and my field guide. He even made an overnight visit to our home in New Jersey so he could have a look at the color renderings Isabelle had finished up to that time. The following morning we had to depart very early for the airport so he could catch a plane to New York and then on to Europe.

Karl Schmidt was a warm, kind person, and the most wonderful thing he did for me was to treat me as an equal, even though I was keenly aware that I could never even remotely approach the lofty heights he had achieved in his chosen profession. He gave me confidence in myself.

Karl knew I was primarily a zoo man, and he strongly and repeatedly urged me to apply for the directorship of the Brookfield Zoo in suburban Chicago after the death of Edward H. Bean. I did not feel that I could fill the shoes of such a distinguished person, and, besides, I didn't want to break the dynasty. Robert Bean succeeded his father. Ironically, Robert tried to draft me, years later, as his assistant.

When I was editing "Fauna," the Philadelphia Zoo's natural history magazine, I solicited an article from Karl on the crocodilians, in which he had long been interested. He produced an excellent review of the group and provided the information we needed to list all the species, their ranges, and their average and maximum total lengths in a table occupying nearly a full page. Modestly, he omitted his adventures afield from the article, but he gave in when I insisted that some should be included. Among other experiences he explained how he managed to subdue a five-foot-plus Morelet's crocodile in knee-deep water in British Honduras by pressing on its eyes with thumb and forefinger. But when he tried to capture a crocodile at Zamboanga, in the Philippines, he sustained severely lacerated fingers from the reptile's sharp teeth. As Karl put it, "My two experiences of grabbing crocodiles with my bare hands neatly cancel out."

While Schmidt was the president of the American Society of Ichthyologists and Herpetologists, he appointed a committee of five to prepare a sixth edition of "A Check List of North American Amphibians and Reptiles." While the committee dragged its feet for some years, we had a lively correspondence about what to do. I declined to become actively involved, and he finally was forced to conclude that he would have to do it himself. With extra time on his hands, he wrote the first draft of it while, because of his fluency with the language, he was a visiting professor in Germany. He had the use of Robert Mertens's fine library to check on innumerable details. He introduced many changes of style and interpretation, dropped the second "i" in every case where such appeared in patronyms, omitted parentheses after the names of authors of scientific names for which the generic name had changed, and he included common names. He thanked me for helping him with those and encouraged me to battle the traditionalists who insisted that common names were useless and confusing, in spite of the fact that the scientific names were constantly changing in one way or another. Karl's encouragement helped influence me into chairing the committee that led to the publication of "Common Names for North American Amphibians and Reptiles," which was published in "Copeia" in 1956. After all, I was a zoo man, and zoos needed common names for the signs posted in front of every animal on exhibition.

Schmidt and I collaborated in print on only one project, the rescue of *sirtalis* from oblivion as the specific name of the common garter snake of the genus *Thamnophis*. It was a long struggle in which, as he put it, we were caught in the toils of the lengthy legalistic procedures of the International Commission on Zoological Nomenclature.

Schmidt was interested in many subjects, including the stability of the continents and ocean basins, a seldom-disputed tenet of his day. He wrote a long and learned paper theorizing that all of the major groups of animals had originated in the Northern Hemisphere, and, as newer and more modern species evolved, the older ones were forced southward into southern continents and peninsulas as relicts. Continental drift was widely discredited back then. If he were still living, Karl's ability to evaluate evidence would quickly convince him that plate tectonics is the correct explanation for a multiplicity of geological and biological anomalies.

Karl received many honors, especially during his later years. He was elected to the prestigious National Academy of Sciences, and he was chosen an Eminent Ecologist by the Ecological Society of America. On the occasion of his retirement at age 65 he was presented with a fat festschrift to which only his colleagues at the museum contributed. It would surely have been several volumes in length had others been permitted to participate. He received a long-overdue honorary doctor of science degree from Earlham College in 1952.

When I learned that Emmett Reid "Dixie" Dunn was dying from cancer, I wrote to Schmidt to give him the sad news. In his response, lamenting the imminent demise of a good friend, Karl used the words, "Death is so terribly final!" Less than two years later, Karl P. Schmidt was laid to rest after a tragic herpetological accident.

Karl died on September 26, 1957. His close associate, Robert F. Inger, wrote immediately giving me the details, which I summarize as follows: A live snake arrived at the museum from the Lincoln Park Zoo with a request that it be identified. Bob reached down into the sack, grasped the snake firmly by the head, and was holding it in one hand while thumbing through keys with the other. Schmidt entered the room and took it. Here I quote, "Unfortunately, he used his usual offhand manner and grabbed it too far behind the head. It immediately turned and bit him on the thumb. I took it back while KP wiped the blood that oozed from the puncture."

Together they identified the snake as *Dispholidus typus*, the rear-fanged boomslang from Africa. A few words were exchanged about treatment, but since the snake was only about 30 inches long, Schmidt just shrugged it off. About a half hour later he returned to Inger's office and said, "Look, I've got a local reaction." There was a bluish spot a centimeter in diameter at the puncture mark on the end of the thumb, which was slightly swollen. There were no other symptoms.

As a dedicated herpetologist, Karl started a careful record of the effects of the bite. When Bob Inger and Dwight D. Davis drove him home later, he became nauseated and had a slight chill. He insisted it was from shock. He had a history of shock after surgery and at other times of stress. The next day he felt much better, talked by telephone with museum people, and told them he was writing a report for a case history. At lunch he still felt good, but a short time later he collapsed. A doctor arrived, took one look at him, and called the police emergency squad. Karl was pronounced dead on arrival at the nearest hospital.

Thus perished a distinguished scientist and close friend in a most dramatic and unexpected fashion. How little was known about the toxicity of the venoms of rear-fanged snakes.

ALBERT SCHWARTZ (1923-1992) had an enduring love affair with the fauna of the West Indies that covered a period of four decades. He collected on all the islands and many of the islets of the archipelago, and he reported on its butterflies, mammals, birds, reptiles, and amphibians in a total of 230 papers, of which 198 were on herpetology. His close colleague Robert W. Henderson stated that these contained the descriptions of 80 new species and about 279 new subspecies of amphibians and reptiles. Al's total output was an incredible 5,100 published pages, including the 580 pages of his "The Butterflies of Hispaniola." Albert Schwartz did virtually everything he attempted with vigor and thoroughness, and he has left us an impressive legacy.

I knew Al best when he was a young man teaching at Albright College in Reading, Pennsylvania. We met many times at the Philadelphia Zoo, and we even took a few field trips together, chiefly in the Pine Barrens of New Jersey. He occasionally dropped in on us at the zoo or at our home at Taunton Lake, and twice he appeared on our doorstep in the late evening and asked if he could spend the night with us. Although our cottage was small and crowded, Isabelle made up a bed for him on the porch couch. In the morning after his first night with us, I passed the bathroom and heard the water running rapidly in the sink. I knocked on the door and said, "Al, please turn off the water." "I'm shaving," he replied. I explained that we had no sewer, only a cesspool. He turned off the tap, but by then it was too late. The overflow fertilized our wildflower garden so well that some of the plants might have qualified for inclusion in the "Guinness Book of Records."

After receiving his Ph.D. at the University of Michigan, Al joined the staff of the Charleston Museum, in South Carolina, and he at one time contemplated doing a herpetology of that state. He advanced far enough to mark a set of county outline maps for me indicating all the many hundreds of localities where he had found herps. Those maps, which I still have, were an invaluable resource when I assembled the distribution maps for the first edition of our field guide.

During our 1952 search through the southern Appalachians for salamanders to illustrate the field guide, Isabelle and I, while in the highlands of western South Carolina, stumbled on a sizable colony of *Plethodon clemsonae* (now regarded as a pattern morph of Jordan's salamander, *P. jordani*). When Al heard about it, he asked for directions on how to find the locality, which he later visited, and he corroborated our conclusion that *P. clemsonae* was far from being the rarity that herpetologists had thought it was.

Schwartz published several papers on the herpetology of the Southeast, including a partitioning of the chicken turtle, *Deirochelys reticularia*, in which he described two new subspecies. His most important contribution in that general area is the lengthy report on the amphibians and reptiles of southern Florida that he wrote in collaboration with William E. Duellman.

When Al turned his attention to the West Indies, after

resigning from Albright College in 1960 and moving to Miami in 1962, our close personal contact was terminated except for occasional meetings, but our correspondence continued apace. Including his letters to me and my carbon-copy responses, there are hundreds of pages in my files, two rather fat folders of them, in fact. We reported our progress to each other in detail, and I was able to look up many references for him at the splendid library of the Academy of Natural Sciences. Al did some preliminary work in Cuba in 1954, and I can well recall his exuberance when he received his first grant from the National Science Foundation in 1957 for fieldwork on the Pearl of the Antilles. Those were the revolution years, however, and he was in Cuba at the end of the Batista regime and after Castro's victory. We worried about him and his companions, especially since part of his fieldwork was conducted at night, when guerrilla patrols were most active. He took it all in stride, however, and assured us that the Cubans were mad at the U.S. government, and not Americans in general. He had several scary episodes, nonetheless, and we were thankful when he returned safely to Key West late in 1960.

Artist David C. Leber, then quite a young man, accompanied Al to Cuba and began the first of his excellent series of watercolors showing the throat fans of lizards of the genus *Anolis*. When Cuba became off-limits and Al decided to expand his studies to encompass the herpetology of the entire West Indian archipelago, Dave Leber was still at Albright, and the problem arose about how to get live specimens from the Lesser Antilles into his hands. Al and I worked out an agreement late in 1961, whereby he shipped live specimens to the Philadelphia Zoo that I, in turn, passed on to Leber. Even in those days the importation of livestock was restricted in part, but we could get things through customs for exhibition at the zoo. To satisfy that requirement, Al sent herps that we could exhibit, along with the lizards he wanted depicted in color. We had numerous difficulties. Somewhere en route, by mail or air freight, packages occasionally were exposed to excessive heat or cold, depending on the season of the year, and some of the animals arrived dead or in poor condition. When the desiderata succumbed, we froze them at once and telephoned Dave, and he came to the zoo within a day or so to get them. He was able to record the colors and salvage many of the carcasses. The final success of this enterprise appeared in 1985 in "A Guide to the Identification of the Amphibians and Reptiles of the West Indies Exclusive of Hispaniola," by Albert Schwartz and Robert W. Henderson. That publication

contains beautiful, large throat fan pictures in full color of more than 100 kinds of anoles. Al sent me a copy of the guide, and I was pleased that he mentioned me in the acknowledgments.

After I retired from the Philadelphia Zoo in 1973 our correspondence dwindled, although we occasionally still kept in touch. I last talked with Al by telephone when I was in Miami on my way to Costa Rica in 1982.

Al Schwartz never married. He lived alone and liked it. Miami-Dade Community College, where he taught for many years, gave its faculty members no time for research, and Al welcomed the hours at night and during weekends when he could pursue his studies. He was also deeply interested in music. He was a splendid pianist, and I recall that he often came to Philadelphia from Reading during the opera season.

Albert Schwartz was an intellectual, a workaholic, and a determined describer of new species. He also produced several general works, often with coauthors on their findings on the archipelago.

When Al retired in 1988 he theoretically had ample time for fieldwork, but he was prevented from attempting any because of the arthritis that nearly crippled his legs. He continued to work, but by that time he had turned his major attention to the butterflies of the Indies. He died in 1992 after a fall in his home that caused injuries requiring surgery.

Albert Schwartz's name is, and always will be, indelibly associated with the herpetofauna of the West Indies. I am proud to have known him and I wish I could have retraced some of his routes. My interests were elsewhere, however, and I didn't set foot in the West Indies until Kathryn and I made our first visit to Puerto Rico in 1991.

CHARLES EDWARD SHAW (1918-1971) spent his entire professional life in association with the San Diego Zoo. Even while he was a student at San Diego State College (now University) he literally haunted the reptile collection at the zoo. He became the protégé of C. B. "Si" Perkins, Curator of Reptiles, and succeeded him in that position. Later he was promoted to Assistant Director of the splendid zoological garden in Balboa Park.

What an outstanding reptile curator Chuck was. During the mid-1960s he won three consecutive Edward H. Bean Awards from the American Association of Zoological Parks and Aquariums. They were for the successful hatching and rearing of the Galápagos tortoise, Gila monster, rhinoceros iguana, and African soft-shelled tortoise. He, like so many of us, was pioneering in attempting to breed reptiles in captivity, and we had our troubles. Herpetoculturalists, with all the knowledge and techniques that are available today, doubtless will raise their eyebrows in surprise when they read that statement. But Chuck and I and the few other reptile curators of that early period were still struggling to find the best ways to incubate reptile eggs and then how to raise the young. My voluminous correspondence with Shaw is studded with letters detailing our successes, or lack of them.

Chuck made many contributions to the scientific literature, and several were reports about his achievements with one species or another. He was especially helpful as an editor when Laurence M. Klauber died after revising only three chapters for the second edition of his monumental two-volume work on the rattlesnakes. Shaw wrote well, and he frequently was tapped for popular articles for publication in the San Diego Zoo's magazine, "ZOONOOZ." He was deeply interested in the longevity of snakes in captivity, and he published annual lists on that subject, thus following in the footsteps of Si Perkins. A major part of their interest, no doubt, was their knowledge that they themselves had established an imposing array of records for many species. There is much in the Shaw-Conant correspondence on that subject, too. The San Diego Zoo always had by far the largest number of snakes holding longevity records. My own Philadelphia Zoo was a distant second for several years. I blamed our comparatively poor showing, in large measure, on the fact that the salubrious California climate was far superior to that of Philadelphia's. Also, the old reptile house in which the keepers and I were forced to operate was a sweltering hothouse in summer, and almost impossible to heat properly during the winter.

I lost track of such things when I retired in 1973, but the old "rivalry" leaped back into mind when I learned about the ball python, that I purchased for the Philadelphia Zoo on April 26, 1945. It lived until October 7, 1992, after residing in the zoo for over 47 years. It was and is the oldest snake on record. So I won on that single point, and I am sure that, if he were still living and I were still in the zoo business, Chuck would be the first to congratulate me.

We traded live snakes. I would send him surplus ones of eastern species, and he would reciprocate by shipping some from California. Because we lived thousands of miles apart, we saw each other rather seldom. We met occasionally at scientific gatherings, and I managed to visit the San Diego Zoo on several occasions during my long zoo career. The first time we met was in the autumn of 1939 when he, a student, accompanied Perkins and Dr. Charles R. Schroeder, then San Diego's veterinarian, when they took me on a trip to Borrego, in the desert east of the mountains. In essence, we were chiefly pen pals.

There was, however, a field trip to northern Baja California that stands out in my memory as my most interesting association with Chuck. In 1955, from July 6 to 8, he and his wife, Joan, took Isabelle and me on an excursion to San Quintín, 225 miles south of the border. The road was paved only about half of the way; the rest was gravel and then dirt. It was an education for us, because, during our subsequent wide travels all over Mexico, we never encountered similar terrain. We saw wild, undisturbed country, and noted how the Mexicans were attempting to cultivate crops and graze cattle in an almost barren desert where much of the moisture came from the fogs that enveloped the area daily. We saw a primitive salt mine, where water from the ocean was allowed to evaporate in settling basins, and the resultant salt was scraped into piles for shipment to market. We were surprised at how cold it was, both air- and waterwise. We donned bathing suits at a time when the sun was shining brightly, but when we waded into the Pacific up to our knees, we nearly froze. Isabelle and I took a hasty dunk and then raced to the leeward side of the nearest dune to warm up and dry off. Chuck explained that cold water welled upward from deep ocean currents near the shore, the source of California's famous (infamous?) fogs. He told us that the phenomenon was under study at the Scripps Institution of Oceanography at La Jolla, near San Diego. We were in a fog desert, the smallest of the world's three. (The others are the Namib Desert along the Atlantic coast in extreme southwestern Africa, and the north-to-south attenuated Atacama-Peruvian Desert of the Pacific coast of South America.)

Chuck and Joan demonstrated how to find the small legless lizards of the genus *Anniella*, seemingly tiny replicas of the glass lizards of the genus *Ophisaurus* that we knew so well from the southeastern United States. We knelt in the coastal sand dunes and, with a short-handled shovel, dug at the bases of clumps of small plants. That's where the lizards lived; they were scarcely ever seen on the surface. We also caught several quadrupedal species out in the open.

Chuck was always patient and helpful and forever willing to share his knowledge with others. He had my profound respect, and I consider him to have been the best curator of reptiles in the country during the period when we both were serving in that capacity.

PHILIP WAYNE SMITH (1921-1986) was both a herpetologist and an ichthyologist. During his younger years he concentrated on the first of those two disciplines, and he published a considerable series of papers that culminated in a master work of some 300 pages entitled "The Amphibians and Reptiles of Illinois" (published in 1961). It was an exhaustive, well-illustrated review of the herpetology of his native state with range maps and keys for the identification of the many species. His maps were innovative. In addition to the customary spots indicating localities from which specimens were examined or authentically reported, he added hatching which, on the basis of his encyclopedic knowledge of the surface features of Illinois, indicated additional suitable habitats where the species in question might be found. He also followed my lead (in the "Reptiles of Ohio") by including a small inset map of the United States showing the range of each species as a whole.

After the appearance of that major opus, Phil directed his attention largely to ichthyology, and, in 1979 his monumental "The Fishes of Illinois" also appeared. Quite a double accomplishment for a quiet, unassuming man who spent a large portion of his time sharing his wealth of information on natural history with colleagues, students, and the lay public. He had a phenomenal comprehension of the cold-blooded vertebrates, and he frequently astounded his associates by identifying specimens on sight from distant parts of the United States.

During his working years Phil was associated with the Illinois Natural History Survey. He advanced steadily upward through the hierarchy of its staff, and served concurrently, for 14 years, as professor of zoology at the University of Illinois. His wife, Dorothy M. Smith, who was also his best friend, was his constant companion, often a coauthor, and a major factor in his success.

I heard it said, more than once, that Phil Smith was too parochial, that his focus was all on Illinois. His home state was certainly his starting point, but when taxonomic or distributional puzzles developed within its borders, he often undertook wider studies. As an example, he and Dorothy examined the chorus frog, now *Pseudacris triseriata*, complex in depth and over a large fraction of its known range. Phil actually did fieldwork in many parts of the country, particularly in the Southwest, and also in Mexico. Whenever he traveled he collected material, including insects, for his associates at the Natural History Survey. His attention to zoogeography enabled him to make a major contribution to science: an interpretation, in several papers, of the relict distributions of terrestrial vertebrates in relation to postglacial history and the warm, dry

Hypsithermal interval of about 8,500 to 5,000 years ago.

My closest contact with Phil Smith was during the years when we were both active in the affairs of the American Society of Ichthyologists and Herpetologists. Also, at about that same time, we both were preparing range maps, mine for the first edition of the "Field Guide to Reptiles and Amphibians," in the Peterson series, and his for his inset maps. It was a productive period of close cooperation.

As the president of the ASIH, it was my prerogative to make appointments to various committees, and I chose Phil to represent us for a four-year term on the National Research Council, which met annually in Washington. I was immediately bombarded with flak. Why did I choose him? So-and-so was much better qualified, which was a subtle way, in some cases, of saying, "Why didn't you appoint me?" My response was that Phil was one of the few persons who could represent both disciplines, and his devotion to the Society was amply demonstrated when he served as editor in chief of its journal, "Copeia," when no one else would undertake that difficult and time-consuming assignment.

Phil's last publication was a charming autobiography entitled "A Naturalist in the Environmental Crisis." In it he chronicled his many activities and also stressed his concern for the alarming decreases in the native fauna of Illinois, mostly because of the activities of mankind and the destruction of habitats. He, with other boys, founded their private zoo, consisting chiefly of herps, but also with a few mammals and even some invertebrates. One of the boys was James A. Peters, who later became another well-known herpetologist who eventually served as curator of the herp collection at the National Museum.

For me, the most amusing anecdote in his book was his account of an adventure I had at his home. While I was in the midst of a long-distance telephone call, their pet flying squirrel, Jo, leaped onto my shoulder, squeezed between the buttons on my shirt, and proceeded to race around my waist inside, just above the beltline.

After his retirement in 1979, Phil served as the scientific leader for two East African safaris. Health-related problems overtook him, and he succumbed in 1986 at the age of 65, after a long bout with cancer.

How proud Philip Wayne Smith would be if he could know that two of his devoted students and disciples, Lawrence M. Page and Brooks M. Burr, recently produced "A Field Guide to Freshwater Fishes," also in the Peterson series. As I write this, the same two persons are working officers, treasurer and secretary, respectively, of the ASIH.

LEONHARD STEJNEGER (1851-1943) was an elderly gentleman when I first met him during the 1930s. His dress was impeccable and his beard and mustache were trimmed to perfection. I knew quite a little about his distinguished career as an ornithologist and herpetologist, that he was a Norseman who migrated to the United States, that he was employed at the Smithsonian Institution under the secretaryship of Spencer F. Baird, and that he had produced a number of very important scientific publications. I approached him with a slight feeling of awe, but he quickly dispelled that with his friendly greeting. Because he was the head curator of biology of the U.S. National Museum, with administrative duties, he referred me to Doris Cochran for any assistance I might need. I already knew Dr. Cochran, who, as she always did with young people, went all out to help me.

Dr. Stejneger remembered me, however, and greeted me warmly each of the few times we saw each other subsequently.

During my long association with the Philadelphia Zoological Garden I visited Washington for a day at least twice a year, normally spending the morning at the National Zoo and the afternoon at the National Museum. One time, when I reversed that order, I met Dr. Stejneger in the hall as he was walking toward his office. He had a big smile on his face and he seemed almost to be chortling to himself. I greeted him and remarked that he seemed especially happy. "Look at this," he exclaimed and showed me a secondhand book dealer's catalogue that offered for sale "The Black List of North American Amphibians and Reptiles," by Stejneger and Thomas Barbour. "Black List," of course, was a misprint for "Check List." After he had picked up his mail near the building's entrance, and while he was waiting for someone else to arrive, he had thumbed through the herpetological titles and discovered the error.

The Stejneger and Barbour check lists were the taxonomic bibles in their day. The senior author was responsible for all the decisions, whereas Dr. Barbour aided and abetted in many ways, including, no doubt, underwriting the cost of publication and any incidental expenses. The fifth edition of the list, which appeared during the same year (1943) that Stejneger died at the age of 92, was largely the work of Barbour (see his vignette in this series of recollections).

Stejneger's contributions to the scientific literature were many, but I didn't fully appreciate his meticulous thoroughness until I made frequent use of his "Herpetology of Japan" during the 1980s while I was working on the Gloyd-Conant monograph on the genus *Agkistrodon* and its allies. It was especially complete because of his fluency in many languages.

His outstanding career would have terminated officially when he reached the age of 70, had not President Herbert Hoover interceded in 1932 and initiated what became a lifetime tenure. Dr. William M. Mann, Director of the National Zoo and himself an employee of the Smithsonian Institution, told me that Dr. Stejneger's annual reappointment required the approval of the U.S. Congress, but it was virtually automatic.

The extraordinary procedure of being retained in office indefinitely was an outstanding honor for Dr. Stejneger, but it exacerbated a situation that thwarted the research efforts of several young herpetologists, notably Norman E. Hartweg.

The massive work by Edward Drinker Cope entitled "The Crocodilians, Lizards and Snakes of North America," published in 1900, did not include the turtles. Stejneger planned to remedy the omission by preparing a complete and definitive work on that group of reptiles. He had long since transferred all the types and unique specimens to his private office, and there they remained for a great many years, unavailable to others. He made some progress on his intended opus, part of which Barbour published for him posthumously, but advancing age and declining energy caused his ambitious project to die with him.

Dr. Hartweg was deeply interested in monographing the Kinosternidae, the musk and mud turtles, and their allies, but he was unable to examine the critical National Museum material without which no general work on the group would be complete. Several other young herpetologists were similarly affected, and two of them told me privately that they were bitter and frustrated by Dr. Stejneger's "dog-in-the-manger" attitude. Dr. Cochran eventually retrieved them all and returned them to the general collection, and the softshell turtles were available for Coleman J. Goin and me when we collaborated on studying the spiny (*spinifera*) group soon after Dr. Stejneger's death.

EDWARD HARRISON TAYLOR (1889-1978) was a superb field man who had an uncanny knack for finding reptiles and amphibians. He seemed instinctively to know which rock to overturn or which pile of debris to search for his quarry. He had the stamina to keep going all night, if necessary, and then teach classes the following morning. He easily wore out anyone who tried to keep up with him. In his prime he was strong and muscular, a large handsome man with a lantern jaw and a keen mind.

He was a strict disciplinarian, but he was so dedicated to his students that those who worked hard and met his standards learned much and revered him as their mentor. He hated hasty, sloppy work, and was outspoken in his criticism, thus earning the enmity of others. The Dunn-Taylor feud was legendary. I never learned the details about that rivalry. Rumor had it, however, that both acquired specimens of the same new species at about the same time. Each of them wrote a description, proposed a new name, and sent his manuscript off to a different journal to be published. Taylor's appeared first, and, under the rule of priority, his new name became the official one, whereas Emmett Reid Dunn's was sunk in synonymy. Dunn accused Taylor of rushing into print to steal his new species, and forever afterward he despised and deprecated him.

After completing his bachelor of arts degree Taylor accepted a civil post in the Philippines, then an American possession. During his relatively long tenure of service he assembled sufficient material to produce a series of technical reports on the mammals, reptiles, and amphibians of the archipelago. He also prepared one on the fishes, but the sole copy of the manuscript was lost at sea. Instead of fretting over that catastrophe, as many of us might have done, he took the loss in stride and put it out of his mind.

During the 1930s Taylor wrote a series of radio talks for personal presentation on KFKU, the station of the University of Kansas, the institution with which he was associated for most of his life. He said the talks were for young people, but they included tales of his hair-raising adventures as he traveled alone among the savages and headhunters of the Philippines. Fortunately for posterity, they were included verbatim in a volume entitled "Recollections of an Herpetologist," which also features detailed biographical sketches of the author and a list of his 198 scientific publications up to that time. The book, which appeared in 1975, served in lieu of a festschrift.

Taylor turned his attention more or less consecutively to the herpetofauna of Mexico, Ceylon (= Sri Lanka), Thailand, and Costa Rica. He lived at a time when many species new to science were still being discovered, and there was much competition among zoologists. The race was still on to describe the world's vertebrate fauna. According to Hobart M. Smith, his student and later his most distinguished colleague, Taylor described more than 500 species and over 25 new genera. His published pages approached 10,000, and a substantial number of his works consisted of long or relatively long papers. Taylor carefully examined and studied the material at hand, and based his conclusions on it. He thus did not follow the practice, developed by Alexander G. Ruthven

and his associates at the University of Michigan, of also studying all the pertinent available specimens, even those in other institutions. As a result, quite a number of Taylor's new taxa eventually were synonymized with forms that had been described earlier.

In 1958 Taylor was the president of the American Society of Ichthyologists and Herpetologists, and I was the secretary charged with keeping things running smoothly. Ed Taylor was off in the field, and, although I tried several times to reach him at the addresses he had given me, my letters failed to catch up with him. I was trying to remind him that a presidential address would be expected at the Society's annual meeting in Bloomington, Indiana. I finally alerted Boyd Walker, the vice president, to be ready to take over if necessary. The banquet was already in progress when Taylor walked in the door unannounced. He gave one of his usual witty presentations, which was highlighted by his statement of, "I am kept very busy trying to describe new species faster than the people at Michigan can knock them down."

Taylor was a superb raconteur, and he was as fully at ease in high society as he was in the muddy environs of a frog pond. He was an excellent dancer and bridge player, and he was accepted everywhere, even in the "Royal Court of Siam." One of his favorite stories was about how he managed to slip away from the armed guards furnished for him by the Thai military. He was fearless and, in general, preferred to work by himself. Once, during an ASIH meeting in California, I was alone with Ed during a brief daytime field trip. He caught at least twice as many herps as I did, but, before we parted, I offered him the few things I had found. He politely declined, stating that he preferred to preserve and catalogue only the animals he had caught personally.

On the other hand, he long maintained a personal collection in collaboration with Hobart M. Smith that was designated by the initials EHT-HMS. It was begun during the early 1930s when they undertook a lengthy and extraordinarily rugged herpetological exploration of Mexico in a cantankerous vehicle over virtually nonexistent roads. The large EHT-HMS collection no longer exists as a separate entity. About two-thirds of it is now at the Field Museum in Chicago; the remainder is at the University of Illinois Museum of Natural History.

Sometimes Ed's field data were difficult to interpret, as I discovered while I was working on the water snakes of Mexico. For example, I could not correlate his Sinaloan locality of "Presidio" with any map I could find, until I discovered that the railroad station at Villa Unión, Sinaloa, had retained the name "Presidio," a hangover from its early use as a military garrison. That made sense when I learned he had traveled by *autovia*, a motor vehicle equipped with wheels to operate on rails. Mexico was replete with duplicate and confusing place-names even during the 1960s when Isabelle and I made the last of our field trips south of the border.

Ed Taylor was an indefatigable worker and writer, and among his many major contributions to science were a lengthy monograph on the skinks of the genus *Eumeces*, published in 1935, and an even longer one on the caecilians of the world (1967). There also were the several lengthy checklists on the herpetofauna of Mexico, by Smith and Taylor (1945, 1948, 1950, and the reprint with a list of subsequent taxonomic innovations published in 1966). As an amusing aside, I heard a number of criticisms of the Smith and Taylor checklists from persons who were familiar only with a few species or genera, but those same detractors carried the lists on field trips to Mexico as indispensable tools.

My personal contacts with Ed were sporadic, aside from formal meetings and the inevitable bull sessions associated with them. He had married in 1916 and subsequently sired three children, but he and his wife separated for life a few years later. In keeping with Catholic dogma there was no divorce, but Ed came east annually to visit his wife, who lived somewhere in the Philadelphia metropolitan area. While he was in the vicinity he dropped in to see me at the zoo for several consecutive years to talk and gossip and to have a look at the live reptile collection. When Isabelle and I were touring European zoos in 1967 we took time out to visit the Senckenberg Museum in Frankfurt, Germany. After chatting awhile with Konrad Klemmer, we went to look at the collection and en route, much to our surprise, discovered Ed seated at a table reading proofs of his caecilian monograph. Konrad had purposely kept Taylor's presence there as a surprise. When we attended a meeting in Dallas during the 1970s, Ed and I were both billeted as overnight house guests in the home of James B. Murphy. Not too long before he died in 1978, I visited Ed in his small apartment in Lawrence, Kansas. He insisted on living alone, but friends kept close watch on him.

Edward H. Taylor was a pioneer in many ways. No herpetologist who ever lived traveled as many miles in pursuit of amphibians and reptiles or spent such a tremendous number of hours in the field.

Zoo Personalities I Have Known

EDWARD HOWARD BEAN (1875-1945) was the dean of American zoo directors when I first met him in 1930. With his snow-white hair, strong features, and erect bearing, he was a handsome man whose very presence commanded respect. Besides, he had an enviable record. He had been the director of the Washington Park Zoo in Milwaukee from 1906 until 1927. He had planned and supervised the construction of the Chicago Zoological Park (the Brookfield Zoo) in suburban Chicago, and he was its distinguished director. Everyone in the business looked up to him, especially a 21-year-old stripling who was in St. Louis attending his first meeting of the American Association of Zoological Parks and Aquariums.

Despite my extreme youth, Ed Bean took a liking to me. He realized that I was deeply interested in the zoo profession, as evidenced by my having prepared a paper to read at the meeting. It was entitled "The Educational Duty of the Zoological Park." A few years later, in Chicago, he came to my rescue. As the delegate from the Toledo, Ohio, Zoo, I was given only 25 dollars with which to attend the meeting, even though at the time I was secretary of the AAZPA. We were still feeling the effects of the Great Depression and, after buying a round-trip railroad ticket, I had little left. My personal funds were so low that I stayed at the YMCA. When Ed Bean discovered that, he promptly bought me a banquet ticket and staked me to several meals. He made me feel as though I were needed and wanted, and not just a poor church mouse hanging on by the proverbial shoestring. We remained good friends, and he was always prompt when I solicited news from him about new exhibits and developments at the Brookfield Zoo for publication in the zoo section of "Parks and Recreation" magazine.

Ed Bean was the first zoo leader to realize that there was big money to be made from the visiting crowds. He learned that at Milwaukee. When the time approached for the opening of the Brookfield Zoo, the matter of concessions for the sale of food and souvenirs came up for attention. Ed stated emphatically that all such activities would be handled by the zoo itself, no matter how much extra work might be required. That policy became a gold mine, just as it did at the Philadelphia Zoo. When I came back from a tour of European zoos in 1937 with that idea, I thought it was brand new. Taking over our own concessions certainly rescued the Philadelphia Zoo from potential bankruptcy. Virtually every zoo nowadays garners much revenue through the sale of food, drinks, and souvenirs, either directly or through associated zoological societies or "friends of the zoo." My superiors, way back then, should have looked to Ed Bean for guidance instead of waiting for me to give it to them.

During his long career, Bean did his best to breed the animals in his care. He had the foresight to predict what was coming. He pointed out, "It is only a matter of a few years until all animals will have to be reared in captivity if we are to preserve the various species for scientific and educational purposes." How prophetic that has turned out to be.

It was Ed's attention to breeding and rearing captive animals that led to the establishment, in 1956, through the AAZPA, of the Edward H. Bean Awards. Many zoos have qualified since then for the distinction it brought to them. At first only one animal was chosen annually, but the concept was expanded long ago to include outstanding propagative achievement in each of a variety of categories—mammals, birds, reptiles, etc.

Easily the most outstanding zoo event in Ed Bean's long career was the acquisition of young Su Lin, the first giant panda ever brought out of China alive. Ruth Harkness, the panda's owner, sought to sell the animal to the highest bidder. After much bickering and a six-week quarantine and study period, the Chicago Zoological Society purchased Su Lin for $14,000. "Panda fever" broke out the moment she was placed on exhibition. On a winter Sunday in February, an amazing 40,000 visitors flocked to the Brookfield Zoo to see her. She earned her purchase price in short order. It was the beginning of the craze that made the giant panda the most beloved of all mammals. I wonder how many millions of panda dolls, books, emblems, and other replicas have been sold.

Why Ed Bean chose Grace Olive Wiley to be his curator of reptiles remains a mystery. She was personable, to be sure, and she certainly was successful in caring for individual snakes over long periods of time. She had a curious quirk, however, that was well known to the few of us who were supervising reptile collections in those days (1933-35). She believed that any kind of snake, even the most venomous ones, could be tamed, and she placed rattlesnakes and cobras, bare-handedly, in her lap or over her shoulders. She trusted them too much, and unreported escapes of highly dangerous snakes at Brookfield caused her to be dismissed summarily. She died more than a decade later after being bitten by a pet cobra.

Edward H. Bean founded a dynasty, although he didn't live long enough to witness the activities of his grandsons. Ed's own son, Robert, when he was 25, was the director of the then relatively small San Diego Zoo, but he resigned to become his father's assistant when Brookfield was opened to the public. Both he and his sister, Mary, literally grew up in the zoo business. Mary looked after Su Lin and many other animals. In 1939 she married George Speidel, who came up through the ranks at Brookfield and was later, and for many years, the director of the Milwaukee County Zoo. Robert's son became a zoo director, and the Speidels' son also served in that capacity for a time.

Robert succeeded his father as head of the Chicago Zoological Park, and he did very well in general. He had a great weakness, however; an addiction to alcohol kept him from being as well-liked and professionally famous as his sire.

Edward Howard Bean was a legend in his time. He had been in the zoo business for 47 years, including a stint at Chicago's Lincoln Park Zoo, before he went to Milwaukee. During almost all of his professional life he was a zoo director. His career was cut short by an automobile accident, while he was still head of the great institution he had created and nurtured, the Chicago Zoological Park.

BELLE J. BENCHLEY (1882-1973) was the only lady zoo director I ever really knew, but she didn't receive that title until just before she retired at the end of 1953. Otherwise, during all the many years she was in office, she was executive secretary of the Zoological Society of San Diego. Afterward, she was listed as director emeritus.

I first met Mrs. Benchley in 1939 after making a transcontinental train trip. That was an eye-opener for me, because I had never previously been farther west than St. Louis. Nowadays, most people fly and thus miss seeing the many exceedingly interesting things that are readily apparent from a train window. I crossed the Appalachians, the prairies of the Midwest, the Great Plains, the Rocky Mountains, the desert, and the Coast Range. I relished them all. What an exciting and educational trip for me, especially since I was so deeply interested in geography. We even stopped in Albuquerque, the city to which I was to retire a great many years later. While the train was standing alongside the station platform, men with long-handled tools washed the windows on the outside to improve visibility. I had never previously experienced such an amenity.

My objective, of course, was to see the San Diego Zoo and to meet the people associated with it. I had corresponded with some of them, and we had exchanged live snakes for several years, mine being sent from both the Toledo and Philadelphia zoos. They greeted me warmly.

Mrs. Benchley was then a motherly middle-aged lady who took an immediate liking to me. She showed me a few highlights of the zoo at once, even though I was groggy after a night in a Pullman lower berth, from which I peered out the window many times to see the scenery lit by a full moon. When she had to depart to cope with her daily desk-load of paperwork, she took me to the reptile house and left me with Curator of Reptiles C. B. "Si" Perkins (no relation to Marlin Perkins) and Charles E. "Chuck" Shaw, who was then still a college student. She said she would pick me up at my hotel to go to dinner with other guests. That first day was an exciting one, but I wisely retreated to my quarters and had a long nap.

That evening, we parked near a seafood restaurant but, in walking to it, Mrs. Benchley tripped at the curb and would have fallen to the pavement if I hadn't caught her in the nick of time. I think that sealed our bond, because it was not too long afterward that she shifted to "Roger" instead of "Mr. Conant," and began to think of me as one of her "boys," as she called her younger staff members. Because of the great difference in our ages, I never had the temerity to address her as "Belle," although some of my less polite colleagues did. The dinner itself was a memorable one, and I ate my first abalone, the delicious shellfish that was then still plentiful and inexpensive on the West Coast.

The San Diego Zoo had a superb setting on a series of small mesas with steep "canyons" between them. Harry Wegeforth, M.D., the zoo's founder, was interested in tropical plants as well as animals. Under his direction as president of the Zoological Society, a large and impressive arboretum was planted in the zoo. Previously, the ground had been covered with low chapparal, just as it was east of the zoo, where I went exploring for lizards early one morning. Incidentally, Mrs. Benchley became Dr. Wegeforth's secretary early during her career at the zoo. She showed such an aptitude for management that she was soon running things, at first for him.

Largely because it was a relatively young institution, the San Diego Zoo, with its fine collection and wonderful vegetation, had the prettiest setting I had encountered in any zoo up to that time. Among the livestock, the most interesting were the two huge mountain gorillas that the explorers Martin and Osa Johnson had imported from Africa for the San Diego Zoo in 1931. Allegedly they were a pair, but they both turned out to be males. Mbongo, the larger of the two, weighed 618 pounds, as I reported in a roundup article on captive gorillas in the Philadelphia Zoo magazine "Fauna" in 1941. Mrs. Benchley took great pride in showing me those two wonderful anthropoids.

My visit to San Diego was also memorable in other ways. I was taken to Tijuana for my first venture into Mexico, and four of us had a wonderful herpetological field trip. Starting late one afternoon, we drove across the mountains and down to Benson's Dry Lake in the desert, collecting and observing as we went. I was accompanied by Perkins, Shaw, and Charles R. Schroeder, the zoo's veterinarian, who later became its director, and was the creator of the vast and famous Wild Animal Park in the San Pasqual Valley.

When I expressed a desire to see the desert in the daylight, the men, unhappily, were tied up with work and school, but Mrs. Benchley told me to take her personal car and stay all day if I wished. Perkins provided me with a 22-caliber rifle and dust-shot cartridges, and I had a glorious day crossing southern California all the way to Yuma, Arizona. En route, I shot a few lizards, which I took back with me to have identified and preserved.

Later, I saw Mrs. Benchley occasionally at zoo meetings, and we kept up a lively correspondence, especially after she was elected chairman of the American Association of Zoological Parks and Aquariums in 1950. That same year, I was a member of the Board of Directors of the American Institute of Park Executives, and I was able to help her in obtaining a little more freedom for the zoo organization. Until many years later, the AAZPA was a subdivision of the parental Park Institute.

Belle Benchley had a flair for popular writing, and she authored several interesting and entertaining books with such intriguing titles as "My Life in a Man-Made Jungle," "My Friends the Apes," and "My Animal Babies."

The San Diego Zoo had a unique name for its official publication, which Mrs. Benchley stoutly defended from everyone, myself included, who wanted to borrow it for one purpose or another. A copyright had been obtained for it immediately after it was introduced. "ZOONOOZ" is a splendid palindrome that reads the same backward and forward, as well as upside down.

Mrs. Benchley was an able administrator for many years, and she was instrumental in getting the talented, dedicated Charles R. Schroeder to succeed her when she retired. I saw her for the last time when Isabelle and I were in San Diego on July 10, 1955. She made a special trip to the zoo to spend an enjoyable few hours with us. Sadly, when we were back there in 1967, she was in a nursing home and her mind had gone to sleep.

W. REID BLAIR (1875-1949) was the veterinarian at the New York Zoological Park under the directorship of the irascible but celebrated William T. Hornaday. Blair, who had been with the organization for many years, was thoroughly familiar with its policies and procedures, and he was chosen to be Hornaday's successor. He served in that office from 1926 to 1940, a particularly difficult period because of the Great Depression and because the officers of the New York Zoological Society, who had been very active in earlier years, were growing

old. Although a few changes and improvements were made during Blair's tenure, his was chiefly a caretaker's administration. The renaissance of the Bronx Zoo was to come after his retirement.

My initial meeting with Reid Blair was in 1930 at the very first session of the American Association of Zoological Parks and Aquariums I ever attended. We were delegates from our respective institutions, mine being the Toledo Zoo. He was dignified and reserved, but seemed quite willing to help the young man from Ohio. At the Bronx Zoo, where I saw him several times during later years, he never failed to admit me to his well-guarded office for a chat.

One winter, long before I became the director of the Philadelphia Zoo, I decided to attend the annual membership meeting of the New York Zoological Society at the Waldorf-Astoria Hotel in New York. William Beebe was to speak. I do not recall whether it was on his tropical explorations or his descent to a great depth into the ocean near Bermuda in the bathysphere. It was a formal affair, so I carefully packed my tuxedo in a small suitcase and took the train to Penn Station, in New York. As I entered the hotel, I met Dr. Blair, who had also just arrived. We exchanged greetings and then I excused myself, saying that I had to change my clothes. "Where are you going to do that?" he asked. Embarrassed, I replied, "In the men's room." "Nonsense," he said. "Come with me." He led me to the elevator and then to his room, which he had engaged for the night. The two of us changed into our formal wear, and soon we entered the grand ballroom together. There we parted, he to the dais and I to a seat in the crowd.

After the lecture was over and William Beebe, who was both an eloquent speaker and an excellent writer, had been properly lionized, I approached Dr. Blair. He handed me his room key and asked me to bring it back to him when I was finished. I followed his instructions, and I was in time to catch the late night train to Philadelphia.

I have never forgotten that spontaneous act of kindness to a young Philadelphia Zoo employee, and W. Reid Blair has always occupied a high position in my mental pantheon of zoo directors.

WILLIAM BRIDGES (1901-1984) was my opposite number at the Bronx Zoo in New York. His first contact with that institution was in late 1933 when a city editor at the "New York Sun" dispatched him to the zoo to gather feature story material for their newspaper. He continued visiting the zoo on a regular basis, and he established such a good reputation with the zoo management that on January 1, 1935, he reported for duty as the New York Zoological Society's curator of publications. He prepared press releases and edited everything that was published by the zoo, including its membership magazine, "Animal Kingdom," the scientific journal "Zoologica," annual reports, guidebooks, pamphlets, and thousands of exhibit labels. In short, his work almost exactly paralleled the duties for which I would soon be responsible at the Philadelphia Zoo.

Bill was adept at writing, and he had an uncanny talent for coming up almost instantly with just the right words to make even the most prosaic sentence flow and sing. Despite his many duties at the zoo, he was much in demand as a writer, and early in 1938 the Appleton-Century publishing company asked him to prepare a book entitled "What Snake Is That?" as a companion volume for their "What Bird Is That?" He agreed. He had accompanied Raymond L. Ditmars to the Tropics in search of snakes and other animals, but when he tackled the new assignment, he soon bogged down while trying to assemble details about our native serpents. So he sought my help. What a human dynamo he was. He kept me jumping and laboring after hours at home until midnight for weeks at a time, preparing copy and then checking and double-checking it. Edmond V. Malnate, who was then my assistant with the zoo reptiles, was engaged to make snake pattern drawings, and in an amazingly short time our material was ready to ship off to the publisher. Bill, who had the original contract, magnanimously insisted that I be the first author, stressing that it was I who had dug out most of the detailed information.

I never assembled another lengthy publication so quickly, and, in comparison with the years of toil and careful work that later were devoted to the preparation of our "Field Guide to Reptiles and Amphibians" (Isabelle's and mine), "What Snake Is That?" seems crude and amateurish. It served its purpose, however, and it had a brisk sale for a while. One of our zoo boys, a lad of perhaps 14, who led ponies around a ring while juvenile visitors rode in the saddles, approached me one day and said, "I think there's a mistake in your book." When I checked, I was mortified to see that, on our map, Oregon was labeled Washington and vice versa.

Bill and I often visited back and forth, and we freely borrowed ideas from each other. For example, we had an annual members' day at our respective institutions, and we often were hard-pressed to find new ways to entertain participants. The chore was made easier by seeing what the other was doing.

We kept in touch even after Bill retired in 1966. I attended his hilarious farewell party in New York, which also attracted some of his other friends from out of town.

Bill helped me hone my writing to convey as much as possible with the written word, but I never came close to achieving his perfection. No one else in my ken ever did either. He was always helpful and thoughtful. A letter written from England where he was visiting at the time, commented warmly on my assumption of the directorship of the Philadelphia Zoo, and it is a cherished treasure in my correspondence files. So also is his extremely kind offer to recommend that I take his place at the Bronx Zoo should he be drafted for service during World War II.

He continued to write long after his retirement, and he authored or coauthored 21 books during his lifetime, among them "Gathering of Animals," a splendid and entertaining history of the New York Zoological Society. His skill and splendid style never diminished, and his pithy vignettes entitled "Out of the Blue Box," some of which he wrote during the last year of his life, are as charming as any of his earlier works. One March night in 1984 he died quietly in his sleep. He was 83.

C. EMERSON BROWN (1869-1949) was a New England taxidermist who earned an excellent reputation for his installation of habitat groups of birds in several museums, including the one in Boston. How and why he was chosen as superintendent (later director) of the Philadelphia Zoological Garden I never learned, but he headed that institution for many years. I first met him when I was a student at the University of Pennsylvania, and I have always felt deeply indebted to him for helping me get started in the zoo business professionally. Without his assistance I would not have obtained my job at the Toledo Zoo. Several times afterward I sought his advice and opinions by mail, and he was always prompt in responding. During the few times I drove east from Ohio, I called on him at his office in the zoo's historic Penn House, little dreaming that eventually I would occupy his chair.

Emerson Brown was one of the founding fathers of the American Association of Zoological Parks and Aquariums, and he served as its chairman for several terms. During the Great Depression he endured the financial pinch that nearly forced the Philadelphia Zoo to close. He worked hard to bring in all the money he could, even pennies from schoolchildren who were worried about the welfare of the animals. He had the strong support of two or three influential zoo board members, but when they died, his detractors forced him to retire. Some of them were still associated with the zoo when I arrived in 1935, soon after he had been replaced by Dr. Roderick Macdonald. They accused

Brown, but could offer no proof, of accepting kickbacks from animal dealers. They pointed to his vanity and his uncanny knack of managing to get into the picture when news photographers came to portray the animals. They sneered at his lack of training in business management and zoology, and said the only reason he lasted at the zoo was because no one else would accept the responsibility at the low pay he received. He obviously had not been popular with several of his associates, but I never forgot how kind he was to me. I saw him a few times later outside the zoo, and I paid him a visit during his terminal illness. Only six persons attended his funeral, including two others from the zoo besides myself. In his heyday everyone knew the name of C. Emerson Brown, and his death would have been front-page news. All he rated were a picture and a few paragraphs on the obituary page. Such is often the reward of local celebrities. I, personally, was saddened by his death, and I will always remember him as my benefactor.

Incidentally, C. Emerson Brown was no relation to Arthur Erwin Brown, the first superintendent of the Philadelphia Zoo, and who served from 1876 until he suffered a fatal heart attack while on duty in the Garden in 1910. A. E. Brown was deeply interested in herpetology, and he described a number of new species of snakes, including the short-tailed snake, *Stilosoma extenuatum;* the Trans-Pecos rat snake, *Bogertophis suboccularis*; and the gray-banded kingsnake, *Lampropeltis alterna.* (The scientific names are those currently in use.) His "Review of the Genera and Species of American Snakes, North of Mexico," published in 1901, was a classic at the time. His career and mine had several parallels. We both published scientific contributions on serpents, we were both dedicated to the zoological garden and worked incessantly for its welfare, and late during our terms of office we each received an honorary Doctor of Science degree, his from the University of Pennsylvania, and mine from the University of Colorado.

LEE SAUNDERS CRANDALL (1887-1969) was one of the most dedicated zoo enthusiasts I ever met. Aside from his daily personal chores, his every moment seemed to be spent on or thinking about his birds, and, later, all the animals under his supervision. His entire professional career of 44 years was with the New York Zoological Park (the Bronx Zoo).

Crandall started at the zoo under unusual circumstances. His father and grandfather were medical doctors, and he was attending Cornell Medical College in 1908 when he was offered a job as a student keeper. He couldn't resist. Many years later, in his 1966 book, "A Zoo Man's Notebook," he wrote that, when he was interviewed for that early assignment, nothing was said about payment, so he assumed that such a glorious opportunity was free, and that he wouldn't have to pay for the privilege! Soon thereafter William Beebe, then the zoo's curator of birds, took Crandall on as a 30-dollar-a-month assistant. "Such happiness comes few times in a lifetime," Crandall commented in his book. Soon afterward he and Beebe departed for British Guiana to collect birds for the zoo. Lee's ability and enthusiasm in the field were quickly proven, and they returned with hundreds of living specimens. He continued as Beebe's assistant until he became curator of birds himself in 1920.

In 1928 Lee Crandall undertook an expedition to New Guinea to collect birds-of-paradise, and he returned with 40, most of species never seen before in any American zoo. His many adventures on the island, such as living with cannibals who helped him catch the birds, were entertainingly recounted in his 1931 book, "Paradise Quest." Incidentally, the vessel on which he left Port Moresby, New Guinea, was wrecked on a reef. When the other passengers were taken off, Crandall elected to stay aboard, despite a bad storm, to care for his cargo of living birds and mammals until he was rescued almost a week later.

Lee Crandall was a prolific writer. He also authored a book (1917) entitled "Pets and How to Care for Them," and he spent 12 years after his retirement assembling facts for an almost 800-page volume on "The Management of Wild Mammals in Captivity," a unique reference work. He also contributed some 300 published notes and papers on birds and mammals, and at least one on snakes.

Fairfield Osborn, President of the New York Zoological Society, interested himself in the daily operation of the Bronx Zoo, and he was actually the "director" for many years. Thus, instead of being given that title, which he richly deserved, Lee Crandall eventually became general curator, a designation that was retired with him when he reached the mandatory age of 65 in 1952.

I recall being invited, during one of my many visits to the Bronx Zoo, to attend a staff meeting. It was an unusual one, inasmuch as we walked rather slowly from place to place, with many stops while Osborn held forth on one subject or another. While we were passing through a building housing many small birds, Crandall whispered to me and pointed out a species that had just hatched young for the first time anywhere in captivity. He was very proud of his accomplishment. Osborn, noting the event, called out loudly, "Lee! Pay attention. We are having a staff meeting." My respect for Osborn vanished instantly. If he felt that Crandall should be reprimanded, why didn't he wait and do it privately? I had long since learned that chastising a person in the presence of others is a major social felony.

Lee Crandall was the oracle to whom we all turned for counsel and advice. He had a phenomenal memory, especially for birds, and virtually everyone in the business respected him as the best zoo man of his time. Unwittingly, he did me a great favor by educating Freeman M. Shelly, my boss for many years at the Philadelphia Zoo. Shelly, a certified public accountant, had been hired in 1936 to save our zoo from bankruptcy. He did extremely well in that respect but, unlike most of us, he had never tended to the needs of an animal of any kind, much less handled a broom and shovel to clean up. He was extremely reluctant to take advice from his underlings, meaning me and the curators of birds and mammals. He was morbidly jealous of his title of Zoo Director Shelly. When two different cub reporters misquoted me as "Director" of the zoo, in the newspapers, during the same month, it precipitated a crisis that earned me a reprimand from the president of our zoo. I was given strict orders to have such things stopped at once.

When Shelly became a member of the International Union of Directors of Zoological Gardens, he and Lee Crandall often traveled together to Europe, where most of the meetings were held. My boss did not consider it infra dig to take advice from someone who was his peer, and so he learned much about the animal side of running a zoo. He also learned that such basic problems as having someone else quoted as the director plagued every zoo in the world.

Lee and I were good friends. Somewhere in his ancestry there was a person named Conant, so occasionally we facetiously called each other "cousin." Once, when I was fed up with Shelly's attitude toward me and the other curators, I asked Lee, at the Bronx, if there might be an opening for me in New York. The position of curator of reptiles, so ably handled for decades by Raymond L. Ditmars, had not yet been filled by a dyed-in-the-wool herpetologist. I asked chiefly with tongue in cheek, because I knew Lee would pass the information on to Shelly almost at once. When the latter heard about it, he quickly mended his ways, at least in part. He didn't want to lose me from the Philadelphia Zoo staff. Once again Lee had befriended me. I had no real intention of moving, and it would have taken a herd of elephants to drag Isabelle and me away from our beautiful retreat, on Taunton Lake, in the New Jersey Pine Barrens.

After the Zoo Board literally forced me to take the directorship of the Philadelphia Zoo when Shelly retired,

we had to ship a camel to the Bronx Zoo. The average person, having seen movies or television programs depicting Bedouins skillfully and effortlessly guiding camels across the sands, usually thinks that moving one of the "ships of the desert" is a simple assignment. "Tain't so," is my emphatic comment. Camels are stubborn beasts and Osa, of the exploring team of Martin and Osa Johnson, considered the camel to be among the stupidest of quadrupeds, second only to the rhinoceros.

For years our camels had resided in pens with wooden shelters, which they usually disdained to use during snow or rain storms. We built a new cinder-block barn in a spacious yard for them, but moving them even a short distance took a whole week of pulling, shoving, and trickery. We didn't beat them unmercifully, as the Bedouins did when they were out of sight of the cameras. When we finally finished, there was one camel left over that was to be shipped to the Bronx. He was as stubborn as the rest, and we had one devil of a time getting him into his shipping crate. The journey to New York was uneventful, the crate was placed in their camel yard, and the wooden guillotine-type door was removed so he could step out whenever he wished.

I no longer have Lee Crandall's correspondence, and his priceless description of what happened has long since been lost. In essence, the camel refused to leave the crate, not even to get the food or water that had been placed nearby. Two or three days later, the keepers took the crate apart, board by board, removing the top, end, and sides. The camel remained standing on the wooden floor for two or three more days before it finally gave up and walked into the yard. When I read Lee's letter to the Philadelphia Zoo keepers who had participated in the "camel maneuver," they were amused but not surprised. They all knew that trying to move and crate animals could be an exasperating chore.

HEINRICH DATHE (1910-1991) was an able zoologist and zoo expert who, in the eyes of those of us who live in the West, was on the wrong side of the line. After World War II, when Germany was partitioned by Great Britain, France, the United States, and the Soviet Union, Dathe found himself in the Russian zone, which eventually became the German Democratic Republic (GDR), known as East Germany in America. It was a lucky break for him, however, because his excellent reputation, as the assistant director of the Leipzig Zoo, made him the logical choice to head a brand-new zoo. That gave him the opportunity to plan, design, supervise the construction, and thus create, from scratch, the Tierpark Berlin, or East Berlin Zoo. It was opened to the public on July 2, 1955. I never saw it myself, but friends and colleagues told me it was a splendid zoo and very different from the Berlin Zoologischer Garten, which I had visited in 1937. When the International Union of Directors of Zoological Gardens met in East Berlin in 1970, I was unable to attend because of a stubborn respiratory infection that my doctors wanted to keep under close observation.

Dathe got along well with the Communists and accepted their dictates. He produced and operated a big zoo that was a real credit to him and to East Berlin. Like many European zoo directors, he lived in a house right on the zoo grounds. Thus, in a sense, he was on 24-hour duty. He had academic standing and was known officially as Professor Doctor sc. Doctor h.c. Heinrich Dathe. In writing to him, especially after we both were getting elderly, I addressed him as "Dr. Dr. Dathe." There was always a thank-you letter for me to send him every year, for the whimsical animal cutouts he sent to his friends and colleagues at holiday times. He found time to edit and write portions of two zoo publications, "Milu" and "Der Zoologische Garten." In one or the other of them, much of what was going on in zoo circles world-wide was chronicled. When the new reptile house at the Philadelphia Zoo was completed in 1972, he accepted an article I wrote about it, which appeared later, in English and with many illustrations, in "Der Zoologische Garten."

Dr. Dathe was a prolific writer. The list of his signed publications numbered well over 1000 titles, including reports and notes about zoos, their livestock, comments about the activities of zoo people, and obituaries. He also contributed parts or chapters to the books of others, such as Grzimek's great 13-volume "Tierleben" (Animal Life Encyclopedia).

The distinguished East Berlin zoo director was permitted to visit other zoos in the Western world, and after he and his wife reached the age of 60, they both could leave East Berlin together. He attended the IUDZG meetings whenever he could, and during 1969 he toured American zoos. He was my guest at the Philadelphia Zoo on October 30, 1969. We spent much of the day together looking at and talking about our exhibits. His English was excellent, although heavily accented, and he was quite complimentary about many of the things he saw. In the evening, I hosted a dinner for him and several staff members of the Philadelphia Zoological Garden at the Philadelphia Art Alliance, a private club to which I belonged by virtue of my position. We had an interesting conversation and discussion of zoos in general. Afterward, I took him to the Philadelphia Airport so he could go on to Washington

or New York, I have forgotten which. In 1981, when he was in California, he received a gold conservation medal from the Zoological Society of San Diego.

My last visit with Heinrich Dathe was in Amsterdam in 1972. It was my swan song as a member of IUDZG, and I was alone. Isabelle, my constant companion all during our married life, had undergone surgery, and the doctors wouldn't permit her to make a trans-Atlantic trip. I vividly recall a dinner party, cohosted by Heini Hediger, director of the Zürich Zoo, and Mario Paulo Autuori, director of the São Paulo Zoo in Brazil. They each had their wives with them, and Dr. and Frau Dathe and I were their guests. It was a memorable occasion with good friends and one of the most enjoyable dinners I ever had. For me, it was a fond, almost affectionate farewell.

Dathe had the respect and admiration of zoo leaders of the Western world. He was able, always helpful, and fully trusted despite his residence in a Communist country. In essence, he was regarded as one of the most distinguished of all zoo persons. As he aged, he continued to be active, and his seventy-fifth birthday celebration was marked by a vast outpouring of praise for what he had accomplished during his busy life.

After the Berlin Wall came down in 1989, Dathe's personal world collapsed. I have no details about the internal politics, but after the reunification of the two Germanys, West Berlin authorities took over the zoo. Dathe was demoted, so to speak, and, late during 1990, he was ordered to get out of his house in the zoo within 30 days. He had lived there for decades, ever since the East Berlin Zoo was opened in 1955. He died on the twenty-ninth day, January 6, 1991.

As an impartial foreign observer, I fail to understand why Heinrich Dathe, a sick old man, was not permitted to die in peace. Why subject him to unnecessary stress? Hadn't the West German authorities ever heard of the "milk of human kindness"?

WILL OJIBWA DOOLITTLE (1878-1965) was the human glue who kept the American Institute of Park Executives and its affiliate, the American Association of Zoological Parks and Aquariums, from disintegrating during their early, formative years.

I first met Will-O, as we all called him, at a combined meeting of the two organizations in St. Louis in 1930, at which time I became a member of the AAZPA. He was then serving as the superintendent of parks in Tulsa, Oklahoma. He had previously held a similar position in Minot, North Dakota, and he had established zoos in both cities. He was an avid bird-watcher, and one of his early objectives was to install a large number of nesting boxes in Minot's Riverside Park.

Will-0 had a flare for public relations and he had a firm belief that publications, especially those containing news and editorial comments about parks and zoos and their operating personnel, were the best way to keep things going. He wrote an article on the value of animal collections in public parks way back in 1918 that appeared in the second number of "Parks and Recreation" magazine. Subsequently, he was a frequent contributor. So it may be said that he had an affiliation with that magazine from its very beginning. He was already the editor in chief in 1930, but seven years later he resigned from his position in Tulsa and moved to Rockford, Illinois, to devote his full time to "Parks and Recreation." It was a financial struggle. When funds were low he cut his own meager salary and took on other part-time jobs. We all admired him for his tenacity and dedication to his chosen objective.

I soon found myself the "editor" of the zoo section, a responsibility I had for two full decades. Actually I was more of a reporter, because I had to rustle up zoo news myself, which required considerable correspondence and the wheedling of information out of zoo people.

In 1932 Will-O found the money to publish a bound book of more than 100 pages featuring papers presented at meetings of the AAZPA, and it included pictures of many of its members. Because I was then the secretary, my portrait was among them. How amusing it is now to see myself, at age 23, with a full head of wavy hair. A comment beneath a set of illustrations of others just getting started in the zoo business reads, "These three young men and Roger Conant of Toledo are examples of future energetic and efficient leadership." Of the four, Marlin Perkins and I stayed in the zoo business throughout our professional careers. The book is labeled "Volume I," but, lamentably, it was the one and only. It served, however, as a splendid well-illustrated record of the AAZPA's early years.

One of the other persons depicted in the special book was Hugh S. Davis. His father had died when he was young, and Will-O became his role model and mentor. Hugh later served as director of the Tulsa Zoo for many years. Also, he had the glorious opportunity, at age 22, of accompanying Martin and Osa Johnson, world-famous explorers and photographers, for almost a full year during their sixth expedition to Africa.

Will-O kept a low profile at our annual meetings, but he was always willing, even eager, to help anyone who sought his assistance or advice. He was the "power behind the throne," to use a hackneyed phrase. He continued as editor until the publication of the June 1953 issue. It truly could be said that he devoted a large part of his life to "Parks and Recreation" magazine.

I have many pleasant memories of Will O. Doolittle, but only one fits the accepted definition of an anecdote: "a short, funny tale." During my wanderings all over the Buckeye State in the early 1930s, as I assembled material for "The Reptiles of Ohio," I sought out every private collection I could find. I heard about a small one belonging to an E. A. Doolittle, of Painesville, Ohio. He greeted me cordially when I called on him, and he permitted me to examine the few specimens he had preserved. In the course of our conversation he told me, with some pride, that he was the best paperhanger in town, and that was how he made his living. I also discovered that he was Will O. Doolittle's brother. When next I saw Will-O, I mentioned the incident and the profession. That was too infra dig for him. He drew himself up to his full height and said, "Please. My brother is an interior decorator."

My last meeting with Will-O was in the autumn of 1959 when the park and zoo people met in convention in Philadelphia. In a speech in which he reviewed many highlights of his career, he thanked me for the help I had given him with "Parks and Recreation" for so many years. At his request, and because I knew about his interest in birds, I arranged to have him driven to and escorted through the Tinicum Wildlife Preserve at the southern end of the city. He had a delightful day and added a species or two to his life list. Despite his advanced age, he continued his interest in birds almost until the time of his death, in 1965, in the home of his niece in Painesville. Could it have been the same house where I met his brother so many years previously?

Will-O's middle name, Ojibwa, was after the Amerindian tribe. He had Indian blood in his veins, and he was proud of it. Lieutenant Colonel James H. "Jimmy" Doolittle who commanded the air raid on Tokyo and other Japanese cities that did so much to restore American morale during the dark and worrisome days soon after we entered World War II, was an illustrious cousin of Will-O's.

BERNHARD GRZIMEK (1909-1987) was an outstanding conservationist and also a resourceful opportunist. He was long the director of the Frankfurt Zoo, and his regular television show about animals made him the best-known naturalist in the German-speaking world. His American friends pronounced his name "Chee'-mek," and he said that was close enough. His family was from Upper Silesia, which had been both German and Polish, depending on the varying fortunes of many wars.

We saw each other several times at international zoo meetings (IUDZG), but it was during our visit to the Frankfurt Zoo in 1967 that he told Isabelle and me, almost with the glee of a mischievous boy, what he had done for his zoo immediately after World War II. Allied planes had flattened much of Frankfurt. Only a few of the original zoo buildings survived, and even they were damaged. The surrounding residential neighborhood was reduced to rubble, and there was no indication of where the streets were. The authorities erected barriers where the presumed boundaries of the zoo had been. Grzimek and his men, on dark nights, repeatedly moved the barriers outward. No one noticed the difference, and they thus enlarged the zoo, gaining a number of hectares as a result.

Word came that a roller coaster from an amusement park had been dismantled and secreted in the Black Forest to avoid destruction. Frankfurt was in the American zone, but the amusement device was in the nearby French zone. Grzimek sought the help of the U.S. military authorities, and they received permission from the French to dispatch a group of troops and sufficient transport vehicles to move the material to the Frankfurt Zoo. There the parts were reassembled, and the resulting structure soon became the mecca for the occupying American soldiers and their German dates. There they could, at least momentarily, forget the massive destruction that surrounded them. The admission fees for the ride accrued to the zoo and helped it to stay in operation during the difficult postwar years. By the time of our visit in 1967 there were several new buildings and exhibits, and the zoo once again was largely surrounded by houses. The roller coaster, having served its purpose, had vanished.

Dr. Grzimek was devoted to the wildlife of Africa, and he did everything in his power to preserve it. In the early days of exploration it teemed with myriads of animals, large and small, furred, feathered, and cold-blooded—and the huge and extremely diverse fauna lived in balance, if not in harmony, with primitive mankind. The partitioning and colonizing of Africa by European nations and the introduction of firearms resulted in disastrous reductions in the numbers of game animals in many parts of the continent. Grzimek focused his attention on the Serengeti, a vast area in Tanzania (then Tanganyika and under British control) that extends from the shore of Lake Victoria south and southeast to and including the Ngorongoro Crater, one of the world's largest calderas. The latter is roughly circular, averages 11 miles in diameter, and is completely surrounded by walls 2,000 feet high, yet it has an amazingly large and varied fauna living within it

The Serengeti, as a whole, is known for the spectacular migration of great herds of animals, notably wildebeests (gnus), zebras, and gazelles, as they seek grass during the seasonal changes in rain patterns. Grzimek felt, and passionately so, that the Serengeti must be preserved for all time as a living remnant of the halcyon days of the Age of Mammals and its associated fauna. He set out, with his son, Michael, to learn everything possible about the region and to make a motion picture that would take his conservation message to millions of persons worldwide.

With a small, highly sophisticated airplane in which they could, when desired, fly at low altitudes and at surprisingly slow speeds, they traveled from Germany to Tanganyika. The plane was gaily painted with zebralike stripes, and with it father and son criss-crossed the Serengeti, using ingenious methods of counting the numbers of animals in its many and diverse parts. They often dropped into the Ngorongoro caldera to compare the fauna there with its counterpart outside. They worked hard for the better part of two years, assembled a mass of useful information, and had many adventures, which Grzimek related in one of his several books. The English edition is entitled "Serengeti Shall Not Die."

After a narrow escape from the treacherous, soda-encrusted border of Lake Natron, where they wished to photograph great flocks of flamingos, they flew back to the caldera where they had been staying for a few days in a hut. Michael then left alone in the plane, promising to bring back two of their collaborators on the morrow. The following morning a native scout delivered a note to Dr. Grzimek from a game warden informing him that the plane had crashed and Michael had been killed. An investigation revealed that a griffon vulture hit and bent a wing, crippling the rudder cables. Michael was buried on the rim of the Crater, and the Tanganyika National Park Administration later erected a stone monument over his grave that bore the inscription:

> MICHAEL GRZIMEK
> 12.4.1934 - 10.1.1959
> He gave all he possessed for the wild
> animals of Africa, including his life.

At least Bernhard Grzimek survived to interpret their voluminous notes and to carry the Serengeti message to the rest of the world.

Isabelle and I stayed for three nights in the tourist lodge on the rim of the Ngorongoro Crater in 1968, and she photographed the memorial inscription. From close by we could look to the east and southeast, however, and, through our binoculars, see large modern farm machinery in operation. No wonder the Grzimeks did their utmost. They wanted to insure that at least one major part of Africa would remain intact, so that future generations of human beings would be awed by the spectacle of the great mammalian migrations.

When Bernhard Grzimek died in 1987, his body was cremated and his ashes were taken to Africa to be interred next to the mortal remains of his son.

HEINI HEDIGER (1908-1992) was director of all three of Switzerland's zoos during his long professional career. He was chosen to head the newly opened animal park, the Dählhölzli, in Berne in 1937. He later became director of the much larger Basel Zoological Gardens in 1944, and then transferred to the Zoo Zürich in 1954, where he remained until his retirement in 1973.

Hediger was deeply interested in the psychology of animals. He studied such topics as defense, the marking of territories, fear, escape, and sleep, and he related his findings to the animals in his care. He applied his knowledge to the construction of new exhibits that were free from such human habitation principles as right angles, straight walls, and plain flat floors. He had the first open-fronted aviary in Europe, an open-fronted tropical terrarium, and he designed the still unique Afrika Haus, where cattle egrets and oxpeckers live in symbiosis with hippos and rhinos, just as they do in nature. Outdoor exhibits that replicated wildlife habitats were part of many zoos at the time, but Hediger succeeded in bringing them indoors, thus making them accessible to the public during the cold Swiss winters. His success with innovations saved him from the jealousy of his zoo's board of trustees, who summarily fired him in 1958. His fame and popularity resulted in an instant clamor and show of support by his students and private citizens. He was promptly reinstated, and the trustees were replaced by a new board.

My first meeting with Heini Hediger occurred on September 26, 1951. He spent the day visiting our Philadelphia Zoo and, in the evening, was the guest of honor at a dinner given by Williams B. Cadwalader, M.D., President of the Zoological Society of Philadelphia. The officers of the zoo board were invited, and so were the zoo director, the three curators, and Dr. Herbert L. Ratcliffe, director of the zoo's Penrose Research Laboratory. Dr. Cadwalader lived well to the west of the city. Because I had to cross the Delaware River on the Benjamin Franklin Bridge to get home

to our sylvan retreat in the New Jersey Pine Barrens, I volunteered to drive Dr. Hediger to his downtown Philadelphia hotel. It was a long ride, and we were blocked by an earlier traffic accident that required a time-consuming detour. It was all to the good for me, because it gave me the opportunity to become better acquainted with our distinguished guest. He told me something about his studies on animal psychology, and I became a convert. Later, I found myself defending him and his views from some of his detractors who refused to part with tradition. When his book entitled "Psychology of Animals in Zoos and Circuses" was translated and published in English in 1955, I bought a copy and devoured it with interest.

Incidentally, during that long drive I also learned that he had started out as a herpetologist and that his doctoral dissertation was entitled (translated) "Contribution to the Herpetology and Zoogeography of New Britain and Some Adjacent Regions." He sent me a copy of it and several of his other publications in that discipline.

Hediger was quite impressed by the revolutionary dietary regimes that Dr. Ratcliffe had originated and which were in use at our zoo. He sent one of his young associates, René E. Honegger, to Philadelphia for two years to learn and practice our methods. René was admitted to the United States on a visa as a student apprentice, and we became good friends during his lengthy stay.

I kept Hediger's tenets in mind when the new Philadelphia Zoo reptile house was in the planning and building stages. I insisted that natural habitats be used virtually throughout the structure. By that time fiberglass was available, a strong, almost indestructible material we could mold into any shape, color, or form desired.

Although we corresponded occasionally, I did not see Hediger again until Isabelle and I attended our first meeting of the International Union of Directors of Zoological Gardens in Barcelona, Spain, in 1967. For a postconference study tour we flew to Zürich and several cities in Germany to see their zoos. Hediger greeted us warmly on his home ground and proudly showed us some of his achievements. He also honored us by taking us to his private club for a sumptuous repast.

During his long career, he had appointments on the faculties of universities in the cities whose zoos he directed. As Professor Dr. Hediger, he actively lectured and conducted classes both in the zoos and in formal classrooms. His warm personality and keen interest in his students' work and welfare were seminal contributions to their future careers.

Hediger helped to host a farewell party for me in Amsterdam in 1972. I was at my last international meeting before my retirement, and I was there principally to say farewell to my foreign colleagues and to several American zoo directors who were also present. Isabelle, for the first time ever, wasn't with me. Because of recent surgery, the doctors would not permit her to go abroad.

My final visit with Heini Hediger occurred long after he also had retired. I stopped off in Zürich after a nonstop flight from Bombay, accompanied by my wife, Kathryn J. Gloyd. We were homeward bound after my initial efforts to learn as much as possible about the venomous snakes of the *Agkistrodon* complex of southeastern and southern Asia. We visited with René Honegger, who was curator of the Vivarium and of reptiles, at the Zoo Zürich, and Heini, despite the fact that his wife was very ill, made a special trip in from the countryside just to see us.

I was fortunate to know Heini Hediger and to meet with him several times at IUDZG meetings. Among all the European zoo directors whom I knew and admired, I had my strongest personal rapport with him. He made his mark in zoo history, and was not afraid to depart from the traditional.

EDMUND H. HELLER (1875-1939) was a distinguished naturalist. He traveled to distant parts of the world to explore, gather information, and collect specimens for such sponsoring institutions as the Field Museum, the American Museum, the Academy of Natural Sciences of Philadelphia, Stanford and Yale universities, and the National Geographic Society. His fieldwork was usually under primitive conditions during his seven long trips to Africa, three to South America, and two to Asia. He was the naturalist with the Theodore Roosevelt party in Africa during 1909-10, and he was the only person with whom the former president ever collaborated in writing a book. Their two-volume "Life Histories of African Game Animals" was a classic of its day. Heller also accompanied such famous explorers as Lincoln Ellsworth, Roy Chapman Andrews, Carl E. Akeley, and Paul Rainey on their expeditions.

In the late 1920s Heller decided to settle down. He placed first in a civil service examination, and was appointed the director of the Washington Park Zoo, in Milwaukee, to begin on January 1, 1928.

My first meeting with Edmund Heller was at the Toledo Zoo during the late summer of 1929. Even though I was a very young newcomer to that institution, I served as his guide. I spent some two hours escorting him through the grounds and talking about the animals on exhibition. Much to my surprise, he

invited me to accompany him to his hotel, the Commodore Perry, to have dinner with him. We taxied to mid-city, and he regaled me, as we ate and then in his room afterward, with tales of his adventures in the wilds. I was an ardent listener. He complimented me on my enthusiasm and deep interest in animals. The name of Heller was well known to me, and there I was, thrilled to the core to be the guest of the great man. I had long dreamed of visiting faraway places, and there I was, just a kid, an audience of one for perhaps the most widely traveled explorer of them all. Some of the things he told me eventually found their way into the weekly scripts I prepared for the "Let's Visit the Zoo" program on Philadelphia's radio station KYW.

From that chance meeting, we developed a rapport that seemed almost miraculous to me. He was old enough to be my grandfather. Once each year thereafter, during my six-year stint at Toledo, he stopped off to see me. He would write ahead, and I would meet his train and drive him to the zoo. He was usually on his way to the East to lecture about his travels. Normally he would stay only a few hours, but one other time we had dinner and spent an evening together as we did the first year we met. I felt extremely flattered to be his friend, and I was grateful to him for defending me when a jealous, obstreperous member of the zoo board tried to insult me in his presence.

Both Heller and I left our respective posts in 1935, he to become director of the Fleischhacker Zoo in San Francisco, and I the curator of reptiles at the Philadelphia Zoo. He, because he acted too independently in the opinion of the Milwaukee Park Board, with inevitable friction developing, was probably glad to make the change.

We corresponded frequently until his death on July 18, 1939. He was felled by a severe heart attack late during 1938 that kept him inactive for months, but, once he was back on his feet, he was soon going full speed. He was stricken again on July 4, but on that very day he wrote to me offering to participate in the annual zoo meetings, and he asked me for information on the births of cat animals at the Philadelphia Zoo. He hoped to write a book on the breeding of captive felines. What a determination to keep going! No wonder Teddy Roosevelt, in writing about their explorations in Africa together, said that "Edmund Heller was the man for any task. No work at any hour of the day or night ever came amiss to him."

During his annual visit to the Toledo Zoo, Heller never forgot to ask me how my work was progressing on my projected book on the "Reptiles of Ohio." He seemed so interested that I sent him a copy when it was published in 1938. How astonished I was, when I opened a newly arrived "Parks and Recreation" magazine, to find a very favorable review he had written. To surprise me, he had sent his manuscript directly to Will O. Doolittle, the editor in chief, instead of to the zoo editor, meaning me. At the time almost all zoo items destined for publication in "Parks and Recreation" passed across my desk.

Edmund Heller's death, in 1939, inadvertently caused a problem for Frederick A. Ulmer, Jr., who later became the Philadelphia Zoo's curator of mammals. Fred was returning from a long stay in the East Indies as a member of the George Vanderbilt Sumatran Expedition. Ulmer's steamer arrived in San Francisco on the very day that funeral services were held for Edmund Heller, and all the important members of the Fleischhacker Zoo staff were away from their posts. Ulmer ran into a king-sized problem that was "solved" by bureaucratic blundering completely lacking in common sense. Fred had two live rarities with him that he wanted to donate to the Philadelphia Zoo: a binturong, the largest member of the civet family, the Viverridae; and a siamang, a vociferous, long-armed ape. An obdurate customs inspector insisted that the binturong was a mongoose, which could not be imported. He got in touch with Washington to check, and someone, probably an underling or political appointee, looked in a natural history book, and saw that the binturong and the mongoose both belong to the civet family. Therefore, the binturong must be a mongoose, which it certainly is not. No amount of reasoning would sway the stubborn inspector, so Ulmer had to euthanize the poor animal and prepare it as a study specimen for the Philadelphia Academy. He didn't want to lose it altogether. If any one of the San Francisco zoo officials had been available, the stupid, tragic situation could have been avoided. There were two binturongs living at the time in the Fleischhacker Zoo, as Ulmer learned later. There was no trouble over the siamang.

One warm August afternoon in 1950, a middle-aged feminine visitor went to the main zoo office, explained that the film had jammed in her camera, and asked if there was anyone who could fix it for her. The telephone operator sent her to my office, and I, in turn, asked Isabelle to help her. In the darkroom the trouble was corrected in a matter of seconds. When the two ladies emerged, the visitor introduced herself. Her name was Hilda Hempl Heller, and she had been married to Edmund Heller for a decade before being divorced many years previously. She was living in Arequipa, Peru, and trying to make a living by selling live animals, chiefly young ones, that she obtained during long journeys into the hinterland, and then writing about them.

During the following two years she shipped quite a number to us, including a spectacled bear, pacarana, culpeo (Andean fox), Humboldt's penguin, and many amphibians and reptiles, among which was a fairly large pit viper of an undescribed species.

What a strange coincidence for me to have met the two Hellers, both by chance, and then to have interesting contacts with them for some years afterward.

Oh, one other thing. Edmund Heller bore a strong resemblance to Will Rogers, and he was occasionally mistaken for that renowned entertainer and humorist.

WILLIAM MONTANA MANN (1886-1960) was an early idol of mine. Not only was he the director of the National Zoo in Washington, he was also one of the most talented raconteurs I ever heard. What stories he had to tell! He had been all over the world, both in the field collecting and hobnobbing with potentates. The National Zoo, a division of the Smithsonian Institution, was frequently visited by foreign dignitaries, and Dr. Mann was the perfect host to help entertain them.

He had humble beginnings. He was born in Helena, Montana, the son of a harness maker, but he quickly developed a deep interest in natural history. He received a good education and eventually earned an Sc.D. at Harvard.

I first met Dr. Mann along with many other zoo directors in St. Louis in 1930 at a gathering of the then-infant American Association of Zoological Parks and Aquariums. When the daily sessions were over and we had eaten dinner, we would repair to a hotel suite. Prohibition was then very much in force, but our host, George P. Vierheller, the Director of the St. Louis Zoo, had a bootlegger friend who supplied a varied array of libations. We were scarcely more than a dozen in number, and, whereas all the conversation was lively, several of us, including Marlin Perkins of later television fame, soon gravitated toward Bill Mann's chair. I would nurse a single highball through the evening until midnight or beyond while I listened spellbound to tales of his adventures.

After I became associated with the Philadelphia Zoological Garden, I visited the National Zoo and the National Museum fairly often to pursue my twin avenues of interest in zoos and herpetology. Bill Mann frequently invited me to lunch at his apartment across the street from the zoo, and his lovely and able wife, Lucille Quarry Mann, was always a gracious hostess. He was forever springing surprises on her, as I soon discovered, because he invited everyone to lunch who was a professional zoo person or well-known naturalist. We would all walk through the door and Lucy would mentally count noses and become a short-order cook. The biggest surprise he ever gave her was when he arrived home in late afternoon one day and announced that the two of them were leaving on the morrow for Europe on the first leg of a trip to Liberia. She remarked that it was good to have a day to get ready. His startling rejoinder was, "But our ship sails tonight at one minute after midnight from New York." Lucy, after long experience as Bill's spouse, kept a set of suitcases all packed in advance for such emergencies. Their train from Washington arrived just in time for a taxi to transport them to a Hudson River pier.

Bill Mann enjoyed life to the full. He was an excellent mixer, and he had the magic knack of making a good impression on almost everyone he encountered. I daresay that he had more friends and acquaintants than anyone else I ever knew.

He was a circus fan, and many a time he played hooky from school and from his job as the "Eminent Zoo Director" to attend a performance and visit with the cast and supportive workers. It didn't have to be the great Barnum and Bailey outfit, "the most colossal, most stupendous, most gargantuan" of them all. Any circus would do. One evening when Isabelle and I were staying overnight in Washington, he invited us and another couple to go to the circus with him. We piled into a taxi. He had no idea where the show was playing, and we had to stop several times while he telephoned from sidewalk phone booths for information and directions. Finally, we arrived at a tiny, one-ring, tented circus set up on an empty lot. The news of his appearance raced from mouth to mouth, and soon there was a procession of personnel, from the star performers to the lowliest roustabouts, enthusiastically waiting to shake his hand. When they reached him they said, "Hello, Doc. It's nice to see you again."

When Mann became the director of the National Zoo in 1925, his main objective quickly became a great effort to increase and improve the animal collection. As a field entomologist, he had worked in many parts of the world, so why not travel and collect himself? In 1926 he persuaded Walter P. Chrysler, the automobile magnate, to donate $50,000 and thus sponsor an expedition to East Africa. Mann returned with a huge collection of mammals, birds, and reptiles, including many kinds that were rarities or previously unknown in captivity.

During the recovery from the Great Depression, Bill Mann's friend Harold L. Ickes, Secretary of the Interior, telephoned to tell him that $870,000 had been granted to the zoo for new construction under the aegis of the WPA, FERA, or whatever relief agency was then in vogue. He soon had a new elephant house, a small mammal house, and a new wing for the bird house. They had to be filled up, of course.

In 1937 the National Geographic Society sponsored an expedition to the East Indies. When the oceangoing freighter bearing Bill's collection returned to the United States, it put in first at Boston before going on to unload the livestock (at Baltimore?). I happened to be in Lexington, Massachusetts, at the time, visiting my Uncle Harold and Aunt Mae, and I read in the newspaper that a ship with Dr. Mann and a menagerie aboard, would be in port for a couple of days. I hastened to the dock the next morning to see what he had. There was a diversity that would make any zoo man drool with envy. After being in the field, Bill had bought many additional treasures in Singapore, which was then the main shipping point for wild animals in the Far East. His greatest prize, in his estimation, was a fairly large Komodo dragon. He told me sadly that he had started out with two, but one had died at sea.

Probably I was less enthusiastic about it than I should have been, because just a short time earlier we had received two much larger dragons at the Philadelphia Zoo through the good offices of the Dutch East Indies government. I told him about it, and he replied that he knew we had them. He then asked why we hadn't let him bring ours back with him. I told him that I hadn't known his plans or when he expected to sail home. I could not help but speculate to myself, however, that if one of the four dragons had succumbed en route, it would have been one of ours, not his. Ironically, his Komodo dragon lived for an exceptionally long time, whereas we lost both of ours two or three years later to amoebiasis, a scourge in our reptile house for which there was no quick and easy cure in those early days.

In 1940 Harvey S. Firestone, Jr., the tire manufacturer, contributed $15,000 for an expedition to West Africa. By the time the Manns returned to the United States, Hitler's Nazi juggernaut had invaded the Netherlands, and World War II was well under way. That was Bill's last great trip.

The National Zoo could never have had a better press agent than Dr. William M. Mann. His personality, his bubbling enthusiasm, and his broad knowledge about zoo animals of all kinds were appreciated by the members of the press and other news media. He also had a mischievous streak. An oft-told tale concerned a routine visit to the zoo by the U.S. Budget Director, General H. M. Lord. Dr. Mann led him past a cage containing a mynah, a bird noted for its ability to mimic the human voice. At precisely the right moment the mynah called out, loud and clear, "How about the appropriation?" General Lord was taken aback and said, "That's impertinent!" Supposedly, the mynah replied, "So's your old man," but that part may have been apocryphal. In any event, General Lord obviously recognized the humor of the situation after he had had time to think about it, and the zoo's appropriation was increased by $30,000. Did Bill Mann instruct the keeper to teach the bird what to say? We never knew for sure, but most of us in the zoo business would have given large odds that he was responsible.

In Bill Mann's later years at the zoo he developed an invariable route along which he escorted his guests. Most of it was to the bird and mammal exhibits. So I worked out a scheme, hoping to get around by myself. I had my taxi driver take me to a side entrance so that I could head directly to the reptile house. It didn't work. The keepers knew me, and they had strict orders to telephone Dr. Mann the minute any zoo person was recognized. I must say, however, that Bill was quite generous. The National Zoo was the constant recipient of live animals from overseas, and he was more than willing to share extra reptiles and amphibians. I seldom went back to my zoo empty-handed. Twice I met his train at a station in Philadelphia when it stopped briefly before going on to New York. Both times he had herpetological goodies for me. In exchange, I sometimes took spare snakes to Washington when I visited there. Bill was always ready and willing to trade surplus animals. He would never sell them. He learned early in his career that any cash received did not help his zoo. It had to be deposited immediately in the U.S. Treasury.

When Bill retired in 1956, at the mandatory age of 70, I took a leading part in making ready for his convivial farewell luncheon that was attended by many of his fellow zoo directors, curators, and friends. I assembled a fat bound book of letters of congratulations from his colleagues, and I also wrote a full-page tribute to him that was printed in "Parks and Recreation."

The Manns continued to live across the street from the zoo after Bill retired, and he haunted his erstwhile "empire," but his decline was rapid. When I saw him for the last time, in 1958 or 1959, he looked old, tired, and dissipated. His long years of being a chain-smoker and enjoying double Scotches had caught up with him. Still, in a small office assigned to the director emeritus, he greeted me warmly, and said he was clearing out his library, and that I should have one of his books. He gave me his copy of "Deutschlands Amphibien und Reptilien," by Bruno Dürigen, published in 1897. I have used it only once or twice, but I still have it as a reminder of a good friend and an entertaining character who enjoyed

regaling his listeners. Regrettably, we were interrupted while I was in his office during that final visit, and I failed to ask him to write his name in my newly acquired book.

Bill was a marvelous animal man and general naturalist. During his younger years he was a leading authority on ants. He had a personal collection of more than 117,000 mounted and labeled specimens from many parts of the world. Just before his retirement he gave it to the National Museum. He was always well liked, he won many honors for himself, and he was mourned by all who knew him well.

The greatest tribute that Bill Mann ever received, in my opinion, was given in Gordon MacCreagh's wonderful book entitled "White Waters and Black," published in 1926. In it, the author recounted the ludicrous events that occurred during a highly touted, million-dollar expedition from La Paz, Bolivia, over the Andes and down into the jungles of the Amazon. It was so poorly planned and directed that MacCreagh's account is truly hilarious in part. No names were mentioned, but Dr. Mann was the Eminent Entomologist who had been assigned to go along to collect insects. He and MacCreagh were the only members of the expedition with enough previous field experience to weather the hardships, frustrations, and vicious backbiting among the expedition's supposedly erudite, authoritative, and dignified scientists. "White Waters and Black" is dedicated to "The Bug-Hunter, Stout Companion of the Trail."

RICHARD MARLIN PERKINS (1905-1986) began his professional zoo career as the superintendent of reptiles at the St. Louis Zoological Park. Later, he became the executive head of three different zoos: Buffalo, then Lincoln Park in Chicago, and finally the St. Louis Zoo, back where he started. It was through the magic of television, however, and his decades-long weekly appearances on the tube that he became the best-known zoo man in America.

I first met Marlin and his assistant, Moody J. R. Lentz, in August 1929 at their home base, where I had gone to see the splendid new reptile house and to garner ideas for the eventual erection of a similar structure back at the Toledo Zoo, where I worked at the time. A month later Marlin spent a day and night visiting me in Ohio. We talked for hours about zoos and herpetology in general, and we became good friends. We frequently exchanged specimens for our respective collections, I visited him in St. Louis several times, and, of course, we met occasionally at national or international zoo conferences. The encounter farthest from home was in the

Kruger National Park, in South Africa, in 1968, where Isabelle and I had dinner with him and Captain Jean Delacour, whose splendid personal game park at Cleres, France, I had visited way back in 1937. Marlin was all set to film wild hippos the next day for his television show.

My most memorable adventure with him took place when he and I and Moody Lentz made a trip to the fabulous snake dens near Murphysboro, in southern Illinois, where great numbers of snakes were then being slaughtered by both local people and so-called sportsmen from far away. Timber rattlesnakes, cottonmouths, and copperheads, as well as many kinds of nonvenomous snakes hibernated in the three-mile-long, westward-facing Horseshoe Bluffs. They migrated in the spring to the nearby lowlands and then, in the autumn, back to the uplands. At the height of the migration, newspapers in St. Louis and Memphis kept track of the numbers of venomous snakes reported killed each week. We were there out of season, fortunately, and were not witnesses to the wanton waste. Nowadays, public attitudes toward snakes have changed. According to my latest information, that area is now under the protection of the Shawnee National Forest, snakes may not be killed, and collecting is allowed only under permits issued for scientific or educational purposes. The access road paralleling the west side of the bluffs is closed to vehicular traffic for several weeks each spring and autumn to permit the snakes to move safely from their overwintering dens and back again.

After he became deeply involved with television, I saw Marlin only occasionally. Being a master showman required too much of his time, yet he took off an evening to entertain me and Isabelle and a few others at a congratulatory dinner after I became president-elect of the American Society of Ichthyologists and Herpetologists in Chicago in 1960. At the time he was in training for his expedition to the Himalayan Mountains in search of the abominable snowman. He told us about his aching muscles resulting from his daily sessions in a gymnasium as he prepared himself physically for climbing.

Our last visit with Marlin was at our dream home, Hyla Holler, on the shore of Taunton Lake in the New Jersey Pine Barrens. We had invited him repeatedly to visit us there, but his busy schedule prevented him from doing so until April 11, 1969, on the very day before we had planned to trade in our Volkswagen Kamper, the wonderful vehicle that had taken us safely through so very many parts of Mexico. We had treated it roughly, of necessity, over difficult and even non-existent roads, and it had become cantankerous and costly to keep in repair. As a "last hoorah," in honor of both our guest

and our faithful vehicle, we took Marlin through the Barrens on a beautiful day and we picnicked at lovely, isolated Oswego Lake in the Penn State Forest. We had the place to ourselves. It was a fitting farewell both to the car and to Marlin. He enjoyed the quiet and solitude where wildlife was king, just as we did, and he relaxed and thoroughly enjoyed himself. At that time the Pine Barrens were still a naturalist's paradise.

I never regretted refusing to become Marlin's competitor when CBS was trying to create a show at the Philadelphia Zoo to air opposite his NBC's "Zooparade," as mentioned elsewhere in these recollections. I would never have achieved Marlin's flare for showmanship, and, although I have always liked to travel, I could not have become a globe-trotter as he eventually did. I would have been totally unable to be away from my home and my beloved wife repeatedly for long periods of time.

CHARLES ROBBINS SCHROEDER (1901-1991) had a reputation for being a contagious enthusiast. He seemed always to be bubbling over with new ideas that ran the gamut from improving the performance of menial tasks to great new projects. When any of us were dining together at zoo meetings, his vivacious manner of speaking invariably engendered a lively conversation, and it had the salutary effect of stimulating our efforts to do bigger and better things when we were back at our own institutions. Leonard J. Goss, his successor as the Bronx Zoo's veterinarian, and later the director of the Cleveland Zoo, said that Schroeder was a perpetual optimist. I heartily agree.

Charlie, as we always called Charles R. Schroeder, migrated virtually from coast to coast a great many times. He attended Washington State University at Pullman, and he made many a trek from there to his native New York. After receiving his D.V.M., he worked twice for Lederle Laboratories, once for the New York Zoological Park in the Bronx, and three times for the San Diego Zoo. It was during the early days of his second stint at the last named when I first met Charlie. He went along on a field trip with me and the zoo's two herpetologists, C. B. Perkins and Charles E. Shaw. The Zoological Society's Executive Secretary, Belle J. Benchley, had wooed Charlie back from the Bronx Zoo, and it was also she who succeeded in having him named to head the San Diego Zoo when she retired at the end of 1953.

Mostly, I saw Charlie at national or international zoo meetings. Only once can I recall entertaining him at Philadelphia, but, of course, his main interest while he was working in the East was as a veterinarian, and we had no regular one. The care of the animals was invested in the curators and pathologists at the Penrose Research Laboratory, the celebrated institution, founded in 1901, right in the Philadelphia Zoological Garden. Local veterinarians were called in when needed.

I remember an amusing incident that occurred when Charlie was the president of the International Union of Directors of Zoological Gardens. He was presiding at a business meeting, and, when the time came for the election of new members, his kindness and friendliness prompted him to remark that they were all fine fellows, and so they were now officially members. I glanced around and saw many raised eyebrows on the faces of some of our more conservative European colleagues. He had cut right through the usual red tape and the often lengthy discussions about each candidate. I was told later that several of those present were upset, and they insisted he had acted out of order. Nothing came of it, because all the newcomers had been carefully screened in advance. That was the only time I ever recall Schroeder's being criticized by any of his peers. Speaking of international meetings, as I was writing this account, I discovered a long-forgotten photograph that was taken at the IUDZG banquet in Pretoria, South Africa, in 1968. In it, Isabelle and I are sitting together, and Charlie is on the other side of her.

It was on his own turf in California that I had the best and most interesting visits with Schroeder. He was always a gracious host, he gave us as much of his time as his duties would permit, and he was even thoughtful enough to make us members of the Zoological Society. That meant we had cards that admitted us to the zoo anytime we wanted to visit by walking from our hotel.

July 10, 1955, was a red-letter day for Isabelle and me. We were at the zoo, and my old friend Belle J. Benchley, who had headed the zoo for many years, came in from her home to visit with us. We also saw the San Diego Zoo's weekly television show, in which Charlie participated. During the late afternoon, I finally met Laurence M. Klauber, the outstanding herpetologist. He and I had corresponded for years, but we had missed seeing each other on several previous occasions. After I became the director of the Philadelphia Zoo, and especially when Isabelle and I were planning our move to a new home in the Southwest, we were in San Diego several times.

Our most memorable visit was during June 1971. We had ample time to "do" the zoo in Balboa Park. The next day, Charlie arranged a special trip for us to see the Wild Animal Park in the San Pasqual Valley, near Escondido, which was then under construction. Many animals had already arrived, including a herd of 20 white rhinoceroses

from South Africa, which were destined to produce almost a plethora of young. During the next two decades, 75 babies were born to that largest of all the rhinos, a species that not too many years ago had seemed headed for extinction.

The Wild Animal Park was Charlie Schroeder's dream, and he had the necessary drive and enthusiasm to see it through to its completion. It was the first such large park associated with any public American zoo. He did it up brown, with massive vistas, novel exhibits, and a monorail that gave visitors an aerial view and saved them from getting foot weary from tramping the long walks through the vast acreage. It was Charlie's masterpiece, and a permanent monument to one of the finest zoo personalities I ever met. He capped it off with a fillip that was fully worthy of all the grand ideas Charlie ever envisioned. Atop a small "mountain" reached by a winding road, he and his wife, Maxine, built a beautiful home, an aerie from which he could look down on the magnificent wildlife panorama below. Almost up to the time of his death, in 1991, he drove down daily to visit with the staff, offer suggestions, and revel in the vast menagerie. Meanwhile, no doubt, he took silent pride in the great Wild Animal Park, his brainchild and finest achievement.

SALVATORE A. STEPHAN (1849-1949) was a zoo man of the old school, who was always known as "Sol." He grew up in Cincinnati, but early came into contact with the famous Hagenbeck organization, which, for a long time, was the largest and most important animal dealership in the world. Its headquarters was in Stellingen, near Hamburg, Germany. Young Stephan successfully delivered a bull elephant to the Cincinnati Zoo, and remained as an employee for 62 years, during the last 51 of which he served as superintendent, the equivalent of director. He retired when he was 88 years old, and lived to celebrate his 100th birthday.

In the general Cincinnati area, Sol Stephan's name was synonymous with the zoo. Everyone knew him, had heard about him, or had seen his picture in the newspaper. He served as Hagenbeck's American agent for several years, and he drew heavily on the experience and teaching he had received from that famous organization. He was very popular, and his skill in caring for animals and his success in getting them to breed in captivity was outstanding. Modern zoo techniques and the enormous advancements in veterinary science were still far in the future.

Sol personally witnessed two extinctions. He was among the last to see a living passenger pigeon. Martha, the sole survivor of a species that once numbered in the billions, died at the Cincinnati Zoo on September 1, 1914. The Carolina parakeet also became extinct on February 21, 1918, with the death of Incas, which, like Martha, had been under Sol's care for many years.

Sol Stephan was already an old man when I first met him in the early 1930s. He was still active, but his son, Joseph, who also had Hagenbeck training, was actually supervising the animal collection in his capacity as assistant superintendent. Joe took his father's place for a few years, and Sol's grandson, Sol G. Stephan, D.V.M., served as the zoo veterinarian for a while, but then went into private practice.

My chief memory of Sol Stephan is of a kindly old gentleman who enjoyed showing a youthful visitor from the Toledo Zoo his outstanding exhibits. Among them were Gimpy, a young forest (pygmy) elephant, and Susie, a young gorilla that ate regularly at a table with her trainer, both of them using cups, plates, and spoons.

If we had lived closer together I doubtless could have learned much from Sol Stephan. All I could contribute was a letter of congratulations when he retired and an article about him in "Parks and Recreation" magazine. I was recently surprised to learn that the letter of congratulations I sent to him on the occasion of his 100th birthday, has survived in the archives of the Cincinnati Zoo and Botanical Garden.

GEORGE PHILIP VIERHELLER (1882-1966) was above all a showman. I know little about his early life or his qualifications for assuming his new responsibilities, but once he became the director of the St. Louis Zoo, things began to happen. A building campaign was launched, and, in rapid succession, new primate, bird, and reptile houses were constructed, as were a series of unique, barless bear dens. Casts were made of limestone bluffs in southeastern Missouri near the Mississippi River, concrete was poured behind the casts, and the result was an excellent replica of a natural background. Gunite, or its equivalent, was soon to come into use, but modern fiberglass construction was still far in the future.

Marlin Perkins, who was then at the St. Louis Zoo, told me that there was some hesitancy about using the zoo's none-too-abundant money for a reptile house. So he set up a good temporary exhibit which, on busy days, was mobbed by long lines of people waiting to see it. All doubts were swept away, and John Wallace, the zoo's architect, with Marlin's help, designed a truly splendid and efficient building.

Vierheller was responsible for introducing the trained animal acts that drew visitors in vast numbers to the zoo. There was an elephant act and a big cat act, but it was the chimpanzee show that became world-renowned. The active, intelligent young apes rode ponies, bicycles, even a unicycle; they performed a variety of tricks, and they had a band, consisting of various percussion instruments with which they kept time to the music played over a loudspeaker. It was the best chimpanzee show by far of any I had ever seen—in circuses or vaudeville shows. (Yes, I am old enough to remember the Keith and Loew circuits of traveling vaudeville acts.) Incidentally, George once told me that circuses did poorly in St. Louis. The public attitude was, "Why should we pay to get in when we can see the same thing for free at our zoo?"

On special occasions or for special visitors, George would light a cigar and then hand it to a huge male orangutan in an outdoor cage, which seated itself and puffed away like a fat old man. George once conveyed a young orang from an animal dealer's headquarters in New York City to St. Louis in his Pullman compartment with him. He kept the animal concealed until his arrival, when the press and newsreels had a field day taking pictures and making a nationwide story of the affair. Neither the railroad nor Pullman company were very happy, but the event boosted attendance at the zoo.

George was a wonderful host. He delighted in showing off his collection and the animal tricks he had developed, such as the orangutan and the cigar. Whenever two or more zoo persons were in town, it was an excuse for a party, to which he always invited some of his cronies on the Zoo Board of Control. Once he did me an unexpected favor. My mother, many years after our early struggles, visited her sister in Houston, Texas, and she had a day's layover in St. Louis between trains. Completely on her own initiative, she taxied to the zoo, found the office and introduced herself, and George took over. Not only did he show her around, but he treated her to lunch and told her what a bright future her young son had ahead of him. He then drove her to a theater, bought a ticket for her, returned to work at his office, but went back to get her when the show was over. Then he took her to dinner with several other persons, and made sure she was at the railroad station in ample time to catch her train. Mother was thrilled to death, but I no longer have the wonderful letter she sent to me about her day in St. Louis. She felt like a queen.

I was often amused by how George murdered the "King's English." When a union managed to establish itself at the zoo, he complained bitterly that, "Them there guys have a new griev′-ee-ance every day." Whatever he may have lacked in education, however, it was George P. Vierheller who put the St. Louis Zoo on the map and made it an extremely popular and outstanding asset for the city of St. Louis.